THE PAPERS OF ULYSSES S. GRANT

THE PAPERS OF

ULYSSES S. GRANT

Volume 9: July 7–December 31, 1863
Edited by John Y. Simon

ASSISTANT EDITORS
John M. Hoffmann
David L. Wilson

————

SOUTHERN ILLINOIS UNIVERSITY PRESS
CARBONDALE AND EDWARDSVILLE

Library of Congress Cataloging in Publication Data (Revised)

Grant, Ulysses Simpson, Pres. U.S., 1822–1885.
    The papers of Ulysses S. Grant.

    Prepared under the auspices of the Ulysses S. Grant Association.
    Bibliographical footnotes.
    CONTENTS: v. 1. 1837–1861—v. 2. April–September 1861.
—v. 3. October 1, 1861–January 7, 1862.—v. 4. January 8–March 31,
1862.—v. 5. April 1–August 31, 1862.—v. 6. September 1–Decem-
ber 8, 1862.—v. 7. December 9, 1862–March 31, 1863.—v. 8.
April 1–July 6, 1863.—v. 9. July 7–December 31, 1863.
    1. Grant, Ulysses Simpson, Pres. U.S., 1822–1885. 2. United
States—History—Civil War, 1861–1865—Campaigns and battles
—Sources. 3. United States—Politics and government—1869–1877
—Sources. 4. Presidents—United States—Biography. 5. Generals—
United States—Biography. I. Simon, John Y., ed. II. Ulysses S.
Grant Association.
E660.G756 1967   973.8′2′0924   67–10725
ISBN 0–8093–0979–3 (v. 9)

To Chapman Grant

Contents

Maps and Illustrations

Introduction

====

O<small>N</small> J<small>ULY</small> 7, 1863, news of the surrender of Vicksburg reached Washington, D. C., arriving soon after word that Major General George G. Meade had repulsed General Robert E. Lee at Gettysburg. President Abraham Lincoln spoke to an exultant crowd from a White House window, mentioning neither Vicksburg nor Ulysses S. Grant by name, but instead groping toward the ideas that he would express so brilliantly a few months later at Gettysburg. The government expressed gratitude to Grant more concretely: Major General Henry W. Halleck notified Grant that he had been appointed a major general in the U.S. Army to date from July 4, the date of the surrender of Vicksburg. The promotion meant that Grant, already a major general of volunteers, would retain his rank when the war ended. Only three other officers on active duty held this rank, none of them commanding in the field.

At Vicksburg, Grant supervised the parole of some 30,000 prisoners while much of his army, led by Major General William T. Sherman, pursued Confederates under General Joseph E. Johnston who had originally come to Mississippi to relieve Vicksburg and who now found themselves outnumbered by the army they had hoped to overwhelm. The garrison of Port Hudson, La., after learning of the fall of Vicksburg, surrendered on July 9 to Major General Nathaniel P. Banks, which completed the opening of the Mississippi River. The availability of this great trade artery encouraged commercial ventures, and Grant spent much of the summer coping with problems of regulating trade so that the enemy would not benefit.

At the end of August, Grant went to New Orleans to confer with Banks about a planned attack on Mobile, Ala. At New Orleans, he fell while on horseback, which revived stories of his drinking, and injured his leg so severely that he did not return to Vicksburg for two weeks. By then, it was too late for him to make his own plans. On September 19, Confederate General Braxton Bragg had defeated Major General William S. Rosecrans at Chickamauga, Ga., and driven him back to Chattanooga, where he was besieged. As the situation at Chattanooga worsened, Grant was first asked to send troops, then to assume command there himself. After relieving Rosecrans and replacing him with Major General George H. Thomas, Grant entered Chattanooga and began to open a supply line and to mass troops for an attack.

On November 21, Grant launched three days of battle as he sent Thomas forward toward Missionary Ridge. On the second day, Major General Joseph Hooker with troops from the Army of the Potomac captured Lookout Mountain while Sherman occupied high ground beyond Missionary Ridge from which Grant expected him to roll up the Confederate line, which proved unrealistic because of intervening natural obstacles. On the third day, Thomas's advance to the foot of Missionary Ridge somewhat unexpectedly led to a gallant charge to the heights that threw Bragg back into Georgia in wild disorder.

Bragg had contributed to his own disaster by detaching troops under Lieutenant General James Longstreet to attack U.S. forces at Knoxville commanded by Major General Ambrose E. Burnside. Although Longstreet's siege of Knoxville caused anxiety, Bragg's defeat enabled Grant to send Sherman to Burnside's relief, and Longstreet retreated before Sherman arrived. Grant devoted the remainder of the year to attempting to complete the task of driving Confederates from Tennessee. After his victories at Vicksburg and Chattanooga, Congress voted him a gold medal and began to discuss a bill to revive the rank of lieutenant general, a rank only Grant seemed to deserve.

Grant's dramatic victory at Chattanooga, following so closely upon his triumph at Vicksburg, coincided with the opening rounds of speculation about the 1864 presidential election. Politicians who hoped to sweep into the White House behind a national hero turned their thoughts to Grant. Because he had favored the Democrats before the Civil War, some believed that they should nominate him, but Republicans who doubted Lincoln's chances for reelection also considered as a possible nominee the man who had done most to prosecute the war successfully. During the winter, Grant's most carefully composed letters were directed toward discouragement of potential political supporters. As usual, Grant meant what he said: he was a soldier who wanted the opportunity to fulfill his responsibility.

We are indebted to W. Neil Franklin and Karl L. Trever for searching the National Archives; to Mary Giunta, Anne Harris Henry, and Sara Dunlap Jackson for further assistance in the National Archives; to Barbara Long for maps; to Sue E. Dotson and Deborah Pittman for typing; to Harriet Simon for proofreading; and to Richard T. Boss, Daniel Doherty, Patrick M. McCoy, Tamara Melia, and Patricia Lynn Walker, graduate students at Southern Illinois University, for research assistance.

Financial support for the Ulysses S. Grant Association for the period during which this volume was prepared came from Southern Illinois University and the National Historical Publications and Records Commission.

JOHN Y. SIMON

December 31, 1979

Editorial Procedure

1. Editorial Insertions

A.   Words or letters in roman type within brackets represent editorial reconstruction of parts of manuscripts torn, mutilated, or illegible.

B.   [. . .] or [— — —] within brackets represent lost material which cannot be reconstructed. The number of dots represents the approximate number of lost letters; dashes represent lost words.

C.   Words in *italic* type within brackets represent material such as dates which were not part of the original manuscript.

D.   Other material crossed out is indicated by ~~cancelled type~~.

E.   Material raised in manuscript, as "4th," has been brought in line, as "4th."

2. Symbols Used to Describe Manuscripts

AD	Autograph Document
ADS	Autograph Document Signed
ADf	Autograph Draft
ADfS	Autograph Draft Signed
AES	Autograph Endorsement Signed
AL	Autograph Letter
ALS	Autograph Letter Signed
ANS	Autograph Note Signed
D	Document
DS	Document Signed

Df	Draft
DfS	Draft Signed
ES	Endorsement Signed
LS	Letter Signed

3. *Military Terms and Abbreviations*

Act.	Acting
Adjt.	Adjutant
AG	Adjutant General
AGO	Adjutant General's Office
Art.	Artillery
Asst.	Assistant
Bvt.	Brevet
Brig.	Brigadier
Capt.	Captain
Cav.	Cavalry
Col.	Colonel
Co.	Company
C.S.A.	Confederate States of America
Dept.	Department
Div.	Division
Gen.	General
Hd. Qrs.	Headquarters
Inf.	Infantry
Lt.	Lieutenant
Maj.	Major
Q. M.	Quartermaster
Regt.	Regiment or regimental
Sgt.	Sergeant
USMA	United States Military Academy, West Point, N.Y.
Vols.	Volunteers

4. *Short Titles and Abbreviations*

ABPC	*American Book-Prices Current* (New York, 1895–)
CG	*Congressional Globe* Numbers following represent the Congress, session, and page.

J. G. Cramer	Jesse Grant Cramer, ed., *Letters of Ulysses S. Grant to his Father and his Youngest Sister, 1857–78* (New York and London, 1912)
DAB	*Dictionary of American Biography* (New York, 1928–36)
Garland	Hamlin Garland, *Ulysses S. Grant: His Life and Character* (New York, 1898)
HED	*House Executive Documents*
HMD	*House Miscellaneous Documents*
HRC	*House Reports of Committees* Numbers following *HED, HMD*, or *HRC* represent the number of the Congress, the session, and the document.
Ill. AG Report	J. N. Reece, ed., *Report of the Adjutant General of the State of Illinois* (Springfield, 1900)
Johnson, Papers	LeRoy P. Graf and Ralph W. Haskins, eds., *The Papers of Andrew Johnson* (Knoxville, 1967–)
Lewis	Lloyd Lewis, *Captain Sam Grant* (Boston, 1950)
Lincoln, Works	Roy P. Basler, Marion Dolores Pratt, and Lloyd A. Dunlap, eds., *The Collected Works of Abraham Lincoln* (New Brunswick, 1953–55)
Memoirs	*Personal Memoirs of U. S. Grant* (New York, 1885–86)
O.R.	*The War of the Rebellion: A Compilation of the Official Records of the Union and Confederate Armies* (Washington, 1880–1901)
O.R. (Navy)	*Official Records of the Union and Confederate Navies in the War of the Rebellion* (Washington, 1894–1927) Roman numerals following *O.R.* or *O.R.* (Navy) represent the series and the volume.
PUSG	John Y. Simon, ed., *The Papers of Ulysses S. Grant* (Carbondale and Edwardsville, 1967–)
Richardson	Albert D. Richardson, *A Personal History of Ulysses S. Grant* (Hartford, Conn., 1868)
SED	*Senate Executive Documents*
SMD	*Senate Miscellaneous Documents*
SRC	*Senate Reports of Committees* Numbers following *SED, SMD*, or *SRC* represent the number of the Congress, the session, and the document.
USGA Newsletter	*Ulysses S. Grant Association Newsletter*

Young	John Russell Young, *Around the World with General Grant* (New York, 1879)

5. *Location Symbols*

CLU	University of California at Los Angeles, Los Angeles, Calif.
CoHi	Colorado State Historical Society, Denver, Colo.
CSmH	Henry E. Huntington Library, San Marino, Calif.
CSt	Stanford University, Stanford, Calif.
CtY	Yale University, New Haven, Conn.
CU-B	Bancroft Library, University of California, Berkeley, Calif.
DLC	Library of Congress, Washington, D.C. Numbers following DLC-USG represent the series and volume of military records in the USG papers.
DNA	National Archives, Washington, D.C. Additional numbers identify record groups.
IaHA	Iowa State Department of History and Archives, Des Moines, Iowa.
I-ar	Illinois State Archives, Springfield, Ill.
IC	Chicago Public Library, Chicago, Ill.
ICarbS	Southern Illinois University, Carbondale, Ill.
ICHi	Chicago Historical Society, Chicago, Ill.
ICN	Newberry Library, Chicago, Ill.
ICU	University of Chicago, Chicago, Ill.
IHi	Illinois State Historical Library, Springfield, Ill.
In	Indiana State Library, Indianapolis, Ind.
InFtwL	Lincoln National Life Foundation, Fort Wayne, Ind.
InHi	Indiana Historical Society, Indianapolis, Ind.
InNd	University of Notre Dame, Notre Dame, Ind.
InU	Indiana University, Bloomington, Ind.
KHi	Kansas State Historical Society, Topeka, Kan.
MdAN	United States Naval Academy Museum, Annapolis, Md.
MeB	Bowdoin College, Brunswick, Me.
MH	Harvard University, Cambridge, Mass.
MHi	Massachusetts Historical Society, Boston, Mass.

MiD	Detroit Public Library, Detroit, Mich.
MiU-C	William L. Clements Library, University of Michigan, Ann Arbor, Mich.
MoSHi	Missouri Historical Society, St. Louis, Mo.
NHi	New-York Historical Society, New York, N.Y.
NIC	Cornell University, Ithaca, N.Y.
NjP	Princeton University, Princeton, N.J.
NjR	Rutgers University, New Brunswick, N.J.
NN	New York Public Library, New York, N.Y.
NNP	Pierpont Morgan Library, New York, N.Y.
NRU	University of Rochester, Rochester, N.Y.
OClWHi	Western Reserve Historical Society, Cleveland, Ohio.
OFH	Rutherford B. Hayes Library, Fremont, Ohio.
OHi	Ohio Historical Society, Columbus, Ohio.
OrHi	Oregon Historical Society, Portland, Ore.
PCarlA	U.S. Army Military History Institute, Carlisle Barracks, Pa.
PHi	Historical Society of Pennsylvania, Philadelphia, Pa.
PPRF	Rosenbach Foundation, Philadelphia, Pa.
RPB	Brown University, Providence, R.I.
TxHR	Rice University, Houston, Tex.
USG 3	Maj. Gen. Ulysses S. Grant 3rd, Clinton, N.Y.
USMA	United States Military Academy Library, West Point, N.Y.
ViHi	Virginia Historical Society, Richmond, Va.
ViU	University of Virginia, Charlottesville, Va.
WHi	State Historical Society of Wisconsin, Madison, Wis.
Wy-Ar	Wyoming State Archives and Historical Department, Cheyenne, Wyo.
WyU	University of Wyoming, Laramie, Wyo.

Chronology

JULY 7–DECEMBER 31, 1863

JULY 7.   USG notified of his appointment as maj. gen. U.S.A. to date from the surrender of Vicksburg on July 4.

JULY 9.   Port Hudson, La., surrendered to Maj. Gen. Nathaniel P. Banks in accordance with terms negotiated the day before. This effectively completed the opening of the Mississippi River.

JULY 11.   USG ordered troops to occupy Natchez, Miss.

JULY 12.   USG sent an expedition to Yazoo City, Miss.

JULY 13.   Draft riots began in New York City.

JULY 13.   U.S. troops occupied Natchez.

JULY 17.   Maj. Gen. William T. Sherman, pursuing C.S.A. Gen. Joseph E. Johnston, occupied Jackson, Miss., which Johnston had evacuated the day before.

JULY 17.   U.S. cav. occupied Canton, Miss., destroying much railroad property.

JULY 26.   C.S.A. Brig. Gen. John Hunt Morgan captured in Ohio.

JULY 30.   Maj. Gen. Henry W. Halleck ordered USG to send an Army Corps to Banks. On Aug. 7, USG selected the 13th Army Corps, commanded by Maj. Gen. E. O. C. Ord.

AUG. 1.   USG and Banks conferred at Vicksburg about an attack on Mobile, Ala. To further this plan, USG asked permission to visit New Orleans.

Aug. 23. USG at Cairo, Ill., having accompanied Julia Dent Grant partway to St. Louis.

Aug. 26. USG at Memphis, where he attended a banquet of loyal citizens.

Aug. 27. USG at Helena, Ark.

Aug. 31. USG left Vicksburg for New Orleans.

Sept. 2. USG arrived at New Orleans.

Sept. 2. U.S. troops under Maj. Gen. Ambrose E. Burnside occupied Knoxville, Tenn.

Sept. 4. USG injured when his horse fell.

Sept. 9. U.S. troops under Maj. Gen. William S. Rosecrans occupied Chattanooga, Tenn.

Sept. 16. USG returned to Vicksburg.

Sept. 19. Battle of Chickamauga began. On the second day, Rosecrans and much of his army fled to Chattanooga, while Maj. Gen. George H. Thomas held his position.

Sept. 22. USG began to send reinforcements to Rosecrans, now besieged at Chattanooga by Gen. Braxton Bragg.

Sept. 29. Halleck ordered USG to Memphis to supervise the transfer of reinforcements to Rosecrans.

Oct. 2. Troops from the Army of the Potomac under Maj. Gen. Joseph Hooker began to arrive at Bridgeport, Ala., to relieve the siege of Chattanooga.

Oct. 3. USG ordered to Cairo.

Oct. 10. USG prepared to leave Vicksburg, placing Maj. Gen. James B. McPherson in command.

Oct. 14. USG at Memphis on his way to Cairo.

Oct. 15. USG at Columbus, Ky.

Oct. 16. USG arrived at Cairo and received orders to proceed to Louisville, Ky.

Oct. 17. USG left Cairo for Louisville, meeting Secretary of War Edwin M. Stanton in Indianapolis. USG received orders to take command of the Military Div. of the Miss., comprising the depts. of the Ohio, Cumberland, and Tenn.

Oct. 18. USG, at Louisville, assumed command of the Military Div. of the Miss.

Oct. 18. USG exercised his option to replace Rosecrans with Thomas.

Oct. 19. USG placed Sherman in command of the Dept. of the Tenn.

Oct. 20. USG left Louisville for Chattanooga.

Oct. 21. USG arrived at Bridgeport.

Oct. 23. USG arrived at Chattanooga.

Oct. 24. Following a survey of the ground, USG ordered the opening of a "cracker line" to Brown's Ferry on the Tennessee River.

Oct. 24. Sherman assumed command of the Dept. of the Tenn.

Oct. 27. Cracker line opened and siege of Chattanooga relieved. Hooker moved from Bridgeport to the foot of Lookout Mountain.

Oct. 28. C.S.A. Lt. Gen. James Longstreet launched an unsuccessful night attack against Hooker at Wauhatchie, Tenn.

Nov. 4. Bragg sent Longstreet to attack Burnside at Knoxville.

Nov. 7. USG planned an assault on Missionary Ridge, but decided against it the next day because of C.S.A. strength and the shortage of supplies and animals in Chattanooga.

Nov. 13. Sherman and the advance of his force reached Bridgeport.

Nov. 15. USG conferred with Sherman in Chattanooga, while four divs. of Sherman's troops camped at Bridgeport.

Nov. 16. Longstreet besieged Burnside at Knoxville.

Nov. 18. USG planned to attack Bragg on Nov. 21.

Nov. 21. Sherman moved to take position on the right of the C.S.A. line.

Nov. 22. Bragg sent forces under Maj. Gen. Simon B. Buckner to aid Longstreet.

Nov. 23. Thomas captured Orchard Knoll as the battle of Chattanooga began. Sherman sent a brigade across the Tennessee River to prepare for an attack the next day.

Nov. 24. Hooker captured Lookout Mountain. Sherman attacked the C.S.A. right.

Nov. 25. Troops under Thomas carried Missionary Ridge, concluding the battle of Chattanooga as Bragg retreated in disorder.

Nov. 25. USG made plans to relieve Burnside.

Nov. 27. USG at Ringgold, Ga., directing the pursuit of Bragg.

Nov. 27. USG sent two divs. under Maj. Gen. Gordon Granger to assist Burnside. On Nov. 29, USG gave Sherman command of the Knoxville expedition.

Nov. 29. Longstreet launched a desperate and unsuccessful assault on Fort Sanders, attempting to take Knoxville before U.S. reinforcements arrived.

Nov. 30. Bragg relieved of command.

Dec. 1. USG again planned an attack on Mobile.

Dec. 3. Longstreet abandoned the siege of Knoxville.

Dec. 6. Sherman and his staff entered Knoxville.

Dec. 8. President Abraham Lincoln issued a Proclamation of Amnesty and Reconstruction.

Dec. 9. Maj. Gen. John G. Foster replaced Burnside in command of the Dept. of the Ohio.

Dec. 14. U.S. Representative Elihu B. Washburne introduced a bill to revive the rank of lt. gen., a rank intended for USG.

Dec. 16. Johnston assigned to command the Dept. and Army of Tennessee. Johnston assumed command on Dec. 22 at Dalton, Ga.

Dec. 17. USG wrote to the chairman of the Ohio Democratic Central Committee that he would not allow his name to be used as a presidential nominee.

Dec. 17. Lincoln signed a joint resolution of Congress thanking USG and his command and providing a gold medal for USG.

Dec. 18. USG went to Nashville.

Dec. 28. USG back in Chattanooga.

Dec. 31. USG reached Knoxville.

The Papers of Ulysses S. Grant
July 7–December 31, 1863

To Maj. Gen. James B. McPherson

————

Head Quarters, Dept. of the Ten
Vicksburg Miss. July 7th 1863.
MAJ. GEN. J. B. MCPHERSON,
COMD.G 17TH ARMY CORPS,
GEN.

Give instructions that no passes are to be given to negroes to accompany their masters on leaving the City.[1] The negroes may be informed that they are free by any one who may choose to give them the information and if they still wish to go no force need be used to prevent.

In the particular case where I gave the reply that force would not be used to prevent negroes accompanying their masters the officer said he had a family and children and could not get along without a nurse. Further that the nurse had been raised in the family and was like one of them and would take it as hard to be seperated as would an actual member of the family.

If there is any indication that a suspicious number of blacks are going to accompany the troops out then all should be turned back except such as are voluntarily accompanying families, not more than one to each family.

Very respectfully
U. S. GRANT
Maj. Gen. Com

ALS, deCoppet Collection, NjP. *O.R.*, I, xxiv, part 3, 483. On July 7, 1863, Maj. Gen. James B. McPherson included the substance of USG's instructions in a letter to Lt. Gen. John C. Pemberton. *Ibid.*, p. 484. In a letter to McPherson the next day, Pemberton protested the instructions. *Ibid.*, p. 487.

1. On July 7, Maj. Gen. John A. Logan wrote to Lt. Col. John A. Rawlins. "I solemnly protest as an officer of the U. S. Army, against the Manner, in which

confederate officers are permitted to intimidate their servants in presence of officers appointed to examine sd. servants, and also against passes worded permitting them to go out with their masters, the manner in which this thing is big done is conniving at furnishing negroes to every officer who is a prisoner in Vicksburg." ALS, DNA, RG 94, War Records Office, Dept. of the Mo. *O.R.*, I, xxiv, part 3, 483.

To Maj. Gen. James B. McPherson

Head Quarters, Dept. of the Ten.
Vicksburg Miss. July 8th 1863.

MAJ. GEN. J. B. MCPHERSON,
COMD.G 17TH ARMY CORPS.
GEN.

There apparently being some misunderstanding between Lt. Gen. Pemberton and the paroling officers as to the method of conducting the paroling of prisoners I will give you the following rules for your guidance. That there may be no misunderstanding no prisoners will be allowed to leave our lines until all are paroled who will accept. Those who decline will be confined on Steamers anchored in the stream until they accept and concent to march out with officers appointed over them. Declining this they will be sent North as prisoners of War to be held for exchange. When all those able to leave the lines are paroled, and the rolls are approved by Gen. Pemberton, or any officer designated by him, the whole will be required to leave our lines. Those declining to leave will be sent out under guard.

Gen. Pemberton's acceptance of the terms proposed to him binds the Confederate Govt. not to accept the services of any man who formed a part of this Garrison on the morning of the 4th inst. until properly exchanged The object of the parole is to make each individual feel the same obligation.

Very respectfully
U. S. GRANT
Maj. Gen.

ALS, Abraham Lincoln Book Shop, Chicago, Ill. On July 8, 1863, Lt. Gen. John C. Pemberton wrote to USG. "I am informed by Col. Henderson, 5th Confed. Reg thro, an asst adjt Genl that the 27th La Regt, a portion of the command surrendered, is now crossing the Miss River in skiffs, I respectfully call your to this and protest against this violation of the terms of the capitulation, entered into between you and myself—" ALS, DNA, RG 94, War Records Office, Dept. of the Tenn. *O.R.*, I, xxiv, part 3, 488. On July 8, Maj. Gen. James B. McPherson wrote to Lt. Col. John A. Rawlins that the river crossings had been stopped. *Ibid.*, p. 489. See following letter.

To Maj. Gen. James B. McPherson

Headquarters Dept of the Tennessee
Vicksburg Miss July 8th 1863

Maj. Genl. J. B. McPherson
Comdg 17th Army Corps.
General:

There apparently being some misunderstanding between Lieut Genl Pemberton and the paroling officers engaged in issuing paroles to the prisoners and Maj. Watts commissioner for the exchange of prisoners, apparently having the idea that his presence here makes it necessary that he should receipt all rolls to make the parole binding, I will give you a line of policy to pursue.

The terms which I proposed to Gen Pemberton were free from ambiguity, and were accepted in unmistakeable language. That acceptance alone made the whole garrison prisoners of war, who could not properly be placed on military duty until properly exchanged, even if they should escape before being paroled or enrolled. No further receipt than Gen Pembertons letter of acceptance of terms is necessary to bind the Confederate authorities to acknowledge the entire garrison of Vicksburg on the morning of the 4th inst. prisoners of war. The only object in issuing paroles to the officers and men, is that they may feel the Same obligation that Southern authorities will in this matter: The object of having rolls made out is that the Government may have something in a compact form which will be recognized to enable them to negotiate for the exchange of prisoners hereafter. I do not regard it as essential that

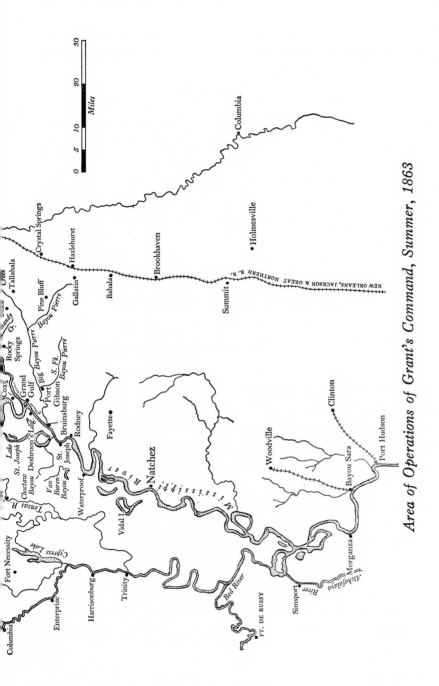

Area of Operations of Grant's Command, Summer, 1863

Maj. Watts should sign the rolls so long as they are signed by
Brigade or regimental commanders   Maj. Watts with the balance
is at present a prisoner of war

U. S. GRANT

Copies, DLC-USG, V, 19, 101, 103; DNA, RG 393, Dept. of the Tenn., Letters
Sent. *O.R.*, I, xxiv, part 3, 488. On July 8, 1863, USG wrote again to Maj. Gen.
James B. McPherson. "Inform Gen. Pemberton that owing to the refusal of Maj.
Watts to countersign rolls of paroled prisoners certified to by Regimental Com-
manders unless the numbers are actually present when passing out of the lines
I would be pleased if all those already paroled be moved out as early as possible
to-morrow. Hereafter require all regiments, or detachments, coming up to be
paroled to come ready to march immediately out as soon as they receive their
paroles." ALS, Lehigh University, Bethlehem, Pa. *O.R.*, I, xxiv, part 3, 489.
See preceding letter.

To Commanding Officer, Bovina, Miss.

———

Headquarters Dept of the Tennessee
Vicksburg, July 8th 1863.

COMMANDING OFFICER, BOVINA
OR BIG BLACK BRIDGE.

Paroled prisoners will be sent out of here tomorrow.[1] They will
be authorized to cross at the Railroad and move from there to Edwards station, and in by way of Raymond East. Instruct the command to be orderly and quiet as these prisoners pass, to make no
offensive remarks, and not to harbor any who fall out of ranks in
passing. After they have passed should any return they will be
sent to the Provost Marshal here.

U. S. GRANT
Major General.

Copies, DLC-USG, V, 19, 101, 103; DNA, RG 393, Dept. of the Tenn., Letters
Sent. A variation of the message, misdated July 10, 1863, probably taken from
Adam Badeau, *Military History of Ulysses S. Grant* (New York, 1868), I, 390,
appears in *Memoirs*, I, 570.

1. The paroled prisoners did not march out of Vicksburg until July 11. See
letter to Maj. Gen. James B. McPherson, July 10, 1863.

To Maj. Gen. Francis J. Herron

———

Head Quarters, Dept. of the Ten.
Vicksburg Miss. July 9th 1863.

MAJ. GEN. F. J. HERRON
COMD.G DIVISION,
GEN.

Make all preparation to move with your Division to Port Hudson as soon as the prisoners of War are turned out of our lines. This will probably enable you to leave on the 11th. Take with ten days rations. Leave your Artillery and Convalescents in charge of such camp & garrison equipage as it will not be necessary to take with you.

It is expected that Port Hudson must fall within a few days and as your Division will return here as soon as possible you will take with you as little baggage as possible and no land transportation.

Very respectfully
U. S. GRANT
Maj. Gen. Com

ALS, NHi. *O.R.*, I, xxiv, part 3, 490–91. See letter to Act. Rear Admiral David D. Porter, July 11, 1863.

To Lt. Gen. John C. Pemberton

———

Head Quarters, Dept. of the Ten.
Vicksburg Miss. July 10th 1863.

LT. GEN. J. C. PEMBERTON,
COMD.G CONFEDERATE FORCES,
VICKSBURG MISS.
GEN.

Yours of this date proposing to leave Maj. Gen. M. L. Smith to arrange for the paroling of the sick and wounded, granting furloughs &c. is received. It will be agreeable to me to have Gen.

Smith remain a proper time for the purposes named.—Whilst here it is not necessary for me to assure you he will receive every courtesy and on leaving will be insured a safe conduit beyond our lines. Four orderlies will be authorized to remain with Gen. Smith. All communications passing between Gen. Smith and outside our lines during his stay will be forwarded, & received, open, through a flag of truce.

> Very respectfully
> U. S. GRANT
> Maj. Gen. Com

ALS, DNA, RG 109, Documents Printed in *O.R. O.R.*, I, xxiv, part 3, 493. On July 10, 1863, Lt. Gen. John C. Pemberton wrote to USG. "I propose designating Maj Genl M. L. Smith to remain after the departure of the army with a view of carrying into effect in conjunction with yourself the terms of the capitulation of my army and this city—In order that he may act understandingly in reference to granting leaves of absence to sick and disabled officers and soldiers and in forwarding the sick and wounded as they may become able to travel, it will probably be ~~un~~necessary for him to communicate with me—under such conditions and at such times as may not interfere with your military movements   it is of course expected that Genl Smith is to be respected and treated according to his rank with the priviledge when he leaves of designating a successor should one be necessary and that he be furnished with transportation to the extent of one wagon & team and a proper escort through your lines when leaving and likewise to have the facilities for getting supplies while here—Please inform me if this designation will be acceptable to you and if what is asked will be accorded—I also ask that Genl Smith be allowed two or three couriers with their horses either from my present command or detailed from yours" ALS, DNA, RG 94, War Records Office, Dept. of the Tenn. *O.R.*, I, xxiv, part 3, 493. On July 11, Pemberton again wrote to USG. "I have the honor to request that a copy of the communications relating to the capitulation of this place, be furnished Maj. Genl. Smith: C. S. A. as the communications were through mistake sent off in my trunk this morning and I am unable to furnish him with a copy." LS, DNA, RG 94, War Records Office, Union Battle Reports. *O.R.*, I, xxiv, part 3, 502. Evidently, USG returned the original of the letters written by Pemberton on July 3. On July 15, Pemberton wrote to USG. "In accordance with an arrangement for communication between Genl. Smith & myself while at Vicksburg, I send an open letter to his address by the hands of Genl. Taylor, a member of my staff—I hope you will facilitate him in his passage in going to and returning from Vicksburg" ALS, DNA, RG 94, War Records Office, Dept. of the Mo. The enclosed letter, from Pemberton to Maj. Gen. Martin L. Smith, July 15, requested a complete list of officers and men paroled from Vicksburg "with the least possible delay." Copy, *ibid.*, RG 94, Dept. of Miss. and East La., Letters and Telegrams Sent. On July 18, Pemberton wrote to USG. "I find it necessary again to communicate with you Gen'l Smith and in pursuance of engagement I send by the hands of Maj H M Mathews an open letter to his address   I hope you will afford him him every facility in going to & returning from Vicksburg" Copy, *ibid*. He probably enclosed a letter asking Smith to inform him of the number of regts. ready for exchange.

To Brig. Gen. William A. Hammond

————

Head Quarters, Dept. of the Ten.
Vicksburg Miss. July 10th 1863.

Brig. Gen. J. H. Hammond,
Surgeon Gen. U. S. Army,
Washington D. C.
Gen.

The siege of Vicksburg having closed I have relieved Surgeon M. Mills as Medical Director of the Dept. and announced Surgeon Jno Moore in his place.[1]

Surgeon Mills has filled the position of Medical Director as it has never before been filled in this Department, and I regreted exceedingly that he should have been relieved by orders from Washington, especially to go before a "Retiring Board" for examination.[2]

Surgeon Mills has performed the duties of his office, in the field and on the march, in the most satisfactory manner and to the great advantage of the service. In correcting some old evils and irregularities he has incured the displeasure of some of the Surgeons of Volunteers who were evidently determined not to follow the prescribed forms for making out requisitions for all supplies drawn by them. You may have seen published some letters addressed by different Surgeons to the Medical Purveyer and published through the agency no doubt of one of the officers whose names appear to these letters.[3] The endorsement of Surgeon Mills to these several letters was evidently what they desired to get before the public to prejudice the public mind against him. Surgeon Mills was only performing a duty and requiring of them what they knew he would require before their letters were written. The fact is there was an evident desire on the part of Surgeons to draw an amount of ice that would enable them to use it freely not only for the sick but for private use, and as the supply was limited and liable to be exhausted before more could be received Dr. Mills prescribed the amount that could be drawn for each patient and would allow the issue only on requitions. There is one of these letters, the one signed by Surgeon Franklin, that is so improper in its tone that I would recommend his dismissal from the service.[4]

> I am Gen. very respectfully
> Your obt. svt.
> U. S. GRANT
> Maj. Gen.

ALS, DNA, RG 94, Medical Officers and Physicians, Personal Papers. See letter to Edwin M. Stanton, Sept. 25, 1863.

1. John Moore, born in Ind. in 1826, was appointed asst. surgeon as of June 29, 1853, and promoted to surgeon as of June 11, 1862. He served as a medical director in the Army of the Potomac before his transfer to the Dept. of the Tenn. See letter to Brig. Gen. Lorenzo Thomas, June 12, 1863. On July 10, 1863, Lt. Col. John A. Rawlins issued Special Orders No. 186. "Surgeon Madison Mills U. S. A is hereby releived from duty as Medical Director of the Department of the Tennessee and will report in person to the Assistant Surgeon General of the Army Saint Louis Mo" Copies, DLC-USG, V, 27, 28; DNA, RG 94, Letters Received; *ibid.*, RG 393, Dept. of the Tenn., Special Orders.

2. On July 23, Brig. Gen. William A. Hammond, surgeon gen., endorsed a copy of Special Orders No. 186. "Respectfully forwarded for the information of the General Commanding Army   Surg Mills was recommended for the Retired List on the 29th of April last" ES, *ibid.*, RG 94, Letters Received, 220D 1863. On the same day, Maj. Gen. Henry W. Halleck endorsed the order. "The recommendation of Surg Genl has been approved by me." AES, *ibid.* USG's letter concerning Surgeon Madison Mills, however, reached Hammond on July 27. *Ibid.*, RG 112, Register of Letters Received. The letter was apparently effective; Mills was not retired. On Aug. 23, Mills wrote to Rawlins. "I am assigned to duty as Medical Director of the Depatment of the Tennessee by order of the Secretary of War, and ordered to report, without delay, to the Major General Commanding. I beg leave to ask that the Major Genl. Comdg will permit me to delay at St. Louis 'till the 1st of October next. Please answer quickly, and direct to St. Louis Mo:" ALS, *ibid.*, RG 94, Staff Papers.

3. Written in the first week of June, the letters concerned ice for the sick and wounded. The letters, first published in the *St. Louis Daily Union*, June 19, appeared in the *Chicago Tribune*, June 26. Mills wanted all surgeons to follow established procedure in requisitioning medical supplies, and the resentment of some vol. surgeons erupted over the matter of ice. Three times on June 5, Surgeon Charles McMillan, medical director, 15th Army Corps, ordered the medical purveyor to issue ice to various hospitals. The procedure used by McMillan was incorrect. Since ice was in short supply and was being depleted by private con-

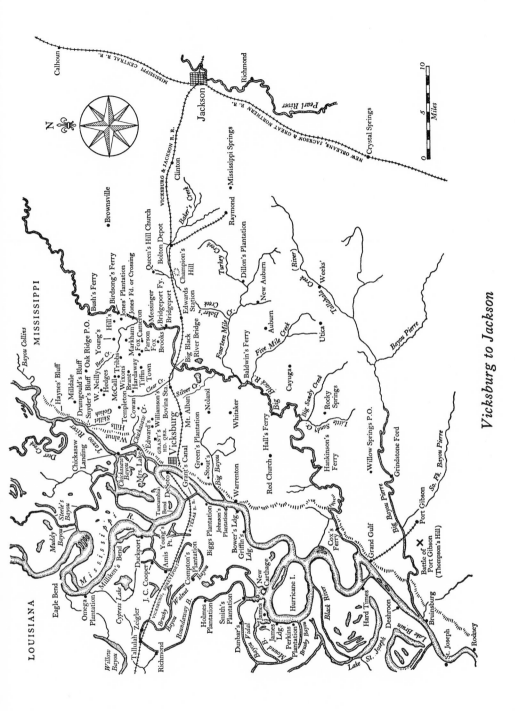

Vicksburg to Jackson

sumption, Mills strictly rationed it. Consequently, Mills endorsed each of Mc-Millan's orders separately. "In future you will not give the Medical Purveyor any order. *He is directed to disregard them.*" "Dr. McMillan cannot give the Medical Purveyor an order. The Medical Purveyor will issue on Surgeon Plummer's order, if it have your approval. Hereafter you will not use the above style to the Purveyor." "Dr. McMillan is directed not to give any more orders to the Medical Purveyor, as an order is one thing, and a request another thing." On June 6, Mc-Millan replied to Mills. "I regret most sincerely that you should have made an insulting indorsement on a most courteous request addressed to the Medical Purveyor for ice, while I was informed he had some in his possession for distribution. . . . You would seem to imply that it would be more proper for the Medical Purveyor to receive an order from Surgeon Plummer than from me; I therefore approve such an order, hoping that no more delays and objections will be imposed, and wounded and sick men be allowed to suffer while the ice is running away on the decks of the Medical Purveyor's boat. I can assure you that not only the medical officers, but the corps and division commanders, look with surprise and regret, not unmingled with anger, at such manifestations of disregard of the welfare of sick and wounded men on the part of the Medical Director and Medical Purveyor." *Chicago Tribune,* June 26, 1863.

On June 6, Surgeon Edward C. Franklin issued a similar order that Mills endorsed. "Surgeon Franklin is notified that on a proper application he can get ice for his sick and wounded. He has no authority over Assistant Surgeon Brewer, and has no right to give him an order." Also included in the printed correspondence was a letter to Franklin conveying the idea that Mills was depriving the sick and wounded of needed supplies that were readily available. Finally, on June 7, Franklin wrote to Asst. Surgeon John W. Brewer, medical purveyor. "Surgeon Franklin's compliments to Assistant Surgeon J. W. Brewer, U. S. A., and requests, if the Assistant Surgeon can spare any ice from his refreshing drinks, that he will be kind enough to furnish some to bearer for the wounded in the 2d division hospital, under his charge. Having sent two applications for ice for the wounded, with the 'request' that the Assistant Surgeon, U. S. A., will 'please furnish,' etc, and *that* not appearing sufficiently obsequious from a volunteer to a regular doctor, he is furthermore willing to beseech, implore and beg, if these terms shall be deemed obsequious enough for the Assistant Surgeon, or to employ, by other solicitations, entreaties and prayes that may be considered becoming language to an Assistant Regular Army Doctor. It is hoped that the heart of the Assistant Surgeon, U. S. A., will be touched with the entreaties set forth before the ice shall have entirely melted away." *Ibid.*

On July 3, McMillan wrote to Maj. Gen. William T. Sherman disclaiming responsibility for the publication of the letters. He indicated that Franklin had been loaned the correspondence briefly for his own use. Even so, he still blamed Mills for the controversy over ice. "It is a matter exceedingly to be regretted on all accounts and more particularly as in an interview with the Medical Director a few days afterward, it was made plain that a misunderstanding as to the Proprietorship of the Ice lay at the bottom of the matter: & for, while it was supposed that the article was sent by the Sanitary Commission, all Surgeons knew that the Regulation system of drawing and accounting for it would be unnecessary, but if it had been communicated to them that it was an article of Hospital supply furnished by the Government it would have been seen at once that the usual Requisitions, approved by Corps & Department Directors must be put in—And

I believe that the chief complaint on the part of the Medical officers concerned is, that in the exigency the informality was not either for the moment ignored, proper papers being allowed to come in subsequently or that they were not informed that it was a Medical supply and directed to make requisition for it—To you, General, I know I need put in no further disclaimer of knowledge or consent to the publication of these papers than is contained in this communication and the note to the Medical Director—and, as the proper statements & corrections have been made both privately, and in the public Press, it is to be hoped the whole matter may now be permitted to rest; especially as it is now known to be the result of an unfortunate misunderstanding of which the most that can be said, is, that it was probably, not corrected at the proper moment and in the proper manner, by the Medical Director and the Medical Purveyor." ALS, DNA, RG 393, Dept. of the Tenn., Letters Received. On July 6, Sherman enclosed this letter in a report to Rawlins on the matter. "I have the honor to acknowlege receipt of your letter of July 1, calling for a Report touching the publication of certain official matters that transpired between Surgeon Mills, Medl Director of the Dept—& Surgeons McMillan & Franklin of my Corps. I enclose the Report of Surgeon McMillan now present, explaining what agency he had in allowing this matter to reach the Public. he seems to have loaned the original notes to Surgeon Franklin of the 2nd Division with the injunction to return them to him at once. He disclaims any knowlege of an intention to publish, and I feel assured that he would have scorned to appeal to the Public in such a matter. Surgeon Franklin is now absent on sick Leave, and I have no means of calling on him for his agency in this transaction. Capt Joel A Q M on General Blairs Staff is also absent. I know not by what authority, certainly not by mine, and I only have incidental knowlege that he is in St Louis. If Captain Joel gave these notes to a printer for publication, I do most assuredly think it a case for dismissal It was none of his business, and he must have known of the orders on this Subject which have been made public, and much discussed in this army. I need not add that publication of official matter are mischiveous in the extreme and no army can maintain a decent discipline or sence of self respect if such publications are tolerated. I therefore hope the order will be strictly enforced if Dr Franklin or Captain Joel admit their instrumentality in the publication. I am in the point of starting east of Black River, and I feel assured Gen Grant will pardon my not followig this enquery further at this time." ALS, *ibid.*

On July 9, Rawlins issued Special Orders No. 185. "All Ice not required by the Medical Department for the sick and wounded here, will be turned over to the parties to whom it belongs for their use but not for sale. Medical Director Mills will be the Judge of the amount required for Hospitals." Copies, DLC-USG, V, 27, 28; DNA, RG 393, Dept. of the Tenn., Special Orders. On July 11, Rawlins wrote to Lt. Col. Judson D. Bingham. "You will please make a payment of five cents per lb. to Alex Kelsey of St. Louis, on a barge of ice, Siezed this morning by Surgeon Moore, Med. Director, for the use of the Med. Director." Copies, DLC-USG, V, 19, 101, 103; DNA, RG 393, Dept. of the Tenn., Letters Sent.

4. Franklin, born in Flushing, N. Y., in 1822, graduated in medicine from the University of the City of New York in 1846. He practiced medicine successfully in N. Y., Calif., Panama, and Iowa before settling in St. Louis in 1860. He was appointed surgeon, 5th Mo., as of May 18, 1861, and surgeon of vols. as of Sept. 30. His resignation was accepted effective Aug. 5, 1863.

To Act. Rear Admiral David D. Porter

———

Head Quarters, Dept. of the Ten.
Vicksburg Miss. July 10th 1863.

Admiral D. D. Porter,
Comd.g Miss. Squadron,
Admiral.

I have directed a Division of troops to be in readiness to go aboard of transports the moment the prisoners are discharged. This will be to-morrow morning. Unless word should be received in the mean time announcing the fall of Port Hudson I will send them to reinforce Gen. Banks.[1] Will these transports require a convoy?

If I can get out of the office I will call and see you this afternoon.

Very respectfully
U. S. Grant
Maj. Gen.

ALS, MdAN.

1. See letter to Act. Rear Admiral David D. Porter, July 11, 1863.

To Maj. Gen. Nathaniel P. Banks

———

Head Quarters, Dept. of the Ten.
Vicksburg Miss. July 10th 1863.

Maj. Gen. N. P. Banks,
Comd.g Dept. of the Gulf,
Gen.

I send Maj. Gen. Herron to Port Hudson with the available Infantry force of his Div.[1] I feel confidant that Port Hudson will be in your possession before these troops reach you, but learning of the position of Gen. Taylors forces I did not know but you might want to make a prompt movement to capture him which could not be done without other forces to take the place of some of yours where they now are.

As I informed you in my letter of the 4th inst. all my ~~availa~~ surplus troops were held in readiness to move on Johnston the moment Vicksburg fell. They started the same day. I have had no word from them since yesterday morning. At that time Gen. Sherman was at Clinton, nine miles from ~~from~~ Jackson. His advance had slight skirmishing with the enemy's cavalry but nothing further at that time.

Gen. Sherman will give Johnston no rest on this side of Pearl River. With the exception of clearing out Kirby Smith's forces on the West side of the Miss. river I have but little idea of what is next to be done with our Western forces. Hope to have instructions from Washington soon however.

On the 4th of July Gen. Prentiss was attacked at Helena by Holmes, Price, Parsons & Marmaduke with a force vastly superior to his own, numerically. Gen. Prentiss writes me that his loss will not exceed 250 killed, wounded & missing. They had picked up about 300 of the enemys dead and had captured 1100 prisoners. He says further that at every house and on every road his troops go they find wounded men left by the enemy.[2]

I received a telegraphic dispatch from the Gen. Supt. of telegraphs, Washington, of the 5th of July stating that Meade had whipped Lee badly and that the latter was retreating and Meade in full pursuits.[3]

The troops I send you General leave behind their baggage, hospitals and Artillery. I hope you will send them back as soon as their services can be dispensed with. I will also ask that Gen. Grierson be sent here as soon as possible. I am very much in want of Cavalry and of Grierson to command them.

Hoping Gen. that you have removed the last barrier to the free navigation of the Mississippi, I remain

your very obt. svt.
U. S. GRANT
Maj. Gen.

ALS, Albany Institute of History and Art, Albany, N. Y. *O.R.*, I, xxiv, part 3, 492–93.

1. See letters to Maj. Gen. Francis J. Herron, July 9, 1863, and to Act. Rear Admiral David D. Porter, July 11, 1863.

2. On July 6, 1863, 8:00 A.M., Maj. Gen. Benjamin M. Prentiss, Helena, wrote to USG. "I had the honor to forward yesterday a preliminary report of the result of the attack on this place, by the enemy's force under command of Lieut. Gen. Holmes, assisted by Generals Price, Marmaduke, Parsons and others. I have the honor to report now that the enemy has not renewed the attack and that our victory is complete and final. Our list of prisoners already exceeds eleven hundred and among them are several field and line officers. The enemy succeeded in taking away some of his killed and wounded but we have already buried nearly 300 of his killed and have captured more than that number of his severely wounded. Our own loss in killed, wounded and missing will not exceed 300. I sent out a small reconnoitering party today which came up with a small party of the enemy's rear guard some six miles out. This party reports the enemy as admitting to the inhabitants along the line of his retreat that he had met with a severe repulse. His wounded are founded in whateve[r] direction we search. The party today paroled over 100 at one place. The enemy is evidently very much demoralized and I much regret that the number and condition of my small force will not warrant a pursuit. I will forward a detailed report as soon as reports are received from subordinate commanders." Copy, DNA, RG 393, District of Eastern Ark., Letters Sent. Printed as written at 8:00 P.M. in *O.R.*, I, xxii, part 1, 387. On July 11, USG endorsed this letter. "Respectfully forwarded to Head Quarters of the Army, Washington, D. C. Report referred to not rece'd." Copies, DLC-USG, V, 25; DNA, RG 393, Dept. of the Tenn., Endorsements. On July 5, Prentiss had written to USG. "I have the honor to report that the enemy's forces, estimated at from 15.000 to 18.000 strong under Lieut. Genl. Holmes and Genls. Price, Marmaduke and others, attacked our lines heavily at 3 o'clock A. M., of July 4th. The engagement lasted till 10.30 A. M., when the enemy retreated, having been repulsed at every point with severe loss, and leaving hundreds of his killed and wounded on the battle field. Occasional skirmishing continued till 1 or 2 o'clock P. M., but the attack in force has not been renewed. We have taken 1000 prisoners, about 1200 stand of arms, and 2 colors. Our loss in killed and wounded is about 250.—the loss of the enemy in killed, wounded and prisoners, as near as we can ascertain, is about 2,500. The soldiers of my command, numbering about 4.000 effective men, are entitled to all credit for their determined and successful defence of this Post. Their bravery and gallantry have not, I think, been surpassed in this war. The Gun. Boat '*Tyler*' rendered valuable assistance in this action. The '*Covington*' has since arrived—and I have applied to Genl Hurlburt for ~~assistance~~ reinforcements, as the enemy is still in superior force, and is still in the vicinity, supposed to be massing his troops for a renewed attack. I will forward a more detailed report as soon as particulars can be received from the various parts of the command. You can rely upon my sparing no exertions nor precautions to hold this point." Copy, *ibid.*, District of Eastern Ark., Letters Sent. *O.R.*, I, xxii, part 1, 386–87. See also Prentiss's report of July 9, *ibid.*, pp. 387–90.

On June 30, Prentiss had written to USG. "I forwarded some days since to your head-quarters my application for leave of absence for 20 days, to visit my home in Illinois—and fearing that it or its answer may have miscarried, in our present defective and unreliable mail arrangements, I venture to renew the application. I find it imperatively necessary to the proper disposition of my business affairs that I should spend 2 or 3 days at home. Gen. Ross is expected here daily, on his return from his leave, and my absence will scarcely be felt in this District. If, therefore, there are no reasons of importance, at Department Head Quarters, why my leave should not be granted, I have the honor respectfully to request that it be allowed at as early a day as possible. I will say, as before, that my business at home shall be closely and strictly attended to, with a view to my returning before the expiration of the leave, if it be possible for me to do so, as I have now no doubt it will. Believe me, Sir, that it is only urgent business that impels me to ask a leave of absence at all—and that I shall be anxious to cut it as short as possible, and return to my post. Trusting that my application directly to your head quarters may not be considered unmilitary under existing circumstances," LS, DNA, RG 94, Generals' Papers and Books, Prentiss. By Special Orders No. 179, July 3, Prentiss's request was granted, although "This leave will not take effect until Brig. General L. F. Ross., arrives at Helena." Copies, DLC-USG, V, 27, 28; DNA, RG 393, Dept. of the Tenn., Special Orders. See letter to Maj. Gen. Stephen A. Hurlbut, Aug. 5, 1863. On Aug. 8, Prentiss wrote to Brig. Gen. Lorenzo Thomas. "I have the honor to tender through you to the President of the United States my commission as Major General of Volunteers. My reasons for so doing are that my private business requires that I relinquish my connection with the service, and now that our armies have achieved such great successes, and there being such bright prospect of a speedy termination of the rebellion my services can be easily dispensed with   I have been without an adequate command since the battle of Helena. I have endeavored to do my whole duty since joining the service. I earnestly ask that the Department give this their prompt attention; and that my resignation may be accepted." LS, DNA, RG 94, ACP, P533 CB 1863. On the same day, Hurlbut endorsed this letter. "Respectfully forwarded   Maj. Genl. Prentiss states to me that his personal affairs are in such a state that his presence & attention are necessary to secure him from pecuniary ruin. He also appears to feel as will be noticed in one paragraph of his letter that his merits & services have not been appreciated by his superior officers. To this he evidently ascribes the alleged fact that he has not been assigned to a command corresponding to his rank. Under the entire case I am satisfied it is to the advantage of the Service that his resignation be accepted" AES, *ibid.* On Aug. 8, USG endorsed this letter. "Approved and respectfully forwarded." AES, *ibid.* See letter to Maj. Gen. Henry W. Halleck, Sept. 30, 1863; *O.R.*, I, xxx, part 4, 118. Prentiss's resignation was accepted as of Oct. 28.

3. The telegram of July 5 has not been located. However, on July 4, 9:40 P.M., Secretary of War Edwin M. Stanton telegraphed to USG and to Maj. Gens. Ambrose E. Burnside, William S. Rosecrans, and John M. Schofield. "After a three days sanguinary battle at Gettysburg General Meade has defeated General Lee who is now in retreat." ALS (telegram sent), DNA, RG 107, Telegrams Collected (Bound); telegram received, *ibid.*, RG 393, Dept. of the Tenn., Telegrams Received. On July 6, 9:10 P.M., Maj. Gen. Henry W. Halleck telegraphed to USG, Burnside, and Schofield. "The three days battles of Major Genl Meade at Gettysburg, Penn, have resulted in in a complete and unequivocal victory. The defeated rebel forces under Lee are in full retreat and will be properly pursued   [The] details of these battles have not been recieved, but enough is known to justify the anouncement of a complete and decided victory by the

Army of the Potomac under Genl Meade." ALS (telegram sent), *ibid.*, RG 107, Telegrams Collected (Bound); telegram received, *ibid.*, RG 393, Dept. of the Tenn., Telegrams Received.

To Maj. Gen. James B. McPherson

Headquarters Dept. of the Tenn
Vicksburg Miss. July 10th 1863

Major Gen J. B. McPherson
Comdg 17th Army Corps.
Gen.

Gen Pemberton desires to commence leaving with his command to night. As the paroling is now about completed, he may be permitted to do so.

In going over the lines the rolls will be called and those not answering to their names will be checked so, that under the head of "Remarks," it can be noted that such persons did not march out with their commands. The rolls will show who are prisoners, and every man named will be acknowledged as such only it is wanted to avoid leaving the same man subject to exchange twice Some named in the rolls may be in Hospital, and no doubt many more will skulk, and be found within our lines after these regiments have left, with or without passes

I told Gen Pemberton that everything would be done on my part to prevent any man being exchanged for twice Accordingly every man sent North whose name appears on the rolls, sent to Washington, will be enrolled again and his name sent forward so that it may be stricken from the Original roll. You will want to appoint officers to be at the line of entrenchments to witness and compare rolls of absentees with the officers appointed by Gen. Pemberton.

Yours &c
U. S. Grant

Copies, DLC-USG, V, 19, 101, 103; DNA, RG 393, Dept. of the Tenn., Letters Sent. *O.R.*, I, xxiv, part 3, 495. On July 10, 1863, Maj. Gen. Cadwallader C.

Washburn telegraphed to USG. "There are a good many paroled confederate
Soldiers here anxious to get beyond our lines   they all have their papers   Shall
I let them go" Telegram received, DNA, RG 393, Dept. of the Tenn., Tele-
grams Received. USG drafted his reply on the bottom of Washburn's telegram.
"We are bound in good faith to see that all paroled prisoners march ~~over~~ out
of our lines with their commands. Send those you have here to be started again."
ANS, *ibid.*

To Maj. N. G. Watts

Vicksburg Mississippi
July 11th 1863

MAJR W. G. WATTS C. S. A.

Your Note of Yesterday enclosing an application of A. K.
Smedes[1] & Bro. for protection to their property near Boltons and
permission for their families to leave our lines &c is just received.

I enclose you the pass desired. Protection cannot be given because to establish the rule would end in a vast amount of labor,
as every family within fifty miles would ask the same thing and
really would receive no benefit from it. Within our lines of Sen-
tinels is as far as we Can really give protection. Beyond those
limits all persons are protected by the most stringent orders against
pillaging and plundering. Parties who will not be governed by
orders when they are out would pay but little attention to a safe
guard.

Majr Gen'l McPherson is placed in immediate Command here,
and will furnish you Majr with all the pass you and your Military
family require.

I will be pleased to see you Major at any time you may see fit
to call.

I am Major
Very Respectfully
Your Obt Servt
U. S. GRANT.
Majr Genl

Copy, Elson's, Atlanta, Ga.

1. On May 29, 1865, Abraham K. Smedes, a forty-six-year-old Vicksburg lawyer, born in N. Y., signed an oath of amnesty. DS, DNA, RG 109, Union Provost Marshals' File of Papers Relating to Individual Civilians.

To Brig. Gen. Lorenzo Thomas

Vicksburg, Mississippi
July 11th, 1863.

Brig.-Genl. L. Thomas,
Adj. Gen. of the Army.
General:

Your letter of the 26th of last month, enclosing a letter from Mrs Duncan,[1] was received on the 9th. I have ordered an investigation of the matters complained of but think there must be some mistake about the acts complained of having been committed. About the date of your letter Mr Duncan the husband of Mrs Mary Duncan, called on me for a permit to ship from the north, supplies of various kinds for the use of his negroes. He then thanked me for the protection and courtesy that had been extended to him by the Federal Authorities in this Department. He made no complaint of even having been annoyed.

All new organizations of negro regiments have been broken up and their men transferred to those regiments for which you had appointed officers. I found that the old regiments never could be filled so long as authority was granted to form new ones. I am anxious to get as many of these negro regiments as possible and to have them full and completely equipped. The large amount of arms and equipments captured here will enable me to equip these regiments as rapidly as they can be formed.

I am particularly desirous of organizing a regiment of Heavy Artillerists from the negroes to garrison this place, and shall do so as soon as possible, asking the authority and commissions for the officers named after it is organized. I will ask now if this course will be approved.

I caused an informal investigation to be had in the case of

Col. Shepard.[2] The result of it was, his release and restoration to duty. I will send the proceedings to your office for your information. I am satisfied that the whole difficulty arose from the outrageous treatment of the Black troops by some of the white ones, and the failure of their officers to punish the perpetrators when they were reported. Becoming exasperated Col. Shepard took the punishment in his own hands.

The long line of Plantations from Lake Providence to Millikens Bend, it has been perfectly impossible to give perfect protection to, during the siege of Vicksburg. Besides the gunboats, negro troops and six regiments of white troops left west of the Mississippi River in consequence of these Plantations being there, I sent an additional Brigade from the investing Army, and that at a time when the government was straining every nerve to send me troops to insure the success of the enterprise against Vicksburg. All has not been availing. I can now clean out the Tensas, and Bayou Macon country so that there will be but little difficulty in protecting what is left of the Plantations.

There are two of the Commissioners appointed by you, Field and Livermore who are doing a great deal of harm. The limits of a private letter would not suffice to describe their character, selfishness misrepresentations and impracticable characteristics for doing good to any cause. I have thought seriously of removing them from my Department and appointing officers to act in their stead until successors could be appointed by proper authority. Capt. Strickle[3] I believe to be honest and enthusiastic in the cause which he is serving. He is probaby influenced by old theories of abolishing slavery and elevating the negro but withal very well qualified to carry out orders as he receives them without reference to his private views. The capture of Vicksburg has proved a bigger thing than I supposed it would. There was over thirty one thousand rebel troops still left when we entered the city. The number of small arms will reach 50,000 stands I think, and the amount of Ordnance and Ordnance stores is enormous. Since crossing the Miss. River an army of (60,000) sixty thousand men has, in the various battles been killed wounded, captured, and scattered so as to be lost to the Confederacy, and an armament for an army of (100,000) one hunderd thousand men has departed from there forever.

My surplus troops were held in a position menacing Johnston ready to move at a moments notice when Vicksburg should fall. The moment a surrendered was agreed upon the order was given. I hope to hear to day that Johnston's forces have been broken to pieces and much of his munition of War abandoned   I have not heard from Sherman since the morning of 9th. He was then near Jackson skirmishing with the cavalry of the enemy. What was intended as a private letter General has spun out into a long semi official one which I hope you will excuse

Thanking you kindly for the assurance given in your letter of the satisfaction my course has given the Administration I remain

> Your very oddt Servt
> U. S. GRANT
> Major General

Copies, DLC-USG, V, 6, 8, 24, 94; DNA, RG 393, Dept. of the Tenn., Letters Sent.

1. On June 26, 1863, Brig. Gen. Lorenzo Thomas, Washington, wrote to USG. "I enclose a letter I a few days since received on my return from the south west, the perusal of which has caused me much regret. Dr Duncan who I had formerly known many years ago at Natchez, is a union man, and when I was on the Mississippi his plantations I understood had not been molested which I was glad to hear   The depredations referred to must have been committed after I left that section of the country   Will you please direct an enquiry into the case. I have also sent a copy of it to General Hawkins   The President and Secretary are highly pleased with your operations, which have been so successful, and they look with interest to your further progress. We hope soon to hear of the fall of Vicksburg, an ~~issue~~ event of the highest importance   A severe spell of sickness at Memphis & Louisville, compelled me to leave the south, before visiting General Rosecrans Army. I am getting well rapidly but am still very weak   I shall go to Tennessee as soon as I am well enough. Say to Col Wilson that the proper correction has been made in the extract 11 of Special Orders No. 227 of May 21st respecting Capt Badeau. I understand a Regiment of blacks (4th Mississippi) is in your rifle pits—will you please direct its commander to send me the roster of the officers that I may send the letters of appointment   I hope a 5th Mississippi may soon be formed and thus have a brigade   I had intended to recommend Col Shepard 1st Mississippi as a brigadier General to command it, but hear he is in some serious difficulty—will you inform me its nature, and whether it should prevent his advancement." ALS, *ibid.*, Letters Received. On

June 2, Mrs. Henry P. Duncan, Staten Island, had written to Thomas. "As well known & acknowledged Unionists—we received strong 'protection papers' from Genls. Grant & McPherson,—& from Admiral Porter:—but despite said 'papers' —our rights as loyal citizens have been rudely violated by certain parties—who visited our several estates, & forcibly removed nearly all the male negroes therefrom. (saving some blacks who managed to *conceal* themselves from the 'pressgang.') . . . Our negroes were freed, & working for us on wages . . . My husband (Mr Henry Duncan of Miss.) writes me of the seizure of his hired blacks & also mentions that the 'pressgang' visited his house at night,—searched the Quarters for their occupants,—& remained on his premises until daylight. . . . We (as a family) have *nine* estates on the Miss. most of them opposite Lake Providence, & they have been literally *rifled* & *stripped*.—" ALS, *ibid.* See letter to Mary Duncan, June 5, 1863. For the investigation of the complaint, see letter to Brig. Gen. Elias S. Dennis, July 11, 1863.

2. Isaac F. Shepard, born in Natick, Mass., in 1816, graduated from Harvard College and was principal of a Boston grammar school (1844–57), editor of the *Boston Daily Bee* (1846–48), and a member of the Mass. House of Representatives (1859–60). An ardent abolitionist, he moved to St. Louis in 1861 and served as aide-de-camp to Brig. Gen. Nathaniel Lyon. Appointed 1t. col., 19th Mo., Aug. 30, he was promoted to col., 3rd Mo., when the two regts. were consolidated on Jan. 18, 1862. He was appointed col., 1st Miss. of African Descent, in May, 1863, and placed in command of all black troops in the District of Northeastern La. during the absence of Brig. Gen. John P. Hawkins. A court of inquiry was ordered for June 1 at Milliken's Bend, La., to investigate charges against Shepard of "causing a soldier to be whipped in violation of law and existing orders." On June 14, the court ordered Shepard released from arrest and restored to command. Special Orders Nos. 143 (May 28), 147 (June 1), 160 (June 14), Dept. of the Tenn., copies, DLC-USG, V, 27, 28; DNA, RG 393, Dept. of the Tenn., Special Orders. For the first, see *O.R.*, I, xxiv, part 3, 356–57. On Aug. 10, Shepard wrote to USG's hd. qrs. requesting that the proceedings be published due to unfavorable accounts in the press, and on Aug. 29, Brig. Gen. John A. Rawlins endorsed the letter. "Respectfully returned. The General Commanding can see no good purpose to be subserved by the publication of the proceedings referred to at this time, and therefore withholds his consent. It should always be sufficient satisfaction for an officer of the Army to know that the result of an investigation fairly made meets with the approval of those above him, regardless of anything said by a partisan press." Copies, DLC-USG, V, 25; DNA, RG 393, Dept. of the Tenn., Endorsements. On Oct. 5, Thomas, Goodrich's Landing, La., wrote to Secretary of War Edwin M. Stanton. "When I first commenced the organization of negro regiments on the Mississippi river, Colonel Isaac F. Shepard, commanding the 3rd regiment Missouri Volunteers, presented himself with high testimonials and requested authority to raise some troops; and expressed a desire, although then a colonel, of a white regiment, to take the command of a colored one; looking forward, of course to further advancement should his zeal activity and services justify a recommendation from his superior officers. I gave him the 1st Mississippi; and he went to work with an energy which showed that his heart was in the business. I should have asked his promotion some time since, but, when in Washington, understood that he had ordered a white soldier to be whipped by blacks, which caused great in-

dignation against him in the army here. You may recollect I personally brought the case to your notice and it was determined not to appoint him brigadier general. Since my return here I have examined the case and find that Colonel Shepard when in command of the colored troops near white regiments, acted with great judgment and forbearance, when the white soldiers committed acts of wantoness against the negroes and their families. To his numerous complaints to the commanding officer no action was had, and, finding it useless to make any more, the flagrant case under consideration coming up, one calling for the severest punishment, even to the loss of life, he had the culprit tied up to a tree to be flogged. The punishment inflicted was very light and Col. Shepard soon stopped it. The Colonel asked for a Court of Inquiry which was granted, the proceedings of which I have seen and they cast no censure upon him. General Grant dismissed the case without notice and ordered the Colonel to duty—I have conversed with the President of the Court, Brigadier General T. Kilby Smith, who speaks in high praise of Colonel Shepard and of his capacity for command. Brigadier General Hawkins, his present commander also commends him for his soldierly bearing military capacity and high moral character. Colonel Shepard was made a colonel by the late lamented General Lyon at the battle of Wilson Creek, in which grade he has continued up to the present time. He was with General Sherman in the first attack upon Vicksburg and received honorable mention from that general. His case is a special one, he being the only Colonel who presented himself for a command in colored troops which gave no additional rank at a time when I needed the support and co-operation of high officers. His services with the negroes have been valuable, and no one has rendered better service in elevating them and fitting them for all the duties of soldiers. I therefore now respectfully recommend him for the appointment of Brigadier General, and, if he be appointed, request that the commission may date from the 7th of June, the day of the battle of Milliken's Bend, where, though in arrest for the case above stated, he accompanied his regiment to the ramparts and encouraged his men during that bloody fight, whilst unable to give a command." ALS, *ibid.*, RG 94, ACP, 1027S CB 1863. On Oct. 9, USG endorsed this letter. "Approved and respectfully forwarded to Hd Qrs. of the Army. Col. Shepard, from the active interest he took in organizing Colored troops, at the begining of their organization, made him prominant at the time for promotion. Although disappointed he has not abated one particle in zeal. I therefore earnestly recommend his promotion and that the recommendation of Gen. Thomas, as to date of Commission, be complied with." AES, *ibid.* Shepard was appointed brig. gen. to date from Oct. 27, but was not confirmed by the Senate, and his appointment expired July 4, 1864. See letter to Charles A. Dana, Aug. 5, 1863.

3. Capt. Abraham E. Strickle died of typhoid July 9, 1863. See letter to Brig. Gen. Elias S. Dennis, June 11, 1863, note 1; letter to Julia Dent Grant, June 15, 1863; letter to Lt. Col. Judson D. Bingham, July 21, 1863.

To Maj. Gen. Henry W. Halleck

———

Vicksburg Miss
July 11th 1863—3 P M

Maj Gen H. W. Halleck
Gen in Chief

Gen Banks writes me that he wants from ten to twelve thousand men to enable him to follow up the Enemy and to move into Texas.[1] Shall I send them? All my spare troops are now with Gen Sherman following Joe Johnston   I have had no news since the morning of the 9th   Sherman was then at Clinton, his advance skirmishing with the Enemys Cavalry

U S. Grant
Maj Genl

Telegram received, DNA, RG 107, Telegrams Collected (Bound); copies, *ibid.*, Telegrams Received in Cipher; *ibid.*, RG 393, Dept. of the Tenn., Hd. Qrs. Correspondence; DLC-USG, V, 6, 8, 24, 94. *O.R.*, I, xxiv, part 3, 498–99. On July 7, 1863, Maj. Gen. Henry W. Halleck telegraphed to USG. "Advices just recieved from New Orleans of the condition of Genl Bank's army, render it important that you send him aid if it be possible for you to do so." ALS (telegram sent), DNA, RG 107, Telegrams Collected (Bound); telegram received, *ibid.*, RG 94, War Records Office, Military Div. of the Miss. *O.R.*, I, xxiv, part 1, 62.

1. See letter to Maj. Gen. Nathaniel P. Banks, July 11, 1863.

To Act. Rear Admiral David D. Porter

———

Head Quarters, Dept. of the Ten
Vicksburg Miss. July 11th 1863.

Admiral Porter
Comd.g Miss. Squadron,
Admiral.

I am just informed that Johnston has sent a dispatch to Yazoo City to press all the negroes in the country and set them to work fortifying.[1] One thousand are said to be already collected, guarded by two regiments of Infantry. Also that their fleet of steamers have come down to that place. Johnston claims to have repulsed Sherman and captured three Brigades. As I have no news from Sherman confirmatory I doubt the truth of this statement.—Gen. Washburn informs me that the Yazoo has risen six feet. Will it not be well to send up a fleet of ~~boats~~ gunboats and some troops and nip in the bud any attempt to concentrate a force there.

I will order troops at once to go aboard of transports.

> Very respectfully
> U. S. GRANT
> Maj. Gen. Com

ALS, MdAN. *O.R.*, I, xxiv, part 3, 499; *O.R.* (Navy), I, xxv, 280–81. On July 11, 1863, Act. Rear Admiral David D. Porter, "off Vicksburg," wrote to USG. "Port Hudson surrendered unconditionally on the 7th inst. The Steamer has just brought the despatches. As Genl. Herron is already allow me to suggest that he move up the Yazoo tomorrow morning when I shall be all ready." ALS, DNA, RG 94, War Records Office, Dept. of the Tenn. *O.R.*, I, xxiv, part 3, 499; *O.R.* (Navy), I, xxv, 281. On the same day, USG wrote to Porter. "The change you suggest will be made and Gen. Herron sent to Yazoo City. Orders are now being sent to him." ALS, Brigham Young University, Provo, Utah. Also on July 11, Lt. Col. John A. Rawlins wrote to Maj. Gen. Francis J. Herron. "The fall of Port Hudson obviates the necessity of your move in that direction. Your orders are, therefore countermanded. You will proceed with your command to Yazoo City, take possession of that place, and drive the enemy from that section. Johnston is reported as having sent orders to have Yazoo City fortified. This we must not permit. Admiral Porter is sending Gun-boats to cooperate. Communicate with him, and move when he is in readiness. Take with you a Battery if you can get it aboard without too much delay" LS, NHi. *O.R.*, I, xxiv, part 3, 500; *O.R.* (Navy), I, xxv, 281.

On July 22, Porter wrote to USG. "In the late expedition up the Yazoo River a question arises with regard to property captured afloat by combined Army and Navy forces. I allude to the boat 'St. Marys' captured at Yazoo City or thereabouts. All guns munitions of war &c captured by the Navy are turned over to the Army, ~~and~~ when acting jointly, the officers and crew get prize money for vessels, to which Sailors attach great importance, even if it is only twenty five cents. The St Mary's might have been a large vessel, and therefore of value, in which case if the Army retained her the Sailors lose their prize money. I do not suppose you have ever thought of the matter, or know of the St. Marys . . ." ALS, DNA, RG 45, Correspondence of David D. Porter, Mississippi Squadron, General Letters (Press). On July 25, Herron, "Steamer Chanceller, En Route to New Orleans," submitted to Rawlins his report on the expedition to Yazoo City. LS, *ibid.*, RG 94, War Records Office, Union Battle Reports. *O.R.*, I, xxiv, part 2, 667–69; *O.R.* (Navy), I, xxv, 286–88. On July 30, USG endorsed the report. "Respectfully forwarded to Hd Qrs. of the Army." AES, DNA, RG 94, War Records Office, Union Battle Reports.

1. On July 10, Maj. Gen. Cadwallader C. Washburn, "Haines Bluff," telegraphed to USG. "An intelligent person who has just came in reports that when he left Yazoo City at five oclock last night a dispatch had been recd there from Johnson saying that he had repulsed our troops & captured three 3 brigades also that orders came there yesterday to press all the negroes to work on fortifications at Yazoo City & that 1000 were at work that two regts of Infy were there but were to march this morning   The Yazoo has risen Six 6 feet at Yazoo City   the large fleet of transports ten 10 in all all had been brought down to near Yazoo City   two other parties who are boatmen left night before last & Confirm the report about the boats   I send them all to you   Should not the gun boats go up at once"   Telegram received, *ibid.*, RG 393, Dept. of the Tenn., Unregistered Letters Received. On July 11, USG responded. "I am sending troops from here to Yazoo City." *O.R.*, I, xxiv, part 3, 502.

To Act. Rear Admiral David D. Porter

Head Quarters, Dept. of the Ten.
Vicksburg Miss. July 11th 1863.

ADMIRAL D. D. PORTER
COMD.G MISS. SQUADRON,
ADMIRAL.

Col. Smith who has just returned from Port Hudson reports that a large number of cattle are now collected at Natchez intended for the rebel army on this side of the river.[1] I have just ordered boats with a proper military force to bring these cattle for our own use. My troops will probably be ready to start in the morning. I am also sending a number of steamers, coal and forage called for by Gen. Banks. Among the many calls made for Gunboats will it be possible for you to furnish a convoy for this?

Very Truly
your obt. svt.
U. S. GRANT
Maj. Gen. Com

ALS, MdAN. *O.R.*, I, xxiv, part 3, 499; *O.R.* (Navy), I, xxv, 262. On July 12, 1863, Act. Rear Admiral David D. Porter wrote to USG. "I have but one gunboat, which was to have gone after the Cattle, and returned with the transports I have written for the Benton to come up from Red River to Natches, to remain there altogether, and this gun boat has the letter. the Benton will be in natches in 4 days from this if the gun boat goes right through with the transports, and by that time or before another one will be in, will that Suit you." ALS, DNA, RG 393, Dept. of the Tenn., Letters Received. See letter to Maj. Gen. James B. McPherson, July 11, 1863.

1. See Walter George Smith, *Life and Letters of Thomas Kilby Smith* . . . (New York and London, 1898), pp. 76–77, 321–22.

To Maj. Gen. Nathaniel P. Banks

Head Quarters, Dept. of the Ten,
Vicksburg Miss. July 11th 1863.

MAJ. GEN. N. P. BANKS,
COMD.G DEPT. OF THE GULF.
GEN.

It is with great pleasure I congratulate you upon your removal of the last obsticle to the free navigation of the Mississippi. This will prove a death blow to Copper headism in the Northwest beside proving to demoralize the enemy. Like arming the negros it will act as a two edged sword cutting both ways.

Immediately on receipt of your dispatches I forwarded them by Col. Riggin of my Staff who will take them as far as Cairo.[1] I ordered the boats and other articles you requested at once and as many of the boats as can be got ready will go down at the same time with this.—I also ordered, on the strength of Col. Smith's report, about 1000 men to Natchez to hold that place for a few days and to collect the cattle that have been crossing there for the rebel Army. I am also sending a force to Yazoo City to gather the heavy guns the rebels have there and to capture, if possible, the steamers the enemy have in the Yazoo.

Sherman is still out with a very large force after Jo Johnston and cannot well be back under six or seven days. It will be impossible therefore for me to send you the forces asked for in your letter until the expiration of that time. I telegraphed to Washington however the substance of your request and the reason for it.[2] So far as anything I know of being expected from my forces I can spare you an Army Corps of as good troops as tread American soil.

No better are found on any other. It will afford me pleasure to send them if I am not called on to do some duty requiring them.

When the news of your success reached me I had Gen. Herron's Division on board transports ready to start for Port Hudson. That news induced me to change their direction to Yazoo City.

> I am General
> Very respectfully
> your obt. svt.
> U. S. GRANT
> Maj. Gen.

ALS, PPRF. *O.R.*, I, xxiv, part 3, 499–500. On July 8, 1863, Maj. Gen. Nathaniel P. Banks, "before Port Hudson," wrote to USG. "It gives me pleasure to inform you that Port Hudson surrendered this day. We are unable to determine the number of prisoners, or extent of the armament. The Commissioners asked for six thousand rations. The surrender is in effect unconditional. I declined to stipulate for the parole of officers or men, but necessity will compel me to parole at once a considerable portion of the prisoners, selecting those representing states mainly in our control, as Louisiana, Arkansas, Etc. About 12 or 15.000 of the enemy have been threatening my communications, and have occupied the Lafourche District   I shall move against them forthwith. My disposable force is about equal to their numbers if I detain General Grierson's cavalry. This I hope to do for a term of not more than two weeks, when I will return him in good condition to your camp. He has been of infinite service, and I know not in what way we could have supplied his place. My thanks are due to Lieutenant Ulffers for valuable services. He is a patient, sound, intelligent and patriotic officer. He returns with Colonel Smith. The enemy in my rear disposed of, I earnestly desire to move into Texas, which is now denuded of troops. The enemy here is largely composed of Texans. We hope to capture them. Will it be possible for you to spare me for this Expedition, which will be closed in two months from this date, a division of ten or twelve thousand men. I know the claims upon your force: I see that you will hope to strengthen our armies in the East, and prefer my request with hesitation; but there is no point where the same number of men could do as much good. I want western men. It was my hope to join you in the contest for Vicksburg, and strengthen your command with what force I have; but it was impossible. Colonel Smith who brought me the welcome message has remained at my command; to convey to you in return the news of the surrender or capture of Port Hudson, which could not have been deferred longer than to-morrow. His visit has given me the greatest pleasure. His effectual destruction of the boats and other means of crossing the Mississippi which the enemy possessed, has been of the greatest service to us and the cause. I hope he may return safely to you." Copy, DLC-Nathaniel P. Banks. *O.R.*, I, xxvi, part 1, 624–25.

1. On July 11, USG telegraphed to Maj. Gen. Henry W. Halleck. "The following dispatch is just received from Gen. Banks. Before Port Hudson July

8th 1863 GENL. The Mississippi is now opened. I have the honor to inform you that the Garrison of Port Hudson surrendered unconditionally this afternoon. We shall take formal possession at seven o'clock in the morning. (signed) N. P. BANKS Maj. Gen" ALS (telegram sent), CSmH; telegram received, DNA, RG 107, Telegrams Collected (Bound); copies (misdated July 10), DLC-USG, V, 6, 8, 24; DNA, RG 393, Dept. of the Tenn., Letters Sent. A copy of the Banks telegram is *ibid.*, Dept. of the Gulf, Letters Sent. *O.R.*, I, xxvi, part 1, 624.

    2. See telegram to Maj. Gen. Henry W. Halleck, July 11, 1863.

To Maj. Gen. James B. McPherson

Vicksburg Miss. July 11th 1863.

MAJ. GENL. J. B. MCPHERSON
COM'DG POST AT VICKSBURG.

I am just informed that Gen. Johnston has sent orders to Yazoo City to impress all the negroes that can be collected and set them to fortifying the place. Also that 1000 are now at work, guarded by two Regiments of troops. Johnson says in his dispatch that he has repulsed Sherman, capturing three Brigades of his troops. I get nothing from Sherman, and as this news comes by way of Yazoo City, cannot believe it. I have asked Admiral Porter, however to send up a fleet of boats and I will send troops to cooperate. Send Gen Smith with as much of his command as can be spared after leaving proper guards over his camps &c. The Yazoo has risen 6 feet, so that good sized steamers can run up. I will order the Quarter Master to have in readiness transportation for 2500 men, including one battery of Artillery. These troops should return as soon as the Rebels are effectually cleaned out.

Very Respectfully
U. S. GRANT
Maj. Genl

Copies, DLC-USG, V, 19, 101, 103; DNA, RG 393, Dept. of the Tenn., Letters Sent. *O.R.*, I, xxiv, part 3, 501. See letter to Act. Rear Admiral David D. Porter, July 11, 1863.

To Maj. Gen. James B. McPherson

———

Headquarters Dept of the Tenn
Vicksburg Miss. July 11. 1863

MAJ. GENL J. B. MCPHERSON
COMDG 17TH ARMY CORPS.
GENERAL.

Col Smith who has just returned from Port Hudson, informs
me that the rebels are crossing a large number of cattle at Natches.
There are several thousand there now which I propose to send and
bring away.

Eight hundred or one thousand men, with one battery of artillery will be sufficient to send.[1] Col Bingham is instructed to furnish the necessary transportation for the troops and to bring the
cattle back. Make the order for this number of men with a discreet
officer to command. Send the officer who will command this expedition to report to me for special instructions.

U S. GRANT
Maj. Genl.

Copies, DLC-USG, V, 19, 101, 103; DNA, RG 393, Dept. of the Tenn., Letters
Sent. On July 11, 1863, Maj. Gen. James B. McPherson issued Special Orders
No. 135. "Brig. Gen. T. E. G. Ransom will detail from his command 800 men
and a battery of artillery, provided with 100 rounds of ammunition and five
days' rations, to be employed on an expedition to Natchez, Miss., for the purpose of collecting beef-cattle, &c. The quartermaster of the department will
furnish transportation. The expedition will be placed in command of a discreet
colonel, who will at once report to Major-General Grant for special instructions."
O.R., I, xxiv, part 3, 501–2. See letter to Act. Rear Admiral David D. Porter,
July 11, 1863.

1. On July 20, Lt. Col. John A. Rawlins wrote to Brig. Gen. Thomas
E. G. Ransom. "You will remain with your command in the occupation of
Natchez until further orders. Lieut. Col. Macfeeley, Chief of Subsistence has
been directed to send forward commissary supplies for you." Copies, DLC-USG,
V, 19, 101, (dated July 21) 103; DNA, RG 393, Dept. of the Tenn., Letters
Sent. For reports by Ransom of activities around Natchez, Miss., see O.R., I,
xxiv, part 2, 680–82, 685–86.

To Maj. Gen. William T. Sherman

Vicksburg Miss, July 11. 1863

DEAR GENERAL

Dispatches just received from Gen Banks announces the good news of the surrender of Port Hudson with 5000 prisoners, and all the armament of the place. News came from the East of the defeat of Lee and his precipitate retreat with Mead in full pursuit.

I have heard nothing definite from you since the morning of the ninth, but not hearing suppose all is right. Is there any probability that Johnson may be securing reinforcements, and intends standing? I have just learned from Yazoo that all the steamers from above have come down there, and that Johnson has sent orders to press all the negroes that can be got to prosecute the work of fortifying with all Vigor. More than a thousand negroes are said to be at work now. I immediately ordered a Division from here to break them up.

The well prisoners have now been paroled, and about all are out of town. The number reached near 25.000. There is still those in hospital near 6000 yet to parole, besides many escaped without paroling.

Hoping to hear of your giving Johnston a good threshing, and driving him beyond Pearl River, with the loss of his artillery, transportation and munitions of war I remain

Yours truly

U. S. GRANT

Maj Genl

Copies, DLC-USG, V, 19, 101, 103; DNA, RG 393, Dept. of the Tenn., Letters Sent. *O.R.*, I, xxiv, part 3, 501. On July 9, 1863, Maj. Gen. William T. Sherman, Clinton, telegraphed to USG. "Steeles advance entered Clinton at 3 oclock last night skirmishing with the enemys cavalry. At Day break this mornig Ords advance arrived and his Corps now 7 A m is passing through Clinton on the Main Road. Generals Steele and Parke are reconnoitrig for a seperate Road north of the Railroad & parallel. We have to march at night—days are intensely hot. Otherwise all well." ALS (telegram sent), DNA, RG 94, War Records Office, Union Battle Reports; telegram received, *ibid.*, Dept. of the Tenn. *O.R.*, I, xxiv, part 2, 521.

On July 11, Sherman wrote to Lt. Col. John A. Rawlins that his "forces arrived before Jackson, yesterday forenoon," and that he wanted "another Division on the Road from Champion hills to Clinton to guard the Communications, and a depot of supplies kept at the Railroad Bridge on Black River." ALS, DNA, RG 94, War Records Office, Dept. of the Tenn. *O.R.*, I, xxiv, part 2, 521–22. On July 12, 10:00 A.M. and noon, Sherman, "Before Jackson," telegraphed to USG. "I gave the Enemys line & town an hours Cannonading this mornig with our Rifled Guns. I have the Canton Road (Parke) about 1½ miles from State House, the Clinton Road to the Hospital (steele) and the Raymond Road & Railroad north to the House where we were May 14th.—all telegraphs & Railroad north & south are broken *good* and Cavalry is out Extending the damage. I am now manoeverig on the Pearl River to reach the East. Will keep troops well in hand. News from all quarters glorious. As usual my 20 pr Parrott Guns use too much ammunition. Please send to Black River Bridge 4000 20 pr Parrott ammunition, 10 000. six pr Shells, and a million of musket cartridges assorted to be sent me in case I call, or you suppose me in want. Events resemble much our position at vicksburg except I have not assaulted, and we have sustained very little loss. Three wagons gatherig forage to our Rear, yesterday were captured by guerillas & burned.—No other losses on the Road." "Port Hudson beig ours, and Holmes repulsed at Helena, the Missouri forces should be pushed to Little Rock at once. Mobile should be attacked also from the direction of New Orleans, and when it is taken we could move on Selma. I fear the weather is too hot for me to march to Grenada. Would it not be better to move on Grenada from Memphis, and on Columbus Mississipi from Corinth, leaving me to fight Johnston according to circumstances and to destroy the Central Road as far as Canton and Black River. . . . Harrisonburg Louisiana—should be attacked by a Brigade. It would parallyse the Washita Country. Cant Grierson join me by Land. . . . All is well with me now. I have ten days supplies. Will send my supply train to Black River under good escort, as soon as unloaded." ALS (telegrams sent), DNA, RG 94, War Records Office, Dept. of the Tenn.; telegrams received, *ibid. O.R.*, I, xxiv, part 2, 522–23. Probably on July 12, Sherman sent another telegram to USG. "If you have not made other arrangements I would be obliged if you would give my Corps the flank of Vicksburg in front of my old Lines, viz Fort Hill resting on the River above town. Especially the Hill in front of Woods Brigade. Order all the Hospitals, Quarter Masters Camps, and all stragglers and persons whatsoever to be assembled inside and under command of some officer to guard the parapet and man the Guns. This arrangemet will make useful a class of men not otherwise of any account. The Hospital at Chickasaw Bayou should also be moved inside. I fear the filling the country with parolled prisoners will do us no good, but I wont let any pass into Jackson." ALS (telegram sent, dated July 14), DNA, RG 94, War Records Office, Dept. of the Tenn.; telegram received (dated July 12), *ibid.* Dated July 14 in *O.R.*, I, xxiv, part 2, 524. In response to the first telegram, Rawlins wrote on the same day to 1st Lt. James H. Burdick. "Send immediately by rail, to Big Black River Railroad Bridge, for Major Genl Sherman, 4000 rounds 20 pdr parrot ammunition, 10.000 rounds 6 pdr shells, and 1,000,000 rounds of musket cartridges. Call of Col. Coolbaugh, Superintendent of Railroad for cars. Quarter Masters Department will furnish teams to move it to the Depot." Copies, DLC-USG, V, 19, 101, 103; DNA, RG 393, Dept. of the Tenn., Letters Sent. On July 13, Sherman, "Before Jackson," telegraphed to USG. "All well with us   all are strengthening

their battery & rifle pits prior to a genl. Cannonade as soon as the train is known
to be near with a re-supply   I will continue to threaten the Rail way beyond
Real [*Pearl*]   Pemberton is crossing with his paroled pisoners about ten miles
below Jackson   Busey has returned   he burned two locomotives & a dozen cars
several bridges & tore up track to Canton but found Canton occupied by a
brigade & deemed it ~~unimpudant to~~ imprudant to attempt it or the brdge beyond   I will destroy this Railroad certain but the Cavalry has not the dash to
do the work   Cannot Grierson be brought up here? In a month he could make
the state of Miss. forever useless to the rebels"   Telegram received, *ibid.*, RG 94,
War Records Office, Dept. of the Tenn. *O.R.*, I, xxiv, part 2, 523–24.

On July 12, Sherman telegraphed to USG. "General Lauman in taking posi-
tion to day got his Line, uncovered by skirmishers too close the enemys Lines and
Suffered considerably. Loss not yet ascertained. Col Gresham is reported Killed.
Lieut Adams of the artillery was Killed the first day, and Lt Nelson of the Regu-
lars   The ground to the Right is so wooded that Gen Ord has been unable to
ascertain Laumans Loss. Johnston evidently intends to make a strong fight at
Jackson, behind his parapet. He may endeavor to operate outside with Cavalry.
With plenty of Rifle ammunition I can make the town pretty hot to live in. I
have published all the good news to our troops." ALS (telegram sent), DNA,
RG 94, War Records Office, Dept. of the Tenn.; telegram received, *ibid. O.R.*,
I, xxiv, part 2, 522. On July 13, Sherman telegraphed to USG. "The paroled
prisoners will go to Brandon via Raymond   Pemberton wrote to Gen Johnstone
reporting his position & line of march & sent a Captain to bear the letter to
Johnstone but I would not let him pass in but sent him back with a short note to
Pemberton saying I could not permit it   I have already broken up the ferry
where that road crossing & dont See how Pemberton can cross Pearl River but
he must Manage that as he best can   Col Gresham was Not Killed yesterday   it
was col Earle   Killed wounded & missing yesterday ~~Amount~~ amount to 350
nearly all confined to Laumans Command who got his line too close to the enemies works   Ord has relieved Lauman & sent him to vicksburg   I approve
because I want the corps Comdrs to be satisfied with their division Comdrs
when McArthur comes up I will press the right & reach the bridge across Pearl
River   the army inside Jackson lays close behind its entrenchments" Telegram
received, DNA, RG 94, War Records Office, Dept. of the Tenn. *O.R.*, I, xxiv,
part 2, 523. On July 12, elements of Brig. Gen. Jacob G. Lauman's div. came
too close to C.S.A. lines at Jackson, sustaining 441 casualties in a few minutes,
forty percent of the casualties suffered by Sherman's forces in the Jackson
campaign. See *ibid.*, pp. 550, 597–99, 603–5. On July 15, Rawlins issued
Special Orders No. 191. "Brig. General J. G. Lauman, U. S. V., will proceed
to the State of Iowa and there await orders. He will take with him his personal
Staff." Copies, DLC-USG, V, 27, 28; DNA, RG 393, Dept. of the Tenn., Special
Orders. *O.R.*, I, lii, part 1, 413. On July 14, and again on July 28, Sherman indicated to USG that confusing orders may have caused Lauman's misadventure,
but he believed it necessary to sustain Lauman's relief by Maj. Gen. Edward
O. C. Ord, commander of the 13th Army Corps. See letters to Maj. Gen. William
T. Sherman, July 13, 17, 1863. Ord, however, believed that Lauman, in addition to being incompetent, had acted in violation of orders. See *O.R.*, I, xxiv,
part 2, 574–76. On July 25, Ord wrote to Rawlins. "The Corps needs efficient
Brigadier Generals *very* much. There are none for the command of Brigades,
or will be none when Genl. Lee is assigned to the command of Genl. Hovey's

Division. Thus I have thirteen Infantry Brigades commanded by Col's and Lieut. Cols.—absent of course from the command of their Regiments,—and on some occasions when a Division is left without a General, or it becomes necessary to remove the General of it, there is absolutely no officer of sufficient rank or experience to assign in his place. The want of one efficient Division Commander has recently resulted in great loss of life and severe disaster." ALS, DNA, RG 393, Dept. of the Tenn., Letters Received. On July 19, Rawlins wrote to Ord, informing him of the assignment of Brig. Gen. Marcellus M. Crocker to command Lauman's div. LS, IaHA. On July 21, Crocker, Vicksburg, wrote to Brig. Gen. Grenville M. Dodge. "I arrived here, day before yesterday, and found the City warm dusty and generally as disagreeable as possible. I have been assigned to the Command of Laumans division (the 4th) at present attached to the 13th Army Corps (Gen Ord's) I have not reported for duty yet but am waiting for the Corps to return from Jackson, will probably start out in that direction to meet it tomorrow. Our old friend Lauman has been relieved for blundering like an old ass, as he is, upon the enemy strongly posted with a battery, his skirmishers being advanced about thirty yards so that he was cut up before he knew what was the matter. he thinks he exercised abundance of caution and that great injustice has been done him. . . ." ALS, *ibid.* On July 20, Maj. Gen. Stephen A. Hurlbut wrote to USG. "I saw Lauman a few minutes on his way home. I judge from all I can learn that a very needless slaughter of good men took place by some one's fault or negligence. I write now to request that in reassigning the troops to the several Corps you would do me the favor of placing the fourth Division in the Corps Commanded by Genl. Sherman. As I suppose they are not likely to return I consider that this will be the best disposition that can be made of them for the public service. The troops know & love Genl Sherman & will do better under him than any other man" ALS, DNA, RG 393, Dept. of the Tenn., Letters Received. On July 28, Maj. Theodore S. Bowers issued Special Orders No. 204 transferring the 4th Div. to the 13th Army Corps. Copies, DLC-USG, V, 27, 28; DNA, RG 393, Dept. of the Tenn., Special Orders. On July 28, Ord apparently preferred formal charges against Lauman. DLC-USG, V, 22; DNA, RG 393, Dept. of the Tenn., Register of Letters Received. On Aug. 31, Rawlins wrote to Lauman. "By direction of Maj. Genl U S. Grant I now send herewith Charges and Specifications preferred against you by Maj Genl E. O. C Ord Commanding 13th Army Corps, with the request that you report in person, as soon as practicable that the investigation or trial may be had before the proper court." Copies, DLC-USG, V, 19, 103; DNA, RG 393, Dept. of the Tenn., Letters Sent. On Sept. 26, Rawlins issued Special Orders No. 264. "Brig General J. G. Lauman with his Staff will proceed without delay to Natchez Miss. and there await the convening of a General Court Martial for his trial on charges preferred against him by Maj Genl. E O. C Ord. The Quartermaster will furnish him transportation." Copies, DLC-USG, V, 16, 28. On Oct. 27, Maj. Robert Williams, AGO, telegraphed to USG. "I am directed to inform you that the order directing General Lauman to relieve General Hatch at Philadelphia has been countermanded—" LS (telegram sent), DNA, RG 107, Telegrams Collected (Unbound); copies, *ibid.*, RG 393, Military Div. of the Miss., Telegrams Received; DLC-USG, V, 40, 94. On Dec. 28, Hurlbut telegraphed to USG. "Genl Lauman is here sick with orders from the Adjutant Generals office to rejoin his command—He does not know that he has any at present will you desegnate what he shall do" Telegram received, DNA, RG 393, Dept. of the Tenn., Telegrams Received;

copies, *ibid.*, 16th Army Corps, Letters Sent; *ibid.*, Military Div. of the Miss., Telegrams Received. Lauman, although mustered out on Aug. 24, 1865, with the bvt. rank of maj. gen. "for gallant and meritorious service during the war," did not hold an active command after the incident during the Jackson campaign.

To Brig. Gen. Elias S. Dennis

Headquarters Department of the Tennessee
Vicksburg Miss. July 11. 1863

BRIG. GENL E. S. DENNIS.
COMDG DIST N. E. LA.
GENL.

I have received a letter from Washington[1] stating that the Duncan estate has been visited by the Press Gang or recruiting parties from your District, and their negroes carried off. The Duncan's have been loyal from the beginning of the rebellion and as loyal persons have had safe guard given them by myself and Admiral Porter;[2] and I have further received instructions from Washington to protect all loyal persons found in the South and mentioning the family of Duncans in particular as being entitled to protection. They have gone so far as to acknowledge the freedom of their slaves, and made as I understand regular contracts with them to pay wages and employ them, just as negroes are being employed on the leased plantations.

I want the matter fully investigated, and a report made to me. Send some officer immediately to Duncans to inquire for the facts. If their negroes have been carried off, find out where they are and who carried them off. Return to them as far as possible everything that has been taken. Arrest the parties engaged in this transaction, and all officers among them send to me under guard.

Very Respectfully
U. S. GRANT
Maj. Gen.

Copies, DLC-USG, V, 19, 101, 103; DNA, RG 393, Dept. of the Tenn., Letters Sent. *O.R.*, I, xxiv, part 3, 500–1. Under orders from Brig. Gen. Elias S. Dennis, 2nd Lt. George C. Lockwood, act. aide-de-camp, proceeded to the Duncan plantation at Skipwith Landing, Miss., and discussed the charges with Henry and Stephen Duncan, Jr. On July 19, 1863, Lockwood reported to 1st Lt. William E. Kuhn, act. adjt. to Dennis, that a number of Henry Duncan's Negroes had been forced into service on April 12 by soldiers of the 8th La. Vols. of African Descent. Lockwood then proceeded to Milliken's Bend, La., where the regt. was stationed, to investigate the matter further. The soldiers in question asserted that they had been forced into service. The co. officer responsible, however, had been killed in action on May 27. Lockwood also learned from the Duncans that the 1st Ark. Vols. of African Descent had stolen a number of hams from the plantation. The offending officer had been arrested at the time of the incident by Brig. Gen. Hugh T. Reid but no charges were preferred. The officer was too ill to be arrested by Lockwood. ALS, DNA, RG 393, Dept. of the Tenn., Letters Received. Also on July 19, Col. Hiram Scofield, 8th La., wrote to asst. adjt., District of Northeastern La. "Enclosed you will please find the statements of officers of this Regmient with regard to a matter the investigation of which has been made ordered by Maj Genl Grant—I refer to the charge of the exercise of undue means to on the part of an officer of this Regmient to procure recruits from the 'Duncan Plantations' In justice to the officer—now deceased having lost his life from wounds received in defence of his country—it is due me to say there was no better officer in the regiment & his personal appearance and known character in the Regmient would go far to disprove any charge of the kind I was with the Regmient at or about the time the recruits were received into the Regmient—concerning the means of getting which there is complaint—no complaints were made to me as it would seem to me there would have been had they (men) been forced into the regmient against their will—for the men were always very free to lay all their complaints before me The negro race—as every one acquainted with it knows—has very strong attachments for family—and a negro will risk his liberty and life for his family—The men now connected with this Regmient are absent from their families and are feeling very desirous of seeing them as they have been unable to do for since the Regmient left Lake Providence—the result is that they will resort to almost any means to get back to see them and in my opinion this motive went far to cause them to make the declarations they did as to their being forced into the service" ALS, *ibid*. USG took no further action on the matter.

1. See letter to Brig. Gen. Lorenzo Thomas, July 11, 1863.
2. On March 14, Act. Rear Admiral David D. Porter wrote to USG. "Major Hammond tells me he is going up on Sunday in a transport. Could I ask of you the favor to let the boat stop at Mrs. Duncan's place, and give her a passage north. This agreeable lady thinks she is under your and my protection, which she assuredly is. If Mrs. Duncan is not ready, I propose placing a Gunboat at her disposal. Will you please allow the transport to deliver a letter to the Gunboat 'Curlew' at Skipwith's Landing." LS, DNA, RG 109, Union Provost Marshals' File of Papers Relating to Individual Citizens.

To Maj. N. G. Watts

Head Quarters, Department of the Tennessee,
Vicksburg, Miss., July 12, 63.

MAJOR N. G. WATTS,
COMMISSIONER FOR EXCHANGE OF PRISONERS OF WAR, &c.,
C. S. A.,
MAJOR:

The acceptance by Lieutenant General Pemberton of the terms proposed to him for the surrender of this City on the 4th inst., making any person in the city connected with the Confederate Army, a Prisoner of War, and desiring as an act of courtesy to release you from the obligation of absaining from further duty until properly exchanged, I wish now to release you unconditionally, from such obligation.

You may then Major regard yourself and the two gentleman now serving with you as assistants, as fully and unconditionally released from the time you pass outside of our lines.

> I have the honor to be
> Very Respectfully
> Your obt. serv't.
> U S GRANT
> Major General.

Copies, DLC-USG, V, 19, 101, 103; DNA, RG 393, Dept. of the Tenn., Letters Sent. *O.R.*, II, vi, 108.

To Maj. Gen. Cadwallader C. Washburn

July 12th 1863

GEN. WASHBURN,

I am compelled to send McArthurs Division forward to join Sherman. I can send but one Brigade from here to relieve him and

must therefore call on you for another. Send as soon as possible
~~reporting~~ the commander reporting by courier in advance to Mc-
Arthur for his location.

U. S. GRANT

Maj. Gen.

ALS, DNA, RG 94, War Records Office, Dept. of the Tenn. *O.R.*, I, xxiv, part 3,
505–6. On July 12, 1863, Maj. Gen. Cadwallader C. Washburn, "Haines Bluff,"
telegraphed to USG. "I shall have a brigade in motion in a few minutes   As I
understand it they are to releive Genl McArthur who I suppose to be at Shermans
crossing of Black River   They will move as rapidly as possible to that point via
Tiffin I have no artillery to send I have despatched a courier to Genl
McArthur"   Telegram received, DNA, RG 393, Dept. of the Tenn., Telegrams
Received.
    On July 11, Lt. Col. John A. Rawlins wrote to Brig. Gen. Elias S. Dennis.
"You will order Mouers. Brigade and the 108th Ill to move to this place at once,
bringing with them their Camp and garrison equipage and Sick. They will report
on arrival here to Maj. Genl. J. B. McPherson for location and orders. The Quartermaster's Dept. will furnish them the necessary transportation." Copies, DLC-
USG, V, 19, 101, 103; DNA, RG 393, Dept. of the Tenn., Letters Sent. On July
12, USG wrote three times to Brig. Gen. John McArthur. "Mouer's Brigade will
leave here at day light in the morning. You will move out as early as possible, leaving an officer to put Mouer's Brigade, when it arrives, in position." "Hold yourself
in readiness to move forward towards Jackson, as soon as troops arrive to relieve
you. Report by courier to Gen. Sherman at once for orders when to go. Troops will
probably reach Black River tonight." "One Brigade goes from here by Railroad
and one Brigade marches from Snyder's Bluff to relieve your Division. They are
ordered to report to you for location. You will designate what they are to guard,
and turn over such orders as you have received from Gen. Sherman"   Copies,
ibid. O.R., I, xxiv, part 3, 505.
    On July 17, USG wrote to Washburn. "Johnstone evacuated Jackson last
night. You need not now move to Black River but may move your command to
any healthy location in this direction leaving a sufficient guard for public property
left behind." ALS, DNA, RG 94, War Records Office, Dept. of the Tenn. *O.R.*,
I, xxiv, part 3, 526. See letters to Maj. Gen. William T. Sherman, July 17, 1863.

To Maj. Gen. William T. Sherman

———

Head Quarters Dept. of the Tenn.
Vicksburg Miss July 13. 1863

MAJ. GEN. W. T. SHERMAN,
COMDG ARMY INVESTING JACKSON, MISS.
GENERAL:

The object of the expedition you are commanding, being to break up Johnstons Army and drive it from our rear, and if possible to destroy the rolling stock, and everything valuable for carrying on War or placing it beyond the reach of the Rebel Army. You may return to Vicksburg as soon as this object is accomplished. Being on the spot, you will know better than I can how far your Cavalry should be sent either east or north. I do not think it necessary to send the Cavalry further than Black River Bridge. In case you send them there after starting back here yourself it might be better to let them return to Vicksburg by the roads west of the Black.

Do you think Johnston is receiving reinforcements? or is he simply holding Jackson until the road east of him is completed, so that he can get off all the rolling stock now on this side? Can you make a safe retreat to the Big Black if it is found Johnston is receiving reinforcements from the East.

I would not advise your Infantry going any further East than they now are, except you should find it advantageous to hasten the retreat of the enemy. Should you find it impossible to drive Johnston from his position and yours, and your remaining to endanger either it or this place, you can then return.

I have sent Mower's Brigade, and one Brigade from Kimballs Division to relieve McArthur, and ordered the latter forward.[1] The remainder of Kimballs Division is still disposable, but there is no other force here to spare well.

I send this by Capt Audenreid[2] of my staff, who will remain with you for a day or two.

An intercepted letter from Jeff Davis to Lee, was sent me from

Washington.³ From that it would seem that Lee has been asking for Beauregard to be sent to Culpepper C. H. with an army of 30.000. Davis speaks of the impossibility of doing so and says Johnston is still calling for more reinforcements though his first requisition had been more than filled. He does not say whether he will still send more troops west—but from the alarm expressed in the letter for the safety of Richmond, I judge Johnston can expect nothing more

Capt Audenried will give you any news there is here.

Very truly yours

U. S. GRANT

Maj. Genl

Copies, DLC-USG, V, 19, 101, 103; DNA, RG 393, Dept. of the Tenn., Letters Sent. *O.R.*, I, xxiv, part 3, 507–8. On July 14, 1863, Maj. Gen. William T. Sherman telegraphed to USG. "Capt Auderied is here   I will answer at length tonight   I think I have troops enough   I don't think Johnston can under present Circumstances get any more reinforcements & with plenty of ammunition I have the town too hot to hold him   In the meantime I am destroying the railroad North & South most effectually"   Telegram received, DNA, RG 94, War Records Office, Dept. of the Tenn. *O.R.*, I, xxiv, part 2, 524. On the same day, Sherman wrote to USG. "Yours of yesterdays date is received and I avail myself of the opportunity to describe more fully, than I have hitherto done, the operations up to this date, and the present attitude of affairs, that you may give me Orders or advice.—The first hint of the Capitulation of Vicksburg reached me from you by Telegraph on the 3d day of July, when I was in person at Tribles place near Bear Creek, with troops disposed from Haines Bluff to the Big Black at the Rail-Road crossing.—I immediately concentrated on the three best points for passing Black River, viz: at the Rail Road crossing, at Messengers Ford and at Birdsongs Ferry.—At the two latter points I had constructed bridges, and by the 6th of July the 13th Army Corps, General Ord, had reached the Rail Road crossing— the 15th Army Corps, General Steele, Messengers,—and the 9th Army Corps, General Parke, Birdsongs.—All the heads of Columns crossed Black River the evening of the 6th and on the 7th marched to Boltons Depot, each keeping different roads.—The weather was so intensely hot, that it would have been fatal to push the Troops.—During the evening and night of the 7th all the Columns marched opposite Clinton, where we rested and formed the Columns for battle, all the evidence being, that General Johnston in strong force was in our front, determined to resist our entering Jackson.—Early the morning of the 9th all moved forward in close supporting distance, Ord on the Right, Steele on the Centre and Parke on the Left.—The enemy had Cavalry videttes and small guards to our front, but they retired rapidly before us and by 9½ A. M. of the 9th we drew the Artillery fire of the Batteries at Jackson.—I soon satisfied myself, that General Johnston had taken refuge in Jackson, that he had resolved to fight behind intrenchments, and that his intrenched position was the same, substantially, that we found last

May, only that it had been much strengthened and extended, so that its flanks reached Pearl River.—The works were too good to be assaulted, and Orders were given to deploy and form lines of circumvallation about fifteen hundred yards from the enemys parapet, with skirmishers close up, and their supports within five hundred yards, also that each Corps should construct covered Batteries for their guns, and trenches for their men. All the troops took up their positions with comparative ease, and little loss, save the Division, Commanded by General Lauman, of Ords Corps, which by the obscure character of the ground, its trees and bushes, advanced too near the enemy's parapet without proper skirmishers deployed and received the cross fire of his Artillery and Infantry, causing considerable loss of life.—The exact extent of this loss has not been reported, but will not fall much short of four hundred.—General Ord has relieved General Lauman of the Command of the Division, and I deem it so important, to support Corps Commanders in their authority, that I must sustain General Ord for the time being.—Having invested the place, I ordered Colonel Bussey, Chief of Cavalry, with his Cavalry Force, numbering about one thousand effectives to proceed to Canton and destroy the Cars, Locomotives, Rail Roads and Machine shops there, and proceed on to the Black River Bridge and destroy that.—He has returned— having found Canton occupied by a force too large for him to attack—and he did not go to the bridge at all, as he deemed it unsafe to pass so considerable a force by the flank—but he destroyed two locomotives and fourteen box Cars at Calhoun Station.—At the same time, the Cavalry Force, attached to Genl. Ords Corps, were despatched South—this party has also returned, having burned five bridges on the road out for fifteen miles.—We have also in our possession here about twenty platform Cars, which will be completely burned; and two Brigades are kept on daily duty, burning the Rail Road ties and iron, North and South, with Orders to completely destroy it for ten miles each way, so that a very fair beginning has been made towards the destruction of this Railway; but I am determined, that it shall be so effectually destroyed that it cannot be repaired during the war.—A force of five hundred Cavalry with four guns and five wagons will start to morrow South for Brookhaven, with orders, to destroy the road at many places, especially at Gallatin and Brookhaven—and Colonel Bussey's Cavalry with Woods Brigade of Infantry, and Landgraebers Battery of Light Artillery will also be despatched again to Canton, to destroy that place with all its machinery and Rail Roads and then to proceed to the bridge, twelve miles beyond, and burn it. Thus I hope to make a break of one hundred miles in this great Central Rail Road, to be so effectually destroyed, that the enemy will not even attempt its reconstruction.—General McArthurs Division is on the road, two Brigades at Clinton and one at the Champion Hills, so disposed, as to insure the safety of our Trains against the enemy's Cavalry, of which I can learn but little.—There is a Division of Cavalry, Commanded by General Jackson, two Brigades, commanded by Whitfield and Cosby, containing I think about three thousand men. Cosby is—I suppose at Canton and the bridge, and Whitfield is East of Pearl River, guarding the Rail Road back to Meridian—with some scattered squads, hanging about the Country. Our foraging parties now go out about fifteen miles but are invariably guarded by a Regiment of Infantry. We are absolutely stripping the Country of Corn, Cattle, Hogs, Sheep, Poultry, every thing and the new growing Corn is being thrown open as pasture fields, or hauled for the use of our animals.—The wholesale destruction, to which this country is now being subjected, is terrible to contemplate; but it is the scourge of war, to which ambitious men have appealed rather than the judgment of the learned and pure Tribunals, which our forefathers had provided for supposed wrongs and injuries.—Therefore so much of my instructions as contemplated destroying and weakening the resources of our enemy are being executed with rigor, and we have also done much towards the destruction of Johnstons Army.—If he waits a day or two, I will so threaten his Rear, that he will be compelled to come out and fight or run, and in either event I feel confident of success.—I know, that much plunder has been sent by him to the East of Pearl River, but his Army is still in Jackson and several very heavy guns are mounted at the Salients, and reply to our fire. Their parapets also are well manned; and our sharpshooters are closing nearer and nearer and becoming familiar with their respective Fronts. We are now ready for a sally—and if he attempts to escape, we ought to detect the movement very early and will of course take advantage of it.—Captain Audenreid of your Staff is here, and will examine our lines to-morrow and carry this Report to you with a map of our position, compiled from partial surveys, and all other available sources.—I will also send by him all the lists of casualties, thus far sustained, that I can obtain of Corps and Division Commanders.—The Field labors of all are so arduous and constant that I know, General Grant will overlook the want of more accurate, detailed Reports till the issue of this Campaign is reached.—" LS, DNA, RG 94, War Records Office, Union Battle Reports; ADfS, Sherman Family Papers, InNd. *O.R.*, I, xxiv, part 2, 525–27. On July 16, USG forwarded the letter to Maj. Gen. Henry W. Halleck. ES, DNA, RG 94, War Records Office, Union Battle Reports.

On July 14, USG telegraphed to Sherman. "Do you think Johnstone is reinforcing so as to require more troops? If it becomes absolutely necessary I will send everything but one Brigade and the Convelescents from here." ALS (telegram sent), *ibid.*, Dept. of the Tenn. *O.R.*, I, xxiv, part 3, 509. On the same day, 8:00 P.M., Sherman answered. "All is well with us   I think I have troops enough   Johnstone is still in Jackson & our skirmishers are engaged all around the lines & but little execution done by either party. Our lines of investment are well covered by rifle trenches. We are now firing every five minutes from four different Batteries day & night & as soon as the ammunition train is up will increase the fire   We now reach Pearl river above & below the town   I do not think Johnstone is receiving reinforcements   at all events he has manifested no intention to sally & has permitted us to Surround him with parapets   a brigade is breaking R R both ways & as soon as I know our Ammunition train is coming I will send a good brigade & arty & Cavalry to complete the destruction of Canton & Black River bridge also a cavalry party to Brookhaven South" Telegram received, DNA, RG 94, War Records Office, Dept. of the Tenn.; copies, *ibid.*, Union Battle Reports; *ibid.*, RG 393, Dept. of the Tenn., Telegrams Sent. *O.R.*, I, xxiv, part 2, 524–25.

On July 11, Maj. Gen. Stephen A. Hurlbut telegraphed to Lt. Col. John A. Rawlins. "A passenger just down on the Graham says that at Columbus Genl. Asboth shewed him a dispatch just recd from Buford in Cairo. 'Genl Dix telegraphs from Fort Monroe that our forces occupy Richmond' " ALS (telegram sent), DNA, RG 393, Dept. of the Tenn., Telegrams Received. On July 14 or 15, Sherman telegraphed to Rawlins. "Good for Richmond   I never attached much importance to the place but tell me the facts of Lee's army the moment you hear   if that can be broken up & destroyed with our sucessess out west will make an impression in Rebeldom & the world   tell the genl I have heard of his appointment as maj gen in Regular army   Of course I congratulate him & hope he may live long to enjoy the Ease & luxury of the position   I think we are doing well out here but wont pay till Johnstone cleans out & stops shooting his big rifle guns at us   If he moves across Pearl River & makes good speed I will let him go   By a flag of truce today I sent him our newspapers of 7th & 8th that with our cannon tonight will desturb his Slumbers" Telegram received (dated July 15), *ibid.*, RG 94, War Records Office, Dept. of the Tenn.; copy (dated July 14), *ibid.*, RG 393, Dept. of the Tenn., Telegrams Sent. Dated July 14 in *O.R.*, I, xxiv, part 2, 527.

1. See letter to Maj. Gen. Cadwallader C. Washburn, July 12, 1863; see also following letter.

2. Joseph C. Audenried of Pa., USMA 1861, was appointed 2nd lt., 1st Cav., June 24, 1861, and had been promoted to 1st lt., 6th Cav., on the same day. He held various staff appointments in the Army of the Potomac and was promoted to staff capt. as of Aug. 20, 1862. On April 21, 1863, USG wrote to Col. John C. Kelton. "Capt. J. C. Audenried Additional Aid de Camp on the Staff of Maj. Gen. Sumner and now with Gen Wool has written letters expressing a desire to be placed on duty in this Dept. If consistant with the interests of the service I would be pleased to have him assigned to me. This Department is deficient in officers eligable for the position of Asst. Com.y of Muster and if in no other way he could be of service in that capacity." ALS, Mrs. Walter Love, Flint, Mich. On June 20, Rawlins issued General Orders No. 39. "Capt. J. C. Audenreid U. S. A. and Aid-de-Camp, appointed under the act July 17th 1862, to Maj. Gen. Sumner, having reported in person to these Headquarters, in pursuance of orders from the Adjutant General's Office, Washington, D. C., is hereby announced as Aid-de-Camp to the Major General Commanding, and will be respected and obeyed accordingly." Copies, DLC-USG, V, 13, 14; DNA, RG 393, Dept. of the Tenn., General and Special Orders; (printed) USGA.

3. On July 4, Kelton wrote to USG. "I am directed by the General-in-Chief to forward to you for your information the enclosed copies of important intercepted letters from President Davis and General Cooper." LS, DNA, RG 94, War Records Office, Dept. of the Tenn. The two letters enclosed, President Jefferson Davis to Gen. Robert E. Lee, June 28, and Gen. Samuel Cooper to Lee, June 29, indicated that C.S.A. resources were stretched to the limit. Copies, *ibid. O.R.*, I, xxvii, part 1, 75–77.

To Maj. Gen. William T. Sherman

July 13th 1863

Gen. Sherman,

McArthur left Black River at 5 this morning. Mowers Brigade and one of Kimballs relieved him. I have written to Banks to send Griersen up but do not believe he will send him.[1] Ransom has gone to Natchez to destroy ferries and bring up beef cattle collected there for Johnston. Herron has gone to Yazoo City to break up that place. On his return I can send you Kimballs Division if you want it.

U. S. GRANT
Maj. Gen.

ALS, DNA, RG 94, War Records Office, Dept. of the Tenn. *O.R.*, I, xxiv, part 3, 508. On July 13, 1863, Brig. Gen. John McArthur telegraphed to USG. "My Command moved from here this morning at five oclock   Chambers brigade crossed at Messengers ferry   will join us at Edwards Depot. I have left an officer to post the other troops as they arrive." Telegram received, DNA, RG 94, War Records Office, Dept. of the Tenn.

1. See letter to Maj. Gen. Nathaniel P. Banks, July 10, 1863.

To Maj. Gen. Francis J. Herron

Head Quarters, Dept. of the Ten.
Vicksburg Miss, July 14th 1863.

MAJ. GEN. HERRON,
COMD.G YAZOO EXPEDITION,
GEN.

You may remain in Yazoo City as long as Admiral Porter thinks it necessary to save all that can be saved from the sunken gunboat, or leave such a force as may be necessary for the protection of those engaged in that work and return with the balance of your command.

Bring with you such Government stores as you can and destroy all others. You may bring also the cotton mentioned in your letter and particularly bring all the negro men you can.

I do not want you to remain longer at Yazoo City than may be absolutely necessary because it may become necessary for me to send all the forces that can be possibly spared to Jackson.

Very respectfully
U. S. GRANT
Maj. Gen. Com

P. S. Two Regiments will be enough to leave at Yazoo City while the gun-boats remain there. You will return here with the remainder of your command, as you may be needed below.

U. S. GRANT
Maj Gen.

ALS, NHi. *O.R.*, I, xxiv, part 3, 509.

To Maj. Gen. William T. Sherman

———

July 14th 1863

MAJ. GEN. SHERMAN.

Two men who left Canton on Saturday morning report but few troops there. A large amount of rolling stock was sent North of the Yalobusha, some on each of the roads. When Johnston went into Jackson he sent all his cattle and wagon train from Canton directly East to the Mobile road. They say he would not have stood in Jackson only his troops said they would not go back.

U. S. GRANT
Maj. Gen.

ALS, DNA, RG 94, War Records Office, Dept. of the Tenn. *O.R.*, I, xxiv, part 3, 509.

To Surgeon John Moore

———

Head Quarters, Dept. of the Ten.
Vicksburg Miss. July 14th 1863

SURGEON J. MOORE
MEDICAL DIRECTOR,
SIR:

Gen. Smith,[1] C. S. A. complains that the prisoners in hospitals, in many cases have not received proper supplies of either medicine or food. In some cases the sick have only had hard bread and pork although requisitions have been sent to the Medical Purveyor for articles required.

I wish you would have this matter inquired into as soon as possible and have every thing necessary for the health and comfort of those confined in hospital supplied. Let me know the facts about these supplies being furnished as soon as you can.

Very Respectfully
U. S. GRANT
Maj. Gen. Com

ALS, PHi. See letters to Maj. Gen. Nathaniel P. Banks, July 16, and to C.S.A. Maj. Gen. Martin L. Smith, July 24, 1863.

1. On July 12, 1863, Maj. Gen. Martin L. Smith wrote to USG. "I am under the impression that parolled or non-parolled prisoners leaving Gen'l. Pemberton's command without authority, will endeavour to cross the Mississippi at or near the following points above and below this city, to wit: Lake Providence, Greenville, Milliken's Bend, Young's Point, Warrenton, Grand Gulf, Port Gibson, Natchez. If orders covering this extent o[f] river, have not been given to arrest all said prisoners, permit me to request that as far as practicable they be given, and that all boats armed and unarmed as well as all officers and men be directed to capture whenever and whereever met and return them to this point." LS, DNA, RG 393, Dept. of the Tenn., Letters Received. On July 14, Smith wrote to USG. "I have the honor to enclose a statement from Surgeon Boyd C. S. A regarding his detention in place of two Surgeons U. S. A thought to be detained in Jackson. I have no knowledge of these cases, but take the liberty of requesting that surgeon Boyd, if to be kept as a hostage, be allowed to report himself at some hospital here, where his services may be of benefit to the sick and wounded, until further investigations may be had. Surgeon Boyd informs me that although permitted to pass around the City during the day, it is on condition of reporting at Short intervals to the jail Guard, by whom he is confined at night subject to great discomfort and exposed to the weather. I do not think injustice would be done any one were he unconditionally released, but should it be deemed your duty to further detain him, I trust the request made in his favor may be complied with" ALS, *ibid.*, RG 94, War Records Office, Dept. of the Tenn.

To Maj. Gen. Henry W. Halleck

Vicksburg Miss
July 15th 1863 10 A M

MAJ GEN H W HALLECK
GEN-IN-CHIEF

Genl Sherman has Jackson invested from Pearl River on the north to the River on the south. This has cut off many Hundred cars from the Confederacy—Sherman says he has force enough and feels no apprehension about the result

Finding Yazoo City was being fortified I sent Gen Herron there with his Division[1] He captured several Hundred prisoners one steamboat five pieces heavy Artillery and all the public stores fell into our hands   The Enemy burned three steamboats on the approach of the Gunboats.

The DeKalb was blown up and sunk in fifteen feet of water by the explosion of a torpedo—Finding that the enemy was crossing cattle for the rebel Army at Natchez and were said to have several thousand there now, I had sent steamboats and troops to collect them and to destroy their boats and all means for making more

Genl Banks has made requisition on me for Steamboats, coal, and forage which I have sent

Shall I send the Ninth Army Corps back to Burnside so soon as Johnston is driven from Jackson?

U. S. GRANT
Maj Genl Comdg

Telegram received, DNA, RG 107, Telegrams Collected (Bound); copies, *ibid.*, Telegrams Received in Cipher; *ibid.*, RG 393, Dept. of the Tenn., Hd. Qrs. Correspondence; DLC-USG, V, 6, 8, 24, 94. *O.R.*, I, xxiv, part 3, 512–13. See telegram to Maj. Gen. Henry W. Halleck, July 18, 1863.

1. See letter to Act. Rear Admiral David D. Porter, July 11, 1863.

To Maj. Gen. Francis J. Herron

Head Quarters, Dept. of the Ten.
Vicksburg Miss July 15th 1863.

MAJ. GEN. HERRON,
COMD.G YAZOO EXPEDITION,
GEN.

The enemy's Cavalry 4000 strong have crossed Pearl River fourteen miles above Jackson evidently with the intention of geting to the rear of Sherman to opperate on his waggon trains. Whilst it is necessary for you to keep a force at Yazoo City move Eastward with all the force not necessary to leave back so as to attract the attention of this Cavalry. It will only be necessary for you to go Eastward about twenty or twenty five miles, or to a point east of Black River where if you can hear of this Cavalry you can threaten them. The entire object of this move is to protect Shermans wagon train from the rebel Cavalry. You will therefore be governed in your movements accordingly. You need not stay out to exceed four or five days.

> Very respectfully
> U. S. Grant
> Maj. Gen. Com

ALS, DNA, RG 94, War Records Office, Dept. of the Tenn. *O.R.*, I, xxiv, part 3, 513. Probably on July 15, 1863, Lt. Col. John A. Rawlins telegraphed to Maj. Gen. Cadwallader C. Washburn. "Is there a steamboat at your landing? Please ascertain immediately and if so detain her until further orders. A̶n̶s̶" Telegram received, DNA, RG 393, Dept. of the Tenn., Telegrams Received. Washburn answered Rawlins on the same day. "There is a boat here that can be had for any service" Telegram received, *ibid.* Also on July 15, USG telegraphed to Washburn. "You will please forward the above dispach by boat immediately to Gen Herron at Yazoo City. *Russh*" Telegram received, *ibid.*; copies, *ibid.*, Letters Sent; DLC-USG, V, 19, 101, 103. Washburn, "Haines Bluff," telegraphed to USG on the same day. "Dispatch for Gen Herron recd   boat tempest will leave Soon as she can get up steam" Telegram received, DNA, RG 393, Dept. of the Tenn., Telegrams Received.

On July 16, Maj. Gen. Francis J. Herron, Yazoo City, telegraphed to USG. "I have just recd your order and will march in one hour taking with me seven regts Infy & four pieces of artillery leaving brig Genl Orme with one regt & f̶i̶ five pieces at this place   my route will be south of Benton crossing Black River at or near warsaw   I shall go to canton or near that place & will c̶o̶m̶e̶ carry out your orders. in regard to the cavalry force there is no force of the enemy near here except a small body of Cavalry at Alexandria   Capt Walker arrived yesterday afternoon with your first order & I had prepared to leave intending to move at 10 oclock this morning. they are making very good progress in getting out the guns from the DeKalb & will finish tomorrow   I send down by this boat the well prisoners I have taken viz: 122 privates & 7 officers   I have paroled One officer and o̶n̶e̶ 146 men from the hospitals   I shall cross Big Black tomorrow." Telegram received, *ibid.*, RG 94, War Records Office, Dept. of the Tenn. *O.R.*, I, xxiv, part 3, 519–20; *O.R.* (Navy), I, xxv, 289.

To Maj. Gen. James B. McPherson

Head Quarters, Dept. of the Ten.
Vicksburg Miss. July 15th 1863.

Maj. Gen. J. B. McPherson,
Comd.g 17th Army Corps.
Gen.

Some ladies just in from eight miles in the country applying for a guard at their house state that guards are at almost every house through the country. That the negroes are armed and wors than the straggling soldiers. I wish you would instruct your Cavalry to patroll the country as much as possible and bring in all guards and send them to their regiments and all stragglers and armed negroes and put them at work in the city. It is highly probable that most of the guards are self constituted guards. In that case they should be punished same as stragglers.

Very respectfully
U. S. Grant
Maj. Gen. Com

ALS, Lincoln Memorial University, Harrogate, Tenn. On July 15, 1863, Maj. Gen. Edward O. C. Ord telegraphed to USG. "Can you collect my stragglers in some suburb under such officers as may be with them & send them out here   twelve hundred 1200 from Laumans Division remained behind four hundred from Smith & Hoveys Each & Several hundred from Bentons" Telegram received, DNA, RG 393, Dept. of the Tenn., Telegrams Received. On July 17, Lt. Col. John A. Rawlins ordered Maj. Gen. James B. McPherson to "assume temporary command of all the troops in the vicinity of Vicksburg, belonging to the 13th, 15th, and 16th Army Corps, left behind when their corps moved against Johnston." All officers and men found in the area without proper authority were to be arrested and put to work cleaning the streets. Copies, DLC-USG, V, 19, 101, 103; DNA, RG 94, War Records Office, 17th Army Corps; *ibid.*, RG 393, Dept. of the Tenn., Letters Sent. *O.R.*, I, xxiv, part 3, 520–21.

To Maj. Gen. John M. Schofield

Head Quarters, Dept. of the Ten.
Vicksburg Miss. July 15th 1863.

MAJ. GEN. J. M. SCHOFIELD,
COMD.G DEPT. OF THE MO.
GEN.

Your letter of the 8th inst. is just received. In answer I will give you a brief statement of the position of affairs here.

During the siege of Vicksburg I had a large surplus of troops over what was required to make the investment complete. These troops occupied a line from Haines Bluff to Black River, across which Johnston would have to move to reach Vicksburg, or the rear of the investing Army. Sherman commanded all these forces and held them in readiness to move the moment Vicksburg should fall into our hands. Accordingly on the 4th inst. he started. As soon as the City capitulated I ordered the whole of Sherman's and Ord's Corps, forming about two thirds of the investing Army, to move out and join Sherman. They started the night of the Fourth. A portion of McPhersons Corps was already with Sherman. This left me at this place but six small Brigades. Hearing that the enemy were fortifying Yazoo City most vigerously I sent two of them to that place. They captured it with conciderable stores, five or six pieces of Artillery and several hundred prisoners, but one of the gunboats accompanying the expedition being sunk by the explosion of a torpedo I shall have to leave them there until the Armament and machinery of the vessel can be got away. I have also sent a Brigade to Natchez to collect a large number of Texas cattle supposed to be there destined for Johnstone's Army. This you will see leaves me no force to move with until Sherman returns. When this will be it is hard to tell. Johnstone commenced to fall back from the Big Black the moment he heard of the surrender of Vicksburg. As all his droves of cattle, and wagon trains that fell back via Canton, were ordered East to the Mobile & Ohio road he could not have intended to make a determined stand. He drew all his troops however inside the entrenchments of Jackson and remains there yet. Sherman has him closely invested from the Pearl River on the North to the river on the South. By this an immense deal of rolling stock has been separated from the Confederacy, both North and South of Jackson, and the roads so completely destroyed as to render them forever useless. How long this siege will last it is impossible to say. When Johnston is driven from his position however I will have troops available for anything that will go to put down the rebellion. I suppose the 9th Army Corps will have to be sent back to Burnside and 10 to 12 thousand effective men sent to Banks. But for the expedition you speak of, unless other orders should come from Washington, I will still have force enough.

Kirby Smith has been hovering around on the opposite side of the river, with his Head Quarters at Monroe, and his force scattered from St. Josephs to Floyd. It has been my intention to pay him a call as soon as possible but I now learn, and I believe reliably, that all his scattered forces are called in and the whole are moving to Schrieveport La. The object of the move I dont see unless it is to avoid being hurt.

I have not paid any special attention to the Geography of the opposite side of the river but suppose that at this season of the year White River would have to be used as a base for supplies to reach Little Rock. The Arkansas can hardly be used until the Fall rains set in. You will see from the foregoing statements that I can give you nothing definite of future opperations yet. As soon as I possibly can I will do so.

Nothing like five hundred wagons will be required with this Army to prepare it for any move and should any be required it would probably be only the wagons and Harness without the animals.

I am General, Very respectfully
your obt. svt.
U. S. GRANT
Maj. Gen.

ALS, St. Louis Public Library, St. Louis, Mo. *O.R.*, I, xxii, part 1, 19–20; *ibid.*, I, xxiv, part 3, 516–17. On July 8, 1863, Maj. Gen. John M. Schofield, St. Louis, wrote to USG. "I congratulate you most heartily upon your glorious triumph at Vicksburg. I desire, General, as soon as possible to commence active operations in Arkansas, now that you have removed the obstacle which has so long stood in our way, and forced us to remain comparatively idle. You are aware that since active operations in this Department ceased last winter nearly all the troops in my Department except those necessary for police duty have been sent to reinforce your Army, with the understanding that as soon as Vicksburg should fall, they, or a sufficient portion of them would be sent back into my Department. It occurs to me that the concentration of the rebel forces near the river in the vicinity of Vicksburg may force you to keep all your present forces on or near the river for some time to come. I do not desire to ask anything which will in any way embarass your operations, but simply to inform you what I am prepared to do, and to gain similar information from you so far as your operations affect mine, and thus be prepared to act promptly in harmony with you. It is very important with reference to my Department to occupy the line of the Arkansas river as soon as possible. This can be done by the use of the Arkansas river if it be navigable at this season, or if not then the White river as far as Duvals Bluff, and the Rail-Road, or even wagon road from that place to Little Rock. The force which will be required for this purpose will depend upon operations up the Ouachita and Red Rivers, but I presume will in no case be very large. I have a Cavalry Division full Five thousand strong now operating in South East Missouri and North East Arkansas, which is ready to move across the Country and join a force of Infantry and Artillery at any point on the Arkansas or White River as soon as you can send such force. I have also small bodies of troops in South West Missouri, and the Indian Country ready to advance and occupy the Country south of them as soon as we get possession of the Arkansas River. I have directed the Quartermaster in St Louis to send you Five hundred wagons and teams for your own operations, and will probably have enough left to supply the forces which are to operate in Arkansas. Please inform me, General, what you will be able to do, and give me details as to time &c, as far as possible   I would like to suggest Maj. Genl. Steele as a suitable officer to command the force to be sent into Arkansas." LS, DNA, RG 393, Dept. of the Tenn., Letters Received. *O.R.*, I, xxii, part 1, 18–19.

On July 10, Schofield wrote to Maj. Gen. Henry W. Halleck enclosing a copy of his letter to USG of July 8. Copy, DNA, RG 393, Dept. of Mo., Letters Sent. *O.R.*, I, xxii, part 2, 361–62. On July 17, Halleck wrote to Schofield. "Your letter of the 10th, enclosing one of the 8th to Genl Grant, is recd. Your views in regard to operations in Arkansas agree mainly with those which I have expressed to Genl Grant, and I hope he has been able to commence carrying them out by this time. Helena has been indicated as the starting point. I shall probably hear from him in a few days." ALS, DNA, RG 108, Letters Sent (Press). *O.R.*, I, xxii, part 2, 379–80. See letters to Maj. Gen. Henry W. Halleck, Maj. Gen. John M. Schofield, and Maj. Gen. Stephen A. Hurlbut, July 21, 1863.

To Maj. Gen. William T. Sherman

———

July 15th 1863

Gen. Sherman,

Some paroled officers who have afflicted families to take out have just been to see me for permission to buy forage from us beyond Jackson saying that we would have the place to-morrow or next day and they might be compelled to go by their private conveyances the whole length of the Southern road. May not Johnstons sending his Cavalry to this side of the river mean a retreat and he adopting this course to cripple you to prevent pursuit? Herron[1] is ordered Eastward towards Canton from Yazoo City but I fear he will be to late to intercept Johnstons Cavalry.

U. S. Grant
Maj. Gen. Com

ALS, DNA, RG 94, War Records Office, Dept. of the Tenn. *O.R.*, I, xxiv, part 3, 514. On July 15, 1863, USG wrote again to Maj. Gen. William T. Sherman. "If the Cavalry of the enemy have crossed to this side of the river cant you throw a force to the East side and destroy their trains?" ALS, DNA, RG 94, War Records Office, Dept. of the Tenn. *O.R.*, I, xxiv, part 3, 513. On the same day, Sherman, "Before Jackson," twice telegraphed to USG, the second time at 8:30 P.M. "A deserter just in reports a heavy cavalry force of four thousand (4000) having crossed Pearl river from the east to the west 15 miles north of us no doubt to operate on our train   If yazoo force moves in direction of Black River bridge It will draw off this force from our roads" "Have sent a brigade to Clinton to protect our trains on the road. Col Woods Brigade & Busseys Cavalry will move up pearl at Daylight to watch the point where this cavalry has crossed & will push up to Canton & Big Black Bridge   Col Woods is notified that Herron is moving out from Yazoo City. If Johnstone is going to make a retrograde movement I hope to detect it promptly. Although the wooded nature of the outskirts covers the interior of the city also the camp fires & Burning Railroad ties have so filled the air with smoke that we see but little I will have the pickets notified to watch close & report any change   All their heavy guns are still in position" Telegrams received, DNA, RG 94, War Records Office, Dept. of the Tenn.; copies, *ibid.*, RG 393, Dept. of the Tenn., Telegrams Sent. *O.R.*, I, xxiv, part 2, 527. Probably on July 15, Sherman telegraphed again to USG. "I have placed a brigade of Infy at Clinton & send before day another brigade up the west side of pearl to destroy the bridge by which they passed & await the trains with artillery ammunition before attempting to pass to the East of Pearl river   the man who brought the news is identified as belonging to our 3d Iowa

& is there for & is Entitled to credit" Telegram received (dated July 15), DNA, RG 94, War Records Office, Dept. of the Tenn.; copy (dated July 17), *ibid.*, RG 393, Dept. of the Tenn., Telegrams Sent. On July 18, 4:00 P.M., Sherman, Jackson, telegraphed to USG. "Just heard from Canton My party was to enter at daylight. Herron was within Six miles of Canton All well" Telegram received, *ibid.*, RG 94, War Records Office, Dept. of the Tenn.; copy, *ibid.*, RG 393, Dept. of the Tenn., Telegrams Sent. *O.R.*, I, xxiv, part 2, 529. On July 19, Sherman telegraphed to USG. "The following is this minute recd from col Bussey all good" Telegram received, DNA, RG 94, War Records Office, Dept. of the Tenn.; copy (incomplete), *ibid.*, RG 393, Dept. of the Tenn., Telegrams Sent. On July 18, Col. Cyrus Bussey, Canton, telegraphed to Sherman. "I entered canton yesterday morning without po opposition we destroyed five Locomotives fifty cars burned 13 machine Shops & rail road buildings & destroyed a large quantity of the rail road track we burned the black River bridge & one mile of trestle work near it & the depot at Ways Bluff we captured 60 prisoners Herron got to Moores ferry on black River night before last but did not come over nor, did nor did he communicate with me we will camp tonight at Grants Mills & reach Jackson tomorrow morning" Telegram received, *ibid.*, RG 94, War Records Office, Dept. of the Tenn.

1. See letter to Maj. Gen. Francis J. Herron, July 15, 1863.

To Act. Rear Admiral David D. Porter

Head Quarters, Dept. of the Ten.
Vicksburg Miss. July 16th 1863.

ADMIRAL D. D. PORTER,
COMD.G MISS. SQUADRON,
ADMIRAL,

Capt. Owens letter of the 15th to you is just received. There will be boats continuously passing from this out between this and New Orleans, one starting in the morning. Such persons as are thought to be proper characters to travel upon them either by Naval or Military commanders will be allowed to do so so far as my command goes. I presume Gen. Banks will admit within his Department such persons as have passes either from the Naval or or Military authority.

Gen. Ransom will be returning from Natchez in a few days and will not fail to make a effort to capture any Artillery he may hear of above that point. Sherman is now sending troops South from Jackson to Brookhaven and will capture any Artillery there may be there.

> Very Truly your obt. svt.
> U. S. GRANT
> Maj. Gen.

ALS, deCoppet Collection, NjP. On July 14, 1863, Act. Rear Admiral David D. Porter wrote to USG. "A party of guerrillas about 1,000 strong have assembled at Ashwood, below Carthage with field pieces, for the purpose of firing into transports; they have their camps at Bayou Bedell, as near as I can ascertain they are engaged in driving in mules and negroes and also calculate to make an attack on Young's Point, and carry off the negroes there. A man by the name of O'harb, acts as a spy for them and comes into Young's Point for rations and keeps the rebels regularly informed of what is going on there: he lives three miles below Bower's Landing. I will endeavor to send a gunboat to protect the Cattle Steamers as they come up. The Carondelet is lying within two miles of Ashwood, and I will move her down closer; though I do not want her to lose sight of the Indianola. If you have a force to spare the Carondelet could ~~carry~~ cover them, if you wish to chase these fellows out." LS, DNA, RG 45, Correspondence of David D. Porter, Mississippi Squadron, General Letters (Press).

To Maj. Gen. Nathaniel P. Banks

Vicksburg Miss July 16th 1863

MAJ. GEN N. P. BANKS
COMD'G DEPT. OF THE GULF.
GENERAL.

The wounded and sick rebels in Hospital here have proven themselves so troublesome, that I acceded with great promptness to the proposition from Gen. M. L. Smith (rebel) to move them all, who may be unable for land carriage, to Mobile, Alabama and Monroe La.[1] I send Col. Lagow of my staff with the first batch. I have nothing but ordinary river steamers to send these Mobile prisoners in, and it may be unsafe for such steamers to run outside the Balize. In this case, General, may I ask that you will authorize the transfer of these prisoners, from the River steamers to suitable vessels for carrying them to Mobile either by Lake Ponchetrain or directly out of the mouth of the river.

All my force except a portion of the 17th Army Corps are with Sherman after Johnston. As soon as Johnston learned of the surrender of Vicksburg, he commenced a retrograde movement. All his beef cattle, and a large part of his wagon train is understood to have fallen back by way of Canton, with orders to push on to the Mobile and Ohio road. This would look as if he had not intended to stop short of that road. He has however drawn all his forces, supposed to be about 45,000 in number inside the fortifications at Jackson, and seems determined to make a stand there   Sherman has entrenched himself outside, and now has Jackson invested from the river above the City to the river below. I sent you all the steamers that could be got ready, as soon as your requisition was received.[2] More can go now as soon as a convoy can be had. Any of the steamers going down with wounded men, suitable to your purposes can be retained if you wish.

> I am, General, very respectfully,
> Your Ob't. Servt.
> U. S. GRANT
> Maj. Genl.

Copies, DLC-USG, V, 19, 101, 103; DLC-Nathaniel P. Banks; DNA, RG 393, Dept. of the Tenn., Letters Sent. *O.R.*, I, xxiv, part 3, 518–19. On July 18, 1863, Brig. Gen. Charles P. Stone, Port Hudson, wrote to USG. "During the temporary absence of the Major General Commanding, I have had the honor to receive Clonel Lagow of your Staff, who arrived here this morning with a steamboat load of sick and wounded prisoners. He was immediately dispatched to New Orleans, where he will doubtless receive all facilities for transporting his charge to Mobile according to your wishes. A portion of Grierson's Cavalry has doubtless arrived today at your Head Quarters, having been sent on the steamer Planet the day before yesterday. General Grierson himself with most of the remainder of his command leaves today on the steamer 'Imperial.' By the same steamer, and under the escort of Grierson's Cavalry, are sent twenty two (22) commissioned officers of the rebel Army, prisoners, including Brigadier-General-Beall and Staff. A list is enclosed. You will greatly oblige Major-General Banks by forwarding these prisoners up the river to such point as may have been disignated by the War Department. A steamboat laden with cattle arrived here this morning from Natchez, forwarded by Brigadier General Ransom. Our forces here are engaged in destroying the works of attack recently constructed for the reduction of the place, and in putting the lines in a state of defence, so that a smaller force can maintain the position. Hoping to soon receive cheering accounts of success on

General Sherman's line of operations, and congratulating you most sincerely on the recent mark of recognition of your services by the Government" LS, DNA, RG 94, War Records Office, Dept. of the Tenn. *O.R.*, I, xxvi, part 1, 644–45. See following letter.

1. See letter to Surgeon John Moore, July 14, 1863. On July 14, Lt. Col. John A. Rawlins wrote to Lt. Col. Judson D. Bingham. "You will get a steamer in readiness as soon as possible, to move six hundred confederate sick to New Orleans, and report here the name of the Boat, and at what hour it will be ready." Copies, DLC-USG, V, 19, 101, 103; DNA, RG 393, Dept. of the Tenn., Letters Sent.

2. See letter to Lt. Col. Judson D. Bingham, July 16, 1863.

To Maj. Gen. Nathaniel P. Banks

Headquarters Dept of the Tennessee
Vicksburg Miss July 16, 1863

MAJ. GEN N. P. BANKS
COMDG DEPT OF THE GULF.

Your letter of the 12th received at the hands of Maj. Lister[1] of your Staff is just at hand. I had written a letter for you which will explain the present position of all my forces and the impossability of sending you any troops just now.

Ten steamers have been sent to Port Hudson and others are about ready, discharged, to send, also all the coal forage and barges that can possibly be spared for the present. Coal and forage are looked for daily however and as soon as it arrives, it shall be forwarded.

I regret, General my inability to send you troops but my letter sent by Col. Lagow will explain to you that if I was to send the last man here it would scarcely make the number you wish. There is no material change in affairs at Jackson except the enemy has crossed a large force of Cavalry to this side of the River which was said this morning to be near a train of ordnance stores and provisions going towards Jackson. It would hurt Sherman materially to loose this train. I have not to exceed 1500 effective Cav-

aly with the whole of the army with me, and all that is now at
Jackson

> I am, General, very respectfully
> Your obt servt
> U. S. GRANT
> Maj. Gen

Copies, DLC-USG, V, 19, 101, 103; DLC-Nathaniel P. Banks; DNA, RG 393,
Dept. of the Tenn., Letters Sent. *O.R.*, I, xxiv, part 3, 519. On July 12, 1863,
Maj. Gen. Nathaniel P. Banks wrote to USG. "I have this evening the first intelligence from New Orleans for more than a week. The enemy, taking advantage of
the preoccupation of my entire available force in the siege of this place, had, as you
are aware, thrown a heavy force, (probably 7000 men, but estimated as high as
13000) into the Lafourche Country, had attacked Donaldsonville meeting a severe
repulse, and had planted batteries on the river some miles below Donaldsonville so
as effectually to interrupt our communication with the City. As soon as possible
after the surrender, I sent the First and Fourth Divisions down the river to land
at Donaldsonville. I have no official reports, but the steamer brings news that the
enemy has spiked his heavy guns and fallen back from the river. It is certain that
the steamers were unmolested. Before the movement I requested Admiral Farragut to send all his light draught gunboats round, by way of the Gulf, into Berwick
Bay to intercept the enemy's retreat, by way of Brashear City, while my troops
occupy and push him in front. My chief embarrassment is the great want of
water transportation. The movement of the two Divisions without their baggage
eighty miles, has occupied nearly three days, and in that time my troops with
all their equipage marched ninety miles from Opelousas to Alexandria. I also
need more troops at once to enable me to follow our success up to the entire destruction of the enemy's forces in this Department. I have the honor to request
that, if you can possibly spare them you will send me as quickly as practicable, a
full Division of Infantry, embarked on two classes of transports; one with strong
decks, for the transportation of Artillery and Cavalry, the other of very light
draught, suitable for the navigation of Bayoux and shallow lakes. I shall be very
glad if you send down with this Division, a small force of cavalry, as I made
arrangements which will enable you to expect the return of Brigadier General
Grierson with his command to your Head Quarters within a week from this time.
I have plenty of Artillery. Barges are also much needed, of a kind which can be
easily towed, transporting Artillery forage and coal; and coal is urgently required
for the steam transports. If twenty good barges could be immediately laded with
hay, oats, corn and coal, bothe the barges and their cargoes would be of great
service. As a matter of secondary importance, I would like to have, very much,
three small steam tug boats of light draught and good speed, to be used as despatch
boats. I trust it will be in your power to send me the troops and steamers at once.
I am much gratified to hear of your continued success and the more than full
confirmation of the mgnitude of your achievement." Copy, DNA, RG 393, Dept.
of the Gulf and La., Letters Sent. *O.R.*, I, xxiv, part 3, 504–5.

On July 18, Banks wrote to USG. "The substance of your communication has
been sent me by telegraph and I shall receive the papers themselves by the first
Transport from Port Hudson—accept my thanks for the Steamers ordered to report

to me. They will be of great service. I am glad to assure you that I can get along, with the force I have for the present without serious difficulty—The enemy is in force—about 8000 probably—in the La Fourche district, but can do no harm. They may escape capture. My troops are too much disabled by a campaign of four months to proceed against them directly. My intention is to get possession of Bewicks Bay and the Atchafaleya River and thus hold them. My troops being concentrated at Donaldsenville on the Mississippi, to prevent their escape in that direction—I can wait I think safely the result of your operations with Johnston. Then I pray you give me your aid. The Corps you propose to send me will be of infinite assistance. It is my belief that Johnston when defeated by you, as I am confident he will be, will fall back upon Mobile—Such is also the expectation of the Rebels. The capture of Mobile, is of importance, second only in the history of the war, to the opening of the Mississippi. I hope you will be able to follow him. I can aid you somewhat by land & sea, if that shall be your destination—Mobile is the last stronghold in the west and south west No pains shd. be spared to effects its reduction. I beg you general to accept my congratulation on the triumphant success of your campaign, and the assurance of my very great pleasure in being able to co operate with you." ALS, DNA, RG 94, War Records Office, Dept. of the Tenn. *O.R.*, I, xxiv, part 3, 527–28. On July 25, Lt. Col. Richard B. Irwin, adjt. to Banks, wrote to USG. "I have the honor to communicate by direction of the Major General Commanding this Department, the following telegram from him. New Orleans July 25th 1863 To COLONEL R. B. IRWIN A. A. G. The enemy having been driven from the Lafourche Country, there is no immediate necessity for General Grants troops. Send word to him that we will rest for the present. (signed) N. P. BANKS M. G. C." Copy, DNA, RG 393, Dept. of the Gulf and La., Letters Sent. *O.R.*, I, xxiv, part 3, 551.

1. G. Norman Lieber, son of the distinguished jurist Francis Lieber, born at Columbia, S. C., in 1837, graduated from South Carolina College in 1856 and received a law degree from Harvard in 1858. He practiced law in New York City until his appointment as 1st lt., 11th Inf., as of May 14, 1861. After serving in the peninsular campaign in Va. in 1862, he served as an aide to Maj. Gen. Henry W. Halleck for three months. Appointed judge advocate of vols. and maj. as of Nov. 13, he transferred to the Dept. of the Gulf.

To Col. Lucius F. Hubbard

———

[*July 16, 1863*]

COL L F HUBBARD
BIG BLACK RIVER BRIDGE
The officer in command of ~~The Officer~~ the Brigade at Messengers had orders to report to Genl McArther. You will send a courier to communicate with him at once, & convey to him my orders, which are that he send all but one Regt of his Brigade to

Big Black Rail road bridge, and send two Regts of your command immediately to Champion Hills, and the remainder of your Brigade to the other side of Big Black when the ~~one~~ fr troops from Messengers arrive to releive you

U. S. GRANT
Maj Genl

Telegram sent (in the hand of Lt. Col. John A. Rawlins), DNA, RG 393, Dept. of the Tenn., Telegrams Received; copies, *ibid.*, Letters Sent; DLC-USG, V, 19, 101, 103. Lucius F. Hubbard, born in Troy, N. Y., in 1836, moved to Chicago in 1854. In 1857, he moved to Minn., where he established the *Red Wing Republican* and participated in the affairs of the Minn. Republican Party. He enlisted as a private, 5th Minn., on Dec. 19, 1861, and was promoted to capt. as of Feb. 4, 1862, lt. col. as of March 24, and col. as of Aug. 30. For a report of his activities during the Vicksburg campaign, see *O.R.*, I, xxiv, part 1, 767–69. On July 16, 1863, Hubbard, "Big Black," telegraphed to Rawlins. "Two of my regts have started for champion Hills I have communicated with the brigade at Messengers three regts from there will be here tomorrow a m how far out do you wish the remainder of my brigade to go" Telegram received, DNA, RG 393, Dept. of the Tenn., Telegrams Received. USG's answer was drafted by Rawlins at the foot of the telegram. "The remainder will go as far as champions Hill to join those now marching there unless other orders should be sent you by Genl sherman" ADf, *ibid.*; telegram received, *ibid.*, 16th Army Corps, 1st Div., 2nd and 3rd Brigades, Telegrams Received. Hubbard telegraphed Rawlins again on July 16. "The Brigade at Messengers has not reported here has any portion of it orders to move to champion Hills The Brigade that has been at champion Hills moved forward this morning with the supply train" Telegram received, *ibid.*, Dept. of the Tenn., Telegrams Received. On July 17, Col. William H. Graves, Big Black Bridge, wrote to Rawlins. "I have the honor to report the arrival at this point of Three (3) regiments of my command, as per telegraph order of Genl Grant, recd. last evening—One regiment remains at Messengers Bridge—If you think it consistent, I should like a section of artillery for Messengers Bridge, and one company of cavalry to patrol the river & carry despatches &c—I understand Col. Hubbard leaves two sections of 'Taylors Battery' here; If so, I think twill be sufficient, but in case it don't remain, should like a battery sent to me—Of which I can send one or two pieces to Messengers—The river can be forded very conveniently above Messengers ford—I should like instructions relative to the issuing of rations to Citizens and negroes—" ALS, *ibid.*, Letters Received.

On July 16, Hubbard telegraphed to Rawlins. "Gen Taylor of the C. S. A parolled at Vicksburg is outside my lines with a flag of truce bearing a letter from Genl Pemberton to Genl Grant requesting permission for the bearer to pass to Vicksburg to communicate with Genl Smith regarding the rolls of parolled prisoners Shall I let him pass" Telegram received, *ibid.*, Telegrams Received. On July 17, Rawlins wrote to Hubbard. "Genl Taylor cannot be permitted to come within our lines. Any communication he may have or desires to send Genl Smith you will forward; open under cover to these Head Quarters, either by telegraph or courier as he may indicate; and the answer will be returned in same manner"

ALS, *ibid.*, RG 94, War Records Office, Dept. of the Tenn. *O.R.*, I, xxiv, part 3, 521. On the same day, USG wrote to Hubbard. "Permit Gen. Taylor to come into the city by the cars." ALS, DNA, RG 393, Dept. of the Tenn., Telegrams Received. *O.R.*, I, xxiv, part 3, 521.

To Lt. Col. Judson D. Bingham

Head Quarters, Dept. of the Ten.
Vicksburg Miss. July 16th 1863.

Lt. Col. Bingham
Chief Q. M. Dept.
Col.

Gen. Banks has sent a letter renewing his requisition for steamers adding to it for coal, forage and barges of light draft suited to the transportation of Artillery. You may send him all those things you can. The General also calls for light draft tugs to be used as dispatch boats. These we have not got.

Some of the boats required are large fine Mississippi River steamers and some of small size and light draft suited to the navigation of bayous and shallow lakes.

Let me know what has been done for Gen. Banks and what can be done.

Yours &c
U. S. Grant
Maj. Gen. Com

ALS, Goodspeed's Book Shop, Inc., Boston, Mass. See letter to Maj. Gen. Nathaniel P. Banks, July 16, 1863.

To Maj. Gen. William T. Sherman

July 17th 1863.

Gen. Sherman,

Dont destroy any cars at Jackson nor the road East near Jackson whilst you occupy ~~Jacks~~ the place. Destroy it far off to the

East if you can. If Johnston was pursued would it not have the effect to make him abandon much of his train and many of his men to desert? I do not favor marching our men much but if the Cavalry can do anything they might do it.

I leave this to your judgement with the superior opportunities you have of knowing what should be done.

U. S. GRANT
Maj. Gen.

ALS, DNA, RG 94, War Records Office, Dept. of the Tenn. *O.R.*, I, xxiv, part 3, 522. On July 17, 1863, Maj. Gen. William T. Sherman, Jackson, twice telegraphed to USG, the second time at 8:00 P.M. "Genl Johnston evacuated Jackson last night I will occupy with one Division of Steele & hasten the enemy on his way but in mean time the weather is too hot for a vigorus pursuit Rail Road north & south is very absolutely annihilated" Telegram received, DNA, RG 94, War Records Office, Dept. of the Tenn. *O.R.*, I, xxiv, part 2, 528. "I have just made the circuit of Jackson we are in full possession & Johnson is retreating east with thirty thousand men who will perish from heat thirst & disappointment the place has been well fortified we have the hevy guns & about 400 prisoners & more being picked up hourly I do not pursue because of the intense heat, & dust & fatigue of the men but I will perfect the work of destruction & await orders Train all safe I propose to break Rail Road ten (10) miles south east & north & out for forty (40) & sixty (60) miles in spots we are in possession of some fifty (50) cars which will be burned what more shall I do" Telegram received, DNA, RG 94, War Records Office, Dept. of the Tenn.; copies, *ibid.*, Union Battle Reports; *ibid.*, RG 393, Dept. of the Tenn., Telegrams Sent. *O.R.*, I, xxiv, part 2, 528. On the same day, USG telegraphed to Sherman. "Continue the pursuit of as long as you have reasonable hopes of favorable results, but do not wear your men out. When you stop the pursuit return by easy marches to the vicinity of this place" Copies, DNA, RG 94, War Records Office, Dept. of the Tenn.; (dated July 18) *ibid.*, RG 393, Dept. of the Tenn., Letters Sent; DLC-USG, V, (dated July 17) 19, 101, 103. Dated July 18 in *O.R.*, I, xxiv, part 3, 528. See following letter. On July 17, 9:00 P.M., Sherman telegraphed to USG. "All my Cav. is off at this time breaking road at & beyond Canton to the north & as Brookhaven south I doubt the policy of holding this place for any length of time all of the Division Brigade & Regiments are so reduced & so many officers of rank sick & wounded determined on furloughs that I doubt if my corps will be kept up to Eight Thousand (8000) men if kept here Every officer & man is an applicant for furlough—At Black River we could better mass our troops & sally forth when the time comes—Here we would have our ranks counted every day—In three days I would complete the destruction of road & reach Black River without renewing supplies Johnston got off his baggage & sick by cars" Telegram received, DNA, RG 94, War Records Office, Dept. of the Tenn.; copy, *ibid.*, RG 393, Dept. of the Tenn., Telegrams Sent. *O.R.*, I, xxiv, part 2, 528.

On July 22, Sherman twice telegraphed to USG, the second time at 8:00 P.M. "If you think my chances reasonably good to have a couple months rest in camp on Black River I would be obliged if you would write a letter to Mrs W T Sherman Lancaster O saying that I have telegraphed to have her pay me a visit to Vicksburg   I think we have made a good winding up of the campaign & that the people of Miss are satisfied & want to be let alone on our own terms" "Thank you for the letter to Mrs Sherman   I will increase my estimates so as to embrace they heavy reinforcements of shermans   we move to Clinton tomorrow next day to Bolton & next day to our camps on black river when I will come to report to you in person at vicksburg   Should you wish to communicate with me I will be at Clinton by 8 a m & stay all day   our been work at Jackson has been thorough   we burned brought some 600 good muskets & some ammunition   have destroyed all else"   Telegrams received, DNA, RG 94, War Records Office, Dept. of the Tenn. See telegram to Maj. Gen. William T. Sherman, July 29, 1863.

To Maj. Gen. William T. Sherman

July 17th 1863

GEN. SHERMAN,

Make such pursuit after Johnston as you deem advisable. and when you cease the pursuit[1] Return the 9th & 13th Corps the former to near your old position the latter to its old position. With your Corps and Smith Division which I will add to it, hold Jackson and such healthy points as you deem advisable between Black river and there. Keep all the Cavalry except that belonging to Ord with you. Grierson will be here in a day or two and I will then add him to your command.

U. S. GRANT
Maj. Gen.

ALS, DNA, RG 94, War Records Office, Dept. of the Tenn. *O.R.*, I, xxiv, part 3, 522. See preceding letter. On July 17, 1863, 9:30 P.M., Maj. Gen. William T. Sherman, Jackson, telegraphed to USG. "I will order Genl Parke to march to Vicksburg the day after tomorrow   I will feel towards the east with Ords Corps & my own await the return of our detachments & then return to Black river. in mean time if you think best I will hold Jackson though as I said before I think it is imprudent   Ords Corps is very much out of order & mine reduced by sickness Casualties & a desire for rest   Genl W. S. Smith is really quite ill & says he must go home   Cols. Giles, Smith, Tupper, Judy, & others are urging their claims to furloughs & I repeat that all the army is clamorous for rest   The constant stretch of mind for the past two months begins to tell on all"   Telegram received, DNA, RG 94, War Records Office, Dept. of the Tenn.; copy, *ibid.*, RG 393, Dept. of the Tenn., Telegrams Sent. *O.R.*, I, xxiv, part 2, 528–29. On the same day, USG telegraphed to Sherman. "You can return slowly to Black River. Let Parke come into the city so that he can be sent back to Ky." ALS (telegram sent), DNA, RG 94, War Records Office, Dept. of the Tenn. *O.R.*, I, xxiv, part 3, 522. On July 19, Sherman telegraphed to USG. "Gen Park is Ordered to begin his march tomorrow back to vicksburg unless Steele & Expedition to Brandon develope some thing unexpected   A deserter from a S. C. Brigade reports that ft Sumter is in possession of the Yankees" Telegram received, DNA, RG 94, War Records Office, Dept. of the Tenn.; copy, *ibid.*, RG 393, Dept. of the Tenn., Telegrams Sent. *O.R.*, I, xxiv, part 2, 530. Probably on the next day, Sherman telegraphed to USG. "Genl Parke started in with two Divisions this morning. Genl. Ord will move to-morrow and I will follow only when order & system are restored to the destracted country. The people are subdued, and ask for reconstruction. They admit the loss of the Southern cause. Expedition from Canton & beyond is back having done their task well, whipping Jackson's Cavalry at Canton. The Cavalry is also in from Brook haven,—burned four Locomotives and many cars. Depots, tracks, bridges &c. &c. so there is a break of one hundred miles in the Great Central Road. Steele was at Brandon last night. The drought is terrible and must tell terribly on the enemy retreating fast to the East through a parched and desert Country. Our march back, will be slow and easy, regulated by water." Copy (undated), DNA, RG 393, Dept. of the Tenn., Telegrams Sent. Dated [July 20, 1863] in *O.R.*, I, xxiv, part 2, 530.

On July 24, Brig. Gen. John McArthur, "Big Black," telegraphed to USG. "Genl Sherman with his comd. is encamped tonight at Champion Hills   He directs me to say to you that he will cross the Big Black at Messengers tomorrow morning early with his comd. & establish his Head Quarters at Parson Foxs   All well" Telegram received, DNA, RG 94, War Records Office, Dept. of the Tenn. *O.R.*, I, xxiv, part 3, 548. On July 26, Sherman wrote to Lt. Col. John A. Rawlins. "I have the honor to report the arrival of my Corps at Black River. I have ordered the Divisions to be disposed as follows. Steeles at Rail Road Bridge. Ewings, late W. S. Smiths at Messengers. Tuttle's at Bear Creek near Markhams Blairs at Foxs. I will make my Head Quarters near Foxs and will extend the wires heretofore constructed so as to place me in Telegraphic Communication with Vicksburg, Haines Bluff, and the Rail Road Bridge. The points I have selected for Camps are believed to be healthy, near good water for washing, bathing, are selected to cover the Bridges across the Big Black, and are within one march of Vicksburg. Having come into Vicksburg for a personal interview with the General in Chief, I will return this afternoon to my Post and remain with my command, ready for any ~~command~~ orders, as to labor in improving the organisation and instruction of my Corps." ALS, DNA, RG 94, War Records Office, Dept. of the Tenn. *O.R.*, I, xxiv, part 2, 532.

1. This six-word phrase is in Rawlins's hand.

To Brig. Gen. Lorenzo Thomas

Head Quarters, Dept. of the Ten.
Vicksburg Miss. July 18th 1863.

Brig. Gen. L. Thomas,
Adj. Gen. of the Army,
Washington D. C.
Gen.

I have the honor to acknowledge the receipt of notice of my appointment as Maj. General in the Army of the United States and my acceptance of the same.

Herewith please find the "Oath of Office," required by law, duly signed and sworn to before Maj. T. S. Bowers, Judge Advocate for the "Army of the Tennessee."[1]

I was born at Point Pleasant, Clermont County, Ohio on the 27th day of April 1822 and was consequently Forty-one years of age on the last 27th of April. I settled in Galena Ill. in the year 1860 and regard that as my permanent home.

I am Gen. very respectfully
your obt. svt.
U. S. Grant
Maj. Gen. U. S. A.

ALS, DNA, RG 94, ACP 4754/1885. Secretary of War Edwin M. Stanton endorsed the letter. "Appoint Major General Grant Major General in the regular army for gallant services for in the on the Mississippi and in the Cap siege and capture of Vicksburg" AES, *ibid.* On July 7, 1863, Maj. Gen. Henry W. Halleck wrote to Stanton. "I respectfully recommend the following appointments: 1st Major Genl Ulysses S. Grant. Vols. to be a Major Genl in the U. S. Army, to date July 4th, the capture of Vicksburg. 2d Major Genl George G. Meade, vols. to be a Brig. Genl in the U. S. Army, to date July 3d the victory of Gettysburg." ALS, *ibid.*, ACP, 335H CB 1863. Stanton endorsed the letter "Approved." AES, *ibid.* On the same day, Halleck telegraphed to USG. "It gives me great pleasure to inform you that you have been appointed a Major Genl in the Regular Army, to rank from July 4th, the date of your capture of Vicksburg." ALS (telegram sent), *ibid.*, RG 107, Telegrams Collected (Bound); telegram received, *ibid.*, RG 94, War Records Office, Military Div. of the Miss. *O.R.*, I, xxiv, part 1, 62.

1. USG signed his oath of office on July 18. DS, DNA, RG 94, ACP 4754/1885. See letter to Maj. Gen. Henry W. Halleck, Aug. 11, 1863.

To Maj. Gen. Henry W. Halleck

Vicksburg Miss
July 18th 1863 12.M

MAJ GEN H W HALLECK
GEN IN CHIEF

Joe Johnston evacuated Jackson the night of the Sixteenth He is now in full retreat east. Sherman says most of his Army would perish from heat, lack of water and general discouragement

The Army paroled here have to a great extent deserted, and are scattered over the country in every direction

Learning that Yazoo city was being fortified I sent Gen Herron there[1]—Five guns were captured, many stores and about three hundred prisoners

Gen Ransom was sent to Natchez[2] to stop the crossing of cattle for the Eastern Army—On arrival he found large numbers had been driven out of the city to be pastured; also that munitions of war had recently been crossed over to wait for Kirby Smith   He mounted about two hundred of his men and sent in both directions   They captured number prisoners and five thousand head Texas cattle—Two thousand head of which were sent to Gen Banks   Balance have been and will be brought here   In Louisiana they captured more prisoners, a number of teams loaded with ammunition—over two million rounds musket ammunition was brought back to Natchez with the teams captured and two hundred sixty eight thousand rounds besides Artillery ammunition destroyed—

It seems to me now that Mobile should be captured, the Expedition starting from some point on Lake Ponchetrain[3]—

There is much sickness in my command now, from long and excessive marching and labor—I will co operate as soon as possible with Gen Schofield so as to give him possession of the line of Arkansas—

Shall I retain or send back the Ninth Army Corps?

U S GRANT
Maj. Genl. Comdg

Telegram received, DNA, RG 107, Telegrams Collected (Bound); copies, *ibid.*, Telegrams Received in Cipher; *ibid.*, RG 393, Dept. of the Tenn., Hd. Qrs. Correspondence; DLC-USG, V, 6, 8, 24, 94. *O.R.*, I, xxiv, part 3, 529–30. On July 22, 1863, 11:30 A.M., Maj. Gen. Henry W. Halleck telegraphed to USG. "Yours of the 15th & 18th just recieved. Should Johnston escape & join Bragg the ninth corps must be sent to Rosecrans by quickest route. If not, it may be used elsewhere. Before attempting Mobile, I think it will be best to clean up a little. Johnston should be disposed of; also Price & Marmaduke so as to hold line of Arkansas river; this will enable us to withdraw troops from Missouri; Vicksburg & Port Hudson remodeled so as to be tenable by small garrisons; also assist Genl Banks in cleaning out Western Louisiana. When these things are accomplished, there will be a large available force to operate either on Mobile or Texas. The navy is not ready for co-operation. Should Fort Sumpter fall, Iron clads can be sent to assist at Mobile. Please send copy to Genl Banks." ALS (telegram sent), DNA, RG 107, Telegrams Collected (Bound); copies, *ibid.*, RG 108, Telegrams Sent; *ibid.*, RG 393, Dept. of the Tenn., Hd. Qrs. Correspondence; *ibid.*, Miscellaneous Letters Received; DLC-Nathaniel P. Banks; DLC-USG, V, 6, 8, 24, 94. *O.R.*, I, xxiv, part 3, 542. See telegram to Maj. Gen. Henry W. Halleck, July 15, 1863; letter to Maj. Gen. Nathaniel P. Banks, July 27, 1863.

1. See letter to Maj. Gen. Francis J. Herron, July 15, 1863.
2. See report by Brig. Gen. T. E. G. Ransom on the occupation of Natchez in *O.R.*, I, xxiv, part 2, 680–82.
3. See letter to Abraham Lincoln, Aug. 23, 1863.

To Maj. Gen. William T. Sherman

Vicksburg July 18th 1863.

GEN. SHERMAN, JACKSON,

It was only on the ground of occupying Jackson for the present that I proposed to spare the cars you had captured. When you leave leave nothing of value for the enemy to carry on war with. I would like the road to be destroyed East of Jackson as far out as possible.

A portion of Grierson's command[1] passed here to-day with rebel officers.[2] The remainder will be up in a day or two and will go on to West Ten. to join their command. Grierson is very anxious to get back there to get his troops together. He has no whole company with him. By having him there I can organize a large cavalry force under his command to make a big raid through the Eastern part of the state or wherever required.

U. S. GRANT
Maj. Gen.

ALS, DNA, RG 94, War Records Office, Dept. of the Tenn. *O.R.*, I, xxiv, part 3, 528. On July 18, 1863, Maj. Gen. William T. Sherman, Jackson, twice telegraphed to USG, first at 11:00 A.M. "Have just returned from a long ride day intensely hot & dust terrific. Heard of Col Woods expedition near Canton last night he had met opposition but expected to enter Canton this morning Gen Steele with 3 brigades will move out to Brandon this eve As soon as I hear satisfactory accounts of these detachments I will despatch Gen Park to Mill Dale via Brownsville & as soon as the detachments are back & rested I will move Ord to Black River via Raymond & 15th A C & Cavalry to Messengers & bear creek via clinton the enemy burnt great part of Jackson & we have done some in that line the place is ruined I am destroying the Northern & Southn R R but according to your orders spare that East & west with the cars Have heard from my cavalry South a prisoner was sent in with a written order on his person dated Brookhaven he states the place contained but two co's & that Grierson was reported coming I do hope Grierson will come by land with his Cavalry & what I have I can clean out all middle Miss." Telegram received, DNA, RG 94, War Records Office, Dept. of the Tenn.; copy, *ibid.*, RG 393, Dept. of the Tenn., Telegrams Sent. *O.R.*, I, xxiv, part 2, 529. "We have made fine progress today in the work of destruction Jackson will no longer be a ~~pont~~ point of danger destroyed much cotton used in Breast works some heavy arty & a large pile shot & shell Will be thrown into the river Steele will ~~be~~ be at Brandon in the morning & I have reason to believe all is working well north & south I hope it will rain tonight in which case I will order Parks two Divisions to march for Mill Dale & Brownsville I will hold the balance till I accomplish all you design. The Enemies cavalry has retreated from Canton across Pearl We have five hundred prisoners & more are being brought in every hour. The Inhabitants are Subjugated they cry aloud for mercy the land is devastated for thirty miles around" Telegram received, USG 3; copy, DNA, RG 393, Dept. of the Tenn., Telegrams Sent. *O.R.*, I, xxiv, part 2, 529.

On July 18, USG telegraphed to Sherman. "send me in the names of such officers as you will recommend for promotion from your Corps. Ask Gens Ord & Park to do the same thing from theirs." ALS (telegram sent), DNA, RG 393, Dept. of the Tenn., Telegrams Received. On the same day, Sherman telegraphed to USG. "I will notify Gens Ord & Park to Send in names for Promotion I will make a short list in short time & transmit it all things working admirably" Telegram received, *ibid.*, RG 94, War Records Office, Dept. of the Tenn.; copy, *ibid.*, RG 393, Dept. of the Tenn., Telegrams Sent. On July 20, Sherman telegraphed to Lt. Col. John A. Rawlins. "I have notified Generals Parke and Ord to send in lists of recommendation for promotion. I name now as eminently worthy of promotion as Brigadier Genl's. Colonel C. R. Wood 76th Ohio Colonel Giles A. Smith 8th Missouri Colonel I. R. Cockell 70th Ohio Colonel John M. Corse 6th Iowa When I make up more detailed reports of escorts, I will add other names which will not conflict with the above." Copy, *ibid.* On July 27, Maj. Gen. Edward O. C. Ord wrote to Rawlins. "I have the honor to recommend for Promotion Brigadier General Alvin P. Hovey Brigadier General P Joseph Osterhaus Colonal W. Q. Gresham—53d Indiana Infantry Colonel R. A. Cameron —34th Inda. Infantry Surgeon Robert B Jessup—24th Inda. Infantry—Major Hugh Fullerton—2d Illinois Cavy—I only know these men from their services, and we want these services in a higer grade" ALS, *ibid.*, Miscellaneous Letters Received. On July 30, USG endorsed this letter. "Approved and respectfully forwarded." AES, *ibid.* On Aug. 7, Maj. Gen. John G. Parke wrote to USG. "In accordance with instructions received from you through Maj. Genl. Sherman, Comdg. late Expeditionary army against Johnston, I have the honor to forward to you the names of the following Officers for promotion to the rank of Brigader General—Col. L. K. Bliss. 7th R. I. Vols. Capt. 8th U. S. Inf.   Col. Hartsaufe 51st Penn. Vols.   Col. Griffin 6th N. H. Vols. There are but four General Officers in the Corps exclusive of the Comdg. General and including one division now on detached duty in the Dept. of Virginia   I take pleasure in recommending the above mentioned Officers to your favorable notice, for their Soldierly qualities, as well as for their gallant Conduct whenever they have met the Enemy"   Copy, *ibid.*, 9th Army Corps, Letters Sent. *O.R.*, I, lii, part 1, 432.

On July 13, Maj. Gen. James B. McPherson wrote to Rawlins. "I have the honor to recommend for promotion on account of gallant conduct, in the several engagements of the recent campaign, the following Colonels, serving in this Corps: Co'l Lyman Ward, 14th Reg't. Wis. Vo'l. In'f.   Co'l Alex Chambers, 16th Reg't. Iowa. Vo'l. In'f. commanding 3d Brig. 6th Division.   Co'l John B. Sanborn, 4th Minn. In'f. Vol's. commanding 1st Brig. 7th Division   Co'l J. J. Alexander, 59th Reg't. In'd. In'f. Vol's.   Co'l M. F. Force, 20th Reg't. Ohio. In'f. Vol's. commanding 2d Brigade, 3d Division." LS, DNA, RG 393, Dept. of the Tenn., Letters Received. On July 30, USG endorsed this letter. "Approved and respectfully forwarded to Hd Qrs. of the Army." AES, *ibid.*

1. On July 16, Brig. Gen. Charles P. Stone, Port Hudson, wrote to USG. "By the steamboat 'Planet' I send a large number of Confederate officers, prisoners captured at this place, (189) according to the list enclosed—These officers have not been paroled, & are placed under the escort of a battalion of General Grierson's cavalry, returning to rejoin your command—General Grierson with the remainder of his cavalry will probably leave this tomorrow on the steamboat 'Imperial,' having in charge Brigr General Beall & certain field & staff officers. May I ask of you, on the part of Major General Banks, who is temporarily absent, to forward these prisoners to the proper destination in the north? Yesterday brought us the welcome intelligence of the occupation of Natchez by General Ransom of your command, and two transports laden with beef cattle captured by him have since been received here—The arrival of this beef is most opportune and acceptable. There is nothing especially interesting to communicate concerning operations in this region since the last communication of the Major General Commanding." LS, *ibid.*, RG 94, War Records Office, Dept. of the Tenn. *O.R.*, I, xxvi, part 1, 643. On the same day, Brig. Gen. Benjamin H. Grierson wrote to Rawlins. "I herewith send on the Steamer 'Planet,' a Battalion of my command in charge of Rebel officers captured at this place. I shall leave on Friday night or Saturday morning with the balance of the command. If consistent with General Grant's views I would urgently request permission to take the command to Memphis or some point where it can readily be united with those now in La Grange Tenn. We have now been absent from Camp, three months, leaving detachments of each company with all books & records behind, and the business of the command is in a bad condition. Our labors in this department have been very severe and on account of a constant scarcity of forage, our horses are in very bad condition. Give my regards to the Gen'l. & Staff." ALS, DNA, RG 393, Dept. of the Tenn., Letters Received. On July 18, Lt. Col. Richard B. Irwin, Port Hudson, issued Special Orders No. 174. "Brigadier General Benjamin H. Grierson, Commanding

Cavalry, will proceed with the 6th & 7th regiments of Illinois Cavalry and the 1st Illinois Battery under his command, to Vicksburg, and will then report in person to Major General Grant, for duty in the Department of the Tennessee. It is with extreme regret that the Major General Commanding sees this gallant officer and his brave cavalry leave this Department, in which they have rendered such brilliant and useful service: but it is due to both commander & command that they should no longer be detained absent from their comrades of the Department of the Tennesee. The Major General Commanding while tendering to General Grierson and his troops the thanks of the 19th Corps, wishes for them in Each future field of duty, opportunities for maintaining the reputation they have so justly won, and for rendering to the Republic services which shall add new lustre to her arms." DS, *ibid. O.R.*, I, xxvi, part 1, 645.

2. On July 18, Rawlins wrote to Maj. Gen. Stephen A. Hurlbut. "The Confederate Officers, Prisoners of War, captured at Port Hudson, by General Banks, and in charge of Major I. M. Graham, 7th Illinois Cavalry Vol's, you will send to Cairo, Ill's, under proper guard, with dispatch to the General-in-Chief, to be telegraphed from Cairo, asking for instructions as to the disposition to be made of them." LS, DNA, RG 393, 16th Army Corps, Letters Received. On July 19, Rawlins wrote to Hurlbut. "Gen. Grierson will deliver to you twenty three officers of the Confederate States Army captured by Maj. Gen Banks at Port Hudson, which you will please take charge of, and forward under proper escort to such point as the Secretary of War may designate." LS, *ibid.*

To Capt. Loyd Wheaton

Headquarters Dept of the Tenn.
Vicksburg Miss July 18. 1863

CAPT L. WHEATON
INSP GEN 3D DIV.
CAPT.

You will proceed to New Orleans on board the Steamer City of Madison in charge of the sick and wounded prisoners of war.[1] On your arrival at New Orleans you will report to the Commanding officer of the Post, to know what disposition is to be made there of the prisoners, to get them on their way to Mobile. If they are to be transferred to Lake Steamers, superintend in person their transfer from the River to the Lake, and if no Federal officer is being sent with them, by Gen Banks direction, you will accompany them to Mobile and return by the same Steamer. Should it be necessary to go from New Orleans by way of the Balize you will accompany the Steamer on the round trip. See Col Lagow of my staff at New Orleans and inform him that I expect him to remain in the City until the last of the prisoners destined for Mobile have passed and to make arrangements for the prompt removal at that place of all the prisoners arriving.

Respectfully &c

U. S. Grant

Maj Genl

Copies, DLC-USG, V, 19, 101, 103; DNA, RG 393, Dept. of the Tenn., Letters Sent. Loyd Wheaton, born in 1838 at Pennfield, Mich., enlisted as 1st sgt., 8th Ill. Commissioned 1st lt. as of July 25, 1861, he was promoted to capt. on March 25, 1862. On July 18, 1863, Lt. Col. John A. Rawlins ordered Maj. Gen. James B. McPherson to secure transportation and supplies for the sick and wounded prisoners. LS, *ibid.*, RG 94, War Records Office, 17th Army Corps. *O.R.*, II, vi, 125. On July 28, Wheaton wrote to Rawlins. "In accordance with orders from Maj Genl Grant I embarked on board Steamer 'City of Madison' on the 18th Inst in charge of two hundred and fifty Sick and wounded prisoners of war. Arrived in New Orleans at 2 O Clock P. M on the 21st Inst. and reported to Brig Genl Emory Comd'g Post and Defences of New Orleans, was ordered by him to report to Genl Bowen Provost Marshal Genl of the Dept of the Gulf. I placed the prisoners in charge of Genl Bowen. by whom they were immediately transfered to the Ocan Steamer 'North America.' The Steamer departing for Mobile at 9 P. M. of the same day. Saw Col Lagow and delivered instructions as required" ALS, DNA, RG 393, Dept. of the Tenn., Letters Received.

1. See letter to Maj. Gen. Nathaniel P. Banks, July 16, 1863.

To Commanding Officer, Clinton, Miss.

July 18th 1863.

Comd.g Officer Clinton Miss.

See Miss Alice Shirley staying at the house of Mrs Shirley Clinton and say her father desires her to come to Vicksburg. You may give Miss Shirley any facility of reaching here.

U. S. Grant

Maj. Gen.

ALS, DNA, RG 109, Union Provost Marshals' File of Papers Relating to Two or More Civilians. James Shirley, a pro-Union planter whose home was located between the siege lines at Vicksburg, gave valuable information to USG about the city. Shirley died at the age of sixty-nine in Aug., 1863. On Sept. 29, 1864, his daughter Alice married Chaplain John Eaton, Jr. See John Eaton, *Grant,*

Lincoln and the Freedmen (New York, 1907), pp. 71–85. On July [13], 1863, Shirley wrote to USG. "Permit me to introduce to you the bearer, Mr. Pyle   Mr Pyle is one who stood by the Stars and Stripes in our most gloomy hours, and if their is a Union man in the United States he is one. He has endured persecution and the pain for his Union sentiment" Copy (faded), letterpress book of Charles W. Montross, Alton Area Historical Society, Alton, Ill. (IHi). On Jan. 28, 1864, USG, St. Louis, endorsed this letter. "Mr James Shirley and his family are well known for their unflinching loyalty throughout the present rebellion   Mr Shirley was to old for the conscription to take him but having a son near grown he sent him north f[ro]m Vicksburg early in the rebellion to join the Union Army where I presume he is now residing   The statements of Mr Shirley can beyond doubt be relied on"   Copy, *ibid.* See letter to Edwin M. Stanton, Feb. 15, 1865.

On Sept. 24, 1863, Lt. Col. John A. Rawlins endorsed a letter of Shirley's widow, Adeline, requesting an investigation of damages to her plantation. "Respectfully referred to Major General McPherson who will appoint a commission to examine and assess the damages done the within named premises by our forces stating particularly the circumstances under which the damage was done and also the value of the personal property lost, and all the circumstances connected therewith"   Copies, DLC-USG, V, 25; DNA, RG 393, Dept. of the Tenn., Endorsements. The commission's figure of $8,348.57—of which $2,254.52 was for q. m. stores and the remainder for damages—was approved by Maj. Gen. James B. McPherson. This claim was approved for payment by the Secretary of War, but Congress disallowed claims of this kind on July 4, 1864. See *U.S. Statutes at Large*, XIII, 381–82. On March 12, 1866, USG endorsed the claim. "The loyalty of the claimant from the beginning of the rebellion to the present is undoubted. I could, therefore respectfully recommend that the sum of $2254.52 for property supposed to have been take for the immediate use of the army be paid, and that the finding of the commission to assess damages be regarded as a voucher for the same. This to be without prejudice to the remainder of the claim, should Congress authorize the payment in full" Copy, DLC-USG, V, 58. On June 17, 1867, Maj. Gen. Edward O. C. Ord, Vicksburg, telegraphed to USG. "Mrs Shirley widow of James Shirley recommended by you as unflinching union during the war is in poverty.   her house was so damaged being in Eighteen sixty four (1864) a Small Pox Hospital for our troops that it is not fit to live in. Can I put five hundred (500) dollars worth repairs on it till her claim now on file is settled?" Telegram received, DNA, RG 108, Telegrams Received; *ibid.*, RG 92, Consolidated Correspondence, Mrs. Shirley; copy, *ibid.*, RG 393, 4th Military District, Civil Affairs Office, Letters Sent. On June 18, USG endorsed the telegram. "Respectfully forwarded to the Secretary of War. I have personal knowledge that the Shirleys were persons of unflinching loyalty, demonstrated at great risk; and earnestly recommend favorable action on this application" AES, *ibid.*, RG 92, Consolidated Correspondence, Mrs. Shirley. On June 29, Bvt. Maj. Gen. Daniel H. Rucker, act. q. m. gen., endorsed the telegram. "Respectfully returned to the Secretary of War. Under the recent enactments of Congress, the proposed expenditure for repair of a house in a state recently in rebellion, rendered necessary by U. S. occupancy, cannot be favorably considered by the Acting Quarter Master General." ES, *ibid.* On Aug. 28, USG, secretary of war *ad interim*, approved Rucker's recommendation, and Ord was informed of the negative decision on Sept. 6. Numerous attempts were made to secure the claim in Congress. See *HRC*, 50-1-1126, 51-1-1288, 52-1-84, 52-1-1657, 54-1-695, 55-2-161; *SRC*, 52-1-574,

54-2-1439, 55-2-544. The 55th Congress finally authorized payment in full to the heirs of Mrs. Shirley thirty-four years after the original claim. *U.S. Statutes at Large*, XXX, 1209. On July 3, 1903, the commissioners of the Vicksburg National Military Park reported that "The Shirley House has been repaired at a cost of $3,000, exclusive of the small cost of supervising the work. Its restoration to the condition and appearance existing at the beginning of the siege preserves a notable landmark of the battlefield, and is gratifying to the veterans of both armies." *HD*, 58-2-2, p. 242.

USG also dealt with other civilians in Vicksburg. On July 15, 1863, he issued a pass for William W. Lord and his family. "Rev. W. W. Lord & family and Miss. Birchett, with their private baggage and personal effects will be permited to accompany wounded Confederate prisoners, via New Orleans to Mobile." ADS (facsimile), USG 3. Lord, born in N. Y. in 1819, was appointed rector of the Episcopal church in Vicksburg in 1854 and became the chaplain of the 1st Miss. Brigade in 1861. During the siege of Vicksburg, many of his possessions were destroyed, reportedly including the largest private library in the Southwest. Although USG urged him to go north to join his brother, a judge in St. Louis, Lord continued his duties as C.S.A. chaplain. See William W. Lord, Jr., "A Child at the Siege of Vicksburg," *Harper's Magazine*, 118 (Dec., 1908), 44–53, and "In the Path of Sherman," *ibid.*, 120 (Feb., 1910), 438–46.

While in Vicksburg, USG lived in the home of Mr. William Lum, a prosperous merchant before the war. See John Y. Simon, ed., *The Personal Memoirs of Julia Dent Grant* (New York, 1975), pp. 120, 122, 143n. On July 23, 1863, Lt. Col. Loren Kent, provost marshal, wrote to USG. "Mrs Lum will apply to you for a permit granting Royal & Lansden the privilige of bringing to this place for use in the washington Hotel $2000 worth of furniture. Mr Merry says that in conversation with Royal, he heard him express disloyal sentiments and that if he could start the Hotel he could assist the rebels more than before, that the surrender of Vicksburg but prolongs the war &c. Royal it seems told this thinking Merry a southern man & rebel" ALS, DNA, RG 109, Union Provost Marshals' File of Papers Relating to Two or More Civilians. On Sept. 28, R. D. Royall, Vicksburg, applied to Maj. Gen. John A. Logan "for the restoration to him of the Washington Hotel   States, that he was the former lessee of that Building and owned nearly all the furniture, fixtures &c, in the House—that he appealed to Mrs. Lum owner of the House who expressed a desire that he should retain possession of the House, she at the same time showing him a permit from General Grant to retain the House and rent it for her own benefit—that he cleaned up said House, and was getting ready to occupy it when a man by the name of John H. Smith presented a permit he had obtained from Brig Genl John E. Smith then Commd'g Post to open the Washington Hotel. Suspects Mr. Smith of being a dishonest unprincipled man and of using deception for the purpose of Swindling him out of the Property mentioned, States during his absence, while the house was in possession of Mr. Smith, his baggage room in the Hotel was Entered, his trunks broken open, and articles of value taken"   Copy, DLC-USG, V, 99. On Sept. 30, Kent, to whom Royall's letter had been referred by Rawlins, reported that "Upon investigation it appears that Mr. Royall is as he states, the original lessee of the Hotel that he at one time owned furniture there to the amount of 9.000\frac{00}{100}$, of which, much has been removed, leaving still about 3.000\frac{00}{100}$ worth of furniture in the House, now owned by Royall, who was denied by General Grant soon after the occupation of the City, the privilege of retaining the Hotel on account of his disloyalty. By order of General Grant, General J E. Smith was directed to put the Hotel in charge of some loyal man. This man Smith was selected. His management has not been very creditable. The trunks mentioned in the petition were robbed as Stated. Under recent orders from Department Headquarters, Mr. Royall is either entitled to the possession of the furniture or proper rent for it   I recommend that he have that privilege. Mr. Smith is now sick, unable to do business or answer questions. But recently he turned Mrs. Watts, a good Union Woman from Louisiana, known to General Grant, out of her room with insulting language, and compelled her to stay in the parlour during the night." Copy, *ibid.*

On Sept. 12, 1866, Lum's widow, Ann, wrote to USG. "Old age feels its troubles since only in times of dependency, thru if independent of others. I am now almost dependent upon my children for the use of their homes—when I ought indeed to have one of my own   I do not ask as much for a favor, as I do for a simple act of kind and considerate justice. The Fort where my dear old home once stood is now abandoned—no longer of use to the Government; and was simply vacated. It stands with its fertile embankments, and magazine half ruined. It is a land mark of War, where my home once stood. And it being all the land I own can you grant me an order, if in your power, requiring the proper officers here to fill up the ditches and level the ground smoothly so that I may build there a simple cotage, in which I can pass the remainder of my days? I trust this will find you and your family well. Let me hear from you soon. Begging to be remembered to all of your family." ALS, DNA, RG 109, Union Provost Marshals' File of Papers Relating to Two or More Civilians. On Nov. 7, Maj. George K. Leet endorsed the letter. "Respectfully referred to Maj. Gen. Geo. H. Thomas, Comdg Dept Tenn., who will give directions to have the request of Mrs Lum complied with, if the Government has no further use for the fort in question." AES, *ibid.*

On Aug. 6, 1863, USG endorsed a letter of July 15 of James Chapin, Saratoga Springs, N. Y., asking permission to return to Vicksburg. "I know nothing about this case and do not see that any order can be made by me effecting Mr Chapin. If deemed advisable by the Secretary of War to permit him to return to Vicksburg I see no objection to it." Copies, DLC-USG, V, 25; DNA, RG 393, Dept. of the Tenn., Endorsements. See *O.R.*, II, ii, 300.

On July 15, USG wrote to Brig. Gen. John McArthur. "Mr. Stout living south of Vicksburg represents that your Division borrowed a waggon and pair of mules which were never returned. Do you know anything about it. Mr. Stout lives where you had Hd Qrs. at one time." ALS, DNA, RG 393, Dept. of the Tenn., Telegrams Received.

To Brig. Gen. Lorenzo Thomas

Head Quarters. Dept. of the Tenn.
Vicksburg. Miss. July. 19. 1863.

Respectfully forwarded. This report contains so many inaccuracies that to correct it, to make it a fair report to be handed down as historical would require the rewriting of most of it.

It is pretentious and egotistical, as is sufficiently shown by my own and all other reports accompanying.

The officers and men composing the 13th Army Corps throughout the campaign endin[g with] the capture of Vicksburg [have done nobly, an]d there are no honors due the Army of the Tennessee in which they do not share equally

U. S. GRANT
Major General

ES, DNA, RG 94, War Records Office, Union Battle Reports. *O.R.*, I, xxiv, part 1, 157. Written on Maj. Gen. John A. McClernand's report of the Vicksburg campaign, submitted to Lt. Col. John A. Rawlins, dated June 17, 1863. DS, DNA, RG 94, War Records Office, Union Battle Reports. *O.R.*, I, xxiv, part 1, 137–57. Although dated June 17, the report was not sent to Rawlins by Lt. Col. Walter B. Scates, adjt., 13th Army Corps, until June 19, after McClernand had left Vicksburg. ALS, DNA, RG 393, Dept. of the Tenn., Letters Received.

On May 30, Rawlins had written to McClernand. "You will please send at once to these Head Quarters an official statement of the casualities in your corps in the several battles in which it has been engaged since its debarkation at Bruinsburg Miss on the 30th of April last up to and including the assault on Vicksburg on the 22nd inst" Copies, DLC-USG, V, 19, 30, 98; DNA, RG 393, Dept. of the Tenn., Letters Sent; *ibid.*, 13th Army Corps, Letters Received. On the same day, McClernand wrote to USG. "I have the honor to transmit herewith a tabular statement of the number of Killed, Wounded and Missing of the several divisions of the 13th Army Corps,—except the 9th,—in the several battles and skirmishes since I crossed the Mississippi River into the State of Mississippi. I can only give a partial report at the present time. I will add a summary of the Casualties of the 9th Division as soon as received. In the more extended, or full reports, which will be ready soon, slight corrections, doubtless of this statement, will be found. The press of public duties must be my apolagy for this delay." LS, *ibid.*, RG 94, War Records Office, Union Battle Reports. *O.R.*, I, xxiv, part 1, 157. The casualty figures appear *ibid.*, p. 158.

USG did not endorse McClernand's report of June 17 until he decided to send Rawlins to Washington to discover firsthand the impact of McClernand's dismissal. See letter to Abraham Lincoln, July 20, 1863. On June 23, McClernand enclosed the report in a letter to Lincoln. ALS, DLC-Robert T. Lincoln. On the same day, he wrote another letter to Lincoln defending his actions in the campaign. ALS, *ibid.* A rough draft of the second letter, dated June 20, is located in the Henry C. Warmoth Papers, Southern Historical Collection, University of North Carolina, Chapel Hill, N. C.

On July 22, Brig. Gen. Eugene A. Carr wrote to Rawlins protesting the treatment of himself and his div. in McClernand's report. LS, DNA, RG 94, War Records Office, Union Battle Reports; *ibid.*, Dept. of the Tenn. *O.R.*, I, xxiv, part 1, 623–24. On Aug. 3, USG endorsed this letter to U.S. Army hd. qrs. ES, DNA, RG 94, War Records Office, Union Battle Reports.

On June 27, McClernand wrote to Secretary of War Edwin M. Stanton requesting "an investigation of General Grant's and my conduct as officers from the battle of Belmont to the assault of the 22d upon Vicksburg, . . ." *O.R.*, I, xxiv, part 1, 166–67. Receiving no reply, McClernand wrote to Stanton again on Aug. 24. *Ibid.*, p. 168. His request denied on Aug. 29, McClernand wrote to Stanton requesting an investigation of his "own conduct." *Ibid.* This request was denied by Stanton on Sept. 14. *Ibid.*, p. 169. On Sept. 28, McClernand, Springfield, Ill., wrote to Maj. Gen. Henry W. Halleck. "I have the honor to enclose, herewith, my Official protest against parts of Maj Genl. Grant's report of the 6th of July ulto." ALS, DNA, RG 108, Letters Received. His polemical defense, addressed to Halleck on Sept. 25, *O.R.*, I, xxiv, part 1, 169–86, made no specific charges, but hinted at misconduct by Grant. "How far General Grant is indebted to the forbearance of officers under his command for his retention in the public service so long, I will not undertake to state unless he should challenge it. None know better than himself how much he is indebted to that forbearance. . . ." After being restored to command of the 13th Army Corps in Jan., 1864, McClernand wrote to U.S. Senator Lyman Trumbull on Feb. 12. "I have been so deeply injured by Grant that I am absolved from all obligations of forbearance towards him. If I can find opportunity, I will prefer charges against him—for incompetency, as proved at Donelson and Shiloh—for shameless desertion of the field at Belmont—for falsification of facts in his report of the Miss. campaign, and for drunkenness." ALS, DLC-Lyman Trumbull. See letters to Maj. Gen. John A. McClernand, June 17, and to Brig. Gen. Lorenzo Thomas, June 26, 1863.

To Abraham Lincoln

Head Quarters, Dept. of the Ten.
Vicksburg Miss July 20th 1863.

His Excellency, A. Lincoln,
President of the United States.
Sir:

The bearer of this, Lieut. Col. J. A. Rawlins, is the Assistant Adj. Gen. of the Army of the Ten. Col. Rawlins has been connected with this Army, and with me in every engagement, from the Battle of Belmont to the surrender of Vicksburg.

Col. Rawlins goes to Washington now by my order as bearer of the reports of the campaign just ended, and rolls, and Paroles, of prisoners captured. Any information desired of any matter connected with this Department, from his official position, he can give better probably than any other officer in it.

I would be pleased if you could give Col. Rawlins an interview and I know in asking this you will feel relieved when I tell you he has not a favor to ask for himself or any other living being. Even in my position it is a great luxury to meet a gentleman who has no "axe to grind" and I can appreciate that it is infinitely more so in yours.

> I have the honor to be
> very respectfully
> your obt. svt.
> U. S. Grant
> Maj. Gen. U. S. A.

ALS, DLC-Robert T. Lincoln. *O.R.*, I, lii, part 1, 416. Lt. Col. John A. Rawlins left for Washington on July 22, 1863. On July 30, Rawlins, Baltimore, Md., telegraphed to Col. John C. Kelton. "I am here under orders from Maj Gen Grant with despatches for Head Quarters of the Army   Have I permission to proceed to Washington?" Telegram received, DNA, RG 107, Telegrams Collected (Bound). On the same day, 9:25 A.M., Kelton telegraphed to Rawlins. "~~You have permission~~ to come to Washington.—" LS (telegram sent), *ibid.* After arriving in Washington on July 30, Rawlins wrote to USG. "I arrived here this evening, after one of the hardest trips one ever experienced I reckon. The boat was awful slow & the Illinois Central was behind time & to cap the whole about noon Monday & 100 miles from Chicago the train ran off the track. I was on the car that was most damaged & the consequence was came nearer being killed than ever before in my life.   had one day that I could scarcely talk, which I suppose would make you think of me as you did of Dick oglesby, that it was terrible punishment. I soon get along first-rate. Have just seen Genl Brains & Col Kelton, It is worth a trip here to see how delighted they are over your successes, There is nothing left undone by them to make me feel that I am here all properly   The general scolds because you have not sent on your recommendations for promotions. I gave him the names of those you would recommend as far as I could recollect. The[y] say there are three vacancies of Brigadiers in the Regular army, [. . .] to have Sherman, McPherson, & Genl. George Thomas fill them, Now do Genl Send forward your recommendations at once. I would send them if I had not already done so to Cairo & from there, by telgraph here, I[t] would be a deserved compliment to Sherman & McPherson   let your list be full & give the 13th a fair proportion   but [I] only mention this, I know you will. He says they have finally concluded to hand McClernand out to grass   the order was made to day mustering his staff out of service   An order is also published asserting clearly the government policy in reference to to black troops for every soldier or officer of ours put to death by the confederates, one of same rank will be put to death of theirs, & for every colored soldier sold into or returned to slavery a Confederate soldier will be put to hard work & so kept until the release of the colored soldier. Halleck says that the army of the Potomac is here and succeeds in getting every vacancy filled almost as fast as they occur. That your army fights and wins seven battles, & no promotions get asked, that the army of the Potomac fights the same number & looses six & before it is really determined that the seventh is won they have all the vacancies filled   This latter of course he did not intend should be repeated   it was spoken in his jubilance of spirits over the Western successes. Your agreement with Pemberton he heartily endorses, as being proper as well as wise. Genl Banks he says has made a great mistake in paroling the garrison of Port Hudson it not being in the terms of capitulation   still he is not inclined to censure for he says many of the officers have done the same thing right here when they had every means of knowing better,   I shall wind up my business here & start back tomorrow   Shall see the President & the secretary of the Treasury in the morning,   Genl Halleck is fully alive to the necessity of your army having rest. give my best regards to all the members of your staff & tell the Major he is continually in my mind. With my regards to yourself & Mrs Grant . . ." ALS, ICHi.

Officially, Rawlins was sent to Washington as the bearer of USG's report of the Vicksburg campaign. See letter to Col. John C. Kelton, July 6, 1863. Unofficially, Rawlins was to gauge the impact on the Lincoln administration of the dismissal of Maj. Gen. John A. McClernand. On July 31, Rawlins presented USG's version of events to a cabinet meeting. Secretary of the Navy Gideon Welles described the meeting: "Colonel Rawlins of General Grant's staff . . . arrived yesterday with the official report of the capture of Vicksburg and Pemberton's army. Was much pleased with him, his frank, intelligent and interesting description of men and of army operations. His interview with the President and Cabinet was of nearly two hours' duration, and all, I think, were entertained and instructed by him. His unpretending and unassuming manners pleased me—the absence of pretension and I may say the unpolished and unrefined deportment of this earnest and sincere patriot and soldier interested me more than that of almost any officer whom I have met. He was never at West Point and has had few educational advantages, yet he is a soldier, and has a mind which has served his general and his country well. He is a sincere and earnest friend of Grant, who I think sent him here for a purpose. It was the intention of the President last fall that General McClernand, an old neighbor and friend of his should have been associated with Porter in active operations before Vicksburg. It was the wish of Porter who made it a special point to be relieved from associations with the West Pointers who were arrogant and assuming and never willing to treat naval officers as equals. The President thought the opportunity a good one to bring forward his friend McClernand who is a volunteer officer of more than ordinary ability, and possesses great political influence in Illinois. Stanton and Halleck entered into his views, for Grant was not a special favorite with either. He had like Hooker the reputation of indulging too freely with whiskey to be always safe and reliable. Rawlins now comes from Vicksburg with statements in regard to McClernand which show him an impracticable and unfit man,—that he has not been subordinate and intelligent, but has been an embarrassment, and instead of assisting has been really an obstruction to, army movements and operations. In his statements there is such candor with such earnest and intelligent conviction, that there can be hardly a doubt McClernand is in fault, and Rawlins has been sent here by Grant to satisfy the President of the fact. In this I think he has succeeded, though the President feels kindly towards McClernand. Grant evidently hates him, and Rawlins is imbued with the feelings of his chief." Howard K. Beale, ed., *Diary of Gideon Welles* (New York, 1960), I, 386–87.

To Maj. Gen. William T. Sherman

July 20th 1863,

GEN SHERMAN.

The heat and dust being suffocating you may take your own time for returning. You can locate your forces on Big Black or return to your former position at your own option. By scattering the troops on high ground it may be more healthy than having them close together. No Eastern news.

U. S. GRANT
Maj. Gen.

ALS, DNA, RG 94, War Records Office, Dept. of the Tenn. *O.R.*, I, xxiv, part 3, 536. On July 20, 1863, 6:00 P.M., Maj. Gen. William T. Sherman, Jackson, telegraphed to USG. "Steele is back   all well   he drove the Cavalry of the Enemy beyond Brandon & then destroyed Depot & 3 miles of road there   I will remain tomorrow Batter down the pearl river piers destroy the bridge we have built & make a good finish to our Job   the enemy is now far beyond Pearl river in full retreat & Jackson is utterly destroyed as military point   If after the day after tomorrow no change occurs I will move my corps slowly back to Black River Camp the Divisions in good locations & then report to you in person   I ask no indulgence for myself but the men & officers need a couple months of rest & relaxation"   Telegram received, DNA, RG 94, War Records Office, Dept. of the Tenn.; copy, *ibid.*, RG 393, Dept. of the Tenn., Telegrams Sent. *O.R.*, I, xxiv, part 2, 530.

On Aug. 16, USG wrote to Col. John C. Kelton transmitting reports of the Jackson campaign. Copies, DLC-USG, V, 6, 8, 24, 94; DNA, RG 393, Dept. of the Tenn., Hd. Qrs. Correspondence. These and other reports are printed in *O.R.*, I, xxiv, part 2, 532–654.

To Maj. Gen. Henry W. Halleck

Vicksburg Miss. July 21st/63

MAJ. GEN. HALLECK, WASHINGTON,

I am sending one Division from here to Helena to move on Price. This is all the troops I have not worn out with fatigue. Troops from Jackson not yet returned. I will send other troops to Helena to release that entire garrison to go after Price.

U. S. GRANT
Maj. Gen.

ALS (telegram sent), DNA, RG 94, War Records Office, Dept. of the Tenn.; telegram received, *ibid.*, RG 107, Telegrams Collected (Bound). *O.R.*, I, xxii, part 2, 384; *ibid.*, I, xxiv, part 3, 539. On July 15, 1863, 10:00 A.M., Maj. Gen. Henry W. Halleck telegraphed to USG and to Maj. Gen. Benjamin M. Prentiss. "It is reported that Genl Price is moving north. All available forces should immediately move on his rear so as to cut off his retreat. The forces in Missouri will prevent his penetrating far into that state, and if he is cut off in rear his forces must disperse or surrender. Apply to the naval commander for cooperation with gun boats on White River—No time should be lost." ALS (telegram sent), DNA, RG 107, Telegrams Collected (Bound); telegram received, *ibid.*, RG 94, War Records Office, Military Div. of the Miss. *O.R.*, I, xxiv, part 3, 513. On July 15, 8:00 P.M., Halleck telegraphed again to USG. "No expedition to Texas will be undertaken at present. First clean out Miss, Ark, and Louisa. I have written fully to you & to Genl Banks by mail" ALS (telegram sent), DNA, RG 107, Telegrams Collected (Bound); telegram received, *ibid.*, RG 393, Dept. of the Tenn., Telegrams Received. *O.R.*, I, xxiv, part 3, 513. See letter to Maj. Gen. Henry W. Halleck, July 24, 1863. On July 15, Halleck telegraphed to Maj. Gen. Stephen A. Hurlbut. "If Genl Sherman's movements have sufficiently occupied the enemy to render your lines safe, send all the forces you can spare to Genl Prentis to operate on Price's rear, if he advances towards Missouri." ALS (telegram sent), DNA, RG 107, Telegrams Collected (Bound); copy, *ibid.*, RG 94, War Records Office, Dept. of the Mo. Printed as sent at 10:24 A.M. in *O.R.*, I, xxiv, part 3, 518.

On July 17, Hurlbut wrote to USG. "I send you dispatches this day received for Gen Prentiss and myself. You will see by their tenor that the General in Cheif expects me to aid in a movement from Helena on the rear of Price. I am not in force enough to do so until I learn more accurately the state of things below. I have no men to spare from this portion of my corps. Asboth reports to me to day that Pillow with 6000 men is at Macedonia near Paris and expects to be reinforced by *Forrest.* I have so little confidence in Asboth's reports that I am at a loss what to do. Still I think from the fact that Col. Jesse Forrest, Col. Biffle, & Newsome & other bands were defeated at Jackson on 13th by Hatch that it is probable that a considerable body of conscripts & others have been gathered at or near Paris with intent to move on Paducah. With this gathering threatening the Ohio & Mississippi Rivers, with Roddy's force at Bear Creek, with Ruggles at Akalona and Chalmers at Panola I am not in condition to spare any force. I am entirely in the dark as to movements below   cannot tell what has become of Johnstone, though I suppose from reports from my spies that he is falling back on the line of the Mobile & Ohio R Road or perhaps the Tombigbee River. In this event my immediate front will be cleared. It is evident to me that the disposable cavalry of Braggs army is to be thrown in marauding expeditions such as John Morgan's— into such points as they can reach. Bragg himself holds his line from Chattanooga to Atlanta, and will operate on Rosecranz line of communications. Under the orders of the General in Chief if the rear of Price's movement is to be attacked, it can only be done by detaching from the Army below a Division, either Herron's Missouri force—or by sending me for that purpose such Division of my Corps as you may choose. If you detach a Division it will be necessary to send them with field transportation & field artillery—I am very light in Batteries for the field. I respectfully ask for such orders from you as may in your judgment be necessary & proper" ALS, DNA, RG 94, War Records Office, Dept. of the Tenn. *O.R.*, I, xxiv, part 3, 526–27. On the same day, Hurlbut telegraphed to Halleck that it was not possible to send reinforcements to Prentiss as requested. Copy, DNA, RG 393, 16th Army Corps, Letters Sent. *O.R.*, I, xxiv, part 3, 526. On July 19, Hurlbut wrote to Col. John C. Kelton describing the disposition of his forces, concluding: "Under these circumstances there is no possibility of sending any force from the remnant of the 16th Army Corps, now here; to Arkansas without serious peril to our hold upon this line. I have requested Genl Grant to return me a Division, and have forwarded the telegram of the General in Chief to him. Memphis requires as Garrison to cover its immense stores, to protect its Hospitals, and not least to prevent smuggling at least eight Regiments, and this necessity will exist until the operations of the Army below shall destroy the basis upon which the advanced line of the enemy now rests. I await this time hopefully, and as soon as I learn that fact shall throw all my Cavalry and mounted Infantry supported by a Brigade from Corinth, first upon Roddy at Bear Creek, and thence on Okolona." Copy, DNA, RG 393, 16th Army Corps, Letters Sent. *O.R.*, I, xxiv, part 3, 535–36.

On July 18, 1:00 A.M., Brig. Gen. Leonard F. Ross, Helena, wrote to USG. "Enclosed I send you a dispatch just recd—You are aware that we have not the requisite force here to move as directed—not having at this time over 3,500 effective men.—From the best information we can get Holmes force amounts to about 12,000 effective men and I should not consider it safe to move against him with less than 6,000 or 7,000—If you could spare 9,000 or 10,000 it would I think insure success—If a force should be sent up White River with gunboats I could take 2,000 men from this place and from the River forces at Des Arcs or Cotton Plant—In retreating from this place the enemy moved up on the East side of White River to Des Arcs where Parsons Brigade crossed over—the balance were seen six miles above Augusta en route for Jacksonport—I think they will remain in the vicinity of Jacksonport for the present—unless forced out by Davidson—" ALS, DNA, RG 94, War Records Office, Dept. of the Tenn. *O.R.*, I, xxii, part 2, 381. For the enclosure, see *ibid.*, I, xxii, part 1, 20–21.

To Maj. Gen. Stephen A. Hurlbut

Headquarters Department of the Tennessee
Vicksburg Miss. July 21. 1863.

MAJ. GENL. S. A. HURLBUT
COMMANDING 16TH ARMY CORPS.
GENERAL:

Sherman has driven Johnston from Jackson. The latter is now retreating eastward with his whole Army much demoralized, and deserting in great numbers, and no doubt many falling by the way side from heat, dust and drought. My Army from long marches, battles and the extraordinary length of the seige is much broken and must have rest. Two Divisions of the 16th Corps, are now at Jackson. The remaining one (Kimballs) is here and is in fact the only troops I have fit to make a move. These I have ordered to be in readiness to go to Helena, as soon as transportation can be proseded [*procured*].¹ This I think will be within two days. Johnston's army is so broken, that no danger need be apprehended from them for the next thirty days or more. I shall as soon as possible send some odd regiments to you, they are weak, ineffective men, but will no doubt recuperate rapidly by the change.

I am sending artillery from here to complete the armament at Helena,² and can send as much as you want for Memphis. Capt. Comstock Engineer, has now gone up to see what is required for both places.

I cannot believe that any portion of your command is in any danger from any thing more than a cavalry raid, but your opportunities are so much better for knowing than mine, that I leave it to you entirely to make the necessary dispositions of the forces at your command.³

If any more troops are required to operate against Price, I will have to send Herron, who is now returning from an exhausting march from Yazoo City to Clinton and return.

The forces going from here will be provided with field transportation and artillery.

It is probable if any move is made against Price, Ord will go in command, but of this I am not yet certain.

Very respectfully
Your obt Servt
U. S. Grant
Maj. Genl.

Copies, DLC-USG, V, 19, 101, 103; DNA, RG 393, Dept. of the Tenn., Letters Sent. *O.R.*, I, xxii, part 2, 384–85; *ibid.*, I, xxiv, part 3, 539–40. See preceding telegram; letters to Maj. Gen. Stephen A. Hurlbut, July 22, 24, 1863; and following letter. On July 25, 1863, Maj. Gen. Stephen A. Hurlbut wrote to USG. "Yours of 21st. has been received   The clearing of the Country about Jackson and Canton has completely relieved my front. Chalmers has retired toward the Mississippi Central R. Road probably to Coffeeville. Ruggles is so far as I can learn disposing his force to cover Columbus. Roddy is said to be falling back through Alabama toward Bragg who is retreating upon Atlanta. I have learned that twenty Locomotives, and two hundred cars are at Water Valley and have sent orders to Dodge to send down and destroy them. This line is entirely quiet now except from Guerrilla parties up above in the neigborhood of Jackson Brownsville and other points who are conscripting   I think that a notice to these men permitting them to return to their homes unmolested on taking the oath, and also that conscription within our lines is in violation of the laws of war, and that persons so found, will not be considered as prisoners of war, would have an effect in bringing these scattering gangs to order, and quieting the Country. I hardly know what course to pursue. If I send Cavalry they break up and scatter, and my own cavalry commits depredations in following them. The people of the Country themselves are more afraid of the Guerrillas than of our troops, and therefore will not report them. If, I was authorized to make serious examples, of such as are caught in acts of robbery, and violence, it would be beneficial. I do not consider them soldiers, but feel, bound by your order recognizing Richardson's band." Copy, DNA, RG 393, 16th Army Corps, Letters Sent. *O.R.*, I, xxiv, part 3, 551–52.

1. On July 21, USG wrote to Maj. Gen. Cadwallader C. Washburn. "Get Kimball's Division in readiness to be moved up the river as soon as possible. Boats will be ordered as soon as coal arrives to furnish fuel. ~~Orders will be prepared before these troops leave.~~ Full instructions will be given before the troops leave." ALS, DNA, RG 94, War Records Office, Dept. of the Tenn. Misdated July 20 in *O.R.*, I, xxiv, part 3, 536. On the same day, Washburn telegraphed to USG. "Cannot a boat be sent here at once for the sick of Kimballs Division   Your despatch ordering that division to be ready was recd." Telegram received, DNA, RG 393, Dept. of the Tenn., Telegrams Received.

2. On July 16, Hurlbut wrote to Lt. Col. John A. Rawlins. "Accompanying this you will find dispatch from Genl. Schofield. He understands Price to be at or near Jacksonport & on his march for Missouri. I this morning received a letter from Genl Ross at Helena asking reinforcements for that point, and stating his apprehension of an attack from a heavy force. Dobbins with two Regiments of Cavalry he says is at LaGrange 15 miles west—and he apprehends a heavy force to be gathering behind him. Ross believes it to be Price's & apprehends attack. If there is any force there it must be from the South in my opinion. I have sent two 12 lb Howitzers to Helena & shall send some Heavy pieces—and in case of necessity can spare a Regiment for a while. My force is too light for many details of this nature, but I will always advance them when necessary" ALS, *ibid.*, RG 94, War Records Office, Dept. of the Tenn.

3. On July 15, Hurlbut wrote to Rawlins. "If it be possible so to do, I request that Kimballs Division may be ordered back to me as soon as practicable. The evident intention of the enemy is to occupy West Tennessee with cavalry and conscripts until they can raise force enough to threaten the Rail Road or the River posts. Col. Forrest's Regular Cavalry 700 Strong with revolving rifles are at or near Jackson and united with Biffles & other bands gave a severe fight to Col Hatchs on the 13th at that place. They were defeated with loss on our side of 30 to 50 killed & wounded, larger on the part of the enemy. Hatch is pursuing them toward Trenton. Asboth has succeeded in losing most of his Cavalry by surprises and sending out light Expeditions under in competent officers. My Cavalry are worked too hard. They have to clear the whole country West of the

Tennessee & North of the Road, as well as watch the front & left of the line.
If Kimball has his transportation he should land about Commerce and march in
toward Coldwater Station clearing Chalmers out & moving thence where he may
be ordered. He should have one good battery, at least. By thus establishing himself,
he can be moved to any point I may wish him. If Johnstone is driven out of the
way East of Pearl, Kimball might land lower down and with his pioneers build
a bridge a cross the Tallahatchie below Panola, taking that place in rear and
be of admirable service and thence move up to me. I hope no cavalry will be withdrawn from me at present as the duty is enormous and the line of country too
heavy for the force I have." ALS, *ibid.*, RG 393, Dept. of the Tenn., Letters
Received. *O.R.*, I, xxiv, part 3, 518.

To Maj. Gen. John M. Schofield

Headquarters Dept. of the Tenn.
Vicksburg Miss. July 21st. 1863.

Maj. Genl Schofield
Comd'g Dept. of the Mo.
General:

I am sending, or will send as soon as transportation can be
provided, one Division, about 5000 effective men, to operate in
Price's rear. These are the only troops I have, not exhausted and
worn down. In addition to this there will probably be 8000 men
to spare from the garrison of Helena, and West Tennessee.

Johnston has been totally routed from Jackson, and will no
doubt lose half his Army from desertion, and the balance will be
so broken down and demoralized, that but little danger need be
apprehended from them, for the for the next sixty days.

My troops are not yet in from Jackson, no part of them. Should
it be necessary to send more troops to Helena, I can send from
here men to hold that place, and relieve the entire garrison to look
after Price. Possibly this will be the best course to pursue.

I am very respectfully
Your obt. Serv't.
U. S. Grant.

Copies, DLC-USG, V, 19, 101, 103; DLC-John M. Schofield; DNA, RG 393,
Dept. of the Tenn., Letters Sent. *O.R.*, I, xxii, part 1, 21–22. On July 21, 1863,

USG telegraphed to Maj. Gen. John M. Schofield. "I will send one Division to Helena to go after Price. I have no more troops here not worn out. I will send other troops to form the garrison so as to releave all the force now at Helena." ALS (telegram sent), DNA, RG 94, War Records Office, Dept. of the Tenn. *O.R.*, I, xxii, part 2, 385. On July 14, Schofield, St. Louis, telegraphed to USG. "Price is in North Eastern Arkansas with about fifteen thousand men moving into Missouri. I have not force enough to drive him out having sent nearly all to Vicksburg. Can you not send a force up White River or the Arkansas immediately? You can capture all of Prices Infantry and Artillery." ALS (telegram sent), DNA, RG 107, Telegrams Collected (Unbound); telegram received, *ibid.*, RG 94, War Records Office, Dept. of the Tenn. *O.R.*, I, xxii, part 2, 374. On July 22, Rear Admiral David D. Porter telegraphed to USG. "Your telegram has been received. I have already sent orders to White River to have four gun boats ready when General Schofield's forces or any others arrive. I received a telegram from the Secretary of the Navy on the subject but he did not say what was going to be done." ALS, DNA, RG 45, Correspondence of David D. Porter, Mississippi Squadron, General Letters (Press).

To Maj. Gen. William T. Sherman

July 21st 1863

GEN. SHERMAN,

I am very much opposed to any trade whatever until the rebellion in this part of the country is entirely crushed out. Sec. Chase differs however and the special Agt. for the West is now on the way here to arrange this matter. I received a letter today from the Spl. Agt. and one from Chase[1] enclosing a copy of his letter to the Agt.

When he arrives we will fix upon some plan by which citizens can get necessary supplies for such produce as they have.[2] I want it arranged so no Citizens shall be allowed to come to trade. I would make no proposition about neutral territory.

U. S. GRANT
Maj. Gen

ALS, DNA, RG 94, War Records Office, Dept. of the Tenn. *O.R.*, I, xxiv, part 3, 539. On July 22, 1863, Maj. Gen. William T. Sherman, Jackson, telegraphed to USG. "All right about trade   I will not promise or do anything except to relieve the immediate wants of suffering humanity   All well   will ride around the city to see all my orders are executed   when I propose to Clinton next day to Bolton next to Black River & then to report to you in person—after which to establish

healthy camps of instruction for my corps   I want 10.000 conscripts two months
& the fifteenth army corps will be ready for Selma & Atlanta   Order Maj Smith
down to help me drill & organize   Also I would like to have a few brigadiers who
know how to drill & instruct   I also want authority to consolidate two three or
even four regts of the Same state into Single regts   The mode prescribed by the
war dept is wrong as it would leave us with little battallions whereas we want
to concentrate the materials in our possession into Simple regts & brigades   my
men are now well rested   have bathed fully in pearl River   the people are
moving from the Terror of the cannonade & we can draw behind black River
with propriety   I still think it would be imprudent to hold Jackson   it is not
a strategic point now that its R R are utterly ruined & demolished & were my
corps to remain here it could do no good where as a few good guerrellas could
constantly attack our trains & keep us uneasy all the time   at Black River we
can draw our lines exclude every body & conceal our strenght plans & purposes
& when you give the word I can in a day ~~relieve~~ recover Jackson or what amounts
to the Same thing a good crossing over Pearl River"   Telegram received, DNA,
RG 94, War Records Office, Dept. of the Tenn. *O.R.*, I, xxiv, part 2, 531–32.

On July 21, Sherman twice telegraphed to USG, the second time at 2:00
P.M. "I will stay here another day & longer if I can do any good   All is working admirably   I believe the people will appreciate the liberal gift of provisions   I ~~a~~ have been compelled to relieve hospitals asylums immediate pressing
wants   would I be Justified in making a distinct proposition to the people that if
Johnston or prest Davis will agree that no Confederate Soldiers or guerrillas will
operate west of Pearl River we will establish at Black River bridge a kind of trading depot where the people of Miss may exchange their cotton corn & produce for
provisions & family Supplies   this would throw on the confederate govt the onus
of relieving the wants of the women & children that are now threatened with
starvation   at Brandon Canton & Jackson all act as though the thing was ended
unless Lee achieves the capture of Baltimore & Washington which they are taught
to believe & Such men as Starkey Young Poindexter & others of good reputation
are actually at work ~~to~~ & appeal for permission to build up a civil Govt Even
the old union as they style it   I profess to know nothing of politics but I think
~~wel~~ we have here an admirable wedge which may be encouraged without committing the prest or war Dept   if prominent men in Miss admit the fact of being
Subdued it will have a powerful effect over the south   all the army except my
corps is en route for Vicksburg & having destroyed the R R & other material I
only remain here to rebel against a Govt which they now feel is unable to protect
them or support them   I cannot learn of an enemy with in 30 miles of me"   "We
have desolated this land for thirty miles round about   there are about 800
women & children who will perish unless they receive some relief   may I promise
the Mayor & Committee say two hundred 200 bbls of flour & one hundred Bbls
of salt Pork if they will send for it to Big Black bridge & give me pledges that it
shall be donated to pure charity   Judge Stanley Dr Poindexter & Mr Young with
many very intelligent & influently men have consulted me as to moving in the
matter of organizing the state to submit to the lawful authority of the United
States   they admit themselves beaten subdued & charge their rulers & agita-
tors with bringing ruin & misery on the State   of course I make no promises
or pledges but merely that I beleived such a movement would be recd with
favor   Since Steele went to Brandon a perfect stream of negroes has been
passing towards vicksburg   I am am battering down the R R piers with artillery"

Telegrams received, DNA, RG 94, War Records Office, Dept. of the Tenn.; copies, *ibid.*, RG 393, Dept. of the Tenn., Telegrams Sent. *O.R.*, I, xxiv, part 2, 530–31. USG answered on the same day. "I will send the flour & pork to Black River as you suggest." ALS, DNA, RG 393, Dept. of the Tenn., Telegrams Received. On July 21, Lt. Col. John A. Rawlins issued General Orders No. 46. "Hereafter no issues of provisions will be made for Contrabands, except those serving in regiments or contraband camps. Issues of provisions will not be made to citizens, except on certificates that they are destitute, and have no means of purchasing the necessary supplies for their families. These certificates must state the number in family; and the time for which they draw, which shall not exceed ten days at any one time. In making issues to citizens, only prime articles of ncessity will be given, i.e., bread and meat and these at the rate of one pound of flour, one-half pound of salt meat or one pound of fresh beef to the ration." Copies, DLC-USG, V, 13, 14; DNA, RG 393, Dept. of the Tenn., General Orders; (printed) USGA.

 1. See letter to Salmon P. Chase, July 21, 1863.
 2. On July 9, Maj. Gen. Cadwallader C. Washburn telegraphed to USG. "Many families are making applications to have rations issued to them representing themselves in a starving condition from having their property taken or destroyed by the army. I have supplied quite a number but they multiply rapidly   shall I ~~find~~ feed such such as appear to be objects of charity" Telegram received, DNA, RG 393, Dept. of the Tenn., Telegrams Received. USG drafted his answer on the bottom of the telegram. "We will have to supply rations for the present to families who are without and have not the means of purchasing." ANS, *ibid.*

To Brig. Gen. Charles P. Stone

Head Quarters, Dept. of the Ten.
Vicksburg Miss. July 21st 1863.

Brig. Gen. J. P. Stone,
Comd.g U. S. Forces,
Port Hudson.
Gen.

 I have just received a letter from the Adj. Gen of the 19th Army Corps asking for the establishment of Mail facilities by this route and to telegraph the Sec. of War for six telegraph operators.

 The Special Agt. of the P. O. Dept. for the West makes his Hd Qrs in Vicksburg. I will instruct him to make the arrangement asked at once.

Having contracted my lines I can spare from here the operators required and have accordingly ordered them to go down with the vessel just up from Port Hudson. In a few days my troops will return from Jackson when the balance of the required number will be sent.

I wish you would say to Gen. Banks that the call for transports has been so great that I could not supply them with the promptness I expected. I am now compelled to send some 10 000 troops to Helena to operate against Price who is said to be moving towards S. E. Mo. The 9th A. C. is to be sent back to Burnside. Many hundreds of my own men are becoming sick and have to be sent to Northern hospitals, and to get clear of the rebel sick and wounded I gladly accepted the opportunity of sending them to Mobile & Monroe.

I will be very glad to facilitate Gen. Bank in getting everything from this direction he requires. There is no coal on hand now but some is expected daily. When it arrives it will be divided with him. Forage, rations an[d] Ordnance stores can be supplied at any time. The 2000 mules called for can also be sent at once.

Sherman has forced Johnston to retreat from Jackson eastward. He will loose half his Army. Johnston's troops burned Jackson, or the most of it, before leaving.

Sherman telegraphs me the people are completely subdued. They acknowledg[e] the loss of the Southern cause. Some of the most prominent citizens of Jackson called on Sherman to know what the citizens of their state could do to get back into the Union and to secure Federal protection. The country from here to Brandon and for ten miles south of the rail-road, for the whole distance, and forty miles North of it, is completely devastated by the two armies living off of it. Thousands of people would now be suffering from starvation if our Com.y supplies were witheld from them.

> I am Gen. Very respectfully
> your obt. svt.
> U. S. GRANT
> Maj. Gen. Com

ALS, CSmH. Charles P. Stone, born in Mass. in 1824, USMA 1845, was appointed bvt. 2nd lt. of ordnance as of July 1, 1845, and resigned as 1st lt. effective Nov. 17, 1856. Appointed col. and inspector-gen. of D. C. vols. as of Jan. 1, 1861, he was promoted to col., 14th Inf., as of May 14, and to brig. gen. as of May 17. Unfairly blamed for the U.S. defeat at the battle of Ball's Bluff, he was imprisoned without charges for over six months, then released and later assigned to the Dept. of the Gulf in May, 1863, where he participated in the siege of Port Hudson, and, on July 25, became chief of staff for Maj. Gen. Nathaniel P. Banks. On July 19, Lt. Col. Richard B. Irwin wrote to USG. "In accordance with telegraphick instructions from the Major General Commanding, temporarily absent in New Orleans, I have the honor to request that you will, by the earliest opportunity ask the War Department in his name, to send at least six skilled telegraph operators to this Department, as a measure almost essential to the efficiency of our operations. During the investment of Port Hudson, on account of the insufficient number of operators, we rarely if ever had communication over the wires at night, and the force we then had has since been reduced by over exertion and the influences of this climate. I am further instructed by the Commanding General to request that you will have the necessary steps taken to secure a regular and frequent mail communication with the North by the Mississippi River. The Commanding General regards this as a matter of no little importance. Trusting that the General's absence and his telegraphic instructions to me, may plead excuse for the irregularity of this communication." Copy, DNA, RG 393, Depts. of the Gulf and La., Letters Sent.

To Lt. Col. Judson D. Bingham

[*July 21, 1863*]

I have relieved Mr. Livermore of his functions as Negro Commissioner and taken from him the controll of the Steamer Patten. It seems one boat has been kept for the use of the Negro Regiments and another for the Commissioners. One it seems to me can do the business for all the contrabands both soldiers and others. There are some rations to go up this morning which will probably be put aboard of the Patten . . . As the Bullet and Patten are both now at the Wharf, please give directions which boat you will have them go on—and order the other boat for general service. . . .

U. S. GRANT

Manuscripts, 16, 1(Winter, 1964), [p. 65]; Paul C. Richards, *Catalogue No. 24*, p. 178. On July 21, 1863, Lt. Col. John A. Rawlins wrote to Lt. Col. Judson D. Bingham. "The Steamer Patten will be immediately released from the employ of the U. S. Commissioners for leasing abandoned Plantations. No boat will be furnished said commissioners until further orders. Rev'd L. S. Livermore has been relieved from duty as U. S. Commissioner." Copies, DLC-USG, V, 19, 101, 103; DNA, RG 393, Dept. of the Tenn., Letters Sent. See letter to Charles A. Dana, Aug. 5, 1863. Capt. Abraham E. Strickle, the only commissioner of abandoned plantations trusted by USG, died on July 9. See letter to Brig. Gen. Lorenzo Thomas, July 11, 1863. USG probably did not learn of Strickle's death until, or shortly before, July 20, when Rawlins issued Special Orders No. 196 directing Lt. Col. Robert Macfeely to arrange for proper disposition of Strickle's official papers and private effects. Copies, DLC-USG, V, 27, 28; DNA, RG 393, Dept. of the Tenn., Special Orders.

To Salmon P. Chase

Head Qrs. Dept. of the Ten.
Vicksburg Miss. July 21st 1863.

Hon. S. P. Chase
Sec. of the Treasury,
Sir:

Your letter of the 4th inst. to me, enclosing copy of letter of same date to Mr. Mellen; Spl. Agt. of the Treasury is just received.—My Asst. Adj. Gen. by whom I shall send this letter is about starting for Washington hence I shall be very short in my reply.

My experiance in West Tennessee has convinced me that any trade whatever with the rebellious states is weakening to us of at least Thirty three per cent of our force. No matter what the restrictions thrown around trade if any whatever is allowed it will be made the means of supplying to the enemy all they want. Restrictions if lived up to make trade unproffitable and hence none but dishonest men go into it. I will venture that no honest man has made money in West Tennessee in the last year whilst many fortunes have been made there during the time.

The people in the Mississippi Valley are now nearly subjugated. Keep trade out for but a few months and I doubt not but that the work of subjugation will be so complete that trade can be opened freely with the states of Arkansas, La. & Mississippi. That the people of these states will be more anxious for the enforcement, and protection, of our laws than the people of the loyal states. They have experienced the misfortune of being without them and are now in a most happy condition to appreciate their blessing.

No theory of my own will ever stand in the way of my executing, in good faith, any order I may receive from those in authority over me. But my position has given me an opportunity of seeing what could not be know by persons away from the scene of War and I venture therefore to suggest great caution in opening trade with rebels.

> I am sir, very respectfully
> your obt. svt.
> U. S. GRANT
> Maj. Gen. Com

ALS, DNA, RG 56, Letters Received from the War Dept. *O.R.*, I, xxiv, part 3, 538. On July 4, 1863, Secretary of the Treasury Salmon P. Chase had written to USG. "I find that the establishment of a rigorous line, within districts occupied by our military forces, from beyond which no cotton or other products can be brought and within which no trade can be carried on, gives rise to serious, and to some extent, apparently, well-founded complaints. I have, therefore, instructed Mr. Mellen, the Supervising Special Agent of this Department for the Mississippi Valley, to confer with you as to the propriety of substituting Bonds, to be given by all parties receiving permits, for the rigorous line now established; or, at least, of substituting them partially. I enclose you a copy of my letter to Mr. Mellen; and, beg you to give it, and any suggestions on the subject he may offer, such consideration as the other great demands upon your time and attention will allow." LS, DNA, RG 393, Dept. of the Tenn., Letters Received. *O.R.*, I, xxiv, part 3, 468. Chase enclosed a copy of his letter of July 4 to U.S. Treasury Agent William P. Mellen stating that civilians engaged in legitimate trade in occupied areas be required to give bonds for compliance with regulations. Copy, DNA, RG 393, Dept. of the Tenn., Letters Received. *O.R.*, I, xxiv, part 3, 468.

Also on July 4, Chase wrote to USG. "It has long been on my mind to express to you my deep sense of your great services to our country; but I have foreborne lest you might think I overstepped a civilians limits. Having occasion now, however, to write you briefly on another subject, I will not deny myself the gratification of adding my personal thanks to the gratitude which the whole patriotic people feel towards you for the patient energy and skilful courage with which you have conducted the military operations under your direction. God has crowned you with success hitherto and will, I trust, continue to prosper our arms under your conduct. Vicksburgh, probably, has already succumbe[d.] Whether so or not its speedy fall can hardly be doubted; and its capture cannot fail to be followed by the rapid and complete suppression of the rebellion in the whole region west of the Mississippi and by the complete control of the river from its mouth to Cairo. It has given me great satisfaction to be somewhat useful in sustaining you here by laying before the President, from time to time the letters of Mr. Mellen, the excellent Supervising Special Agent of the Department for the Valley of the Mississippi. He has taken every pains to inform himself accurately and has constantly defended you against the assaults sometimes of slanderous malice & sometimes of mistaken honesty & has as constantly awarded to you the praise of doing all that ability, zeal & fidelity could accomplish." ALS, DNA, RG 393, Dept. of the Tenn., Letters Received. *O.R.*, I, xxiv, part 3, 469. On July 10, Mellen, Cincinnati, at Chase's direction, wrote to USG to arrange a meeting with him regarding regulations for marketing cotton. LS (partly illegible), DNA, RG 366, First Special Agency, Letters Sent (Press).

On July 27, USG issued a pass. "Mr. T. H. Yeatman, Spl. Agt. of the Treasury Dept. will be permitted to pass through all parts of this Department at all times. Good until countermanded." ANS, NjP. On Aug. 1, Thomas H. Yeatman, Memphis, wrote to USG. "The bearer of this, Mr Chas. A. Montross, goes to Vicksburg, as the Treasury Agent, to collect all the seized, or abandoned, Cotton, or other property, in the vicinity of Vicksburg. Mr Montross, will require the assistance, of hands, and teams;—may I ask the favor, that you detail, what may be necessary, and such further facilities, as to you shall seem proper." Copies, DNA, RG 36, Special Agents, Reports and Correspondence; *ibid.*, RG 366, Correspondence of the General Agent.

On Aug. 7, USG wrote to Maj. Gen. William T. Sherman. "Send in the loose & abandoned cotton from about Black River bridge   there is a Treasury agent here to receive it now & send it north." Telegram received, DLC-William T. Sherman; copies, DLC-USG, V, 19, 101, 103; DNA, RG 393, Dept. of the Tenn., Letters Sent. On Aug. 13, USG telegraphed to Sherman. "Have the cotton about your Camp, and in the fortifications east of Black River, not the property of private individuals, sent here to Mr. Montrose, Special Agent of the Treasury Department." Copies, *ibid.* On the same day, Sherman telegraphed to USG. "I ordered Gen Dennis Some days ago to Send in all the loose cotton about the bridge & will renew the order   there is no Confederate cotton hereabouts   we could get plenty of cotton by opening a store to barter for it   the people East of the Big black have all more or less private cotton that they want to Exchange for Shoes & groceries—Farrars regt will come to Vicksburg in the 4 P m train" Telegram received, *ibid.*, RG 94, War Records Office, Dept. of the Tenn.; copy (undated), *ibid.*, RG 393, Dept. of the Tenn., Telegrams Sent. *O.R.*, I, xxx, part 3, 19. See letter to Brig. Gen. Marcellus M. Crocker, Aug. 28, 1863.

To Abraham Lincoln

Head Quarters, Dept. of the Ten.
Vicksburg Miss. July 22d 1863.

His Excellency, A. Lincoln,
President of the United States.
Sir:

I would most respectfully but urgently recommend the promotion of Maj. Gen. Wm. T. Sherman, now commanding the 15th Army Corps, and Maj. Gen. J. B. McPherson, commanding the 17th Army Corps to the positions of Brig. Gen. in the regular Army.

The first reason for this is their great fitness for any command that it may ever become necessary to intrust to them. Second, their great purity of character and disinterestedness in everything except the faithful performance of their duty and the success of every one engaged in the great battle for the preservation of the Union. Third they have honorably won this distinction upon many well fought battle fields. I will only mention some of their services since serving under my command.

To Gen. Sherman I was greatly indebted for his promptness in forwarding to me, during the siege of Fort Donelson, reinforcements and supplies from Paducah. At the battle of Shiloh on the first day he held, with raw troops, the key point to the landing. To his individual efforts I am indebted for the success of that battle. Twice hit and several, I think three, horses shot on that day he maintained his position with his raw troops. It is no disparagement to any other officer to say that I do not believe there was another Division commander on the field who had the skill or experience to have done it. His services as Division Commander in the advance on Corinth I will venture were appreciated by the, now, Gen. in Chief beyond those of any other Division commander. Gen. Sherman's management as commander of troops in the attack on Chickasaw Bluffs last December was admirable. Seeing the ground from the opposite side from the attack I see the impossibility of making it successful. The conception of the attack on Arkansas Post was Gen. Sherman's. His part of the execution, no one denies, was as good as it possibly could have been. His demonstration on Hain's Bluff in April to hold the enemy about Vicksburg whilst the Army was securing a foot hold East of the Miss.; his rapid marches to join the Army afterwards,; his management at Jackson, Miss., in the first attack; his almost unequaled march from Jackson to Bridgeport and passage of ~~that stream~~ Black River; his securing Walnut Hills on the 18th of May and thus opening communication with our supplies, all attest his great merit as a soldier. The siege of Vicksburg and last capture of Jackson, and dispersion of Johnston's Army, entitle Gen. Sherman to more credit than it usually falls to the lot of one man to earn.

Gen. McPherson has been with me in every battle since the commencement of the rebellion except Belmont. At Henry, Donelson, Shiloh and the siege of Corinth, as a Staff officer and Engineer, his services were conspicuous and highly meritorious. At the second battle of Corinth his skill as a soldier was displayed in successfully carrying reinforcements to the besieged garrison when the enemy was between him and the point to be reached. In the advance through Central Mississippi last November & December Gen. McPherson commanded one Wing of the Army with all the ability possible to show, he having the lead on the advance and the rear returning.

In the campaign and siege terminating with the fall of Vicksburg Gen. McPherson has filled a conspicuous part. At the battle of Port Gibson it was under his immediate direction the enemy were driven late in the afternoon from a position they had suceeded in holding all day against an obstinate attack. His Corps, the advance always under his immediate eye, was the pioneer in the advance from Port Gibson to Hankersons Ferry. From North Fork of Bayou Pierre to Black River it was a constant skirmish the whole skilfully managed. The enemy was so closely pressed as to be unable to destroy their bridge of boats after them. From Hankersons Ferry to Jackson the 17th Army Corps marched upon roads not traveled by other troops fighting the battle of Raymond alone and the bulk of Johnston's Army at Jackson also was fought by this Corps entirely under the management of Gen. McPherson. At Champion Hill the 17th Corps and Gen. McPherson were conspicuous. All that could be termed a battle there was fought by two Divisions of Gen. McPherson's Corps and Hovey Division of the 13th Corps.

In the assault of the 22d of June on the fortifications of Vicksburg and during the entire siege, Gen. McPherson and his command won unfading laurels. He is one of our ablest Engineers and

most skilfull Generals. The promotion of such men as Sherman
and McPherson always add strength to our Arms.

> I have the honor to be
> very respectfully
> Your obt. svt.
> U. S. GRANT
> Maj. Gen. U. S. A.

ALS, DNA, RG 94, Letters Received, 502T 1863. *O.R.*, I, xxiv, part 3, 540–42.
An identical letter was sent to Brig. Gen. Lorenzo Thomas. LS, DNA, RG 94,
ACP, H1125 CB 1863. On July 11, 1863, Maj. Gen. Henry W. Halleck wrote
to USG. "Genl G. G. Meade has been appointed a Brig Genl in the regular Army
at the same time that you were made a Major Genl. There is still one vacant Brig
Generalcy & I hope that Harney, Anderson & Cooke will soon be retired, making
three more vacancies. The most prominent candidates at present for Brig Genls
in regular army are W. T. Sherman, McPherson, G. H. Thomas, Sedgwick &
Hancock. I am of opinion that Sherman & McPherson have rendered the best
service & should come in first. If you think so, write an official letter to that
effect, urging their appointment to the first vacancies. State their services pretty
fully & mention the battles they have been in under your command. The feeling
is very strong here in your favor & there will be a strong disposition to grant
any favor you may ask for your generals. We are anxiously waiting to hear
the fall of ~~Vicksburg~~ Port Hudson & the entire opening of the Miss. River.
The Prest will then issue a genl order congratulating the armies of the east &
west on their recent victories. This consideration has prevented me from issueing
one myself for your army. I prefer that it should come from the Prest. Meade
has thus far proved an excellent general, the only one in fact who has ever
fought the army of the Potomac well. He seems the right man in the right
place. Hooker was worse than a failure. Had he remained in command he would
have lost the army & the capital. Give my kindest regards to my old friends
among your officers. I sincerely wish I was with you again in the west. I am
utterly sick of this political Hell." ALS, Oglesby Papers, IHi. *O.R.*, I, xxiv,
part 3, 498.

On Aug. 4, Halleck reported to USG the appointments of Maj. Gen. William
T. Sherman and Maj. Gen. James B. McPherson as brig. gen. in the regular
army. See letter to Maj. Gen. Henry W. Halleck, Aug. 11, 1863, note 1. On
Aug. 15, Sherman, Big Black, wrote to USG. "I had the satisfaction to receive,
last night, the appointment as brigadier-general in the Regular Army, with a
letter from General Halleck, very friendly and complimentary in its terms. I
know that I owe this to your favor, and beg to acknowledge it, and to add that
I value the commission far less than the fact that this will associate my name
with yours and McPherson's in opening the Mississippi, an achievement the importance of which cannot be overestimated. I beg to assure you of my deep
personal attachment, and to express the hope that the chances of war will leave
me to serve near and under you till the dawn of that peace for which we are
contending, with the only purpose that it be honorable and lasting." *O.R.*, I, xxx,
part 3, 31. Sherman and McPherson were nominated on Jan. 7, 1864, and confirmed on March 1.

To Maj. Gen. Stephen A. Hurlbut

———

Head Quarters, Dept. of the Ten.
Vicksburg Miss. July 22d 1863.

Maj. Gen. S. A. Hurlbut,
Comd.g 16th Army Corps,
Gen.

Furloughs may be given to soldiers on Surgeons Certificates, for thirty days. These furloughs will only be given to such soldiers as are not likely to be fit for Military duty for the time their furloughs are for and at the same time to men who are likely to recover so as to be fit for Field service. All others will either be placed in the Invalid Corps or be discharged.

I have directed the Med. Director to instruct Surgeons how certificates are to be given.

Very respectfully
U. S. Grant
Maj. Gen. Com

ALS, DNA, RG 393, 16th Army Corps, Letters Received. *O.R.*, I, xxiv, part 3, 544.

To Maj. Gen. Stephen A. Hurlbut

———

Head Quarters, Dept. of the Ten.
Vicksburg, Miss. July 22d 1863.

Maj. Gen. S. A. Hurlbut,
Comd.g 16th Army Corps,
Gen.

I am sending Kimballs Division to Helena and shall send to you some five or six ~~weak~~ regiments now weakened by sickness. These latter will be able to do garrison duty in Tennessee and release other troops that are fully rested to join the expedition after Price.

Unless Ord chooses to go on this expedition himself, in person, I think I shall add the Dist. of N. E. Ark. to your Corps and leave it optional with you who shall command.

I will send you an officer to command the Dist. of Columbus but cannot say just yet who it will be. I would send Gen. Smith (W. S.) but his health is so broken that he must go North. How would Hovey or Morgan L. Smith do?

> Very respectfully
> Your obt. svt.
> U. S. GRANT
> Maj. Gen. Com

ALS, DNA, RG 94, War Records Office, Union Battle Reports. *O.R.*, I, xxii, part 2, 386–87; *ibid.*, I, xxiv, part 3, 544. See *ibid.*, I, xxii, part 2, 407; letters to Maj. Gen. Stephen A. Hurlbut, July 21, 24, Aug. 5, 1863.

To Maj. Gen. James B. McPherson

———

July 22d 1863.

DEAR MC

I send you a private letter just received from "Old Brain" which I send for your perusal. Return it by bearer. There is a portion of the letter which probably should not be repeated. The whole letter is *private* & *confidential* but I know there is no objection to you and Sherman seeing it.

So far as you and Sherman are concerned I will do my part this very day.

> Yours,
> U. S. GRANT
> Maj. Gen.

ALS, deCoppet Collection, NjP. See letter to Abraham Lincoln, July 22, 1863. On July 22, 1863, Maj. Gen. James B. McPherson wrote to USG. "I appreciate most highly the favor you have shown me in sending 'Old Brains,' letter for perusal—It is another of the repeated acts of kindness which you have always shown me, and it will ever be my duty as well as pleasure to try to merit your confidence   I certainly had no idea before, that my name was thought of in connection with a Brigr-ship in the Regular Army, though of course it is very gratifying to know that it is so, Sherman richly deserves the position and I earnestly hope he will get it—" ALS, DNA, RG 393, Dept. of the Tenn., Letters Received.

To Maj. Gen. John G. Parke

July 22d 1863

GEN. PARKE,

Encamp your Corps where it will be pleasant and healthy until further orders. I have not got the transportation to move you now owing to the unexpected calls that have been made for boats and have no instructions yet from the Gen. in Chief. I telegraphed him to know if your Corps was to return to Burnside's Dept.[1]

U. S. GRANT
Maj. Gen.

ALS, DNA, RG 94, War Records Office, Dept. of the Tenn. *O.R.*, I, xxiv, part 3, 543. On July 21, 1863, 2:00 P.M., Maj. Gen. John G. Parke, "Messengers," telegraphed to USG. "My advance reached this point this P M   Gen Sherman Ordered us to return to our old camp at Milldale & report by letter in advance   our men suffered today from the heat but will probably be able to move tomorrow   In case we are to take transports shall we march to Snyders Bluff or Vicksburg   the courier will wait a reply at the telegraph office" Telegram received, DNA, RG 94, War Records Office, Dept. of the Tenn. *O.R.*, I, xxiv, part 3, 539. On July 25, Maj. Gen. Ambrose E. Burnside telegraphed to USG. "When may we expect the 9th Corps up. I congratulate you upon your continued success." Copies, DNA, RG 393, Dept. of the Ohio (Cincinnati), Telegrams Sent; *ibid.*, Dept. of the Ohio and Cumberland, Telegrams Sent. On July 31, Maj. Theodore S. Bowers issued Special Orders No. 207. "The 9th Army Corps, General J. G. Park, Commanding will return to the Department of the Ohio, as rapidly as transportation can be provided. On arriving at Cairo, General Parke, will telegraph to the General-in-Chief of the Army, and to Major General Burnside for further instructions   The Provost Marshal General of this Army, will send North all prisoners of war not authorized to be paroled, in charge of the 9th Army Corps. They will be left at Indianapolis or such other point as the General-in-Chief, may direct. In returning the 9th Army Corps, to its former command, it is with pleasure that the General Commanding acknowledges its valuable services in the campaign just now closed. Arriving at Vicksburg opportunely, taking position to hold at bay Johnstons army then threatening the forces investing the City, it was ready and eager to assume the aggressive at any moment. After the fall of Vicksburg it formed a part of the army which drove Johnson from his position near the Big Black River into his intrenchments at Jackson, and after a siege of eight days compelled him to fly in disorder from the Mississippi Valley. The endurance, valor, and general good conduct, of the 9th Corps are admired by all, and its valuable co-operation in achieving the final triumph of the campaign is gratefully acknowledged by the Army of the Tennessee. Major General Parke will cause the different regiments and batteries of his command to inscribe upon their banners and guidons 'Vicksburg' and 'Jackson.' " Copies, DLC-USG, V, 27, 28; DNA, RG 393, Dept. of the Tenn., Special Orders. *O.R.*, I, xxiv, part 3, 565–66. On Aug. 4, Parke, "Haines Bluff," telegraphed to Bowers. "Since we have commenced embarking my troops I have recd. transportation for less than two thousand (2000) men   Graham has since taken the Gladiator from me by order of Genl Grant   Can you do anything to forward our movements   It would seem that we are destined to remain here for some time" Telegram received, DNA, RG 393, Dept. of the Tenn., Telegrams Received. Bowers, Vicksburg, answered the same day. "Boats are on their way here from Port Hudson and from Memphis for the purpose of moving your command and are hourly expected. No pains shall be spared to furnish you transportation with the least possible delay." Copies, DLC-USG, V, 19, 101, 103; DNA, RG 393, Dept. of the Tenn., Letters Sent. Parke telegraphed again to Bowers on Aug. 4. "Many thanks for your despatch & for your interest in receiving transportation   You must excuse our apparent impatience to return to our Dept. I think Genl Burnside is equally anxious for our return" Telegram received, *ibid.*, Telegrams Received. On Aug. 7, Parke, "Mill Dale," telegraphed to USG. "One Division with ~~five~~ all the sick & wounded have been embarked & gone up the river—One Division Genl Potters remains. I will leave Capt Van Ness my Q. M. to attend to the transportation   I will embark my Hd Qrs this evening on the Groesbeck & start as soon as she is loaded   I will take great pride in showing your Order to Gen Burnsides with many thanks for your kindness & consideration" Telegram received, *ibid.*, Unregistered Letters Received.

On July 20, USG telegraphed to Maj. Gen. Edward O. C. Ord. "You can encamp your Corps any place on the peninsular between the Black & Miss. South of the rail-road you choose." ALS (telegram sent), *ibid.*, Telegrams Received. On July 23, Ord, "Big Black," telegraphed to USG. "I shall get in three Divisions to Vicksburg today the other two tomorrow. Had I not better turn my cavalry over to genl McArthur who is garrison here   he has but small detachment   I have about three thousand (3000) sick & wounded many of whom ought to go north at once." Telegram received, *ibid.* On the same day, Bowers telegraphed to Ord. "Turn your Cavalry over to Gen McArthur, as you suggest. Arrangements will be made for your sick" ALS (telegram sent), *ibid.*

1. See telegrams to Maj. Gen. Henry W. Halleck, July 15, 18, 1863; letter to Halleck, July 24, 1863.

To Maj. Gen. Cadwallader C. Washburn

July 22d 1863

GEN. WASHBURN,

The boats of the Marine Brigade will be up to-morrow. They will be able to take five or six regiments with five or six wagons to each regiment. Have that number of Kimballs[1] troops ready to embark and start off immediately to debark at Helena. The scarsity of transports is such that we will have to send the Division off by Brigades if we can do no better. Price is said to be moving towards S. E. Mo. Schofield is moving a force to drive him back. I am ordered from Washington to send a force from Helena to cut off all retreat.

U. S. GRANT

AL (signature clipped), DNA, RG 393, 13th Army Corps, Letters Received. *O.R.*, I, xxiv, part 3, 543–44; *O.R.* (Navy), I, xxv, 319. On July 22, 1863, Maj. Gen. Cadwallader C. Washburn, Snyder's Bluff, telegraphed to USG. "There is but one battery of four guns attached to Kimballs division. Sands eleventh 11 Ohio   This Battery did belong to the seventeenth 17th Corps   shall I send that with Kimballs Division"   Telegram received, DNA, RG 393, Dept. of the Tenn., Telegrams Received. USG's answer was noted on the bottom of the telegram. "Yes send it along & if I can I will attach another battery to that brigade" Copy, *ibid*.

On July 23, Washburn telegraphed to USG. "How many of the marine boats will be sent here   if as many as five I can send the entire division provided I can have a suitable boat for the sick   These are here four hundred 400 sick belonging to Kimballs & Smiths Divisions that should be sent up   the steamer Kennett is here ready empty   If I could have her for the sick I could send them all away"   Telegram received, *ibid*. USG answered Washburn on the same day. "All the marine boats will be up. Gen Ellet does not concent to leave his boats but takes up his whole command, horses and all, hence the limited number of men they can take. They are not subject to my orders or it would be different. I will make enquiries about the Kennett and let you know as soon as possible." ALS, *ibid*., RG 94, War Records Office, Dept. of the Tenn. *O.R.*, I, xxiv, part 3, 546; *O.R.* (Navy), I, xxv, 319–20.

1. See letter to Maj. Gen. Stephen A. Hurlbut, July 24, 1863.

To Maj. Gen. Nathaniel P. Banks

Head Quarters, Dept. of the Ten
Vicksburg Miss. July 23d 1863.

MAJ. GEN. N. P. BANKS,
COMD.G DEPT. OF THE GULF,
DEAR GEN.

The bearer of this, Mr. W. C. Graham,[1] is the son of a gentleman from Ohio who, at the begining of the rebellion was doing business in New Orleans, in connection with a house in Cairo. On account of his strong outspoken Union sentiments his place of business was closed before Steamers had yet seased to run between New Orleans and the North and everything, debts and personal property, confiscated to the so called Confederacy.

Young Mr. Graham goes to New Orleans to look after the business of his father & Uncle. I do not know what your policy is about allowing, or aiding in, the collection of Northern debts. But being personally acquainted with Graham and Bro, I can vouch for their loyalty and more than ordinary Commercial honesty.

They will not ask anything more than is allowed to other loyal Northern creditors and I of course would ask nothing more for them.

I am Gen. very respectfully
your obt. svt.
U. S. GRANT
Maj. Gen.

ALS, DLC-Nathaniel P. Banks.

1. William Cary Graham of New Orleans, presumably George W. Graham's nephew, married Ellen Duncan of Newark, Ohio, on Jan. 11, 1860. The 1860 U.S. Census listed W. C. Graham as a twenty-two-year-old commission merchant of Cairo, born in Ohio. Ellen's sister, Mary, lived in their house. The Duncan family of Ohio was related to the Duncans of Natchez, Miss. See *PUSG*, 2, 278–79; Katherine D. Smith, *The Story of Thomas Duncan and His Six Sons* (New York, 1928), p. 20; letter to Brig. Gen. Lorenzo Thomas, July 11, 1863.

To Maj. Gen. Francis J. Herron

Head Quarters, Dept. of the Ten.
Vicksburg Miss. July 23d 1863.

MAJ. GEN. HERRON,
COMD.G DIV.
GEN.

You will proceed as early as practicable with your Division to Port Hudson, La, and there report in person, or by telegraph to Maj. Gen. Banks Comd.g Dept. of the Gulf.

You will take with you all the baggage and transportation of your Division, thirty days rations, five hundred rounds per man of Inf.y Ammunition, and Artillery Ammunition to refill boxes once.

Should no orders reach you before arriving at Port Hudson you will go on to that point and await orders there.

Should Gen. Banks give you service to perform in co-operation with movements in other parts of his Dept. and which require a greater force than you have with you call upon me and I will endeavor to reinforce you to the necessary extent. All the troops left with me are exhausted and unfit for immediate service. It is hoped therefore that no call will be made for more troops except in case of great necessity.

Very respectfully
U. S. GRANT
Maj. Gen. Com

ALS, NHi. *O.R.*, I, xxiv, part 3, 545. On Aug. 4, 1863, USG wrote to Maj. Gen. Francis J. Herron. "Except such boats as have been ordered to New Orleans, or elswhere, by Gen. Banks, send all boats at Port Hudson to this place. We are much in want of boats to transport troops now under orders and have been looking for those taken by your command back." ALS, NHi. On Aug. 7, Herron, Port Hudson, wrote to USG. "I have the honor to acknowledge the receipt of your letter of the 4th inst. received late last night. About a week since— I received an order by telegraph—from Lt Col Irwin, Asst Adjt Gen of this Department (a copy of which is enclosed) to turn over all the transports of this fleet to the Chief Quarter Master of the Department at New Orleans—which was done with the exception of two Hospital and one Commissary & Quarter Master boat. Since that time the boats have all been under his orders—and have been and are being used as he directs. I am in receipt of no orders or official communications from Maj Gen Banks, since his visit to Vicksburg, & have no intimation as to the final disposition to be made of my command. Though from my previous interview with Gen Banks at New Orleans—I certainly expected to have seen him, as he passed down the river, or have heard on his return to New Orleans. My Division, is encamped below the town, and outside of the line of works—with the exception of one Brigade—now absent escorting an Artillery Regemint from this Post to Baton Rouge, by order of Gen Banks. Brig Gen Andrews, is in command of the post and fortifications. Brig Gen Vandever, Comdg my 1st Brigade is absent, at New Orleans, as President of a Court Martial, by order of Gen Banks. Left as I am in this Department—without orders of any kind—I find myself placed in a very unpleasant position. These boats having been taken possession of by Col Holabird, Chief Quarter Master of this Department, it will probably require an order from you, to enable me to return them as you desire. I should prefer to send them up the river, and as most of them are lying here, will do so, if armed with authority from you. Assuring you that no effort shall be spared to serve your wishes—and trusting to hear from you by return mail." ALS, DNA, RG 393, Dept. of the Tenn., Letters Received. *O.R.,* I, xxiv, part 3, 581. Herron enclosed a copy of an Aug. 3 telegram from Lt. Col. Richard B. Irwin, New Orleans. "The Comdg General in accordance with his understanding with General Grant, directs that you cause the transport fleet which brought your division to be turned over to the Quarter Masters Department And reported to Col Holabird Chief Q. M. for orders." Copy, DNA, RG 393, Dept. of the Tenn., Letters Received.

To Maj. Gen. Martin L. Smith

—————

Headquarters Dept. of the Tenn.
Vicksburg Miss. July 24th 1863.

MAJ. GEN. M. L. SMITH C. S. A.

Your note of this date is just received. I have directed the Provost Marshal General, to authorize the furloughing of all paroled prisoners who have returned to our lines, when it is their desire to receive furloughs. It will be optional with these prisoners however, to go North as prisoners of War if they prefer it.

It is impossible to furnish boats any farther than they are now being furnished. It is not probable that any boats can now be furnished for several days.

Respectfully &c
U. S. GRANT
Maj. Genl. U. S. A. Comdg.

Copies, DLC-USG, V, 19, 101, 103; DNA, RG 393, Dept. of the Tenn., Letters Sent. *O.R.*, I, xxiv, part 3, 550.

On July 27, 1863, C.S.A. Maj. Gen. Martin L. Smith, Vicksburg, wrote to USG. "The condition of the Confederate sick in hospital here, compels me to attempt their relief, which must be my excuse for addressing you at this time. I would respectfully enquire if while waiting for more boats to be disposable, a wagon train could not be obtained for taking those sick as far as Brandon, most able to be transported in that way. I would prefer boats altogether, but the Surgeons report that in a week more the list of those unable to be removed under any circumstances, must largely increase, unless steps are taken to dispose of the convalescents. If a train can be obtained please inform me of what probable number of wagons it will consist" ALS, MH. On July 29, Maj. Theodore S. Bowers issued Special Orders No. 205. "Capt. Audenried, A. A. D. C. will proceed in charge of Steamer 'St Maurice,' loaded with sick and wounded of the Confederate States Army to New Orleans, and report to the commanding officer at that place, upon whose advice he will proceed from there to Mobile and deliver said sick and wounded to the Confederate Authorities there. Upon the execution of this order he will report to these Head Quarters." Copies, DLC-USG, V, 27, 28; DNA, RG 393, Dept. of the Tenn., Special Orders. See letter to Capt. Loyd Wheaton, July 18, 1863; to Maj. Gen. James B. McPherson, Oct. 10, 1863.

To Maj. Gen. Henry W. Halleck

Head Quarters, Dept. of the Ten.
Vicksburg Miss. July 24th 1863.

MAJ. GEN. H. W. HALLECK,
GEN. IN CHIEF, WASHINGTON D. C.
GEN.

Your letter of the 11th inst. is just received. Since that date you must have received a number of dispatches from me and before this reaches you you will receive my official report of the Campaign & sieges just ended.[1]

I have sent Banks one Division numbering full 4000 effective men. About 7000 are going up the river over 5000 of them to Helena and the remainder enfeebled regiments to West Tennessee to do garrison duty there and release fresh troops for the field. I have turned over to Gen. Hurlbut all the directions for the expedition against Price. He is nearer and has better and speedier means of getting information than I have.

I hear from Gen. Banks every few days. He feels no alarm, or expresses none to me now for the safety of his position. With the troops and transports I have sent him he will find no difficulty in keeping the river clear from Port Hudson down. Above that I will take care of the river.

My troops from Jackson are now arriving. The rail-roads in every direction from there are destroyed beyond repairs for this summer. The enemy have lost an immense amount of rolling stock by Sherman's expedition. Johnston's Army was much demoralized and deserted by the hundreds. I do not believe he can get back to Mobile or Chatanooga with an effective force of 15000 men. The Army paroled here were virtually discharged the service. At last accounts Pemberton had but 4000 left with him and they were no doubt men whos homes are in states East of here and are only waiting to get near them to desert too.

The country is full of these paroled prisoners all of them swearing they will not take up arms again if they are exchanged. Thousands have crossed the Miss. River and gone West. Many beg passages North and quite a number expressed a strong anxiety to enlist in our service. This of course I would not permit.

The 9th Army Corps has just returned from Jackson and will return to Burnside as fast as transportation can be provided.

My troops are very much exhausted and entirely unfit for any present duty requiring much marching. But by selecting any duty of immediate pressing importance could be done.

It seems to me that Mobile is the point deserving the most immediate attention. It could not be taken from here at this season of the year. The country through which an Army would have to pass is poor and water scarce. The only present route it seems to me would be from some point on Lake Ponchertrain. I have not studied this matter however it being out of my Department.

Either Sherman or McPherson would be good men to entrust such an expedition to. Between the two I would have no choice and the army does not afford an officer superior to either in my estimation. With such men commanding Corps or Armies there will never be any jealousies or lack of hearty co-operation. I have taken great pleasure in recommending both these officers for promotion in the regular service.

Immediately on taking possession of Vicksburg I directed Capt. Comstock, Chief Eng. to lay out a line of works suitable for a Garrison of 5000 men. The work will necessarily progress slowly for I do not want the White men to do any work that can possibly be avoided during the hot months.[2] I also authorized the raising of a regiment of twelve companies of 150 men each to be used as Artillerists and also to be drilled as Infantry to garrison the place. I selected one of the Colored regiments that had been officered by Gen. Thomas for this purpose. The regiment selected had but few men in it at the time. It is now filled to nearly a complete Infantry regiment. Should my course not be sustained all the surplus men can be transfered to other organizations.[3]

The negro troops are easier to preserve discipline among than our White troops and I doubt not will prove equally good for garrison duty. All that have been tried have fought bravely.

Before raising any new regiments of Colored troops I think it advisable to fill those already organized. Gen. Herron's trip to Yazoo City gave us a great many recruits and Gen. Ransoms expedition to Natches has given and will give several thousand.

The absence of Gen. Hawkins has been a great drawback to the perfect organization of the Black troops. I have no one to fully take his place.

Should Schofield require more troops than are already sent him, (I do not believe he will) to drive Price south of the Arkansas River, I will furnish them. Kirby Smith's forces now occupy Delhi, Monroe & Harrisonville, besides points on the Red River. They are represented as being in a demoralized condition requiring one half to hold the other in service. I may, when my troops are a little rested, clear out the Harrisonville & Monroe forces, but I do not think this of sufficient importance to allow it to interfere with any movement East of the river.—sending a force to Natchez was a heavy blow to the enemy. At this point the troops West of the river cross their munitions of War and cattle for the Eastern army cross at the same place.

Ransom secured 5000 head of Texas cattle, nearly 500000 rounds of Infantry ammunition some Artillery ammunition, many mules and horses, prisoners and small Arms. A part of the cattle were sent to Banks. He also called on me for 2000 mules which we are able to supply as fast as transportation can be provided.

The wounded and sick prisoners, of which there was about 5000 who would not bear land transportation I am sending to Mobile & Alexandria. Pemberton's Army may be regarded as discharged the service and we stand credited with about 31000 of them paroled and 7 or 8 thousand sent North since the 1st of April.

I am Gen. Very respectfully
your obt. svt.
U. S. GRANT
Maj. Gen. Com

ALS, IHi. *O.R.*, I, xxiv, part 3, 546–47. On July 11, 1863, Maj. Gen. Henry W. Halleck wrote to USG. "I am anxiously waiting for more definite information of the capture of Vicksburg than that contained in your brief telegram of July 4th. I am also exceedingly anxious about General Banks' command, having heard nothing from him since June 29th. I hope you have reenforced him sufficiently to secure the capture of Port Hudson and to enable him to reopen his communications with New Orleans. I also hope you will send north the 9th Corps as early as possible, for if Johnson should now send reenforcements to Bragg, I must add that Corps to Rosecrans' command. Unfortunately Burnside's army is employed in repelling petty raids instead of advancing into east Tennessee to cooperate with Rosecrans. Your idea of immediately driving Johnson, out of Mississippi is a good one. But it will not be safe to pursue him into alabama, nor will it be best at present to hold the line of the Tombigbee, even after he has been driven east of that river. The Mississippi should be the base of future operations, east and west. When Port Hudson falls the fortifications of that place as well as of Vicksburg should be so arranged as to be held by the smallest possible garrisons, thus leaving the mass of the troops for operations in the field. I suggest that colored troops be used as far as possible in the garrisons. If this meets your approval, raise and arm as many as you can and send on the names of suitable persons for their officers and I will submit them to the War Department for appointments. Name none but those known to be competent and reliable, and of good moral character. I will suppose these preliminary measures—the expulsion of Johnson's army, the capture of Port Hudson, and the proper security of that place and Vicksburg—to be all accomplished, what is to be done with the forces available for the field? This is an important question which should be carefully considered. If Johnson should unite with Bragg, we may be obliged to

send Rosecrans more troops than the 9th Corps. Some reenforcements will soon
go to Banks from the north, but he will probably require troops from you, even
after the fall of Port Hudson, to drive Magruder and Taylor from Louisiana.
Large forces are comparatively neutralized in Missouri by the forces of Price
and Marmaduke threatening the southern frontier of that state. If Little Rock
and the line of the Arkansas river were held by us, all of Arkansas north of
that river would soon be cleared of the enemy, and all the troops in Missouri
except the militia could join your army in its operations at the south. If driven
from northern Arkansas and Southern Louisiana, the enemy would probably
operate on the Tensas, Washita, and Red rivers; but with the gunboats and forces
you could send against him I do not believe he could accomplish anything of
importance. If the organized rebel forces could be driven from Arkansas and
Louisiana these states would immediately be restored to the Union. Texas would
follow almost of its own accord. I present these general views for your consideration. Circumstances may compel you to pursue a course entirely different
from the one suggested. For example, Johnson may be so reenforced as to require
all your means to oppose him. In that case Rosecrans should be able to occupy
east Tennessee without any additional forces. And east Tennessee being once occupied, Burnside's forces in Kentucky can be sent to you or to Rosecrans. In
other words wherever the enemy concentrates, we must concentrate to oppose
him." LS, DNA, RG 94, War Records Office, Dept. of the Tenn. *O.R.*, I, xxiv,
part 3, 497–98.

1. See letter to Col. John C. Kelton, July 6, 1863.
2. On July 22, Maj. Theodore S. Bowers wrote to Maj. Gen. James B.
McPherson. "No more details of white troops will be made for works on the
fortifications in the vicinity of Vicksburg, at present. Negro troops will be
brought here for that purpose. During the present hot weather it is necessary
to save our men as much as possible from fatigue duty in the sun." Copies, DLC-
USG, V, 19, 101, 103; DNA, RG 393, Dept. of the Tenn., Letters Sent. *O.R.*,
I, xxiv, part 3, 542.
3. On Aug. 3, 12:15 P.M., Halleck telegraphed to USG. "Your views in regard to organizing negro troops are approved. Adjt Genl Thomas is now on
his way to Vicksburg to assist in the organization & to put some officer in place
of Genl Hawkins, now absent sick. If, in your opinion, it be deemed advisable,
you are authorised to enlist & organise into regiments deserters & citizens of
Mississippi. It will be well to keep up the impression in your army that Mobile
will be the next point of attack." ALS (telegram sent), DNA, RG 107, Telegrams
Collected (Bound); telegram received, *ibid.*, RG 393, Dept. of the Tenn., Telegrams Received. *O.R.*, I, xxiv, part 3, 571.

To Maj. Gen. Francis J. Herron

Vicksburg Miss.
July 24th 1863.

MAJ. GEN. HERRON,
DEAR SIR:

Permit me to introduce you to Col. Markland, Spl. Agt. of the
P. O. Department for the Southwest.—Col. Markland goes to New
Orleans on business connected with his Dept. and will be pleased
to go, with Mrs. Markland, on one of the vessels taking your command.

The Ocean Steamer is probably the only one with you that will
be going immediately through.

Any attention to Col. & Mrs. Markland will be appreciated by
him and will be regarded as a personal favor to myself.

Very respectfully
your obt. svt.
U. S. GRANT
Maj. Gen. U. S. A.

ALS, NHi. See letter to Brig. Gen. Charles P. Stone, July 21, 1863.

To Maj. Gen. Stephen A. Hurlbut

Head Quarters, Dept. of the Ten.
Vicksburg Miss. July 24th 1863.

MAJ. GEN. S. A. HURLBUT,
COMD.G 16TH ARMY CORPS,
GEN.

I am sending Kimballs Division to Helena.[1] These are the only
troops I have not worn out with long and fatiguing marches
through the dust and heat. In addition to this Div. I will send several regiments that are the most reduced by sickness to Memphis
thus enabling you to take well regiments for field service.

I am so far away, and know nothing of Price's movements except what is contained in the dispatches forwarded by you that I shall instruct the troops going to Helena, and those now there, to report to you for orders. In fact I think it will be best to add all territory in the Department, as far South as the Arkansas River, to the 16th Army Corps. You may give directions accordingly.

Telegraph directly to Washington the number of troops you can send after Price and whatever of the orders you give them you deem necessary. I do not know anything of Kimball's merits as a commander and have no officer here senior to him to send in his stead. Steele would probably be the best man but he is not here and cannot well be spared. I will however see Sherman by tomorrow night and if Steele can be got will send him up at once.[2]

I send two batteries from here with Kimball. More could be sent but I doubt the necessity for it. If you deem more necessary send them and I will replace all you send from here.

> I Am Gen. very respectfully
> your obt. svt.
> U. S. GRANT
> Maj. Gen. Com

ALS, DNA, RG 94, War Records Office, Union Battle Reports. *O.R.*, I, xxii, part 2, 394–95; *ibid.*, I, xxiv, part 3, 550. On July 29, 1863, Maj. Gen. Stephen A. Hurlbut wrote to USG. "I received your letter instructing me to add all of the Department North of Arkansas River to my Command. I have this day issued the necessary orders. I have sent a telegraphic message to Genl Schofield desiring to know his plan of operations so as to put myself in communication with his force & sustain his movement. There will be vast difficulty in obtaining supplies for so large a body in that country until the corn crop hardens so as to be fit for use, and of course I cannot select any route for supplies or any depôt until I learn the probable route. I suppose the base of operations will be on White River which I am informed is now navigable   I shall probably run up to Cairo to consult with Genl Schofield & shall do every thing in my power to make the movement effective   Price's where abouts is very uncertain. If Morgan L. Smith is fit for duty he would probably be the best man for Columbus. Chalmers with about two thousand men is back again at Panola and seems disposed to stay there. I will reach him soon from Helena in rear and by Cavalry in front. You would much oblige me by sending me the Northern limit of your Department and the line between yourself & Schofield" ALS, DNA, RG 393, Dept. of the Tenn., Letters Received.

On Aug. 1, Hurlbut wrote to USG. "Maj Genl. Steele has reported to me from Helena. I have directed him to take all the effective force of Kimballs Di-

vision and ten thousand men from Helena Garrison, open Communications with
Davidson now at Madison, and establish a junction at Clarendon, thence to move
on Little Rock where Price is reported to be. Marmaduke is at Jacksonport. I
have also directed him to establish a temporary depôt of supplies at Clarendon
to which access is easy by White River and if the Arkansas is navigable at this
time to seize another point on that river below Little Rock for a second Depôt.
The Country from Helena to Clarendon is reported to be utterly desolate and exceedingly dry. I have directed Gen Steele to ascertain if it be practicable by
Land—if so to march the troops and send supplies &c round by the River. Upon
uniting at Clarendon the force will be over 10000 men five thousand of whom
will be mounted, more than enough to meet the entire force in Arkansas. I think
the occupation of Little Rock will be simply a question of marching and the holding of it merely a question of supplies   It is evidently the intention of the General in Chief to hold the line of Arkansas River which again depends upon the
water. I take this occasion to remind you that several important Court Martials
are in your hands and to ask their return" ALS, *ibid.*, RG 94, War Records
Office, Dept. of the Tenn. *O.R.*, I, xxii, part 2, 424–25.

On Aug. 4, Hurlbut wrote to USG. "I am now about to start for Cairo to
meet Genl Schofield & arrange the plan of campaign in Arkansas. So far as I can
ascertain Davidson has committed a very serious blunder in coming down Craw-
ley's Ridge leaving Marmaduke with 7 Regiments at Jacksonport. He should
have struck them. By his proposed movement to Des Arc or Clarendon he opens
Missouri to a Raid. I had already sent him my views, and to day send him Schofield's order directing him to strike for Jacksonport. Steele is pressing the formation of his expeditionary Corps. Prentiss is disappointed in not having the
command. I have ordered him to report here. Kimball will scarce bear the trip
& if he makes up his mind that he cannot go—is to report to me & be assigned
to Columbus. Hatch is now returning from a splendid march of ten days through
west Tennessee. Every thing in force has been driven out up to Fort Heiman. If
I relieve Asboth which I must do where shall I send him. I congratulate you on
the highly worded reply of Genl Halleck on acceptance of your report. It was all
thoroughly deserved" ALS, DNA, RG 94, War Records Office, Dept. of the
Tenn. *O.R.*, I, xxiv, part 3, 575–76. See letters to Maj. Gen. Stephen A. Hurlbut,
July 21, 22, Aug. 5, 1863.

On July 27, USG telegraphed to Maj. Gen. John M. Schofield. "Steele will
take command of troops at Helena, receiving instructions from Hurlbut." *O.R.*,
I, xxii, part 2, 402. On the same day, 11:00 A.M., however, Maj. Gen. Henry W.
Halleck telegraphed to USG. "The troops sent into Arkansas will act under the
orders of Major Genl Schofield. This, however, will not prevent you from recalling them to your command if you should find it necessary to do so." ALS
(telegram sent), DNA, RG 107, Telegrams Collected (Bound); telegram received, *ibid.*, RG 393, Dept. of the Tenn., Telegrams Received. *O.R.*, I, xxii,
part 2, 402; *ibid.*, I, xxiv, part 3, 554. See *ibid.*, I, xxii, part 2, 376, 398. On
July 27, 11:30 A.M., and July 30, 6:35 P.M., Halleck telegraphed to Schofield.
"The expeditionary corps in Arkansas will act under your general orders. Genl
Grant will garrison Helena with his troops so as to render present garrison available for the field." ALS (telegram sent), DNA, RG 107, Telegrams Collected
(Bound); copy, *ibid.*, RG 108, Telegrams Sent. *O.R.*, I, xxii, part 1, 22. "General Hurlbut has been placed in command of a column of 6,000 men, to move
from Helena against Price. The forces which you may send down will unite with

Hurlbut's corps, and be temporarily under his command. Telegraph to him your plans and how you can best cooperate." *Ibid.*, I, xxii, part 2, 409. See *ibid.*, I, xxii, part 1, 22–24. On Aug. 8, Schofield wrote to USG. "I have the honor respectfully to request a list of the Regiments, Batteries &c. serving in the Department of the Tennessee. This request is made in view of the numerous Official Communications forwarded to these Head Quarters from the Bureaus of the War Department, the Hospitals &c. and in order to facilitate the return of Deserters. A corresponding list of Regiments &c. now within this command will be furnished if desired." Copy, DNA, RG 393, Dept. of the Mo., Letters Sent. On Aug. 21, Hurlbut wrote to USG. "I forgot to mention to you a matter as to which I am not sure what to do. Steele reports to me—I have your order to organize &c the Arkansas Expedition. The Infantry is from my Corps—but you have also sent me a dispatch from Genl Halleck that troops serving in this Expedition shall be under command of Maj Genl Schofield. Will you please inform me whether I am responsible for the Expedition & if so how far—" ALS, *ibid.*, RG 94, War Records Office, 16th Army Corps. *O.R.*, I, xxii, part 2, 464. USG endorsed this letter. "The troops with Steele are in Schofields Dept. and will be subject to his orders, according to Gen. Halleck's dispatch. But being nearer Steele than the Hd Qrs. of the Dept. in which he is serving any aid you can give him it is advisable you should give whether it is men or supplies he may require." AES, DNA, RG 94, War Records Office, 16th Army Corps. *O.R.*, I, xxii, part 2, 465. See *ibid.*, pp. 469, 506–7, 539–41, 573.

On Aug. 1, Brig. Gen. John W. Davidson, "Crowleys Ridge Arkansas," wrote to USG. "I have moved this far on a plan of operations adopted by General Schofield Comm'dg Dept of the Mo. and shall now proceed to White River to throw a bridge across at Clarendon. I ask the co-operation of two or more Gun boats at that point as my force is all Cavalry. I have 6000 Sabres. My latest information is that Marmaduke's cavalry is near Jacksonport across the river, that Price's Infantry Division is part at Searcy, and part at Des Arc, and that Holmes is at Little Rock, with but few troops, & that the Rebels are preparing to move into Texas. I think they should be pursued with rapidity—I don't know whether I come under your orders or not. If I do, if I cannot command the expedition, by reason of rank, at least give me the advance" ALS, DNA, RG 94, War Records Office, Dept. of the Mo. *O.R.*, I, xxii, part 2, 424; *O.R.* (Navy), I, xxv, 349. On Aug. 4, Davidson, "Camp near Marianna L'Anguille River," wrote to USG. "I wrote you some days ago, that I was here with a force of six thousand cavalry, in pursuance of a plan approved thus far by General Schofield. I am on my way to White river to throw a bridge across at Clarendon, and hope I am doing right. You should know the character of my force. I have three batteries, and my regiments are Dragoons, taught by me to use the Carbine dismounted when necessary and after a march of three hundred miles from Pilot Knob to this point are better fitted—men—horses—and transportation—to strike the enemy than when they started. I am in an anomalous position here. The Commander of the N. E. Dist. of Arkansas is my junior—and the troops in the District are ordered to report to General Hurlbut. May I not have some infantry and be pushed to Little Rock before Kirby Smith can join Holmes and Price. I believe they are trying to get into Texas, unless they fight in Arkansas, possibly into Mexico. They are said by the people of the country to have much stock and negroes with them." ALS, DNA, RG 94, War Records Office, Dept. of the Mo. *O.R.*, I, xxii, part 2, 430. See *ibid.*, I, xxii, part 1, 483. On Aug. 14, Maj. Gen. Frederick Steele,

Helena, wrote to USG. "I enclose herewith copy of my final dispatch to Genl. Hurlbut before taking the field. My Troops are now Enroute to Clarendon. I have not determined positively whether to take the road from Du Val's Bluff, or the Southern route from Clarendon. That will be determined by the reports of scouts after we reach Clarendon. Each route has peculiar advantages. The former is shorter and shady; with not so many flies to trouble the animals. The latter passes through an extensive prairie, but is better supplied with water. If we go by Duval's Bluff, we shall stop their opperations on the railroad at oncce, which, it said they are using to get supplies to Little Rock from the Black river Country. The Rebels . . ." AL (incomplete), DNA, RG 94, War Records Office, Dept. of the Ohio. According to USG's register entry for a letter of Aug. 13 (probably 14), Steele also referred "to his troops—bad, management on the part of some Commanders of regements Etc." DLC-USG, V, 23. Apparently Steele enclosed his letter of Aug. 13 to Hurlbut, although the copy was addressed to USG. "To day I received Despatches from Davidson. The Escort captured a Rebel captain and one man. The Captain, Witherel, has been a great annoyance to this Post. The Gun Boats are reconnoitering up white, and Bache intends going to Jacksonport to ascertain what has become of Marmaduke. Davidson writes, that he did not go there because he heard that Marmaduke was crossing the river and that it was too late for such a movement at the time Schofields despatches were received. He has scouts on the other side of white. The Gun boats are towing Coal barges up to be used for making a flying bridge. My other Division under Col. McLean 43d Ind. marched from here to day. I kept a Regiment of Cavalry here to escort the last of the supply train which will be ready tomorrow morning. I reviewed and inspected both Divisions before they marched, and must confess that I was very much disapointed in regard to the numbers that they turned out, as well as in their general appearance; with the exception of very few Regiments. In Kimball's old Division, there is but one really live Regiment—The 3d Minn. The latter had about 300. and appeared well in every respect. Some of the Regiments that reported 300 & 500 for duty did not turn out but about 125 & 150. Regiments were commanded by Captains and Companies by Sergeants. In one Regiment there were but two non-commissioned officers in the rank of File closers. In some instances the officers were ignorant of their duties and the men slovenly and indifferent. I presume that most of these Regiments will turn out better on the march than they did on review. I have 'pidgeon-holed' a number of Leaves of Absence issued from your Head quarters and hope you will approve of my action under the circumstances. The manner in which the marching Regiments left thier sick and convalescents, especially the Iowa Regiments, shows that they are badly commanded. Notwithstanding I had issued definite orders on the subject, they were simply abandoned, without orders and without subsistence, thier Rations having been carried off in the Regimental trains. It was officially reported to me that the abandoned Camps and the town were full of stragglers and convalescents, belonging to the Regiments that had marched. I immediately ordered the Post Commander to send out Patrols and collect them together. There are now over a thousand convalescents here, besides, three supply boats have been loaded with all they would hold, to go up white and join thier commands. Some of my personal friends here tell me that I am going to meet with a much stronger apposition at Little Rock than I anticipate. Judge Sebastian & Mr Underwood say that the Rebels are determined to make a desperate fight before they will give up the Capitol. Kirby Smith is no doubt at Little Rock, and they say that his troops are now marching towards that place. He found, that they could not stay in La—. Three of our men who were carried away from here on the 4th of July have returned. They left Little Rock just a week ago. The Rebels say that I am comming with 12000. men half Infty and half Cavly. I asked one of the men if he thought that would be enough, to go to Little Rock with; and he replied in the negative. They saw no fortifications at Little Rock, but one of my spies reports that they are throwing up entrenchments on the roads approaching the city both above and below. There is also a work at Bayou Metre. I still have doubts about thier making a stand, but hope you will be prepared to send me support at once in case of necessity. I think it will be rather a difficult trip for cavalry through from Clarendon to Memphis along the Rail Road line, but will order it on my arrival at the former place. Our men say the people are running thier negroes and all thier property S. W. from little Rock. they are constantly playing off Flags of Truce on us." LS, DNA, RG 94, War Records Office, Dept. of the Ohio.

On Aug. 15, Sept. 2, and 3, Hurlbut wrote to Lt. Col. John A. Rawlins regarding Steele's expedition and the need for reinforcing it. *O.R.*, I, xxii, part 2, 453; *ibid.*, I, xxx, part 3, 295, 320. On Sept. 9, Hurlbut wrote to Rawlins. "I send a copy of Genl Steele's last communication. You will perceive he recommends change of base to the Mississippi at Napoleon. If this meets the views of the Major Genl Commanding I would respectfully recommend that the Division just returned from Monroe be ordered up to Napoleon, to communicate with Steele moving either on Pine Bluff or such other point as he may direct"   Copies, DNA, RG 94, War Records Office, Dept. of the Cumberland; *ibid.*, RG 393, 16th Army Corps, Letters Sent. *O.R.*, I, xxii, part 2, 520. See *ibid.*, p. 506. On Sept. 13, Rawlins wrote to Hurlbut. "Yours of the 9th inst., endorsing copy of Genl. Steele's communication of date the 2d inst., is just received. General Grant has not returned from his visit to General Banks at New Orleans but is hourly expected. On the receipt of your communications of the 2d & 3d inst., relative to the probable necessity of reinforcements for Genl. Steele, I called on General McPherson who ordered forward to him the Division of Brigr. Genl. John E. Smith which, owing to the want of river transportation, did not get off until yesterday. It has no doubt reported at Helena and become subject to your orders for any destination you may deem best. The making of Napoleon the basis for General Steeles operations and supplies seems to be the best move that can be made. Whatever you do, I am sure General Grant will approve and know it is his desire that you give direction to this movement against Little Rock. A few more troops may be spared from here if absolutely required for the success of the expedition. When General Grant returns he will write you fully." LS, DNA, RG 393, 16th Army Corps, Letters Received. *O.R.*, I, xxx, part 3, 594. On Sept. 10, Hurlbut had written to USG. "I inclose with this a Telegram from Maj Genl Halleck. Steele has not called for any more men—though I hold a Brigade 'Fullers Ohio' in readiness to move when he does so. I refer to my letter of yesterday as to Steele's plans. There seems no doubt but that Johnston's force has mainly gone to the Chattanooga line. I still think that there will be an abandonment of Arkansas & the collection of as many men as they can take South in Texas & N. W. Louisiana. The mere march of troops from Napoleon on the south side of Arkansas River will be a great lever of power over that region which has been intensely secesh, and is the wealthiest portion of the State. I shall expect to hear from you soon, as my position is exceedingly embarrassing

in relation to this Arkansas Expedition. Schofield does not give any order &
Genl Halleck telegraphs to me as if I were responsible. I do nothing but advise
Steele & leave him to his own devices which after all I fancy is the best way."
ALS, DNA, RG 108, Letters Received. *O.R.,* I, xxii, part 2, 522. See *ibid.,*
pp. 513–14; letter to Maj. Gen. Henry W. Halleck, Aug. 31, 1863. On Sept. 13,
Rawlins telegraphed to Col. John C. Kelton. "A communication from Maj. Genl.
S. A. Hurlbut of date the 10th inst and enclosing copy of despatch from the
General in Chief, of date Washington D. C. Septr. 6th 1863, relative to rein-
forcements for General Steele is just received. Major General Grant being still
absent I take the liberty of enclosing for your information communication from
General Hurlbut and copy of my letter in reply to him on same subject showing
action here also please find herewith General Crockers Official report, and sub-
reports of the expedition to Harrisonburg La. General Grant is expected every
hour." Copies, DLC-USG, V, 6, 8, 24, 94; DNA, RG 393, Dept. of the Tenn.,
Hd. Qrs. Correspondence.

On Sept. 11, Lt. Commander S. Ledyard Phelps, *Hastings,* "Duvall's Bluff,
White River," wrote to USG. "A dispatch reached me to day announcing the
Capture of 'Little Rock' and the retreat of the enemy pursued by Davidson's
Cavalry force. I have forwarded General Steele's dispatches to the Govt: by the
Gunboat taking this to the mouth of this river, and have thought this informa-
tion might be of sufficient importance in the operations in Red River to justify
sending down a bearer of the 'news' to the Admiral, as well as this letter to
you. There appears to have no severe fighting if any; the dispatch of the A. A.
Genl. is brief." ALS, DNA, RG 94, War Records Office, Dept. of the Tenn. *O.R.,*
I, xxx, part 3, 527. See *O.R.* (Navy), I, xxv, 393, 403. On Sept. 10, 5:00 P.M.,
Steele, Little Rock, had written to USG. "We have taken Little Rock. The
Enemy is retreating & Davidson is pursuing" ALS, DNA, RG 94, War Records
Office, Dept. of the Tenn. *O.R.,* I, xxx, part 3, 640. On Sept. 15, Hurlbut sent
a copy of this letter to Rawlins, adding: "In view of the above I have ordered
Brig. Gen. J. E. Smith to hold his division at Helena, Ark., awaiting advices
from Maj. Gen. Steele" LS, DNA, RG 393, Dept. of the Tenn., Letters Re-
ceived. *O.R.,* I, xxx, part 3, 640. See *ibid.,* pp. 661–62; letter to Maj. Gen.
Henry W. Halleck, Sept. 19, 1863.

1. On July 24, USG wrote to Brig. Gen. Nathan Kimball. "You will
proceed with your command to Helena with as little delay as practicable, on
your arrival at Helena, you will report by letter to Maj. Genl. Hurlbut at Memphis, Tenn. Gen Hurlbut has been directed to give instructions for the expedition to be started after Price I have ordered another Battery from here to
report to you at Helena." Copies, DLC-USG, V, 19, 101, 103; DNA, RG 393,
Dept. of the Tenn., Letters Sent. On the same day, Maj. Theodore S. Bowers
wrote to Lt. Col. Judson D. Bingham. "Kimball's Division of the 16th Army
Corps and four Companies of the 10th Illinois Cavalry have been ordered to
proceed to Helena, Ark. the 108th, 113th, 120th and 131st Regiments Illinois
Infantry Vols. have been ordered to Memphis, Tenn. And the 9th Army Corps,
Maj. Gen J. G. Parke, commanding has been ordered to report to Maj. Gen.
Burnside. You will provide transportation for these troops in the order in which
they are here stated with the least possible delay." Copies, *ibid.* On July 25,
USG wrote to Maj. Gen. Cadwallader C. Washburn. "Send all the boats that
are loaded immediately to Helna. There is no necessity of waiting to get all

the troops embarked." ALS, *ibid.*, RG 94, War Records Office, Dept. of the Tenn. *O.R.*, I, xxiv, part 3, 551.

2. On July 27, USG wrote to Maj. Gen. William T. Sherman. "I think I will have to send Steele with the command from Helena after Price. Will you send him in to see me to-day. I have a letter from ~~you~~ Mrs. Sherman asking you and her brothers to come home on account of the dangerous sickness of her mother" ALS, DNA, RG 94, War Records Office, Dept. of the Tenn. See *O.R.*, I, xxiv, part 3, 553; *ibid.*, I, xxx, part 3, 145–46; letter to Maj. Gen. William T. Sherman, July 17, telegram to Sherman, July 29, 1863.

To Brig. Gen. Robert Allen

Vicksburg Miss July 24th 1863.

Brig. Genl. R. Allen.
Chief Qr. Mr. &c.
St. Louis Mo.
General,

The bearer of this, Capt. H. McDougall has been on constant duty here with his Steamer, the "Diligent." from the time the army first came to Young's Point. Constantly the "Diligent" has been used as a messenger boat leaving no time for rest or repairs. All difficult navigation, such as that up Steel's Bayou &c, this boat has been ready for. Up to this time from Capt. McDougals statement, he has received no pay and cannot settle with the hands or his boat longer. He now goes to St Louis for a settlement. I can say that Capt McDougal with his boat has done more actual service than any other Steamboat Man with this Army. He does all that he is called on to do cheerfully and promptly. I hope the settlement he asks may be promptly made

Very truly your obt. Sevt.
Maj. Gen. U. S. Grant.

Copy, Parsons Papers, IHi.

To Brig. Gen. Robert Allen

———

Head Quarters, Dept. of the Ten.
Vicksburg Miss. July 25th 1863.

BRIG. GEN. R. ALLEN,
ST. LOUIS MO.
GEN.

The bearer of this, Capt. McMellen is Master of the steamer Silver Wave, one of the Vessels that run the Vicksburg batteries and done service below the city of inestimable value. All the steamers that run the batteries were hit more or less frequently by the enemy's shell and injured. It is due the owners of these boats now that they should be put in as good repair, at Government expense, as they were in before running the blockade and without loss of time. In other words their charters should continue until the repairs are made.—It might prove more economical to Government to pay damages and loss of time in making repairs to the owners at once and let them superintend and contract for their own work.

The names of the steamers that run the blockade and are entitled to a settlement covering damages and loss of time in making repairs are the Silverwave, Forest Queen, Moderator, Cheesman, Anglo Saxon & Empire City. The Tigress[1] & Henry Clay were destroyed in runing the blockade and the Horizon sunk by collision after passing the Grand Gulf batteries.[2]

In making the settlement for the services of these boats should you require my signature to make a satisfactory voucher I will freely give it.

I am Gen. very respectfully
your obt. svt.
U. S. GRANT
Maj. Gen.

ALS, Parsons Papers, IHi. Brig. Gen. Robert Allen endorsed the letter. "Respectfully referred to Col Parsons, who will take measures to have the Boat repaired" AES, *ibid.*

1. See letter to Brig. Gen. Montgomery C. Meigs, Aug. 10, 1863.

2. On Aug. 11, 1863, USG endorsed a letter of 1st Engineer John N. McCurdy, U.S. Navy, owner of the *Horizon*, wanting to buy the wreck or to obtain its machinery to build another steamer. "Make application through Brig Genl. Allen Chief Quartermaster of the West, Saint Louis, Mo." Copies, DLC-USG, V, 25; DNA, RG 393, Dept. of the Tenn., Endorsements. See *O.R.*, I, xxiv, part 1, 634, 643.

To Brig. Gen. Joseph D. Webster

Headquarters Dept. of the Tenn.
Vicksburg Miss. July 26th 1863

BRIG. GENL. J D. WEBSTER
SUPT. MILITARY RAILROADS.
GENERAL:

Your two letters of the 20th are just received. In regard to opening the Road East from Corinth, I am not yet prepared to say, whether any move will be made requiring it. With the present force in West. Tennessee, it would not be possible to give adequate protection to extension beyond Corinth.

I am anxiously waiting for some general plan of operations from Washington. It is important that the troops of different Departments should act in concert. Hence the necessity of general instructions coming from one head

Nothing is required from above for the road here. We captured five locomotives in Vicksburg and a number of cars. Only eleven miles of the road is being used, and that only for army purposes. All that will have to be supplied hereafter by this road, will be two or three thousand men.

Very respectfully
Your obt Servt
U. S. GRANT
Maj Genl.

Copies, DLC-USG, V, 19, 101, 103; DNA, RG 393, Dept. of the Tenn., Letters Sent. *O.R.*, I, xxiv, part 3, 552–53.

To Brig. Gen. Lorenzo Thomas

Head Quarters, Dept. of the Ten.
Vicksburg Miss. July 27th 1863.

Brig. Gen. L. Thomas,
Adj. Gen. of the Army,
Gen.

I would respectfully call attention of the War Department to the case of Brig. Gen. J. M. Thayer whos rank among the Brigadiers seems to be anomilous. He was appointed Brigadier General to take rank from the 4th day of October 1862. As soon as notice of the appointment was received he vacated his commission as Col. of the 1st Nebraska Regiment of Infantry and the place was filled by the appointment of his successer. Gen. Thayer though never rejected, I believe, by the Senate was not confirmed until the 13th of March 1863, and now appears on the official list of Brigadiers to take rank from that date. The same rule does not seem to have applied to others who had been serving as Generals previous to the meeting of Congress.

Gen. Thayer has served constantly from the begining of the rebellion, I believe without a days leave of absence. He has been in command of a Brigade constantly since the summer, or Fall, of 1861 giving entire satisfaction, and received his promotion for meritorious services at Donelson and Shiloh.

It seems to me but a simple act of justice to Gen. Thayer to date his rank back to the date of his first appointment and thus restore him to the same relative rank he had before confirmation by the Senate.

I am Gen. Very respectfully
your obt. svt.
U. S. Grant
Maj. Gen.

ALS, RPB. On July 25, 1863, Brig. Gen. John M. Thayer wrote to Lt. Col. John A. Rawlins requesting a twenty-day leave of absence. LS, DNA, RG 94,

ACP, T334 CB 1863. On July 27, USG endorsed this letter. "Approved & respectfully forwarded to Head Quarters of the Army." AES, *ibid*. On the same day, USG telegraphed to Maj. Gen. William T. Sherman. "Gen. Thayer has applied for leave of absence; approved by Gen. Steele, but without passing through you. As there is a boat leaving at 5 this evening, I have granted it, and report to you the fact." Copies, DLC-USG, V, 19, 101, 103; DNA, RG 393, Dept. of the Tenn., Letters Sent. On the same day, Sherman telegraphed to USG. "I report [*regret*] that the leave to Gen Thayer was granted   Gen Steele is now ordered away & it leaves a Div without a commander   I h We should make an inflexible rule that at least one Genl officer should be with a division one field officer with a Regt & one Commissioned officer with a Co   If we dont look out our army will take leave en masse" Telegram received, *ibid.*, RG 94, War Records Office, Dept. of the Tenn. *O.R.*, I, xxiv, part 3, 554.

To Brig. Gen. Lorenzo Thomas

Head Quarters, Department of the Tennessee,
Vicksburg, Miss., July 27th 1863.

BRIGADIER GENERAL L. THOMAS,
ADJUTANT GENERAL OF THE ARMY.
GENERAL:

I would very respectfully recommend for gallant and meritorious services, and for extreme fitness for command, corresponding to the increased rank, the following promotions, to wit: Brig.-Gen'l., Granville M. Dodge, Brig.-Gen'l. Alvin P. Hovey, Brig.-Gen'l. John E. Smith, and Brig.-Gen'l. W. S. Smith to be Major Generals of Volunteers.[1]

And Col. Charles R. Woods, 76th Ohio, Col. Alexander Chambers, 16th Iowa, Lieut Col Jno. A Rawlins, A. A. General, Col. Giles A. Smith 8th Mo., Col. John M. Corse 6th Iowa,[2] Col. R. A. Cameron 34th Indiana, Col. John B. Sanborn 4th Minnesota, Col. W Q. Gresham 53rd Ind., Col. M. F. Force 20th Ohio, and Col. T. Kilby Smith 54th Ohio, to be Brigadier General's of Volunteers.[3]

These officers have all rendered valuable services in the field, and will fill the places for which they are recommended, well.

Lieut Col. Jno. A. Rawlins has been my Assist Adjutant General from the beginning of the rebellion. No officer has now a more

honorable reputation than he has won, and I think I can safely say
that he would make a good Corps Commander. This promotion I
would particularly ask as a reward of merit.

> I am, General, Very Respectfully,
> Your ob'd't. servant.
> U. S. GRANT
> Major General.

LS, DNA, RG 94, ACP, G232 CB 1863. *O.R.*, I, lii, part 1, 419. On Aug. 3,
1863, Maj. Gen. Henry W. Halleck wrote to Secretary of War Edwin M. Stanton. "I respectfully recommend the following promotions of officers serving in
the army of Major Genl Grant, to date from July 4th/63, the time Vicksburg
capitulated. Major F. E. Prime, Engrs. to be Brig. Genl. Vols.   Col. Chs R.
Wood 76th Ohio Vols. to be Brig. Genl. Vols. Col. Giles Smith 8th Mo. Vols
to be Brig. Genl. Vols. Col. J. A. Maltby 45th Ill. Vols to be Brig. Genl.
Vols.   Col. J. B. Sanborn 4th Minn. Vols. to be Brig. Genl. Vols." LS, DNA,
RG 94, ACP, H391 CB 1863. Stanton endorsed this letter: "Appointments
Ordered" AES, *ibid.* See letter to Abraham Lincoln, July 20, 1863; letter to
Col. John C. Kelton, Aug. 17, 1863, note 1. On Aug. 10, Halleck wrote to
Stanton. "I respectfully forward with approval the following recommendations
of Genl Grant for promotion: Brig Genl Granville M. Dodge, Brig Genl Alvin
P. Hovey, Brig Genl John E. Smith & Brig Genl W. S. Smith, to be Major Genls
of volunteers; Col. Alexander Chambers, 16th Iowa, Lt Col John A. Rawlins,
A. A. Genl, Col John M. Corse, 6th Iowa, Col. R. E. Cameron, 34th Indiana,
Col W. Q. Gresham 53d Indiana, Col M. F. Force, 20th Ohio & Col T.
Kilby Smith, 54th Ohio, to be Brig Genls of Volunteers." ALS, DNA, RG 94,
ACP, H401 CB 1863. Stanton endorsed this letter: "Approved" AES, *ibid.* On
Aug. 28, Halleck wrote to USG. "Immediately on the receipt of your recommendations for promotion dated July 27th, I approved and submitted them to
the Secty of War. All vacancies of Major Genl had been previously filled. I tried
all I could to keep some open for your army, but failed. Only a part of those
recommended for Brig Genls could be appointed at present. My object in getting the appointments on Col Rawlins statement, without waiting for your
official letter, was to prevent everything from being gobbled up, before your
army could get a chance." LS, *ibid.*, RG 393, Dept. of the Tenn., Letters Received. *O.R.*, I, lii, part 1, 442; (misdated Aug. 20) *ibid.*, I, xxx, part 3, 82.

On Aug. 18, Asst. Secretary of War Charles A. Dana wrote to USG listing
the new brig. gens. on the adjt. gen.'s register from USG's command, including Lt. Col. John A. Rawlins and the five officers recommended by Halleck on
Aug. 5, but noting that Maj. Frederick E. Prime had declined the appointment. See letter to Charles A. Dana, Aug. 5, 1863. On Aug. 30, USG wrote
to Col. John C. Kelton. "I would respectfully recommend the promotion of Maj.
Theodore S. Bowers, Judge Advocate, to Lieutenant Col. & Asst. Adj. Gen.
vice Lt. Col. Rawlins appointed Brigadier Gen. Maj. Bowers has been with me
since the Fall of 1861, is thoroughly acquainted with the duties of the office
and is a most deserving officer." ALS, DNA, RG 94, ACP, G273 CB 1863.
On Sept. 7, Halleck endorsed this letter "Approved," and the appointment was

made as of Aug. 30. AES, *ibid.* Also on Aug. 30, USG wrote to Kelton. "Capt. F. E. Prime, who has rendered distinguished services in this Department as Chief Engineer, has frequently expressed a desire to be assigned to duty on permanent fortifications. The Capt. was forced to leave here before the surrender of Vicksburg in consequence of extreme debility since which time his place has been most ably filled by Capt. Comstock. Feeling that Capt. Prime would regard it as a complement to be assigned to duty on permanent works I would respectfully request that the option be given him either to be placed on such duty or to return to this Department." ALS, IHi. Prime, on sick leave from June 27 to Oct. 5, was then assigned to fortifications in the East.

1. Of those recommended for promotion to maj. gen., only Brig. Gen. Grenville M. Dodge was nominated, on May 26, 1864, and confirmed, as of June 7. On Aug. 20, 1863, Brig. Gen. Alvin P. Hovey, Mount Vernon, Ind., wrote to USG. "I hope you will pardon me for troubling you personally with official business—I wrote to you from Cleavland asking an extension of my leave for twenty days and have not as yet recd an answer—The extreme feebleness of my wife would make it nothing less than cruelty to leave her in her present condition—I hope you will favor me as far as the service will permit—Your report has been published and is the subject of universal praise—The press too, has changed its tone, and instead of censuring the paroling of the Vicksburgh prisoners is loud in the praise of the policy which caused you to accept Pemberton's offer—Your campaign rises still above all other war news and the people are unbounded in your praise" ALS, USG 3. Hovey was given twenty-day leaves of absence by Special Orders No. 199 and 226, July 23 and Aug. 19, 1863. Copies, DLC-USG, V, 27, 28; DNA, RG 393, Dept. of the Tenn., Special Orders. On Sept. 18, Brig. Gen. John A. Rawlins issued Special Orders No. 256 ordering Hovey to procure "conscripts and volunteers" in Ohio, Ind., and Ill. "for the respective Regiments and batteries from said States now in the Department" Copies, DLC-USG, V, 16, 28. On Nov. 19, Hovey wrote to USG. "On yesterday I had the misfortune to bury my wife—I assure you, I shall never forget your great favor in permitting me to be near her in her dying hours—I now await your Orders for service—Where shall I report, and to what Command shall I be assigned? As my horses and baggage are here it will save me much trouble to know where I am to go before I leave this place—You know how much I desire to serve under your command and I trust you will be able to give me some position where I can serve you and my country—I presume your new organization is complete and that I will have but little chance to be assigned to a command with the army at Chatanooga—If such should be the case I would be highly gratified to be assigned to the command of the new levies now being raised in Indiana. By the time this reaches you from six to 10,000 will be mustered into the service—I think if I had command of these forces that I could discipline and drill them So as to be ready to use them successfully in the Spring campaign—A soldier has no right to dictate or even suggest to his superior officer—his simple duty is to obey and I assure you that no officer in your command will submit to your commands more willingly—Do with me what you think best for the service and I shall be content. I received a letter from a member of the Cabinet—(Sec Usher of the Interior) a few days ago in which he says—'The President anticipats that Genl Grant will reccommend you for promotion and he looks forward with the plasure of doing so—&c' From

this letter I am fearful that by some means your reccommendation has never reached the President—Would it be asking too much to request you to inform the Presdent that the reccommendation was long since made?" ALS, DNA, RG 94, Generals' Papers and Books, Hovey. On Dec. 20, Lt. Col. Theodore S. Bowers issued Special Orders No. 24. "Brigadier General A. P. Hovey, U. S. Volunteers, will proceed to Indianapolis Indiana, to take command of all troops now being raised in the state of Indiana, as fast as they are turned over to the United States Government. He will locate them in proper camps, organize them into brigades and divisions, and prepare them for the field as rapidly as practicable." Copy, DLC-USG, V, 38. *O.R.*, I, xxxi, part 3, 455. See letter to Brig. Gen. Alvin P. Hovey, Feb. 9, 1864.

2. On July 19, 1863, Brig. Gen. William Sooy Smith, Jackson, Miss., wrote to Bowers recommending Col. John M. Corse for brig. gen. LS, DNA, RG 94, ACP, 641S CB 1863. On Aug. 4, USG endorsed this letter. "~~Respect~~ Approved and respectfully forwarded to Head Quarters of the Army Washington D. C." ES, *ibid*. On July 20, Col. William W. Sanford, 48th Ill., wrote to Capt. Thomas J. Loudon recommending Corse and others for promotion. LS, *ibid.*, 650S CB 1863. On Aug. 10, USG endorsed this letter. "Respectfully forwarded to Headquarters of the Army, Washington, D. C." ES, *ibid*.

3. On Sept. 15, 11:00 P.M., Lt. Col. James H. Wilson, Memphis, wrote to Capt. Adam Badeau. "I see General Grant has allowed himself, from modesty, to be furnished with a batch of self recommended Brigadiers. He's an unsuspicious scalawag and needs watching a little—but withal manages to get along fairly." Typescript, WyU. For Cols. Charles R. Woods, John B. Sanborn, and Giles A. Smith, see letters to Col. John C. Kelton and Brig. Gen. Lorenzo Thomas, Aug. 17, 1863. The others recommended for promotion to brig. gen. were nominated on Jan. 7, 1864, and confirmed on April 5, to date from Aug. 11, 1863. See letter to Maj. Gen. Henry W. Halleck, Feb. 20, 1864.

To Maj. Gen. Nathaniel P. Banks

Vicksburg Miss.
July 27th 1863,

MAJ. GEN. N. P. BANKS
COMD.G DEPT. OF THE GULF,
GEN.

Herewith I send you dispatch just received from Washington. In consequence of Prices movements I am called upon to send forces to Helena to move against him. I am also compelled to send the 9th Army Corps back to Ky. These moves are taking all the transportation that can be raised and I fear that a week more will not see the last of these troops off. Should I hear in the mean time that the forces sent you are not sufficient for the services required I will send the freshest Division I have although all of them are much in need of rest.

Sickness is showing itself to a very great extent in this command though there is but little fatal diseas. I am inclined to believe that Kirby Smith has withdrawn most of his forces that were at Monroe, and thereabouts, to Schrievesport, or at least taken them from where they were. I have taken no pains however to find out about them not being prepared to make any move against them just now.—By the time transportation can be got I will be ready to co-operate with an Army Corps, if necessary, for the extinction of Smiths forces should no move be ordered from Washington requiring my troops elswhere.

If my troops are to rest for some time I shall send an Army Corps to Natchez instead of keeping them all here. In that case there will always be a force there, disposable, to give very great assistance should you require it.

> I am Gen. very respectfully
> your obt. svt.
> U. S. GRANT
> Maj. Gen

By telegraph from Port Hudson

ALS, DLC-Nathaniel P. Banks. *O.R.*, I, xxiv, part 3, 553. See telegram to Maj. Gen. Henry W. Halleck, July 15, 1863. On July 27, 1863, USG wrote again to Maj. Gen. Nathaniel P. Banks. "The bearer of this, C. Newcomb, has been employed by me in secret service. I now wish to send him to Mobile to pass through the interier of rebeldom. You will oblige me very much by furnishing him a pass through your lines." ALS, DNA, RG 393, Dept. of the Gulf, Letters Received. On June 27, USG issued a pass for Charles Newcomb. "Pass the bearer, Chas. Newcomb, out our lines towards Hankerson's Ferry, on public service." ANS, DLC-USG.

To Maj. Gen. William T. Sherman

July 28th 1863

GEN. SHERMAN,

It will be ten days or more before transportation can be provided to move troops to Natchez. Ord is now here and could be sent off at any time. You can take your choice between staying where you are and going below.

U. S. GRANT
Maj. Gen.

ALS, DNA, RG 94, War Records Office, Dept. of the Tenn. *O.R.*, I, xxiv, part 3, 557. On July 28, 1863, Maj. Gen. William T. Sherman telegraphed to USG. "Under the circumstances I think Ord ought to be sent—My Corps is now in good healthy camps convenient for instruction or service. I prefer to remain here to going to Natchez. I think Harrisonburg should be attacked at once.—The Road from Natchez is good, distance not to exceed 45 miles, and it is near the confluence of Washita, Tensas, and Bayou Macon; but it can be done by a detachment from here or Natchez as you may prefer   Despatch received. I will await your Report." Copy, DNA, RG 393, Dept. of the Tenn., Telegrams Sent. *O.R.*, I, xxiv, part 3, 557. On July 29, Maj. Theodore S. Bowers issued Special Orders No. 205. "The 13th Army Corps Maj. General E. O. C. Ord, Commanding will be held in readiness to move to and take post at Natchez, Miss, as soon as transportation can be furnished. On the arrival of one Division of the 13th Army Corps at Natchez the troops now there will return to Vicksburg. The Commander at Natchez, will be charged with keeping the River open to navigation from Rodney, Miss., to Louisiana and Mississippi State line." Copies, DLC-USG, V, 27, 28; DNA, RG 393, Dept. of the Tenn., Special Orders. *O.R.*, I, xxiv, part 3, 560; *ibid.*, I, xxvi, part 1, 661.

To Maj. Gen. William T. Sherman

July 28th 1863.

GEN. SHERMAN,

The Confederates at Raymond have sent in for medicines and provisions for their sick left there about 150 in number. Having stripped the country thereabouts of course we can do no less than to supply them. But they have brought no teams the country having been stripped of them also. I will have to call on you to forward these things from Big Black as soon as I can get them there and if you have captured teams and carriages you may send them in ~~the~~ place of our own and they need not be returned.

AL (signature clipped), DNA, RG 94, War Records Office, Dept. of the Tenn. *O.R.*, I, xxiv, part 3, 557. See telegram to Maj. Gen. William T. Sherman, July 29, 1863.

To Charles W. Ford

———

Vicksburg Mississippi,
July 28th 1863.

DEAR FORD,

It will soon be time now for schools to open and as I am entirely broken up of a home from which to send my children I must look around for a place for them in time. If possible I would rather place my two oldest boys with Mr. Wyman of St. Louis.[1] Not knowing his initials or address I want to ask the favor of you to see Mr. Wyman for me and know if he can take them and his conditions.

The oldest boy is thirteen years old and the other eleven. I want them to board with Mr. Wyman and have their washing done there also. My little girl I will send to Mrs. Boggs.

If you will attend to this for me you will place me under renewed obligations.

This breaking up of families is hard. But such is War. I have much less to complain of however than the majority. In this worlds goods I had nothing to loose, and in escaping wounds, or loss of health, I have been so far fortunate.

Everything is now quiet along the Mississippi. But there is still work for the Army. Little side expeditions will be required to clean out the country West of the Miss.—The state of Miss. is now completely subjugated. It would be easyer to preserve law and order in this state now than in Mo. or Ky. so far as the inhabitants are concerned. Ark. & Louisiana will soon be in the same happy frame of mind.

I shall hope to hear from you soon.

Yours Truly
U. S. GRANT
~~Maj. Gen.~~

ALS, USG 3.

1. Edward Wyman, born in Charlestown, Mass., in 1815, educated at Amherst, operated "E. Wyman's English and Classical High School" in St. Louis 1843–53, then opened his City University in 1861. Pupils wore uniforms and drilled while receiving an otherwise standard education.

To Maj. Gen. William T. Sherman

July 29th 1863,

GEN. SHERMAN,

I will go out and see you soon. Mrs. Grant will go out when Mrs Sherman arrives. Nothing new. Did you receive a dispatch from me about furnishing transportation for supplies to Raymond?[1] Our troops passing through there have left the country destitute both of transportation and subsistence. I am sending the required supplies out and authorized you to turn over to them to keep transportation taken from the country if you have it   if not send the stores out by our teams they to be returned.

U. S. GRANT
Maj. Gen. Com

ALS (telegram sent), DNA, RG 94, War Records Office, Dept. of the Tenn. Incomplete in *O.R.*, I, xxiv, part 3, 559. On July 29, 1863, Maj. Gen. William T. Sherman, "Big Black," telegraphed to USG. "Am at R R bridge   is there anything new   Rain washed away our bridges over Clear Creek but will repair at once   if you Mrs Grant & children will visit me I can meet you here at any time appointed with Carriage & Saddle horses." Telegram received, DNA, RG 94, War Records Office, Dept. of the Tenn. On Aug. 1, Sherman telegraphed to USG. "I will meet you at 9. a. m. at the R. R. Bridge, with led horses. Will Mrs. Grant come? I can have an elegant carriage for her and children, and our Palace will accommodate a retine of any size. If convenient I would advise you to spend some days out here as the Country is beautiful. Telegraph me how many will come that I may order the necessary transportation." Copy, *ibid.*, RG 393, Dept. of the Tenn., Telegrams Sent. See *Memoirs of Gen. W. T. Sherman* (4th ed., New York, 1891), I, 373.

1. See telegram to Maj. Gen. William T. Sherman, July 28, 1863.

To Maj. Thomas Hendrickson

Headquarters Department of the Tennessee
Vicksburg, Miss. July 30th, 1863

MAJOR HENDRICKSON
COMD'G ALTON, ILL.
MAJOR:

Please release W. Williams, R. Murdock and T. P. Farran who it seems were confined in Alton Prison, by my order, but without my knowledge. If you have any more prisoners with you, known to have been arrested by Col. Clark J. Wright, of the 6th Mo. Cavalry, please release them also. I find that it is almost proof positive of the innocence of a man, to have been arrested by that Officer.

Very respectfully
Your Obt. Servt.
U. S. GRANT
Maj. Genl.

Copies, DLC-USG, V, 19, 101, 103; DNA, RG 393, Dept. of the Tenn., Letters Sent. On July 22, 1863, USG had written to Maj. Thomas Hendrickson. "Enclosed I send you a list of prisoners, who it seems have been confined in Alton by my order, but without my authority. If you will please release them, and return them to their homes on their paroles you will much oblige me." Copies, *ibid.* On Aug. 19, USG endorsed the proceedings of a board of examiners at Vicksburg inquiring into the conduct of Col. Clark Wright, 6th Mo. Cav. "Approved: and respectfully forwarded to Head Quarters of the Army Washington D. C. for the action of the President" Copies, *ibid.*, Endorsements; DLC-USG, V, 25. On Sept. 7, USG's name was endorsed on a letter of Aug. 28 of Wright, Vicksburg, stating his case, requesting a copy of the charges against him, and asking to be relieved from arrest. "Respectfully forwarded to Head Quarters of the army Washington D. C. Col. Wright was ordered before a Military Board of Examiners to examine into his qualifications and competency as a Cavalry Officer and the proceedings of said Board in his case were forwarded to the Adjt. Generals Office on the 19th day of August 1863. There is no doubt entertained of his loyalty and devotion to his country   I have ordered his release from arrest." Copies, *ibid.* On the same day, Brig. Gen. John A. Rawlins wrote to Maj. Gen. James B. McPherson regarding Wright. "You will order his release from arrest, but he will not return to duty with his command until a dicision is had in his case from the proper authority." Copies, *ibid.*, V, 19, 103; DNA, RG 393, Dept. of the Tenn., Letters Sent. Wright was discharged on Sept. 16.

On Oct. 17, Lt. Col. Loren Kent was sent to Alton to ". . . report in detail the names of all prisoners from the Department of the Tennessee now confined there, the date they were sent, for what time, by whose order, the nature of their offence, and all other facts and circumstances that he may deem important . . ." Special Orders No. 283, copies, DLC-USG, V, 16, 28. On Nov. 1, Kent, Vicksburg, sent Lt. Col. Theodore S. Bowers a list of soldiers confined at Alton recommending that many of them should be released and returned to duty. ALS, DNA, RG 393, Military Div. of the Miss., Letters Received. On Dec. 14, USG endorsed this letter. "The recommendation of Col. Kent is approved, and will be put into execution w[it]hout delay—" ES, *ibid.*

General Orders No. 50

[*Aug. 1, 1863*]

GEN. ORDERS.

The State of Mississippi ~~South of Yazoo City, to the state line of Louisiana~~, throuhout its length and West of the Miss. Central rail-road being now free from the presence of any armed force of the enemy are called upon to pursue their peaceful avocations in obedience to the laws of the United States.—Whilst doing so, in good faith, all United States forces are prohibited from molesting in any way the citizens of the country. It is earnestly recommended that ~~all~~ negroes, who can, will make contracts to labor for their former owners, ~~Where contracts~~ and ~~do so~~ that they labor in good faith. When such contracts cannot be made then to hire themselves to such persons as are willing to employ their services. Their private property will be respected except where the use of it is necessary for the Government, in which case it must be taken ~~by the order of a commanding officer of a Corps, District, Post or Expedition.~~ under the direction of Corps Commanders. In all cases where it becomes necessary to take private property for public use a detail will be made, under a Commissioned officer, to take specified property, and none other. A staff officer of the Quartermaster or Subsistence Dept. will, in all cases, be designated who ~~is to~~ will give receipts for all property taken, to be paid at the end of the war, on proof of loyalty or on proper adjustment of claim under any regulation hereafter established. All property so seized must be taken up, on returns by the officers giving receipts. Persons having Cotten or other products of the southern soil not ~~used~~ consumable, or not required, by the Army, will be allowed to bring the same into any Military post within the state of Mississippi, and abandon ~~the same~~ it to the Agt. of the Treasury Department at said Military post, to be dealt with according to such regulations as the Treasury Department may establish. At posts where there is no Treasury Agt. ~~has~~ the Post Quartermaster will receive all such property and hold it for the arival of a Treasury Agt. or ship it, to Memphis to the care of Capt. A. R. Eddy to be turned over to the Treasury Agt. at that place, at the option of the owner of the property.

Within the County of Warren, which has been laid waste by the long presence of contending Armies, the following rules will be observed to prevent ~~actual starvation or~~ suffering.

Maj. Gen. Sherman and Maj. Gen. McPherson will each designate a Com.y of Subsistence who will issue articles of prime necessity to all destitute families who call on them, under such restrictions for the protection of Government as they may deem expedient to establish. Families who are able to pay for the provisions drawn from the subsistence Dept. will, in all cases, be required to do so.

ADf, DLC-USG, III. This draft, with minor revisions, became sections II–IV of General Orders No. 50, issued by Maj. Theodore S. Bowers on Aug. 1, 1863. Sections I and V of these orders read: "All regularly organized bodies of of the enemy having been driven from those parts of Kentucky and Tennessee west of the Tennessee river: and from all of Mississippi, west of the Mississippi Central Railroad: and it being to the interest of those districts not to invite the presence of armed bodies of men among them, it is announced that the most rigorous penalties will hereafter be inflicted upon the following classes of prisoners, to wit: All irregular bodies of Cavalry not mustered and paid by the Confederate authorities: all persons engaged in conscripting, enforcing the conscription, or in apprehending deserters, whether regular or irregular; all citizens encouraging or aiding the same; and all persons detected in firing upon unarmed transports. It is not contemplated that this order shall effect the treatment due to prisoners of war, captured within the districts named when they are members of legally organized companies, and when their acts are in accordance with the usages of civilized warfare. . . . Conduct disgraceful to the American name has been frequently reported to the Major General Commanding, particularly on the part of portions of the Cavalry. Hereafter if the guilty parties cannot be reached, the commanders of Regiments and detachments will be held responsible, and those who prove themselves unequal to the task of discipline in their commands, will be promptly reported to the War Department for 'muster-out.' Summary punishment will be inflicted upon all officers and soldiers apprehended in acts of violence or lawlessness." Copies, *ibid.*, V, 13, 14; DNA, RG 94, War Records Office, Union Battle Reports; *ibid.*, RG 393, Dept. of the Tenn., General and Special Orders; (printed) USGA. *O.R.*, I, xxiv, part 3, 570–71. On Aug. 23, Maj. Gen. William T. Sherman telegraphed to Lt. Col. John A. Rawlins. "Is there any Regulation permitting citizens living within our lines to sell a bale of cotton   I am called on every day by persons for permission to sell cotton as they have been stripped of everything else & have no means of support" Telegram received, DNA, RG 94, War Records Office, Dept. of the Tenn.; copy, *ibid.*, RG 393, Dept. of the Tenn., Telegrams Sent. On the same day, Rawlins wrote to Sherman. "The orders of Adjutant Gen'l Thomas prohibit the shipment of Cotton North and substantially, declares all Cotton abandoned to the Government. Gen'l Grant's Gen'l Order No 50 permits persons well disposed to the Government to bring their cotton in an abandon it to the government, with a view of receiving pay for it from the Treasury Agent at Memphis. In some instances he has, where they have done so, auterized them to purchase from the Commissary supplies on the credit of such abandonment. This order is made to try and afford releif to Citizens, without violating those of the Adjt Genl. The General has not returned." Copies, DLC-USG, V, 19, 103; DNA, RG 393, Dept. of the Tenn., Letters Sent. On Dec. 30, 1865, USG wrote: "The object of General order No 50 of Aug 1st 1863 was to prevent captures of private property by the troops under my command within the District of country named in said order; to protect peaceable citizens therein from molestation in their lawful pursuits; and to enable the owners of southern products, especially Cotton, to get them to market for their own benefit, in accordance with law and the regulations of the Treasury Department. Any property taken by my troops under the supposed authority of said order No 50 was merely in aid of the operations of the Treasury Department" DS, *ibid.*, RG 200, Stidham Collection.

On Aug. 10, 1863, Bowers issued General Orders No. 51. "At all military posts in States within the Department, where slavery has been abolished by the Proclamation of the President of the United States, camps will be established for such freed people of color as are out of employment. Commanders of Posts or Districts will detail suitable officers from the Army as Superintendents of such camps. It will be the duty of such Superintendents to see that suitable rations are drawn from the Subsistence Department for such people as are confided to their care. All such persons supported by the Government will be employed in every practicable way, so as to avoid, as far as possible their becoming a burthen upon the Government. They may be hired to planters or other citizens, on proper assurances that the negroes so hired will not be run off beyond the military jurisdiction of the United States; they may be employed on any public works; in gathering crops from abandoned plantations; and generally, in any manner local commanders may deem for the best interests of the Government in compliance with law and the policy of the Administration. It will be the duty of the Provost Marshal at every military post, to see that every negro within the jurisdiction of the military authority, is employed by some white person, or is sent to the camps provided for freed people. Citizens may make contracts with freed persons of color for their labor, giving wages per month in money, or employ families of them by the year on plantations, &c., feeding, clothing, and supporting the infirm as well as the able bodied, and giving a portion, not less than one twentieth, of the commercial part of their crops, in payment for such service. Where negroes are employed under this authority, the parties employing will register with the Provost Marshal their names, occupation and residence, and the number of negroes employed. They will enter into such bonds as the Provost Marshal, with the approval of the local commander, may require, for the kind treatment and proper care of those employed, and as security against their being carried beyond the employers jurisdiction. Nothing in this order is to be construed to embarrass the employment of such colored persons as may be required by the Government." Copies, DLC-USG, V, 13, 14; DNA, RG 393, Dept. of the Tenn., General and Special Orders; (printed) USGA. *O.R.,* I, xxiv, part 3, 585. See *Memoirs,* I, 577.

On Aug. 23, Rawlins issued General Orders No. 53. "Hereafter, negroes will not be allowed in or about the camps of white troops, except such as are properly employed and controlled. They may be employed in the Quartermaster's department, Subsistence department, Medical department, as hospital nurses and laundresses, in the Engineer department, and as Pioneers. As far as practicable, such as have been, or may be rejected as recruits for colored regiments by the examining surgeon, will be employed about hospitals and in Pioneer Corps. In Regiments and Companies, they may be employed as follows: One cook to each fifteen men, and one teamster to each wagon. Officers may employ them as servants, but not in greater numbers than they are entitled to commutation for. Commanders of Regiments and detachments, will see that all negroes in or about their respective camps, not employed as provided in this order, are collected and turned over to the Provost Marshal of the Division, Post, or Army Corps, to which their regiment or detachment belongs. Provost Marshals will keep all negroes thus coming into their hands, from straggling and wandering about, until they can be put in charge of the Superintendent of the camp for colored people nearest them; and all negroes unemployed in accordance with this or previous orders, not in and about camps of regiments and detachments, will be required to go into the camps established for negroes, and it is enjoined upon Provost Marshals to see that they do so. Recruiting for colored regiments in negro camps, will be prohibited, except when special authority to do so is given. All able bodied negro men who are found, ten days after the publication of this order, without a certificate of the officers or persons employing them, will be regarded as unemployed, and may be pressed into service. Certificates given to negroes must show how, where, and by whom they are employed, and if as officers servants, that the officer employing them has not a greater number, than by law he is entitled to commutation for." Copies, DLC-USG, V, 13, 14; DNA, RG 393, Dept. of the Tenn., General and Special Orders; (printed) USGA. On Sept. 12, Rawlins issued Special Orders No. 250. "Major William Tweedale Engineer Regiment of the West is hereby authorized to take up and press into the public service as laborers all idle and unemployed freedmen he may require, in the vicinity of and in rear of Vicksburg, including those in Contraband Camps. They will be organized by him into working parties under charge of competent commissioned and non commissioned officers   They will be borne on returns as similar as may be to report of persons and things form two, Quartermasters Department, and paid by the Quartermasters Department monthly the sum of ten dollars per month, three dollars of which shall be in clothing   one ration daily will be allowed them" Copies, DLC-USG, V, 16, 28.

On Aug. 31, Brig. Gen. John P. Hawkins, Goodrich's Landing, La., wrote to Rawlins. "The condition of the contrabands a loose in this District is deplorable   I understood there is an officer, Capt Anderso[n] detailed to attend to them, and that a plan has been adopted for taking care of them, but as far as developed here, it amounts to nothing more than giving them rations, and letting them live in demoralizing idleness, what is wanted more is some system of labor for them, by which they can at least partly support themselves. The plan of having them cut Steamboat wood is good if only carried out. There are a large number now here available for that purpose if taken to 'Pau-Pau' Island. The officer above mentioned, talked of it the other day while here, but not was done. One and the principal difficulty in their case is that there are not enough persons detailed for this service. Before winter sets in they should be settled some where, and earning something. I could have made this letter shorter by simply saying that the persons in charge of Contrabands are not attending to their business." Copy, DNA, RG 393, District of Northeastern La., Letters Sent. On Sept. 21, Rawlins endorsed this letter. "Respectfully referred to chaplain Eaton Supt. of contrabands" Copies, DLC-USG, V, 25; DNA, RG 393, Dept. of the Tenn., Endorsements. See letters to Brig. Gen. Marcellus M. Crocker, Aug. 28, 30, 1863.

To Maj. Gen. Henry W. Halleck

Vicksburg, Miss. Aug 1 [*1863*]

Maj. Gen. Halleck
Gen'l in Chief—

Everything indicates a withdrawal of Kirby Smith's troops to Natchetoches and Shreveport—

Mobile can be taken from the Gulf department, with only one or two gunboats to protect the debarkation. I can send the necessary force, with your leave—I would like to visit New Orleans, particularly if the movement against Mobile is authorized—[1]

U. S. GRANT
Maj. Gen'l

Telegram received, DNA, RG 107, Telegrams Collected (Bound); copies, *ibid.*, Telegrams Received in Cipher; *ibid.*, RG 393, Dept. of the Tenn., Hd. Qrs. Correspondence; DLC-USG, V, 6, 8, 24, 94. *O.R.*, I, xxiv, part 3, 569. On Aug. 1, 1863, Maj. Gen. Nathaniel P. Banks conferred with USG at Vicksburg regarding plans for an expedition against Mobile, Ala. See *ibid.*, I, xxvi, part 1, 666. On July 29, Brig. Gen. Grenville M. Dodge, Corinth, Miss., conveyed to Maj. Gen. Stephen A. Hurlbut's adjt. information gained from scouts regarding C.S.A. fortifications at Mobile. Copies, DNA, RG 94, War Records Office, Dept. of the Mo. *O.R.*, I, xxiv, part 3, 561. Hurlbut forwarded this report to USG on July 31, who forwarded it to army hd. qrs. on Aug. 5. AES and ES, DNA, RG 94, War Records Office, Dept. of the Mo.

1. On Aug. 9, Maj. Gen. Henry W. Halleck telegraphed to USG. "There is no objection to your visiting New Orleans, leaving an officer at Vicksburg to recieve & carry out any orders that are sent from Washington. The orders sent through you to Genl Banks will indicate what operation is next to be undertaken." ALS (telegram sent), *ibid.*, RG 107, Telegrams Collected (Bound); copy, *ibid.*, RG 108, Telegrams Sent. *O.R.*, I, xxiv, part 3, 584. See letters to Maj. Gen. Nathaniel P. Banks, Aug. 7, 1863, note 1, and to Maj. Gen. Henry W. Halleck, Aug. 31, 1863.

To Lt. Commander John G. Walker

Head Quarters, Dept. of the Ten.
Vicksburg Miss. Aug. 3d 1863.

CAPT J. G. WALKER U. S. N.
COMD.G STEAMER RATTLER,
SIR:

It is impossible to furnish a steamer on which to ship troops to Yazoo City. I am now compelld to ship off the 9th & 13th Army Corps and as fast as steamers are unloaded they go to one or other of those Corps. Can the Navy not furnish the steamer Champion or some other vessel suitable for the transportation of a regiment?

Very respectfully
U. S. GRANT
Maj. Gen. Com

ALS, Mrs. Walter Love, Flint, Mich. John G. Walker, born in N. H. in 1835, graduated first in his class from the U.S. Naval Academy in 1856. Promoted to lt. commander as of July 16, 1862, and capt. of the *Baron De Kalb* in the Mississippi Squadron, he commanded a land battery during the siege of Vicksburg. On Aug. 3, 1863, Walker, Vicksburg, wrote to USG. "I will have the Champion at any point most convenient for your troops as soon as I can get orders to her, (probably a couple of hours). My messenger tells me you spoke of sending some cavalry. By pushing up above Yazoo City with cavalry they might capture or destroy the remainder of the transports." ALS, DNA, RG 393, Dept. of the Tenn., Letters Received. On the same day, Maj. Theodore S. Bowers wrote to Maj. Gen. James B. McPherson, Vicksburg. "Order one Regiment of your command to embark on the Steamer Champion No 3, and proceed at 4 Oclock tomorrow morning to Yazoo City, under convoy of the U. S. Steamer Rattler, Lieut Commander Walker, to occupy that place, during the attempt to raise the vessel DeKalb, and to render the navy such assistance as may be necessary. Ten days rations and the necessary amunition will be taken. The Regiment selected, should be one possessed of a discreet and competent officer." Copies, DLC-USG, V, 19, 101, 103; DNA, RG 393, Dept. of the Tenn., Letters Sent. See *O.R.* (Navy), I, xxv, 368.

To Maj. Gen. Stephen A. Hurlbut

Head Quarters, Dept. of the Ten
Vicksburg Miss. Aug. 4th/63

MAJ. GEN. S. A. HURLBUT,
COMD.G 16TH ARMY CORPS.
GEN.

The destruction of the rail-road at Jackson Miss. has cut off a large amount of rolling stock from the enemy. This stock numbering from forty to seventy locomotives and several hundred Cars is now North of Grenada. If the labor of reconstructing the bridges on the Mississippi & Memphis rail-road will not be too great it might pay to rebuild them for the purpose of geting the stock into Memphis. An expedition sent out for the purpose of collecting it, if rightly conducted, might have a beneficial effect.

In this part of Miss. the people acknowledge themselves subjugated, the southern cause lost, and are holding meetings to ~~know~~ devise plans for coming back into the Union. If we can send troops through the state who will respect the property of the people and advise them what is being done about Jackson & Natchez, and that saving this stock and repairing the road might lead to the opening of trade with them the effect might be good.

I will send cavalry from here to collect all the rolling stock and take it as far North as the road is in running order. You can send troops from Memphis to meet them and repair the road Northward sufficiently to pass the cars.

You will want to get these troops off as early as possible. The troops from here will be all Cavalry, one thousand in number, and can remain with the party until they get through to Memphis, if necessary, and return by water.

I will start the Cavalry from here on the 8th.

> Very respectfully
> your obt. svt.
> U. S. Grant
> Maj. Gen. Com

ALS, DNA, RG 393, 16th Army Corps, Letters Received. *O.R.*, I, xxiv, part 3, 575. See following letter. On Aug. 8, 1863, Maj. Gen. Stephen A. Hurlbut, Memphis, wrote to USG. "I will be ready to move a force down on the line of the Memphis & Grenada Rail Road so as to cooperate with the force you send up. My information is that the Engines & Cars are held by a light guard with instructions to destroy them in case any of our troops appear and they will do so. I fear the amount of repairs necessary to transport the stock will exceed its value, as there will be three bridges to repair or reconstruct between this point and Panola. My opinion is that the Rolling Stock will have to be destroyed. If the stock was as I supposed it near Water Valley it might be brought to LaGrange with much less expence, but I understand from your letter that it is on the other road. Steele is pushing his preparations for his movement. He thinks Kirby Smith is reinforcing Holmes & Price—This is doubtful, but in any event I consider him strong enough for their combined force. The President & Genl in Chief have fairly complimented me into a withdrawal of my resignation until better times. I will send to you by next mail a copy of the President's letter which contains his views on questions of great public importance. Genl Prentiss has tendered his resignation. I think it should be accepted. He thinks himself undervalued & in all such cases it is well to relieve the army & make way for men who are not plagued in that way." ALS, DNA, RG 393, Dept. of the Tenn., Letters Received. *O.R.*, I, xxiv, part 3, 583–84. Regarding the resignations of Hurlbut and of Maj. Gen. Benjamin M. Prentiss, see letters to Maj. Gen. Nathaniel P. Banks, July 10, note 2, and Aug. 14, 1863. On Aug. 10 and 15, Hurlbut wrote to USG. "I am fully informed that the Rolling Stock & cars are just below Watervalley, the whole are covered with fence rails ready to be set on fire. An attempt is now being made to work them off South by reparing the road temporarily. An Expedition is on the point of starting from LaGrange to save them if practicable to bring them in. I am satisfied they will be destroyed by the enemy, before we can reach them. I inclose you copy of the President's letter to me. You will see his views. In connection with this I would state that a large number some 50 very prominent men in Miss. apply for leave to hold a meeting in North Miss—to consider the ways & means of bringing the state into the Union. I propose to give them such permission considering it the inauguration of an important movement. If they are not interrupted by the Confederate authorities, I shall consider the future of Miss—as fixed and shall at their request give them my personal views as to the present necessities of their condition. I shall carefully decline any official or representative capacity but as a citizen place before them what I understand to be their proper course for their own salvation. I will send you a copy of my letter as soon as I can find time to write it." ALS, DNA, RG 393, Dept. of the Tenn., Letters Received. *O.R.*, I, xxiv, part 3, 586. "I have the honor to inclose for your consideration my communication to S B Walker   I hope it may meet your approbation. He is the agent of prominent parties in Miss. and I believe this to be a bonâfide movement toward reconstruction. As such I have acknowledged it, but not *officially*, so that it is perfectly competent to disavow my personal advice" ALS, DNA, RG 94, War Records Office, Military Div. of the Miss. Hurlbut enclosed a copy of his letter of Aug. 10 to S. B. Walker stating at length his views regarding Reconstruction. Copy, *ibid.*

To Maj. Gen. James B. McPherson

[*Aug. 4, 1863*]

Some difficulty seems to have arisen between the Post Commander and the P. O. Dept. growing out of authority given some Jews to search the P. O. building for private property . . . There is always military authority at every military post to control all matters at the post, but when there are H'd Q'rs above that of post commander there are always staff officers, and, it may be, civil departments who are only under the control of these higher military authorities.

U. S. GRANT

Anderson Galleries Sale No. 2146, March 16, 1927, p. 7.
On Aug. 9, 1863, Lyman & Cooledge, St. Louis, wrote to USG. "We are Pained to hear from Many prominent Officers, That there are a very numerous number of Israelites who are Landing & Storeing Goods in Vicksburg Contrary to your orders—And Those who are storeing are Taking Soldiers Officers & Citizens in their Back doors and selling Goods contrary to your orders—Now are such things Tolerated By you and of your knowledge. As I well know Two of my American friends who have pressed you hard for the Same Privilege and have been flatly denied, for whish I at the time gave you credit   Please inform

me of the facts." ALS, DNA, RG 393, Dept. of the Tenn., Letters Received. On Aug. 12, USG endorsed this letter. "Refered to Col. Kent Provost Marshal Gen. who will have the matter herein mentioned investigated and if as represented confiscate all property so stored and arrest owners or representatives of such property." AES, *ibid.* On Aug. 13, Lt. Col. Loren Kent endorsed this letter. "Respectfully returned   I have made very careful inquiry and do not learn that abuses of the kind mentioned now exist. Such violations of orders have been corrected. I will have more attention given to such things in future by the officer in charge." AES, *ibid.* On the same day, Kent wrote to Lt. Col. James H. Wilson. "I am informed by Major Bowers: that there is a man here who has landed and stored a large stock of goods for sale to Sutlers. He is an unauthorized trader and must be sent North. I do not know his name, but was told that he was a tall man, from Saint Louis. I am also informed that 'Isralites' closed, are selling at the 'back door'   Your Attention is called to these statements. If found true you will apply the penalty." Copy, *ibid.*, Provost Marshal, Letters Sent.

On Aug. 30, Kent referred to Wilson "for investigation and full report" a letter of Northrup & Co., St. Louis, stating "That no matter what action was taken in reference to his order issued against Jews, that seven eights of the business men uphold and sustain him in it, but many of them are pained to hear that Jews are permitted to Land and store Goods in Vicksburg, when Americans are obliged to ship back, and furthermore there are a large number of these 'Jews' shipping Goods south on old Sutler Commissions, which have expired, and still represent themselves as Sutlers, with a view of Smuggling goods through the lines, for instance Aaron Meyers & Co & many others are shipping to Vicksburg." DLC-USG, V, 99. On Aug. 31, Wilson wrote to Kent. "The communication of Northop & Co. St Louis in relation to Jews &c, which has been referred to me by you was duly received, and in regard to the matter I respectfully submit the following report:—Upon a careful examination of the Books of the River and Shipping Department of this office, I find that no persons have been permitted to land or store, merchandise, at this place, except those who gave evidence of being authorized Sutlers: *and in no case have any been obliged to ship their goods back again*—There are a few instances where sutlers having unsaleable remnants of stocks, have had permission to ship the same North—If any persons not properly authorized, have been permitted, through misrepresentations of theirs, to land goods, a plan has just been adopted at this Office which will effectually prevent a similar occurrence   A. Meyer, had permission to land and take, 102 packages Sutlers goods, to the 12th Regt Mo. V. I, of which regiment he claimed to be sutler, and as it is reported in the communication referred to me, that he has used deception, an investigation will be made at once. It is difficult to determine from the records who are Jews; but judging from the names it is to be presumed that out of about a hundred sutlers who have received goods at this place only four are five are of that class." LS, DNA, RG 393, Dept. of the Tenn., Letters Received. On Sept. 2, Kent endorsed this letter. "Respectfully forwarded to Head Quarters Dept of the Tenn" AES, *ibid.*

To Maj. Gen. William T. Sherman

Headquarters Dept. of the Tenn
Vicksburg, Miss Aug. 4th 1863

MAJ. GENL. W. T. SHERMAN,
GENERAL.

I had determined to direct Hurlbut to send a force down the Mississippi & Memphis Road, and if there would not be too much labor in repairing the Road, to collect all the rolling stock cut off from the South, and take it into Memphis. I think therefore two or three days hence will be early enough for our Cavalry to start. The bridges at Grenada must not be destroyed, otherwise the rolling stock on the Central Road cannot be got on to the other. A Regiment with one Gun Boat leaves here today for Yazoo City with ten day's rations.

U. S. GRANT
Maj. Genl.

Telegram, copies, DLC-USG, V, 19, 101, 103; DNA, RG 393, Dept. of the Tenn., Letters Sent. *O.R.*, I, xxiv, part 3, 574. See preceding letter. On Aug. 4, 1863, Maj. Gen. William T. Sherman had telegraphed to USG. "I can make up a party of about one thousand Cavalry to go up to Grenada. I would suggest that a gunboat and one light transport go to Yazoo City with provisions, to communicate with this Cavalry and await its return, that the officer in Command be ordered to strike the Rail-road above the Bridge & follow it to Grenada. The Bridge at Grenada to be burned, so that the Locomotives & Cars can alone be taken Northwards. If you think proper the Road could be repaired from Memphis to Grenada and all these Cars taken to Memphis, and our Cavalry could go into Memphis and return by water." Copy, DNA, RG 393, Dept. of the Tenn., Telegrams Sent. *O.R.*, I, xxiv, part 3, 573. On the same Tuesday, Sherman telegraphed to USG. "I will order my Cavalry to be ready on Short notic[e] subject to your orders. I did not propose to burn the Grenada Bridg[e] until after the Locomotives and Cars were above the Yalabusha. I think the Yalabusha is as far as the Memphis forces should attempt to operate South   All below that point will be of no importance to us in a military sense. The Yazoo Country will hereafter be absolutely at our mercy—with water communication. All quiet here as Sunday and I begin to feel like doing something but until recruits arrive and our furloughed men get back I suppose we had bett[er] keep quiet." Copy, DNA, RG 393, Dept. of the Tenn., Telegrams Sent. *O.R.*, I, xxiv, part 3, 574. See telegram to Maj. Gen. William T. Sherman, Aug. 6, 1863.

To Edward Salomon

———

Head Quarters, Dept. of the Ten
Vicksburg Miss. Aug. 4th 1863,

His Excellency, Edward Salomon,
Governor of Wisconsin,
Sir:

Your letter of the 24th of July in relation to Col. Anneke is just rec'd. The case of Col. Anneke is not one probably that will have to be refered to me, but a final decission will be made by his Corps Commander, Maj. Gen. Hurlbut. I have therefore refered your letter to Gen. Hurlbut with directions to him to answer it if there are reasons why Col. A. should not be continued in the service. I know none myself.

Thanking you kindly for your congratulations to the Army which I have the honor to command I remain,

very respectfully
your obt. svt.
U. S. Grant
Maj. Gen. U. S. A.

ALS, WHi. Edward Salomon, born near Halberstadt, Prussia, in 1830, emigrated to Wis. in 1849, becoming a prominent lawyer. Elected lt. gov. in 1861, he became gov. upon the death of the incumbent the following year, and was active in recruiting. On Aug. 14, 1863, Maj. Gen. Stephen A. Hurlbut, Memphis, wrote to Salomon. "In reply to your communication of July 24th, 1863 in relation to Col F. Anneke 34th Wis Inftry. referred to me by Maj Gen Grant I have the honor to state. That Col Anneke has been tried by a Court Martial for grave military offences principally for gross insubordination. The *sentence* was approved by me on full examination and forwarded to Maj Genl Grant, from whom it has not yet returned. Since the session of that Court Martial and while under arrest other *charges* have been filed against him for sending a challenge to fight a duel. Conviction under this as well as upon the first charges compels dismissal from the service. I know nothing of Col Anneke's military history or qualifications, but it is evident from the testimony that from defect of temper or some other cause he is unable to command himself, and consequently, unable to command others. I hope if the Regiment is not reorganized that a portion of the men may enlist in the 32d Wisconsin. We do not want new *Regiments* or more *Officers*, we want the men for the old Regiments" Copy, DNA, RG 393, 16th Army Corps, Letters Sent. On Sept. 10, the proceedings in the court-martial of Col. Fritz Anneke, 34th Wis., were endorsed in USG's name. "Respectfully forwarded to Head Qrs. of the Army, Washington D. C. For confirmation see inside" ES, *ibid.*, RG 153, NN 230; copies (dated Sept. 15), *ibid.*, RG 393, Dept. of the Tenn., Endorsements; DLC-USG, V, 25. On Sept. 15, a letter of Aug. 22 of Anneke protesting his arrest was also endorsed in USG's name. "Respectfully returned to Head Quarters of the Army Washington D. C. with copy of order promulgating findings and sentence the Court Martial before which this Officer was tried. The original proceedings have just been forwarded   a copy of Order was sent some days ago to Col. Anneke through the proper Military Channel" Copies, *ibid.* See *Calendar*, Oct. 7, 1862.

On Feb. 25, 1863, Maj. Gen. John A. McClernand wrote to USG. "Col. Fritz Anneke Comdg. a Wisconsin regiment, lately, reported to be *en route* for your Department is desirous, and so are the authorities of that State, as I am informed, that he should join my command. I hope it will be consistent and agreeable for you to so order. I so request not only at my own instance but for the accommodation of others." ALS, McClernand Papers, IHi. On Feb. 26, Lt. Col. John A. Rawlins endorsed this letter. "Respectfully returned to Maj. Gen McClernand. On the arrival of Col. Anneke's regiment in this Department, he will be assigned to your command, unless the exigencies of the service should require otherwise." ES, *ibid.* On March 28, McClernand, Milliken's Bend, wrote to USG. "You will, probably, reccollect that I stated to you, in conversation, sometime since that an order has been applied for by the Wisconsin Authorities to send Col Anneke's regiment of Wis. drafted militia to your Department, in order that he should have an opportunity of joining my command. An order, as you are doubtless aware, was accordingly made, and I learn that Col Anneke with his regiment is now at Columbus Ky. If you can put him under orders to join me, without interfering with more important purposes, it would, doubtless, be agreable to his friends and to him." Copies, *ibid.*; DNA, RG 393, 13th Army Corps, Letters Sent. On April 2, Rawlins endorsed this letter. "Respectfully referred to Maj. Gen Hurlbut who will report whether this Regt. has reached Columbus, Ky:" Copies, DLC-USG, V, 25; DNA, RG 393, Dept. of the Tenn., Endorsements. On April 7, Hurlbut wrote to Rawlins. "I have the honor to acknowledge receipt of communication of Major General John A. McClernand referred to me by yourself in relation to Col Anneke's ( ) Wisconsin Infantry Regiment at Columbus Ky, and further that having thought it necessary to occupy Fort Heinman, since its abandonment by order of Maj Gen Rosecrans, I deem it impracticable at present to send forward the Regiment, unless by order." Copy, *ibid.*, 16th Army Corps, Letters Sent.

To Charles A. Dana

Vicksburg Mississippi,
August 5th 1863.

MAJ. C. A. DANA,
DEAR SIR:

Your letter of the 22d of July is just received and it needs no assurance from me to inform you how glad I am to hear from you and to learn so much from the vicinity of Hd Qrs. Gen. Halleck and yourself were both very right in supposing that it would cause me more sadness than satisfaction to be ordered to the command of the Army of the Potomac. Here I know the officers and men and what each Gen. is capable of as a separate commander. There I would have all to learn. Here I know the geography of the country, and its resources. There it would be a new study. Besides more or less dissatisfaction would necessarily be produced by importing a General to command an Army already well supplied with those who have grown up, and been promoted, with it.

I am very anxious to take Mobile while I think it can be done with comparative ease. But this would have to be done from Pascagoula, or even a point further along on the coast, and through Banks' Dept. He has not the troops to do it. I am sending one Army Corps, Ord's, to Natchez so that if authorized they can be sent under Banks' direction on this enterprise. In the mean time there are two little bodies of rebel Cavalry in the Mississippi valley, one on the East bank under Logan, and one on the West Bank under Harrison which can be cleaned out from Natchez and leave the river free.[1]

Ord placed in the command of the 13th Army Corps has proven a very great relief to me. The change is better than 10 000 reinforcements.

I have been surprized at the health of this command after so long a campaign, and so much time in the trenches. When we first came into the city the sick report increased at so alarming a rate that I feared the whole command had to go through a spell of sickness after their relaxation. But the Army is now in very good trim for another campaign. Our Artillery however is in bad trim. Some of the pieces have been fired from over 3000 times and the brass rifled guns are entirely used up for present purposes.

With the present Army Corps Commanders nothing but entire harmony can ever exist throughout all parts of the Army of the Ten. The 13th Army Corps has been so long governed by Ambition, ignorance and insubordination however that Ord may make some enemies among his Generals, particularly among his Brigade Commanders, by drawing them up suddenly to a proper standard. I can relieve him some by changes.

I feel very greatful to you for your timely intercession in saving me from going to the Army of the Potomac. Whilst I would disobey no order I should beg very hard to be excused before accepting that command.

I should like very much to see Gen. Thomas out here. Since Hawkins absence there is no one with the negro troops to organize them effectively. Shepard is not fit and Col. Wood,[2] I believe next in command, is absent without leave and I understand took off with him a lot of cotton picked up on the Miss. shore and several thousand dollars worth of ~~prop~~ furnature taken from the houses of two of the Gov't. lesees. Wood is a preacher.

Two of the Commissioners appointed by Gen. Thomas, Field & Livermore are, in my opinion, great rascals. They are undoubtedly very unfit for their present places.

It is about time for the mail to close and I must do the same thing. I intended writing much more when I commenced but have been interrupted every thirty seconds and forget what I intended saying.

yours very truly
U. S. GRANT
Maj. Gen.

ALS, DLC-Charles A. Dana. See letter to Elihu B. Washburne, Aug. 30, 1863. On Aug. 18, 1863, Asst. Secretary of War Charles A. Dana, Washington, wrote to USG. "Yours of the 5th inst. has been read with great satisfaction not only by myself, but by the Secretary of War and the President. I need not assure you that you will continue to receive the entire confidence of the administration & that any suggestion of yours will be received with the utmost consideration. I have not seen your list of recommendations for promotion & cannot say how completely it has been complied with. As there are no vacancies in the list of major generals, it has not been practicable as yet to appoint any new officers of that grade, either from the candidates proposed by you, or by Gen. Meade, with the single exception of Gen. G. K. Warren, who was promoted not only on account of his own extraordinary merits, but because he was needed to take command of an army corps in the army of the Potomac. It is not impossible that a number of major generals who have been tried (I don't mean by court martial) and have proved wanting may be dismissed,—there are about a dozen such who will not again be called into active service,—and in that case I have no doubt the men you have recommended will receive their commissions. Of new brigadier generals I find in the register of the adjutant general the names of Prime, Woods, G. Smith, Maltby, Sanborn & Rawlins, all of whom I know belong to your command. (Prime has declined, for what reason I do not know: his health I understand to be much improving.) I judge that these are all that you have recommended for appointment to that grade, as I am sure your wish would be followed, wherever it is practicable to do so. There is no news here of any importance aside from that published in the papers. The grand combined attack on Charleston will be made between Thursday of this week & Thursday following. Gen. Gillmore and Gen. Foster are both confident of success. There is no probability of any change in the command of the army of the Potomac, nor of any immediately, in that of the army of the Cumberland. There is however, much dissatisfaction with the present state of things, but it takes a long time to make any movement at Hd Qrs. I am about leaving to go down to Winchester, and shall probably remain with that army for several weeks. The question of transferring the Marine Brigade to your command has lately been acted upon here, and was negatived by the general in chief. I have had no opportunity of speaking with him on the subject and cannot say what were his reasons. I find that the Secy of War is pretty strongly convinced that the M. B. is a good institution, and though he is in favor of putting it under your authority, he will not think that it ought to be abolished altogether. I have however told him that in my judgment that ought to be done. I hope you will do the utmost to second the efforts of Gen. Thomas to raise negro troops. It is of great importance that the army should be as much strengthened from this source as possible, with a view to the contingency of a partial failure to raise men enough by the conscription. So far, the number of conscripts who pay commutation, & of those who are exempted by physical disability is much larger than was expected, & the number of valid soldiers smaller. The obstacles thrown in the way by the Copperheads are also numerous, cunning, & effective to a considerable degree. Besides, there is a large party whose effort is to bring the seceded states back with the same leaders & the same slavery with which they went out, and as an offset to their plot it is desirable to enlist a powerful negro force, from among the former slaves especially of the states of Arkansas, Lousiana, & Mississippi. If I find anything at Winchester or Nashville which I think likely to interest you, I will communicate it. . . . P. S. I can tell you in confidence that the report of the McDowell Commission bears very hard on Curtiss." ALS, USG 3.

1. On Aug. 5, USG endorsed a report of July 31 of Brig. Gen. Thomas E. G. Ransom to Lt. Col. William T. Clark, adjt., 17th Army Corps, regarding a skirmish near Natchez with a force under C.S.A. Col. John L. Logan. "Respectfully forwa[rded] to Hd Qrs. of the Army. Cavalry have gone t[o] Natchez and have bee[n] ordered to clear the Co[un]try of Logan's Cavalry and then direct thei[r] attention to Harrison['s] on the Louisiana sid[e.]" AES, DNA, RG 94, War Records Office, Union Battle Reports. *O.R.*, I, xxiv, part 2, 686.

2. William F. Wood, formerly lt. col., 1st Ind. Cav., then col., 1st Ark. A. D. On Aug. 10, Lt. Col. James H. Wilson wrote to Maj. Theodore S. Bowers extracting and then endorsing a report of Capt. Asa C. Mathews, 99th Ill., act. asst. inspector-gen., detailing the charges against Wood. "Capt. Mathew's's report is

full and unequivocal in the case of Colonel Wood and leaves no reasonable room to doubt that the service would be benefitted by the prompt dismissal of the officer complained of.—" ALS, DNA, RG 393, Dept. of the Tenn., Letters Received.

To Maj. Gen. Stephen A. Hurlbut

Head Quarters, Department of the Tennessee,
Vicksburg, Miss. August 5th 1863.

MAJ.R GENL. S. A. HURLBUT,
COMDG. 16TH ARMY CORPS.
GENERAL,

I have ordered Brig. Genl. A. J. Smith to proceed without delay to Columbus Kentucky and releive Brig. Genl. Asboth from his command. The latter will report to you; he need not be assigned to duty till the result of the inspection which I have ordered is known. If Colonel Thurston has not already started to Columbus when this is received, be good enough to see that he proceeds at once, and is supplied with such special instructions as you may think advisable.[1]

Should the inspection result as I anticipate or as facts seem to indicate I shall order Genl. Asboth to report to the Secretary of War.

The steamer now plying between Helena & Memphis as a special packet must be discontinued—the mail facilities afforded by the steamers to this place being sufficient for all way points.

Very Respectfully,
U. S. GRANT
Maj. Genl. Com

P. S. Since writing the above your communication of July 31st has been rceivd,[2] Genl. Kimball will have to be retained in his present command, and Genl. Ross having tendered his resignation will be excused from taking command of troops in the field.[3]

Very Respectfully
U. S. GRANT.
Maj. Genl.

LS, DNA, RG 393, 16th Army Corps, Letters Received. *O.R.*, I, xxiv, part 3, 576-77. On July 18, 1863, Maj. Gen. Stephen A. Hurlbut, Memphis, wrote to Lt. Col. John A. Rawlins. "I enclose telegraphic report from Genl Dodge of Hatch's movement upon Rebel force at Jackson Tenn. It is very serious labor for my cavalry to cover this whole region, but I think they do it with singular success. If by any possibility I could induce or compel similar activity in Asboth's command it would relieve me very much, but he is constantly the victim of false & alarming reports. His last report is that he is informed by 'reliable citizens' that Pillow with 6,000 men is at or near Paris. This is out of whole cloth & is I think a story got up in Mayfield to influence the coming elections. The District of Columbus is a very important one both in a military & political point of view— and it is necessary that it should be commanded by a different officer. I require for that post a man of sense and judgment of courage and discretion, who will handle affairs with coolness and with knowledge of the peculiarities of the people and of the position. If you have such an officer I desire that Genl Asboth may be relieved. This District gives me more trouble than all the rest. I forwarded to you the Dispatch from the General in Chief, and await orders. A very considerable force is gathering along the line of Bear Creek and down to Okalona, which in my judgment indicates the abandonment of Miss. west of M. & Ohio Rail Road" ALS, DNA, RG 94, War Records Office, Military Div. of the Miss. *O.R.*, I, xxiv, part 3, 530. See telegram to Maj. Gen. Henry W. Halleck, July 21, 1863; letter to Maj. Gen. Stephen A. Hurlbut, July 24, 1863.

1. William H. Thurston, appointed capt., 52nd Ind., as of Feb. 1, 1862, and lt. col. and asst. inspector gen., 16th Army Corps, as of Feb. 28, 1863. On Aug. 14, Thurston wrote to Capt. Henry Binmore, Hurlbut's adjt. "Brig. Genl. Asboth has issued many extravagant orders and caused the Quarter Master to expend a large amount of money, at Columbus Ky—unnecessarily   He has been under the *impresssion* that Columbus was to be made a permanent, Military Post, or Garrison, and has ordered improvements to be made in accordance with his impressions. By the estimate furnished by the Quarter Master, (a copy of which find enclosed) he has expended Six Hundred Dollars ($600.) upon the Head Quarters occupied by him. He has shown a reckless expenditure of Government funds in the erection of buildings, grading the Streets and Side-walks of the town and in his general management. . . . His general, management is bad, not having proper control over the officers and men under him, is constantly fearful that by Some of his acts, he will injure the feelings of Officers under him, and therefore has lost that command, which he as Superior Officer should have, and exercise in his command. Captain McKay has also been very reckless in his Department, and as I have before recommended his accounts should be fully investigated by some one conversant with Quarter Masters' duties before he is permitted to serve with any other Division. He has been releived from duty at Columbus. . . . In the Provost Marshall's Office, the accounts have the appearance of correctness. Maj. Rowley, A. D. C. Maj Genl. Grant, is Provost Marshal of the District or Division. Capt. I. Williams Co __ Regt. Ill. Vol. Inft. is the Local. Capt Williams reputation is not good with Officers or citizens but in my investigation I could not detect him in any illegality and although a sharp Detective and in some respects a good man for the position I cannot but beleive that there is ground for some of the many reports against him. There are reported to be a large number of Prostitutes in Columbus, and has caused much disease of a

private nature among the troops Stationed there" LS, DNA, RG 393, Dept. of the Tenn., Letters Received. On Aug. 18, Hurlbut endorsed this letter. "Respy forwarded for information of Genl Comg Department $40,000 of Govt funds has been used in permanent improvements for which $5000 would have been ample" AES, *ibid*. USG also endorsed the letter. "File sending Extract of that rlating to Provost Marshal & Prostitutes to Comd.g Officer Columbus." AE, *ibid*. On Aug. 25 or 26, USG gave Hurlbut verbal orders to have Brig. Gen. Alexander Asboth report to Maj. Gen. William T. Sherman. See *O.R.*, I, xxx, part 3, 170. See also *ibid*., p. 198. On Aug. 29, Sherman wrote to USG. "Flag of Truce not yet in—. Gen'l Asboth reported and assigned to the 3rd Division late Tuttle— Nothing new—all quiet" Copy, DNA, RG 393, Dept. of the Tenn., Telegrams Sent. *O.R.*, I, xxx, part 3, 211. See *ibid*., p. 504.

On Sept. 18, Sherman telegraphed to Rawlins. "I fear I will be embarrassed by having more generals of divisions than I have commands for. I want my division commanders as near permanent as possible   Osterhaus has Steeles old Division   asboth now has Tuttles old Division & Tuttle is nowhere   Asboth ranks Tuttle but Tuttle ranks Osterhaus   I do think General Asboth should have some fixed command say the fortifications of Vicksburg as independent of any Davison or Brigade   I want Morgan L Smith to have his old Division second but Blair will soon be here to command it & W S Smith is daily expected & will want his old Division fourth. The Brigades are all so small now that they do not satisfy a Brigadier. Can you suggest any relief for the dilemma   Will be at Oak Ridge tomorrow." Telegram received, DNA, RG 94, War Records Office, Dept. of the Tenn.; copy, *ibid*., RG 393, Dept. of the Tenn., Telegrams Sent. *O.R.*, I, xxx, part 3, 719–20. On the same day, Rawlins wrote to Sherman. "Will assign Gen'l Tuttle to command of fortifycations here:" Copies, DLC-USG, V, 19, 103; DNA, RG 393, Dept. of the Tenn., Letters Sent. *O.R.*, I, xxx, part 3, 720. On Sept. 20, however, Rawlins wrote to Sherman. "Genl Tuttle will be assigned to the command of his old Division. Gen'l Asboth will be ordered to report to Maj Genl N P Banks for assignment to a command in the 13th Army Corps under Ord. The destination of the expedition from New Orleans is such that the Gen'l will be pleased to accompany it. Gen'l. Tuttle will be out tomorrow." Copies, DLC-USG, V, 19, 103; DNA, RG 393, Dept. of the Tenn., Letters Sent. *O.R.*, I, xxx, part 3, 747. See *ibid*., I, lii, part 1, 450.

2. On July 31, Hurlbut wrote to Rawlins. "I have the honor to report that upon his own request I have relieved Brig Gen N Kimball from command of the Division of 16th Army Corps at Helena Arkansas. It is my intention to order him to Columbus Ky. to relieve Brig Gen. A. Asboth and I ask instructions as to order for him. Brig Gen L. F. Ross will command Kimball's Division. I cannot possibly get along with Brig Gen A Asboth and suggest that if you have any place to which you can assign him you will send orders accordingly" Copy, DNA, RG 393, 16th Army Corps, Letters Sent.

3. On July 18, USG endorsed a letter of resignation of July 8 of Brig. Gen. Leonard F. Ross, who had previously submitted and withdrawn his resignation. "Respectfully forwarded and approved. Many reasons have conspired to make Gen. Ross' absence from his duties during a great part of the time he has been in service. For this reason I would urge the acceptance of his resignation." AES, *ibid*., RG 94, ACP, 154R CB 1863. See Ross to Brig. Gen. Lorenzo Thomas, April 19, and to Secretary of War Edwin M. Stanton, June 9, July 28, ALS, *ibid*. Ross's resignation took effect on July 22.

To [Col. William Myers]

Head Quarters, Dept. of the Tenn.
Vicksburgh, Miss. Aug. 5th, 1863

The within statement shews the necessity that has existed, and still exists, for transports at this place. Since the occupation of Vicksburgh by our forces the Levee has been used to the fullest extent of its capacity in discharging boats and none have been detained unnecessarily. Whilst Col. L. Parsons may be working zealously for the interests of the public service I think many of his efforts tend to no good results, and in some instances amount to impertinent interference   There has been so many boats sent up the river that there can be no difficulty in supplying this army if the Government is to have the preference over private individuals. The present system of convoying leads to much detention and in my opinion is entirely unnecessary. I wrote Admiral Porter on the subject more than one month ago, but received no reply; and as no change has been made I infer the communication may not have been received by him. The Adml. is now absent from here so that I will not be able to communicate with him on this subject for some days and do not know that a change will be made on my suggestion

U. S. GRANT
Maj. Gen.

Endorsement, copies, Parsons Papers, IHi; DNA, RG 92, Consolidated Correspondence, Vicksburg. William Myers, born in Pa. in 1830, USMA 1852, asst. q. m. at St. Louis from Oct., 1861, was promoted to col. as of June 14, 1862. USG's endorsement was written on a letter of Aug. 4, 1863, from Lt. Col. Judson D. Bingham, Vicksburg, to Myers, St. Louis. "I am directed by Major Gen. Grant to reply to a letter received today by him from Col. Parsons, in relation to detention of boats at this place and points below. On the 8th of July, preparations having been completed for discharging freight, the unloading of the transports was commenced. Since that date the following requisitions have been made for transports. To transport Gen. Herron's Division to Yazoo city and back to this place: Gen. Ransom's Brigade to Natchez: 5000 Beef Cattle from Natchez to New Orleans and this place; 3 Regiments to Memphis; Gen. Kimball's Division to Helena, Ark.; 22 Boats to Gen. Banks; Coal, Grain and Hay to New Orleans: Gen. Herron's Division to Port Hudson: Ninth Army Corps to Cairo: 5 per cent of the army of the Tennessee to Memphis and Cairo on furlough: removal of the

Brigade from Lake Providence, and troops from Goodrich's Landing to this place; about 4.000 rebel prisoners to Mobile, Ala.: two Boat loads of rebel prisoners to Monroe, La. removal of the troops and supply train of 13th army corps from Young's Point to this place: two Boat loads of rebel prisoners to Cairo and St. Louis. 13th Army Corps to Natchez: Supplies to the troops at Haine's Bluff and Natchez: 500 Mules and 1.600 Bales Cotton, (captured), from Yazoo City to this place: Seven hundred head of unserviceable Stock to St. Louis. Two Boats have been discharged for repairs, and as many Boats have been sent up the river as have brought supplies to this place during that time: the distance for transporting supplies has been reduced by removing from Chickasaw Bayou to this place. The Steamer Planet arrived here yesterday, partially loaded with private freight for New Orleans, and Sutlers' goods are arriving by Boats at the present time, when our supply of forage is exhausted, notwithstanding requisitions for the same were sent forward three weeks ago. The number of transports here not being sufficient for all demands, we have been compelled to apply for and use the Boats of the Marine Brigade, with Barges." LS, *ibid*.

On July 18, Col. Lewis B. Parsons, asst. q. m., St. Louis, wrote to USG. "Is it not possible to send up some of the Steam boats—As yet scarse one has reported since the fall of Vicksburgh and over 60 are below Cairo—The river is so low boats cant take large loads and more are required—We are called upon to send you large stores and supplies which it is *impossible* to do because the boats are not in the harbour   I most sincerely congratulate you and your gallant army on your great and eventful successes—God save the Country—now the d——l catch the Copper heads.—I hope your successes have improved Col Rawlins piety!!—" ALS, *ibid.*, RG 393, Dept. of the Tenn., Letters Received. On July 25, Parsons wrote to USG. "I enclose copy of a letter to the Quartermaster General. You cannot conceive the trouble we now have to get forward supplies. The river is so low that boats can't take out over one third to one-half-a load, and it is still falling. This, with the continued detention of boats in large numbers below, renders it impossible now for me to send Stores as fast as hitherto, and as they are required. Add to this the detention of Boats, days and days for Convoys, beside the very great expense of say $200. to $300. per day for such Boats, and I fear you will soon have to 'make war support war.' I can't see from this point any necessity for any convoy. Our Boatman and Merchants are a unit against it, so far as I can learn; at least they think it should be optional with Boats to wait or go on. It seems to me that if Gun Boats were 75 or 100 miles apart it would do better, service at less Cost. I assure you that in my opinion, this order if not construed merely as optional, will cause great embarrassment and expense. Already here our Contractors notified me that they shall demand pay for each day their boats are detained for Convoys." LS, *ibid*. Parsons enclosed his letter of the same day to Brig. Gen. Montgomery C. Meigs objecting to a "notice of Admiral Porter, relative to convoys" on the Mississippi River. LS, *ibid*. On Aug. 22, Parsons wrote to USG enclosing copies of communications from Meigs indicating that Secretary of the Navy Gideon Welles had essentially adopted Parsons's suggestion. ALS (press), Parsons Papers, IHi.

In an undated letter, possibly never sent, Parsons wrote to USG. "I have just read with the greatest surprise and regret a letter of Col. Bingham to Col Myers of the 4th inst in reply to a letter of mine to you together with your endorsement. It is impossible for me to comprehend the cause of the following: 'while Col. Parsons may be working zealously for the interests of the public service I think many of his efforts tend to no good results and in some instances amount to impertinent interference.' I can but feel certain that you never penned these lines except under an entire misapprehension of my conduct as well as my motives, caused as I must believe by misrepresentations wilfully or ignorantly made. I think I know your sense of justice too well to believe you would under any other circumstances have so treated one who since he has known you personally has had no *greater object*, no stronger desire than to promote your wishes and success and thereby promote the welfare of the country,   Not a single effort has been spared by day or by night to comply with every requisition you have made and I apprehend you cannot be well advised of the difficulties with which I have many times been surrounded in doing so. I had supposed you both knew and appreciated my efforts to serve you and can but painfully feel a result so different from my anticipations. Concious, however, no less of the rectitude of my motives than of the general propriety of my conduct, and that with more accurate information you will do me full justice," Copy, *ibid*. On Aug. 16, Brig. Gen. Robert Allen, q. m., St. Louis, wrote to USG. "Colonel Parsons feels very much agrieved at an endorsement made by you on a Letter of Lt Col Bingham addressed to Col Myers. He appears unconscious of having in any thing he has written, transgressed the bounds of military propriety, & is deeply wounded by the term 'impertinent' which you apply to him, being keenly alive to rebuke, as he has always been one of your warmest friends. If he has sinned against martial etiquette or been intrusive in suggestions, most assuredly he did not mean to encroach upon any military prerogative, but was actuated solely by what he considered the best interest of the service. In his zeal to conduct the affairs of the transportation branch of the service with *economy*, he has drawn down upon him the whole power of the Steamboat interest, & by those representing this interest he has been vilified & abused without stint   In those his honest efforts to discharge his duty as he understood it, reckless of his personal popularity, is it not hard that he should be rewarded by a sneer from his commanding general? I ask my dear General your reconsideration of this subject satisfied that you have pronounced a hasty judgement, & knowing that you will not deliberately do injustice to a highly meritorious officer & personal friend—" Copy, *ibid*. On Sept. 19, USG wrote to Allen. "Your letter of Aug. 16th reached me while in New Orleans, and unable to write, and I do so now, only through the medium of another. In regard to the endorsement referred, I have to say, Col. Parsons had in some instances taken a course that interfered with the Department and perhaps the remark I made was rather hasty   I have always esteemed Col. Parsons, did while he was with me and have always looked upon him as an officer who had his whole heart in the cause, and cannot say I have had reason to change my opinion of him,   if I have done him injustice and I think I did in using the term impertinent, I shall be happy to correct it, and shall take pains to do so" Copies, DLC-USG, V, 94; Parsons Papers, IHi. See letter to Brig. Gen. Lewis B. Parsons, May 20, 1865. Probably in 1885, Parsons endorsed a summary of his letter of Aug. 31, 1863, to USG. "See Gen Grants letter to me on leaving service   He was greatly imposed upon by some scoundrel—Lyman, A Q, . . ." AE, Register of Letters Sent, Parsons Papers, IHi. See letter to Brig. Gen. Robert Allen, Aug. 15, 1863; letter to Brig. Gen. Montgomery C. Meigs, Aug. 18, 1863.

On March 19, 1864, Allen wrote to USG. "Col L. B. Parsons has tendered his resignation as Asst Qr M and I have forwarded it to Washington recomending that it be accepted. As Col Parsons is in Earnest in his desire to be relieved from quarter Master duty I hope you will throw the weight of your high influence in favor of the acceptan of his Q. M. ~~Resignation~~ Commission Col Parsons does not propose to abandon the Service by dropping his lesser Commission but retains his A. D. C rank and is desirous of entering upon a kind of Service more congenial with his feelings—and more promising of promotion. His predilections incline him to line Service and I have no doubt he would distinguish himself at the head of a brigade and he would be pleased to Serve near your person.—Col Parsons services in the Q. M Dep are known to you ~~yourself~~ and I hope that whatever of Merit there has been in them will have due consideration in appointing him to a new sphere of action." Copy, Parsons Papers, IHi.

To Maj. Gen. William T. Sherman

Vicksburg, Miss. Aug. 6. 1863

GENL. SHERMAN:

I have instructed Genl Hurlbut to send a force from Memphis, to meet one from here to collect rolling stock on Central Memphis Roads, and repair roads and take it to Memphis if possible. Start your Cavalry on Monday next.[1] Let them collect the stock on Central Road, and get it on to the Memphis road. Then push North until they meet the party from Memphis. If the whole force is necessary for security, the Cavalry from here can remain with that from Memphis until they get through, then return by the River. Impress upon the men the importance of going through the State in an orderly manner, abstaining from taking anything not absolutely necessary for their subsistence whilst travelling. They should try to create as favorable an impression as possible upon the people and advise them if it will do any good, to make efforts to have law and order established within the Union.

It should be our policy now to make as favorable an impression upon the people of this State as possible.

U. S. GRANT
Major General

Telegram, copies, DLC-USG, V, 19, 101, 103; DNA, RG 393, Dept. of the Tenn., Letters Sent. O.R., I, xxiv, part 3, 578. See telegram to Maj. Gen. William T. Sherman, Aug. 4, 1863. On Aug. 4, 1863, Maj. Gen. William

T. Sherman, "Camp on Black River," wrote to Lt. Col. John A. Rawlins deploring recent acts of vandalism by U.S. soldiers. ALS, DNA, RG 94, War Records Office, Dept. of the Tenn. *O.R.*, I, xxiv, part 3, 574–75. See General Orders No. 50, Aug. 1, 1863; *Memoirs*, I, 577. On Aug. 6, Sherman telegraphed to USG. "Your instructions about the Cavalry Expeditio[n] is received. It will give me excessive pleasure to instruct the Cavalry as you direct, for the Policy you point out meets every wish of my heart. I have seen Gentlemen from Clinton. Some of Wirt Adams' Cavalry are about Jackson and the rascals ate some of our bread under protest of the People! It is said Johnston is at Morton at a Station East of Brandon, his Cavalry near Brandon.—Why he stays there I cant imagine. his advance had got out to Chunky 68 from Jackson but it seems have moved back this way. My informa[nt] says, he thinks Johnston hates to give up Mississippi and remains as near Jackson as he has Rail-road, but his men are dispirited and are deserting." Copy, DNA, RG 393, Dept. of the Tenn., Telegrams Sent. *O.R.*, I, xxiv, part 3, 578. On Aug. 13, Sherman telegraphed to USG. "The telegraph wire was put up to Haines Bluff & out on the ridge road as far as Neelys ~~when Genl Parke~~ at the time Gen Parke was there ~~at~~ I advise it be extended one mile to oak Ridge Post office where I have two regts commanded by Col Corse 6th Iowa   it happens that telegraphic communication with that point will be of advantage & therefore I think it advisable   I had several persons in yesterday from as far as brandon   Johnston Has gone east doubtless to explain matters   he still commands and enjoys the confidence of the army & people   Hardee commands the camp at Morton   A court of enquirty is to examine Pembertons case at Montgomery   Wirt Adams & Starks Cavalry are west of Pearl & have behaved so that I have forbidden any more rations being issued to people east of black. I have also put a picket of one 1 Regt of Infy with at amsterdam & sent the second 2d Wis cavalry belonging to McPherson with his approval to red bone church to watch the crossings at Baldwins Halls & Hankinsons   it is represented that Chalmers is coming south towards Brandon with his cavalry moving cotton & gathering conscripts & negroes as he comes along   I suppose the enemy has established telegraphic Communication between Canton & Panola but this will be broken by Col Winslows Cav which I suppose to be now well towards Grenada   his orders are to communicate as often as possible with me ~~and~~ or you direct   if he writes to you please let me have the ~~sta~~ substance that I may keep pace with his movements   I take it for granted he will reach Memphis before his return   A man residing near Bolton who is I think in our interest says he knows the enemies cav 8000 Strong are to cross pearl river today in spite of the earnest protestations of all the people   of course they have not eight thousand but ~~th~~ doubtless they wish to counteract the back sliding of the people of Miss   in stead of checking such a tendency they will expedite it by their Cavalry" Telegram received, DNA, RG 94, War Records Office, Dept. of the Tenn. Dated Aug. 12 in *O.R.*, I, xxx, part 3, 8. Also on Aug. 13, USG telegraphed to Sherman. "The extension of the telegraph to Oak Ridge will be made immediately." Copies, DLC-USG, V, 19, 101, 103; DNA, RG 393, Dept. of the Tenn., Letters Sent. Regarding the cav. expedition ordered by USG, see *O.R.*, I, xxiv, part 3, 579, 582–83; *ibid.*, I, xxx, part 1, 5–24. See also letter to Maj. Gen. Henry W. Halleck, Aug. 11, 1863.

On Aug. 7, Sherman telegraphed and wrote to USG. "A flag of truce in from Genl Jackson at Brandon   nothing important   inquires about young Maury   I send the bearer back & the Communication to you by the cars this P M" Telegram received, DNA, RG 94, War Records Office, Dept. of the Tenn. "I happened at the Bridge this a m when a flag was reported. I admitted the Bearer Capt Moorman. he had a letter to me from Gen W H Jackson dated Aug 5, 1863 at Brandon, with several newspapers of Aug 3, which I send you herewith. I have opend this Communication, and will send Capt Moorman back with an answer that the letter is sent to you, and that I know you will make the inquiry after young Maury and will reply. When you reply I will send out the Answer to Brandon, by a small escort and a staff officer." ALS, *ibid.*, RG 393, Dept. of the Tenn., Letters Received. On the same day, Sherman telegraphed to USG. "I am satisfied from a chance word from an officer that Price has resigned & that it is so understood among the Confederates" Telegram received, *ibid.*, RG 94, War Records Office, Dept. of the Tenn. On Aug. 7, USG endorsed a letter of C.S.A. Maj. Gen. Dabney H. Maury inquiring about his aide, John H. Maury. "Refered to Col. Linsey 22nd Ky Vols, who will please report what he knows of the capture of Lt. Maury, of the Confederate Army, and return this letter, with his report," Copy, DLC-USG, V, 99. On Aug. 8, this letter was endorsed at hd. qrs., 4th Brigade, 1st Div., 13th Army Corps. "Col. D W Linsey, 22nd Ky Infty Reports that his advance guard on march from Port Gibson to Willow Springs, captured a Confederate, on the 4th of May, 1863 who called himself Maury, & stated that he acted as aid to Genl Bowen, in the fight near Port Gibson   Said Maury was turned over to Maj L. Hommedieu, Pro Mar 13th Army Corps." Copy, *ibid.* See *O.R.*, I, xxiii, part 2, 819. On Aug. 14, Sherman telegraphed to USG. "I will send out the flag of Truce to morrow morning.—Telegraph to Genl. Dennis, to send the letter up to me, as I want to get the flag of truce out by a route, where it will not be ~~not be~~ met for as great a distance as possible.—" Copy, DNA, RG 393, Dept. of the Tenn., Telegrams Sent.

1. Aug. 10.

To Maj. Gen. Nathaniel P. Banks

Headquarters Dept. of the Tenn.—
Vicksburg Miss. Aug 7th 1863

MAJ. GENL. N. P. BANKS
COMD.G DEPT. OF THE GULF
GEN,

I have just reccd a dispatch from the Genl. in Cheif directing me to send you an Army Corps of from 10 to 12 thousand Men.[1] I have made the order designating the 13th Army Corps Maj Gen. E. O. C. Ord Commanding. I take from it one Division recently attached, to form the garrison at natches and to hold the River from Rodny to the La. state line, and attach the Div. of Gen. Herron, previously sent to your Darpt.[2] This gives, I think, a force of full 12 000 well effective men present for duty exclusive of furloughed men who will return soon. Gen. Ord will be directed to report by telegraph from Port Hudson.

Moving so many men north I am almost entirely without transportation to move these troops with. If you can send any boats from below it will expedite the movement materialy.

Gen. Hallecks dispatch does not seem to be in responce to any dispatch received from you or myself, I cannot tell therefore whether this looks to any immediate movement.

I am Sir very Respectfuly
your obt. svt.
U. S. GRANT,
Maj Gen. Com

Copies, DNA, RG 393, Dept. of the Gulf, Letters Received; *ibid.*, Dept. of the Tenn., Letters Sent; DLC-USG, V, 19, 101, 103. *O.R.*, I, xxiv, part 3, 580. On Aug. 10, 1863, Maj. Gen. Nathaniel P. Banks, New Orleans, wrote to USG. "I have the honor to acknowledge the receipt of your letter dated the 7th of August, by the hand of Captain Hudson. General Ord has reported to me, and I have directed his Corps to be camped near the City of New Orleans. I think he will find everything to his satisfaction, and I do not anticipate any important movements which will put his men to great labor. His transportation will be used to bring his command here, and will be returned immediately for the troops he has left behind. I have read General Halleck's despatch, with attention. Some information has been received at Washington in regard to the sailing of the iron-clads from Liverpool. The conversation of Southern men, overheard in the shipyards, indicated that their destination will be the Southwest, and a possible attack on New Orleans. I do not apprehend any danger from this source, but the Government deems it worthy attention, and the positions indicated will be strengthened. It is quite possible the movement of troops, not having reference to your despatch, nor to my own, might have been caused by the information received. I have the honor to enclose to you some memoranda concerning Mobile. I still think it of the utmost moment that that port should be in our hands. Except for Johnston's army, we should have no difficulty. He seems to occupy a position intended to cover Mobile, and if he is in force 30,000, or 40,000. strong, as I suppose, he could embarass operations against that point very seriously. I am unable however, to see how he can hold his position in the Southwest, with Rosecrans' army pressing down upon ~~his~~ the rebel centre. A line extending from Mobile to Richmond, in the present shattered condition of the Rebel armies, the right, centre, and left, having all been disastrously defeated, it seems to me impossible that they can maintain their positions if Rosecrans with a heavy force pushes down upon their centre, or if Charleston shall fall into our hands through the operations of the fleet and army combined. A successful movement in either direction, from Charleston, or by Rosecrans, will cut their centre, and place Bragg and Johnston with their forces, between the troops under Rosecrans, ~~and myself~~ at your own and mine New Orleans. I do not believe that that condition of things, can be maintained. All the information we receive here, points to a change in their operations. For instance, we hear that the guns are removed from the Forts at Mobile to the town. This indicates that their ordnance is deficient, or that they may be intending to remove them to a distance. The Catholic Priests there, write to their friends here, that they are in daily anticipation of an order for the evacuation of the city. This is said with reference to the supply of provisions, and for the purpose of assuring the friends here that their supplies from the Government of the United States, may be expected very soon. The Mobile papers in speaking of Johnston's visit, though apparently denying the possibility of evacuation, actually evade the question. Johnston is made to say, that if he had intended to evacuate, he should not have shown himself there; and after an examination of the works, he is said to have pronounced the opinion, that the post was one of the strongest on the Rebel seaboard. This is undoubtedly true, but it does not effect the question of maintaining a line extending from Mobile to Richmond. It is important that as much information as possible should be had of Johnston's movements. I shall be greatly indebted to you for any information you may gain upon this subject, and will also transmit to you without delay, memoranda, or information that may fall into our hands. Until we have further orders from the Government, active operations will of course be suspended. I am greatly indebted to you for the promptness with which you have sent the reinforcements to this Department." LS, DNA, RG 94, War Records Office, Dept. of the Mo. *O.R.*, I, xxvi, part 1, 673–74. On the possible attack on New Orleans should the C.S.A. obtain the Laird rams from Liverpool, see *ibid.*, pp. 658–59. On Aug. 11, Banks wrote to USG. "The Army Corps of Major General Ord is arriving in this Department, greatly to my satisfaction. The presence of this additional force cannot fail to produce beneficial results as my command is almost destitute of Cavalry and that in a region where the cavalry arm is most necessary—I hope that you will, if practicable, do me the favor to attach to General Ord, some additional troops of that character." Copies (2), DLC-Nathaniel P. Banks.

1. On July 30, 4:30 P.M., Maj. Gen. Henry W. Halleck telegraphed to USG. "You will send to Major Genl Banks a corps of ten or twelve thousand men, to report at such point as he may designate, probably at New Orleans." ALS (telegram sent, dated July 30), DNA, RG 107, Telegrams Collected (Bound); telegram received (dated July 31), *ibid.*, RG 94, War Records Office, Military Div. of the Miss.; copies, *ibid.*, RG 108, Telegrams Sent; *ibid.*, RG 393, Dept. of the Tenn., Hd. Qrs. Correspondence; DLC-USG, V, 6, 8, 24, 94. Dated July 30 in *O.R.*, I, xxiv, part 3, 562; *ibid.*, I, xxvi, part 1, 664. On Aug. 6, 12:30 P.M., Halleck telegraphed to USG. "Please send a special messenger to Major Genl Banks with the following telegram, and also give him all necessary assistance for its execution. 'Major Genl BANKS New Orleans, There are important reasons why our flag should be restored in some point of Texas with the least possible delay. Do this by land, at Galveston, at Indianola, or at any other point you may deem preferable. If by sea Admiral Farragut will cooperate. There are reasons why the movement should be as prompt as possible.' " ALS (telegram sent), DNA, RG 107, Telegrams Collected (Bound); telegram received, DLC-

Nathaniel P. Banks; LS, *ibid*. *O.R.*, I, xxiv, part 3, 578; (incomplete) *ibid*., I, xxvi, part 1, 672. See letter to Maj. Gen. Nathaniel P. Banks, Aug. 13, 1863. On the decision to send an expedition to Tex., see *O.R.*, I, xxvi, part 1, 652–53, 659, 673, 675; Lincoln, *Works*, VI, 364; letter to Abraham Lincoln, Aug. 23, 1863. USG, forgetting Lincoln's explanation of this matter to him and not informed of the other dispatches, later supposed that Halleck unilaterally overruled USG's proposal to attack Mobile. *Memoirs*, I, 578–80.

    2. See Special Orders No. 214, Aug. 7, copies, DLC-USG, V, 27, 28; DNA, RG 393, Dept. of the Tenn., Special Orders. *O.R.*, I, xxiv, part 3, 581–82. By these orders, the 4th Div., 13th Army Corps, Brig. Gen. Marcellus M. Crocker commanding, was transferred to the 17th Army Corps and sent to Natchez.

To Maj. Gen. Henry W. Halleck

Vicksburg Miss.
6. P. M. Aug. 8. 1863,

MAJOR GEN H W HALLECK
GENL-IN-CHF

    Your dispatches of the first & third rec'd.[1] Ord's Corps goes immediately to Genl Banks' Department. Will send a list of candidates for cadetship on Monday, after giving them an examination.[2]

U. S. GRANT
Maj. Genl.

Telegram received, DNA, RG 107, Telegrams Collected (Bound); copies, *ibid*., Telegrams Received in Cipher; *ibid*., RG 393, Dept. of the Tenn., Hd. Qrs. Correspondence; DLC-USG, V, 6, 8, 24, 94. *O.R.*, I, xxiv, part 3, 582. This telegram was received in Washington on Aug. 26 or 27, 1863, 4:00 P.M.

    1. For the telegram of July 30 or 31, which USG believed to be dated Aug. 1, see preceding letter, note 1; for the telegram of Aug. 3, see letter to Maj. Gen. Henry W. Halleck, July 24, 1863, note 3.

    2. See letter to Brig. Gen. Lorenzo Thomas, Aug. 11, 1863.

To Maj. Gen. Stephen A. Hurlbut

Head Quarters, Dept. of the Ten.
Vicksburg Miss. Aug. 8th 1863

Maj. Gen. S. A. Hurlbut
Comd.g 16th Army Corps,
Gen.

I have been directed to nominate from soldiers of this Department, between the ages of Sixteen & Twenty one, a number for cadetships at West Point, to fill vacancies from Mississippi & Arkansas.[1] The number of vacancies I suppose to be equal to the number of Congressional Districts in the two states. Please make the nominations from your Corps, one fourth of the whole number, and send direct to the secretary of War without sending through these Hd Qrs. Studies commence the 1st of Sept. and as these appointments have to be made at Washington and the Cadets appear for examination before that time there is no time to loose.

Very respectfully
your obt. svt.
U. S. Grant
Maj. Gen. Com

ALS, DNA, RG 393, 16th Army Corps, Letters Received. On Aug. 7, 1863, USG telegraphed to Maj. Gen. William T. Sherman. "If you have any deserving young men in your command between the ages of 16 & 21 fit for a Cadetship, send in the names of five or six of them to be forwarded, to receive appointments from the state of Miss." Copies, *ibid.*, Dept. of the Tenn., Letters Sent; DLC-USG, V, 19, 101, 103. *O.R.*, I, xxiv, part 3, 580. On Aug. 8, USG wrote a similar letter to Maj. Gen. James B. McPherson. Anderson Galleries Sale No. 2146, March 16, 1927, p. 8. On Aug. 7, Sherman telegraphed to USG. "I will make it my personal business to select 5 or 6 boys out of my command for West Point   it is an admirable Idea   I have just learned from a most intelligent citizen just in from Canton that it is reported & universally believed that Yancey is dead   our forces were still hammering away at Charleston"   Telegram received, DNA, RG 94, War Records Office, Dept. of the Tenn.; copy, *ibid.*, RG 393, Dept. of the Tenn., Telegrams Sent. On Saturday, Aug. 8, Sherman telegraphed to USG. "Am busy examining applicants for West Point   Amased at the no & high qualification of the applicants   I could select fifty fine subjects but will narrow down the number to six   give me till monday to get the list & I will certify to the qualifications of all   Nothing new out here   all quiet & the Cavalry is inspected ready for the start on Monday" Telegram received, *ibid.*, RG 94, War Records Office, Dept. of the Tenn.; copy (misdated Aug. 10), *ibid.*, RG 393, Dept. of the Tenn., Telegrams Sent. See letter to Brig. Gen. Lorenzo Thomas, Aug. 11, 1863.

1. On July 27, 3:45 P.M., Maj. Gen. Henry W. Halleck telegraphed to USG and to Maj. Gen. Stephen A. Hurlbut. "Send the names of any young men serving in your command, between the ages of sixteen and twenty one, suitable for appointment as cadets to West-Point, for the vacant districts of Mississippi and Arkansas." ALS (telegram sent), DNA, RG 107, Telegrams Collected (Bound); copy, *ibid.*, RG 108, Telegrams Sent. See preceding telegram.

To Brig. Gen. Montgomery C. Meigs

Head Quarters, Dept. of the Ten.
Vicksburg Miss. Aug. 10th 1863.

BRIG. GEN. M. C. MEIGS,
QUARTERMASTER GEN. U. S. ARMY,
GEN.

This will probably be forwarded to you with the papers intended to secure payment for the Steamer "Tigress," lost in running the Vicksburg Batteries.[1] I wish to urge prompt payment because I know the boat & owner well and the merits of the owner to receive this concideration.

Mr. Graham has been Asst. Master of transportation most of the time since September 1861, and at the time I ordered a certain number of boats to be selected and barricaded to run the Vicksburg batteries he was acting in that capacity, and was ordered to select the boats. He took his own as one to prevent dissatisfaction among other owners, all, or most of whom, would have prefered being excused from this duty.—I ordered a Board to appraise these boats, before starting to run the batteries, so that something might be had, official, upon which to base a settlement. In this appraisment stores on board, and which were necessary for the boat after passing the batteries, were not included.—I now understand, for the first time, that the fix value fixed on the Tigress was $22500. I do not know that Mr. Graham complains of this but I am satisfied that a higher price could have been obtained for the boat from parties who wished to purchase. I am further satisfied that Mr. Graham is now paying interest on a part of the money borrowed to purchase this boat. He is now out of the use of the boat and it would seem that as prompt payment should be made as possible.

I know that Mr. G. W. Graham has always been one of our most patriotic Steamboat owners, Always ready to make any sacrifice either of his own time or money for the Government. For the loss sustained by him, in the Steamer "Tigress" $26000 would not leave him as well off, pecuniarily, as if this boat had been one of the fortunate ones that passed through the ordeal of the Vicksburg Batteries without total destruction.

I am Gen. very respectfully
your obt. svt.
U. S. GRANT
Maj. Gen Com

ALS, ICarbS. See letters to Maj. Gen. John C. Frémont, Sept. 18, 1861, and to Brig. Gen. Robert Allen, July 25, 1863. On Sept. 22, 1863, Col. Robert E. Clary, Q. M. Dept., wrote to Third Auditor Robert J. Atkinson, Dept. of the Treasury, forwarding USG's letter and related papers in the case. LS, DNA, RG 92, 4th Div., Letters Sent (Press). On April 20, a military commission convened at Milliken's Bend, La., to assess the value of steamers ordered to run the blockade of Vicksburg. USG endorsed the findings of the commission on Feb. 8, 1864. "Respectfully forwarded to Head Quarters of the Army Washington D. C. Of the boats within named the 'Tigress' sunk below Vicksburg from damage received whilst passing the Batteries: and the 'Horizon' collided with the 'Moderator.' between Bruinsburg and Grand Gulf on the first day of May and sunk." Copies, DLC-USG, V, 39; DNA, RG 393, Military Div. of the Miss., Endorsements. Payment in full of claims for the *Tigress* and the *Horizon* is noted in *HED*, 40-2-337, pp. 114, 184.

On Aug. 4, 1863, George W. Graham, *J. H. Groesbeck*, at Vicksburg, wrote to USG. "I recd. an order this evening, from Col. Bingham, through Capt Lyman, by your order, to send this steamer to Hains Bluff at once—This has been the Quarter Masters Dept for Chief & Transportation for several months—It has been my home—and has become almost a part and parcel of the army—The Captain, Engineers, & Pilot—were sent down to *Port Hudson* with Genl Herrons Command—the Pilot was brought back by Genl Banks and taken back, with his ship as he had no Pilot—a number of our Engineers and Pilots are sick, and have been sent home, consequently it requires considerable trouble to keep the boats going—My object in writing this letter is simply to have her remain here, until I c[an] returns, and give me time to settle up what River business remains—I have sent one boat to Capt Van Ness to-day & will send another in the morning,

& one the next day" ALS, Edward C. Gumprecht, Cheshire, Conn. On the same day, USG endorsed this letter. "Refered to Col. Bingham. If the Groesbeck is unable to run from any fault of the officers of the boat it deduction should be made from the charter for the time so lost." AES, *ibid*.

On July 9, Capt. Alexander Doyle, *Moderator*, wrote to USG asking for seven men by name to help run his ship. ALS, DNA, RG 393, Dept. of the Tenn., Letters Received. On July 7, Capt. Moses N. Twiss, Co. K, 30th Ill., Vicksburg, of the *Moderator*, wrote to USG listing the men who had run the blockade on April 22 in place of the civilian crew which had deserted. LS, *ibid*. On the same day, Lt. Col. John A. Rawlins issued Special Orders No. 183 restoring control of the *Moderator* to one of her owners, Alexander Doyle, "unless there is some good reason to the contrary." Copies, DLC-USG, V, 27, 28; DNA, RG 393, Dept. of the Tenn., Special Orders.

1. See letter to Act. Rear Admiral David D. Porter, April 21, 1863.

To Capt. Charles Parsons

————

Headquarters Dept. of the Tenn.
Vicksburg Miss. Aug 10. 1862 [*1863*]

CAPT. C. PARSONS: A. Q. M.
SIR.

Your letter of the 1st inst enquiring if certain cars will be required for this Dept. is just received. The cars will not be required and I shall be glad to know that they are of service elsewhere. Should a a greater number be requires anywhere in the South than those mentioned by you, I think they might be supplied by this Dept. The length of road now is materially shorter than formerly, and the troops to be supplied fewer. In addition to this a large number of locomotives and cars have been cut off from the South by the destruction of the Railroad at Jackson Miss. These cars I am making an effort to get into Memphis, and if successful will have about one hundred locomotives and fifteen hundred cars of all classes.

Respectfully &c
U. S. GRANT
Maj. General

Copies, DLC-USG, V, 101, 103; (dated Aug. 11, 1863) *ibid.*, V, 19; DNA, RG 393, Dept. of the Tenn., Letters Sent. On Aug. 1, Capt. Charles Parsons, St. Louis, had written to Brig. Gen. Joseph D. Webster, superintendent, military railroads, Memphis, a letter forwarded to USG. "By Order of Genl Grant of Dec 28, 1862 I contracted for 100 R R freight Cars 5 foot guage for use of R R,s in his Dept— J. B. Andersen sup mil R R at Louisville wishes to get them if they are not needed in your Dept—Please advise me—a part of them are now at Cairo & Balance at Michigan City—" ALS, *ibid.*, Letters Received. See letter to Maj. Gen. Stephen A. Hurlbut, Aug. 4, 1863.

On June 10, Col. Lewis B. Parsons, St. Louis, had written to Lt. Col. John A. Rawlins. "Last Winter Genl. Grant ordered the purchase of a large number of Railroad cars; no destination having been given for them, they have been held at Cairo and north of there; There are now nearly 200 box and flat cars at Cairo St Louis and near Chicago belonging to the Government and ready for delivery; I write as above to advise you of our ability to Supply any necessities of this nature that may arise in the progress of an army south" LS, DNA, RG 393, Dept. of the Tenn., Letters Received. See telegram to Col. Lewis B. Parsons, Nov. 17, 1862.

On Aug. 24, Maj. Gen. William S. Rosecrans, Stevenson, Ala., telegraphed to USG. "Have you not some locomotives which you can spare for use in my Department, we are in great need of five or six immediately." Copy, DNA, RG 393, Dept. of the Cumberland, Telegrams Sent. Printed as sent at 11:20 in *O.R.*, I, xxx, part 3, 144. On the same day, 7:00 P.M., Capt. Parsons telegraphed to Capt. Walworth Jenkins, Louisville. "General Grant Writes me that General Rosecrans can have all the Cars necessary for his use I have more of them at Cairo Please show this to Capt John Steward—" ALS (telegram sent), DNA, RG 107, Telegrams Collected (Unbound). Rosecrans's request was also sent to USG's hd. qrs., Vicksburg. See *O.R.*, I, xxx, part 3, 145.

To Thomas Carney

Headquarters Dept. of the Tenn.
Vicksburg Aug. 10th 1863

HIS EXCELLENCY T. CARNEY GOVERNOR OF KANSAS.

SIR:—

Your letter of July 30th 1863., asking to have the 1st Kansas Vols. returned to Kansas to recruit their health, is just received. It is impossible for me to comply with your request. In fact I have not the authority to do so.

The Regiment as all others left on the West bank of the River here has suffered severely from sickness, and I have therefore removed them to the highlands on the East bank, where all our troops are doing much better, than I had any reason to hope they would do after the exposure of the past winter & spring.

> Very respectfully
> your Obt Servt
> U. S. GRANT
> Major Genl

Copies, DLC-USG, V, 19, 101, 103; DNA, RG 393, Dept. of the Tenn., Letters Sent. Thomas Carney, born in 1824 in Delaware County, Ohio, was a prosperous merchant of Leavenworth when elected gov. of Kan. in 1862.

On July 30, 1863, Gov. Samuel Kirkwood of Iowa wrote to USG urging at length the removal of "sick & wounded soldiers from this State, . . . to the U. S. Military Hospital at Keokuk" where they would be closer to family and friends and in a more healthful climate "than below." ALS, *ibid.*, Letters Received. USG endorsed this letter. "Refered to the Med. Director. I think it will be advisable to send as many sick & wounded who are unlikely to be fit for duty for two or three months to Hospitals in their own states. If practicable such orders will be given." AES, *ibid.* On Aug. 11, Surgeon John Moore also endorsed the letter. "With the approbation of Maj. Genl. Grant, instructions were given three weeks ago to Regimental Surgeons, to send to Hospital[s] 'North' all wounded or sick men, who were not likely to recover in six weeks. Under these instructions about 2000 men have gone mostly to St. Louis. Four Hospital transports are running regularly for this purpose. It was hoped that many of these men might be furloughed from St Louis Hosp. Instructions were sent to the Superintendt. of Hospital[s] at Memphis on the 22nd of July, to furlough all men not likely to be well in six weeks; and to discharge or send to the Invalid Corps, all, that were permanently unfitted for active field-service. This morning 400 sick were sent on the Hosp. Steamer 'McDougall', with instructions to go to Keokuk Iowa. But the sending of men to their respective states can be more readily accomplished from the Hospitals further north than from here. During low stages of water in the Ohio it is impracticable, to send the sick of Ohio or Indiana to their respective States; and to select those of Iowa or Illinois only, would for obvious reasons create discontent and be detrimental to the servic[e.]" ES, *ibid.*

On the same day, Maj. Theodore S. Bowers wrote to Maj. Gens. James B. McPherson, Edward O. C. Ord, and William T. Sherman, and to Moore. "All men now in Hospital who can be restored to active duty by a furlough of thirty days, may be furloughed in excess of the five per cent heretofore ordered. No furloughs will be granted however to men who are not likely to be returned to duty thereby. These latter will be transferred without delay to northern Hospitals, into the Invalid Corps, or discharged the service on certificates of disability." Copies, DLC-USG, V, 19, 101, 103; DNA, RG 393, Dept. of the Tenn., Letters Sent.

To Brig. Gen. Lorenzo Thomas

Head Quarters, Dept. of the Ten.
Vicksburg Miss. Aug. 11th 1863,

BRIG. GEN. L. THOMAS,
ADJ. GEN. OF THE ARMY,
GEN.

Herewith I forward applications of young men of this army for Cadet appointments. As soon as it was known to be possible for soldiers to get such an appointment it is astonishing the number and qualifications of the applicants. If there was not a Cadet at West Point the whole number of vacancies could be filled from young men, under twenty-one, of this army who would do credit to the institution and to their friends. I would respectfully suggest whether it would not be a great incentive to good conduct if young men were to know that all Cadetships during the rebellion were to be given to soldiers alone.[1]

All the applications are in the handwriting of the applicants themselves except in the case of Private Jas. Rawlins, Private of Co. "D" 45th Illinois Infantry. Private Rawlins is on detached service as Mail Messenger and is now some place between here and Cairo with a Mail. He is under twenty years of age, is a young man of good character and I would be pleased to have him one of those appointed to a Cadet ship. He has been in in the service since the organization of the 45th regiment in 1861 and I will venture has never been so much as repremanded since that time.

I am Gen. very respectfully
your obt. svt.
U. S. GRANT
Maj. Gen.

ALS, IHi. See letter to Maj. Gen. Stephen A. Hurlbut, Aug. 8, 1863. On Aug. 10, 1863, Maj. Theodore S. Bowers wrote to USG urging the appointment to USMA of Private James S. Rawlins, "a brother to your Assistant Adjutant General. Lieut. Col. Jno. A. Rawlins; was born and resides in Jo. Davies County, Illinois; is in his nineteenth (19) year; of vigorous constitution; good character

and habits; of more than ordinary intelligence, and of moderate education. . . ."
ALS, DNA, RG 94, Cadet Applications. On Aug. 11, USG endorsed a letter of
the same day of Private Francis E. Lovejoy, Co. A, 4th Ill. Cav., to Lt. Col.
John A. Rawlins requesting appointment to USMA. "This applicant for a Cadetship has been for a long time a Clerk at these Hd Qrs. I know him to be an
exemplary young man and am satisfied he would do well at West Point and make
a good officer after graduating." AES, *ibid.* On Aug. 15, Maj. Gen. James B.
McPherson, Vicksburg, wrote to USG recommending the appointment to USMA
of Private J. W. Moore, Co. E, 78th Ohio; 1st Sgt. Robert F. Lowe, Co. D, 13th
Iowa; Rawlins; Q. M. Sgt. Joseph C. Glenat, 45th Ill., of Galena, Ill.; and
Corporal John L. Maxwell, Co. H, 17th Ill. LS, *ibid.* On Aug. 18, USG tele-
graphed to Col. John C. Kelton. "I would recommend the following named
Enlisted men for appointment as Cadets in the Mil. Academy at West Point. . . .
Please telegraph appointments to Cairo." USG listed, in order, Rawlins; Lovejoy;
Corporal Clinton B. Sears, Co. G, 95th Ohio; Sgt. Luke Clarke, Co. A, 13th U.S.;
Musician Jacob E. Goodman, 116th Ill.; Corporal Charles L. Arnold, Battery A,
1st Ill. Art.; 1st Sgt. John D. Major, 53rd Ohio; Corporal Horace S. Callender,
Co. K, 26th Iowa; Private James L. Sherrer, 54th Ohio; Moore; Lowe; and
Maxwell. Telegram received, *ibid.*, Letters from USMA Superintendent; *ibid.*,
RG 107, Telegrams Collected (Bound).

On Aug. 23, 3:00 P.M., Maj. Gen. Henry W. Halleck telegraphed to USG.
"Please telegraph the names of some young men in your army suitable for cadets
to West-Point. All vacancies will be filled in a day or two." ALS (telegram sent),
ibid.; telegram received, *ibid.*, RG 393, Dept. of the Tenn., Telegrams Received.
On Aug. 24, Halleck received and endorsed USG's telegram to Kelton of Aug. 18.
"Respectfully recommended to the Secty of War." AES, *ibid.*, RG 94, Letters
from USMA Superintendent. On the same day, 11:00 A.M., Halleck telegraphed
to USG. "The horse equipments have been ordered to Vicksburg. As soon as cadet
appointments are made I will telegraph names, when you will order them to
immediately report to West-Point for examination. Should they fail to pass, they
will return to their regts. They will recieve public transportation to & fro. Their
warrants will be sent to West-Point to await their arrival. I hope to give you a
list of names by to-morrow morning." ALS (telegram sent), *ibid.*, RG 107,
Telegrams Collected (Bound); telegram received, *ibid.*, RG 393, Dept. of the
Tenn., Telegrams Received.

On Aug. 26, 1:50 P.M., Halleck telegraphed to USG. "The following named
persons in your command will be immediately sent to West-Point, N-Y, for
examination as cadets. They will report to the supt. of the Military Academy, &
if they do not pass examination, they will be ordered back to their regts. They
will be given public transportation. Clinton B. Sears, Robert Law, Horace S.
Callender, Jacob E. Goodman, Francis E. Lovejoy, & James A. Rawlings.
Acknowledge receipt." ALS (telegram sent), *ibid.*, RG 107, Telegrams Collected
(Bound); telegram received, *ibid.*, RG 393, Dept. of the Tenn., Miscellaneous
Letters Received. On Sept. 2, USG telegraphed to Halleck. "Your dispatch
naming six (6) enlisted men of my command to be sent forward to West Point
for examination as cadets, is just received and will be complied with" Telegram
received, *ibid.*, RG 107, Telegrams Collected (Bound); *ibid.*, (Press). On the
same day, Rawlins wrote to Maj. Gen. William T. Sherman ordering Sears,
Callender, and Goodman to report to USMA for examination as cadets. Copies,
ibid., RG 393, Dept. of the Tenn., Letters Sent; DLC-USG, V, 19, 103. Also on

Sept. 2, Sherman telegraphed to Rawlins. "Have recd the Message for the Cadets I will send three named at once   I am sorry the whole six were not appointed but I will Soften the blow to the disappointed"   Telegram received, DNA, RG 94, War Records Office, Dept. of the Tenn.; copy (misdated Aug. 30), *ibid.*, RG 393, Dept. of the Tenn., Telegrams Sent. On Sept. 29, USG telegraphed to Halleck. "Private Francis E Lovejoy having declined appoentment to Cadetship to Military Academy at West Point, I have ordered forward in his stead Lieut John, W. Griffiths, of 22d Regt Iowa Vols Infy. The sergeant who particularly distinguished himself in the assault of the 22d May & mentioned in my Official report. Notice of his appointment if made will reach him at West Point"   Telegram received, *ibid.*, RG 107, Telegrams Collected (Bound); *ibid.*, RG 94, Cadet Applications. Secretary of War Edwin M. Stanton endorsed this telegram. "Approved, & appointment ordered"   AES, *ibid.* See letter to Col. John C. Kelton, July 6, 1863, note 5.

1. On Sept. 1, Halleck wrote to USG. "Your letter of Aug 11th in regard to the appointment of cadets to the Military Academy, is just received. Ten cadets from your army have already been appointed, and it is possible that some more may be. I shall immediately submit the applications forwarded by you. I have been urging upon the Government for several months the policy of filling cadet vacancies in the rebel states by appointing from refugee Union families, and from young men serving in our armies in the rebel states. No decision was arrived at till the last moment, or I should have sooner called for recommendations from the Generals in the field. I shall urge upon the President and Seretary of War that *all* appointments to West Point for the coming year be made from the forces serving in the field, and from sons of Officers who have themselves rendered meritorious services in the Army, Navy or Volunteers." LS, DNA, RG 94, War Records Office, Dept. of the Mo.

To Col. William Hoffman

Head Quarters, Dept. of the Ten.
Vicksburg Miss. Aug. 11th 1863,

COL. WM HOFFMAN
COM.Y OF PRISONERS,
COL.

Among the prisoners of War sent from this Department there was a Maj. M. Simmes, registered or enrolled as a Staff officer of Brig. Gen. P. O. Hebert's,[1] C. S. A. Maj. Simmes was captured at or Near Natchez and sent North the latter part of July.

Gen. Hebert has conditionally released one of the Govt. Lesees of La. Plantations who had been captured by Confederate Cavalry and asks the release of Maj. Simmes in exchange. He states that Maj. Simmes is a citizen and not an officer of the Confederate Army.

The Conscript act is so rigidly enforced in the South that every one, to be secure, must enroll themselves in some capacity. Many whos interests and inclination incline them to remain at home enroll themselves as Volunteer Aid on the Staff of some Gen. and this I understand to be the case with Maj. Simmes.

I would respectfully ask that Maj. Simmes be released and returned to his home in exchange for Judge L. Dent who has been released by Gen. Hebert and allowed to return to his plantation.

> I am Col. Very respectfully
> your obt. svt.
> U. S. GRANT
> Maj. Gen.

ALS, DNA, RG 249, Letters Received. *O.R.*, II, vi, 194. See letters to Julia Dent Grant, June 15, July 1, 1863. On July 2, 1863, Brig. Gen. Elias S. Dennis signaled to USG. "Judge Dent is safe at Providence." Copy (intercepted), DNA, RG 109, Pemberton Papers. See *Calendar*, June 24, 1863. On July 19, C.S.A. Brig. Gen. James C. Tappan, Delhi, La., wrote to USG. "Your verbal proposition made through Capt Freeman U S A., as to the exchange of Judge Dent and captured citizens, has been submitted to the Lieut Genl. Comdg this Department; a response will be made immediately upon hearing from him. As a connection of Judge Dent's, it may be gratifying to you to learn that he was placed upon parol within our lines and treated with kindness and courtesy." ALS, DNA, RG 393, Dept. of the Tenn., Letters Received. On July 27, C.S.A. Lt. Gen. Edmund Kirby Smith, Shreveport, La., wrote to USG. "I am informed that Mr Simms, a Volunteer aid de camp of Brig Genl P. O. Hebert, was captured by a part of your forces at Natchez Miss, and is now held a prisoner of war. This gentleman is a citizen of the Confederate States without commission or rank in the army, and ought therefore to be dealt with by your Government as any other citizen of the Confederacy not in the military service. I have released Mr Lewis Dent a citizen of the United States, who was captured by a part of my troops near the Mississippi. He has been permitted to return within your lines, notwithstanding he was in the military employment of your Government in managing the plantations of Confederate citizens on the Mississippi. Other citizens of the United states who have been captured while employed by your Government as Mr Dent was, have been sent to the Rio Grande, there to be released for obvious military reasons. They number 52. Some were captured on the Mississippi and others on the Lafourche. I have about forty officers of the United States Army and Navy whom I hold prisoners of war. I propose to exchange them with you according to the cartel agreed upon by our respective Governments." LS, *ibid.*, RG 94, War Records Office, Dept. of the Tenn. On Aug. 1, Col. Isaac F. Shepard, Goodrich's Landing, La., wrote to USG. "A flag of truce, borne by Lt. Col. F. C. Zacharie, Lt. J. W. Sparks, and Lt. Conrad, has arrived here, being improperly passed through the pickets. Judge Dent accompanies them. They bear two despatches from Gen. Hebar to yourself. They are instructed to deliver them to yourself *in person*, if possible,—and if not allowed this deliver them *only* to Gen. Reid, or the officer in Command at Lake Providence. I do not feel at liberty to allow them to proceed to either place,—to you, because it is evidently improper to suffer them to pass inside our lines without your order,—and to allow them to go to Lake Providence now, as I know orders have been given to evacuate that post, I have thought to be quite unwise, as they may find no one there. Judge Dent will explain why they came here instead of going direct to Lake Providence. I have, therefore decided to retain them at my head quarters, (outside and out of sight of our forces and works here,) while I forward to you the facts for your instructions." ALS, *ibid.*, RG 393, Dept. of the Tenn., Letters Received. On Aug. 2, Maj. Theodore S. Bowers wrote to Shepard, Milliken's Bend, La. "I am directed by the Major General Commanding, to acknowledge the receipt of your communication of date the 1st inst. and to respectfully say in reply, that you did right in detaining the officers and men bearing the flag of Truce, from the Confederate States Authorities. You will not permit them to visit this place or Lake Providence. Should they desire to deliver their despatches, you may receipt for them, and send the bearers beyond our lines immediately. Any reply will be sent to the lines of the enemy, under our own flag of truce. Should they refuse to deliver their despatches upon these terms, you will direct them to return immediately." Copies, DLC-USG, V, 19, 101, 103; DNA, RG 393, Dept. of the Tenn., Letters Sent. On Aug. 29, Mrs. Lewis Dent, Memphis, sent a telegram asking "if Lewis Dent is living and where" DLC-USG, V, 23; DNA, RG 393, Dept. of the Tenn., Register of Letters Received.

On Aug. 6, Lt. Col. Loren Kent, provost marshal, wrote "To all whom it may concern." "It is hereby ordered that Major. Simms, taken prisoner of war near Natchez Miss, be released, and permission granted him to return to his home. This Order is made, as it has been discovered that Major Simms his not been in the Confederate Army, and that he duly [e]ntitled to all the privileges of non-combatant citizens." Copy, *ibid.*, Provost Marshal, Letters Sent. On Aug. 8, Kent wrote to Bowers. "As directed by the General, I have the honor to report as follows. The name of the man arrested as a prisoner of war, whose release is now desired, M. Simms, captured near or at Natchez, Mis[s] enrolled as Major, on Genl P. O. Hebert's Staff, C. S. A. and sent to Memphis with other prisoners of war on July 17th 1863. At that place they were turned over to other Officers, so that I cannot designate their present whereabouts." Copy, *ibid.* On Sept. 5, Col. William Hoffman, commissary gen. of prisoners, wrote to USG. "I have the honor to inform you in reply to your letter of the 11th inst that by direction of the secretary of war Maj M. Simmes A. D. C on Genl Herberts staff, a prisoner of war at Johnsons Island has been this day ordered to be sent to report to you at Vicksburg, to be disposed of by exchange as indicated by you in your letter   An officer will be detailed to accompany him from the Island who will report to you in person" Copy, *ibid.*, RG 249, Letters Sent. On Sept. 24, Kent wrote to Brig. Gen. John A. Rawlins. "I respectfully call the attention of the Major General Commanding to the case of one Major — Sims of Genl' Herberts Staff C. S. A. who with Lt' Sparks, also of Genl Herberts Staff, is charged with ordering the *murder* of two Federal Officers, taken prisoner by them near Lake Providence

La' in the month of June last'—from sworn statements made before Capt' W. H. Wellman 59th Ind Vols'.—by Citizens of Monroe and vicinity it appears, that Maj' Sims & Lt' Sparks did cause two Federal Officers, to be taken into the woods, at night, and then shot and *partially* buried.—Statements are also made, that it is well known by the Citizens of Monroe and vicinity that Maj' Sims' caused four ministers to be dragged from their beds, and brutally murdered, also, that he hung a Negro' soldier, near Delhi La'—in the month of June.—Maj' Sims is now in confinement at this place.—" LS, *ibid.*, RG 393, Dept. of the Tenn., Letters Received. *O.R.*, I, xxiv, part 3, 590. On Oct. 18, B. F. Sims, Meridian, Miss., wrote to C.S.A. Gen. Joseph E. Johnston seeking the release of Maj. M. W. Sims, who had been captured on July 13 after delivering messages from Smith to Johnston, ordered to Vicksburg in the belief that he would be exchanged, but then jailed there "on the charge of having ordered the execution of two Federal prisoners at the engagement at Milliken's Bend." *Ibid.*, II, vi, 394. See *ibid.*, I, xxiv, part 3, 537.

1. Paul O. Hébert, born in La. in 1818, graduated first in his class, USMA 1840, and resigned effective March 31, 1845. He served as lt. col., 14th Inf., during the Mexican War, and was elected governor of La. in 1852. He was appointed C.S.A. brig. gen. on Aug. 17, 1861, serving mostly in La. until the end of the Civil War.

To Maj. Gen. Henry W. Halleck

Head Quarters, Dept. of the Tn.
Vicksburg Miss. Aug. 11th 1863.

MAJ. GEN. H. W. HALLECK,
GEN. IN CHIEF,
GEN.

Your two dispatches announcing the appointment of Sherman & McPherson as Brigadiers in the regular army and the non-receipt of my acceptance of promotion, and approval of my ~~course~~ recommendations as to organization of Colored troops &c are received.[1] As soon as notified of of my appointment I filled out the the required oath of office and forwarded it to the Adj. Gen. of the Army.[2] If this has not been received I will be glad to fill out a duplicate and forward as soon as notified of the nonreceipt.

I took great pleasure in notifying Sherman and McPherson of their appointments. These appointments could not have been more worthily bestowed, and however much others may desire the same honors I am sure they will acknowledge the merits of these two.[3]

I feel under many obligations to you General for the interest you have ever taken in my welfare and that of the Army I have the honor to command. I will do the best I know how to satisfy you that your confidence has not been misplaced.

Although this letter is intended as private I will mention some matters which might be regarded as semi official at least.—I have no doubt movements here, since the fall of Vicksburg, appear slow. But this could not possibly be helped. As soon as Port Hudson fell Gen. Banks made requisition on me for twenty-two steamers, coal, forage &c. I supplied him all the boats then possible and all the other articles. Sick and wounded had to be sent North, wounded rebels sent South, troops sent to Helena and to Banks; an expedition to Yazoo City seemed to be highly necessary, and was sent, and Natchez had to be occupied. Under all these circumstances I am only now getting of the last of the 9th Army Corps, and moving at the same time the 13th Corps to New Orleans.

There are said to be about eighty locomotives and six or eight hundred cars on the two roads North of Grenada. These I am trying to save by having them all worked through to Memphis, but hardly hope to succeed. A Cavalry force is now on its way North to where they are, and another coming South to meet them, for the purpose of taking these cars through. But I understand the rebels have a small force guarding them and in all probability will burn them rather than let them fall into our hands. This will be better than to risk them falling into the hands of the enemy.[4]

As soon as transports can be had I shall drive what forces Kirby Smith has near me back to the Red River. Forces will move from Natchez to Trinity & Harrisonburg and from here, by Lake Providence, or Goodriche's Landing, to Floyd and Monroe. This I think will force the few troops left by Smith, to annoy the plantations, across the desert country between the Ouchita & Red River to Schrieveport where they will remain.

This state and Louisiana would be ~~easyer~~ more easily governed now than Kentucky or Missouri if armed rebels from other states could be kept out. In fact the people are ready to accept any thing. The troops from these states too will desert and return so soon as they find that they cannot be hunted down.

I am informed that movements are being made through many parts of Mississippi to unite the people in an effort to bring the state into the Union. I receive letters and delegations on this subject myself and believe the people are sincere.

Ords Command will probably all be off in one week.

The health of this Army is much better than there was any reason to hope for. The troops are physically ready for another campaign. The Artillery is, very much of it, entirely worn out, many of the pieces having been fired over three thousand times. Some I have been able to replace here, from captured guns, and other requisitions have gone in to replace.

The total at of guns captured at this place proves to have been 171, and since leaving Millikin's Bend, I believe, 268.

I am Gen. very respectfully
your obt. svt.
U. S. GRANT
Maj. Gen

ALS, University of Texas, Austin, Tex. *O.R.*, I, xxiv, part 3, 587–88. On Aug. 22, 1863, Maj. Gen. Henry W. Halleck wrote to USG. "Your letter of the 11th inst is just recieved. The acceptances of yourself Sherman & McPherson have now all been recieved. I have heard of no complaints whatever about the movements of your army since the fall of Vicksburg. On the contrary every body supposed that it would require some rest before undertaking new operations. Your plan of moving against Kirby Smith from Natchez by Harrisburg & Monroe will agree very well with the line of operations suggested to Genl Banks, viz: to ascend the Red River to Schreveport & move on Marshall, Tex., or to move from Nachetoches on Nacodaches, Texas. This will make your two lines near enough together to assist each other. In case Banks adopts this plan, Kirby Smith & Magruder must abandon either Texas or Arkansas; or they will be obliged to wage a mere guerrilla war. Genl Banks has been left at liberty to select his own objective point in Texas, and may determine to move by sea. If so, your movement will not have his support, & should be conducted with caution. You will confer, on this matter, freely with Genl Banks. The Government is exceedingly anxious that our troops should occupy some points in Texas, with the least possible delay. In your contemplated operations in Arkansas & Louisiana you will probably require additional cavalry. You are authorised to mount any of your infantry regiments, making requisitions on the proper departments for horses & equipments. Your forces should move as much as possible by water transports, in order to save land transportation through a country where the roads are few & bad." ALS, DNA, RG 393, Dept. of the Tenn., Letters Received. *O.R.*, I, xxx, part 3, 108–9. See letters to Maj. Gen. Nathaniel P. Banks, Aug. 7, 13, 14, 1863.

1. On Aug. 4, 2:40 P.M., Halleck telegraphed to USG. "I send by mail to day appointments as Brig Generals in the Army for W. T. Sherman & J. B. McPherson. You have not acknowledged my telegram notifying you of your appointment as Major Genl in the Army." ALS (telegram sent), DNA, RG 107, Telegrams Collected (Bound); telegram received, *ibid.*, Telegrams Collected (Unbound). For the other telegram from Halleck which USG acknowledged, see letter to Maj. Gen. Henry W. Halleck, July 24, 1863, note 3.
2. See letter to Brig. Gen. Lorenzo Thomas, July 18, 1863.
3. See letter to Abraham Lincoln, July 22, 1863.
4. See telegram to Maj. Gen. William T. Sherman, Aug. 6, 1863; telegram to Maj. Gen. Henry W. Halleck, Aug. 23, 1863.

To Maj. Gen. Nathaniel P. Banks

Head Quarters, Dept. of the Ten.
Vicksburg Miss. Aug. 13th 1863.

Maj. Gen. N. P. Banks,
Comd.g Dept. of the Gulf,
Gen.

The enclose, dispatch from the Gen. in Chief of the Army is just received.[1] I send it to you in all haste. Lack of boats prevents me getting the 13th Corps to you promptly. Can you not send me some boats from below for them?

Call on me for anything it is possible to serve you in.

Very respectfully
your obt. svt.
U. S. Grant
Maj. Gen. Com

ALS, DLC-Nathaniel P. Banks; telegram received, DNA, RG 393, Dept. of the Gulf, Letters Received. *O.R.*, I, xxvi, part 1, 680. On Aug. 16, 1863, Maj. Gen. Nathaniel P. Banks, New Orleans, wrote to USG. "I have the honor to acknowledge the receipt of your letter enclosing—a despatch from Major General Halleck—by the hand of Colonel T. Kilby Smith—last evening at 9 o'clock. Colonel Smith had considerately forwarded a copy of the despatches from Port Hudson by telegraph which were received at 9 a. m. I beg you will accept my thanks for the tender of your assistance—I shall call upon you freely, assured as I am from our intercourse since I have been in this Department that whatever you can you will do to assist us. There will be no delay in making the movement suggested by the Government. As soon as General Ord's command can reach us we shall be ready. I shall move I hope within a week. I hope to concentrate with your Corps (20.000) Twenty Thousand men. Our great want will be in Cavalry—If you can send us any assistance in this I shall be greatly indebted— General Grierson expressed a strong desire to join us in this expedition but it opens sooner than either of us expected—If he can be spared I hope he will be permitted to join us. I forward a despatch to him by way of information. Cavalry is of the highest importance in the country to which we are ordered. I am sorry that I cannot now send transports to expedite General Ord's movements. The Steamers sent north have not yet returned. We have not one to send you, but as soon as they arrive will urge them forward. The vessels fit for sea navigation only can be used by us in this Expedition. If you can spare any of the Tug Boats temporarily, I shall be greatly obliged and will return them as soon as they can be spared. We shall be compelled to use Sailing vessels from the deficiencies of our transportation. I will keep you advised of all our movements and shall be indebted to you for any suggestions which you make upon the matter in hand. . . . Light Draft Tin Clads of which there are many on the Upper River as I am informed by Commodore Graham will be of great service to us in the waters connecting with New Orleans   If they can be spared I beg you to send them to us without delay" LS, DNA, RG 94, War Records Office, Dept. of the Mo. *O.R.*, I, xxvi, part 1, 686–87.

1. See letter to Maj. Gen. Nathaniel P. Banks, Aug. 7, 1863, note 1.

To Maj. Gen. John A. Logan

Headq'rs Department of Tennessee,
Vicksburg, Miss., August 13, 1863.

MAJOR GENERAL JOHN A. LOGAN:

DEAR SIR: I sent you ten days' extension of leave, and will give you as many more as you require. I have read your speeches in Illinois, and feel that you are really doing more good there than you can possibly do whilst the army of your command is lying idle.

Stay while you feel such good results are being worked by your absence, and I will extend your leave to cover your absence. In the meantime, should any movement of your command be contemplated I will notify you as early as possible of it.

Yours, truly,
U. S. GRANT,
Major General.

Washington Chronicle, Nov. 7, 1867. On Aug. 11, 1863, 11:10 A.M., Col. Edward D. Townsend, AGO, telegraphed to USG. "The Secr'y of War has Extended the leave of Genl John A Logan twenty (20) days" LS (telegram sent), DNA, RG 107, Telegrams Collected (Unbound); telegram received, *ibid.*, RG 94, Generals' Papers and Books, Logan. This telegram was received at Memphis on Aug. 16. See Lincoln, *Works*, VI, 382–83.

To William P. Mellen

Headquarters Dept. of the Tenn
Vicksburg Miss. Aug 13th 1863

WM. P. MELLEN
SUPERVISOR, SP'L AGENT OF THE TREAS:
SIR:

Your letter of the 5th of Aug. together with the letter of A Pearce and B. Able,[1] and copy of one to yourself from Business men of St. Louis, and Ills. is received. My own opinion is that all trade with an enemy with whom we are at war, is calculated to weaken us. Individually I am opposed to selling to, or buying from them whilst war exists, except from those actually within our lines. From them I would purchase enough only to enable them to purchase the absolute necessaries of life. The moment purchases of Cotton are allowed in the Market, that moment, all the cotton in the Southern States, becomes the property of that class of persons, who are authorized to sell and receive pay. More than half the cotton now in the South, is the property of the so called Confederate States. This of all other will find its way to market, and will be sold by actual agents of the so called Confederate Government, for their benefit. Thus while we are making much efforts to close their Ports, we will be opening a better market for them. Our money being always worth a known price in New York City, will have a commercial value in Europe. This will enable the South to Ship at much less risk the means of exchanging for imported articles, than by sending the bulky article of Cotton.

I do not however pretend to set up my views against those of any body else. If therefore the Treasury Department of the Government thinks the advantages to us of getting out the cotton of the South, outweighs the disadvantages, I will interpose no obsticle. I would suggest however that no person be permitted to purchase cotton, or other articles in a Southern Market, except under stringent rules, and these, that none but responsible parties, under heavy bonds be allowed permits to purchase.

If the Treasury Department decides to grant permits, I will publish an order, requiring all Military Commanders to respect all permits properly given.

> I am Sir
> Very respectfully
> Your Obt. Servt.
> U. S. GRANT.
> Maj. Genl.

Copies, DLC-USG, V, 19, 101, 103; DNA, RG 393, Dept. of the Tenn., Letters Sent. On Aug. 5, 1863, U.S. Treasury Agent William P. Mellen, St. Louis, had written to USG. "Enclosed herewith I hand you copy of a letter I have received from H. E. Bridge & Co. The names of the firm are given and I am assured that they are respectable and reliable gentlemen some of them known to you personally. Of course no *exclusive* privileges can be given to these men, any license which can be given to them must be given to all men of the same character subject to compliance with the same terms. It seems to me that with sufficient bonds that no party connected with the boat shall leave the shore, and that no purchases shall be made except from citizens who come there from the country to sell their Cotton or other property, and make such affidavit as may be required before an authorized officer of the Government to be placed on every such boat, licenses of the kind asked might be given without injury to the public interests. But I am instructed by the Secretary of the Treasury to be governed entirely by your judgement and wishes in regard to *trade* throughout your Department. None will be licensed by him except upon your expressed assent and approval. In my recent interview with you, you assented to permitting shipments by the residents, and planters, upon taking the oath of allegiance. If the proposed arrangement can safely be made to work in with that, so that the parties can bring in their property to the River and sell it there instead of shipping it to a loyal state to be sold, it seems to me desirable that it should be done. Mr Butler, one of the partners in this application, visits you hoping for a favourable decision, and I send this by him. Please give me your views and wishes in reply to this and they shall be strictly observed." LS, *ibid.*, RG 366, First Special Agency, Letters Sent (Press). On Aug. 6, Mellen wrote to Secretary of the Treasury Salmon P. Chase. "Immediately after the sale of Government Cotton in Cincinnati on the 3d Monday of July, in pursuance of your instructions I visited General Grant to present your wishes and views as to adopting a more liberal policy in permitting trade in his Department. He informed me that he had received a letter from you upon the same subject, and that he did not agree with you in the views expressed, and had written to you stating his feelings and opinions upon the subject. He is disposed to do what is best for the success of the great cause in which his army is engaged, but thinks his position enables him to judge more correctly of the effects of trade in his Department, than you can do in Washington. He says commerce should not be conducted in the midst of contending Armies and that if traders at home are impatient of the delay to their money making in such districts they had better do as his Army has done, volunteer and aid it in the more speedy accomplishment of its purpose. He says that the trade within his lines previous to the restrictions of last spring was demoralizing to his whole Army, Officers and men, and that he will not willingly consent to a repetition of it. That as to supplying the people within our lines, the loyal among them should be satisfied with the fare of our soldiers and the treasonable should be kept upon 'hard tack and side meat.' This he is dealing out in rations to those who come in and apply for it, through the Commissary Department. He objects to any other supplies being brought to Vicksburg. I assured him that you would do nothing in the way of trade in his Department without his approval. I told him of the outside pressure upon the administration. He replied 'I am afraid they will force me into it.' He says the accounts of Cotton burning are great exaggerations got up by traders for effect, that comparatively little is being burned so long as it is held by those who own it there. This is the substance of his general conversation. His sincerity and patriotism, and earnestness as well as his sound judgement and intelligent comprehension of 'the situation' impressed me even more forcibly than in any previous interviews   He is willing that residents of his Department may bring in their Cotton or other property and ship it to market in the loyal states for sale, and that parties who purchased under licenses and made payment previous to the revocation thereof, may have their Cotton. Provided that such safeguards are placed upon such transactions as will prevent abuse. He is also willing that Memphis and Paducah may be placed upon the same trade footing as other Cities. I prepared the provisions under which this may be done and submitted them for his consideration. He approved them. I enclose them herewith. If you approve them please so inform me and I will publish them and instruct the proper officers to commence acting under them at once. I have assumed that General Rosecrans wil be willing to have Nashville placed in the same position a[s] Memphis and to save delay and dissatisfaction there, have inclosed it in the rule. Several gentlemen of Illinois and this City are anxious to be permitted to go with their Steamers down the River and without leaving the shore purchase from residents who may bring it there for sale. I cannot see how a regulation permitting this, if carefully guarded by bonds or otherwise, will not be substantially the same as to permit residents to take it there and ship it. They addressed a letter to me stating their proposition. I enclose it herewith. I sent a copy of it to Genl. Grant with a letter of which the enclosed is a copy. Mr. Butler, one of the parties visits General Grant to endeavor to get his consent to their proposition. If it is given, I will prepare rules under which it can be done and submit them for your consideration." LS, *ibid.*

1. Barton S. Able, born in Ill. in 1823, moved to St. Louis in 1845, becom-

ing a steamboat capt. in 1847, retiring in 1858 to enter into various business enterprises. In 1860, he was a delegate to the Republican National Convention.

To Brig. Gen. Lorenzo Thomas

———

Head Quarters, Dept. of the Ten.
Vicksburg Miss. Aug. 14th 1863.

BRIG. GEN. L. THOMAS,
ADJ. GEN. OF THE ARMY,
GEN.

Enclosed I send you a letter directed to Gen Ransom from A. T. Bowie. This is but one of numerous complaints made of the conduct of the Marine Brigade under Gen. Ellet.[1]

I think it highly probable the charges brought against the Marine Brigade are exagerated. But that their conduct is bad and their services but very slight in comparison to the great expence they are to Govt. and the injury they do, I do not doubt. Seven of the finest boats on the Miss River are kept for the use of this Brigade, the Brigade, I understand, not numbering over 800 effective men. They live on board their boats keeping Cavalry horses and all with them I should think very much to the prejudice of their effectiveness and the good of the service.

These boats, in charge of the Department commander, might be made very useful in transporting troops from one place to another, within the Dept, and in carrying troops to opperate agains[t] guerrillas. But then the troops should be selected with reference to their commanding officer, and the numbers necessary with reference to the service to be performed.

If there is nothing in the terms of the enlistment of the Marine Brigade to prevent it I would earnestly recommend that they be transfered to the land service and their boats to the Quartermaster's Dept. to be used as suggested above. If they cannot be so transfered I would as earnestly recommend that the whole Brigade be mustered out of service and the boats be taken for general use. I am fully satisfied the boats are worth much more to the service than the boats and men.

> I am Gen. very respectfully
> your obt. svt.
> U. S. GRANT
> Maj. Gen.

ALS, IHi. *O.R.*, I, xxx, part 3, 24; *O.R.* (Navy), I, xxv, 297–98. On July 13, 1863, Act. Rear Admiral David D. Porter, off Vicksburg, similarly wrote to Secretary of the Navy Gideon Welles regarding charges against the Mississippi Marine Brigade and recommending its reorganization. *O.R.*, I, xxiv, part 3, 565; *O.R.* (Navy), I, xxv, 293–94. On July 22, Porter wrote to Brig. Gen. Alfred W. Ellet, commanding Marine Brigade. "As General Grant is pressed for transportation and has requested the assistance of the boats under your command, you will proceed to such point as he may designate and take on board what troops you can carry, transporting them to such places as he may designate. . . ." *Ibid.*, p. 319. See letter to Maj. Gen. Cadwallader C. Washburn, July 22, 1863. Also on July 22, Porter wrote to USG. "I have received your communication in relation to the Marine Brigade boats, and have sent down to Rockwood for [*them all*] to come up without delay. Harrison came in there with his cavalry and commenced burning up the cotton. Burnt a large amount. . . . I have written to the department expressing your views in relation to these vessels, and expect the next mail will bring an order to transfer them all to you. [*If*] you would write a letter to the Secty of War it would settle the matter. I do not see how you can do without them. they are just what you want" LS (partly illegible), DNA, RG 45, Correspondence of David D. Porter, Mississippi Squadron, Letters Sent (Press). On Aug. 14, Brig. Gen. Lorenzo Thomas, Vicksburg, telegraphed to Secretary of War Edwin M. Stanton. "Major Genl Grant is very desirous of having transferred to him Brig Genl Ellett's command which is is in accordance with the wishes of Admiral Porter. Genl Ellett has seven of the largest and finest boats on the western waters for a command not exceeding eight hundred (800) effective men. Genl Grant constantly requires transports for troops and if this transfer is made he will land Genl Ellet's command and thus be enabled fully to avail himself of the transports, Besides he can give Genl Ellet when on shore a command more suitable to his rank." Copy, *ibid.*, RG 107, Letters Received from Bureaus. *O.R.*, I, xxx, part 3, 25; *O.R.* (Navy), I, xxv, 298.

On Aug. 5, Stanton wrote to Welles concurring in the decision of the Cabinet and of Maj. Gen. Henry W. Halleck not to reorganize the Marine Brigade. *O.R.*, I, xxiv, part 3, 576. See letter to Charles A. Dana, Aug. 5, 1863. On Aug. 24 and 27, Halleck wrote to USG. "Adjt. Thomas has telegraphed to the War Dept. asking that Brig. Genl. Ellet's Marine Brigade be placed on Shore duty and his Ram boats be turned over to you as transports. The Secty. of War does not approve the conversion of this Marine or River Brigade into a land brigade, but authorises you to use any of Genl. Ellet's brigade for temporary shore duty, and any of his boats for temporary transports whenever the exigencies of the service require this use. This brigade was organized & the men enlisted especially for service as river-men, in conjunction with either the Military or Naval forces, as circumstances might require. They have already proved themselves valuable auxilliaries, and can probably be used to great advantage against guerrilla parties on the Mississippi, and with expeditions up the Arkansas and Red Rivers. Moreover as the men have been enlisted for a special service, if that service were entirley changed, it might be claimed that they were released from their contract. Alternate employment, on land and water, as circumstances may require, is deemed within the object of the organization, you are therefore authorized to so employ the boats, and the men, as you may require their services. It is said by Adjt. Genl. Thomas that Admiral Porter wishes you to take charge of these boats and the brigades" LS, DNA, RG 94, War Records Office, Dept. of the Tenn. *O.R.,* I, xxx, part 3, 144; *O.R.* (Navy), I, xxv, 298–99. "Your despatch of the 14th in regard to Ellett's brigade has been recieved & shown to the Secty of War. He directs that you assume command of this brigade & take proper measures to reduce it to discipline, trying & punishing the guilty parties. For reasons given in my letter of the 24th inst., it is not deemed advisable at present to break up this brigade, but you can detach & place on shore such portions of it as you may deem necessary for the good of the service." LS, DNA, RG 108, Letters Sent (Press). *O.R.,* I, xxx, part 3, 183; *O.R.* (Navy), I, xxv, 299.

On Sept. 25, USG ordered the Marine Brigade to encamp near Vicksburg and its boats turned over to the q. m. dept. "for the immediate transportation of troops." Special Orders No. 263, copies, DLC-USG, V, 28; DNA, RG 393, Dept. of the Tenn., Special Orders. See letter to Maj. Gen. James B. McPherson, Oct. 10, 1863; *O.R.* (Navy), I, xxv, 370, 524, 558, 693–94. On Oct. 12, Halleck endorsed a proposal of Act. Lt. J. S. Hurd for better patrolling the Mississippi River. "This is precisely what was intended to be accomplished by Brigadier General Elletts Brigade and boats. It was proposed, that each boat should carry a company of Cavalry and a piece or section of Artillery to land and pursue the guerilla bands from the river. It is still believed, that this will be found the most effectual method of keeping the Missisippi open. Respectfully referred to Major General Grant." Copy, DNA, RG 107, Letters Received from Bureaus. *O.R.* (Navy), I, xxv, 300.

On Aug. 31, Ellet, Cairo, wrote to USG. "I have the honor to report in accordance with instructions this day rec'd, from the Hon. Sec. of War (informing me that my command was placed by the War. Department under your orders) that I came to this place for the purpose of repairing several of my boats that are badly out of repair and also to make some arrangment to obtain a supply of coal for my fleet the whole of my large supply having been consumed during my recent engagement transporting troops from your department. I had made application to the Hon Sec. of War for special authority to appoint recruiting officers for my command, which has suffered very greatly during the past season. The Secretary of War refers me to you. I should have no difficulty in obtaining all the men wanted if my recruiting is done under such authority as will enable the States from which the recruits are obtained to have credit for the number, against the draft. I desire to call your attention to this matter of recruits especially. I will proceed with my repairs and await your orders at this place." LS, DNA, RG 94, Generals' Papers and Books, A. W. Ellet. On Nov. 9, USG endorsed a letter of Oct. 22 of Ellet relative to recruiting his brigade to the maximum. "Approved and respectfully forwarded to Head Quarters of the Army Washington D. C." Copies, *ibid.,* RG 393, Military Div. of the Miss., Endorsements; DLC-USG, V, 39.

1. For the charges of A. T. Bowie, Natchez, Aug. 4, and of John Routh, of Tensas Parish, La., Aug. 7, against the Marine Brigade, see *O.R.*, I, xxx, part 3, 25; *O.R.* (Navy), I, xxv, 696–97. For replies, see *ibid.*, pp. 726–27, 729–30. For other charges and replies, see *ibid.*, pp. 302–3, 429, 550–52, 697–98, 727–28.

To Maj. Gen. Nathaniel P. Banks

Head Quarters, Dept. of the Ten.
Vicksburg Miss. Aug. 14th 1863,

MAJ. GEN. N. P. BANKS,
COMD.G DEPT. OF THE GULF,
GEN.

Gen. Ord is now here and not having heard from his family for forty days, and when he did hear from them they were among strangers, his wife & two little children sick. He has asked me for permission to go up the river to Cairo to learn something from them by telegraph if he can and if not he will go on, or send an aid, until something can be learned. Gen. Ord will not absent himself except in case of the most imperative necessity, and in that case will endeavor to return before any field opperations can possibly take place with his Corps.

Capt. Audenried has just returned bringing your dispatches of the 10th inst.[1]

Johnston's forces, under the immediate command of Hardee are still on the Southern rail-road, the Cavalry at Branden principally, and the balance scattered from there to Enterprise on the Mobile & Ohio road, most of them however in one camp in the Pine woods some forty or fifty miles East of Jackson. Their principle occupation seems to be to collect deserters & conscripts. Johnsto[n's] force after his retreat from Jackson is said to have fallen off to 10 000 men and no doubt they were so demoralized that half their number could have ~~been~~ put them to flight. Now he must be better off both as to numbers and Morale. I do not believe however that he could get together 30 000 men exclusive of the Mobile forces.

Johnston's Cavalry were to have crossed to the West side of Pearl River yesterday. Probably did. Their object is to suppress a movement now being made by the Citizens to bring their state back into the Union, to pick up deserters, and to run off negroes. The Citizens of all classes are beging the rebel Cavalry to keep away.

I have no Cavalry here to opperate with. My whole Cavalry force with this Army, including escort Companies with General Officers, and that belonging to the 13th Corps going to your Department, does not exceed 2000 effective men. Over 1000 of these are penetrating North, in co-operation with a force I ordered to be sent from Lagrange, Ten. for the purpose of collecting and saving, if possible, the rolling stock cut off from the enemy by the destruction of Big Black Bridge. They will go on through to Memphis and will not probably return here for a month. I am much in need of Cavalry and regret exceedingly that I have not got more to send to you.

> I am General, very truly
> your obt. svt.
> U. S. GRANT
> Maj. Gen.

ALS, DNA, RG 393, Dept. of the Gulf, Letters Received. *O.R.*, I, xxvi, part 1, 680–81. On Friday, Aug. 28, 1863, Maj. Gen. Nathaniel P. Banks, New Orleans, wrote to USG. "Your despatch of the 14. instant I received today. The absence of General Ord, has not delayed the—re-organization of the 13th Corps. General Washburne has been most assiduous in his attention to the troops, and they are daily improving. I reviewed General Herrons', General Lee's, and General   Divisions last week, and tomorrow a Review of the Corps is ordered. Their appearance is in the highest degree gratifying. I regret that you are unable to strengthen our cavalry, but appreciate the heavy demands made upon this arm of the service. The deficiency of Cavalry, is the great mis fortune of our army organization. I hope to correct it here—but want it much as a means of increasing the force. A Deserter from Mobile came in today. He reports the greatest confusion there, and much conflict among the troops. They are ill fed and greatly discontented. The naval offices report the capture of one or two prizes, loaded with Beef and Pork, from which they conclude there is a greater scarcity of provisions than has been reported. General Johnston is reported above Mobile with his force greatly weakened by Desertion. The enemy under Taylor in Western Louisiana is reported in movement towards the Mississippi about (8000) Eight thousand strong. They are likely to debouch between Plaquemine, and Morganzia—possibly to attack our forces in the Lafourche district. To defend this department, we need light draft Gun Boats. It is impossible for us to intercept the enemy and cut off his retreat except by naval occupation of Berwicks Bay, and the Atchafalya. This is the best method of protecting the River—I beg you to urge upon Admiral Porter the necessity of assisting us in this if it be only temporarily. The first movement in the expedition before referred to will probably take place by wednesday." ALS, DNA, RG 393, Military Div. of the Miss., Letters Received. *O.R.,* I, xxvi, part 1, 701.

1. See letter to Maj. Gen. Nathaniel P. Banks, Aug. 7, 1863.

To Maj. Gen. Stephen A. Hurlbut

Head Quarters, Dept. of the Tennessee
Vicksburg, Miss. Aug. 14, 1863

MAJ. GEN. S. A. HURLBUT,
COMMD. 16TH ARMY CORPS.
GEN.

Your letter enclosing Copy of President Lincoln's letter to you is received. I am very glad that you received that evidence of the President's and Gen. in Chief appreciation of your services and still more so that you have concluded to withdraw your resignation. I have every reason to believe that entire harmony exists between all parts of my command, and feeling the confidence I do in all the *present* corps commanders, I would regret any change.

Whether you know it or not Gen. I do not know, but I have been your warm admirer, as a military man, from the time I fell under your command in North Mo. to the present, and I have ever expressed myself so, when occasion required it, in the most substantial manner I knew how.

Very truly your obl. svt.
U. S. GRANT
Maj. Gen.

Stephen A. Hurlbut, ed., *Between War & Peace* . . . (Charleston, S. C., 1953), p. 22. On July 7, 1863, Maj. Gen. Stephen A. Hurlbut, Memphis, wrote to President Abraham Lincoln. "I respectfully tender to your Excellency the Commission of Major General of Volunteers. My first Commission as Brig General was received direct from yourself in June 1861, and throughout the period of my service I have always received the kindest assistance from the Commander in Chief as well as from all the officers under whom I have been in actual service. I have served according to my ability during the dark hours of the Country's danger. Now that the successes at Vicksburgh, in Tennessee and in Pennsylvania have brought the clear dawning of a brighter day for the Republic—I ask to be relieved from military duty. My reasons are, that I feel myself rapidly becoming unfitted for civil life and yet requiring that fitness when this war shall close, to enable me by my own exertions to provide for and support my family. Many officers have, by the experience of the past two years, been prepared to fill with ability, higher than my own, the place left vacant & the Executive without any injury to the service can thus promote some eminently deserving man. I earnestly ask that my Resignation may be accepted at as early a date as the Exigencies of the public service will permit" ALS, DNA, RG 94, ACP, 375H CB 1863. On the same day, Hurlbut wrote to USG. "I forward with this letter my Resignation. It is due to you & to myself that I should acknowledge the invariable kindness I have received from you. I feel as if the Country did not now need my services, and I know they are required at home. I have the fortune good or bad to be decently poor, have nothing but my profession, have thought of nothing for two years but the war and am rapidly losing both the knowledge & the temper necessary for successful practice. Now that the long course of brilliant Achievements of the Army of the Tennessee and its commander have been crowned by the triumph at Vicksburgh, now that Bragg is dropping back to Georgia and Johnstone undoubtedly making for the same new base—now that the Army of the Potomac once more alive is forcing the retreating columns of Lee back to Virginia, while Dix is threatening the Rebel Capital—I see an honorable time to resign. I beg that you will do me the favor of indorsing this application, for I think you know that I make it from sincere motives. I have no ambition to subserve, and sank the politician if I ever was one in the officer. I can recommend very earnestly in my place the appointment of Genl Dodge who is the best officer I have ever had." ALS, *ibid.*, Generals' Papers and Books, Hurlbut. On July 9, USG endorsed Hurlbut's letter to Lincoln. "Gen Hurlbut has sustained his position as Corps Commander and as Commander of an important District, with great credit to himself and advantage to the service. He has always had my entire confidence, and it affords me great pleasure to state that during the time I have been out of telegraphic communication with him, and with a large part of the force of the Department with me, I have felt a security that I could not have enjoyed with many others in General Hurlbut's place. I regret the necessity which Gen. Hurlbut feels for resigning his commission, but at his request, as expressed in a private letter accompanying his resignation, I approve it, and respectfully request its acceptance." ES, *ibid.*, ACP, 375H CB 1863. On July 27, USG wrote to Brig. Gen. Lorenzo Thomas. "Maj. Gen. S. A. Hurlbut having tendered his resignation I would respectfully recommend, in case of its acceptance, the appointment of Maj. Gen. F. Steele to the command of the 16th Army Corps." ALS, Goodspeed's Book Shop, Inc., Boston, Mass.

On July 10, Hurlbut wrote an "unofficial letter" to Lincoln elaborating his reasons for resigning. ALS, DLC-Robert T. Lincoln. See Lincoln, *Works*, VI, 359. Maj. Gen. Henry W. Halleck on July 30 and Lincoln on July 31 wrote to Hurlbut urging him not to resign. *O.R.*, I, xxiv, part 3, 563–64, 566–67; Lincoln,

Works, VI, 358. On Aug. 10, Hurlbut wrote to Lincoln withdrawing his resignation. *O.R.*, I, lii, part 1, 436–37. See letter to Maj. Gen. Stephen A. Hurlbut, Aug. 4, 1863.

To Brig. Gen. Robert Allen

Head Quarters Dept of the Tenn.
Vicksburg Miss Aug. 15, 1863.

BRIG GEN ROBT ALLEN
CHF. QR. M. OF THE WEST
GEN.

My father has come down here at the instance of the owners of the Sunny South" to effect a settlement for her Services.[1] I know nothing of the merits of the Case, or what the services of this Boat ought to command. This I do know however. The course pursued by Col Parsons in taking up Boats, without any agreement and settling with them arbitrarily, and in annulling Charters and paying for services already rendered, has resulted in very great dissatisfaction, and constant references to me of matters which I really have nothing to do with.—

I hope you will give this matter a few moments of your time and enable my father to transact all he has to do in the matter.

Yours truly.
U. S. GRANT.
Maj. Genl

Copy, Parsons Papers, IHi. On Aug. 31, 1863, Col. Lewis B. Parsons, asst. q. m., St. Louis, wrote to USG. "A copy of your letter of the 15th inst. to Gen. Robert Allen in reference to a claim of the Steamboat 'Sunny South' presented by your father has been referred to me. Gen. Allen is sick at Milwaukie, hence the informality of my replying direct to you. In your letter is the following language;— 'The course pursued by Col. Parsons in taking up boats, without any agreement, and settling with them arbitrarily, and in anulling charters and paying for services already rendered has resulted in very great dissatisfaction, and constant reference to me of matters which I really have nothing to do with.' Waving the Justice of condemning me unheard, I will only seek to correct eroneous impressions produced by the misrepresentations of others, I have *very seldom* taken boats without agreement except in three (3) instances: Once on orders of Major Gen. Halleck, to send twenty seven Boats without delay to move Gen. Popes army up the Tennessee, and in both the other cases on your own order. 1st Your order of the 9th of December last, received on the 11th requiring transportation for 40.000 men at Memphis on the 19th which took about sixty boats, and second your order of March 5, 1863 for 30 boats for the Yazoo Pass Expedition; In each of these cases there were not onethird Boats enough in our harbor for the purpose, and I had to send every way and gather them in great haste as fast as I could; I think you will admit that in all these cases there was no time for negotiation or regular charter, and even if there had been, it must be plain that negotiation would simply end in extortion. Aside from these; the cases of seizure by me amount to nothing and have *never* been made, when they could be reasonably avoided. As to 'settling arbitrarily'; On the first seizure the cases were referred to Captain Moore President of the Chamber of Commerce, Captain Blood President of the Boatmen's Savings Institution, (both Veteran Steamboat men) Jas. H. Lightner, President of County Court, and Gen. A. G. Edwards, one of our best Merchants,—Than whom there are not four purer and more just men in St. Louis; They fixed the price to be paid every boat, I thought two cases too low, and asked the right of the Q M. Gen'l. to increase the rate, but was refused; In both seizures on your order it was agreed the Steamboat owners should select one umpire, the Gov't. one and they two a third, whose report should be subject only to the decission of the Chief Quartermaster or Quarter master General. A Committee was so selected, and I think fully five sixths of their awards were passed and settled. From six I appealed, Gen. Allen sustained my appeal, and another Committee was selected in the same way, consisting of Capt. Throckmorton, John How, and Carlos Greeley, whom I presume you will recognize as fair men. They patiently heard full testimony, and reduced every case appealed from, and in the aggregate nearly $20.000—In illustration, the first Committee gave that old hulk the 'Daniel G. Taylor' lying at the shore merely as a store boat $90- per day, the Gov't. to pay *all expenses*. She was sold about a year ago for $6000—and had been in service some 200 days—say $18.000 —for 200 days. Would I be justified in allowing that if I could prevent it? There is no Civil Court in Christendom which would not have set aside such an award, I am not aware, that any boat seized by orders from this Office has ever been refused a reference, but many have prefered to settle direct with me; and to conclude this point, I would suggest that, hard as I may have served boats it is universally admitted, that *never* have our steamboat owners made money *near so fast as during the last year*, their 'dissatisfaction' to the contrary not withstanding.—As to 'annulling charters and paying for services already rendered.' About six or eight months since Vouchers for Transportation at so extraordinary rates came Gen. Allen for payment as to induce him to make inquiries before paying. Such enquiries satisfied him that certain officers ignorantly or wilfully allowed rates entirely inequitable, and he simply refused to pay such vouchers; Subsequently he referred all such claims to me for investigation and ordered me to report on them to him; *This and no more have I done.* General Allen's conduct was not only sustained by the War Dept, but certain Officers were directed from Washington not to fix rates at all. Gen. Allen could not according to General Orders have been called on to pay these vouchers, but if he did pay, he certainly had a right to try and discover whether they were just, and to refuse them if they were unjust; He has done no more. I have spent many laborious days and nights in patient investigation of most disagreeable subjects, and have marked in pencil on these Vouchers my opinion, as I was ordered by my superior Officer to do;

and then the owners have settled or not with Gen. Allen as they pleased. *These are the facts and he who informs you differently informs you falsly.* The seizure of Boats except in the cases alluded to has been mainly by *Officers in your own department, and then the odium of settling has been referred here.* I hardly think any one would knowingly be willing to assume the defence of *many* Vouchers given or of prices now paid in some cases as I am advised, which I think exceed the notorious 'Catalonia' case and which I hope to be investigated. In conclusion I have only to add, that I have been shamefully misrepresented and traduced, by certain persons, but I did not suppose my reputation could suffer at the hands of such men, or certainly that I should be condemned unheard   I have, however, an abiding faith in the ultimate triumph of Justice on a full knowledge of facts." ALS (press), *ibid.* On Sept. 4, Parsons wrote to Maj. Gen. William T. Sherman similarly defending his dealings with steamboatmen and also criticizing Capt. Charles W. Lyman, asst. q. m. LS, DNA, RG 94, Staff Papers. See letter to Brig. Gen. Montgomery C. Meigs, Aug. 18, 1863. Probably in 1885, Parsons endorsed a copy of USG's letter of Aug. 15, 1863, to Allen. "Unscrupulous men not unfrequently employed Gn Grants old father—in his dotage to prosecute claims against the Govt & secure the aid thereby of Gen Grant—It had been better to repel—the robbers by declining to consider claims pushed through his father—than to help him collect them—at least so it seems to me"   AE, Parsons Papers, IHi. See endorsement to Col. William Myers, Aug. 5, 1863. On Oct. 3, 1885, Parsons endorsed a copy of USG's letter of Sept. 19, 1863, to Allen. "Gen Grant in both these letters did me the greatest injustice—but has repeatedly since admited it—and sent me a letter just before leaving the army—recognizing my services—(*see it among my papers*)   He has since the war also given me many evidences of his haveing done me a wrong—which arose from false statements made by a class of unscrupulous men whom I had often thwarted in their efforts to rob the Govt—My promotion over Several Regular Army officers—who were near Gen Grant and my far wider sphere of action—and influence greatly annoyed them and I had their influence always against me as my brother Charles was well advised of—Hence tho *deeply* hurt at the time subsiquent events have fully vindicate me." AE, Parsons Papers, IHi.

On July 30, Maj. Theodore S. Bowers issued General Orders No. 49 establishing "rules to protect" military personnel "against the exorbitant charges and other impositions daily practiced by steamboats of this Department:" Copies, DLC-USG, V, 13, 14; Drish Papers, IHi; DNA, RG 393, Dept. of the Tenn., General and Special Orders; (printed) USGA. On Aug. 10, Parsons wrote to USG. "I am very glad to hear you have issued an order requiring boats to transport furloughed Soldiers at reasonable rates. I have Sought in many ways to get at this result; but from lack of power have only succeeded with Such boats as had to settle at my office. I however made a provision in a Contract some weeks ago, Covering over 30 boats at rates about half what they have been charging; and which rates are not far from fair; and would be $12,00 from Vicksburg to Cairo, Cabin passage and Sub[s]istence included. I have not yet Seen your order, but am told it is about the Same rate when the [S]ubsistence is added. If I had power to Controll, [I] think I should have made it lower than the Contractors were willing to do in my Contract   I hope the first boat violating the order may be Severely dealt with, and there would be no trouble after that. I am excessively weary of the disagreeable drudgery, I have been kept at since I left you. I have repeatedly solicited other duty, and have made a formal application for transfer to the line; which I hope to get with the privelege of reporting to you. I am willing to labor continually, but really think it is hardly just to Confine me perpetually to the most laborious and disagreeable duty in the Service." LS (press), Parsons Papers, IHi. On Aug. 14, Parsons wrote to USG. "You will see by the within table from a contract I made at what rates officers and soldiers can be transported—and that they are less than your order gives—I have transported many thousands by contract at still less rates—I have no idea Steamboat owners will become bankrupt   The fact is that though I have been *well abused* by them as unjust and illiberal they have as a whole made much more than was just—I have often wished some one would delegate me a little power on this subject." ALS (press), *ibid.* On Sept. 16, Capt. Charles Parsons, asst. q. m., St. Louis, wrote to USG. "I have read a petition addressed you by the principal Steamboat owners running Boats South—The prices named were a concession on their part for all soldiers, officers & employees of the army not travelling under orders with passes for Govt. Transpn. By this, the Government was not bound to see them paid these rates, but they were bound not to charge more than such prices—This was a concession of from 30 to 50 per cent from rates charged before the war, and as Col Parsons possessed no power to compel a Less rate he thought it our object to obtain this concession. At same time it was understood that Soldiers travelling on Deck should pay but (½¢) one half a cent pr mile & for any meals taken 50¢ each—I also enclose a copy of rates to & from Various points between here and New Orleans for your information,   These are the prices paid at the present time by Contract with C. S. Rogers & Co—I have written this to prevent any misapprehension which seemed likely to occur from the petition of the Steamboat owners, & Not to express any opinion for or against their petition—"   ALS (press), *ibid.* On Sept. 29, Brig. Gen. John A. Rawlins issued General Orders No. 59 substituting "the rates of Military transportation and subsistence established by Col. Lewis B. Parsons" for those set by General Orders No. 49. Copies, DLC-USG, V, 13, 14; DNA, RG 393, Dept. of the Tenn., General and Special Orders; (printed) USGA.

On Aug. 6, USG wrote to Maj. Gen. John M. Schofield. "The enclosed petition has been examined. I have no doubt of the disloyalty of a great number of the Steamboat men now employed in the Government Service. I would favor anything you might deem proper to reach this case, and to give the Government patronage to those who are loyal. But I do not see how it can be done effectually." Copies, DLC-USG, V, 19, 101, 103; DNA, RG 393, Dept. of the Tenn., Letters Sent. On Dec. 14, USG endorsed a draft of orders regulating the pay of pilots on the Mississippi River, which Schofield had forwarded. "The within order is highly approved. I would further recommend a severe and stated penalty be affixed for each and every violation of the provisions of the order." Copies, *ibid.*, Military Div. of the Miss., Endorsements; (attributed to USG's adjt.) DLC-USG, V, 39. On Feb. 6, 1864, Bowers issued General Orders No. 4 regulating the pay of pilots and providing penalties for violations. Copies, *ibid.*, V, 14; DNA, RG 393, Military Div. of the Miss., General Orders; (printed) RG 217, Miscellaneous Records; USGA. *O.R.*, I, xxxii, part 2, 346–48.

1. On Aug. 19, 1863, Jesse R. Grant, Vicksburg, wrote to Maj. Gen. Nathaniel P. Banks. "The bearer Mr L. Block is one of a firm of five Brothers doing business in Cincinnati—They possess a heavy capital, & are regarded as fine & honorable dealers. And are true & loyal Citizens—Mr Block is desirous of open-

ing a Mercantile operation in the south if a favorable oportunity presents itself—
Trade not being opened here in my sons Dept he preposes to visit your Dept   My
son Gen Grant has gone up to Memphis. I am a resident of Ky, & am on a visit
here, but will return to day—I am of course an *unconditional* Union man—I must
congratulate you on your great & valuable success in La generally, & Fort Hudson
particularly—With sentiments of the highest regard for you politically . . ." ALS,
DLC-Nathaniel P. Banks.

To Brig. Gen. Lorenzo Thomas

                                          Headqrs Depart of the Tenn
                                          Vicksburg Miss Aug 17 1863

BRIG GEN. L. THOMAS.
ADJT GENL OF THE ARMY
GENERAL!

Commissions for the promotion to Brig. General of Colonels
Sanborn, Maltby, Giles Smith and Wood are just received. The
name of Col Maltby was not on the list submitted by me but I am
very glad to see his promotion. There is no more gallant or deserving Officer named for advancement   The only reason why Col.
Maltby's name was left off the list submitted by me was that more
recommendations were in from the 17th Army Corps to which he
belonged than any other Corps. and again he is from Galena, the
same place with myself and I felt a delicasy about so many promotions coming from one locality.

I return herewith the appointment of J. B. Sanborn and hope
it will be recalled.[1] Col Sanborn tendered his resignation as Colonel, knowing that he had been recommended for promotion. The
principal ground for doing so was evidently because he had not
been promoted before. I send also copy of Special Order, accepting the resignation of Col Sanborn.[2]

                                          I am, General!
                                          Very Respectfully
                                          Your obedt Servant
                                          U. S. GRANT
                                          Maj. General.

LS, DNA, RG 94, ACP, 5054/1884. Dated Aug. 10, 1863, in *O.R.*, I, lii, part 1, 436. On Sept. 1, Maj. Gen. Henry W. Halleck endorsed this letter. "Respectfully recommended that the appt be cancelled, this officer having resigned." AES, DNA, RG 94, ACP, 5054/1884. On Sept. 4, Lt. Col. James A. Hardie wrote to USG. "In reply to your letter of the 17th ulto. returning the letter of appointment of Col. Sanborn, as Brig. Gen'l. of Volunteers, and recommending that it be recalled, I have to inform you that the appointment has been, this day, revoked, by order of the Secretary of War." Copies, *ibid.*, Letters Sent, Commissions and Returns; *ibid.*, RG 393, Military Div. of the Miss., War Dept. Correspondence. On Sept. 12, Hardie wrote to USG. "You will please return to this office, the letter of the 4th instant, informing you of the revocation of the appointment of Gen'l. Sanborn, as Brig. Gen'l. of Volunteers, the order revoking that appointment having been cancelled by the Secretary of War." Copy, *ibid.*, RG 94, Letters Sent, Commissions and Returns. On Sept. 24, USG endorsed this letter. "Respectfully returned to Head Quarters of the Army Washington D. C. with the letter requested enclosed. No copies of said letter have been sent from these Head Quarters" Copies, *ibid.*, RG 393, Dept. of the Tenn., Endorsements; DLC-USG, V, 25. On Oct. 2, Halleck telegraphed to USG. "Brig Genl J. R. Sanborn will be ordered to report for duty to Major Genl Schofield at St Louis" ALS (telegram sent), DNA, RG 107, Telegrams Collected (Bound); copies, *ibid.*, RG 94, Letters Received; *ibid.*, RG 393, Dept. of the Tenn., Letters Sent; DLC-USG, V, 6, 8, 24, 94. *O.R.*, I, xxx, part 4, 27. Col. John B. Sanborn, confirmed as brig. gen. on April 7, 1864, to rank from Aug. 4, 1863, assumed command of the District of Southwest Mo.

1. See following letter.
2. On Aug. 5, Lt. Col. John A. Rawlins issued Special Orders No. 212. "The resignation of Colonel John. B Sanborn 4th Regt Minesota Infantry Volunteers, is hereby accepted, to take effect *this day*" Copies, DNA, RG 108, Letters Received; *ibid.*, RG 393, Dept. of the Tenn., Special Orders; DLC-USG, V, 27, 28.

To Col. John C. Kelton

Head Quarters, Department of the Tennessee
Vicksburg, Miss., August 17th 1863.

COLONEL J. C. KELTON,
A. A. GENERAL,
WASHINGTON, D. C.
COLONEL:

Yours of the 4th inst., inclosing the appointments of Colonels C. R. Wood, 76th Ohio, Giles A. Smith, 8th Missouri, J. A. Maltby, 45th Illinois, and John B. Sanborn 4th Minnesota as

Brigadier Generals of Volunteers, made on the statement of Lieut Colonel Jno. A. Rawlins, A. A. G., is received.[1]

I am gratified with these promotions. The names of all these officers, I repeatedly stated to Col. Rawlins would be among those whom I should recommend, hence, his giving in their names, was entirely proper and meets my approval.

When I wrote my letter of recommendation,[2] the name of Colonel J. A. Maltby was left out, not, that he was less deserving, for no man has now greater distinction throughout the entire campaign, than he; but I felt a delicacy in recommending him for this reason, he being from Galena, my own place of residence. With no appointment, however, am I more pleased.

The promotion of Wood and Smith, I particularly desired. Sanborn's I also desired, but the next day after I recommended him, he tendered his resignation, knowing at the time of his recommendation. I have therefore returned his appointment to the Adjutant General of the Army and asked that it be recalled.

I send herewith a copy of my letter to the Adjutant General of recommendations, also a copy of the one returning the appointment of Colonel Sanborn.[3]

I trust, however, the original of my letter of recommendations has reached the General-in-Chief before this, as I am anxious prompt attention should be given it, as I know will be the case when it comes before him.

> I am, Colonel, very respectfully,
> Your obedient servant.
> U. S. GRANT
> Major General.

LS, DNA, RG 108, Letters Received; copies (dated Aug. 10, 1863), *ibid.*, RG 393, Dept. of the Tenn., Letters Sent; DLC-USG, V, 6, 8, 24, 94. Dated Aug. 10 in *O.R.*, I, lii, part 1, 435–36. The promotions to brig. gen. of Col. Charles R. Woods, 76th Ohio, and Col. Giles A. Smith, 8th Mo., were confirmed on April 7, 1864; that of Col. Jasper A. Maltby, 45th Ill., was confirmed on April 21; all to rank from Aug. 4, 1863.

1. On Aug. 4, Col. John C. Kelton wrote to USG. "The appointments herewith enclosed were made on the statement of Lt Col. Rawlins that you had recom-

mended these officers for promotion. Your official recommendations have not
been recd. The only letter recd from you since June 19th is dated July 24th. But
one despatch has been recd since that announcing the fall of Vicksburg, dated
July 21, recd 26th." ALS, DNA, RG 393, Dept. of the Tenn., Letters Received.

    2. See letter to Brig. Gen. Lorenzo Thomas, July 27, 1863.

    3. See preceding letter.

To Brig. Gen. Montgomery C. Meigs

Headquarters Dept. of the Tenn.
Vicksburg, Miss. Aug. 18, 1863

BRIG. GEN. M. C. MEIGS,
QUARTERMASTER GENERAL U. S. A.
GENL.

    Captain Lyman, A. Q. M. who has been on duty in this De-
partment, or with my command, since 1861, is now relieved from
duty, by orders from the Chief Quartermaster in St. Louis.

    Most of the time Captain Lyman has been on duty in charge of
transportation—In that capacity he can, and always has, dispatched
business with more promptness, than any other officer who has
ever had the same duties to perform in this Department.

    I do not know the reasons for General Allen's course towards
Capt. Lyman nor do I desire to shield him if his course has not
been strictly right—I hope however, a prompt examination will be
had, and if Capt. Lyman's course is sustained, that he will be returned for duty here—I do know that his promptness and enery are
of great service to the country and cannot well be spared.

I am, General, Very Respectfully,
Your Obd't Servt.
U. S. GRANT.
Maj. Gen.

Copy, DNA, RG 92, Consolidated Correspondence, Lyman. On June 30, 1863,
Brig. Gen. Montgomery C. Meigs ordered Brig. Gen. Robert Allen, q. m., St.
Louis, to relieve Capt. Charles W. Lyman, asst. q. m., Memphis, and have him
report to Lt. Col. Judson D. Bingham, dept. q. m., Vicksburg. *Ibid.*, "Brief of
papers connected with charges against Capt. C. W. Lyman, . . ."; *ibid.*, Register
of Letters Received, Vol. 54, A235, B481. On Aug. 11, at Allen's request,

Lyman was ordered to report to him "for settlement of his accounts." Special
Orders No. 218, copies, DLC-USG, V, 27, 28; DNA, RG 393, Dept. of the Tenn.,
Special Orders. On Aug. 18, Col. William Myers, asst. q. m., St. Louis, tele-
graphed to USG. "If Col Bingham can be spared please order him here to confer
in reference to the business of the Quarter Masters Department, by order Chief
Quarter Master" Telegrams received (2), *ibid.*, Letters Received; *ibid.*, RG 107,
Telegrams Collected (Unbound). On Aug. 23, Lyman was given a twenty-day
leave of absence "to proceed beyond the limits of the Department to commence
September 1st 1863, with leave to apply by letter for permission to visit Washington" Special Orders No. 230, copies, DLC-USG, V, 27, 28; DNA, RG 393,
Dept. of the Tenn., Special Orders. On Aug. 29, Col. Lewis B. Parsons, asst.
q. m., St. Louis, sent copies of Meigs's correspondence regarding Lyman to USG
"for your information, and action if deemed necessary." ALS (press), Parsons
Papers, IHi. On Aug. 31, Parsons wrote to Meigs. "As it has been reported for
some days that Capt. Lyman was ordered to report here, and was on his way up,
it was deemed best not to arrest him till he arrived here, so as to get his books,
papers, clerks, &c. Captain Woolfolk telegraphed me on Saturday that Captain
L. was then at Cairo enroute for St Louis, but he has not arrived, and I am advised has gone East—probably to Washington and that he has letters of strong
commendation from General Grant, Sherman, &c. If so they are simply deceived. . . . This man has traduced General Allen and myself beyond measure,
and I feel it is right to ask a *full* investigation." Copy, *ibid*. On Sept. 7, Brig.
Gen. John A. Rawlins endorsed a letter of Parsons reporting that Lyman had
received bribes from steamboat owners. "Respectfully referred to Lt. Col. Bingham Chief Quarter Master" Copies, DLC-USG, V, 25; DNA, RG 393, Dept. of
the Tenn., Endorsements. See endorsement to Col. William Myers, Aug. 5, 1863;
letter to Brig. Gen. Robert Allen, Aug. 15, 1863. For additional charges against
Lyman, and documents in his support, see DNA, RG 92, Consolidated Correspondence, Lyman.

To Abraham Lincoln

Cairo Illinois
August 23d 1863,

His Excellency A. Lincoln
President of the United States,
Sir:

Your letter of the 9th inst. reached me at Vicksburg just as I
was about starting for this place. Your letter of the 13th of July
was also duly received.[1]

After the fall of Vicksburg I did incline very much to an immediate move on Mobile. I believed then the place could be taken

with but little effort, and with the rivers debouching there, in our possession, we would have such a base to opperate from on the very center of the Confederacy as would make them abandon entirely the states bound West by the Miss. I see however the importance of a movement into Texas just at this time.

I have reinforced Gen. Banks with the 13th Army Corps comprising ten Brigades of Infantry with a full proportion of Artillery.

I have given the subject of arming the negro my hearty support. This, with the emancipation of the negro, is the heavyest blow yet given the Confederacy. The South rave a greatdeel about it and profess to be very angry. But they were united in their action before and with the negro under subjection could spare their entire white population for the field. Now they complain that nothing can be got out of their negroes.

There has been great difficulty in getting able bodied negroes to fill up the colored regiments in consequence of the rebel cavalry runing off all that class to Georgia and Texas. This is especially the case for a distance of fifteen or twenty miles on each side of the river. I am now however sending two expeditions into Louisiana, one from Natchez to Harrisonburg and one from Goodriche's Landing to Monroe, that I expect will bring back a large number. I have ordered recruiting officers to accompany these expeditions. I am also moving a Brigade of Cavalry from Tennessee to Vicksburg which will enable me to move troops to a greater distance into the interior and will facilitate materially the *recruiting service*.

Gen. Thomas is now with me and you may rely on it I will give him all the aid in my power. I would do this whether the arming the negro seemed to me a wise policy or not, because it is an order that I am bound to obey and do not feel that in my position I have a right to question any policy of the Government. In this particular instance there is no objection however to my expressing an honest conviction. That is, by arming the negro we have added a powerful ally. They will make good soldiers and taking them from the enemy weaken him in the same proportion they strengthen us. I am therefore most decidedly in favor of pushing this policy to the enlistment of a force sufficient to hold all the South falling into our hands and to aid in capturing more.

Thanking you very kindly for the great favors you have ever shown me I remain, very truly and respectfully

> your obt. svt.
> U. S. Grant
> Maj. Gn.

ALS, DLC-Robert T. Lincoln. USG marked the envelope *"Private."*

1. On July 13, 1863, President Abraham Lincoln wrote to USG. "I do not remember that you and I ever met personally. I write this now as a grateful acknowledgment for the almost inestimable service you have done the country— I wish to say a word further—When you first reached the vicinity of Vicksburg, I thought you should do, what you finally did—march the troops across the neck, run the batteries with the transports, and thus go below; and I never had any faith, except a general hope that you knew better than I, that the Yazoo Pass expedition, and the like, could succeed—When you got below, and took Port-Gibson, Grand Gulf, and vicinity, I thought you should go down the river ~~to~~ and join Gen. Banks; and when you turned Northward East of the Big Black, I feared it was a mistake—I now wish to make the personal acknowledgment that you were right, and I was wrong." ALS, PHi. *O.R.*, I, lii, part 1, 406; Lincoln, *Works*, VI, 326. On Aug. 9, Lincoln wrote to USG. "I see by a despatch of yours that you incline quite strongly towards an expedition against Mobile. This would appear tempting to me also, were it not that in view of recent events in Mexico, I am greatly impressed with the importance of re-establishing the national authority in Western Texas, as soon as possible. I am not making an order, how-ever—That I leave, for the present at least, to the General-in-Chief—A word upon another subject. Gen. Thomas has gone again to the Mississippi Valley, with the view of raising colored troops. I have no reason to doubt that you are doing what you reasonably can upon the same subject. I believe it is a resource which if vigorously applied now, will soon close the contest—It works doubly, weakening the enemy & strengthening us.—We were not fully ripe for it, until the ~~opening of the river~~ river was opened.—Now, I think at least a hundred thousand can, and ought to be rapidly organized along ~~the river~~ it's shores, reliev-ing all white troops to serve elsewhere. Mr. Dana understands you as believing that the emancipation ~~proclation~~ proclamation has helped some in your military operations—I am very glad if this is so—Did you receive a short letter from me dated the 13th of July?" ADfS, DLC-Robert T. Lincoln. *O.R.*, I, xxiv, part 3, 584; Lincoln, *Works*, VI, 374.

To Maj. Gen. Henry W. Halleck

Cairo Ill.
Aug 23, 1863.

MAJ. GEN'L HALLECK.
WASHINGTON—

All quiet at Vicksburg—Crocker will lead an expedition against ~~Stevenson~~ Trinity and Harrisonburg from Natchez, and Stevenson, one from Goodrich's landing, against Monroe, starting about Wednesday[1] or thursday next. This, with Steele's move, I think will clean Louisiana side of the river to mouth of Red river—It is so secure on the river now, that I think the Mississippi river might be declared opened for through trade. The expedition through central Mississippi was compelled to burn the cars they had gone to save. The enemy run them south of Grenada and destroyed the bridges—There were 57 Locomotives & about 400 cars.[2] I would like 3000 set of horse Equipments ordered to Vicksburg, to enable me to mount Infantry, in case of emergency—[3]

U. S. GRANT
Maj. Gen'l.

Telegram received, DNA, RG 107, Telegrams Collected (Bound); copies, *ibid.*, Telegrams Received in Cipher; *ibid.*, RG 393, Dept. of the Tenn., Hd. Qrs. Correspondence; DLC-USG, V, 6, 8, 24, 94. *O.R.*, I, xxx, part 3, 129. On Aug. 23, 1863, 6:00 A.M., USG, Columbus, Ky., had telegraphed to Maj. Gen. Henry W. Halleck. "I will be here and [at] Cairo until tomorrow when I will leave on first boat down the river" Telegram received, DNA, RG 107, Telegrams Collected (Bound). *O.R.*, I, xxx, part 3, 128.

1. Aug. 26.
2. See telegram to Maj. Gen. William T. Sherman, Aug. 6, 1863.
3. See letter to Maj. Gen. Henry W. Halleck, Aug. 11, 1863. On Aug. 24, Halleck wrote to Brig. Gen. James W. Ripley, chief of ordnance. "Major Genl Grant asks that three thousand sets of horse equipments be immediately sent to Vicksburg to be used, if necessary, in mounting Infantry." ALS, DNA, RG 108, Letters Sent (Press). On Aug. 27, Ripley wrote to USG. "I have to acknowledge the receipt of your letter of the 18th inst. with the accompanying requisitions for Ordnance for filling up the 17th Army Corps; which requisitions will receive the earliest possible attention. This Department concurs fully in your views as respects the reduction of the number of different calibres, and has made all its recent arrangements with that intent. It has suggested the use of the light 12

pounders and the 3 inch rifled guns, only, for field service, and the composition of batteries of these pieces, either mixed or separate, as the character of the operations and the nature of the service may, in the opinion of the Commanding General, render most advisable. While it has not been possible, heretofore, in consequence of the great demand for artillery rendering it necessary to avail ourselves of all on hand or at once procurable, to carry out this suggestion and desire, the opportunity of so doing, in replacing batteries worn out in service, has not been lost, and our arrangements have been made with that end in view, which it is believed will accomplish the object deemed so desirable by this Department, and which it is pleased to learn meets your concurrence, and has the sanction of practical experience." LS, *ibid.*, RG 393, Dept. of the Tenn., Letters Received.

To Maj. Gen. Francis P. Blair, Jr.

————

Cairo Ill.
Aug. 23d 1863.

MAJ. GEN. F. P. BLAIR,
DEAR SIR;

Your letter from New Port R. I.[1] has just reached me at this place. So long as your Division is laying idle there will be no particular necessity of your presence with it.

I have sent one entire Army Corps to Banks. In a day or two from now four Brigades will start for Monroe La. by way of Goodriches Landing. An another expedition starts at the same time from Natchez for Harrisonburg. These expeditions cannot accomplish their work and be in readiness for any move much before the expiration of the time the President has extended your time to include. Should any move be contemplated I will inform you of it as early as possible.[2]

I feel under many obligations to you General for the very flattering way in which you spoke of me in your St. Louis speach[3] and also for the kindness expressed in your letter.

Very Truly
your obt. svt.
U. S. GRANT
Maj. Gen.

ALS, IHi.

1. On Aug. 19, 1863, Maj. Gen. Francis P. Blair, Jr., wrote to USG. "The President extended my leave of absence to the 1st day of October next, on the condition that I would inform you of the fact, and if you desired me to report for duty sooner than that date I should do so immediately. I am, therefore, waiting orders. If any movement is to be made by the corps to which I belong before that time, I shall be very glad to be informed of it, as I do not desire to be absent under such circumstances. My understanding, however, from General Sherman, was that no movement would probably be made prior to that time. I feel, therefore, like availing myself of the President's kindness, if it meets with yours and General Sherman's approbation. General, allow me to observe to you that the entire people of the loyal States are filled with admiration and gratitude to you and your army for the glorious achievements of your arms. Among the best and most intelligent people especially does this feeling predominate. This recognition by our loyal countrymen of the great services you have rendered is especially gratifying to your friends and to no one more than to your friend and servant, . . . P. S.—Any communication addressed to me will reach me at St. Louis, Mo." *O.R.*, I, xxx, part 3, 73.

2. Blair returned to the field on Oct. 4, joining Maj. Gen. William T. Sherman's march to Chattanooga. *Ibid.*, I, xxx, part 4, 73, 433–34; *ibid.*, I, xxxi, part 2, 570.

3. USG referred to Blair's speech of Aug. 4. (St. Louis) *Daily Missouri Democrat*, Aug. 5, 1863.

To Maj. Frederick T. Dent

Cairo Ill.
Aug. 23d 1863.

DEAR DENT,

Your letter was duly received, at Vicksburg, and not answered at once because I was about coming this far on the route my letter would have to travel. I wanted a little recreation and as Julia has to go to St. Louis for the purpose of placing the three oldest children at school I concluded to come this far with her. I return to Vicksburg by the first boat. The health of my command is remarkably good concidering all they have gone through. Myself I feel younger than I did six years ago.

My Staff is entirely filled up so there would be no place except as addition Aid and I do not suppose you would like such a position. If you have command of your regiment I would think it probably a better place to win promotion. If however you think differently I will apply to have you assigned to duty with me. One difficulty, or at least annoyance to you, would be that I have men on my Staff much younger than yourself, with the rank of Col. who have none of your experiance, and who I am sorry to say are of but little assistance.

Julia will return to Vicksburg in a few weeks. She will spend but a few days in the country. The children will go to school in the city and Julia will want to spend all the time she is at home with them.

Yours
U. S. Grant

P. S. I will apply to Gen. Halleck to assign you to me and then you can exercise your judgment about what is best to be done. Your own advancement is what I look to.[1]

ALS, Mrs. Gordon Singles, Arlington, Va. See letter to Frederick Dent, April 19, 1861, note 4. On Aug. 30, 1863, USG, Vicksburg, wrote to Col. John C. Kelton. "Maj. F. T. Dent, 4th U. S. Infantry, has written to me expressing a desire to serve on my Staff, stating at the same time that his regiment is reduced to a mere handfull of men, scarcely sufficient for a good company. If consistent with the good of the service therefore I would respectfully request that he be ordered to report to me for duty." ALS, deCoppet Collection, NjP. On Sept. 10, Kelton wrote to USG. "In reply to your application of August 30, just recd. for the services of Major Dent 4th U. S. Infty on your staff, I have the honor to inform you that that officer is now in command of his regiment and cannot be spared for staff duty. The regular regiments are being filled up rapidly with conscripts." ALS, DNA, RG 108, Letters Sent (Press).

1. Manuscript torn.

To Edwin M. Stanton

Memphis Ten.
August 26th 1863,

Hon. E. M. Stanton,
Secretary of War,
Washington D. C.
Sir:

Since the forces under my command ~~leave~~ moved south of Helena, Ark, I have prohibited trade with citizens entirely, and believe it would be better for our cause if this prohibition was general with all the states in rebellion. Trade however has been opened, under restrictions, I believe, in all the Depts. except this, and in this as far down as Helena. Under these circumstances I do not know but it would be advisable to open up means for those persons living within our lines in the states of Miss. and Louisiana to obtain the necessaries of life and indispenseble articles of clothing &c.—If trade is opened under any general rule all sorts of dishonest men will engage in it, taking any oath or obligation necessary to secure the privilege. Smuggling will at once commence, as it did from Memphis, Helena and every place where trade has been allowed within the disloyal states, and the armed enemy will be enabled to procure from Northern markets every article they require.—In view of all these facts therefore I would recommend the appointment of a Post Sutler for each post occupied in those parts of the country where trade has not been opened, and authorize them to keep such articles as it is desirable should be supplied to citizens within our lines. Such persons would be under Military controll and being limited in number such precautions might be taken as would prevent improper trade.

> I have the honor to be
> very respectfully
> your obt. svt.
> U. S. GRANT
> Maj. Gen.

ALS, James S. Schoff, New York, N. Y. *O.R.*, III, iii, 721. See letter to Salmon P. Chase, Sept. 26, 1863.

To Ruel Hough and Others

————

Memphis, Tenn., Aug. 26, 1863.
GENTLEMEN: I have received a copy of resolutions passed by the "loyal citizens of Memphis at a meeting held at the rooms of the Chamber of Commerce, August 25, 1863," tendering me a public reception.[1]

In accepting this testimonial, which I do at a great sacrifice of my personal feelings, I simply desire to pay a tribute to the first public exhibition in Memphis to the Government which I represent in the Department of the Tennessee. I should dislike to refuse, for considerations of personal convenience, to acknowledge, anywhere or in any form, the existence of sentiments which I have so long and so ardently desired to see manifested in this Department. The stability of this Government and the unity of this nation depend solely upon the cordial support and the earnest loyalty of the people. While, therefore, I thank you sincerely for the kind expressions you have used toward myself, I am profoundly gratified at this public recognition, in the city of Memphis, of the power and authority of the Government of the United States.

I thank you, too, in the name of the noble army which I have the honor to command. It is composed of men whose loyalty is proved by their deeds of heroism and their willing sacrifices of life and health. They will rejoice with me that the miserable adherents of the rebellion, whom their bayonets have driven from this fair land, are being replaced by men *who acknowledge human liberty as the only true foundation of human government.* May your efforts to restore your city to the cause of the Union be as successful as have been theirs to reclaim it from the despotic rule of the leaders of the rebellion.

> I have the honor to be, gentlemen,
> Your very obedient servant,
> U. S. Grant, Major General.

Messrs. R. Hough, and Others, Committee, Memphis, Tennessee.

Missouri Democrat, Sept. 2, 1863. Ruel Hough, merchant and newspaperman in Memphis, was surveyor of customs. This letter may not have been written by USG. *Richardson*, p. 347. At the banquet on Aug. 26, 1863, Surgeon Henry S. Hewit responded to the first toast offered to USG; USG responded to the second. "I thank you, gentlemen, for your kindness. All that will add to your prosperity, that it is in my power to do, I will grant you." *Missouri Democrat*, Sept. 2, 1863.

1. For the resolutions, see *Memphis Bulletin*, Aug. 26, 1863.

To Maj. Gen. Frederick Steele

Head Quarters, Dept. of the Ten.
Helena Ark, Aug. 27th 1863,

MAJ. GEN. F. STEELE
GEN

The 3d Iowa Cavalry, Col. Bussy[1] Comd.g has been divided six Comps being with me and six in the Dept. of the Mo, now with you. I have brought the six companies belonging to this Dept. to this place with the view of getting the regiment together again. As Schofield has so much more Cavalry than me I think the whole should come to me, but rather than to keep them separated I will give up the six companies. You will find the six companies at this place. Make such orders with regard to them as you deem advisable. Should you want the entire regiment with you order these six companies out. Can you spare the six companies with you order them to Helena. It may be advisable for you to have a regiment of Cavalry in the rear to act against guerrillas. Of this however you are the judge.

I will order these six companies to report to the Commanding officer of this place to await your orders.

Very respectfully
U. S. GRANT
Maj. Gen. Com

ALS, CSt. On Aug. 27, 1863, USG, Helena, Ark., issued special orders. "The detachment of the 3d Iowa Cavalry Commanded by Maj. J. W. Noble, will debark his command at Helena Ark. and report for duty to the Comdg officer of the post. He will also report by letter to Maj. Gen. F. Steele, Comd.g Expedition against Little Rock, Ark. for orders." ADS, MH. See following letter.

1. Cyrus Bussey, born in Ohio in 1833, moved to Bloomfield, Iowa, in 1855, where he was successful in business and was elected to the Iowa Senate in 1858 as a Democrat. Appointed col., 3rd Iowa Cav., as of Sept. 5, 1861, he commanded a cav. brigade during the Vicksburg campaign. On Aug. 29, 1863, 10:45 A.M., Maj. Thomas M. Vincent, AGO, telegraphed to USG. "The Secretary of War desires you to grant Colonel Bussey third (3rd) Iowa Cavalry, leave for thirty (30) days." ALS (telegram sent), DNA, RG 107, Telegrams Collected (Unbound); copies (misdated Aug. 20), *ibid.*, RG 393, Dept. of the Tenn., Hd. Qrs. Correspondence; DLC-USG, V, 6, 8, 24, 94.

To Maj. Gen. William T. Sherman

Vicksburg Miss Aug 28, 1863

Maj Genl. W. T. Sherman

Send 'Flag of truce" to the Southern lines, and enquire if Gen'l S. D. Lee has been exchanged. I have received no notice of the fact.[1] Order all the Camp and garrison equpage men &c of the 3d Iowa Cavly, to Helena. I stopped the Six companies that went with Col Winslow, there, to get the regiment together.[2] One Brigade of Cavalry 2200 strong besides Winslows command will come here from West Tennessee. I have also 3000 Horse equipments ordered which will, enable us to mount that number of Infantry.

U. S. Grant Maj Genl

Copies, DLC-USG, V, 19, 103; DNA, RG 393, Dept. of the Tenn., Letters Sent. *O.R.*, I, xxx, part 3, 197. On Aug. 28, 1863, Maj. Gen. William T. Sherman telegraphed to USG. "Glad you are back—will order the 3d Iowa Cav. to Helena   also will send the flag of truce out   Capt Audenried Col Coolbayh & others have just gone into Vicksburg   they wanted much to go out along with the next flag   if you think it proper please notify them to come out as I will start the flag for Canton at or afternoon tomorrow"   Telegram received, DNA, RG 94, War Records Office, Dept. of the Tenn.; copy, *ibid.*, RG 393, Dept. of the Tenn., Telegrams Sent. *O.R.*, I, xxx, part 3, 197. On the flag of truce and its results, and for similar information from a Mobile paper, see Sherman to Brig. Gen. John A. Rawlins, Aug. 27, 29, 30, *ibid.*, pp. 183, 211, 227.

1. Stephen D. Lee, born in S. C., USMA 1854, promoted to 1st lt. as of Oct. 31, 1856, resigned on Feb. 20, 1861. Appointed C.S.A. capt. in the S. C. Vols., he participated in the bombardment of Fort Sumter, and later served as an art. officer in the Army of Northern Va. Promoted to brig. gen. as of Nov. 6, 1862, he commanded C.S.A. art. during the siege of Vicksburg. After his exchange, he was promoted to maj. gen. as of Aug. 3, 1863, and assigned to command of C.S.A. cav. in Miss. See following letter.

2. Edward F. Winslow, born in Me. in 1837, moved to Mount Pleasant, Iowa, in 1856, becoming involved in railroad construction. Appointed capt., 4th Iowa Cav., on Nov. 23, 1861, he was promoted to maj. as of Feb. 6, 1863, and to col. as of July 4, commanding the cav. of the 15th Army Corps.

To Maj. Gen. William T. Sherman

Vicksburg Miss Aug 28, 1863

MAJ GENL. W. T SHERMAN

I do not think Gen'l Lee would act in bad faith, but I would like to know if he has been notified of his exchange. I am particularly desirous be cause some of the Southern papers, have contended for the right of setting aside the Parole given at Vicksburg. You may telegraph me the substance of your letter, as you propose, or send a copy by morning train, and I will telegraph back my opinion on it. I have no doubt but what your action will be just right.

U. S. GRANT Maj Gen'l

Copies, DLC-USG, V, 19, 103; DNA, RG 393, Dept. of the Tenn., Letters Sent. *O.R.*, I, xxx, part 3, 197. On Aug. 28, 1863, Maj. Gen. William T. Sherman had telegraphed to USG and to Brig. Gen. John A. Rawlins. "In drawing up my letter for the flag of truce I was led to Examine more critically the Dix Hill Cartel Genl Orders no 14 of 1862 by article five (5) Each of the parties has the right to release from their paroles any of their Exchanged prisoners Simply furnishing to the adverse party a list of the prisoners released it does not appear that we must have notice of such release Lee may Simply answer that he has notice from Richmond & dont care whether we have notice or not If you say so I will prepare a letter & telegraph you for Approval before dispatching it—I dont want these fellows to get an advantage on us on paper as I think they are great braggarts & would make the most of it" "Genl Dennis reports as information recd from a Gentleman just from Demapolis that Breckenridge & Walkers division Eighteen thousand 18000 Strong have been sent to Bragg have you recd any notice of the exchange of any of the officers captured at Vicksburg I notice that Gen stephen D. Lee is in Command of the Confederate Cavalry in the interior he was one of the Vicksburg Generals & the most enterprising of all in their army. If not properly exchanged I would send him word that the exercise of any Command by him would be a breach of the terms of capitulation & would Justify us in resorting to measures of extreme retaliation I should have notice of all exchanges as I am determined they shall respect their paroles given at Vicksburg I need much a Topographical Engr & Draftsman I want to compile a good map to connect my present one with Mobile & Montgomery I have many scattered data that ought to be united now All my engrs are used up & gone Could you spare me Ulfers or any enterprising officer to take Charge of a party" Telegram received, DNA, RG 94, War Records Office, Dept. of the Tenn.; copies, *ibid.*, RG 393, Dept. of the Tenn., Telegrams Sent. *O.R.*, I, xxx, part 3, 197–98; *ibid.*, II, vi, 233–34. Possibly on the same day, Rawlins wrote to Sherman. "Have no notice of the exchange of the Vicksburg prisoners. Gen'l Halleck said to me that those who had been paroled, would be exchanged first. Capt

Comstock is out, will answer as to Engineers when he returns." Copies (dated Sept. 21), DLC-USG, V, 103; (undated) *ibid.*, V, 19; DNA, RG 393, Dept. of the Tenn., Letters Sent. See letter to Maj. Gen. Henry W. Halleck, Aug. 31, 1863. For Sherman's letter of Aug. 28 regarding C.S.A. Brig. Gen. Stephen D. Lee and C.S.A. Brig. Gen. William H. Jackson's reply of Aug. 30, see *O.R.*, II, vi, 234; *ibid.*, I, xxx, part 3, 228–29. On Sept. 17, Sherman wrote to Rawlins. "Enclosed please find the answer made by Brig Gen W. H. Jackson C. S. A. to my communication of Aug 30 a copy of which was submitted on its day of date to General Grant. It is plain that Gen Lee was notified by the authorities at Richmond of his exchange which according to the Cartel releases him of his parole, but notice of such release should have been sent to our Commissioner at Washington. It might be well to refer this letter to the adj General with the Inquiry if the notice has been received. I do think if the Dix Hill Cartel is ever remodelled it should require Notice to be given the Agent of the adverse party, and his assent obtained *before* the Prisoner of War is released of his parole and allowed to resume his hostile character. As the case now stands the Confederate Governmt at Richmond can release all their Prisoners of War, and we could not punish them, but would merely have new Cause of grievance against the Southern Confederacy. I do not presume that Davis would commit so gross a breach of honor, but I beleive when we impose a parole not to serve against us until exchanged, our Governmt should not only have notice of the Exchange, but should assent to it before it goes into Effect. For otherwise in case of our taking a prisoner recognized as havig been released on Parole how could we arraign him for a breach of his Parole? What evidence should we demand that he has been Exchanged? I think no Evidence could be entertained Except our consent, by ourselves or proper agent that we have received his Equivalent." ALS, DNA, RG 94, Letters Received, 372T 1863. *O.R.*, II, vi, 296–97. On Sept. 21, USG forwarded Sherman's and Jackson's letters to U.S. Army hd. qrs. ES, DNA, RG 94, Letters Received, 372T 1863.

To Brig. Gen. Marcellus M. Crocker

Head Quarters, Dept. of the Tn
Vicksburg Miss. Aug. 28th/63

BRIG. GN. CROCKER,
COMD.G NATCHEZ MISS.
GEN.

Col. Farrar has just called on me for instructions with regard to recruiting for his regiment.[1] I have just returned from Cairo and not yet reached my Hd Qrs. When I get there I will prepare fuller instructions and only give some general rules to be observed here.

In the first place it is the intention of the Sec. of War that all able bodied negroes that can be reached shall be taken to fill up the Colored regiments. At the same time it is desirable that we should make a wide distinction between Southern Citizens who have been loyal and those who have not; also a distinction between those who have not been loyal but now, express a voluntary willingness to return to their allegiance and employ their negroes in accordance with existing orders and those who hold out in their acknowledgment of a Souther Confederacy.

I would lay down these, as a rule, that negroes who have belong to persons of known loyalty only be recruited as free white persons are. That is when they come and offer themselves. Of the second class they may be visited by recruiting officers and the option given them to enlist; and the able bodied negroes of the third class of citizens may be taken possession with or without their own concent. All negroes who have not been employed in accordance with published orders may be taken to put in the ranks. In hunting them up the plantations of persons of known loyalty should not be visited. Indeed I think it advisable that a list of planters and Citizens should be made out whos premisis should not be visited for the purpose of securing negroes.—I am desirous of seeing the two organizations now being raised in Natchez filled up as soon as possible. I hope you will give both of them every facility to do so within these meager instructions.—I want the expedition against Harrisonburg to start as soon as possible. I will see the Naval Commander here at once and secure his cooperation.

Very respectfully
U. S. Grant
Maj. Gen. Com

ALS, DNA, RG 94, War Records Office, 17th Army Corps. *O.R.*, III, iii, 735. On Aug. 12, 1863, Col. Isaac F. Shepard, Goodrich's Landing, La., wrote to USG. "The bearer, Maj. J. E. Bryant, together with Captains Palmer, Lemert and Wolff of the 1st Mississippi Regiment, are the parties selected to proceed on recruiting service, under protection of Gen. Crocker, as arranged with yourself at my last interview. Maj. Bryant has the honor to wait upon you in person for the instructions you expressed a wish and a purpose to give." ALS, DNA, RG 393, Dept. of the Tenn., Letters Received. On Aug. 13, Lt. Col. John A. Rawlins issued Special Orders No. 220. "Major J. E. Bryant, Captains Palmer, Lemert and Wolf 1st Regt Mississippi Vols. of African Descent, will hold themselves in readiness to accompany an Expedition, which will shortly leave Goodrich's Landing for the interior, for the purpose of enlisting Negroes into the United States Service. The Commanding Officer of the Expedition will afford them every facility in his power for the purpose indicated in this order." Copies, DLC-USG, V, 27, 28; DNA, RG 393, Dept. of the Tenn., Special Orders. On Sept. 15, Col. Edward D. Townsend, AGO, wrote to USG. "In compliance with the request of Brig Gen L. Thomas Adjt. Genl. U. S. Army, that the drafted colored men of the west be sent to the Dept. of the Tennessee, in order that non-commissioned officers for colored troops organizing in the South-west might be selected from among such drafted men, orders are about to be issued directing that all such drafted men be sent to Memphis Tennessee; and I am directed by the Secretary of War to request you to detail a suitable officer to take charge of such men on their arrival, and make the necessary provision for their quarters, subsistence &c. General Thomas will assign them to such organizations as he may think the interests of the service demands." LS, *ibid.*, Unregistered Letters Received. On Oct. 28, Lt. Col. Theodore S. Bowers endorsed this letter. "Respectfully forwarded to Maj. Gen. W. T. Sherman, Com'd'g Depart. of the Tennessee, with the information that official copies of the within letter have been furnished to Maj. Gen. S. A. Hurlbut and Maj. Gen. Jas. B. McPherson." AES, *ibid.*

1. Bernard G. Farrar, born in St. Louis in 1831, was appointed maj. and provost marshal of Mo. on May 12, 1861, and col., 30th Mo., as of Oct. 29, 1862. See John Y. Simon, ed., *The Personal Memoirs of Julia Dent Grant* (New York, 1975), pp. 81–82. On Aug. 12, 1863, USG had telegraphed to Maj. Gen. William T. Sherman. "Order Col. Farrar, 30th Missouri Volunteers to move in with his regiment, baggage, sick and all to ship for Natchez. The regiment will be detached from the 15th Army Corps." Copies, DLC-USG, V, 19, 101, 103; DNA, RG 393, Dept. of the Tenn., Letters Sent. *O.R.*, I, xxx, part 3, 8–9.

To Eliza W. Smith

Vicksburg, Miss., August 28, 1863.

Mrs. Smith,

My Dear Madam: I have received two letters from you heretofore, and told your son, T. Kilby Smith, that I should write to you in answer. But I am generally so busy with matters that I am bound to give attention to, that to this time I have neglected it.

I have just returned from a visit to the northern end of my department, and am happy to learn that in my absence Col. T. Kilby Smith has received the appointment of Brig.-Gen. in the Volunteer service. I congratulate you and him sincerely upon this promotion. You will believe me when I say sincerely, because it was on my recommendation that he has been promoted. I do not

know that Colonel Smith was aware of my having recommended
him for this appointment. At all events, I did not tell him so.

You will excuse me for writing a very short letter and a very
uninteresting one, except for the announcement it makes.

Believe me most sincerely the friend of yourself and your son,
with whom I have become intimately acquainted, and to say that
acquaintance with him only ripens friendship.

U. S. GRANT,
Maj.-Gen.

Walter George Smith, *Life and Letters of Thomas Kilby Smith* . . . (New York
and London, 1898), p. 80.

To Maj. Gen. Henry W. Halleck

Head Quarters, Dept. of the Ten.
Vicksburg Miss. Aug. 29th 1863.

MAJ. GEN. H. W. HALLECK,
GEN. IN CHIEF OF THE ARMY,
GEN.

Your letter of the 12th inst. owing to my absence from Hd
Qrs. for a few days, is just received. The letter refered to contains
an extract from the Mo. ~~Republican~~ Democrat, entirely sensational
I think, detailing horrors said to have been committed upon officers
and soldiers captured at Millikin's Bend in June last. Enclosed I
send copy of correspondence which ensued.[1]

I have no evidence of ill treatment to any prisoners captured
from us further than the determination to turn over to Governor's
of states all colored soldiers captured.

Owing to movements now going on West of the Mississippi
I cannot communicate well with either Gen. E. Kirby Smith or
Gen. Taylor. As soon as I can however I will do so and enclose a
copy of the Presidents retaliatory Order.[2] I am also in hopes of
having on hand by that time a number of prisoners of War from

Smith's command which would add great force to anything I might say.

The expedition from Goodriche's Landing is now five days out. Between Steeles movement and this one it will confuse the enemy so as to make Banks entry into Texas easy.

> I am Gen. very respectfully
> your obt. svt.
> U. S. GRANT
> Maj. Gen. Com

ALS, Schoff Collection, MiU-C. *O.R.*, I, xxiv, part 3, 590.

1. On Aug. 12, 1863, Maj. Gen. Henry W. Halleck wrote to USG. "I enclose herewith a slip taken from the Missouri Democrat. The Secty of War directs that you report any answer you may have recieved from Genl Taylor to your communication to him on the treatment of colored troops & of white officers of such troops. You will also report any reliable evidence you may have of the alleged ill-treatment of any of our troops by the enemy." ALS, DNA, RG 393, Dept. of the Tenn., Letters Received. *O.R.*, I, xxiv, part 3, 589. For Halleck's enclosure, see *ibid.*, pp. 589–90. See letters to Maj. Gen. Richard Taylor, June 22, July 4, 1863; *O.R.*, I, xxiv, part 1, 7.

2. For the order of July 30, see Lincoln, *Works*, VI, 357.

To John G. Thompson

> Head Quarters, Dept. of the Ten.
> Vicksburg Miss. Aug. 29th 1863,

JNO. G. THOMPSON, ESQ.
SIR:

Your letter of the 10th inst. asking if "Democratic" newspapers, pamphlets &c. will be allowed to circulate within this Army, and stating that it is reported that such documents are destroyed by Postmasters, Provost Marshals &c. is received.

There can scarsely be a foundation for the report you speak of. If such a thing has ever been done in any one instance it has been without authority and has never been reported to me. This Army is composed of intelligent, reading, thinking men, capable of forming their own judgement, and acting accordingly. Papers of all pursuasions, political and religious, are received and freely read. Even those from Mobile & Selma are some times received and no effort is made to keep them out of the hands of soldiers. I will state however that whilst the troops in this command are left free to vote the ticket of their choice no electioneering or circulation of speaches of a disloyal character, or those calculated to create dissentions, will be tolerated if it can be avoided.

Disloyalty in the North should not be tolerated whilst such an expenditure of blood and treasure is going on to punish it in the South.

> I have the honor to be
> very respectfully
> your obt. svt.
> U. S. GRANT
> Maj. Gen Commanding

ALS, IHi. John G. Thompson, born in 1833 in Union County, Ohio, moved to Columbus in 1854. A successful merchant, he served as county treasurer, on the city council, and on various Democratic Party committees. On Aug. 10, 1863, Thompson, chairman, and four other members of the Democratic State Central Committee of Ohio, Columbus, wrote to USG. "You are no doubt aware that the General Assembly of Ohio at its last session passed a law providing for a vote for civil officers of the State, counties, &c. by such qualified electors of the State as may be in the Military service of the Republic. And you doubtless recognize the fact that every elector ought to enjoy all reasonable opportunities to ascertain the views of the respective parties in the country, and the opinions and merits of their candidates. This we beg leave to say, is of peculiar and national importance at this time. The opponents of the Democratic party are industriously engaged in representing it as sympathizing with the rebellion, and if this charge is untrue, as we affirm it to be, the best interests of the Republic require that it should be corrected. For it is obvious, that nothing could encourage the Southern people to persistency in the rebellion more than the belief that at least one half, if not a majority, of the people of the north are their aiders and abettors. And of the evil effects upon the army of such a belief, it is surely unnecessary for us to speak. Now, the Democratic party of Ohio has pronounced its views, in an authoritative form, by its State Conventions every year since the war began, and we can safely challenge its opponents to point out one word in any of its platforms, that sanctions the idea of disunion or is wanting in sympathy with our soldiers in the field. On the contrary, the fact is, that no stronger Union sentiments nor any stronger expressions of admiration and gratitude for the army, have ever been uttered than are found in these platforms. We make these remarks not to elicit any expression of your own views, but as an act of justice to the party to which we belong, and to explain why we are desirious that its opinions and motives shall be truly understood. They cannot be so understood if nothing but the representations of its adversaries be heard; and manifestly, the public welfare and justice to a party that has furnished, we believe, as many soldiers as any other party, require that it should be allowed to speak for itself. It is with this view we write to respectfully request you to state what, if any, regulations you have established in referrence to the circulation of newspapers and other political matters in the army under your command. Having entire confidence that you are incapable of knowingly prescribing any unfair regulation on the subject, we make this request in order that we may conform to such as you may have prescribed. And we do so the more earnestly because, while we have heard not a word of complaint against you on this subject it is yet currently reported that Democratic newspapers, pamphlets and speeches sent to the army are destroyed on the way by Provost Marshals and Military Post Masters & do not reach their destination, while Republican newspapers &c. pass on and are freely circulated among the soldiers. Whether this report is true or not, we do not certainly know, but if true, great injustice is done to the Democratic party, and a proceeding so unfair ought at once to be stopped. The Democracy of Ohio wish their brethren in the field to be truly informed of their views, and for this purpose to send them newspapers and pamphlets, and, at the proper time, tickets. They ask nothing more in this respect than is or may be accorded to their political opponents and their self respect forbids them to ask less. Trusting, General, that you will excuse the length of this communication, we have the honor to subscribe ourselves, with the highest consideration." LS, DNA, RG 393, Dept. of the Tenn., Letters Received.

On Aug. 4, USG wrote to LeGrand Byington, an Iowa City lawyer, unsuccessful candidate in 1863 for the Democratic nomination for governor, and chairman of the Democratic State Central Committee. "Your letter of the 6th July, asking if citizens of the State of Iowa will be allowed to visit this army and distribute tickets when the election is held for soldiers to vote, etc., is just received. In reply I will state that loyal citizens of Northern States will be allowed to visit the troops from their States at any time. *Electioneering, or any other course calculated to arouse discordant feelings, will be prohibited.* The volunteer soldiers of the army will be allowed to hold an election, if the law gives them the right to vote, and no power shall prevent them from voting the ticket of their choice." *Missouri Republican*, Jan. 23, 1868; typescript, LeGrand Byington Papers, State Historical Society of Iowa, Iowa City, Iowa.

To Maj. Gen. William T. Sherman

Vicksburg Miss Aug 30, 1863

MAJ GENL. W. T SHERMAN

Send in the prisoners you have taken without uniform, to be confined in Jail, until their case can be made the subject of a communication. I shall leave here tomorrow for New Orleans. In my

absence you can send the communication. I will probably be gone
ten days

U. S. Grant Maj Gen'l

Copies, DLC-USG, V, 19, 103; DNA, RG 393, Dept. of the Tenn., Letters Sent.
O.R., I, xxx, part 3, 226. On Aug. 30, 1863, Maj. Gen. William T. Sherman had
telegraphed to USG. "We have taken two men in arms who profess to belong to
Pinsons Cavalry detached they say along with eleven others who escaped into
the canebrake   These men have no uniform no marks of a solders dress, are not
even dressed alike & are clothed as citizens   we should not treat such men as
soldiers   we should insist on their soldiers wearing an uniform something to
distinguish them from the common Citizen   shall I proceed against them as
spies   at the time of capture they were fully equipped were outside our lines
dogging one of our mounted parties coming back from a regular scout   I wish
I had made this point by the flag of truce yesterday but it will do for the next"
Telegram received, DNA, RG 94, War Records Office, Dept. of the Tenn.; copy,
ibid., RG 393, Dept. of the Tenn., Telegrams Sent. *O.R.*, I, xxx, part 3, 226.
Later on the same day, Sherman telegraphed to USG. "I will send in the two
prisoners with written charges list of witnesses &c   I will prepare with great
care after reading all of Hallecks orders on the subject a letter to Genl Lee and
take the plain ground that the Confederate solders must have some uniform
disticnt from the dress of the citizen or else be treated as spies & guerrellas   this
is a good time for you to go to New Orleans   Please say to Genl Banks that I
regret that I have never met him   him & my bro. John are stong frieds &
I hope to meet him at some future time when events are further advanced   I
might be of good service on red river where I have a large & influential acquantance   Judge Boyce of Rapids should be won over to our cause as soon as possible   Give my special regards to Genl. Stone & Franklin   we begin division
drills immediately after muster & will keep up my corps well in hand" Telegram received, DNA, RG 94, War Records Office, Dept. of the Tenn.; copy, *ibid.*,
RG 393, Dept. of the Tenn., Telegrams Sent. *O.R.*, I, xxx, part 3, 226–27.
    On Sept. 2, Sherman wrote to Brig. Gen. John A. Rawlins. "The 113th
Reg.t. Ill. Vols. Infty. has been separated from this Command for some time past.
No Order detaching the Regiment from the Corps has been received at these
Head Qrs.—nor have I any official information of its whereabouts.—If it is the
intention of the General Commanding to permanently detach the Regiment, will
you please to furnish a Copy of the Order—in which case I would ask, that another Regiment be assigned me, that the organisation of the 2d Division may be
kept complete.—The 3d Brigade of the 3d Division of this Corps is composed of
but Three Regiments. It was the intention of the General Commanding, expressed
some time since, to assign another Regiment, to fill the Brigade to Four Regiments,—If this be practicable, I would wish, that it may be done as soon as
possible, as we are now engaged in drilling and organising for the coming Campaign.—" LS, DNA, RG 94, War Records Office, Dept. of the Ohio. Rawlins
noted on this letter, "see order detaching this regt, it has been since July 21st,"
and sent a copy of the order to Sherman on Sept. 8. AN, *ibid.* On Sept. 9, Sherman telegraphed to Rawlins. "The company of the 27th Mo is wanted with the
regt Simply because the regts is very much reduced in strength & in danger of

being wiped out by Consolidation I think that all regts brigades & divisions should be kept entire for the reason that by detaching parts the remainder lose their interest & consequently fall off My experience is that the small regts fall away by discharges faster than the larger regts because the officers lose interest in their regt when they see it small I would prefer the co should be in its regt & if we must work our white soldiers which I think wrong I would prefer to detach a whole brigade to work by the week" Telegram received, *ibid.*, Dept. of the Tenn.; copy (dated Sept. 10), *ibid.*, RG 393, Dept. of the Tenn., Telegrams Sent. Dated Sept. 9 in *O.R.*, I, xxx, part 3, 475.

On Sept. 12, Sherman twice telegraphed to Rawlins. "I have send in by Dr. Hewitt two Newspapers, Mobile and Meridian which I want you to read to Catch the tone.—Notice that Hardee is to assemble the Vicksburg Army at Enterprise instead of Demopolis.—I want to know of the Generals arrival when he comes.—Weather is hot and Country dried up,—As soon as it Changes I want to begin to strike at the Interior.—The success at Harrisonburg is a real advantage as it gives us the Washita as soon as the Water rises" Copy, DNA, RG 393, Dept. of the Tenn., Telegrams Sent. *O.R.*, I, xxx, part 3, 557. "I have Mobile papers of 9th The enemy evacuated all of Morris Island including Batteies Wagner & Gregg Sumpter though in ruins is still in their possession of it & Beauregard answerd Dahlgrens demand for its surrender by saying the demand was puerile—from these papers Kingston Tenn is held by Burnside & I infer that Knoiville is also at all events these papers treat east Tenn. as occupied by the Yankees but a great & terrific battle is predicted between Bragg & Rosecrans the object of the flag of truce is to send in proof that a certain negro was killed in war & not murdered" Telegram received, DNA, RG 94, War Records Office, Dept. of the Tenn.; copy (dated Sept. 13), *ibid.*, RG 393, Dept. of the Tenn., Telegrams Sent. Dated Sept. 12 in *O.R.*, I, xxx, part 3, 557. See letter to Maj. Gen. Henry W. Halleck, Sept. 19, 1863.

To Brig. Gen. Marcellus M. Crocker

Head Quarters, Dept. of the Ten.
Vicksburg Miss. Aug. 30th 1863,

BRIG. GEN. M. M. CROCKER,
COMD.G DIST. OF NATCHEZ.
GEN.

You will please direct the Supt. of Contrabands[1] to hire to Mr. Merrill,[2] for wages, any number of Contrabands necessary for securing his crops. This rule may be regarded as general and where it can be done without prejudice to the service Military protection may be given to hands so employed.

Negroes hired out to gather crops may work for days wages,

by the month or job, at the discretion of the Superintendent. Money received for such services will be divided two thirds going to the negroes who perform the work and the balance will be held as a fund for the benefit of the Contrabands by the Superintendent. Funds so received will be reported to J. Eaton, Gen. Superintendent, and only expended according to his directions.

> Very respectfully
> U. S. GRANT
> Maj. Gen. Com

ALS, DNA, RG 94, War Records Office, 17th Army Corps.

1. J. M. Anderson, superintendent of contrabands at Vicksburg.

2. Ayres P. Merrill, Jr., born in Natchez, graduated from Harvard in 1845, and studied law before becoming a planter and acquiring—through marriage—Elmscourt, a Natchez estate. Biographical sketch, MH. On Aug. 29, 1863, Merrill, Natchez, wrote to USG. "I write to solicit your permission to ship & sell my cottons, and also, to request the privilege of accompanying, or following, said shipments with my family. My *growing* crops of cotton (if they could be harvested) would probably yield 1000 Bales or more, but for want of laborers they are now wasting in the fields. Is it permissible for me to procure such laborers from the cont[ra]band Camps, by paying them [*good*] wages for balance of current year?" ALS, DNA, RG 109, Union Provost Marshals' File of Papers Relating to Individual Civilians. On the same day, Brig. Gen. Thomas E. G. Ransom, commanding post of Natchez, endorsed this letter. "Respectfully ~~refered~~ forwarded to the Genl Comdg Department with the recommendation that the request of Mr Merrill be granted   Genl Grant will recollect Mr Merrill as one of the Gentlemen who called on him at Vicksburg & as one of the few sound union men of this region—being a young man he has passed through great trials and dangers & suffered great pecuniary loss—during all of his difficulties he has brav[ely] maintained his position and pistol in hand defied the mob that had threatened to burn his residence and hang him" AES, *ibid.* On Jan. 14, 1864, USG endorsed a letter of Merrill regarding depredations of his property by guerrillas. "Respectfully referred to Maj. Genl. Sherman. I know the writer to be thoroughly loyal and reliable. You will therefore give such attention to his case as you can. Assess the rebels in the vicinity for the full amount of the damage inflicted on Mr. Merrill if you think best." Copies, *ibid.*, RG 393, Military Div. of the Miss., Endorsements; (attributed to USG's adjt.) DLC-USG, V, 39.

On June 20, 1865, Merrill, Washington, wrote to President Andrew Johnson. "Although a loyal southerner, and having always opposed, to the full extent of my power & influence, the enemies of my government, yet I respectfully beg to receive from your hands the full benefit of your amnesty proclamation, in order to protect, save & enjoy my property in the south, which was large before the war, and now exceeds in taxable value the sum of $20.000 00   By the rebellion, I have suffered much in 'mind, body & estate,' but the glorious triumph of our arms, and the restored integrity of our country more than repays me for all that I have endured." ALS, DNA, RG 94, Amnesty Papers, 1865, No. 180. On the same day, USG endorsed this letter. "Respectfully recommended that Amnesty be extended to A. P. Merrill Jr. His known loyalty from the begining of the rebellion to the present I presume makes it unnecessary for him to take any oath to secure what may be left of his property in the South, but to save possibility of trouble hereafter he has adopted this cours. I vouch personally for Mr. Merrills loyalty to the Government." AES, *ibid.* Merrill was pardoned on July 1. *Ibid.*

On June 27, 1864, USG, City Point, endorsed a statement of June 20 of Merrill's father, Dr. Ayres P. Merrill. "Respectfully returned with the recommendation that ~~some~~ ~~private~~ ~~extention~~ ~~be~~ ~~given~~ ~~Mr.~~ Merrill be released from all obligation to return to Memphis and that the bonds executed by him, herein described, be canceled. Mr Merrill and family are among the few influential and wealthy Southerners who have stood out firmly for the Union from the first. As a consequence of their loyalty they are now practically exiles from rich and valuable estates in the state of Miss." AES, *ibid.*, RG 109, Union Provost Marshals' File of Papers Relating to Individual Civilians. The second word of this endorsement is in another hand.

To Elihu B. Washburne

———

Vicksburg Mississippi
August 30th 1863.

HON. E. B. WASHBURN,
DEAR SIR;

Your letter of the 8th of August, enclosing one from Senator Wilson to you, reached here during my temporary absence to the Northern part of my command; hence my apparent delay in answering. I fully appreciate all Senator Wilson says.[1] Had it not been for Gen. Halleck & Dana I think it altogether likely I would have been ordered to the Potomac. My going could do no possible good. They have there able officers who have been brought up with that army and to import a commander to place over them certainly could produce no good. Whilst I would not possitively disobey an order I would have objected most vehemently to taking that command, or any other except the one I have. I can do more with this army than it would be possible for me to do with any other withou[t] time to make the same acquaintance with others I have with this. I kno[w] that the soldiers of the Army of the Ten. can be relied on to the fullest extent. I believe I know the exact capacity of every General in my comm[and] to command troops, and just where to place them to get from them thei[r] best services. This is a matter of no small importance.

Your letter to Gen. Thomas has been delivered to him. I will make an effort to secure a Brigadiership for Col. Chetlain with the colored troops   Before such a position will be open however more of these troops will have to be raised. This work will progres[s] rapidly.

The people of the North need not quarrel over the institution of Slavery. What Vice President Stevens acknowledges the corner stone of the Confederacy is already knocked out. Slavery is already dead and cannot be resurrected. It would take a standing Army to maintain slavery in the South if we were to make peace to-day guaranteeing to the South all their former constitutional privileges.

I never was an Abolitionest, [n]ot even what could be called anti slavery, but I try to judge farely & honestly and it become patent to my mind early in the rebellion that the North & South could never live at peace with each other except as one nation, and that without Slavery. As anxious as I am to see peace reestablished I would not therefore be willing to see any settlemen[t] until this question is forever settled.

Rawlins & Maltby have been appointed Brigadier Generals. These are richly deserve[d] promotions. Rawlins especially is no ordina[ry] man. The fact is had he started in this war in the Line instead of in the Staff there is every probability he would be to-day one of our shining lights. As it is he is better and more favorably know than probably any other officer in the Army who has filled only staff appointments. Some [m]en, to many of them, are only made by their Staff appointments whilst others give respectability to the position. Rawlins is of the latter class.

My kind regards to the citizens of Galena.

Your sincere friend
U. S. GRANT

ALS, IHi. See letter to Charles A. Dana, Aug. 5, 1863. On Aug. 29, 1863, Asst. Secretary of War Charles A. Dana wrote to U.S. Representative Elihu B. Washburne. "Many thanks for your letter & especially for the enclosure. I am very glad to have a copy of that speech. My impressions concerning Grant do not differ from yours. I tell every body that he is the most modest, the most disinterested, and the most honest man I have ever known. Since my return I have met hundreds of prominent and influential men to whom I have said that, and other things in the same direction. To the question they all ask: 'Doesn't he drink?'—I have been able, from my own knowledge to give a decided negative.—When do you expect to be here? What are the prospects in Illinois? And how will the elections generally go in the North West?" ALS, DLC-Elihu B. Washburne.

1. On July 25, U.S. Senator Henry Wilson of Mass. wrote to Washburne. "I con[g]ratulate you on the brilliant success of your friend Gen. Grant. When others censured, denounced or defamed him you stood by him, and he has nobly justified your confidence. I honor you for your fidelity to a man you knew and in whom you had the fulliest confidence. In this hour when the nation acknowledges his great services it must be a source of gratification to you to feel that in the day of trial you stood by your friend. A day or two ago I had a long talk with Dana late of the Tribune who has spent four months with Grant. Dana you know is a man of talent and a good judge of men. He speaks in the most glowing terms of Grant. You would be gratified to hear him talk. He tells me that Grant is modest, true, firm, honest and full of capacity for war. He says that he is in favor of destroying the cause of this civil war—of overthrowing Slavery and that his army is deeply imbued with the same feeling. I am glad to hear from so good a judge such an account of Grant and his noble army. It is reported that Grant has been invited to take command of the army of the Potomac. I do not believe it, but if it should be made to him I hope he will not for a moment think of it. He has a splendid and a united army. He can render great service to the country with that army. I fear if he should take the Potomac army that he would be ruined by a set of men in and out of that army. I am confident his great success has excited envy, and that if an oppotunity should offer he would be sacrificed. . . ." ALS, ibid.

To Maj. Gen. Henry W. Halleck

Head Quarters, Dept. of the Ten.
Vicksburg Miss. Aug. 31st 1863.

MAJ. GEN. H. W. HALLECK
GEN. IN CHIEF OF THE ARMY,
GEN.

I shall start this evening on a short trip to New Orleans, remaining there but a day or two. Gen. Banks is not yet off and I am desirous of seeing him before he starts to learn his plans and see how I may help him. The General is very anxious for more Cavalry but I have none whatever here at present. I am looking for the return of that sent North to save, if they could, the rolling stock near Grenada, daily, and also for 2000 more which Hurlbut says he can spare me. If they arrive in time I will send a portion to Banks though I cannot well spare them.

S. D. Lee, who was one of the Generals paroled here, is in command of all the Cavalry in my front. I am somewhat at a loss to know by what means he has been released from the obligations of his Parole, but suppose it must be all right. I have taken measures to ascertain if he has been exchanged.

I have heard nothing from the expedition which left Goodriches Landing yet though they have been gone seven days. I feel no apprehension for their safety.

The river is generally quiet, but one case of firing into steamers having been reported for several weeks. That occured yesterday at Morganza, below here. No Artillery was used. The party who fired a is said to be headed by a prisoner who escaped recently from New Orleans. They are a party of robbers who prey upon all parties alike knowing no friends.

Signs of negro insurrection are begining to exibit themselves. Last week some armed negroes crossed the Yazoo in the neighborhood of Haine's Bluff and went up into the Deer Creek Country where they murdered several white men. I cannot learn the full particulars of this occurrence. The negroes who committed this act however are not soldiers but were probably some men from a negro camp occupying plantations near Haine's Bluff. It seems that some of the citizens in that country have attempted to intimidate the negroes by whipping and in a few instances by shooting them. This probably was but a case of retalliation.

The enemy seems to have withdrawn most, if not all, his force from my front, except their Cavalry, and gone to the vicinity of Mobile. Movements in Banks' Dept. evidently indicates to them an early attack on that city.

The health of the troops of this com[mand] is as good as it could be in camp in any part of the Country. Shermans Corps is in condition to move on the shortest notice. McPherson's would be just as ready but is scattered on different expeditions and in Garrisoning this City and Natchez.

> I am Gen. very respectfully
> your obt. svt.
> U. S. Grant
> Maj. Gen. Com

ALS, ICHi. Dated Aug. 30, 1863, in *O.R.*, I, xxx, part 3, 224–25. On Sept. 9, Maj. Gen. Henry W. Halleck wrote to USG. "Your letter of Aug 31st is just recieved. Neither Genl S. D. Lee nor any other officer or man paroled by you has been exchanged. If any such are recaptured they should be immediately placed in close confinement, until their cases can be determined on. It is reported that Kirby Smith's forces have been withdrawn from northern Louisiana & southern Arkansas to reenforce Price. If so & Steele is in any danger he must be reenforced. On Genl Hurlbut's representations I ordered two regiments, all that could possibly be spared, and directed him to assist Steele to the best of his ability. So long as Rosecrans and Burnside occupy the enemy in East Tennessee there can be little danger of raids in west Tennessee. I wish you to watch Genl Steele's movements and give him all necessary assistance. His expedition is a most important one and must not fail. With the occupation of Little Rock & the line of the Arkansas river, all the country north is secure to us. If Steele & Banks succeed, all Trans-Mississippi must return to the union." LS, DNA, RG 94, War Records Office, Dept. of the Mo. *O.R.*, I, xxx, part 3, 474–75; (incomplete) *ibid.*, II, vi, 273.

To Maj. Gen. Henry W. Halleck

Vicksburg Miss Sept. 19th 1863

My Dear General

I have returned from New Orleans, arriving here on the 16th inst. and am still confined to my bed, lying flat on my back.[1]—my injuries are severe, but still not dangerous. my recovery is simply a matter of time. Although fatiguing I will still endeavor to perform my duties, and hope soon to recover, that I may be able to take the field, at any time I may be called upon to do so.

I have just read Genl. Shermans private letter to you,[2] but do not fully coincide, with the General, as to the policy that should be adopted towards these people, while I believe with him, that every

effort, should be made, to fill up our thinned ranks, and be prepared to meet and destroy their armies wherever found. I think
we should do it, with terms held out, that by accepting, they could
receive the protection of our laws—There is certainly, a very fine
feeling existing in the State of Louisiana, and in most parts of this
State, towards the Union. I enclose you copies of Resolutions sent
me, by Citizens of both Louisiana and Mississippi,[3]—showing
something of this feeling.

If able to write myself, I should write much more at length on
this subject, but being compelled to dictate for another to write,
I will be brief, and should I recover in a short time sufficient to
write, I will address you again.

Yours Truly
U. S. GRANT
Maj. Gen.

To MAJ GENL H. W. HALLECK
COMM' IN CHIEF U. S. FORCES
WASHINGTON D C

LS, La. Collection, NjP. *O.R.*, I, xxx, part 3, 732.

1. On Sept. 2, 1863, USG had reached New Orleans. See preceding letter.
On Sept. 5, Maj. Gen. Cadwallader C. Washburn, Carrollton, La., wrote to U.S.
Representative Elihu B. Washburne. ". . . Gen. Grant reviewed this Corps
yesterday accompanied by Genl. Banks & Thomas. We had a fine review & all
passed off well until the review was over   The Soldiers received Gen. Grant
very enthusiastically—After the review was over and Gen Grant was returning to the city his horse fell with, and injured him severly. . . ." ALS, DLC-
Elihu B. Washburne. On the same day, Brig. Gen. Lorenzo Thomas, New Orleans, wrote to Evan Randolph, Philadephia. "Returning from the review General
Grant met with an accidant which will detain us two or three days. His horse,
a hard mouth beast became restive, and a carryall driving up at the moment
struck the horse in the shoulder and threw him over with great violence. The
General who is a splendid rider maintained his seat in the saddle, and the horse
fell upon him; injuring the muscles of the right leg from the knee to the hip.
Doctor Alexander was at hand and soon ascertained that no bones were broken.
He was taken into the Carrollton Hotel, where he now is unable to move his
leg. He suffered much pain last night; and had some fever   To day he has no
fever, and is decidedly better. Our steamboat the Ben Franklin will go up to
Carrollton, and when judged proper to move him, he will be carried on board
and we will go up the river. . . ." ALS, PHi. See Thomas to Secretary of War
Edwin M. Stanton, Sept. 5, *O.R.*, III, iii, 770; Maj. Gen. Nathaniel P. Banks to
Maj. Gen. Henry W. Halleck, Sept. 5, *ibid.*, I, xxx, part 3, 359. On Sept. 4,

Lawrence Van Alstyne noted in his diary that, "We were up early and at the St. Charles to see General Grant and staff start for Carrolton. General Banks has his headquarters in Julia Street, and soon after we got to the St. Charles he and his staff rode up. A horse was led out for General Grant, which took two men to hold. He was in full uniform now and made a better appearance mounted than on foot. It was a fine sight to see them ride off up St. Charles Street, and I wished I could see the review." Lawrence Van Alstyne, *Diary of an Enlisted Man* (New Haven, Conn., 1910), p. 176. The horse which USG rode had become "frightened by the letting off of steam, with a shrill whistle, by a railroad locomotive, . . ." Henry Coppée, *Grant and his Campaigns* . . . (New York, 1866), p. 207. See *Memoirs*, I, 581–82. For suggestions by Banks, Maj. Gen. William B. Franklin, and Sylvanus Cadwallader that USG was drunk at the time of the accident, see Bruce Catton, *Grant Takes Command* (Boston, 1969), p. 26; Benjamin P. Thomas, ed., *Three Years with Grant as Recalled by War Correspondent Sylvanus Cadwallader* (New York, 1955), p. 117.

On Saturday, Sept. 12, USG telegraphed to Halleck. "I will leave for Vicksburg on Monday. Am improving rapidly but not yet able to leave my room." Telegram received, DNA, RG 107, Telegrams Collected (Bound); copies, *ibid.*, RG 393, Dept. of the Tenn., Hd. Qrs. Correspondence; DLC-USG, V, 6, 8, 24, 94. *O.R.*, I, xxx, part 3, 735. On Sept. 17, Brig. Gen. John A. Rawlins, Vicksburg, wrote to Col. John C. Kelton. "General Grant has returned from New Orleans and, though unable to walk from the effects of injuries received while there, by the falling of his horse, his general health is good and he is able for duty. General Steele dispatches from Little Rock, date 10th inst., the enemy's evacuation of that place, his retreat south and Genl. Davidson's in pursuit. Orders have been issued for the return of the Division sent from here to reinforce Genl. Steele. Everything here is quiet. The health of the troops is good." LS, DNA, RG 108, Letters Received. *O.R.*, I, xxx, part 3, 694. See James Harrison Wilson, *The Life of John A. Rawlins* (New York, 1916), pp. 154–55.

On Sept. 19, Maj. Gen. William T. Sherman telegraphed to Rawlins. "My little daughter Minnie is sick, very sick—, still I will go up to Oak Ridge to day and return by 4. P. M.—We are somewhat troubled by Citizens, insisting to pass in and out on that flank and I must see Gen'l Buckland about it. Though it is not our interest to Exclude all people, yet I wish to show them that we are military and dont care one way or the ~~other~~ other what the people wish   They must Confirm to our policy" Copy, DNA, RG 393, Dept. of the Tenn., Telegrams Sent. On Sept. 19 and 20, Sherman telegraphed to Rawlins regarding a rumored C.S.A. attack on Vicksburg. Telegrams received, *ibid.*, RG 94, War Records Office, Dept. of the Tenn.; copies, *ibid.*, RG 393, Dept. of the Tenn., Telegrams Sent. *O.R.*, I, xxx, part 3, 735, 747–48. See Rawlins's reply of Sept. 20, copies, DLC-USG, V, 19, 103; DNA, RG 393, Dept. of the Tenn., Letters Sent. *O.R.*, I, xxx, part 3, 747. See also Sherman's subsequent reports, Sept. 20 and 21, on this matter and on the war elsewhere, *ibid.*, pp. 747, 748, 758. The three dispatches of Sept. 20 were evidently printed in reverse order. The original telegrams received (except for the second dispatch on Sept. 20) are in DNA, RG 94, War Records Office, Dept. of the Tenn.; copies, *ibid.*, RG 393, Dept. of the Tenn., Telegrams Sent.

2. On July 30, 11:30 A.M., Maj. Gen. Henry W. Halleck telegraphed to USG. "I am very desirous of recieving your views in regard to the policy of attempting to organize a civil government in Mississippi, to be in subordination,

however, for the present to the military authorities." ALS (telegram sent), *ibid.*, RG 107, Telegrams Collected (Bound); copy, *ibid.*, RG 108, Telegrams Sent. *O.R.*, I, xxiv, part 3, 562. On Aug. 29, not yet having received an answer from USG, Halleck wrote to Sherman seeking his views on reconstruction in La., Miss., and Ark. ALS, DLC-William T. Sherman; *Memoirs of Gen. W. T. Sherman* (4th ed., New York, 1891), I, 363. On Sept. 17, Sherman wrote to Halleck at length on this matter. *Ibid.*, I, 363–70; *O.R.*, I, xxx, part 3, 694–700. Sherman enclosed his reply in a letter of the same day to Rawlins. ALS, DNA, RG 94, War Records Office, Dept. of the Tenn. *Memoirs of Gen. Sherman*, I, 370–71.

3. Resolutions of Sept. 3 from Parish of Winn, La., and of Sept. 4 from the Oak Ridge and Milldale Precincts, Miss., ADS, DNA, RG 94, War Records Office, Dept. of the Tenn. *O.R.*, I, xxx, part 3, 732–35. See *ibid.*, pp. 401–4.

To Maj. Gen. Nathaniel P. Banks

———

Head Quarters Dept. of the Tenn
Vicksburg Miss. Sept. 21st 1863

GENERAL

Capt. Robert T. Dunn,[1] of your Staff, has arrived, and has shown me his instructions. I regret to say that I am still confined on my back, as much as when I left New Orleans, but hope for a pemanent cure in the course of time.

The Cavalry which I ordered from West Tennessee, to this place before my departure for New Orleans, has not yet arrived— it should have been here by the third of this month, at the latest. Finding that it was not arriving as expected, my Adjutant General reiterated the order, for this Cavalry, to be sent at once. I am now daily expecting it, until it does arrive, it will be totally impracticable for me to spare from my command any Cavalry. there is to my front a Rebel Cavalry force, under Genl. Stephen. D. Lee. To watch, and counteract their movements, I have a Cavalry force, at present of scarce, twelve hundred effective men. when my Cavalry, does arrive, I will endeavor, to clean out the country east of Pearl river, and south of Bayou Pierre, as far south, as Port Hudson, of all bands of Rebel Cavalry.[2]

I have received official information, from Genl. Steele, of the evacuation of Little Rock,[3] by the enemy. I dont think that this action of the enemy, had any reference to your movements into Texas, but no doubt, when your movements are discovered by them, they will abandon Arkansas, and northern Louisiana to concentrate against you,   if my forces, with General Steele, are returned to me, I could reinforce you largely, without interfering with my Army Corps, that have been in the field. These forces however, are operating in another Department, and are for the present, beyond my control.   as it is, I will have to send you for the present emergency: *one Division*, from the 17th Army Corps —as it reduces this Army Corps, very much to make this draft upon it, I hope this Division, will be returned, as soon, as the good of the public service will admit.

I find on inquiring of my Ordnance Officer, that we have not got here the class of Guns, you desire, after supplying the Forts at this place, and at Natchez.   I can spare you the following Guns, *"towit'*   2 Two ten inch Columbiads   3 Three ten inch Sea-coast Guns   7 Seven ten inch Mortars   6 Six eight inch Mortars   4 Four nine inch Navy Guns   2 Two Rifle Guns, 650 Calibre, and quite a large number of Guns, of a smaller Calibre, some of which I presume are rifled.   any thing you call for, on this list, will be promptly furnished

As I am compelled to dictate for anothers writing, to which I am unaccustomed, I make my letter brief.   should write more fully could I write my self.

Instead of sending you a Division as I spoke of, in the first part of this letter, I will hold one in readiness here, with sufficient transportation and fuel, to send you, on receipt of orders, in accordance with the understanding, I had of our conversation in New Orleans.

Should you require them at once, please inform me—The Division, I desire to send you, has not yet returned from Helena, where it was ordered to reinforce the Little Rock Expedition.   orders have gone for its return.

I am, General Very Respectfully
Your Obedient Servant
U. S. GRANT
Maj. Gen

LS, DNA, RG 393, Dept. of the Gulf, Letters Received. *O.R.*, I, xxvi, part 1, 730–31. See *ibid.*, pp. 731–32.

1. Robert T. Dunham, 1st lt. and adjt., 3rd N. J., as of May 31, 1861, confirmed as capt. and asst. adjt. on July 14, 1862.

2. Evidently on Aug. 25 or 26, 1863, when returning from Cairo to Vicksburg, USG verbally ordered Maj. Gen. Stephen A. Hurlbut to send cav. On Sept. 6, Brig. Gen. John A. Rawlins wrote to Hurlbut. "None of the Cavalry expected under Col. Hatch has yet arrived. It is greatly needed here and could be used to good purpose—You will please send it forward without delay. If you have not the transportation to move it all at once send part at a time, by such boats as can be made available for the purpose." LS, DNA, RG 393, 16th Army Corps, Letters Received. *O.R.*, I, xxx, part 3, 380. On Sept. 16, 9:00 P.M., Lt. Col. James H. Wilson, Memphis, wrote to Rawlins. "I saw Mr. Sargent this afternoon, and learned from him the purport of your dispatch concerning the cavalry—and the satisfaction given him by Col. Binmore. It seems from all I can learn by conversing with Genl. Grierson and Col. Binmore, that it was agreed by Genl. Grant and Genl. Hurlbut, that the 4th Illinois Cavalry, 11th Ill. and 10th Missouri cavalry should go—This arrangement don't seem to meet the case at all—for in the first place you get no colonel, who is worth more than Mudd, Clark Wright or Mussy—in fact neither of these regiments has a colonel—So that your cavalry simply becomes an armed mob, with no one to control it. Neither of the three regiments selected is in any thing like a creditable state of organization, discipline or equipment—In the secondplace, My understanding of the case was that you wanted a cavalry commander quite as badly as the cavalry itself—and I have only to say on that head that I always thought Hatch Grierson's superior—and to day I became thoroughly convinced that my judgement was properly founded. I inspected the 2nd Iowa this afternoon, and I say to you what I said to Hatch, that: though it is not all that cavalry *should* be, it is by far the best cavalry regiment in the Department of the Tennessee. And what's more Hatch is the best officer and ought to be sent down. From what Sargeant said you probably take the same view of the case, and therefore wish Hatch's regiment to be sent—Hurlbut (who by the way, between me & you, is *small* enough to be *envious and Jealous* of Genl. Grant) knows fully the worth of Hatch's regiment and will retain it here unless you order it down; I don't like this 'part of the Machine': we have too many generals engaged in semi-civil affairs, to the utter neglect of their military duties. I have not yet seen a *general* but he was commanding a 'post' or 'district' or 'a city.' I have reviewed and inspected nearly all of the 16th A. C. and have not yet seen any part of the troops on the parade ground commanded by a general. This may be a little surprising to you, but is ne'ertheless, true! These distinguished gentlemen should be required to assume command of their men as their first duty, and dispose of civil and *trade* business afterwards. They should be held responsible for the dicipline, order, and instruction of their *troops* and give their *first* attention to these matters—rather than devote their undivided time to cotton—confederates and corruption. I tell you Sir, the Government of the United States cannot be upheld in purity and honesty by hands that lay aside the sword for instruments of trade & peace. We want soldiers, not traders—Generals not governors and civil agents. A few hundred thousand bayonets led by clear heads and military rules, can crush the rebellion—but a million without *Military* Generals can do nothing, except by main

strength and awkwardness. The system of occupying undisputed territory is all wrong—we must put our armies in the field, and compel our generals to lead them against the Enemy—And if they faiil from ignorance put them aside. I am disgusted with the whole system—I've heard things of you, My dear General I never expected to hear! But then this is a *horrible* war and I see no sign of Peace! I shall probably see you again before I die and may revert to these matters again—What shall I hear next? I am very sorry to learn from Colonel Mussy that the General's injury was much greater than first supposed. Remember me to him Very Kindly—I hope I shall find him at Vicksburg when I return; which may be any time during the approaching month. Love to all, who on earth do dwell—*and who do care for me*." ALS, DNA, RG 94, War Records Office, Military Div. of the Miss. Incomplete in *O.R.*, I, xxx, part 3, 664. On Sept. 30, Rawlins wrote to Brig. Gen. James M. Tuttle. "Can you give me names of Cavalry regiments, and their respective Commanders, who lately arrived at your station from Memphis." Copies, DLC-USG, V, 19, 103; DNA, RG 393, Dept. of the Tenn., Letters Sent. See letter to Maj. Gen. Nathaniel P. Banks, Oct. 3, 1863.

On Aug. 1, Maj. Theodore S. Bowers had issued Special Orders No. 208 ordering Hurlbut to send Cos. B, C, D, L, and M, 2nd Ill. Cav., to Vicksburg. Copies, DLC-USG, V, 27, 28; DNA, RG 393, Dept. of the Tenn., Special Orders. On Aug. 4, USG wrote to Maj. Gen. James B. McPherson. "You will please order all detached members of the 2d Illinois Cavalry Vols. to report at once for duty with their regiment, which goes to Natchez this day." Copies, DLC-USG, V, 19, 101, 103; DNA, RG 393, Dept. of the Tenn., Letters Sent. On the same day, Brig. Gen. John D. Stevenson, Vicksburg, wrote to USG. "I have recd your order of this date ordering Company A 2d Ills Cavalry to report to their Regt. This company is the escort co of Maj Genl Jno A Logan—I know that Genl Logan from long service of the co with him—is much attached to it and would with great reluctance see it taken from him—particularly during his temporary absence from his command—Taking the company away leaves the Div without a solitary mounted orderly and will seriously interrupt the ordinary business of the Division—Unless there is an imperative military necessity for the order—In the name of Maj Genl Logan, I would ask that the co be permitted to remain with the Div—" ALS, NHi. On Aug. 10, Hurlbut wrote to Rawlins. "I received order in relation to moving the Battalion of 2d Ills Cavalry from Fort Pillow to Vicksburgh. In a few days I shall be able to do so, but at present they are necessary for repressing guerillas in that neighborhood.—I have just been much shocked in hearing that Col. Cornyn was shot & killed to day by his Lt. Col. Bowen at Corinth   Genl. Dodge is reported dangerously sick. I hope it is not serious as I cannot well spare him" ALS, DNA, RG 94, War Records Office, Dept. of the Cumberland. On Aug. 31, Rawlins wrote to Hurlbut. "If Brig Genl E. A. Carr. has not yet passed Memphis, enroute for this place—detain him for the command of Corinth until the return of Gen'l. Dodge." Copies, DLC-USG, V, 19, 103; DNA, RG 393, Dept. of the Tenn., Letters Sent. Dated Aug. 30 in *O.R.*, I, xxx, part 3, 229. See *ibid.*, p. 320. On Aug. 20, Hurlbut wrote to Rawlins. "I exceedingly dislike breaking up Cavalry Regiments and for this reason take the liberty of suggesting that as Genl Grant has withdrawn one Battalion of the 4th Ills from me, that he order the balance of the Regiment down, and send me the remaining companies of the 2nd Illinois. This will unite both regiments in Regimental formation. I further recommend the consolidation of the 11th Ills with the 4th thus making a strong and effective Regiment out of the old 4th" Copy, DNA, RG 393, 16th Army Corps, Letters Sent. On Sept. 1, Rawlins endorsed Hurlbut's second letter. "Respectfully returned to Major General Hurlbut. It is impracticable to at this time to make the transfers requested, the 2nd Illinois Cavalry having gone to New Orleans" Copies, DLC-USG, V, 25; DNA, RG 393, Dept. of the Tenn., Endorsements. See Samuel H. Fletcher, *The History of Company A, Second Illinois Cavalry* (n.p., [1912]), pp. 65, 114.

On Aug. 30, Maj. Gen. William T. Sherman telegraphed to Rawlins. "Colonel McConnell 5th Ills Cavalry late Major of the 3rd Ills Cavalry has reported for muster in   His Regiment is below the Minimum and he is not fairly entitled to muster in except on the theory that he was actually commissioned prior to the receipt of the order   I dont want any Colonels unless they are super extra; Do you know Col. McConnell. Is he such an officer that we should strain the order to accept him. Unless he is far superior to other Colonels, I prefer to get along with Majors & Captains to command" Copy, DNA, RG 393, Dept. of the Tenn., Telegrams Sent. *O.R.*, I, xxx, part 3, 227. On the same day, Rawlins wrote to Sherman. "The Col. is a stranger to me and at Head Quarters we have no knowledge of his qualifycations. He called here on his way to join his regiment, and speaking of his muster, I informed him that I did not think the regiment had the requisite number to entitle it to a Colonel, under Gen'l Orders Adj't Gen'ls Office No 110. & 182 current series. In absence of good evidence that he is a better officer than any of the other Field officers, of the regiment, my opinion is the orders should be strictly adhered to. If he was known to be a superior man, steps might be taken to secure his muster. Col Hatch a good Officer will be here to command the Cavalry." Copies (dated Aug. 31), DLC-USG, V, 19, 103; DNA, RG 393, Dept. of the Tenn., Letters Sent. Dated Aug. 30 in *O.R.*, I, xxx, part 3, 228. Also on Aug. 30, Sherman telegraphed to Rawlins. "Have recd your despatch & that of Genl Grants   I will not muster in Me Col McConnell   with a good cavalry leader some three or four young Majors such as I have in Winslows noble will break up Lees forces or make them concentrate   They are without uniforms   please notify me when any Cavalry comes from Memphis   I need it all the time"   Telegram received, DNA, RG 94, War Records Office, Dept. of the Tenn.; copy, *ibid.*, RG 393, Dept. of the Tenn., Telegrams Sent. *O.R.*, I, xxx, part 3, 228.

On Aug. 27, Sherman telegraphed to Rawlins. "Do you think there is any chance of my getting the other Regts of Sandfords Brigade or should I break up that Brig. & organize my 4th Brigade 4th Div so as to have only three (3) Brigades in that Division"   Telegram received, DNA, RG 94, War Records Office, Dept. of the Tenn.; copy, *ibid.*, RG 393, Dept. of the Tenn., Telegrams Sent. On Aug. 29, USG endorsed a letter of July 26 of Col. William W. Sanford, commanding 4th Brigade, 4th Div., 15th Army Corps, requesting the 49th and 119th Ill. "Referred to Maj. Gen Hurlbut. Whilst these troops are required at Memphis it is not desirable that they should be brought here, but when no longer required send them." Copies, DLC-USG, V, 25; DNA, RG 393, Dept. of the Tenn., Endorsements.

On Sept. 19, Rawlins endorsed a letter of Brig. Gen. John McArthur requesting that the 12th Ill. be ordered to the 6th Div., 17th Army Corps, and that the 15th Mich. be returned. "Respectfully returned to Brig. Genl J McArthur. The 12th Ills Infty and 32d Wisconsin will be ordered to report to you" Copies, *ibid.* On Sept. 21, Rawlins wrote to Hurlbut. "You will please detach from your command, and send forward to this place the 12th Regt. Ills. Inf. Vol and 32d

Regt. Wisconsin Inf. Vol. to report to Maj Genl J. B. McPherson Comm'd'g 17th Army Corps if their services can be possibly spared" Copies, *ibid.*, Letters Sent; DLC-USG, V, 19, 103. *O.R.*, I, xxx, part 3, 757.

    3. See letter to Maj. Gen. Stephen A. Hurlbut, July 24, 1863.

To Maj. Gen. Henry W. Halleck

Vicksburg Miss
Via Memphiss Sept 22nd 10 30 A m

MAJ GEN H W HALLECK
GENL IN CHIEF

    Your dispatch to Maj Gen Hurlbut of the Fifteenth (15th) inst directing reinforcements to be sent Maj Gen Rosecrans is just received. I have ordered two (2) Divisions from here, one from each the Fifteenth (15th) and Seventeenth (17) Army Corps The one from the Seventeenth (17th) Army Corps is already on Steamboats between Vicksburg and Helena, having been previously ordered to Steele   Hurlbut should be able to send one full Division, if not two besides the troops that may return from the Expedition against Little Rock and I have so directed. Genl Banks has asked for another Division. This of course I cannot send him in view of what you require for Rosecrans. Should more troops be required from here for Rosecrans there is sufficient time for orders to reach before transportation can be had—An Army Corps Commander will be sent in command of all troops from here—

U. S. GRANT
Maj Genl Comdg

Telegram received, DNA, RG 107, Telegrams Collected (Bound); copies, *ibid.*, Telegrams Received in Cipher; *ibid.*, RG 393, Dept. of the Tenn., Hd. Qrs. Correspondence; DLC-USG, V, 6, 8, 24, 94; DLC-Nathaniel P. Banks. *O.R.*, I, xxx, part 1, 162. On Sept. 22, 1863, Brig. Gen. John A. Rawlins wrote to Maj. Gen. William T. Sherman. "The following dispatch is just recd   'Head Qr's U. S. Mil Telegraph   Dept of the Tenn   Memphis   Sept 18th 1863   4 P. M.   Telegraph from Washington City   Sept 15th 5 P M for Maj Gen S A HURLBURT   Memphis. All the troops that can possible be spared in Western Tenn & on the Mississippi River should be sent without delay to assist Gen Rosecrans on the Tennessee River. Urge sherman to act with all possible promptness   If you have boats send them down to Bring up his troops. Information just received indicates that a part of Lees army has been sent to reinforce Bragg (signed) H. W. HALLECK Gen in chief' Official (signed) Henry Binmore A A G   Please order at once one Division of your army Corps to proceed to reinforce Rosecrans moving from here by Brigades as fast as transportation can be had. Orders have been given to detain all steamers available for such purpose   McPherson will send one Division by" Copies, DLC-USG, V, 19, 103; DNA, RG 94, War Records Office, Dept. of the Tenn.; *ibid.*, RG 393, Dept. of the Tenn., Letters Sent. *O.R.*, I, xxx, part 1, 161–62. See *ibid.*, I, xxx, part 3, 720–21. On the same day, Sherman, in camp on the Big Black River, Miss., issued orders for Brig. Gen. Peter J. Osterhaus's div. to report at Vicksburg. *Ibid.*, pp. 772–73. Also on Sept. 22, Sherman telegraphed to Rawlins. "By my orders a copy of which we resent you by telegraph you will see that I have detailed Osterhaus division my first the same that was Commanded by Steele   Genl Wood & Col Williamson are the Brig Commanders   They can be moved into Vicksburg quicker than any other   The For prudential reasons I leave the designation of the destination & route to you   The easiest way to relieve pressure on Rosecrans would be for that Texas expedition to be directed on Mobile & all our available forces including those of Steele moving on Meridean & Selma uniting at Pascagoula with the new orleans force. Or in other words leave the trans mississippi alone for a while till Red River rises & using the interior to attack the line of the Alabama destroying in passing the Mobile & Ohio Road   This would force force Joe Johnston to make very heavy detachments from Bragg   I doubt if our reinforcements to Rosecrans can reach him in time to do good   He is not going to push into Georgia & his force is ample to cover the line of the Tennessee" Telegram received, DNA, RG 94, War Records Office, Dept. of the Tenn.; copy, *ibid.*, RG 393, Dept. of the Tenn., Telegrams Sent. *O.R.*, I, xxx, part 3, 773. On the same day, USG telegraphed to Sherman, alluding to Eleanor Maria (Minnie) Sherman. "If the health of your daughter will permit your leaving her, I would like to have you come in, in the morning." Copies, DLC-USG, V, 19, 103; DNA, RG 393, Dept. of the Tenn., Letters Sent. *O.R.*, I, xxx, part 3, 772. The two gens. conferred the following day. *Memoirs of Gen. W. T. Sherman* (4th ed., New York, 1891), I, 375. On Sept. 23, Rawlins issued orders for Osterhaus's div. to report to Maj. Gen. Stephen A. Hurlbut and to Maj. Gen. William S. Rosecrans, Dept. of the Cumberland. Copies, DLC-USG, V, 16, 28; DNA, RG 108, Letters Received. *O.R.*, I, xxx, part 3, 787–88. On Sept. 22, Sherman telegraphed to USG. "Chambers is not, and never has been in my Corps—He belongs to McPherson   he is doubtless in Vicksburg" Copy, DNA, RG 393, Dept. of the Tenn., Telegrams Sent.

Also on Sept. 22, Rawlins wrote to Maj. Gen. James B. McPherson, Vicksburg. "Enclosed find copy of despatch from Genl Halleck. You will please send orders to Genl. Smith to proceed with his Division to reinforce Genl. Rosecrans, reporting to Genl. Hurlbut at Memphis for instructions as to the most practicable route. Genl. Sherman will send one Division from his Corps" LS, *ibid.*, RG 94, War Records Office, 17th Army Corps. *O.R.*, I, xxx, part 3, 773. On the same day, Rawlins issued orders for Brig. Gen. John E. Smith's 2nd Div., 17th Army Corps, to report to Hurlbut and to Rosecrans. Copies, DLC-USG, V, 16, 28; DNA, RG 108, Letters Received. *O.R.*, I, xxx, part 3, 774. Also on Sept. 22, Rawlins wrote to Hurlbut. "Yours of the 18th inst encosing dispatch from the Gen'l in Chief of date the 15th inst ordering reinforcements. Sherman has been ordered to get one Division in readiness to move from here as soon as transportation can be had. Smith Division of McPhersons Corps has been ordered to reinforce Rosecrans, reporting to you at Memphis for the most practicable route by which to reach him, or rather route by which it is intended re-inforcements should go. The General in chief has been telegraphed the above, also that you ought to be able to spare one full Division if not two besides such troops as may return from the Little Rock expedition. It is desirous that an Army Corps Commander should go in command of all the reinforcements from here, and that as many of one Corps be sent as soon as possible. If therefore they are to move east from Corinth, You will please put your entire Corps in motion, and proceed with it in person to join Rosecrans, directing the troops from here to relieve yours in their present duties. If they are not to move by that route, please send word by dispatch boat, at once to these Head Quarters." Copies, DLC-USG, V, 19, 103; DNA, RG 108, Letters Received; *ibid.*, RG 393, Dept. of the Tenn., Letters Sent. *O.R.*, I, xxx, part 3, 774. On the same day, USG wrote to Maj. Gen. Nathaniel P. Banks, New Orleans. "Enclosed I send you dispatches from the Genl-in-Chief—also my reply. This will necessarily prevent further reinforcements being sent from here to you until word is had from the Genl-in-Chief. We must make no disposition of troops that will endanger the success of Rosecrans." LS, DLC-Nathaniel P. Banks. *O.R.*, I, xxx, part 3, 772. See letters to Maj. Gen. Nathaniel P. Banks, Sept. 21, Oct. 3, 1863.

On Sept. 22 (not 27, as printed in *Memoirs*, I, 582), USG had only received a copy of Maj. Gen. Henry W. Halleck to Hurlbut, Sept. 15, not Halleck's dispatches of Sept. 13 and 14. See telegram to Maj. Gen. Henry W. Halleck, Sept. 25, 1863; letter to Maj. Gen. Henry W. Halleck, Sept. 30, 1863.

To Edwin M. Stanton

Head Quarters, Dept. of the Tn.
Vicksburg Miss. Sept. 25th 1863.

HON. E. M. STANTON
SEC. OF WAR,
WASHINGTON D. C.
SIR:

Seeing that the Surgeon Gen. of the Army has been removed from his position, temporarily or otherwise, permit me to recommend for assignment as Acting Surgeon Gen. for the time being, Surgeon Madison Mills of the Army.

Knowing the vast importance of having the proper person at the head of each of the Departments at Washington there is not the man living I would recommend for any one of them without first giving them a trial in the position. I believe sincerely that Surgeon Mills would sustain himself well if he could have such trial.

My services in Mexico brought me in contact with many of the older officers of the Medical Dept. There is not one of them who I believe possesses all the qualifications for an executive office in an equal degree with Surgeon Mills. He is active, intelligent, and perfectly firm. No amount of personal friendship for an officer of his Dept. could turn him from enforcing perfect discipline. He would perform all his duties without partiality or favor but with perfect fairness towards all.

I am induced to make this recommendation in behalf of an experienced and able officer because I believe I know what I say of him to be strictly true. He served as Asst. Surgeon with my regiment before, and during a portion of the Mexican War. Since he has served for a few months as Medical Director, and the accidents of life in the interval between these two services have occationally thrown us together, so that I am as capable of judging of the merits of Surgeon Mills as I am to judge of the merits of almost any other man.

Hoping that this voluntary suggestion may not be regarded as an intrusion I remain with great respect

Your obt. svt.

U. S. GRANT

Maj. Gen.

ALS, ICarbS. See letter to Brig. Gen. William A. Hammond, July 10, 1863. On Jan. 24, 1864, Surgeon Joseph B. Brown, Louisville, wrote to USG urging him to use his influence to promote Col. Robert C. Wood, asst. surgeon gen., to surgeon gen. "Dr. Hammond will undoubtedly be superceded, and an immense effort will be made by the insatiable politicians of Massachussetts to put a doctor from the 'hub of the universe' at the head of our Corps. I *know* that the old officers of of the line of the Army, wish well to the old Medical Corps, and now in the time of our trial, I hope they will sustain us. The appointment of an 'outsider' as Surgeon General at this time would destroy all 'esprit de corps' among us, & complete the disorganization which has already commenced. It would establish a precedent, which would make the Surgeon Generalship, like the Attorney Genlship, or the Postmaster Genlship, a political appointment to be scrambled for with every change of Administration. *Next* to Dr. Satterlee, under the old organization of the Corps, & under the new, the *first* for promotion, stands Dr. Wood. Dr. Satterlee, I am assured, cannot under any circumstances receive the nomination of the President, but I am confident that a few decided words from *you* would at this time turn the scale against the outsiders, and in favor of Dr. Wood and the integrity of the Medical Corps. . . ." ALS, USG 3. On Aug. 22, Brig. Gen. Joseph K. Barnes became surgeon gen.

To Maj. Gen. Henry W. Halleck

Vicksburg Sept 25th 12 M 1863

MAJ GEN H. W. HALLECK
GEN IN CHIEF.

Your dispatches of the 13th are just this moment received. Have been detained between Cairo and Memphis from the 14th to the 22nd.[1] Under more recent dispatches troops have been moved up the Mississippi.[2] As per dispatch sent 22nd Inst. I will now send Sherman to West Tennessee with two more divisions of his corps.[3] This leaves one division of Shermans corps here but is replaced by one of McPhersons already above. I send this to Cairo by a Staff Officer who will await dispatches[4]

U. S. GRANT
Maj Genl

Telegram received, DNA, RG 107, Telegrams Collected (Bound); copies, *ibid.*, Telegrams Received in Cipher; *ibid.*, RG 393, Dept. of the Tenn., Hd. Qrs. Correspondence; DLC-USG, V, 6, 8, 24, 94. *O.R.*, I, xxx, part 3, 840–41.

1. On Sept. 22, 1863, Capt. Henry Binmore, adjt. for Maj. Gen. Stephen A. Hurlbut, wrote to USG. "I enclose herewith telegrams *nine days on their way* from Cairo to this place. Gen'l Hurlbut is absent at Cairo in consultation with Gen'l Halleck by telegraph" ALS (telegram sent), DNA, RG 94, War Records Office, Dept. of the Tenn. *O.R.*, I, xxx, part 3, 775. On Sept. 13, 1:30 P.M., Maj. Gen. Henry W. Halleck had telegraphed to USG or Maj. Gen. William T. Sherman. "It is quite possible that Bragg & Johnston will move through northern Alabama to the Tennessee river to turn Genl Rosecrans' right & cut off his communications   All of Genl Grant's available forces should be sent to Memphis, thence to Corinth & Tuscumbia to cooperate with Rosecrans should the rebels attempt that movement." ALS (telegram sent), DNA, RG 107, Telegrams Collected (Bound); copies, *ibid.*, RG 94, War Records Office, Dept. of the Tenn.; *ibid.*, RG 393, Dept. of the Tenn., Hd. Qrs. Correspondence; DLC-USG, V, 6, 8, 24, 94. *O.R.*, I, xxx, part 1, 36; *ibid.*, I, xxx, part 3, 592. On Sept. 14, Halleck had telegraphed to Hurlbut. "There are good reasons why

troops should be sent to assist Genl Rosecrans right wing with all possible des-
patch   Communicate with Genl Sherman to assist you and Hurry forward re-
inforcements as previously directed." Copy (dated Sept. 13, 1:30 P.M.), DNA,
RG 94, War Records Office, Dept. of the Tenn. Dated Sept. 14, 3:00 P.M., in
O.R., I, xxx, part 1, 36; *ibid.*, I, xxx, part 3, 620. These telegrams, according to
Binmore's note on the copies received by USG, had "left Cairo Sept 14th on the
Steamer Minnehaha Marked 'Important Govt dispatches to be delivered imme-
diately.' She failed to deliver the package." ANS (2), DNA, RG 94, War
Records Office, Dept. of the Tenn. *O.R.*, I, xxx, part 1, 36*n*.

On Sept. 17, Halleck wrote to USG. "You will perceive from my telegrams
to Generals Sherman and Hurlbut (in your absence), that I wish all available
troops on the Mississippi sent to Tuscumbia or further up the Tennessee river
to cover General Rosecrans right and secure his communications. It was early
apparent that while you and General Banks were operating west of the Mississippi, the enemy would concentrate his available forces on General Meade or
General Rosecrans. It was believed, from all the information we could obtain,
that Lee's army was to be greatly reenforced. It now appears that all of Johnson's
forces and at least three large divisions of Lee's army have joined Bragg—
Probably the advance of Burnside and Rosecrans into east Tennessee and the
danger of the rebel arsenals at Atlanta have changed their plans. At any rate
Rosecrans is now the main object of their attack, and he must be strengthened by
all the means in our power. Burnside is joining him with all the available troops
in Kentucky, and I wish you to afford him all possible aid. Vicksburg and other
places on the river cannot require large garrisons under present circumstances.
The Rebel Government has announced that some sixteen thousand of the
prisoners paroled by you at Vicksburg are released from their paroles and will
return to duty. None of them have been exchanged. It is also understood that they
intend to put in the ranks against Rosecrans, *without exchange*, all the prisoners
paroled by you and Genl Banks. Such outrageous conduct must cause very serious
difficulties. After violating the Cartel in every possible way, they now violate the
plainest laws of war and principles of humanity. We must nevertheless prepare
for this, and I think we may expect all their paroled prisoners that they can
collect will be put in the field against us *without exchange*. It is understood that
the orders issued to them state that they have been exchanged. This is utterly
false. Not one of them have been exchanged." LS, DNA, RG 94, War Records
Office, Dept. of the Tenn. *O.R.*, I, xxx, part 3, 693–94. On Sept. 19, Halleck
wrote to USG. "I enclose herewith what purports to be *an exchange* of the rebel
prisoners taken at Vicksburg. No such exchange has been made. The act of
Commissioner Ould is entirely *ex parte*, and in violation of the cartel. Our Commissioner has protested against this act of bad faith and deception on the part
of the rebel authorities." ALS, DNA, RG 94, War Records Office, Dept. of the
Tenn. *O.R.*, II, vi, 303. Halleck enclosed C.S.A. Exchange Notice No. 6, Richmond, Sept. 12, *ibid.*, pp. 295–96; see also *ibid.*, pp. 279–80. On Nov. 6, Col.
William Hoffman, commissary gen. of prisoners, wrote to USG. "I have the
honor to enclose herewith a declaration of Exchanges made by Mr Ould Confed.
Agt. for exchanges and a statement giving the names of officers and the strength
of commands covered by this Declaration   These will be some assistance to you
in distinguishing among Prisoners of War who may fall into your hands. those
who have violated their paroles if there be any such . . . It is contemplated that
Prisoners of War will be generally held at the Depots established North of the

Ohio, but there must necessarily be a great many captured in small parties and many wounded must fall into our hands as the Army advances, who should be collected at some convenient point from which they can be transferred to the principal depots, and I have respectfully to request that you will have Nashville or other suitable place designated as a temporary depot . . ." Copies, DNA, RG 109, Union Provost Marshals' File of Papers Relating to Two or More Civilians; *ibid.*, RG 249, Letters Sent. *O.R.*, II, vi, 470. See letter to Maj. Gen. James B. McPherson, Oct. 10, 1863; *Calendar*, Jan. 20, 1864.

2. See telegram to Maj. Gen. Henry W. Halleck, Sept. 22, 1863.

3. On Sept. 25, Brig. Gen. John A. Rawlins telegraphed to Sherman. "Despatches from Genl Halleck of Date the thirteenth inst show that the forces from here are to move via Corinth & Tuscumbia to Cooperate with Rosecranz— You will be a therefore hold two 2 of the remaining Divisions of your corps in readiness to move to this place for embarkation to Memphis on receipt of notice that transportation is provided. You will go in command. The division you leave will report to Genl McPherson in place of smiths Division of his corps which will accompany you. You will take no cavalry" Telegram received, DNA, RG 94, War Records Office, Dept. of the Tenn.; copies (misdated Sept. 26), *ibid.*, RG 393, Dept. of the Tenn., Letters Sent; DLC-USG, V, 19, 103. *O.R.*, I, xxx, part 3, 842; (misdated Sept. 26) *ibid.*, p. 864. On Sept. 25, Sherman telegraphed to USG, then to Rawlins. "Your despatch received The preliminary orders will be issued the moment Col Coolbough is outside our lines with his flag of truce. It is best that the with drawal of my Corps be kept secret from the enemy as long as possible" "I have just inspected & reviewed my 4th Division I will take the 2d & 4th Division & leave Tuttles This Division & the Cavalry can cover the points of Big Black. McPhersons will be out tomorrow & I will show him everything & leave him to dispose of the force left behind. I have ordered the sick & all surplus baggage to be sent in by cars & will hold the troops to march at an hours notice having their wagons ready to load up I can easily start on sunday & embark by monday if you have the boats" Telegrams received, DNA, RG 94, War Records Office, Dept. of the Tenn.; copies, *ibid.*, RG 393, Dept. of the Tenn., Telegrams Sent. *O.R.*, I, xxx, part 3, 842. On Sept. 26, Sherman telegraphed to Rawlins. "I expect Gen McPherson out this mornig shall I turn over to him the division of infantry & five Regts of Cavalry & let him give directions as to the positions they shall take up confinig my attention to the movement contemplated of my two Divisions preparing for embarkation to Memphis" Telegram received, DNA, RG 94, War Records Office, Dept. of the Tenn.; copy, *ibid.*, RG 393, Dept. of the Tenn., Telegrams Sent. *O.R.*, I, xxx, part 3, 865. On the same day, Rawlins telegraphed to Sherman. "You can turn over the command of that part of your Corps, that will be left, to General McPherson, and have them so posted as to cover the country between the Yazoo as is now covered by you" Copies, DLC-USG, V, 19, 103; DNA, RG 393, Dept. of the Tenn., Letters Sent. *O.R.*, I, xxx, part 3, 866. See *ibid.*, pp. 844–45.

On Sept. 25, Rawlins wrote to Capt. Greenbury L. Fort. "Transportation for two Divisions of the 15th Army Corps to Memphis is required at once. You will therefore collect all the boats available for that perpose detaining too, those now here except the one bound for New Orleans, and a swift light draught dispatch boat for Cairo, which you will get in readiness to start by the time dispatches are prepared. It will be subject to the order of Lt Col J. H. Wilson, Asst Inspec-

tor Genl. Please report here at once the number of boats now available for transports and their capacity." Copies, DLC-USG, V, 19, 103; DNA, RG 393, Dept.
of the Tenn., Letters Sent. On Sept. 26, Fort sent to Rawlins a list of the boats
available. *O.R.*, I, xxx, part 3, 864–65. On Sept. 28, Fort sent to Rawlins another list of boats at Vicksburg available to carry troops to Memphis. *Ibid.*, p.
908. On the same day, Rawlins wrote to Brig. Gen. John M. Corse. "Since General Shermas dispatch to you, the Quartermaster has reported that a sufficient
number of Boats will be in readiness to embark your Division by 6. O. clock P. M.
to.-day. You will therefore put your Division in motion at once for this place.
Your entire Division should leave here by Wednesday morning." Copies, DLC-
USG, V, 19, 103; DNA, RG 393, Dept. of the Tenn., Letters Sent. *O.R.*, I, xxx,
part 3, 909. On Oct. 2, Col. Lewis B. Parsons, St. Louis, wrote to Rawlins. "I
understand there was some surprise at so many boats being sent to move troops
from Vicksburg to Memphis. It was with extreme regret, I gave orders to Boats to
turn back from Memphis and Cairo, and sent others down from here, as it put
it out of my power to fill requisitions; but the order of Gen'l. Halleck to Gen'l.
Allen was such, that Gen'l. Allen felt; he had no discretion, and ordered me to
send boats, to move from 20 to 25000 men. I have now in my Office, requisitions
for transportation, for over 8000 animals, 600 Wagons, and 5000 tons of freight,
mostly for Gen'l. Banks, and there are scarce boats enough here to perform
our daily requisitions. The great trouble is in the low water, say 4 to 5 feet,
owing to which boats can take but trifling loads." ALS (press), Parsons Papers,
IHi. *O.R.*, I, xxx, part 4, 28.

4. On Oct. 2, Lt. Col. James H. Wilson, Cairo, telegraphed to Col. John
C. Kelton. "I have just arrived here with the dispatches of Genl. Grant dated
Vicksburg 25th, delayed by difficulties & accidents of navigation Can give the
present distribution of our forces Shall wait dispatches for the General."
Telegram received, DNA, RG 107, Telegrams Collected (Bound). *O.R.*, I, xxx,
part 4, 27. On Oct. 3, Wilson twice telegraphed to Kelton, the second time at
5:00 P.M. "Gen Grant directed me to say that the special messengers between
Memphis and Cairo having been discontinued great delays have arisen in transmitting important dispatches. Suggests that hereafter the operators here be
notified when matters of great interest are involved so that the Post Commander
can send an officer with the dispatches. Have just mailed a letter of Genl Grant's
explaining the disposition of troops under the recent orders of Maj. Gen Halleck
and enclosing copies of orders." "On Twenty Second (22d) Sept J E Smiths
Division of the Seventeenth Corps then at Helena was ordered to proceed to
Department of the Cumberland reporting at Memphis for instructions and the
route by which they should march; is now at Memphis and moves at once to
Corinth—On Twenty Third (23d) Osterhaus—15th Corps received the same
order and is now at Corinth The balance of the 15th Corps under Sherman
with exception of one Division to replace Smiths in the 17th follows as soon as
transportation could be obtained Transportation had arrived and was arriving
on the Twenty fifth Genl Hurlbut was ordered on the Twenty Second to send
one Division at least and two if possible on the supposition that they might have
to move through Kentucky, but in case the movement was via Corinth his instructions were to move his entire Corps, leaving the places vacated to be filled
up as far as necessary by troops from elsewhere. Sherman to command the whole
force—Gen Hurlbut has not however made any material alteration in his position.
A J Smith is still at Columbus, his troops at Paducah, Union City, Columbus,
and Fort Pillow—Veatche's Division is at Lebanon and vicinity—Carr at Corinth

and on the Rail Road   Seventeenth Corps at Vicksburg and Natchez—" Telegrams received, DNA, RG 107, Telegrams Collected (Bound). *O.R.*, I, xxx, part 4, 56.

To Col. John C. Kelton

Head Quarters, Dept. of the Tn.
Vicksburg Miss. Sept. 25th/63

COL. J. C. KELTON
WASHINGTON D. C.
COL.

The dispatch of the Gen. in Chief to Maj. Gen. Hurlbut for reinforcements for Rosecrans was received here on the 22d inst. The enclosed are the orders made.[1]

The Division ordered from the 17th Corps is one that had been ordered to further reinforce Gen. Steele's Column. On arriving at Helena dispatches were received from Gen. Steele announcing the retreat of Price, hence their services were not required there.[2] Supposing this Division to be about embarking for their return to this place, and being already far on their way in the direction troops must travel in obedience to the dispatch of the Gen. in Chief, one of my staff was immediately dispatched with orders to turn them Northward. The Division of the 15th Army Corps ordered (Osterhaus) was at Big Black River Bridge. They received their orders in the fore noon of the 22d, all reached here during the night of the same day and embarked and most of them got off on the 23d. What was left of this Division got off yesterday. I would much prefer sending an Army Corps to sending detachment from each. But this could not be done without much delay unless the route to be taken is by Corinth and the 16th Corps is sent. This contingency you will see is provided for in the orders enclosed.

Should detachments from all the Corps of my command go to reinforce the Army of the Cumberland Gen. Sherman will be sent in charge of them.

Gen. Banks is now calling on me for another Division of troops. It will be impossible for me to supply them.

I regret not having a force now to move against Mobile with. I am confident that Mobile could now be taken with a comparatively small force. At least a demonstration in that direction would either result in the abandonment of the city or force the enemy to weaken Braggs Army to hold it. I see by a paper published at Meridian Miss. that Gen. Jo Johnston has been relieved from duty.

There is no Infantry force to my front now except Lorings Division. A portion of the Cavalry has also been withdrawn. Logan & Wirt Adams infest the country from about Rodney to Port Hudson. I shall put my Cavalry in that country in a few days and endeavor to clear them out.[3]

I am just out of bed and find that I can write only with great difficulty. During the twenty days that I have been confined to one position, on my back, I have apparently been in the most perfect health. But now that I am up, on crutches, I find myself very weak.[4]

> Very respectfully
> U. S. GRANT
> Maj. Gen.

ALS, deCoppet Collection, NjP. *O.R.*, I, xxx, part 3, 841.

1. See telegram to Maj. Gen. Henry W. Halleck, Sept. 22, 1863.
2. See letter to Maj. Gen. Stephen A. Hurlbut, July 24, 1863.
3. See telegrams to Maj. Gen. William T. Sherman, Sept. 26, 1863.
4. On Sept. 28, 1863, USG telegraphed to Maj. Gen. Henry W. Halleck. "I am fully able now for field or any other service" Telegram received, DNA, RG 107, Telegrams Collected (Bound); copies, *ibid.*, Telegrams Received in Cipher; *ibid.*, RG 393, Dept. of the Tenn., Hd. Qrs. Correspondence; DLC-USG, V, 6, 8, 24, 94. *O.R.*, I, xxx, part 3, 908.

To Capt. Gilbert A. Pierce

> Head Quarters, Dept. of the Ten.
> Vicksburg Miss. Sept. 25th 1863.

CAPT. PEARCE A. Q. M.
CAPT.

Mrs. Wright has just called representing that our troops on coming to this place rifled her house completely not leaving any of the necessaries for housekeeping. As payment can not be made for articles taken in this way I would direct that if you, or any other Asst. Qr. Mr. have such articles of household goods as she requires, from abandoned or captured property, such articles as Mrs. Wright requires be given to her.

Mrs. Wright also owns a house which I understand is now occupied by Govt. employees. She being a widow, without any member of her family in the Southern Army, this house should be given up to be rented out for her own benefit.

Respectfully &c.

U. S. GRANT.

Maj. Gen. Com

ALS, IHi. Gilbert A. Pierce, born in N. Y. in 1839, moved to Ind. in 1854, enlisted in Co. H, 9th Ind., was appointed capt. and asst. q. m. as of Aug. 3, 1861, and was promoted lt. col. *ex officio* as of Sept. 12, 1863. See *Calendar*, June 12, 1863. By Special Orders No. 263, Sept. 25, Mrs. E. D. Wright was issued "one barrell of Molassess and one barrell of Sugar." Copies, DLC-USG, V, 16, 28.

On Aug. 5, USG telegraphed to Maj. Gen. William T. Sherman. "Where families have been deprived of all their subsistence by our troops, other articles than those specified in orders may be issued at the discretion of Corps commanders. Judge Brian is now here and states, that all the necessaries for comfortable living, including Coffee, have been taken from him by our troops. It is only fair the same articles should be given in return." Copies, *ibid.*, V, 19, 101, 103; DNA, RG 393, Dept. of the Tenn., Letters Sent. On Oct. 3, USG wrote to Brig. Gen. James M. Tuttle. "You will please have the guard placed at Judge Brien's house replaced by a guard from your Division. You will also direct your Com.y to issue to or sell to the Judge the necessary supplies for his family until such time as other arrangements for procuring them can be made." ALS, IaHA.

On Aug. 3, Sherman telegraphed to USG. "Families east of Big Black ask to come to Vicksburg   do you want them   The case now in hand is a Mrs Lightcap who has a daughter there   Now that your town is pretty well clear it might save a world of trouble to keep it so" Telegram received, DNA, RG 94, War Records Office, Dept. of the Tenn.; copy, *ibid.*, RG 393, Dept. of the Tenn., Telegrams Sent. On the same day, USG telegraphed to Sherman. "I do not want families to move into town. When they are divided, a portion in town, and a portion out, they may unite, either by those out coming in, or vice versa." Copies, DLC-USG, V, 19, 101, 103; DNA, RG 393, Dept. of the Tenn., Letters Sent. By Special Orders No. 252, Sept. 14, "Mrs. F. Lightop and Daughter" were furnished public transportation from Vicksburg to New York City "on account of public service." Copies, DLC-USG, V, 16, 28.

On Sept. 28, Brig. Gen. John A. Rawlins issued Special Orders No. 266. "A Military Commission is hereby appointed to meet at Vicksburg Miss. on the first day of October 1863. or as soon thereafter as practicable, to examine into the claims of owners of property in Vicksburg Miss and report their right to possession of the same. The Commission may take the testimony of loyal citizens of this place for the purpose of better ascertaining the true owner ship of property and the character of owners. All property owned by parties of decided disloyalty will be condemned to the use of the United States. That belonging to widows who have no male members of their family in the Southern Army or otherwise assisting the rebellion, will be entitled to be placed in possession of their property, or in case it is necessary for the use of the Government, to receive rent for the same on taking an oath of future loyalty to the Government. All other citizens who can show loyalty to the Government or that they have given neither aid nor countenance to the rebellion voluntarily, or who have voluntarily taken the oath of allegiance to the Government prior to the date of this order and since Federal occupation, will be entitled to the same restoration of property. Detail for the Commission   Brigadier General M D. Loggett U. S. Volunteers   Lieutenant Colonel J H Howe 124 Regiment Illinois Infantry Vols. Captain Chauncey Black 17th Regiment Illinois Infantry Vols." Copies, *ibid*. On Oct. 7, Lt. Col. Theodore S. Bowers wrote to the Commission. "The Commission will condemn property of Disloyal persons without referance to the Confiscation act. The object is to have a record of property in the City that Can be used for Govermnt purposes when necessary without remunerations   even when property is condemd it, does not follow that the present occupant must vacate it unless until the Military authorities require it for Goverment use"   Copy, DNA, RG 393, 17th Army Corps, Claims before Leggett Commission in Vicksburg, Case No. 14. For other cases initiated by petitions addressed to USG and routinely referred to the commission, see *ibid*. Most of these cases involved residences or places of business in Vicksburg. On Oct. 17, however, J. D. O'Leary, cashier, Franklin Bank of Ky., Louisville, wrote to Brig. Gen. Mortimer D. Leggett seeking payment on bonds held by the bank of the Southern (Miss.) Railroad Co. Copy, USG 3. On Oct. 28, Leggett wrote to O'Leary acknowledging that the government used the railroad out as far as Black River but stating that the "commission will only extend its inquiries to such property as may be needed for use of the Government in its occupancy of this Post." LS, *ibid*. On Nov. 11, O'Leary wrote to USG protesting this decision. ALS, *ibid*.

On Oct. 14, R. A. Hill, judge of the probate court, Tishomingo County, Miss., wrote to USG suggesting that a commission be appointed to hear claims of civilians, including widows and minors, whose property had been taken for military purposes and for whom necessities should be provided. ALS, DNA, RG 393, 16th Army Corps, Letters Received. Although forwarded by Col. Patrick E. Burke and Brig. Gen. Grenville M. Dodge on Oct. 19 and 20, this letter apparently did not reach USG. AES, *ibid*.

To Salmon P. Chase

Head Quarters, Dept. of the Ten.
Vicksburg Miss. Sept. 26th 1863.

Hon. S. P. Chase
Sec. of the Treasury,
Washington D. C,
Sir:

Mr. Mellen, Supervising Agt. of the Treasury Dept. for the West, was here a few days since and upon consultation together we agreed upon the following plan for opening trade within this Department, South of Helena; towit: No purchasers of Cotton were to be allowed within the district named. Owners of Cotton, within said district, favorable to the Government, are to be allowed to bring the same in to any Military post or station and on a permit from the Commanding officer, or Provost Marshal, of the post, to ship it to Memphis or New Orleans for sale for their benefit.[1]

To supply the necessaries of life, both provisions & clothing, to persons within our lines, and deserving persons without, on proper permits, I authorized Mr. Mellen to appoint two loyal Citizens for this place, two for Natche[z] and one for Goodriches Landing to keep for sale such articles as were authorized to be sold.[2]

I am now satisfied that this regulation, approved by myself, will, if carried out, lead to a world of trouble and discontent. I believe the only remedy is in total prohibition or free trade in articles not contraband of War. If the latter policy is adopted I will make stringent regulations to prevent improper persons from being benefited by it and enforce such regulations with great upon Merchants who are caught violating such regulations.

By free trade I do not intend to say that persons should be allowed to come into this Department indiscriminately with their wares and set up at any point they please. Trade should be confined to Military Posts or stations. All goods brought should have a

Treasury permit obtained at the place from which the goods are brought, and require that they be taken to a specified place for sale.

Purchasers of Cotton, or other southern products, I would also like to be required to obtain Treasury authority to do so.

Hereafter I will raise no objection to any regulation made by the Treasury Department but will enforce the regulations made to the best of my ability. To establish business within the district named the only enquiry hereafter will be, has Treasury authority been obtained? Should I find that any system adopted works badly I will write you freely on the subject, or inform you through the Supervising Agt. pointing out such defects and make suggestions, if I have any to make, for their correction.

I am thoroughly satisfied that no perfect system can be devised. There is too much corruption in the country for it. Our country, I believe, is not peculiar in this respect. The same spirit has been shown in all countries, in all ages during time of war.

> I have the honor to be
> with great respect
> your obt. svt.
> U. S. GRANT
> Maj. Gen Com

ALS, DNA, RG 56, Letters Received from Executive Officers. *O.R.*, III, iii, 841–42.

On Oct. 1, 1863, U.S. Treasury Agent William P. Mellen, Cincinnati, wrote to Secretary of the Treasury Salmon P. Chase describing the trade district in USG's dept. LS, DNA, RG 366, First Special Agency, Letters Sent (Press). On Oct. 19, Mellen wrote to USG about the Treasury regulations of Sept. 11, asked USG to designate places of trade in his dept., and suggested that trading privileges be limited to U.S. citizens. LS, *ibid.*, RG 393, Military Div. of the Miss., Letters Received. *O.R.*, III, iii, 895–97. Writing to Chase on Oct. 23, Mellen mentioned that he planned to see USG. LS, DNA, RG 366, First Special Agency, Letters Sent (Press). On Oct. 25, having reached Nashville after USG had left for Chattanooga, Mellen again wrote to USG, outlining his understanding of the Treasury regulations and USG's views on the matter, and commenting on the overlapping departmental jurisdictions. "I know that notwithstanding every safeguard abuses will occur. But if the Military and Civil authorities combine harmoniously for the execution of the Regulations in conducting an honest trade by honest men, I shall hope that but little supplies will reach the enemy, or little interference with military operations will occur in the carrying on of the trade so authorized. I will feel very much obliged to you for such suggestions as may from time to time occur to you calculated to correct any abuses which may come to your knowledge, either as to the general system adopted or as to any individuals, officers or traders, acting under it. If you will issue such a general order under which, this system may be faithfully carried out throughout your Department, as you shall think sufficient for the purpose, I will be much obliged to you, and I feel certain that it will do very great good in producing harmony of action between the Civil and Military officers of the Government." ALS, *ibid.*, RG 393, Military Div. of the Miss., Letters Received. *O.R.*, III, iii, 922–23. On Oct. 29, Mellen, Cincinnati, again wrote to Chase about trade in Tenn. and his failure to see USG. "I regret very much that I could not have seen General Grant in order to have had a perfect understanding with him, and such an order as would have insured harmonious action throughout his Department. But I shall do as well as I can untill I can find time to see him." LS, DNA, RG 366, First Special Agency, Letters Sent (Press).

On Nov. 16, Mellen telegraphed to USG. "Did you receive my letter of October twenty-fifth? Do you approve the action proposed therein? Shall I limit the number of stores at Vicksburg, Little Rock, and such places, or authorize any reasonable number asked? Please reply by telegraph, and also write fully, sending me copy order you issue on the subject." ALS (telegram sent), *ibid.*; copy, *ibid.*, RG 393, Military Div. of the Miss., Telegrams Received. On the same day, USG telegraphed to Mellen. "Your letter was received and is approved. I would recommend that all loyal men be put on the same footing, giving as many as desire the privilege of trading" Copies, *ibid.*, RG 56, Div. of Captured and Abandoned Property, Letters Received; *ibid.*, RG 393, Military Div. of the Miss., Letters Sent; DLC-USG, V, 34, 35; CSmH.

USG's dissatisfaction with the system that evolved is apparent in a letter from Mellen to Chase, Feb. 27, 1864. "While at Nashville yesterday I conferred with General Grant about matters of trade in the Department of the Cumberland. Authorities to purchase products at all places within our lines in that Department have been given as provided in the regulations. Under these authorities persons have gone south of Nashville and into Northern Ala, and made purchases. It is charged by General Logan that some of them have gone beyond our lines, and that when acting within them, the whole tendency is mischievous. He therefore ordered them all North of Nashville. General Grant has approved the order. Men now complain as they did down the Mississippi last spring under similar circumstances. They have paid their money and must now lose it they say, and all under authorized officers of the Government. General Grant thinks no trade whatever near the front should be allowed, and that Congress should enact that all the cotton can be bought by the Government and by it only, in the same way as the law approved March 12/63 originally provided. This would prevent all the confusion, and corruption, and dissatisfaction of military men, and it seems to me be generally advantageous." ALS, DNA, RG 56, Div. of Captured and Abandoned Property, Letters Received. On March 5, Chase sent copies of this letter to U.S. Senator Zachariah Chandler and U.S. Representative Elihu B. Washburne, chairmen of the congressional committees on commerce. Copy, *ibid.*, Letters Relating to Restricted Commercial Intercourse.

1. On Sept. 22, 1863, Brig. Gen. John A. Rawlins issued General Orders No. 57. "All actual residents within this Department, well disposed to the Govern-

ment of the United States, will hereafter be permitted to bring into any Military Post or Station on the Mississippi river, Cotton or other Southern products of which they are the bona fide owners, and on the permits of the Military Commander of such Posts or Stations, or the local Provost Marshals thereof, ship the same to Memphis, Tenn., or New Orleans, La., for sale on their own account. All Cotton belonging to the States in rebellion, to the Confederate States or to persons in arms against the United States, will be seized for the benefit of Government and disposed of under existing orders. No person or persons speculating in Cotton will be permitted to remain in this Department South of Helena, Arkansas, and all persons South of the latter place against whom there is, or may be, grounds of suspicion that they are so engaged, either directly or indirectly, will be regarded as unauthorized persons and sent beyond the limits of the Department." Copies, DLC-USG, V, 13, 14; DNA, RG 393, Dept. of the Tenn., General and Special Orders; (printed) USGA. *O.R.* (Navy), I, xxv, 428. These orders were issued in light of Chase's trade regulations of Sept. 11. *HED*, 38-1-6, No. 3, pp. 410–22.

Throughout this period, USG was involved in the cotton claims of individual Southerners. On Aug. 4, he approved the shipment of nine bales of cotton claimed in lieu of wages by Nicholas W. Halligan, former overseer on G. Mallory Davis's plantation, Concordia Parish, La. "Permission is granted to ship the cotton to Mr. Thos. H. Yeatman Agent of the Treasury Dept., to accompany it, & accept the action of the Agent." Copy, DNA, RG 366, First Special Agency, Book Records. On Oct. 2, USG endorsed a letter of Sept. 14 of W. H. Womble, Corinth, Miss., who had lost two bales of cotton while serving as a guide for Maj. Gen. Don Carlos Buell. "The commanding officer Corinth Miss. will turn over to W. H. Womble two bales of cotton from any abandoned or captured cotton that may be in possession of Govt. I remember the circumstances related within. This man did render service to the union forces and whilst doing so his cotton was taken by Govt." Copies, DLC-USG, V, 25; DNA, RG 393, Dept. of the Tenn., Endorsements. Womble had also petitioned USG for this cotton on Feb. 13, providing particulars in the case which USG had requested when Womble saw him the preceding Sept. ALS, *ibid.*, Letters Received. On Oct. 6, Mrs. Susan Bolls, Warren County, Miss., petitioned USG for the replacement of seven bales of cotton seized for fortifications, a claim allowed on Oct. 9. LS, *ibid.*; Special Orders No. 277, Dept. of the Tenn., copies, DLC-USG, V, 16, 28. On Oct. 17, USG signed a report to Secretary of War Edwin M. Stanton regarding the cotton of Mrs. Mary B. Woods and F. Carpenter seized by military authorities at Bolivar, Tenn., in 1862. DS, DNA, RG 107, Letters Received. On Nov. 27, 1862, Maj. Gen. James B. McPherson, La Grange, Tenn., had written to John H. Bills, father of Mrs. Woods, that USG allowed her to retain six bales of cotton for her own use. ALS, *ibid.* She had not, however, retained the cotton or received the proceeds from it. DS (3), *ibid.* On Sept. 8, 1863, former Postmaster General Horatio King, Washington, D. C., had written to Stanton in her behalf, a letter which Rawlins had referred to McPherson on Oct. 1. ES, *ibid.* On Oct. 10, McPherson had reported that USG had given the cotton to Mrs. Woods, whose husband served in the C.S. Army, not as a right but as an act of humanity, to purchase necessities for herself and her children. AES, *ibid.* On Nov. 19, however, William Whiting, solicitor for the War Dept., ruled that there was no appropriation from which the claim could be paid. AES, *ibid.* On Dec. 30, Chase wrote to Treasury Agent Thomas H. Yeatman, Memphis, approving his release to Miss Carrie E.

Martin of three bales of cotton which had been shipped with USG's approval from Vicksburg in early Aug. but seized in Memphis due to the informality of the permit. Copy, *ibid.*, RG 56, Letters Relating to Restricted Commercial Intercourse.

On Oct. 7, Mellen wrote to USG. "I have this day made a contract with Mr. James B. Peabody, to bring out about 550 Bales of Cotton, which he represents as forsaken and abandoned by the owners. I believe Mr Peabody to be truthful in his statement and disposed to do every thing correctly, and if upon your sending any one with him to ascertain exactly the situation of this cotton, you find that he has not made any misrepresentation in the matter, I should be pleased if you would give him every facility you can consistently to aid him in getting it out. I have granted him this contract only to be executed with your full approbation and approval and not in any case without it." LS, *ibid.*, RG 366, First Special Agency, Letters Sent (Press).

2. See letter to William H. H. Taylor, Oct. 6, 1863. On Oct. 12, Brig. Gen. Lorenzo Thomas, Vicksburg, wrote to USG. "I understand that a few individuals will be authorized to open stores at proper places for the sale of goods to plantations, &c. I have a son who lost his all by our own troops in Virginia, who I would like to see in a position where he might have an opportunity of redeeming his losses Natchez I suppose would be one of the positions designated; and may I ask your recommendation for him to Mr. Mellen as one of the persons to operate at that place He is of business habits, and of high moral character. His name is Henry C. Thomas, at present residing in the District of Columbia" ALS, DNA, RG 366, Correspondence of the General Agent. On Oct. 30, USG endorsed this letter. "Respectfully refered to Mr. W. P. Mellen, Supervising Agt. Treas. Dept. I decline making any recommendations whatever for persons to trade within my command but if I was doing anything in that line would most certainly accomodate Gen. Thomas with whom I have had most pleasant official relations." AES, *ibid.* On June 12, 1864, Asst. Secretary of War Charles A. Dana telegraphed to Stanton that USG suspected Thomas's son of being involved in "knavish speculations" at Vicksburg. Telegram received, DLC-Edwin M. Stanton. *O.R.*, I, xxxvi, part 1, 96.

Although trade applications were routinely handled by Treasury agents and district military officials, USG was occasionally involved. On Sept. 19, Samuel L. Casey, Vicksburg, wrote to Mellen. "I find my Brother James with my application and Genl Grants approval I also find a list of good that we want to come down first I think Mr Moore had better buy them in St Louis as we can get them here so much sooner—still Mr Moore can use his discretion in the matter but I think he had better buy the first lot in St Louis—every thing is going on very well—" ALS, DNA, RG 366, Correspondence of the General Agent. On Sept. 24, Rawlins wrote to Casey & Vance, Vicksburg. "Your authority from the Treasury Department only extends to the sale of goods at this place, under such restrictions as the Military authorities may establish, and not to the purchase of Cotton, the receiving of it on Commission, or the shipment of it. You will therefore desist from any further handling of Cotton, either with or without an interest in it within this Military Department from this date." Copies, DLC-USG, V, 19, 103; DNA, RG 393, Dept. of the Tenn., Letters Sent. For a possibly distorted account of the background of this letter, see James Harrison Wilson, *The Life of John A. Rawlins* (New York, 1916), pp. 155–57. On April 6, U.S. Treasury Agent W. D. Gallagher had written to Chase protesting reported permission to purchase cotton given to James F. Casey, USG's brother-in-law. ALS, DNA, RG 36, Special Agents, Reports and Correspondence.

On Oct. 20, W. H. Settle, Louisville, wrote to Mellen. "Your valued favor of 16th inst came duly to hand. I had an interview with Genl Grant yesterday in regard to opening trade at Osceola Ark. He informed me the matter was altogether with the Treasury Department—That if it choose to open trade at that point he had no objection—I told him what you had said about its being under his jurisdiction—He said if you required the sanction of the Military authority, I might apply to Genl Hurlburt. Genl Grant, also in the same interview, informed me that there would be two trade stores allowed at Natchez. He could not tell whether they had been authorized yet by you, but stated, the application for that purpose would also have to be made to the Treasury Department, as he did not wish to interfere at all. The Genl states that he exercises the same control in his old Department that he always has—Now if there is a vacancy at Natchez nothing could please me better than to get it   I have spent an entire year trying to get a trading privilege below, and have obtained several, without ever being permitted to ship a dollars worth of goods, as some New Order would come out just about the time I would get to market to make my purchases. I most respectfully submit my claims for a place at Natchez and in case that point is filled, then I must stand for Osceola. If anything further is necessary for me to do, in expediting, matters, please be so good as to point it out. Hoping to hear from you at any early day . . . Vicksburg would likewise be a most acceptable point" ALS, *ibid.*, RG 366, Correspondence of the General Agent.

On Nov. 28, M. M. Yeakle, Memphis, wrote to Mellen applying for a permit to open a store at Little Rock, Ark. ". . . having received from Maj. Genl. F. Steele, Commdg. U. S. Forces in Arkansas, his reccommendation (on file in Office of Geo. N. Carleton Esq.) of myself for such appointment, he having reccommended me to your Department on the reccommendation of Maj. Gen. U. S. Grant, and Maj. Genl. S. A. Hurlbut. . . ." ALS, *ibid.*

On Dec. 22, USG, Nashville, telegraphed to Maj. Gen. George H. Thomas, Chattanooga. "Post and other commanders are giving trade permits so says the Treasury Agent for carrying goods to points in this state where trade has not been established   There is also a Capt Mills who seems to exercise the functions of inspector to pass such goods as he thinks proper & in violation of law." Copies, *ibid.*, RG 393, Dept. of the Cumberland, Telegrams Received; *ibid.*, Military Div. of the Miss., Letters Sent; DLC-USG, V, 34, 35.

To Maj. Gen. William T. Sherman

Vicksburg Miss Sept 28th [*26*] 1863

MAJ GENL. W. T SHERMAN

I am told that there is a small camp of rebel cavalry near Burton,[1] committing depredations. Have you got three or four hundred fresh cavalry to send in there, rapidly to try and pick them up. I think they should start in the afternoon, and travel at night so as to come upon them early in the morning. They might then go down to Yazoo City and return by way of Satartia.

U. S. GRANT Maj Genl.

Telegram, copies, DLC-USG, V, 19, 103; DNA, RG 393, Dept. of the Tenn., Letters Sent. *O.R.*, I, xxx, part 3, 866. On Sept. 26, 1863, Maj. Gen. William T. Sherman twice telegraphed to USG. "I have the Cavalry and can send it out. The Cavalry back of Yazoo City is not in Camp. Their Camp is near Vernon east of Black River, and they are engaged in getting Cattle from the Yazoo. I doubt if we can catch them but I will try tomorrow afternoon" Copy, DNA, RG 393, Dept. of the Tenn., Telegrams Sent. *O.R.*, I, xxx, part 3, 866. "In preparing orders & instructions for Col. Winslow for the movement of cavalry it seems to me that the risk of sending only four hundred (400) cavalry above Vernon exceeds the advantantages to be expected   Vernon is the head quarters of a brigade of confederate cavalry & should our party pass up as high as Benton & return would be intercepted from Vernon unless the movements were covered by Infantry   would it not be better to send a large force around by Browsville Vernon & Benton with an infantry force as far out as Brownsville   I am satisfied Crosby can assemble One thousand (1000) Confederate cavalry at Vernon in twenty four (24) hours" Telegram received, DNA, RG 94, War Records Office, Dept. of the Tenn.; copy, *ibid.*, RG 393, Dept. of the Tenn., Telegrams Sent. *O.R.*, I, xxx, part 3, 867. See following telegram.

1. Benton, Miss.

To Maj. Gen. William T. Sherman

Vicksburg Miss Sept 26th 1863

MAJ GEN'L. W. T. SHERMAN

I was not aware that Vernon was the Head Quarters of a Cavalry Division. You may send a Brigade of Infantry as you propose, or as much of it as you deem necessary, and all the Cavalry that can be spared and see if we cannot break up their present Cavalry arrangement. The rebels have at present a small force over on Silver Creek collecting cattle and negroes & burning cotton. They might be intercepted, and this stock taken from them; by going down to Yazoo City and returning by the river route. You have studied the Geography of the route to be traversed more than I have, and can give the specific directions.

U. S. GRANT Maj Gen'l.

Telegram, copies, DLC-USG, V, 19, 103; DNA, RG 393, Dept. of the Tenn.,

Letters Sent. *O.R.*, I, xxx, part 3, 866. See preceding telegram. On Sept. 26, 1863, Maj. Gen. William T. Sherman telegraphed three times to USG. "I will start in the 2d Division tomorrow, and organize the Cavalry and some Infantry of the reserve Division to clean out the Enemy near Vernon and Benton to start to morrow" Telegram received, DNA, RG 94, War Records Office, Dept. of the Tenn.; copy, *ibid.*, RG 393, Dept. of the Tenn., Telegrams Sent. *O.R.*, I, xxx, part 3, 867. "Genl. McPherson has been out with me all day He is just starting back We have arranged all things & I am now ready to move I will undertake to put my men on board as fast as boats are provided in giving notice remember that we have twenty miles to march" Telegram received, DNA, RG 94, War Records Office, Dept. of the Tenn.; copy, *ibid.*, RG 393, Dept. of the Tenn., Telegrams Sent. *O.R.*, I, xxx, part 3, 868. "My aid Capt McCoy just arrived says there are eleven boats at Vicksburg & more close at hand when do you want my two Divs. to march in for embarkation I understand they are not to march until I am notified from your HdQrs I am embarrassed to embark those two Divisions & at the same time to send out the expedition to the Northeast which should be done & if the steamboats are there we ought to be in motion" Telegram received, DNA, RG 94, War Records Office, Dept. of the Tenn.; copy, *ibid.*, RG 393, Dept. of the Tenn., Telegrams Sent. *O.R.*, I, xxx, part 3, 865. See Sherman's orders for the expedition to Yazoo City, Miss., Sept. 26. *O.R.*, I, xxx, part 3, 869. See also telegram to Maj. Gen. Henry W. Halleck, Sept. 25, 1863, note 3. On Sept. 26, USG telegraphed to Sherman. "There are Steamers enough here now and to arrive by the time your command could march in, to take the whole of them, but the difficulties of obtaining fuel, are such, that not more than one Division can be got off now. One Division may be started in tomorrow, and the other, on further notice from here. Will not two Regiments of Infantry from the Division intended to be left, be sufficient to go with the Cavalry." Copies, DLC-USG, V, 19, 103; DNA, RG 393, Dept. of the Tenn., Letters Sent. *O.R.*, I, xxx, part 3, 865.

On Sept. 27, Sherman twice telegraphed to Brig. Gen. John A. Rawlins. "My second Division is now marching & the last Reg of it can embark by (9) nine A m tomorrow I will go to Memphis with with this division & be in town during the night the 4th Div. can start at a moments notice One Brig of it will march out to Brownsville to cover the Cavaly movement which strike Vernon tomorrow moring I will also send up two Regts of Infy from Oak Ridge to Mechanicsburg to receive the Cavalry on its way in I will move my HdQrs tonight & go at once on board" Telegram received, DNA, RG 94, War Records Office, Dept. of the Tenn.; copy, *ibid.*, RG 393, Dept. of the Tenn., Telegrams Sent. *O.R.*, I, xxx, part 3, 884. "Every thing is now done which should be done here The Expedition for Brownsville Vernon Benton & Yazoo City have gone out The Brigade of Infantry at noon & cavalry one thousand men at 3 P M The flag of truce is not back. Gen Tuttle has moved to my Hd Quarters. The 2d Division is all gone & the 4th is ready to start at a moments notice. I shall now start for Vicksburg & report in person early in the morning prepared to go to Memphis. All is well out here" Telegram received, DNA, RG 94, War Records Office, Dept. of the Tenn. *O.R.*, I, xxx, part 3, 884. See letter to Maj. Gen. William T. Sherman, Sept. 30, 1863. On the same day, Sherman telegraphed to USG, probably referring to USG's five-year-old son Jesse. "Giles Smiths Div. marched at daylight this A M & are doubtless in possesson of many cows I know that nearly all their hospitals had cows write a note to Genl Giles Smith saying your boy is sick & needs milk & send it to him as he comes into Vicksburg & he will surely find one in his column   I doubt not the head of his column will enter Vicksburg by 4 P M   Should you not get one by 5 P M telegraph me & I will have my camp scoured & confiscate one for you   cows in all this region have been used as beef or are in possession of the Regt hospitals"   Telegram received, DNA, RG 94, War Records Office, Dept. of the Tenn.; copy, *ibid.*, RG 393, Dept. of the Tenn., Telegrams Sent. *O.R.*, I, xxx, part 3, 883. On Sept. 29, USG wrote to Absalom H. Markland, special agent of the Post Office Dept. "Having exhausted every other resource for procuring a cow I now send to you to get one of those at the Qr. Mr. & Com.y's quarters" ALS (facsimile), Frank A. Burr, *Life and Deeds of General Ulysses S. Grant.* . . . (Philadelphia, 1885), p. 411. See letter to Absalom H. Markland, Feb. 13, 1862.

To Abraham Lincoln

Head Quarters, Dept. of the Ten.
Vicksburg Miss. Sept. 28th 1863

HIS EXCELLENCY, A. LINCOLN
PRESIDENT OF THE UNITED STATES,
SIR:

Permit me to recommend for an appointment at large, to West Point, John B. R. Hoff of Albany N. Y.

This young man is now sixteen years of age. His father is a surgeon of Volunteers with this army and one of the most worthy of his profession. He has been for many months in direct charge of one of the Hospital Boats used in tranfering sick from the camps to Northern Hospitals and has general charge over all boats so used. In this capacity Surgeon Hoff has won for himself golden opinions both from officers of his own profession and from all who have had the misfortune to require his aid.

I do not know the young man for whos benefit this application is made, but the father is highly deserving of the compliment which he would regard as being paid him if this appointment was given to his son.

I have the honor to be
Your very respectful
& obt. svt.
U. S. GRANT
Maj. Gen. U. S. A.

ALS, DNA, RG 94, Cadet Applications. On April 8, 1864, USG endorsed a letter of March 23 from Surgeon Alexander H. Hoff, New York City, asking USG
to inquire regarding the application of his son John V. R. Hoff to USMA. "Respectfully forwarded to the Sec. of War. Dr. Hoff has been one of our most valuable surgeons. I have previously recommended his son for an appointment to
West Point and unless these appointments are confined to young soldiers in the
Army should like to see him get it." AES, *ibid*. In 1874, the younger Hoff began
a career as army surgeon.

To Commanding Officer, Cairo

Vicksburg Miss Sept 28th 1863

Com'dg Officer Cairo Illinois

Direct the Post Quarter Master at Cairo, to call upon the United
States Sanitary Agent, at your place, and see exactly what building
they require to be erected for their charitable and humane purposes.
The Commission has been of such great service to the country, and
at Cairo are doing so much for this army at this time, that I am
disposed to extend their facilities for doing good, in every way in
my power. You will therefore cause to be put up at Government
expense, suitable buildings for the Sanitary Commission, connecting those they already have, and also put up for them necessary
out buildings

In doing this work, all economy should be observed, bearing
in mind that these buildings are not likely to be required for any
great length of time for public service, and when no longer required, will revert to the owner of the land on which they are built.
If the barracks erected in 1861, have not been disposed of, material
can be taken from them, to put up the necessary buildings.

U. S. Grant Maj Gen'l

Copies, DLC-USG, V, 19, 103; DNA, RG 393, Dept. of the Tenn., Letters Sent.
On Sept. 16, 1863, Chauncey N. Shipman, sanitary agent, Cairo, wrote to
Surgeon Henry S. Hewit, Vicksburg, urging that the government construct a
new building, "about 60 by 75 ft, two stories," adjacent to two other buildings
adapted for the Sanitary Commission's use. ALS, *ibid*., Letters Received. For
USG's undated special orders to carry out the earlier plan to expand the Soldiers'
Home at Cairo, see J. S. Newberry, *The U. S. Sanitary Commission in the Valley
of the Mississippi* . . . (Cleveland, 1871), p. 390. On Oct. 7, Col. William F.

Lynch, Cairo, wrote to USG. "Your communication relative to the erection of buildings for Sanitary commission at this Post is received—Your instructions have been complied with" Copy, DNA, RG 393, Dept. of Ky., Letters Sent, Cairo.

On July 25, Lt. Col. John A. Rawlins endorsed a letter of the same day from A. W. Plattenburg, sanitary agent, Vicksburg, stating that a house intended for the Sanitary Commission's use was otherwise occupied. "Respectfully referred to Lieut Col. J. D. Bingham, Chief Quartermaster for report. If the building was assigned for a 'Soldiers Home' as herein stated; it should be turned to Mr Plattenburg at once." Copies, DLC-USG, V, 25; DNA, RG 393, Dept. of the Tenn., Endorsements. On Aug. 4, Plattenburg wrote to USG requesting a detail of three men at the Soldiers' Home. ALS, *ibid.*, Miscellaneous Letters Received. On Aug. 6, USG endorsed a letter of the same date from Brig. Gen. John E. Smith to Maj. Theodore S. Bowers regarding a dispute between Smith, who required a building in Vicksburg for a soldiers' home, and the medical director, who wanted the same building for a hospital. "Refered to Gen. McPherson who is authorized to examine the merits of this case and settle it in his own way. It is singular that no town can be found in the Southern country sufficiently capacious to supply the wants of the Medical and Staff Departments. There has been difficulties every place I have yet been from Corinth to Vicksburg. I am almost begining to doubt the propriety of allowing the use of any house, other than temporary structures put up by the Army itself, for any purpose whatever. When I was spoken to about the house in question as a place suitable for the 'soldiers Home' I certainly understood that it was not being used for any other purpose. I now as distinctly understand that it has been all the time used as a Hospital. A proper decission I suppose would rest entirely upon which of these statements prove to be the fact." AES, Ritzman Collection, Aurora College, Aurora, Ill. On Sept. 13 and 14, Robert K. Foster, superintendent, Vicksburg Soldiers' Home, wrote to USG regarding another detail of three men. ALS, DNA, RG 393, Dept. of the Tenn., Miscellaneous Letters Received.

To Maj. Gen. Henry W. Halleck

Head Quarters, Dept. of the Ten.
Vicksburg Miss. Sept. 30th 1863.

MAJ. GEN. H. W. HALLECK,
GEN. IN CHIEF, WASHINGTON D. C.
GENERAL.

I regret that there should be such apparent tardiness in complying with your orders. But I assure you that as soon as your wishes were known troops were forwarded as rapidly as transportation could be procured. As previously reported your dispatches of the 13th were not received for several days after those of the 15th. The latter did not explain your wishes further than that you wanted Rosecrans reinforced with all my available forces, leaving the Mississippi Valley secure. Although the troops sent under the dispatches of the 15th were fifteen miles off most of them were embarked within twenty-four hours of the receipt of the order, and all of them were sailing up the river within forty-eight hours. The receipt of your dispatches of the 13th explained everything and Sherman was immediately ordered up the river with the remainder of his Corps, substituting one Division of the 17th Corps, already forwarded to Memphis, for one here. This reduces me to the smallest possible number for holding this ~~this~~ Valley.

There is to my front now four Brigades of Cavalry with at least twenty pieces of Artillery that I know of. The Brigades are commanded as follows. Cosby,[1] Whitfield, Logan & Chalmers. S. D. Lee commands the whole.

A letter just received from Hurlbut states that he can send but one Brigade from his Corps.[2] An Inspection Report. of the 20th of August shows him to have over 23 000 well men for duty exclusive of Extra Duty men. From this he should spare at least 8000 men and a large portion of Artillery. Gen. Hurlbut's letter seems to ignore my orders to him and show an evident inclination to set up a sort of independent command receiving orders only from Washington. He passes over my orders to him quietly and tells me that he will send Prentiss in command of forces going Eastward.

All I believe is now moving according to your wishs. I have about 10.500 men to hold the river from here to Bayou Sara. This is exclusive of colored troops mostly used in guarding the West Bank of the river with the special view of protecting the leased plantations. Citizens of the country, in various parts, express great anxiety to have our troops among them. I have received applications to send troops to Monroe to hold the place with the assurance that we should be supplied with beef & corn for nothing. There has also been application made to send troops to Yazoo City. I will not, of course, scatter my forces having already few enough at the points, Vicksburg & Natchez, necessary to hold.

I have heard nothing recently from Steele's Expedition nor do I learn much of the movements of the enemy West of the river.[3]

I regret that I have not got a movable force with which to attack Mobile, or the river above. As I am situated however I must be content with guarding territory already taken from the enemy. I do not say this complainingly but simply regret that advantage cannot be taken of so fine an opportunity of dealing the enemy a heavy blow.

> I am Gen. very respectfully
> your obt. svt.
> U. S. GRANT
> Maj. Gen.

ALS, DNA, RG 94, War Records Office, Dept. of the Tenn. *O.R.*, I, xxx, part 3, 944. On Oct. 11, 1863, Maj. Gen. Henry W. Halleck wrote to USG. "Yours of Sept 30th is just received. Although the reinforcements from your army for Genl Rosecrans did not move as soon or as rapidly as was expected, no blame whatever attaches to you. I know your promptness too well to think for a moment that the delay was any fault of yours. In regard to Genl Hurlbut, I have given no orders to him except when the urgency of the case was great and he could not communicate with you. He may have ref[erred] matters here, when he could have consulted you, but I think he did so from no improper motives. It takes a long time for civilians to learn & practice strict military subordination. I regret equally with yourself that you could not have forces to move on Mobile; but there were certain reasons, which I cannot now explain which precluded such an attempt. You need not fear being left idle. The moment you are well enough to take the field you will have abundant occupation. I hope to soon hear of your arrival at Cairo, as directed through Col Wilson of your staff." LS, DNA, RG 108, Letters Sent (Press); copies, *ibid.*, RG 393, Dept. of the Tenn., Hd. Qrs. Correspondence; DLC-USG, V, 6, 8, 24, 94. *O.R.*, I, xxx, part 4, 274. See General Orders No. 61, Oct. 10, 1863.

1. George B. Cosby, born in Ky., USMA 1852, resigned as capt., 2nd Cav., on May 10, 1861, becoming a C.S.A. cav. capt. As a staff maj., he carried C.S.A. Brig. Gen. Simon B. Buckner's letter to USG opening negotiations for the surrender of Fort Donelson. Cosby was promoted to brig. gen. as of Jan. 20, 1863, and commanded a cav. brigade in the C.S.A. attempt to relieve Vicksburg.

2. On Sept. 27, Maj. Gen. Stephen A. Hurlbut, Memphis, had written to Brig. Gen. John A. Rawlins. "I send you the correspondence between myself & the Genl in Chief. Like every thing else connected with the River this correspondence has been delayed. It is evident that the Genl in Chief does not expect the troops forced forward beyond our reachs into Middle Tennessee & that he did expect that Sherman's Corps was to be moved up. If I correctly understand the nature of things in the Army of the Cumberland, the extreme urgency of the case has passed. An accumulation of force from East & West was suddenly thrown upon Rosecrans to destroy his Army thence intended to strike with like effect & the same purpose on Burnside. Genl. Thomas by his heroic resistance has saved the Army of the Cumberland from actual destruction & the enemy are too severely

crippled to pursue the advantages gained. Burnside has probably joined before this and is safe. Meade is moving on Richmond & the Eastern force must return and that rapidly to save the Capital. Rosecrans should be reinforced to enable him to profit by the reflux of this tide. The movement was a dash & has failed. Osterhaus has reported to me to day & moves out to & beyond Corinth tomorrow by Rail. John E Smith will be up to morrow. In four days these Divisions will be in readiness to move wherever directed. My entire Corps is to day ready to move. I have only two Divisions of Infantry excluding Colored Troops on this line, & cannot in my judgment spare more than one Brigade (four Regiments) — I am very strong in artillery & have now 4500 cavalry. The line cannot be abandoned & it is far easier to send ~~new~~ troops to the Country through than to relieve these on guard. I am perfectly willing & ready to go, but unless ordered so to do, do not propose to leave my own Army Corps & assume command of strange & fragmentary troops, when the good of the service will be promoted as well by putting them under command of a Maj. Genl.   Prentiss is here & if the troops move at all I shall assign him to command. The expedition as prepared will consist of Osterhaus Divn—John E Smiths Division & Bane's Brigade from Corinth consisting of about 9000 Infantry. If relief is given by proper officers & command to hold Memphis & its line & I can take my own Command as it stands I am ready to move with 11,000 Infantry & 4500 Cavalry leaving to my successor whoever he may be 1500 Cavalry & the Negro Regiments say 4,000. I dare not leave this line until adequate force is provided to hold it. The Maj. Genl thinks I can spare one or *two Divisions*   I have but *two*. I still insist that a Corps established East & South of Corinth will cover Vicksburgh better than at the Big Black, and will give a better hold for future movements. In any event I shall have here when Osterhaus & Smith are fully in place 12,000 disposable men to be moved wherever the exigency of the service demands and will await orders from the Commander in Chief to whom I report the substance of the above. The Route proposed for the Troops to Rosecrans is to Tuscumbia—thence crossing the Tennessee by Jackson's ford near Florence through Athens to Fayetteville & Decherd. If I take my Corps complete I shall move by Huntsville to Stevenson keeping nearer the River than with a smaller force. Smith's Division reports only 2000 men. I send the substance of this to Maj Genl Halleck by Telegraph from Cairo & wait his orders"   ALS, DNA, RG 393, Dept. of the Tenn., Letters Received. *O.R.*, I, xxx, part 3, 888–89. On Sept. 29, Hurlbut wrote to Rawlins. "I have waited to the last moment that I might send the very latest dispatches but none come. The River above is so low as very seriously to impede navigation. Osterhaus' Division is moving by Rail to Corinth & will get through by to night or tomorrow. I have filled all his requisitions & he is in order for the field. Jno. E. Smiths Division comes up without Camp or Garrison Equipage—Shelter Tents or Blankets, all of which he informs me are below. I hold them near Memphis until these necessaries are supplied. I have a heavy supply and ordnance train organized, and ready to move whenever directed. It is manifestly of no special advantage to move now unless it be to cover Nashville & the communications. At all events as I understand Genl Hallecks wishes we are to hold on until ordered. I dislike to throw troops from this line to Rosecrans because they will be lost forever. Nothing returns from the Cumberland Army. If not ordered off I shall move in a few days to Columbus Miss & thence or rather under cover of that move, send Spencer with the Alabama Cavalry to Montgomery to destroy the Montgomery & West Point Road & the steamers between Selma & Montgomery. This is all prepared for if we are not ordered away. Lee is raising quite a force from

Columbus to Grenada & needs breaking up. I shall smash him effectually when we go on the Columbus Expedition" ALS, DNA, RG 393, Dept. of the Tenn., Letters Received. *O.R.*, I, xxx, part 3, 924.

3. On Sept. 28, Halleck sent to USG a memorandum based on C.S.A. dispatches, Aug. 1–18, regarding enemy activities and plans west of the Mississippi River. DS, Schoff Collection, MiU-C. *O.R.*, I, xxx, part 3, 908–9. Copies of this memorandum went to Maj. Gen. Nathaniel P. Banks and to Maj. Gen. Frederick Steele. *Ibid.*, I, xxii, part 2, 578–79; *ibid.*, I, xxvi, part 1, 739–40.

To Maj. Gen. William T. Sherman

Vicksburg Miss Sept 30th 1863.

MAJ GEN'L. W. T. SHERMAN

The Flag of truce has returned,[1] and gives the following summary of news. Genl Rosecrans still occupies Chattanooga, Longstreet Lookout Mountain twelve miles South. Longstreet advanced on Sunday morning but was repulsed. Burnside was coming up, but with what force not known. Our loss was fifty four peices of artillery and from 15 to 20. thousand men killed wounded and missing. Rebels loss about the same. We lost one Genl. Lytle killed & Hood lost a leg, and since reported dead. Rebels lost five or six Generals killed, among them Generals Smith, Helm, Adams, Brown and Gregg, killed. Breckenridge is reported mortally wounded.[2] Johnson received Col Coolbaugh at his quarters in Canton, and communications freely given, his last dispatch which to 8. O clock 28th inst. as he received it. He claims a great victory but says the loss on both sides was great, and about equal. Thus they have no advantage in that respect. Their Papers claim that Wheeler is to the rear of Rosecrans, but Johnson does not know this to be a fact. A large force went out on the 28th to meet ours, sent out by you, Corby [*Cosby*] undertook to cut ours off, but was repulsed and sent for reinforcements. Jackson afterwards joined him. Our forces are not yet in but I presume are all safe.[3] The Brigade sent east stampeded the enemy completely causing them to send their wagon train back to Pearl River in great disorder. A letter just received from General Hurlbut shows, that he can send you a much less force, than I had expected.[4] What troops you have are good however, and will be a powerful reinforcement to any army. I will send you with this a Southern Paper of the 27th   You will see that it gives a more favorable Southern view than is contained in this summary, this is to be expected however. No doubt Johnsons account will prove the most correct.

I hope you will be in time to aid in giving the rebels the worst or best thrashing they have had in this war. I have constantly had the feeling that I shall leave you from this command entirely. Of course I do not object to seeing your sphere of usefulness enlarged and think it should have been enlarged long ago, having an eye to the public good alone. But it needs no assurance from me General that taking a more selfish view, while I would heartily approve such a change, I would deeply regret it on my own account. I have no intentions in the world upon which to base the idea of such a change, as is referred to being made, except my own feeling. I may be wrong and judge Rosecrans from rather a prejudical view instead of impartially as I would like, and try to do. The last of Smiths Division will be off this evening if the boats get their fuel. I have it seriously in contemplation to keep Smith here, to take Tuttles command, and send Tuttle to command some Post in West Tennessee. I will make up my mind on this point before evening.[5]

U. S. GRANT, Maj Gen'l

Copies, DLC-USG, V, 19, 103; DNA, RG 393, Dept. of the Tenn., Letters Sent. *O.R.*, I, xxx, part 3, 945.

1. Carried by George Coolbaugh. See telegram to Maj. Gen. Henry W. Halleck, Sept. 25, 1863, note 3.
2. Brig. Gen. William H. Lytle was mortally wounded Sept. 19, 1863, during the battle of Chickamauga. During the same battle, C.S.A. Maj. Gen. John B. Hood was severely wounded, losing a leg; Brig. Gen. Preston Smith died of wounds on Sept. 19; Brig. Gen. Benjamin H. Helm was wounded Sept. 19, and died the next day; on Sept. 20, Brig. Gen. Daniel W. Adams was wounded and captured; Brig. Gen. John C. Brown was slightly wounded; Brig. Gen. John Gregg was severely wounded; Maj. Gen. John C. Breckinridge was unharmed.
3. For the expedition to Yazoo City, Miss., Sept. 27–Oct. 1, see telegrams to Maj. Gen. William T. Sherman, Sept. 26, 1863, and Col. Edward F. Winslow's report, *O.R.*, I, xxx, part 2, 660–61.
4. See preceding telegram, note 2.
5. For the moment, Brig. Gen. James M. Tuttle remained in command on the Big Black River. See *O.R.*, I, xxx, part 3, 868–69.

To Brig. Gen. John P. Hawkins

Head Quarters, Dept. of the Ten,
Vicksburg Miss. Oct. 2d 1863,

BRIG. GEN. J. H. HAWKINS
COMD.G DIST N. E. LA,
GEN.

The small force now left here is so occupied with details for unloading boats, guarding an extended line, policing the city &c. that it is impossible to furnish a sufficient force for work on the fortifications. If you can furnish one regiment at a time from your command, detailing them for one week at a time, without detriment to the service it would help out very much.

I do not wish to order this not knowing how well able you may be to spare the troops. If they can come I want the first detail made on Monday next details to be relieved each Monday thereafter.

Please inform me if they can be sent and if so a boat will be sent for them.

Very respectfully
U. S. GRANT
Maj. Gen. Com

ALS, DNA, RG 393, District of Northeastern La., Letters Received. *O.R.*, I, xxx, part 4, 28. On Oct. 4, 1863, Brig. Gen. John P. Hawkins, commanding the District of Northeastern La., Goodrich's Landing, La., replied to USG. "I have the honor to acknowledge the receipt of your letter of 2d inst, come to hand to-night. As soon as you can send a boat up here a Regt will be ready to go to Vicksburg according to your wishes, Much time will be taken in travelling, perhaps it would be better to retain the Regt ten days. I respectfully request that whoever has them in charge for work will use towards them the same treatment as would be shown white soldiers" ALS, DNA, RG 94, War Records Office, Dept. of the Tenn.

On Oct. 2, Brig. Gen. Lorenzo Thomas, Goodrich's Landing, wrote to USG. "The time is approaching when the plantations on this side of the river held by the government will have to be re-leased. It is important that the two cuts, one at Lake Providence (the most important) and the other known as the Bissell cut, should be filled up, as otherwise a large district of country will, on the next rise of the river, be overflowed; including not only the government plantations but also that part of the parish over which the railroad running from opposite Vicksburg passes. As I have no funds at my command to do this work I request that you will authorise the stationing of some one of the negro regiments now at this place at Lake Providence, as well to fill up that cut as to give protection to lessees of plantations in that neighborhood in gathering their crops. It is estimated that five hundred men will complete the work in ten days after they shall have fairly commenced. If this is done I request that the necessary spades, wheelbarrows, gang planks, and other utensils be furnished. After the completion of the work at Lake Providence the same body of men can be taken to the Bissell cut—" ALS, *ibid.*, 17th Army Corps. *O.R.*, I, xxx, part 4, 27. On Oct. 30, Capt. Ely S. Parker referred this letter to Maj. Gen. William T. Sherman. AES, DNA, RG 94, War Records Office, 17th Army Corps. *O.R.*, I, xxx, part 4, 27–28. On Oct. 8, Hawkins wrote to Brig. Gen. John A. Rawlins. "I would respectfully request that the following changes of troops be made   viz Col. W. F. Woods' 1st Ark. Vols (Colored) to be ordered to Helena Ark.   The Missouri Regt of Colored troops, (The Colored troops sent from St Louis to Helena) to be ordered from Helena to Goodrichs Landing. The 1st Ark was raised at Helena and have left behind them their wives and children and naturally they are very anxious about them as to how they are getting on. If their husbands can be near their families they will do a great deal towards taking care of them and thus relieve the Gov,ment of their support. I think it would be a matter of humanity to let this change be made. The Missouri Regiment has or should have no local attachments there. If the change can be ordered, it would be better the 1st Ark did not leave here till the arrival of the 1st Mo. . . . I have spoken to Genl Thomas on the subject, who says he has no plans involved in the stay of the Regt at Helena." ALS, DNA, RG 393, 17th Army Corps, Letters Received. Parker referred this letter to Sherman on Oct. 30. ES, *ibid.* On Nov. 2, Parker endorsed another letter from Hawkins in regard to filling up the canal at Lake Providence and repair of levees. "Respectfully returned to Maj. Genl. McPherson. No military authorities are permitted to engage in repairing or working upon any of the levees of the Mississippi." Copies, *ibid.*, Military Div. of the Miss., Endorsements; DLC-USG, V, 39. See second telegram to Maj. Gen. Henry W. Halleck, Oct. 27, 1863.

On Oct. 9, Hawkins wrote to Rawlins. "A nice and peculiar question has come up in this District as to the rights of a Negro, coming into our lines from the country occupied by the enemy, to the property he may bring with him, such as mules oxen or wagons. When the case has been brought up before me I have decided the right of property in favor of the Negro. President Lincoln's Proclamation gives legal freedom to the slaves. The masters in the lines of the enemy deprive them of this right and attempt to hold them contrary to law; I hold it no crime that the slave should attempt to escape this wrong and in so doing has a right to make use of the facilities that might assist him in his escape by taking horse, mule or any thing else of his masters that might help him to get away. We have a distinguised precedent for this when the children of Israel went out fugitive slaves from the Egyptians. Again, I think the negro should hold the property as his own, which he has secured by his energy and effort, and that it is a very small thing on the part of a Government, that should be magnanimous towards such persons to take it away from him. By letting the property remain in their possession, they will be enabled next year to cultivate a few acres of ground and the Government be relieved of their support. By taking it away they or their families are made paupers for perhaps all time to come. The immediate gain to government by the seizure is very small, compared to with the great loss to them. As the wealth of a government consists in the prosperity of its Citizens, and as these people have been declared citizens of the United States nothing is gained to government by interfering with the individual prosperity of any one of them. Many of them now use their property to make a living. When planting season comes they will be able to do a great deal better; if they have half a chance. I am willing to run this District without instructions, without troubling the Dept. Commander on delicate questions that may arise, and would not write now only that Genl. Thomas intends to refer the matter to Dept. Hd Qrs. for decision, and I wished to present my views of the question." LS, DNA, RG 393, Dept. of the Tenn., District of Northeastern La., Letters Sent. On Oct. 30, Parker referred this letter to Sherman. Copies, *ibid.*, Military Div. of the Miss., Endorsements; DLC-USG, V, 39.

To Maj. Gen. Nathaniel P. Banks

Head Quarters, Dept. of the Tn.
Vicksburg Miss. Oct. 3d 1863.

MAJ. GEN. N. P. BANKS,
COMD.G DEPT. OF THE GULF,
GEN.

I regret that recent events in Northern Georgia and consequent orders to me from Hd Qrs. of the Army, prevents me entirely from keeping any portion of my promises to you in regard to furnishing you with further aid. I am left in a condition that I cannot even send the cavalry force which I intended to clear out the country between the Miss. River & the New Orleans & Jackson Road, as far South as Port Hudson. The Brig. which I ordered from West Ten. never came, but in lieu of it Gen. Hurlbut sent parts of three regts. numbering about 1000 men. I have sent to Rosecrans aid an entire Army Corps, from here, and part of the 16th from West Ten. This leaves me a force of little over 16000 men, of all arms, to guard the whole country from Helena to your lines. I have in my immediate front four Brigades of rebel Cavalry that I know of, and some twenty, or more pieces of Artillery. I assure you Gen. this is no less a disappointment to you than to me. I was anxious to give you the aid to make your expedition a certain success. By my orders from Washington were preemptory to send every man I could East from Corinth. I informed the Gen. in Chief that you had made a call upon me to furnish one Division more[1] but received no reply.

I am very glad to say that I have so far recovered from my injuries as to be able to move about on crutches. It will probably be some time yet before I will entirely recover.

> I am Gen. very respectfully
> your obt. svt.
> U. S. GRANT
> Maj. Gen. Com

ALS, DNA, RG 393, Dept. of the Gulf, Letters Received. *O.R.*, I, xxvi, part 1, 752–53; *ibid.*, I, xxx, part 4, 50–51.

On Sept. 29, 1863, Maj. Gen. Henry W. Halleck telegraphed to USG. "Genl Banks has made requisition on Quarter Dept for six hundred wagons & teams. The wagons & harness will be sent from Philadelphia. Send all the teams you can spare & Genl Allen will replace them as soon as possible." ALS (telegram sent), DNA, RG 107, Telegrams Collected (Bound); telegram received, *ibid.*, RG 393, Dept. of the Tenn., Telegrams Received. *O.R.*, I, xxx, part 3, 923. See *ibid.*, p. 922. On Oct. 9, Brig. Gen. John A. Rawlins, Vicksburg, sent a copy of this telegram to Lt. Col. Judson D. Bingham, chief q. m., Dept. of the Tenn., adding: "In obedience to the above dispatch you will send to Gen'l Banks every mule that can possiby be spared from the Quarter Masters Department. You will provide immediate transportation, and have the mules sent to Gen'l Banks with the least practicable delay" Copies, DLC-USG, V, 19, 103; DNA, RG 393, Dept. of the Tenn., Letters Sent. On Oct. 17, USG, Cairo, wrote to Bingham, Memphis. "You will send all wagons you can spare from Vicksburg and Natchez to General Banks." Copies, *ibid.* On the same day, USG telegraphed to Brig. Gen. Robert Allen, St. Louis. "From ten to twelve hundred good mules have been sent from Vicksburg to Banks Department. Fifty wagons can be sent if you direct it but they will have to be replaced. The mules we do not require, being able to keep up the supply by capture." Copies, *ibid.* Also on Oct. 17, Allen telegraphed to USG. "Very glad you have sent the mules to Genl. Banks. Please order the wagons down also   I will replace them." LS (telegram sent), *ibid.*, RG 107, Telegrams Collected (Unbound).

1. See telegram to Maj. Gen. Henry W. Halleck, Sept. 22, 1863.

To Maj. Gen. Henry W. Halleck

Vicksburg
Oct 5th 1863 5 P M

MAJ GEN H. W. HALLECK
GEN IN CHIEF

Your despatch of 29th Sept just received.¹ Before moving from here I will await the return of Col Wilson from Cairo. He may have direct orders for me²

U S. GRANT
Maj Genl

Telegram received, DNA, RG 107, Telegrams Collected (Bound); copies, *ibid.*, Telegrams Received in Cipher; *ibid.*, RG 393, Dept. of the Tenn., Hd. Qrs. Correspondence; DLC-USG, V, 6, 8, 24, 94. *O.R.*, I, xxx, part 4, 97.

1. For Maj. Gen. Henry W. Halleck's dispatch, suggesting that USG go to Memphis, see letter to Maj. Gen. William T. Sherman, Oct. 8, 1863.
2. See General Orders No. 61, Oct. 10, 1863.

To Maj. Gen. Henry W. Halleck

Head Quarters, Dept. of the Ten
Vicksburg, Miss, Oct. 5th/63

MAJ. GEN. H. W. HALLECK
GEN. IN CHIEF, WASHINGTON D. C.
GENERAL,

The Army & Navy Gazette of the 22d of Sept. just received here, contains a "Notice to Delinquents," of same date, requiring them to report to the "Military Commission" now in session in Washington City, within fifteen (15) days from the date of the notice, or stand dismissed. Surgeon H. S. Hewitt's name I see is on the list.¹ I have ordered him to report forthwith and he will leave here in compliance with the order this evening.

Surgeon Hewitt is now well and ready for any duty assigned to him. As I understand his case it stands thus. On the march from

Bruinsburg to this place it was necessary to leave Surgeons in charge of such of our men as were wounded in the different battles and would not bear moving. In this way Surg. Hewitt was left at Jackson Miss.[2] When the wounded in his charge had so far recovered as to require his services no longer he was released but required to return North via Richmond. Privations and exposure made him sick and on his arrival North he obtained sick leave. Before the expiration of his leave he recovered sufficiently to do duty and reported for orders. He received his orders to report here and on his way out received the order to report at Annapolis, Md.[3] Thinking the order to report there was given under the supposition that he was unfit for duty he continued on in obedience to the previous order.

I was not aware of the existence of the order for Surgeon Hewitt to report at Annapolis and am not entirely prepared to say whether, under the circumstances, he should have reported there or simply report the facts to Washington for further instructions. The latter I rather think would have been the proper course. I do not know whether this was done or not. I am satisfied however the Dr. intended no disobedience or neglect of orders and if an error has been committed it has been one of judgement only.

I hope the penalty of this notice will be set aside in this case.

I am Gen. Very respectfully
your obt. svt.
U. S. GRANT
Maj. Gen. Com

ALS, ViU. On Oct. 12, 1863, Surgeon Henry S. Hewit, Cairo, telegraphed to Col. Edward D. Townsend, AGO. "I have an orde from Gen. Grant to report in Washington also dispatches from Genl. Thomas for your office. Shall I proceed?" Telegram received, DNA, RG 94, Letters Received, 604H 1863.

1. Hewit was charged with "*Failing to report at Annapolis, Maryland, as ordered. . . .*" *Army and Navy Journal*, I, 5 (Sept. 26, 1863), 77. See letter to Col. Robert C. Wood, March 6, 1863, note 6. On Oct. 3, however, Hewit's name appeared in a list of officers "*exempt from being dismissed . . .* having made satisfactory defence . . ." *Army and Navy Journal*, I, 6 (Oct. 3, 1863), 91. By War Dept. special orders of Oct. 26, Hewit was directed to return to the Dept. of the Tenn., but within two weeks he was ordered to report instead to the Army of the Cumberland. *Ibid.*, I, 10 (Oct. 31, 1863), 149; I, 12 (Nov. 14, 1863), 188.

On Jan. 13, 1864, by Special Orders No. 8, Military Div. of the Miss., Hewit was assigned as medical director, Dept. of the Ohio. Copy, DLC-USG, V, 38.
2. See letter to Lt. Col. Grantham I. Taggart, May 17, 1863.
3. To appear before the board for examination of sick officers.

To Maj. Gen. Henry W. Halleck

Headquarters Department of the Tennessee,
Vicksburg, Miss., October 5, 1863.

MAJ. GEN. H. W. HALLECK,
GENERAL-IN-CHIEF, WASHINGTON, D. C.:
GENERAL:

The bearer of this, L. Trager, is the person who has been traveling through the Southern States for several months, having been sent from La Grange, Tenn., by General W. S. Smith, and whose report was sent to you from Memphis by General Hurlbut about the 1st of this month.

Mr. Trager's account is full, and no doubt reliable, on account of his knowledge of the topography of the country throughout the South, the preparations made by the enemy to receive us at different points, the locality of all their armories, machine-shops, &c. I thought it would probably be well for him to visit Washington, and see you in person.

I am, general, very respectfully, your obedient servant,

U. S. GRANT
Major-General.

Incomplete in *The Collector*, 842 (1975), p. 10. *O.R.*, I, xxx, part 4, 97. On Oct. 1, 1863, Maj. Gen. Stephen A. Hurlbut wrote to Maj. Gen. Henry W. Halleck enclosing a copy of Louis Trager's report. *Ibid.*, p. 4. On Oct. 2, Hurlbut also sent Brig. Gen. John A. Rawlins a copy of the report. Copy, DNA, RG 393, 16th Army Corps, Letters Sent. Trager's undated "Statement before Maj Genl U. S. Grant" is substantially the same as his report to Hurlbut. Of the dozen points at which they differ, the most significant involve Trager's suggestions to USG concerning the possible raid on Mobile. Copies, *ibid.*, RG 94, War Records Office, Dept. of the Tenn.; DLC-Nathaniel P. Banks. *O.R.*, I, xxx, part 4, 4–8. On Nov. 30, 1865, Bvt. Col. Theodore S. Bowers wrote a letter of recommendation. "At the request of the bearer, Mr. L. Tregar, I state that he was employed by Gen. Grant during the year 1863 in secret service; that he was regarded faithful, intelligent and reliable.—During one of his trips into the enemy's country, he reached Charleston and other important points, and his information was so valuable that Gen Grant sent him to report in person to the General-in-chief at Washington. Since that time I have known but little of him." ALS, DNA, RG 109, Union Provost Marshals' File of Papers Relating to Two or More Civilians, 18632. On Aug. 3, 1897, former Brig. Gen. William Sooy Smith, Chicago, wrote to Secretary of the Treasury Lyman J. Gage. "In the year 1862 Louis Trager was sent by me from La Grange, Tennessee, through our lines under promise that he would visit as many of the Confederate Armies as he could and get the strength and organization of each one of them and all other facts and figures that might be important or valuable to us. He was to ascertain if possible any proposed movement of a Confederate army threatening any of our positions and to send timely information of the same to the point threatened. And when his work was completed he was to make a full report to the first of our Commanding Generals whom he could reach. He performed the service with great skill and made his final report to General Grant through General S. A. Hurlbut who was then in command at Memphis, Tennessee. I have never seen his report but it was said to be of very great value, and Trager himself informed me that he had been paid ten thousand dollars in compensation for his work. He now says that he has been prominent at the south since the war; but that the prejudice created against him by the knowledge that crept out of the services he rendered our Government has been such as to rob him of all chances of permanent success in business. And so he turns to the government asking employment in some position that he may be able to fill satisfactorily. Of course he must expect to furnish evidence of his fitness in point of honesty and capacity. . . ." LS, *ibid.*, RG 56, Appointment Div.

On June 24, 1864, U.S. Treasury Agent William Burnet, Natchez, wrote to Treasury Agent William P. Mellen. "While forwarding the statement of the case of seizure of Merchandize and liquors from Louis Trager, it seems proper to say a few words as to his personal claims and pretensions. He has been in the habit heretofore of assuming a very self important and dictatorial tone, in his intercourse with this office, and with the Military Authorities. He claims to be the particular and *trusted* friend of Genl Grant and of Mr Chase as well as of yourself, and that his word is authoritative, throughout the Departments in Washington. He was considerate enough to advise me, through a third party, that if I gave him trouble, I would be removed from office. It is *hardly possible* he may have imposed on General Grant and on Mr Chase, but it is certain, that his arrogance of manner, has made him a perfect nuisance in all the offices in this place. To relieve ourselves, and show his true character to you, and to Mr Chase, if you are not already acquainted with it, I send herewith copies of Statements filed in this office, which show clearly his true character, and together with the fraudulent invoices in this office, prove him entirely unworthy of trust, and it is to be hoped, will relieve us of his pertinacity hereafter. It is perhaps due to him to say, that for a day or two-past, he wears the appearance of the humblest and meekest of Men. It is to be desired, that the change may work inwardly as well as outwardly." LS, *ibid.*, RG 366, Correspondence of the General Agent. In 1872, Trager, then of Black Hawk Point, Concordia Parish, La., was a delegate-at-large to and a vice-president of the Republican Convention. Francis H. Smith, reporter, *Proceedings of the National Union Republican Convention* . . . (Washington, D. C., 1872), p. 22; (Appendix) p. 11. On April 2, 1873, Collector of Customs James F. Casey, New Orleans, wrote to USG. "Mr. Louis Trager, one of the most pronounced republicans of this state is very anxious to be appointed Consul in some good and pleasant City in Europe. Mr. Trager's claims are such that the representative men of the party feel that they should make every effort in their power to get this appointment for him, as by his active support and his self sacrificing spirit he gave force and strength to the party when many who now hold position were determined to have office at the risk of utter defeat to the whole party. It would not only be agreeable to those of the party with whom I come in daily contact, but would be a personal favor to me could Mr. Trager have the position he seeks." ALS, DNA, RG 59, Letters of Application and Recommendation. Writing on April 4 to USG's secretary, Orville E. Babcock, Trager enclosed this letter and copies of telegrams urging his appointment from Governor William P. Kellogg, U.S. Representative Frank Morey, and U.S. Marshal Stephen B. Packard. ALS, *ibid.* On May 5, Packard wrote to Secretary of State Hamilton Fish in Trager's behalf. ALS, *ibid.* Nominated and confirmed as consul at Boulogne, France, Trager served until his post was abolished in 1874, at which point Morey repeatedly, but unsuccessfully, wrote to Fish to secure another appointment for him. *Ibid.*

To Maj. Gen. Nathaniel P. Banks

Vicksburg Miss.
October 5th 1863.

MAJ. GEN N. P. BANKS,
COMD.G DEPT. OF THE GULF,
DEAR GEN.

I send by Capt. Dunham of your staff copy of a report made by a man sent from this Department five months ago and who has been traveling in the South ever since.[1] Although there is no information in it that can benefit you in your present move yet I thought it might prove of interest. I sent a dispatch from here some ten days ago stating that I was ready for the field or any other service.[2] As my dispatches were sent to Cairo by a Staff Officer, with instructions to remain there for rep[ly] from Washington, I will not move until he returns.

I am Gen with great respect
your obt. svt.
U. S. GRANT
Maj. Gen.

ALS, IC.

1. See preceding letter.
2. See letter to Col. John C. Kelton, Sept. 25, 1863.

To Lt. Commander Francis M. Ramsay

Head Quarters Dept of the Tenn.
Vicksburg Miss Oct 6th 1863

Capt Ramsay
U. S. Navy
Capt.

Learning of the stoppage of the Steamer Empress by the Navy, on her way to New Orleans I have concluded that you have not yet been made acquainted with the new Treasury Regulations of I believe the 16th of Sept. I enclose you copies of my orders made in conformity with these regulations[1] and respectfully request that you instruct all officers within your District to pass all boats conforming with these orders. At least pass them until further instructions can be received from Admiral Porter who I shall write to on the same subject

It was my understanding with Admiral Porter that during his absence the Navy within this Dep't and out of his reach, would always act on my suggestions as he, the Admiral has ever done. Should there be anything wrong in any orders made by me governing Commerce on the river the Navy can in no manner be held responsible

Renewing the request that you permit the Steamer Empress to pass, and all other boats conforming to the enclosed order

I remain,
Your Obt Serv't
U. S. Grant
Maj Gen.

Copy, DNA, RG 45, Correspondence of David D. Porter, Officers' Letters, Mississippi Squadron. *O.R.* (Navy), I, xxv, 446. Francis M. Ramsay, born in D. C., graduated from the U.S. Naval Academy in 1856. Promoted to lt. commander as of July 16, 1862, he was capt. of the *Choctaw* during the Vicksburg campaign. In July, 1863, he was assigned to command the 3rd District, Mississippi Squadron. On Oct. 4, Ramsay wrote to Rear Admiral David D. Porter that he had turned back to Natchez, Miss., the *Empress*, with about 2,800 bales of cotton on board, because the shipment lacked Treasury Dept. approval, although the owners did have permits given by order of USG and Brig. Gen. Marcellus M.

Crocker. *Ibid.*, pp. 444–45. On the same day, Ramsay reported his action to Crocker. *Ibid.*, p. 445. On Oct. 6, Crocker, Natchez, wrote to Brig. Gen. John A. Rawlins. "Enclosed I send you one of my cotton permits, with the endorsement of Capt. James P. Conchony, of the Gun Boat 'Osage.' This is one of the passes that I gave before I received Gen. Grant's order upon the subject, and is objectionable in this, that it does not designate the military Post or station. However, that was not the objection to it. I sent to you by Gen. Stewart the note received from the naval commander at the mouth of Red River, which I suppose you have received before this. My object in sending this is, to explain that the permit was granted under the verbal order received from Gen. Grant while at this place, and before receiving the written order, and to call your attention to this Capt. ~~Concon~~ Conchony, of the 'Osage,' whose conduct is highly objectionable, and disrespectful to Gen. Grant, and who appears to be a drunken loafer of the lowest type." Copies, DNA, RG 393, 13th Army Corps, 3rd Div., Miscellaneous Records; *ibid.*, 17th Army Corps, 4th Div., Letters Sent.

On Oct. 17, Porter wrote to USG. "I enclose you a letter I wrote to Capt Ramsay, in relation to the late transaction about stopping the cotton, and boarding the steamer. I don't know that I exactly understand the case or have stated it right, still my letter will bring out the facts. I think with the enclosed General Order distributed that we may hope at length to get the cotton trade regulated. The orders have reached all the vessels before this time." L (signature clipped), *ibid.*, Military Div. of the Miss., Letters Received. Porter enclosed a copy of his letter of Oct. 17 to Ramsay. "General Grant reports to me that one of the Gunboats under your command (a 'tin clad') stopped some Steamer that was bound to New Orleans loaded with Cotton and caused her to be turned back to Vicksburg, putting army officers and others to great inconvenience, notwithstanding the Steamer had regular permits, which were properly endorsed by an army officer Commanding a Post or District. I am moreover informed that when the officer went on board he behaved in a most ungentlemanly manner. He first went to the bar and tried to get some whiskey, which was very properly refused him, and when told that tho vessel was going down by authority of General Grant made use of the most offensive, and ungentlemanly language against General Grant and disgusted every one with his behavior. I do not know the officers name or I would arrest him at once, and try him by Court Martial. General Smith will however send me the charges against him, and he shall be dismissed at once. I thought I understood his name to be Shilleto, if so he is on board the 'New Era,' and not in your District. There is but one man of that name in the Fleet. I wish however you would make enquiries and let me know all you can ascertain about the matter   The Commander of 'Tin clads' have no judgement at all, and they must be allowed no discretion. They must be taught that they have no business to interfere with trade on these Rivers, beyond carrying out the orders they receive, and preventing gross violations of Treasury Laws, when there is no doubt of an intention to supply the Rebels with contraband of war. It is the policy of the Government to open trade, and get out the Cotton, and I must look to the Commanders of Divisions, to see that the Volunteer Officers are not interfering improperly and that they give aid and protection where it is properly due. Moreover that they pay due respect to the permits granted by Officers Commanding Posts or Districts, and to the endorsements of Generals Grant and Banks, in their respective Departments. This is required by the late Treasury Orders. I wish you would run up along your whole line and look into these matters, and those that you cannot trust to execute an order, keep them within hailing distance and look after them." Copy, *ibid.* On Nov. 7 and 8, Ramsay wrote to Porter regarding his action in the case and defending Act. Lt. Joseph P. Couthouy against the charges of former Brig. Gen. David Stuart, one of the cotton traders. *O.R.* (Navy), I, xxv, 447–49. On Oct. 31, U.S. Treasury Agent Benjamin F. Flanders, New Orleans, wrote to Secretary of the Treasury Salmon P. Chase. "Enclosed herewith I hand you copy of Genl Orders No 57, issued by Maj Genl Grant concerning the shipment of Cotton and other products to Memphis and New Orleans. Owing to a seeming want of harmony between the Army and Navy this order is not effective, Boats having Cotton on board loaded in conformity therewith are turned back by the commanders of the Gunboats who say that they do not acknowledge Gen Grants authority over the Mississippi river and commerce thereon but only the orders from Com.e Porter permitting shipments. In some instances said Commanders speak of a Treasury permit as sufficient authority for them to allow cotton &c to pass, but in other instances when a permit has been issued by the proper Treasury officer they disregarded it. The Steamer Empress from Natchez with (2711) two thousand seven hundred and eleven bales of Cotton shipped this month in conformity with Genl Grants order about the 1st of this month was sent back by the Gunboats and detained several days and only after great difficulties was she allowed to come to New Orleans and her officers were given to understand by the naval officers that the thing would not be allowed again. There is a great deal of Cotton upon and near the banks of the river which if proper facilities are allowed, will come to market" ALS, DNA, RG 36, Special Agents, Reports and Correspondence.

On Oct. 4, Porter wrote to USG. "I received a note today from Col. Wilson, to the following effect—'in one or two instances recently, special permits to loyal citizens of Mississippi to take out the products of their plantations, have not only been disregarded by naval officers, but the parties prohibiting from acting under the permits till the guerrillas had had time to destroy the cotton.' 'The General mentions with great satisfaction the assurances you have always given him of your willingness to have your authorities accord with him in every problem, and feels confident that little annoyances are done inadvertently, and without your sanction.' While you may rest assured of the above mentioned disposition on my part, I hope you will not always place faith in what the cotton owners say in relation to these little Transactions, and I enclose you the report of Capt Greer in relation to this affair. Capt Wright the commander of the 'Forest Bee' is a very upright officer, and was very doubtful about a person who offered to bribe him, and who did not come down with a Treasury Agent as the law requires   The permit was brought to me, and I endorsed on the back of it for a Gun boat to protect the vessel while she was loading. I think I can say that there is every disposition on the part of the Gun boats to help any of these people, when they come with their papers properly endorsed by yourself, or the Treasury Agent; but so many attempts have been made to bribe the officers, by parties who really own no cotton, but who are buying on speculation, that the officers are a little suspicious, and they have been so cautioned by me, not to let the Navy get mixed up in any illegal transactions that they keep the xiv, xxi, and xxv sections of Treasury regulations, approved March 12 1863 before their eyes. I do not see how the officers at the different stations can very well give protection to persons who do not comply with the laws or regulations   I was much grieved to hear of your accident at New Orleans, and hope that this will not long keep you confined to your chair. I may be down to Vicksburg soon if I can get away, and the water don't all run out of the river. The guerrillas are very thick about Rodney and came in and captured 15 of the officers and men of one of the Gun boats who were at church, at the time. It would be rather a bad place to go cotton hunting just now." ALS, *ibid.*, RG 45, Correspondence of David D. Porter, Mississippi Squadron, General Letters (Press). For Porter's general views on trade, see his letter to Maj. Gen. William T. Sherman, Oct. 29. *O.R.* (Navy), I, xxv, 520–24.

1. See letter to Salmon P. Chase, Sept. 26, 1863, note 1.

To William H. H. Taylor

Vicksburg Miss. October 6th 1863.

Col W. H. H. Taylor
Dear Sir,

Your letter of the 29th of September, is just this moment recieved. In reply I will state that trade with this part of this Dept. has not yet been opened. Mr Mellen Supervising agt. of the Treasury Dept. and myself however agreed that facilities should be given loyal persons, and those within our lines, the means of procuring the necessaries of life. For this purpose the Treasury Dept. are to license two firms for Vicksburg, two for Natchez, and one for Goodrich's Landing. I have nothing under the sun to do with these appointments, and told the agt. expressly, that I would not have anything to do even with the recommendation of suitable persons for the appointments. I will try to regulate the sales, but nothing more. Since this plan was agreed upon, however I have thought it over well, and concluded it would look too much like a monopoly, and have so written to the Sec. of the Treasury, sending a copy of my letter to Mr Mellen.

The whole matter of trade in this Dept. is left entirely with the Treasury Department. I refer you to Mr Mellen, who will be found a great part of the time in Cincinnati.

With Great respect
your obt. Svt.
U. S. Grant
Maj. Gen. U. S. A.

Copy, DNA, RG 366, Correspondence of the General Agent. On Oct. 19, 1863, former Col. William H. H. Taylor, Memphis, wrote to U.S. Treasury Agent William P. Mellen. "Enclosed, I have the honor to send you a copy of a letter I have just recd. from Maj. Gen. U. S. Grant, upon which, I respectfully ask a permit to ship ($50.000) fifty thousand dollars worth of assorted merchandise to Vicksburg, Miss, to-wit: Dry Goods, Groceries and Hardware." LS, *ibid.* See letter to Salmon P. Chase, Sept. 26, 1863.

To Col. John Riggin, Jr.

Vicksburg Miss.
October 7th 1863.

Dear Riggin,

I have this day sent Harry Boggs[1] a draft for $200 00 with directions that he should turn over to you so much of it as you may call for. If Nicholson[2] has not been paid his bill, which is about $80 00, will you please pay it and collect as above. I also owe you for the crutches you paid for in New Orleans, and other bills for ought I know. Please collect any difference there may be.

All are well here. My respects to your father.

Yours Truly
U. S. Grant
Maj. Gen.

ALS, ICarbS. On Oct. 3, 1863, Col. John Riggin, Jr., wrote a letter of resignation to Brig. Gen. Lorenzo Thomas, which USG endorsed on Oct. 4. "Col. Riggin has served on my staff almost continuously from the breaking out of the rebellion to the present day, first as a volunteer aid, without compensation, and since as an additional A. D. C. His private affairs and the health of his father's family now requiring his personal attention I approve and recommend the acceptance of his resignation." AES, DNA, RG 94, ACP, R66 CB 1867. On Oct. 9, Brig. Gen. John A. Rawlins, writing to his fiancée, Mary E. (Emma) Hurlbut, noted the departure of Riggin and Surgeon Henry S. Hewit. "At their withdrawal from Genl Grants staff I have no regrets and shall express none." ALS, ICHi.

1. For a brief time in 1859, USG and Harry Boggs, Julia Dent Grant's cousin, had a real estate partnership in St. Louis. *PUSG*, 1, 346n–47n. On Oct. 6, 1863, USG wrote to Maj. George Browne, paymaster. "I would like an Eastern draft for $200 00 made payable to Harry Boggs and the remainder of my pay in large bills, say 50s & 100s." ALS, William A. Margeson, West Dundee, Ill.

2. Probably David Nicholson, a leading St. Louis grocer, from whom Harry and Louisa Boggs may have secured provisions used in boarding the Grant children at this time. J. Thomas Scharf, *History of Saint Louis City and County* . . . (Philadelphia, 1883), II, 1241–43.

To Maj. Gen. Stephen A. Hurlbut

Head Quarters, Dept. of the Ten.
Vicksburg Miss. Oct. 8th 1863,

MAJ. GEN. S. A. HURLBUT,
COMD.G 16TH ARMY CORPS,
GENERAL,

There is every indication that the enemy will make an effort to cut the line of communication between Memphis and Corinth, and also that he will endeavor to prevent Sherman from joining Rosecrans or geting near enough to support him. The Cavalry to my front have evidently gone North, from 3 to 4 thousand strong, and have been reinforced by two Brigades of Infantry. I am also informed, and I believe reliably, that two Divisions from Braggs Army have gone up the Mobile & Ohio Road. Johnston is now with these troops in person. He was at Oxford a few days ago but has gone around to Oakalona.

I am just sending out all the force that can be spared from here to drive the enemy from ~~Clinton~~ Canton and Jackson, with instructions to remain at Canton for a few days and scout with the Cavalry as far Eastward as possible. Columbus Miss. is a point of vast importance to the enemy and if threatened would necessarily cause the enemy to detain a large force at that point. The Cavalry will try to create the impression that they are going there. I presume you have full information of the movements of the enemy and are acting accordingly.

I further learn from Braggs Army that since the fight it has been reduced largely by sending off detachments first to prevent reinforcements being sent to Rosecrans from Corinth, and second, to push a force across the Tennessee West of any forces Rosecrans has with the view of getting to his rear. I do not know how reliable this may be but send the information as I receive it.

I wish you would forward this letter, or a copy, to Sherman with the private letter for him accompanying.[1]

> I am Gen. Very respectfully
> your obt. svt.
> U. S. GRANT
> Maj. Gen. Com

ALS, DLC-Stern Collection. *O.R.*, I, xxx, part 4, 170–71.

On Oct. 2, 1863, Maj. Gen. Stephen A. Hurlbut, Memphis, twice wrote to Brig. Gen. John A. Rawlins, the second time at 5:00 P.M. "I avail myself of the present opportunity to communicate such matters as are of importance   The Division of Genl Osterhaus is now at Camp Davis six miles South East of Corinth   The Division of Brig Genl John E. Smith is encamped near Memphis waiting for Camp & Garrison Equipage of which part only has yet arrived the remainder being on the Steamer Adriatic aground near Helena. I have ordered Genl Webster to prepare every thing for opening the M & C Rail Road to Decatur. The Coal ordered by Lt Col Wilson in your name is very difficult to procure, but I have sent two Barges in tow of the Rocket with 22,000 bushels. My scouts just in from Alabama report Bragg fallen back to Rome. Stories from Alabama conflict. Most say that his victory has crippled him. It may be if he has strength enough that he will advance through Northern Alabama toward Huntsville & Decatur. But with Rosecrans powerful cavalry so far as I know unhurt he should be kept in check from any flank march of that kind   From the gross neglect of the St Louis Depôt we are short of forage, and in the present stage of water are likely to be more so. It is therefore desirable that our troops move soon into the Tuscumbia Valley. I keep up a good system of intelligence in Northern Alabama, and have just received 120 recruits from that region who fought their way in handsomely bringing 10 prisoners." ALS, DNA, RG 393, Dept. of the Tenn., Letters Received. *O.R.*, I, xxx, part 4, 29. "I have this moment learned that Loring is up at Okalona with his Division—The Cavalry from below are uniting with Chalmers & Richardson. They aim for our Rail Road & to prevent reinforcements. We are ready but if attacked will lose some small posts   There are not less than 15000 all told & of all arms threatening the Road" ALS, DNA, RG 94, War Records Office, Dept. of the Tenn. *O.R.*, I, xxx, part 4, 30; (misdated Oct. 20) *ibid.*, I, xxxi, part 1, 673. On Oct. 5, Hurlbut wrote to Rawlins. "Sherman's troops are arriving and moving out. Two Divisions are beyond Corinth. Johnston has been organizing & reviewing troops. Stephen D. Lee has command of the Cavalry about 6000 strong. They are massing near Wyatt with eight peices of artillery   Lorings Division is at or near Okalona and every thing indicates a dash on the Road. My Cavalry is on the line from Salem across by the Coldwater, to observe & repel the movement as well as to forage   They are too late to stop Sherman but unless withdrawn will annoy me very much when he moves on. The line of Telegraph has been cut twice in two days and is now down. I exceedingly dislike this flank march of Sherman's but suppose it will turn out right. It is said Pemberton's 'Exchanged men' supply

Lorings place at Meridian   I have yet no knowledge that they are exchanged except a printed notice in the Mobile papers   We are prepared here for any thing—The whole line is rigidly closed & we watch for what may turn up"   ALS, DNA, RG 393, Dept. of the Tenn., Letters Received. *O.R.*, I, xxx, part 4, 98.

1. See following letter.

To Maj. Gen. William T. Sherman

[*Vicksburg, Miss., Oct. 8, 1863*]

The following is copy of a dispatch received a few days since.[1] Washington Sept. 28th 63. MAJ. GEN. GRANT. The enemy seems to have concentrated on Rosecrans all his available forces from every direction. To meet him it is necessary that all the forces that can be spared in your Dept. be sent to Rosecrans assistance. He wishes them sent by Tuscumbia, Decatur & Athens as he requires the opening of the Nashville (Memphis probably intended) & Charleston road East of Corinth. An able commander like Sherman or McPherson should be selected.[2] As soon as your health will permit I think you should go to Nashville[3] & take the direction of this movement. Should Bragg move by Rome through Northern Alabama to turn Rosecrans right your forces on that line may require all your assistance. Longstreet's Corps I believe is the only one withdrawn from Lee's Army, but almost everything has been taken from other places   (signed H. W. HALLECK, Gen.-in-Chief).[4] I telegraphed Halleck about the time you were leaving that I was ready for the field or any other duty.[5] I shall not act therefor on this suggestion to go to Nashville but await orders before going. Wilson may be looked for now almost any day and may have orders for me. I have written Hurlbut all the official news and requested him to send you my letter, or a copy of it.[6] All well here. I am able to ride now on horseback as well as ever only requiring a little assistance in mounting and dismounting.

U. S. GRANT

Collection of George W. Childs, Samuel T. Freeman & Co., Dec. 10, 1928. On Oct. 9, 1863, Brig. Gen. John A. Rawlins wrote to Mary E. (Emma) Hurlbut.

"The prospects now are that within a few days Department HeadQuarters will be changed from here to some place nearer the Mass of troops and it may be to Nashville Tenn in which event Genl Grant will have the directions of the entire operations on Genl Rosecrantz lines . . ." ALS, ICHi.

On Oct. 1, 4:00 P.M., Maj. Gen. William T. Sherman, Helena, wrote to USG. "My Boat arrived here an hour ago and the Pilots are gone to sound the bar—River very low. and we will surely have to land our men & stock & pass round the Bar and even then it is doubtful if this Boat can pass. River is lower than ever known before.—I have sent one of my staff up to Gen Buford to learn the news. I have papers of the 25th   Rosecrans is at Chattanooga awaiting reinforcemts   Bragg threatens him close at hand. The newspapers announce that Rosecrans is already reinforced by Burnside and Sherman. They will doubtless hold us accountable for not passing by Magic from Black River to Chattanooga   It will be as much as I expect to get to Memphis tomorrow & all the 2nd Div is behind me. We found plenty of wood at Griffins Landing 10 miles below Greenville, and plenty here. The wood at Griffins is about a mile back, and is represented by one of my staff at 4000 cords. It would well pay to send up and haul it to the Bank. To move troops along the River woodyards must be established. It would be better for the 4th Division to come on without waiting for the return of those boats and work their way up in small boats as best they can. I will send your letters up to Cairo by a staff officer. Minnie is much better but Willy, my oldest boy is *very* sick—I will push matters from Memphis with all possible energy, but no amount of energy will move a sandbar." ALS, DNA, RG 94, War Records Office, Dept. of the Tenn. *O.R.*, I, xxx, part 4, 3. On Oct. 4, Sherman, Memphis, wrote to USG. He wrote *"Private"* at the top of the first page, and crossed out eleven lines at the end. The dispatch from Maj. Gen. Henry W. Halleck to which Sherman refers is quoted in the letter to Sherman, above. "Willy my oldest and healthiest boy, came on board the Atlantic at Vicksburg complaining of a Diarrhea. Dr Roler took him in hand at once, and he was feverish. He became rapidly very ill, and sank from the begining. We reached Memphis at 10 ½ P M. Friday night, and I brought him up to the Gayoso, when by Rolers advise I called in two other good physicians but he sank surely & rapidly dying at 5 P M yesterday. At noon today I dispatched his body and all my family up the River in the War Eagle & for home. This is the only death I have ever had in my own family, and falling as it has so suddenly & unexpectedly on the one I most prised on earth has affected me more than any other misfortune could. I can hardly compose myself enough for work but must & will do so at once. Hallecks despatches all look to pushing all available forces East to Decatur repairing the road & looking to supplies.—I never liked this Eastern & Western Road for supplies   It is too easily cut by small parties of Guerillas. The Columbus Road is better and is better covered. This Road works very slow. Only one Brigade of Jno E Smith is yet out. Another goes tonight and the last tomorrow. I will push out my 2nd Division Morgan L Smith & before he gets off Corse will be up. I will move all troops east from Corinth by marching and use the Railroad as repaired to carry supplies. Hurlbut has apparently well authenticated reports that Joe Johnston & Stephen D Lee have all of Long's Division up the Ohio & Mobile Road about Okalona, and any quantity of the new Levees especially of Cavalry movig north in Mississippi. This if corroborated dont show that there is the Concentration against Rosecrans which is reported. From the news north to Oct 1, Rosecrans was at Chattanooga, Burnside at Knoxville and all other armies in about the situation at the time of my leavig Vicksburg. I understand Hallecks plan is now strongly offensive at all points—but more especially on the line of Rosecrans now, using all Railroads & the Tennessee as the Base line. I infer from a despatch which Hurlbut shew me that he wants you at Nashville to control the whole thereby consolidating under you all of Burnside, Rosecrans and your own forces not necessary to guard the Mississippi. I suppose it to be an order. Of course I would be pleased to know such is the case though I leave the Line of the Mississippi with Regret. Sooner or later we must penetrate inland and it may be the time is come. I expect to go to Corinth with the 2nd Division as soon as my 4th begins to arrive, and I need not assure you that I will use all possible energy to put my force just where it is ordered and at the same time watch any side movemt of the enemy. I repeat you cannot decline to go to Nashville which seems to be the strategic Grand Center from which to control all movemts forward from the valley of the Tennessee. It will be a pity to leave McPherson out, but a good officer will be needed there to watch the country east, and the Washita west. We are on the outside of a tremendous circle giving our enemy the inside track all the time, but this we cant help. I sent your despatch to Halleck announcing your recovery. . . ." ALS, USG 3. On Oct. 10, Sherman, Memphis, wrote to USG, whom he "Expected hourly at Memphis." "I should have gone out today but am delayed for want of cars, but am assured a train will be disposable tomorrow. We have been delayed more than I calculated 1st by low water some of the 4th Division still beig on the River below we know not where, & 2nd the capacity of the Railroad hence to Corinth is far less than we estimated as it is I moved nearly all the wagons & mules by Land, & propose to let the 4th Division march, the Rail cars taking their knapsacks &c. I now have Genl Blair at Corinth, Jno E Smith's Division at Glendale, and Osterhaus at Iuka. The 2nd Division Morgan, L Smith is at this moment at Lagrange in consequence of a Reported threat of the Rail road at that place, but it will be moved forward at once. The 4th Division will march and should overtake us at Bear Creek. I dont like this Railroad, it lies parallel to an enemys country, and they can break it when they please   Hurlbut's Cavalry under ~~Genl~~ Col Hatch encountered the enemy's Cavalry at Salem yesterday & retired as I infer worsted. I await momentary information from them. My own opinion is that we will have to rely on the Tennessee River, or reopen the Road from Corinth to Columbus. I have advised Genl Webster at once to look to that Road, for it is certain this one from Memphis will be cut the moment I get east of Bear Creek. I feel sure you will be ordered to Nashville to assume a General Command over all the forces operating to the South East—Say Rosecrans your Center, Burnside Left wing & Sherman Right—I have no knowledge of the strength of the other parts but mine is too small to attempt to divide up to cover a long line of Railway, and I would prefer to move about & learn to live on the corn & meat of the country. To depend on a Road so precarious as this, would tie us down to localities that can have no material influence on events. I was in hopes to see you, but of course I must move on, and shall proceed on the plan to cross the Tennessee at Florence and move to Athens as well supplied as possible. Here at Memphis you will learn all material facts and can make the necessary orders, or recommendations to General Halleck." ALS, DNA, RG 94, War Records Office, Dept. of the Tenn. *O.R.*, I, xxx, part 4, 236.

1. USG here copied Maj. Gen. Henry W. Halleck to USG, which Halleck

telegraphed on Sept. 29, 11:00 A.M. ALS (telegram sent), DNA, RG 107, Telegrams Collected (Bound); copies, *ibid.*, RG 393, Dept. of the Tenn., Hd. Qrs. Correspondence; DLC-USG, V, 6, 8, 24, 94. *O.R.*, I, xxx, part 3, 923.

2. These two sentences were inaccurately deciphered; Halleck punctuated them differently, and correctly named the railroad. "He wishes them sent by Tuscumbia, Decatur & Athens. As this requires the opening and running of the Memphis & Charleston R. R. east of Corinth, an able commander, like Sherman or McPherson should be selected."

3. Halleck wrote "Memphis," but a telegrapher transmitted it as "Nashville."

4. On "Oct. 1/63" (probably Oct. 5), USG sent another copy of Halleck's telegram to the "Comdg. Officer Mississippi Squadron off Vicksburg Miss.," prefacing it with the sentence "I have just received the following dispatch from the Gen. in Chief." ES, Lincoln Memorial University, Harrogate, Tenn.; ALS, IC.

5. See letter to Col. John C. Kelton, Sept. 25, 1863.

6. See preceding letter.

General Orders No. 61

Headquarters Department of the Tennessee.
Vicksburg, Miss., October, 10, 1863.

GENERAL ORDERS, NO. 61,

I. . . "In addition to the command of the 17th, Army Corps, Major General J. B. McPherson will assume command of all the United States Forces, including the Mississippi Marine Brigade, within this Department south of the Arkansas river, and all reports and returns will be made to him at Vicksburg, Miss.

II. . . The Chiefs of the several Staff Departments of the Army of the Tennessee, will proceed without delay to Memphis, Tenn., where they will establish their offices until further orders.

By order of Maj. Gen. U. S. Grant
T. S BOWERS
Asst Adjt. Gen'l

Copies, DLC-USG, V, 13, 14; DNA, RG 393, Dept. of the Tenn., General and Special Orders; (printed) USGA. On Oct. 3, 1863, Maj. Gen. Henry W. Halleck had telegraphed to Lt. Col. James H. Wilson, Cairo. "Telegraph in General terms disposition of Gen Grants forces. Convey as soon as possible to Gen Grant the following: 'General, it is the wish of the Secretary of War, that as soon as Gen Grant is able to take the field he will come to Cairo and report by telegraph.'"
Copies, DLC-USG, V, 6, 8, 24, (misdated Oct. 3, 1864) 94; DNA, RG 393,

Dept. of the Tenn., Letters Sent. Printed as sent at 11:00 A.M. in *O.R.*, I, xxx, part 4, 55. Wilson delivered this telegram to USG on Oct. 10, 1863, submitting on the same day a report of his trip to Cairo as dispatch bearer. DLC-USG, V, 23; DNA, RG 393, Dept. of the Tenn., Register of Letters Received.

To Maj. Gen. James B. McPherson

[*Vicksburg, Miss., Oct. 10, 1863*]

MEMORANDA FOR GEN. McPHERSON.

Hd Qrs. will be removed to Nashville Ten. All forces South of Helena, black & white, will be under Gen. McPherson as Commander of the Dist. of Vicksburg. Complaints are made that raids go out from the West bank of the river into the Macon Country and bring in cotton thus endangering the crops & personal property of the inhabitants there to seizure and destruction by the rebels. This is unauthorized and Gen. Hawkins should be instructed to use every effort to put a stop to it.

It would be advisable to send Osbands Cavalry to Skipwith's Landing to remain for a few weeks to give protection to the few deserving people in that Country and also to fill up his regiment from plantations owned by persons of disloyalty. Send them through by land, crossing the Yazoo about the mouth of Sun Flower.

They should be instructed to treat the people with kindness. A few on that side have protection papers. Such persons should receive the full benefit of them.

When planters have hired their negroes in accordance with established regulations recruiting officers should refuse to receive them or harbor them about their camps.

The Duncans[1] have hired theirs in that way.

Head Quarters may be established in Louisville for the purpose of receiving all reports &c. This will be fully determined probably at Cairo.

In regard to the expedition going out to Canton special directions cannot be given for it after reaching that place. I would like however that every thing possible should be done to create the impression that the O. & M road[2] was in danger.

The commanding Gen. will of course keep ~~Hd Qrs~~. Dept. Hd Qrs. informed, by letter, of all movements of the enemy coming to his knowledge. He will also make such moves with his troops as the protection of territory entrusted to his charge may require. The Marine fleet will habitually be kept on shore and only go on their boats when sent for special duty. Details can be made from other forces to accompany them when necessary. The boats of the Marine fleet can be used for transportation of troops when required; but habitually they will be kept ready to send to threatened points on the river.

U. S. GRANT.
Maj. Gen. Com

ALS, USMA. *O.R.*, I, xxx, part 4, 233–34.

On Oct. 12, 1863, Maj. Gen. James B. McPherson wrote to USG. "I am all ready to start on the expedition to Canton and only awaiting the arrival of the Brigade from Natchez   Rumors come in through contrabands and from other sources that the Enemy is concentrating a very respectable force for the purpose of making an attack on this place   I do not place much faith in the reports as yet, but will probably find out something definite in a few days. I have directed Brig Genl. Hawkins to send two Regiments of his Command to this place as soon as Boats can be furnished. The Cavalry Expedition across the 'Big Black' at 'Hankerson's Ferry' had quite a spirited skirmish with about two hundred of Wirt Adams Cavalry, chased them about ten miles, breaking and scattering them in every direction. Our forces consisted of Maj. Osband's Battalion 4th Ill. Cavalry, and two Battalions of the 2nd Wis. Cavalry, the whole under the Command of Major Eastman. I have not yet received Maj. Eastmans report, but he states they counted fifteen dead rebels in the road and knows that a good many were wounded, and they brought in four prisoners. Our loss was one killed and two wounded. They came up with the rebels at Mr. Ingerham's place, near Willow Springs" Copies, DNA, RG 393, 13th and 17th Army Corps, Letters Sent; *ibid.*, 17th Army Corps, Letters Sent. Printed as written at 10:00 A.M. in *O.R.*, I, xxx, part 2, 797. See *ibid.*, pp. 797–800.

On Oct. 20, McPherson wrote to USG. "I returned yesterday from the reconnoissance in the direction of Canton, the particulars of which will be found in the report sent this day to Brig Genl. Rawlins   After reaching Robinson's Mills near Livingston, I was satisfied that the Enemy would have a force of Infantry superior to mine, besides their Cavalry, and under the circumstances, considering the defenceless state of Vicksburg, I deemed it best to return, which I did via Clinton and 'Big Black Bridge.' On returning I found Genl. Hawkins at 'Goodrich's Landing' had reported that four thousand had assembled in the vicinity of Delhi, and were coming across Bayou Macon to attack him, and had called for reinforcements—2.000 Infantry and a Battery of Artillery   The Marine Brigade was sent up to his support, and the Commander of a Gun Boat at Lake Providence notafied and requested to send him assistance if required   This was four days ago, since which I have heard nothing from him in regards to the movements of the Enemy, and am decidedly of the opinion that the Enemy's force was greatly exaggerated, and that it consisted of a Reg't of Cavalry which has infested that country ever since we came down the river. A Boat came down last night. Everything was all right then." Copies, DNA, RG 393, 13th and 17th Army Corps, Letters Sent; *ibid.*, 17th Army Corps, Letters Sent. *O.R.*, I, xxx, part 2, 804–5; *ibid.*, I, xxxi, part 1, 679–80. McPherson's report of Oct. 20 to Brig. Gen. John A. Rawlins, copies, DNA, RG 393, 13th and 17th Army Corps, Letters Sent; *ibid.*, 17th Army Corps, Letters Sent. *O.R.*, I, xxx, part 2, 802–4.

On Oct. 26, McPherson wrote to USG, apparently having received USG's letter of Oct. 17 to Maj. Gen. Stephen A. Hurlbut. "I am just in receipt of your letter of the 17th and am gratified to hear of your safe arrival at Cairo. I presume ere this you have recd. a full account of the reconnoissance towards Canton as I sent you a full report the day I returned. I am satisfied the Rebels have a much larger force of *mounted men* in this State than we have given them credit for. If Chalmers had from 3000, to 4000, at Collierville, and Lee 4000, at Tuscumbia, they have not less than 10.000, as I know there were fully 2.500 with six pieces of artillery in front of me when I was near Livingston all cavalry *and well armed.* We got some few of their arms, *short Enfield rifles* with *sword bayonets*, an excellent weapon for fighting on foot or on horseback. I started the Cavalry off several times on side roads to make a detour, and come in on the rear or flank of the enemy, but they invariably got stopped, and sent back for Infantry and Artillery to assist in dislodging the enemy. It is well they did not strike off for the Mobile and Ohio Road   if they had, they would have stood nine chances out of ten of being cut off   There is no disguising the fact that the cavalry of *Cosby's* and *Whitfield's* is far superior to ours under *Winslow*. Winslow himself is a very good Officer though somewhat lacking in spirit and dash, but many of his subordinate Officers are of no account whatever. Even the horses have caught the timidity of the men, and turn round involuntarily and break for the rear as soon as a cannon shot is fired. This occurred twice on the expedition and before any one was hurt. Winslow is doing his best to get the Cavalry in shape and make up a proper spirit. I am going to give him two rifled guns and two twelve p'd'r howitzers in the place of his mountain howitzers and I hope to see some signs of improvement. All the information I can get confirms the report sent you by *Capt. Gile* A. D. C. that the rebels have a very respectable force of Infantry at Canton, Brandon and other points towards Maridean. *Davis* was as far west as Jackson with Joe. *Johnston*. If they attempt to retake this place, I don't think they will find us unprepared, and they may expect to fight, and fight hard and long before they get it. I have not had anything alarming from *Hawkins* for several days. I learned today that an expedition of about 2.500 mounted men with a battery of artillery was organizing at some point N. W. of Monroe, with a view of making a raid on the River, though I do not place much reliance on the information. It would be however in accordance with the instructions of the rebel Secretary of War as contained in the letter which was captured. The fact is General I believe the rebels have more men in the Field east of the Mississippi River to day than we have, and they are able to concentrate them more rapidly than we can possibly do. What shall I do with the confederate prisoners who were left here in hospitals. There is one hundred and thirteen, and three surgeons, all of them are convalescent and can be moved, except twelve. They ought to be disposed of in some way, and I do not feel like sending them out of the lines here until I hear from you. I have presented your regards to all, and they all unite in sending their best wishes for your success. I assure you General nothing would give me more pleasure than to be near you, and to assist to the best of my ability in rendering your operations successful." Copies, DNA, RG 393, 13th and 17th Army Corps, Letters Sent; *ibid.*, 17th Army Corps, Letters Sent. *O.R.*, I, xxxi, part 1, 748–49. See Edwin C. Bearss, "Misfire in Mississippi: McPherson's Canton Expedition," *Civil War History*, VIII, 4 (Dec., 1962), 401–16.

On Nov. 13, USG telegraphed to McPherson. "Release all the Vicksburg prisoners according to agreement. We will not violate good faith if the rebels do. Parole the Surgeons." Copies, DLC-USG, V, 34, 35; DNA, RG 393, Military Div. of the Miss., Letters Sent. *O.R.*, II, vi, 511. See *ibid.*, p. 646. See telegram to Maj. Gen. Henry W. Halleck, Sept. 25, 1863. On Oct. 24, C.S.A. Lt. Col. N. G. Watts, agent for the exchange of prisoners, at Vicksburg, wrote to McPherson. "My object in visiting this place under Flag of Truce, is to effect an arrangement with you for the exchange of any officers who have been or may captured by your command—giving officer for officer of equal rank. This proposition is made in consequence of there being some difficulty existing between the Federal & Confederate Governments in regard to a general exchange of prisoners of War—the place of exchange to be at or near Big Black River, or such other point as may be agreed upon. My Head Quarters at present, are at Mobile Ala.— and any communication sent me through the Confederate pickets beyond Big Black River will reach me promptly." ALS, DNA, RG 94, War Records Office, 16th Army Corps. *O.R.*, II, vi, 418. On the same day, McPherson endorsed this letter to USG "for his action in the matter" AE (signature clipped), DNA, RG 94, War Records Office, 16th Army Corps. *O.R.*, II, vi, 419. On Nov. 2, Capt. Ely S. Parker endorsed the letter. "Respectfully returned. In the exchange of Prisoners of War you will be governed only by such regulations as are authorized from Washington" AES, DNA, RG 94, War Records Office, 16th Army Corps. *O.R.*, II, vi, 419. On Dec. 22, McPherson forwarded to USG another letter on the same matter from Watts which McPherson had answered. *Ibid.*, pp. 738–39. On Dec. 26, Col. William Hoffman, commissary gen. of prisoners, wrote to USG. "Some time in July last the war Dp't. found it necessary to suspend the operation of so much of Genl orders No 60, of June 6th 62, and No. 90. of July 26th 62, as direct that medical officers and chaplains who may be captured shall be unconditionally discharged, they being non-combatants but recently the cause of the suspension having been removed, the orders above alluded to have again been put in full force" Copies, DNA, RG 249, Letters Sent; *ibid.*, RG 393, Military Div. of the Miss., War Dept. Correspondence. *O.R.*, II, vi, 762.

1. See letter to Brig. Gen. Lorenzo Thomas, July 11, 1863, note 1.
2. Mobile and Ohio Railroad.

To Maj. Gen. William T. Sherman

By Telegraph from Head Quarters Memphis [*Oct.*] 14 [*1863*]
MAJ GEN SHERMAN

Arrived this morning   will be off in a few hours   my orders
are only to go to Cairo & report from there by Telegraph   Mc-
Pherson will be in Canton today   he will remain there until Sunday or monday next & reconnoitre as far eastward as possible with
Cavalry in the meantime

U S GRANT
Maj Gen

Telegram received, DLC-William T. Sherman; copy (misdated Oct. 14, 1873),
ibid. Printed as sent at 11:00 A.M. in *O.R.*, I, xxx, part 4, 354. On Oct. 12, 1863,
Brig. Gen. John A. Rawlins, aboard the *Metropolitan* at the mouth of White
River, Ark., wrote to Mary E. (Emma) Hurlbut. "We are now enroute for Cairo
Ills where we expect orders in writing for General Grant. what they will be is
not certainly known, but will probably be such as indicated in my letter of the
ninth inst. Where our next Head Quarters will be I cannot tell but more than
likely they will be in Nashville." ALS, ICHi. On Oct. 14, Rawlins again wrote
to Emma Hurlbut. "Thus far our trip from Vicksburg has been pleasant and
speedy. I am inclined to believe you were right about clearing out this 'little
stream' as you passed up for we have not struck a snag nor stuck on a sand bar
since starting and are now some sixty miles north of Memphis and if we meet
with no more detention than we have thus far will reach Cairo tomorrow night,
making the trip from Vicksburg in five days, which at this stage of water is remarkably quick. . . . As we near Cairo I am more and more uncertain as to the
orders Genl Grant may receive, . . ." ALS, *ibid.*
On Oct. 14, Maj. Gen. William T. Sherman, Corinth, telegraphed to USG.
"Railroad repaired to Bear Creek. Osterhaus at Iuka. John E Smith at Burnsville. All my troops in motion by land. It is raining & roads heavy. I am collecting
provisions & forage to the fullest capacity of the Road & will move on to Tuscumbia at the earliest possible momt. Stephen J Lee at Tuscumbia with about
4000 of the Mississippi Cavalry. Accept the Command of the Great Army of the
Centre. Dont hesitate. By your presence at Nashville you will unite all discordant
elemts, and impress the Enemy in proportion. All success and honor to you." ALS
(telegram sent), DNA, RG 107, Telegrams Collected (Unbound); copy, *ibid.*,
RG 94, War Records Office, Dept. of the Tenn. *O.R.*, I, xxx, part 4, 354–55.
Also on Oct. 14, Sherman wrote to Rawlins discussing local military affairs. ALS,
DNA, RG 94, War Records Office, Dept. of the Tenn. *O.R.*, I, xxx, part 4, 355–
56.
On Oct. 15, 7:30 A.M., Sherman wrote to USG. "Yesterday I got your dispatch from Memphis and answered it instanter. I hope my answer got to you
quick, though these operators take their time in making up the 'ciphers.' I am
afraid you got off before you heard from me. I now send by young Dunn some
letters I had written yesterday which contain about all the facts I can now obtain

reliable. The railroad has a kink somewhere, and it seems our horses and men eat up rations and forage as fast as they come forward. But I will manage to stop the leak somehow. Again, my troops were directed after they left Memphis to protect the road, and two of the regiments are still off with Sweeny. Nevertheless, the head of my column is now at Bear Creek and Eastport, and it won't take long to get to Tuscumbia. I am a little uneasy about the means of crossing, as General Osterhaus reports a good wide and deep channel at Eastport, with a 'strong current.' If this be so, the Tennessee is rising from rains in the Alleghanies, and once up a few feet it may be relied on for six months sure. I have written to Admiral Porter on this subject, but hope you will take it in hand. Boat communication being once established with me at Eastport I will be all right. I don't believe Hurlbut's force will keep this road open long, though I do believe from present appearances that there is no enemy near it but the guerrillas and Chalmers' force, which is being pushed down beyond the Tallahatchie. Hatch ought now to make up old scores with that whole band. Their attack on Collierville was very weak. They had artillery, but did not get it in any position where a shot could do but one execution. No enfilading fire attempted, though one or two solid shots tearing through our train would have demolished it. I was glad to be at Collierville, for it has given heart to these railroad guards that don't know the value of the defenses they have all made. I am very anxious you should go to Nashville, as foreshadowed by Halleck, and chiefly as you can harmonize all conflicts of feeling that may exist in that vast crowd. Rosecrans and Burnside and Sherman, with their subordinates, would be ashamed of petty quarrels if you were behind and near them, between them and Washington. Next, the union of such armies and the direction of it is worthy your ambition. I shall await news from you with great anxiety." *Ibid.*, pp. 380–81.

For reports by Sherman and Maj. Gen. Stephen A. Hurlbut of the action at Collierville, Tenn., Oct. 11, see *ibid.*, I, xxx, part 2, 731–33, 734.

Endorsement

―――――

[*ca. Oct. 15, 1863.*]

I have read the within letter of Col. J. Eaton Jr. Supt. of Freedmen for the Dept. of the Ten. and respectfully invite special attention to it. Col. Eaton has worked most faithfully as Supt. of these people for more than one year studying the most practicable means of ameliorating the condition of Freedmen and ~~to h~~ how to relieve the Govt. as far as practicable of the expence of their maintainance. ~~I He believe he is more practical in his ideas, and more~~ He is more conversant with this subject than any man I know in the Dept. of the Ten. and is practical in his ideas. He is perfectly sincere in his labors and has no ~~un~~selfish ends to accomplis and therefore his views are entitled to ful weight. The regulations of Freedmen within the different Departments I propose to leave entirely to Commanders of Departments, so far as the Military are left to controll, but ~~this subject~~ the importance of an early settlement of the policy to be pursued so as to secure the labor of Freedmen for the coming season being iminent, and Gen. Sherman being off where his attention can not be called to the matter, I make this endorsment. Col. Eaton will also forward within a day or two regulation, which he ~~would~~ propose will prepare for the leasing of abandoned plantations and for the employment of colored people

AE (facsimile), John Eaton, *Grant, Lincoln and the Freedmen* (New York, 1907), between pp. 114–15. Eaton believed, but without certainty, that USG drafted the endorsement while traveling from Vicksburg to Cairo. *Ibid.*, pp. 113–14. USG's statement that Col. John Eaton, Jr., had served as superintendent for "more than one year" is either inaccurate or indicates that the endorsement was written later. See telegram to Maj. Gen. Henry W. Halleck, Nov. 15, 1862.

To Maj. Gen. Henry W. Halleck

Cairo Ills.
11 30 a. m. Oct. 16, 1863.

MAJ GEN H. W. HALLECK
GENL-IN-CHF

Rebels seem~~ed~~ to have moved north with most of the Cavalry in Mississippi & also with Loring's Division.

Loring & a portion of the Cavalry moved up the Mobile Railroad. Chalmers & others with from three to five thousand Cavalry & some artillery up the Mississippi Central. Their place back of Vicksburg is filled by two brigades of Infantry.

Genl McPherson moved out with all the force he could take on the 12th intending to drive the enemy from the Mississippi Central Railroad. He will stay several days at Canton & send the Cavalry as far to the east as they can safely go.

The Charleston Railroad was attacked at Collierville on the eleventh. They were repulsed with a loss to us of about one hundred killed & wounded, but after destroying one bridge & the Camp and Garrison equipage of the 66th Indiana Hatch got south of

this force, & when I left Memphis had been fighting them for two days. Br Gen Sweeney was near him with an Infantry force & I am in hopes before this, Chalmers force is entirely broken up. &
If the Columbus Railroad is opened it will be necessary to abandon the Rail road from Memphis.

I would rather advise depending on the Country, the Tennessee River, & the Nashville & Chattanooga Railroad for supplying our armies.

The Charleston Railroad is completed to I-u-k-a and the work progressing eastward.

Gen. Sherman was at Corinth as I passed, with a portion of his force to the east of him.[1]

Price is reported to have left Arkadelphia and gone to Washington.

I directed Gen Hurlbut to advise Steele to send a Cavalry force to Arkadelphia & destroy the salt works, powder mills &c.

Is it not practicable to withdraw a portion of Steele's force?[2]

U. S. GRANT

Major Genl.

Telegram received, DNA, RG 107, Telegrams Collected (Bound); copies, *ibid.*, Telegrams Received in Cipher; *ibid.*, RG 393, Dept. of the Tenn., Letters Sent; DLC-USG, V, 6, 8, 24, 94. *O.R.*, I, xxx, part 4, 403.

On Oct. 15, 1863, USG, Columbus, Ky., telegraphed to Maj. Gen. Henry W. Halleck. "Your despatch of 3rd directing me to report at Cairo was received at 11.30 A. M the 9th Inst. I left same day with my staff and Head Quarters and have just reached here enroute for Cairo." Telegram received, DNA, RG 107, Telegrams Collected (Bound); copies, *ibid.*, Telegrams Received in Cipher; (dated Oct. 16) *ibid.*, RG 393, Dept. of the Tenn., Hd. Qrs. Correspondence; DLC-USG, V, 6, 8, 24, 94. *O.R.*, I, xxx, part 4, 375. USG's letterbook copies of this telegram correctly give Oct. 10 as the date on which he received Halleck's dispatch. On Oct. 16, 9:00 A.M., USG, Cairo, telegraphed to Halleck. "I have just arrived & report in pursuance with instructions of the 3rd inst. The staff & Head Qrs are with me." Telegram received, DNA, RG 107, Telegrams Collected (Bound); copies, *ibid.*, Telegrams Received in Cipher; *ibid.*, RG 393, Dept. of the Tenn., Hd. Qrs. Correspondence; DLC-USG, V, 6, 8, 24, 94. *O.R.*, I, xxx, part 4, 403. In his *Memoirs* (I, 583–84; II, 17), USG treated as a single communication these two telegrams to Halleck.

1. On Oct. 17, 11:00 A.M., USG relayed to Halleck information just received from Maj. Gen. William T. Sherman. "On the Fourteenth (14th) part of Shermans forces were at Bear Creek—Rail Road then completed to that point. S. D. Lee with four thousand men was at Tuscumbia" Telegram received, DNA,

RG 107, Telegrams Collected (Bound); copies, *ibid.*, Telegrams Received in Cipher; *ibid.*, RG 393, Dept. of the Tenn., Letters Sent; DLC-USG, V, 6, 8, 24, 94. *O.R.*, I, xxx, part 4, 429. See telegram to Maj. Gen. William T. Sherman, Oct. 14, 1863.

2. See letter to Maj. Gen. Stephen A. Hurlbut, Oct. 17, 1863, note 3.

To Maj. Gen. Henry W. Halleck

Head Quarters, Dept. of the Ten.
Cairo, Ill. Oct. 16th 1863.

MAJ. GEN. H. W. HALLECK,
GEN. IN CHIEF, WASHINGTON,
GENERAL.

In my recommendations for promotion[1] after the fall of Vicksburg I neglected the names of two worthy officers who should not have been neglected. They are Col. Jas. B. Slack, 46th Ia Vols. and Col. E. Hatch, 2d Iowa Cavalry.

Col. Slack has been commanding a Brigade for more than one year. In battle he is one of our very best commanders. His name was sent in by his Corps Commander but left out by me through mistake. Col. Hatch belonging to the 16th Army Corps, which was not engaged in the battles about Vicksburg, was not thought of at the time. As a Cavalry officer he has done most valuable service, second to no other officer in the Dept. The discipline of his Brigade is higher than that of any other Cavalry Command under me.

I would respectfully request that these two officers be appointed Brigadier Generals, and, if consistent, that their appointments be dated back to the same time with those whose names were sent in in July last.

I am Gen. very respectfully
your obt. svt.
U. S. GRANT
Maj. Gen.

ALS, DNA, RG 94, ACP, S1177 CB 1866. Col. Edward Hatch, 2nd Iowa Cav., was promoted to brig. gen. as of April 2, 1864. See Lincoln, *Works*, VII, 279. Col. James R. Slack, 47th Ind., was promoted to brig. gen. on Feb. 14, 1865, to date from Nov. 10, 1864. On July 28, 1865, Secretary of the Treasury Hugh McCulloch wrote to Secretary of War Edwin M. Stanton recommending that Slack be appointed bvt. maj. gen. of vols., stating that Slack broke with the Democratic Party to support the war and that his appointment would "gratify a great many friends of the Administration, in Indiana." LS, DNA, RG 94, ACP, S1177 CB 1866. On Nov. 15, Maj. Gen. Philip H. Sheridan, commanding the Dept. of the Gulf, in which Slack had served since the Vicksburg campaign, endorsed this letter. "The political reasons for this Brevet are stronger, than the military—I cannot recommend the brevet." AES, *ibid.* On Jan. 11, 1866, USG disapproved Slack's appointment. ES, *ibid.* On June 23, however, USG wrote to Stanton. "I would respectfully recommend the Appointment, by Brevet, of Brig. Gen. Jas. R. Slack, U. S. Volunteers, to be Maj. General. General Slack served during the entire war and all, or nearly all the time in the field." ALS, *ibid.*, ACP, 781S CB 1866. Slack was so appointed, as of March 13, 1865.

1. See letter to Brig. Gen. Lorenzo Thomas, July 27, 1863.

To Maj. Gen. Henry W. Halleck

> Head Quarters, Dept. of the Ten.
> Cairo, Ill. Oct. 16th 1863.

MAJ. GEN. H. W. HALLECK,
GEN. IN CHIEF, WASHINGTON D. C.
GENERAL,

This will be handed to you by Mr. E. E. G. Barney, of Holly Springs Miss.

Mr. Barney is a Northern man but has resided in the south for a number of years, and having been largely connected with the railroad interest of the South is extensively acquainted with that portion of our country. Mr. Barney took occation to show his devotion to the Union long before our forces reached his home and property. He has, I believe, never failed to get information to commanders at Memphis when he thought it important.

I have no hesitation in saying that I believe the most implicit confidence can be placed in Mr. B. and in all his statements.

> I am Gen. very respectfully
> your obt. svt.
> U. S. GRANT
> Maj. Gen.

ALS, DNA, RG 156, Letters Received, OCO File 1867–76.

On Oct. 14, 1865, Bvt. Maj. Gen. Joseph D. Webster, Washington, wrote
to USG. "On behalf of Messrs. E. G. Barney and W. S. McElwain, late of Holly
Springs, Miss, I beg leave to submit the following statement and request. Previous to the late war these gentlemen were engaged in partnership, in operating
a foundry and machine shop in Holly Springs.' Shortly after the breaking out of
the rebellion their buildings and machinery, largely new, were taken by the rebel
authorities to be converted into a manufactory of small arms. When it became
apparent that the national forces would soon take possession of that part of the
country, the machinery was removed further South, and is now understood to be
in the Armory at Macon, Georgia, which is in custody of officers of the U. S.
Ordnance Corps. After the removal of the machinery from Holly Springs Mr.
McElwain went into Alabama and engaged in the iron business, thus continuing
to secure exemption from the rebel 'conscription' by his character of 'skilled
mechanic.' These gentlemen are now about engaging in the manufacture of iron
in Alabama, and desire (1) that such of the machinery, above referred to, as
can be identified by Mr. McElwain may be directed to be restored to him by the
Officers in charge at Macon. 2. They further desire to purchase such *other* machinery in the rebel Armory or Arsenal at Macon, as may be useful in their
present business, on a credit of 12, 18, & 24 months with interest, giving therefor *security*, which shall be certified to, as *ample*, by the District Attorney or
other U. S. Officer at Cincinnati, Ohio; so as to make the Government safe against
loss. 3. They also desire to *purchase*, on same terms as above, twenty miles of
Rail-road iron, now in charge of Officers of the Quarter Master's Department at
Chattanooga, and in course of disposal. It is proper to state that Messrs. Barney
and McElwain received no compensation from the rebel authorities for the
machinery taken as above stated,—and further, that for any seeming acquiescence
(compulsory) by Mr. McElwain in the rebellion, he has received the President's
full pardon. It will be readily understood that all the cash means at the disposal
of the parties is needed for necessary preliminaries to the commencement of
business; hence their request for the favor of credit. But it is thought that the
active prosecution of this enterprise in Alabama will be of public utility by providing compensated labor for many of the freedmen, and will tend to promote
the restoration of prosperity, and kindly and patriotic feeling in that region. With
the character and conduct of Mr. E. G. Barney during the early periods of the
rebellion you have considerable personal acquaintance. No man is more patriotic
or better fitted to carry a good influence into the Southern Country. His past services and present enterprise deserve well of the National Government. I beg
leave to say that all possible avoidance of delay is highly important in the present
stage of the proposed business, and to request that such orders may be given to
the proper officers of the Ordnance and Quarter Master's Department as may
secure the promptest action consistent with the observance of the necessary
forms." ALS, *ibid*. On Oct. 17, USG endorsed this letter. "Respectfully referred
to the Secretary of War. It is recommended that the within named parties be
allowed to receive such of their machinery as is in the possession of the U. S. on
making proper proof of property; and be allowed to purchase such other arsenal
machinery at Macon as is not needed by the U. S. and against which there are no
rightful claims by other parties, on properly secured credits, provided the Gov't.
is making such sales on credit." ES, *ibid*. Secretary of War Edwin M. Stanton
also endorsed the letter. "Approved so far as relates to thier own machinery; and
so far as relates to other arsenal machinery reference is made to the Chief of
Ordnance." AES, *ibid*. On Oct. 26, Col. Edward D. Townsend, AGO, wrote to

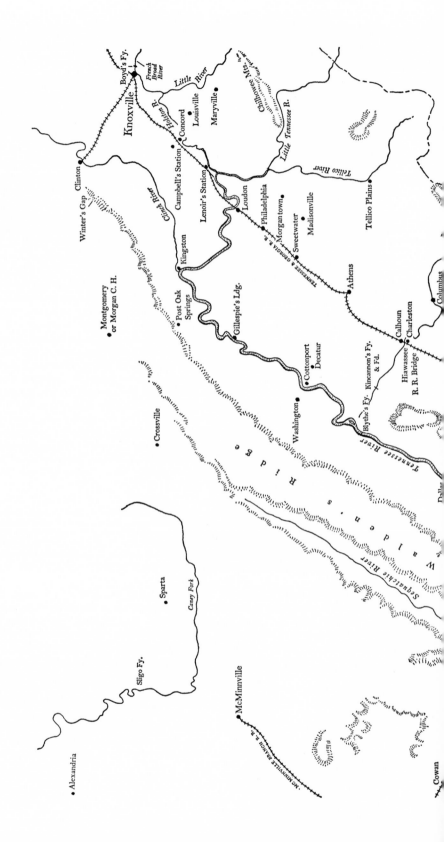

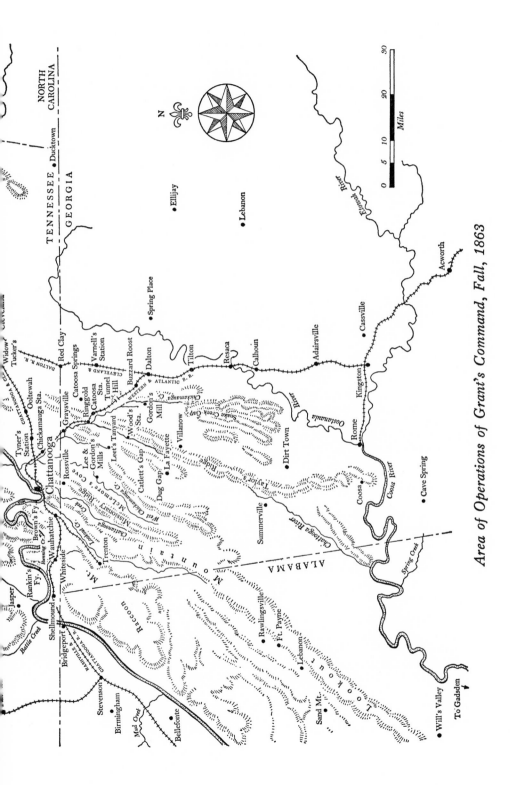

Area of Operations of Grant's Command, Fall, 1863

Brig. Gen. Alexander B. Dyer, chief of ordnance, stating that Stanton had received Dyer's recommendation of Oct. 24 that the additional machinery be sold and authorized him to do so "on credit not to exceed six months—" LS, *ibid.*

On Nov. 6, Webster, Cincinnati, wrote to USG. "I take the liberty to inclose to you a letter to Gen. Dyer with a bond signed by Mr. A. D. Breed and Mr. M. H. Crane of this city, guaranteeing the performance of any obligations Messrs Barney and McElwain and myself may enter into about the machinery &c. at Macon. . . . What we desire is that instructions be sent at once to Lieut. Webb, acting Ordnance Officer at Macon to let us have the machinery we want, both the reclaimed and the purchased portions, upon *our* (B. McE. and W.) obligation guaranteed by the bond. . . ." ALS, *ibid.* On Nov. 8, Bvt. Col. Ely S. Parker endorsed this letter for USG. "Respectfully referred to the Chief of Ordnance, with the recommendation that the order requested by Gen. Webster be made, and the within bonds accepted." AES, *ibid.* On Nov. 10, Act. Asst. Secretary of War Thomas T. Eckert approved a bond for $100,000, guaranteeing that Webster, Wallace S. McElwain, and Elijah G. Barney, doing business as the Cahawba Iron Co., Irondale, Ala., would prove ownership of machinery later appraised at $9,741.38 and would pay for additional machinery later appraised at $17,730. AES, *ibid.*

On Feb. 10 and 15, 1866, Lt. H. P. Webb, act. ordnance officer, Macon, Ga., wrote to Dyer enclosing statements of former C.S.A. Lt. Col. William LeRoy Brown of Jan. 28 and of James H. Burton, former superintendent, C.S.A. Armory, Macon, of Jan. 26 regarding a C.S.A. contract with Jones, McElwain & Co., Holly Springs, Miss., and its purchase of their machinery. ALS, *ibid.* On June 8, both Barney and McElwain wrote to Stanton, denying that they willingly cooperated with the C.S.A. Copies, *ibid.* On the same day, Webster and his partners, Irondale, wrote to Stanton seeking an extension of six months for payment of their debt. ALS, *ibid.* On July 2, Webster, Washington, wrote to Stanton. "In December last certain machinery in the 'confederate' Arsenal at Macen, Georgia, was by your order, delivered to E. G. Barney, W. S. McElwain and myself on condition secured by bond that it should be paid for at an appraisal, or payment remitted on proof of former ownership by the first two of the abovementioned parties. The sworn statements of Messrs. Barney and McElwain, and of Mr. J. F. Humphrey, late Acting Asst. Engineer U. S. Navy, herewith submitted will fully explain the facts in relation to the property in question. Constant intercourse with these gentlemen for almost a year has fully convinced me that they have been truly loyal to the Government of the United States, and that any acts of theis of seeming conformity to the Authority of the late 'Confederate' government were done under what amounted to stringent cumpulsion. During the war Mr. Barney, to my official knowledge, gave very important information to Officers of our Army, and did also, as I fully believe, *several times risk his life*, within the rebel lines, to procure such information. For more full accounts of his services in this regard I refer to Lieutenant General Grant. The amount of property now reclaimed is only a small part of that on which a lien of nearly one hundred thousand dollars still exists. The remainder can probably never be traced or recovered. For these reasons I beg leave to request that the obligation and bond, for payment for this machinery, be remitted." ALS, *ibid.* On the same day, USG endorsed this letter. "Mr. Barney was an active Union man during the rebellion and from his social standing in the South was enabled to collect valuable information which he always communicated to the nearest Union commander,

not as a paid spy, but for the benefit of the cause deepest in his heart." AES, *ibid.*
On July 7, Dyer wrote to Stanton doubting that the iron co. had proven its ownership to any machinery and objecting to Webster's request that its debt to the U.S.
be remitted. LS, *ibid.* On Aug. 25, Webster wrote to Stanton affirming Barney's
loyalty and stating that he only sought to have remitted the debt for machinery
of the predecessor co. which, in effect, had been seized and, in large part, never
paid for by the C.S.A. ALS, *ibid.* On Aug. 27, USG endorsed this letter. "Knowing the loyalty of Mr. Barney, and his services to the Union cause, without wanting compensation for it I would recommend the restoration to him of all captured
property in possession of the Government which previously belonged to him, and
the cancelling of [all] claims for money the Government may have against him
for such property (that previously belonging to him) as he may have purchased
and not yet paid for." AES, *ibid.* On Oct. 19, however, the War Dept. Claims
Commission decided "that the whole of the machinery was the property of the
rebel government, and that any interest which the claimants might have had in
it has been parted with by them. The Commission recommend that the Government assert its right to the whole of this machinery, and in default of payment by
the claimants that the bond be enforced." Copy, *ibid.*

On June 17, 1868, Webster, Chicago, wrote to Secretary of War John M.
Schofield, reviewing his partnership with "Barney and others," protesting the
Claims Commission decision, and stating that, nevertheless, "We went on with
our enterprise. Some of the parties interested took a contract for extending the
Alabama & Tennessee River Railroad from Blue Mountain, its late terminus, to
Dalton in Georgia, thus furnishing a wanting link in a line shorter than any other
existing between New York and New Orleans. The execution (fulfillment) of
[the] contract was impeded for many months by various causes, among which
jealousy of Northern men and influence had a large place. The business activity
which sprung up at the South directly after the war did not continue—our expenses had been very heavy and we were unable to pay. After an arduous struggle with many difficulties the Railroad (now called the Selma, Rome and Dalton
R. R.) is going on well, under the auspices of men of ample capital in New York
& the Iron Works are thus finding a market for castings &c. which they can supply. But just as we are beginning to make a little progress we are served with a
notice from the Ordnance Department that unless immediate payment is made for
the machinery, suit will be instituted on the bond given for it. The sureties on
the bond are among the most substantial men in Cincinnati, worth many times
the amount of the debt, making the U. States amply secure in the matter. We
now ask for an extension, such as will enable us to work out the payments and
save our selves and sureties from annoyance and loss. We think we can pay say
five hundred dollars ($500) per month for six months, and, after that, one thou-
sand ($1000) per month. . . ." ALS, *ibid.* On July 27, USG endorsed this letter.
"I am personally acquainted with Genl. J. D. Webster, who makes the within
application and am satisfied he would prefer no request in a business matter of
this kind that might not be with propriety granted, and do therefore recommend
that the relief asked for by him be granted." ES, *ibid.* On Oct. 10, a new bond
for $60,000 guaranteed that Webster, McElwain, and Barney would pay the
government, by such monthly installments as Webster had proposed, $27,471.98,
"together with interest at six per cent per annum on each instalment from June
25th 1865." Copy, *ibid.* On June 13, 1871, Solicitor Gen. Benjamin H. Bristow
wrote to Warner M. Bateman, U.S. Attorney, Cincinnati, requesting that he sue

the guarantors. ALS, *ibid.* On Feb. 18, 1873, Attorney General George H. Williams wrote to Secretary of War William W. Belknap stating that the sureties, Abel D. Breed and Martin H. Crane, had paid $37,448.83 "in full satisfaction of the judgment obtained against them." LS, *ibid.*

To Brig. Gen. Marcellus M. Crocker

Head Quarters, Dept. of the Ten.
Cairo, Ill. Oct. 16th 1863,

BRIG. GEN. CROCKER,
COMD.G NATCHEZ, MISS.
GENERAL.

There is an estate in Louisiana called "Ravenswood" situated about twenty miles above Natchez, in Tensas Parish belonging to a Mrs. Ignaga[1] of New York City. The overseer living on the place is named M. M. Beaver. I have been written to by the father-in-law of Gen. Halleck[2] who is acquainted with this lady requesting a protection for this property. If you have an opportunity of sending Mr. Beaver a protection paper for what still remains on this place you may do so, exercising your own judgement however whether they are entitled to it from the lights you may have.

I am here by order of the Gen. in Chief to receive orders. What they will be I dont know.

yours Truly
U. S. GRANT
Maj. Gen.

ALS, ICHi.

1. Ellen Yznaga del Valle, born in La. in 1822, the only child of Samuel Clement, who developed Ravenswood plantation, married Don Antonio Yznaga del Valle, owner of sugar plantations in Cuba and La. She spent the early Civil War years in New York City, publicly supported the C.S.A., and moved to London after the death of her husband.
2. John Church Hamilton (1792–1882), son and biographer of Alexander Hamilton, was the father of Elizabeth Hamilton Halleck and of Maj. Gen. Schuyler Hamilton.

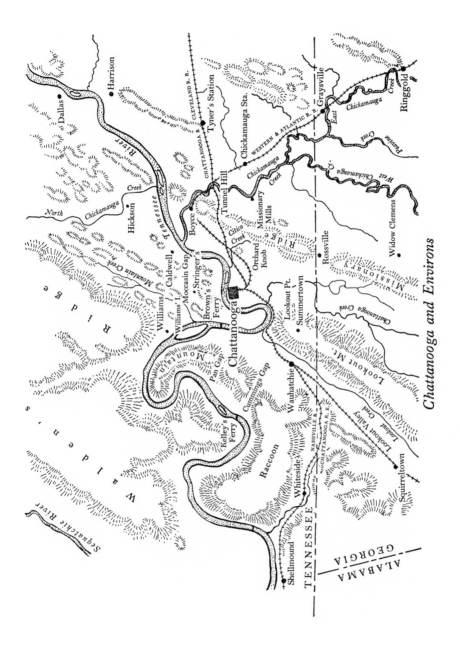

Chattanooga and Environs

To Maj. Gen. Stephen A. Hurlbut

———

Head Quarters, Dept. of the Ten.
Vicksburg Miss.[1] Oct. 17th 1863,

MAJ. GEN. S. A. HURLBUT,
COMD.G 16TH ARMY CORPS,
GENERAL.

I arrived here yesterday morning and immediately reported by telegraph to Washington. Answer is just received for me to proceed to Louisville, Ky.[2] For the present address all communications to me at that place. I will inform you as soon as my Head Quarters are located.

Nothing is received from the East to suggest any change of orders you already have. Continue to forward to Sherman all that you receive effecting the movement of his column. Should the enemy be so effectually driven from North Mississippi as to enable you to do so extend your command Eastward and protect all the road you can. If possible Sherman should have at least the force he now has with him compact and ready to move in any direction without detaching rail-road guards.

I have telegraphed Gen. Halleck the information I obtained at Memphis with regard to movements of the enemy in Arkansas, and on your line, and asked if Steeles force could not be withdrawn. I also told him that I had advised that Steele send his Cavalry as far as Arkadelphia and destroy the saltworks, powder Mills &c.[3]

There is nothing in this of special interest to Gen. Sherman, but I wish you would send him a copy. It will serve to show him that I have no orders controlling his movements not already in his possession.

I Am Gen. Very respectfully
your obt. svt.
U. S. GRANT
Maj. Gen. Comd.g

ALS, DNA, RG 393, 16th Army Corps, Letters Received. *O.R.*, I, xxx, part 4, 430–31.

1. Corrected by Maj. Gen. Stephen A. Hurlbut to read "Cairo Ills."

2. On Oct. 16, 1863, 9:00 P.M., Maj. Gen. Henry W. Halleck had tele-graphed to USG. "Private & confidential . . . You will immediately proceed to the 'Galt House' Louisville, Ky, where you will meet an officer of the War Dept with your orders & instructions. You will take with you your staff, &c., for immediate operations in the field. Wait at Louisville for officer of War Dept" ALS (telegram sent), DNA, RG 107, Telegrams Collected (Bound); copies, *ibid.*, RG 393, Dept. of the Tenn., Hd. Qrs. Correspondence; DLC-USG, V, 6, 8, 24, 94. *O.R.*, I, xxx, part 4, 404. On Oct. 17, 11:00 A.M., USG telegraphed to Halleck. "Your dispatch of 9 P M yesterday just received. I will start for Louisville by rail im-mediately." Telegram received, DNA, RG 107, Telegrams Collected (Bound); copies, *ibid.*, Telegrams Received in Cipher; *ibid.*, RG 393, Dept. of the Tenn., Hd. Qrs. Correspondence; DLC-USG, V, 6, 8, 24, 94. *O.R.*, I, xxx, part 4, 429.

3. See telegram to Maj. Gen. Henry W. Halleck, Oct. 16, 1863. On Oct. 17, Hurlbut wrote to Brig. Gen. John A. Rawlins. "Genl. Sherman has called for force enough from me to cover the Rail Road to Buzzard Roost. I have therefore ordered Fuller's Brigade from Memphis to Big Bear Creek which leaves me very light handed here. I have written to Steele asking True's Brigade to be sent back, but do not know that it will be done. I request an order for that purpose. I desire that you obtain from Maj. Genl. Grant or Genl. Halleck, some definite instructions as to my limits of authority. The troops which I have furnished Steele are borne on my books as *detached* and do not report to me but, I suppose, to Schofield. I do not like to lose them, but do not like either to issue any orders about them. Col. Manter, who is Chief of Staff for Steele, is a little disposed to consider any call made by me for information as to these troops, an interfer-ence The Okalona force, I am inclined to think, is moving into N. E. Alabama. Hatch has returned having killed about 75 and wounded many of the enemy. His report is not in. I will send it as soon as it comes. We will probably have quiet for a few days in which time supplies are being pushed forward." Copy, DNA, RG 393, 16th Army Corps, Letters Sent. *O.R.*, I, xxx, part 4, 431. See *ibid.*, p. 407. On Oct. 19, 1:00 P.M., Halleck telegraphed to USG. "Genl. Schofield tele-graphs that he will send one regiment & a battery from St Louis to Louisville, and that troops not required by Genl Steele to hold Arkansas river will be sent to Memphis to reenforce Genl Sherman's column." ALS (telegram sent), DNA, RG 107, Telegrams Collected (Bound); copies, *ibid.*, RG 393, Military Div. of the Miss., Hd. Qrs. Correspondence; DLC-USG, V, 40, 94. *O.R.*, I, xxx, part 4, 470.

General Orders No. 1

Head Quarters Military Division of the Mississippi,
Louisville, Ky., Oct 18. 1863

GENERAL ORDERS No. 1.

In compliance with General Orders No. 337, A. G. O., of date Washington D. C., Oct. 16. 1863, the undersigned hereby assumes command of the "Military Division of the Mississippi" embracing the Departments of the Ohio, of the Cumberland and of the Tennessee.

The Head-Quarters of the Military Division of the Mississippi will be in the field, where all reports and returns required by Army Regulations and existing Orders will be made.[1]

U. S. GRANT.
Major General.

Copies, DNA, RG 94, Generals' Papers and Books, U. S. Grant; *ibid.*, RG 393, Military Div. of the Miss., General Orders; DLC-USG, V, 14; (printed) USGA. *O.R.*, I, xxx, part 4, 450–51.

On Oct. 16, 1863, Maj. Gen. Henry W. Halleck wrote to USG, Louisville. "You will recieve herewith the orders of the President of the United States placing you in command of the Depts of the Ohio, Cumberland & Tennessee. The organization of these Depts will be changed as you may deem most practicable. You will immediately proceed to Chattanooga & relieve Genl Rosecrans. You can communicate with Genls Burnside and Sherman by telegraph. A summary of the orders sent to these officers will be sent to you immediately. It is left optional with you to supercede Genl Rosecrans by Genl G. H. Thomas or not. Any other changes ~~you wish~~ will be made on your request by telegram. One of the first objects requiring your attention is the supply of your armies. Another is the security of the passes in the Georgia mountains to shut out the enemy from Tennessee and Kentucky. You will consult with Genl Meigs & Col Scott in regard to transportation and & supplies. Should circumstances permit I will ~~see~~ visit you personally in a few days, for consultation." ALS (telegram sent), DLC-William T. Sherman; copies, *ibid.*; DNA, RG 108, Letters Sent (Press); *ibid.*, RG 393, Dept. of the Tenn., Letters Sent; DLC-USG, V, 6, 8, 24, 94. *O.R.*, I, xxx, part 4, 404. Pursuant to conversations on Oct. 18 between Secretary of War Edwin M. Stanton and USG on a train between Indianapolis and Louisville, War Dept. General Orders No. 337, dated Washington, Oct. 16, were issued. "By direction of the President of the United States the Departments of the Ohio, of the Cumberland, and of the Tennessee will constitute the Military Division of the Mississippi. Maj. Gen. U. S. Grant, U. S. Army, is placed in command of the Military Division of the Mississippi, headquarters in the field. Maj. Gen. W. S. Rosecrans, U. S. Volunteers, is relieved from the command of the Department and Army of the Cumberland. Maj. Gen. G. H. Thomas is hereby assigned to that command." *Ibid.* See *Memoirs*, II, 18–19. As USG remembered it, he accepted command of the Military Div. of the Miss. and sent these War Dept. orders to Chattanooga on the same night as his Oct. 19 telegram to Maj. Gen. George H. Thomas, but the change of command actually occurred the day before. See *ibid.*, p. 26.

On Oct. 18, Brig. Gen. John A. Rawlins issued Special Orders No. 1, Military Div. of the Miss. "Major General W. S. Rosencrans having been relieved from the command of the Department of the Cumberland by direction of the President of the United States by General Orders. No. 337, of date October 16th 1863, and Major General G. H. Thomas having been assigned to the command, he will at once enter upon the duties thereof, and Major General Rosencranz will turn over to him all books, papers, maps, and other property pertaining to said command. All Staff Officers, except personal Aides-de-Camp, now on duty with

General Rosencrans, will report at once to General Thomas for orders. Major General Rosencrans, on turning over his command to Major General Thomas may proceed to Cincinnati, Ohio, and from there report by letter to the Adjutant General of the Army, Washington D. C., for orders." Copy, DLC-USG, V, 38. A copy of these orders, dated Oct. 20, signed by Capt. Ely S. Parker, and addressed jointly to Maj. Gen. William S. Rosecrans and Thomas, is in *O.R.*, I, xxxi, part 1, 669.

On Oct. 19, 8:00 A.M., Stanton, Louisville, telegraphed to Halleck. "Gen Grant accepted the command at once and has already issued his orders to Thomas. He considers it indispensible that Rosecrans should be relieved because he would not obey orders. His health and spirits are very good but is still quite lame and moves with difficulty on a crutch. Meigs is here." Telegram received, DNA, RG 107, Telegrams Collected (Bound). Writing to Mary E. (Emma) Hurlbut on Nov. 23, Rawlins discussed USG's reasons for relieving Rosecrans. "There has been much less said in what is termed the radical papers of the North than I had expected to see and there would be much less I am sure if they were advised as to all the facts. One thing is very certain   while General Grant is no enemy of Genl Rosecrans as some of our papers seem to be impressed he is, he could not in justice to himself and the cause of his country think of again commanding General Rosecrans, after his experience with him in the summer and fall of 1862. Of this the Authorities at Washington were fully advised, in General Grants Reports of the battles of Iuka and Corinth, in the former of which in consequence of his (Genl Rosecrans) deviation from the entire plan and order of battle the enemy was enabled to escape and by his tardiness in pursuit in the latter allowed to get off with much less loss than he should. To this might also be added his general spirit of insubordination toward General Grant. Although to his face he professed for him the highest regards both as a Man and Officer. Knowing these facts the government could not consistently with the good of the service retain General Rosecrans in command under Genl Grant. That it was necessary for some one other than Genl Rosecrans to have the direction of matters here was too apparent to every military mind in this army to elicit question" ALS, ICHi. Possibly at the same time or earlier, Rawlins drafted a ten-page memorandum which may at first have been intended for publication in response to newspaper criticism of Rosecrans's removal. Contrary to the view that Rosecrans and USG were "enemies," Rawlins noted that USG spoke of Rosecrans as his "warm personal friend" and "one of the ablest & purest of men, both in motive and action." When Rawlins first saw Rosecrans in May, 1862, he was "not surprised" that the two gens. greeted each other with "how are you Grant, how are you Rosey." Furthermore, when Maj. Gen. John Pope was given the command of the Army of Va. "over his seniors in rank," Rawlins heard USG remark that he would "willingly serve under" but two junior officers in his dept., Rosecrans and Maj. Gen. William T. Sherman. But in July when Halleck, appointed gen.-in-chief, was about to transfer to USG the command of the Dept. of the Miss., Rosecrans reportedly told Halleck that "whatever you do with me for Godsake dont place me under Grant, and this while he was ~~stating~~ manifesting for Grant every evidence of friendship for him personally and confidence in him as an Officer." Rawlins then reviewed at length USG's dissatisfaction with Rosecrans's generalship at the battle of Iuka. ADf, USG 3. In *Memoirs*, II, 19–22, 28, USG limited criticism of Rosecrans to his record in 1863.

On Oct. 19, 6:30 P.M., Rosecrans telegraphed to USG. "Genl. Order No. 1: Division of the Mississippi just recd. and shall be executed to night" Copies,

DNA, RG 393, Dept. of the Cumberland, Telegrams Sent; *ibid.*, Military Div. of the Miss., Telegrams Received. *O.R.*, I, xxx, part 4, 478. On Oct. 20, Thomas assumed command of the Dept. and Army of the Cumberland. *Ibid.*, I, xxxi, part 1, 669. On Oct. 19, Maj. Gen. Ambrose E. Burnside, Knoxville, telegraphed to USG. "Your telegraph order received assuming command of Division of Mississippi. Please rely upon my full and cordial support. Will send you during the night a full statement in cipher of my position and numbers." Telegram received, DNA, RG 393, Military Div. of the Miss., Telegrams Received. *O.R.*, I, xxx, part 4, 488.

On Oct. 20, Halleck wrote to USG. "In compliance with my promise, I now proceed to give you a brief statement of the objects aimed at by Genl. Rosecrans & Genl Burnsides movement into East Tennessee, and of the measures directed to be taken to attain these objects. It has been the constant desire of the government from the beginning of the war to rescue the loyal inhabitants of East Tennessee from the hands of the rebels, who fully appreciated the importance of continuing their hold upon that country. In addition to the large amount of agricultural products drawn from the upper valley of the Tennessee, they also obtained iron and other military materials from the vicinity of Chattanooga. The possession of East Tennessee would cut off one of their most important Rail Road communications, and threaten their manufactories at Rome, Atlanta, &c. When Genl Buell was ordered into East Tennessee in the summer of 1862, Chattanooga was comparatively unprotected; but Bragg reached there before Buell, and, by threatening his communications, forced him to retreat on Nashville and Louisville. Again, after the battle of Perryville, Genl Buell was urged to pursue Bragg's defeated army & drive it from East Tennessee. The same was urged upon his successor, but the lateness of the season or other causes prevented further operations after the battle of Stone River. Last Spring, when your movements on the Mississippi river had drawn out of Tennessee a large force of the enemy, I again urged Genl Rosecrans to take advantage of that opportunity to carry out his projected plan of campaign, Genl Burnside being ready to cooperate, with a diminished but still efficient force. But he could not be persuaded to act in time, preferring to lie still till your campaign should be terminated. I represented to him, but without avail, that by this delay, Johnston might be able to reenforce Bragg with the troops then operating against you. When Genl Rosecrans finally determined to advance, he was allowed to select his own lines & plans for carrying out the objects of the expedition. He was directed, however, to report his movements daily till he crossed the Tennessee, and to connect his left, so far as possible, with Genl Burnside's right. Genl Burnside was directed to move simultaneously, connecting his right, as far as possible with Genl Rosecrans' left, so that if the enemy concentrated upon either army the other could move to its assistance. When Genl Burnside reached Kingston & Knoxville, and found no considerable number of the enemy in East Tennessee, he was instructed to move down the river & cooperate with Genl Rosecrans. These instructions were repeated some fifteen times, but were not carried out, Genl Burnside alleging as an excuse that he believed that Bragg was in retreat & that Genl Rosecrans needed no reinforcements. When the latter had gained possession of Chattanooga he was directed not to move on Rome as he proposed, but simply to hold the mountain passes so as to prevent the ingress of the rebels into East Tennessee. That object accomplished, I considered the campaign as ended, at least for the present. Future operations would depend upon the ascertained strength and movements of the enemy. In other words, the main objects of the campaign were the restoration of East Tennessee to the Union, and, by holding the two extremities of the valley, to secure it from rebel invasion. The moment I recieved reliable information of the departure of Longstreet's corps from the Army of the Potomac, I ordered forward to Genl Rosecrans every available man in the Dept of the Ohio, & again urged Genl Burnside to move to his assistance. I also telegraphed to Genls Hurlbut & Sherman & yourself to send forward all available troops in your Dept. If these forces had been sent to Genl Rosecrans by Nashville, they could not have been supplied. I therefore directed them to move by Corinth and the Tennessee river. The necessity of this has been proved by the fact that the reinforcements sent to him from the Army of the Potomac have not been able, for the want of rail road transportation, to reach Genl Rosecrans' army in the field. In regard to the relative strength of the opposing armies it is believed that Genl Rosecrans when he first moved against Bragg, had double if not treble his force; General Burnside also had more than double the force of Buckner; and even when Bragg & Buckner united, Rosecrans' army was very greatly their superior in numbers. Even the eighteen thousand men sent from Virginia under Longstreet would not have given the enemy the superiority. It is now ascertained that the greater part of the prisoners paroled by you at Vicksburg & Genl Banks at Port Hudson were illegally & improperly declared exchanged & forced into the ranks to swell the rebel numbers at Chickamauga. This outrageous act, in violation of the laws of war, of the cartel entered into by the rebel authorities, and of all sense of honor, gives us a useful lesson in regard to the character of the enemy with whom we are contending. He neither regards the rules of civilized warfare, nor even his most solemn engagements. You may, therefore, expect to meet in arms thousands of unexchanged prisoners released by you and others on parole not to serve again till duly exchanged. Although the enemy by this disgraceful means have been able to concentrate in Georgia & Alabama a much larger force than we anticipated, your armies will be abundantly able to defeat him. Your difficulty will not be in the want of men, but in the means of supplying them, at this season of the year. A single track rail-road can supply an army of sixty or seventy thousand men, with the usual number of cavalry & artillery; but beyond that number, or with a large mounted force, the difficulty of supply is very great. I do not know the present condition of the road from Nashville to Decatur, but if practicable to repair it, the use of that triangle will be of great assistance to you. I hope also that the recent rise of water in the Cumberland and Tennessee rivers will enable you to employ water transportation to Nashville and Eastport or Florence. If you reoccupy the passes of Lookout Mountain, which should never have been given up, you will be able to use the rail road and river from Bridgeport to Chattanooga. This seems to me a matter of vital importance, & should recieve your early attention. I submit this summary in the hopes that it will assist you in fully understanding the objects of the campaign, & the means of attaining these objects. Probably the Secty of War in his interviews with you at Louisville has gone over the same ground. Whatever measures you may deem proper to adopt under existing circumstances, you will recieve all possible assistance from the authorities at Washington. You have never heretofore complained that such assistance has not been afforded you in your operations, and I think you will have no cause of complaint in your present campaign." LS, DLC-William T. Sherman. *O.R.*, I, xxxi, part 1, 667–69. From Louisville on Oct. 18, Rawlins wrote to Mary E. (Emma) Hurlbut, describing USG's new command and plans to go to Chattanooga. "how long we will remain there I am at present unable to say, it will be I have no doubt several weeks, sufficiently long at any rate to attack and drive Bragg from his position in that immediate front, or to at least see to the securing of the safety of our position there; . . ." By the first of the year, he added, "either a decisive battle will be fought or the rainy weather will bar active operations in the field." ALS, ICHi.

1. On Oct. 30, Parker, Chattanooga, wrote to Burnside, Sherman, and Thomas, requesting regular monthly and trimonthly reports of officers and units in their commands. ALS, DNA, RG 393, Dept. of the Tenn., Unregistered Letters Received; copies (by USG), *ibid.*, Military Div. of the Miss., Letters Sent; DLC-USG, V, 34, 35. On Nov. 20, 11:35 A.M., Maj. Samuel Breck, AGO, telegraphed to USG. "Please forward a Return of your command, to this Office, as early as practicable—No Return yet received—" Telegram received, DNA, RG 107, Telegrams Collected (Unbound); copies, *ibid.*, RG 94, Enlisted Branch, Letters Sent; *ibid.*, RG 393, Military Div. of the Miss., War Dept. Correspondence; DLC-USG, V, 40, 94. On the same day, 10:00 P.M., USG telegraphed to Breck. "Since my assignment to the command of the military Division time enough has not elapsed for the order to have reached all parts of the command & returns get to me. If they had been already made out." Telegram received, DNA, RG 107, Telegrams Collected (Bound); copies, *ibid.*, RG 393, Military Div. of the Miss., War Dept. Correspondence; DLC-USG, V, 40, 94. On Nov. 24, USG wrote to Sherman. "You will please furnish to these Head Quarters as soon as practicable, a list of the Regiments and Batteries of your command now at this place, also a list of the troops now serving with General Dodge" Copies, *ibid.*, V, 34, 35; DNA, RG 393, Military Div. of the Miss., Letters Sent. On Dec. 3, Capt. George K. Leet wrote to Sherman and to Thomas, again requesting their monthly and trimonthly reports. Copies, *ibid.*

On Nov. 6, Maj. Gen. John M. Schofield, St. Louis, wrote to USG. "I have the honor to respectfully request a list of the Regiments, Batteries &c. serving in the Military Division of the Mississippi. This request is made in view of the numerous Official Communications forwarded to these Head Quarters from the Bureaus of the War Department the Hospitals &c. and in order to facilitate the return of deserters. A corresponding list of Regiments &c. now within this command will be furnished if desired." Copy, *ibid.*, Dept. of Mo., Letters Sent. On Nov. 5, Schofield had telegraphed to USG. "Please inform me where the 2nd Wisconsin Cavalry and 6th Wisconsin Cavalry are. I want to send two battalions which I have to join them." Telegram received, *ibid.*, RG 107, Telegrams Collected (Unbound); copy, *ibid.*, RG 393, Dept. of Mo., Telegrams Sent.

On Nov. 13, 1:00 P.M., USG telegraphed to Halleck. "I respectfully recommend that Medical Inspectors in this military Division be ordered to report to me so that their labor may be divided more equally, than by assigning them to Departments." Telegram received, *ibid.*, RG 107, Telegrams Collected (Bound); copies, *ibid.*, RG 393, Military Div. of the Miss., War Dept. Correspondence; DLC-USG, V, 40, 94. On Sept. 20, USG endorsed a letter of Act. Asst. Surgeon Gen. D. O. McCord seeking authorization to pay act. hospital stewards for contrabands an extra $17 per month. "Respectfully forwarded to Head Quarters of the Army Washington D. C. with the request that the enclosed Special Order No 9. of date Lagrange, Tenn. Nov. 27th 1862 from these Head Quarters be approved and the Quarters Masters Department directed to pay the amount, up to the time of the passage of the act, cutting off extra duty for Special Service, if it cannot be approved generally. The order was a necessity at the time to assure the proper attention to these people nor has any expedient, been since adopted to obviate the necessity that prompted its issue" Copies, *ibid.*, V, 25; DNA, RG 393, Dept. of the Tenn., Endorsements. On Nov. 6, Breck wrote to USG approving such payment for the period before March 3, when Congress prohibited extra-duty pay. Copies, *ibid.*, RG 94, Enlisted Branch, Letters Sent; *ibid.*, RG 393, Military Div. of the Miss., War Dept. Correspondence.

On Nov. 5, Col. Edward D. Townsend, AGO, wrote to USG. "I have the honor to request you will please cause twenty copies of all *printed* orders, issued and to be issued by you as Commander of the Division of the Mississippi, to be furnished for the files of this Office" Copy, *ibid.* On Dec. 30 and Jan. 15, 1864, USG, Chattanooga and Nashville, wrote to the AGO. "I have the honor to transmit herewith copies of Special Field Orders issued from my Head Quarters, commencing with No. 1, of date October 25th 1863, and ending with No. 44, of date December 29th 1863." "I have the honor to transmit herewith copies of Special Orders, from No. 1, of date Oct 18th 1863, to No. 34, of date Dec. 30th 1863, inclusive, issued from my Head Quarters." Copies, *ibid.*, War Dept. Correspondence; DLC-USG, V, 40, 94.

To Maj. Gen. George H. Thomas

Louisville Oct. 19th 11.30. P. M. [*1863.*]

MAJOR GENL. G. H. THOMAS.

CHATTANOOGA

Hold Chattanooga at all hazards. I will be there as soon as possible. Please inform me how long your present supplies will last and the prospects for keeping them up.

U. S. GRANT
Major General.

Telegram, copies, DLC-USG, V, 34, 35; DNA, RG 393, Military Div. of the Miss., Letters Sent. *O.R.*, I, xxx, part 4, 479. On Oct. 19, 1863, Maj. Gen. George H. Thomas telegraphed to USG. "Two hundred four thousand four hundred Sixty two (204,462) rations in Storehouses. Ninety thousand to arrive tomorrow and all the trains were loaded which had arrived at Bridgeport up to the Sixteenth, probably three hundred wagons. I will hold the town till we Starve" Telegram received, DNA, RG 107, Telegrams Collected (Bound); copies, *ibid.*, RG 393, Dept. of the Cumberland, Telegrams Sent; *ibid.*, Military Div. of the Miss., Telegrams Received. *O.R.*, I, xxx, part 4, 479. On Oct. 20, 1:00 A.M., Thomas telegraphed to USG. "If the wagons now on the road arrive Safe, we are all right till the first of November at least" Telegram received, DNA, RG 107, Telegrams Collected (Bound); copies, *ibid.*, RG 393, Dept. of the Cumberland, Telegrams Sent; *ibid.*, Military Div. of the Miss., Telegrams Received. *O.R.*, I, xxxi, part 1, 669. Also on Oct. 20, Thomas telegraphed to USG. "No change to report—Five days rations issued to troops to day—three hundred wagons between here and Stevenson with provisions. Genl. Rosecrans left this morning Communicated with Burnside to day. He is moving toward Kingston. His couriers connect with mine near Washington." Copy, DNA, RG 393, Dept. of the Cumberland, Telegrams Sent. *O.R.*, I, xxxi, part 1, 825. On the same day, Tuesday, 3:00 P.M., Secretary of War Edwin M. Stanton telegraphed to Maj. Gen. Henry W. Halleck. "Sunday night General Grant issued his orders taking command. Gen'ls Burnside, Rosecrans, and Thomas reported last night. Gen Grant has gone forward with Genl Meigs and will reach Chattanooga tonight or tomorrow Thomas says if the supply wagons now on the road arrive safely they will be all right to the first of November at least. Genl Grant ordered him to hold Chattanooga at all hazards; he replied: 'I will hold the town till we starve!' Genl Meigs has taken with him a large supply of tools for blasting and opening the road across the mountains and everything possible has been done for Rail Road transportation." Telegram received, DNA, RG 107, Telegrams Collected (Bound). *O.R.*, I, xxxi, part 1, 666.

On Oct. 19, Brig. Gen. Hugh T. Reid, Cairo, telegraphed to USG. "There are despatches here from Gen'l. Hurlbut shall they be forwared to you at Louisville and if so by mail or by special bearer." Copies, DNA, RG 393, Military Div. of the Miss., Telegrams Received; *ibid.*, Dept. of Ky., Letters and Telegrams Sent. On the same day, USG telegraphed to Reid. "Communications for Genl Grants Head Qrs will be forwarded to him by mail. to. Chattanooga Ga via Nashville Tenn. Notify Post Master at Cairo accordingly" Telegram received, *ibid.*, RG 107, Telegrams Collected (Unbound).

On Oct. 21, USG, Murfreesboro, telegraphed to Stanton. "I will feel obliged if you will order Lieut J. R. Meigs Engineer Dept to report to me." Telegram received, *ibid.*, RG 94, ACP, M1003 CB 1863. On Oct. 28, USG, Chattanooga, telegraphed to Halleck. "I would respectfully ask that Lt J R Meig be ordered to report to me for duty" Telegram received, *ibid.*, RG 107, Telegrams Collected (Bound); copies, *ibid.*, RG 393, Military Div. of the Miss., Hd. Qrs. Correspondence; DLC-USG, V, 40, 94. Halleck denied USG's request, leaving Lt. John R. Meigs, USMA 1863, son of Brig. Gen. Montgomery C. Meigs, an engineer on the staff of Brig. Gen. Benjamin F. Kelley, Dept. of West Va. See telegram to Maj. Gen. Henry W. Halleck, Oct. 30, 1863.

To Edwin M. Stanton

Nashville October 20 1863

HON. E. M. STANTON
LOUISVILLE KY.

Just arrived. I will leave here early in the morning and get through to Chattanooga as soon as possible. I presume you saw Gen Thomas' dispatch to me on the subject of rations.[1]

U S. GRANT
Major General

Telegram, copies, DLC-USG, V, 40, 94; DNA, RG 393, Military Div. of the Miss., Hd. Qrs. Correspondence. *O.R.*, I, xxxi, part 1, 825. See *ibid.*, p. 684.

On Oct. 20, 1864, Brig. Gen. John A. Rawlins, Nashville, wrote to Mary E. (Emma) Hurlbut. "I reached here with General Grant this evening enroute for Chattanooga, will continue on to that place in the morning. We will be three days in reaching there from here. One on cars and two on horse back, over a road not void of dangers, . . . The prospects of affairs here are not so cheering as I had hoped to find them, General Grants presence will tend I am sure greatly to allay any animosities existing between our generals & harmonise all into *one purpose namely* the *defeat* of the *enemy*. No one possesses higher characteristics to that end than he. Unostentatious in his manners ambitious only for his countrys success, he renders powerless to harm him the jealousys of those who should be his friends, and wins success where others fail, in the field. . . ." ALS, NHi.

During the evening of Oct. 20, USG reportedly remarked to a crowd gathered in front of the St. Cloud Hotel in Nashville that he had "never made a speech in his life, and was too old to learn now." Governor Andrew Johnson of Tenn. then addressed the crowd at length. *Missouri Democrat*, Nov. 3, 1863; *Memphis Bulletin*, Oct. 29, 30, 1863. See *Memoirs*, II, 27.

1. See preceding telegram.

To Rear Admiral David D. Porter

By Telegraph from Nashville 11 P. M. [*Oct.*] 20th *186*[*3*]
To Adm'l Porter

Gen'l Shermans advance was at Eastport on the fifteenth—The sooner a gunboat can be got to him the better—

Boats must now be on the way from St Louis with supplies to go up the Tennessee for Sherman—

U. S. Grant

Telegram received, DNA, RG 45, Correspondence of David D. Porter, Telegrams Received; copies, *ibid.*, RG 393, Military Div. of the Miss., Letters Sent; DLC-USG, V, 34, 35. *O.R.*, I, xxxi, part 1, 825; *O.R.* (Navy), I, xxv, 470. On Oct. 21, 1863, Rear Admiral David D. Porter telegraphed to USG. "Three Gunboats are now on their way up the Tennessee, and four up the Cumberland. My intention is to send up every Gunboat I can spare, up the Tennessee. I have also sent below for Light drafts to come up. Am sorry to say that the River is at a stand." LS, DNA, RG 45, Correspondence of David D. Porter, Mississippi Squadron, General Letters (Press); telegram received, *ibid.*, RG 393, Dept. of the Tenn., Telegrams Received. *O.R.*, I, xxxi, part 1, 689; *O.R.* (Navy), I, xxv, 471.

To Maj. Gen. Ambrose E. Burnside

Nashville Tenn. October 20. '63 11.30 P. M.
MAJOR GENERAL. A. E. BURNSIDE
KNOXVILLE TENN.

Telegraph me the quantity of clothing you want, and what point you will have it shipped to. There is enough here to supply you. Repairing the road to McMinnville[1] is right. All roads that can be used to get to supplies should be put in order as far as possible. Can you not lay in large supplies of forage, bacon, and other supplies by purchase? If so, do it. Have you tools for fortifying? Important points in East Tennessee should be put in condition to be held by the smallest number of men, as soon as possible. Please inform me what you regard as the key position in your Department. I suppose Kingston[2] to be the most important but do not know. I will be in Stevenson[3] tomorrow night and Chattanooga the next night.

U. S. GRANT
Major General.

Telegram, copies, DLC-USG, V, 34, 35; DNA, RG 393, Military Div. of the Miss., Letters Sent. Printed as received at 11:30 P.M., Oct. 21, 1863, in *O.R.*, I, xxxi, part 1, 681. On Oct. 22, USG, Jasper, Tenn., telegraphed to Maj. Gen. Ambrose E. Burnside. "Every effort should be made to increase your small arm ammunition to 500 rounds per man and artillery to 300 rounds." Copies, DLC-USG, V, 34, 35; DNA, RG 393, Military Div. of the Miss., Letters Sent. Printed as sent from Chattanooga in *O.R.*, I, xxxi, part 1, 701. On Oct. 20, 12:30 A.M., Burnside, Knoxville, had telegraphed to USG. "Following is the disposition of the forces in this Department,   3000 Cavalry & 1000 Infantry and 10 pieces of Artillery at Jonesboro with advanced posts at the ford of the Poland [*Holston*]— scouting well out on the north side of the Holston   one thousand (1000) Cavalry & 4 pieces of Artillery at Rogersville scouting in the direction of Kingsport   forces [*four*] new Indiana Regts. with about 3000 men for duty with 10 pieces of Artillery at Greenville   one Regt. of Infantry 400 strong & a six gun battery & 250 cavalry at Morristown   Two regiments new Ohio troops & one six gun battery & a Battalion of cavalry 300 strong at Cumberland Gap with 13 captured pieces in position   1200 infantry three (3) batteries of Artillery & 1000 cavalry at Knoxville   900 infantry at Concord   2700 infantry 3 batteries of artillery at Loudon   1200 cavalry & four mountain howitzers under col Wolford with Head qrs. at Philadelphia & outposts & scouting parties attending (——) the Hiawatchie River   1500 cavalry & one battery of artillery with Headquarters at Post oak spring nine miles below Kingston on the north side of the river picketing down to Blythes Ferry connecting with Rosecrans besides these we have a column of 4500 infantry 18 pieces of artillery & 350 cavalry of the 9th Corps near this place under orders for Kingston   these estimates are given in round numbers rather than by regiments as it will give you a better idea of our real strength   Some two or 3000 Home guards have been armed in different parts of the state & we have over two thousand recruits for the three years troops all of whom are armed but not (——)   we have on hand twelve days half rations of small stores & a good supply of beef cattle & salt with an abundance of bread stuffs in the country for present use   we have over one hundred rounds of ammunition per man and one hundred & fifty rounds per gun   our horses are in fair condition considering the amount of work they have done   We are suffering for want of clothing for recruits as well as for old troops and also for want of horses shoes & nails but we have commenced to manufacture the latter here   we find great difficulty in transporting supplies over the long line between here & camp Nelson & unless there is a fair prospect for driving the Enemy below Dalton so that the Rail Road can be opened I think it would be well to establish communication by wagon train between Kingston & McMinnville   I have already taken steps to repair the road from Clinton to the mouth of the Big South Fork on the Cumberland to which point stores can be transported by water and soon as that river becomes navagable which may not be till January"   Telegram received, DNA, RG 94, War Records Office, Dept. of the Ohio; copy, *ibid.*, RG 393, Military Div. of the Miss., Telegrams Received. *O.R.*, I, xxxi, part 1, 680. Also on Oct. 20, Burnside had telegraphed to USG. "The indications from the front confirms me in the belief expressed in my despatch of last night that the enemy are falling back from in front of Rosecrans"   Telegram received, DNA, RG 94, War Records Office, Dept. of the Ohio; copy, *ibid.*, RG 393, Military Div. of the Miss., Telegrams Received. *O.R.*, I, xxxi, part 1, 681.

On Oct. 21, 1:30 P.M., Maj. Gen. Henry W. Halleck telegraphed to Burnside. "Having by a demonstration forced General Meade to retreat, and having destroyed all his line of supply, General Lee will probably send a part of his army to the Southwest. Whether to Bragg or by Abingdon is uncertain. I think your available forces at Kingston and above should be held in readiness to move up the valley, should the enemy appear in force in Southwestern Virginia. A copy of this is sent to General Grant. Communicate with him." *Ibid.*, p. 687. Although no copy of this telegram as sent to USG has been found, Burnside referred to it in two telegrams to USG on Oct. 22, the first at 3:00 A.M. "Your despatch rec'd. It is owing altogether to the circumstances as to which is the key point in East Tenn—If we are here with a view to cooperate with the army of the Cumberland alone and *uniting* (?) with that Army in case of any reverse ~~of~~ to either a point opposite Kingston on the north side of the Tenn. river is certainly the key point   if we are expected to hold the line between Southwest Kentucky & Chattanooga with a view to creating diversion in favor of or rendering assistance to either the Army in Ky or the army of the Cumberland then it is [*plain*] to me that Loudon Knoxville & some point as far up the road as possible should be strongly held   A despatch from Halleck today a copy of which he sent to you would indicate that he now regards the latter place as the proper one which I did not understand be his position before   if Kingston is regarded as the key point the line of Rail road from Bristol to Loudon should be held I think by just force enough to completely destroy upon the approach of the enemy and fall back upon Kingston evacuating the entire country east of it except such portions of it as could be held by small bodies of cavalry   I have already taken steps for the improvement of the road from Clinton to the mouth of the Big south fork steps taken by me towards building a rail road from Cumberland to this   I will have working parties put on the road at once from Kingston to McMinnville by way of Crossville & Sparta   Cannot working parties be sent out from McMinnville to meet our   We need about 25000 suits of clothing   We have been on half rations ever since our arrival of every thing except fresh beef & bread   in fact we have had no small rations except sugar coffee & salt but the command is in good condition and ready for any ordered emergency"   "The following dispatch was sent to Genl Halleck last night. your dispatch recd. all portions of this Command have been kept in readiness to move at a moments notice ever since our arrival & in fact have kept on moving nearly all the time   our last move up the country was made with a view to discovering Enemy above the Va line & showing him that we were ready to meet any force that he might send against us in that direction & possibly creating a diversion in favor of Meade's Army. had I felt that Rosecrans Army was perfectly secured, I should have pushed the movement farther with a view to the destruction of the Salt works but my instructions & Rosecrans call for assistance forbid   I will communicate fully with Genl Grant & hope to be able to successfully meet any emergency that may arise. the enemy attacked our cavalry under Col Wolford yesterday at Philadelphia driving them back upon Loudon capturing six mountain Howitzers & a portion of the wagon train & camp Equipage—today we have driven them back beyond Philadelphia. it is reported that the attacking column Composed of Infy artillery & cavalry under command of Buckner but I am disinclined to believe it—we are ready however to make a good defense. Loudon has been pretty well fortified & has been considerably reinforced   I hope to report more definitely tomorrow the nature of the attacking force. the indications now are that the enemy is advancing in considerable force on to Loudon & it is also reported that they are crossing between Post oak springs and Cottonport   this last report is not well defined." Telegrams received, DNA, RG 94, War Records Office, Military Div. of the Miss.; copies, *ibid.*, RG 393, Military Div. of the Miss., Telegrams Received. *O.R.*, I, xxxi, part 1, 702–3.

On Oct. 23, Burnside telegraphed to USG. "On the 20th Inst. Col Wolford's Cavalry brigade at Philadelphia was surprised by Ewing's Cavalry & driven back to Loudon with a loss of six mountain howitzers & a considerable number of men   Col Wolford reports his loss at one hundred   the Enemy has been driven back again beyond Philada & are said to be concentrating at Sweetwater A heavy force of Infantry cavalry & Artillery   the reports of the number of the enemy are indefinite except as to the presence there of Stevensons—of Infantry of some 3 or 4000 cavalry   I have reinforced the garrison at Loudon & shall leave for there at once   from there I will endeavor to telegraph you more definitely   we have had a great deal of rains   Trains late & I fear much of our supplies will be very badly delayed by high water & bad roads   it is reported from several sources that a considerable force under Joe Johnson has left Braggs army" Telegram received, DNA, RG 94, War Records Office, Military Div. of the Miss.; copy, *ibid.*, RG 393, Military Div. of the Miss., Telegrams Received. *O.R.*, I, xxxi, part 1, 5.

1. McMinnville, Tenn., the terminus of the McMinnville and Manchester Railroad, approximately fifty-five miles northwest of Chattanooga.

2. Kingston, Tenn., on the Tennessee River, approximately thirty miles southwest of Knoxville.

3. Stevenson, Ala., at the junction of the Memphis and Charleston Railroad and the Nashville and Chattanooga Railroad, approximately thirty-five miles southwest of Chattanooga.

To Maj. Gen. George H. Thomas

———

Nashville Tenn. Oct. 20th 1863.

MAJOR GEN. GEO H. THOMAS
CHATTANOOGA

I will leave here in the morning and push through Chattanooga as soon as possible. Should not large working parties be put upon the road between Bridgeport and Chattanooga at once? General Meigs suggests this and also that depots of forage be established on each side of the mountain.

U. S. GRANT
Major General.

Telegram, copies, DLC-USG, V, 34, 35; DNA, RG 393, Military Div. of the Miss., Letters Sent. *O.R.*, I, xxxi, part 1, 670.

To Maj. Gen. Henry W. Halleck

———

Chattanooga Tenn.
9.30 P. M. Oct. 23, 1863.

MAJ GEN H. W. HALLECK,
GEN-IN-CHF

Have just arrived. I will write tomorrow. Please approve order placing Genl Sherman in command of Dept. & army of the Tennessee with Hd. Qrs. in the field.

I think it much preferable to leave Departments as they are to consolidating the three into one.

U. S. GRANT
Maj. Gen. Comdg

Telegram received, DNA, RG 107, Telegrams Collected (Bound); copies, *ibid.*, RG 393, Military Div. of the Miss., Hd. Qrs. Correspondence; DLC-USG, V, 40, 94. *O.R.*, I, xxxi, part 1, 706.

On Oct. 19, 1863, Brig. Gen. John A. Rawlins, Louisville, wrote to Maj. Gen. William T. Sherman. "Your dispatch of the 14th inst. by Lieut Dunn, is received.—Enclosed herewith find General Orders, No. 2 from these Headquarters assigning you to the command of the Department, and Army of the Tennessee, also copy of dispatch of this date, from the General-in-Chief, relating to the movements of troops, by Genl. Schofield, and the return of those, not required by Genl. Steele, to hold Arkansas, to reinforce your column—The command of the entire forces of the Department of the Tenn. being now in you, you will make such disposition of them, as to increase to the greatest possible strength, your moving column, and at the same time, secure your communications to your base of supplies. Communicate with Genl. Steele, and urge the necessity of his sending you the Division of Kimball of the 16th Army Corps, and with it when it arrives, relieve one of the Divisions of that Corps, now maintaining, the line of Rail Road from Memphis to Corinth, and the Division thus relieved, bring forward under Genl. Dodge to the front—He is an able Officer, one whom you can rely upon, in any emergency. The 111th Regiment Ills. Infty Vols., is stationed at Paducah Ky. and numbers over eight hundred effective men. If it is necessary, to keep troops there at all, a Regiment one third as large, would be ample.—It should be moved forward, together with anyother, Regiments, that can be spared from Memphis and the line of the Rail Road, and assigned to strengthen Divisions already to the front. The Chiefs of Departments for the West, at St Louis Mo. have been instructed, to shove forward by the Tennessee, and Cumberland rivers, when they rise, supplies for the troops operating, on the Chattanooga, and Tennessee line. Admiral Porter is watching both these rivers, and will the moment, there is a sufficient rise in either, send in his Gun-Boats, and as far up as possible, for the convoying of supply-boats, and protection of navigation. You will please put yourself, in communication, with him at once, as Commander of the Dept. of the Tenn.—You are aware of his good feelings towards, and cordial co-operation with the Army—receiving any suggestions, for the good of the service, in the most courteous, and friendly manner, and carrying them out, when possible, promptly, and willingly. *You* will have no difficulty with him. A proper activity on the part of your Cavalry, ought to enable it, to disperse, and drive out, of West Tennessee, and from the immediate neighborhood of the Memphis, and Charleston R. R. any considerable organized body of the enemy, that may be there. The General Commanding, will, leave here, tomorrow morning, for Chattanooga, Ga. where he will establish for the present his Head.quarters, and until you can communicate with him by a more direct route, you will do so, there, Via. Nashville Tenn." LS, DNA, RG 94, War Records Office, Military Div. of the Miss. *O.R.*, I, xxx, part 4, 475–76. Rawlins enclosed General Orders No. 2, Oct. 19. "Subject to the approval of the President, Maj. General W. T. Sherman, U. S. Volunteers, is hereby assigned to the command of the Department of the Tennessee, Headquarters in the field." Copies, DLC-USG, V, 14; DNA, RG 393, Military Div. of the Miss., General Orders; (printed) USGA. *O.R.*, I, xxx, part 4, 476. On Oct. 24, Sherman, Iuka, Miss., received these orders and assumed command of the Dept. and Army of the Tenn. *Ibid.*, I, xxxi, part 1, 712. On Oct. 26, 2:30 P.M., Maj. Gen. Henry W. Halleck telegraphed to USG. "Orders will be issued placing Genl Sherman in command of the Army & Dept of the Tennessee." ALS (telegram sent), DNA, RG 107, Telegrams Collected (Bound); copies, *ibid.*, RG 393, Military Div. of the Miss., Hd. Qrs. Correspondence; DLC-USG, V, 40, 94. *O.R.*, I, xxxi, part 1, 738.

On Oct. 26, USG telegraphed to Halleck. "I would respectfully reccommend

Maj Genl John A Logan as a suitable commander for Shermans Corps" Telegram received, DNA, RG 107, Telegrams Collected (Bound); copies, *ibid.*, Telegrams Received in Cipher; *ibid.*, RG 94, Letters Received, 506T 1864; *ibid.*, RG 393, Military Div. of the Miss., Hd. Qrs. Correspondence; DLC-USG, V, 40, 94. *O.R.*, I, xxxi, part 1, 739. On Oct. 27, 2:15 P.M., Halleck telegraphed to USG. "Genl John A Logan has been placed in command of Sherman's Corps. Genl G. H. Thomas has been appointed a Brig General U. S. Army, in place of Genl R. Anderson, retired. Three western batteries from here and a heavy battery from Wisconsin, have been ordered to Chattanooga. They can be used as garrison artillery if required. I fear Genl Thomas' plan of raising a veteran regiment of artillery is impracticable, as the men would be drawn from different states, & therefore in violation of law & General orders. An Infantry regiment, or several batteries from the same state can be organized as a regt of Heavy Artillery. Had not any additional troops we can obtain better be sent to Corinth & Eastport to secure Genl Sherman's rear?" ALS (telegram sent), DNA, RG 107, Telegrams Collected (Bound); copies (datelined 2:30 P.M.), *ibid.*, RG 393, Military Div. of the Miss., Hd. Qrs. Correspondence; DLC-USG, V, 40, 94. *O.R.*, I, xxxi, part 1, 751–52. See *ibid.*, p. 759. On Oct. 28, Capt. Ely S. Parker issued Special Field Orders No. 4 directing Maj. Gen. John A. Logan to assume command of the 15th Army Corps. Copy, DLC-USG, V, 38. *O.R.*, I, xxxi, part 1, 768. Meanwhile, Sherman had given this command to Maj. Gen. Francis P. Blair, Jr., who kept it through the Chattanooga and Knoxville campaigns. *Ibid.*, pp. 714, 730–32; letter to Maj. Gen. Francis P. Blair, Jr., Aug. 23, 1863, note 2; letter to Maj. Gen. William T. Sherman, Dec. 11, 1863, note 2. On Oct. 27, USG wrote to Maj. Gen. George H. Thomas. "Allow me to congratulate you on your appointment as Brig. Gen. in the regular Army for the battle of Chickamauga. I have just recieved a dispatch announcing the fact." ALS (facsimile), Stan. V. Henkels & Son, Catalogue No. 1379, Oct. 15, 1925.

To Maj. Gen. Henry W. Halleck

Chattanooga Tenn
8 P M Oct 24th 1863

MAJ GEN H W HALLECK
GEN IN CHIEF

All animals that can be spared will go back tomorrow to forage —One Division of troops started this evening to *Dave Rankin*[1] to seize that place to enable Hooker to possess the roads to Mountain Creek.[2] Once there we will have water communication to within four miles of ~~this place~~ here and can supply this place with beef cattle or driven here as required   Rations have been reduced—the Enemy is closely watched but if he should move against Burnside or break through our lines between here and Burnside, it would be difficult in the present condition of the roads to follow—

I will however do the best possible—

U. S. GRANT

Maj Genl

Telegram received, DNA, RG 107, Telegrams Collected (Bound); copies, *ibid.*, Telegrams Received in Cipher; *ibid.*, RG 393, Military Div. of the Miss., Hd. Qrs. Correspondence; DLC-USG, V, 40, 94. *O.R.*, I, xxxi, part 1, 712. On Oct. 22, 1863, 1:10 P.M., Maj. Gen. Henry W. Halleck had telegraphed to USG. "I would suggest that Genl Sheridan is one of the best men in the army to organize & regulate transportation & supplies. He fully supplied Genl Curtis army in mid-winter, over the most horrible roads. Should not all animals, not absolutely re-quired at Chattanooga, be sent to the rear? Cannot a part of the troops be sent nearer the depôts of provisions? As at Pittsburg, short forage can be sent forward on the backs of artillery & cavalry horses. Men can be successively detailed to carry forward provisions on the backs. Beef on the hoof can be driven over the mountain, & the rations of bread reduced. The issue of small rations can be temporarily suspended" ALS (telegram sent), DNA, RG 107, Telegrams Col-lected (Bound); copies, *ibid.*, RG 393, Military Div. of the Miss., Hd. Qrs. Cor-respondence; DLC-USG, V, 40, 94. *O.R.*, I, xxxi, part 1, 698. On Oct. 24, 11:40 A.M., Halleck had telegraphed to USG. "From advices recieved last night, it is pretty certain that Ewell's corps, from twenty to twenty five thousand men, has left Lee's army, and gone to Tennessee, probably by way of Abingdon. As Burn-side will be obliged to move all his forces up the valley, you must guard against Bragg's entrance into East Tennessee above Chattanooga." ALS (telegram sent), DNA, RG 107, Telegrams Collected (Bound); copies, *ibid.*, RG 393, Military Div. of the Miss., Hd. Qrs. Correspondence; DLC-USG, V, 40, 94. *O.R.*, I, xxxi, part 1, 712.

1. Rankin's Ferry, near the point at which Running Creek enters the Ten-nessee River, about sixteen miles upstream from Bridgeport, Ala.

2. Mountain Creek enters the Tennessee River opposite Williams' Island, about seven miles downstream from Chattanooga. See telegram to Maj. Gen. Henry W. Halleck, Oct. 28, 1863.

To Maj. Gen. William T. Sherman

Chattanooga Oct 24 [*1863*]

MAJ GENL SHERMAN
CARE GENL CROOK[1]

Drop everything east of bear Creek & move with your entire force towards stevenson until you receive further orders—The enemy are evidently moving a large force towards cleveland[2] & may break through our lines & move on Nashville in which event your troops are the only force at command that should be at them there,—with your forces here before the enemy cross the Tennessee we could turn their position so as to force them back & save the probability of a move northward this winter

U. S. GRANT
Maj Genl

Telegram received, DNA, RG 94, War Records Office, Military Div. of the Miss.; (dated Oct. 25, 1863, and sent to the "Commanding Officer at Brownsboro Paint Rock or extreme point of telegraph Line Towards General Crook   forward following to Gen Sherman with all possible dispatch,") *ibid.*, RG 393, Dept. of the Tenn., Telegrams Received; copies (dated Oct. 25 and sent via Cairo to Maj. Gen. William T. Sherman and to Maj. Gen. Stephen A. Hurlbut), *ibid.*, RG 94, War Records Office, Military Div. of the Miss.; (dated Oct. 24) *ibid.*, RG 393, Military Div. of the Miss., Letters Sent; DLC-USG, V, 34, 35. *O.R.*, I, xxxi, part 1, 713. On Oct. 26, 2:00 P.M., USG telegraphed to Maj. Gen. Henry W. Halleck. "I have sent orders to Gen'l Sherman to move East towards Stevenson, leaving everything unguarded except by the way of the army of the Cumberland East of Bear Creek   The possibility of the Enemy breaking through our lines East of this, and present inability to follow him from here if he should, is the cause of this order. Shermans forces are the only troops I could throw in to head such a move" Telegram received, DNA, RG 107, Telegrams Collected (Bound); copies, *ibid.*, Telegrams Received in Cipher; *ibid.*, RG 393, Military Div. of the Miss., Hd. Qrs. Correspondence; DLC-USG, V, 40, 94. *O.R.*, I, xxxi, part 1, 738.

On Sunday, Oct. 25, Brig. Gen. George Crook, Maysville, Ala., telegraphed to USG. "I sent your communication by a courier with instructions not to sleep until he finds Gen'l. Sherman. My expedition to the Tenn. report no rebel Cavalry on this side. The Citizens here report that Gen. Wheeler has been skirmishing with Sherman at or near Bear Creek on Tuesday, Wednesday and Thursday. I have the honor to report that my Cavalry have been on a constant go & the cold drenching rains we have had since this last raid have so completely used up my horses that there are scarcely any of them fit for service   I would like any of them sent to me by way of Decherd also have shoes that are not set sent me. Have no Forge to work rough shoes here. I have been trying to get these things ever since I arrived here" Copy, DNA, RG 393, Military Div. of the Miss., Telegrams Received. *O.R.*, I, xxxi, part 1, 836. On Oct. 26, Crook telegraphed to USG. "A wounded prisoner captured yesterday and brought in to day states he was wounded at Bear Creek & reports Gen. Sherman had completed the bridge across the Bear Creek & part of his force had crossed. I expect to hear very soon from him as I sent escort to find him some days ago"   Copy, DNA, RG 393, Military Div. of the Miss., Telegrams Received. *O.R.*, I, xxxi, part 1, 839. On the same day, 7:00 P.M., USG telegraphed to Crook. "Send some of your men to Nashville for the horses. Shoes &c they require. There is now over 900 Cavalry horses for issue at Nashville and more to arrive. The broken down horses should all be sent to Nashville to recuperate." Copies, DLC-USG, V, 34, 35; DNA, RG 393, Military Div. of the Miss., Letters Sent. On Oct. 27, 9:00 A.M., USG telegraphed to Maj. Gen. Henry W. Halleck. "Four thousand (4000) sets horse equipment are required for the Dept of the Cumberland as soon as they can be had. They should be sent to Nashville" Telegram received, *ibid.*, RG 107, Telegrams Collected (Bound); copies, *ibid.*, RG 393, Military Div. of the Miss., Hd. Qrs. Correspondence; DLC-USG, V, 40, 94. *O.R.*, I, xxxi, part 1, 752. On Oct. 28, 11:50 P.M., Brig. Gen. George D. Ramsay, chief of ordnance, telegraphed to USG. "Your telegraphic requisition to General Halleck for four thousand (4000) sets of horse equipments has been referred to this office. Two thousand sets (2000) left Allegheny Arsenal on the sixteenth (16) instant for Nashville and one thousand (1000) more have to day been ordered to the same place, with quick despatch from each of the following arsenals. New York, Allegheny and St Louis, or three thousand (3000) in addition to the first log. Are you in need of more immediately?" ALS (telegram sent), DNA, RG 107, Telegrams Collected (Unbound); copies, *ibid.*, RG 156, Letters Sent; *ibid.*, RG 393, Military Div. of the Miss., Hd. Qrs. Correspondence; DLC-USG, V, 40, 94.

On Oct. 20, Maj. Gen. Stephen A. Hurlbut, Memphis, telegraphed to USG. "Genl. Sherman will have two Divisions at or near the [*Tuscumbia*] today   The Tennessee is rising   fords are bad and growing worse   I have [*sent*] to Genl Allen today for a steam ferry boat to go up the Tennessee   there is three feet water. Chalmers & Richardson are said to be *troops* but it is doubtful   my Cavalry is well out to the front   the danger to this line will be from Forrest & Lee   when drawn out of Middle Tennessee their [*attack*] may be serious with my thin lines" Telegram received, DNA, RG 393, Dept. of the Tenn., Telegrams Received; copy, *ibid.*, Military Div. of the Miss., Telegrams Received. *O.R.*, I, xxxi, part 1, 673. On Oct. 21, 11:30 A.M., Hurlbut telegraphed to USG. "The following recd from Corinth—'All troops at Mobile except provost guard have gone to Bragg   No troops at Okalona have gone to Roddy at Chickasaw   Much of Prestons army is with Bragg   the rest of Longstreets corps have arrived   Southern papers of 10th state that Bragg draws one hundred & eighty thousand rations   this is published for effect evidently   Wheeler is reported to be concentrating his whole cavalry claiming eighty thousand (8000) at the Tennessee above and below Florence   Sherman will make his hospital depot at Iuka   Blair crossed Bear Creek with two Divisions yesterday & will be near Tuscumbia today   one other division of Sherman is beyond Bear Creek and one will be kept on this side until a brigade sent from Memphis can relieve it   It will take five days longer to repair bridge at Bear Creek for trains   The Tennessee must be our main dependencies   it is now rising   I need two thousand horse equipments to mount infantry   they were promised some weeks since but have not arrived   As soon as the force comes from Steele I shall strike for Columbus Mississippi   at present I have no disposable infantry" Telegram received, DNA, RG 94, War Records Office, Military Div. of the Miss.; copy, *ibid.*, RG 393, Military Div. of the Miss., Telegrams Received. *O.R.*, I, xxxi, part 1, 689. On Oct. 24, 9:30 P.M., USG telegraphed to Hurlbut. "There are 3000 horse equipments in the hands of Lieut Barker Ordnance Officer. You can get them to mount your Infantry." Copies, DLC-USG, V, 34, 35; DNA, RG 393, Military Div. of the Miss., Letters Sent. On Oct. 21, 5:00 P.M., Hurlbut telegraphed to USG. "Sherman telegraphs from Bear Creek— 'My advances found Jesse Forrests Cavalry four hundred strong at Prestons [*Barton*'s] station & whipped them handsomly yesterday killing two & taking nine prisoners—our loss one killed three wounded slightly   The 5th Ohio cavalry behaved most handsomly   The Tennessee is up eight feet on the shoals   I must cross over to communicate with Nashville & Chattanooga and must have a steam ferry boat   I I will keep a regiment at Eastport   wheeler 10 000 strong is near Decatur   I hope he will oppose my advance but think he will swing up on my flank   my advance is at cane creek—Signed SHERMAN'   Send by this boat despatch to Porter and to Col Allen for ferry boat to be sent up and hope it may be hurried forward   otherwise after crossing Sherman will be beyond reach of supplies of which he has now fifteen days on ~~hand~~ wagon train"   Telegram received, *ibid.*, RG 94, War Records Office, Military Div. of the Miss.; copy, *ibid.*, RG 393, Military Div. of the Miss., Telegrams Received. *O.R.*, I, xxxi, part 1, 16. On Oct. 22, 3:30 P.M., Hurlbut telegraphed to USG. "Sherman telegraphs that Wheelers Cavalry are on the south side of the Tennessee River & cut off by high water from Bragg   he urgently asks for a steam ferry boat   A pretty heavy force is opposing his advance   Osterhaus had a pretty severe fight yesterday losing eight killed and twenty wounded   Col Lorenz 30th Iowa is killed   Dodge telegraphs from Corinth that Loring went to Grenada to check McPhersons movements from Vicksburg   Few troops on Mobile & Ohio R R   Davis reviewed Braggs troops on 11th & 12th & has gone back to Richmond   Chalmers is south of the Tallahatchee recruiting for another move on R R"   Telegram received, DNA, RG 94, War Records Office, Military Div. of the Miss.; copy, *ibid.*, RG 393, Military Div. of the Miss., Telegrams Received. *O.R.*, I, xxxi, part 1, 703.

On Oct. 24, Sherman, Iuka, Miss., wrote to Brig. Gen. John A. Rawlins. "I have this moment received at the hands of Lt Dunn A D C. copies of your Genl Orders Nos 1 & 2, and your communication of of Oct 19, which shall have my immediate and undivided attention. Two Gunboats under Lt Comd Phelps arrived at Eastport and that officer is now with me and I will proceed at once to p[a]ss a Division over the Tennessee to move to Florence, and I have three Divisions in front of Bear Creek that have had several sharp encounters with the Enemy's Cavalry. I have ordered them tomorrow to drive them beyond Tuscumbia. The Railroad is now in fine order from Memphis to Bear Creek, but the break in the Road beyond is serious & repairs proceed too slow, but I hope to have the head of my column so advanced that it will influence your Enemy in front of Chattenooga. I will persevere to reach the neighborhood of Athens the point designated in Gen Hallecks Order. I see no reason for a large Regimt at ~~Eastport~~ Paducah and will order it up in Boats to Eastport & Waterloo. I will order Genl Smith at Columbus to make a force of Cavalry or Mounted Infantry sweep down from Columbus to Grand Junction, taking all the available horses in the Country. It is useless to be too delicate on this score. Either the U. S. or Guerillas must have all the horses in that Region and we might as well act on that supposition. I will also instruct Genl A. J. Smith to instruct the officer in Command to notify the Union People that they must now take sides and expel the Guerillas else their Country will be constantly liable to the destruction of passing parties of Cavalry. The Tennessee river is now available to us for supplies and if necessary we could absolutely abandon the Railroad, but as Corinth Lagrange and other points have formed so effectual a barrier in the Past I would like Genl Grant to order in the case. If information from Chattanooga indicated any danger to your army I would drop every thing & hasten forward, but Genl Hallecks orders were positive to mend road and look to supplies as I progressed, and this has delayed me. I wish if you have not already done so that you would open communication with me at Florence. I will write Genl Steele and do all that is pointed out in your letter." ALS, DNA, RG 393, Military Div. of the Miss., Miscellaneous Letters Received. *O.R.*, I, xxxi, part 1, 713–14. On Oct. 26, Col. Thomas J. Haines, chief commissary, St. Louis, telegraphed to USG. "I have sent a commissary to Eastport with 250 000 rations five hundred thousand more and two hundred & fifty head of cattle will follow this week   There will I presume be sufficient for Shermans force unless you desire a permanent depot of supplies forwarded thence in the direction of Chattanooga   shall a depot at Eastport be established" Telegram received, DNA, RG 94, War Records Office, Military Div. of the Miss.; copy, *ibid.*, RG 393, Military Div. of the Miss., Telegrams Received. *O.R.*, I, xxxi, part 1, 740. On Oct. 28, Sherman telegraphed to USG. "Genl Blair entered Tuscumbia yesterday & Genl Ewing will be in Florence tomorrow having crossed at Eastport   I tried to get a boat over Culbert Shoals to enable Blair to cross over but failed   water good up to Eastport but not above   I will push the whole 15th Army Corps at Eastport & occupy Florence at once   met Wheeler & Fergusons cavalry in my front & Right flank   Blair drove them beyond Town creek   Ferguson rebel encountered the first Alabama union Regement on its return from a raid & routed ~~them~~ it   details not yet recd in full   at all other points we got decidedly the advantage   RailRoad across bear creek done but useless   I can go back to Tuscumbia so as to cross over   we gain nothing by repairing any more of it   Tenn. River in full stage up to Culbert Shoals" Telegram received, DNA, RG 94, War Records Office, Military Div. of the Miss.; *ibid.*, RG 107, Telegrams Collected (Unbound); copies, *ibid.*, RG 393, Dept. of the Tenn., Telegrams Sent; *ibid.*, Military Div. of the Miss., Telegrams Received. *O.R.*, I, xxxi, part 1, 766.

On Oct. 30, Brig. Gen. Hugh Ewing, Florence, Ala., telegraphed to USG. "My Division the head of Shermans column is here   Your Dispatches via Huntsville will reach here to night. Courier reports but few Rebels us & Huntsville" Copies, DNA, RG 393, 15th Army Corps, 4th Div., Letters Sent; *ibid.*, Military Div. of the Miss., Telegrams Received. *O.R.*, I, xxxi, part 1, 791. On the same day, Sherman, Waterloo, Ala., telegraphed to USG. "the Tennessee is impassible except by ferrying. anticipating this I ordered a Fery boat before I left Corinth and I am officially informed that one was ordered up from Paducah on the 20 4th, but it is not yet come. there is plenty of water in the Tenn   2 gun Boats have come up and one has returned to see what causes delay to the others. I have but one gun Boat and one coal barge to pass my troops and heavy rains having set in our progress is slow. we work day and night. one Division is forward at Florence, another is crossing and I will do all that man can to hasten forward. I have received your dispatch by way of Cairo and through gen crook" Telegrams received (2), DNA, RG 107, Telegrams Collected (Unbound); copies, *ibid.*, RG 393, Dept. of the Tenn., Telegrams Sent; *ibid.*, Military Div. of the Miss., Telegrams Received. *O.R.*, I, xxxi, part 1, 789.

On Oct. 31, Sherman, Eastport, Miss., telegraphed to USG. "I have your despatch of twenty fourth through General Crook. I had two divisions in Tuscumbia and drove his cavalry beyond Town Creek but the Muscle Shoals had too much water for us and I had to fall back to Eastport & Chickasaw where I had crossed one Division Ewings which is now at Florence another John E. Smiths is nearly over and it will go forward at will   I will start tomorrow morning with these two divisions rapidly for Athens. The effect of which will be to make the enemy believe all my army is there   I have heretofore been working in foul weather with a single coal barge decked over—but this moment have arrived a ferry boat three transports and two more gunboats so that my progress will be more rapid   I think I can have all the 15th Army Corps over tomorrow and Dodge ought to follow with his division the day after. I can only carry ten days rations and will draw liberally of meats & corn of the country   The country is full of cavalry & guerrillas   we have had numerous skirmishes and thus far have had the advantage"   Telegram received, DNA, RG 94, War Records Office, Military Div. of the Miss.; *ibid.*, RG 108, Letters Received; copies (dated Oct. 30), *ibid.*, RG 393, Dept. of the Tenn., Telegrams Sent; (dated Oct. 31) *ibid.*, Military Div. of the Miss., Telegrams Received. Dated Oct. 30 in *O.R.*, I, xxxi, part 1, 789.

On Nov. 5, Crook telegraphed to USG. "The following Despatch has just been received from Genl Sherman. Hd Qrs Army of the Tenn Waterloo Ala Oct 31st 63. SIR   Corp'l Vike came through safe also a private today   Lt Fitz Gerald came through with your letter of the 22d   One of my Divisions is Nearly over the Tennessee & will be at Florence tomorrow night. two more Divisions are on the other side of the Tennessee & will cross as fast as possible   Dodge's Division will be all ready to follow as soon as the 15th Army Corps is across. I will hurry forward as fast as possible   at first I only had a coal Barge to Cross the Command But today a ferry Boat Arrived & 3 Transports & the work moves faster. We have also had some villianous weather but this is also over & now I hope to be in Athens in four Days. we drove the Enemy's cavalry below the Tennessee Beyond town Creek but Roddys cavalry returned and is Hanging around Iuka. I think wheeler has gone back to Bragg & that Lee has gone back to okolona. There are small bands of Guerrillas in every location but give us a wide Birth as soon as the Head of my column reach Athens. I will send forward to Advise you & would be pleased if you would advise me in the meantime of your whereabouts also what is the best road from Athens to the Stevenson   that from Huntsville via Bellefonte to Stevenson used to be very bad. I have received General Grants Dispatch of Oct 27th enclosed in yours   Signed W T SHERMAN Maj Genl'   If tools & workmen were sent at once to Paint Rock Creek that Bridge could be repaired by the time Genl Sherman arrives here which would be of great assistance to Him when He Arrives. my men have all the timber Cut necessary for the Bridge with what Axes they could get a Hold of But cannot go any further for want of proper tools." Telegram received, DNA, RG 94, War Records Office, Military Div. of the Miss.; copy, *ibid.*, RG 393, Military Div. of the Miss., Telegrams Received. *O.R.*, I, xxxi, part 1, 797–98; *ibid.*, I, xxxi, part 3, 54. On Nov. 4, Crook telegraphed to USG. "I have just heard from Gen'l Sherman   he says that he received your order and is carrying it out. Courier says that he was crossing the river at East port & expected his advance would be at Rogersville by this time. Elk River yesterday was not fordable   I fear he will have some trouble, & delay in crossing it   There are no regular troops of rebels on this side of the river but small [b]ands of guerrillas and Conscripting parties.   I am fast cleaning the country of them"   Telegram received, DNA, RG 94, War Records Office, Military Div. of the Miss.; copy, *ibid.*, RG 393, Military Div. of the Miss., Telegrams Received. *O.R.*, I, xxxi, part 3, 39.

1. George Crook of Ohio, USMA 1852, was promoted to capt., 4th Inf., as of May 14, 1861. Appointed col., 36th Ohio, as of Sept. 12, he was wounded in

action at Lewisburg, Va., on May 23, 1862. Appointed brig. gen. as of Sept. 7, he participated in the battle of Antietam. In Oct., 1863, he commanded the 2nd Cav. Div., Army of the Cumberland.

2. Cleveland, Tenn., on the East Tennessee and Georgia Railroad, approximately twenty-five miles northeast of Chattanooga.

To Julia Dent Grant

———

Chattanooga Oct. 24th *1863.*

Dear Julia,

We arrived here in the night last night after a horse-back ride of fifty miles through the rain over the worst roads I ever saw. A discription of the roads over the mountains would give you no conception of them. I stood it very well however but was very much fatigued. The enemy are here close to us our pickets being within a hundred or two yards of each other. Our camps are but a few miles apart.

Ross remained back at Nashville to lay in supplies. Bowers remained there to establish Hd Qrs. office. Hudson on arrival at Bridgeport found that all his things had been stolen or left back and he returned to Nashville to look after them.[1]

Have you heard anything from the children? I am very anxious to hear from them. You had better start at once to make your visit in Ohio. You will find the weather much more pleasant now than later in the season. Did Jess get his pony? Kiss the little rascal for me. Kisses for yourself dear Julia. Write soon and direct your letters to Chattanooga Ten.

Ulys.

ALS, DLC-USG. Also on Oct. 24, 1863, Surgeon Edward D. Kittoe, Chattanooga, wrote to Julia Dent Grant. "I have not had an opportunity to write until now since we left Louisville   from that place to Bridgeport (the part of the journey that we came by Rail) the General was recieved by hundreds at each station and cheered most heartily   in fact it was a perfect ovation,   from Bridgeport to this place a distance of sixty two miles we came on horseback   we came about halfway the first day and the balance yesterday   the roads are the worst I ever saw and beggar description,   it rained in torrents all day yesterday and we arrived a little after dark wet and hungry   just as we got into Chattanooga the Generals horse fell flat on his side but luckily did not hurt the General at all, he stood the journey very well and does not seem at all the worse or even fatigued. We have not as yet gone into quarters and it will take several days for our baggage to get over the mountain. The General is staying with Maj. Gen Thomas, and his staff are scattered about among the other officers here. I am staying with Major Gen Reynolds   This is a rough and wretched looking place as can well be imagined. I hope that you and your little pet Jess are well and agreeably situated   I will endeavour to keep you posted in regard to the General's health   he is in fine spirits." ALS, USG 3.

1. At this point, twenty-one lines have been heavily cancelled, the first nine so heavily that it is only possible to determine that USG states that Col. Clark B. Lagow was lost and that cav. had been sent to search for him. The final lines read: "But when I left at twelve o'clock in the morning [———] got out to look for him. I presume he will find it necessary to go back to Louisville to look for his horses. If he does go back before rejoining he will never return. I [presume] before you get this you will have seen Lagow." ALS, DLC-USG. See letter to Maj. Gen. William T. Sherman, Nov. 29, 1863.

To Henry T. Blow

———

Chattanooga, Tenn, October 25, 1863.

HON. HENRY T. BLOW, MEMBER OF CONGRESS:

DEAR SIR: Your letter of the 21st inst., asking for copy of document referred to by Gen. Blair, charging you with joining in an effort for my removal from command, is just received. I did not save that, nor do I save any document not having direct reference to my duties. If, however, Franklin A. Dick has preserved copies of all his letters, written to the Attorney General, Mr. Bates, during the summer of '62, he can furnish you with the document I presume General Blair referred to. At all events, I know of no other.

> With great respect,
> Your obedient servant,
> U. S. GRANT,
> Major General, U. S. A.

Missouri Democrat, Nov. 14, 1863. For the letter of Sept. 28, 1862, from Franklin A. Dick, a prominent St. Louis lawyer, to Attorney General Edward Bates, see telegram to Maj. Gen. Henry W. Halleck, Sept. 25, 1862. Henry T.

Blow, born in Va. in 1817, moved to St. Louis in 1830, becoming a businessman. After serving as a state senator and as U.S. minister to Venezuela, he entered the U.S. House of Representatives in 1863. For Maj. Gen. Francis P. Blair, Jr.'s charges against him and Blow's defense, see *Missouri Democrat*, Oct. 28, 1863; William Ernest Smith, *The Francis Preston Blair Family in Politics* (New York, 1933), II, 257. On Oct. 21, Blow, St. Louis, wrote to USG. "General Blair has published me as making an effort, or assisting in an effort to have you removed, by vouching for some charges made against you and says that you have the document proving this, in your possession. As you were kind enough to consider me your friend sometime since, may I beg of you to let me have a copy of this letter at once that I may be able to do justice to all concerned." *Missouri Democrat*, Nov. 14, 1863. On the same day, Blow wrote to Secretary of War Edwin M. Stanton. "General Blair, in answer to a speech of mine, writes as follows: 'Would any one believe that General Grant (that glorious war Democrat so deeply loved by Mr. Blow) has at this moment in his possession *a letter asking for his removal from the head of the Army of the Tennessee, upon information furnished and vouched for by Henry T. Blow*, in which that war Democrat is charged with the grossest improprieties, which I will not name, but which, having served under his command, I know to be false, although vouched for by Mr. Blow?' Will you do me the favor to let me know if any such letter has ever been addressed to the President or the War Department, or any letter in which my name has been used as authority, or I vouch for statements made in relation to General Grant, and to send me at once copies of same? I have no recollection of anything in this connection, and the only means of doing justice, if I have made the slightest error in any way, will be to receive the copy of this document." *Ibid.* On Oct. 31, Stanton wrote to Blow. "Your letter of the 21st inst. reached here during my absence in the West, and being brought to my attention this morning, I hasten to reply, that I have no knowledge of any such letter as that referred to in your inquiry, either addressed to the President, or to the War Department, or to any one else. I never heard of any such letter, or of any letter from you, respecting General Grant, until I read your letter this morning." *Ibid.* On Nov. 5, Blow wrote to Dick, Philadelphia. "General Grant writes me that the letter he supposed General Blair referred to was one written by yourself to Judge Bates in 1862. Will you do me the favor to let me know so much of the contents of that letter as refers to me, and oblige" *Ibid.* On Nov. 8, Dick wrote to Blow. "Your letter of the 5th received. In reply to your inquiry I state that I have not seen the letter referred to, nor any copy of it since it was written; nor have I any sufficient recollection of its contents to attempt to state what you ask of me. I would give you the information you ask, if in my power to do so. I will be in St. Louis in a few days." *Ibid.* On Nov. 5, Blow wrote to Bates. "General Grant writes me that Colonel F. A. Dick, of this city, wrote you a letter in which my name is used in connection with his (General Grant's.) Will you do me the favor, sir, to enclose me a copy of that letter at your earliest convenience, and very much oblige." *Ibid.* On Nov. 9, Bates wrote to Blow acknowledging his letter. "I have not received any such letter from Mr. Dick, nor, indeed, any letter from any man associating your name with General Grant's. But if I had, I should be reluctant to give out copies, without some reason assigned, to excuse such use of private correspondence." *Ibid.*

To Maj. Gen. Henry W. Halleck

Head Quarters Military Div. of the Miss.
Chattanooga Ten. Oct. 26th 1863.

MAJ. GEN. H. W. HALLECK,
GEN. IN CHIEF, WASHINGTON,
GENERAL,

I arrived here in the night of the 23d inst. after a ride on horse-back of fifty miles, from Bridgeport, over the worst roads it is possible to concieve of, and through a continuous drenching rain. It is now clear and so long as it continues so it is bearly possible to supply this Army from its present base. But when Winter rains set in it will be impossible.—To guard against the possible contingency of having to abandon Chattanooga for want of supplies every precaution is being taken. The fortifications are being pushed to completion and when done a large part of the troops could be removed back near to their supplies. The troops at Bridgeport are engaged on the rail-road to Jaspar[1] and can finish it in about two weeks. Rails are taken from one of the branch roads which we do not use. This shortens the distance to supplies twelve miles and avoids the worst part of the road in wet weather. Gen. Thomas had also set on foot, before my arrival, a plan for geting possession of the river from a point below Lookout Mountain to Bridgeport. If successful, and I think it will be the question of supplies will be fully settled.[2]

The greatest apprehension I now have is that the enemy will move a large force up the river and force a passage through our line between Blyhe's Ferry[3] and ~~Kingston~~ Cotton Port.[4] Should he do this our Artillery horses are not in a condition to enable us to follow and neither is our larder. This part of the line is well watched but I cannot say guarded. To guard against this, in addition to the troops now on that part of the river, I have directed Gen. Thomas to increase the force at McMinnville immediately by one regiment of Cavalry with instructions to collect all the provisions and forage which the enemy would have to depend on for his subsistence, giving vouches payable at once when taken from loyal citizens, and payable at the end of the war, on proof of good conduct, when disloyal. As soon as the fortifications here are sufficiently defensable a Division will be sent there. I have also ordered Sherman to move Easward towards Stevenson until he recieved further orders, guarding nothing this side of Bear Creek, with the view of having his forces in a position to use if the enemy should attempt this move.[5] Should this not be attempted when Sherman gets well up there will be force enough to insure a line for our supplies and enable me to move Thomas to the left thus securing Burnside's position and give a strong hold upon that part of the line from which I suppose a move will finally have to be made to turn Bragg. I think this will have to be done from the Northeast.

This leaves a gap to the West for the enemy to get into Middle Tennessee by, but he has no force to avail himself of this opportunity with except Cavalry, and our Cavalry can be held ready to oppose this.

I will endeavor to study up my position well and post the troops to the best of my judgement to meet all contingencies. I will also endeavor to get the troops in a state of readiness for a forward movement at the earlyest possible day.

What force the enemy have to my front I have no means of judging accurately. Deserters come in every day but their information is limited to their own Brigades or Divisions at furthest. The camps of the enemy are in sight and for the last few days there seems to have been some moving of troops. But where to I cannot tell. Some seem to have gone towards Cleveland whilst others moved in exactly an opposite direction.

I am Gen. very respectfully
your obt. svt.
U. S. GRANT
Maj. Gen.

ALS, Schoff Collection, MiU-C. *O.R.*, I, xxxi, part 1, 739–40.

1. Jasper, Tenn., approximately ten miles west of Chattanooga.
2. See telegram to Maj. Gen. Henry W. Halleck, Oct. 28, 1863.

3. Blythe's Ferry on the Tennessee River, approximately thirty-two miles
northeast of Chattanooga.
4. Cotton Port Ferry on the Tennessee River, approximately twelve miles
north of Blythe's Ferry.
5. See telegram to Maj. Gen. William T. Sherman, Oct. 24, 1863.

To Maj. Gen. Henry W. Halleck

Head Qrs. Mil. Div. of the Miss.
In the field, Chattanooga Oct. 26th 1863
Respectfully forwarded to Head Qrs. of the Army, Washington
D. C. On taking command of the Military Division of the Miss.
I found Maj. Gen. Hooker in command of the 11th & 12th Army
Corps. His position is one that rather embarrasses the service than
benefits it, inasmuch in detaching one of these Corps would leave
two commanders for one small Army Corps. As Gen Slocum[1] ob-
jects to serving under Gen Hooker, who has been assigned to his
present command by the President, I would respectfully recommend that Gen. Hooker be assigned to the command of the 12th
Army Corps and Gen. Slocum relieved from further duty

U. S. GRANT
Major General

AES, DNA, RG 107, Letters Received, Irregular Series. *O.R.*, I, xxxi, part 1,
740. Written on a letter of Oct. 19, 1863, from Maj. Gen. Henry W. Slocum,
Wartrace, Tenn., to Maj. Gen. William S. Rosecrans, which Maj. Gen. George
H. Thomas had forwarded to USG. "On the 25th of Sep I was placed under command of Gen Hooker, and ordered to move my Corps at once to this Department.—
Having no confidence in Gen Hooker as a military man, and no respect for him
either as an officer or a Gentleman, I at once tendered a resignation of my commission to the President—My resignation was not accepted, but a letter addressed
to you by the President, very earnestly requesting you to relieve me from his
command, was read to me by Mr Lincoln, and I finally consented to continue in
command of my Corps—confidently beleiving that I should soon be releived from
serving under Genl Hooker. I have now served under him nearly a month, during which time I have refrained from importuning you on the subject,—and have
quietly waited for your action—To day I have received an order from Gen Hooker,
indicating that my Corps is soon to take the feild, and that I am to remain under
his command,   I feel therefore that it is time for me to take some action in the
matter, because I do not intend under any circumstances, to again take my command on to the feild under this officer   I respectfully ask you to inform me

whether or not it is in your power to comply with the request of the President, and relieve me from my present position—I have long been the senior officer in the Army of the Potomac—Senior in rank as well as in length of service in that Army—I bring you a Corps which has never faltered in the field—a Corps against which no word of condemnation has ever been uttered.—I ask no other command —but I do ask as an act of justice, not only to myself but to my command, that we shall not be compelled to serve under an officer, who commands neither our confidence or our respect" LS, DNA, RG 107, Letters Received, Irregular Series. For Slocum's resignation of Sept. 25 and President Abraham Lincoln's telegram of Sept. 28 to Rosecrans, see Lincoln, *Works*, VI, 486. See also *O.R.*, I, xxxi, part 1, 715, 741.

On Oct. 29, Asst. Secretary of War Charles A. Dana, Chattanooga, telegraphed to Secretary of War Edwin M. Stanton. "Genl Grant desires me to request for him that Lieut Col J. H. Wilson of his Staff Capt of Engineers be appointed Brigadier General Volunteers. Gen Grant wants him to command cavalry for which he possesses uncommon qualifications Knowing Wilson thoroughly I heartily endorse the application. Gen Grant also wishes to have both Hooker and Slocum removed from his command, and the Eleventh (11th) and Twelfth (12th) Corps consolidated under Howard. He would himself order Hooker and Slocum away, but hesitates because they have just been sent here by the President, besides I think he would rather prefer that so serious a proceeding should come from Head Quarters. Hooker has behaved badly ever since his arrival, and Slocum has just sent in a very disorderly communication, stating that when he came here, it was under promise that he should not have to serve under Hooker whom he neither regards with confidence as an Officer, nor respect as a man Altogether, Gen Grant feels that their presence here is replete with both trouble and danger, besides the smallness of the two (2) Corps requires their consolidation, and even after that it will be necessary to add troops to make the numbers of the new consolidated Corps respectable" Telegrams received (2), DLC-Edwin M. Stanton. *O.R.*, I, xxxi, part 1, 73. Slocum remained in command under Maj. Gen. Joseph Hooker until April, 1864. See endorsement to Maj. Gen. Henry W. Halleck, Feb. 9, 1864.

The command of Thomas's own 14th Corps fell vacant when he was assigned the command of the Dept. and Army of the Cumberland. See General Orders No. 1, Oct. 18, 1863. On Oct. 27, he telegraphed to Maj. Gen. Henry W. Halleck. "General Grant has placed General Palmer in command of the Fourteenth Army Corps, subject to the approval of the President." *O.R.*, I, xxxi, part 1, 842. War Dept. General Orders No. 350, Oct. 28, assigned Maj. Gen. John M. Palmer to this command. *Ibid.*, p. 847. On Oct. 27, USG wrote to Thomas. "General Palmer having sent in a certificate of disability and application for leave of absence, I am inclined to the opinion that it would be advisable to telegraph the fact to Washington and name another Commander or suitable person for Commander of the 14th Army Corps." Copies, DLC-USG, V, 34, 35; DNA, RG 393, Military Div. of the Miss., Letters Sent. Palmer, wounded in a skirmish near Chattanooga, Sept. 25, was granted a ten-day leave of absence. George Thomas Palmer, *A Conscientious Turncoat: The Story of John M. Palmer 1817–1900* (New Haven, 1941), pp. 116–17, 122. On Nov. 1, noon, Dana telegraphed to Stanton noting the locations of Palmer's brigades. "Palmer himself is sick from exposure on his recent march, and the effects of a wound here received here a month since. Genl Grant has assigned him to command Fourteenth Corps, and he has accepted, although three weeks ago, he put his resignation in hands of Rosecrans, for the reason, that he was not then made a Corps Commander   He is a good Division General, and a sensible man, but hardly equal to this new position   Rosseau is deeply grieved because Palmer is put over him. . . ." Telegram received, DLC-Edwin M. Stanton. *O.R.*, I, xxxi, part 2, 53–54. See also Dana to Stanton, Oct. 23, 4:00 P.M. Telegrams received (2), DLC-Edwin M. Stanton. *O.R.*, I, xxxi, part 1, 69. On Nov. 10, USG telegraphed to Halleck. "Has a Commander been assigned to the 14th Corps? Rosseau is senior Maj'r Gen'l not commanding a Corps—" Telegram received, DNA, RG 107, Telegrams Collected (Bound). On the same day, Halleck telegraphed to USG. "At your request, Genl J. M. Palmer was appointed to the command of the 14th Army corps." ALS (telegram sent), *ibid.*; copies, *ibid.*, RG 393, Military Div. of the Miss., Hd. Qrs. Correspondence; DLC-USG, V, 40, 94. See *O.R.*, I, xxxii, part 2, 377, 387.

On Nov. 17, Lt. Col. James H. Wilson received notice of an interim appointment as brig. gen. of vols. and was sworn in by USG. James Harrison Wilson diary, Nov. 17, 1863, Historical Society of Delaware, Wilmington, Del. Brig. Gen. John A. Rawlins and USG had already told Wilson of Dana's telegram to Stanton which led to this appointment. See *ibid.*, Nov. 3, 1863; Wilson to Capt. Adam Badeau, Nov. 5–6, 1863, typescript, WyU. On May 18, 1864, Wilson was confirmed as brig. gen. to rank from Oct. 30, 1863. On Sept. 21, USG had written to Brig. Gen. John G. Barnard. "I desire permission for Lieut J. H. Wilson of Corps of Engineers and Asst. Inspector Genl. U. S. Vols. to be examined by letter by the Board of Examiners of which you are President for promotion to a Captaincy of Engineers. his duties are such that he cannot well be spared"   Copies, DLC-USG, V, 6, 8, (misdated Sept. 2) 24, (dated Sept. 21) 94; DNA, RG 393, Dept. of the Tenn., Letters Sent. On Oct. 1, Barnard telegraphed to USG. "Lieut. Wilson will be examined by letter" ALS (telegram sent), *ibid.*, RG 107, Telegrams Collected (Unbound). On May 28, 1864, Wilson was confirmed as capt. to rank from May 7, 1863. On Oct. 17, Rosecrans telegraphed to Halleck requesting that Wilson be made col. of a proposed veteran engineer regt. *O.R.*, I, xxx, part 4, 435; Wilson diary, Oct. 20, 1863; Wilson to Badeau, Oct. 24, 1863, typescript, WyU. USG, however, contemplated giving Wilson a cav. command. See letter to Julia Dent Grant, Nov. 14, 1863; letter to Maj. Gen. William T. Sherman, Dec. 1, 1863; Wilson to Badeau, Nov. 18, 1863, typescript, WyU; Wilson diary, Nov. 28, Dec. 7, 1863. Yet, in diary entries for Dec. 9–11, 1863, Wilson wrote: "Genl declines to assign me to Cavl Comd permanently—wishing me to remain with him.—" *Ibid.* See telegram to Charles A. Dana, Jan. 18, 1864.

1. Henry W. Slocum of N. Y., USMA 1852, resigned as 1st lt. on Oct. 31, 1856, and began a new career as lawyer-politician. Appointed col., 27th N. Y., as of May 21, 1861, brig. gen. as of Aug. 9, and maj. gen. as of July 4, 1862, he served in the Army of the Potomac. Sent to Chattanooga in command of the 12th Army Corps, Slocum submitted his resignation because he objected to serving under Maj. Gen. Joseph Hooker. Lincoln, *Works*, VI, 486. See endorsement to Maj. Gen. Henry W. Halleck, Feb. 9, 1864.

To Maj. Gen. Ambrose E. Burnside

Chattanooga Oct. 26th [*1863*] 6 P. M.

MAJOR GENERAL, A. E. BURNSIDE
KNOXVILLE TENN.

Have you indications of a force coming from Lee's Army by way of Abingdon[1] towards you? Do you hear of any of Braggs army threatening you from the southwest? Thomas command is in bad condition to me for want of animals of sufficient strength to move his Artillery and for want of rations. If you are threatened with a force beyond what you can compete with, efforts must be made to assist you. Answer.

U. S. G.
Major General.

Telegram, copies, DLC-USG, V, 34, 35; DNA, RG 393, Military Div. of the Miss., Letters Sent. Printed as sent at 2:00 P.M. in *O.R.*, I, xxxi, part 1, 745. On Oct. 25, 1863, 11:30 P.M., Maj. Gen. Ambrose E. Burnside, Loudon, Tenn., had telegraphed to USG and to Maj. Gen. Henry W. Halleck. "Evidence still seems to indicate that the enemy are concentrated in considerable force on the souh side of the river   we can easily give up this place & take up the bridge but it seems advisable to hold it and not release the enemys force to join the army in front of Thomas & Information from Genl Shackleford on our left seems to corroborate the report of considerable concentration by the enemy in the neighborhood of Abingdon"   Telegram received, DNA, RG 94, War Records Office, Military Div. of the Miss.; copy, *ibid.*, RG 393, Military Div. of the Miss., Telegrams Received. *O.R.*, I, xxxi, part 1, 729–30. On Oct. 27, 7:00 P.M., Burnside telegraphed to USG and to Halleck. "We have had many reports here with reference to Ewells Corps coming from Lees army against us by way of Abingdon but the indications are that no such force has yet made its appearance at Abingdon and I am inclined to believe the reports to be incorrect but there is a considerable force from Bragg's army on this side of the Hiawassa One Division at SweetWater and two others said to be approaching there   we have had constantant cavalry skirmishing for several days   The first day's resulting in a loss to us of ~~over~~ over four hundred prisoners from Walfords Brigade but since that day the results have been in our favor   The morning I came here I determined that the position held by our troops on the Rail Road side of the river was not a good position for defense, except for a larger force than can possibly be spared for this place   I ordered what I considered to be sufficient reinforcements to make an offensive move towards the Hiawassa but I am now satisfied that no decisive result ~~will~~ would follow a movement of that kind particularly as Thomas army is not ready for a movement   We might drive the enemy to the Hiawassa river but as their cars run up to the crossing a sufficient force could be concentrated against us by them no doubt to drive us back & no good would result from the movement   I have been warned by Halleck not to be caught on the south side of the river & nothing but a strong desire to attack a force from the front of the Army of the Cumberland ever kept me on that side because I am not strong enough to attack them in the flank although I was at one time favorable to passing their flank & assaulting their communication   I have therefore thought it best to withdraw the from the south side of the river & only attempt to hold that part of the country south of the Charleston & east of little Tennessee & all of that part of the state north of the big Tennessee   neither the little Tennessee or the Holston are now fordable & I shall now move the ponton bridge to some point above the junction of these rivers & hold Kingston & Knoxville as strongly as possible   We are building ponton Boats as rapidly as possible at Kingston for a bridge across the Tenn river just below the mouth of the Clinch which with a flank movement, in case they attempt to move up the Rail Road to Loudon in force   I telegraphed you some days ago in reference to the construction of road which we propose to draw our supplies on   If the RailRoad to MacMinnville is in operation it is possible that supplies might be drawn from there but it is reported as almost impracticable particularly at the crossing of the Carry [*Caney*] river   I am satisfied that if the enemy hold the country about Chattanooga so that we cannot command the rail road we shall have to draw our supplies from the head of navigation on the Cumberland near the mouth of the big South Fork   Steps have been taken to to put the road in condition for winter travel from that place   The only Indiana Regts we have are on the extreme front   details will be sent as soon as possible   our necessities for subsistence and clothing will prevent us from accumulating our supply of ammunition as rapidly as you order unless Capt Irwin can furnish wagon transportation from McMinnville for the clothing which he proposes to send up from Nashville   we can probably get it sooner from Camp Nelson   if he could possibly send the amount you ordered to Kingston it would be of very great service to us   if the disposition of my forces are not satisfactory to you I shall be very glad to receive from you specific instructions   If it becomes necessary to evacuate this country in order to reinforce Thomas we hold our selves ready to do it though it would be a sad thing for this country   While I do not believe that Ewells Corps is at Abingdon I am satisfied that all the rebels forces of west Virginia are being concentrated in that neighborhood & will probably amount to fifteen thousand"   Telegram received, DNA, RG 94, War Records Office, Military Div. of the Miss.; *ibid.*, RG 107, Telegrams Collected (Bound); copy, *ibid.*, RG 393, Military Div. of the Miss., Telegrams Received. *O.R.*, I, xxxi, part 1, 756–57.

1. Abingdon, Va., on the Tennessee and Virginia Railroad, approximately ten miles north of the Tenn. border.

To Maj. Gen. George H. Thomas

Chattanooga Oct 26, 1863

MAJOR GENERAL GEO. H. THOMAS
CHATTANOOGA

The Quartermaster General suggests that Col Buell[1] be detailed to take general supervision of all the troops between here and Bridgeport, and Stevenson and direct the repairs on the roads over which supplies are now brought. Col Buell is an engineer and even with the small force on the road could repair the worst places so as to materially faciliatate the transportation of supplies. I would also direct that a call be made for ship carpenters and such mechanics as can work on the building of a steamboat and that thirty if that number can be got, be detailed on extra duty and ordered to report to Capt. A. Edwards[2] A. Q. M. Bridgeport Ala.

U. S. GRANT
Major General

Copies, DLC-USG, V, 34, 35; DNA, RG 393, Military Div. of the Miss., Letters Sent. *O.R.*, I, xxxi, part 1, 741. On Oct. 26, 1863, Maj. Gen. George H. Thomas, Chattanooga, wrote to USG. "Your communication directing the detail of Col Buell to superintend the repairs of the road hence to Bridgeport has just been received. I will have Col Buell detailed for that duty. have already sent the order detailing Ship Carpenters to work on the Steamers at Bridgeport." Copy, DNA, RG 393, Dept. of the Cumberland, Letters Sent.

On Oct. 24, 11:00 A.M., USG telegraphed to Maj. Gen. Joseph Hooker. "What amount of rations is there now at Stevenson and how much forage? Report immediately approximately" Copies, DLC-USG, V, 34, 35; DNA, RG 393, Military Div. of the Miss., Letters Sent. On the same day, 12:30 P.M., Hooker, Stevenson, Ala., telegraphed to USG. "Despatch recieved—In round numbers we have (540.000) Five Hundred & forty thousand Rations—No forage except 100 bales of hay—" ALS (telegram sent), NRU; copy, DNA, RG 393, Military Div. of the Miss., Telegrams Received. Also on Oct. 24, 11:00 A.M., USG telegraphed to Maj. Gen. Oliver O. Howard. "What amount of rations and forage is there at Bridgeport.—ask with the view of using the road in transporting animals from Louisville, if it can be spared for the purpo[se] for a few days. Answer quick." Copies, *ibid.*, 11th Army Corps, Telegrams Received; *ibid.*, Military Div. of the Miss., Letters Sent; DLC-USG, V, 34, 35. On the same day, Howard, Bridgeport, Ala., telegraphed to USG. "Only three days rations for the Corps and Post and eight thousand sacks of corn and twenty five thousand lbs of Hay. We have no coffee and sugar. A train is coming from Stevenson with Commissary Stores. Amount not known." Copies (2), DNA, RG 393, 11th Army Corps,

Telegrams Sent. On Oct. 22, Lt. Col. Theodore S. Bowers, Nashville, wrote to Capt. Samuel J. Little. "Major General U. S. Grant, commanding directs me by telegraph from Bridgeport to order you to send to the front as speedily as possible vegetables for the Army. Beans and Hominy are especially required." Copies, *ibid.*, Military Div. of the Miss., Letters Sent; DLC-USG, V, 34, 35. On the same day, Bowers telegraphed to USG. "Capt Little depot commissary has a quantity of vegetables on hand and will send them forward at once   Heretofore He has been unable to procure necessary transportation   The road requires more rolling stock"   Telegram received (misdated Nov. 22), DNA, RG 94, War Records Office, Military Div. of the Miss.; copy (misdated Nov. 22), *ibid.*, RG 393, Military Div. of the Miss., Letters Sent.

On Nov. 1, 4:00 P.M., Asst. Secretary of War Charles A. Dana, Chattanooga, telegraphed to Secretary of War Edwin M. Stanton. "Having got short and rapid transportation for subsistence a new difficulty suddenly appears. It seems that we have no subsistence stores at Stevenson and that our Steamboats actually have to come up the river with light loads. The fault is with Lieut Col. Simmons Commissary of the Department and Capt Little, depot Commissary at Nashville. There is no excuse for them, for even the universal intermeddling and non action of Gen Rosecrans cannot have prevented the bringing forward of rations. They should in my judgement be at once dismissed from the service, but when I told Genl Thomas that I should ask you to dismiss them he desired that such punishment might not be inflicted since it was not certain that the fault was not with Genl Rosecrans. Genl Reynolds however thinks both ought to be summarily dealt with. I promised Thomas that I would make no recommendation with respect to Simmons but would simply report the facts. Thomas applies today for a new Chief Commissary. I recommend Col Clarke B. Lagow and Col Joseph C. McKibbin additional aides be mustered out. The first belongs to Gen'l Grant who wishes to get rid of him. The second Genl Rosecrans sent away for drunkenness. Both are worthless fellows who earn no part of their pay. Gen'l Grant has despatches from Gen'l Sherman dated 27th at Florence. One brigade was at Tuscumbia and would have to march back to Eastport to cross the river. A regiment of Alabama Cavalry which Sherman had sent south to cut the Rail Road had been worsted. Shermans advance is necessarily slow, much as he is needed here. Gen Burnside desires a diversion to be made by Thomas but as I have before reported this army is immovable for want of animals, forage, and subsistence   Bridge nearly repaired"   Telegram received, DLC-Edwin M. Stanton. *O.R.*, I, xxxi, part 2, 54. See telegram to Maj. Gen. William T. Sherman, Oct. 24; letter to Sherman, Nov. 29, 1863. Lt. Col. Samuel Simmons served as chief commissary, Dept. of the Cumberland, until Nov. 25; Little was retained as depot commissary, Nashville.

On Oct. 31, 11:55 A.M., Lt. Col. James A. Hardie, AGO, telegraphed to USG. "Please forward any recommendations you may have for the Staff of the Fourth Corps." Telegram received, DNA, RG 107, Telegrams Collected (Bound); copies, *ibid.*, RG 94, Commissions and Returns, Letters Sent; *ibid.*, RG 393, Military Div. of the Miss., Hd. Qrs. Correspondence; DLC-USG, V, 40, 94. On Nov. 1, noon, USG telegraphed to Hardie. "The following staff officers are recommended for the fourth army corps—Maj J. S. Fullerton A A G   Maj Robert. O. Selfridge Inspector Genl   Capt Hiatt Ranasen Chf Q M   Lt Thos G Benham Senior Aid   A D Taylor, Wm L Avery Aids"   Telegram received, DNA, RG 94, ACP, 322G CB 1863; (dated Nov. 2) *ibid.*, RG 107, Telegrams Collected (Bound); copies, *ibid.*, RG 393, Military Div. of the Miss., Hd. Qrs. Correspondence; DLC-USG, V, 40, 94. On Oct. 19 and 29, Maj. Gen. Gordon Granger, 4th Army Corps, Chattanooga, had telegraphed to Brig. Gen. Lorenzo Thomas making the same recommendations but also proposing Capt. David Remick for commissary and Maj. John Mendenhall for judge advocate. Telegrams received, DNA, RG 94, ACP, 324G, 325G CB 1863. On Oct. 10, Maj. Gen. William S. Rosecrans, Chattanooga, had retained Lt. Col. Gilbert C. Kniffin, commissary, 21st Army Corps (which was merged into the 4th Army Corps), to assist Simmons. *O.R.*, I, xxx, part 4, 245. On Nov. 2, Hardie telegraphed to USG. "No recommendation for Commissary of the Fourth Corps.—Do you recommend Lieut. Colonel Kniffin to be retained as such?" Telegram received, DNA, RG 107, Telegrams Collected (Unbound); copies, *ibid.*, RG 94, Commissions and Returns, Letters Sent; *ibid.*, RG 393, Military Div. of the Miss., Hd. Qrs. Correspondence; DLC-USG, V, 40, 94. On Nov. 4, 10:00 A.M., USG telegraphed to Hardie. "Capt David Reneyck C S is recommended as Chief Commissary for fourth (4) army corps" Telegram received, DNA, RG 94, ACP, 325G CB 1863; *ibid.*, RG 107, Telegrams Collected (Bound); copies, *ibid.*, RG 393, Military Div. of the Miss., Hd. Qrs. Correspondence; DLC-USG, V, 40, 94. On Nov. 6, Hardie noted Stanton's approval of this recommendation. AES, DNA, RG 94, ACP, 325G CB 1863.

1. Col. George P. Buell, 58th Ind.
2. Capt. Arthur Edwards, 5th Mich. Cav.

To Lt. Col. Charles L. Kilburn

Chattanooga Oct. 26, 8.30 A. M. [*1863*]

COLONEL C. L. KILBURN
CARE CAPT LITTLE NASHVILLE

Your dispatch received. The Departments will remain as they were, each one through their Staff Officers providing themselves I have no expectation of returning to Nashville. Would have been glad to see you on my way here.

I recieved a letter from you about the time of starting from Vicksburg which I will attend to as soon as I can get hold of it. The letter was put in my private desk, which with other baggage has not yet arrived, and will not for several dates owing to the desperate state of the roads between here and Bridgeport.

Write to me your views as to how Department Chief Commissaries should obtain their supplies

U. S. GRANT
Major General

Telegram, copies, DLC-USG, V, 34, 35; DNA, RG 393, Military Div. of the
Miss., Letters Sent. Charles L. Kilburn of Pa., USMA 1842, served with the 3rd
Art. during the Mexican War. He was promoted to lt. col., asst. commissary gen.
of subsistence, as of Feb. 9, 1863. On Oct. 25, Kilburn, Nashville, had telegraphed to USG. "Please General let me know how are going to organize the
Commissary Department in your division   shall I write you   I am waiting here
on Floyds & other business   would like to see you   Are you coming up here
soon"   Copy, *ibid.*, Telegrams Received.

On Oct. 30, USG wrote to Secretary of War Edwin M. Stanton. "Believing
as I do that officers occupying the responsible places that Lieut. Col. C. L. Kilburn and Col. Haines, supplying Commissaries at Cincinnati & St. Louis, do
should have more rank than they now have I would earnestly recommend them
for promotion to the rank of Brig. Gen of Vols. Both these officers have filled
their present places to the great satisfaction of those troops supplied by them
and to the best interests of the Government." ALS, *ibid.*, RG 94, ACP, K30 CB
1863. Promoted to col. as of June 29, 1864, Kilburn, like Col. Thomas J. Haines,
only became bvt. brig. gen. on March 13, 1865. On Oct. 26, 1863, USG wrote
to John How, businessman and former mayor of St. Louis, regarding the promotion of Haines, USG's recent interview with Stanton, and other matters.
American Antiquarian, IV, 9 (April, 1887), 393; Stan. V. Henkels, *A Choice
Collection of Autographs* . . . Feb. 20–21, 1902, p. 57.

To Maj. Gen. Henry W. Halleck

Chattanooga Tenn
7 P M Oct 27/63

Maj Gen H W Halleck
Gen in Chief

Thomas Crutchfield[1] is here and reported to be a strong union
man   Thompson I do not know. I have ordered the immediate
arrest of both and will send them under guard to Louisville for
trial—

U S Grant
Maj Genl

Telegram received, DNA, RG 107, Telegrams Collected (Bound); copies, *ibid.*,
Telegrams Received in Cipher; *ibid.*, RG 393, Military Div. of the Miss., Hd.
Qrs. Correspondence; DLC-USG, V, 40, 94. *O.R.*, I, xxxi, part 1, 752. On Oct.
27, 1863, 4:00 P.M., Maj. Gen. Henry W. Halleck had telegraphed to USG.
"It is reported from Atlanta that Thomas Crutchfield & Dean Thompson, pretended Union men & in the confidence of General Rosecrans, are really spies &
furnish information to Genl Bragg." ALS (telegram sent), DNA, RG 107, Telegrams Collected (Bound); copies, *ibid.*, RG 393, Military Div. of the Miss., Hd.

Qrs. Correspondence; DLC-USG, V, 40, 94. Probably on the same day, USG endorsed this telegram to Maj. Gen. George H. Thomas. "Have these men arrested and sent under guard to Louisville Ky and closely confined for trial. When arrested I will report the fact to Washington." Copies, *ibid.* On Oct. 28, 10:00 A.M., Halleck telegraphed to USG. "I have no evidence against Crutchfield & Thompson, only a rumor. I did not desire their arrest on that rumor, but merely to put you on your guard against them. Horse equipments will be forwarded as soon as possible." ALS (telegram sent), DNA, RG 107, Telegrams Collected (Bound); copies, *ibid.*, RG 393, Military Div. of the Miss., Hd. Qrs. Correspondence; DLC-USG, V, 40, 94. See telegram to Maj. Gen. William T. Sherman, Oct. 24, 1863.

On Nov. 20, Capt. George K. Leet wrote to Lt. Col. William M. Wiles, provost marshal, Dept. of the Cumberland. "Miss Boyer has permission from the General Com'dg to come to Chattanooga, for the purpose as she represents of obtaining pay from the proper authorities for services rendered Maj Genl Rosecranz in secret service. The General Com'dg, knowing nothing of her, or of the justice of her claims, and in fact, having nothing to do with the matter in any event refferred her to you, who, he supposed, might have some knowledge of her case." Copies, DLC-USG, V, 34, 35; DNA, RG 393, Military Div. of the Miss., Letters Sent. On Dec. 12, USG telegraphed to Lt. Col. Theodore S. Bowers. "I have recd a letter from Miss Boyer asking for leave to go to Cincinnati before commencing on here new duties I told Rawley to call on her and say that since the late battles I shall not want her to make a trip south If Rawley has not communicated this tell him to do so or send some one to communicate it" Telegram received, *ibid.*, Dept. of the Tenn., Telegrams Received; copy, *ibid.*, Military Div. of the Miss., Telegrams Received.

1. Thomas Crutchfield and his brother William were hotelkeepers and prominent businessmen in Chattanooga. Johnson, *Papers*, IV, 166–67. On Dec. 4, Thomas Crutchfield wrote to USG requesting that his house not be used as a U.S. hospital. ALS, DNA, RG 109, Union Provost Marshals' File of Papers Relating to Individual Civilians. On Dec. 5, Capt. Ely S. Parker wrote to Surgeon William W. Bridge. "You are hereby directed to remove the sick and wounded soldiers out of the house owned by Thomas Crutchfield and which you now use as a hospital, to some other convenient place near or into the nearest buildings near by. You will also restore all the furniture, cooking utensils and the stove of Mr Crutchfield" Copies, DLC-USG, V, 34, 35; DNA, RG 393, Military Div. of the Miss., Letters Sent. On March 2, 1864, William Crutchfield wrote to Thomas asking permission to bring in goods for sale in partnership with his brother and his brother-in-law John King. LS, *ibid.*, RG 366, First Special Agency, Nashville District, Letters Received. On March 15, USG endorsed this letter. "Mr. Cruchfield is a Tennesseean of undoubted loyalty from the begining of the rebellion to the present. He has made large sacrifices of property on account of his opinions and has been of great service to the union cause. I would like to see the greatest priviliges extended to him that can be legally extended." AES, *ibid.*

To Maj. Gen. Henry W. Halleck

Chattanooga Tenn
Oct 27 1863 9 P M

MAJ GEN H W. HALLECK
GEN IN CHIEF

I have ordered McPherson to send one Division of troops to Sherman   This will leave him a present effective force of at least thirteen thousand (13 000) White troops   These will go by way of Corinth   I think it advisable to send all troops intended to join Sherman from the north up Tennessee River to Eastport

U S GRANT
Maj Genl

Telegram received, DNA, RG 107, Telegrams Collected (Bound); copies, *ibid.*, Telegrams Received in Cipher; *ibid.*, RG 393, Military Div. of the Miss., Hd. Qrs. Correspondence; DLC-USG, V, 40, 94. *O.R.*, I, xxxi, part 1, 752. On Oct. 27, 1863, USG wrote to Maj. Gen. James B. McPherson. "Send Tuttle's Division forward with all possible haste via Corinth to report to General Sherman." Copies, DLC-USG, V, 34, 35; DNA, RG 393, Military Div. of the Miss., Letters Sent. On the same day, 2:00 P.M., USG telegraphed via Brig. Gen. George Crook, Maysville, Ala., to Maj. Gen. William T. Sherman. "I have ordered McPherson to send forward Tuttles division to report to you   repeat the order stating how you wish it to come   the order placing you in Command of the department & army of the Tennessee has been made in washington"   Telegram received, *ibid.*, RG 94, War Records Office, Dept. of the Tenn.; copies, *ibid.*, RG 393, Military Div. of the Miss., Letters Sent; DLC-USG, V, 34, 35. *O.R.*, I, xxxi, part 1, 759. See telegram to Maj. Gen. Henry W. Halleck, Oct. 23, 1863.

On Nov. 2, Brig. Gen. John A. Rawlins wrote to McPherson. "While the General believes that the forces collected at Canton to resist you were much less than reported, still he approves of your action in returning to Vicksburg for he says it will not do to hazard a defeat of the Vicksburg forces. He has ordered forward Tuttle's Division to join General Sherman; but if the enemy are really and in earnest assembling an Army to operate against Vicksburg desires me to say you are authorized, if you deem it necessary to retain Tuttle at least until you can communicate with Sherman. The repairing of levees on the Mississippi by the military authorities he deems inadvisable and therefore disapproves of it. In fact the propriety of permitting them to be repaired at all, even by citizens or those who desire to leave them, he regards as exceedingly questionable, for certainly the flooding of the country will, during the winter and spring tend greatly to the security of navigation. He is pleased to know that you are pushing the work on the fortifications and desires you to put to work on them every available man you have and push them with all possible haste to completion, so that with three Divisions of your Corps and the Colored troops of General Hawkins, you can hold Vicksburg and Natchez against any possible combination of force the enemy can make. The Natchez fortifications ought now to be finished. If Tuttle's Division can be spared without too much endangering Vicksburg's safety, you will send it forward via the Tennessee river. The General desires to know if two full regiments and the Colored troops would be sufficient garrison for Natchez, and if so he will try and have sent you two such regiments from the North and thereby enable you to relieve Crocker and bring him to Vicksburg for when a forward movement is to be made from here he wishes to have you in such condition as to move with a respectable force in point of numbers, as he knows they will be in point of fighting material, east from Vicksburg to Alabama or as far in that direction as as practicable so as to compel the enemy to detach forces to oppose you, or, failing to do so have his rear exposed to attack from you. Owing to the difficulties of getting forward supplies and the poverty of the animals, a forward movement from here before spring is exceedingly problematical— Gen Sherman's advance was at Florence on the 30th ult. He is expected to reach Stevenson by the last of this week or first of next. The information latest from the enemy would indicate they were moving their Divisions East from here [*to*] Cleveland, one of which is known to be there under General Stevenson. This may be with a view of attacking Burnside, or it may be to watch and prevent him from moving to the South of the Tennessee River. We have hopes on General Sherman's arrival to be able to drive the enemy from our immediate front here and getting possession of Lookout Mountain. This with little repairs, would give us the Rail Road to this place and also uninterrupted use of the river. Anything else that may be of interest Captain Gill, who will be the bearer of this, can communicate to you—" Copies, DLC-USG, V, 34, 35; DNA, RG 393, Military Div. of the Miss., Letters Sent. *O.R.*, I, xxxi, part 3, 22–23. See letter to Brig. Gen. John P. Hawkins, Oct. 2, 1863. On Oct. 24, McPherson, Vicksburg, had written to USG. "I enclose herewith a letter just received from Brig. Genl. Tuttel Comdg on line of 'Big Black,' giving the report brought in by one of his scouts. From this you will see that there is some talk and even probability of the Enemy trying to retake this place. I think their number is greatly exaggerated, but from what I learned during the recent reconnoissance the force they can concentrate is quite formidable. President Davis has been with Genl Johnston at Meridian, and whether he came any farther west or not I have not learned. I am pushing the new line of defenses forward as rapidly as possible, but it will require a vast amount of work to complete it. I have some scouts out, and will endeavor to keep you advised of any decided movement of the Enemy." Copies, DNA, RG 393, 13th and 17th Army Corps, Letters Sent; *ibid.*, 17th Army Corps, Letters Sent. *O.R.*, I, xxxi, part 1, 721. On Nov. 15, McPherson wrote to Rawlins. "Captain Gile has just returned bringing your letter of the 2nd inst and I need not say to you that it gave me the greatest satisfaction   Shortly after your departure, I sent to Genl. Crocker at Natchez to see Lieut Harris in charge of the constuction of Fortifications at that place, and arrange the permanent Garrison, assigning the two colored Regiments to a part of it, and organize the balance of his Command into a movable force to operate as circumstances may require. I had not seen a plan of the new works and my surprise was great when I found that they would require a garrison of over seven thousand.(7000) men. I immediately directed Genl. Crocker to inform Lieut. H— that this was a much larger garrison than could be assigned to that post, and to finish up the work to accommodate about two thousand five hundred men, (including the colored troops.) As soon as the order was received directing Genl Tuttle's Division to be sent to

Sherman, I made arrangements to have Crocker's Division moved up here, and one Brigade has already arrived. I propose to move the whole Division up here, which will give me Logan's and Crocker's Divisions to operate with, leaving McArthur's Division and the colored troops to garrison this place and Natchez. I would like very much to have two Regiments sent if possible as it would let me out of a difficulty in making these dispositions. I have it upon good authority that the Rebels are repairing the Railroad north from Brandon, and getting out timber to construct a temporary bridge across Pearl River at Jackson, and repairing the Road from Canton to Jackson. I shall keep a close watch upon them, and try and break up their arrangments if they are really in earnest about carrying it out . . .P. S. Tuttle's Division left here a week ago today." Copies, DNA, RG 393, 13th and 17th Army Corps, Letters Sent; *ibid.*, 17th Army Corps, Letters Sent. *O.R.*, I, xxxi, part 3, 161.

To Julia Dent Grant

Chattanooga Tennessee
October 27th 1863.

Dear Julia,

The very hard ride over here and necessary exercise since to gain a full knowledge of location instead of making my injury worse has almost entirely cured me. I now walk without the use of a crutch or cane and mount my horse from the ground without difficulty. This is one of the wildest places you ever saw and without the use of rail-roads one of the most out-of-the way places. To give you an idea of its inaccessibility I have only to state that the waggons with our baggage left Bridgeport, the present rail-road turminus, fifty miles distant by the road they have to travel, on the 23d inst. It is now 10 O'Clock at night of the 27th and they have not yet arrived and I hardly expect them to-morrow. Then too six-mule teams are not loaded with what two would easily pull on ordinary dirt roads. We have not consequently been able to start Messes.—Ross remained back at Nashville to lay in supplies but as he has not yet come up to Bridgeport I suspect he has had to go, or send, to Louisville for them. When they will get up is hard to surmise. I am making a desperate effort however to get possession of the river from here to Bridgeport and if I do it will facilitate bringing supplies very much.

There are but very few people here and those few will have to leave soon. People about Vicksburg have not seen War yet, or at least not the suffering brought on by war.

I have received no line from you yet. I feel very anxious to hear from the children. Tell Fred and Buck they must write at least one letter each week to you or me.

Kisses for yourself and Jess.

ULYS.

When do you think of starting on your trip to Ohio? You ought to start soon or you will not be able to go this Fall.

U.

ALS, DLC-USG.

To Maj. Gen. Henry W. Halleck

Chattanooga 8 P M. Oct 28 63

MAJ. GEN HALLECK WASHINGTON.

Gen Thomas' plan for securing the river and south side road hence to Bridgeport has proven iminently successful. The question of supplies may now be regarded as settled. If the rebels give us one week more time I think all danger of losing territory now held by us will have passed away, and preparations may commence for offensive opperations

U S. GRANT
Maj Gen.

Telegram received (incomplete), DNA, RG 107, Telegrams Collected (Bound); copies, ibid., Telegrams Received in Cipher; ibid., RG 393, Military Div. of the Miss., Hd. Qrs. Correspondence; DLC-USG, V, 40, 94. O.R., I, xxxi, part 1, 56. On Oct. 27, 1863, 9:00 A.M., USG had telegraphed to Lt. Col. James H. Wilson, Bridgeport, Ala. "Telegraph me progress made by Gen Hooker's expedition   Also ask the General to say what he may require to insure success in order that you may let me know his exact wants. Gen Hooker will of course telegraph Gen Thomas for all he requires but by me being informed also, additional facilities may be given." Copies, DLC-USG, V, 34, 35; DNA, RG 393, Military Div. of the Miss., Letters Sent. On the same day, Lt. Col. William G. Le Duc, q. m., 11th Army Corps, telegraphed to USG. "Your dispatch to Lt. Co'l. Wilson of date 27th received by me this morning at 11 o'clock. Co'l. Wilson having gone with General Hooker this morning the expedition with 3 days cooked rations and 3 days forage marched at daylight: the rear passing the river at 9 30 A. M. I think there is a reasonable probability that the Steamer will leave here tomorrow morning with either forage or rations or both. I will order her to the mouth of Sequatchie or Landing opposite Shell Mound unless otherwise ordered   will it be safe to run her up the suck." Copy, *ibid.*, Telegrams Received.

On Oct. 27, Brig. Gen. John A. Rawlins wrote to Mary E. (Emma) Hurlbut. "The river from here to near Bridgeport a distance of twenty eight miles, when we arrived, which was on the evening of the 23rd inst., was commanded by the enemy from the south side and cut off from us, compelling the transportation of supplies for the entire army by wagons fifty miles over muddy mountainous roads, this General Grant took immediate steps to obviate by the moving of a sufficient force south of the river at Bridgeport and points between here and there to seize the mountain passess to the river and drive out the enemy, to day the crossings were made and as far as heard from have been a success, should the whole move result in the success it now promises, it will give us the use of the river to the foot of Lookout Mountain; leaving but five miles and that too over good roads to haul our supplies by wagons. and will secure us against the elements destroying our lines of communications and against any efforts the enemy may make to dislodge us from here." ALS, ICHi. For reports of the opening of the "cracker line," Oct. 26–27, and the battle to retain it at Wauhatchie, Tenn., Oct. 28–29, see *O.R.*, I, xxxi, part 1, 39–235; letter to Col. John C. Kelton, Dec. 23, 1863; *Memoirs*, II, chap. xli.

On Oct. 28, USG wrote to Maj. Gen. George H. Thomas. "It seems to me the Steamer 'Paint Rock' should by all means be got down to Browns ferry before morning, even if a house has to be torn down to provide the necessary fuel. There is every probability that the enemy will make every preparation possible before to morrow night to prevent our accomplishing this." Copies, DLC-USG, V, 34, 35; DNA, RG 393, Military Div. of the Miss., Letters Sent. *O.R.*, I, xxxi, part 1, 60. On Oct. 29, Capt. Ely S. Parker issued Special Field Orders No. 5. "Lieutenant Colonel J. H. Wilson, Assistant Inspector General, and Captain of Engineers, will report, without delay to Major General G. H. Thomas, commanding Army of the Cumberland, to take charge of the laying out and construction of the defences of the passes on the southside of the Tennessee River, through which the enemy might reach it. Major General Thomas will direct the Commanding Officers of troops defending such passes to furnish him such details of men for the prosecution of said work as he may require." Copy, DLC-USG, V, 38. *O.R.*, I, xxxi, part 1, 775. On Nov. 1, USG telegraphed to Lucius B. Boomer, Bridgeport, Ala., regarding work on the railroad bridge over Running Water Creek. "I will order General Thomas to furnish the men you require at once" Copies, DLC-USG, V, 34, 35; DNA, RG 393, Military Div. of the Miss., Letters Sent.

To Maj. Gen. Henry W. Halleck

———

Chattanooga Tenn,
11.30 P. M. Oct. 28. 1863—

Maj. Gen'l Halleck
Gen'l in Chief—

Gen'l Burnside thinks troops from Western Virginia are concentrating about Abingdon, to the number of 15,000 men—Also towards Loudon,[1] from Bragg's army—Present lack of supplies and poverty of stock will prevent effective assistance being given from here for a few days—Can Gen'l Kelly[2] do anything towards Abingdon from his position?—I want to hold all the ground Burnside now has, but if any must be given up, think it should not be that between him and Thomas—

U. S. Grant.
Maj. Genl

Telegram received, DNA, RG 107, Telegrams Collected (Bound); copies, *ibid.*, Telegrams Received in Cipher; *ibid.*, RG 393, Military Div. of the Miss., Hd. Qrs. Correspondence; DLC-USG, V, 40, 94. *O.R.*, I, xxxi, part 1, 767–68.

1. Loudon, Tenn., on the Tennessee River and the East Tennessee and Georgia Railroad, approximately seventy miles northeast of Chattanooga.
2. Benjamin F. Kelley, born in N. H. in 1807, moved to Wheeling, Va., when nineteen, becoming freight agent of the Baltimore and Ohio Railroad in 1851. Appointed col., 1st W. Va., as of May 22, 1861, he was wounded during the battle of Philippi on June 3. He was nominated as brig. gen. on July 31, confirmed on Aug. 3 to rank from May 17, and served mostly in W. Va.

To Maj. Gen. Ambrose E. Burnside

———

Chattanooga 11:30 P. M. 28th Oct. 1863.
Major General. A. E. Burnside
Knoxville Tenn.

The positions taken by you are I suppose the best that could be taken under the circumstances. I would like however if you could [*hold*] the line of the Hiawassee   It is particularly desirable that all the territory you now have should be held, but if any portion must be given up, let it be to the east, and keep your Army so that it and Thomas Army can support each other. It is better that you should be forced from the Eastern end of the valley than from the west.[1] Thomas is in no condition to move from his present position. He has succeeded however in getting possession of the river and roads south of it from Browns ferry to Bridgeport. It is to be hoped with this line open and Sherman up here, as he may be expected to be in a few days, Thomas will be able to place one Division, at McMinnville and the remainder of the Corps, between here and you. I have telegraphed Genl. Halleck to know if Gen. Kelly cannot move out from Western Virginia to threaten any force collecting about Abingdon.[2]

U. S. G.

Major General.

Telegram, copies, DLC-USG, V, 34, 35; DNA, RG 393, Military Div. of the Miss., Letters Sent. *O.R.*, I, xxxi, part 1, 770. On Oct. 29, 1863, Maj. Gen. Ambrose E. Burnside, Lenoir's Station, Tenn., telegraphed to USG and to Maj. Gen. Henry W. Halleck. After reporting information from Col. Robert K. Byrd, Kingston, Tenn., about the advance of C.S.A. troops, he concluded: "I cannot vouch for the truth of these statements but they agree with substantially with the reports that I have been getting for some days   That there is a considerable force of moving in this direction there can be no question   If such is the case the force in front of Thomas must be materially weakened   I have removed the forces at Loudon to this side of the River holding the heights commanding the town—If the enemy were to succeed in crossing the river below it would be impossible for me to concentrate the forces that are now in the eastern part of the state to join Thomas but unless they have ponton trains with them I can probably prevent them from crossing   I am drawing the forces back from the eastern part of the state gradually and the enemy's cavalry follows on after them. A rapid move of our forces in the eastern part of the state would probably cause us to lose our communication with Cumberland gap and also many trains now on that route and as [no] other route is now practicable without troops to assist over the bad parts   If you should think it desirable at any time for us to order all the trains back that have not yet arrived at Cumberland Gap and make a rapid concentration at Kingston I think it can be done if the enemy's movements are not too far advanced and even should he be he could not will prevent us from getting there unless he had a very large force or we can concentrate and fight him at a point where we can meet him under the most favorable circumstances and do our best to hold him in check until Thomas can attack Bragg and probably defeat him but in case of disaster we could try to make our way to some of the mountain passes which we could hold until supplies could come to us   The concentration would probably be at Knoxville   Our great trouble lies in the shortness of supplies but we have nearly Ten (10) day's salt on hand and probably as many day's of beef cattle and will probably receive more before an attack can be made   Our Cavalry has suffered a great deal from constant service along so extended a line but I have held this long line in accordance with what I considered to be the spirit of the instructions from Washington as well as their wishes & it would be a sad thing indeed to have to give up this country   I had already designated Genl Wilcox for the command in Louisville but if you direct it Major General Rosseau can be ordered to the command   I beg to say that I very much regret the ordering of Genl Boyle from his present work as he seems to me almost essential to its prosecution as he is so intimately identified with the work now being carried on under previous orders in Kentucky   I have always regarded him as a most fearless & efficient officer and in all my intercourse with him I have never discovered any disposition to meddle with politics except that he ran for congress"   Telegram received, DNA, RG 94, War Records Office, Dept. of the Ohio; *ibid.*, RG 107, Telegrams Collected (Bound); copy, *ibid.*, RG 393, Military Div. of the Miss., Telegrams Received. *O.R.*, I, xxxi, part 1, 778–79. Regarding the command of Brig. Gen. Jeremiah T. Boyle, see telegram to Maj. Gen. Ambrose E. Burnside, Nov. 1, 1863, note 3.

1. See telegram to Maj. Gen. Ambrose E. Burnside, Oct. 26, 1863.
2. See preceding telegram.

To George W. Childs

———

Chattanooga Tennessee,
October 29th 1863,

GEO. W. CHILDS, ESQ.
DEAR SIR:

Your letter of the 21st of Sept. asking for drawings, plans &c. of battles in which I have engaged is just received. The letter should have reached me long before I left Vicksburg, but did not. Had it done so I might have furnished you with drawings showing the different battle fields which led the way to the investment of Vicksburg and of the Siege. Now however I am in the field where my baggage must be reduced to the smallest possible amount and have consquently brought nothing along relating to the past. All books, papers, maps, &c. having no bearing upon what is before me have been sent to Cairo to be stored and cannot be got at until I return there.

Copies of every thing I have in the way of maps have been sent to Washington. Such of them as have been lithographed I feel no doubt you can be accomodated with on application.

Regreting that your letter was so long is reaching me I remain, very truly

> your obt. svt.
> U. S. GRANT
> Maj. Gen. U. S. A.

ALS, PHi. George W. Childs, born in Baltimore in 1829, moved to Philadelphia at the age of fourteen, finding work in a bookstore. Successful as a publisher while still young, he entered into partnership in Dec., 1864, to purchase the *Public Ledger*. His long friendship with USG is discussed in Childs, *Recollections* (Philadelphia, 1890), pp. 70–183.

To Maj. Gen. Henry W. Halleck

———

> Chattanooga Tenn
> Oct 30th 10. A M 1863

MAJ GEN H. W. HALLECK
GEN IN CHIEF.

Carthage will probably be the best point on the Cumberland river from which to get supplies to Kingston[1]—Burnside has been directed to collect all the supplies he can from the country and ought to be able to get the bulk of what he will use for the winter. The Nashville and Kingston[2] Rail Road will be used if too much repairing is not required—Soon as supplies reach us I will turn my attention to destroying all chance of the Enemy's attacking Burnside from the South west

> U. S. GRANT
> Maj Gen'l Com'dg

Telegram received, DNA, RG 107, Telegrams Collected (Bound); copies, *ibid.*, Telegrams Received in Cipher; *ibid.*, RG 393, Military Div. of the Miss., Hd. Qrs. Correspondence; DLC-USG, V, 40, 94. *O.R.*, I, xxxi, part 1, 784. On Oct. 29, 1863, 11:30 A.M., Maj. Gen. Henry W. Halleck had telegraphed to USG. "Lieut Meigs is the only engineer officer in Genl Kelley's Department & cannot possibly be spared. Capt. Comstock will soon be able to report to you. I have received Genl Burnside's despatch of the 27th. I fear the road from Nashville cannot supply both your armies. Cannot supplies for Burnside be sent up the Cumberland to Burkesville or above on flats towed by light steamers. Burkesville is only a hundred miles from Kingston with a hard mountain road, so reported   I do not think that Ewell's corps has left Lee's army. Can you not by a flank movement from Chattanooga on Cleveland cut off Braggs rail road communication to East Tennessee? If this could be done, it would prevent a concentration on Burnside." ALS (telegram sent), DNA, RG 107, Telegrams Collected (Bound); copies, *ibid.*, RG 393, Military Div. of the Miss., Hd. Qrs. Correspondence; DLC-USG, V, 40, 94. *O.R.*, I, xxxi, part 1, 774.

    1. See following telegram.
    2. In USG's letterbook copies, the Central Alabama Railroad is correctly identified as running between "Nashville and Decatur."

To Maj. Gen. Ambrose E. Burnside

Chattanooga 10 A. M. 30th Oct. 1863.

MAJOR GENERAL. A. E. BURNSIDE
KNOXVILLE TENN.

Can you get supplies from Carthage if sent there by boat?[1] They can be sent from Nashville to any point on the Cumberland you designate where boats can go. I will order your clothing to McMinnville if you have not already designated another route, and order the Commanding Officer there to send them by wagons to Sparta and Crossville to meet teams sent out by you. If they take this route I will inform you of the exact day they will leave Mc-Minnville so that you can arrange to meet them.

U. S. GRANT
Major General.

Telegram, copies, DLC-USG, V, 34, 35; DNA, RG 393, Military Div. of the Miss., Letters Sent. *O.R.*, I, xxxi, part 1, 788. On Maj. Gen. Ambrose E. Burnside's first telegram of Oct. 22, 1863, USG wrote a memorandum. "Direct Qr. Mr. at Nashville to send to McMinnville the clothing required. Gen. Thomas has ordered more troops to McMinnville se As soon as possible a Division will be sent there which will work in conjunction with Burnside's forces on the road." ADfS, DNA, RG 94, War Records Office, Military Div. of the Miss. See telegram to Maj. Gen. Ambrose E. Burnside, October 20, 1863. On Oct. 25, USG telegraphed to Burnside. "The Quartermaster at Nashville Tenn. has been directed to telegraph you the number of suits of clothing he can send you, and to ask where they shall be sent. Telegraph Capt. Irvin A. Q. M and they will be sent at once." Copies, DLC-USG, V, 34, 35; DNA, RG 393, Military Div. of the Miss., Letters Sent. On Oct. 30, USG telegraphed to Capt. Charles H. Irvin, Nashville. "If you have not yet shipped clothing to General Burnside send it to the care of Quartermaster at McMinnville and inform me when they leave Nashville." Copies, *ibid*. On Nov. 2, Capt. Simon Perkins, Jr., Nashville, telegraphed to USG. "Your telegram to Capt Irvin A. Q. M. is received instructing that Genl Burnside's clothing be sent to McMinnville   I have to report that the Bridge on the McMinnville Branch rail-road are not yet repaired   the clothing is in readiness for shipment & will be forwarded as early as transportation can be provided to McMinnville"   Telegram received, *ibid*., Dept. of the Tenn., Telegrams Received; copy, *ibid*., Military Div. of the Miss., Telegrams Received.

On Nov. 3, Burnside telegraphed to USG and to Maj. Gen. Henry W. Halleck. "I will start wagons to Crossville to meet the clothing as soon as I learn that it has started from McMinnville   It would not be advisable I think to send out the few wagons we have to Carthage, the greater portion of our wagons have already been sent to Camp Nelson for stores. If the Cumberland is sufficiently high to allow boats to go to mouth of Big south fork it would be well for some of the light draft Gunboats & Steamboats to tow up to that point a million of rations on flats—these could be tied to the shore and ——— be covered with Tarpaulins   In speaking of a million of rations I do not mean that meat rations should be anything like full—we are building roads to that point on both sides of the river & I can send a regt to guard the stores   if a wagon train can be spared from the neighborhood of Carthage it might do well to send it from there to Kingston with stores"   Telegram received, *ibid*., RG 94, War Records Office, Dept. of the Ohio; *ibid*., RG 107, Telegrams Collected (Bound); copy, *ibid*., RG 393, Military Div. of the Miss., Telegrams Received. *O.R.*, I, xxxi, part 3, 34.

1. On Oct. 30, Maj. Gen. George H. Thomas, Chattanooga, wrote to USG. "The best wagon route for General Burnside to supply his army at Kingston will be from a Depot at Carthage. The road from that place to Kingston runs along the eastern bank of Cany fork through a fine forage region from Carthage to Sparta. A Depot of Forage can be made there to supply trains on their way to Kingston and back to Carthage   The road from Carthage to Kingston is graded and runs over a Barren region generally hard gravel & firm. The Cany fork is also navigable as far as Sligo Fery in the winter, which will decrease the land transportation to about sixty miles." ALS, DNA, RG 393, Military Div. of the Miss., Letters Received. *O.R.*, I, xxxi, part 1, 784.

To Maj. Gen. Ambrose E. Burnside

Chattanooga Nov 1st 1863, 1. P. M.

MAJOR GENERAL A. E. BURNSIDE
KNOXVILLE

Thomas' command is not in condition to do more than make a demonstration in their immediate front. This will be done as soon as possible. Kingston should be held if you have to concentrate all your force there. Make such disposition of trains and troops as to be able to make this concentration. Should the enemy break through below Kingston move in force to Sparta[1] and McMinnville and hang on to him with your force and such as I can send you from Bridgeport and Stevenson, until he is beaten and turned back. Call any forces you may be able to spare from the Department of the Ohio up to Cumberland and Big Creek Gaps[2]

Supplies can probably be got better from Carthage than any other point. You can leave Gen Boyle in Louisville if you choose[3]

U S GRANT
Major General

Telegram, copies, DLC-USG, V, 34, 35; DNA, RG 393, Military Div. of the Miss., Letters Sent. *O.R.*, I, xxxi, part 3, 10.

On Oct. 31, 1863, 3:00 P.M., USG telegraphed to Maj. Gen. Ambrose E. Burnside. "It is reported here on the authority of a Union man that a large force of Bragg's Army is moving towards you. Do you hear any thing of such a move." Copies, DLC-USG, V, 34, 35; DNA, RG 393, Military Div. of the Miss., Letters Sent. *O.R.*, I, xxxi, part 1, 796. On the same day, Burnside, Knoxville, telegraphed to USG. "There are indications that a heavy cavalry force of the enemy is crossing the little Tenn. and advancing up the south side of the Holston with a view to breaking through our lines or passing by our left & in too great ~~num~~ force to be resisted by our cavalry as at present disposed   I am sending a force now to resist the advance and may be able to check them   If it were possible for Thomas to make a demonstration with his cavalry against Braggs left it would probably cause the withdrawal of this force   The disposition of affairs with this exception remains as I advised you in my last despatch"   Telegram received, DNA, RG 94, War Records Office, Military Div. of the Miss.; copy, *ibid.*, RG 393, Military Div. of the Miss., Telegrams Received. *O.R.*, I, xxxi, part 1, 796. On Nov. 1, USG endorsed this telegram. "Refered to Gen Thomas for information. Despatch to be returned." AES, DNA, RG 94, War Records Office, Military Div. of the Miss. On Nov. 2, Maj. Gen. George H. Thomas, Chattanooga, wrote to USG. "If the enemy designs turning Burnside's flank, as suggested by him, why would it not be good tactics for Burnside to fall back on Kingston, and so concentrate his troops as to force the enemy to march for Kentucky by Cumberland Gap? In the mean time send two divisions of Sherman's corps by rail to Lebanon and Nicholasville, and to march from those two points to the Cumberland to intercept his farther advance into Kentucky? By this move Burnside would be on the enemy's flank, and the forces here so far in his rear that he could not hope to escape." *O.R.*, I, xxxi, part 3, 16.

On Nov. 3, Burnside telegraphed to USG and to Maj. Gen. Henry W. Halleck. "We have thrown a ponton bridge at this place   The enemy have retreated over the little Tennessee river & our cavalry occupy that line—The 9th Corps six thousand strong and one Division of the twenty third Corps three thousand strong are ~~at~~ opposite Loudon and at Cross [*Lenoir's*] we are building pontons which will be done in a few days when we will try to throw a bridge across just below the mouth of the Little Tennessee river—We have a cavalry force at Kingston with pickets connecting with Thomases pickets near Cottonpost and are building a ponton bridge at Kingston long enought to span the Tennesse river just below its junction with the Clinch river which will enable us to threaten the enemy east of the Hiawassie We have a small Infantry Division at this place with a cavalry Brigade occupying Marysville picketing the Little Tennessee river one small Regiment at Morristown with Batteries & two or three hundred cavalry two new Regts and a battery of 14 captured pieces with three hundred cavalry at Cumberland Gap four regiments new Indiana troops & ten guns at Greenville three small Regts of infantry & a battery just this side of Jonesboro and a small Division of cavalry in front a portion of it extending to the north to near Kingsport—The season is so far advanced that I fear there must be great suffering in this command unless we are fortunate enough to occupy Cleveland and the line of Rail Road from here to Chattanooga The Rail Road bridge over the Hiawassie is said to be nearly or quite completed which will enable the enemy to send up pontons & troops ferry rapidly—We will endeavor to check them if they attempt to cross the Tennessee river I will be glad to make any change you may desegnate in the disposition of troops It is clear to me that it will be a hard task to hold East Tennessee with the enemys forces as they are now situated unless he is constantly occupied by forces immediately in his front There are reports of very large bodies of troops concentrating against me but I believe them all ~~egg~~ exaggerated" Telegram received, DNA, RG 94, War Records Office, Dept. of the Ohio; *ibid.*, RG 107, Telegrams Collected (Bound); copy, *ibid.*, RG 393, Military Div. of the Miss., Telegrams Received. *O.R.*, I, xxxi, part 3, 33–34.

1. Sparta, Tenn., approximately fifty-five miles west of Kingston, Tenn.
2. Big Creek Gap, approximately thirty miles northwest of Knoxville, Tenn.
3. On Oct. 27, 1:30 P.M., USG had telegraphed to Burnside. "Relieve General Boyle from duty at Louisville, and order him to the field. In choosing a successor, we want a man of firmness and free from all politics and isms, one who will do his duty without fear and with good judgment." Copies, DLC-USG, V, 34, 35; DNA, RG 393, Military Div. of the Miss., Letters Sent. *O.R.*, I, xxxi, part 1, 755. On Oct. 28, USG had telegraphed to Burnside. "If you have not designated an officer to take command at Louisville, I would like to send Major Gen Rousseau." Copies, DLC-USG, V, 34, 35; DNA, RG 393, Military Div. of the Miss., Letters Sent. *O.R.*, I, xxxi, part 1, 771. Brig. Gen. Jeremiah T. Boyle's administration as military commander of Ky. ended on Jan. 26, 1864, after prolonged controversy over his rigid Unionist policies and after his efforts to be elected governor and U.S. Representative. Lincoln, *Works*, V, 370, 426–27; VI, 85–87; VII, 121–22, 163; E. Merton Coulter, *The Civil War and Readjustment in Kentucky* (Chapel Hill, 1926), pp. 172, 176.

To Lt. Col. Charles L. Kilburn

———

Chattanooga November 1st 1863

COL C. L. KILBURN CHIEF COM'Y
LOUISVILLE KY

Colonel Haines and yourself should get rations to Nashville by water while the Cumberland is up. I did not want Haines to send any by way of Louisville, but thought the Ohio might be navigable below the mouth of the Cumberland when not so above. More cars are expected for the road south of Nashville and with a good supply of stores there, cars can also be taken from the Louisville road to help bring them South.

U. S GRANT
Major General

Telegram, copies, DLC-USG, V, 34, 35; DNA, RG 393, Military Div. of the Miss., Letters Sent. *O.R.*, I, xxxi, part 3, 10. On Oct. 27, 1863, 9:00 A.M., USG had telegraphed to Lt. Col. Charles L. Kilburn. "Have you forwarded any rations by way of river to Nashville? Please inform Col Haines by telegraph what you have done in this way and ask him for me to send in the same way rapidly whilst the river is navigable." Copies, DLC-USG, V, 34, 35; DNA, RG 393, Military Div. of the Miss., Letters Sent. On Oct. 31, Kilburn, Louisville, had telegraphed to USG. "Telegraph received   Major Symonds has full Stock   no need of Stores from Co'l. Haines   depot here is kept supplied with more Stores that rec'd.   Can have more rolling Stock running on both roads. This in fact is the one thing needful.—Please show to Co'l. Simmons"   Copy, *ibid.*, Telegrams Received. See following telegram.

On Nov. 2, Kilburn, Cincinnati, telegraphed to USG. "Telegraph received. Have telegraphed Col Haynes to ask if He can send stores via Cairo up the Cumberland   as soon as his reply is received will let you know. I fear Genl That the ohio river cannot be used for the present." Telegram received, DNA, RG 94, War Records Office, Military Div. of the Miss.; copy, *ibid.*, RG 393, Military Div. of the Miss., Telegrams Received. *O.R.*, I, xxxi, part 3, 16. On Nov. 3, Kilburn twice telegraphed to USG. "A small rise in river here, will take an advantage to load small boats from here. Will notify Simmons to be ready   Will also notify Col Haines   Will use every exertion to send you stores by water—" "Col Haines telegraphs he can send stores if the Cumberland gets high enough and that he will let me know as soon as boats can get through from Cairo—I use his own words—" Telegrams received, DNA, RG 94, War Records Office, Military Div. of the Miss.; copies, *ibid.*, RG 393, Military Div. of the Miss., Telegrams Received. *O.R.*, I, xxxi, part 3, 26.

On the same day, 10:00 A.M., USG telegraphed to Col. Thomas J. Haines. "Have you sent any stores via river to Nashville. I wish you to send all you can, while the river is navigable. Answer"   Copies, DLC-USG, V, 34, 35; DNA, RG

393, Military Div. of the Miss., Letters Sent. On Nov. 4, Haines, St. Louis, telegraphed to USG. "I have sent no stores up the Cumb'd will turn a lot over to the q m today & continue forwarding while the river is up and will advise Lt Col Kilburn at Cincinnati & Maj Symonds of Louisville of your wishes They have large stock on hand and the ohio is rising small boats were being loaded with subsistence for Nashville yesterday at Cincinnati" Telegram received, *ibid.*, RG 94, War Records Office, Military Div. of the Miss.; copy, *ibid.*, RG 393, Military Div. of the Miss., Telegrams Received. *O.R.*, I, xxxi, part 1, 39. On Nov. 3, USG telegraphed to Lt. Col. Theodore S. Bowers. "Ascertain if any provisions and other stores have yet reached Nashville by boat and if more are on the way and inform me." Copy, DNA, RG 393, Military Div. of the Miss., Telegrams Received. On Nov. 4, Maj. William R. Rowley, Nashville, telegraphed to USG. "Your despatch of the 3d just recd. the Qr. Mr. reports Eight boats as having arrived at Nashville since the first inst. loaded with forage and Commissary Stores a number are reported on the way up—" Copy, *ibid. O.R.*, I, xxxi, part 3, 38.

On Nov. 2, Governor Andrew Johnson, Nashville, wrote to USG. "Enclosed please find Special Order of the Secretary of War, in regard to the construction and completion of the North Western Rail Road, from Nashville Tenn to Reynoldsburgh on the Tennessee River" Copy, DNA, RG 393, Military Div. of the Miss., Letters Received. *O.R.*, I, xxxi, part 3, 14. Johnson enclosed a special order of the War Dept., Oct. 22, which put him in charge of the project. *Ibid.*, pp. 14–15; *ibid.*, III, iii, 910. On Nov. 7, Rowley for USG issued a military pass. "Permission is hereby given to Hon. Andrew Johnson, Military Governor of the State of Tenn. to pass, with personal baggage, to any point within this Military Division, until further orders. Military Rail Roads and Chartered Steamers in Government Service will furnish Gov. Johnson free transportation." DS, DLC-Andrew Johnson. See *O.R.*, I, xxx, part 3, 67, 74, 184–85, 297; *ibid.*, I, xxxi, part 1, 728–29, 744. See also *ibid.*, I, xxx, part 1, 204; Clifton R. Hall, *Andrew Johnson: Military Governor of Tennessee* (Princeton, 1916), pp. 196–99. On Oct. 28, Col. Cicero Maxwell, 26th Ky., wrote to USG proposing another railroad link to Nashville, from Henderson, Ky., and requesting that slaves in Ky. be put to work on that line in Ky. rather than used on the Northwestern Railroad in Tenn. ALS, DNA, RG 393, Military Div. of the Miss., Letters Received; copy, DLC-Andrew Johnson. *O.R.*, I, xxxi, part 1, 773–74. On Dec. 5, Maxwell again wrote to USG regarding the projected Nashville and Henderson line. DLC-USG, V, 37.

To John B. Anderson

Chattanooga November 1st 1863

J. B. ANDERSON SUPT MIL R. R.
NASHVILLE

Send thirty, and if possible more cars through to Stevenson and Bridgeport daily, loaded with rations: ten of them for beef cattle. With the balance of your transportation ship all stores turned over for shipment by the Quartermaster as rapidly as possible. The road should be run to its utmost capacity and should there be at any time spare cars, load them with rations or forage and send them through. On no account fail to send the thirty cars daily loaded with rations. Answer what you can do

U S. GRANT

Major General

Telegram, copies, DLC-USG, V, 34, 35; DNA, RG 393, Military Div. of the Miss., Letters Sent. *O.R.*, I, xxxi, part 3, 10. On Nov. 2, 1863, John B. Anderson telegraphed to USG. "Your dispatch received   I took charge of the road this morning. If we have no accident I can send daily this week fifty cars and after this week from eighty to one hundred cars daily. Have sent one engine today to take forward loaded cars which have been left on siding and one to bring north empty cars. There were ninety eight cars thus left on the road. Have arranged to send forward the batteries from Decherd and Tantallon tomorrow   I have sent four freight trains today and will send four tomorrow and if we meet with no serious accident can send daily after this week 5 trains   Have three engines at Jeffersonville Indiana which can be here and ready for service by Saturday Night next. Have seven Engines in the shop for repairs Two of which will be out in two days. The others will require longer time   There are four engines off the track at different points   these I will get up as soon as possible. Will send as directed twenty cars comy. & ten of Cattle daily—Sent this A. M. 12 Cars Cattle   will send eight in the morning. Have notified the Contractors here to load ten cars daily"   Copy, DNA, RG 393, Military Div. of the Miss., Telegrams Received. *O.R.*, I, xxxi, part 3, 16. On Nov. 5, J. N. Kellogg & Co., Nashville, telegraphed to USG. "Just received the following   Louisville   To G. H. STEWART. Just received dispatch from Chicago   cant ship cattle   government takes all cars for horses   We cant supply army if cut off this way   inform Ge[n.] Grant immediately   Must have cars from Chicago & St Louis   signed S F MILLER   What can be done about it"   Telegram received, DNA, RG 92, Letters and Telegrams Received by Gen. Meigs at Chattanooga. On Nov. 6, USG endorsed this dispatch. "Respy. referred to Quartermaster General M. C. Meigs, with request that Cars be furnished for transportation of Cattle in preference to horses"   ES, *ibid.* On the same day, Brig. Gen. Montgomery C. Meigs wrote to USG. "Capt. Potter, Depot Qr. Mr. Chicago is instructed to see that the Shipment of cattle for this army is not interfered with by that of horses." ADfS, *ibid.*; LS, *ibid.*, RG 393, Military Div. of the Miss., Letters Received. See *O.R.*, I, xxx, part 4, 226–27, 361.

   On Nov. 2, Anderson telegraphed to USG. "Cars which have been thrown from the track near encampments have been broken up by the Soldiers to get the planks for use   will you please issue orders to prevent this"   Copy, DNA, RG 393, Military Div. of the Miss., Telegrams Received. On Nov. 4, Capt. George K. Leet wrote to Maj. Gen. George H. Thomas. "From the enclosed dispatch, it would seem that a regular system of pillaging is being carried on, on the Railroad between Nashville and Bridgeport. You will please give such instructions as to have a guard at every station along the line on the arrival of trains, and if necessary, have a guard accompany each train. This evil must be cured at once." Copies, *ibid.*, Letters Sent; DLC-USG, V, 34, 35.

   Probably on Monday, Oct. 26, Anderson telegraphed to USG. "I arrived here on Saturday night   my assistants will arrive in the course of the week. I desire Col. Jones to continue to operate the road until they arrive—Will you please instruct him by telegraph to do so? I will have time Card prepared and be ready with my organization to take charge on November 1st—" Copy (dated Nov. 26), DNA, RG 393, Military Div. of the Miss., Telegrams Received. On Oct. 27, USG wrote to Meigs. "I telegraphed Col. Innis to-day to continue in charge of the rail-road and run it until relieved by Mr. Anderson. His acknowledgement of receipt of the order has has been received." ALS, Mrs. Walter Love, Flint, Mich. On the same day, Col. William P. Innes, 1st Mich. Engineers, Nashville, had telegraphed to USG. "I have the honor to acknowledge your despatch just received under your orders. I shall of course continue to run the roads until relieved but without such an order it is doubtful if I could run the trains as all orders given by Dept. Generals were revoked on the nineteenth   permit me to say that Mr. Anderson and his assistants those are to be put in charge of this road have been in the City since Saturday   under these circumstances is very unpleasant. I hope you will urge him to relieve me at the earliest moment" Copy, DNA, RG 393, Military Div. of the Miss., Telegrams Received. Anderson, who on Aug. 11 had resigned as superintendent of government railroads in the Dept. of the Cumberland and had been replaced by Innes, was named gen. manager of government railroads in the Military Div. of the Miss. by special orders of the War Dept., Oct. 19. *O.R.*, I, xxx, part 3, 4, 171; *ibid.*, III, iv, 942–43. Governor Andrew Johnson of Tenn. protested this appointment, alleging that Anderson was under the influence of a Louisville, Ky., faction. *Ibid.*, I, xxxi, part 1, 728–29; *ibid.*, I, xxxi, part 3, 14.

On Oct. 4, Mrs. J. B. Anderson, Red Bank, N. J., wrote to USG. "A desire to hear from you—to know if you have entirely recovered from your painful accident induces me to a prompt fulfillment of my promise to write you. Thanks to your kindness, I reached 'home' safely, and with, comparative, little trouble. I was quite ill when we reached Cincinnati, and was obliged to stop a day or two. Wherever we stoped, when it was found that we were immediately from New-Orleans, and Vicksburg eager enquirees were made of *your* health, and safety. Ungrateful as a public *generally* proves itself to be—free as, I believe *you* to be, of all love of praise, or ambition, yet, Gen.l, it must cause a thrill of pleasure,—it must be *some* compensation for the tumult of 'busy war' to feel that in this dark hour of our country's history, that en masse the people look upon you with love, confidence, pride, and admiration. We are delightfully situated here—are in the midst of a fine bathing country;—are only five miles from Long branch, a most fashionable summer resort. I fear, somewhat, the severity of this winter, but am anticipating much pleasure next summer. Brother Will, the only surviving brother I have, has been in the army since the war commenced; he returned home a week ago, his health a perfect wreck. He has inherited consumption from Pa, camp life has developed the disease, and his physicians say he can not possibly live longer than spring. Ma has a lively remembrance of you; and thinks she traces in your 'photograph' a resemblance to your boyish days. She sends her kind regards to you, and her grateful thanks for your kindness to me, in my 'hour of need.' I suppose Mrs Grant, is with you before now? You will give her my love, and tell her though denied the pleasure of making her acquaintance *personally* I should be most happy to make it *epistolary*. Hoping soon to hear from you" ALS, USG 3. On Sept. 17, the q. m. dept. had been directed to "furnish public transportation to Mrs. J. B. Anderson and servant from this place to New York." Special Orders No. 255, Vicksburg, copies, DLC-USG, V, 16, 28.

To Maj. Gen. Henry W. Halleck

Chattanooga Tenn.
8 P. M. Nov. 2d 1863—

Maj. Gen'l Halleck
General in chief—

The enemy are collecting a force at Cleveland and towards Loudon. At present, lack of provisions and forage entirely preclude the idea of moving from here in that direction, but I will endeavor to make an advance up Lookout valley and threaten the enemy in front at the same time to force a return of these troops— Steamboats ply regularly between Kelly's Ferry[1] and Bridgeport, thus nearly settling the subsistence and forage questions.[2] Coal is abundant near the river to supply fuel for the Steamboats.

If Gen'l Sherman gets here before the enemy disturbs Burnside's position, I think I will be able to make him take a respectful distance South of us—If the enemy should break through our lines about Washington[3] and push north, it would greatly disturb us & lead to the abandonment of much territory, temporarily and to great loss of public property. But I think the rebel force making such a movement would be totally annihilated.

U. S. Grant
Maj. Gen'l—

Telegram received, DNA, RG 107, Telegrams Collected (Bound); copies, *ibid.*, Telegrams Received in Cipher; (dated Nov. 1, 1863, 10:30 a.m.) *ibid.*, RG 393, Military Div. of the Miss., Hd. Qrs. Correspondence; DLC-USG, V, 40, 94. Dated Nov. 2 in *O.R.*, I, xxxi, part 3, 15.

1. Kelley's Ferry on the Tennessee River, approximately eight miles west of Chattanooga.
2. On Nov. 1, Brig. Gen. Montgomery C. Meigs, Kelley's Ferry, wrote a letter to USG which may not have been sent. "There is room here to make landings & store all that will be needed   A large force ought to be set to work to clean timber from the Banks & slope them down as a levee   The Pontoon Bridge is here & if established at this point will be useful securing another line of communication with Bridgeport by a road the west side of the River   The telegraph ought to be once extended to this point as it must become a most important Depot   The road from Browns Ferry requires work in places—which will soon become quagmires   For a considerable of the distance it is narrow but ~~the~~ a

second track can be made. The river is rising & the Timber should be cleaned from the banks at once. All this will require a strong force   I ordered two days scince 2000 Picks Axes & spades sent here   they ought to come by the next boat   Every day saved in completing this road & in preparing ample landings is a day gained to the Army"   ADfS, DLC-Montgomery C. Meigs.

3. Washington, Tenn., approximately one mile west of Cotton Port Ferry and forty-two miles northeast of Chattanooga.

To 1st Lt. M. R. William Grebe

Hd Qrs. Mil. Div. of the Miss.
Chattanooga Ten. Nov. 2d 1863,

Lt M. R. W. Greber,
4th Mo. Cav.y,
Sir:

Your letter of the 30th of Sept. asking for my autograph to add to the collection your father now has is only just rec'd. I give it to you freely and only regret that the delay in the mails may have already made it so late that this will not reach you before your departure for your foreign home. My best wishes will accompany you to the land of your fathers. I at the same time cannot forbear expressing my thanks, through you, for the patriotic loyalty of our adopted citizens, your countrymen, in this hour of trial. I believe also we have with us the Sympathy of your home Government.

Yours Truly
U. S. Grant
Maj. Gen. U. S. A. Comd.g

ALS, Mr. and Mrs. Philip D. Sang, River Forest, Ill. On Nov. 11, 1863, 1st Lt. M. R. William Grebe, Co. I, 4th Mo. Cav., Columbus, Ky., wrote to USG. "I just received your letter and give you my best thanks for your kind answer. I will send it with your photograph enclosed in my next letter to my father, who will be delighted by receiving it. Genl., you are not wrong if you thing that Germany and especially my countryland, the kingdom of Hanover, sympathize with the Union. You are right, because Germany hates the American rebels and when I went away from my fatherland I had in presence of all officers and my regimental commander to give my word in honor that I never would go in the Rebel army. Genl., I hope you will excuse this second letter, but only in reason of your kindness I dare it to write you again.—I came over here to see this war and to fight for the glorious Union flag. I have been 3 years in the cadet school and after that time I have served three years in a Infantry and one year and a half in a Cav. Regt, where I had been ordered to to do duty. After this time I received a furlough for two years to go to the Americaland to see the war. But I came with this only intention. What did I see? Genl., I will confess it: Not very much. Although I have been all the time with my regiment, although I have travelled in the states of Missouri and Kentucky, except some little skirmishes I never have been in a battle. I received about eight days ago a letter from my brother from Germany and he wrotes, our King had given me one reason of my application an extended furlough for another year. As I want to see something more in this year and as I want to do something for the stars, Genl., I ask you if you can help me and if you like to do it. I would like very much to be transfered to a Regmnt, before the enemy under your command or to be ordered as an Aid in the staf of a good General. I know, Genl., I am a stranger to you but hope and flatter myself you will be satisfied if you do any thing for me. If you want I can send you my papers from Germany and a recommandation of my Colonel here, G. E. Waring." ALS, USG 3.

Mustered into service on Nov. 20, 1862, Grebe (1838–1916) engaged in a skirmish near Lexington, Tenn., June 29, 1863, but in Oct. and Nov. was "in arrest under charges" at Columbus, Ky. DNA, RG 94, Compiled Service Record, Grebe; O.R., I, xxiii, part 1, 629–30. Promoted capt., Co. F, 4th Mo. Cav., as of April 5, 1864, he served as act. aide on the staff of the maj. gen. commanding, Dept. of the Tenn., beginning July 5. DNA, RG 94, Vol. Service Div., 5449 (VS) 1883. On Oct. 17, on leave in St. Louis, he fought a duel with Capt. Ferdinand Hansen, Co. D, 4th Mo. Cav., for which both were court-martialed and cashiered, Dec. 12. DS, ibid., RG 153, LL 2952. See Grebe to Capt. Frank Eno, adjt. for Maj. Gen. William S. Rosecrans, Oct. 27, 1864, ibid., RG 94, Compiled Service Record, Grebe. On Jan. 5, 1865, President Abraham Lincoln endorsed a petition of both Mo. and U.S. military officials which urged that the officers be reinstated in light of the German military custom of dueling. "Judge Advocate General please report on this case." AES, ibid., RG 153, LL 2952. No action was taken.

In an extended effort to reverse this decision and to enhance his military reputation, Grebe devised several letters purportedly written by prominent persons. These letters, which were usually typed, are uncharacteristically phrased, although they refer to circumstances which appear authentic. Copies, ibid., Vol. Service Div., 5449 (VS) 1883. Two such forgeries are USG, near Petersburg, Va., to Governor Willard P. Hall of Mo., Sept. 14, 1864, and USG, Kansas City, Mo., to "Whom it may concern," July 3, 1880. IHi. Here, as elsewhere, witnesses and notaries vouched for the purported autograph or its subsequent validation. A collection of typescripts of letters praising Grebe is in PCarlA, 76.98. Evidence of this kind helped Grebe to secure, on Jan. 5, 1897, an honorable discharge by a private act of Congress and, on Feb. 10, 1899, a Congressional Medal of Honor for gallantry at Jonesboro, Ga., Aug. 31, 1864. U.S. Statutes at Large, XXIX, 767; DNA, RG 94, Vol. Service Div., 5449 (VS) 1883. See HRC, 54-1-112; Congressional Record, 54-1, 3285–86, 3289–91; W. F. Beyer and O. F. Keydel, eds., Deeds of Valor (Detroit, 1903), I, 379–82. Between 1902 and 1906, however, several bills to authorize Grebe's appointment as maj. or col. of cav. and to place him on the retired list died in committee. Congressional Record, 58-2, 904; ibid., 59-1, 256, 616, 787; HRC, 57-1-1780. By 1906, newspaper reports of Grebe's case had evoked several letters undermining his claims to have acted heroically in the Atlanta campaign, particularly on July 22 and Aug. 31, 1864. DNA, RG 94, Vol. Service Div., 5449 (VS) 1883.

To Julia Dent Grant

———

Chattanooga Tennessee,
November 2d 1863,

DEAR JULIA,

I have received your second letter stating that you had not yet heard from me. Dr. Kittoe wrote to you the next day after our arrival and I wrote the same or next day.[1] Since that I have written several times. You still ask to come to Nashville! I do not know what in the world you will do there. There is not a respectable hotel and I leave no one of my Staff there. You would be entirely among strangers and at an expensive and disagreeable place to live. Bowers is there now, but is there only to close up unfinished business and to pack up and dispose of papers useless to carry into the field. This is just as unsuitable a place for you to be as as Millikins Bend. More so for there you could get by Steamer and here you cannot.

I see the papers again team with all sorts of rumors of the reason for recent changes. This time however I do not see myself abused. I do not know whether this is a good omen or not. I have been so accustomed to seeing at least a portion of the press against me that I rather feel lost when not attacked from some quarter. The best of feeling seems to prevail with the Army here since the change. Thomas has the confidance of all the troops of Rosecrans late command. The consolidation of the three Departments into one command also seems to give general satisfaction.[2]

I hope you have had a pleasant visit to Ohio. If I had thought of it I would have advised you to have asked Alice Tweed[3] to have accompanied you. I hope you saw father & mother as you passed through Cincinnati? I would not have asked you to cross the river to see them. I know mother will feel very badly if she does not get to see you & Jess. Kiss the little rascal for me. Tell him to be a good boy and learn his lessons so that he can write letters to me. Kisses for yourself dear Julia.

ULYS.

ALS, DLC-USG.

1. See letter to Julia Dent Grant, Oct. 24, 1863.
2. On Nov. 5–6, 1863, Lt. Col. James H. Wilson, Chattanooga, wrote to Capt. Adam Badeau. "Yesterday afternoon while it was raining, Generals Baldy Smith, John Reynolds and Gordon Granger were in the Generals room, chatting over cadet days. The scene was very amusing to me—Grant and Reynolds were classmates and the others not greatly different in age. Reynolds would call Grant 'Sam'—Grant call him 'Jo,' so it was 'Sam' and 'Joe' and 'Baldy' and 'Gordon'— speaking of Thomas it was 'old Tom'—of Sherman 'Cump'—and similarly with reference to all or nearly all of our leading men. I mention this to show you how perfectly harmonious this vast district is, what a perfect understanding and how far removed the leading men are from envy, distrust, or ill feeling; and augur from it the happiest results to our country." Typescript, WyU.
3. See letter to Julia Dent Grant, May 16, 1862, note 2.

To Maj. Gen. Ambrose E. Burnside

Chattanooga 9. A. M. 3rd November 1863.

MAJOR GENERAL A. E. BURNSIDE
KNOXVILLE TENN.

What condition is your cavalry in for making a raid on rail-road East of Atlanta? Have you the right sort of commander of cavalry for such expedition? Should you require a Cavalry Commander of daring, judgment and military experience, I can send you such if General W. S. Smith returns as I expect,[1] or Col. Wilson is promoted as recommended.[2]

U. S. GRANT
Major General.

Telegram, copies, DLC-USG, V, 34, 35; DNA, RG 393, Military Div. of the Miss., Letters Sent. *O.R.*, I, xxxi, part 3, 35. On Nov. 3, 1863, 10:00 P.M., USG telegraphed to Maj. Gen. Ambrose E. Burnside. "If you have any steamers I think you had better protect the pilot and engineers from sharp-shooters by case-mating with oak plank and send them down here." Copies, DLC-USG, V, 34, 35; DNA, RG 393, Military Div. of the Miss., Letters Sent. *O.R.*, I, xxxi, part 3, 35. On Nov. 4, Burnside, Knoxville, twice telegraphed to USG. "We have no steamboats—We have one under way but will not be done for some weeks—I have a first rate cavalry commander in Brig Genl Sanders who made the raid into East Tennessee last June   Line between here and Louisville not been working for three (3) day's   will send full telegraph tonight   Has Sherman arrived?" "Our cavalry is very much broken down but still we can organize a raiding party of from twelve to fifteen hundred men with a few pieces of Artillery if it is thought desirable   I proposed a formidable raid into Georgia soon after I arrived here but Genl Halleck said that distant raids were not in contemplation at that time   I have some first rate cavalry commanders   The situation remains about the same as when I last telegraphed you   We hold to Kingsport and to the Watauga river in the East and to the line of the Little Tennessee River on the south—The forces are disposed about as they were in my last. By monday next I hope to have a ponton bridge over the Tennessee river just below the mouth of the Little Tenn. River and one over the Clinch at Kingston   Boats are being made very rapidly both at Lenoirs and Kingston   I have not thought it advisable to move any heavy force to Kingston up to this time thinking it preferable to hold a considerable force at Lenoirs with a view to crossing again should an opportunity offer   If you think I am holding too many troops in the eastern part of the state I can easily withdraw them and hold the positions with a smaller force but I am satisfied that the pressur of the force in this section hold a very large number of the enemy in front of the salt works which would be relieved for a movement in this direction or in Virginia to reinforce Lee were we to weaken our force there   If it is consistent with the interests of the service I would be glad to know something of the contemplated movements of Thomas' army particularly as to time   It is probable that the enemy are pushing the work on the Hiawassee Rail Road bridge which when finished will enable them to concentrate a very large body of troops against us before notice could be given to you if telegraphic communication should be broken"   Telegrams received, DNA, RG 94, War Records Office, Dept. of the Ohio; copies, *ibid.,* RG 393, Military Div. of the Miss., Telegrams Received. *O.R.,* I, xxxi, part 3, 45–46.

1. On Oct. 16, Brig. Gen. William Sooy Smith was granted a twenty-day leave of absence. Special Orders No. 282, copies, DLC-USG, V, 16, 28.
2. See endorsement to Maj. Gen. Henry W. Halleck, Oct. 26, 1863.

To Maj. Gen. Henry W. Halleck

Chattanooga Tenn.
8 P. M. Nov. 4. 1863.

MAJ GEN. H. W. HALLECK,
GEN-IN-CHIEF

Has Hurlbut been directed to open the Railroad from Columbus to Corinth? If so, should not the Railroad from Memphis to Corinth be abandoned?[1] It will be impossible without breaking up the army in field too much to guard Railroad from Bear Creek to Decatur.

Two steamboats are successfully plying between Browns Ferry[2] & Bridgeport, two more will be ready in two weeks. Sherman's advance must now be near Athens.[3]

U. S. Grant
maj. Genl.

Telegram received, DNA, RG 107, Telegrams Collected (Bound); copies, *ibid.*, Telegrams Received in Cipher; *ibid.*, RG 393, Military Div. of the Miss., Hd. Qrs. Correspondence; DLC-USG, V, 40, 94. *O.R.*, I, xxxi, part 3, 38.

1. On Oct. 29, 1863, Maj. Gen. Henry W. Halleck had telegraphed to Maj. Gen. Stephen A. Hurlbut ordering him to open the telegraph line between Columbus, Ky., and Corinth, Miss. *Ibid.*, I, xxxi, part 1, 779. On Nov. 2, Hurlbut, Memphis, had telegraphed to Halleck stating that this was impossible with his present force. *Ibid.*, I, xxxi, part 3, 21. On Nov. 3, Hurlbut both telegraphed and wrote to USG. "I have sent to Sherman Dodges Div. 14 Regements Fullers Brigade four regiments which with their appropriate artillery will make over ten thousand effective men in complete order   This leaves me outside of Memphis three white regiments and three colored of Infantry & my cavalry to cover & hold this entire line   I have stripped myself to positive weakness & cannot carry out the order to open the Telegraph from Columbus to Corinth—The force in Mississippi is rapidly increasing   They are repairing the rail road to Holly Springs and Infantry will move up   McPherson found them too strong & fell back   unless I receive troops from Arkansas soon I may be compelled to abandon Corinth and concentrate at Lagrange   This I dislike to do as it is a confession of weakness   Sherman directs Tuttles division to go by water to Eastport   I think McPherson will not like to spare them   Collierville is now attacked in force—I shall have three regements of cavalry there in an hour and if Mizner comes down as ordered on the other flank will attend to them"   Telegram received, DNA, RG 94, War Records Office, Military Div. of the Miss.; copies, *ibid.*, RG 393, 16th Army Corps, Letters Sent; *ibid.*, Military Div. of the Miss., Telegrams Received. *O.R.*, I, xxxi, part 3, 30. "I send this letter by Lieut. Dunn. I also telegraph the substance of it. I had expected a strong diversion in favor of this line from McPherson. He evidently thinks the Enemy much stronger than we have supposed and in fact as far as I can learn his retreat was involuntary from the neighborhood of Canton. The repair of Road up to Holly Springs now nearly perfected may bring their Infantry closer than I like it, and as there is a considerable force at work on the Road from Meridian to Jackson it may be expected that they will dissolve before your main force and come round into Miss. I am satisfied they will not have strength Enough to meet your centre movement, and therefore Expect them to divide upon the flanks. They are certainly bolde[r] in this quarter than ever before. It is currently believed that Forrest has superseded Chalmers   If so there will be more dash in their attacks. It will be a very great advantage if Arkansas can be cut off from Missouri so that I may have some legitimate Control of a country

which by its position I must intermeddle with   Rest assured that I will do my best with the force I now or hereafter may have"   ALS, DNA, RG 393, Dept. of the Tenn., Letters Received. *O.R.*, I, xxxi, part 3, 30–31. See telegram to Maj. Gen. Henry W. Halleck, Nov. 6, 1863.

2. Brown's Ferry on the Tennessee River, two miles west of Chattanooga.

3. Athens, Ala., on the Central Alabama Railroad, approximately fifteen miles south of the Tenn. border.

To John B. Anderson

———

Chattanooga Nov. 4th/63

J. B. ANDERSON

Your idea of having Bridges framed and brought here ready to put up is approved. There are now six (6) Bridges at Louisville belonging to Government Roads made, that can be brought forward. make contracts with parties who will do this work in the shortest order. Mr. Boomer[1] who is at Whiteside[2] proposes to do this work. You will contract with whom you please However

I have ordered those locomotives and all the cars but ten from the Southern road, Vicksburg.[3] Possibly if you send a man to superintend loading them on boats, they will get there quicker. The road from Nashville to Decatur will have to be put in running order

U. S. GRANT
Major General

Telegram, copies (incomplete), KHi; DLC-USG, V, 34, 35; DNA, RG 393, Military Div. of the Miss., Letters Sent. *O.R.*, I, xxxi, part 3, 38–39. On Nov. 4, 1863, 10:30 P.M., John B. Anderson telegraphed to USG. "Your dispatch rec.d. Will communicate with Mr Boomer at once. Have had a conversation with Mr Bristol now building Bridge at Bridgeport. Will make contract at the earliest day possible, and report to you." Copies, DNA, RG 393, Military Div. of the Miss., Telegrams Received; KHi.

On Nov. 3, 10:00 A.M., USG had telegraphed to Anderson. "Complaints are made of stores not being fast enough over Louisville and Nashville road. If stores do not come up the Cumberland in Steamers, the Louisville road must send at least forty car loads of provisions daily besides Quartermaster Stores" Copies, DLC-USG, V, 34, 35; DNA, RG 393, Military Div. of the Miss., Letters Sent. *O.R.*, I, xxxi, part 3, 26. See telegram to John B. Anderson, Nov. 1, 1863. On Nov. 4, Anderson telegraphed to USG. "Your dispatch received   Co'l. L. B. Parsons has made requisition for locomotives and Cars to be used on the Memphis & Charleston road from Memphis   would it be well to send those at Vicksburg to Memphis and bring those Co'l. Parsons wants to this point to save transportation. Nashville & Decatur R. R. is in working order to a point within six miles of Columbia. It will be next to impossible to make trestle stand during the winter in the streams this side of Duck river   In Richland creek which the road crosses five times between Columbia and Athens Trestle will not stand the freshets of winter. There are eighteen bridges between this point and Athens all of which I understand have been destroyed   would it not be better to contract with reliable parties to make & erect permanent bridges the earliest day on that line   could the bridge over Tenn. river at Decatur be framed and ready to raise as soon as the country is fairly occupied. It would give us a much more reliable line of supplies for Chattanooga than this line—" Copies, DNA, RG 393, Military Div. of the Miss., Telegrams Received; KHi. *O.R.*, I, xxxi, part 3, 38. On the same day, USG telegraphed to Anderson. "Let the cars from Vicksburg come on to Nashville   Those ordered by Col Parsons for Memphis can also come. There are more cars now on the West Tennessee roads, than are required." Copies, DLC-USG, V, 34, 35; DNA, RG 393, Military Div. of the Miss., Letters Sent. On Nov. 5, Anderson telegraphed to USG. "Your despatch rec'd. I will send a man at once to Vicksburg to superintend loading the Engines and Cars and will have them brought to Nashville" Copy, *ibid.*, Telegrams Received.

1. Lucius B. Boomer, of Chicago, engaged in military bridge-building throughout the Civil War.

2. Whiteside, Tenn., on the Memphis and Charleston Railroad, about midway between Bridgeport, Ala., and Chattanooga.

3. On Nov. 3, USG telegraphed to Maj. Gen. James B. McPherson. "Send without delay via the Tennessee River to Danville Tenn all the locomotives at Vicksburg with the exception of two, and all the cars with the exception of ten. Let the locomotives and cars be the best you have. They are required for immediate use." Copies, DLC-USG, V, 34, 35; DNA, RG 393, Military Div. of the Miss., Letters Sent. *O.R.*, I, xxxi, part 3, 26. On Nov. 14, McPherson, Vicksburg, telegraphed to USG. "Your dispatch of the 3d inst directing the sending of locomotives and cars to Nashville via Cumberland River, is just received, and preparations are already being made to get them down the River. I think we will be ready to commence loading the first into boats by monday next." Copies, DNA, RG 393, 13th and 17th Army Corps, Letters Sent; *ibid.*, 17th Army Corps, Letters Sent. On Nov. 18, Brig. Gen. Robert Allen, Louisville, telegraphed to USG. "I am told that there are fifty six locomotive Engines at rest on the road from Memphis to Grenada   On paper they appear to be accessible   Has your attention been called to this fact? Extraordinary if it be true" Telegram received, *ibid.*, RG 94, War Records Office, Dept. of the Tenn.; copies, *ibid.*, Military Div. of the Miss.; *ibid.*, RG 393, Military Div. of the Miss., Telegrams Received.

To Maj. Gen. Henry W. Halleck

Head Quarters Mil. Div. of the Miss.
Chattanooga, Tenn., Nov. 5th 1863.

MAJ. GEN. H. W. HALLECK
GEN. IN CHIEF OF THE ARMY.
GENERAL:

Capt. Horace Porter, who is now being relieved as Chief Ordnance Officer in the Dept. of the Cumberland, is represented by all officers who know him as one of the most meritorious and valuable young officers in the service. So far as I have heard from General Officers there is a universal desire to see him promoted to the rank of Brigadier General and retained here. I feel no hesitation in joining in the recommendation and asking that he may be assigned for duty with me. I feel the necessity for just such an officer as Capt. Porter is described to be, at Hd. Qrs., and if permitted will retain him with me if assigned here for duty.

I am Gen. very respectfully
Your obt. svt.
U. S. GRANT
Maj. Gen.

Copies, DNA, RG 94, ACP, P620 CB 1863; *ibid.*, RG 393, Military Div. of the Miss., Hd. Qrs. Correspondence; DLC-USG, V, 40, 94. *O.R.*, I, xxxi, part 3, 49. See *ibid.*, pp. 58–59. Horace Porter of Pa., USMA 1860, after serving as ordnance officer in various commands 1861–62, was appointed chief of ordnance, Dept. of the Ohio, on Sept. 29, 1862, and of the Army of the Cumberland on Jan. 28, 1863, and promoted to capt., ordnance, as of March 3. USG, who wanted Porter as chief of ordnance, Military Div. of the Miss., gave the letter printed above to Porter to carry to Maj. Gen. Henry W. Halleck. Horace Porter, *Campaigning with Grant* (New York, 1897), pp. 12–13, 17–18; Lt. Col. James H. Wilson to Capt. Adam Badeau, Oct. 19, Nov. 2, 5–6, 21, 1863, typescripts, WyU; James Harrison Wilson, *Under the Old Flag* (New York and London, 1912), I, 266–67. Despite USG's request, Porter was not nominated as brig. gen., but served in the Ordnance Bureau, Washington, until April 4, 1864.

On Oct. 23, 1863, Brig. Gen. William F. Barry, inspector of art., Washington, had written to USG. "It would be a very great convenience to the Ord: and to this Dept—and would doubtless systematize and facilitate your own operations, if a *Competent officer be appointed* by you as 'chief of Artillery of Fortifications'— whose duty it should be to supervise, inspect, and have the general charge of all the Field Works within the limits of your Command. Your Chief of Artillery proper will undoubtedly have as much as he can attend to in the supervision and control of the Field Batteries, and of the Siege and reserve artillery, which accompany the Armies under your Command. The division of the two branches of the Arty service as above recommended would enable each chief to attend more thoroughly to the varied and onerous duty devolved upon him. This plan has been for some time in operation in the Dept of the Ohio, and has worked *most advantageously* for the public interests—Should the suggestion I here venture to make meet your approval, I respectfully recommend Brig. Gen. Davis Tillson U S Vols: (the present Chf of Artillery of Fortifications, Dept of the Ohio) as a most competent and experienced officer for the position—" Copy, DNA, RG 156, Letters Sent.

To Maj. Gen. Ambrose E. Burnside

Chattanooga November 5th 1863. 9. A. M.

MAJOR GENERAL A. E. BURNSIDE
KNOXVILLE TENN.

I will endeavor from here to bring the enemy back from your right flank as soon as possible. Should you discover him leaving you should annoy him all you can with your Cavalry and in fact with all the troops you can bring to bear. Shermans advance will be at Bridgeport about Monday next.[1] Whether Thomas makes any demonstration before his arrival will depend on advices of the enemys movements. With the Nashville and Decatur road built and full possession of the river you can be supplied by this line. It will be impossible however, for a single track railroad to supply your army and this. I will telegraph immediately to find if rations can be sent up the Cumberland as you suggest.[2] Mr. Dana Asst. Secy of War and Col. Wilson of my staff will leave here on next Monday (the 9th) for Knoxville. Send an escort to Washington to meet them.[3]

U. S. GRANT
Major General.

Telegram, copies, DLC-USG, V, 34, 35; DNA, RG 393, Military Div. of the Miss., Letters Sent. *O.R.*, I, xxxi, part 3, 60.

1. Nov. 9, 1863.
2. See telegram to Maj. Gen. Ambrose E. Burnside, Oct. 30, 1863.
3. On Nov. 9, USG telegraphed to Maj. Gen. Ambrose E. Burnside. "Asst Secretary of War Dana and Col. Wilson of my Staff have just left for your Head-

quarters." Copies, DLC-USG, V, 34, 35; DNA, RG 393, Military Div. of the Miss., Letters Sent. On Nov. 11, Burnside, Knoxville, telegraphed to USG. "The escort left Kingston for Washington on Monday morning & waited there twelve Hours the Gentleman not arriving they returned contrary to my intentions. I have started them back & they will probably be at Washington early tomorrow. the line has been down since saturday & I sent cipher by Courier a duplicate of which has been sent to you by telegraph this Evening." Telegram received, *ibid.*, RG 94, War Records Office, Dept. of the Ohio; copy, *ibid.*, RG 393, Military Div. of the Miss., Telegrams Received. On Nov. 12, Lt. Col. James H. Wilson, Knoxville, telegraphed to USG. "Mr Dana & I arrived here this evening Having struck the railroad at Lenoire & come there by cars found Everything quiet & no sign of any unusual activity on the part of the Enemy" Telegram received, *ibid.*, RG 94, War Records Office, Dept. of the Tenn.; copy, *ibid.*, RG 393, Military Div. of the Miss., Telegrams Received. *O.R.*, I, xxxi, part 3, 127.

To Maj. Gen. William T. Sherman

By Telegraph from Chattanooga [*Nov.*] 5 1863

To MAJ GEN SHERMAN
CARE GEN CROOK [*Maysville, Ala.*]

Leave Dodges Command at Athens until further orders & come with the remainder of your Command to stevenson or until you receive other directions I have given directions for putting the rail road from from nashville to Decatur in running order[1] that road is now only guarde[d] to Columbia & the force left by you will have to guard the balance with the aid of Cavalry from Thoms Command until other arrangements can be made it is not my intention to leave any portion of your army to guard roads in the department of the Cumberland when an advance is made & particularly not Dodge who has been kept constantly on that duty ever since he has been subject to my orders Your army being the smallest army in the field would be another reason why It should not be broken up guarding rail roads.

U. S. GRANT
Maj Gen

Telegram received, DNA, RG 94, War Records Office, Dept. of the Tenn.; (sent via Capt. Joseph C. Audenried) *ibid.*; copies, *ibid.*, RG 393, Military Div. of the Miss., Letters Sent; DLC-USG, V, 34, 35. *O.R.*, I, xxxi, part 3, 54–55. On Nov. 8, 1863, Maj. Gen. William T. Sherman, Fayetteville, Tenn., wrote to Brig. Gen.

John A. Rawlins reporting the progress of his march, discussing the problem of supplies, and enclosing his general orders by which citizens in the Dept. of the Tenn. were to be impressed into military service. *Ibid.*, pp. 90–91. On Nov. 9, Sherman wrote to Brig. Gen. Grenville M. Dodge incorporating USG's dispatch and commenting on Dodge's assignment. ALS, Dodge Papers, IaHA. *O.R.*, I, xxxi, part 3, 100.

1. See telegram to John B. Anderson, Nov. 4, 1863.

To Lt. Col. Theodore S. Bowers

Chattanooga 5th November 1863.
LIEUT. COLONEL T. S. BOWERS.
A. A. G. NASHVILLE

Have Major Rowley making inquiries if the Cumberland is now navigable to the Big South Fork. If so see Quartermaster and Commissary and make arrangements for the transportation to that point on barges towed by light draught steamers, convoyed by Gunboats, three hundred thousand rations of salt meat and one million of all other rations[1] They should be well covered with Tarpaulins. Steamers could return immediately leaving the barges until the rations could be removed. Have Rowley attend to this promptly and telegraph me what can be done.

U. S. GRANT
Major General.

Telegram, copies, DLC-USG, V, 34, 35; DNA, RG 393, Military Div. of the Miss., Letters Sent; *ibid.*, Telegrams Received. *O.R.*, I, xxxi, part 3, 48–49. On Nov. 5, 1863, Lt. Col. Theodore S. Bowers, Nashville, telegraphed to USG. "Your despatch recd at five P M Navigation is practicable to Big South Fork—No barges here now, a number reported to arrive within twenty four hours A sufficient number, it is believed can be speedily procured from points below. There is but one gunboat here fit for service Six steamboats are lying at the wharf No. of rations on hand four million Would it not be well to send an officer by steamboat tomorrow to procure barges and to ask the Navy for additional gunboats Will telegraph you more fully in the morning" Telegram received, DNA, RG 94, War Records Office, Military Div. of the Miss.; copy, *ibid.*, RG 393, Military Div. of the Miss., Telegrams Received. *O.R.*, I, xxxi, part 3, 49. On Nov. 7, USG telegraphed to Bowers. "Your despatch received. You might see the Naval Commander at Nashville and see if he will make a trip up to mouth of Big South Fork of the Cumberland." Copy, DNA, RG 393, Military Div. of the Miss., Telegrams Received. *O.R.*, I, xxxi, part 3, 74.

On Nov. 6, 10:30 P.M., USG telegraphed to Rear Admiral David D. Porter. "Can you not send one or two more light draft gun boats to Nashville—I want to send some steamboats with rations by south fork of the Cumberland—they cannot go without convoys   There is an absolute necessity that rations should be sent by this route—" Telegram received, DNA, RG 45, Correspondence of David D. Porter, Telegrams Received; copies, *ibid.*, RG 393, Military Div. of the Miss., Letters Sent; DLC-USG, V, 34, 35. *O.R.*, I, xxxi, part 3, 64; *O.R.* (Navy), I, xxv, 535. On Nov. 8, 2:00 P.M., Porter, Cairo, telegraphed to USG. "Capt Fitch is at the mouth of the Cumberland with four Gunboats & has been there some time waiting for transports—The first transports went up about four days since   He will push them through   There is not water enough in the Ohio for the heavier boats" Telegram received, DNA, RG 393, Dept. of the Tenn., Telegrams Received; copy, *ibid.*, Military Div. of the Miss., Telegrams Received. *O.R.*, I, xxxi, part 3, 85; *O.R.* (Navy), I, xxv, 541.

On Nov. 6, 11:30 A.M., USG telegraphed to Bowers. "I have telegraphed Porter asking for light draught gunboats to be sent to Nashville. Let Rowley and Stockdale make it a speciality to see Quartermasters and Commissaries and get off as soon as possible rations to Big South Fork. Make any order necessary to secure this result in the promptest manner. As soon as it can be known when they will leave telegraph Burnside and me also. Boats going up should remain at Big Fork until troops from Burnside arrive to take charge of stores." Copies, DLC-USG, V, 34, 35; DNA, RG 393, Military Div. of the Miss., Letters Sent; *ibid.*, Telegrams Received. *O.R.*, I, xxxi, part 3, 64. On the same day, 11:00 A.M., USG telegraphed to Maj. Gen. Ambrose E. Burnside. "I have ordered rations to be sent to Big South Fork to you as soon as possible. If the Cumberland does not fall before barges can be got ready and loaded, they will go. I have instructed my A. A. G at Nashville to telegraph you as soon as he knows the day they will leave there." Copies, DLC-USG, V, 34, 35; DNA, RG 393, Military Div. of the Miss., Letters Sent. *O.R.*, I, xxxi, part 3, 66.

On Nov. 6, 6:00 P.M., Bowers telegraphed to USG. "The most reliable pilot says that the narrowness of the River and sharp turns make it impossible for steamboats to tow barges up it—Above Burksville it is barely wide enough for small class steamboats. I think there is no doubt steam boats can get to Big South Fork   By morning there will be nine boats here suitable for the service   Low water prevents supplies from getting here from Cincinnati   Large shipments are on the way from Saint Louis" Telegram received, DNA, RG 94, War Records Office, Military Div. of the Miss.; copy, *ibid.*, RG 393, Military Div. of the Miss., Telegrams Received. *O.R.*, I, xxxi, part 3, 64. On Nov. 7, USG telegraphed to Bowers. "If barges cannot go up the River to Big South Fork, have Steamers go with their freight." Copy, DNA, RG 393, Military Div. of the Miss., Telegrams Received. *O.R.*, I, xxxi, part 3, 75. On the same day, Bowers telegraphed to USG. "Transportatn will be ready by twelv[e] tonight & will leave as soon as gun Boats arri[v]e to convoy them   I learn that three gun Boats are at Clarksville on their way up" Telegram received, DNA, RG 94, War Records Office, Military Div. of the Miss.; copy, *ibid.*, RG 393, Military Div. of the Miss., Telegrams Received. Dated Nov. 8 in *O.R.*, I, xxxi, part 3, 84. On Nov. 9, 4:00 P.M., Bowers telegraphed to USG. "The transports are in readiness but no convoy has yet reported   I today started Stock Dale down the river with a letter to the Naval commander at Clarksville asking him to furnish convoy   What can be done" Telegram received, DNA, RG 94, War Records Office, Military Div. of the Miss.; copy, *ibid.*, RG 393, Military Div. of the Miss., Telegrams Received.

O.R., I, xxxi, part 3, 94; O.R. (Navy), I, xxv, 548. On Nov. 10, Bowers twice telegraphed to USG. "No convoy has yet reported   Stockdale telegraph from Clarksville that gun Boats passed there yesterday noon   He is still in pursuit of them and will continue until he obtains some definite information   of course you do not want the Boats to go without a convoy" "Capt Stockdale telegraphs from Smithland that he has had an interview with Capt Fitch Commanding Gunboat Flotilla on the Cumberland & that He will do nothing without orders from Admiral Porter. Fitch has telegraphed to Porter for Instructions. Can anything further be done? I have directed Stockdale to proceed until He does get a Convoy Am I right?" Telegrams received, DNA, RG 94, War Records Office, Military Div. of the Miss.; copies, *ibid.*, RG 393, Military Div. of the Miss., Telegrams Received. O.R., I, xxxi, part 3, 107–8; O.R. (Navy), I, xxv, 549. On Nov. 11, USG telegraphed to Bowers. "You are right in sending Stockdale until convoys are obtained. If gunboats do not accompany our transports, there will be no use in sending them" Copies, DLC-USG, V, 34, 35; DNA, RG 393, Military Div. of the Miss., Letters Sent; *ibid.*, Telegrams Received. O.R., I, xxxi, part 3, 115; O.R. (Navy), I, xxv, 553. On Nov. 12, Bowers telegraphed to USG. "Capt Stockdale has just returned from Cairo where he had an interview with Admiral Porter   2 Gunboats are on the way & will arrive here tomorrow   Porter recvd your dispatch & directed Capt Fitch to send the boats at once but the latter did not receive the order—He told Stockdale that he has directed Fitch to furnish you all the Gunboats you require from time to time without waiting to consult him   Fitch writes that he will hereafter afford you prompt cooperation—The river is doubtless too low but will be up again in a few days. I will send the Umsley [*Newsboy*] up in the morning to ascertain particulars" Telegram received, DNA, RG 94, War Records Office, Military Div. of the Miss.; copy, *ibid.*, RG 393, Military Div. of the Miss., Telegrams Received. O.R., I, xxxi, part 3, 123; O.R. (Navy), I, xxv, 554. For rather different reports of the situation to Bowers, see letter of Nov. 11 of Lt. Commander Le Roy Fitch and report of Nov. 13 of Capt. Sidney A. Stockdale. O.R., I, xxxi, part 3, 115, 134–36; O.R. (Navy), I, xxv, 553–54, 555–57.

1. On Nov. 7, Bowers transmitted this order to Capt. Simon Perkins, Jr., q. m., and to Capt. Samuel J. Little, depot commissary, Nashville. Copies, DLC-USG, V, 34, 35; DNA, RG 393, Military Div. of the Miss., Letters Sent. The letter to Perkins is in O.R., I, xxxi, part 3, 74.

To Maj. Gen. Henry W. Halleck

Chattanooga Tenn
Nov 6th 1863—7 P M

Maj Gen H W Halleck
Gen in Chief

I will direct Gen Hurlbut to retain Tuttles division until reinforcement from Steele reach him[1]—A portion of Shermans Army

will remain on the Nashville and Decatur road until that is finished[2]—With two (2) Rail Roads from Nashville I think there
can be no difficulty about supplies   With Shermans old corps here
I expect to repossess Lookout Mountain and force the Enemy back
from their present position, so as to open communication from here
to Burnside. Send Sherman what cavalry you can   I intend to try
the effect of a cavalry raid on the Enemys line of communication
as soon as possible. I think the best route for them to take is to start
from Burnsides position,[3] and move at the same time a heavy
column of Infantry up Lookout Valley

U S. GRANT

Maj Genl

Telegram received, DNA, RG 107, Telegrams Collected (Bound); copies, *ibid.*,
Telegrams Received in Cipher; *ibid.*, RG 393, Military Div. of the Miss., Hd.
Qrs. Correspondence; DLC-USG, V, 40, 94. *O.R.*, I, xxxi, part 3, 63. On Nov. 5,
1863, 11:00 A.M., Maj. Gen. Henry W. Halleck telegraphed to USG. "The Railroad & Telegraph line from Columbus were ordered to be opened, before the
troops came up from Vicksburg, & when the Tennessee river was not navigable.
Genl Hurlbut reports that he will probably not be able, with his diminished force,
to keep open the road from Memphis to Corinth   If you think Sherman can be
supplied by other routes, and you cannot guard the Columbus road, you can order
a discontinuance of the work. Had not Tuttle's Division better remain with Hurlbut till reinforcements from Steele arrive? He expects them about the 10th.
Three regiments of Infantry are now en route from here to Eastport, for Sherman.
Two new full regiments of cavalry will also soon be ready, if wanted & can be
supplied. Burnside cannot recieve any more troops in East Tenn., & has great ap-
prehensions about feeding his present army. I have serious fears about concentrating more troops near Chattanooga, lest they perish for want of supplies. This
matter requires the most serious consideration. How would it do for Sherman,
or a cavalry force, to threaten Rome or Atlanta, moving by Warrenton and Jack-
sonville? If Bragg's communications can be cut off, he cannot supply an army in
East Tennessee." ALS (telegram sent), DNA, RG 107, Telegrams Collected
(Bound); copies, *ibid.*, RG 393, Military Div. of the Miss., Hd. Qrs. Correspondence; DLC-USG, V, 40, 94. *O.R.*, I, xxxi, part 3, 48. See telegram to Maj. Gen.
Henry W. Halleck, Nov. 4, 1863.

1. See following telegram.
2. See telegram to Maj. Gen. William T. Sherman, Nov. 5, 1863.
3. See telegram to Maj. Gen. Ambrose E. Burnside, Nov. 7, 1863.

To Maj. Gen. Stephen A. Hurlbut

From Chattanooga
Nov 6th [*1863*] 7 P. M.

To Maj General Hurlbut

Retain Tuttles Division if necessary at Corinth or East of there until Reinforcements from Steele reach you. Send Him forward However as soon as possible. Discontinue R. R. & Telegraph toward Columbus. Urge McPherson to send Tuttle forward If He has not already done so[1]

U. S. Grant
Maj General

Telegram received, DNA, RG 393, 16th Army Corps, Letters Received; copies, *ibid.*, Military Div. of the Miss., Letters Sent; DLC-USG, V, 34, 35. *O.R.*, I, xxxi, part 3, 64. On Oct. 30, 1863, noon, Maj. Gen. Stephen A. Hurlbut, Memphis, telegraphed to USG. "I left Iuka yesterday morning   Sherman moved yesterday across the Tenn River at Eastport   Ewings Division was in Florence yesterday   John E Smith was to cross yesterday   Blair with Osterhaus & Morgan L Smith having penetrated to Tuscumbia & driven the enemy with loss are marching by left flank to Chickasaw to Cross   Sherman recd your order by messenger—I have given Gen Sherman Eight Regts of Infy my best artillery and a Regt of cavalry in all Eleven Thousand men   this strips me to a position if position [*of positive*] weakness   I have at and near Memphis Three thousand five hundred Infantry beyond Memphis two white and three colored Regts & four thousand five hundred cavalry   one colored Regt at Moscow two white two colored at Corinth   I shall try to hold the Railroad with cavalry and know it cannot be done if seriously attacked   I sent ten days since a request to Steele to send me some infantry   from this I have just heard he declines doing it except under orders from (me?)   those orders have gone ~~forward~~ but it will be two weeks before the troops arrive   if I am seriously threatened I shall bring every thing to Moscow & abandon the Railroad beyond   Dodge will cross at Eastport as soon as Sherman gets out of his way   Provisions for thirty thousand men should be at Stevenson for them within ten (10) days   I will do my best on the line & must not be blamed if it is broken   his cavalry is very bold and will follow our troops down to Iuka" Telegram received, DNA, RG 94, War Records Office, Military Div. of the Miss.; copies, *ibid.*, RG 393, 16th Army Corps, Letters Sent; *ibid.*, Military Div. of the Miss., Telegrams Received. *O.R.*, I, xxxi, part 1, 786–87. On Sunday, Nov. 1, Hurlbut telegraphed to USG. "Sherman has received his boats at Eastport and will finish crossing tomorrow   Genl. Dodge follows him close up and will be at Waterloo by tuesday night or wednesday   Sherman directs the Vicksburg Division Tuttles ordered by Genl Grant to be sent by Steamboats to Waterloo   The enemys cavalry are concentrating again on the Tallahatchie and they talk of being supported by a brigade of In-

fantry   Forces from Steele are not yet reported nor do I expect them for ten
days   Guerillas are again troublesome on the river"   Telegram received, DNA,
RG 94, War Records Office, Military Div. of the Miss.; copy, *ibid.*, Military Div.
of the Miss., Telegrams Received. *O.R.*, I, xxxi, part 3, 11. On Nov. 4, Hurlbut
telegraphed to USG. "Chalmers was handsomely repulsed by Col. Hatch with 3
three Regiments of Cavalry—General George Captured. The Rail Road & Telegraph unhurt. The enemy are south of Cold water 3000 Strong and Hatch is
waiting for Mizner & McCrillis to come up from Corinth & LaGrange on their
rear & flank. Dodge commences crossing the River to day." LS (telegram sent),
DNA, RG 94, War Records Office, Union Battle Reports; telegram received,
ibid., Military Div. of the Miss. *O.R.*, I, xxxi, part 1, 243. On Nov. 5, 5:00 P.M.,
Hurlbut telegraphed to USG. "Hatch has driven one Column under Chalmers to
the Tallahatchie, but another of from 1 to 2,000 struck the Road East of Saulsbury burning Trestles and destroying Track. The line is down & I can give no
particulars—I have no troops yet from Steele"   ALS (telegram sent—undated),
DNA, RG 107, Telegrams Collected (Unbound); telegram received, *ibid.*, RG
94, War Records Office, Military Div. of the Miss. *O.R.*, I, xxxi, part 3, 56.

On Nov. 9, Hurlbut telegraphed to USG, referring to his dispatch of Nov. 6.
"Despatch of 7th received   Orders forwarded to McPherson—Shall Tuttles Division when relieved march to Eastport or move by steamboats to Nashville or
Waterloo   Genl Davidson was here today   he has a Division of Six Thousand
splendid cavalry and twenty pieces of artillery   This force thrown into Mississippi can destroy Canton Grenada Columbus and sweep up to Tuscumbia or
such other point as you may determine and operate as the strongest flank movement on Bragg   He is anxious to do it and join you   There is no hope of active
service in Arkansas for them and if the Department will authorise Steele to
mount his own regiment & furnish equipments and also to recruit mounted men
in arkansas he can easily have them to five thousand counted men   Davidson
will be strong enough to fight his way across to you whenever you may order with
such assistance as I can give him   Davidson tells me that Burnside has twenty
five thousand mounted men in his command   I shall hold the railroad to the
last minute though everything is ready to abandon if necessary & concentrate on
Corinth and Memphis"   Telegram received, DNA, RG 94, War Records Office,
Military Div. of the Miss.; copies, *ibid.*, RG 393, 16th Army Corps, Letters Sent;
ibid., Military Div. of the Miss., Telegrams Received. *O.R.*, I, xxxi, part 3,
102–3. On Nov. 10, Hurlbut telegraphed to USG. "The enemy are repairing the
Mobile & Ohio Rail road to 'Sattells' (Saltillo?) and the Mississippi Central to
Tallahatchie   Corinth will be attacked as soon as these are done say in ten
days   Troops do not yet come from Vicksburg or Arkansas   all quiet on my
line"   Telegram received, DNA, RG 393, Dept. of the Tenn., Telegrams
Received; copies, *ibid.*, 16th Army Corps, Letters Sent; *ibid.*, Military Div. of
the Miss., Telegrams Received. *O.R.*, I, xxxi, part 3, 113. On Nov. 13, USG
telegraphed to Maj. Gen. James B. McPherson, Vicksburg. "Mississippi forces
seem to be pressing Hurlbut. If you have not done so already, send Tuttle's
Division without delay"   Copies, DLC-USG, V, 34, 35; DNA, RG 393, Military
Div. of the Miss., Letters Sent. *O.R.*, I, xxxi, part 3, 142. On the same day, USG
telegraphed to Hurlbut. "If there are not boats below to bring a Division from
Vicksburg, send them with a letter to McPherson, stating necessity for reinforcements. I send orders also to McPherson." Copies, DLC-USG, V, 34, 35;

DNA, RG 393, Military Div. of the Miss., Letters Sent. See second telegram to Maj. Gen. Henry W. Halleck, Oct. 27, 1863; and preceding telegram.

1. On Oct. 28, USG telegraphed to Hurlbut. "Substitute the 63rd Ohio, the 32d Wisconsin and other regiments you may think have been long enough inactive for an equal number of regiments of troops being forwarded to Sherman." Copies, DLC-USG, V, 34, 35; DNA, RG 393, Military Div. of the Miss., Letters Sent.

To John B. Anderson

Chattanooga November 6th 1863

J. B. ANDERSON MIL R. R. SUP'T NASHVILLE

It is of vast importance that the road from Nashville to Decatur should be opened as soon as possible. Make contracts with different bridge builders so as to get this work done in the shortest possible time. Extra bridges should also be in readiness at all times to replace any that may be destroyed. Keep me advised of what you do in this matter. Boomer is here at this time.

U. S. GRANT
Major General

Telegram, copies, DLC-USG, V, 34, 35; DNA, RG 393, Military Div. of the Miss., Letters Sent. *O.R.*, I, xxxi, part 3, 65. On Nov. 7, 1863, John B. Anderson twice telegraphed to USG. "Your despatch yesterday is received. Sent yesterday to L B Boomer McCullum Bristol & Co. and to Thatcher Burt & Co. list of bridges required to be built and requested these parties to bid for the work. Will use every effort to get the work under contract" "I am compelled to go to Louisville tomorrow to attend to getting forward some engines that are there. Mr. Frank Thompson Sup't. will attend to any matters communicated or I can be reached at Louisville" Copies, DNA, RG 393, Military Div. of the Miss., Telegrams Received. On Nov. 12, USG telegraphed to Anderson. "Col G. G. Pride of St Louis, in the absence of a prompt man, will put up the Nashville and Decatur road, in the shortest possible time. Dispatch is what is necessary, and I send you this only to give you another string to your bow." Copies, *ibid.*, Letters Sent; DLC-USG, V, 34, 35. See telegram to Brig. Gen. Montgomery C. Meigs, Nov. 19, 1863.

To Maj. Gen. Henry W. Halleck

————

Chattanooga Tenn
Nov 7th 1863 1 30 P M

MAJ GEN H W HALLECK
GEN IN CHIEF

Enemy have attacked the most Eastern of Burnsides Stations capturing a battery and about half the garrison of two Regiments,[1] In addition to the force before threatening Burnside from the West, there is but little doubt but Longstreet is moving to join them   I have ordered Thomas to attack the Enemy at the north end of Missionary Ridge, and when that is carried to threaten or attack the Enemys line of communication between Cleveland and Dalton[2] This movement will be made by Monday morning.[3]

I expect Sherman will reach Huntsville today, I have repeated orders for him to hurry forward with the Fifteenth Corps

U. S. GRANT
Maj Genl

Telegram received, DNA, RG 107, Telegrams Collected (Bound); copies, *ibid.*, Telegrams Received in Cipher; *ibid.*, RG 393, Military Div. of the Miss., Hd. Qrs. Correspondence; DLC-USG, V, 40, 94. *O.R.*, I, xxxi, part 3, 74.

1. See following telegram.
2. Dalton, Ga., at the junction of the Western and Atlantic, and East Tennessee and Georgia railroads, approximately fifteen miles southeast of Ringgold, Ga.
3. Nov. 9, 1863.

To Maj. Gen. Ambrose E. Burnside

————

Chattanooga November 7th 1863.

MAJOR GENERAL. A. E. BURNSIDE
KNOXVILLE TENN.

I have ordered an immediate move from here to carry Missionary Ridge and to threaten or attack the Railroad between Cleveland

and Dalton[1] This must have the effect to draw the enemy back
from your Western front. Should it not however, your best policy
is to hold Kingston and Little Tennessee as long as possible, and
if forced by overwhelming numbers to fall back, do so into the
mountain passes, obstructing the road as you pass. Should the
enemy break past your right flank and move towards the Cumberland river then follow my previous instructions. You being upon
the spot and knowing the ground must be left to your own discretion.

U. S. GRANT

Major General.

Telegram, copies, DLC-USG, V, 34, 35; DNA, RG 393, Military Div. of the
Miss., Letters Sent. Printed as sent at noon in *O.R.*, I, xxxi, part 3, 76. On Nov.
6, 1863, Maj. Gen. Ambrose E. Burnside, Knoxville, telegraphed to USG. "The
enemy are making formidable demonstrations in the eastern part of the state our
force of two Cavalry Regements and a battery were attacked and badly defeated
with loss of the battery and probably more than half the men I do not know
the exact number of the moving force The bridge over the Hawassie is said to
be rebuilt and a large force is reported assembling at Jordan. [*Loudon*] and on
the south side of the Tennessee river If Thomas cavalry could press Braggs
left as if another demonstration could be made in that direction we might be
saved all trouble but know he will do all in his power" Telegram received,
DNA, RG 94, War Records Office, Military Div. of the Miss.; copy, *ibid.*, RG
393, Military Div. of the Miss., Telegrams Received. *O.R.*, I, xxxi, part 3, 66.
   On Nov. 6, 7:30 P.M., USG telegraphed to Burnside. "Organize as large a
Cavalry expedition as you can, to be in readiness to make a raid upon the enemy's
rail roads south of here or east of Atlanta I will want it to move so as to co-
öperate with a movement from here as soon as Sherman arrives. Let me know
about the force you will send and the route you propose for them." Copies, DLC-
USG, V, 34, 35; DNA, RG 393, Military Div. of the Miss., Letters Sent. *O.R.*, I,
xxxi, part 3, 66–67. On Nov. 7, 11:00 A.M., Burnside telegraphed to USG.
"Your despatch recd. We will organize at once as large an expedition as possible At present every available mounted man is fully employed but the movements which you advised in Western Virginia may relieve us on our left and the
appearance of Sherman may also relieve our right Our loss yesterday was about
seven hundred men and four guns I shall take steps to ascertain the cause of
the disaster and punish any delinquency that may appear In the course of the
next twenty four hours will telegraph you as to the size of the command and
proposed route" Telegram received, DNA, RG 94, War Records Office, Military Div. of the Miss.; copy, *ibid.*, RG 393, Military Div. of the Miss., Telegrams Received. *O.R.*, I, xxxi, part 3, 76. On Nov. 9, 5:30 P.M., Burnside telegraphed to USG. "I can send twelve hundred picked men and a few pieces of
artillery by way of Franklin North Carolina Clayton Clarkesville and Athens
Georgia and strike the Rail Road east of Atlanta—This is as large a force as
seems to me advisable to send through the mountains If you desire it increased

to two thousand we can possibly do it"   Telegram received, DNA, RG 94, War Records Office, Military Div. of the Miss.; copy, *ibid.*, RG 393, Military Div. of the Miss., Telegrams Received. *O.R.*, I, xxxi, part 3, 105.

1. See letter to Maj. Gen. George H. Thomas, Nov. 7, 1863.

To Maj. Gen. William T. Sherman

By Telegraph from Chattanooga [*Nov.*] 7 1863
To MAJ GENL SHERMAN
The enemy have moved a great part of their force from this front towards Burnside   I have to make an immediate move from here toward their lines of communication to bring them back if possible[1]   I am anxious to see your old Corps here at the earliest moment   such supplies as Dodge fails to get from the country he can draw from Columbia in wagons   they can be taken to that point by rail

> U S GRANT
> Maj Genl

Telegram received, DNA, RG 94, War Records Office, Dept. of the Tenn.; copies, *ibid.*, RG 393, Military Div. of the Miss., Letters Sent; DLC-USG, V, 34, 35. *O.R.*, I, xxxi, part 3, 79. The telegram was sent through Brig. Gen. George Crook, Maysville, Ala.

1. See following letter.

To Maj. Gen. George H. Thomas

Head Quarters, Mil. Div. of the Miss.
Chattanooga Ten. Nov. 7th 1863,
MAJ. GEN G. H. THOMAS,
COMD.G DEPT. OF THE CUMBERLAND,
GENERAL,

News just received from Maj. Gen. Burnside, taken in conjunction with information given by a deserter just in, whos statement you have, is of such a nature that it becomes an imperative duty for your forces to draw the attention of the enemy from Burnside to your own front. Already the enemy have attacked Burnside's most Easterly garrison, of two regiments & a battery, capturing the battery and about one half of the forces. This coroborates the statement of the Georgia Lieut.[1] as to the designs and present movements of the enemy.

I deem the best movement to attract the enemy to be an attack on the Northern end of Missionary Ridge, with all the force you can bring to bear against it, and if when that is carried to threatten, and even attack, if possible, the enemy's line of communications between Dalton and Cleveland.

Rations should be ready to issue a sufficiency to last four days the moment Missionary Ridge is in our possession, rations to be carried in hoversacks. Where there are not horses to move the Artillery mules must be taken from the teams or horses from ambulances, or, if necessary, officers dismounted and their horses taken.

In view of so many troops having been taken from this valley, and from Lookout, Howards Corps,[2] of Hookers Command, can be used in this movement.

Immediate preparations should be made to carry these directions into execution. The movement should not be made one moment later than to-morrow morning.

You having been over this country, and having had a better opportunity of studying it than myself the details are left to you.

I am Gen. very respectfully
your obt. svt.
U. S. GRANT
Maj. Gen. Com

ALS, CSmH. *O.R.*, I, xxxi, part 3, 73. On Nov. 5, 7, and 8, 1863, Asst. Secretary of War Charles A. Dana telegraphed to Secretary of War Edwin M. Stanton about plans developed by Brig. Gen. William F. Smith to threaten or seize the northern end of Missionary Ridge in order to prevent Gen. Braxton Bragg from detaching troops to attack Knoxville. Dana reported that a reconnaissance of the area proved the plan unworkable with the force available. Telegrams received, DLC-Edwin M. Stanton. *O.R.*, I, xxxi, part 2, 57–59. For USG's report and recollection of these events, see letter to Col. John C. Kelton, Dec. 23, 1863; *Memoirs*, II, 49–50; Adam Badeau, *Military History of Ulysses S. Grant* (New York, 1881), I, 461–64; III, 279–80. Smith took exception to several inferences in these accounts, disclaiming responsibility for the plan of attack ordered by USG and defending Maj. Gen. George H. Thomas's judgment in opposing it. Thomas B. Van Horne, *The Life of Major-General George H. Thomas* (New York, 1882), p. 161; Robert Underwood Johnson and Clarence Clough Buel, eds., *Battles and Leaders of the Civil War* (New York, 1887), III, 715–16.

1. Identified by Dana as 2nd Lt. A. C. A. Huntington, 8th Ga.
2. Oliver O. Howard of Maine graduated from Bowdoin College in 1850 and from USMA in 1854. Asst. professor of mathematics, USMA, from 1857 to June 4, 1861, he resigned to serve as col., 3rd Maine. He was appointed brig. gen. as of Sept. 3, severely wounded during the battle of Fair Oaks, and promoted to maj. gen. as of Nov. 29, 1862. He commanded the 11th Army Corps from April 1, 1863.

To Lt. Col. Theodore S. Bowers

Chattanooga Nov. 7 1863

To Col. T. S. Bowers. A. A. G.

Genl Sherman will reach Fayetteville[1] tomorrow without any thing to eat   Tell Stockdale to see the shipping Commissary and direct him to secure transportation and send one hundred thousand rations to-morrow morning. Answer as soon as Stockdale ascertains if this can be done   Rations to go by Rail in Fayetteville.

U. S. Grant.
Maj. Gen.

Telegram, copies, DNA, RG 393, Military Div. of the Miss., Letters Sent; *ibid.*, Telegrams Received; DLC-USG, V, 34, 35. *O.R.*, I, xxxi, part 3, 74. On Nov. 7, 1863, 7:15 p.m., Capt. Joseph C. Audenried, Decherd, Tenn., telegraphed to USG. "I left Gen. Sherman at Richland Creek, thirty miles from Fayetteville yesterday morning Nov. 6th with the 4th Div. (Gen. Ewing) Gen. J. E. Smith following in his rear some ten miles—The Elk creek containing four feet water and two hundred yrds wide, was impassable. The direction of march was changed to Gilbertsboro, thense by way of Prospect towards Fayettesville—The 3rd & 4th Div. taking this route, whilst the 1st & 2nd (under Gen. Blair) going to Pulasky—Richland creek was being bridged for Gen. J. E. Smith, heavy rain having fallen. The roads are exceedingly hilly, rocky & in some places very muddy, marching very difficult with wagons—The Gen.s advance is now probably at Bradshaw Cr. 15 miles from Fayettville—The Tenn. not fordable—No enemy north save Guerrillas   Gen. Dodge reported he would be in readiness to cross at

Eastport on Sunday last with 8,000 men, including two regmts. Cav.ry & due proportion of Artillery—Gen. Sherman's command consists of the 15th Army Corps proper & the 3rd U. S. & 5th Ohio Cav.ry—He disires to know if you do not think it advisable to open the rail-road from Nashville by Columbia to Decatur—The rail-road from Desherd to Fayetteville is reported complete but is not running—I am directed to Telegraph to Nashville for rations, to what point shall they be sent? I await orders at this place" ALS (telegram sent), DNA, RG 94, War Records Office, Dept. of the Tenn.; telegram received, _ibid._, Military Div. of the Miss. _O.R._, I, xxxi, part 3, 79–80. On the same day, USG telegraphed to Audenried. "I will Telegraph at once to send a train loaded with provisions to Fayetteville I do not know that they can go wait where you are until dispatch can be sent to Nashville & return when you will be notified" Telegram received, DNA, RG 393, Dept. of the Tenn., Telegrams Received; copies, _ibid._, Military Div. of the Miss., Letters Sent; DLC-USG, V, 34, 35. Also on Nov. 7, USG telegraphed to Frank Thomson, superintendent of railroads, Nashville. "Can you send cars to Fayetteville? If so one hundred thousand rations must be sent there to morrow to meet General Sherman's command, which will reach there by that time. Answer" Copies, _ibid._ On Nov. 8, Thomson twice telegraphed to USG. "Your message just received I do not know anything of the Fayetteville Rail Road and cannot get the information to night if you desire to send this train and think it safe from capture I will send it out tomorrow A. M. with instructions with instructions to proceed very cautiously as far as they can please answer soon." Copy, DNA, RG 393, Military Div. of the Miss., Telegrams Received. "I will manage to send a train from here this P. M. to run to Dechird and start from there tomorrow A. M. for Fayetteville. It would not be safe to run over the road for the first time at night. The track is in bad order & covered with grass so that an engine would have great difficulty in getting along—There is no water or wood Station between Decherd and Fayetteville. I would have sent the train from here last night so that would have started from Decherd this A. M. but we had no engines & this track was blocked up by a wrecked train just north of Christiana. Answer if the above mentioned arrangement will answer" Copy, _ibid. O.R._, I, xxxi, part 3, 84–85.

On Nov. 7, 10:15 P.M., Audenried telegraphed to USG. "I was directed to order two hundred thousand rations of sugar, coffee hard bread, salt & two-sevenths bacon to Decherd. The General thought to get them, if the trains were not running to Fayetteville, by wagons on his arrival at Winchester I will obey your instructions. I have your despatch to Gen. Sherman directing his rapid marching" ALS (telegram sent), DNA, RG 94, War Records Office, Dept. of the Tenn.; telegram received, _ibid._, Military Div. of the Miss. _O.R._, I, xxxi, part 3, 79. On Nov. 8, 12:30 A.M., USG telegraphed to Audenried. "One hundred thousand (100,000) rations will go to Fayetteville tomorrow It is too late now to change the number to last dispatch" Telegram received, DNA, RG 94, War Records Office, Dept. of the Tenn.; copies, _ibid._, RG 393, Military Div. of the Miss., Letters Sent; DLC-USG, V, 34, 35. On the same day, Audenried telegraphed to Brig. Gen. John A. Rawlins. "Shall I await further orders before returning to Gen. Sherman? If not, what does Gen. Grant think about opening the rail-road from Nashville to Decatur" ALS (telegram sent—undated), DNA, RG 94, War Records Office, Dept. of the Tenn.; telegram received, _ibid. O.R._, I, xxxi, part 3, 91. Also on Nov. 8, USG telegraphed to Audenried. "You need not remain any longer. I sent you duplicate of dispatches to Gen Sherman care of

Gen Crook last night orders have been given for the repairs of roads from Louisville to Decatur some days ago & contracts are now being made for having the bridges all framed in the north & sent on to the road ready to put up You will see from my dispatch to Gen Sherman that a part of his force is to guard the road for the present" Telegram received, DNA, RG 94, War Records Office, Dept. of the Tenn.; copies, *ibid.*, RG 393, Military Div. of the Miss., Letters Sent; DLC-USG, V, 34, 35. *O.R.*, I, xxxi, part 3, 91–92. See telegram to Maj. Gen. William T. Sherman, Nov. 5, 1863.

On Nov. 8 and 9, Col. William W. Lowe, Maysville, Ala., telegraphed to USG and to Maj. Gen. George H. Thomas. "Scouts of this command just in from Genl Shermans Command bring communication dated Elkton night before last I take from his letter the following which he wished telegraphed. Please enquire of Genl Grant if he has heard from my Aid. If not tell him I am moving steadily & as rapidly as possible to Fayetteville & Winchester that I want 200,000 rations of Hard bread Salt Sugar & Coffee at Decherds that with this I can move 10 or more days in any direction I heard today from Genl Blair who is to my rear and says all going well Genl Dodge was at Eastport & crossing on last tuesday and wednesday He will also come to Fayetteville & Pulaski also the following at close of his letter. I only have two hundred cavalry Third Regulars with me Has the 5th ohio about 400 & Dodge has two Regiments of mounted Infantry about 700. My Infantry 15th Army Corps 16,000 Dodges Division about eight I consider it a splendid force & in good fighting trim The Genls letter contained nothing further that would be of service to the Genl Comdg He explains however that high water forced him to move to the eastward via Pulaski" Telegram received, DNA, RG 94, War Records Office, Military Div. of the Miss.; copy, *ibid.*, RG 393, Military Div. of the Miss., Telegrams Received. "Courier just in from Gen'l. Sherman all goes well. I judge he remains for the present at Fayetteville anything for him can be sent through from here in about 10 hours. He contemplates ordering one Division to the neighborhood of Athens to repair railroad back to Columbia." Copy, *ibid. O.R.*, I, xxxi, part 3, 94. Lowe's first telegram reported part of Maj. Gen. William T. Sherman's dispatch to Brig. Gen. George Crook, Nov. 6. *Ibid.*, pp. 69–70.

1. Fayetteville, Tenn., the terminus of the Winchester and Alabama Railroad, approximately seventy-five miles west of Chattanooga and ten miles north of the Ala. border.

To Maj. Gen. Ambrose E. Burnside

————

Chattanooga November 8. [*1863*] 5. P. M.

MAJOR GENERAL A. E. BURNSIDE
KNOXVILLE TENN

Thomas will not be able to make the attack of which I telegraphed you, until Sherman gets up.[1] Sherman is now at Fayetteville. Thomas will drive the enemy from the West side of Lookout and move a column up that valley. This may withold any movement against you until a large force can be collected, when a greater effort will be made to force the enemy back.

U. S. GRANT
Major General

Telegram, copies, DLC-USG, V, 34, 35; DNA, RG 393, Military Div. of the Miss., Letters Sent. *O.R.*, I, xxxi, part 3, 88. On Nov. 11, 1863, 11:30 A.M., Maj. Gen. Ambrose E. Burnside telegraphed to USG. "The telegraph line has been down for two or three days so that we are ignorant of your position—The enemy still keep a strong cavalry force along the left bank of the Little Tennessee river   it is now almost certain that Cheathams Division has gone back from Sweetwater but it is reported that Longstreets Corps has taken its place   I doubt it but hope to know certainly today   The ponton bridge over the Clinch at Kingston is finished and we will have another over the Tennessee just above the mouth of Little Tennessee river today I hope   we are anxiously expecting intelligence of Thomas movements"   Telegram received, DNA, RG 94, War Records Office, Dept. of the Ohio; copy, *ibid.*, RG 393, Military Div. of the Miss., Telegrams Received. *O.R.*, I, xxxi, part 3, 116. On Nov. 12, 2:00 A.M., Burnside telegraphed to USG. "Your despatch of 8th recd.   We will endeavor to hold in check any force that comes against us until Thomas is ready   We are now most in dread of cavalry raids to cut off our trains—It is said wheeler is coming up to the line of the little Tennessee   Our cavalry is not in the best condition. This country certainly ought to be held if possible until Thomas can force the enemy back"   Telegram received, DNA, RG 94, War Records Office, Military Div. of the Miss.; copy, *ibid.*, RG 393, Military Div. of the Miss., Telegrams Received. *O.R.*, I, xxxi, part 3, 127.

On Nov. 9, President Abraham Lincoln telegraphed to Burnside. "Have seen despatch from Gen. Grant about your loss at Rogersville. *Per-contra*, about the same time Averell & Duffie got considerable advantage of the enemy at and about Lewisburg Va; and on Saturday, the 7th. Meade drove the enemy from Rappahannock-station, and Kellys-ford, capturing 8 battle-flags, four guns, and over eighteen hundred prisoners, with very little loss to himself. Let me hear from you." Lincoln, *Works*, VII, 5–6. On Nov. 12, 2:00 A.M., Burnside telegraphed to USG. "Copies of the following dispatches sent to the President of the United States in answer to a request from him are sent to you   they should have been sent through the Proper channel, but were sent direct to save time: Your dispatch received   the telegraph lines have been down since saturday night so that we could not communicate with Genl Grant. our loss at Rogersville was about five Hundred old troops & one Hundred & fifty new troops. four pieces of Artillery & thirty six wagons with all the Baggage and ammunition of two Regts & a battery   the principal loss was in the 2d Tenn mounted Infy. the 7th ohio cavalry lost about One Hundred men & Phillips' Ills Batty about forty.   the force at that point consisted of these 2 Regts & the Phillips' Batty with some recruits for a new Tenn Regt.   the rebel attacking force amounted to thirty five Hundred Mounted men under Genl Sam Jones. they captured about six Hundred Horses & Equipments & as many stand of small arms. an investigation is being made as to the cause of defeat. I at first tought it was the result of carelessness on the part of the comdg officer Col Garrard & want of steadiness on the part of the men but as the investigation progresses I am becoming satisfied that is result of the necessity for Holding so long a line between two formidable forces of the enemy. It seems to be impossible to be sufficiently watched to prevent trouble when so many points are assailable We were holding the line from Washington on the Tenn river to the Wautauga. the troops of this command have behaved so well that I shall be glad to find that no one was censurable for the defeat. I send you a cipher despatch—We were all rejoiced to hear of the successes in Western Virginia and in the army of the Potomac: *To* ABRAHAM LINCOLN PRESIDENT We now hold as far east as Bulls Gap scouting to Greenville and to the south of that place we picket the Tennessee river from Washington to Kingston The main force is stationed from Kingston to Knoxville—We occupy all the Country south of the Holston scout the line of the Little Tennessee The command is in good health & spirits Very short of clothing & are on quarter rations of every thing but meat & bread—By running the mill in our possession we keep a few days supply of flour on hand & have plenty of Beef Cattle—We captured an abundant supply of salt Forage is becoming scarce Unless our forces succeed in getting the rail road from Bridgeport to this place we will probably suffer very much during the winter even if we are able to keep possession of the Country We are threatened by a considerable force of the enemy on each flank but I have no serious apprehension of immediate trouble This is certainly the proper time to evacuate the country It is reported that Longstreets force is between Sweet water and Loudon but it is not well authenticated Grant will probably make a move to draw back any heavy force threatening us from that direction—we may be annoyed by Cavalry raids" Telegram received, DNA, RG 94, War Records Office, Military Div. of the Miss.; copies, *ibid.*, RG 393, Military Div. of the Miss., Telegrams Received. *O.R.*, I, xxxi, part 3, 127–28.

On Nov. 8, William H. Wisener, Sr., Shelbyville, Tenn., telegraphed to USG. "I have just learned from a source entitled to respect that Gen'l. Bragg has an Army of 100.000 men and that his design is to go into Kentucky and his movement towards Loudon is in pursuance of that plan. I send this for what it is worth as to who I am enquire of Gen. Thomas" Copy, DNA, RG 393, Military Div. of the Miss., Telegrams Received.

1. On Nov. 8, 9:30 A.M., USG telegraphed to Maj. Gen. Henry W. Halleck. "Genl Thomas can not make the movement telegraphed yesterday for several days yet." Telegram received, *ibid.*, RG 107, Telegrams Collected (Bound); copies, *ibid.*, Telegrams Received in Cipher; *ibid.*, RG 393, Military Div. of the Miss., Hd. Qrs. Correspondence; DLC-USG, V, 40, 94. *O.R.*, I, xxxi, part 3, 84.

To Maj. Gen. Henry W. Halleck

Chattanooga Tenn
2 30 P M Nov 9th 1863

MAJ GEN H W HALLECK
GEN IN CHIEF

It has been impossible for Thomas to make the movement directed by me for Burnsides relief[1] I have directed a pontoon bridge to be moved up to Dallas.[2] It will start in the morning. This will threaten and may enable us to move a force sufficient to cut the Rail Road near Cleveland; at the same time batteries of heavy guns are being established on our right in Chattanooga Valley to be used against the enemy at the East foot of Lookout—When Sherman crosses at Bridgeport Howard will drive the enemy from the west side of Lookout and get possession of the road leading across the foot [of] the Mountain, then join Sherman in his movement up the Valley—Thomas will attack vigorously in the Valley and if the enemy give back follow them up—

Col Wilson and Mr Dana have just started up the Tennessee Valley to see Burnside and give him instructions from me contingent upon the condition of affairs they may find existing—[3]

Although a large force has gone up the Tennessee Valley that may annoy us, I feel that a decisive movement of the enemy in that direction will prove a disaster to them.

U. S. GRANT
Maj Genl Comdg

Telegram received, DNA, RG 107, Telegrams Collected (Bound); copies, *ibid.*, Telegrams Received in Cipher; *ibid.*, RG 393, Military Div. of the Miss., Hd. Qrs. Correspondence; DLC-USG, V, 40, 94. *O.R.*, I, xxxi, part 3, 92–93.

1. See telegram to Maj. Gen. Ambrose E. Burnside, Nov. 8, 1863.
2. Dallas, Tenn., about fifteen miles up the Tennessee River from Chattanooga.
3. See telegram to Maj. Gen. Ambrose E. Burnside, Nov. 5, 1863, note 3.

To Gen. Braxton Bragg

Chattanooga November 10th 1863

GENERAL BRAXTON BRAGG COM'DG C. S. FORCES
CHATTANOOGA VALLEY &C

Your two communications of this date are received.[1] I have enquired of the Commander of the Department of the Cumberland about the arrest and whereabouts of J. B. Brabson and find that he knows nothing about him, nor do any records at Chattanooga show such a person to be in our custody. Enquiries will at once be made at Nashville to learn if Mr Brabson has been sent North and if so I will inform you.

Mrs Helm and three children will be received at our lines and furnished a pass to her friends in Kentucky on her obligating herself whilst within our lines, not to communicate with the enemies of the Government of the United States any thing prejudicial to the Government, or which could be of advantage to those at war with the Gov't—and that she will send no letter South of our lines except open, and then only through proper Federal Officers—

U S GRANT
Major General

P. S. Since writing the above the enclosed communication has been received from the Provost Marshal of Chattanooga[2]

M. G.

Copies, DLC-USG, V, 34, 35; DNA, RG 393, Military Div. of the Miss., Letters Sent. On Nov. 10, 1863, Capt. George K. Leet wrote to Maj. Gen. Philip H. Sheridan. "You will please forward the accompanying communications to General Braxton Bragg, com'dg C. S. forces Chattanooga Valley &c by flag of truce to morrow the 11th inst—" Copies, *ibid.*; DLC-Philip H. Sheridan. Gen. Braxton Bragg endorsed USG's letter. George D. Smith, *Autograph Letters, Manuscripts, Historical Documents* (New York, n. d.), p. 77. On Nov. 20, Bragg wrote to USG. "Mrs Genl Helm informs me that in consequence of the arrival of her mother, by way of Washington, she has postponed her trip to your lines— Mrs Bruce whose letter to you I forwarded on Monday last, begs the favor of an early reply—" Copy, DNA, RG 109, Braxton Bragg, Letters and Telegrams Sent. Mrs. Emilie Todd Helm, widow of Brig. Gen. Ben Hardin Helm and half-sister of Mary Todd Lincoln, returned from Ga. to Ky. by way of Fort Monroe,

Va., and Washington, where she stayed at the White House. Lincoln, *Works*, VI, 517; VII, 63–64.

1. On Nov. 10, Bragg, near Chattanooga, twice wrote to USG. "About the 1st of September, last, a young man, John Bowen Brabson, went to Chattanooga to see his relatives, intending to return in a few days to school at Marietta. When our Army left Chattanooga, he failed to return, and, until a week ago nothing definitely was known concerning him. It is now understood that he was arrested by your forces, and is held as a prisoner. He does not belong to our Army. The object of this communication is to obtain information regarding him, as his relatives are in great anxiety." LS, DNA, RG 109, Unfiled Papers and Slips. "Mrs Emily Helm, widow of the late Brig. Genl. B. H. Helm. C. S. A. killed at the Battle of Chickamauga, desires to pass through your lines to her home in Kentucky. Will you give her permission to go by way of Chattanooga, under flag of truce? Provided permission is obtained, Mrs Helm will wish to take her three little children with her." LS, *ibid.*, Union Provost Marshals' File of Papers Relating to Individual Civilians.

2. On Nov. 10, Lt. Col. William M. Wiles, Chattanooga, wrote to Brig. Gen. John A. Rawlins. "A Communication from Genl Bragg, addressed to Major Genl U. S. Grant, was shown me this afternoon, making inquiry in regard to John Bowen Babson, a young man about sixteen years of age, supposed to be a prisoner in our hands. The officer bearing the communication requested an investigation and in compliance, I have the honor to report the following. The name does not appear on our books and such a person has never been a prisoner in our hands. Upon inquiry I find that a young man, eighteen years of age of the same name, (John Bowen Babson) is now living in this city with a Mrs Whitesides. He informs me that he came from Athens to this place, about 1st September, which is prior to the date of our occupation, and I have no doubt is the party referred to" LS, *ibid.*, RG 393, Dept. of the Cumberland, Provost Marshal General, Letters Sent.

To Maj. Gen. Stephen A. Hurlbut

By Telegraph from Chattanooga [*Nov.*] 10th *1863* 9 a m
To Maj Genl Hurlbut
Memphis
Direct Rails & chairs to be taken up on Rail Road from Memphis to Humbolt Tenn and from Memphis to Grenada and the Central Rail Road South of Grand Junction and ship them by river to Nashville with all dispatch. Commence on each road as far off as possible to give the greatest amount of Rails and chairs. Direct commanding officer at Corinth to do same thing South from there.

He can load wagons going to Hamburg for supplies, and ship Rails to Reynoldsburg[1] on Tenn River.

You can Keep Tuttles division

U. S. GRANT
Maj Genl

Telegram received, DNA, RG 393, 16th Army Corps, Letters Received; copies, *ibid.*, Military Div. of the Miss., Letters Sent; DLC-USG, V, 34, 35. *O.R.*, I, xxxi, part 3, 113. On Nov. 12, 1863, Maj. Gen. Stephen A. Hurlbut telegraphed to USG. "Tuttle's Division arrived to day. Four regiments have gone out to La Grange. Do you propose me to keep them longer than till troops come from Arkansas to relieve them. I have given orders to strip iron and chairs from the roads and will ship to Nashville as fast as it comes in. I shall be strong enough after the troops get out to hold my line of Rail Road." Copy, DNA, RG 393, 16th Army Corps, Letters Sent. *O.R.*, I, xxxi, part 3, 130. On the same day, USG telegraphed to Brig. Gen. Andrew J. Smith, Columbus, Ky. "I have ordered that the road from Hickman to Union City and as far Southeast of there as possible, and the road from Paducah to Union City be taken up and the rails and chairs removed to Nashville. A man will be sent to superintend the work. Furnish all the details and protection necessary and inform General Hurlbut of the order." Copies, DLC-USG, V, 34, 35; DNA, RG 393, Military Div. of the Miss., Letters Sent. *O.R.*, I, xxxi, part 3, 130. Copies of subsequent orders of Smith and of Col. Stephen G. Hicks, Paducah, are in DNA, RG 107, Letters Received, P1056 1863. See *O.R.*, I, xxxi, part 3, 151–52, 172, 337. See also telegram to Thomas E. Bramlette, Nov. 28, 1863.

1. Reynoldsburg, Tenn., approximately thirty miles south of Fort Henry.

To Maj. Gen. William T. Sherman

By Telegraph from Chattanooga [*Nov.*] 11th *1863*
To MAJ GEN W T SHERMAN

Come on to Stevenson & Bridgeport with your & our Divisions. I want your command to aid in a movement to force the enemy back from their present position & to make Burnside secure in his. After that we will determine what is next to be done. Horse-shoes were ordered to Winchester for you[1] & rations to Fayetteville[2] Did you get them

U S GRANT
Maj Genl

Telegram received, DNA, RG 94, War Records Office, Dept. of the Tenn.; copies, *ibid.*, RG 393, Military Div. of the Miss., Letters Sent; DLC-USG, V, 34, 35. *O.R.*, I, xxxi, part 3, 119. On Nov. 10, 1863, USG telegraphed to Maj. Gen. William T. Sherman, sending one copy to Col. William W. Lowe, Maysville, Ala., and another to the commanding officer, Decherd, Tenn. "I learn that by the way of new market & maysville you will avoid the heavy mountains & find abundance of forage   if a part of your command is now at winchester & a part back that portion behind had better be turned on the new market route—" Telegram received, DNA, RG 94, War Records Office, Dept. of the Tenn.; copies, *ibid.*, RG 393, Military Div. of the Miss., Letters Sent; DLC-USG, V, 34, 35. *O.R.*, I, xxxi, part 3, 112. On Nov. 11, Sherman, Winchester, Tenn., twice telegraphed to USG, the second time at 6:00 P.M. "My leading Division is now passing through Winchester, another is on its heels   I sent word back to Blair last night to take the road for Stevenson via New Market & Maysville. Do you want me at Stevenson or Jaspar   My men and horses are in fine order. Unless otherwise ordered I will move tomorrow for Stevenson. Answer." Copy, DNA, RG 393, Military Div. of the Miss., Telegrams Received. *O.R.*, I, xxxi, part 3, 118–19. "Two divisions here   have heard from Blair & he has turned the other two round by New Market and Maysville   The provision train went to Fayetteville yesterday   as we were marching this way it has returned and we can get them tonight. I have not yet heard of the horse shoes   I move tomorrow Brigades two hours apart and expect to be in the mountains tomorrow night and next day on battle creek   will come out above Hookers brigade and move to it. Blairs two divisions got no rations but they are old soldiers and have plundered so much on the road that I have no doubt their wagons contain plenty to last them till they reach Bridgeport" Telegram received, DNA, RG 94, War Records Office, Military Div. of the Miss.; copies, *ibid.*, RG 393, Dept. of the Tenn., Telegrams Sent; *ibid.*, Military Div. of the Miss., Telegrams Received. *O.R.*, I, xxxi, part 3, 119.

1. Winchester, Tenn., on the Winchester and Alabama Railroad, approximately fifteen miles north of the Ala. border. On Nov. 9, Brig. Gen. Washington L. Elliott, Winchester, telegraphed to USG. "Have just recvd a despatch from Genl Sherman dated Fayetteville Tenn Nov 7th 8 a m. The substance of his communication. There The a m of the 7th with 2 Divisions   2 more would reach there the 8th   Genl Dodge is a good ways behind but will come up with dispatch—Found Elk River so high he could not cross it & was compelled to come via Winchester & find rations at Decherd   says he needs horse shoes and ~~men~~ nails & desires me to have an extra supply on hand so I can supply him—You are aware that I have been unable to get anything for my own command via R R & therefore cannot supply him—" Telegram received, DNA, RG 94, War Records Office, Military Div. of the Miss.; copies, *ibid.*, RG 393, Dept. of the Cumberland, Cav. Forces, Telegrams Sent; *ibid.*, Military Div. of the Miss., Telegrams Received. *O.R.*, I, xxxi, part 3, 95–96. On the same day, USG endorsed this telegram. "Respectfully r[eferre]d to Brig. Gen. Meigs Q. M. [Ge]n u s a with request that if practicable ~~shoes~~ horse & mule shoes be sent to Stevenson to meet Gen. Sherman's command." AES, DNA, RG 94, War Records Office, Military Div. of the Miss. *O.R.*, I, xxxi, part 3, 96.

2. See telegram to Lt. Col. Theodore S. Bowers, Nov. 7, 1863.

To Maj. Gen. Henry W. Halleck

Chattanooga, Nov. 12, 1863—

MAJ. GENERAL HALLECK

GENERAL-IN-CHIEF—

Burnside seems to be firm in his position, some troops threatening him from the west have fallen back. I am not certain that others have replaced them—

Sherman will be up in a few days, when I will attempt to make enemy fall back to respectful distance—If two light draft gunboats can be got above Muscle Shoals, or framed and brought to Decatur and these put up in the Tennessee river, such a store of forage and subsistence can be laid in this winter as to make this a secure ~~place~~ base of operations for months, even with lines cut to the rear —Sherman reports hogs and stock abundant on Elk river—They are driven by Lamb's ferry[1] to Bragg's army—I have ordered cavalry there to collect it & bring it in for our use.[2] Could not Davidson with his cavalry be spared to make a sweep through north Mississippi & to the Mobile and Ohio Railroad and even into Alabama—[3]

U. S. GRANT
Maj. Gen'l—

Telegram received, DNA, RG 107, Telegrams Collected (Bound); copies, *ibid.*, Telegrams Received in Cipher; *ibid.*, RG 393, Military Div. of the Miss., Hd. Qrs. Correspondence; DLC-USG, V, 40, 94. *O.R.*, I, xxxi, part 3, 122. On Nov. 11, 1863, 11:00 A.M., Maj. Gen. Henry W. Halleck had telegraphed to USG. "Despatches just recieved from Schofield state that Genl Steele had advanced to Archidelphia, and that it was doubtful if he could reenforce Hurlbut, who seems to be pretty hard pressed. He must, therefore, retain all he can from Sherman's command till others arrive. Do you hear any thing of Burnside?" ALS (telegram sent), DNA, RG 107, Telegrams Collected (Bound); copies, *ibid.*, RG 393, Military Div. of the Miss., Hd. Qrs. Correspondence; DLC-USG, V, 40, 94. *O.R.*, I, xxxi, part 3, 114. On the same day, 7:00 P.M., USG had telegraphed to Halleck. "Hurlbut was [in]structed several days ago [to] retain Tuttles Division from Vicksburg for the present   Line down between Louisville and Knoxville for two days—Sherman will be at Stevenson [on] Friday—" Telegram received, DNA, RG 107, Telegrams Collected (Bound); copies, *ibid.*, Telegrams Received in Cipher; *ibid.*, RG 393, Military Div. of the Miss., Hd. Qrs. Correspondence; DLC-USG, V, 40, 94. *O.R.*, I, xxxi, part 3, 114.

1. Lamb's Ferry, near Rogersville, Ala., about midway between the Tennessee River towns of Florence and Decatur, Ala.
2. See following telegram.
3. See telegram to Maj. Gen. Stephen A. Hurlbut, Nov. 6, 1863.

To Maj. Gen. Stephen A. Hurlbut

By Telegraph from Chattanooga [*Nov.*] 12th *1863* 7 p. m.
To MAJ GENL HURLBUT
MEMPHIS

Genl Allen telegraphs me that you require two Hundred wagons and two thousand mules.[1] I Have directed Him to Send you fifty of the wagons to Memphis, and wait until I hear from you for the balance. do you want the whole two Hundred wagons Sent to Memphis or Hamburg Landing   Can you not Supply yourself with mules from west Tennessee and North Mississippi. Mules is only a question between us and Rebels, which will get them.

U. S. GRANT
Maj Genl

Telegram received, DNA, RG 393, 16th Army Corps, Letters Received; copies (dated Nov. 10, 1863), *ibid.*, Military Div. of the Miss., Letters Sent; DLC-USG, V, 34, 35. Dated Nov. 12 in *O.R.*, I, xxxi, part 3, 130. On Nov. 7, 4:00 P.M., Maj. Gen. Stephen A. Hurlbut telegraphed to USG. "In conformity with instructions from Genl. Sherman I this day abandon the line of rail road through to Corinth holding only to Moscow with infantry and LaGrange with Cavalry   All troops from LaGrange east are ordered to Corinth   This is compelled by the reduction of my infantry force and the concentration of the enemy from Tuscumbia & Okalona on Corinth   There is abundance of rations & ammunition in Corinth but no forage   Forage should be sent to Hamburg for two thousand animals and a gunboat lie off that point as a means of Communication— General Steele has not sent any troops and I do not think he will as, up to his last report—recd today—, he had not been able to decipher Schofields Telegram   It is of positive necessity that a division should be added to this force   A bold attack from below by infantry & cavalry would lose this city & its stors   Ten thousand men would drive me into the forts and cause the destruction of the city   If Tuttles division can be stopped here it will be sufficient, if not they must be furnished from some other Command to control expected movements of the enemy on the Mississippi and Tennessee rivers   I have now no means of relieving Corinth if attacked in force and the troops there must work out their own defense"   Telegram received, DNA, RG 94, War Records Office, Military Div. of the Miss.; copies, *ibid.*, RG 393, 16th Army Corps, Letters Sent; *ibid.*,

Military Div. of the Miss., Telegrams Received. *O.R.*, I, xxxi, part 3, 81. On Nov. 9, USG twice telegraphed to Hurlbut. "Collect Mules & Horses in West Tennessee & Northern Mississippi to supply all required in your command, from North Mississippi collect all Serviceable animals & Beef Cattle you can reach, giving [*vouchers*] to be paid on proof of Loyalty not transferable, that county ought to be put in such condition that it will not support Chalmers command any longer." Telegram received, DNA, RG 393, 16th Army Corps, Letters Received; copies, *ibid.*, Military Div. of the Miss., Letters Sent; *ibid.*, RG 94, War Records Office, Dept. of Ky.; DLC-USG, V, 34, 35. *O.R.*, I, xxxi, part 3, 103. "I have telegraphed Allen to send forage to Hamburg Landing. Direct your Quarter master and Commissary to make requisition for the necess[ar]y supplies for that place." Telegram received, DNA, RG 393, 16th Army Corps, Letters Received; copies, *ibid.*, Military Div. of the Miss., Letters Sent; DLC-USG, V, 34, 35. *O.R.*, I, xxxi, part 3, 103. On the same day, USG telegraphed to Brig. Gen. Robert Allen, Louisville. "The road from Corinth to Grand Junction has been abandoned by our forces leaving the former an isolated Post to be supplied by the river Tennessee. They are in immediate want of forage, to be sent to Hamburg Landing. Will you please order it." Copies, DLC-USG, V, 34, 35; DNA, RG 393, Military Div. of the Miss., Letters Sent. *O.R.*, I, xxxi, part 3, 97.

On Nov. 10, Allen telegraphed to USG. "Am obliged for the order forbidding interference with transportation   will send immediately a Cargo of forage to Hamburgh   have shipped largely to Eastport." Telegram received, DNA, RG 94, War Records Office, Military Div. of the Miss.; copy, *ibid.*, RG 393, Military Div. of the Miss., Telegrams Received. *O.R.*, I, xxxi, part 3, 108. On Nov. 8, Allen had telegraphed to Brig. Gen. Montgomery C. Meigs. "The interference of Gen'l. Boyle the Local commander here with the transportation is operating to the prejudice of the public service. I ask that an order be issued forbidding his exercise of any control over the shipment of supplies not intended for his own district   will forward by by mail particulars on the subject—" Copy, DNA, RG 393, Military Div. of the Miss., Telegrams Received. Meigs had forwarded this dispatch to USG on Nov. 9. LS, *ibid.*, Letters Received. On the same day, USG telegraphed to Brig. Gen. Jeremiah T. Boyle. "You will not in future interfere with transportation for the Dept of the Cumberland nor permit interference by any officers in your District" Telegram received, *ibid.*, Dept. of Ky., Telegrams Received; copies, *ibid.*, Military Div. of the Miss., Letters Sent; *ibid.*, RG 92, Letters and Telegrams Received by Gen. Meigs at Chattanooga; DLC-USG, V, 34, 35. On Nov. 9 and 10, Boyle telegraphed to USG. "I have just returned today after more than two weeks absence in execution of orders of Genl Burnside in regard to his transportation   I have never interfered with transportation to the Army of Cumberland except ~~by~~ in execution of orders of Genl Rosecrans. No interference by officers in my command known to me and will see there is none except on your order—" Telegram received, DNA, RG 94, War Records Office, Military Div. of the Miss.; copies, *ibid.*, RG 92, Letters and Telegrams Received by Gen. Meigs at Chattanooga; *ibid.*, RG 393, Military Div. of the Miss., Telegrams Received. "Only interference with transportation to the Army of the Cumberland was an order given by Adgt during my absence for 3 batteries & their trains to go by river being loaded on boats as the supt of R R stated He could not send them for a week & it was believed to be important to throw them forward. no orders were given for transportation except for supplies for troops at Bowling Green Mumfordville & Russellville   have directed there is to be no interference except by your order and Genl Thomas." Telegram received, *ibid.*, RG 94, War Records Office, Military Div. of the Miss.; copy, *ibid.*, RG 393, Military Div. of the Miss., Telegrams Received. *O.R.*, I, xxxi, part 3, 108.

1. On Nov. 10, Meigs received a telegram from Allen referring to Hurlbut's requisition. "Col Myers telegraphs me from St Louis that the requisition by Genl McPherson for mules appears to be urgent and that Genl Sherman had taken all the Local wagons & teams from Memphis" Copy, DNA, RG 393, Military Div. of the Miss., Letters Received. On Nov. 11, Meigs wrote to USG. "The enclosed telegram from Genl Allen is herewith respectfully referred to your   I had informed Gen Allen that you were of opinion that it was not necessary to send mules to Memphis, as they could supply themselves by impressment." LS, *ibid.* See following telegram.

To Brig. Gen. Robert Allen

Chattanooga November 12th 1863

BRIG GENL ROBT ALLEN CHF Q. M.
LOUISVILLE KY

Your dispatch received.[1] I have instructed General Hurlbut to take from West Tennessee and North Mississippi what horses and mules he requires. It is only a question between us and the guerrillas which will get them, and if [we] supply our deficincies the rebels will buy them from our men at a trifle. All our troops except at Corinth are supplied by railroad and cannot require a great number of wagons. Should wagons be required there, they would go to Hamburg Landing. Send fifty wagons to Memphis and I will enquire of Hurlbut if more is required at that point—[2]

U S GRANT
Major General

Telegram, copies, DLC-USG, V, 34, 35; DNA, RG 393, Military Div. of the Miss., Letters Sent. *O.R.*, I, xxxi, part 3, 122. On Nov. 13, 1863, Brig. Gen. Robert Allen telegraphed to USG. "I am at a loss to know what the requirements are in the Tenn river having no advices. Shall I continue to forward supplies to Eastport   what is the strength in men & annimals dependant upon Hamburg Landing." Copy, DNA, RG 393, Military Div. of the Miss., Telegrams Received. *O.R.*, I, xxxi, part 3, 134. On the same day, USG telegraphed to Allen. "I do not know what force Sherman, who now commands the Department of the Tennessee left at Corinth. I think there are no forces to be supplied from Eastport. Hurlbut telegraphed me that there were plenty of provisions at Corinth for the present, but no forage. Sherman will be through to Stevenson to morrow, and I will instruct him then to telegraph you just what will be required." Copies, DLC-USG, V, 34, 35; DNA, RG 393, Military Div. of the Miss., Letters Sent. *O.R.*, I, xxxi, part 3, 134.

1. See preceding telegram, note 1.
2. See telegram to Maj. Gen. William T. Sherman, Nov. 13, 1863.

To Brig. Gen. William Sooy Smith

Chattanooga November 12th 1863

Brig Genl W. S. Smith Chf Cav. (Gen Grants Staff)
Nashville

On assuming the duties of Chief of Cavalry: you will acquaint yourself as soon possible with the organization, location and condition of the different Cavalry commands. You will endeavor to supply all deficiences in arms, equipments and horses at the earliest moment, and hold the Cavalry always ready for active service. As far as practicable horses should be obtained traversed by the Cavalry. Where taken from loyal oweners, vouchers should be given payable at once; where taken from persons whose status is not known, vouchers should be given (not transferable) payable on proof of loyalty, and where taken from persons of known disloyalty, simple receipts only will be given. These should show the standing of the parties from whom stock is taken. The object in giving receipts at all in the latter case—is, that there may be a system of accountability for all property taken, and that the Government may get the benefit of it—

Department Commanders will locate the Cavalry of their respective commands, but general directions for foraging, disciplining &c. may be given by the Chief of Cavalry. Where an enemy makes his appearance, in any way threatening our lines of communication, Cavalry commanders should never wait orders to pursue, but should start at once simply reporting what they are doing. When the appearance of the enemy is in such numbers and in such direction as to bring Cavalry of two or more Armies in pursuit, the Military Division Chief of Cavalry should, if practicable, take command in person.

Further instructions will be given in orders or otherwise from these Headquarters, as the necessities of the service may suggest—

U S GRANT
Major General

Copies, DLC-USG, V, 34, 35; DNA, RG 393, Military Div. of the Miss., Letters Sent. *O.R.*, I, xxxi, part 3, 122–23. On Nov. 11, 1863, Brig. Gen. William Sooy Smith, chief of cav., Dept. of the Tenn., was named chief of cav., Military Div. of the Miss. General Orders No. 5, copies, DNA, RG 393, Military Div. of the Miss., General Orders; (misdated Nov. 11, 1864) DLC-USG, V, 14. Printed in part in *O.R.*, I, xxxi, part 3, 115.

On Nov. 17, 21, and 26, Smith telegraphed to Brig. Gen. Montgomery C. Meigs, to Brig. Gen. Washington L. Elliott, and to Maj. Gen. George Stoneman regarding the great number of unserviceable horses at Nashville. *Ibid.*, pp. 176, 218, 254. On Dec. 11, Bvt. Lt. Col. James L. Donaldson, Nashville, wrote to Meigs that Brig. Gen. Robert Allen, St. Louis, had reported that such horses had been furnished by the Cav. Bureau, not the Q. M. Dept., and concluding: "I have called on Gen'l. Allen to furnish me as soon as he can with two thousand artillery and eight thousand Cavalry horses." Copies, Atwood Collection, InU; (incomplete) Kenneth W. Rendell, Inc., *Autographs and Manuscripts: The American Civil War*, Catalogue No. 98, 1974, p. 44. On Dec. 13, Meigs endorsed this letter to USG "with the request that he will advise me whether 8,000 Cavalry horses can be needed by this army from the North. If so, the Cavalry Bureau should be notified of the probable wants." Copies, *ibid.* On the same day, USG endorsed this letter to Meigs. "I do not think it possible to require such a number of Cavalry horses in this Command unless it may be to mount recruits for its Cavalry Rgts. I will instruct the chief of Cav'y. to make a requisition through the Chief of the Cavalry Bureau for what he will probably need." Copies, *ibid.* On Dec. 21, USG, Nashville, telegraphed to Allen, Louisville. "Colonel Donaldson I presume will require at least 4000 Artillery and Ambulances horses to fill all requisitions on him between this and spring. I have directed the Chief of Cavalry to make requisitions on the Cavalry Bureau for horses required in that branch of service." Copies, DLC-USG, V, 34, 35; DNA, RG 393, Military Div. of the Miss., Letters Sent. *O.R.*, I, xxxi, part 3, 458–59. Apparently after reading USG's telegram of Dec. 21, Maj. Gen. George H. Thomas, Chattanooga, telegraphed to USG. "Your telegram in reference to transportation recd   Col Eastons Estimate was made on the supposition that this Army might be filled up to the maximum strength but we shall need nearly all the horses Estimated for as the Cavalry has been on constant duty all fall & winter and is now almost Entirely broken down   the Estimate for mules can be reduced by dispersing with the greater part of the transportation for troops at Depots & guarding rail Roads—"   Telegram received (undated), DNA, RG 393, Dept. of the Tenn., Telegrams Received.

To Edwin M. Stanton

———

Head Quarters, Military Division of the Miss.
Chattanooga Ten. November 13th 1863.

HON. E. M. STANTON,
SECRETARY OF WAR,
SIR:

Some of the citizens of Northern Illinois have expressed the conviction that a regiment of Cavalry can be raised in a short time from that section of the State if special authority be given the Governor to accept them, and have desired that I obtain the authority for them. I want no special favor for myself and cannot ask the desired authority on that ground. If however it is the policy of the Government to accept new organizations I would recommend that authority be given Governor Yates to accept a regiment of Cavalry to be raised in Northern Illinois.

I have the honor to be,
Very respectfully, your obt. svt.
U. S. GRANT
Maj. Gen.

ALS, IHi. On Nov. 14, 1863, Brig. Gen. John A. Rawlins, Chattanooga, wrote to U.S. Representative Elihu B. Washburne. "Enclosed please find the letter you asked, from Gen. Grant to the Secretary of War, relative to the recruiting of a Cavalry regiment in Northern Illinois. It is not just what you desired however, the General having some delicacy in asking for anything that looks like being personal to himself. I know what you propose meets with his cordial approval and nothing would gratify him more than to have the regiment raised as you propose. The General is all himself and in splendid health. Renewing my thanks for your many kindnesses and continued remembrance of these Head Quarters" LS, DLC-Elihu B. Washburne. On Nov. 19, Lorenzo H. Whitney, Dixon, Ill., wrote to Washburne. "I trouble you once more to enquire whether you have yet recieved an answer from Gen Grant. If he writes favorable, or if he does not, in either case when you go to Washington, if it is not ~~too~~ going to be too much in the way of your own projects I hope you will not forget to mention it to the War Department & see what Stanton will do. I see by the papers that your chances for the speakership are brightening. I hope you will obtain it. If Grant has written you please let me know what he says." ALS, *ibid.* See Whitney to Washburne, Nov. 30, *ibid.* On June 18, 1864, Whitney, formerly capt., 8th Ill. Cav., became col., 140th Ill., a hundred-day regt. which was mustered out on Oct. 29. *Ill. AG Report,* VII, 3, 141; VIII, 111. On Jan. 2, 1865, Whitney wrote

to Washburne. "As there is no good opportunity for again going into the army,
& as yet I have labored so far, for country & not for self; I propose now to
change the Programme. I want to go to *buying Cotton*: & I want a *permit from
the President to do* so. I write you to see if you cannot get me a Permit for twelve
hundred Bales—I want the Permit something like this: 'Col. L. H. Whitney,
late of the 140th Ills Regt ~~having se~~ is hereby permitted to purchase upon any of
the roads leading from Memphis Tenness, & within five miles of that City Cotton
to the amount of twelve hundred bales: & to this effect the Pickets will allow
him to pass ~~beyond~~ on horseback beyond their lines.' Now Mr. Washburn if you
can get the Presidents signature to such a document it will be worth several thousand to me; & I do think I ought to have the same chance that *rebels* & *Jews have*—
I was in Memphis lately & found out to my certain knowledge that those classes
of persons are getting all the favors of the government. I think that is wrong;
& I make this application to you to see if I cant have a hand in. If you think it
advisable for me to come there & apply for myself, I will do so; but if you can
get it for me, without too much trouble you will greatly oblige Your true
friend . . . P S. Please write me at once what can be done in the case." ALS (misdated Jan. 2, 1864), DLC-Elihu B. Washburne.

To Maj. Gen. William T. Sherman

By Telegraph from Chattanooga [*Nov.*] 13th *1863*
To MAJ GEN SHERMAN

Assemble the 15th Corps at Bridgeport & get ready for moving
as soon as possible. Leave directions for your command and come
up here yourself. Telegraph when you start & I will send a horse
to Kellys Ferry for you. Hurlbut Telegraphs that road is gone up
between Grand Junction & Corinth. The latter place must be supplied from Hamburg. I ordered forage to be sent there immediately.[1] Allen sent it but wants to know what number of men and
horses he has to provide for at that place   I could not tell him but
replied that as soon as you reached Stevenson I would get you to
inform him.[2] Hurlbuts Q. M & commissary should look after that
command. Hurlbut also states that rebels are building road to
Saltilla & Tallahatchie with view of attacking Corinth   I have
sent McPherson another dispatch to forward. Tuttles Division to
Hurlbut[3]   Have you still got troops coming up the Tenn   All
now to arrive had better be left with Dodge on the Decatur road
for the present. Those troops should collect all the forage & sup-

plies they can & mules & horses from the country. What we do not get the Rebels will & ~~these~~ those entitled to pay will get it

U. S. GRANT
Maj Gen'l

Telegram received, DNA, RG 94, War Records Office, Dept. of the Tenn.; copies, *ibid.*, RG 393, Military Div. of the Miss., Letters Sent; DLC-USG, V, 34, 35. *O.R.*, I, xxxi, part 3, 140. On Nov. 13, 1863, 6:15 P.M. and 10:30 P.M., Maj. Gen. William T. Sherman, Bridgeport, Ala., telegraphed to USG. "Am just in Ewings Division ought to be at Stevenson John E. Smith is coming across the mountains by Battle Creek but cannot be here till the day after tomorrow I have not yet heard of the progress of Blair But he must be this side of Paint Rock creek & may be near Bellefonte Shall I assemble the 15th A Corps here" "I will come up tomorrow after looking over the ground so as to place my troops as they arrive—No troops are coming up the Tennessee except Tuttle whose division I ordered to come up the Tennessee to Eastport and follow Dodge I heard from Dodge at Pulaski I ordered him to repair the bridges south of Pulaski & move to Athens I have telegraphed him via Columbia that you had ordered the bridge at Columbia to be built. The timber to come from the north I will order him to gather all serviceable mules & horses in his reach —I ordered all the ordnance at Corinth not needed in its defence to be sent to Memphis & a garrison left sufficient to defend its work Hurlbut knows its exact garrison about three thousand (3000)—" Telegrams received, DNA, RG 94, War Records Office, Military Div. of the Miss.; copies, *ibid.*, RG 393, Dept. of the Tenn., Telegrams Sent; *ibid.*, Military Div. of the Miss., Telegrams Received. *O.R.*, I, xxxi, part 3, 139–41. On Nov. 14, Sherman telegraphed to USG. "I understand a Steamboat will be down this Afternoon and leave for Kelly's ford tonight I will come to Chattanooga in her & bring with me Maj. Sawyer & one Servant. Would like to have 3 Saddled horses sent to me at Kellys ford tomorrow I expect Ewings division to be up to day & Mrs. [*John*] E. Smith should reach the mouth of Battle Creek tonight. Blair is reported at Maysville with two other division but he should be far on this side. I can make no estimate of the time he should reach Bridgeport. He ought to make fifteen or twenty miles a day. I am uneasy about Corinth but presume Hurlbut will reach it via Hamburg. There are plenty of stores at Eastport." Copies, DNA, RG 393, Dept. of the Tenn., Telegrams Sent; *ibid.*, Military Div. of the Miss., Telegrams Received. *O.R.*, I, xxxi, part 3, 152. On the same day, USG telegraphed to Sherman. "I have sent one of my horses to Bridgeport for you. Would have gone myself but dispatches received last night & this morning make it necessary for me to remain at home." Telegram received, DNA, RG 94, War Records Office, Dept. of the Tenn. Sherman took the steamboat to Kelley's Ferry, Tenn., then rode to Chattanooga, where he conferred with USG and other gens. *Memoirs*, II, 58; *Memoirs of Gen. W. T. Sherman* (4th ed., New York, 1891), I, 400–1; *Autobiography of Oliver Otis Howard* (New York, 1907; reprinted, Freeport, N. Y., 1971), I, 473–76. For a description of a reconnaissance made by USG and Sherman on Nov. 16, see William Wrenshall Smith, "Holocaust Holiday: The Journal of a Strange Vacation to the War-torn South and a Visit with U. S. Grant," *Civil War Times Illustrated*, XVIII, 6 (Oct., 1979), 31–32.

1. See telegram to Maj. Gen. Stephen A. Hurlbut, Nov. 12, 1863.
2. See telegram to Brig. Gen. Robert Allen, Nov. 12, 1863.
3. See telegram to Maj. Gen. Stephen A. Hurlbut, Nov. 6, 1863.

To Maj. Gen. Ambrose E. Burnside

Chattanooga November 14th 63

MAJOR GENERAL A. E BURNSIDE
KNOXVILLE TENN

Your dispatch and Dana's just received.[1] Being there you can tell better how to resist Longstreet's attack than I can direct. With your showing you had better give up Kingston at the last moment and save the most productive part of your possessions. Every arrangement is now made to throw Sherman's force across the river just at and below the mouth of Chicamauga Creek, as soon as it arrives. Thomas will attack on his left at the same time and together it is expected to carry Missionary Ridge and from there push a force on the the Rail road between Cleveland and Dalton. Hooker will at the same time attack and if he can, carry Lookout Mountain. The enemy now seem to be looking for an attack on his left flank. This favors us. To further confirm this Sherman's advance Division will march direct from Whiteside to Trenton. The remainder of his force will pass over a new road just made from Whiteside to Kelly's Ferry, thus being concealed from the enemy and leave him to suppose the whole force is going up Lookout Valley. Sherman's advance has only just reached Bridgeport. The rear will only reach there on the 16th. This will bring it to the 19th as the earliest day for making the combined movement as desired. Inform me if you think you can sustain yourself until this time. I can hardly conceive of the enemy breaking through at Kingston and pushing for Kentucky. If they should however, a new problem would be left for solution. Thomas has ordered a Division of Cavalry to the vicinity of Sparta. I will ascertain if they have started and inform you. It will be entirely out of the question to send you ten thousand men, not because they cannot be spared, but how would they be fed, after they got even one day east from here.

U S GRANT
Major General

Telegram, copies, DLC-USG, V, 34, 35; DNA, RG 393, Military Div. of the Miss., Letters Sent. *O.R.*, I, xxxi, part 2, 30. Also on Nov. 14, 1863, USG telegraphed to Maj. Gen. Ambrose E. Burnside. "Can you hold the line from Knoxville to Clinton for seven days. If so I think the whole Tennessee Valley can be secured from all present danger" Copies, DLC-USG, V, 34, 35; DNA, RG 393, Military Div. of the Miss., Letters Sent. *O.R.*, I, xxxi, part 3, 145.

1. On Nov. 13, Burnside telegraphed to USG. "It is reported by General White who occupies the heights opposite Loudon that the enemy are placing guns in position this evening in the works on the south side of the river I am satisfied that Longstreet is on that side with his corps and probably a considerable portion of wheelers cavalry and intends to cross either the Big or Little Tennessee In either case I think it would be advisable to concentrate the force in East Tennessee and risk a battle if we concentrate in the neighborhood of Loudon (?) the enemy will have the advantage of being able to reinforce from the rear whereas if we concentrate near this place not only the present force of the enemy but all reinforcements would have to march forty (40) miles before fighting—In view of this condition of affairs I would be glad to withdraw the Brigade of Infantry that is now at Kingston Should he cross either river and move up to attack us in this neighborhood he will be so far from the main body of Bragg's army that he cannot be recalled in time to assist it In case Thomas finds himself in condition to make an attack after Sherman gets up I take it that Sherman is at Chattanooga now—Col Wilson and Mr Dana sent you a long cipher despatch this evening which will explain to you the situation of affairs here as also my views in regard to the campagn I should be glad to have as early an answer as possible to both these despatches" Telegram received, DNA, RG 94, War Records Office, Military Div. of the Miss. *O.R.*, I, xxxi, part 3, 138.

Also from Knoxville on Nov. 13, 4:00 P.M., Asst. Secretary of War Charles A. Dana telegraphed to Secretary of War Edwin M. Stanton and to USG reporting at length Burnside's preference for concentrating his forces at Knoxville and abandoning Kingston if C.S.A. forces under Lt. Gen. James Longstreet continued their advance. Telegram received, DNA, RG 94, War Records Office, Dept. of the Ohio; copy, *ibid.*, RG 393, Military Div. of the Miss., Letters Sent. *O.R.*, I, xxxi, part 1, 258–59. On the same day, Lt. Col. James H. Wilson telegraphed to USG to the same effect. ALS (telegram sent), DNA, RG 393, Military Div. of the Miss., Letters Received; telegram received, *ibid.*, RG 94, War Records Office, Dept. of the Tenn. *O.R.*, I, xxxi, part 1, 265–67.

To Maj. Gen. Ambrose E. Burnside

———

Chattanooga November 14th 1863.
MAJOR GENERAL A. E. BURNSIDE
KNOXVILLE TENN.

Shermans advance has reached Bridgeport. His whole force will be ready to move from there by Tuesday,[1] at furthest. If you can hold Longstreet in check until he gets up, or by skirmishing and falling back can avoid serious loss to yourself and gain time, I will be able to force the enemy back from here and place a force between Longstreet and Bragg that must inevitably make the former take to the mountain passes by every available road to get back to supplies. Sherman would have been here before this but for high water in Elk river, driving him some thirty miles up that river to cross.

U. S. GRANT
Major General.

Telegram, copies, DLC-USG, V, 34, 35; DNA, RG 393, Military Div. of the Miss., Letters Sent. Printed as sent at 10:00 A.M. in *O.R.*, I, xxxi, part 3, 145–46.

1. Nov. 17, 1863.

To Maj. Gen. Ambrose E. Burnside

———

Chattanooga 10 P. M. Nov. 14th 1863
MAJOR GENERAL A. E. BURNSIDE
KNOXVILLE

Colonel Wilsons dispatch is just coming,[1] cannot be deciphered before morning. I will answer in full as soon as received. It is of the most vital importance that East Tennessee should be held: Take immediate steps to that end. Evacuate Kingston if you think best. As I said in a previous dispatch, I think seven days more will enable us to make such movements here as to make the whole valley secure if you hold on that time.

U. S. GRANT
Major General

Telegram, copies, DLC-USG, V, 34, 35; DNA, RG 393, Military Div. of the Miss., Letters Sent. Printed as sent at 10:30 P.M. in *O.R.*, I, xxxi, part 3, 146.

1. Earlier on Nov. 14, Lt. Col. James H. Wilson, Knoxville, had telegraphed to USG. "The enemy [*threw*] two bridges across the Tennessee near Loudon last night under cover of a strong position on the opposite side, and is making preperation to cross his force. Burnside has ordered Ninth Corps & Whites Division of the 23d to fall back from Lenoires detaining the enemy as much as possible & destroying Cotton factory at Lenoires. Burnside has decided to collect his forces here & if pushed too hard to move towards the Gaps through he feels greatly relieved to cross his whole force to the East side of the Holston where he can get supplies and endeavor to baffle the enemy in his attempt to dislodge him. It seems to me his decision to fall back up the Valley is the best step now left open for doing so he can save at least his Cavalry & Artillery but may be compelled to destroy his Wagons   at all events he can hold the enemy so strongly as to allow himself six days between here and the mountain passes & meanwhile something may be done near Chattanooga to call Longstreet back   If Longstreets force is three Divisions of Infantry and all Wheelers Cavalry this is the best step left open for this Army. I shall start back this morning Via Lenoire and hope to cross the Clinch somewhere between Kingston and Clinton. Shall telegraph to you from Lenoire if wires are undisturbed when I arrive there." Copy, DNA, RG 393, Military Div. of the Miss., Telegrams Received. *O.R.*, I, xxxi, part 3, 146. Asst. Secretary of War Charles A. Dana also reported on the situation faced by Maj. Gen. Ambrose E. Burnside in a series of telegrams to Secretary of War Edwin M. Stanton. See *ibid.*, I, xxxi, part 1, 258–61. On Nov. 18, Wilson, Chattanooga, wrote to Capt. Adam Badeau, commenting on the trip to Knoxville. ". . . found Burnside anxious to see us—had a very remarkable series of interviews or night councils, left him with his forces moving to repel Longstreet's crossing the Tennessee, and had barely time left for effecting our escape from East Tennessee by way of Kingston." Typescript, WyU. Both Dana and Wilson later recalled various details of their interviews with Burnside at this time. Charles A. Dana, *Recollections of the Civil War* (New York, 1898), pp. 138–40; James Harrison Wilson, *The Life of Charles A. Dana* (New York and London, 1907), pp. 286–87; James Harrison Wilson, *Under the Old Flag* (New York and London, 1912), I, 283–85.

To Maj. Gen. Ambrose E. Burnside

Chattanooga November 14th '63

MAJOR GENERAL A. E. BURNSIDE
KNOXVILLE

If General Judah desires to be ordered here in person for the purpose of being assigned to duty, I do not see how to accomodate him. The consolidation of two Corps into one here,[1] has reduced the number of Divisions three, and Brigades nine, and Corps one, thus taking away thirteen commands for General Officers, while but three General Officers have been ordered away. Four not here before have been ordered here, and there has been one promotion. There are now seven General Officers doing Staff duty and several not assigned   If it is for any other purpose General Judah desires to come here I have no objections to his being ordered

U S GRANT
Major General

Telegram, copies, DLC-USG, V, 34, 35; DNA, RG 393, Military Div. of the Miss., Letters Sent. On Nov. 12, 1863, 1:00 A.M., Maj. Gen. Ambrose E. Burnside had telegraphed to USG. "Genl Judah has requested me to order Him to report to you in person for duty and I would be glad to gratify Him with your permission   shall I issue the order?" Telegram received, *ibid.*, RG 94, War Records Office, Dept. of the Ohio; copy, *ibid.*, RG 393, Military Div. of the Miss., Telegrams Received. See *O.R.*, I, lii, part 1, 471. Brig. Gen. Henry M. Judah, who had commanded the 3rd Div., 23rd Army Corps, June 24–Aug. 6, 1863, during C.S.A. Brig. Gen. John H. Morgan's raid into Ohio, served on courts-martial from Nov. to Jan. 20, 1864.

1. On Sept. 28, 1863, the 20th and 21st Army Corps were consolidated into the 4th Army Corps, Dept. of the Cumberland. *Ibid.*, I, xxx, part 3, 911.

To Julia Dent Grant

Chattanooga Nov. 14th/63

DEAR JULIA,

I have not heard from you since you left Louisville except through the Georgetown paper which announced your being there. I have received a letter from Mr. Page however saying that Sis was with you.[1] I know you had a nice pleasant plain visit which both of you enjoyed very much. How long did you stay in Cincinnati? who did you see? and who did you find to abuse me half as much as you do when you are mad.

Things will culminate here within ten days in great advantages with one or other parties.—I am certainly hapily constituted. At present I am confronting a large force here. The enemy are at work on the Mobile & Ohio road towards Corinth; on the Mississippi Central towards Holly Springs; moving a force up East of me towards Knoxville, thus threatning Memphis, Corinth, East Tennessee & Chattanooga: and the responsibility of guarding all, to a great extent, devolves upon me. With all this I loose no sleep, except I do not get to bed before 12 or 1 o'clock at night, and find no occation to swear or fret. I am very hopeful and fully believe, if not failed by any officer in immediate command, that all will show the Union forces in a more favorable position twenty days hence than they have been in since the begining of the rebelion. Some small point may give way, possibly Corinth. That will depend on who Sherman left in command.[2] I will know to-morrow all about this; but Sherman is so fine an officer, and possessed of such fine judgement that he will leave no point in improper hands. You know Sherman now commands the Department of the Tennessee? my old Department. William Smith is here.[3] He will probably stay a couple of weeks or more.—Tell Mr. Page his letter was duly received and I feel much obliged to him for writing. If I do not answer it now I shall write to him after you leave. While you are there he will hear from me every few days.—Wilson has been made a Brigadier Gen. At present I have him, and Dana, (that you did not like) at Knoxville. I shall put Wilson in command of a large Cavalry force and fully expect he will eclipse all Cavalry officers the war has produced.[4] I did not intend writing to you thus when I commenced but we are on the point of important events and I have been receiving, and answering, important dispatches, bearing on the subject, and whilst I write, long after 12 o'clock, other dispatches are being disciphered which I have to answer.—Since Vicksburg fell this has become really the vital point of the rebellion and requires all the care and watchfulness that can be bestowed upon it. It has all mine. and no fault shall rest upon me if we are not successful.

The Staff with me are well. I have but few however and none but thinking working men are necessary. Bowers and Rowley are still at Nashville and I do not know but I will have to keep them there for several weeks. There is so much dependent upon geting up everything promptly, (and all the means of carrying on War here have to pass through Nashville,) that I have found it necessary to keep some one there, that I could order by telegraph, to attend in person to see that every order is carried out. Bowers and Rowley are the best of men for this.

Do you think of going to St. Louis? or will you remain in Louisville for a while? If you are so inclined you might remain where you are until the result of impending events ends. Give my love to your Uncle, Aunt[5] and family.—Kisses for Jess and yourself.

ULYS.

P. S. Endorse your note against Orvil[6] and send it to J. R. Jones, Chicago Ill. for collection. I will write to Mr. Jones[7] and Orvil about it. I am going to invest my savings in Chicago Horse railroad stock. Also write to Mr. J. the name of the Banker with whom our Bonds are deposited. I presume the first interest $150 00 in gold has been collected. This will sell for about $220 00 at present rates and pay that much towards the stock I am going to purchase.

ULYS.

ALS, DLC-USG.

1. Charles A. and Ellen Page were cousins of Julia Dent Grant. See letter to Julia Dent Grant, April 3, 1862, notes 1 and 2.

2. Brig. Gen. John D. Stevenson commanded at Corinth, Miss.

3. On Oct. 4, 1863, USG, Vicksburg, had written a pass. "Pass W W Smith of Pittsburg Pa. to any part of the Department he may desire. Pass good until 1st of Jany 1864." ALS, DLC-USG. USG added: "We will be glad to see you here. My three oldest children are in St. Louis at school. Mrs. Grant and the youngest boy are with me. All send respects to what remains of your family." ALS, *ibid.* In his diary for Nov. 13, William W. Smith wrote of his arrival in Chattanooga. "In a short time the General arrives. He greets me cordially, and takes me into his room. He puts his quarters and horses at my disposal and makes me feel altogether comfortable. We have a long talk. He tells me all about his children,

about his purchases since he has been in the army—his saving all the money he could for the future, not knowing when his fortunes might change, and he be thrown out of his office—Besides buying the ground and beautiful English Villa in which he lived when I was with him 5 years ago in ~~four~~ Missouri, from Fred Dent,—he has invested five thousand Dollars in U. S. 5/20's. He now wants to buy five thousand Dollars worth of Chicago city passanger Rail Way Stock, and concludes to send his note for that amount—with the U. S. 5/20's as collateral—for discount, to secure the stock. We have a long pleasant talk ~~untill~~ Dinner—which is at 6 oclock. The dinner is very plain—consisting of Roast Beef, ~~and~~ Boiled Potatoes, Bread and Butter. The mess consists of the General Dr. Kittoe, Col Lagow, Capt Hudson ~~and Capt. Ross (who is in Ohio)~~ and (now is added) myself. The General at the head of the table ~~dose~~ does the carving." AD, Mrs. John W. McIlvaine, Washington, Pa. See letter to Julia Dent Grant, May 24, 1862, note 1.

4. See endorsement to Maj. Gen. Henry W. Halleck, Oct. 26, 1863.

5. Samuel K. Page and Emily Wrenshall Page. See letter to Julia Dent Grant, April 3, 1862, note 4.

6. USG's brother, Orvil L. Grant.

7. See letter to J. Russell Jones, Nov. 17, 1863.

To Brig. Gen. Montgomery C. Meigs

By Telegraph from Chattanooga [*Nov.*] 15 1863
To BRIG GEN M. C. MEIGS

I have received the following from Anderson Cincinnati 14th
To MAJ GEN GRANT.

Two of the parties decline to bid for the bridge work in less than four months   L B Boomer bids for the whole work to be completed in ninety (90) days at prices varying from twenty one (21) to eighty five (85) dollars per foot averaging for the whole work sixty three (63) dollars per foot   If not impeded by the elements the united states Gov't or the enemy he will pay a forfiet of seventy five dollars per day for every day over one hundred ~~can~~ consumed in the work & to be paid a bonus of two hundred dollars per day for every day less than ninety in which he may complete the work   Other terms of contract to be similar to those in the contract for running water bridge   if you approve please inform Gen Meigs & Telegraph me at Louisville that I may notify Mr Boomer at Chicago

(signed) J. B. ANDERSON[1]

Have answered him that the object is to have the bridge built in the shortest possible time & to make the best possible contract with that object in view[2]

U. S. GRANT
Maj Gen'l

Telegram received, DNA, RG 92, Letters and Telegrams Received by Gen. Meigs at Chattanooga. On Nov. 16, 1863, Brig. Gen. Montgomery C. Meigs endorsed this telegram. "Telegraph Col Anderson Gen Grant has tonite instructed you in regard to bids for Bridges on the Nashville & Decatur R R" AES, *ibid.* On Tuesday, Nov. 17, John B. Anderson, Nashville, telegraphed to USG. "I telegraphed you on Saturday from Cincinatti stating L. B. Boomer's proposition have not yet received your answer. Boomer telegraphs that he can secure all the timber required please let me know your decision." Copy, *ibid.*, RG 393, Military Div. of the Miss., Telegrams Received, where the sender's name is given as J. B. Donaldson. On Nov. 20, USG telegraphed to Anderson. "What steps have you taken for the completion of the Nashville and Decatur Railroad? Answer immediately" Copies, *ibid.*, Letters Sent; DLC-USG, V, 34, 35. On the same day, Anderson telegraphed to USG. After quoting his dispatch of Nov. 14 to USG, he concluded. "I asked operators to get an answer at Louisville on Monday on this & on Wednesday I telegraphed you from this place asking for an answer to none of these did I receive any reply. Boomer telegraphs that he can contract for all the lumber required—I agreed to make contract with him if approved by you. Shall I instruct Boomer to go ahead with the work? please answer." Copy, DNA, RG 393, Military Div. of the Miss., Telegrams Received.

1. Copy, *ibid.* See telegram to Brig. Gen. Montgomery C. Meigs, Nov. 19, 1863.
2. On Nov. 15, USG telegraphed to Anderson. "The object is to build the bridge in the shortest possible time. Make the best possible contract having that object in view" Copies, DNA, RG 393, Military Div. of the Miss., Letters Sent; DLC-USG, V, 34, 35.

To Maj. Gen. Henry W. Halleck

Chattanooga Tenn
Nov 15/63 10 A M

MAJ GEN H W HALLECK
GENL IN CHIEF

Col Wilson of my Staff and Mr Dana are in Knoxville and will not leave until present dangers are over[1] Burnside can certainly detain Longstreet in the Tennessee Valley until we can make such moves here as will entirely free him from present danger. I have asked him if he cannot hold the Knoxville and Clinton line for one week.[2] If so we can make moves here that will save all danger in East Tennessee   Sherman is now at Bridgeport   He will commence moving tomorrow or next day, throwing one brigade from Whiteside into Trenton, thus threatening enemy's left flank—Remainder of his force will pass over by Kellys Ferry, leaving [*evading*] view from Lookout, and march up to Mouth of Chickamauga Pontoons are made and making to throw across at that point, over which it is intended Shermans force ~~passes~~ & One Division of Thomas shall pass.

This force will attack Missionary Ridge with the left flank, and Thomas supporting from here—In mean time Hooker will attack Lookout and carry it if possible—

If Burnside can hold the line from Knoxville to Clinton as I have asked him, for six days, I believe Bragg will be started back for South side of Oostenaula[3] and Longstreet cut off   I have been anxious for earlier movements here, but the condition of transportation of ~~of~~ the command would not admit of it—

U. S. GRANT
Maj Genl

Telegram received, DNA, RG 107, Telegrams Collected (Bound); DLC-Robert T. Lincoln; copies, DNA, RG 107, Telegrams Received in Cipher; *ibid.*, RG 393, Military Div. of the Miss., Hd. Qrs. Correspondence; DLC-USG, V, 40, 94. *O.R.*, I, xxxi, part 3, 154–55. On Nov. 14, 1863, 2:00 P.M., Maj. Gen. Henry W. Halleck telegraphed to USG. "Advices recieved from East Tennessee indicate that Burnside intends to abandon the defence of Little Tennessee & fall back before Longstreet towards Cumberland Gap & the upper valley. I am pretty certain that no reenforcements have been sent by Lee to the Virginia valley, & that Jones has only a small force there. He cannot seriously threaten Burnside on that side. Longstreet is said to be near the Little Tennessee with from twenty to forty thousand men. Burnside has about thirty thousand in all and can hold his position; he ought not to retreat. Cannot Thomas move on Longstreets rear and force him to fall back. A mere demonstration may have a good effect. I fear further delay may result in Burnsides abandonment of East Tennessee. This would be a terrible misfortune and must be averted if possible." ALS (telegram sent—incomplete), DNA, RG 107, Telegrams Collected (Bound); copies, *ibid.*, RG 393, Military Div. of the Miss., Hd. Qrs. Correspondence; DLC-USG, V, 40, 94. Printed as sent at 2:20 P.M. in *O.R.*, I, xxxi, part 3, 145.

1. See telegram to Maj. Gen. Ambrose E. Burnside, Nov. 17, 1863, note 1.
2. See telegram to Maj. Gen. Ambrose E. Burnside, Nov. 14, 1863.
3. The Oostanaula River flows from near Resaca, forty miles from Chattanooga, to Rome, in northwestern Ga.

To Maj. Gen. Ambrose E. Burnside

Chattanooga November 15th 1863.

MAJOR GENERAL. A. E. BURNSIDE
KNOXVILLE

I do not know how to impress on you the necessity of holding on to East Tennessee, in strong enough terms. According to the dispatches of Mr. Dana and Col. Wilson it would seem that you should if pressed to do it hold on to Knoxville and that portion of the valley which you will necessarily possess holding to that point. Should Longstreet move his whole force across the Little Tennessee, an effort should be made to cut his pontoons on that stream even if it sacrificed half the cavalry of the Ohio Army. By holding on and placing Longstreet between the Little Tennessee and Knoxville he should not be allowed to escape with an army capable of doing any thing this winter. I can hardly conceive the necessity of retreating from East Tennessee. If I did so at all it would be after losing most of the Army, and then necessity would suggest the route. I will not attempt to lay out a line of retreat. Kingston, looking at the map, I thought of more importance than any other point in East Tennessee. But my attention being more closely called to it, I can see that might be passed by and Knoxville and the rich valley around it possessed, ignoring that place entirely. I should not think it advisable to concentrate a force near Little Tennessee, to resist the crossing of it would be in danger of capture, but I would harass and embarrass progress in every way possible reflecting on the fact that the army of the Ohio is not the only army to resist the onward progress of the enemy.

U. S. GRANT
Major General

Telegram, copies, DLC-USG, V, 34, 35; DNA, RG 393, Military Div. of the Miss., Letters Sent. *O.R.*, I, xxxi, part 2, 30. On Nov. 14, 1863, Maj. Gen. Ambrose E. Burnside telegraphed to USG. "The enemy are reported by Genl White to have thrown a regiment of Infantry across in Boats at Hoff's ferry six miles below Loudon & to be engaged in throwing a Pontoon Bridge at that place. It is almost definitely ascertained that Longstreet is at or near Loudon with the Main body of his force." Telegram received, DNA, RG 94, War Records Office, Military Div. of the Miss.; copy, *ibid.*, RG 393, Military Div. of the Miss., Telegrams Received. *O.R.*, I, xxxi, part 3, 147. On the same day, Burnside telegraphed to USG a copy of the report of Nov. 13 of Brig. Gen. Robert B. Potter, Lenoir's Station, Tenn., regarding the C.S.A. advance. Telegram received, DNA, RG 94, War Records Office, Dept. of the Ohio; copy, *ibid.*, RG 393, Military Div. of the Miss., Telegrams Received. *O.R.*, I, xxxi, part 3, 147.

To Maj. Gen. Ambrose E. Burnside

Chattanooga November 15th 1863.

MAJOR GENERAL. A. E. BURNSIDE
KNOXVILLE.

Boats have been laying at Nashville loaded with rations to take to Big South Fork ever since you asked to have them sent there, a waiting for convoy. I had to send all the way to Cairo for orders before gunboats could be got. They have now arrived at Nashville and will go up by the first rise. Col. Donaldson[1] is sending you clothing by wagons from Nashville. He sends by way of Sparta to Kingston. You will have to send out and direct the course of the train. The clothing will leave Nashville on two trains one leaving there on the 18th the other on the 20th

U. S. GRANT
Major General.

Telegram, copies, DLC-USG, V, 34, 35; DNA, RG 393, Military Div. of the Miss., Letters Sent. *O.R.*, I, xxxi, part 3, 156. On Nov. 16, 1863, USG telegraphed to Maj. Gen. Ambrose E. Burnside. "Col. Donaldson will start one hundred wagons on the 18th inst. and about the same number on the 20th loaded with clothing for your command. They will go to Sparta at which place you will have to send teams to meet them and let those sent from Nashville return." Copies, DLC-USG, V, 34, 35; DNA, RG 393, Military Div. of the Miss., Letters Sent. *O.R.*, I, xxxi, part 3, 165. On Nov. 17, USG telegraphed to Lt. Col. James L. Donaldson, Nashville. "I will telegh Gen Burnside to answer your dispatch as to the best place to send rations." Telegram received, DNA, RG 393, Dept. of the Cumberland, Telegrams Received; copies, *ibid.*, Military Div. of the Miss., Letters Sent; DLC-USG, V, 34, 35. Also on Nov. 17, USG telegraphed to Burnside. "Col. Donaldson wishes to know if rations now on Steamer for your Army had better be taken to the mouth of Obeys river. Please answer" Copies, *ibid. O.R.*, I, xxxi, part 3, 177. On the same day, 10:00 A.M., Burnside, Knoxville, telegraphed to USG. "Do not send the clothing at present It will be impossible for me to meet it" Telegram received, DNA, RG 94, War Records Office, Dept. of the Ohio; copy, *ibid.*, RG 393, Military Div. of the Miss., Telegrams Received. *O.R.*, I, xxxi, part 3, 177. Later on Nov. 17, USG telegraphed to Donaldson. "Gen Burnside is now engaged with the enemy you need not start the clothing for him until the result is known and further Orders are received from here" Telegram received, DNA, RG 393, Dept. of the Cumberland, Telegrams Received; copies, *ibid.*, Military Div. of the Miss., Letters Sent; DLC-USG, V, 34, 35. *O.R.*, I, xxxi, part 3, 174. Again on Nov. 17, Donaldson telegraphed to USG. "Genl Burnside telegraphs me as follows from Knoxville: do not want the clothing. I cannot send to meet the trains at present. The first hundred wagons were to have started tomorrow—The rations ordered to Big South Fork are still here awaiting a rise in the River—Would it not be best for them to go to Celina, Mouth of Obey River and thence by Jamestown & Montgomery better road, and saves one hundred and fifty (150) miles difficult River transportation" LS (telegram sent), DNA, RG 393, Dept. of the Cumberland, Q. M. Dept., Telegrams Sent (Press); copy, *ibid.*, Military Div. of the Miss., Telegrams Received. *O.R.*, I, xxxi, part 3, 174. On Nov. 18, USG telegraphed to Brig. Gen. Montgomery C. Meigs, Bridgeport, Ala. "Col Donaldsons views are Right about supplying the army at Chattanooga first the Rations for Genl Burnside could not be sent now even if there was water enough in the Comberland until the Result of present movements by Longstreet are known I think it better therefore to let the boats now loaded discharge & Return I have directed Col Donaldson not to send clothing to Genl Burnside for the present" Telegram received, DNA, RG 92, Letters and Telegrams Received by Gen. Meigs at Chattanooga; copies, *ibid.*, RG 393, Military Div. of the Miss., Letters Sent; DLC-USG, V, 34, 35. Incomplete in *O.R.*, I, xxxi, part 3, 182.

1. James L. Donaldson of Md., USMA 1836, served as q. m. in the Mexican War. Promoted to maj. and staff q. m. as of Aug. 3, 1861, he held the rank of bvt. lt. col. from May 14. He became chief q. m., Dept. of the Cumberland, on Nov. 10, 1863.

To Maj. Gen. Henry W. Halleck

––––

Chattanooga Tenn.
3 P. M. Nov. 16. 1863.

MAJ. GEN. H. W. HALLECK
GEN-IN-CHIEF

I am pushing everything to give Gen. Burnside early aid. I have impressed on him in the strongest terms the necessity of holding on to his position.

Gen. Sherman's troops are now at Bridgeport. They will march tomorrow and an effort will be made to get a column between Bragg and Longstreet as soon as possible.

U. S. GRANT,
Maj. Genl. Cmd'g—

Telegram received, DNA, RG 107, Telegrams Collected (Bound); copies, *ibid.*, Telegrams Received in Cipher; *ibid.*, RG 393, Military Div. of the Miss., Hd. Qrs. Correspondence; DLC-USG, V, 40, 94. *O.R.*, I, xxxi, part 3, 163. On Nov. 16, 1863, 10:30 A.M., Maj. Gen. Henry W. Halleck had telegraphed to USG. "Dana left Burnside on the 14th to return to you. Burnside was then hesitating whether to fight or retreat. I fear he will not fight, although strongly urged to do so. Unless you can give him immediate assistance, he will surrender his position to the enemy. I have offered to give him more troops from Kentucky, but he says he cannot supply them. Immediate aid from you is now of vital importance." ALS (telegram sent), DNA, RG 107, Telegrams Collected (Bound); copies, *ibid.*, RG 393, Military Div. of the Miss., Hd. Qrs. Correspondence; DLC-USG, V, 40, 94. *O.R.*, I, xxxi, part 3, 163.

To Maj. Gen. Ambrose E. Burnside

––––

Chattanooga November 17th 63

MAJOR GENERAL A. E. BURNSIDE
KNOXVILLE

I have not heard from you since the 14th. What progress is Longstreet making, and what are your chances for defending yourself? Sherman's forces commenced their movement from Bridgeport threatening the enemy's left flank. This alone may turn Longstreet back, and if it does not, the attack will be prosecuted until we reach the roads over which all their supplies have to pass while you hold East Tennessee. Is Dana and Wilson with you?[1]

U S Grant
Major General

Telegram, copies, DLC-USG, V, 34, 35; DNA, RG 393, Military Div. of the Miss., Letters Sent. Printed as sent at 10:00 A.M. in *O.R.*, I, xxxi, part 3, 177.

1. On Nov. 15, 1863, USG twice telegraphed to Maj. Gen. Ambrose E. Burnside. "Say to Mr Dana and General Wilson that I desire them to remain with you until they are otherwise directed." "If General Wilson and Mr Dana have started back, you will please send by telegraph or by courier for them to return to you, as I am desirous they should remain with you for the present" Copies, DLC-USG, V, 34, 35; DNA, RG 393, Military Div. of the Miss., Letters Sent. USG did not know that Asst. Secretary of War Charles A. Dana and Lt. Col. James H. Wilson had already left Knoxville on Nov. 14, arriving in Chattanooga on Nov. 17.

To Maj. Gen. Ambrose E. Burnside

9. P. M. Chattanooga November 17th 1863

Major General A. E. Burnside
Knoxville

Your dispatch received.[1] So far you doing exactly what appears to me right. I want the enemies progress retarded at every foot all it can be only giving up each place when it becomes evident that it cannot longer be held without endangering your force to capture. I think our movements here must cause Longstreet's recall within a day or two if he is not successful before that time. Sherman moved this morning from Bridgeport with one Division. The remainder of his command moves in the morning. There will be no halt until a severe battle is fought, or the railroads cut supplying the enemy.

U. S. Grant
Major General

Telegram, copies, DLC-USG, V, 34, 35; DNA, RG 393, Military Div. of the Miss., Letters Sent. *O.R.*, I, xxxi, part 3, 177.

1. Apparently USG received a copy of Maj. Gen. Ambrose E. Burnside's telegram to President Abraham Lincoln, Nov. 17, 1863, 1:30 A.M. *O.R.*, I, xxxi, part 1, 268. See telegram to Maj. Gen. Henry W. Halleck, Nov. 18, 1863.

To J. Russell Jones

Chattanooga Ten.
Nov. 17th 1863,

J. R. JONES,
DEAR SIR:

I have written a letter to Mrs. Grant[1] directing her to send you a note I have against J. R. Grant, for collection, and to be applied on the rail-road stock which you have been kind enough to say I could have.[2] I have also written to my brother Orvil to pay it as soon as presented. I hold also $5000 00 worth of 5/20 bonds which are in the hands of some banker, I do not know who, in Chicago. These bonds I will have to predicate to borrow about $3000 00 of the money until I can save that much from my pay. Mr. Antrobus[3] left here will pleased with his success. I hope you will be equally pleased.—One week more will decide a greatdeel here. Within that time either the position of the enemy will be greatly worse than at present or our will not be so good. When I got here it was impossible to move a peg. The army[4]   of the worst roads you can concieve of. There was not another trip left in the mules and already about 10 000 had died or totally given out. Soldiers were on short rations and Artillery horses had become so reduced that it would take all belonging to a battery to move one piece. Gaining possession of the river below Lookout Mountain has remedied this so far as to enable to hold on here.

Rawlins and staff are well and wish to be remembered[5]   this place to-morrow. I recommended him for promotion after the siege of Vicksburg. But at present there are no vacancies.

Yours Truly
U. S. GRANT

ALS, USG 3.

1. See letter to Julia Dent Grant, Nov. 14, 1863.

Portrait of Maj. Gen. Ulysses S. Grant, 1863, by John Antrobus.
Courtesy Chicago Public Library.

Photographer and guard at Strawberry Plains, Tenn.
Courtesy Library of Congress.

2. Chartered in 1861 and reorganized in 1863 with J. Russell Jones as president, the Chicago West Division Railway Co. on July 30 bought the road and franchises of the Chicago City Railway Co. in the West Division of Chicago. Among the investors were several Galena businessmen and U.S. Representative Elihu B. Washburne. A. T. Andreas, *History of Chicago from the Earliest Period to the Present Time* (Chicago, 1884–86), II, 121.

3. Painter John Antrobus, born in England in 1837, and sculptor Leonard W. Volk opened a gallery in Chicago in Dec., 1862. *Ibid.*, p. 557. Regarding Antrobus's full-size portrait of USG, exhibited in Chicago and Washington, see letter to Barnabas Burns, Dec. 17, 1863; (Galena) *Weekly Northwestern Gazette*, Jan. 26, 1864; P. J. Staudenraus, ed., *Mr. Lincoln's Washington: Selections from the Writings of Noah Brooks* . . . (New York, 1967), pp. 288–89. A lithographic copy of this portrait is in the Print Div., DLC. For the other portrait, which Jones retained and later donated to the Chicago Public Library, see Chicago *Times-Herald*, April 1, 1900.

4. Two lines missing.

5. Two lines missing, although an attached note of Mrs. Frederick Dent Grant suggests that USG referred at this point to Brig. Gen. William F. Smith. ALS, USG 3.

To Maj. Gen. Henry W. Halleck

Chattanooga Tenn
Nov 18/63 9 P M

Maj Genl H W Halleck
Genl in Chief

Dispatches from Burnside received to ten (10) P M yesterday Troops had got back to Knoxville. Shermans advance reached Lookout Valley today movement will progress, threaten enemys left flank until forces can be got up and thrown across the river to attack their right flank and Missionary Ridge—A battle or a falling back of enemy is inevetable by Saturday at farthest—Burnside speaks hopefully

U S Grant
Maj Genl

Telegram received, DNA, RG 107, Telegrams Collected (Bound); copies, *ibid.*, Telegrams Received in Cipher; *ibid.*, RG 393, Military Div. of the Miss., Hd. Qrs. Correspondence; DLC-USG, V, 40, 94. *O.R.*, I, xxxi, part 3, 181. On Nov. 17, 1863, 10:00 P.M., Maj. Gen. Ambrose E. Burnside, Knoxville, telegraphed to President Abraham Lincoln and to USG. "Since I reported to you at 1 o. c. this morning our troops ~~trains & b~~ batteries & trains have all arrived. The enemy did not press us during the night—The troops ~~have been~~ were placed in position, intrenchments thrown up where none existed & every exertion made to render the position secure—The enemy have made no serious demonstrations during the day—Our cavalry on the Kingston road have been skirmishing all the afternoon & have been pressed slowly back—and the enemy's pickets are now about two miles from town—His advance today has not been vigorous & he is evidently holding back for the arrival of his artillery ~~or rein~~ or the developement of some flank movement—If he should assault our position here I think we can give a good account of ourselves—They still have a force on the other side of the river with pickets in sight of ours but have made no demonstrations to day." ALS (telegram sent), DNA, RG 94, Generals' Papers and Books, Burnside; telegram received, *ibid.*, War Records Office, Dept. of the Ohio. *O.R.*, I, xxxi, part 1, 268.

To Maj. Gen. William T. Sherman

Head Quarters, Mil. Div. of the Miss.
Chattanooga Ten. Nov. 18th 1863.
MAJ. GEN. W. T. SHERMAN,
COMD.G DEPT. & ARMY OF THE TEN.
GENERAL,

Enclosed herewith I send you copy of instructions to Maj. Gen. Thomas.[1] You having been over the ground, in person, and having heard the whole matter discussed,[2] further instructions will not be necessary for you.

It is particularly desirable that a force should be got through to the rail-road between Cleveland and Dalton and Longstreet thus cut off from communication with the South, but being confronted by a large force here, strongly located, it is not easy to tell how this is to be effected until the result of our first effort is known. I will add however what is not shown in my instructions to Gen. Thomas that one Brigade of Cavalry has been ordered here which, if it arrives in time, will be thrown across the Tennessee, above Chickamauga, and may be able to make the trip to Cleveland or thereabouts.[3]

I am Gen. Very respectfully
your obt. svt.
U. S. GRANT
Maj. Gen. Comd.g

ALS, DLC-William T. Sherman. *O.R.*, I, xxxi, part 2, 32.

1. See following letter.
2. See telegram to Maj. Gen. William T. Sherman, Nov. 13, 1863.
3. Between Nov. 24 and 27, 1863, Col. Eli Long, 4th Ohio Cav., commanding 2nd Brigade, 2nd Cav. Div., Army of the Cumberland, under orders from Maj. Gen. George H. Thomas, crossed the Tennessee River and South Chickamauga Creek and, damaging or destroying track, lines, and military stores, advanced to Tyner's Station, Cleveland, and Charleston, Tenn., before turning back. *O.R.*, I, xxxi, part 2, 74–75, 97, 561.
On Nov. 11, USG had endorsed a letter of Oct. 30 from Brig. Gen. George Crook, Maysville, Ala., to Secretary of War Edwin M. Stanton urging the promotion of Long. "Recommended and respectfully forwarded to Hd Qrs. of the Army Washington D. C." AES, DNA, RG 94, ACP, 239L CB 1863. Long was appointed brig. gen. as of Aug. 18, 1864.

To Maj. Gen. George H. Thomas

Head Quarters Mil. Div. of the Miss.
Chattanooga, Ten., November 18th 1863.

Maj. Gen. Geo. H. Thomas
Comdg. Dept. & Army of the Cumberland
General,

All preparations should be made for attacking the enemys position on Missionary Ridge by Saturday morning, at daylight.[1] Not being provided with map giving names of roads, spurs of the Mountain and other places such definite instructions cannot be given as might be desirable. However, the general plan you understand is for Sherman, with the force brought with him, strengthened by a Division from your command[2] to effect a crossing of the Tennessee River just below the mouth of Chicamauga; his crossing to be protected by Artillery from the hights on the north bank of the river, (to be located by your Chief of Artillery) and to carry the hights from the northern extremity to about the rail-road tunnel before the enemy can concentrate a force against him

You will co-operate with Sherman. The troops in Chattanooga Valley should be well concentrated on your left flank,[3] leaving only the necessary force to defend fortifications on the right & center and a movable column, of one Division, in readiness to move wherever ordered. This Division should show itself as threateningly as possible, on the most practicable line for making an attack up the Valley. Your effort ~~will~~ then will be to form a junction with Sherman, making your advance well towards the North end of Missionary ridge, and moving as near simultaneously with him as possible. The junction once formed, and the ridge carried, communications will be at once established between the two Armies by roads on the south bank of the river. Further movements will then depend on those of the enemy.

Lookout Valley I think will be easily held by Geary's[4] Division and what troops you may still have there belonging to the old Army of the Cumberland. Howards Corps can then be held in readiness to act either with you at Chattanooga or with Sherman. It should be marched on friday night to a position on the north side of the river, not lower down than the first pontoon bridge and there held in readiness for such orders as may become necessary. All the troops will be provided with two days cooked rations in their haversacks and one hundred rounds of ammunition on the person of each Infantry soldier. Special care should be taken by all officers to see that ammunition is not wasted or unnecessarily fired away. You will call on the Engineering Dept. for such preparations as you may deem necessary for crossing your Infantry and Artillery over Citico Creek.[5]

> I am Gen. Very respectfully
> Your obt. svt.
> U. S. GRANT
> Maj. Gen. U. S. A. Commdg.

Copies (2), DLC-William T. Sherman; DLC-USG, V, 34, 35; DNA, RG 94, War Records Office, Union Battle Reports; *ibid.*, 20th Army Corps; *ibid.*, RG 393, Military Div. of the Miss., Letters Sent; Tulane University, New Orleans, La.; Oliver O. Howard Papers, MeB. *O.R.*, I, xxxi, part 2, 31. See *ibid.*, p. 60.

1. Nov. 21, 1863.
2. Brig. Gen. Jefferson C. Davis's 2nd Div., 14th Army Corps.
3. Under Maj. Gen. Gordon Granger, 4th Army Corps.
4. John W. Geary, born in Pa. in 1819, attended Jefferson College, studied civil engineering and law, and eventually passed the bar. He attained the rank

of col. during the Mexican War, was elected the first mayor of San Francisco in 1850, and was territorial governor of Kan. (1856–57). Appointed col., 28th Pa., as of June 28, 1861, he was promoted to brig. gen. as of April 25, 1862.

5. Citico Creek enters the Tennessee River about one mile east of Chattanooga.

To Col. John Riggin, Jr.

[Chattanooga, Tenn., Nov. 18, 1863]

... When I arrived here everything was in a desperate situation. The Army was being supplied with wagons over a desperately bad mountain road seventy miles in length. Teams could not get through with more than six hundred pounds each and but very few mules even lived to make the second trip. Artillery horses were entirely gone or so reduced that all left could not more than move one piece to each battery. The enemy staring us in the face, with their pickets and ours not one hundred yards apart, have been able to send Longstreet off, before my eyes, and I have not been able to move a foot to stop his advance up the Tennessee Valley against Burnside.

Things have changed now however. We have got the river below Lookout Mountain and steamer to bring up supplies from the railroad terminus to within eight miles of Chattanooga. If Burnside can hold out a few days longer, we will be all right. The wires are cut between Louisville and him, so that I have not heard from him since yesterday morning.

There will be a big fight here, of general skeedadle of the enemy before you receive this. I am tired of the proximity of the enemy and do not intend to stand it if it can be helped. . . . And one more good whiping will virtually end the war. Unfortunately I am not in a condition to give them that, . . .

U. S. GRANT

Incomplete in Doris H. Hamilton, "Letters of U. S. Grant," *Hobbies—The Magazine for Collectors*, 62, 2 (April, 1957), 106; Anderson Auction Co., Sale No. 1115, Dec. 11, 1914. See letter to Col. John Riggin, Jr., Oct. 7, 1863.

To Brig. Gen. Montgomery C. Meigs

Chattanooga November 19th 1863

GENERAL M. C. MEIGS Q. M. G.

BRIDGEPORT ALA

General Dodge telegraphs that no work is being done on Columbia and Decatur road. No directions have been given to the Pioneers at Columbia. If Mr Anderson will send a man to direct the work there is 8000 troops South of Columbia that can be set to work at once. This work should not be delayed a moment—

U. S GRANT

Major General

Telegram, copies, DLC-USG, V, 34, 35; DNA, RG 393, Military Div. of the Miss., Letters Sent. On Nov. 19, 1863, Maj. Gen. William T. Sherman, Bridgeport, Ala., had telegraphed to USG. "Gen'l Dodge reports no work in progress on the road between him and Nashville and says the Pioneer Corps at Columbia had no orders. Had you not better send some officer to Nashville to pass along the lines and put every body to work on the smaller bridges, leaving the large ones to be finished by Anderson or give Dodges command of every thing between Nashville & Decatur" Copies, *ibid.*, Telegrams Received; *ibid.*, Dept. of the Tenn., Telegrams Sent. *O.R.*, I, xxxi, part 3, 195. See Brig. Gen. Grenville M. Dodge, Pulaski, Tenn., to Sherman, Nov. 16, DNA, RG 393, Dept. of the Tenn., Telegrams Received. Dated Nov. 15 in *O.R.*, I, xxxi, part 3, 161–62. On Nov. 19, USG telegraphed to Sherman. "The trestle work for the road is being made in the North and will be brought out and put up rapidly. I will direct Mr Anderson to commence operations as soon as possible." Copies, DLC-USG, V, 34, 35; DNA, RG 393, Military Div. of the Miss., Letters Sent.

On Nov. 21, USG telegraphed to John B. Anderson. "Drop the whole subject of Nashville and Decatur Railroad. The single road from Nashville to Stevenson will require the entire attention of one person. I will put other parties on the other road to build it" Copies, *ibid. O.R.*, I, xxxi, part 3, 219. On Nov. 22, Anderson, Nashville, telegraphed to USG. "Your despatch is received. L. B. Boomer has contracted to build the Bridges to Decatur Junction and expects to build the work. He is the only builder who could procure the timber   shall I notify him that you will not approve the contract with him   do you propose to make a seperate organization to work the Nashville & Decatur R. R. and am I to understand your despatch as relieving me in so far from the duty to which I was appointed by the War Dept. under date Oct. 19th 1863—" Copy, DNA, RG 393, Military Div. of the Miss., Telegrams Received. *O.R.*, I, xxxi, part 3, 230. On Nov. 23, USG telegraphed to Anderson. "I mean by my dispatch that I think the Nashville & Stevenson road in its present condition is enough for one man to attend and I shall put some one else, whose exclusive duty it will be to look after the construction of the other road. Already several weeks of valuable time has been lost. I presume we will want Boomer to make the bridges you contracted for, but in the mean time I want trestles built and the road running" Copies, DLC-USG, V, 34, 35; DNA, RG 393, Military Div. of the Miss., Letters Sent. *O.R.*, I, xxxi, part 3, 237. On Nov. 21, 9:30 A.M., Asst. Secretary of War Charles A. Dana, Chattanooga, telegraphed to Secretary of War Edwin M. Stanton regarding work on the Nashville and Decatur Railroad. "Genl. Grant has relieved Anderson from all connection with that road, on the ground, that having ordered him three weeks ago to get it done soon as possible, he should have got further on with the work, than now to refer the question of Contracts to him. Genl. Dodge is ordered to proceed with all dispatch, opening the road, and Col. Pride formerly serving with Genl. Grant on west Tennessee, Railroads, and before Vicksburg, has been sent for to take direction of the work. . . ." Telegram received, DLC-Edwin M. Stanton. *O.R.*, I, xxxi, part 2, 63; see *ibid.*, p. 61. George G. Pride was not retained as railroad superintendent. See Special Orders No. 29, Dec. 9, copy, DLC-USG, V, 38; letter to Julia Dent Grant, Nov. 30, 1863.

On Nov. 19, Stanton telegraphed to USG. "The power and authority conferred on J B Anderson as ~~Special~~ rail road Superintendent is Subject to your control. Although appointed directly by the Department he is Subordinate to you and the Commander of the Military Department the appointment being only designed to aid in the management of the road and transportation. ~~If On~~ To any failure or neglect of duty on his part you will therefore apply such remedy as you deem proper. I have no reason to doubt that he is doing every thing in his power or in the power of any to improve and stock the road but if you think differently you and also the Quarter Master General are authorized to make such changes as you or he may deem proper for the Service." Telegram received, DNA, RG 107, Telegrams Collected (Bound); copies, *ibid.*, RG 393, Military Div. of the Miss., Hd. Qrs. Correspondence; DLC-USG, V, 40, 94. For a similar telegram on the same day from Stanton to Brig. Gen. Montgomery C. Meigs, see *O.R.*, I, xxxi, part 3, 190–91.

On Nov. 21, USG telegraphed to Dodge. "Put all the force you can at work repairing rail road. Impress negroes for all the work you want from them. I will send a Superintendent as soon as I can" Copies, DLC-USG, V, 34, 35; DNA, RG 393, Military Div. of the Miss., Letters Sent. *O.R.*, I, xxxi, part 3, 220. On Nov. 23, USG sent to Dodge via Brig. Gen. George Crook, Maysville, Ala., an identical telegram, adding a final phrase regarding the railroad superintendent he would send: "and until one arrives it will be under your superintendence." Copies, DLC-USG, V, 34, 35; DNA, RG 393, Military Div. of the Miss., Letters Sent. On the same day, Dodge telegraphed to USG. "I have heavy details at work on all bridges from Elk River to Columbia and I am using Every tool in the Country between Columbia & end of R. R. Duck River is very important work & nine other bridges out a pioneer corps is stationed at Smiths station but have no orders & last I heard from them were doing nothing I have tried to find some one who had authority to set them to work They should be at work on bridges up to and include Duck River I will have my work done before that is and then move south & build to Decatur I hold the road to that point now" Telegram received, *ibid.*, RG 94, War Records Office, Military Div. of the Miss.; copy, *ibid.*, RG 393, Military Div. of the Miss., Telegrams Received. Dated Nov. 21 in *O.R.*, I, xxxi, part 3, 220. On Nov. 23, Capt. George K. Leet endorsed this telegram. "Respectfully referred to Maj. Genl.

G. H. Thomas Comd'g Dept. of the Cumberland who will direct the Pioneer Corps within mentioned and any other troops within reach of Genl. Dodge's orders to report to him to work on the road under his direction." ADf (incomplete), DNA, RG 94, War Records Office, Military Div. of the Miss.; copies, *ibid.*, RG 393, Military Div. of the Miss., Endorsements; DLC-USG, V, 39. On Nov. 26, Dodge telegraphed to Brig. Gen. John A. Rawlins. "Gen Thomas has ordered away the Pioneer Corp, that is repairing the Road North of Columbia. As I judge from Gen Shermans and Gen Grants dispatches to me, they consider workmen are on that end of line. I report the fact, that there may be no misunderstanding of my former dispatches. I send to you as Gen'l Sherman is away." Copy, DNA, RG 393, 16th Army Corps, Left Wing, Telegrams Sent. On Dec. 9, Dodge telegraphed to USG. "In pursuance of your instructions I pressed all the negroes in this country and put them to work on bridges cutting wood for R R ballasting up R R &C so as to have it not only ready to run but also to have material to run it with which it is now entirely destitute of   The recruiting officers for colored troops claim the right to open recruiting offices along my line. If this is done I lose my negroes which at this time would be very detrimental to the service. so far I have refused to allow them to recruit. They have now recvd positive orders from the Comd'r of colored troops for Tennessee to come here [and] recruit—I dont want any [t]rouble with them & have assured them that when we were through with the negroes I would see that they go into the service—Unless you order otherwise I shall continue to refuse to allow them to recruit along my line—Please advise me" Telegram received, *ibid.*, RG 94, War Records Office, Military Div. of the Miss.; copies, *ibid.*, RG 393, 16th Army Corps, Left Wing, Telegrams Sent; *ibid.*, Military Div. of the Miss., Telegrams Received. *O.R.*, I, xxxi, part 3, 366–67. On the same day, USG telegraphed to Dodge. "Your action in prohibiting the recruiting of Negroes from those you have pressed into service for repairing railroad and providing fuel for trains is approved. Put in arrest any one who disobeys your order" Copies, DLC-USG, V, 34, 35; DNA, RG 393, Military Div. of the Miss., Letters Sent. *O.R.*, I, xxxi, part 3, 367. See telegram to Brig. Gen. Grenville M. Dodge, Dec. 2, 1863; *Memoirs*, II, 46–48.

To Maj. Gen. Stephen A. Hurlbut

By Telegraph from Chattanooga [*Nov.*] 19 *1863*
To MAJ GENL HURLBUT
MEMPHIS

If you have given up a portion of the road to Corinth cannot a large portion of the rolling stock be shipped to Nashville   Send all you can and as rapidly as possible   if not indespensible to the Service to return [*retain*] it to [*send*] the rolling stock used from Columbus and Paducah. It is almost impossible to get sufficient to supply this army. I have directed Genl Allen to send you Wagons and Harness and what mules he can   it is becoming almost impossible to supply animals and transpotation as fast as called for.

U. S. GRANT

Maj Genl

Telegram received, DNA, RG 393, 16th Army Corps, Letters Received; copies, *ibid.*, Military Div. of the Miss., Letters Sent; DLC-USG, V, 34, 35. *O.R.*, I, xxxi, part 3, 196. On Nov. 17, 1863, Maj. Gen. Stephen A. Hurlbut telegraphed to USG. "All my transportation was given to Sherman to take him through   I want three hundred wagons and harness   I may get mules from the Country. Tuttles Division is here unfit for the field & not over Thirty three hundred men   I expect a Brigade from Arkansas daily, & shall commence the offensive when they come. There are about four thousand Rebels on the Tallahatchie and about Twenty five hundred in West Tennessee" Telegram received, DNA, RG 94, War Records Office, Military Div. of the Miss.; copies, *ibid.*, RG 393, 16th Army Corps, Letters Sent; (misdated Dec. 17) *ibid.*, Military Div. of the Miss., Telegrams Received. Dated Nov. 17 in *O.R.*, I, xxxi, part 3, 179. On Nov. 19, Brig. Gen. Robert Allen, Louisville, telegraphed to USG. "The following Dispatch from Genl Hurlbut comes round from St Louis. I turned over from this Corps a full transportation train to Genl Sherman leaving us helpless. we must have the wagons & Harness & ought to have the mules. I am ordered to haul from Hamburg to Corinth & this will require two Hundred & fifty teams & I have only ninety. this comes in a Despatch to Col Meyers. I ordered fifty wagons with Harness to be sent as you directed   shall I send more   wagons are getting scare." Telegram received, DNA, RG 94, War Records Office, Dept. of the Tenn.; copies, *ibid.*, Military Div. of the Miss.; *ibid.*, RG 393, Military Div. of the Miss., Telegrams Received. *O.R.*, I, xxxi, part 3, 196. See telegram to Maj. Gen. Stephen A. Hurlbut, Nov. 12, 1863, note 1; telegram to Brig. Gen. Robert Allen, Nov. 19, 1863.

On Nov. 15, USG telegraphed to Hurlbut and to Maj. Gen. James B. McPherson, Vicksburg. "From all that can be derived from the statements of deserters and Scouts all of Johnsons forces are being sent from Mississippi here to reinforce Bragg. a large number have already arrived." Telegram received, DNA, RG 393, 16th Army Corps, Letters Received; copies, *ibid.*, Military Div. of the Miss., Letters Sent; DLC-USG, V, 34, 35. *O.R.*, I, xxxi, part 3, 158.

To Maj. Gen. William T. Sherman

———

Chattanooga November 19th '63

MAJOR GENERAL W. T. SHERMAN

BRIDGEPORT ALA

   The Chief Engineer reports that he will require 750 oarsmen to carry out the programe of effecting the crossing of the river.

Of this number he has received all he can from Genl Thomas command 375: and will require the balance from your forces. As these men and the Brigade who are to fill its boats, have to march about five miles higher up the river than the balance of the command, I would suggest that the detail be made to night, and they placed in advance for the remainder of the march. The Commanding Officer of this Detatchment can be instructed to report to General W F Smith for a guide to conduct his march from Brown's Ferry to their place of embarkation.

U S GRANT
Major General

Telegram, copies, DLC-USG, V, 34, 35; DNA, RG 393, Military Div. of the Miss., Letters Sent. *O.R.*, I, xxxi, part 2, 37. See letter to Maj. Gen. William T. Sherman, Nov. 24, 1863.

To Brig. Gen. Robert Allen

Chattanooga November 19th 1863

BRIG GENL ROBT ALLEN CHF Q M
LOUISVILLE KY

Under the circumstances send the wagons and harness to Hurlbut, and a portion of the mules, if you can.[1] By all means stop work at the machine shops for Elletts rams. and set their whole force at work for engines on our roads.[2]

If Hurlbut gives up a portion of the road from Memphis to Corinth, a number of cars and locomotives can be brought there and also all used between Columbus, Union City and Paducah can be brought. I will telegraph Hurlbut at once to send all he can.[3]

U S GRANT
Major General.

Telegram, copies, DLC-USG, V, 34, 35; DNA, RG 393, Military Div. of the Miss., Letters Sent. *O.R.*, I, xxxi, part 3, 195.

1. See telegram to Brig. Gen. Robert Allen, Nov. 12, 1863.
2. On Nov. 19 and 20, 1863, Brig. Gen. Robert Allen telegraphed to USG.

"The machine shops at New Albany are employed in Building Enjines for some of Genl Ellett's Rams. to facilitate the Building of the Enjines required by Genl Meigs cannot the works on thise rams be suspended. I imagine when completed they will not be wanted." "You do not understand me   I mean to ask if you would not order the suspension of the buildings of machinery for Ellets Rams If we found it necessary to employ the new albany foundries in assisting in building engines for steamboats to be constructed at Bridgeport" Telegrams received, DNA, RG 94, War Records Office, Military Div. of the Miss.; copies, *ibid.*, RG 393, Military Div. of the Miss., Telegrams Received. *O.R.*, I, xxxi, part 3, 195, 200. On Nov. 20, USG telegraphed to Allen. "Certainly I will order the discontinuance of work at the New Albany Founderies for Ellets rams, whenever you require them to work on other machinery. You are authorized to use this dispatch for that purpose if it is necessary to have these Foundries before the mail can carry the written order." Copies, DLC-USG, V, 34, 35; DNA, RG 393, Military Div. of the Miss., Letters Sent. *O.R.*, I, xxxi, part 3, 200.

3. See telegram to Maj. Gen. Stephen A. Hurlbut, Nov. 19, 1863.

To Maj. Gen. James B. McPherson

Chattanooga Ten.
Nov. 20th 1863,

DEAR GENERAL,

This will be handed to you by Mr. A. Burwell, formerly a resident of Vicksburg, but, since early in the rebellion, of St. Louis, Mo. Mr. Burwell is a man of the most undoubted loyalty and also a man of standing and influance. I was very glad to receive a letter from him thisevening stating that he purposed returning to Vicksburg to remain and practice his profession, the law.

Mr. Burwell will exert an influance in restoring order in the state of Miss. and will, beyond doubt, do all in his power to mould the public mind in that state to desire a speedy restoration of the Union.[1]

I bespeak for Mr. B. all the privileges extended to the most loyal citizens.

Yours Truly
U. S. GRANT
Maj. Gen

To MAJ. GEN. J. B. McPHERSON,
COMD.G 17TH ARMY CORPS.

ALS, DLC-Caleb Cushing. On Dec. 30, 1863, Armistead Burwell, Vicksburg, wrote to USG thanking him for the letter of introduction. "I have been here since the 16th instant but so far have been unable to procure an Office. Even if I did, I am doubtful whether I could pay the rent as there seems to be little or no business by which I can realise any thing. My own affairs, my claims for property and debts, I am informed must be postponed until the close of the war, or referred for adjudication to the court of claims or to Congress. . . . I claim the sum of $12.298 for the 'Castle' which has been totally destroyed and the grounds appropriated to a fort: a lot of sugar, and other articles found in the store of Cobb Manlove & Co and in military possession of about the value of $16.000 as near as I can estimate: . . . In the winter & spring of 1860-1, I was compelled to sell property: to go away: the money was left with Cobb Manlove & Co, who had been my Merchants & Bankers, to be remitted to me. Events took such a turn that they could not do so: they got sugar &c, and kept it for me. . . . The sugar is not captured property within Mr Chase's definition. It was not seised or taken from hostile possession by the military forces of U. S. It was in a warehouse and subject to my rights. There is no pretence of any fraud or evasion. The treason of one partner cannot operate on all the others and through them on an innocent third person. I appeal to you, as *able* & *willing* to do what is right & equitable, to relieve me. . . ." ALS, DNA, RG 393, Military Div. of the Miss., Letters Received. On Jan. 15, 1864, Lt. Col. Cyrus B. Comstock, Nashville, wrote to Maj. Gen. William T. Sherman. "Gen Grant desires me to enclose the accompanying letter from Mr Burwell, and to state that he is one of our most undoubtedly loyal men, forced early in the war to flee from Mississippi. He also requests that the sugar referred to, seized for the use of our army, may if possible be paid for by your Cheif Commissary, and that you will give him any assistance in your power toward getting possession of his other property, or compensation therefor." ALS, *ibid.*, RG 109, Union Provost Marshals' File of Papers Relating to Two or More Civilians.

On Jan. 4, Burwell, New Orleans, again wrote to USG regarding his claim. ALS, *ibid.*, Union Provost Marshals' File of Papers Relating to Individual Civilians. On Jan. 23, Lt. Col. Theodore S. Bowers endorsed this letter to Maj. Gen. James B. McPherson. "There is no record of this transaction or papers connected with it, at these Headquarters" AES, *ibid.* On Jan. 14, Lt. Col. John C. Cox, commissary, 17th Army Corps, wrote to USG explaining his disposition of several lots of sugar, including that claimed by Burwell. LS, *ibid.*, RG 393, Military Div. of the Miss., Letters Received. On Jan. 31, McPherson, Vicksburg, wrote to USG. "I have the honor to forward herewith the report of Lt. Col: J. C. Cox Chf. Commissary 17th Army Corps, in relation to sugar taken possession of by the U. S. authorities, after the surrender of this place, with the action in each case—You will also find letters of *Mr. Burwell* in relations to claims of his against certain parties, *viz Messrs Cobb, Manlove & Co* and Mr. Latham— I have not considered it within my jurisdiction to order the transfer of property to him to satisfy his *claims*, leaving these matters for a competent court to decide —I have however given him every facility in my power to take possession of any property which belonged to him, and which came into our hands on the surrender of this place—" ALS, *ibid.*, RG 109, Union Provost Marshals' File of Papers Relating to Two or More Civilians. On Feb. 17, S. M. Breckenridge, St. Louis, wrote to USG in support of Burwell's claim. ALS, USG 3.

In 1879, payment was made on this claim. *HRC*, 47-1-728; 50-1-635; *SRC*,

48-1-114; Frank W. Klingberg, *The Southern Claims Commission* (Berkeley and Los Angeles, 1955), pp. 136–37. For other claims by Burwell or his estate, see *HED*, 44-1-189, p. 32; *HRC*, 43-2-287; *SRC*, 45-3-849; 48-1-115; 51-1-932. In the last report, the committee noted among the papers supporting the claim a copy of a letter of April 19, 1871, of USG "certifying to the loyalty of Mr. Burwell." *Ibid.*

1. On Aug. 28 and Oct. 10, 1863, Burwell wrote to President Abraham Lincoln regarding the political situation in Miss. and Mo. ALS, DLC-Robert T. Lincoln.

To Maj. Gen. William T. Sherman

Head Quarters, Mil. Div. of the Miss.
Chattanooga Ten. Nov. 20th 1863.

MAJ. GEN. W. T. SHERMAN,
COMD.G DEPT. & ARMY OF THE TN.
GEN.

To-morrow morning[1] is the time I had first set for your attack. I see now it cannot possibly be made then, but can you not get up for the following morning? Order Ewing down immediately fixing the time for his starting so that the roads and bridge will be full all the time. I see no necessity for him moving by a circuitous route, but you can bring him as you deem proper reflecting that time is of vast importance to us now that the enemy are undeceived as to our move up to Trenton.[2]

Every effort must be made to get up in time to attack on Sunday morning.

Very respectfully
U. S. GRANT
Maj. Gen. Com

ALS, PHi. *O.R.*, I, xxxi, part 2, 37. On Thursday, Nov. 19, 1863, Maj. Gen. William T. Sherman, Bridgeport, Ala., had telegraphed to USG. "Genl Ewing arrived at Trenton yesterday at 10 A. M. John E. Smiths Div. is all on the march and the two other Divisions and the two other Divisions are crossing the river now. I start myself to day. It is rather slow work crossing the Bridge here but we worked almost all night. I will be at Shell. Mound or Whitesides tonight & about Gen'l. Hookers tomorrow. I will keep the column closed up & reach the camp opposite Chattanooga soon as possible—" Copies, DNA, RG 393, Dept.

of the Tenn., Telegrams Sent; *ibid.*, Military Div. of the Miss., Telegrams Received. *O.R.*, I, xxxi, part 2, 37.

   1. See letter to Maj. Gen. George H. Thomas, Nov. 18, 1863.
   2. Brig. Gen. Hugh Ewing's 4th Div., 15th Army Corps, had been sent to Trenton, Ga., to threaten Gen. Braxton Bragg's left flank from the south. *O.R.*, I, xxxi, part 2, 583–87, 630–31.

To Maj. Gen. George H. Thomas

Head Quarters, Mil. Div. of the Miss.
Chattanooga Ten. Nov. 20th 1863.

MAJ. GEN. G. H. THOMAS,
COMD.G DEPT. & ARMY OF THE CUMBERLAND,
GENERAL,

On reflection[1] I think it would be better to let Howard start as soon as possible, making his march and crossing of the river by daylight. Our forces will be seen by the enemy coming out of Lookout Valley and seeing this force cross into Chattanooga will have a tendency to conceal from them Sherman's movement.[2]

If it is not practicable to make this change now without interfering too much with uses it was previously intended to put the bridge to I do not insist on the change being made.

I am General, very respectfully
your obt. svt.
U. S. GRANT
Maj. Gen. Com

ALS, deCoppet Collection, NjP. *O.R.*, I, xxxi, part 2, 38. On Nov. 20, 1863, Maj. Gen. George H. Thomas wrote to USG. "Your letter of this morning suggesting that General Howard pass across the river in day light was hand-to me at Fort Wook [*Wood*], & I have taken the earliest oportunity to reply after returning to my quarters. I did not give the order to Genl Howard, because by an arrangement with Genl Smith Chief Engn. he is to have the exclusive use of the bridge all afternoon to enable him to pass across the river the *balks* & cheess [*chesses*] for the pontoon bridge to be thrown across the river above." AL (signature clipped), DNA, RG 94, War Records Office, Union Battle Reports. *O.R.*, I, xxxi, part 2, 38.

   1. See letter to Maj. Gen. George H. Thomas, Nov. 18, 1863.
   2. See *O.R.*, I, xxxi, part 2, 62.

To Maj. Gen. George H. Thomas

Chattanooga Ten.
November 20th/63

MAJ. GEN. THOMAS
COMD.G DEPT. OF THE CUMBD
GEN.

A note just received from Gen. Sherman giving present position of his forces[1] showes an entire impossibility for him to get all his troops up, and over, Brown's Ferry before to-morrow night. His attack can not be made therefore before Sunday morning,[2] if then. I have written to him to use all disppatch to be ready by that time. You can make your arrangements for this delay.

You can exercise your own judgement about bringing Howard across to-night, as previously directed.[3] The only advantage in it will be in getting continuous use out of the bridges.

Very respectfully
U. S. GRANT
Maj. Gen.

ALS, deCoppet Collection, NjP. *O.R.*, I, xxxi, part 2, 38. For an account of activities at USG's hd. qrs. on Nov. 20, 1863, see William Wrenshall Smith, "Holocaust Holiday . . ." *Civil War Times Illustrated*, XVIII, 6 (Oct., 1979), 32–33.

1. See letter to Maj. Gen. William T. Sherman, Nov. 20, 1863.
2. Nov. 22.
3. See preceding letter.

To Brig. Gen. Orlando B. Willcox

Chattanooga November 20th 1863

BRIG GENL O. B. WILCOX
BEANS STATION[1] E. TENNESSEE

If you can communicate with General Burnside, say to him that our attack on Bragg will commence in the morning   If successful, such a move will be made as, I think, will relieve East

Tennessee, if he can hold out.[2] Longstreet passing through our lines to Kentucky, need not cause alarm. He would find the country so bare that he would lose his transportation and Artillery before reaching Kentucky and would meet such a force before he got through, that he could not return.

U S GRANT

Major General

Telegram, copies, DLC-USG, V, 34, 35; DNA, RG 393, Military Div. of the Miss., Letters Sent. *O.R.*, I, xxxi, part 3, 207. On Nov. 18, 1863, Maj. Gen. Ambrose E. Burnside, Knoxville, telegraphed to President Abraham Lincoln and to USG. "Heavy skirmishing commenced about ten o. c. & continued all day, principally on the Kingston road. We have lost but little ground perhaps a quarter of a mile. Our troops are all within our fortifications—with skirmishers to the front. We have every hope of repelling an assault if one be made—There is a bare chance that ~~this~~ Longstreet may be simply covering a movement into Kentucky His feeble advance would seem to indicate something of that kind. No demonstrations by the Enemy across the river" ALS (telegram sent), DNA, RG 94, Generals' Papers and Books, Burnside; telegram received, *ibid.*, War Records Office, Military Div. of the Miss. *O.R.*, I, xxxi, part 3, 182. See telegram to Maj. Gen. Henry W. Halleck, Nov. 18, 1863.

Orlando B. Willcox of Mich., USMA 1847, served in the war with Mexico and on frontier and garrison duty before resigning in 1857 to practice law in Detroit. Commissioned col., 1st Mich., as of May 24, 1861, he was wounded at the first battle of Bull Run, and captured and imprisoned for over a year. Appointed brig. gen. as of July 21, he held commands in east Tenn. starting Sept. 17, 1863. On Nov. 21, Willcox, Cumberland Gap, telegraphed to USG. "Interpretation of Cipher Despatch of yesterday just rec'd. telegraph your success today & if advisable to march from here to Knoxville, I will try it & endeavor to subsist on the Country. it would be a desperate attempt, as the roads are bad & the country pretty much fed out along the route. the firing last heard by my advanced Scout was about five miles below Knoxville. The rebels may be trying to Draw Burnside out of his works. will get your message to Him if possible." Telegram received, DNA, RG 94, War Records Office, Dept. of the Tenn.; copy, *ibid.*, RG 393, Military Div. of the Miss., Telegrams Received. *O.R.*, I, xxxi, part 3, 214–15. See first telegram to Maj. Gen. Henry W. Halleck, Nov. 23, 1863.

On Nov. 20, Willcox, Bean's Station, Tenn., telegraphed to USG. "I was instructed by Gen'l. Burnside that the security of the retreat of my forces to Cumberland Gap was the first object in case my communication by telegraph was cut off from him. On the evening of the 17th the telegraph communication was was stopped I was then at Bulls Gap the time of leaving there was left to my own judgement. I made a demonstration on Rogersville & sent scouting parties on Greenville Strapps Ferry and and Babbs Mill roads secured the fords below Rogersville with my Cavalry and moved my Infy. to Russellville at the same time ordered scouts and telegraph line repairers from Morristown toward Knoxville. I waited at Russellville until noon of 18th. Reports are current that a heavy force of rebel Cavalry crossed at Strawberry Plains. I then determined to concentrate my force near this point. I ordered my troops to abandon Morristown but the telegraph wires were left connected at Morristown from Knoxville though still cut off   on arriving here I found the line had been cut six miles from Knoxville and was repaired. Sent a force under Col. Davis to Morristown with an operator and established communication with Cumberland Gap and Knoxville. Genl. Burnside instructed me that when it was important to Gauard The Rogersville road it was more important to secure Cumberland Gap and this has determined my prisent move Tazwell. I hope it will meet with your approval." Copy, DNA, RG 393, Military Div. of the Miss., Telegrams Received. Printed as addressed to Maj. Gen. Henry W. Halleck in *O.R.*, I, xxxi, part 3, 206. See Burnside to Willcox, Nov. 17, *ibid.*, p. 177. On Nov. 20, USG telegraphed to Willcox. "If you receive no further instructions from General Burnside, follow those he has given you. Retreat should not be allowed cut off, but can you not concentrate your forces and raise the seige at Knoxville? This I know would close the route to Cumberland Gap for us, and would probably not compensate unless entirely successful in expelling Longstreet." Copies, DLC-USG, V, 34, 35; DNA, RG 393, Military Div. of the Miss., Letters Sent. *O.R.*, I, xxxi, part 3, 207. On Nov. 21, 5:00 P.M., Willcox, Cumberland Gap, telegraphed to USG. "Your dispatch of yesterday was not recd till 3 30 this p m   I regret I did not receive it at Bean Station   It is now too late & something else must be decided upon Tonight if possible as there is neither a forage nor bread stuff for the command   A heavy rain has fallen 24 hours & broken up the roads" Telegram received, DNA, RG 94, War Records Office, Dept. of the Tenn.; copy, *ibid.*, RG 393, Military Div. of the Miss., Telegrams Received. *O.R.*, I, xxxi, part 3, 214. See telegrams to Brig. Gen. Orlando B. Willcox, Nov. 23, 1863.

1. Bean's Station, Tenn., about twenty-three miles southeast of Cumberland Gap.
2. For delivery of this message, see W. F. Beyer and O. F. Keydel, eds., *Deeds of Valor* (Detroit, 1903), I, 280–81.

To Maj. Gen. Henry W. Halleck

Chattanooga Tenn
2 P M Nov 21st 1863

MAJ GENL H W HALLECK
GENL IN CHIEF

Despatches just received from Genl Wilcox. He was at Tazwell[1] this morning but retreating towards Cumberland Gap   His cavalry attempted to communicate [with] Burnside but could not effect it. A severe fight took place on Nineteenth (19th). Enemy carrying two (2) Intrenchments with heavy loss.[2] Our attack on Enemy's right has not yet commenced   Troops have been moving night and day ever since Sherman appeared at Bridgeport, but narrow and bad roads has made an earlier attack impossible   Shermans advance Division moved [up] to Trenton several days since and advanced their position south each day, keeping up their old camp fires at night and building new ones where they were to give the appearance [of] concentrating a large force in [that] direction. A portion of this [division] ascended the south end [of] Lookout Mountain.³ Owing to heavy [rain] last night it will be impossible [to] attack Bragg before Monday⁴

> U S. GRANT
> Maj Genl Comdg

Telegram received, DNA, RG 107, Telegrams Collected (Bound); copies, *ibid.*, Telegrams Received in Cipher; *ibid.*, RG 393, Military Div. of the Miss., Hd. Qrs. Correspondence; DLC-USG, V, 40, 94. *O.R.*, I, xxxi, part 3, 215.

1. Tazewell, Tenn., about ten miles southeast of Cumberland Gap.
2. On Nov. 20, 1863, 9:00 P.M., Brig. Gen. Orlando B. Willcox, Tazewell, telegraphed to USG. "My cavalry penetrated the enemy's line of pickets around Knoxville this morning. from prisoners & other Sources they learn that the enemy made an assault upon Genl Burnside's position yesterday & carried two entrenchments. the enemy lost heavily in the assault: our men reserving their fire till close up them. our men fought well & still determined. wheeler's whole corps & one Div. of Longstreet's is reported this side of town. my Cavalry have been unable to effect Communication with Genl Burnside. firing has been heard at Knoxville today, but not as heavily as yesterday. the enemy have blockaded the roads approaching from the north." Telegram received, DNA, RG 94, War Records Office, Dept. of the Tenn.; copy, *ibid.*, RG 393, Military Div. of the Miss., Telegrams Received. Earlier on the same day, 8:00 A.M., Willcox, Bean's Station, Tenn., telegraphed to USG. "The following just recd. Hd Qrs 2d Brig Blaine Crossroads 20th. 5 A. M. BRIG GENL WILCOX. A Despatch from the front says the advance scouts is within five miles of Knoxville & within quarter of a mile of rebel pickets   It is reported that the road from this side is blocked   signed T. W. GRAHAM Col Comdg" Telegram received, *ibid.*, RG 94, War Records Office, Dept. of the Tenn.; copy, *ibid.*, RG 393, Military Div. of the Miss., Telegrams Received. On the same day, 9:00 A.M., Willcox telegraphed to USG. "My advance commenc'd moving on Taswell at 12 M last night   if nothing happened Co'l. Foster will arrive there about noon. my movement from this place from Bulls Gap was covered by a Demonstration on Rogersville which seems to have checked the advance of the enemy on that road. I have heard of but two Regts. of the enemy making down on the Rogersville road. Dont know where the main body is   Jones Cavalry forces reported at Bulls Gap yesterday. I dont know how strong   Scouts from Cumberland Gap on Jonesville road have not reported any movement in that direction yet. I think the main body of Jones Cavalry which defeated Gariard at Rogersville on the sixth inst. is moving in a body but cannot tell where. At Knoxville

some shelling reported yesterday afternoon by telegraph operator at 2 P. M. I have no particulars. Morristown telegraph station was abandoned by Co'l. Davis last night at dark. Have sent Co'l. Graham to Blaines Crossroads hoping to open communication with Knoxville by by Cavalry but a force of Rebels is reported on the north side of Knoxville. Cannonading was thought to be heard there at daylight in the direction of Knoxville. Clinch mountain gap is very bad but I hope and the Clinch river ford is bad but I hope my rear Guard will get over Clinch river this evening." Copy, *ibid.* Also on Nov. 20, Willcox, Clinch Mountain, Tenn., telegraphed to USG. "The following just received Blaines Crossroads seven (7) A. M. To BRIG GENL WILCOX—Citizens report that there are from eight thousand to One hundred thousand rebels around Knoxville. Firing ceased at dark last evening. Steady firing and heavy during afternoon rebel pickets all round the town very respectfully. (Signed) T. W. GRAHAM. Later another dispatch states that firing ceased at dark last evening. It is possible that Genl. Burnside is overwhelmed. Co'l. Graham says no firing heard this morning. I do not credit Citizens, as to numbers but it is possible that Bragg is shifting his base of operations but probably you know best my train is nearly through Clinch Gap. no signs of an attack in rear. I shall go forward" Copy, *ibid.* These four telegrams are printed as addressed to Maj. Gen. Henry W. Halleck in *O.R.*, I, xxxi, part 3, 205–7. On Nov. 21, 11:30 A.M., Halleck telegraphed to USG. "Telegrams from Genl Wilcox dated yesterday at Bean's station & Clinch mountain contain rumours that Burnside is surrounded in Knoxville. At any rate we have no communication with him. The President seems very anxious that some immediate movement should be made for his relief. You, however, as fully understand the exigencies of the case, as any one here possibly can. Longstreet's force may be larger than was supposed." ALS (telegram sent), DNA, RG 107, Telegrams Collected (Bound); copies, *ibid.*, RG 393, Military Div. of the Miss., Hd. Qrs. Correspondence; DLC-USG, V, 40, 94. *O.R.*, I, xxxi, part 3, 215–16.

On Nov. 20, Willcox, Tazewell, telegraphed to USG. "I have the honor to report every thing cames through in good order the rebel force that was at Kingsport seems to have been concentrating towards several days towards Cumberland Gap. At Mulberry Gap Sneedsville it is reported that a considerable force was crossing Clinch River at Wallens ford to day. Seven miles about Sneedsvlle that is probably the force that moved down towards Rogersville. A small scouting party under command of Capt Hammond 65th Ind. Mounted charged through the camp of a rebel Regt. Sixth Virginia and scattered it at Mulberry Gap last night killing (3) wounding one capturing our prisoners, some horses and arms We now hold Mulberry Gap with small force there are two rebel regiments at Sneedsville. I expect to move to Cumberland Gap tomorrow." Copy, DNA, RG 393, Military Div. of the Miss., Telegrams Received. *O.R.*, I, xxxi, part 1, 570–71.

On Nov. 19, Col. Robert K. Byrd, Kingston, Tenn., telegraphed to USG. "Two reliable gentlemen have just arrived from Knoxville and inform me that General Burnside has fallen back to Knoxville, and that Longstreet's forces have him almost surrounded. I think it would be well for him to have assistance, if possible. Of course you know his situation better than [I] do, unless communication is cut between you and him, [which] I think very likely, as they have near 10,000 cavalry, besides about 20,000 infantry. A courier of mine corroborates the statement made above. I sent him to Knoxville day before yesterday morning, and he tried to get into Knoxville yesterday morning and he could not succeed

for the rebel cavalry. He states that they were all around Knoxville, and he returned. General Burnside fought Longstreet at Campbell's Station on last
Monday, and it is said he had the best of the fight. On the same night he fell back
to Knoxville, where he was yesterday morning. My courier states that they were
skirmishing all around Knoxville. I fear the general will be starved out, as all
the supplies will be cut off from him. Wheeler's, Dibrell's, and Biffle's commands
went up across Little Tennessee River through Blount County. Two officers
of Wolford's cavalry, who were taken prisoners in Blount County on last Saturday morning, state that they had then in Blount County about from 12,000 to
15,000 mounted men and nine pieces of artillery, and about 20,000 infantry on
the north side of Tennessee, under Longstreet. I thought it was my duty to communicate to you, general, as we are now cut off from General Burnside. The
last order he gave me was to hold this point if I could. He said in five days he
thought all would be well. The time will be out to-morrow at 10 o'clock. We are
guarding the river for 25 miles, and a pontoon bridge and steamboat hull, &c."
Ibid., I, xxxi, part 3, 193–94.
    3. See letter to Maj. Gen. William T. Sherman, Nov. 20, 1863, note 2.
    4. Nov. 23.

To Maj. Gen. Henry W. Halleck

Chattanooga Tenn
8 P M Nov 21/63

MAJ GENL H W HALLECK
GENL IN CHIEF

I ordered an attack here two (2) weeks ago but it was impossible to move Artillery[1]—Now Thomas's Chief of Artillery says
he has to borrow teams from Sherman to move a portion of his
Artillery to where it is to be used   Sherman has used almost super-
human efforts to get up even at this time, and his force is really the
only one I can move   Thomas can take about one (1) gun each
battery, and go as far with his Infantry as his men can carry rations
to keep them and bring them back.

I have never felt such restlessness before as I have at the fixed
and immovable condition of the Army of the Cumberland. Genl
Meigs states, that the loss of animals here will exceed ten thousand.
Those left are scarcely able to carry themselves—

U S GRANT
Maj Genl Comdg

Telegram received, DNA, RG 107, Telegrams Collected (Bound); copies, *ibid.*, Telegrams Received in Cipher; *ibid.*, RG 393, Military Div. of the Miss., Hd. Qrs. Correspondence; DLC-USG, V, 40, 94. *O.R.*, I, xxxi, part 3, 216.

1. See letter to Maj. Gen. George H. Thomas, Nov. 7, 1863; telegram to Maj. Gen. Ambrose E. Burnside, Nov. 8, 1863.

To Maj. Gen. George H. Thomas

———

Chattanooga November 21st 1863

MAJOR GENERAL GEO. H. THOMAS
CHATTANOOGA

I have just received a report of the position of Sherman's forces. The rain last night has thrown them back so much, that it will be impossible for him to get into position for action to morrow morning. He will be up however against all calamities that can be foreseen to commence on Monday morning

U. S GRANT
Major General

Copies, DLC-USG, V, 34, 35; DNA, RG 393, Military Div. of the Miss., Letters Sent. *O.R.*, I, xxxi, part 2, 39. On Nov. 21, 1863, Brig. Gen. John A. Rawlins wrote to Maj. Gen. William T. Sherman. "I am directed by the General Commanding to say that in order to avoid delay, you will have your troops pass your transportation and move up at once, leaving only a sufficient force to guard your trains" Copies, DLC-USG, V, 34, 35; DNA, RG 393, Military Div. of the Miss., Letters Sent. *O.R.*, I, xxxi, part 2, 39. See *ibid.*, pp. 64–66; *Memoirs*, II, 59.

To Brig. Gen. Robert Allen

———

Chattanooga November 21, 63

BRIG GENL ROBT ALLEN CHF Q. M.
LOUISVILLE KY

Wagons and mules going to Hurlbut at the present time, had better go to Memphis. That is where most of them will be wanted. I do not know the exact condition of the road between Memphis and Corinth. Hurlbut telegraphed me that the road had been cut, and in pursuance of previous instructions from General Sherman Department Commander, he had ordered garrison's on the road between Corinth and Grand Junction and Corinth must be supplied from Hamburg Landing. Also that they were out of forage but had plenty of rations.[1] Subsequently, he informed me the roads were running and all quiet in his command.[2] I directed him to require his Chief Commissary and Quartermaster to call direct for what they want.[3]

U S GRANT
Major General

Telegram, copies, DLC-USG, V, 34, 35; DNA, RG 393, Military Div. of the Miss., Letters Sent. *O.R.*, I, xxxi, part 3, 221. On Nov. 21, 1863, Brig. Gen. Robert Allen telegraphed to USG. "am I to understand that the communication by rail from Memphis to Corinth is closed should the wagons & mules for Gen Hurlbut be sent to Hamburg" Telegram received, DNA, RG 94, War Records Office, Dept. of the Tenn.; copies, *ibid.*, Military Div. of the Miss.; *ibid.*, RG 393, Military Div. of the Miss., Telegrams Received. *O.R.*, I, xxxi, part 3, 221.

    1. See telegram to Maj. Gen. Stephen A. Hurlbut, Nov. 12, 1863.
    2. See telegram to Maj. Gen. Stephen A. Hurlbut, Nov. 6, 1863.
    3. See telegram to Maj. Gen. Stephen A. Hurlbut, Nov. 12, 1863.

To Maj. Gen. William T. Sherman

———

Head Quarters, Mil. Div. of the Miss
Chattanooga Ten. Nov. 22d 1863.

MAJ. GEN. W. T. SHERMAN,
COMD.G ARMY OF THE TEN.
GENERAL,

Owing to the late hour when Ewing will get up, if he gets up atal tonight and the entire impossibility of Wood reaching in time to participate to-morrow, I have directed Thomas that we will delay yet another day.[1]

Let me know to-morrow at as early an hour as you can if you will be entirely ready for Teusday morning.[2] I would prefer Wood should be up to cross with the balance of your command, but if he can[*not*] be up in time to cross as soon as your pontoons are laid I would prefer you should commence without him to delaying another day.

Very respectfully
U. S. GRANT
Maj. Gen Com

ALS, DLC-William T. Sherman. *O.R.*, I, xxxi, part 2, 39. See letter to Brig. Gen. Charles R. Woods, Nov. 22, 1863. On Nov. 23, 1863, Maj. Gen. William T. Sherman, in camp opposite South Chickamauga Creek, wrote to USG. "I received your letter at the hands of Captain Audenried, and immediately made the orders for the delay of twenty hours. I need not express how I felt, that my troops should cause delay, but I know Woods must have cause, else he would not delay. Whitaker's and Cruft's troops fill the road, doubtless, and it must be a ditch full of big rocks. But Ewing is up, and if possible Woods or Osterhaus (for I got an orderly in the night announcing that he had overtaken and would resume command to-day) will be also. But in any event we will move at midnight, and I will try the Missionary Ridge to-morrow morning, November 24, in the manner prescribed in my memorandum order for to-day. I will use the Second Division in place of the First as guide, and Jeff. C. Davis' division will act as reserve, and bring me forward the artillery as soon as the bridge is put down. I will try and get out at least six guns in the first dash for the hills. As you ask for positive information, I answer: No cause on earth will induce me to ask for longer delay, and to-night at midnight we move. What delays may occur in the pontoons I cannot foretell. I will get Jeff. C. Davis to make some appearances opposite Harrison, to make believe our troops are moving past Bragg to interpose between him and Longstreet. Every military reason now sanctions a general attack. Longstreet is absent, and we expect no more re-enforcements, therefore we should not delay another hour, and should put all our strength in the attack." *O.R.*, I, xxxi, part 2, 41. On Nov. 23, Asst. Secretary of War Charles A. Dana, Bald Mountain Signal Station, wrote to USG. "Sherman has four divisions across. General Woods has come up and is now embarking. Six pontoons more will complete the bridge. Howard has halted about half a mile from Sherman, and made his men lie down. The rebels have men behind the railroad bank to right of the tunnel. Cannot see whether few or many." *Ibid.*, p. 42.

1. See following letter.
2. Nov. 24.

To Maj. Gen. George H. Thomas

———

Head Quarters, Mil. Div. of the Miss.
Chattanooga, Ten. Nov. 22d 1863.

MAJ. GEN. G. H. THOMAS,
COMDG ARMY OF THE CUMB.D
GENERAL.

The bridge at Brown's Ferry being down to-day, and the excessively bad roads since the last rain, will render it impossible for Sherman to get up either of his two remaining Divisions[1] in time for the attack to-morrow morning. With one of them up, and, which would have been there now but for the accident to the bridge I would still make the attack in the morning, regarding a day gained as of superior advantage to a single Division of troops. You can make your arrangements for this delay.

Very respectfully
U. S. GRANT
Maj. Gen. Com

ALS, IHi. *O.R.*, I, xxxi, part 2, 40. Also on Nov. 22, 1863, USG wrote to Maj. Gen. George H. Thomas. "Up to the hour I left Gen. Sherman's Hd Qrs. 3.30 this afternoon, General Davis had not reported to him. If Davis has not received orders to report to Sherman, and to receive his directions directly from him during the present movement, please so instruct him at once." ALS, deCoppet Collection, NjP. *O.R.*, I, xxxi, part 2, 40. See letter to Maj. Gen. George H. Thomas, Nov. 18, 1863.

1. Brig. Gen. Peter J. Osterhaus's 1st Div., Brig. Gen. Charles R. Woods commanding, and Brig. Gen. Hugh Ewing's 4th Div., both 15th Army Corps.

To Maj. Gen. George H. Thomas

———

Chattanooga November 22d 63

MAJOR GENERAL GEO. H THOMAS
CHATTANOOGA

You will please have the Steamer "Dunbar" wooded by 10 oclock this P. M. with dry wood sufficient to run her tonight and to morrow. If dry wood cannot be obtained in any other way, you will take old buildings. You will also have her manned with a crew of soldiers who have had experience in Steamboating. Place her subject to the orders of Brig Genl W. F Smith, Chief Engineer.

U S GRANT
Major General

Copies, DLC-USG, V, 34, 35; DNA, RG 393, Military Div. of the Miss., Letters Sent. *O.R.*, I, xxxi, part 3, 222. See *ibid.*, I, xxxi, part 2, 64.

To Brig. Gen. Charles R. Woods

Chattanooga November 22d 63

BRIG GENL C. R. WOOD COM'DG 1ST DIV. ARMY TENN. NEAR CHATTANOOGA

You must get up with your force tomorrow without fail. Pass the wagon train and leave it to follow with rear guard. If you cannot get up with your Artillery, come without it, leaving it to follow, I will expect the head of your column at Brown's Ferry by 10 A. M. tomorrow, (23d) without fail.

U S GRANT
Major General

Copies, DLC-USG, V, 34, 35; DNA, RG 393, Military Div. of the Miss., Letters Sent. *O.R.*, I, xxxi, part 2, 39. Copies of this letter were sent to the commanding officers at Whiteside's, Tenn., and at Bridgeport, Ala., with directions to forward by courier. See letter to Maj. Gen. William T. Sherman, Nov. 23, 1863, note 2.

To Maj. Gen. Henry W. Halleck

Chattanooga Tenn.
6. A. M. Nov. 23, 1863

MAJ GEN H W HALLECK.
GENL-IN-CHF.

Genl Willcox dispatch of yesterday to you was repeated to me from Louisville. From the time communication was cut off with

Gen. Burnside till the present I have been sending dispatches to Willcox giving him all the instructions necessary. He has been retreating too fast to get them at the points to which they were directed.

His dispatch to you was for effect.

U. S. GRANT

Maj. Genl.

Telegram received, DNA, RG 107, Telegrams Collected (Bound); copies, *ibid.*, Telegrams Received in Cipher; *ibid.*, RG 393, Military Div. of the Miss., Hd. Qrs. Correspondence; DLC-USG, V, 40, 94. *O.R.*, I, xxxi, part 3, 233. On Nov. 22, 1863, 8:00 P.M., Brig. Gen. Orlando B. Willcox, Cumberland Gap, telegraphed to Maj. Gen. Henry W. Halleck. "I do not hear from Genl Grant   Will you decide whether I shall run the risk of sacrificing all my cavalry in demonstration below Clinch River in an attempt to aid Burnside. If so, I am ready. Please answer to-night   Firing at Knoxville heard up to Eleven (11) Oclock today" Telegram received, DNA, RG 107, Telegrams Collected (Bound). *O.R.*, I, xxxi, part 3, 226. See telegrams to Brig. Gen. Orlando B. Willcox, Nov. 23, 1863.

To Maj. Gen. Henry W. Halleck

———

Chattanooga Tenn.

3 P. M. Nov. 23, 1863.

MAJ GEN H. W. HALLECK,

GENL-IN-CHF

Gen Thomas' troops attacked the Enemy's left at 2. P. M. today carried first line of rifle pits, running over the knoll twelve hundred yards in front of wood's fort & low ridge to the right of it, taking about two hundred prisoners, besides killed and wounded. Our loss small. The troops moved under fire with all the precision of veterans on parade. Thomas' troops will entrench themselves and hold their position until daylight when Sherman will join the attack from the mouth of the Chicamauga & a decisive battle will be fought.

U. S. GRANT Maj. Genl

Telegrams received (2), DNA, RG 107, Telegrams Collected (Bound); DLC-Robert T. Lincoln; copies (dated Nov. 23, 1863, 3:15 P.M.), DLC-USG, V, 40,

94; DNA, RG 393, Military Div. of the Miss., Hd. Qrs. Correspondence. Printed
as sent at 3:00 P.M. in *O.R.*, I, xxxi, part 2, 24. For an eyewitness account of the
attack on Nov. 23, see William Wrenshall Smith, "Holocaust Holiday . . ." *Civil
War Times Illustrated*, XVIII, 6 (Oct., 1979), 33. See also *O.R.*, I, xxxi, part 2,
64–66, 94–95; *Memoirs*, II, 62–64.

On Nov. 23, 3:30 A.M., Brig. Gen. Thomas J. Wood had written to Lt. Col.
Joseph S. Fullerton, adjt. for Maj. Gen. Gordon Granger, stating that two deserters reported C.S.A. forces retreating to Chickamauga Station, Tenn. *O.R.*, I,
xxxi, part 2, 40. On the same day, USG, to whom this letter was forwarded,
wrote to Maj. Gen. George H. Thomas. "The truth or falsity of the deserter who
came in last night stating that Bragg had fallen back should be ascertained at
once. If he is really falling back Sherman can commence at once laying his pontoon trains, and we can save a day." ALS, Abraham Lincoln Book Shop, Chicago,
Ill. *O.R.*, I, xxxi, part 2, 41. On Nov. 22, Gen. Braxton Bragg had detached the
divs. of Maj. Gen. Patrick R. Cleburne and Brig. Gen. Simon B. Buckner to assist Lt. Gen. James Longstreet's forces in east Tenn. On Nov. 23, Bragg, re-
sponding to the U.S. advance, recalled Cleburne's div. and Brig. Gen. Alexander
W. Reynolds's brigade of Buckner's div. *Ibid.*, pp. 659n, 745–46. See letter to
Col. John C. Kelton, Dec. 23, 1863.

To Maj. Gen. William T. Sherman

Hd. Qrs. Mil. Div. of the Miss.
Chattanooga Ten. Nov. 23d 1863.

MAJ. GEN. SHERMAN,

Gen. Rawlins wrote you a note this afternoon, by my directions,
which answer your questions[1]—Wood, if he can get across here in
time, will be sent up on this side of the river, with Howard, to assist
you. I have but little hope however of him being able to do anything, to-morrow, unless it is to help Hooker.[2]

I presume you have given directions for the necessary signal
fires to guide in the landing of boats?

Thomas' loss is about 75. Prisoners taken by us 169. This does
not include wounded prisoners of whom there is quite a number.

yours truly,
U. S. GRANT
Maj. Gen,

ALS, DLC-William T. Sherman.

1. On Nov. 23, 1863, Brig. Gen. John A. Rawlins wrote to Maj. Gen. William T. Sherman. "General Thomas today advanced his lines about twelve hun-

dred yards, carrying the Enemys first line of rifle pits, and now occupies Orchard Knoll in front of Fort Wood and the rifle pits and range of hills to the right of it; He will fortify and hold the ground thus taken. General Howard's corps is advanced to the Rail Road bridge next to the river and to the left of Fort Wood and will occupy this advanced position tonight and from there move early in the morning, hugging the river closely, to form a junction with you. Our loss was light; the enemys in killed and wounded supposed to be small. We captured full two hundred prisoners" LS, DNA, RG 94, War Records Office, Union Battle Reports. *O.R.*, I, xxxi, part 2, 41–42. On Nov. 24, Maj. Gen. Oliver O. Howard, accompanied by Col. Adolphus Buschbeck's brigade, 2nd Div., 11th Army Corps, made contact with Sherman just as he was completing the pontoon bridge across the Tennessee River near South Chickamauga Creek. Howard then returned to his corps, leaving part of Buschbeck's brigade with Sherman. *Ibid.*, pp. 346–48, 573–74. See letter to Maj. Gen. Oliver O. Howard, Nov. 24, 1863.

2. On Nov. 23, USG wrote to Brig. Gen. Charles R. Woods, care of Maj. Gen. Joseph Hooker. "If the bridge is in readiness for you to cross between now and 8. A. M. to morrow, cross over, and come immediately to Chattanooga, in the absence of further orders. Should you not be able to cross by that time, report to General Hooker, to join him in any effort he may be called on to make" Copies, DLC-USG, V, 34, 35; DNA, RG 393, Military Div. of the Miss., Letters Sent. *O.R.*, I, xxxi, part 2, 42. On Nov. 23, 10:00 P.M., and Nov. 24, 12:30 A.M., Maj. Gen. Joseph J. Reynolds, chief of staff for Maj. Gen. George H. Thomas, ordered Hooker to take Lookout Point, the northern promontory of Lookout Mountain, if practicable and if reinforced (as he was) by the 1st Div., 15th Army Corps. *Ibid.*, pp. 105, 106. See *ibid.*, p. 314. USG regarded Missionary Ridge as the main object, with Lookout Point to be taken or bypassed as circumstances might dictate, a view which led Hooker to believe that he was "shut . . . out of the fight" by USG's battle plan, "Grant's object being to give the éclat to his old army . . ." *Ibid.*, I, xxxii, part 2, 468. See letters to Maj. Gen. George H. Thomas, Nov. 18, 20, 1863; *Memoirs*, II, 53–54, 55, 56–58, 64, 66, 88.

To Brig. Gen. Orlando B. Willcox

Chattanooga November 23rd 63

BRIG GENL O. B WILCOX
CUMBERLAND GAP

Your dispatch of yesterday to General Halleck has just been repeated to me.[1] If you had shown half the willingness to sacrifice yourself and command at the start, you do in your dispatch, you might have rendered Burnside material aid. Now I judge you have got so far to the rear, you can do nothing for him. Act upon the instructions you have, and your own discretion, and if you can do any thing to relieve Burnside, do it. It is not expected you will try to sacrifice your command, but that you will take proper risks.

U S GRANT
Major General

Telegram, copies, DLC-USG, V, 34, 35; DNA, RG 393, Military Div. of the Miss., Letters Sent. *O.R.*, I, xxxi, part 3, 233.

On Nov. 21, 1863, 11:30 A.M., Brig. Gen. Orlando B. Willcox, Tazewell, Tenn., telegraphed to USG. "Col Graham finding it impossible to communicate with Gen Burnside has just returned   He reports that Gen Williams has been ordered to Knoxville and says this is reliable. A rebel scouting party that came up as far as Mainerdsville told the citizens that as soon as Knoxville was secured that Wheeler was going to Ky and that they meant to capture this comd   I shall leave in a few minutes for Cumberland Gap   My infy is nearly there"   Telegram received, DNA, RG 94, War Records Office, Dept. of the Tenn.; copy, *ibid.*, RG 393, Military Div. of the Miss., Telegrams Received. Printed as addressed to Maj. Gen. Henry W. Halleck in *O.R.*, I, xxxi, part 3, 213. On the same day, 10:30 P.M., Willcox, Cumberland Gap, telegraphed to USG. "Couriers just in report firing continued at Knoxville at 2 o clock this morning." Telegram received, DNA, RG 94, War Records Office, Dept. of the Tenn.; copy, *ibid.*, RG 393, Military Div. of the Miss., Telegrams Received. *O.R.*, I, xxxi, part 3, 214. On Nov. 21, 11:00 P.M., Willcox telegraphed to USG. "Heavy & regular firing at Knoxville till noon today   But none since noon up to the time the Messenger left." Telegram received, DNA, RG 94, War Records Office, Dept. of the Tenn.; copies, *ibid.*, RG 393, Dept. of the Ohio (Cincinnati), Telegrams Sent; *ibid.*, Military Div. of the Miss., Telegrams Received. Printed as sent at 1:10 P.M. in *O.R.*, I, xxxi, part 3, 213.

On Nov. 22, 2:00 P.M., Willcox telegraphed to USG. "The following information just recd   A reliable Officer Lt Stanley Adjt 12th Ky Cav who left Strawberry Plains on 20th inst bringing hopeful news of the situation at Knoxville   Gen Burnside still holds out & had notified the citizens of Knoxville that he holds the place   The rebel force opposing him is estimated by scouts who have been through their lines Several times to be 36000   Brig Gen Sanders was wounded   has since died   Col Wolford is slightly wounded   The artillery fighting was very heavy on 19th & 20th   The enemy admit a heavy loss   They have withdrawn his force south side of the river   we forage there"   Telegram received, DNA, RG 94, War Records Office, Dept. of the Tenn.; copy, *ibid.*, RG 393, Military Div. of the Miss., Telegrams Received. On the same day, 7:30 P.M., Maj. Gen. John G. Foster, Cincinnati, transmitted this telegram to USG. Telegram received, *ibid.*, RG 94, War Records Office, Dept. of the Tenn.; copy, *ibid.*, RG 393, Military Div. of the Miss., Telegrams Received. Printed as addressed to Maj. Gen. Henry W. Halleck in *O.R.*, I, xxxi, part 3, 225. Also on Nov. 22, 6:15 P.M., Willcox telegraphed to USG. "Firing was heard all day yesterday at Knoxville. No rebel troops had passed down through Morristown or Bean station up to noon yesterday & none heard of advancing that way   williams force must therefore be still above me"   Telegram received, DNA, RG 94, War Records Office, Dept. of the Tenn.; copy, *ibid.*, RG 393, Military Div. of the Miss., Telegrams Received. *O.R.*, I, xxxi, part 3, 225. Later the same day, Willcox telegraphed to USG. "News from the front up to Eleven oclock today   firing still heard at Knoxville" Telegram received, DNA, RG 94, War Records Office, Dept. of the Tenn.; copy (dated Nov. 23), *ibid.*, RG 393, Military Div. of the Miss., Telegrams Received. *O.R.*, I, xxxi, part 3, 225. Also on Nov. 22, Brig. Gen. Jeremiah T. Boyle, Louisville, telegraphed to USG. "Despatch dated today eight P. M. from Gen. Wilcox Cumberland Gap just recd says it is important that my line of Communication with Camp Nelson should be strongly guarded, especially at Loudon near which there is a large quantity of good Stores   Gen'l Burnside is holding out heroiacally and I hope will hold Knoxville. Firing was going at 11 o'clock to day. Is there any news from Gen'l. Grant (Signed) O. B. WILCOX B. Gen'l. No Communication between the Gap and Knoxville." Copy, DNA, RG 393, Military Div. of the Miss., Telegrams Received. Printed as addressed to Foster in *O.R.*, I, xxxi, part 3, 226. On Nov. 23, USG telegraphed to Boyle. "I am much obliged to you for sending Gen Wilcox dispatch. I had sent him repeated dispatches with such instructions as I could give at this distance." Copies, DLC-USG, V, 34, 35; DNA, RG 393, Military Div. of the Miss., Letters Sent.

1. See telegram to Maj. Gen. Henry W. Halleck, Nov. 23, 1863; following telegram.

To Brig. Gen. Orlando B. Willcox

Chattanooga Novembr 23rd 1863

BRIG GENERAL O. B WILCOX
CUMBERLAND GAP

Your dispatches just received.[1] Leave force enough in Cumberland Gap to hold it and if you cannot move to Abingdon and Saltville[2] with your Cavalry and mounted Infantry, fall back until you can supply yourself. We want to hold all the territory possible and be prepared to advance and retake that already abandoned—

U S GRANT
Major General

Telegram, copies, DLC-USG, V, 34, 35; DNA, RG 393, Military Div. of the Miss., Letters Sent. *O.R.*, I, xxxi, part 3, 232. See preceding telegram. On Nov. 24, 1863, 10:00 A.M., Brig. Gen. Orlando B. Willcox telegraphed to USG, evidently referring to USG's two telegrams of Nov. 23. "Your dispatches of 22d & 23d rec'd   The first is unjust as I will show you by my orders from Burnside   I will commence the movement directed in the 2d & if there is the least chance of success will make the demonstration towards abingdon with mounted force which Col Honley [*Harney*] considers too unserviceable for the expedition   Williams troops stationed above watching me & I will hold him as

long as possible by my movement   firing heard in direction of Knoxville last
night" Telegram received, DNA, RG 94, War Records Office, Dept. of the
Tenn.; copy, *ibid.*, RG 393, Military Div. of the Miss., Telegrams Received.
O.R., I, xxxi, part 3, 239. See telegram to Brig. Gen. Orlando B. Willcox, Nov.
24, 1863.

 1. On Nov. 22, Willcox telegraphed to USG. "I have not heard from you
since the 20th   I am holding my troops in position to move on either route
mentioned in my last dispatch   Must move soon for subsistence   No further
news from Burnside" Telegram received, DNA, RG 94, War Records Office,
Dept. of the Tenn.; copy, *ibid.*, RG 393, Military Div. of the Miss., Telegrams
Received. *O.R.*, I, xxxi, part 3, 225. On Nov. 21, midnight, Willcox had telegraphed to USG. "I wouldnot have you understand from my despatch that a
small command could not remain at Cumberland Gap & hold it with the rations
on hand but I have concentrated here 3 times the force that would be necessary
for that purpose which would soon eat up everything here which are only small
stores & no forage   if my communication are cut off with Ky Cumberland Gap
would be starved out & this whole Command sacrificed beside the great quantity
of clothing & other Qr Mr stores accumulated here & all the artillery. clinch
river is passed fording & I do not see any way in which it could assist Genl
Burnside beyond covering his retreat from that river, if he Escapes. a force is
moving down by Moris [*Moore's*] Creek today   this is undoubtedly William's
Command. if you can operate against Longstreet's so that I can continue my communication with Ky I might advance towards Abington by way of Jonesville
but if Knoxville falls & wheelers Cavalry is thrown into Ky my only resource
would be to throw my Cavalry down along the line of communication & move
into Ky the best way I can. cumberland river is up & if we have more rain ~~here~~
there is no Danger of wheeler getting into Kentucky" Telegram received,
DNA, RG 94, War Records Office, Dept. of the Tenn.; copy, *ibid.*, RG 393,
Military Div. of the Miss., Telegrams Received. *O.R.*, I, xxxi, part 3, 214. See
telegram to Brig. Gen. Orlando B. Willcox, Nov. 20, 1863.
 2. Saltville, Va., approximately eighteen miles northeast of Abingdon.

To Maj. Gen. Henry W. Halleck

Chattanooga Tenn
6 P M Nov 24/63

Maj Gen Halleck

 The fight today progressed favorably   Sherman carried the
end of Missionary Ridge and his right is now at the Tunnel and
left at Chicamauga Creek[1]   Troops from Lookout Valley carried
the point of the Mountain and now hold the Eastern slope and point
high up   I cannot yet tell the amount of casualties but our loss is

not heavy   Hooker reports 2000 prisoners taken besides which a small number have fallen into our hands from Missionary Ridge[2]

U S GRANT
Maj Genl

Telegram received, DNA, RG 107, Telegrams Collected (Bound); copies, *ibid.*, RG 393, Military Div. of the Miss., Hd. Qrs. Correspondence; DLC-USG, V, 40, 94. *O.R.*, I, xxxi, part 2, 24. For a contemporary account of the action on Nov. 24, 1863, see William Wrenshall Smith, "Holocaust Holiday . . ." *Civil War Times Illustrated*, XVIII, 6 (Oct., 1979), 33, 35. On Wednesday, Nov. 25, President Abraham Lincoln telegraphed to USG. "Your despatches as to ~~movements~~ fighting on Monday & Tuesday are here—Well done. Many thanks to all. Remember Burnside." ALS, RPB. *O.R.*, I, xxxi, part 2, 25. Lincoln, *Works*, VII, 30. See telegram to Maj. Gen. Henry W. Halleck, Nov. 23, 1863. On the same day, 11:30 A.M., Maj. Gen. Henry W. Halleck telegraphed to USG. "I congratulate you on the success thus far of your plans. I fear that Genl Burnside is hard pressed, and that any further delay may prove fatal. I know that you will do all in your power to relieve him." ALS (telegram sent), DNA, RG 107, Telegrams Collected (Bound); copies, *ibid.*, RG 393, Military Div. of the Miss., Hd. Qrs. Correspondence; DLC-USG, V, 40, 94.

1. See letter to Maj. Gen. William T. Sherman, Nov. 24, 1863.
2. See letter to Maj. Gen. William T. Sherman, Nov. 24, 1863.

To Maj. Gen. Oliver O. Howard

Nov. 24th/63 12.40 p. m.

GEN. HOWARD,
    resist but bring on no attack until otherwise directed unless troops to right or left of you become engaged. In that case push your line forward or to the right or left as circumstances may require. The open spaces between you & Sherman can not be closed until Sherman advances to shorten it. Gen Thomas is not here but I will communicate to him this order as soon as he can be found.

U. S. GRANT
Maj Gen

ALS, IHi. *O.R.*, I, xxxi, part 2, 43. For Maj. Gen. Oliver O. Howard's location, see following letter, note 1.

To Maj. Gen. William T. Sherman

Nov. 24th/63 11.20 a. m.

GEN. SHERMAN,

Thomas' forces are confronting enemy's line of rifle pitts which seem to be but weakly lined with troops   conciderable movement has taken place on top of the ridge towards you. Howard has sent a force to try and flank the enemy on our left and to send through to communicate with you.[1] Until I do hear from you I am loth to give any orders for a general engagement.—Hooker seems to have been engaged for some time but how I have not heard. Does there seem to be a force prepared to receive you East of the ridge? Send me word what can be done to aid you.

Yours

U. S. GRANT

Maj Gen

ALS, DNA, RG 94, War Records Office, Dept. of the Tenn. *O.R.*, I, xxxi, part 2, 42.

On Nov. 24, 1863, Maj. Gen. William T. Sherman's main force crossed the Tennessee River, but, contrary to the reports of Asst. Secretary of War Charles A. Dana and USG, did not advance as far as the tunnel of the Chattanooga and Cleveland Railroad through Missionary Ridge. See *ibid.*, pp. 66–67, 73–75, 571–74; telegram to Maj. Gen. Henry W. Halleck, Nov. 24, 1863, and the following two letters.

Also on Nov. 24, in the evening, Brig. Gen. John A. Rawlins wrote to Sherman, alluding to the orders in USG's second letter to Maj. Gen. George H. Thomas, Nov. 24, 1863. "You will attack the enemy at the point most advantageous from your position, at early dawn tomorrow morning, the 25th inst. General Thomas has been instructed to commence the attack early tomorrow morning; he will carry the enemy's rifle pits in his immediate front, or, move to the left to your support as circumstances may determine best. General Hooker carried the point and Eastern slope of Lookout Mountain today and now holds the line from the White House to the point where the Rail Road passes beneath the Mountain down the river on the Chattanooga side. He reports that his men are unflinching and cannot be driven from their position which they are strengthening every moment; that the enemy still hold the top of Lookout Mountain and he cannot prevent it until he can get around and take possession of the Summertown road, which he is informed will require him to descend into the Valley. He has captured two guns and he thinks full two thousand prisoners, Our loss he says is not severe. Carlins Brigade crossed over Chattanooga Creek from here to Lookout late this afternoon to Hookers support, it has had considerable fighting. The enemys wagon trains were seen passing between two and three P. M. today down the Summertown road from the top of the Mountain to Chattanooga Valley" LS, DNA, RG 94, War Records Office, Military Div. of the Miss. *O.R.*, I, xxxi, part 2, 43–44.

On Nov. 24, 1:25 P.M. and 4:00 P.M., Maj. Gen. Joseph Hooker had written to Maj. Gen. Joseph J. Reynolds, Thomas's chief of staff, reporting his success in taking Lookout Point. *Ibid.*, pp. 109, 111. For accounts of the battle "above the clouds," as Brig. Gen. Montgomery C. Meigs called it, see *ibid.*, pp. 77–78, 315–17; letter to Col. John C. Kelton, Dec. 23, 1863; *Memoirs*, II, 69–73. Although the battle grew in renown, USG considered it an extended skirmish. *Young*, II, 306. For events precipitating the battle, see letter to Maj. Gen. William T. Sherman, Nov. 23, 1863, note 2.

1. On Nov. 24, Maj. Gen. Oliver O. Howard reported to Sherman and left him three regts. See letter to Maj. Gen. William T. Sherman, Nov. 23, 1863, note 1. On Nov. 25, having received orders to reinforce Sherman, Howard moved the balance of the 11th Army Corps to Sherman's left. *O.R.*, I, xxxi, part 2, 113–14, 349.

To Maj. Gen. George H. Thomas

Chattanooga November 24th 1863 1. P. M

MAJ GENL G. H THOMAS

CHATTANOOGA

Shermans bridge was completed at 12. M at which time all his force was over except one Division. That Division was to cross immediately when his attack would commence. Your forces should attack at the same time and either detain a force equal to their own or move to the left to the support of Sherman if he should require it.

U S GRANT

Major General

Copies, DLC-USG, V, 34, 35; DNA, RG 393, Military Div. of the Miss., Letters Sent. *O.R.*, I, xxxi, part 2, 43. On Nov. 24, 1863, 12:40 P.M., USG wrote to Maj. Gen. George H. Thomas. "Gen Howard reports enemy moving on Shurtz front Hold reserves of Granger or a portion of his force if there are no reserves to spare, to be in readiness to move to Howards assistance if he is attacked." Copies, DLC-USG, V, 34, 35; DNA, RG 393, Military Div. of the Miss., Letters Sent. *O.R.*, I, xxxi, part 2, 43. See letter to Maj. Gen. Oliver O. Howard, Nov. 24, 1863.

To Maj. Gen. George H. Thomas

Chattanooga November 24th 1863

MAJOR GENERAL GEO H THOMAS

CHATTANOOGA

General Sherman carried Missionary Ridge as far as the tunnel with only slight skirmishing. His right now rests at the tunnel and on top of the hill; his left at Chickamauga Creek. I have ordered General Sherman to advance as soon as it is light in the morning,[1] and your attack, which will be simultaneous, will be in cooperation. Your command will either carry the rifle pits and ridge directly in front of them, or move to the left as the presence of the enemy may require. If Hooker's present position in the mountain can be maintained with a small force, and it is found impracticable to carry the top from where he is, it would be advisable for him to move up the valley with all the force he can spare, and ascend by the first practicable road.[2]

U S GRANT

Major General

Incomplete in Doris H. Hamilton, "Letters of U. S. Grant," *Hobbies—The Magazine for Collectors*, 62, 2 (April, 1957), 106; copies, DLC-USG, V, 34, 35; DNA, RG 393, Military Div. of the Miss., Letters Sent. *O.R.*, I, xxxi, part 2, 44.

1. See Brig. Gen. John A. Rawlins's orders in letter to Maj. Gen. William T. Sherman, Nov. 24, 1863.
2. On Nov. 24, 1863, 9:30 P.M., and Nov. 25, 7:00 A.M., Maj. Gen. Joseph J. Reynolds, Maj. Gen. George H. Thomas's chief of staff, wrote to Maj. Gen. Joseph Hooker directing his advance into Chattanooga Valley to cooperate with Thomas against Missionary Ridge. *O.R.*, I, xxxi, part 2, 112, 113. By sunrise, Nov. 25, the 8th Ky., the first regt. sent by Hooker to raise the U.S. flag on Lookout Mountain, reached the top, the C.S.A. having abandoned it. *Ibid.*, pp. 317, 399.

To Brig. Gen. Orlando B. Willcox

Chattanooga November 24th 1863

BRIG GENL O. B WILCOX
CUMBERLAND GAP

Telegraph General Boyle to make such disposition of his forces as may be necessary to guard your line of supplies.[1] Can you not now move a mounted force on Abingdon and Saltville? Fighting has been going on here for two days, and as soon as possible I shall send a force up the Valley sufficient to relieve Burnside, if he holds out. If you can communicate this fact to him, do so.

U S GRANT
Major General

Telegram, copies, DLC-USG, V, 34, 35; DNA, RG 393, Military Div. of the Miss., Letters Sent. *O.R.*, I, xxxi, part 3, 240. On Nov. 25, 1863, 1:30 P.M., Brig. Gen. Orlando B. Willcox telegraphed to USG. "Your dispatch of yesterday received. I am making preparations for the mounted expedition towards Abington. Genl Burnside in His dispatch that I recd last night said I should place my Infy in striking distance of Cumberland Gap & send the cavalry down to Harrass the enemies left & rear the impassable state of Clinch river has hitherto prevented any occasion in that direction it is now falling & will be fordable tomorrow unless there should be another rain the stage of water at Clinch river in the Direction of Abington would have great influence in determining the success of the move on abington while my Cavalry preparations are continuing. I telegraph to please decide what line of operations I shall pursue. I have started a courier to Genl Burnside with your message & sent word to Him of the Abington expedition." Telegram received, DNA, RG 94, War Records Office, Dept. of the Tenn.; copy, *ibid.*, RG 393, Military Div. of the Miss., Telegrams Received. *O.R.*, I, xxxi, part 3, 247–48. On Nov. 26, 10:30 A.M., Willcox telegraphed to USG. "Another of my Couriers from Gen Burnside has just got in Tazewell from a house in the mountains where he lay concealed last night he learned from the family that the rebels where they had crossed the mountain went towards Rogersville This indicates rather a want of confidence in Longstreets success or a fear of movement in salt work. His dispatches from Gen. Burnside are on the way to me—" Telegram received, DNA, RG 94, War Records Office, Dept. of the Tenn.; copy, *ibid.*, RG 393, Military Div. of the Miss., Telegrams Received. *O.R.*, I, xxxi, part 3, 254. On Nov. 27, 11:30 A.M., Willcox telegraphed to USG. "In accordance with Gen Burnsides suggestion I have ordered the cavalry down to ~~Har~~ harass the enemys left & rear & sent a brigade of infantry to Tazewell—The rivers are fordable again No further news from Knoxville No trains have arrived here with subsistence—Troops & animals cannot subsist here from the rear in winter—News of Jones movement confiding [*conflicting*]—" Telegram received, DNA, RG 94, War Records Office, Dept. of the Tenn.; copy, *ibid.*, RG 393, Military Div. of the Miss., Telegrams Received. Printed as addressed to Maj. Gen. Henry W. Halleck in *O.R.*, I, xxxi, part 3, 259.

1. On Nov. 24, 11:15 A.M., Willcox telegraphed to USG. "A deserter came into my pickets at walkers ferry   He left the rebel army on friday   His information is not accurate   He says Burnside has a very strong position & that Longstreets force Estimated at fifty thousand men   the rebels are at Evans ford on Clench river today   This is probably the rodgersville force   There is also a force at Jonesville   Two hundred reported at Harlin Court house   what force is there in Ky to guard my line of communication & supplies"   Telegram received, DNA, RG 94, War Records Office, Dept. of the Tenn.; copy, *ibid.*, RG 393, Military Div. of the Miss., Telegrams Received. *O.R.*, I, xxxi, part 3, 239. On Nov. 25, Brig. Gen. Jeremiah T. Boyle, Louisville, telegraphed to USG. "I have sent sixth Ind Cavalry as escort for Maj Gen Foster to Cumberland Gap   I have ordered fifty first (51) N Y little over two hundred (200) strong and one (1) company of fourteenth (14) Ky Cavalry to London and two (2) companies of fourteenth (14) Ky Cavalry to Barbourville   I have sent 91st Ind to Camp Nelson & can send that regiment or forty seventh (47) Ky to Richmond or Big Hill with part of 40th Ky mounted   I fear to withdraw too much of force from line of L & N R R   I have asked Gen Wilcox to advise freely as he knows position of enemy   I will see any orders you give executed—The seventh (7)th Indiana cavalry is still at Indianapolis   could it be sent here temporarily for duty—"   Telegram received, DNA, RG 94, War Records Office, Military Div. of the Miss.; copy, *ibid.*, RG 393, Military Div. of the Miss., Telegrams Received. *O.R.*, I, xxxi, part 3, 249. For the 7th Ind. Cav., see telegram to Maj. Gen. Stephen A. Hurlbut, Nov. 29, 1863, note 1.

On Nov. 24, 7:00 P.M., Willcox telegraphed to USG. "Two of my scouts got into Sycamore from Knoxville at noon today   left Knoxville at 4 P M yesterday   The town was closely invested on north side of river   Rebel forces six hundred (600) yards from ours   firing from rifle pits on both sides incessant   Shells throw into the town especially at night   south side of river open to us and we forage on that side   Burnside is confident of holding his position   He has rations for thirty five or forty (40) days   Rebels are using mortars   scouts saw Gen Burnside in person   He is on his way with a despatch for me from the General   I will telegraph you at once when he arrives—A rebel force of infantry is passing down by Dandridge road as I learn through citizen   the scouts also report Williams passing down through Clinch mountain yesterday with mounted force"   Telegram received, DNA, RG 94, War Records Office, Dept. of the Tenn.; copy, *ibid.*, RG 393, Military Div. of the Miss., Telegrams Received. *O.R.*, I, xxxi, part 3, 238–39.

To Maj. Gen. Henry W. Halleck

Chattanooga Tenn
Nov. 25th 1863 7.15 P M

MAJ GEN H W HALLECK,
GEN'L IN CHIEF

Although the battle lasted from early dawn till dark this evening I believe I am not premature in announcing a complete victory over Bragg. Lookout Mountain top, all the rifle pits in Chattanooga Valley Missionary Ridge entire have been carried and now held by us.

I have no idea of finding Bragg here tomorrow

U. S GRANT
Maj Genl Comdg

Telegram received, DNA, RG 107, Telegrams Collected (Bound); William H. Seward Papers, NRU; DLC-Robert T. Lincoln; copies (dated Nov. 25, 1863, 7:00 P.M.), DLC-USG, V, 40, 94; DNA, RG 393, Military Div. of the Miss., Hd. Qrs. Correspondence. Printed as sent at 7:15 P.M. in *O.R.*, I, xxxi, part 2, 25. See *ibid.*, I, xxix, part 2, 489. On Nov. 26, 11:15 A.M., Maj. Gen. Henry W. Halleck telegraphed to USG. "I congratulate you and your army on the victories of Chattanooga. This is truly a day of Thanksgiving." ALS (telegram sent), DNA, RG 107, Telegrams Collected (Bound); copies, *ibid.*, RG 393, Military Div. of the Miss., Hd. Qrs. Correspondence; DLC-USG, V, 40, 94. *O.R.*, I, xxxi, part 2, 26.

Early on Nov. 25, USG wrote to Maj. Gen. William T. Sherman. "If you can without interfering with the disposition of your troops for the attack, put in the Brigade of Howards Corps now with you, on your right, so that it may fall in on the left of its own Corps, as soon as the condition of affairs will permit, you will please do so, as his Corps is small." Copies, DLC-USG, V, 34, 35; DNA, RG 393, Military Div. of the Miss., Letters Sent. *O.R.*, I, xxxi, part 2, 45. On the same day, Sherman signaled to USG. "Howard's corps should unite with mine along the railroad, toward Tunnel Hill. A deep ravine still exists between my hill and that occupied by the enemy." J. Willard Brown, *The Signal Corps, U. S. A. in the War of the Rebellion* (Boston, 1896; reprinted, New York, 1974), p. 520. *O.R.*, I, xxxi, part 2, 596. Previously neither Sherman nor USG knew of this ravine, which cut through Missionary Ridge just north of Tunnel Hill. See *ibid.*, p. 573; letter to Maj. Gen. William T. Sherman, Nov. 24, 1863. For Maj. Gen. Oliver O. Howard's 11th Army Corps, see *ibid.*, note 1. At 12:45 P.M., Sherman, Mission Ridge Station, signaled to USG. "Where is Thomas?" *O.R.*, I, xxxi, part 2, 44. At 1:00 P.M., Maj. Gen. George H. Thomas, Orchard Knob, signaled to Sherman. "Am here. My right is closing in from Lookout Mountain, toward Mission Ridge." Brown, *Signal Corps*, p. 520. *O.R.*, I, xxxi, part 2, 44,

596. Maj. Gen. Joseph Hooker's forces were delayed in reaching Missionary Ridge due to the destruction of the bridge across Chattanooga Creek. *Ibid.*, pp. 68–69, 318.

About 2:00–2:30 P.M., USG, believing that Sherman's position was "critical," that Gen. Braxton Bragg was weakening his center to resist Sherman on his right, and that Hooker's appearance was imminent, ordered Thomas to "carry the rifle pits at the foot of Missionary Ridge. . . . and then it was my intention to order the assault upon the rifle pitts in the Center and on top of the ridge." See letter to Col. John C. Kelton, Dec. 23, 1863; *Memoirs*, II, 78 and *n.* See also *Richardson*, p. 365; Thomas J. Wood, "The Battle of Missionary Ridge," *Sketches of War History* . . . ed., W. H. Chamberlin (Cincinnati, 1896), IV, 34; Bruce Catton, *Grant Takes Command* (Boston, 1970), p. 501*n*; *O.R.*, I, xxxi, part 2, 68, 96, 189, 195, 209, 301. USG evidently repeated this order because Maj. Gen. Gordon Granger, 4th Army Corps, did not promptly convey it to his div. commanders. See *ibid.*, p. 68; *ibid.*, I, xxxi, part 1, 264–65; *Memoirs*, II, 79. For evidence of USG's remarks at the time and later, see *Richardson*, pp. 367–68; Benjamin P. Thomas, ed., *Three Years with Grant as Recalled by War Correspondent Sylvanus Cadwallader* (New York, 1955), pp. 153–54; Horace Porter, *Campaigning with Grant* (New York, 1897), pp. 25–26.

About 3:30 P.M.–4:00 P.M., USG gave the signal to advance: six guns fired in rapid succession. *O.R.*, I, xxxi, part 2, 132. The troops carried the rifle-pits at the base of Missionary Ridge and proceeded to the crest "without awaiting further orders." *Memoirs*, II, 79–80. See letter to Col. John C. Kelton, Dec. 23, 1863. Lack of such orders caused some confusion among corps, div., and brigade commanders. See *O.R.*, I, xxxi, part 2, 132–33, 190–91, 209, 230, 258, 264, 281–82, 301. Later accounts portray USG as surprised by the advance beyond the first rifle-pits and critical of anyone who may have ordered it, but it accorded with his general intentions. See *ibid.*, p. 69; Joseph S. Fullerton, "The Army of the Cumberland at Chattanooga," *Battles and Leaders of the Civil War*, eds., Robert Underwood Johnson and Clarence Clough Buel (New York, 1887), III, 725; telegram to Maj. Gen. Henry W. Halleck, Nov. 15, 1863; letters to Maj. Gen. George H. Thomas, Nov. 18, 24, 1863. During the advance, USG twice signaled to Sherman, the first time at 4:00 P.M. "Thomas Has engaged the enemy along his whole front—& is driving him up—" Signal received, Justin G. Turner, Los Angeles, Calif. "Thomas has carried the hill and line in his immediate front. Now is your time to attack with vigor. DO SO!" Brown, *Signal Corps*, p. 520. *O.R.*, I, xxxi, part 2, 596.

Brig. Gen. Montgomery C. Meigs, who witnessed this advance from Orchard Knob, wrote in his journal of the battle of Chattanooga: "General Grant repeated his order for a general advance, now making it an order that all the troops in sight should advance, drive back the rebel pickets and following them closely, run them into and over their breast-works, which solidly constructed of logs and earth, extended in nearly continuous lines for two miles along the base of the Ridge. The troops were impatient for work. They were formed; a strong line of skirmishers, a line of battle deployed behind them:—the signal six cannon shots from 'Orchard Knob' was given and forward they sprang with a cheer. With a quick step not a run, they crossed the space between us and the breast-works. The rebels fired a volley, our men fired at will, and the rebels swarming out of the rifle-pits covered the lower slopes behind them turned to look at our advance and firing a few shots, again turned and swarmed up the steep roads, which, by oblique ascents led to the summit. Mission Ridge is 500 feet high its sides nearly denuded of timber cut for Camp fires but still with many oaks upon the slopes. The order was to form on our side of the breast-works, and then send a regiment or two to wheel to the right and sweep the rebels out of their works and capture as many as possible. Every gun on Mission Ridge broke out with shell and shrapnell upon the heads of our gallant troops, who never halted till they reached the breastworks. Most of them halted there; but the colors of three Regiments pushed on and up the slopes of a projecting spur, too steep to be seen from the summit. Mission Ridge is here five hundred feet in height. Slowly the three red silken flags ascended and the regiments swarmed up after them. General Grant said it was contrary to orders, it was not his plan—he meant to form the lines and then prepare and launch columns of assault, but, as the men; carried away by their enthusiasm had gone so far, he would not order them back. Presently he gave the order for the whole line, now well formed to advance and storm the ridge. It extended some two miles in length, and it pressed forward with cheers. Shot and shell and cannister poured into it right and left, our guns, 10 pdr rifles, on 'Orchard Knob' responded firing into the batteries, exploding a caisson, and disturbing the gunners. The line ceased to be a line. The men gathered towards the points of least difficult ascent, for very steep is this hill-side, a horse cannot ascend or descend except by the obliquely graded roads. The three colors approach the summit, another mass, gathered gradually into a confused column or stream, at another point directly, in our front, reaches the summit, the color bearer springs forward and plants his flag upon the crest, a gun gallops wildly to the right, cheer upon cheer rings out from actors and spectators. The men swarm up, color after color reaches the summit, and the rebel line is divided and the confused, astonished and terrified rebels fly this way and that to meet enemies, every way but down the rear slope of the ridge and by this open way they mostly escape. . . ." DS, DLC-Montgomery C. Meigs. See *O.R.*, I, xxxi, part 2, 78–79. See also William Wren-shall Smith, "Holocaust Holiday . . ." *Civil War Times Illustrated*, XVIII, 6 (Oct., 1979), 35–36.

As soon as U.S. troops reached the crest of Missionary Ridge, which from Orchard Knob appeared to happen "simultaneously at six different points," USG, Thomas, and Granger rode to the front to consolidate their scattered forces and overcome C.S.A. resistance, especially on Bragg's right. *O.R.*, I, xxxi, part 2, 96. See *Memoirs*, II, 82. As night fell, USG returned to hd. qrs. in Chattanooga. For Maj. Gen. Philip H. Sheridan's immediate pursuit of the enemy, lasting until Nov. 26, 2:00 A.M., see *O.R.*, I, xxxi, part 2, 192; *Personal Memoirs of P. H. Sheridan* (New York, 1888), I, 312–18; *Memoirs*, II, 81; *Young*, II, 626–27.

On Nov. 25, in the evening, Brig. Gen. John A. Rawlins wrote to Thomas. "I am directed by the General Commanding to say that you will start a strong reconnoisance in the morning at 7. A. M. to ascertain the position of the enemy. If it is ascertained that the enemy are in full retreat, follow them with all your force, except that which you intend Granger to take to Knoxville. This will make sufficient force to retain here. I have ordered Sherman to pursue also, he taking the most Easterly road used by the enemy, if they have taken more than one. Four days rations should be got up to the men, between this and morning, and also a supply of ammunition. I shall want Grangers expedition to get off by the day after to morrow" Copies, DLC-USG, V, 34, 35; DNA, RG 393, Military Div. of the Miss., Letters Sent. *O.R.*, I, xxxi, part 2, 45. On the same day, 8:00 P.M., Brig. Gen. James H. Wilson wrote to Thomas. "General Grant directs me to request you to notify him as soon as the troops have put their position in a defencible condition and properly picketed their front." Copies, DLC-USG, V, 34, 35; DNA, RG 393, Military Div. of the Miss., Letters Sent. See letter to Maj. Gen. William T. Sherman, Nov. 25, 1863. For unsuccessful efforts of Col. Clark B. Lagow and Wilson to ascertain the disposition of Thomas's troops during the night of Nov. 25–26, see James Harrison Wilson, *Under the Old Flag* (New York and London, 1912), I, 302–3.

To Maj. Gen. Henry W. Halleck

Chattanooga Tenn
7 30 P M Nov 25/63

MAJ GEN H W HALLECK
GEN IN CHIEF

I have heard from Burnside to the 23d when he had rations for ten or twelve days. He expected to hold out that time[1] I shall move the force from here on to the Rail Road between Cleveland and Dalton and send a column of twenty thousand men up the south side of the Tennessee without wagons carrying four days rations and taking a Steamboat loaded with rations from which to draw on the route. If Burnside holds out until this force gets beyond Kingston I think Enemy will fly and with the present state of the roads must abandon almost every thing. I believe Bragg will lose much of his Army by desertion in consequence of his defeat in the last three days fight.

U S GRANT
Maj Gen Comdg

Telegram received, DNA, RG 107, Telegrams Collected (Bound); William H. Seward Papers, NRU; DLC-Robert T. Lincoln; copies, DNA, RG 107, Telegrams Received in Cipher; *ibid.*, RG 393, Military Div. of the Miss., Hd. Qrs. Correspondence; DLC-USG, V, 40, 94. *O.R.*, I, xxxi, part 2, 25.

1. On Nov. 23, 1863, Maj. Gen. Ambrose E. Burnside, Knoxville, telegraphed to USG. "The enemy are still in our front. They have not yet invested the place but hold all our line here and—other side of the river Our defenses are comparatively strong the men in good spirits we have provisions for say ten (10) or (12) days longer & will hold out as long as we can It is

possible the enemy are strong enough to carry the place by assault. The enemy have last night atempted to break one ponton Bridge by floating rafts down against it But didnt succeed—We have taken precautions which we hope will defeat any future attempt" Telegram received, DNA, RG 94, War Records Office, Military Div. of the Miss.; copy, *ibid.*, RG 393, Military Div. of the Miss., Telegrams Received. *O.R.*, I, xxxi, part 1, 269. On Nov. 21, Burnside had telegraphed to USG. "The enemy has not yet attempted an assault; he is, however, busily engaged throwing up batteries and making approaches. We have the town completely surrounded by a continuous line of rifle-pits and batteries, and hold the heights on the opposite side of the river. A desultory fire is kept up along our skirmish line, which is from 500 to 1,000 yards beyond our line of rifle-pits. The enemy thus far has not attempted a complete investment. His main body seems to occupy the ground extending from the river below town around to the Clinton road. There has been occasional cannonading since the 18th. Our loss has been trifling. The death of General Sanders is a serious loss, and keenly felt by us all. We have on hand eight days' bread, half rations; fifteen days' beef, and of fresh pork full rations, and an abundance of salt. Our forage trains cross the river daily, and have so far been successful. The cavalry force that threatened us on the opposite side of the river have retired from that immediate front and gone certainly beyond Little River, and there is but a small force between Little River and the Little Tennessee. The rains of last night and this morning will render the streams unfordable. We have a reasonable supply of ammunition, and the command is in good spirits. The officers and men have been indefatigable in their labors to make this place impregnable." *Ibid.*

To Maj. Gen. John G. Foster

Chattanooga November 25th 1863

Maj General J. G. Foster
Cumberland Gap

The great defeat Bragg has sustained in the three days battle terminating at dusk this evening, and a movement which I will immediately make, I think will relieve Burnside, if he holds out a few days longer. I shall pursue Bragg to morrow, and start a heavy column up the Tennessee Valley, the day after. Use your force to the best advantage for Burnside's relief, and for regaining what has been lost in East Tennessee.

U S. Grant
Major General

Telegram, copies, DLC-USG, V, 34, 35; DNA, RG 393, Military Div. of the Miss., Letters Sent. *O.R.*, I, xxxi, part 3, 247. John G. Foster of N. H., USMA

1846, served in the Mexican War and held various assignments in the Corps of Engineers before the Civil War. In charge of fortifications in Charleston harbor before the surrender of Fort Sumter, he rose to the command of the Dept. of Va. and N. C., becoming maj. gen. of vols. as of July 18, 1862. On Nov. 16, 1863, he was ordered to relieve Maj. Gen. Ambrose E. Burnside in command of the Dept. and Army of the Ohio. *Ibid.*, p. 166. On Nov. 24, 8:30 P.M., USG telegraphed to Foster, Cincinnati. "Do you hear any thing from Burnside? Battle has been raging since 2. P. M. yesterday. So far we have captured many prisoners and a part of Missionary Ridge, and the point of Lookout Mountain—" Copies, DLC-USG, V, 34, 35; DNA, RG 393, Military Div. of the Miss., Letters Sent; *ibid.*, Dept. of the Ohio (Cincinnati), Telegrams Received; *ibid.*, Telegrams Sent. *O.R.*, I, xxxi, part 3, 239. On Nov. 25, Maj. Nathaniel H. McLean, Foster's adjt., Cincinnati, telegraphed to USG. "Gen'l Foster left yesterday for Knoxville your telegram received and telegraphed forward. Nothing heard from Gen'l Burnside, since Gen'l Foster left." Copies, DNA, RG 393, Dept. of the Ohio (Cincinnati), Telegrams Sent; *ibid.*, Military Div. of the Miss., Telegrams Received. On Nov. 25, Foster, Camp Nelson, Ky., telegraphed to USG. "Your despatch forwarded to me—No late news from Burnside—I am on my way to Knoxville by way of Cumberland Gap If I find Burnside invested shall take troops from the Gap & try to break the investment" Telegram received, *ibid.*, RG 94, War Records Office, Dept. of the Tenn.; copy, *ibid.*, RG 393, Military Div. of the Miss., Telegrams Received. *O.R.*, I, xxxi, part 3, 247.

To Maj. Gen. William T. Sherman

Head Quarters, Mil. Div. of the Miss.
Chattanooga Ten. Nov. 25th 1863,

MAJ. GEN. SHERMAN,
GENERAL,

No doubt you witnessed the handsome manner in which Thomas' troops carried Missionary Ridge this afternoon, and can feel a just pride too in the part taken by the forces under your command in taking first so much of the same range of hills, and then in attracting the attention of so many of the enemy as to make Thomas' part certain of success. The next thing now will be to relieve Burnside. I have heard from him to the evening of the 23d. at that time he had from ten to twelve days supplies and spoke hopefully of being able to hold out that length of time.

My plan is to move your forces out gradually until they reach the rail-road between Cleveland & Dalton. Granger will move up the South side of the Tennessee with a column of 20.000 men taking no wagons, or but few, with him. His men will carry four days rations and the steamer Chattanooga,[1] loaded with rations, will accompany the expedition.

I take it for granted that Braggs entire force has left. If not of course the first thing is to dispose of him. If he has gone the only thing necessary to do to-morrow will be to send out a reconnoisance to ascertain the whereabouts of the enemy.

yours truly

U. S. GRANT

Maj. Gen.

P. S. On reflection I think we will push Bragg with all our strength to-morrow and try if we cannot cut off a good portion of his rear troops and trains. His men have manifested a strong disposition to desert for some time past and we will now give them a chance. I will instruct Thomas accordingly. Move the advance force early on the most Easterly road taken by the enemy.

U. S. G.

ALS, DLC-William T. Sherman. *O.R.*, I, xxxi, part 2, 45–46. On Nov. 26, 1863, Brig. Gen. John A. Rawlins wrote to Maj. Gen. George H. Thomas. "Sherman put Jeff. C. Davis Division in motion to pursue the enemy about midnight last night—Howards Corps followed at 4. a. m. this morning, and ordered his other three Divisions to close up by Chickamauga Depot. He crossed on Pontoon bridge at mouth of Chickamauga and goes up on east side all the way. You will please move in the direction of the enemy all the force indicated for the pursuit in your orders of last night, with all possible despatch." Copies, DNA, RG 393, Dept. of the Cumberland, Letters Received; (entered as written by USG) *ibid.*, Military Div. of the Miss., Letters Sent; DLC-USG, V, 34, 35. Printed as written by Rawlins in *O.R.*, I, xxxi, part 2, 46. On the same day, Rawlins wrote to Maj. Gen. William T. Sherman. "Your despatch received. Thomas was ordered to pursue with all his force, except Granger's, on the road the enemy retreated, and is no doubt in motion before this. The General Commanding will be with the pursuing column, that he may give such general direction on the field, as circumstances may suggest. Until you receive other orders, you will follow up the enemy on the most easterly road he may have taken, as directed in dispatch of last evening, being governed by your own judgement and the enemy's movements, the object being to bring him to battle again if possible." LS, DNA, RG 94, War Records Office, Union Battle Reports. *O.R.*, I, xxxi, part 2, 46. For USG's order to Thomas, conveyed by Rawlins, see telegram to Maj. Gen. Henry W. Halleck, Nov. 25, 1863, 7:15 P.M.

1. On Nov. 17, USG telegraphed to Brig. Gen. Montgomery C. Meigs. "I have just seen a letter to General Wilson from Col La Duck to the effect that

he believes the management of the Steamer 'Chattanooga' is in exceedingly incompetent hands, and so much so as to very much endanger the loss of the boat—" Copies, DLC-USG, V, 34, 35; DNA, RG 393, Military Div. of the Miss., Letters Sent.

To Maj. Gen. George H. Thomas

Nov. 26th [*1863*] 6 P. M.

GEN. THOMAS,

Sherman is now with his advance about 2 miles North of Graysville.[1] Had some skirmishing all day with the rear guard of the enemy which seems to be protecting a large wagon train. If Sheridan had been where his advance at 12 O'clock indicated he would be at this time the enemy rear would have been cut off.[2] Sherman will push forward to Graysville in the morning. ~~Let~~ Direct your troops to push forward to the same point as early in the morning as possible.

Yours
U. S. GRANT
Maj. Gen.

ALS, deCoppet Collection, NjP. See *O.R.*, I, xxxi, part 2, 576, and following telegram. See also William Wrenshall Smith, "Holocaust Holiday . . ." *Civil War Times Illustrated*, XVIII, 6 (Oct., 1979), 36–38.

1. Graysville, Ga., on the Western and Atlantic Railroad, about twelve miles from Chattanooga.
2. In his journal of the battle of Chattanooga for Nov. 25, 1863, 11:00 P.M., Brig. Gen. Montgomery C. Meigs wrote: "I have just returned from Gen. Grant's. Granger will, if the rebels have run, march to-morrow with 20.000 men to relieve Burnside beseiged in Knoxville." DS, DLC-Montgomery C. Meigs. See *O.R.*, I, xxxi, part 2, 67; *Memoirs*, II, 84, 89–90. Accordingly, Maj. Gen. Gordon Granger's 4th Army Corps was excepted in orders for Maj. Gen. George H. Thomas's troops to pursue Gen. Braxton Bragg's forces after their flight from Missionary Ridge. See telegram to Maj. Gen. Henry W. Halleck, Nov. 25, 1863, 7:15 P.M., and preceding letter. On Nov. 26, Capt. William L. Avery, adjt. for Granger, ordered Maj. Gen. Philip H. Sheridan's 2nd Div., 4th Army Corps, to prepare to march to Knoxville, and Sheridan, who had followed Bragg the preceding night, brought his troops back to Chattanooga. See *O.R.*, I, xxxi, part 2, 97, 134–35, 138, 192.

To Maj. Gen. Henry W. Halleck

Chattanooga Tenn
1. A M Nov 27 63

MAJ GEN H W HALLECK
GEN IN CHIEF

I am just ~~informed~~ in from the front[1] The rout of the Enemy is most complete Abandoned waggons, caissons, and occasional pieces of Artillery are everywhere to be found—I think Braggs loss will fully reach sixty (60) pieces of Artillery A large number of prisoners have fallen into our hands The pursuit will continue to Red Clay in the [morning] for which place I shall start [in] a few hours—[2]

U. S. GRANT M. G

Telegram received, DNA, RG 107, Telegrams Collected (Bound); (incomplete) *ibid.*; *ibid.*, Telegrams Collected (Unbound); (incomplete) William H. Seward Papers, NRU; DLC-Robert T. Lincoln; copies, DLC-USG, V, 40, 94; (incomplete) DLC-Edwin M. Stanton; DNA, RG 94, War Records Office, Army of the Potomac; *ibid.*, RG 393, Military Div. of the Miss., Hd. Qrs. Correspondence. *O.R.*, I, xxxi, part 2, 26.

1. See *ibid.*, pp. 70, 350, 491–93. See also William Wrenshall Smith, "Holocaust Holiday . . ." *Civil War Times Illustrated*, XVIII, 6 (Oct., 1979), 37–38.
2. On Nov. 27, 1863, USG rode by way of Rossville, Ga., to Maj. Gen. Joseph Hooker's front at Ringgold, Ga. Smith, "Holocaust Holiday," p. 38. On the same day, Maj. Gen. William T. Sherman, pursuant to conversations with USG late the preceding day, sent Maj. Gen. Oliver O. Howard's 11th Army Corps to destroy the East Tennessee and Virginia Railroad between Dalton, Ga., and Cleveland, Tenn., near Red Clay, Ga., on the Tenn. state line. See *O.R.*, I, xxxi, part 2, 350–51, 576. This operation severed the line of communication between Gen. Braxton Bragg and Lt. Gen. James Longstreet. See *ibid.*, 495; letter to Col. John C. Kelton, Dec. 23, 1863. On Nov. 27, 3:30 P.M., Maj. Gen. Henry W. Halleck telegraphed to USG. "No news from Knoxville for several days. If Longstreet should be cut off from Bragg & forced to leave Knoxville he will probably retreat into Western Virginia, to threaten East Tenn. on that side, or to rejoin Lee near Richmond. It is hoped that Meade will fight Lee before he can be reenforced. Genl Hurlbut is again apprehending an attack in West Tennessee." ALS (telegram sent), DNA, RG 107, Telegrams Collected (Bound); copies, *ibid.*, RG 393, Military Div. of the Miss., Hd. Qrs. Correspondence; DLC-USG, V, 40, 94. *O.R.*, I, xxxi, part 3, 256–57. See telegram to Maj. Gen. Stephen A. Hurlbut, Nov. 29, 1863.

To Maj. Gen. Henry W. Halleck

Chattanooga Tenn
Nov. 27th 1863 1 P M[1]

MAJ GEN H W. HALLECK
GEN IN CHIEF

Several prisoners state that Longstreet was ordered back from Knoxville the first or second day of the fight. It is positively known ~~that~~ both from citizens and prisoners that Buckner was ordered to the support of Longstreet and that one train load left the first day of battle and [more] were just ready to start when the battle commenced. These troops were all brought back & participated in the defeat—

Granger will be all ready to start for Knoxville this evening and will go unless it is positively learned that Longstreet has fled

U. S. GRANT
Maj Genl Comdg

Telegram received, DNA, RG 107, Telegrams Collected (Bound); DLC-Robert T. Lincoln; copies, DLC-USG, V, 40, 94; DNA, RG 393, Military Div. of the Miss., Hd. Qrs. Correspondence. *O.R.*, I, xxxi, part 3, 256. See *ibid.*, I, xxxi, part 2, 69.

1. 1:00 A.M. in USG's letterbook copies.

To Maj. Gen. Henry W. Halleck

Ringgold[1] Ga. 2 P M
Nov 27/1863

MAJ GEN H W HALLECK
GEN IN CHIEF

The pursuit has continued to this point with continuous skirmishing—It is asserted by citizens that Longstreet is expected tomorrow and that the Enemy will make a stand at Dalton   [I] shall

not take their word [howe]ver but will start Granger [this even]ing
to Burnsides relief   [I] am not prepared to continue pursuit further

U. S. GRANT, M. G. C

Telegrams received (2), DNA, RG 107, Telegrams Collected (Bound); DLC-
Robert T. Lincoln; copies, DNA, RG 107, Telegrams Received in Cipher; *ibid.*,
RG 393, Military Div. of the Miss., Hd. Qrs. Correspondence; DLC-USG, V,
40, 94. *O.R.*, I, xxxi, part 2, 26. See William Wrenshall Smith, "Holocaust
Holiday . . ." *Civil War Times Illustrated*, XVIII, 6 (Oct., 1979), 38–40.

1. Ringgold, Ga., on the Western and Atlantic Railroad, about eighteen
miles by rail southeast of Chattanooga.

To Maj. Gen. William T. Sherman

Ringgold Georgia.
Nov. 27th/63. 12:30 p m.

GEN.

Hooker has engaged the enemy here strongly posted in the
hills. It looks as if it will be hard to dislodge them. If you can move
down with a force East of the ridge, on the East side of the railroad it will effectually turn the enemy's position. I do not care about
the pursuit being continued further south. I am anxious however
to have the Cleveland & Dalton rail-road effectually destroyed. I
think one Brigade will be sufficient to do this. They can move on
any road most direct and should go without a wagon.

If you know any reason why one Brigade will not be sufficient
for the duty indicated, or why a force sufficient for it should not
be detached at this time, you need not send them until you can
communicate with me

Yours
U. S GRANT
Maj. Gen. Com

To MAJ. GEN SHERMAN
COMD.G ARMY OF THE TENN

ALS, DNA, RG 94, War Records Office, Union Battle Reports. *O.R.*, I, xxxi, part 2, 46–47. Earlier on Nov. 27, 1863, Maj. Gen. William T. Sherman had sent Maj. Gen. Oliver O. Howard's 11th Army Corps to cut the East Tennessee and Virginia Railroad between Dalton, Ga., and Cleveland, Tenn. See telegram to Maj. Gen. Henry W. Halleck, Nov. 27, 1863, 1:00 A.M., note 2. This operation helped to turn the C.S.A. position in the gap just east of Ringgold, Ga. *O.R.*, I, xxxi, part 2, 577; see preceding telegram. USG and Sherman conferred at Ringgold on Nov. 27, early afternoon, and at Graysville, Ga., on Nov. 28, also early afternoon. *O.R.*, I, xxxi, part 2, 577; William Wrenshall Smith, "Holocaust Holiday . . ." *Civil War Times Illustrated*, XVIII, 6 (Oct., 1979), 39, 40. On Nov. 28, "10h 10m" (P.M.), Sherman, Graysville, wrote to USG. "I have been over to to See Genls Davis & Howard and will start tomorrow for Cleveland, will be tomorrow night near a point marked Tuckers on the Coast Survey Map—Gen Howard moves by the old Alabama Road and Davis & Blair by the Ringgold & Ooltawah Road. Now I hear that the Cavalry have already destroyed a large part of the Railroad about Cleveland, and I infer from the Despatches that Col Duff has shown me that Longstreet is yet (27th) at or Near Knoxville passing rather above Knoxville & that Sam Jones is comig to him from Abington. Gnl Hooker also has sent me a copy of his Report to you that Bragg is collecting his Army at Tunnel Hill and that he has held on to Palmer. Now these may change your plans. If so send me orders via Tyners & Ooltawah. It may be imprudent to spread too much. That was Rosecrans mistake, and we should not commit it. Unless I recive orders I will go to Calhoun, and find out something definite about Longstreet and if he is coming down we must thwart him. I dont like to See Hooker alarmed, but it would be prudent to have the Road cleared of all the trains, ambulances, caissons & C that are now sticking in the mud. Hooker also has too much artillery to move with anything like expedition." ALS, DNA, RG 393, Military Div. of the Miss., Letters Received. *O.R.*, I, xxxi, part 2, 47–48. On Nov. 29, to protect Maj. Gen. Gordon Granger's column as it proceeded toward Knoxville, Sherman concentrated his inf. at Cleveland, marching the next day to the Hiwassee River near Calhoun and Charleston, Tenn. *Ibid.*, p. 577; *ibid.*, I, xxxi, part 1, 433. See letter to Maj. Gen. William T. Sherman, Nov. 29, 1863.

To Maj. Gen. George H. Thomas

Ringgold Ga November 27. 1. P. M.

MAJOR GENERAL GEO H THOMAS
NEAR CHATTANOOGA

Hooker has just driven the enemy from this place, capturing three pieces of Artillery and some prisoners. Sherman is near by. It is reported by citizens that Longstreet is expected to morrow and that the enemy will make a stand at Dalton. I do not intend to pursue further however. I think it best not to rely on statements of citizens altogether. You will direct Granger therefore, to start at once marching as rapidly as possible to the relief of Burnside. Should he obtain satisfactory evidence that Longstreet has abandoned the seige of Knoxville, he will return at once.

U S GRANT
Major General

Copies, DLC-USG, V, 34, 35; DNA, RG 393, Military Div. of the Miss., Letters Sent. *O.R.*, I, xxxi, part 2, 47. Although USG initiated preparations for the relief of Maj. Gen. Ambrose E. Burnside's forces previous to this letter, he had given Maj. Gen. George H. Thomas verbal orders not to start Maj. Gen. Gordon Granger's column toward Knoxville until it was clear that Gen. Braxton Bragg's army was completely defeated and unable to join Lt. Gen. James Longstreet's troops. See letter to Maj. Gen. George H. Thomas, Nov. 26, 1863, note 2; *Memoirs*, II, 90.

To Maj. Gen. Henry W. Halleck

———

Chattanooga Tenn
Nov. 28th 1863 9 20 P. M.

MAJ GEN H W. HALLECK
GEN IN CHIEF

The pursuit of the Enemy to beyond Ringgold shows their great defeat and demoralization. Prisoners taken must amount to six thousand or more. Over forty pieces of Artillery have fallen into our hands. The roads everywhere are strewn with wagons, caissons, small arms & ammunition. Troops are now on their way to the relief of Burnside.

Granger goes to Knoxville or until he knows Longstreet has left East Tennessee.

Sherman goes to the Hiawassie and will be sent further if it becomes necessary

U. S. GRANT
Maj Genl

Telegram received, DNA, RG 107, Telegrams Collected (Bound); copies (datelined 8:30 P.M.), *ibid.*, Telegrams Received in Cipher; *ibid.*, RG 393, Military Div. of the Miss., Hd. Qrs. Correspondence; DLC-USG, V, 40, 94. Printed as sent at 9:20 P.M. in *O.R.*, I, xxxi, part 2, 26. For USG's activities on Nov. 28,

1863, see William Wrenshall Smith, "Holocaust Holiday . . ." *Civil War Times Illustrated*, XVIII, 6 (Oct., 1979), 40. Smith wrote that USG said: "If I had amunittion and horses, I could now march to Mobile, Chaston & Richmond. . . ." AD, Mrs. John W. McIlvaine, Washington, Pa. In *Memoirs*, II, 92, USG confused the exact sequence and timing of events on his return from Ringgold, Ga., to Chattanooga, Nov. 28.

To Maj. Gen. John G. Foster

Chattanooga November 28th 1863

MAJOR GENERAL J. G FOSTER
CUMBERLAND GAP

After three days fighting we have defeated Bragg and driven him completely out of this portion of the country. Captured near 7000 prisoners, forty two Cannon and many Colors. Our forces are still in pursuit beyond Ringgold. The 4th Corps Major General Granger commanding, left here to day with orders to push with all possible speed through to Knoxville. Sherman is already in motion for Hiwassee and will go all the way if necessary. All the Cavalry has been ordered to march into East Tennessee by the most practicable routes joining with yours to harrass the enemy.

Communicate this information to Burnside as soon as possible, and at any cost; with directions to hold to the very last moment, and we shall not only relieve him, but destroy Longstreet.

U S GRANT
Major General

Telegram, copies, DLC-USG, V, 34, 35; DNA, RG 393, Military Div. of the Miss., Letters Sent. *O.R.*, I, xxxi, part 3, 266. On Nov. 29, 1863, 8:30 P.M., Maj. Gen. John G. Foster, Barboursville, Ky., telegraphed to USG. "Your despatch is received   the roads are so bad that I have only got this far but hope to be at Cumberland Gap tomorrow night   I will do all I can to aid in Crushing Longstreet & thus add another to the already great results of your glorious victories   I propose to cut the Virginia Rail Road if possible   the Cavalry will then try to unite with your Cavalry as soon as it arrives   I have directed Gen Wilcox to send yours order to Gen Burnside with all dispatch" Telegram received, DNA, RG 94, War Records Office, Dept. of the Tenn.; copy, *ibid.*, RG 393, Military Div. of the Miss., Telegrams Received. *O.R.*, I, xxxi, part 3, 273. On Nov. 29, 12:15 P.M. (possibly Nov. 30, 12:15 A.M.), Brig. Gen. Orlando B. Willcox, Cumberland Gap, telegraphed to USG. "Dispatch of seven fifty a m Nov 28th to

Gen Foster Received   Genl Foster not arrived   I started a copy by a trusty courier to Gen'l Burnside   Hope it will get through"   Telegram received, DNA, RG 94, War Records Office, Dept. of the Tenn.; copy, *ibid.*, RG 393, Military Div. of the Miss., Telegrams Received. *O.R.*, I, xxxi, part 3, 273. The time of USG's dispatch to Foster was probably 7:50 P.M.; see preceding telegram.

To Maj. Gen. Joseph Hooker

Graysville Ga 28th November 1863

MAJOR GENERAL J HOOKER

COMD'G RIGHT WING, ARMY IN THE FIELD

General Sherman will start with his force for Loudon leaveing to morrow morning. You will remain where you are during the 29th and 30th, or advance towards Dalton, if you find it practicable to do so without a battle. Should you be able to get a force into Dalton, destroy all materials that might be used in the support of an Army.

The object in remaining where you are is to protect Shermans flank while he is moving towards Cleveland and Loudon. If there fore you should become satisfied that a force of the enemy move up the Dalton and Cleveland road, you will either attack them or move into Dalton behind them after they have passed, as you may regard most favorable.[1]

U S GRANT
Major General

Copies, DLC-USG, V, 34, 35; DNA, RG 393, Military Div. of the Miss., Letters Sent. *O.R.*, I, xxxi, part 2, 48. On Nov. 28, 1863, 5:00 P.M., Maj. Gen. Joseph Hooker, Ringgold, Ga., wrote to USG. "I have recieved your note regarding Genl Shermans movement & my remaining here &c—This noon an orderly of Genl. Johnstons as he represented himself came in to our lines & reports the enemy reinforcing & entrenching at Tunell Hill—a column of troops from Genl Joe Johnston he reports sent to reinforce Bragg—That Genl. Cheathams Division was marching back to Tunnell Hill this morning—& that the enemy were advancing this side of Tunnell Hill   There has no opportunity occured yet for me to ascertain the truth of this report—~~The~~ Genl Thomas has ordered Genl Palmers Corps back to Chattanooga—I have taken the liberty of detaining Genl Palmer until I can send a copy of your order to Genl Thomas—" ADf, Julia L. Butterfield Memorial Library, Cold Spring-on-Hudson, N. Y.; copy ("for Maj. Genl Sherman"), DNA, RG 94, War Records Office, Military Div. of the Miss. *O.R.*,

I, xxxi, part 2, 48–49. On Nov. 29, 7:00 A.M., Brig. Gen. James H. Wilson, Chattanooga, wrote to Hooker. "I am directed by the Major General commanding to acknowledge the receipt of your note of Nov 28th 5. P. M. and to say, that your detention of Palmers Corps is approved, and in view of the bare probability that the enemy may have assumed a menacing attitude in your front, you are authorized to detain Palmer, as long as you may think necessary. In anticipation of your return in a few days, and the probable continuance of bad roads, the General thinks you had better send back your extra Artillery and wagons at once" Copies, DLC-USG, V, 34, 35; DNA, RG 393, Military Div. of the Miss., Letters Sent. *O.R.*, I, xxxi, part 2, 50. On the same day, 1:00 P.M., Hooker wrote to USG. "Your despatch of 7 a m Recd   I notified Gel Thomas of my detention of Palmers Corps last evening by the same courier that ~~bore~~ carried the dispatch to you   At the same time Gel Palmer notified Gel Thomas asking for orders in view of his having been ordered to Chattanooga by Gnl Thomas—Gel Thomas reply dated at midnight to Gel Palmer ordered him to return at once   Upon Gel Palmers shewing me this order I ~~direct~~ of course directed his compliance with it—He has been gone some three hours with his command—The enemy are unquestionably prepared to make a defence at Tunnel Hill—but the only force that has shewn itself in front of my advance pickets has been abody of about 50 cavalry—I do not think it is their intention to make an advance movement—I will know more ~~of~~ concerning their position & movements as soon as my detachment of cavalry left in direction of Trenton comes up—I expect them every moment—All the wagons, except those required to take back two steam-engines, have been returned. We have only two batteries here. I inclose copy of a letter captured here, written by one of General Hardee's staff." ADfS (incomplete), Butterfield Library. *O.R.*, I, xxxi, part 2, 50–51. Regarding Maj. Gen. John M. Palmer's 14th Army Corps, see *ibid.*, pp. 120, 123; *ibid.*, I, xxxi, part 3, 262. See also *ibid.*, I, xxxi, part 2, 456.

1. On Nov. 27, USG ordered Hooker to discontinue his pursuit of C.S.A. forces. *Ibid.*, p. 322. See telegram to Maj. Gen. Henry W. Halleck, Nov. 27, 1863, 2:00 P.M. On the same day, USG instructed Hooker to make a reconnaissance toward Tunnel Hill, Ga., about six miles southeast of Ringgold, on the enemy's line of retreat. *O.R.*, I, xxxi, part 2, 322–23. On Nov. 27, 7:30 P.M., Hooker wrote to USG. "Colonel Grose, commanding brigade sent toward Tunnel Hill, reports that Bragg and Breckinridge staid last night at a house 2 miles from here, on the left of the road; Hardee and Cleburne about a mile from here; that the enemy are in strong force about 2 miles from here. They have burned a long railroad bridge about 2¼ miles distant, the second bridge from here. Hardee made remark at breakfast this a. m., 'Longstreet was in extremely critical position.' The road good, and no evidence of any train stalled. Citizen said no heavy train passed since 9 a. m. They had 2 of our wounded prisoners, which Colonel Grose brought in." *Ibid.*, p. 47. See *ibid.*, p. 172.

On Nov. 29, 10:45 A.M., Hooker wrote to Maj. Gen. Joseph J. Reynolds, chief of staff for Maj. Gen. George H. Thomas, regarding USG's orders not to advance unless it could be done without fighting. "This puts me in the condition of the boy who was permitted to learn to swim provided he would not go near the water. . . ." Misdated Nov. 27, *ibid.*, p. 120. On Feb. 25, 1864, Hooker wrote to Secretary of War Edwin M. Stanton. "The great mistake of all was in checking the pursuit at Ringgold, for if one-half of the marching had been done there that was done in going to Knoxville the greater part of Bragg's army, and certainly all of its material, would now have been ours. . . ." *Ibid.*, I, xxxii, part 2, 469. See telegram to Maj. Gen. Henry W. Halleck, Nov. 28, 1863; letter to Col. John C. Kelton, Dec. 23, 1863.

To Thomas E. Bramlette

Chattanooga 9.40 P. M. 28 Novemb: [*1863*]

GOVERNOR BRAMLETTE OF KENTUCKY
FRANKFORT KY

Your dispatch received.[1] My experience satisfies me, that the citizens of Paducah almost to a man are disloyal and entitled to no favor from the Government. The President of the road and no doubt nine tenths of the Paducah stockholders, are disloyal men. The road never was completed by them but if I am not mistaken some eight or ten miles was built by Government, to connect it with the Ohio and Mobile road. I will however, suspend taking up the track, except the portion laid by Government, until the matter can be referred to higher authority.[2]

U S GRANT
Major General

Telegram, copies, DLC-USG, V, 34, 35; DNA, RG 393, Military Div. of the Miss., Letters Sent. *O.R.*, I, xxxi, part 3, 263. On Dec. 5, 1863, Governor Thomas E. Bramlette of Ky. wrote to Secretary of War Edwin M. Stanton. "A few days since Maj. Genl Grant suspended an order previously issued by him for taking up the rails upon the Railroad from Paduacah to Union City, until he could hear from the authorities at Washington. I understand that the road so far as constructed is entirely by private enterprise; and that Genl Grant is mistaken in supposing that part of the material belonged to the Gov.t—A portion of the rails was purchased of the Govt. to be paid in transportation &c; but the road was constructed without the aid of the Gov.t—Another reason offered by Genl. Grant (viz) is the disloyalty of the Presdt. & majority of the stockholders & the community interested in the road, I am advised is an error.—The President, Judge Trumble—was a Douglass democrat, and is perhaps somewhat copperheadish, but not disloyal; the citizens now remaining there though not perhaps up to the measure of my loyalty, cannot be called disloyal; and there are large interests of other communities connected with the road as well as stockholders who are of unquestionable loyalty, that deserve consideration.—It occurs to me that it should be a very imperious military necessity to warrant the destruction of private interests which will result from the execution of this order. I hope therefore that the order may be revoked; unless that degree of necessity exists which must force the sacrifice of this interest to the public benefit. Gentleman familiar with the extent of private fortune invested in the road, and the interests which it subserves, together with the irreperable injury that the execution of the order will work will explain the same to you. I ask for them a fair hearing." ALS, DNA, RG 107, Letters Received, Registered Series. See John Brough, Columbus, Ohio, to Stanton, Dec. 11, and Lucian Anderson, Washington, D. C., to Stanton, Dec. 15, also protesting USG's orders to dismantle the railroad between Paducah and Union City, Tenn. ALS, *ibid.* On Dec. 5, Bramlette telegraphed to USG. "Your Attention is invited to the following communication. 596 rails were furnished by ordered War Dept to complete Paducah Rail-road. There is due the Company for transportation for the Army and Mail service More money than will be required to pay for that iron. Signed L. S. TRIMBLE, Prest. New Orleans & O. R. R.—" Copy, *ibid.*, RG 393, Military Div. of the Miss., Telegrams Received. On Dec. 10, Governor Oliver P. Morton of Ind. wrote to USG. "At the request of several prominent citizens of this State, I address you in reference to a recent order, issued in obedience to your orders by Brigadier-General Smith, commanding the District of Columbus, Ky., under which the rails and chairs of the railroad from Paducah, Ky., to Union City, Tenn., are to be taken up and sent to Nashville. The following objections urged against the execution of said order by the parties interested are respectfully submitted for your consideration: First. The road (59 miles in length) is immediately needed to carry to market a very large crop of tobacco just gathered along its whole line, the more necessary in the almost total absence of horses and mules. Second. It being the Ohio branch of the Mobile and Ohio Railroad, as contradistinguished from the Mississippi branch of that road terminating at Columbus, Ky., on the Mississippi, its present destruction seems an invidious discrimination against the trade of the Ohio River and its tributary railroads and in favor of the trade of the Mississippi and its railroad connections, a discrimination which the commanding general would certainly not willingly make. Third. The direct and immediate effect of this act will be to greatly damage existing Ohio River and especially Indiana interests by cutting off much of the trade from an existing mail-boat line running between Evansville, Paducah, and Cairo, and of the Indiana railroad lines terminating on the Ohio at Evansville, to which, as a tributary, the Paducah railroad is of vital importance. Fourth. That whilst most American railroads have been constructed to a great extent on foreign capital, this Paducah road has been laboriously, painfully, and slowly built by local subscriptions, taxation, and credit, thereby rendering the loss of the road a serious personal grievance to every member of the communities through which it runs. Fifth. In view of these considerations it would seem that material for repairs of military railroads might be obtained from less objectionable sources and at rates ultimately more favorable to the country. And it is suggested that should the taking up and removal of the rails be already in progress, the military necessity may possibly be satisfied for the present with a few hundred tons, which the Government can speedily replace, and in time for the removal of the tobacco crop." *O.R.*, I, xxxi, part 3, 375.

1. On Nov. 28, Bramlette telegraphed to USG. "Your attention respectfully invited to following communication: To HIS E T E BRAMLETTE, I am Deputed by the Citizens of Paducah to lay before you the following facts & ask your in-

tervention or remonstrance with Genl Grant or the chf executive of the Govt in the matter. Gen Grant has issued orders to commander of the Post at Paducah to take possession of the Paducah rail road & take up & remove the rails to some point in Tenn. the road was built & owned by the citizens of that section. There is a mortgage indebtedness on the road of four Hundred thousand Dollars & a corporate indebtedness of City & Country of three Hundred thousand. The Loss of the use of the road will fall heavily on the Citizens of Paducah and those interested in the road. we would not complain of the use of the road for military purposes whenever deemed necessary, but the Entire loss of the road is ruinous to our community. if rails are wanted to make new roads to facilitate army operations we suggest that they be taken from roads not in use & not liable to be used for several years, for instance the road running from Birds Point opposite Cairo in Missouri, the road opposite Memphis in Arkansas, the road running from Clarksville to Memphis & other Southern roads not in use. we believe the suggestion to Genl Grant that He could procure rails as quickly and conveniently from other roads would prompt him to countermand His order. Signed L M FLOURNEY   Answer"   Telegram received, DNA, RG 94, War Records Office, Military Div. of the Miss.; copy, *ibid.*, RG 393, Military Div. of the Miss., Telegrams Received. *O.R.*, I, xxxi, part 3, 263. See telegram to Maj. Gen. Stephen A. Hurlbut, Nov. 10, 1863.

2. On Nov. 29, USG telegraphed to Brig. Gen. Andrew J. Smith, Columbus, Ky. "Until further orders you need not take up any rails on the road from Paducah to Union City, except such as have been put down by Government." Copies, DLC-USG, V, 34, 35; DNA, RG 393, Military Div. of the Miss., Letters Sent. See *O.R.*, I, xxxi, part 3, 337. On the same day, 11:40 A.M., Maj. Gen. Henry W. Halleck telegraphed to USG. "Gov. Bramlette of Ky has sent to the President a protest against your taking rails from the Paducah road & suggests that they be taken from some Miss, Louisiania or Arkansas Road. I communicate the Governor's suggestion, but do not ask you to adopt it." ALS (telegram sent), DNA, RG 107, Telegrams Collected (Bound); copies, *ibid.*, RG 393, Military Div. of the Miss., Hd. Qrs. Correspondence; DLC-USG, V, 40, 94. *O.R.*, I, xxxi, part 3, 270. On Jan. 11, 1864, Lt. Col. Theodore S. Bowers issued Special Orders No. 6. "The military authorities of the Department of the Tennessee, will release control of, and turn over to the owners thereof, the Paducah Branch RailRoad, and all the property thereto belonging." Copy, DLC-USG, V, 38.

To Maj. Gen. Henry W. Halleck

Chattanooga Tenn
8 P M Nov 29/1863

MAJ GENL H. W. HALLECK
GEN IN CHIEF

The Fourth Corps started yesterday for relief of Burnside. Sherman was sent to the Hiawassie, and I have sent orders to him to take command of the whole and organize a sufficient force for the object to be accomplished and send the remainder of troops here.

I made this change knowing Shermans promptness and ability —If Burnside holds out short time he will be relieved. Should Longstreet succeed in capturing Knoxville, he himself will be captured I think.

U S Grant M. G. C

Telegram received, DNA, RG 107, Telegrams Collected (Bound); copies, *ibid.*, Telegrams Received in Cipher; *ibid.*, RG 393, Military Div. of the Miss., Hd. Qrs. Correspondence; DLC-USG, V, 40, 94. *O.R.*, I, xxxi, part 3, 270.

To Maj. Gen. Ambrose E. Burnside

Head Quarters
Mil. Div. of the Mississippi
Chattanooga Tenn.
Nov 29. 1863.

Maj. Genl Burnside,
Comdg Army of the Ohio
General

I congratulate you on the tenacity with which you have thus far held out against vastly Superior forces. Do not be forced into a Surrender by Short rations. Take all the citizens have, to enable you to hold out yet a few days longer. As soon as you are relieved from the presence of the enemy, you can replace to them everything taken from them. Within a few days you will be relieved. There are now three columns in motion for your relief. One from here moving up the South bank of the River under Sherman, One from Decherd, under Elliott, and one from Cumberland Gap under Foster. These three columns will be able to crush Longstreets forces, or drive them from the valley, and must all of them be within twenty four hours march of you by the time this reaches you, supposing you to get it on Thursday the 1st Inst.

Very Respectfully
U. S. Grant
Maj. Genl Comdg

Copies, IHi; DNA, RG 233, 42A-D1; *ibid.*, RG 393, Military Div. of the Miss., Letters Sent; DLC-USG, V, 34, 35. *O.R.*, I, xxxi, part 3, 273. On Nov. 29, 1863, Brig. Gen. John A. Rawlins wrote to Col. Robert K. Byrd. "Enclosed please find dispatch in duplicate of Major General Burnside comdg at Knoxville. The one in General Grants own handwriting and marked 'A' you will send by some one whom you can trust with instructions to let it fall into the hands of the enemy without fail. The other marked 'B' and not in the Generals hand writing though signed by him, you must get to General Burnside at all hazzards, and at the earliest possible moment." Copies, DLC-USG, V, 34, 35; DNA, RG 393, Military Div. of the Miss., Letters Sent. *O.R.*, I, xxxi, part 3, 273. As directed, USG's letter fell into Lt. Gen. James Longstreet's hands. He reported its capture on Dec. 1 and gave orders to lift the siege of Knoxville the following day. *Ibid.*, I, xxxi, part 1, 462. Meanwhile, Byrd dispatched five copies of USG's letter to Maj. Gen. Ambrose E. Burnside, who received at least one copy on Dec. 2. Deposition of Robert K. Byrd, Jan. 23, 1871, DNA, RG 233, 42A-D1; *O.R.*, I, xxxi, part 1, 278.

While one of Byrd's couriers lost his life, another, Miss Mary Love, who lived near Kingston, Tenn., and who, with a brother in the C.S. Army, was "less exposed to suspicion by the confederate guards," reached Louisville, Tenn., about twenty-six miles east of Kingston, going part of the way with Reverend Thomas F. Carter. *SRC*, 42-3-271; *HRC*, 44-1-670. There her copy of USG's letter was "sewed up in the lining" of the jacket of John T. Brown, a thirteen-year-old, who carried it to Knoxville, about eleven miles northeast of Louisville. Deposition of John T. Brown, Oct. 22, 1870, DNA, RG 233, 42A-D1; *HRC*, 44-1-669. On Dec. 5, 1863, Brown returned to Louisville, reporting Longstreet's retreat to Maj. Gen. Oliver O. Howard. *O.R.*, I, xxxi, part 2, 353; *ibid.*, I, lii, part 1, 500. On Jan. 16, 1873, Congress authorized a payment of $2,000 to Miss Love "for services in carrying despatches . . . through the confederate lines." *U.S. Statutes at Large*, XVII, 719. See petitions in DNA, RG 233, 42A-D1; *CG*, 42-3-521. Subsequent bills to pay Brown and Carter $250 each and then Brown $2,000 did not pass. *Congressional Record*, 44-1-333, 551, 3814; *ibid.*, 45-1-622; *HRC*, 52-1-971.

On Sept. 14, 1869, Burnside, New York City, endorsed a copy of USG's letter, noting that he had received it "in duplicate" during the siege of Knoxville. ES, DNA, RG 233, 42A-D1. The second courier may have been Sgt. Cornelius M. Hadley, Co. F, 9th Mich. Cav., who, on April 5, 1898, was awarded a Congressional Medal of Honor, dated Nov. 20, 1863, and carrying the citation: "With one companion, voluntarily carried through the enemy's lines important dispatches" from USG to Burnside, "and brought back replies, his comrade's horse being killed and the man taken prisoner." *The Medal of Honor of the United States Army* (Washington, 1948), p. 147. In *Memoirs*, II, 94, USG recalled his letter to Burnside, one copy of which was for Longstreet, but the context of his remarks inaccurately suggests that he had entrusted the matter to Asst. Secretary of War Charles A. Dana and Brig. Gen. James H. Wilson.

To Maj. Gen. Gordon Granger

Chattanooga November 29th 1863

Major General Gordon Granger
Comdg 4th Corps

It is now ascertained that up to the 26th inst Longstreet had not abandoned the seige of Knoxville.[1] Now that Bragg's Army has been driven from Chattanooga there is no reason to suppose he will abandon the seige, until forced to do so by reinforcements sent to Burnside's aid, when he will probably take up his march Eastward, to rejoin Lee about Richmond, or halt when he comes to Railroad communications with Richmond, but where he can still threaten East Tennessee. On the 23d inst Gen Burnside telegraphed that his rations would hold out ten or twelve days,[2] at the end of this time unless relieved from the outside, he must surrender or retreat. The latter will be an impossibility. You are now going for the purpose of relieving this garrison. You see the short time in which relief must be afforded or be too late and hence the necessity for forced marches. I want to urge upon you in the strongest possible manner, the necessity of reaching Burnside in the shortest possible time. Our victory here has been complete, and if Longstreet can be driven from E. Tennessee, the damage to the Confederacy will be the most crushing they have experienced during the war.

This important task is now entrusted to you, and it is expected that you will do your part well.

Use as sparingly as possible of the rations you take with you. Replenish all you can from what you find on the road, giving receipts in order that settlements may be made with loyal persons hereafter.

Deeming what is here said to show you the importance of great promptitude in the present movement, I subscribe myself

U. S Grant
Major General

Copies, DLC-USG, V, 34, 35; (2) DLC-William T. Sherman; DNA, RG 393, Military Div. of the Miss., Letters Sent. *O.R.*, I, xxxi, part 2, 49. On Nov. 30, 1863, Maj. Gen. Gordon Granger, Kincannon's Ferry, Hiwassee River, Tenn., wrote to USG. "Reached this point at 3 P. M. Roads horrid, & marches difficult & laborious. The steamer (with flats) has just arrived. We are crossing as rapidly as possible. I expect to get every thing over by 12 M tomorrow. I have no news whatever from Knoxville or elsewhere. In fact this country is depopulated My programme is as follows: To move directly to Kingston, cross the Tennessee River, and attack Longstreets right flank. I am in hopes to reach Kingston on the 3rd proximo & be in front of Knoxville by the fifth or sixth at the latest. I have ordered Spear's Brigade to join me at Kingston also all the Cavalry and troops at that point to be in readiness to move at a moments warning. I have been seriously Embarassed for want of cavalry and was fired into on our arrival here, by the rebel cavalry on the opposite side of the Hiawasse. Please inform me if any movement is being made on my right flank by our troops above Calhoun. If not, Longstreet can easily cross the Tennessee River near Knoxville and escape southward by roads a short distance east of the Cleveland and Dalton Rail Road. Upon my arrival at Kingston I propose to send the steamboat back to Chattanooga for additional supplies as there is little or nothing to be gleaned from the Country. Please give orders to have them forwarded with the least possible delay. We were detained ten hours yesterday constructing a bridge over Ooltewah River above Harrison. When will Elliott's cavalry be at Kingston?" Copy, DNA, RG 393, 4th Army Corps, Letters Sent. *O.R.*, I, xxxi, part 3, 279–80. See letter to Maj. Gen. William T. Sherman, Nov. 29, 1863.

1. On Nov. 26, Col. Robert K. Byrd, Kingston, Tenn., wrote to USG. "I learn this morning from a reliable source that The Rebels from below are Comeing up from below to reinforce Longstreet who is at this time near Knoxville if not all arround it I saw a man this morning who is from Lowdon and he says he saw five Car Loads arrive at Lawdon he also says they Crossed the Pontoon Bridge and went in the direction of Knoxville. We Whiped Wheeler and drove him Back he had with him Ten Rigts of Mounted Men and some Artillery We took 18 Prisoners We buried twenty on the Ground and Wounded about 40 I learn he has gone back to Knoxville we Cant get any reliable news from Genl Burnside I am allarmed for him I hope all is wright. I have no paper nor envelopes . . . P S I sent the steam Boat Hull to Chattanoga" ALS, DNA, RG 393, Military Div. of the Miss., Letters Received. *O.R.*, I, xxxi, part 3, 255. On Nov. 27, Maj. Gen. George H. Thomas endorsed this letter. "This has just been received. I respectfully forward. Have ordered Elliott to move to Kingston as rapidly as possible join Byrd & fall upon the flanks of the enemy. Will get Granger ready as soon as possible if you desire he should go—" AES, DNA, RG 393, Military Div. of the Miss., Letters Received. *O.R.*, I, xxxi, part 3, 255.

On Nov. 24, 4:30 P.M., Byrd had written to USG. "A Rebel force Attact us this morning about day light and we drove them back taking 12 Prisoners killing 8 of them The force is said to be from 5 to six thousand strong we saw a large number Wheeler is in Command I sent the Hull of a steam Boat last night I hope it will arrive safe I heard of 20 mules below here all safe Genl Burnside is still in Knoxville said to be surrounded we have no Communication with him" ALS, DNA, RG 94, War Records Office, Union Battle Reports. *O.R.*, I, xxxi, part 1, 422. On Friday, Nov. 27, Brig. Gen. Orlando B. Willcox, Cumberland Gap, telegraphed to USG. "Prisoners captured on wednesday & from Wheelers Cavaly reports that Wheeler was moving towards Kingston   I congratulate you on Your Victory"   Telegram received, DNA, RG 94, War Records Office, Dept. of the Tenn. *O.R.*, I, xxxi, part 3, 259.

2. See telegram to Maj. Gen. Henry W. Halleck, Nov. 25, 1863, 7:30 P.M., note 1.

To Maj. Gen. Stephen A. Hurlbut

By Telegraph from Chattanooga Nov 29th [*1863*]

FOR MAJ GENL HURLBUT
MEMPHIS

I have directed all the organized force that can be spared from Springfield Chicago and Indianapolis to be ordered immediately to Columbus Ky.[1]

A force of some four regiments have been ordered from Eastport to Nashville by River.[2] orders have gone to Commanding officer at Pulaski[3] to turn them to Columbus also if they have not already passed that place.[4] When you get these reinforcements, make your own disposition of them.

U. S. GRANT
Maj Genl

Telegram, copies, DLC-USG, V, 34, 35; DNA, RG 393, Military Div. of the Miss., Letters Sent; *ibid.*, 16th Army Corps, Letters Received; *ibid.*, District of Western Ky., Unentered Letters Received. *O.R.*, I, xxxi, part 3, 276. On Nov. 23, 1863, Maj. Gen. Stephen A. Hurlbut telegraphed to USG. "Steele has sent me two regts and does not intend to send any more   Tuttles Division can be moved to Eastport but it will take every spare man from this road   if Corinth is held I must hold the road and can only hold it with Tuttles command   if I am authorized to abandon Corinth I can draw my force to LaGrange or Moscow & be strong enough for the present   The rebels are repairing the road to Tupelo Oxford and Panola and we may expect them in force   Iron will be forwarded as fast as ~~possible~~ we get it but we have no trains from Corinth to Hamburg & are informed will get none from Saint Louis   The 15th Corps has all my trains—I will send four or six engines to Nashville as requested   I have not now twenty five hundred disposal Infantry   My cavalry is now at work   West Tenn is full of Rebel Cavalry   I *want* (?) preemptory orders to move Tuttle to Eastport because it involves of necessity the abandonment of Corinth or its capture if attempted to be held   as soon as the vessels of the Marine Brigade report they will be sent forward but they are too deep for the Tenn and A J Smith has his hands full behind Columbus & Paducah" Telegram received, DNA, RG 94, War Records Office, Military Div. of the Miss.; copy, *ibid.*, RG 393, Military Div. of the Miss., Telegrams Received. Printed as addressed to Maj. Gen. William T. Sherman in *O.R.*, I, xxxi, part 3, 234. On Nov. 24, Hurlbut telegraphed to USG. "Forrest is now at Okalona—He will have in all seven thousand men he will start in a few days to break the line & move into West Tenn. This I consider reliable & am preparing for it My cavalry moves tomorrow towards Okalona one Brigade & one north I notify Smith today if Forrest crosses the road I shall throw all the cavalry & some infantry on his track & I do not think he will get back with the force Smith has at Columbus The Genl in Cheif has ordered Steele to Red River which of course cuts off any further supply from him I recommend the reinforcing of Genl Smith at Columbus by at least three good regiments his position with sufficient force will cover everything north of Jackson Tenn but he has not proper force now I have nothing further to report" Telegrams received (2), DNA, RG 94, War Records Office, Military Div. of the Miss.; copies, *ibid.*, RG 393, 16th Army Corps, Letters Sent; *ibid.*, Military Div. of the Miss., Telegrams Received. *O.R.*, I, xxxi, part 3, 242–43. On Nov. 27, Brig. Gen. Grenville M. Dodge, Pulaski, Tenn., telegraphed to Sherman and to USG. "Roddy has crossed Tennessee near Florence and communications captured from Wheeler to him show that Wheeler with Hill intends to unite and make a raid in our rear. I have no mounted force of much account except that watching the Tenn. river. Do you know where Wheeler now is. I should judge he intended to cross the Tenn. near Florence and go north of Duck River and if you have any knowledge of his where abouts please inform me I have taken measures to ascertain full facts and check all movements" Copy, DNA, RG 393, Military Div. of the Miss., Telegrams Received. *O.R.*, I, xxxi, part 3, 261. On Nov. 28, USG telegraphed to Dodge. "At last accounts Wheeler was in the vicinity of Kingston. He attacked our forces there a day or two since, and was repulsed." Copies, DLC-USG, V, 34, 35; DNA, RG 393, Military Div. of the Miss., Letters Sent. *O.R.*, I, xxxi, part 3, 264.

1. On Nov. 29, USG sent identical telegrams to Brig. Gen. Jacob D. Cox, commanding District of Ohio, Cincinnati; Brig. Gen. Jacob Ammen, commanding District of Ill., Springfield; and Col. John S. Simonson, commanding District of Ind. and Mich., Indianapolis. "You will send all the organized forces in your District that can possible be spared to Columbus Ky at once Telegh the number you will probably send" Telegram received, DNA, RG 393, Commands of J. D. Cox, Telegrams Received; copies, *ibid.*, Military Installations, Indianapolis; *ibid.*, Military Div. of the Miss., Letters Sent; DLC-USG, V, 34, 35. *O.R.*, I, xxxi, part 3, 277. On Nov. 30, Cox telegraphed to USG. "There are no troops in the District except the Prison Guards &c raised and enlisted to serve within the State. There is apart of a Regt. here doing guard duty about four hundred effective men. Shall I send them?" Copy, DNA, RG 393, Military Div. of the Miss., Telegrams Received. On the same day, Ammen's adjt., Capt. William P. Ammen, telegraphed to USG. "There are only one hundred troops in this Dist. besides those necessary to guard Prisoners of War & the Provost Marshals Dept. are using those to quiet disturbance at Manchester Ills. I will send these as soon as circumstances permit—" Copy, *ibid.* Printed as signed by Jacob Ammen in *O.R.*, I, xxxi, part 3, 285. On Nov. 30 and Dec. 2, Simonson telegraphed to USG. "No forces in this District except one Regt. the seventh Ind. Cavalry which the Sec'y

of War has stationed under control of Gov. O. P. Morton. Gov. Morton is absent in New York City but has been Telegraphed to know if he will send them will telegraph you again as soon as he is heard from—" Copy, DNA, RG 393, Military Div. of the Miss., Telegrams Received. *O.R.*, I, xxxi, part 3, 285. "The seventh Ind Cavly Eleven hundred strong fully armed and equipped have been ordered to Columbus Ky They will be forwarded as fast as transportation can be furnished" Telegram received, DNA, RG 94, War Records Office, Military Div. of the Miss.; copy, *ibid.*, RG 393, Military Div. of the Miss., Telegrams Received. On Dec. 5, Governor Oliver P. Morton of Ind. telegraphed to USG. "Major S. E. W. Simonson, 7th Ind. Cavalry is here sick. Will you grant him leave of absence of twenty days. He is not able to travel, and the regiment leaves to night for Cairo." Copy, Morton Papers, In. On the same day, USG telegraphed to Morton. "Leave of absence for twenty (20) days is granted Major S. E. W Simonson, 7th Ind. Cavalry" Copy, *ibid.*

2. On Nov. 16, Col. John I. Rinaker, 122nd Ill., commanding at Eastport, Miss., telegraphed to Brig. Gen. John A. Rawlins. "I would respectfully report Col. Cladek 35th N. J. Vols arrived here last night aboard transports from Washington D. C. with three regiments of Infantry numbering twenty two hundred (2200) men with orders to report here to Maj Genl. Sherman He has no land transportation and there is none for him here There has been no communication from or to this place with Genl Sherman for ten (10) days It is impossible for the colonel to cross the country from here to Genl. Sherman He has transportation enough here to take him down the river which I have retained until further orders can be had will you please give the necessary orders Please answer through Admiral Porter through whom this is forwarded" Telegram received, DNA, RG 94, War Records Office, Dept. of the Tenn.; copy, *ibid.*, RG 393, Military Div. of the Miss., Telegrams Received. *O.R.*, I, xxxi, part 3, 173; *O.R.* (Navy), I, xxv, 487–88. On Nov. 18, Brig. Gen. Robert Allen, Louisville, telegraphed to USG. "Is there no mistake in the sending of troops to Eastport now that Gen Sherman has left Three reg'ts of infy passed here ten days ago bound for Eastport thirteen hundred cavalry passed here this morning for the same place nine hundred cavalry & one (1) reg't infy yet to arrive destination same steamer 'arizona' has returned from Eastport to Cairo with cargo of forage no one knowing what was to be done after the departure of Gen Sherman" Telegram received, DNA, RG 94, War Records Office, Dept. of the Tenn.; copies, *ibid.*, Military Div. of the Miss.; *ibid.*, RG 393, Military Div. of the Miss., Telegrams Received. *O.R.*, I, xxxi, part 3, 185. On the same day, USG telegraphed to Allen. "There is no mistake in sending troops to Eastport. Those you mentioned as having gone, have reached there." Copies, DLC-USG, V, 34, 35; DNA, RG 393, Military Div. of the Miss., Letters Sent. Also on Nov. 18, USG telegraphed to the commanding officer, Eastport. "Return [*Retain*] the troops already and to Arrive until further orders—Relieve the Transports on which they Arrive—" Telegram received, DNA, RG 45, Correspondence of David D. Porter, Telegrams Received; copies, *ibid.*, RG 393, Military Div. of the Miss., Letters Sent; DLC-USG, V, 34, 35. *O.R.* (Navy), I, xxv, 488. On Nov. 19, Rear Admiral David D. Porter, Mound City, Ill., telegraphed to USG. "Your Dispatch is on the way to Eastport. shall I send the transports to Nashville from Paducah. your Despatch was not plain." Telegram received, DNA, RG 393, Dept. of the Tenn., Telegrams Received; copy, *ibid.*, Military Div. of the Miss., Telegrams Received. *O.R.*, I, xxxi, part 3, 191. On

Nov. 21, USG telegraphed to Porter. "I meant to let transports return and go about their business or wherever the Quartermaster might have previously directed them. Now I want to change that order. Please send this immediately up and direct all transports turned back to Eastport and take on board all the troops there except the garrison left by Genl Sherman and bring them to Nashville with all dispatch." Copies, DLC-USG, V, 34, 35; DNA, RG 393, Military Div. of the Miss., Letters Sent. *O.R.*, I, xxxi, part 3, 222; *O.R.* (Navy), I, xxv, 489. On the same day, Porter, Cairo, telegraphed to USG. "Your despatch of the 21st recd & on the way" Telegram received, DNA, RG 393, Dept. of the Tenn., Telegrams Received; copy, *ibid.*, Military Div. of the Miss., Telegrams Received. *O.R.*, I, xxxi, part 3, 222. On Nov. 21, Col. Thomas J. Haines, commissary, St. Louis, telegraphed to USG. "There are at here Eastport on str some five hundred thousand rations   shall they be burned [*landed*] there or sent to Nashville?" Telegram received, DNA, RG 94, War Records Office, Military Div. of the Miss.; copy, *ibid.*, RG 393, Military Div. of the Miss., Telegrams Received. *O.R.*, I, xxxi, part 3, 221. On the same day, USG telegraphed to Haines. "There is a force of seven or eight regiments at Eastport and of course no necessity for burning rations. I have however ordered all the troops there except three regiments, to come by water to Nashville, and any surplus rations should be sent to that place. General Sherman commands that Department." Copies, DLC-USG, V, 34, 35; DNA, RG 393, Military Div. of the Miss., Letters Sent. *O.R.*, I, xxxi, part 3, 222.

3. Pulaski, Tenn., on the Nashville and Decatur Railroad, approximately forty miles north of Decatur, Ala.

4. On Nov. 29, 11:10 A.M., USG telegraphed to Col. Stephen G. Hicks, commanding at Paducah. "If the troops ordered from Eastport Tennessee to Nashville have not yet passed Paducah, turn them to Columbus Ky. Answer whether they have passed, and if so, when." Copies, DLC-USG, V, 34, 35; DNA, RG 393, Military Div. of the Miss., Letters Sent. On Nov. 30, Hicks twice telegraphed to USG. "The troops ordered from Eastport to Nashville not passed here   when they get here I will send them to Columbus Ky as you direct above" "There has been no despatches recd here indicating a return from Eastport of the troops that have gone up Tenn river   There is part of a cavalry regt here at this time waiting for the Colonel Colonel & resdue of the regt subject to orders from here   shall I send a gunboat to Eastport Miss to order them down" Telegrams received, *ibid.*, RG 94, War Records Office, Military Div. of the Miss.; copies, *ibid.*, RG 393, Military Div. of the Miss., Telegrams Received. *O.R.*, I, xxxi, part 3, 284–85. On Dec. 1, Hicks telegraphed to USG. "All the transports that were at Eastport (14) in number have just arrived at this place   come down empty. shall I send them back for the troops there. please tell me what to do   I will fill the Bill   I have rec'd your dispatch ordering all the troops to Nashville." Telegram received, DNA, RG 94, War Records Office, Military Div. of the Miss.; copy, *ibid.*, RG 393, Military Div. of the Miss., Telegrams Received. *O.R.*, I, xxxi, part 3, 305. On the same day, USG telegraphed to Hicks. "Send the transports back to Eastport to remove the troops there to Columbus Ky. The following order which was sent in care of Admiral Porter to commanding Officer at Eastport you will send up by an officer of your command with the transports . . ." Copies, DLC-USG, V, 34, 35; DNA, RG 393, Military Div. of the Miss., Letters Sent. *O.R.*, I, xxxi, part 3, 305; *O.R.* (Navy), I, xxv, 494. USG copied his telegram of Nov. 30 to the commanding officer,

Eastport. "You will evacuate Eastport and move all the forces at that place to Columbus Key, reporting to Brig Genl A. J. Smith. Send all the Quartermaster, Commissaries and Ordnance Stores not required for immediate use for your command, to Nashville Tenn via Cumberland River." Copies, DLC-USG, V, 34, 35; DNA, RG 393, Military Div. of the Miss., Letters Sent. *O.R.*, I, xxxi, part 3, 278; *O.R.* (Navy), I, xxv, 494. Also on Nov. 30, USG had telegraphed to Porter. "Please send above dispatch by Gunboat to Eastport with instructions to turn back all transports it may meet, to Eastport for the transportation of troops at that place, and if you are of opinion that there are not sufficient boats in Tennessee River to transport the troops, You will please advise General Reid at Cairo, who will order forward sufficient for that purpose—" Copies, DLC-USG, V, 34, 35; DNA, RG 393, Military Div. of the Miss., Letters Sent. *O.R.*, I, xxxi, part 3, 278; *O.R.* (Navy), I, xxv, 494. On Dec. 1, Porter telegraphed to USG. "Your telegraph of the 30th received & Sent through." Telegram received, DNA, RG 393, Dept. of the Tenn., Telegrams Received; copy, *ibid.*, Military Div. of the Miss., Telegrams Received. On Nov. 24, Porter had telegraphed to USG. "A number of cavalry have arrived at Paducah with orders to wait there until more arrived and then go up the Tennessee   They are without equipments or anything   what do you wish them to do"   Telegram received, *ibid.*, Dept. of the Tenn., Telegrams Received; copy, *ibid.*, Military Div. of the Miss., Telegrams Received.

To Maj. Gen. William T. Sherman

Head Quarters, Mil. Div. of the Miss.
Chattanooga Ten. Nov. 29th 1863.

MAJ. GEN. W. T. SHERMAN,

News is received from Knoxville to the morning of the 27th. At that time the place was still invested but the attack on it was not vigerous, Longstreet evidently having determined to starve the garrison out.[1] Granger is on the way to Burnsides relief but I have lost all faith in his energy or capacity to manage an expedition of the importance of this one.[2] I am inclined to think therefore I shall have to send you.—Push as rapidly as you can to the Hiwassee and determine for yourself what force to take with you from that point. Granger has his Corps with him from which you will select in conjunction with the force now with you. In plain words you will assume command of all the forces now moving up the Tennessee, including the garrison at Kingston, and from that force organize what you deem proper to relieve Burnside. The balance send back to Chattanooga. Granger has a boat loaded with provisions which you can issue and return the boat. I will have another loaded to follow you.[3] Use of course as sparingly as possible from the rations taken with you and subsist off the country all you can.

It is expected that Foster is moving by this time from Cumberland Gap on Knoxville. I do not know what force he will have with him but presume it will range from 3500 to 5000. I leave this matter to you knowing that you will do better acting upon your discretion than you could trammeled with instructions. I will only add that the last advices from Burnside himself indicated his ability to hold out, with rations, only to about the 3d of December.

> Very respectfully
> U. S. GRANT
> Maj. Gen. Comd.g

ALS, DLC-William T. Sherman. *O.R.*, I, xxxi, part 2, 49–50. See *ibid.*, p. 72; letter to Maj. Gen. Gordon Granger, Nov. 29, 1863; *Memoirs*, II, 92–94. On Dec. 1, 1863, 7:00 A.M., Maj. Gen. William T. Sherman, "Charleston on the Hiwassee," wrote to USG. "Genl Wilson & Mr Dana arrived last night and brought me yours of Nov 29.—I have already crossed the Hiwassee & am marching for Loudon & Knoxville. I have sent a messenger down to mouth of Hiwassee to communicate with Granger, but I think I can beat him in Moving fast.—I will have *if possible* Burnside hear my Guns on the 3rd or 4th at furthest. Recollect that East Tennessee is my horror. That any military man should send a force into East Tennessee puzzles me. Burnside is there & must be releived but when releived I want to get out and he should come out too. I think of course its Railroad should be absolutely destroyed, its provisions eaten up or carried away and all troops brought out. Cumberland Gap should be held simply as an outpost of Kentucky. But Burnside must be releived first & these other things *after*." ALS, DNA, RG 393, Military Div. of the Miss., Letters Received. *O.R.*, I, xxxi, part 3, 297. See *ibid.*, I, xxxi, part 2, 577; *Memoirs of Gen. W. T. Sherman* (4th ed., New York, 1891), I, 394–95.

1. On Nov. 28, 4:00 P.M., Brig. Gen. Orlando B. Willcox, Cumberland Gap, telegraphed to USG. "Negro left Rebel Camp at Knoxville yesterday morning says fighting has not been very heavy principally artillery and sharp shooters Longstreets hoped to reduce Knoxville by starvation" Telegram received, DNA, RG 94, War Records Office, Dept. of the Tenn.; copy, *ibid.*, RG 393, Military Div. of the Miss., Telegrams Received. *O.R.*, I, xxxi, part 3, 266. On Nov. 29, 1:30 P.M., Maj. Gen. Henry W. Halleck telegraphed to USG. "Advices from Knoxville on Wednesday last are that Burnside is still hardpressed. Reenforcements should be pushed forward as rapidly as possible till it is positively known that Longstreet has fallen back." ALS (telegram sent), DNA, RG 107, Telegrams Collected (Bound); copies, *ibid.*, RG 393, Military Div. of

the Miss., Hd. Qrs. Correspondence; DLC-USG, V, 40, 94. *O.R.*, I, xxxi, part 3, 270.

2. USG expected Maj. Gen. Gordon Granger's expedition to leave for Knoxville on Nov. 27 in the evening. See telegrams to Maj. Gen. Henry W. Halleck, Nov. 27, 1863. On the same day, 7:00 P.M., Maj. Gen. George H. Thomas transmitted orders for Granger's departure. *O.R.*, I, xxxi, part 2, 139; letter to Maj. Gen. George H. Thomas, Nov. 27, 1863. Granger's column finally left Chattanooga during the afternoon of Nov. 28. *O.R.*, I, xxxi, part 2, 70–71, 91, 139.

One reason for this delay was the six-hour lapse between USG's and Thomas's orders for Granger to start, occasioned in large part by time lost in conveying USG's letter to Thomas from Ringgold, Ga., to Chattanooga. This dispatch was carried by "a staff officer," almost certainly Col. Clark B. Lagow, who had accompanied USG in the field after the battle of Chattanooga until this point and who had gone on a similar errand the previous day. *Memoirs*, II, 91; William Wrenshall Smith, "Holocaust Holiday . . ." *Civil War Times Illustrated*, XVIII, 6 (Oct., 1979), 37. On Nov. 26, in the evening, Lagow had caused USG's party some delay in returning to Chattanooga by erroneously reporting the reconstruction of a bridge over Chickamauga Creek. *Ibid.*, p. 38; diary of James Harrison Wilson, Nov. 26, 1863, Historical Society of Delaware, Wilmington, Del.

Lagow was, according to Charles A. Dana, "a worthless, whisky-drinking, useless fellow" who, by Nov. 1, USG had decided to dismiss. *Recollections of the Civil War* (New York, 1898), p. 74; see letter to Maj. Gen. George H. Thomas, Oct. 26, 1863. In his diary for Nov. 14 and 15, Smith wrote: "Quite a disgracefull party—friends of Col Lagow, stay up nearly all night playing &c. The Gen breaks up the party himself about 4 oclock in the morning. . . . Lagow don't come to table to-day. He is greatly mortified at his conduct last night. Grant is much offended at him and I am fearful it will result in his removal. . . ." AD, Mrs. John W. McIlvaine, Washington, Pa. On Nov. 17, Brig. Gen. John A. Rawlins wrote to Mary E. (Emma) Hurlbut. ". . . Matters have changed and the necessity of my presence here made almost absolute, by the free use of intoxicating liquors at Head Quarters which last nights devellopements showed me had reached to the General commanding. I am the only one here (his wife not being with him) who can stay it in that direction & prevent evil consequences resulting from it. I had hoped but it appears vainly his New Orleans experience would prevent him ever again indulging with this his worst enemy; . . ." ALS, Warren A. Reeder, Hammond, Ind. On the same day, Rawlins wrote to USG. "I again appeal to you in the name of every thing a friend, an honest man, and a lover of his country holds dear, to immediately desist from further tasting of liquors of any kind no matter by whom asked or under what circumstances, not even under the delusive belief that it will aid you now to recover your wonted vitality and energy. If you do not the bitterest imprecations of an outraged and deceived people struggling in blood to preserve their liberties and their nationality, will be invoked from every loyal home that looks toward the tented field for the ones they love, and the God of justice will answer that invocation throughout the 'Eternity of ages,' I tell you General, of indulgence in intoxicating liquors when it becomes criminal, as is the case where it unfits one for the discharge of the obligations he owes his country, family and friends. In all humanity or heaven there is no voice of palliation or excuse. This very moment every faculty of your mind should be clear and unclouded, the enemy threatens your lines with immediate attack, Burnsides one of your Generals trembles where he stands, the authorities at Washington fear he will yield, they look to you to save him,   Since the hour Washington crossed the icefilled Delaware with his bare-footed patriots to the attack of Trenton, so much of weighty responsibility, has not been imposed by your Government upon one man as it has now imposed upon you. Nor has the man lived since then from whom so much is expected,   Do you realise this? If so, you will drink not another drop of that which unmans you. Two more nights like the last will find you prostrated on a sick bed unfit for duty. this must not be,   You only can prevent it, and for the sake of my bleeding country and your own honor I pray God you may." ALS, OCIWHi. Rawlins endorsed this letter. "This letter was written hastily with a view to handing to the one to whom it is addressed but on reflection it was not given to him, but I talked to him upon the subject to which it relates, ~~with~~ which had the desired effect." AES, *ibid.*

On Nov. 18, Lagow wrote to Brig. Gen. Lorenzo Thomas. "I have the honor to tender my resignation as Colonel & A. A. D. C. U. S. A. to take effect December 1st 1863, on account of disability and respectfully urge its acceptance." LS, DNA, RG 94, ACP, L243 CB 1863. On Nov. 30, USG endorsed this letter. "Approved and respectfully forwarded to Hd Qrs. of the Army, Washington, D. C." AES, *ibid.* On Nov. 18, 7:30 P.M., Dana had telegraphed to Secretary of War Edwin M. Stanton. "Col Lagow, additional A D C having resigned Genl Grant would prefer that he should not be dismissed." Telegram received, DLC-Edwin M. Stanton. *O.R.*, I, xxxi, part 2, 60. See *Memoirs*, I, 255. In his diary for Nov. 30, Smith wrote: "Lagow sent in his resignation a few days before the battle. He saw Gen Rawlins wanted him off the staff, and after the unfortunate spree that the General himself broke up, he saw that he was treeted coldly by him. He today heard ~~that~~ his resignation had been approved and sent to Washington for acceptance, and he resolved to go home immediately. He went with a sore, depressed spirits. . . ." AD, Mrs. John W. McIlvaine. See letter to Julia Dent Grant, Feb. 17, 1864.

On Dec. 14, Maj. Gen. David Hunter, Louisville, telegraphed to Stanton. "I arrived at Chattanooga a month since, and was received by General Grant with the greatest kindness. He gave me his bed, shared with me his room, gave me to ride his favorite warhorse, read to me his dispatches received and sent, accompanied me on my reviews, and I accompanied him on all his excursions and during the three days of the battle. In fact, I saw him almost every moment, except when sleeping, of the three weeks I spent in Chattanooga. I mention these, to you otherwise very unimportant facts, to show you that I had a first-rate opportunity of judging of the man. He is a hard worker, writes his own dispatches and orders, and does his own thinking. He is modest, quiet, never swears, and seldom drinks, as he only took two drinks during the three weeks I was with him. He listens quietly to the opinions of others and then judges promptly for himself; and he is very prompt to avail himself in the field of all the errors of his enemy. He is certainly a good judge of men, and has called round him valuable counselors. . . ." *O.R.*, I, xxxi, part 3, 402. In his draft autobiography, former Maj. Gen. William F. Smith, who had become bitterly critical of USG, wrote of seeing USG take a drink from "a bottle of whiskey" which Sherman brought to a meeting at Thomas's hd. qrs. when Sherman first arrived in Chattanooga. Typescript, Smith Papers, Vermont Historical Society, Montpelier, Vt.

3. On Nov. 29, Capt. George K. Leet wrote to Thomas. "You will please have the Steamer 'Chattanooga' loaded with rations to her full capacity, and sent up the river to report to Major General W. T Sherman" Copies, DLC-USG, V, 34, 35; DNA, RG 393, Military Div. of the Miss., Letters Sent.

To Abraham Lincoln

Head Quarters, Military Div. of the Miss.
Chattanooga Ten. Nov. 30th 1863.
HIS EXCELLENCY A. LINCOLN,
PRESIDENT OF THE UNITED STATES,
SIR:

In a previous letter addressed to the Sec. of War I recommended Brig. Gen. Wm F. Smith for promotion.[1] Recent events have entirely satisfied me of his great capabilities, and merits, and I hasten to renew the recommendation and to urge it. The interests of the public service would be better subserved by this promotion than the interests of Gen. Smith himself.

My reasons for writing this letter now is to ask that Gen. W. F Smith's name be placed first on the list for promotion of all those previously recommended by me.

I have the honor to be
Very respectfully
your obt. svt.
U. S. GRANT
Maj. Gen.

ALS, Mrs. Walter Love, Flint, Mich. *O.R.*, I, xxxi, part 3, 277. On Dec. 14, 1863, President Abraham Lincoln endorsed this letter. "And I incline to concur—" AES, Mrs. Walter Love, Flint, Mich. Brig. Gen. William F. Smith was nominated maj. gen. on March 10, 1864, and confirmed on March 23.

On Dec. 9, 1863, USG endorsed a letter of the same day from Smith to Brig. Gen. Lorenzo Thomas. "Approved and respectfully requested that Lt. Duer be assigned as Aid to Gen. W. F. Smith." AES, DNA, RG 94, ACP, 891S CB 1863. 1st Lt. Edward A. Duer, 1st U.S. Art., was assigned as aide-de-camp to Smith on Dec. 28. *Ibid.*

1. On Nov. 12, USG had written to Secretary of War Edwin M. Stanton. "I would respectfully recommend that Brig. Gen. Wm. F. Smith be placed first on the list for promotion to the rank of Major General. He is possessed of one of the clearest Military heads in the Army, is very practical, and industrious. No man in the service is better qualified than he for our largest command." ALS, *ibid.*, S327 CB 1864. *O.R.*, I, xxxi, part 3, 122. On the same day, Smith was named chief engineer, Military Div. of the Miss., by General Orders No. 6. Copies, DNA, RG 393, Military Div. of the Miss., General Orders; DLC-USG, V, 14; (printed) USGA. *O.R.*, I, xxxi, part 3, 123. For USG's suggestions of

possible commands for Smith, see letter to Maj. Gen. Henry W. Halleck, Dec. 7, 1863; telegram to Maj. Gen. Henry W. Halleck, Jan. 13, 1864.

To Julia Dent Grant

Chattanooga November 30th/63

DEAR JULIA,

The fighting at this place, as you will know before you receive this, is all over at Chattanooga. I went with the advance, in pursuit over twenty miles. Every mudhole for that distance showed evidence of the utter route and demoralization of the enemy. Wagons, & Caissons would be found stuck in the mud and abandoned in the haste of the enemy to get away. Small arms were found every where strewn. We have now forty-two pieces of Artillery taken from the enemy and over six thousand stand of small arms and no doubt many more will be found. The number of prisoners taken is about seven thousand.

Your letter speaking of Col. Pride being with me is received. How did you hear he was with me? He is not nor have I any intention of ever having him at Head Quarters again. There is a rail-road to be put in running order from Nashville to Decatur which I wanted him to superintend the building of but I do not suppose he will do it. The job would be simply to superintend workmen whilst they were building bridges and when that is done he would be relieved.[1] Tell me how he has offended you?

I shall not probably remain in Chattanooga many weeks longer. Where I expect to go would not be proper for me to state, but I have no expectation of spending a winter in idleness.

I will send with this some of the Photographs taken here, also photographs of two General officers that you have not yet got, and one of Deshon, a classmate of mine who is now a Catholic priest.[2] Remember me to your Uncle & his family. Kisses for you and Jess.

ULYS.

ALS, DLC-USG.

1. See telegram to Brig. Gen. Montgomery C. Meigs, Nov. 19, 1863.

2. George Deshon of Conn., USMA 1843, served in ordnance and taught at
USMA before resigning from the army in 1851. He became a member of the
Congregation of Redemptorists the following year and one of the first four Paulists
in 1859. On Dec. 7, 1863, Deshon wrote to USG. "Mr Mullaly the Editor of the
Metropolitan Record has requested me to use my influence with you, to allow
the free circulation of his paper in your department. As he has obliged me in
some respects I cannot entirely refuse his request. I therefore transmit his letter,
and say that I detest his paper and its tone and spirit, and that I hope that no
personal considerations will ever induce either of us to swerve a hairs breadth
from what seems to us the line of duty. I congratulate you on your success and
shall always rejoice at its continuance . . . P. S. Mr Mullaly gives his own reasons
for his request." ALS, USG 3. On March 29, 1864, Deshon, New York City,
wrote to USG. "I am afraid you will think me rather obtrusive in writing this
letter but I can not well avoid complying with the request of an old and esteemed
friend, Agnel who has written me to request me to write to you in behalf of a son
of his who has been found deficient in the Naval academy. He thinks your influence would be great in getting him another chance. I told him you would be
as glad to do him a favor as to do me one, and he writes me he has applied to
you   Poor Agnel has had trouble in losing his son Vincent—Vinny we used to
know and Frank (the one now in question) is the only remaining boy. He tells
me there is nothing vicious about him, and that he could get along better if he
could have another trial—I do not doubt it and wish with all my heart that the
Academic Board of the Naval academy would revise their opinion or the Secretary
of the Navy would reappoint or reinstate him. Of course you will do what you
think right and proper in the case. I repeat I dislike to trouble one who has so
much to do and think about as you have with any private affairs, but I trust to
your kindness of heart to excuse me under the circumstances. You promised
to send me your picture but I did not find it in the letter. You have my warmest
and most sincere wishes for your success and welfare." ALS, *ibid.*

To Jno. J. Speed

[*Chattanooga, Nov. 30, 1863*]

Dear Sir,

Permit me to express through you to the Ladies of Louisville
and all over the North, my Admiration of the patriotic steps taken
by them to provide for the wants of those unfortunate Women and
Children whose natural Protectors have offered up their Lives, a
Sacrifice for the Preservation of our Free and United Government.
. . . To further stimulate the loyal citizens of Louisville to attend
and patronize liberally, the Ladies Fair on that day, I hope the most
cheering news may be heard, from all our Armies. This Army has
rendered a good account of itself in the last week, driving a big

nail in the coffin of rebellion. Burnside, to last accounts, has held out manfully, for many days, against vastly superior forces, numerically, and already good news is beginning to be heard from the Army of the Potomac . . .

U. S. GRANT

Incomplete in George D. Smith, *Autograph Letters, Manuscripts, Historical Documents* (New York, n. d.), p. 77; Swann Galleries, Inc., Rare Books & Autographs, 600th Sale. . . , Sept. 27, 1962, p. 24. On Dec. 8, 1863, Jno. J. Speed, president of the Louisville Fair for the Benefit of the Widows and Orphans of Deceased Soldiers, wrote to USG. "In the name of the Ladies who are conducting the Fair for the Poor I tender thanks for your letter of Sympathy. It had been determined to put the manuscript on Sale & I shall venture to say to a modest man that there is perhaps no other name just now prominently before the Kentucky people which would command as many dollars & cents as that of U. S. Grant   May you be as successful as your Cause & your Capacity deserve—& at the end of this 'Cruel war' may you have many years of happiness in a restored Country." ALS, USG 3.

To Maj. Gen. James B. McPherson

Private & confidential.
Chattanooga Tennessee,
December 1st 1863,

DEAR MC.

I have told Rawlins to write you a long letter giving all the news from here. I shall write but a short one myself, leaving out the past and only speak of what is before us.—It will be impossible to make a Winter Campaign from here and so far as the authorities at Washington are concerned I think they expect nothing of us but to make ourselves comfortable this Winter and to get ready for moving in the Spring. I do not feel satisfied though giving the rebels so much time for reorganizing, nor in keeping so large a force idle. If permitted to do so, and I think there is no doubt but I will be, I want to make the line of the Tennessee secure, then organize a force to go by water to Pascagoula[1] from which to opperate against Mobile and the interior of Alabama & Georgia. To do this I can take from here all of Sherman's force, and possibly a small Corps besides. From the troops in Ohio, Indiana & Ill. with a few old regiment that can be spared from Ky. I can garrison Vicksburg & Natchez and take all the White troops of your command. To get ready for this it will take fully to the middle of January before we could leave New Orleans if the authority is promptly granted. I write this merely to ~~know~~ let you know what to expect.[2]

Sherman is now after Peter Longstreet who has been besieging Knoxville for the last ten days. If he gets hold of him it will pretty well wind up the Army Bragg had here with him.

All the staff are well and desire to be remembered. I wish you would call on Mrs. Lumm[3] and present my respects to her and the family.—I am now free from all inconvenience from the hurt I received in New Orleans.

My kindest regards to your staff

> Yours Truly
> U. S. GRANT
> ~~Maj. Gen.~~

ALS, NjR.

1. Pascagoula, Miss., in the southeast corner of Miss. about thirty-eight miles from Mobile.
2. See letter to Maj. Gen. Henry W. Halleck, Dec. 7, 1863.
3. See letter to commanding officer, Clinton, Miss., July 18, 1863.

To Maj. Gen. William T. Sherman

Head Quarters, Mil. Div. of the Miss.
Chattanooga Ten. Dec. 1st 1863.

MAJ. GEN. W. T. SHERMAN,
COMD.G E. TEN. EXPEDITION,
GENERAL,

When you start upon your return to this place, after it is known that East Tennessee is cleared of all formidable bodies of the enemy, if you deem it atal feasable start a Cavalry expedition to strike through into South Carolina to destroy their East & West roads. A force going in this way should move without transportation and live entirely upon the Country. They ought to do all the harm to the roads they can, burn stores accumulated along them, and take all the good horses they find. If they should succeed in what they go for it would make but little difference where within our lines they should return. The Cavalry for such an expedition can be taken either from Foster or Thomas, or a part from each.—I think twelve or fifteen hundred men will be enough. They do not go to fight but to avoid fighting if possible. Crooke or Wilson would be the best men I know of to command such an expedition.

All the Cavalry of the Cumberland Army with you, not taken for the expedition refered to above, bring back to Chattanooga with you. I do not want them to go back where they started from.

I do not insist upon this expedition being started but if you deem it atal practicable start it. I leave this matter to you because you are where the troops start from and can learn more of the practicability of the roads than I know. You see the condition of men and horses and also know better what the enemy are doing in that direction either to defeat such a move or to make our cavalry necessary elswhere.

Yours Truly
U. S. Grant
Maj. Gen. Com

ALS, DLC-William T. Sherman. *O.R.*, I, xxxi, part 3, 297–98. Probably after Dec. 12, 1863, Brig. Gen. James H. Wilson wrote in his diary entry for Dec. 7: "Genl Grants' letter to Sherman directing him to start a cavalry expedition not complied with on account of Elliott's failure to arrive. Long started towards Murphy via Tellico plains." Diary of James Harrison Wilson, Historical Society of Delaware, Wilmington, Del.; see letters to Maj. Gen. William T. Sherman, Dec. 11, 12, 1863.

To Abraham Lincoln

Head Quarters, Mil. Div. of the Miss.
Chattanooga Ten. Dec. 2d 1863,

HIS EXCELLENCY A. LINCOLN
PRESIDENT OF THE UNITED STATES.
SIR:

Permit me earnestly to recommend Col. A. L. Chetlaine, 12th Ill. Vols. for promotion to the rank of Brig. Gen. to command Colored troops. Col. Chetlaine has commanded a regiment, and part of the time a Brigade, under me for a long time, in fact from the begining of the War. Since the siege of Corinth however his command has not been immediately with me his regiment having formed a part of the garrison of Corinth from its capture until recently.

Col. Chetlaine is a soldierly man and attentive to his duties. He will take great pride in bringing a brigade of troops entrusted to him to the highest possible standard of discipline.

Should you see fit to confer this appointment I would recommend that Col. Chetlaine be ordered to report to Brig. Gen. L. Thomas for duty on the Miss. river where nearly all the Colored troops now are.

I have the honor to be,
very respectfully,
your obt. svt.
U. S. GRANT
Maj. Gen.

ALS, DNA, RG 94, ACP, C156 CB 1883. On Dec. 12, 1863, President Abraham Lincoln endorsed this letter. "Unless there be some objection unknown to me, the Secretary of War please carry out the within recommendation of Gen. Grant at once—" AES, *ibid.* Col. Augustus L. Chetlain, 12th Ill., was appointed brig. gen. "to command colored troops." *Army and Navy Journal*, I, 17 (Dec. 19, 1863), 263. On Dec. 31, Lincoln nominated Chetlain to rank from Dec. 18, but on April 1, 1864, the Senate returned the nomination "with the suggestion that the words 'to command colored troops' be stricken . . ." *Senate Executive Journal*, XIII, 470. Accordingly resubmitted, it was confirmed on April 14. On Feb. 15, Chetlain had written to U.S. Representative Elihu B. Washburne. ". . . I had rec'd. orders placing me in command of all the colored Troops now organized or hereafter to be raised—organized in the State of Tenn. with Head Quarters at Memphis. They number now over 10.000—I am pleased with my command, but would have preferred to have had a smaller command or been permitted to go to the front with them. Gen Grant through Adj Gen Thomas assigned me to the above named command. . . ." ALS, DLC-Elihu B. Washburne. See Chetlain to Washburne, Dec. 21, 1863, Jan. 13, 15, 1864, ALS, *ibid.*; Chetlain, *Recollections of Seventy Years* (Galena, 1899), pp. 99–101. See letters to Elihu B. Washburne, Dec. 2, 12, 1863.

To Maj. Gen. Henry W. Halleck

Chattanooga Tenn
8 P M Dec 2nd 1863

MAJ GEN H. W. HALLECK
GEN IN CHIEF

Sherman writes me that he will reach Knoxville on third or fourth.[1] Foster is in position to come into the Valley as soon as it is safe to do so, with his force.[2]

If not already retreating, Longstreet must do so, and with great loss. I see no route for him but up the Valley into Western Va.

Is there any force in Western Va that can head him or cut the road in his front?

U. S. GRANT
Maj Genl

Telegram received, DLC-Robert T. Lincoln; DNA, RG 107, Telegrams Collected (Bound); copies, *ibid.*, Telegrams Received in Cipher; *ibid.*, RG 393, Military Div. of the Miss., Hd. Qrs. Correspondence; DLC-USG, V, 40, 94. *O.R.*, I, xxxi, part 3, 312. On Dec. 3, 1863, 11:30 A.M., Maj. Gen. Henry W. Halleck telegraphed to USG. "The forces in West Virginia are not strong enough to cut off Longstreet's retreat. Orders were given to Genl Meade some time ago, to cut the Rail Road at Lynchburg so as to separate Longstreet from Lee, but nothing has been done, and it does not appear that anything is likely to be done by the Army of the Potomac in this campaign." ALS (telegram sent), DNA, RG 107, Telegrams Collected (Bound); copies, *ibid.*, RG 393, Military Div. of the Miss., Hd. Qrs. Correspondence; DLC-USG, V, 40, 94. *O.R.*, I, xxxi, part 3, 315.

1. See letter to Maj. Gen. William T. Sherman, Nov. 29, 1863.
2. See following telegram.

To Maj. Gen. John G. Foster

Chattanooga 8 P. M. 2. Dec 1863

MAJOR GENERAL FOSTER
TAZEWELL TENN

Sherman will reach Knoxville to morrow or the day following. His force is large and Longstreet must retreat before it without much fighting. I do not see how his route can be any other than up the Valley. You will no doubt be able to inflict a heavy blow upon his retreating column.

U S GRANT
Major General

Telegram, copies, DLC-USG, V, 34, 35; DNA, RG 393, Military Div. of the Miss., Letters Sent. *O.R.*, I, xxxi, part 3, 310–11. On Nov. 30, 1863, 10:00 P.M., USG had telegraphed to Maj. Gen. John G. Foster, Cumberland Gap. "Have you any news from Knoxville to day? If Longstreet is retreating up the Valley would it not be well to strike for Abingdon. Troops have now been out three days from here on their way to Burnside." Copies, DLC-USG, V, 34, 35; DNA, RG 393, Military Div. of the Miss., Letters Sent. *O.R.*, I, xxxi, part 3, 283. On Dec. 1, 9:00 P.M., USG telegraphed to Foster, Tazewell. "Troops from here were crossing the Hiwassee yesterday. They may be looked for confidently on the 5th and I think the 4th at Knoxville. Be prepared to give the best support you can." Copies, DLC-USG, V, 34, 35; DNA, RG 393, Military Div. of the Miss., Letters Sent. *O.R.*, I, xxxi, part 3, 296. For Foster's reports, see telegram to Maj. Gen. John G. Foster, Dec. 6, 1863.

On Nov. 29, 6:00 P.M., Brig. Gen. Orlando B. Willcox, Cumberland Gap, telegraphed to USG. "Col Crawford has just reached here from Knoxville sent through by Gen Burnside   he says that he left Knoxville wednesday night   Burnside is almost entirely surrounded by the rebels who are in heavy force & are busy entrenching themselves around him   He can defend himself against any assault but for want of supplies may have to surrender bu   Burnside thought he could hold out six or eight days from the time Crawford left"   Telegram received, DNA, RG 94, War Records Office, Dept. of the Tenn.; copy, *ibid.*, RG 393, Military Div. of the Miss., Telegrams Received. Printed as addressed also to Maj. Gen. Henry W. Halleck, and sent 4:30 P.M., Nov. 28, in *O.R.*, I, xxxi, part 3, 265. See *ibid.*, pp. 271–72. On Nov. 29, 9:00 P.M., Foster, Barboursville, Ky., telegraphed to USG. "The following dispatch is just received from Gen Wilcox: From Cumberland Gap 29th 7.15 P M   To MAJ GEN FOSTER. My scouts in the direction of Knoxville report that Cannonading has been heard at the rate of forty shots per minute from twelve oclock last night to ten oclock this morning   heretofore the firing has been slow & seldom so that I suppose Longstreet must have his Batteries in position & is now trying to bring things to a rapid close. signed O B WILCOX Brig Gen"   Telegram received, DNA, RG

94, War Records Office, Dept. of the Tenn.; copy, *ibid.*, RG 393, Military Div. of the Miss., Telegrams Received. Printed as addressed to Halleck in *O.R.*, I, xxxi, part 3, 272. On Nov. 30, 9:30 P.M., Foster, Cumberland Gap, telegraphed to USG. "I arrived here two hours since I find here a small moveable force three thousand infantry and two thousand cavalry with which I propose to march towards Knoxville on the direct road to Tazwelle & Maynardsville. I shall thus be in good position to worry the enemys flanks if he retreats or to fall back safely if attacked by much superior force I have no direct information from Gen Burnside since last wednesday when he said he could hold out for six or eight days I have no explanation of the rapid firing on Saturday at night and Sunday morning at Knoxville No firing has been heard since. Telegraphic communication extends from this point to Tazewell from which place couriers will bring my messages to me. Gen Wilcox has opened communication with Col Byrd at Kingston. Col Byrd repulsed wheelers attack on wednesday last. Wheeler then retired towards Knoxville and is now said to be moving towards Louisville Gen Ransom with six thousand infantry is now near Kingsport" Telegram received, DNA, RG 94, War Records Office, Dept. of the Tenn.; copy, *ibid.*, RG 393, Military Div. of the Miss., Telegrams Received. Printed as addressed to Halleck, 11:50 P.M., in *O.R.*, I, xxxi, part 3, 283. On Dec. 1, 7:00 A.M., USG telegraphed to Foster, evidently referring to the two preceding dispatches, the telegram of Nov. 30 having reached USG first. "Your dispatches of Yesterday received move as indicated in your first dispatch or as may be modified by your own judgment." Telegram received, DNA, RG 94, War Records Office, Dept. of the Ohio; copies, *ibid.*, RG 393, Military Div. of the Miss., Letters Sent; DLC-USG, V, 34, 35. *O.R.*, I, xxxi, part 3, 296.

On the same day, 6:00 P.M., Foster, Tazewell, telegraphed to USG. "The reports of Scouts sent out from the advanced Cavalry posts indicate that Genl Longstreet has commenced to retreat from his positions around Knoxville a large force of Cavalry is now advancing on Maynardsville which [*I*] think is the flanking column of main body probably moving off on the Rutledge road If this proves to be correct I shall harrass his flanks and rears as much as possible" Copy, DNA, RG 393, Military Div. of the Miss., Telegrams Received. Printed as addressed to Halleck in *O.R.*, I, xxxi, part 3, 296. Also on Dec. 1, USG wrote to Maj. Gen. George H. Thomas. "If the Steamer Dunbar is not provided with a piece of Artillery she should be and with a detail of men to work the gun. A dispatch just received from Foster states that a large force of rebel Cavalry has shown itself about Maynardsville which is believed to be Longstreet's flanking column to protect his march by the Ruteledge road." ALS, MH. *O.R.*, I, xxxi, part 3, 293.

To Brig. Gen. Grenville M. Dodge

Chattanooga 6.30. P. M. Dec 2d 63

Brig General G. M Dodge
Pulaski Tenn

Mr Boomer is to build the bridge for Duck river as well as the permanent bridges for the whole road.¹ A trestle bridge however, should be built for temporary purposes, at once if it can be done. I expected to have a Superintendent on the road before this time but have failed to get one.² I will telegraph the Commanding Officer at Columbia to put his troops at work on the bridge at once, and for fear no one there knows anything about that kind of work,³ to obey instructions from you.

U S Grant
Major General

Telegram, copies, DLC-USG, V, 34, 35; DNA, RG 393, Military Div. of the Miss., Letters Sent. On Dec. 2, 1863, 6:30 P.M., USG telegraphed to the commanding officer, Columbia, Tenn. "Put your force at work building a trestle rail road bridge over Duck river at once. Obey any instructions you may receive from Brig General Dodge, in this matter." Copies, *ibid.* On Dec. 3, Col. Henry R. Mizner, 14th Mich., Columbia, telegraphed to USG. "Telegram received Directing me to put my force to Building trestle R R Bridge over Duck River & to obey instructions from Brig Genl Dodge in this matter. my force is only three Hundred men having yesterday relieved Pioneers at Smiths Station & having two Companies at Franklin daily details to be deducted. I can work fifty soldiers & one Hundred negroes I have plenty of good mechanics & 2 officers practical Engineers I shall send to Nashville at once for axes & tools & push the work with all possible dispatch." Telegram received, *ibid.*, RG 94, War Records Office, Military Div. of the Miss.; copy, *ibid.*, RG 393, Military Div. of the Miss., Telegrams Received. *O.R.*, I, xxxi, part 3, 325. On the same day, Brig. Gen. Grenville M. Dodge telegraphed to USG. "I start one hundred bridge builders for Duck River this morning, but I would suggest that as the bridge for Duck River is on the Cars in Nashville, and has been for three weeks, that Mr Boomer send a Sup't to take charge of putting it up. I will furnish him the men. It is an endless job at this stage of water to put in a Trestle, and we can run the Truss right up. Between Duck River and Smiths Station (end of the Cars) are five small bridges that should be put in, so as to get the Cars to Duck River. If Gen Rousseau would detail two hundred men and put them to work on these bridges, it would help us. There are hundreds of men in every regiment that can build a common Trestle. I will have thirteen bridges finished in a week, when I ought to move South of Elk River, and finish the road to Decatur. There is as many more out South of Elk River, some very large ones. Every bridge on the road is entirely destroyed. Please answer about Boomer and Duck River, so I may know what to do. I will go up there tomorrow." Copy, DNA, RG 393, 16th Army Corps, Left Wing, Telegrams Sent. Also on Dec. 3, 6:45 P.M., USG telegraphed to John B. Anderson, Nashville. "I send you copy of dispatches just received from Genl Dodge. Please see Gen Rousseau and ask for the detail of men he wants and have the Duck River bridge sent out. Telegraph Mr Boomer to send a man to superintend the work." Copies, DLC-USG, V, 34, 35; DNA, RG 393, Military Div. of the Miss., Letters Sent. On the same day, USG telegraphed to Dodge. "I have sent copy of your dispatch to Mr Anderson Supt Military Railroads and told him to call on Gen Rousseau for the detail you ask and to telegraph Mr Boomer to send a man to superintend the work at Duck river. I have also directed him to send the bridge out from Nashville" Copies, *ibid.*

On Dec. 20, USG, Nashville, telegraphed to Brig. Gen. Robert Allen, Louisville. "Mr Boomer of Chicago, Bridge contractor, complains of difficulty in procuring transportation for his material from Chicago. It is of vast importance that we get the bridges he is to put up, at the earliest day. Can you not urge the Illinois Central Road to give his freight preference to all other until the whole is through." Copies, *ibid.* On Dec. 21, Allen telegraphed to USG. "Dispatch rec'd do you not mean Mich. Central of instead of Ills Central R. R. it is over the former that Mr. Boomer is shipping An agent has been sent to hurry forward the lumber to the exclusion of everything else. Mrs. Grant will leave in the morning—" Copy, *ibid.*, Telegrams Received. Regarding Julia Dent Grant's trip to Nashville, see John Y. Simon, ed., *The Personal Memoirs of Julia Dent Grant* (New York, 1975), pp. 124–25.

1. See telegram to John B. Anderson, Nov. 4, 1863. On Nov. 27, Dodge telegraphed to Brig. Gen. John A. Rawlins. "Please inform me if any orders have been issued in relation to the building of the bridge across Duck River at Columbia—Nothing as yet has been done on it You know it is not in my command & it is the largest bridge on the road I have been told that a bridge was building in Cincinnati for that stream but I have failed to find any one who was posted or had any interest in the matter I am also told that a large number of bridge builders are returning to Cincinnati for want of work They could be used to advantage at that point" Telegram received, DNA, RG 94, War Records Office, Military Div. of the Miss.; copies, *ibid.*, RG 393, 16th Army Corps, Left Wing, Telegrams Sent; *ibid.*, Military Div. of the Miss., Telegrams Received. *O.R.*, I, xxxi, part 3, 261. On Nov. 30, Mizner telegraphed to USG. "I examined bridge this morning will camp working force close by it am in communication with Brig Gen Dodge. He will send me one hundred (100) mechanics Capt Donahugh just returned to me from Gen Mortons pioneer Brigade will go to Nashville tomorrow to secure everything necessary Boom will be arranged to protect trestle work against drift wood bridge is 2 miles from town" Telegram received, DNA, RG 94, War Records Office, Military Div. of the Miss.; copy, *ibid.*, RG 393, Military Div. of the Miss., Telegrams Received. *O.R.*, I, xxxi, part 3, 286.

2. See telegram to Brig. Gen. Montgomery C. Meigs, Nov. 19, 1863. On Dec. 14, Brig. Gen. Joseph D. Webster, general superintendent of military railroads, Memphis, wrote regarding "the dishonesty of W. J. Stevens, late Mil. Supt. R. R." Nashville. DLC-USG, V, 37. See *O.R.*, I, xvii, part 2, 185. On Dec. 24, USG, Nashville, telegraphed to Anderson, Louisville. "I understand

J. W. Stevens has been appointed to manage some portion of the roads in your
charge. He was turned out of the Department of the Tennessee for dishonesty
and until cleared by a competent court, he cannot serve in this Military Division."
Copies, DLC-USG, V, 34, 35; DNA, RG 393, Military Div. of the Miss., Letters
Sent. On Dec. 22, Maj. Gen. Stephen A. Hurlbut, Memphis, telegraphed to USG.
"Mr. A. B. Goodhue has reported here to take charge of Railroads under orders
from Mr Anderson   Shall Genl. Webster be releived   I do not like these civilian
Railroad men"   Telegram received, *ibid.*, RG 109, Union Provost Marshals'
File of Papers Relating to Individual Civilians; *ibid.*, RG 393, Dept. of the Tenn.,
Telegrams Received; copies, *ibid.*, 16th Army Corps, Letters Sent; *ibid.*, Mili-
tary Div. of the Miss., Telegrams Received. *O.R.*, I, xxxi, part 3, 469. Although
A. F. Goodhue became superintendent of military railroads, West Tenn. and
Ark., Webster continued in Jan., 1864, to receive orders regarding military railroads. *Ibid.*, I, xxxii, part 2, 76, 125, 157, 213, 217, 243; *ibid.*, III, v, 63–64,
592, 1005. On Feb. 7, USG wrote to W. J. Stevens. "My telegram disabling you
from accepting a place in Govt. employ within my command was in consequence
of Gen. Webster ~~having~~ Gen. Supt. having discharged you. As Gen Webster no
longer occupies the position of Gen Supt. of Mil. rail-roads, and being fully satisfied of your competancy and fitness for the position of rail-road supt. all disabling
orders to your accepting such position are hereby revoked." ALS, IHi. Stevens
served as superintendent of the Nashville and Chattanooga Railroad, becoming
general superintendent of military railroads, Military Div. of the Miss., in 1865.
O.R., I, lii, part 1, 622; *ibid.*, III, v, 84, 993.

On Feb. 18, 1864, Brig. Gen. James H. Wilson, Washington, wrote to USG.
"A few days ago while at Mr. Washburn's quarters I chanced to see a letter from
Genl. Webster, in which he complained bitterly of his inactivity. He expressed
the warmest regard and respect for you but his sense of duty would not allow
him to appeal directly for employment. Mr. W. did not wish to annoy you with
a case of this kind—felt a delicacy any how, and therefore showed me the letter.
Couldn't General Webster go to Thomas—or wouldn't he be better than quite a
number of Sherman's division commanders? Your sly note enclosing the billet-
doux of Miss Letcher was received a few days ago—I duly appreciate the favor;
but having met quite a number of young ladies, all as pretty as she, and talked
rather indiscriminately of Western heros, I am assailed on all sides for autographs and photographs. As you know I am quite a good friend of yours but
can't quite write your name as well as Jo Bowers—therefore I have to beg of you
to sign your name five or six times to the next letter you write me—and enclose
several copies according to agreement, of your *cartes* d. V.—As a matter of course
this all for benevolent purposes. Col. Hatch is in town, quite active, and will soon
be well of his wound. He could take Kautz's place organizing the Tenn. cavalry.
I am getting along pretty well—and think I can begin to see the light—Mr. Dana
and I both think there is no doubt I can join you when spring operations begin.
We are delighted at the good news from the railroad west." ALS, USG 3. Webster became Maj. Gen. William T. Sherman's chief of staff, as Sherman had contemplated on Nov. 16, 1863. *Memoirs of Gen. W. T. Sherman* (4th ed., New
York, 1891), II, 22; *O.R.*, I, xxxi, part 3, 169.

3. On Nov. 28, Maj. Gen. John M. Schofield, St. Louis, telegraphed to
USG. "I have an order from the war dept to consolidate the twenty fifth Mo Vols
with Col Flids Missouri Vol Engineer Regt   the former is in my dept & the
latter in yours   if you will order Col Flid to come to St Louis with the rolls of

his regt I will arrange the ~~col~~ consolidation [*and*] if you desire submit [*it*] to you for your approval   I will then send you the part of the new regt now here"   Telegram received, DNA, RG 107, Telegrams Collected (Unbound); *ibid.*, RG 393, Dept. of the Tenn., Telegrams Received; copies, *ibid.*, Dept. of Mo., Telegrams Sent; *ibid.*, Military Div. of the Miss., Telegrams Received. On Nov. 30, USG telegraphed to Schofield. "Colonel Flad has been ordered to St Louis as you requested in your dispatch of 28th inst, and will take the rolls of his regiment with him, for the purpose of arrangeing for the consolidation of the 25th Missouri with his own regiment. If the services of the Regiment are absolutely required in your Department, I will send the portion of the new regiment here, to you. If not, I can make it very useful in the repairing and construction of rail roads in this command." Copies, DLC-USG, V, 34, 35; DNA, RG 393, Military Div. of the Miss., Letters Sent. On Dec. 7, Schofield telegraphed to USG. "Please inform me if Col Flad of the Mo Engineer regiment has been ordered to St Louis and when he started—"   Telegram received, *ibid.*, RG 107, Telegrams Collected (Unbound); *ibid.*, RG 393, Dept. of the Tenn., Telegrams Received; copies, *ibid.*, Dept. of Mo., Telegrams Sent; *ibid.*, Military Div. of the Miss., Telegrams Received. On the same day, USG telegraphed to Schofield. "Orders have been sent Col Flad to proceed to St Louis   I cant say whither he has started or not"   Copies, DLC-USG, V, 34, 35; DNA, RG 393, Military Div. of the Miss., Letters Sent; *ibid.*, Dept. of Mo., Telegrams Received. On Dec. 21, USG telegraphed to Hurlbut. "Send the Western Engineer Regiment Maj Tweedale commanding to Nashville with directions to report to these Hd Qurs his arrival there   send this despatch to McPherson that he may order forward the part serving with him"   Telegram received, *ibid.*, 16th Army Corps, Letters Received; copy, *ibid.*, 17th Army Corps, Telegrams Received (Unarranged). On Dec. 31, Schofield and Col. John B. Gray, Mo. AG, wrote to USG regarding the consolidation of the Engineer Regt. of the West and the 25th Mo. Copy and ALS, *ibid.*, Military Div. of the Miss., Letters Received. On Jan. 21, 1864, 2:00 P.M., Maj. Gen. James B. McPherson, Vicksburg, telegraphed to USG. "The engeneer detachment under Maj Tweedale with the exception of the Company with the ponton train was ordered to report to you at Nashville on the 30th of December but it was not until the 18th instant that transportation could be furnished & then they had to be sent up on the U. S. hospital steamer Woodford" Telegram received, *ibid.*, Dept. of the Tenn., Telegrams Received; copy, *ibid.*, Military Div. of the Miss., Telegrams Received.

To Elihu B. Washburne

Chattanooga Tennessee,
December 2d 1863,

HON. E. B. WASHBURN,
DEAR SIR:

Enclosed please find a letter to the President recommending Chetlains promotion.[1] For the last three weeks I have not only been busy but have had company[2] occupying my room making it almost impossible for me to write any thing.—Last week was a stiring time with us and a magnificent victory was won. I am sorry you could not be here. The specticle was grand beyond anything that has been, or is likely to be, on this Continent. It is the first battle field I have ever seen where a plan could be followed and from one place the whole field be within one view. At the Commencement the battle line was fifteen miles long. Hooker on our right soon carried the point of Lookout Mountain, and Sherman the North end of Missionary ridge thus shortening the line by five or six miles and bringing the whole within one view. Our troops behaved most magnificently and have inflicted on the enemy the heavyest blow they have received during the war.

Your Galena friends with me are all well and desire to be remembered.

Yours Truly
U. S. GRANT

ALS, IHi. On Dec. 4, 1863, 4:40 P.M., U.S. Representative Elihu B. Washburne, Washington, telegraphed to Brig. Gen. John A. Rawlins. "Give names and dates of late battles at Chattanooga to put on Grant's sword. Did he receive my letter from Odin in regard to Chetlain?" ALS (telegram sent), DNA, RG 107, Telegrams Collected (Unbound). On the same day, Rawlins telegraphed to Washburne. "Battle of Chattanooga twenty third to twenty seventh November inclusive. Letter from Adna received & answered" Telegram received, DLC-Elihu B. Washburne. See letter to Elihu B. Washburne, Dec. 12, 1863; speech, March 18, 1864.

1. See letter to Abraham Lincoln, Dec. 2, 1863.
2. See letter to Maj. Gen. William T. Sherman, Nov. 29, 1863, note 2.

To Brig. Gen. Grenville M. Dodge

Chattanooga 6.45 P. M. Dec 3d 1863

BRIGADIER GENERAL G. M DODGE
PULASKI TENN

General Hurlbut reports a large force approaching Corinth with the probable view of attacking the place.[1] I had previously ordered boats to Eastport to move that garrison to Hurlbut.[2] If you can I wish you would send a messenger through to Eastport instructing the Commanding Officer, if he has not yet left, to stop at Hamburg Landing and if Corinth is still threatned, to march out there, and remain until the place is relieved from danger. Should they go to Corinth, the Commanding Officer should report to Genl Hurlbut for orders, and if not required to move by water release the steamers.

U S GRANT

Major General.

Telegram, copies, DLC-USG, V, 34, 35; DNA, RG 393, Military Div. of the Miss., Letters Sent. *O.R.*, I, xxxi, part 3, 332–33. On Dec. 4, 1863, Brig. Gen. Grenville M. Dodge, Columbia, Tenn., telegraphed to USG. "I have just received your dispatch and will send it through very fast. Co'l. Rowett just returned overland from Corinth says that fourteen (14) Steamers went up to Eastport three days ago   says that one brigade had been up and went down again   met the rest at Paducah and all returned to Eastport. The force threatening Corinth, is Forest Cavalry five Brigades & rumor said some Infantry   Your dispatch will get to Eastport tomorrow"   Copy, DNA, RG 393, Military Div. of the Miss., Telegrams Received. *O.R.*, I, xxxi, part 3, 333. On Dec. 11, Dodge, Athens, Ala., telegraphed to USG. "The dispatches I sent for you to Eastport got there the 6th & found all troops on board of transports including the one hundred twenty second Ills which I left to garrison the place   They had received your order by way of Paducah & construed it to take everything   that leaves no troops at Eastport   I suppose all stores went with them   They went to Hamburg the same day & would report to Corinth for orders." Telegram received, DNA, RG 94, War Records Office, Military Div. of the Miss.; copy, *ibid.*, RG 393, Military Div. of the Miss., Telegrams Received. *O.R.*, I, xxxi, part 3, 380. On Dec. 7, Col. Stephen G. Hicks, Paducah, telegraphed to Lt. Col. Theodore S. Bowers. "All the troops from Eastport will be here tonight or tomorrow   there is no convoy here for the Steamer loaded with Com. stores ordered up the Tennessee   Shall I send her up"   Telegram received, DNA, RG 94, War Records Office, Military Div. of the Miss.; copy, *ibid.*, RG 393, Military Div. of the Miss., Telegrams Received. *O.R.*, I, xxxi, part 3, 354. On Dec. 8, Rear Admiral David D. Porter, Cairo, telegraphed to USG. "I have already ordered Capt. Shirk to get the Gunboats over the shoals the moment he can do so"   Copy, DNA, RG 393, Military Div. of the Miss., Telegrams Received.

On Dec. 3 and 7, Maj. Gen. Stephen A. Hurlbut, Memphis, telegraphed to Maj. Gen. William T. Sherman through USG, reporting the C.S.A. descent on Saulsbury, Tenn., and the action near Moscow, Tenn. Telegrams received, *ibid.*, RG 94, War Records Office, Military Div. of the Miss.; copies, *ibid.*, RG 393, Military Div. of the Miss., Telegrams Received. *O.R.*, I, xxxi, part 1, 576–77. A similar telegram of Dec. 5 from Hurlbut to Sherman may also have been sent through USG. *Ibid.*, p. 577. On Monday, Dec. 7, Brig. Gen. Hugh T. Reid, Cairo, telegraphed to USG. "Corporal Wilkins of Engineer Corps just from Memphis reports that Chalmers with from three to four thousand men entered Salisbury on Memphis & Charleston R. R. on Wednesday last burned a quantity of cotton, two or three cars, tore up the track for a mile fired into a train coming from Corinth with thirty five rebel prisoners on board who called out come on we will get loose. Train backed out and escaped without injury. On Thursday same force made three desperate charges on our forces at Wolf River bridge but were repulsed with considerable loss   one rebel Colonel reported killed. Co'l Hatch severely wounded. Shot through right lung   Sixth Ills. Cavalry suffered severely   lost many of their horses   Second Tenn. colored fought well. Chalmers retreated towards Brownsville burning depot and tank at Lafayette. Co'l. Misner pursued. The road repaired & trains running to Memphis"   Copies, DNA, RG 393, Dept. of Ky., Telegrams Sent; *ibid.*, Military Div. of the Miss., Telegrams Received.

1. On Nov. 28, Hurlbut telegraphed to USG. "Lee with six thousand (6000) men and artillery and wagon trains was at Pontiac yesterday   Chalmers will join him at New Albany they say near Corinth   I think it is a move on West Tennessee   Winters [*Mizner's*] cavalry is on this front and Right flank   Hatch is moving from Somerville to LaGrange to close up   Tuttle is ordered with six (6) Regiments to close from LaGrange up on them or get to Corinth   Morgan with two Regiments and Battery moves to LaGrange today   I will try and force them to fight"   Telegram received, *ibid.*, RG 94, War Records Office, Military Div. of the Miss.; copies, *ibid.*; *ibid.*, RG 393, Military Div. of the Miss., Telegrams Received. *O.R.*, I, xxxi, part 3, 266–67. On Nov. 30, Hurlbut telegraphed to Sherman through USG. "Roddey is on Bear Creek   Lee near Okalona fronted by our Cavalry   Forrest and Richardson are near New Albany   They meant to attack Corinth in force but have stopped in their march   I have a strong force at LaGrange with orders to move to Corinth if an attack is made there   Their activity has compelled me to abandon the work of taking up iron and be ready for a fight   Their forces if united will be about six thousand (6000) unless they bring infantry by railroad from below which I do not expect. Scout just in from Rome reports that Bragg has been moving ordnance and incumbrances back for two weeks—No further news"   Telegram received, DNA, RG 94, War Records Office, Military Div. of the Miss.; copy, *ibid.*, RG 393, Military Div. of the Miss., Telegrams Received. *O.R.*, I, xxxi, part 3, 287. On Dec. 1, 7:00 P.M., Hurlbut telegraphed to Sherman through USG. "Mizner at Ripley at two (2) is in   Reports enemy advancing in force—There are rumors of infantry in heavy force at Oxford   I am massing from La Grange on Corinth   Cannot yet tell what it is but think the Cavalry advance covers infantry movements   Genl Dodge should be notified in case of a strong movement towards the muscle shoals"   Telegram received, DNA, RG 94, War Records Office, Military Div. of the Miss.; copy, *ibid.*, RG 393, Military Div. of the Miss., Telegrams Received. *O.R.*, I, xxxi, part 3, 300.

2. See telegram to Maj. Gen. Stephen A. Hurlbut, Nov. 29, 1863.

To Maj. Gen. Henry W. Halleck

Chattanooga Tenn
Dec 5th 1863—5 P M

MAJ GEN H W HALLECK
GEN IN CHIEF

Nothing has been heard directly from Sherman since the First (1st)   He was expected to reach Knoxville by Third or Fourth.[1] His force is full thirty thousand (30000) exclusive of Cavalry   Reposing full confidence in him and his command I feel no apprehension for the result except as to Gen Burnsides ability to hold out until he reaches

Dispatch from Gen Burnside on the Thirtieth (30th) stated that enemy had attacked him and been repulsed with great slaughter   His supplies were then still up—[2]

U. S GRANT M G. C

Telegram received, DLC-Robert T. Lincoln; DNA, RG 107, Telegrams Collected (Bound); copies, *ibid.*, Telegrams Received in Cipher; *ibid.*, RG 393, Military Div. of the Miss., Hd. Qrs. Correspondence; DLC-USG, V, 40, 94. *O.R.*, I, xxxi, part 3, 339.

1. See letter to Maj. Gen. William T. Sherman, Nov. 29, 1863.
2. On Nov. 30, 1863, Maj. Gen. Ambrose E. Burnside, Knoxville, telegraphed to USG. "On the evening of the twenty eighth about eleven P M The enemy made an attack in force upon our picket line to the right of the Kingston road and forced us back some distance in front of Fort Saunders the work commanding that road   We afterwards regained a portion of the distance   sharp skirmishing continued nearly all night   About half past six yesterday moring they moved a column of assault of Three brigades against Fort Sanders. In spite of our heavy fire a portion of two brigades succeeded in gaining the ditch but were unable to ascend the parapet   We swept the ditch with an enfilading fire with much slaughter   The rest of the attacking column retreated in confusion   We sent out a detachment to whom the rebels in the ditch surrendered   about three hundred men and three stand of colors were taken   Their killed and wounded amount to about five hundred—Our entire loss was about twenty   The morning being very cold and frosty and the enemys wounded in our ditch and in front of the fort crying for help I sent out a flag of truce offering the opportunity of caring for their wounded and burying their dead   Genl Longstreet gratefully accepted the offer and a cessation of hostilities till five P M was agreed upon   Their lightly wounded were exchanged for our slightly wounded lost in previous affairs and their dead sent to their lines   Ninety eight (98) dead passed through our hands among them Col Rongh Commanding Warfords Brigade which led the assault Col. McElroy and Lieut Col Thomas   A simultaneous

assault was made upon the right of our line on the other side of the river by a rebel brigade   They carried our first line of Rifle pits but were soon after driven from them and the whole line regained and held   Our loss on that side was about forty (40)   That of the enemy is thought to be greater   Our supply of provisions continues the same   The men are in the best of spirits   We have nothing definate of your movements and are very anxious   I have information that on the twenty seventh (27) the enemy received reinforcements of one Division perhaps two (2) Bushrod Johnsons and Cheathams   Some of Buckners troops are certainly here as some of our officers saw the Rebel General Gracie during the flag yesterday   Let us hear from you soon"   Telegram received, DNA, RG 94, War Records Office, Military Div. of the Miss.; copies, *ibid.*, Union Battle Reports; *ibid.*, RG 393, Military Div. of the Miss., Telegrams Received. *O.R.*, I, xxxi, part 1, 270–71. This telegram was received in Chattanooga on Dec. 3.

On Nov. 28, Burnside had telegraphed to USG. "I despatched you last on the twenty third—During that night a body of the enemy crossed the river about three miles below our lines and established themselves on a high point just beyond our picket line & threw up Rifle pits facing our position on that side. During that day and the forenoon of the twenty fifth continual skirmishing went on and on that afternoon they assaulted our right on that side of the river with two Brigades   Col Cameron who held that position with his brigade held his ground in the most gallant manner and finally repulsed them and drove them half way up the apposite hill inflicting severe loss upon them. Our loss was about fifty (50) that of the enemy about one hundred & fifty (150)   Appearances indicating that the enemy were concentrating a heavy force there for another attack our position was strengthened and reinforcements placed at the disposal of Genl Shackleford who commanded the forces on the south side of the River   No further serious demonstrations has been made on that side and we still hold the same skirmish line as at the close of the fight   The enemy are still at work on the hill held by them   On this side of the river the situation is nearly the same as at last accounts. The enemy have thrown up some new works but have not extended their lines and no enemy is visible on our right except cavalry   Skirmishing is continual on our left but we still hold the same line   By sending out trains on the roads still open to us we have been enabled to keep up a fair supply of forage and subsistence"   Telegram received, DNA, RG 94, War Records Office, Military Div. of the Miss.; copies, *ibid.*, Union Battle Reports; *ibid.*, RG 393, Military Div. of the Miss., Telegrams Received. *O.R.*, I, xxxi, part 1, 269–70.

To J. Russell Jones

Chattanooga Dec. 5th 1863,

DEAR JONES,

Your letter of the 25th reached here about the time closing scenes of the late battles were taking place. I regret that you could not be here to witness the grand panorama. I presume a battle never took place on so large a scale where so much of it could be seen, or where every move proved so successful; and out of doors where there was an outlet to retreat by. An Army never was whipped so badly as Bragg was. So far as any opposition the enemy could make I could have marched to Atlanta or any other place in the Confederacy. But I was obliged to rescue Burnside. Again I had not rations to take nor the means of taking them and this mountain country will not support an Army. Altogether I feel well satisfied and the Army feel that they have accomplished great things. Well they may. By the end of this month I will have enough due me to pay you what you have laid out for me.[1] In the mean time can you borrow, at my expense, the amount? It is rather hard to ask a friend to make an investment for you and then get him to borrow the money to make it. But I am so situated that I cannot attend to my own private affairs and hope I am not giving you too much trouble.

J. E. Smith, Rawlins, Dr. Kittoe, and the Galenaites are well and desire to be remembered.

Yours Truly

U. S. GRANT

Maj. Gen.

ALS, ICHi.

1. See letter to J. Russell Jones, Nov. 17, 1863.

To Maj. Gen. John G. Foster

Chattanooga [*Dec.*] 6th [*1863*] 4 15 p m

MAJ GENL. FOSTER

Instruct your Cavalry to follow Longstreet to the last moment. it is not necessary that they should attack the main force but follow up the rear hasten the retreat pick up Stragglers and distroy the roads as far East as possible   if your troops can get as far as Saltville & distroy the works there it will be an immese loss to the enemy

U. S. GRANT M G

Telegram received, DNA, RG 94, War Records Office, Dept. of the Ohio; copies, *ibid.*, RG 393, Military Div. of the Miss., Letters Sent; DLC-USG, V, 34, 35. *O.R.*, I, xxxi, part 3, 345.

On Dec. 1, 1863, Maj. Gen. John G. Foster, Cumberland Gap, telegraphed to USG. "Gen'l Wilcox has just rec'd from Co'l Graham Comdg. his advanced Cavalry force near Maynardsville a Despatch stating that it is reported in that Neighborhood that Burnside had a successful fight with the enemy on the morning of the 29th in which he inflicted severe loss upon them. It is also reported that Buckner had joined Longstreet. I give the reports for what they are worth: a Brigade of Gen'l Wilcox Cavalry moved within 8 miles of Knoxville yesterday but met the enemy in two strong force to risk an engagement   all the available Infy. have moved from this point. I shall be in Tazwell tonight—"   Copy, DNA, RG 393, Military Div. of the Miss., Telegrams Received. *O.R.*, I, xxxi, part 3, 297. On Dec. 2, 7:30 A.M., Foster, Tazewell, Tenn., telegraphed to USG. "A courier came in from the front last night with the report that heavy firing was heard at Knoxville from 3 oclock P. M. yesterday to the time he left. Can this be Granger attacking Longstreets rear. I am posting my small force on the Clinch River in good positions for defence or offense—"   Copy, DNA, RG 393, Military Div. of the Miss., Telegrams Received. *O.R.*, I, xxxi, part 3, 310. On the same day, noon, Foster telegraphed to USG. "A party of eight men One of which is an officer have arrived   left Knoxville on Monday night. They report that Gen'l. Burnside was strongly entrenched sufficiently supplied and confident of holding out any reasonable length of time. Midnight of Saturday Longstreet made a desperate assault on Fort Sanders with picked Com'd. The engagement lasted all night until seven o'clock next A. M. The rebels were completely repulsed with a loss of eight thousand men of which two hundred and forty were killed   Gen'l B—— loss 45 killed & wounded   Some of the prisoners reported that Buckners forces had joined Longstreets whose entire force is estimated 3800 men. One of the party brought a dispatches to you which I have not yet seen. Giving full report of operations up to time of writing; the Genl impression which I rec'd from the officer who gives this information is that Gen. Burnside & his men are in excellent spirits & confident of their ability to defeat the efforts of the enemy"   Copy, DNA, RG 393, Military Div. of the Miss., Telegrams Received. Printed as addressed to Maj. Gen. Henry W. Halleck in *O.R.*, I, xxxi, part 3, 311. See telegram to Maj. Gen. Henry W. Halleck, Dec. 5, 1863, note 2. Also on Dec. 2, 12:10 P.M., Foster telegraphed to USG, possibly answering his dispatch of Dec. 1, 9:00 P.M. "Your despatch received—My force is so small, being only 5000 men of the 6 months troops that I shall not be able to do a great deal, still you may rely upon our doing something at at the most possible right time— A brigade of cavalry in front towards Maynardsville skirmished all day yesterday with a superior force and is still engaged,—being forced to retire towards the clinch River—The iny artillery & infantry are now taking positions to command the fords—"   ALS (telegram sent), DNA, RG 107, Telegrams Collected (Unbound); copy (misdated Nov. 2, 1:10 P.M.), *ibid.*, RG 393, Military Div. of the Miss., Telegrams Received. Printed as addressed to Halleck in *O.R.*, I, xxxi, part 3, 311–12. See telegram to Maj. Gen. John G. Foster, Dec. 2, 1863.

On Dec. 2, 9:00 P.M., Foster telegraphed to USG. "Heavy skirmishing has been continued all day between our advance cavalry and the enemy in the direction of Maynardsville which has resulted in Co'l. Graham Com'dg. the Cavalry being driven back to the Infantry supports on Clinch River   all attempts to force a passage were repulsed. Ransoms Division of three brigades of Infy. en-route for Knoxville is reported near Bean Station" Copy (dated Dec. 3), DNA, RG 393, Military Div. of the Miss., Telegrams Received. Printed as addressed to Halleck in *O.R.*, I, xxxi, part 3, 311. On Dec. 3, 3:00 P.M., Foster twice telegraphed to USG, the first time evidently referring to Halleck's dispatch of Dec. 1, midnight. "Your dispatch is recd. I am at present completely held in check by Wheelers and Jones Cavalry which is stronger than my force with which we are engaged all day yesterday and by Ransoms Div. on the road near Beans Station   shall send courier through to Clinton and tell Gen. Granger that I have doubt Longstreet will retreat by the road leading through Rutledge or Rogersville and that if Granger will advance to Blaines Cross Roads he will strike Longstreets flanks or failing in that we can catch Wheelers Ca'vy. between us—" "Wheelers Cavalry were repelled at the Clinch river and have retired towards Knoxville. A union Citizen over the mountains reports that a large force of Infantry & Cavalry probably Ransoms force passed Bean Station this morning to Knoxville" Copies, DNA, RG 393, Military Div. of the Miss., Telegrams Received. Printed as addressed to Halleck in *O.R.*, I, xxxi, part 3, 315–16. See *ibid.*, p. 295. On Dec. 4, 10:15 A.M., Foster telegraphed to USG. "The enemys Cavalry retired yesterday toward Knoxville closely followed by our Cavalry. Our Scouts went Seven (7) miles beyond Maynardsville. Heavy firing was heard all day yesterday at Knoxville   I have ordered a detachment of Cavalry to Blockade the Valley road from Spring House to Bean Station—" Copy, DNA, RG 393, Military Div. of the Miss., Telegrams Received. Printed as addressed to Halleck in *O.R.*, I, xxxi, part 3, 327. On Dec. 6, noon, Foster telegraphed to USG. "The cavalry scouts just returned from the vicinity of Blain's Cross-Roads report a rebel column passing all last night from Knoxville to Blain's Cross-Roads. They heard the men say that they were going to Virginia; that the Yankees had them surrounded, but that they were going to fight their way out. My scouts on the top of Clinch Mountain say large camp-fires were seen last night on the road from Blain's Cross-Roads to Rutledge. I have no doubt that Longstreet is retreating. My division of cavalry is moving on his rear through Maynardville and Blain's Cross-Roads." Printed as addressed to Halleck, *ibid.*, p. 344.

On Dec. 6, 4:30 P.M., USG telegraphed to Halleck. "Dispatch just received from Gen Foster indicates beyond doubt that Longstreet is retreating towards Virginia   I have directed him to be well followed up—" Telegram received, DLC-Robert T. Lincoln; DNA, RG 107, Telegrams Collected (Bound); copies, *ibid.*, Telegrams Received in Cipher; *ibid.*, RG 393, Military Div. of the Miss., Hd. Qrs. Correspondence; DLC-USG, V, 40, 94. *O.R.*, I, xxxi, part 3, 345. See General Orders No. 7, Dec. 8, 1863. On Dec. 8, 3:00 P.M., Halleck telegraphed to USG. "Do you propose to pursue Longstreet into Virginia? That line of operations is a good one, if the army can be supplied on it. The matter of supplies requires careful consideration. Please give me your views in regard to such a movement." ALS (telegram sent), DNA, RG 107, Telegrams Collected (Bound); copies, *ibid.*, RG 393, Military Div. of the Miss., Hd. Qrs. Correspondence; DLC-USG, V, 40, 94. *O.R.*, I, xxxi, part 3, 357. On the same day, 10:30 P.M., USG telegraphed to Halleck. "The Army pursuing Longstreet can only pursue as far as the country will supply them, which I think cannot be beyond Bristol. I tried very hard to get Wilcox to push from Cumberland Gap to Abingdon and Saltville, whilst Longstreet was at Knoxville, but could not get him off—Not knowing the feisability of the plan I did not make the order imperative." Telegram received, DNA, RG 107, Telegrams Collected (Bound); copies, *ibid.*, Telegrams Received in Cipher; (datelined 10:20 P.M.) *ibid.*, RG 393, Military Div. of the Miss., Hd. Qrs. Correspondence; DLC-USG, V, 40, 94. Printed as sent at 10:30 P.M. in *O.R.*, I, xxxi, part 3, 357. See telegrams to Brig. Gen. Orlando B. Willcox, Nov. 23, 24, 1863.

On Dec. 6, 6:00 P.M., Foster telegraphed to USG. "There seems no doubt that Longstreet is in full retreat   a deserter that came in today reports that he came out with the column from Knoxville on the fourth   The infantry & transportation moving up the valley on the other side of the holston & the cavalry ~~one~~ on this side to cover from my attack   the talk among the soldiers was that they were going to virginia or north Carolina   Fosters cavalry division was four miles this side of Maynardsville at two P M when the courier left preparing to attack the enemies cavalry"   Telegram received, DNA, RG 393, Dept. of Mo., Telegrams Received. Printed as addressed to Halleck in *O.R.*, I, xxxi, part 3, 344. On Dec. 7, 7:00 A.M. and 9:00 P.M., Foster telegraphed to USG. "Longstreet is in full retreat up the valley. Your orders about following with cavalry shall be carried out   My division of Cavalry attacked the enemy's cavalry in one of the passes of the Clinch mountain yesterday P. M. and are pushing them Vigorously   I have not yet heard of the approach of our Cavalry from Knoxville   I have sent Gen'l Wilcox with his Infantry and Artillery towards the mountains and Attack the enemy's flank at Bean Station. Couriers from Knoxville arrived last night. The road is clear. Sherman arrived there yesterday—"   Copy, DNA, RG 393, Military Div. of the Miss., Telegrams Received. Printed as addressed to Halleck in *O.R.*, I, xxxi, part 3, 351. "I have returned from the Clinch river where I expected to join a brigade of Infantry and drive the enemy from the summit of Clinch Mountain so as to play on the flanks of the retreating enemy with artillery but the troops were so weakened by the one quarter rations that they had for some months that they did not get to the position in time   the Cavalry have skirmished with the enemy all day   upon my return here I find a dispatch from Gen'l. Burnside desiring me to join him with my whole force. this I shall do as my force is too small to do much by itself. Gen'l Burnside thinks Longstreet is not defeated but is merely falling back to avoid Sherman—"   Copy, DNA, RG 393, Military Div. of the Miss., Telegrams Received. *O.R.*, I, xxxi, part 3, 351. See telegrams to Maj. Gen. Ambrose E. Burnside, Dec. 10, 1863, and to Maj. Gen. John G. Foster, Dec. 15, 1863.

On Dec. 2, Capt. John C. Van Duzer, asst. superintendent, U.S. Military Telegraph, Nashville, telegraphed to USG. "Gov. A. Johnson makes daily enquiries at this Office for latest intelligence from East Tenn.   will you permit me to give him information derived from Gen'l. Fosters Messages to you which pass this office"   Copy, DNA, RG 393, Military Div. of the Miss., Telegrams Received.

To Maj. Gen. Henry W. Halleck

Head Quarters, Mil. Div. of the Miss.
Chattanooga Ten. Dec. 7th 1863.

MAJ. GEN. H. W. HALLECK,
GEN. IN CHIEF, WASHINGTON, D. C.
GENERAL,

It may now safely be assumed that the enemy are driven from this front, or at least that they no longer threaten it in any formidable numbers. The country South of this is extremely mountainous, affording but little for the support of an Army; the roads are bad, at all times, and the season is so far advanced that an extensive campaign from here this Winter may be looked upon as impossible. Our supplies and means of transportation would not admit of a very early Campaign if the season did. Not feeling willing, or rather desiring to avoid, keeping so large a force idle, for months, I take the liberty of suggesting a plan of Campaign that I think will go far towards breaking down the rebellion before Spring. It will at least keep the enemy harrassed and prevent that reorganization which could be effected by Spring if left uninterrupted.

The rainy season will soon set in. The roads will then be so bad that the enemy cannot move a large Army into Tennessee. A comparatively small force will be able to hold the present line and thereby relieve the rail-roads and enable them to accumulate supplies by the time the roads become passable. With the force thus relieved, and what can be gathered from other parts of this Military Division, I propose, with the concurrence of higher authority, to move by way of New Orleans and Pascagoula on Mobile. I would hope to secure that place, or its investment, by the last of January. Should ~~they~~ the enemy make an obstinate resistence at Mobile I would fortify outside and leave a garrison sufficient to hold the garrison of the town and with the balance of the Army make a campaign into the interior of Alabama, and, possibly, Georgia. The campaign of course would be suggested by the movements of the enemy.—It seems to me this move would secure the entire states of Alabama & Mississippi, and a part of Georgia or force Lee to abandon Virginia & North Carolina. Without his force the enemy have not got Army enough to resist the Army I can take.

There is no necessity for me enlarging upon this because I could say nothing in favor of it that will not suggest itself to you. Hoping an early reply, by telegraph, this is respectfully submitted.

> I am General, very respectfully
> your obt. svt.
> U. S. GRANT
> Maj. Gen.

ALS, Schoff Collection, MiU-C. *O.R.*, I, xxxi, part 3, 349–50. On Nov. 29, 1863, 11:00 A.M., Asst. Secretary of War Charles A. Dana had telegraphed to Secretary of War Edwin M. Stanton outlining USG's plans. *Ibid.*, I, xxxi, part 2, 72. See letter to Maj. Gen. James B. McPherson, Dec. 1, 1863.

On Dec. 17, Maj. Gen. Henry W. Halleck telegraphed to USG. "Your letter of the 7th is just recieved, & will, on the first opportunity, be brought to the attention of the Secty of War. The first object to be accomplished now is the expulsion of the enemy from East Tennessee and the repair & security of the lines of supply for our troops there. Next to secure the points of access of the enemy to East & Middle Tennessee. I agree with you that all troops not required for these purposes, and for cleaning out West Tennessee & the Mississippi can operate with greater advantage during the winter in the South. From present appearances Genl Banks will need all the assistance you can give him just now on the lower Mississippi & in Louisiana, as I telegraphed you a few days ago. I will answer your letter more fully as soon as I learn the wishes of the War Dept & the President." ALS (telegram sent), DNA, RG 107, Telegrams Collected (Bound); copies, *ibid.*, RG 393, Military Div. of the Miss., Hd. Qrs. Correspondence; DLC-USG, V, 40, 94. *O.R.*, I, xxxi, part 3, 454. See telegram to Maj. Gen. Henry W. Halleck, Dec. 11, 1863. On Dec. 18, midnight, Dana, who had left Chattanooga on Dec. 12, telegraphed from Washington to USG. "Have just arrived, but have not seen any one, nor learned any ~~things~~ thing." ALS (telegram sent), DNA, RG 107, Telegrams Collected (Bound); copies, *ibid.*, RG 393, Military Div. of the Miss., Hd. Qrs. Correspondence; DLC-USG, V, 40, 94. See *O.R.*, I, xxxi, part 1, 264; *ibid.*, I, xxxi, part 2, 73.

On Dec. 21, 4:30 P.M., Halleck telegraphed to USG. "As I understand from your despatch of the 7th and from conversations with Mr. Dana, you propose: *first*, to expel the enemy from East Tennessee, & to provide against his return into the valley; *second*, to either force the rebels further back into Georgia, or to provide against their return by that line into Tennessee; *third*, to clean out West Tennessee; *fourth*, to move a force down the Mississippi & operate against Mobile. The importance ~~importance~~ of these objects is considered to be in the order above stated. It is thought that the fourth should not be definitively determined upon till the other three are accomplished, or their accomplishment made reasonably certain. Moreover, circumstances may be such, by the time that your spare forces reach Port Hudson or New Orleans, as to require their services West of the Mississippi. If so the latter part of the plan would be somewhat varied, or its execution delayed." ALS (telegram sent), DNA, RG 107, Telegrams Collected (Bound); copies, *ibid.*, RG 393, Military Div. of the Miss., Hd. Qrs. Correspondence; DLC-USG, V, 40, 94. *O.R.*, I, xxxi, part 3, 458. On the same day, 6:00 P.M., Dana telegraphed to USG. "I have had detailed conversations with the President, the Secretary of War and Gen Halleck with respect to your project of a campaign in Alabama. It meets the full approval of them all in every respect, not only because it keeps your army active during the otherwise useless weather of the winter, but because it appears to them well conceived and as certain of producing the desired effect as any plan can be. 'If it succeed' said Secretary of War 'Braggs Army become prisoners of War without our having the trouble of providing for them.' You would be authorized to proceed immediately with its execution but for the anxiety which seems to exist respecting East Tennessee. If Longstreet were expelled from that country, you could start for Mobile at once. I suppose Gen Halleck will communicate with you fully on this subject. I judge from my conversation with him that he does not understand clearly how an army, large enough to make Longstreets dislodgement certain can be supplied while operating against Rogersville & Bristol and accordingly I presume that first, as soon as it is settled that he must be left in that region, you will be allowed to proceed South with the main body of your forces, leaving of course a sufficient number of troops to observe Longstreet and prevent his getting hold of Knoxville, Cumberland Gap or any other controlling point now in our hands. To my suggestion that the surest means of getting the rebels altogether out of East Tennessee is to be found in the Army of the Potomac the reply is that that is true but from that Army nothing is to be hoped under its present commander. This naturally led to your second proposition, namely that either Sherman or W. F Smith should be put in command of that Army. To this the answer is such as to leave but little doubt in my mind that the second of these officers will be appointed to that post. Both Secretary of War and Gen Halleck said to me that as long as a fortnight before my arrival they had come to the conclusion that when a change should be made Gen W. F. Smith would be the best person to try. Some doubts which they seemed to have respecting his disposition and personal character I think I was able to clear up. Secretary of War has also directed me to inform him that he is to be promoted on the first vacancy. President, Secretary of War and Gen Halleck agree with you in thinking that it would be, on the whole much better to select him than Sherman. As yet however nothing has been decided upon and you will understand that I have somewhat exceeded my instructions from the Secretary of War in his communication, especially in the second branch of it but it seems to me necessary that you should know all these particulars. I leave for New York tonight to remain till after Newyears." Copies, DLC-USG, V, 40, 94; DNA, RG 393, Military Div. of the Miss., Hd. Qrs. Correspondence. *O.R.*, I, xxxi, part 3, 457–58. See Dana, *Recollections of the Civil War* (New York, 1898), pp. 156–57; *Memoirs*, II, 100–1. These sources do not support Brig. Gen. James H. Wilson's later assertion that the plan to strike Mobile had been "originally brought forward" by Brig. Gen. William F. Smith. Wilson, *The Life of Charles A. Dana* (New York and London, 1907), p. 300.

On his trip east, Dana was accompanied by Brig. Gen. John A. Rawlins, who proceeded to Danbury, Conn., where he married Mary E. (Emma) Hurlbut on Dec. 23, returning to USG's hd. qrs. on Jan. 15, 1864. James Harrison Wilson, *Under the Old Flag* (New York and London, 1912), I, 317, 321; James Harrison

Wilson, *The Life of John A. Rawlins* (New York, 1916), p. 384. See *ibid.*, pp. 150–51; Rawlins to Mary E. (Emma) Hurlbut, Dec. 3, 7, 8, 1863, ALS, ICHi.

General Orders No. 7

————

Headquarters Military Division of the Mississippi
In the Field Chattanooga, Tenn., Dec. 8th 1863

GENERAL ORDERS, NO. 7.

The General Commanding takes great pleasure in publishing to the brave Armies under his command, the following telegraphic dispatch just recieved from the President of the United States:—

"Washington Dec. 8th. 1863

To MAJOR GENERAL GRANT:—Understanding that your lodgement at Chattanooga and Knoxville is now secure, I wish to tender you, and all under your command, my more than thanks, my profoundest gratitude, for the skill, courage and perseverance with which you, and they, over so great difficulties, have effected that important object. God bless you all!"

A. LINCOLN."

By order of Major General Grant

T. S. BOWERS

Asst. Adjt. Gen'l

Copies, DLC-USG, V, 14; DNA, RG 393, Military Div. of the Miss., General Orders; (printed) USGA. *O.R.*, I, xxxi, part 2, 51. See Lincoln, *Works*, VII, 35, 53; *O.R.*, I, xxxi, part 2, 12. On Dec. 10, 1863, Lt. Col. Theodore S. Bowers issued General Orders No. 9 congratulating the forces under USG for recovering "the control of the Tennessee River, from Bridgeport to Knoxville;" dislodging the C.S.A. from Lookout Mountain, Chattanooga Valley, and Missionary Ridge; and repelling "repeated assaults upon Knoxville,—" Copies, DLC-USG, V, 14; DNA, RG 393, Military Div. of the Miss., General Orders; (printed) USGA. *O.R.*, I, xxxi, part 2, 51–52.

On Dec. 11, 1:20 P.M., U.S. Representative Elihu B. Washburne telegraphed to USG. "Resolution giving thanks to you and your soldiers, and for medal for you, passed House Unanimously and will pass Senate Unanimously, next week. Have received no ~~letter from~~ answer to my letter from Odin" ALS (telegram sent), DNA, RG 107, Telegrams Collected (Unbound). See letters to Elihu B. Washburne, Dec. 2, 12, 1863. Washburne had introduced Joint Resolution No. 1 on Dec. 8 and the House of Representatives passed it on the same day. *CG*, 38-1, 9, 12. The resolution passed the Senate, after reference to committee, on

Dec. 16, and was approved by President Abraham Lincoln on Dec. 17. *CG*, 38-1, 12–13, 36; War Dept. General Orders No. 398, copies (printed), DLC-USG; *ibid.*, U.S. Army: Civil War Miscellany. *O.R.*, I, xxxi, part 2, 52. On Dec. 21, Secretary of War Edwin M. Stanton wrote to USG. "I take great pleasure in sending you General Orders No. 398, publishing to the Army the joint resolution of Congress thanking you and the officers and soldiers who have fought under your command during this rebellion. The gold medal provided for in the resolution will be duly prepared and presented to you." Copies, DNA, RG 94, Letters Sent; *ibid.*, RG 107, Letters Sent, Military Affairs.

On Dec. 18, Lincoln wrote to Washburne asking him "to superintend the getting up of the Medal" for USG, as well as the preparation of an engrossed parchment copy of the joint resolution. Lincoln, *Works*, VII, 79. On Dec. 23, James Pollock, director, Mint of the United States, Philadelphia, wrote to Washburne projecting a design for the medal, estimated to cost $2,000, which featured a "Representation of Major General Grant, (in full uniform) Mounted" and, on the reverse side, "a shield surmounted by an Eagle." ALS, DLC-Elihu B. Washburne. On Dec. 24, Alexander Kann, a lithographer in New York City, wrote to Washburne proposing a design which included "busts of Lincoln, Grant & Washington," and the figure of Liberty to symbolize emancipation. ALS, *ibid.* However, the painter Emanuel G. Leutze, speaking for a committee, proposed a design consisting of "a profile likeness of the hero" and the "figure of Fame seated . . . on the American eagle," against which rested "the emblematical shield of the United States." Julian K. Larke, *General Grant and his Campaigns* (New York, 1864), p. 432. On Jan. 2, 1864, Leutze, New York City, wrote to Washburne asking to have USG's profile photographed. ALS, DLC-Elihu B. Washburne. On Jan. 5, Washburne telegraphed to Bowers. "Please have photograph taken of Genl. Grant ~~immediately~~ a profile, both right and left side, untouched by the artist, simple impression for medal. Send to me immediately. Designer is waiting." ALS, DNA, RG 107, Telegrams Collected (Unbound). On Jan. 20, Bowers, Nashville, wrote to Washburne regarding such photographs. "I have taken advantage of the *first clear weather* since our return to have the General sit for them, and herewith forward to you the best profiles that could be taken in this city." ALS, DLC-Elihu B. Washburne. On March 3, Leutze applied for $250 "For Design of a medal for General Grant," an application fully certified by March 22. ADS, DNA, RG 217, Office of the First Auditor, Miscellaneous Treasury Accounts, 149-511. Meanwhile, on March 1, John Antrobus, who apparently took primary responsibility for perfecting the design and who saw it through production, received in Washington $50 for "Executing a design for Medal for General Grant." ADS, *ibid.*, 149-132. Antrobus than arranged for A. C. Paquet, asst. engraver to the Mint, to prepare the medal, projecting a cost of $3,500. The design, the subject of some criticism, was evidently very much simplified for casting. Antrobus to Washburne, March 8, 23, 1864, ALS, DLC-Elihu B. Washburne; J. F. Loubat, *The Medallic History of the United States of America, 1776–1876* (New York, 1878), I, 362, 370; II, plate lxxiii; copy of medal stamped on cloth covers of *Memoirs*. On Jan. 6, 1865, Pollock wrote to Washburne forwarding the completed medal and enclosing a bill for "Material & Manufacture of Medal amounting to $660. (payable in *gold* coin)" ALS, DLC-Elihu B. Washburne. See letter to Elihu B. Washburne, Jan. 24, 1865.

To Maj. Gen. William T. Sherman

Chattanooga 5.30 P. M. 8th Dec '63

MAJOR GENERAL W. T. SHERMAN
KNOXVILLE TENN

Keep your troops in the valley of Upper Tennessee until it seems clear that the enemy have entirely abandoned the State. It may be possible that Longstreet may be reinforced about Bristol[1] and return. Two boats unloaded rations near Kingston and more will be sent in a day or two. Two more boats will be running in a few days, when we will be able to feed your Army to a great extent from here.[2]

U. S. GRANT
Major General

Copies, DLC-USG, V, 34, 35; DNA, RG 393, Military Div. of the Miss., Letters Sent. *O.R.*, I, xxxi, part 3, 356. On Dec. 8, 1863, 6:00 P.M., USG telegraphed to Maj. Gen. Henry W. Halleck. "May it not be possible that Lee will reinforce Longstreet about Bristol and return to Knoxville? I have sent Sherman orders to remain in the upper Valley until it is fully believed that it is clear of an enemy. It may prove difficult to feed a large Army there for any length of time" Telegram received, DNA, RG 107, Telegrams Collected (Bound); copies, *ibid.*, Telegrams Received in Cipher; (misdated Dec. 7) *ibid.*, RG 393, Military Div. of the Miss., Hd. Qrs. Correspondence; DLC-USG, V, 40, 94. Dated Dec. 8 in *O.R.*, I, xxxi, part 3, 356.

On Dec. 5, Maj. Gen. William T. Sherman, Maryville, Tenn., telegraphed to USG. "I put my cavalry into Knoxville during the night of Dec 3d My head of columns are now here in communication with Knoxville Enemy retreated last night moving eastward I have sent a staff officer to Burnside & by daylight will determine what to do Elliott is not up But Cav must pursue & harrass the rear We have relieved Knoxville & will soon decide what next A Stern Chase is a long one especially by my advance that have now marched five hundred miles" Telegram received, DNA, RG 94, War Records Office, Military Div. of the Miss.; copy, *ibid.*, RG 393, Military Div. of the Miss., Telegrams Received. *O.R.*, I, xxxi, part 3, 339. See *ibid.*, I, xxxi, part 1, 262–63, 430–32; *ibid.*, I, xxxi, part 2, 577–79. On Dec. 5, 11:00 P.M., Brig. Gen. James H. Wilson, Knoxville, telegraphed to USG. "I arrived here tonight having lef Shermans advance Two Divisions at Marysville sixteen miles distant and all the troops this side of the Little Tenn Granger Davis & Blair on the road from Morgantown to Marysville Howard on united road he having crossed at Davis Ferry we lost time in bridging the little Tennessee Genl Sherman having heard this P. M. of Longstreets retreat towards Bristol sent orders to stop the various columns He & Burnside will confer in the moring & adopt a policy It seems to be quite clear that Longstreet has too much the start to allow of any successful pursuit & therefore they will probably decide to put all the cavalry in motion & follow with infantry enough to push the rebels entirely out of Tennessee   All of Shermans men not necessary will be started back at once   Nothing yet heard from Elliott or Foster   Spears & Byrd were twelve miles from Kingston on the Knoxville road last night pushing on—all probably within ten (10) miles of here tonight—The Paint Rock was twenty miles below Kingston when last heard from   couldnt pass the cars   Burnsides situation was by no means desperate he having had at the termination of the seige more meat & breadstuffs than when it began   thinks he could have held on fifteen or twenty days longer without starvation   supplies were drawn from the French, Miss and Sumerville roads   loyal people sent in cart loads of subsistence stores voluntarily   Burnside does not know anything official of his having been relieved and naturally feels quite anxious concerning it   It seems to me very cold comfort after he has done all the work & maintained himself with so much honor to be relieved and ordered to rear in such an equivocal manner"   Telegram received, DNA, RG 94, War Records Office, Dept. of the Tenn.; copy, *ibid.*, RG 393, Military Div. of the Miss., Telegrams Received. On Dec. 6, 8:00 A.M., Maj. Gen. Ambrose E. Burnside, Knoxville, telegraphed to USG. "Genl Wilson has arrived here & has informed you in detail by telegraph of our present position   the seige was raised yesterday morning & our cavalry is pushing the enemy as rapidly as possible under the circumstances   The horses are in bad condition & the men very much fagged by constant work in the trenches   The infantry are not in good condition for pursuit for the same reason and the artillery can scarcely be moved for want of animals   The advance of Shermans columns are near & he will be here in person in a few hours when we will try & organize a pursuing force large enough to either overtake the enemy & beat him or drive him out of the state—The main body of his force is moving towards Morristown & the indications are that he will try to reach the terminus of their R R line at Bristol   We have saved all our rolling stock on the Railroad but will not be able to use it further than ~~Strat~~ Strawberry Plains as the bridge at that place has been destroyed   We have heard nothing from Foster or Elliott but hope to this morning   Will telegraph you more fully after seeing Sherman   We thank you for the prompt aid rendered as but for the approach of Sherman the siege would not have been raised"   Telegram received, DNA, RG 94, War Records Office, Military Div. of the Miss. *O.R.*, I, xxxi, part 1, 271. These three telegrams were received in Chattanooga on Dec. 7. See telegram to Maj. Gen. Ambrose E. Burnside, Dec. 10, 1863.

1. Bristol, Tenn., on the Va. border on the East Tennessee and Virginia Railroad.

2. On Dec. 8, 10:30 A.M., USG telegraphed to Burnside. "How are you off for medical supplies? I will try to send you from here two steamers loaded with articles you most need and let the steamers return with wounded and sick men, who are unable to travel in ambulances. Give me a list of articles most required." Copies, DLC-USG, V, 34, 35; DNA, RG 393, Military Div. of the Miss., Letters Sent. On the same day, 8:00 P.M., Maj. Gen. John G. Foster, Tazewell, Tenn., telegraphed to USG. "Your despatch of this date to Gen Burnside is recvd   I leave for Knoxville tomorrow & will deliver it in person"   Telegram received, *ibid.*, Dept. of Mo., Telegrams Received; copy, *ibid.*, Military Div. of the Miss., Telegrams Received. Also on Dec. 8, USG wrote to Maj. Gen. George H. Thomas. "Please direct General Slocum to detail from twenty to thirty ship car-

penters, from his command and order them to report to Capt Edwards at Bridge-port. I am anxious to know if General Elliott has gone to East Tennessee. It will probably be necessary to keep his command South of the Holsten for a time until two Steamers can be sent to Knoxville with medical stores and return with wounded men." Copies, DLC-USG, V, 34, 35; DNA, RG 393, Military Div. of the Miss., Letters Sent.

To Edwin M. Stanton

Head Quarters, Mil. Div. of the Miss.
Chattanooga Ten. Dec. 9th 1863,

HON. E. M. STANTON,
SEC. OF WAR, WASHINGTON D. C.
SIR:

I would most respectfully, and earnestly, recommend Surgeon E. D. Kittoe, U. S. Vols. for the position of Medical Inspector, to fill any existing vacancy, or if no such vacancy exists, then to fill the first vacancy that occurs. I will also ask that Surgeon Kittoe be transfered from the volunteer service to the regular Army.

Dr. Kittoe has won golden opinions from officers of his profession in the the Army, and from all officers with whom he has served, for his skill as a Surgeon and Physician, for his ability as a man, his zeal and untiring energy in the discharge of his duties, and his qualities as a gentleman.

Dr. Kittoe has served with the Army under me from his entrance into service to the present time. I know his social and professional standing also before entering the service, and none stands better. I do not hesitate therefore in giving to this recommendation all the strength and earnestness I can.

Hoping it is practicable both to transfer Dr. Kittoe from the Volunteer to the regular service, and to promote him in Inspector's Department, and that he will receive the transfer, and promotion,

I remain, very respectfully
your obt. svt.
U. S. GRANT
Maj. Gen.

ALS, DNA, RG 94, ACP, K199 CB 1863. See letter to Elihu B. Washburne, Nov. 26, 1862. On Dec. 7, 1863, Surgeon Henry S. Hewit wrote to U.S. Representative Elihu B. Washburne recommending Surgeon Edward D. Kittoe's promotion. ALS, DLC-Elihu B. Washburne. On Dec. 9, Kittoe wrote to Washburne enclosing USG's letters to Secretary of War Edwin M. Stanton, Dec. 9, and, apparently, to Washburne, Dec. 2, and adding: "The General is in excellent health and of course feels highly gratified with the results of his recent brilliant and masterly movements. I had the honor of being by his side during the recent battles and as usual he was in the hottest of the fray it was enough to elate any one to hear the boys cheer him as he rode along the front on the top of misionary Ridge . . ." ALS, *ibid.* See Kittoe to Washburne, Dec. 24, ALS, *ibid.*

On Jan. 5, 1864, Surgeon Gen. William A. Hammond, Louisville, telegraphed to USG. "It is understood that Me'd Insp'r Mussay has resigned will you recommend Dr Kittoe for the vacancy." Copy, DNA, RG 393, Military Div. of the Miss., Telegrams Received. On Jan. 13, USG telegraphed to Maj. Gen. Henry W. Halleck. "I am informed by Telegraph that a vacancy in the Medical Inspector Generals Dept has occurred by the resignation of Col Mussey—Having previously requested the promotion of Dr E. D. Kittoe Surgeon of Volunteers for that position I have again most respectfully to call your attention to his claims— He is a faithful & accomplished Officer and deserves the promotion" Telegram received, *ibid.*, RG 107, Telegrams Collected (Bound); copies, *ibid.*, RG 393, Military Div. of the Miss., Hd. Qrs. Correspondence; DLC-USG, V, 40, 94. On Jan. 14, Lt. Col. James A. Hardie, AGO, telegraphed to USG. "With reference to the vacancy occasioned by Dr Muzzy's resignation among the Medical Inspector Generals alluded to in your despatch to General Halleck of yesterday, I beg to inform you that Dr Kittoe has been nominated to the vacancy, and that his name is now before the Senate for that place." ALS (telegram sent), DNA, RG 107, Telegrams Collected (Unbound); copies, *ibid.*, RG 393, Military Div. of the Miss., Hd. Qrs. Correspondence; DLC-USG, V, 40, 94. On the same day, Halleck telegraphed to USG. "Dr. Kittoe has been promoted as you requested. Orders were issued some time since that Brig Genl George Crook report for duty to Genl Kelley, Dept of West Virginia. As he may never have recieved it, please give him such orders" ALS (telegram sent), DNA, RG 107, Telegrams Collected (Bound); copies, *ibid.*, RG 393, Military Div. of the Miss., Hd. Qrs. Correspondence; (misdated Jan. 12) *ibid.*, RG 94, Letters Received, 20A 1864; DLC-USG, V, 40, 94. *O.R.*, I, xxxii, part 2, 88. On Aug. 18, 1863, 12:45 P.M., Halleck had telegraphed to USG. "Brig Genl George Crooke will repair to the Dept of West Virginia and report for duty to Brig Genl Kelley." ALS (telegram sent), DNA, RG 107, Telegrams Collected (Bound); telegram received, *ibid.*, RG 393, Dept. of the Tenn., Telegrams Received. *O.R.*, I, xxix, part 2, 72; *ibid.*, I, xxx, part 3, 65. See *ibid.*, p. 291. On Jan. 16, 1864, USG telegraphed to Halleck. "I have directed General Thomas to relieve General Crook and order him to report to General Kelly I would respectfully ask that General Ransom now in the Department of the Gulf be ordered here to take his place" Telegram received, DNA, RG 107, Telegrams Collected (Bound); copies, *ibid.*, RG 393, Military Div. of the Miss., Hd. Qrs. Correspondence; DLC-USG, V, 40, 94. *O.R.*, I, xxxii, part 2, 109. See second telegram to Maj. Gen. George H. Thomas, Jan. 16, 1864.

On Jan. 15, Maj. Roswell M. Sawyer, Huntsville, Ala., adjt. for Maj. Gen. William T. Sherman, telegraphed to Lt. Col. Theodore S. Bowers. "Gen'l Crook with his Cavalry has arrived at this place. they are stationed in and around town will you please inform me if they are to remain here long the difficulty of procuring supplies to forage prompts this inquiry. We have been attempting to supply the fifteenth Corps with forage from this neighborhood and the condition of our Stock will not at present allow us to send a great distance from this point but we have hauled forage from the immediate country and ship it back to the other Divisions by R. R. if a force of Cavalry is placed here to forage the country also we would soon be in want this Cavalry belongs to another command and do not appear to be subject to orders from this post and difficulties unpleasantly arise in this respect also—" Copy, DNA, RG 393, Military Div. of the Miss., Telegrams Received. *O.R.*, I, xxxii, part 2, 103–4. On Jan. 16, Bowers, Nashville, telegraphed to Sawyer. "Gen'l Crooks Cavalry has been ordered away from Huntsville" Telegram received, DNA, RG 94, War Records Office, Dept. of the Tenn. *O.R.*, I, xxxii, part 2, 112.

To Rear Admiral David D. Porter

Head Quarters, Mil. Div. of the Miss.
Chattanooga Ten. Dec. 9th 1863.

ADML. D. D. PORTER,
COMD.G MISS. SQUADRON,
ADMIRAL,

During the season of navigation on the Tennessee River I am anxious to get to Nashville a very large supply of provisions, forage and quartermaster stores. To do this it is highly important that full protection should be given transports and at the same time that they should not be delayed. I do not know the best way to accomplish both these objects but believe the course you are pursuing on the Mississippi River the most advisable: that is to divide the river into beats and and each boat to patroll its beat every day. Boats, I think, would then be safe in passing without convoy. I do not think any regular boat will be required below Fort Donelson.

Col. Parsons, of the Quartermaster's Dept. will deliver this in person and consult with you in this matter.[1]

Very truly your obt. svt.
U. S. GRANT
Maj. Gen—

ALS, DNA, RG 45, Correspondence of David D. Porter, Mississippi Squadron, Letters Received. *O.R.* (Navy), I, xxv, 630.

On Dec. 8, 1863, noon, and Dec. 9, USG telegraphed to Lt. Col. Charles L. Kilburn, commissary, Cincinnati. "I shall want twenty seven millions rations delivered in Nashville during the winter navigation. Make calculations to send forward as rapidly as possible by boat. I will order from St Louis also" "Twenty seven millions is the sum total of rations I think required at Nashville this winter." Copies, DLC-USG, V, 34, 35; DNA, RG 393, Military Div. of the Miss., Letters Sent. On Dec. 8, noon, USG telegraphed to Col. Thomas J. Haines, commissary, St. Louis. "Send rations as rapidly as possible to Nashville by boat. During navigation I shall want to get there twenty seven million rations from St Louis and Cincinnati." Copies, *ibid.* On Dec. 10, Haines telegraphed to USG. "Am sending stores to Nashville as fast as possible to procure transportation   Water in the Mississippi very low   About 4 feet   Have turned over to Q M about two millions rations since Nov 26th"   Telegram received (misdated Nov. 10), *ibid.*, RG 94, War Records Office, Military Div. of the Miss.; copy (dated Dec. 10), *ibid.*, RG 393, Military Div. of the Miss., Telegrams Received. Misdated Nov. 10 in *O.R.*, I, xxxi, part 3, 108.

On Dec. 11, USG telegraphed to Bvt. Lt. Col. James L. Donaldson, q. m., Nashville. "A very large amount of storage will be required in Nashville this winter & I think it advisable to prepare now for it   I would suggest your taking possession of all storehouses in the city at once & notify occupants of all that you are likely to require to vacate"   Telegram received, DNA, RG 393, Dept. of the Cumberland and Tenn., Telegrams Received; copies, *ibid.*, Military Div. of the Miss., Letters Sent; DLC-USG, V, 34. On Nov. 28, USG telegraphed to John B. Anderson, Nashville. "Build a track from Depot to the river at Nashville and make such other improvements as you may deem fit, for the purpose of facilitating the loading of supplies." Copies, *ibid.*, V, 34, 35; DNA, RG 393, Military Div. of the Miss., Letters Sent. On Nov. 29, Anderson telegraphed to USG. "Your Despatch rec'd   I have consulted Colonel Donaldson who thinks the present facilities for loading all that will be required   a forage house and stock yard are being built with sidings. I will examine the ground and report as to the possibility of making a track £ to the river"   Copy, *ibid.*, Telegrams Received.

On Nov. 23, USG telegraphed to Donaldson. "Load all the cars tomorrow exclusively with forage if possible   If not load as many as you can do and make up the balance the day after—"   Telegram received, *ibid.*, Dept. of the Cumberland and Tenn., Telegrams Received. On the same day, Donaldson telegraphed to USG. "Telegram received. Only Thirty five Cars today—tomorrow I Hope to have sixty if no accident happens with seven Thousand sacks of Forage   Telegraphed General Reynolds this morning that two Cars with heavy Parrott guns off the tracks near Nashville on their way to Bridgeport, and carriages injured had to be brought back to Nashville"   ALS (telegram sent), *ibid.*, Dept. of the Cumberland, Q. M. Dept., Telegrams Sent (Press); copy, *ibid.*, Military Div. of the Miss., Telegrams Received. On Nov. 30, 10:00 P.M., USG telegraphed to Anderson. "Discontinue the passenger train South from Nashville for the present. Prohibit passengers riding in the cars carrying the Mails"   Copies, *ibid.*, Letters Sent; DLC-USG, V, 34, 35. On Dec. 1, Anderson telegraphed to USG. "Your Despatch rec'd. will discontinue passenger train after today   will observe the order in relation to passengers in mail room   Many officers are daily going to join their commands who without the the Post train would have no means of going except on top of freight Cars. 2 passenger Cars might be at-

tached to the Hospital train which runs alternate days if you approve." Copy,
DNA, RG 393, Military Div. of the Miss., Telegrams Received. On Dec. 2,
Donaldson telegraphed to USG. "Coal miners & mechanics are accumulating
here, and I cannot send them to Bridgeport, as the passenger train is taken off.
I dare not put them on freight trains as they are already overloaded. I would like
to restore the passenger train if it does not conflict with your orders, as the freight
trains are not assisted by discontinuing the passenger trains." ALS (telegram
sent), *ibid.*, Dept. of the Cumberland, Q. M. Dept., Telegrams Sent (Press);
copy, *ibid.*, Military Div. of the Miss., Telegrams Received. On the same day,
USG telegraphed to Donaldson. "My only objection in in discontinuing the passenger train was to increase the supplies if necessary start it again" Telegram
received, *ibid.*, Dept. of the Cumberland and Tenn., Telegrams Received; copies,
ibid., Military Div. of the Miss., Letters Sent; DLC-USG, V, 34, 35. On Dec. 3,
Donaldson telegraphed to USG. "Passenger train continued. Relieves us very
much, as we have small engines suitable for nothing else. I leave nothing undone
to push forward supplies; but forage distresses me. If could only send Quarter
rations to the animals I would be satisfied. I am not without hopes, however, as
the road has improved the last few days. Mr Anderson is on it now and the Engineer troops ordered to it will help it materially. The road is my only anxiety." ALS
(telegram sent), DNA, RG 393, Dept. of the Cumberland, Q. M. Dept., Telegrams Sent (Press); telegram received, *ibid.*, RG 94, War Records Office, Military Div. of the Miss. On Dec. 4, Donaldson telegraphed to USG. "Fifteen bales
of Hay for your head quarters, go forward tomorrow. Have directed the qr mr at
Bridgeport to send it on. I shall ship 8000 sacks of grain tomorrow" ALS
(telegram sent), *ibid.*, RG 393, Dept. of the Cumberland, Q. M. Dept., Telegrams
Sent (Press).

On Dec. 14, USG wrote to Brig. Gen. Montgomery C. Meigs. "I have given
directions to Gen. Thomas to have 15000 Cords of wood and 15.000 ties cut by
the troops between here and Bridgeport as soon as possible. The General reported to me this morning that he had given the directions to have it done." ALS,
Mrs. Walter Love, Flint, Mich. On Dec. 15, Brig. Gen. William F. Smith, Nashville, telegraphed to USG. "The condition of affairs on the Railroad from here
to Bridgeport seems to me to demand an immediate and and thorough inspection
and I respy. recommend that orders be given to Brig. Gen'l. Dodge to make such
an examination at once & report to you the condition of the road The energy
with which repairs are pushed forward the urgency of repairs as well as the
administration of the road generally having in view the speed of the trains the
frequent & unecessary delays the condition & police of the cars & the matter of
forces collected and accounted for—Very many cars have been run off the track
and upset & no attempt seems to have been made to get them back into service
and I think every thing and every-body connected with the road need overhaul-
ing—" Copy, DNA, RG 393, Military Div. of the Miss., Telegrams Received.
O.R., I, xxxi, part 3, 414.

On Dec. 4, Donaldson telegraphed to USG. "Robberies on the road have
comparitively ceased. There is really no improvement: I think if the road was
patrolled along its length by cavalry & Infantry each day, the train guards of 25
men & an officer with each train could be dispensed with. An officer would be required to visè passes as heretofore. This would give us six more cars, or the capacity of thirty six thousand rations. The experiment is worth trying" ALS
(telegram sent), DNA, RG 393, Dept. of the Cumberland, Q. M. Dept., Tele-

grams Sent (Press). On Dec. 3, USG's adjt. endorsed a similar letter from Donaldson to Maj. Gen. George H. Thomas, "who if he deems it advisable will try the experiment suggested by Colonel Donaldson." Copies, DLC-USG, V, 39; DNA, RG 393, Military Div. of the Miss., Endorsements. On Dec. 15, Brig. Gen. Grenville M. Dodge, Pulaski, Tenn., telegraphed to USG. "I captured a party of Rebels today under command of Maj Jo Fontaine, Gen'l Roddy's Adjutant. They have been on a Reconnoisance along line of Chattanooga and Nashville R. R, and along line of this. They ~~stopped~~ tapped the Telegraph and took off a No of Dispatches, and I guess got pretty well posted. Their orders were to examine thoroughly the R. R. between Columbia and Nashville, and also to endeavor to capture a train loaded with prisoners from Chattanooga. They are evidently posted on weakness of force between Columbia and Nashville, and no doubt will endeavor to burn those bridges. I have a man in from Montgomery, Ala, eight days on road. All troops in Ala. picking up Conscripts, are ordered to Hardee. All men between 16 and 60 are called out to replace them. Two Brigades last of Nov. went through to Bragg. this is all the force that so far has gone up. The boys met large numbers of Deserters left since last fight." Copy, *ibid.*, 16th Army Corps, Left Wing, Telegrams Sent. *O.R.*, I, xxxi, part 3, 412. See telegrams to Brig. Gen. Grenville M. Dodge, Dec. 2, 3, 1863. On Dec. 23, Lt. Col. Theodore S. Bowers, Nashville, issued Special Orders No. 27. "Major General Rousseau, Commanding District of Nashville, will make such disposition as to have patrols of at least three men pass over each point of the RailRoad between this city and Murfreesboro as nearly as may be, once in two hours, both by day and night. The duties of these patrols will be to arrest any person tampering with the Road, to remove any obstacles, and warn trains of all danger, and in case of accident to give assistance to the conductor in charge of the train." Copy, DLC-USG, V, 38. *O.R.*, I, xxxi, part 3, 473–74.

1. On Dec. 19, Rear Admiral David D. Porter, Cairo, telegraphed to USG. "Col. Parsons has just left me. I will order the Gunboats to carry out his wishes. Nothing is detained." ALS (telegram sent), DNA, RG 45, Correspondence of David D. Porter, Mississippi Squadron, Letters Sent (Press); telegram received, *ibid.*, RG 393, Dept. of the Tenn., Telegrams Received. *O.R.*, I, xxxi, part 3, 452; *O.R.* (Navy), I, xxv, 497.

On Nov. 20, Col. Lewis B. Parsons wrote to USG requesting that 2nd Lt. Quincy J. Drake, 12th Ill., be detailed for service in St. Louis to "facilitate our large requisitions up the Tennessee and Cumberland." ALS (press), Parsons Papers, IHi. On Dec. 15, Drake was so assigned. Special Orders No. 21, copy, DLC-USG, V, 38.

To Maj. Gen. Ambrose E. Burnside

By Telegraph from Chattanooga [*Dec.*] 10th 10 P M *186*[*3*]
To MAJ GENL BURNSIDE

You telegraphed Halleck[1] whilst you were beseiged asking to have Kelly cut the R R East of Abingdon. He replied that he had not force enough but that Meade had been ordered to cut the R R at Lima[2] but failed   Keep Granger with you until ~~you until~~ your forces are relieved   If you can get orders to Elliott direct him to take the line of the Hiawasse   When he is through with any thing you may find for him to do and to report his arrival there   Will it not be necessary to keep a heavier force near the Eastern End of the valley than you have had heretofore. When the River rises and we get the banks more securely I will try to send you a boat load of supplies weekly.

U S GRANT M. G

Telegram received, DNA, RG 94, War Records Office, Dept. of the Ohio; copies, *ibid.*, RG 393, Military Div. of the Miss., Letters Sent; DLC-USG, V, 34, 35. *O.R.*, I, xxxi, part 3, 369. On Dec. 9, 1863, 4:00 P.M., Maj. Gen. Ambrose E. Burnside, Knoxville, had telegraphed to USG. "The pursuing column has continued to press on the Enemys Rear   Daily skirmishing between our Cavalry and their rear guard   Our cavalry advance is now between Rutledge & Bean-Station   the main body of the enemys infantry is undoubtedly going up the main valley towards Virginia   Indications are that the Division of Buckners Corps that joined Longstreet and part of Wheelers Cavalry are endeavoring to rejoin Bragg by way of North Carolinia through the French broad Gap   I have been ill for two days confined to my room and Genl Parke is at the front conducting the pursuit   He will take care not to involve himself in any disaster   Genl Foster was at Tazwell at last accounts but my advices from him are meagre: he will probably reach here within a day or two   Would it not be well for the forces in the east to make a serious & desperate attempt to break the Virginia R. R. in Longstreets rear"   Telegram received, DNA, RG 94, War Records Office, Military Div. of the Miss.; copy, *ibid.*, RG 393, Military Div. of the Miss., Telegrams Received. *O.R.*, I, xxxi, part 1, 272.

On Dec. 7, 10:30 A.M., Burnside had telegraphed to USG. "I have just written the following letter to Genl Sherman who at day light this morning reviewed all his troops with the exception of Grangers and started them back to you   Elliott has not yet reported   when he does I shall put him upon the right flank of the enemy   Our troops are in pursuit of Longstreet & I shall join them today unless Foster arrives. he was at Tazwell last night   I have been able to organize a column of pursuit of about Eight thousand men   Granger is crossing little river now and will probably be here tonight   The rear guard of the enemy is at Blains Cross roads   I can scarcely express to you my obligations for the prompt assistance rendered by you to my command   'Dec. 7th 1863   MAJ GENL SHERMAN   General: I desire to express to you and to your command my most hearty thanks and gratitude for your promptness in coming to our relief during the seige of Knoxville and I am satisfied that your approach ~~saved~~ served to raise the siege—The emergency having passed I do not deem for the pursuit any other portion of your command but the Corps of Genl Granger necessary for operations in this section & in-as much as Genl Grant has weakened the forces immediately with him in order to relieve us; thereby rendering portions of Genl Thomas less secure I deem it advisable that all of the troops now here except those commanded by Genl Granger should return at once to within reporting distance of the forces in front of Braggs army. In behalf of my command I again desire to thank you & your command for the kindness you have done us' " Telegram received, DNA, RG 94, War Records Office, Military Div. of the Miss.; copy (incomplete), *ibid.*, RG 393, Military Div. of the Miss., Telegrams Received. *O.R.*, I, xxxi, part 1, 271. Copies of Burnside's letter to Maj. Gen. William T. Sherman are in DNA, RG 393, Military Div. of the Miss., Telegrams Received; *ibid.*, Dept. of the Tenn., General and Special Orders. *O.R.*, I, xxxi, part 2, 579; *ibid.*, I, xxxi, part 3, 424. For the decision to have Sherman's forces, except those of Maj. Gen. Gordon Granger, return to Chattanooga, see reports of Asst. Secretary of War Charles A. Dana, Burnside, Maj. Gen. Oliver O. Howard, and Sherman, *ibid.*, I, xxxi, part 1, 263, 278; *ibid.*, I, xxxi, part 2, 354, 579. See also Rachel Sherman Thorndike, ed., *The Sherman Letters* . . . (New York, 1894), p. 217; *Memoirs of Gen. W. T. Sherman* (4th ed., New York, 1891), I, 410–11; James Harrison Wilson, *Under the Old Flag* (New York and London, 1912), I, 315; *Memoirs*, II, 105–6. These references indicate that Sherman, Knoxville, had telegraphed to USG on Dec. 6. "I leave Granger at Knoxville and with my command start tomorrow for the Hiawassee—" Telegram received (dated Dec. 8), DNA, RG 94, War Records Office, Military Div. of the Miss.; copy, *ibid.*, RG 393, Military Div. of the Miss., Telegrams Received. *O.R.*, I, xxxi, part 3, 356. See letters to Maj. Gen. William T. Sherman, Dec. 11, 12, 1863.

1. In USG's letterbooks, this clause reads: "I telegraphed Halleck twice . . ." See telegrams to Maj. Gen. Henry W. Halleck, Oct. 28, 1863, 11:30 P.M., Dec. 2, 1863.
2. Maj. Gen. Henry W. Halleck's reply on Dec. 3, 11:30 A.M., *ibid.*, referred to the railroad at Lynchburg, Va., not Luna, as was entered in USG's letterbooks, or Lima, as USG understood it.

To Maj. Gen. Henry W. Halleck

Chattanooga Tenn
Dec 14th [*11*] 1863 10 30 P M

MAJ GEN H W HALLECK
GEN IN CHIEF

Two Regiments of Cavalry and four of Infantry fifty five hundred men have been sent to Genl Hurlbut within a week.[1] I am also making preparations for a heavy cavalry raid through Mississippi to free that State entirely if possible from rebels.[2] I will instruct McPherson to use his force to best advantage to keep open the Mississippi either in or out of the Department[3]

U. S. GRANT

Telegram received, DNA, RG 107, Telegrams Collected (Bound); copies (dated Dec. 11, 1863), *ibid.*, Telegrams Received in Cipher; *ibid.*, RG 393, Military Div. of the Miss., Hd. Qrs. Correspondence; DLC-USG, V, 40, 94. Dated Dec. 14 in *O.R.*, I, xxxi, part 3, 404. On Dec. 11, 12:40 P.M., Maj. Gen. Henry W. Halleck had telegraphed to USG. "Genl Steele reports that the rebel forces under Price & from Texas are advancing upon Little Rock. It is also reported that they are seriously threatening West Tennessee & the Mississippi river. Admiral Porter reports that Port Hudson is also threatened. Would it not be well under these circumstances to send back some troops to Hurlbut, so that the troops detached from Steele & Schofield to West Tennessee may be returned? And also to instruct Genl McPherson to assist, if necessary, Genl Banks forces on the lower Mississippi? Rebel papers recieved here indicate that an effort will be made to reclose the Mississippi river during the absence of your army & that of Genl Banks. The movement of the latter on the Rio Grande was unexpected & contrary to the advice of the government." ALS (telegram sent), DNA, RG 107, Telegrams Collected (Bound); copies, *ibid.*, RG 393, Military Div. of the Miss., Hd. Qrs. Correspondence; DLC-USG, V, 40, 94. *O.R.*, I, xxii, part 2, 739; *ibid.*, I, xxxi, part 3, 376.

On Dec. 15, Rear Admiral David D. Porter, Cairo, wrote to USG. "If I have not sooner congratulated you, on your splendid victory at Chattanooga, it was not because I did not share in the joy of your triumph, for you have no greater well wisher than myself. I congratulate you now, with all my heart, and now that you have finished that business so well, I must tell you, that the Guerrillas are kicking up the mischief on the River, especially about Natches, and down about Red River. Dick Tayor has come in with 4000 men, and 22 pieces of artillery, and has planted them behind the Levee, to great advantage. He dont trouble the Gun Boats, which have driven him away, twice, but the transports get badly cut up, even when they are convoyed. Natches is threatned by a large force, and I think they must have had a hard fight there, three or four days ago, as our despatch boats, just arrived to day, reports heavy firing, after she left there, on the way up. Banks has left the country about Red River, without any troops, and the Rebels have it all their own way. Cant you send to our assistance some of your good fellows?.—The Red River may be blocked again, if we dont look out. The troops arrived at Natches, as the transports left, bound to the mouth of Red River, but they were stopped at Natches, owing to the troubles there   The 'Von Phuel' has just arrived, with 40 Shot holes in her, Captain, and clerk killed; some of the light clads, are badly cut up, but held their own. The whole party can be bagged, with four thousand troops." LS, DNA, RG 393, Military Div. of the Miss., Letters Received. *O.R.*, I, xxxi, part 3, 421–22; *O.R.* (Navy), I, xxv, 636.

1. On Dec. 11, USG telegraphed to Maj. Gen. Stephen A. Hurlbut, Memphis. "If Steele requires troops and you can possibly relieve him, do so to the extent of your ability." Copies, DLC-USG, V, 34, 35; DNA, RG 393, Military Div. of the Miss., Letters Sent; (dated Dec. 12) *ibid.*, 16th Army Corps, Register of Letters Received. *O.R.*, I, xxxi, part 3, 385. On Dec. 19, Hurlbut telegraphed to USG. "Despatch of twelfth received today. Steel has asked for no troops and I think does not need any. Price is on Red River much reduced   recruiting going on vigorously in Arkansas. Forrest is at Jackson. Forces estimated about four thousand. Grierson moves tomorrow on Purdy and Bolivar and Smith from Columbus on monday. Forrest must fight or run. Roads dreadful, from rain. I think we shall cure Forrest of his ambition to command West Tennessee" Telegrams

received (2—dated Dec. 21), DNA, RG 94, War Records Office, Military Div. of the Miss.; copies (2), *ibid.*, RG 393, Military Div. of the Miss., Telegrams Received; (dated Dec. 19) *ibid.*, 16th Army Corps, Letters Sent. *O.R.*, I, xxxi, part 3, 449.

2. See telegram to Brig. Gen. William Sooy Smith, Dec. 17, 1863.

3. On Dec. 11, USG telegraphed to Maj. Gen. James B. McPherson, Vicksburg. "General Halleck informs me that the enemy threaten to close the river, and are now threatening Port Hudson. Give all the assistance you can in or out of the Department. I shall start a Cavalry force through Mississippi in about two weeks, to clean out the State entirely of all rebels." Copies, DLC-USG, V, 34, 35; DNA, RG 393, Military Div. of the Miss., Letters Sent. *O.R.*, I, xxxi, part 3, 386. On Dec. 22, McPherson telegraphed and wrote to USG. "Despatch of the (11th) Elevnth recd. Steamer Hannibal up from below reports every thing quiet   Will give all the assistance I can and do all in my power to keep the river open" Telegram received, DNA, RG 393, Dept. of the Tenn., Telegrams Received; copies, *ibid.*, Military Div. of the Miss., Telegrams Received; *ibid.*, 13th and 17th Army Corps, Letters Sent; *ibid.*, 17th Army Corps, Letters Sent. "Your dispatch of the 11th inst has just been received. The Steamer Hannibal came up from New Orleans this morning, and reports every thing quiet. That efforts have been made, and undoubtedly will continue to be made by the Rebels, to render the Navigation of the Miss River useless for commercial purposes I am well aware. So far they have accomplished Very little. A portion of Dick Taylors force, which was firing into Boats from the West bank of the River near 'Morganza' appears to have left. Brig Genl. Wirt Adams with about Two thousand men and four ps. of Artillery is between Fayette & Gallatin, and a portion of Harrisons Command is on the west side of the River back of Lake St. Joseph. They are evidently trying to act in concert, and the presumption is that Adams has some ammunition which he is trying to get over. This we gather from Captured dispatches, and the fact that he has a Train of about Fifty Covered Waggons, which he keeps with him. Gresham is at Natchez with Four Regts of Infantry (White Troops) one Regt. of Cavalry, Six ps of Light Artillery and Two Regts of Colored Troops, and the Marine Brigade is cruising between Grand Gulf and Natchez with directions to act in concert with the force at the latter place. Gresham has tried several times to get a fight out of Adams, but he keeps out of the way—If he does not succeed in getting a fight out of him, I think he will effectually prevent him from getting anything across the River—Col: Osband at Skipwiths Landing reported three days ago that Fourteen hundred men under 'Forrest' were crossing the 'Sun flower' at Bucks Ferry East of Green Ville for the purpose of making a demonstration on the River, but Boats came down from there this morning, without bringing any information, so that I am inclined to think the report false, or very much exaggerated. I find it necessary to keep boats enough at the Levee all the time to move a Brigade, and in case the Enemy does come to the River at any point within my jurisdiction, will endeavor to dislodge them quickly" ALS, *ibid.*, Military Div. of the Miss., Letters Received. *O.R.*, I, xxxi, part 3, 471–72. On Dec. 9 and 16, McPherson had written to USG regarding operations near Natchez, Miss. ALS (one with signature clipped), DNA, RG 94, War Records Office, Union Battle Reports. *O.R.*, I, xxxi, part 1, 594–96.

To Maj. Gen. William T. Sherman

Head Quarters, Mil. Div. of the Miss.
Chattanooga Ten. Dec. 11th 1863.

MAJ. GEN. W. T. SHERMAN,
COMD.G ARMY OF THE TEN.
GENERAL,

Start your command, with the exception of Granger's Corps, back to their former Camps by the most practicable routes. As soon as they are on the way you can return yourself leaving the troops to follow.

Elliott, I have just learned, did not leave Alexandria[1] until last Friday. He will probably be in to Kingston before this reaches you. If the enemy are any place where he can yet harrass ~~them~~ him you may order such expedition as you deem best. If it is now too late to do any service direct Elliott to take up a position on the line of the Hiwassee and await further orders. Logan[2] has gone to Bridgeport with the two Divisions that were here. I do not suppose it will be necessary to order him up to where you are.

Very respectfully
your obt. svt.
U. S. GRANT
Maj. Gen. Comd.g

ALS, deCoppet Collection, NjP. *O.R.*, I, xxxi, part 3, 380–81. See letter to Maj. Gen. William T. Sherman, Dec. 8, 1863. On Dec. 12, 1863, noon, Maj. Gen. William T. Sherman, Athens, Tenn., wrote to USG. "I am in receipt of yours by Courier Line from Washington and answer by same Line. I have heretofore reported that I left Gen Grangers Command with Gen Burnside and Spears Command with all the Cavalry to arrive all to push Longstreet on his rear, with Gen Foster on his flank from Cumberland Gap. We have rumors of large captures and though not confirmed by any thing official I think it highly probable. Col Longs Cavalry passed the mountains from Telico four days ago, and I have Morgan Smiths Division in Support with Lightburns Brigade well up the mountain in Support. I hope he will capture a train of 300 wagons which dodged us on our way up, and produce consternation in North Georgia. Davis is at Columbus on the Hiwassee, Howard at Charleston & Cleveland, & Ewings Division here. I think I am bound to remain here till the Cavalry returns. In the mean time we are faring well, plenty of Forage & Provisions & we need only Shoes & small stores to go anywhere. From yours of yesterday I supposed you will not wish to push Hardee back of the Etowah & therefore in the absence of other orders, when Long is back & rested I will move slowly back to our Camps at Chattanooga. I cannot hear a word of Elliott. Had he been near Knoxville at the right time Longstreet could not have carried away a single gun or wagon. Even as it is I think he will be forced to drop almost evry thing. I have despatches from Columbus & Telico up to last night   all well. I can only hear of fragments of men seeking to escape, and a small force of Cavalry at the Council Ground, Red Clay on the Dalton Road. I will Send to Kingston the orders you indicate for Genl Elliott." ALS, DNA, RG 393, Military Div. of the Miss., Letters Received. *O.R.*, I, xxxi, part 3, 388–89.

On Nov. 28, Brig. Gen. John A. Rawlins wrote to Maj. Gen. George H. Thomas to have Col. Eli Long, commanding 2nd Brigade, 2nd Cav. Div., Army of the Cumberland, ordered to report to Sherman, and Long reached Knoxville on Dec. 4. LS, DNA, RG 393, Dept. of the Cumberland, Miscellaneous Letters Received. See *O.R.*, I, xxxi, part 3, 263–64; *ibid.*, I, xxxi, part 2, 561–63; *ibid.*, I, xxxi, part 1, 435. On Dec. 15, having failed to overtake a C.S.A. wagon train which he had pursued as far as six miles beyond Murphy, N. C., Long reported his arrival near Calhoun, Tenn. *Ibid.*; *ibid.*, I, xxxi, part 3, 416–17. On Dec. 17, Capt. Ely S. Parker wrote to Long ordering his return to Chattanooga when relieved by Brig. Gen. Washington L. Elliott's cav. command. ALS, DNA, RG 94, War Records Office, Cav. Corps; copies (attributed to USG), *ibid.*, RG 393, Military Div. of the Miss., Letters Sent; DLC-USG, V, 34, 35. *O.R.*, I, xxxi, part 3, 430. See *ibid.*, p. 417. Long, however, remained near Calhoun, defeating an attack by Maj. Gen. Joseph Wheeler's cav. on a U.S. wagon train on Dec. 28. *Ibid.*, I, xxxi, part 1, 435–36, 641–44; *ibid.*, I, xxxi, part 2, 563–64. Regarding Elliott's cav., see *ibid.*, I, xxxi, part 3, 390; following letter, note 5.

1. Alexandria, Tenn., about ten miles south of the Cumberland River and forty-three miles east of Nashville.

2. Maj. Gen. John A. Logan, detained in Miss. by the Canton expedition of mid-Oct., reached Tenn. too late to participate in the battle of Chattanooga and the relief of Knoxville, and therefore did not supersede Maj. Gen. Francis P. Blair, Jr., in command of the 15th Army Corps until Dec. 10. See telegram to Maj. Gen. Henry W. Halleck, Oct. 23, 1863; *O.R.*, I, xxx, part 2, 808–9; *ibid.*, I, xxxi, part 1, 264; *ibid.*, I, xxxi, part 2, 22, 584; *ibid.*, I, xxxi, part 3, 353–54; Special Field Orders No. 30, Dec. 10, copy, DLC-USG, V, 38; Logan to Rawlins, Dec. 10, copies (2), DNA, RG 393, 15th Army Corps, Letters Sent; Lincoln, *Works*, VI, 554–55; James P. Jones, *"Black Jack:" John A. Logan* ... (Tallahassee, Fla., 1967), pp. 184–86; William Ernest Smith, *The Francis Preston Blair Family in Politics* (New York, 1933), II, 171–72.

To Maj. Gen. William T. Sherman

Head Qrs. Mil. Div. of the Miss.
Chattanooga Ten. Dec. 12th/63

MAJ. GEN. W. T. SHERMAN,
COMD.G ARMY OF THE TEN.
GENERAL,

Your letter of the 11th is received.[1] Whilst I would like exceedingly to force Hardee[2] beyond the Oostenaula I do not deem it altogether safe to attempt it now. There is no force here to cooperate with yours nor the means of transportation, nor the rations to carry along. The 4th & 11th Corps of Thomas' Command are absent and the two Divisions of your Command are at Bridgeport.

I sent you orders to return as soon as possible but of course do not want you to start until you know Long[3] to be safe.—Elliott has been directed to take up the line of the Hiawassee. But judging from his efforts there is no telling when he will reach there. His orders were sent to him at Alexandria on the 26th to strike for Kingston and go in pursuit of Longstreet. On the 1st he reached Sparta with one Brigade. On the 9th he reported from Crossville[4] and said he would reach Kingston on the 11th.[5] I hope he succeeded in coming up to time.

If Long should be with you, on your return, you might send him towards Dalton as far as you deem it safe for him to go, and let him destroy any rail-road bridge he may pass on the Cleveland & Dalton road. After going as far as you ~~might~~ choose to send him he could take the most direct road for Chattanooga.

I do not think it advisable to destroy Mills, or any property in East Tennessee, except what may be required for Military purposes.

yours Truly
U. S. GRANT
Maj. Gen.

ALS, DLC-William T. Sherman. *O.R.*, I, xxxi, part 3, 388.

1. On Dec. 11, 1863, Maj. Gen. William T. Sherman, Athens, Tenn., wrote to USG. "I have reported to you the successful relief of General Burnside, my leaving him the two divisions, commanded by General Granger, and my return to the Hiwassee. But a dispatch I made you, and intrusted to General Howard to be carried by an officer going to Chattanooga on business, was lost by the officer from his exceeding care to keep it safe by separating it from other letters. This is just reported to me and I will send this through by some of my own men. On the 7th I left Knoxville, and on the 8th I dispatched Colonel Long with the cavalry through the gap at Tellico Iron-Works, with orders to overtake a certain wagon train and destroy it, to make his appearance in North Georgia, and stampede the people, capture horses, mules, &c. I followed him to Tellico with Morgan L. Smith's division, which I left there in support and came here. Jeff. C. Davis is at Columbus, on the Hiwassee, and is building a bridge; has three mills going and plenty to eat; he needs shoes, sugar, and coffee, to be happy. Howard has one brigade at Charleston, and is repairing the railroad bridge which the rebels damaged after we passed north; it must be ready now. Howard will move to-morrow to Charleston with his corps, and advance one division to Cleveland and open communication with you. I must cover Long, but the moment he returns I can return to Chattanooga or move on Dalton. There is a good road from Columbus, or Cleveland, or Spring Place, which completely turns Dalton. I think we should now compel Hardee to fall back of the Etowah River, giving us Rome and the Oostenaula. Of course we must fight if Hardee gives us battle, but he will not. Longstreet is off and can not do harm for a month. Lee, in Virginia, is occupied, and Hardee is alone. We know that it is all nonsense to blame Bragg; it was his army, his men that broke. Bragg, Hardee, or no man could have held his army after our combinations were made. If you move all your army to Ringgold and Varnell's Station, and I pass along down east of the Oostenaula, we can whip Hardee in no time, and we can enter Rome. Rome, you know, is not on the main railroad, but on a side road, just where the Oostenaula and Etowah unite (I have been there), and is a great manufacturing depot. I find this country full of mills, but have destroyed none, because we hold and may hold the country. I have about thirty cars on the railroad and have destroyed none. General Burnside requested me to destroy none, as he could cross a locomotive at Loudon, and use the road down as far as Hiwassee. We have eaten and are eating up much meat, meal, flour, &c., and though we try to forage on the enemy, I fear we take much of Union people. But we try and discriminate by receipts. I sent word by Wilson to have, say, 50,000 rations of sugar, coffee, salt, and bread, sent me to Cotton Port. We can live well enough anyhow, and I won't complain if you send nothing, for the men are shining fat, but these things are asked for. Shoes are in great demand. Unless otherwise ordered, as soon as Long comes in and is rested, I will march slowly and deliberately for Cleveland and Chattanooga. I cannot hear of Elliott and presume he is where he should be, up the Clinch, on the flank of Longstreet. I saw Burnside's troops march out in pursuit before I left. I suppose Wilson has given you a copy of Burnside's letter to me. If you want me to destroy railroad, mills, machinery, or anything, send me word, for I am sparing all these on your verbal order to spare the railroad from Tyner's to Charleston. The bridge at Charleston could be easily fixed, leaving no break from Tyner's to Knoxville but the bridge at Loudon. Burnside has 5 locomotives and 20 cars. I have saved 30 cars between Charleston and Loudon. I expect to hear from Long in three days. The truth is, we are flourishing up here, and in no particular hurry to come to

Chattanooga. So if you want us, send the order, or if you want to push the enemy beyond Dalton, I am also 'in position.' Send me orders by the party that bears this, who is an expert scout. After to-morrow, the road via Harrison and Cleveland will be safe." *Ibid.*, pp. 381–82. See *ibid.*, I, xxxi, part 1, 265.

2. C.S.A. Lt. Gen. William J. Hardee assumed temporary command of Gen. Braxton Bragg's forces on Nov. 30. *Ibid.*, I, xxxi, part 2, 682; *ibid.*, I, xxxi, part 3, 764–65.

3. Eli Long, born in Ky. in 1837, graduated from a military academy in Frankfort, Ky., in 1855. Appointed 2nd lt., 1st Cav., as of June 27, 1856, he became col., 4th Ohio Cav., as of Feb. 23, 1863. See preceding letter.

4. Crossville, Tenn., about twenty-six miles east of Sparta, nearly halfway from there to Kingston, Tenn.

5. Regarding Brig. Gen. Washington L. Elliott's cav. command, Army of the Cumberland, see *O.R.*, I, xxxi, part 3, 253, 257–58, 320, 365. On Dec. 10, Capt. George K. Leet wrote to Maj. Gen. George H. Thomas. "The General Comm'dg directs that an immediate report be had from Brig Genl W. L Elliott, as to the delay in moving with his command for [*from*] Alexandria" Copies, DLC-USG, V, 34, 35; DNA, RG 393, Military Div. of the Miss., Letters Sent. *O.R.*, I, xxxi, part 3, 368. On Dec. 11, Elliott, Kingston, Tenn., wrote to Maj. Gen. John G. Parke. "Impassable streams, bad roads, and scarcity of forage have delayed me." *Ibid.*, p. 379. See *ibid.*, I, xxxi, part 1, 437.

Also on Dec. 11, Thomas telegraphed to Elliott. "If you do not reach East Tennessee in time to join in the pursuit of Longstreet, you will take up a position on the northeast side of the Hiwassee, . . ." *Ibid.*, I, xxxi, part 3, 378. See *ibid.*, pp. 397–98, 418. On Dec. 14, however, Maj. Gen. John G. Foster ordered Elliott to report to Knoxville, evidently on the basis of USG's instructions of Dec. 12 to drive off C.S.A. forces under Lt. Gen. James Longstreet. *Ibid.*, pp. 387, 401, 403, 406–7; *ibid.*, I, xxxi, part 1, 281.

To Elihu B. Washburne

Chattanooga Tennessee,
December 12th 1863.

HON. E. B. WASHBURN,
DEAR SIR:

Your letter of the 4th inst. is just received.[1] My answer to your letter from Odin was sent but not for several days after it was written and after I supposed it had been mailed. The letter got under ~~my~~ some papers on my table and remained there for several days before I discovered it supposing that it had been mailed when written. I hope, and presume you have, received it before this. I preserved no copy but will write another if it has not reached you.

This I believe is the third recommendation I have given Col. Chet-laine for promotion none of which seem to reach their destination.[2]

I cannot recommend Gen. Carr for promotion. It would be manifest injustice to other Brigadiers of much more merit to do so.

All is well with me. Every thing looks bright and favorable in this command.—I feel under many obligations to you for the interest you have taken in my welfare. But recollect that I have been highly honored already by the government and do not ask, or feel that I deserve, any thing more in the shape of honors or promotion.[3] A success over the enemy is what I crave above every thing els and desire to hold such an influance over those under my command as to enable me to use them to the best advantage to secure this end.

Yours Truly

U. S. GRANT

ALS, IHi.

1. See letter to Elihu B. Washburne, Dec. 2, 1863. On Dec. 12, 1863, 12:05 P.M., U.S. Representative Elihu B. Washburne, Washington, telegraphed to USG. "Yours of Dec. 2, received. All right. Chetlain appointed." ALS (telegram sent), DNA, RG 107, Telegrams Collected (Unbound). See letter to Abraham Lincoln, Dec. 2, 1863.

2. See letter to Abraham Lincoln, Feb. 9, 1863.

3. On Dec. 7, Washburne had given notice that he would soon "introduce a bill to revive the grade of Lieutenant General in the United States Army." He did so on Dec. 14, and the ensuing debate assumed that USG would be named lt. gen., whether or not Washburne's bill as amended recommended USG by name. *CG*, 38-1, 9, 21, 111–12. The matter became entwined with talk of running USG for president. See letter to Barnabas Burns, Dec. 17, 1863. On Jan. 24, 1864, Washburne wrote to USG. "Yours of the 14th inst. was only received yesterday, enclosing the letter to the President in behalf of the appointment of your young friend. I took great pleasure in placing it in his hand myself a few hours only after its reception, and took occasion to add an expression of my own hope that the appointment would be made. The President said he would answer your letter himself. He said to me, 'there are only *ten* places and tens of hundreds of applicants, but I guess we shall have to squeeze Grants' man in.' No man can feel more kindly and more grateful to you than the President. I have never asked anything in regard to you, but what he has most promptly and cheerfully granted. But most of all, and for which he will have my ever lasting gratitude, when the torent of obloquy and detraction was rolling over you, and your friends, after the battle of Shiloh, Mr. Lincoln stood like a wall of fire between you and it, uninfluenced by the threats of Congressmen and the demands of insolent cowardice. The Jo Daviess County sword will be done in about two weeks. It must be brought here, before it goes to Galena, so I can see it. I am greatly indebted to Mr. Rogers of N. Y. (the old partner of Corwith in Galena) for his

aid in getting it up. Mr. Lincoln has entrusted me with the whole duty of getting up the medal. It is much more of a job than I at first supposed. It will take nearly three months to cut the dye. I intend it shall be finest medal ever got up in this country. The artist in N. Y. is now waiting to get a profile likness of you, which I sent to Bowers for. The whole cost of the medal will be betwean $4000.00 & $5000.00, though the bullion itself will not be more than $500.00. I have neither written you or consulted you in regard to my bill to revive the grade of Lieut. Genl. I have acted from a sense of public duty as well as the promptings of personal friendship. I have an abiding conviction that this war will never be closed till our armies are all under one general and that general in the field wherever his services are the most needed.—The bill has been before the Military Committee of the House and they have ordered it to be reported and I have no doubt in due time it will become a law, though it is threatened there will be opposition to it in certain quarters. You cannot have failed to observe that certain parties are attempting to make your name a foot ball for the Presidency, all of which is for more for the accomplishment of certain objects for themselves than for any good will or benefit to you. Some of the men who are now clamoring the loudest in that regard, were the most bitter in your denunciation, eighteen months, or two years ago. I hope you will always feel free to write me whenever I can serve you. I am always glad to hear from you." ALS, USG 3. Regarding USG's letter, which Washburne gave to President Abraham Lincoln, the Jo Daviess County sword, and the medal, see speech, March 18, 1864; General Orders No. 7, Dec. 8, 1863.

On Feb. 1, 1864, in debating the lt. gen. bill, Washburne publicized USG's attitude toward his probable promotion. CG, 38-1, 429. See James G. Blaine, Twenty Years in Congress . . . (Norwich, Conn., 1884–86), I, 509–11; Noah Brooks, Washington in Lincoln's Time (New York, 1895), pp. 139–44. Washburne's speech was read at USG's hd. qrs. Brig. Gen. Augustus L. Chetlain to Washburne, Feb. 15, 1864, ALS, DLC-Elihu B. Washburne; Maj. William R. Rowley to Washburne, Feb. 17, ALS, ibid. On Jan. 18, Lt. Col. Theodore S. Bowers, Nashville, had written to Washburne. "Your prominent and zealous devotion to the great interests of the country, and your heroic and successful defense and advocacy of Gen. Grant have endeared you to the army, and inspired a desire in all Grant's friends to serve the man whose sagacity events have so triumphantly vindicated." ALS, ibid.

Having passed the House of Representatives on Feb. 1, the lt. gen. bill was amended in the Senate and debated on Feb. 11 and 24, at which point it passed. CG, 38-1, 233, 427–31, 539, 586–94, 789–98. On Feb. 26, both houses approved a compromise bill, which followed the Senate version in omitting the express recommendation that USG be named lt. gen., and on Feb. 29, Lincoln signed the bill into law. Ibid., pp. 842, 850–51, (misdating Lincoln's signature) 888, 936. See first letter to Maj. Gen. William T. Sherman, March 4, 1864.

To Jesse Root Grant

————

Chattanooga Tennessee,
December 13th 1863,

DEAR FATHER,

Your letter of the 8th inst. giving a plan by which some citizens propose to crush the rebellion, by a Winter Campaign, with the aid of six months volunteers, and desiring my views, is just received. It is not proper that I should give my views as to policy except directly to the War Dept. through the General-in-Chief of the Army. This I have done.[1] I feel however that there need be no apprehension now but that peace will be speedily restored and the Union, stronger than ever, saved.

My health continues good.

Affectionately &c.
U. S. GRANT

ALS, Cincinnati Historical Society, Cincinnati, Ohio.

1. See letter to Maj. Gen. Henry W. Halleck, Dec. 7, 1863.

To Mrs. Isaac F. Quinby

————

Chattanooga Tennessee,
December 13th 1863,

MRS. I. F. QUINBY,
MY DEAR MADAM,

The letter of my old friend and classmate, your husband, requesting a lock of my hair, if the article is not growing scarse, from age, I presume he means, to be put in an ornament, (by the most delicate of hands no doubt) and sold at the Bazaar for the benefit of disabled soldiers and their families, is just received. I am glad to say that the stock is yet as abundant as ever though time, or other cause, is begining to intersperse here and there a reminder that Winters have passed.

The object for which this little request is made is so praiseworthy that I can not refuse it even though I do, by granting it expose the fact to the ladies of Rochester that I am no longer a boy. Hoping that the citizens of your city may spend a happy week, commensing to-morrow, and that their Fair may remunerate most abundantly, I remain,

> Very truly your friend,
> U. S. GRANT
> Maj. Gen. U. S. A.

ALS, Buffalo Historical Society, Buffalo, N. Y. The Christmas 1863 bazaar of the Ladies Hospital Relief Association, Rochester, N. Y., raised over $10,000, the city's most successful wartime charity appeal. Blake McKelvey, *Rochester: The Flower City 1855–1890* (Cambridge, Mass., 1949), pp. 79–80.

On Dec. 3, Brig. Gen. Isaac F. Quinby, on recruiting duty in Elmira, N. Y., had written to USG. "The congratulations of your humblest friends cannot be unacceptable to you, as being the index of the feelings of a grateful people for the services you have rendered them. I do not intend however to go into any laudation for I do not believe that would be agreeable to you nor am I given to, or apt at, such things. It is enough for me to say that in your recent victory over Bragg you have more than realized my anticipations though I was fully persuaded that you would retrieve the disaster of Rosecrans and drive the rebels in disgrace from before Chattanooga. I did not however think it possible for you to achieve so decisive a victory in so short a time. All honor to you my dear friend and prepare yourself to recieve in due time substantial proofs of the estimation in which you are held by the whole Country. I predict for you a future as bright as the past has been glorious. I will not express any vain regrets for the causes which have kept and probably will still keep me from being with you. In your Military operations I could be no more than an instrument in your hands but in other respects I could play the part of a devoted friend and perhaps guard you from the dangers with which you are now, and must be hereafter surrounded. I need not be more explicit for you know what I mean   I have not yet tendered my resignation but shall do so in a few days, and if accepted expect to resume my duties in the University of Rochester on the 1st of January next. My health is nearly as good as ever and I cannot make it a reason for leaving the service, but the state of my Department in the University is such that it becomes necessary for me either to return to it at once or vacate my chair to enable the Trustees to appoint some one permanently in my place. With my large and dependent family it would be unwise in me to resign my Professorship even though the salary be small to retain my Commission in the Army for the present, with the almost certain prospect of being thrown out at the end of this war, without position or means of support. If you have not changed your determination about your son send him to me whenever you please, and I promise that I will spare no pains with him. Do not take the trouble to answer this unless you feel so inclined and you should have what is not likely to be the case, unoccupied time on your hands. Remember me most kindly to Colonel Duff who I presume is still with you   His letter to me has been in some way mislaid.—With kind regards to Mrs Grant and the children in which Mrs Quinby joins" ALS, USG 3. Quinby's resignation on grounds of ill health was accepted on Dec. 31, enabling him to resume his professorship of mathematics at the University of Rochester.

To Maj. Gen. Henry W. Halleck

Chattanooga Tenn
Dec 14th 2 P M 1863.

Maj Gen H. W. Halleck
Gen in Chief.

Have heard nothing definite from Genl Foster for several days. Sherman sends me word[1] that he hears that Longstreet has lost most of his artillery and Baggage and many prisoners, not certainly known however. Sherman has one division at Tellico Plains[2] one at Sparta and Howards Corps on the Hiawassie. Granger is at Knoxville. Colonel Long has gone through the gorge at Tellico Iron Works into Georgia in pursuit of a portion of Longstreets force. Elliott must be in East Tennessee somewhere with his division of cavalry but I do not know where His start and progress as long as heard from having been slow beyond any apparent excuse. Granger will remain where he is until all danger has passed, also Elliott.[3] I do not think the accounts from Richmond papers can be correct or I would have heard it

U. S. Grant
Maj Genl Comdg

Telegram received, DNA, RG 107, Telegrams Collected (Bound); copies, *ibid.*, Telegrams Received in Cipher; *ibid.*, RG 393, Military Div. of the Miss., Hd. Qrs. Correspondence; DLC-USG, V, 40, 94. *O.R.*, I, xxxi, part 3, 403. On Dec. 13, 1863, 2:30 p.m., Maj. Gen. Henry W. Halleck had telegraphed to USG. "We have heard nothing from Genl Foster for some days. Richmond papers of yesterday say that Longstreet is preparing to hold Rutledge; that his cavalry passed through Pound Gap & penetrated Kentucky to Mount Sterling burning that place and capurting money & supplies; and that Cumberland Gap is threatened. If this be true & Longstreet is establishing himself in East Tennessee, will it not be unsafe to withdraw Sherman's forces till the enemy is driven out of the state? The holding of East Tennessee and of preventing the enemy from getting supplies there is deemed of the greatest importance. Please give this suggestion your careful attention. Moreover, as Genl Meade's operations have failed to produce any results, Lee may send by Rail Road reinforcements to Longstreet without our knowing it. This contingency must also be considered." ALS (telegram sent), DNA, RG 107, Telegrams Collected (Bound); copies, *ibid.*, RG 393, Military Div. of the Miss., Hd. Qrs. Correspondence; DLC-USG, V, 40, 94. *O.R.*, I, xxxi, part 3, 396. On Dec. 16, 10:10 P.M., Maj. Thomas T. Eckert for Secretary of War Edwin M. Stanton telegraphed to USG a dispatch from Maj. Gen. Benjamin F. Butler, Fort Monroe, Va., which quoted newspaper reports of Lt. Gen. James Longstreet's position as of Dec. 8. LS (telegram sent), DNA, RG 107, Telegrams Collected (Bound); copies, *ibid.*, RG 393, Military Div. of the Miss., Hd. Qrs. Correspondence; DLC-USG, V, 40, 94. *O.R.*, I, xxxi, part 3, 422.

1. See letters to Maj. Gen. William T. Sherman, Dec. 11, 12, 1863.
2. Tellico Plains, Tenn., a crossroads village about thirty-seven miles south of the junction of the Holston and Little Tennessee rivers.
3. See letter to Maj. Gen. William T. Sherman, Dec. 12, 1863, note 5.

To Maj. Gen. Henry W. Halleck

Headquarters &c
Chattanooga Dec 14 1863

MAJ GEN H. W. HALLECK
GENL. IN CHIEF—WASHINGTON.

Having been requested by the Chief Signal Officer Department of the Tennessee, to address you a letter expressing my opinion upon the value of the Signal Corps, its services in my Departm't and the conduct of the Officers composing it, I deem it my duty to say that I do not regard its separate existence as either necessary or desirable, though the Officers serving with it in my command have generally been skilful, energetic and efficient. This is particularly true of the officers who have served under my immediate observation, many of them have rendered valuable service at different times and under different organization the system of signalizing might become very useful. Instead, however, of the present organization I would suggest that several officers of the regiments of the Regular Army, be instructed and when deemed necessary, assigned to duty accordingly.

I am, General &c
U S. GRANT
Major General

Copies, DLC-USG, V, 40, 94; DNA, RG 393, Military Div. of the Miss., Hd.
Qrs. Correspondence. *O.R.*, I, xxxi, part 3, 403. This letter met the request of
Capt. Ocran H. Howard who, on Dec. 12, 1863, had written to USG. "The corps
is in its infancy, it is struggling for recognition and for a position in the army
as an organization. Upon the opinions of the generals commanding in the field,
at this time, depends the existence or non-existence of the corps, . . ." *Ibid.*,
pp. 386–87. The U.S. Signal Corps had sought testimonials for its work after
Secretary of War Edwin M. Stanton on Nov. 10 had favored the rival claims
of the U.S. Military Telegraph Corps. See Paul J. Scheips, "Union Signal Communications: Innovation and Conflict," *Civil War History*, 9, 4 (Dec., 1963),
399–421. On Dec. 10, Capt. Lucius M. Rose, Vicksburg, had written to Col.
Albert J. Myer, chief signal officer. "Your communication wishing me to obtain letters from the different Generals here, was duly received and will be
attended to immediately—Gen McPherson is very favorable to the Corps, as you
may have seen by his Official Report—The detachment under my command was
the only one that was noticed officially—If Gen Grant said to the Secretary
what is reported—I do not know that I can blame him, as he was sorely tried by
that worse than wooden-man (Capt Deford) who was then in command—The
Corps was no more nor less than an armed mob—while he was in command—
He was placed over us, and none of us felt like taking the responsibility of running the thing—and I know of one instance that Gen Grant had Aids looking
for three hours for a Signal Officer—That is 'what's the matter' with the Genl—
. . ." ALS, DNA, RG 111, Letters Received. See *O.R.*, I, xxiv, part 1, 130–37,
641. USG may have expressed dissatisfaction with the Signal Corps during his
discussions with Stanton, Oct. 18–19. On Feb. 14, 1864, USG endorsed Myer's
report of Dec. 26, 1863, proposing a line of signal stations about nine miles
apart from Cairo to Memphis. "My opinion in regard to the establishment of
Signal Stations on the Mississippi, is that it would be an expense for which
the government could receive no adequate benefits. The force it would require
to protect these stations would guard the river perfectly without them, and
could be used much more effectively by having it free to move from one place
to another instead of requiring it to guard stationary objects. Communication
with Memphis has no special object now further than ~~that~~ it would bring points
below in nearer telegraph connections" ES, DNA, RG 107, Letters Received.
See endorsement to Andrew Johnson, June 28, 1865.

To Maj. William H. Sidell

———

Chattanooga December 14th 1863

MAJOR H. H. SIDELL
A A. PROVOST MARSHALL OF KENTUCKY.

Your letter of the 9th inst, enclosing copy of Governor Bramlette of the 8th relating to Major General Hurlbut's late order affecting conscriptions in that part of his District embraced in the

State of Kentucky is just received.[1] Major General Sherman commands the Department embracing General Hurlbuts command, and the matter should be reffered to him, or at least through him, but the General being now in East Tennessee, and rather inaccessible, I will correct any abuse that may have already occurred, and give proper directions for future action.

The State of Kentucky having civil laws and officers to enforce them, should not be interfered with any more than any other loyal State, except when it may become necessary to maintain peace and order, at a Military Post. The towns of Columbus, Paducah and Hickman have no doubt become places of refuge for disreputable persons, from all parts of the country. Genl Hurlbuts order was intended or ought to intend to correct this evil. Further than to collect these people, I will direct him to desist from the execution of his order in the State of Kentucky. Actual citizens of the towns named who have committed no act against Military law, shall not be molested by the Order.

U S GRANT

Major General

Copies, DLC-USG, V, 34, 35; DNA, RG 393, Military Div. of the Miss., Letters Sent; Kentucky State Archives, Frankfort, Ky. *O.R.*, I, xxxi, part 3, 411. William H. Sidell of N. Y., USMA 1833, resigned immediately after graduation to pursue a career as an engineer. Appointed maj., 15th Inf., as of May 14, 1861, he served in various staff positions before assignment in March, 1863, as act. asst. provost marshal gen. for Ky. On Dec. 14, Capt. George K. Leet wrote to Maj. Gen. Stephen A. Hurlbut. "Copy of letter from Governor Bramlette to the Provost Marshal General of Kentucky and by him referred to the General commanding the Military Division of the Mississippi, is herewith enclosed to you. Not having received your order refferred to by the Governor the General commanding is ignorant of its full purport, and does not know whether or not it is your intention to impress into the military service of the United States, all the able bodied citizens of Kentucky, embraced within your District. Kentucky however being a loyal State and having furnished her quota of men already in the field, and being also at present engaged in perfecting measures to enforce the General Conscription Act, within her borders, the General desires that the operation of your order may be limited to such citizens in your District as have escaped from or left other States to avoid the Draft, at home, and to such resident citizens as may have violated Military Law. Loyal citizens and Union refugees from the States in rebellion should be excluded from the operation of your order. So far as Tennessee is concerned, the impressment order is approved." Copies, DLC-USG, V, 34, 35; DNA, RG 393, Military

Div. of the Miss., Letters Sent. Printed as written by Capt. Ely S. Parker in *O.R.*, I, xxxi, part 3, 410. On Dec. 28, Hurlbut wrote to Lt. Col. Theodore S. Bowers enclosing Special Orders No. 328, Dec. 22, suspending the operation of his former orders in Ky. *Ibid.*, p. 522. See *ibid.*, pp. 180, 442, 470–71.

On Dec. 17, Governor Thomas E. Bramlette of Ky. telegraphed to USG. "It is rumored that Gen. Boyle is to be relieved of command in Ky. I hope not; no man can so well aid me in enforcing the conscription. I beg for his retention in command." Copy, DNA, RG 393, Military Div. of the Miss., Telegrams Received.

1. See *O.R.*, I, xxxi, part 1, 767; *ibid.*, I, xxxi, part 3, 160–61, 375–76. On Dec. 8, Bramlette wrote to Sidell. "Under Some order of Genl Hurlburt, the counties lying below the Cumberland and Tennessee rivers in Kentucky which are embraced in his Military district, are being much disturbed by an arbitrary Military conscription. Kentucky is your district, and if I understand it properly, the conscription can only be enforced through you. If Genl Hurlburt proceeds to Supercede you in that district, other Generals and Subordinates may in other Districts, and our whole plans in Kentucky become utterly confused. I have letters and information from citizens and Representations, from these, which leave no doubt but that a regular Military conscription is being carried out in that District. We want these men for our old Regiments, and to be organized as agreed between the Secty of War and myself." Copy, DNA, RG 393, Military Div. of the Miss., Letters Received. *O.R.*, I, xxxi, part 3, 411. On Dec. 9, Sidell wrote to USG. "I have the honor to send herewith copy of a letter recieved by me today from the Governor of this State, His Excy. Thos. E. Bramlette, in regard to the reported action of Major General Hurlbut, but of which action I have no official knowledge. It appears to me that the whole matter of raising forces is comprehended in the Recruiting regulations, the President's late call for volunteers and the Enrolment act; and that it belongs exclusively to the Department of the Provost Marshal General wherever a branch of his bureau is established   I am ~~his~~ Acting Assistant Pro. Marshal General for Kentucky and it is in this capacity that the Governor addresses me & that I send this communication to you for your consideration and action in the case presented by the Governor." ALS, DNA, RG 393, Military Div. of the Miss., Letters Received.

To Maj. Gen. John G. Foster

Chattanooga [*Dec.*] 15th [*1863*] 10 30 A M

MAJ. GENL FOSTER

I will try and Send you Stores to Loudon.[1] you must get them from there by rail   Collect all the Stores you can in East Tennessee this Winter   a great battle may be fought in East Tennessee Next Spring, and Stores Must be Collected for the

Subsistence of a large Army   We are building Boats here Which will enable Me, I hope to Send many Stores from here

U. S. GRANT

Maj Genl

Telegram received, DNA, RG 94, War Records Office, Dept. of the Ohio; copies (dated Dec. 17, 1863), *ibid.*, RG 393, Military Div. of the Miss., Letters Sent; DLC-USG, V, 34, 35. Dated Dec. 17 in *O.R.*, I, xxxi, part 3, 433.

On Dec. 10, 8:00 P.M., Maj. Gen. John G. Foster, Knoxville, telegraphed to USG. "I have just arrived—Gen. Sherman has gone—Gen. Granger is here but importunate to return to you—Longstreet has given out that he will make a stand at Bristol. I propose to advance will all available ~~men~~ force to attack him there—shall I do it, and retain Granger for that purpose—" ALS (telegram sent), DNA, RG 107, Telegrams Collected (Unbound); copy, *ibid.*, RG 393, Military Div. of the Miss., Telegrams Received. *O.R.*, I, xxxi, part 3, 372. On Dec. 12, 8:00 A.M., USG telegraphed to Foster. "Drive Longstreet to the farthest point East you can—Retain Granger as long as may be necessary" Telegram received, DNA, RG 94, War Records Office, Dept. of the Ohio; copies, *ibid.*, RG 393, Military Div. of the Miss., Letters Sent; DLC-USG, V, 34, 35. *O.R.*, I, xxxi, part 3, 387. On Dec. 13, 3:20 P.M., Foster telegraphed to USG. "Telegram rec'd. Will do all I can. The weather & want of supplies are serious obstacles—my arrangements for getting supplies by the roads are not yet complete and I shall have to ask you to give me all you can by river & Rail road   Have ordered the river bridge rebuilt as soon as possible   Longstreet has halted eight miles beyond Rogersville. I cannot now move in force until I get the Cars running which will be in a few days and also collect some rations. The state of the roads & lack of supplies may force me to take a position, and wait a little time until I get in better condition" Copies, DNA, RG 393, Military Div. of the Miss., Telegrams Received; (2) *ibid.*, Dept. of the Ohio (Cincinnati), Telegrams Sent. Printed as sent at 2:30 P.M. in *O.R.*, I, xxxi, part 3, 401.

On Dec. 12, 7:00 P.M., Foster telegraphed to USG and to Maj. Gen. Henry W. Halleck. "Longstreet is moving liesurely up the Valley foraging as he goes— There are no indications (certain) that he will stand a fight if we follow him in force. Our Cavalry is constantly harrassing his rear supported by the Infantry under Gen'l. Park which is now at Rutledge   The Infantry is not in a physical condition to follow rapidly. The supplies which are mainly obtained by foraging being very scanty the roads which are bad are fast becoming impassible for trains by reason of the rain now falling—These obstacles interfere very much in my desire to go up in force and engage Longstreet whenever he may halt, and may render it impossible in a short time. In that case I will establish a line of entrenched Infantry posted from Bulls Gap to Mulbury Gap & with the Cavalry holding the Country to the Holston river Wait for a favorable opportunity for making a dash at Saltville with the whole mounted force. Please notify me if this meets the approval" Telegram received, DNA, RG 107, Telegrams Collected (Bound); copies, *ibid.*, RG 393, Military Div. of the Miss., Telegrams Received; (2—addressed to USG) *ibid.*, Dept. of the Ohio (Cincinnati), Telegrams Sent. Addressed to Halleck and USG in *O.R.*, I, xxxi, part 3, 391. On Dec. 14, 9:00 P.M., USG telegraphed to Foster, evidently referring to the preceding dispatch. "Your dispatch of the 14th recd And propositions approved. do all you can to harass the enemy. drive him as far to the east as possible" Telegram received (dated Dec. 15), DNA, RG 94, War Records Office, Dept. of the Ohio; copies (dated Dec. 14, 9:00 P.M.), *ibid.*, RG 393, Military Div. of the Miss., Letters Sent; DLC-USG, V, 34, 35. Dated Dec. 15 in *O.R.*, I, xxxi, part 3, 415.

On Dec. 10, Maj. Gen. Gordon Granger, Knoxville, telegraphed to USG. "We are here and will stay here till hell freezes over tight" Telegram received, DNA, RG 393, Dept. of Mo., Telegrams Received; copy, *ibid.*, Military Div. of the Miss., Telegrams Received. According to Brig. Gen. James H. Wilson, Foster inserted the last word of this telegram to signify that Granger wrote it "under the influence of liquor" and that therefore it should not be sent, but the telegrapher, not understanding this, dispatched every word. Although Wilson misdated Granger's indiscretion as occurring during "the usual holiday jollification" at Christmas time, his story may be substantially true, for the telegram seems to parody Maj. Gen. George H. Thomas's celebrated dispatch from besieged Chattanooga. James Harrison Wilson, *Under the Old Flag* (New York and London, 1912), I, 305. See telegram to Maj. Gen. George H. Thomas, Oct. 19, 1863. On Tuesday, Dec. 10, 2:00 P.M., and Dec. 11, noon, Asst. Secretary of War Charles A. Dana, having returned from Knoxville to Chattanooga, telegraphed to Secretary of War Edwin M. Stanton. "Granger grumbled and complained so much about the destitution of his men that Burnside drew his two divisions into Knoxville, and, with all his own troops, moved out on Monday morning to pursue Longstreet. . . ." "Grant is very angry with Granger for misconduct in the Chattanooga battle, and now for unwillingness to march after Longstreet. Granger will probably be removed and Sheridan assigned to succeed him, subject to approval of Government. Granger is certainly unfit to command." *O.R.*, I, xxxi, part 1, 264–65. See Granger to Thomas, Dec. 9, 3:30 P.M., *ibid.*, I, xxxi, part 3, 365; *Memoirs of Gen. W. T. Sherman* (4th ed., New York, 1891), I, 396. On Dec. 12, Granger telegraphed to USG. "I have the honor to enclose to you the within copy of a dispatch submitted to Major Genl. Burnside, and to solicit your immediate attention to the statement of facts which it embodies. I cannot too strongly urge the necessity of a prompt withdrawal of the troops under my command from this place to Chattanooga. Besides the loss of Transportation, Artillery, and other public property which must attend a march through these mountains after the winter rains have set in, simple justice to the men requires that they should be sent back where they can obtain the greatly needed supplies of clothing, subsistence & shelter. As for Longstreet there is no doubt in my mind that he is making his way to Virginia as rapidly as possible, and even if he were not it is impossible to pursue him and subsist the troops upon his track. The steamboats with our rations are unable to get up further than Gallispos [*Gillespie's*] Landing, twenty miles below Kingston." Copies, DNA, RG 94, War Records Office, Union Battle Reports; *ibid.*, RG 393, 4th Army Corps, Letters Sent. *O.R.*, I, xxxi, part 3, 393. For the enclosure, see DNA, RG 94, War Records Office, Union Battle Reports. *O.R.*, I, xxxi, part 3, 358. On Dec. 15, USG twice telegraphed to Foster. "As soon as you deem your position secure, order the 4th Corps to return to Chattanooga. They will return by the easiest and most practicable route, taking as much time for the march as the condition of the roads, men and animals may make necessary." Copies, DLC-USG, V, 34, 35; DNA, RG 393, Military Div. of the Miss., Letters

Sent. *O.R.*, I, xxxi, part 3, 415. "Keep Genl Granger forces as long as it may be necessary to do so but order them back when you feel your position perfectly secure, if you find it necessary for the effencey of his command relieve him from duty and order him to Cincinnati to report to Me by letter and place Sheridan in command of his troops" Telegram received, DNA, RG 94, War Records Office, Dept. of the Ohio; copies (dated Dec. 17), *ibid.*, RG 393, Military Div. of the Miss., Letters Sent; DLC-USG, V, 34, 35. Dated Dec. 17 in *O.R.*, I, xxxi, part 3, 433.

On Dec. 12, Brig. Gen. Edward E. Potter, Foster's chief of staff, telegraphed to USG. "Gen Burnside left Knoxville this morning for Washington via Cincinnati" Telegram received, DNA, RG 94, War Records Office, Dept. of the Ohio; copy, *ibid.*, RG 393, Military Div. of the Miss., Telegrams Received. For the change of command on Dec. 11 from Burnside to Foster, see *O.R.*, I, xxxi, part 1, 278–79, (misdated) 281; *ibid.*, I, xxxi, part 3, 384–85, 391.

1. On Dec. 17, USG telegraphed to Rear Admiral David D. Porter, Mound City, Ill. "Can you send two or three light draft Gunboats over the shoals if the water gets up sufficiently high to do so, to be used in the Upper Tennessee? They will be of immense service here" Copies, DLC-USG, V, 34, 35; DNA, RG 393, Military Div. of the Miss., Letters Sent. *O.R.*, I, xxxi, part 3, 430; *O.R.* (Navy), I, xxv, 497. On Dec. 18, Porter, Cairo, telegraphed to USG. "I have already ordered Capt Shirk to get the Gunboats over the shoals the moment he can do so" LS (telegram sent), DNA, RG 45, Correspondence of David D. Porter, Mississippi Squadron, General Letters (Press); telegram received, *ibid.*, RG 393, Dept. of the Tenn., Telegrams Received. *O.R.*, I, xxxi, part 3, 444; *O.R.* (Navy), I, xxv, 497. See telegram to Brig. Gen. William Sooy Smith, Dec. 17, 1863.

To Maj. Gen. Henry W. Halleck

Head Quarters Mil. Div. of the Miss.
Chattanooga Ten. Dec. 17th 1863.

MAJ. GEN. H. W. HALLECK,
GENERAL IN CHIEF, WASHINGTON,
GENERAL,

Sherman's command has just returned from East Tennessee. There is left there now besides the force Burnside had, Granger with about 11000 Infantry & Artillery, and Elliotts Division of Cavalry. This will be as much force as can be subsisted for the present and I think abundantly sufficient to keep the enemy from making any inroad and possibly to drive him entirely out.

The rains have already set in making it almost impossible to subsist the Army at any distance from steamboat landings or rail-road depots. To avoid all trouble, and to economize transportation over the rail-road, I have ordered Sherman to Belfont.[1] He will there be able to supply all his forage from the country, and nearly all of his bread and meat. All the Cavalry will be so disposed as to draw forage, and most of their rations from the country. By this means, and with the use of the Nashville and Decatur road, which I hope will be ready for use by the 1st of February, I expect to be able to accumulate a large Magazine of supplies here by spring.

We now have three steamers runing and will have two more in a few days. Still two others are in progress of construction. By the means of these boats, and such portions of the rail-road as can be used, I will endeavor to accumulate supplies in East Tennessee to enable me to fight a battle there, with a large Army, if the spring movements of the enemy should make it necessary.[2] If Longstreet is not driven from the valley entirely, and the road destroyed East of Abingdon, I do not think it unlikely that the last great battle of the war will be fought in East Tennessee.

Reports of deserters and citizens show the Army of Bragg to be too much demoralized and reduced by desertion to do any thing this Winter.

I will get everything in order here in a few days and go to Nashville and Louisville, and if there is still a chance of doing anything against Longstreet, to the scene of opperations there. I feel deeply interested in moving the enemy beyond Saltville this Winter, so as to be able to select my own Campaign in the spring instead of having the enemy dictate it for me.

> I am Gen. very respectfully
> your obt. svt.
> U. S. GRANT
> Maj. Gen.

ALS, Schoff Collection, MiU-C. *O.R.*, I, xxxi, part 3, 429–30. On Dec. 26, 1863, Maj. Gen. Henry W. Halleck wrote to USG. "Your letter of the 17th is just recieved. The views which you express in that letter agree essentially with those expressed in my telegrams sent to you since its date. The force to be retained in East Tennessee must, of course, be limited by your means of supplying it. I only wish to convey to you the anxiety of the President that the enemy should, if possible, be prevented from laying waste that country and gathering up its products for his own subsistence during the winter. As the roads from Kentucky become difficult or impassable over the mountains during the winter, I presume that the smaller rations, [c]lothing and ammunition for Foster's army must go by Chattanooga. Cattle and hogs may be driven over the mountain roads till late in the winter. At least it is so represented here. Your plan of diminishing the forces at Chattanooga so as to increase the supplies seems perfectly correct. If you can carry into effect your idea of forcing the enemy to fight you in the next campaign on ground of your own selection, it will be a great gain. In most of our operations heretofore the rebels have had an advantage of us in this respect." LS, DNA, RG 108, Letters Sent (Press). *O.R.*, I, xxxi, part 3, 496–97. See letter to Maj. Gen. Henry W. Halleck, Dec. 7, 1863.

1. Bellefonte, Ala., between the Tennessee River and the Memphis and Charleston Railroad, about fourteen miles southwest of Stevenson, Ala. On Dec. 17, Capt. George K. Leet issued Special Field Orders No. 37. "Major General W. T. Sherman, Commanding Department of the Tennessee, will immediately take that portion of his command now in the field, and proceed to some convenient point on the Tennessee River west of Bridgeport, and there encamp until the RailRoad from Nashville to Decatur has been completed. Upon the completion of the road, or on the receipt of orders all of the force will be moved to Decatur or as near there as may be convenient, excepting only such troops as may be employed in guarding lines of communication and there remain until further orders. General Sherman will collect all the Quartermaster's and Commissary Stores in the District through which he passes, not only for the subsistence of his command, but for storage, and no receipt for property taken, will be given except to loyal citizens." ADS, DNA, RG 94, War Records Office, Military Div. of the Miss. *O.R.*, I, xxxi, part 3, 431–32.

On Dec. 25, USG, Nashville, telegraphed to Maj. Gen. George H. Thomas, Chattanooga. "I have suspended the order to Capt Stokes to send batteries to front on account of lack of transportation & forage   will be in Chattanooga on the 27th." Copies, DNA, RG 393, Dept. of the Cumberland, Telegrams Received; *ibid.*, Military Div. of the Miss., Letters Sent; DLC-USG, V, 34, 35. USG went from Chattanooga to Nashville on Dec. 18, returning on Dec. 28.

2. See letter to Rear Admiral David D. Porter, Dec. 9, 1863.

To Brig. Gen. William Sooy Smith

Chattanooga 9.30 A. M. 17th Dec 1863

BRIG GENL W. S. SMITH CHF OF CAV. MIL DIV MISS.
NASHVILLE TENN

The following dispatch is just received from General Dodge: "One of the scouts has just come in from Jackson Tenn. He went with Forrest from Mississippi up there, and says General Forrest with 3500 to 4000 men is now there and collecting what force he can, and thinks he will go into Kentucky and also says he will try and cross Tennessee river. Scout left Jackson on Thursday"[1] (S'gd G. M. Dodge B. G.)

In your move try and rake this force clear before going further South. Dodge will probably be in Nashville to morrow.[2] Learn from him all the particulars you can. To make your force what it should be, call on Bowers to order up all the available Cavalry from Kentucky to such point as you determine to cross the Tennessee river at.[3] If you can get force enough, and can get on the enemy once, never drop him while there is a chance of taking one. From the country that supports this class of the enemy, take all that you want in the shape of horseflesh, provisions and all that goes to support war. Leave no formidable enemy in Tennessee when you go into Mississippi

U S Grant
Major General.

Telegram, copies, DLC-USG, V, 34, 35; DNA, RG 393, Military Div. of the Miss., Letters Sent. *O.R.*, I, xxxi, part 3, 431. See telegram to Maj. Gen. Henry W. Halleck, Dec. 11, 1863. On Dec. 16, 1863, Brig. Gen. William Sooy Smith had telegraphed to Brig. Gen. John A. Rawlins. "On my arrival here I found the enclosed report of Cavalry serving in the District of Kentucky, awaiting me. I have telegraphed for a similar report of the Mounted Infantry, and will forward a copy as soon as I recieve it, accompanied by a recommendation as to the movements of such commands as can be spared from the District, to participate in the contemplated movements of our cavalry in West Tennessee, and North Mississippi. I have already informed Gen. Crook of what is designed, and this morning I recieved a telegram from him, a copy of which I enclose, and request that the concentration of his command may be ordered immediately if practicable. The ordnance he requires is already drawn and will go forward today. There are on hand here and ready to issue about five hundred cavalry horses; these I will have drawn and sent forward immediately, and in addition to those already supplied I think they will be sufficient. Gen. Hurlbut should be actively engaged in preparing his cavalry, and I would request that he be instructed accordingly. When our preparations are a little further advanced, a steamboat suitable for ferrying the Command over the Tennessee river, should be ordered to Eastport for that purpose properly convoyed. This boat can take up supplies of rations and forage. May I ask that any important information relating to the Cavalry may be forwarded to me by mail or telegraph." Copy, DNA, RG 393, Military Div. of the Miss., Chief of Cav., Letters Sent. *O.R.*, I, xxxi, part 3, 423. See *ibid.*, p. 387.

On Dec. 17, 12:40 P.M., Smith telegraphed to Rawlins. "Have the orders been given for the concentration of General Crooks div" Telegram received,

DNA, RG 393, Dept. of the Cumberland, Miscellaneous Letters Received; copies, *ibid.*, Military Div. of the Miss., Chief of Cav., Letters Sent; *ibid.*, Telegrams Received. *O.R.*, I, xxxi, part 3, 431. On the same day, USG telegraphed to Smith. "General Elliott is ordered to relieve Col Long and Col Long is to report for further orders to General Thomas. You will send to General Crook such orders as you wish to effect a concentration." Copies, DLC-USG, V, 34, 35; DNA, RG 393, Military Div. of the Miss., Letters Sent. On Dec. 18, Smith sent this telegram to Brig. Gen. George Crook, Huntsville, Ala. Copies (2), *ibid.*, Chief of Cav., Letters Sent. *O.R.*, I, xxxi, part 3, 437. Regarding the cav. commands of Brig. Gen. Washington L. Elliott and Col. Eli Long, see letters to Maj. Gen. William T. Sherman, Dec. 11, 12, 1863. Also on Dec. 18, Smith telegraphed to USG. "I have telegraphed Crook to concentrate his command except Longs brigade at Huntsville immediately   He will have to cross Elk River at the crossing of the Tenn & Ala R R   He can then reach Savannah much easier than Eastport & Dodge thinks we had better cross there   If Gen Wilson can be spared I very much desire that he should proceed to West Tennessee to push forward the movement in that quarter—Forrest will gather up all the conscripts deserters & stock that he can & escape as soon as possible into Missisipi if he is permitted to do so   Dodge will spare us two regiments of mounted Infantry temporarily   If we can have two (2) or three (3) covered barges for ferrying purposes on the Tennessee they will aid greatly   I believe they can be had at Paducah" Telegram received, DNA, RG 94, War Records Office, Military Div. of the Miss.; copies (2), *ibid.*, RG 393, Military Div. of the Miss., Chief of Cav., Letters Sent; *ibid.*, Telegrams Received. *O.R.*, I, xxxi, part 3, 438. On Dec. 20, USG, Nashville, telegraphed to Maj. Gen. George H. Thomas. "I have ordered Gen Crook to assemble his command at Huntsville and proceed to Brospect [*Prospect*] with a view of operating against Forrest. Gen Sherman has been directed to supply the places now garrisoned by Crook with Infantry." Copies, DLC-USG, V, 34, 35; DNA, RG 393, Military Div. of the Miss., Letters Sent. *O.R.*, I, xxxi, part 3, 455. On the same day, USG telegraphed to Maj. Gen. John A. Logan, Bridgeport, Ala. "Relieve General Crook at Huntsville with a Brigade of troops or mounted Infantry as soon as possible. Crook is ordered off on an expedition and I want him to start as soon as he can." Copies, DLC-USG, V, 34, 35; DNA, RG 393, Military Div. of the Miss., Letters Sent. On Dec. 20 and 21, Logan telegraphed to USG. "Have no mounted Infantry save one Regiment, but will send a Brigade of Infantry through as soon as they can make the march the present State of the Roads, Streams &C. considered. They will move in the morning Early" Copies (2), *ibid.*, 15th Army Corps, Telegrams Sent. "Col Alexander of 3d Division with five Regts of Infty and two Companies of Cavalry started at daylight this morning, without camp equipage &C. to Huntsville, with instrictions to get through as quick as posssable." Copies (2), *ibid. O.R.*, I, xxxi, part 3, 462. See *ibid.*, p. 461. On Dec. 27, Logan telegraphed to Lt. Col. Theodore S. Bowers. "My Hd. Qrs at Scottsboro. The roads almost impassable, forage scarce, will have to send animals some distance and have them hearded soon. Condition since return from Knoxville bad, can you not send me a Telegraph operater for the Paint Rock end of the line—have not heard from troops at Huntsville—ought to be there—" Copies, DNA, RG 393, Military Div. of the Miss., Telegrams Received; (2) *ibid.*, 15th Army Corps, Letters and Telegrams Sent. On Dec. 31, Logan telegraphed to Bowers. "I have just returned from Paint River Rock, horse back, find roads very bad   will move forward Genl. John E Smiths Division to

Huntsville as soon as it is possible to get transportation through the Flint River and Paint Rock Swamps—am having wagon road repaired as rapidly as possible will send forward and commence work on Limestone bridge between Huntsville and Decatur as soon as I can do so—the roads from Woodville to Gunters Ferry are at present impassable—Col Alexander at Huntsville reports to me this morning that he has captured Rebel Pickets on the Huntsville and Guntersville road also herd of cattle and hogs intended to be crossed over at that point" Copies, *ibid. O.R.*, I, xxxi, part 3, 543. On Jan. 4, 1864, Logan sent to Bowers a lengthy report that emphasized problems of transportation and supply. Copies (2), DNA, RG 393, 15th Army Corps, Letters and Telegrams Sent. *O.R.*, I, xxxii, part 2, 23–24.

On Dec. 18, 1863, 12:30 P.M., USG, Chattanooga, telegraphed to Rear Admiral David D. Porter, Mound City, Ill. "If you have not already sent your boats up the Tennessee be good enough to send one at once to escort two transports from Paducah to Savannah. They are sent by Col Hicks to ferry Crook's Cavalry across the river." Copies, DLC-USG, V, 34, 35; DNA, RG 393, Military Div. of the Miss., Letters Sent. *O.R.* (Navy), I, xxv, 497. See telegram to Maj. Gen. John G. Foster, Dec. 15, 1863, note 1. On Dec. 21, Porter telegraphed to USG. "Your telegraph received. The Gunboats are thereabouts—" ALS (telegram sent), DNA, RG 45, Correspondence of David D. Porter, Mississippi Squadron, Letters Sent (Press). On Dec. 24, USG, Nashville, telegraphed to Porter. "Will you have the kindness to direct a Gun Boat Number 12 Twelve to convoy Steamer Masonic Gem Now at Paducah to Savannah" Telegram received, *ibid.*, Area 5; copies, *ibid.*, RG 393, Military Div. of the Miss., Letters Sent; DLC-USG, V, 34, 35. *O.R.*, I, xxxi, part 3, 485; *O.R.* (Navy), I, xxv, 497. See *ibid.*, p. 498. On Dec. 25, Porter twice telegraphed to USG. "The Gunboat you mentioned was ordered to proceed yesterday with the transports to Savannah Capt Shirk is at Savannah" ALS (telegram sent), DNA, RG 45, Correspondence of David D. Porter, Mississippi Squadron, Letters Sent (Press); telegram received, *ibid.*, RG 393, Dept. of the Tenn., Telegrams Received. *O.R.*, I, xxxi, part 3, 496; *O.R.* (Navy), I, xxv, 498, 658. "Capt Shirk has just arrived from Savannah. The Gunboats are there, but no troops have arrived. The transports will be at savannah tonight." ALS (telegram sent), DNA, RG 45, Correspondence of David D. Porter, Mississippi Squadron, Letters Sent (Press). On Dec. 26, Porter wrote to USG, evidently having received a copy of USG's telegram to Maj. Gen. Henry W. Halleck, Dec. 20. "I was glad to receive yours of the 20th instant and to hear that I was soon to see my old friend Sherman, whom I esteem as you do. Indeed we have been so much together and in so many hard places, that we look upon him as the property of the Navy. I must make you an apology for not getting the two (2) steamers up to Savannah sooner, but they arrived there in full time. Lieut. Commander Shirk had been there a week waiting for the troops which had not arrived on the 23d. The two (2) boats arrived at Paducah and Colonel Hicks did not report it to me by telegraph. Shirk left them there as he did not get my telegraphic dispatch, and did not know that it was intended that he should convoy the boats up, and the people on board told him nothing. It all turned out right. Shirk could have ferried them all over, having four gunboats with him. Matters are getting quiet below. I sent a crowd of gunboats to Red River, and they have driven General Dick Taylor back from the levee. The latter has 12.000. men in and about the country, and twenty two (22.) pieces of artillery, but is in want of ammuntion. General Dick Taylor has just returned from Mobile, where he went to arrange a system of couriers and signal corps. He left Alexandria on the first of September, and crossed the river at Bruinsburg, on a float, with an ambulance and two horses. With these he travelled to Brandon, where he took the cars. He returned three weeks ago last Thursday, and finding his float broken up, crossed over himself, in a 'dug out,' when one of the gunboats captured his ambulance, horses, papers, arms and his body servant, who is now my valet. General Dick Taylor had a narrow escape, as did also Colonel Patten, Colonel Ward and Colonel Ruth, of the Rebel army. They had to foot it without clothes, back to their troops at Red River. I have not heard of General Dick Taylor's having arrived there yet. I have not yet received the papers and hope they may contain some valuable news. The boy who is very intelligent, says that only one brigade has been left at Mobile, the rest having been sent to reinforce Bragg, arriving there just in time to catch a thrashing. I am now, besides my other duties, equipping ten gun boats for Farragut and have to stop my own affairs, to attend to his. I shall be ready with a fine lot of boats, by the time Sherman can get ready for Red River." LS, *ibid.*, RG 393, Military Div. of the Miss., Letters Received. *O.R.*, I, xxxi, part 3, 498–99; *O.R.* (Navy), I, xxv, 662.

On Dec. 27, Smith telegraphed to USG, Chattanooga, apparently referring to USG's schedule for preparing a cav. force for operations in west Tenn. and northern Miss. "The two weeks are up today   Crooks has reached Pulaski & my regiments that are here are moving this morning   I go to Columbia by rail tomorrow"   Telegram received, DNA, RG 393, Dept. of the Cumberland, Miscellaneous Telegrams Received; copies (2), *ibid.*, Military Div. of the Miss., Chief of Cav., Letters Sent; *ibid.*, Telegrams Received. *O.R.*, I, xxxi, part 3, 512. On Dec. 19, Smith had telegraphed to Brig. Gen. James H. Wilson. "The Steamers should not leave Paducah until our preparations are further advanced. They should cause twenty thousand rations of provision and as many of forage and if possible two (2) covered barges each. Gen'l Brook [*Crook*] gives a very discouraging account of the condition of his divisions and it may take longer than was anticipated to supply indespensable articles. Sorry you cannot go along." Copy, DNA, RG 393, Military Div. of the Miss., Telegrams Received. Printed as sent at 10:00 A.M. in *O.R.*, I, xxxi, part 3, 445. See *ibid.*, pp. 466, 499. On Dec. 29, Smith, Columbia, Tenn., telegraphed to Capt. George K. Leet. "Please see Capt Settle Postcommissary at Nashville immediately & get him t[o] send twenty thousand rations of every thing but meat to this post by train tomorrow if possible   a portion of my command will have to await their arrival here"   Telegram received, DNA, RG 393, Dept. of the Tenn., Telegrams Received; copies, *ibid.*, Military Div. of the Miss., Chief of Cav., Letters Sent; *ibid.*, Telegrams Received. On the same day, Smith telegraphed to Porter. "Gen. Grant's order directing the boats to proceed to Savannah was countermanded, and they were ordered to remain at Paducah subject to my orders. I sent Capt. Hudson, Gen. Grant's aide to Paducah with amunition for my command, which he was ordered to bring up the river with him, also twenty thousand rations of provisions and forage. If these stores have gone up to Savannah on board the boats they can await my arrival there; if not please order them to return to Paducah and get them. I expect to reach Savannah about the 1st or 2nd day of January." Copy, *ibid.*, Letters Sent. Also on Dec. 29, Porter telegraphed to Smith. "The boats are now at Savannah in charge of the Gun boats, awaiting for the troops. Gen. Grant's orders were that they should go to Savannah. Do you wish them to return to Paducah?" Copies (2), *ibid. O.R.*, I, xxxi, part 3, 528.

On Dec. 31, Smith telegraphed to Leet. "Telegraph the following to Genl Grant in cipher in my name. intercepted rebel dispatches indicate that Forrest intends crossing the Tennessee somewhere below the mouth of Duck river at an early day. I have sent one regt to watch the Tenn carefully & have sent scouts across the river have Communicated with Genl Hurlbut & Admiral Porter I will delay my movement alittle & move down on this side if He makes the attempt in forces in west Tenn can prevent his escape to the south until I can get information it will not do to let him into middle Tenn or Ky with my forces withdrawn" Telegram received, DNA, RG 94, War Records Office, Military Div. of the Miss.; copies, *ibid.*, RG 393, Military Div. of the Miss., Chief of Cav., Letters Sent; *ibid.*, Telegrams Received. *O.R.*, I, xxxi, part 3, 542.

1. USG omitted the concluding words of the Wednesday, Dec. 16, dispatch of Brig. Gen. Grenville M. Dodge, Pulaski, Tenn.: "& says Forrests future movements are camp talk" Telegram received, DNA, RG 94, War Records Office, Military Div. of the Miss.; copies, *ibid.*, RG 393, 16th Army Corps, Left Wing, Telegrams Sent; *ibid.*, Military Div. of the Miss., Telegrams Received.

2. On Dec. 16, USG telegraphed to Dodge, Pulaski. "Have you an Officer in your command with whom you can leave your troops for about a week. If so you will please report in person without delay to these Headquarters." Copies, *ibid.*, Letters Sent; DLC-USG, V, 34, 35. On the same day, Dodge telegraphed to USG. "I will leave Gen'l Sweeny in command and start tomorrow." Copies, DNA, RG 393, 16th Army Corps, Left Wing, Telegrams Sent; *ibid.*, Military Div. of the Miss., Telegrams Received.

3. On Dec. 19, Smith, Nashville, telegraphed to Wilson. "Please cause the following regiments to report to me here immediately for orders to join in our movement; 2nd Tenn Cavy. Lebanon. 3d Tenn Cay. 5th Ky Cavy 28th Ky mounted Infty. Last 3 Regiments now at Nashville 4 Tenn Cavy Murfreesboro The 8th Iowa Cavy. now on the North Western R. R. should also be placed subject to my orders—" Copy, *ibid. O.R.*, I, xxxi, part 3, 446. On Dec. 21, Smith's request was met by Special Orders No. 25. Copy, DLC-USG, V, 38. On the same day, Brig. Gen. Jeremiah T. Boyle, Louisville, pursuant to Special Orders No. 23, Dec. 17, telegraphed to USG. "I ordered the third Ky. Cavalry & thirteenth Ky Cavalry to report to Gen. W. S. Smith at Nashville as you ordered. I ought to state that the thirteenth Ky. Cavalry is a twelve months regt. raised under recent act of Congress to raise twenty thousand troops in Kentucky to serve in the State unless the President orders them out as will be seen in Gen'l Order forty (40) A. G. O Current Series" Copy, DNA, RG 393, Military Div. of the Miss., Telegrams Received. *O.R.*, I, xxxi, part 3, 465.

To Barnabas Burns

———

Chattanooga Tennessee,
December 17th 1863.

B. BURNS, ESQ.
CHAIRMAN DEM. CEN. COM.
DEAR SIR:

Your letter of the 7th inst. asking if you will be at liberty to use my name before the convention of the "War Democracy", as candidate for the office of the Presidency is just received.—The question astonishes me. I do not know of anything I have ever done or said which would indicate that I could be a candidate for any office whatever within the gift of the people.

I shall continue to do my duty, to the best of my ability, so long as permitted to remain in the Army, supporting whatever Administration may be in power, in their endeavor to suppress the rebellion and maintain National unity, and never desert it because my vote, if I had one, might have been cast for different candidates.

Nothing likely to happen would pain me so much as to see my name used in connection with a political office. I am not a candidate for any office nor for favors from any party. Let us succeed in crushing the rebellion, in the shortest possible time, and I will be content with whatever credit may then be given me, feeling assured that a just[1] public will award all that is due.

Your letter I take to be private. Mine is also private. I wish to avoid notoriety as far as possible, and above all things desire to be spaired the pain of seeing my name mixed with politics. Do not therefore publish this letter but wherever, and by whatever party, you hear my name mentioned in connection with the candidacy for any office, say that you know from me direct that I am not "in the field," and cannot allow my name to be used before any convention.

I am, with great respect,
your obt. svt.
U. S. GRANT

ALS, IHi; ADfS (dated Dec. 16, 1863), USG 3. On Dec. 7, Barnabas Burns, formerly col., 86th Ohio, a three months regt. which served in 1862, had written to USG from Mansfield, Ohio. "You will be, no doubt surprised to find yourself addressed by a stranger, upon a subject somewhat foreign to one which has so fully occupied your attention for the last two years or more. A portion of the Democracy of this, and other states of the North West finding it impossible to co-operate with that portion of the party which oppose the war, and everything which looks to a speedy termination of the war by military power, have formed a separate organization. In Ohio we have fully organizd by the appointment of a State Central Committee & of which I have the honor to be Chairman   We have a Mass Convention in Columbus Ohio on the 8th of January A. D 1864, to appoint Delegates to a National Convention to be held in Cincinnati in May next, the same steps have been taken in all the North wstern States, & portions of the Middle and Eastern States. At the Convention to be held on the 8th Prox. in Columbus, O it may be desireable to express the preference of the 'War Democracy,' for some Gentleman for the Presidency. Your Successful military career, your unfaltering devotion to your Country in its darkest hours of trial, your indomitable energy in overcomeing all obstacles, your Consumate skill and dauntless courage on the field of battle, have all combined to call the public mind to you as the man to whom the affairs of this great Nation should be committed at the close of the present incumbents term of office. I therefore as chairman of the Central Committee of the 'War Democracy' of Ohio beg leave to inquire, Very Respectfully, whether you will permit your name to be used at the 8th of January Convention spoken of, as a candidate for the Presidency at the approaching Presidential Elections? Your Early answer will be looked for with great anxiety. In the mean time may I be permitted to indulge the hope that your answer will be favorable." ALS, *ibid.* USG's success at Chattanooga prompted considerable correspondence about him as a presidential candidate, and much of it is in DLC-Elihu B. Washburne.

On Jan. 14, 1864, J. Russell Jones, Chicago, wrote to USG. "The finishing touch has been put to the Portrait and if anything in this country beats it, I have yet to see it. Antrobus' Studio is constantly thronged by people desiring to see it, but only the favored few get in. On Monday it is to be placed on exhibition, the proceeds to go to the Soldiers Home—and as soon as I am well enough & can leave, we shall take it to Washington—Rawlins saw & will tell you all about it. I took the liberty of saying in a recent letter to Mr. Washburne that if Lincoln & his friends would have you made Lieut Genl. They might have your interest in the Presidency for four years longer. And in a line from Washburne recd today, he says 'that is just the programme I desire. Lincoln will then go in easy, and Grant must be made Lieut Genl.' Dont understand that I spoke *for you,* or as one having authority to speak—I only indicated what *I* should like, and stated that I believed you would be satisfied with this arrangement. I hope for Gods sake you will not commit yourself by letter or otherwise *to anything or anybody* until this question of your promotion is settled—As things now stand, you could get the nomination of the Democracy, but could not be elected as against Lincoln. I tell everybody that I know nothing whatever of your views, but that I am satisfied that all you care for at present is to whip the Rebels and put down the Rebellion— unless things change wonderfully, Lincoln will be re-elected, and I want him & his friends to unite and secure your promotion, first and then the balance will take care of itself   I have been having a pretty tough time lately—Had the

Varioloid, but did not know it until it was all over. one of my children took it from me but is now nearly well. My youngest child is very ill, but I think better to-day—There many things I should like to say but have not now time—Are your letters marked private ever opened by any one but yourself?" ALS, USG 3. For public interest in the Antrobus portrait, see *Chicago Tribune*, Jan. 15, 16, 18, 22, 25, 31, 1864. Probably after this, Jones wrote to USG "substantially" as follows. "I have no disposition to meddle with your affairs, but cannot resist saying that I very much hope you will pay no attention to what is being said about your being a presidential candidate to succeed Lincoln." James Harrison Wilson, "Joseph Russell Jones," typescript, p. 11, George R. Jones, Chicago, Ill. USG then wrote to Jones. "I am receiving a great deal of that kind of literature, but it very soon finds its way into the waste basket. I already have a pretty big job on my hands, and my only ambition is to see this rebellion suppressed. Nothing would induce me to think of being a presidential candidate, particularly so long as there is a possibility of having Mr. Lincoln re-elected." *Ibid.* According to Jones, he received this letter as he entrained for Washington, summoned by President Abraham Lincoln, who had wanted to learn more about USG than U.S. Representative Elihu B. Washburne knew, and who had been told by Washburne that Jones knew USG best. Lincoln, suspecting that the "presidential grub" was gnawing at USG, was gratified when Jones showed him USG's letter. Similar versions of Jones's story (*ibid.*, pp. 11–12) are in George R. Jones, *Joseph Russell Jones* (Chicago, 1964), p. 43; *Richardson*, pp. 380–81; Ida M. Tarbell, *The Life of Abraham Lincoln . . .* (New York, 1900), II, 187–89.

On Jan. 20, Brig. Gen. John A. Rawlins, Nashville, wrote to Washburne. ". . . I see by the papers the bill creating a Lieutenant Generalcy is still undesposed of—So far as General Grant may be regarded in connection with it, I can only say that if the confering of the distinguished honor upon him would be the taking him out of the field, or with a view to the superceding of General Halleck, he would not desire it, for he feels that if he can be of service to the Government in any place it is in command of the Army in the field, and there is where he would remain if made a Lieut. General; besides he has great confidence in and friendship for the General-in-Chief, and would without regard to rank be willing at all times to receive orders through him. The advocacy of the New York Herald and other papers of the General for the Presidency gives him little concern; he is unambitious of the honor and will voluntarily put himself in no position nor permit himself to be placed in one he can prevent that will in the slightest manner embarrass the friends of the Government in their present grand effort to inforce it's rightful authority and restore the Union of the States. Of his views in this matter I suppose he has fully acquainted you. The presence of Longstreet in East Tennessee is much to be regretted. Had General Grants orders been energetically, and with a broader judgement, executed by General Burnside, Longstreet would have been forced to have continued his retreat from Knoxville to beyond the Tennessee line. . . . I met Russell Jones in Chicago and he had me go & see Mr. Antrobus' painting of the General—They are both very fine and the full size one I regard as the finest likeness I ever saw. I am no judge of paintings but I examined this one closely and compared it in my own mind with the General & pronounced it like him and since my return I have looked at and watched the General with interest and compared him with the picture and am sure he is like it. . . ." LS, DLC-Elihu B. Washburne. Printed in James Harrison Wilson, *The Life of John A. Rawlins* (New York, 1916), pp. 387–89; (incomplete and dated Jan. 30) *ibid.*, pp. 433–34. On March 3, Rawlins wrote to Brig. Gen. James H. Wilson. "I cannot conceive how the use of General Grant's name in connection with the Presidency can result in harm to him or our cause, for if there is a man in the United States who is unambitious of such honor, it is certainly he, yet the matter is not in such a shape as to justify him in writing a letter declining to be a candidate for the Presidency. The nomination for the office has not been tendered him by the people; nor has it by either of the great political parties or any portion thereof. . . . To write a letter of declination now, would place him much in the position of the old maid who had never had an offer declaring she 'would never marry;' besides it would be by many construed into a modest way of getting his name before the country in connection with the office, having, as he always has, avoided public notice or newspaper talk relating to him. His letter to the Democratic Committee of the State of Ohio, he says was written in the strictest confidence and he wishes it still to be so considered. Any use of it by his friends would, if known—and that it would be known scarcely admits of a doubt—remove from it the curtain of privacy and might give occasion for discussing it in the public press which of all things you know he would most avoid; hence I do not send it. The Honorable E. B. Washburne I am sure is not in favor of Grant for the Presidency. He is for Mr. Lincoln, and if he has made use of the language imputed to him, it has been to further the passage of his Lieutenant-Generalcy bill; nothing more I am certain. This is my own opinion. That Washburne should seemingly arrogate to himself the exclusive championship of the General, is not at all strange when we reflect upon the fact that two years ago he was the only man in Congress who had a voice of condemnation for the General's maligners. His defence of Grant aided to keep him in his position . . ." *Ibid.*, pp. 184–85.

1 . In his draft, USG here used the word "grateful."

To Maj. Gen. Henry W. Halleck

Chattanooga Tenn
Dec 18th 9 30 A M 1863

Maj Gen H. W. Halleck
Gen'l in Chief

Sherman has returned. Granger and Elliott are in pursuit of Longstreet. I go tomorrow to Nashville. If appearances do not improve East, will go to Knoxville in person about the 27th. I want, before starting, to organize and start a heavy Cavalry force— to move against Forrest who seems to be collecting in West Tennessee to interrupt our communications

U. S. Grant
Maj Gen'l Com'dg

Telegram received, DNA, RG 107, Telegrams Collected (Bound); copies (misdated Dec. 10, 1863, 11:00 A.M.), *ibid.*, Telegrams Received in Cipher; *ibid.*, RG 393, Military Div. of the Miss., Hd. Qrs. Correspondence; DLC-USG, V, 40, 94. *O.R.*, I, xxxi, part 3, 436.

To Maj. Gen. Henry W. Halleck

Nashville Tenn
Dec 20. 1863 2 15 P M

MAJ GEN HALLECK
GEN IN CHIEF

Despatches just received from Gen Foster say Longstreet will probably attempt to hold east end of the Valley[1] Our troops require many articles of clothing, Ordnance stores &c which I must get through by way of Chattanooga Guerrillas are growing troublesome on the Tennessee. I can attend to all these matters better from here than from Chattanooga and will remain unless I go in person to Knoxville I will send Sherman down the Mississippi I will write you the plans at present determined upon.[2]

U. S. GRANT
Maj. Genl

Telegram received, DNA, RG 107, Telegrams Collected (Bound); copies, *ibid.*, Telegrams Received in Cipher; *ibid.*, RG 393, Military Div. of the Miss., Hd. Qrs. Correspondence; DLC-USG, V, 40, 94. *O.R.*, I, xxxi, part 3, 453–54.

1. See following telegram.
2. See letter to Maj. Gen. Henry W. Halleck, Dec. 23, 1863.

To Maj. Gen. John G. Foster

Nashville Tenn Dec 20th 63

MAJOR GENERAL J. G. FOSTER
BLAIRS CROSS ROADS[1]

I will send you the articles called for as fast as possible. Supplies from the country must be collected as rapidly as possible and

every effort made to drive Longstreet from the valley. It is not
practicable to send Grangers other Division. If you require more
forces can they not be taken from your command in Kentucky?[2]

U S GRANT

Major General

Telegram, copies, DLC-USG, V, 34, 35; DNA, RG 393, Military Div. of the
Miss., Letters Sent. Printed as sent at 11:00 A.M. in *O.R.*, I, xxxi, part 3, 452–53.
   On Dec. 15, 1863, and Dec. 17, 11:30 A.M., Maj. Gen. John G. Foster,
Knoxville, telegraphed to USG. "It is evident that I cannot perfect my arrangements for supplies by trains in time to meet the wants of this army for the next
month: I have therefore to ask that you will order supplies of bread stuffs and
small stores to be sent by the River and that orders be given to get steamers
over the Shoals in the Tennessee River to be used for that purpose. The information from above is of such a nature though conflicting that I am now pushing the
fourth (4) Corps to Blains CrossRoads to meet any demonstration or advance
from Longstreet and to cover and protect our trains coming from Cumberland
Gap. Should it appear that Longstreet has been reinforced from Virginia We will
take up the most advantageous position and accept battle. In case he is retreating
or attempting to cover his movement into Carolina we shall endeavor to punish
him to the extent of our ability" Copy, DNA, RG 393, Military Div. of the Miss.,
Telegrams Received. Printed as sent at 4:00 P.M. in *O.R.*, I, xxxi, part 3, 415–16.
"Longstreet has taken the offensive against Gen Parke who has fallen back to
Blairs ~~crossing~~ cross roads where Granger is now concentrating his corps   I
intend to fight there if Longstreets comes. it is reported that he is reinforced by
a portion of Ewells corps. Ellicott arrived yesterday & I have ordered him towards
Morristown to meet Wheelers Cavalry and operate on Longstrets flank   This
question of supplies is very serious & cramps military operations   having to concentrate & call in the foraging parties it is with great difficulty that I can get
quarter rations of meal or flour from day to day   it is very important therefore
to get boats running on the Tennessee river so as to supply us this winter with
bread small stores & ammunition   Beef & Hogs can be driven to us   I have sent
orders to Capt Dickerson to this effect but ask that you will also give such orders
as will put the thing through. One boat has just arrived at Loudon with timely
supplies which have been brought up on the train. Please order Medicines &
hospital stores to be brought up on the next boat" Telegram received, DNA,
RG 393, Dept. of Mo., Letters Received; copy, *ibid.*, Military Div. of the Miss.,
Telegrams Received. *O.R.*, I, xxxi, part 1, 284.
   On Dec. 18, USG, Chattanooga, wrote to Maj. Gen. George H. Thomas. "I
shall start on the steamer to-day for Nashville. Will probably be gone until the
26th inst. I will instruct my Adj. Gen. to refer all matters requiring immediate
action to you, and request that you will act in all matters, particularly in supply-
ing anything wanted by Foster, without waiting to hear from me." ALS, de-
Coppet Collection, NjP. *O.R.*, I, xxxi, part 3, 437. On the same day, Brig. Gen.
James H. Wilson wrote to Thomas. "General Grant directs that the Steamer
'Chattanooga' be immediately loaded with assorted ammunition, hospital stores
Coffee and Sugar, and sent back to Loudon. Also that as soon as she has dis-
charged her cargo, that she be instructed to move all the stores previously sent

from here and left at Kingston and below, to the same point for the use of General Fosters command   After having done this work to return here without delay." Copies, DLC-USG, V, 34, 35; DNA, RG 393, Military Div. of the Miss., Letters Sent. *O.R.*, I, xxxi, part 3, 437. Also on Dec. 18, USG telegraphed to Foster. "You can build two or three hulls for steamers & float them down here   we will put engines in them & send them to you loaded   I will go to Nashville tomorrow at which place you can communicate with me for a few days   A boat will leave here for Loudon with medical stores ammunition & small rations at once"   Telegram received, DNA, RG 94, War Records Office, Dept. of the Ohio; copies, *ibid.*, Military Div. of the Miss., Letters Sent; DLC-USG, V, 34, 35. On Dec. 19, Foster telegraphed to USG, evidently referring to two of USG's dispatches of Dec. 15 in addition to the one of Dec. 18. "I have just returned from the front to find your telegrams of the 15th, 16th & 18th. Longstreet is near Rutledge with a force equal to my own but shows no disposition to attack us in our position. Had circumstances been favorable I intended to attack him acting in accordance with what I understand to be the wishes of Gen'l. Halleck but I am not sure that it would prove a good operation   at any rate the freshet in the river from the recent rains has delayed operations for some days. I would like to confer with you in order to understand more fully what operations will lead to the first results. Can I do this by Telegraphing from Tazwell to which place I can go for the purpose or will it be better to come to Chattanooga by boat"   Copy, DNA, RG 393, Military Div. of the Miss., Telegrams Received. *O.R.*, I, xxxi, part 1, 284.

Earlier on Dec. 19, Foster, Blain's Cross-Roads, Tenn., twice telegraphed to USG. "I am here in force. The high waters from rains and the state of the roads impede operations very much. The men are suffering for want of shoes and clothing. Amunition is also becoming scarce and of some arms entirely expended. Please to send by Steamer to Loudon as soon as possible five thousand pairs of Shoes ten thousand pairs Socks five thousand shirts five thousand blouses ten thousand over-coats ten thousand shelter tents one Million rifle cartridges caliber fifty-eight, Eight thousand rounds for three inch ordnance field piece four thousand rounds for twelve pounder Napoleon Guns fifteen hundred rounds for twenty pounder parrotts two thousand rounds for ten pound parrotts. Three thousand Spencer rifle cartridges Six thousand sharps rifle cartridges five thousand Burnside rifles cartridges Six thousand Colts revolving rifle cartridges. We need all the above as soon as it can be sent   The appearances are that the enemy intend to try and hold a portion of East Tenn. If this proves true we have sharp work before us   the men and animals are in poor condition which must be improved before I can move with the necessary effect   I desire that you will send up the camp and garrisson equippage of Gen'l Granger two divisions and also that you may give me the service of his third division for a little time. I sent dispatch from Knoxville asking for Medicines and Hospital Stores. Skirmishing goes on almost constantly with little effect. Longstreet is near Rutledge." Copy, DNA, RG 393, Military Div. of the Miss., Telegrams Received. *O.R.*, I, xxxi, part 1, 284–85. "I forgot to include the want of axes and tools in my dispatch of this morning. We are entirely destitute and need them very much. Please send me soon as possible one thousand axes one thousand shovels and spades one hundred augurs different sizes twenty cross cut Saws twelve broad Axes one hundred Kegs spikes and large nails six coils large rope for bridges. these should come up in the boats to Loudon"   Telegram received (misdated Dec. 29), DNA, RG 393, Dept. of Mo., Telegrams Received; copies, *ibid.*, Military Div. of the Miss., Telegrams Received; (dated Dec. 19) *ibid. O.R.*, I, xxxi, part 3, 447. On Dec. 20, USG, Nashville, telegraphed to Wilson, Chattanooga. "I send you dispatches just recd from Foster   Tell Genl Thomas to have the clothing Camp Equipage ordnance stores &c called for forwarded as rapidly as possible with the two new Boats nearly ready   We must send these things" Telegram received, DNA, RG 393, Dept. of the Cumberland, Miscellaneous Letters Received; copy, *ibid.*, Military Div. of the Miss., Telegrams Received. *O.R.*, I, xxxi, part 3, 452. On the same day, Wilson, who had already received Foster's first telegram of Dec. 19 from Blain's Cross-Roads and referred it to Thomas, sent Thomas a copy of USG's telegram, adding: "I have just sent you the telegram referred to from which you will see what General Foster requires. Be good enough to let me know how long it will take to procure and forward these articles, and what part can be sent at once." Copies, DLC-USG, V, 34, 35; DNA, RG 393, Military Div. of the Miss., Letters Sent. See *O.R.*, I, xxxi, part 1, 285. On Dec. 21, USG telegraphed to Thomas. "Please direct your Ordnance officer to ship to Loudon the stores called for by Genl. Foster   If additional transportation is wanted on R. R. to enable him to comply with this requisition promptly let me know & I will order additional cars for Ord. stores." Copy, DNA, RG 393, Dept. of the Cumberland, Telegrams Received. On the same day, Thomas telegraphed to USG. "Capt Baylor ordnance Officer will ship the greater part of the Ordnance stores called for by Genl Foster tomorrow. it will be necessary to have about one car each day from Nashville to Bridgeport to keep up the supply of Ordnance stores for this post & Knoxville. we have no clothing or camp Equipage here. have ordered supply for Foster to be sent forward and will ship to Him immediately on its arrival in about four days." Telegram received, *ibid.*, Dept. of the Tenn., Telegrams Received; copies, *ibid.*, Dept. of the Cumberland, Telegrams Sent; *ibid.*, Military Div. of the Miss., Telegrams Received. *O.R.*, I, xxxi, part 3, 461.

On Dec. 21, USG telegraphed to Foster, Knoxville. "I am pushing forward everything possible for you with all rapidity. As soon as all things are complete in the rear (which I think will be by the 26th) I shall start from here and go to Knoxville." Copies, DLC-USG, V, 34, 35; DNA, RG 393, Military Div. of the Miss., Letters Sent. *O.R.*, I, xxxi, part 3, 463. On Dec. 22, USG telegraphed to Foster. "Advise me of the position of affairs with you now. Everything called for by you is being sent forward as rapidly as possible." Telegram received (in cipher), DNA, RG 94, War Records Office, Dept. of the Ohio; copies, *ibid.*, RG 393, Military Div. of the Miss., Letters Sent; DLC-USG, V, 34, 35. On Dec. 24, USG telegraphed to Foster. "There are two steamers here with three more to arrive loaded with stores for you   the boats destined for Carthage   telegraph if you have made arrangements to receive them   I will detain the boats to hear from you" Telegram received, DNA, RG 94, War Records Office, Dept. of the Ohio; copies, *ibid.*, RG 393, Military Div. of the Miss., Letters Sent; DLC-USG, V, 34, 35. On Dec. 25, Foster telegraphed to USG. "Your dispatch of yesterday received   Ordered Genl Boyle to have arrangements made for a Depot at Carthage & at Point Isabella at the mouth of the Big South Fork   I dont know what he has done at Carthage But at Point Isabella everything is ready I believe for the reciept of Stores   I prefer to have the Boat supply Point Isabella first if they can get up there. If not to unload at Carthage & notify Genl Boyle to have a guard there" Telegram received, DNA, RG 393, Dept. of Mo., Telegrams Received; copy, *ibid.*, Military Div. of the Miss., Telegrams Received. *O.R.*, I, xxxi, part 3, 488. On the same day, USG telegraphed to Foster. "Two Steamers loaded with Sub stores for you leave here this morning to reach Carthage if possible under charge of Gunboats & guards" Telegram received, DNA, RG 94, War Records Office, Dept. of the Ohio; copies, *ibid.*, RG 393, Military Div. of the Miss., Letters Sent; DLC-USG, V, 34, 35. On Dec. 28, Act. Lt. Henry A. Glassford, commanding gunboat *Reindeer*, off Carthage, Tenn., telegraphed to USG. "I reached here safely with my convoy. Since my arrival I have learned from Lieut Garrett 1st Tenn: Guards that a large quantity of Coal is now lying ready mined upon the bank of Obey River about 50 miles from its mouth—near Olympus in Overton County—of which Lieut Garrett is a native Nothing he says is required but Coal Boats and labor.—Timber can be had in plenty—and Saw-Mills are to be found above about seven or eight miles. The Obey empties into the Cumberland near Celina abt 210 miles from Nashville—at the present stage he tells me that coal Barges could come out. A land force of probably 200 or 300 men would be required to clear the County of Hamilton's Guerillas which at present are devastating it and murdering the loyal among its inhabitants. Lt Garrett is engaged in raising a Battallion of Cavalry for home defence, and if sent into Overton County could enlist 150 men. The Coals are reported to be of excellent quality fully equal to that produced from the Coalfield further up the Cumberland River—. . . I leave at daylight tomorrow for up the river." Copy, DNA, RG 94, War Records Office, 5th Army Corps. On Jan. 4, 1864, Lt. Col. Andrew J. Cropsey, 129th Ill., Nashville, wrote to Lt. Col. Theodore S. Bowers reporting the role of his 140 sharpshooters in the expedition. *O.R.*, I, xxxi, part 1, 644–45; *O.R.* (Navy), I, xxv, 650–51.

1. Blain's Cross-Roads, Tenn., about eighteen miles northeast of Knoxville.
2. On Dec. 21, 1863, Foster telegraphed to USG. "Your dispatch of 11 A. M. yesterday is rec'd. I am using every effort to collect supplies and have ordered forward every available man in Ky. I applied to Gen'l Halleck for my old Division of the 9th Corps one brigade of which is available at Newport News Va. but have recd no answer. I regret that I have no cipher in which to communicate fully with you If you are to return to Chattanooga soon I think it will be better to see it out before I move on the enemy" Copy, DNA, RG 393, Military Div. of the Miss., Telegrams Received. *O.R.*, I, xxxi, part 3, 464.

To Maj. Gen. George H. Thomas

Nashville December 22d 1863

MAJ GENERAL G. H THOMAS
CHATTANOOGA

There is immense difficulty in travelling under Provost Marshals General Wiles[1] regime. My orders are not respected by his appointees. Sherman this morning had almost to force a passage on the cars, while Jews and citizens generally find no difficulty in going where they please.

I would direct that Col Wilds be ordered to his regiment immediately,[2] and would suggest a new deal all the way through.

U S GRANT
Major General

Telegram, copies, DLC-USG, V, 34, 35; DNA, RG 393, Military Div. of the Miss., Letters Sent; *ibid.*, Dept. of the Cumberland, Telegrams Received. On Dec. 4, 1863, Bvt. Lt. Col. James L. Donaldson telegraphed to USG. "I have authority from Maj. Genl Thomas to pass my employers on the railroad, but Lt Col Wiles tells his officers here, that I must get general passes from him. This is not always practicable, as I work day & night, and I ask that he be ordered to recognize my passes and that no obstacle be put in my way, to act promptly & efficiently." ALS (telegram sent), *ibid.*, Q. M. Dept., Telegrams Sent (Press). On the same day, Lt. Col. Theodore S. Bowers wrote to Maj. Gen. George H. Thomas. "Enclosed please find telegram from Lt Colonel J L Donaldson Chf Q M. Nashville in reference to passes for his employees. Col Wiles must either be removed or instructed in his duties. This is not the first time of unwarrantable misconception of duty, on his part, if it is a misconception in this particular case. Passes and permits from these Headquarters have, under his instructions, been disregarded and persons having them put to inconvenience, while in one instance, a servant of a Staff Officer of the General Commanding, having a pass signed by the Officer, stating by whom he was employed, and approved by the General Commanding, was notwithstanding arrested and put in the guard house. The orders, passes and permits of the General Commanding must not in future be disregarded, nor persons holding them, be they Officers, Enlisted men, servants, or citizens subject to insult by the Provost Marshals under him" Copies, *ibid.*, Military Div. of the Miss., Letters Sent; DLC-USG, V, 34, 35. On Dec. 21, Surgeon George S. Kemble, Nashville, complained of a military railroad conductor who collected fares from soldiers. *Ibid.*, V, 37. On the same day, Bowers wrote to Frank Thompson, superintendent, military railroads, Nashville. "You will direct the Conductor and the Military Officer in charge of passes on the train that left Stevenson, on the morning of the 20th and arrived in this city last night, to report at these Headquarters in person immediately." Copies, *ibid.*, V, 34, 35; DNA, RG 393, Military Div. of the Miss., Letters Sent. Lt. Col. William M. Wiles and others engaged in operating the military railroads of the Military Div. of the Miss. evidently maintained that they were responsible solely to John B. Anderson, manager of the railroads. Anderson had been appointed by War Dept. special orders of Oct. 19, which assigned certain duties to the Q. M. Dept. but revoked all authority relative to the railroads previously conferred by the War Dept. or by the gens. commanding the several military depts. *O.R.*, III, iv, 942–43. See telegram to John B. Anderson, Nov. 1, 1863. On Dec. 24, Bowers issued General Orders No. 13 which replaced this last provision by giving the Q. M. Dept. "control of Military Railroads so far as relates to the transmission of military freight and military passengers, with power to exclude such other freight and passengers as may be deemed necessary." These orders also regulated the use of the railroads by officers and soldiers, specifying that they not be charged fares. Copies, DLC-USG, V, 14; DNA, RG 393, Military Div. of the Miss., General Orders; (printed) *ibid.*, RG 92, Orders Relating to Military Railroads; (printed) USGA. *O.R.*, III, iv, 943.

1. Wiles, capt., 22nd Ind., was promoted to maj., 44th Ind., as of April 24, 1863, and appointed lt. col., 22nd Ind., as of Aug. 13. He had been announced as provost marshal on the staff of Maj. Gen. William S. Rosecrans on July 8, 1862, and continued in the same capacity with the Army of the Cumberland. *Ibid.*, I, xvii, part 2, 86.

2. Wiles later returned to the 22nd Ind. *Ibid.*, I, xxxii, part 2, 370.

To Maj. Gen. Henry W. Halleck

Head Quarters, Mil. Div. of the Miss.
Nashville Ten. Dec. 23d 1863.

MAJ. GEN. H. W. HALLECK,
GEN. IN CHIEF, WASHINGTON,
GENERAL,

I am now collecting as large a cavalry force as can be spared, at Savanna Ten. to cross the Tennessee River and co-operate with the Cavalry from Hurlbut's command in clearing out entirely the forces now collecting in West Tennessee under Forrest.[1] It is the design that this Cavalry, after finishing the work they first start upon, shall push South through East Mississippi and destroy the Mobile road as far South as they can. Sherman goes to Memphis & Vicksburg, in person, and will have Grenada visited, and such other points on the Miss. Central road as may require it. He will also take effectual measures to secure the quiet and safe navigation of the Mississippi.[2] I instructed McPherson to pay no attention to Department or District limits in his opperations against parties threatning the security of river navigation.

It was not my desire to move against Mobile until ends suggested in your dispatch are all secured.[3] I want East Tennessee, as far as Bristol, free from any threat from a rebel force; I want West Tennessee & the state of Mississippi so visited that large Armies cannot traverse them this Winter, and would like to see the Army in front of Chattanooga pushed further south. This latter however I do not now expect to accomplish   The roads about Chattanooga have become perfectly impassable. This however obviates to a great extent the necessity for driving the enemy further back at that point.

My advices from East Tennessee are not satisfactory. Gen. Foster telegraphs me however that having no cypher he cannot telegraph particulars as he otherwise would.[4] If Longstreet retains his present position until the 28th I shall leave Chattanooga on that day for Knoxville and the scene of opperations in East Tennessee.[5]

> I am General, very respectfully
> your obt. svt.
> U. S. GRANT
> Maj. Gen.

ALS, Schoff Collection, MiU-C. *O.R.*, I, xxxi, part 3, 473.

On Dec. 20, 1863, "12 a m," Brig. Gen. James H. Wilson, Chattanooga, telegraphed to USG. "A Weston representing himself as employed by N P Banks for state dept is here in close keeping   says since 19th sept he has travelled all over the confedcy & is now direct from Richmond Atlanta, and some [*Rome*] estimates rebel loss in recent battles 18 or 20.000 including deserters and wounded. Longstreet had when he went to Knoxville from 12 to 14000 infy 3 to 4000 cavly. Whole cav force Braggs army does not exceed 9.000. Braggs entire strength today 70.000, a large estimate, Entire rebel strength including every man and home guards east of Miss two hundred thousand. Says Bragg is to be chief of staff to Gen Johnson. Joe Johnson has not arrived yet   Rebels he says posted from Tunnell Hill to Dalton Ga. Home guards & Georgia troops Sextoning Bridge from there to Atlanta   Thinks Braggs troops are disaffected and ⅓ of them would not fight. People of northern Ga. loyal and throughout the south begin to hear them say we have no appearance of peace twelve months even if the confedcy should succeed. This man proposes to open a daily line of scouts to Bragg through Ducktown & Murray County or to burn Hightown Bridge. Foster telegraphed this morning for Axes Shovels and various tools   Sent request Thomas   if He cant supply them will get Q M Genl to order them at once. C. A. Dana arrived in Washington but has seen no one yet. Halleck teleghs yesterday . . . Prest U States teleghs following 'Washn 19th   For GRANT—The Indiana delegation in congress or at least a large part of them are very anxious that Genl Milroy shall enter active service & I ~~shall~~ share in this feeling   He is not a difficult man to satisfy sincerity & courage being his strong traits. Believing in our cause and wanting to fight in it is the whole matter with him. Could you without embarrassment assign him a place if directed to report to you   (signed) A LINCOLN Prest'   Seems to me we have quite a number of Brigadiers competent any place Genl Milroy could possibly be assigned   Everything here goes smoothly"   Copies, DNA, RG 393, Dept. of the Cumberland, Miscellaneous Letters Received; *ibid.*, Military Div. of the Miss., Telegrams Received. *O.R.*, I, xxxi, part 3, 454–55. For Maj. Gen. Henry W. Halleck's telegram of Dec. 17, omitted from the telegram above, see letter to Maj. Gen. Henry W. Halleck, Dec. 7, 1863. On Dec. 31, USG, Knoxville, telegraphed to President Abraham Lincoln. "I cannot give Gen Milroy a command without prejudice to the service nor without doing injustice to other officers"   Copies, DLC-USG, V, 40, 94; DNA, RG 393, Military Div. of the Miss., Hd. Qrs. Correspondence. See Lincoln, *Works*, VII, 80; telegram to Maj. Gen. William T. Sherman, April 9, 1864.

On Dec. 24, 1863, Brig. Gen. Grenville M. Dodge, Pulaski, Tenn., telegraphed to USG. "A Considerable Cavalry force is being collected opposite Florence & there is a move on foot of some kind in connection with Forrest. Three
regiments from Hardee went through Somerville to join that force" Telegram
received, DNA, RG 94, War Records Office, Military Div. of the Miss.; copy,
ibid., Military Div. of the Miss., Telegrams Received. Dated Dec. 23 in *O.R.*, I,
xxxi, part 3, 473. On Dec. 26, Dodge telegraphed to USG. "There are two (2)
men here who left Rome eight (8) days ago they say most of Hardees Army is
at that place and falling back to it also his stores and that he has an advance at
Dalton One brigade of Cavalry is camped at Cave Springs a few miles this side
of Rome" Copies, DNA, RG 393, 16th Army Corps, Left Wing, Telegrams
Sent; *ibid.*, Military Div. of the Miss., Telegrams Received. *O.R.*, I, xxxi, part 3,
499. On the same day, Brig. Gen. William Sooy Smith, Nashville, telegraphed to
USG. "The within dispatch just received from Genl Dodge." Copy, DNA, RG
393, Military Div. of the Miss., Telegrams Received. On Dec. 28, Dodge telegraphed to USG. "One of our men has come in lift Cave Springs the 19th says
in the 16th Hardee had his H'd. Qrs. at Dalton with his Army near there one
brigade of Infantry at Ressaca. Kellys Division of Cavalry was with Hardee at
Cave Springs. There was a brigade of cavalry of Martins Division the 1st 2nd
and 3d Tenn. under Command of Co'l. Wheeler of 1st Tenn. They were building barracks and expected to stay the winter in Rome. There was a large force of
State troops estimated at 15000. Martins other ten brigades of Cavalry were with
Longstreet on his way here. He passed through Godsend Somerville Courtland
&c. No troops at those places of any account." Copies, *ibid.*; *ibid.*, 16th Army
Corps, Left Wing, Telegrams Sent. *O.R.*, I, xxxi, part 3, 521. On Dec. 29, Dodge
twice telegraphed to USG. "We captured a mail today from Braggs army The
letters all speak of going into winter quarters at Dalton Ressac & Rome also of
appointment of J E Johnson to Command of that army The Chattanooga Rebel
of the 20th announces his appointment & states he would take command the next
week" "My scouts captured despatches today from Roddy to Forrest in which
he says he has sixteen (16) boats below Florence ready to cross on There is no
doubt from all I can learn that there is some move in contemplatio[n] by Forrest
Roddy & Lee" Telegrams received, DNA, RG 94, War Records Office, Military
Div. of the Miss.; copies, *ibid.*, RG 393, 16th Army Corps, Left Wing, Telegrams
Sent; (1) *ibid.*, Dept. of the Cumberland, Telegrams Received; *ibid.*, Military
Div. of the Miss., Telegrams Received. *O.R.*, I, xxxi, part 3, 530.

On Dec. 19, Maj. Gen. James B. McPherson, Vicksburg, wrote to USG en-
closing a report of Eugene Hill on C.S.A. naval construction and plans to retake
New Orleans. ALS, MH. *O.R.*, I, xxxi, part 3, 451. See *ibid.*, pp. 451–52. On
Jan. 18, 1864, USG, Nashville, forwarded this letter to Rear Admiral David D.
Porter "for his information." ES, MH.

1. See telegram to Maj. Gen. Stephen A. Hurlbut, Nov. 29, 1863; telegram
to Brig. Gen. William Sooy Smith, Dec. 17, 1863.
2. On Dec. 19, 10:30 A.M., Maj. Gen. William T. Sherman, Bridgeport,
Ala., telegraphed to USG, Nashville. "I have seen enough of my official papers
from the Mississippi to satisfy me I should be there. I propose first, Genl Logan
to take the 15th Corps as already arranged. Second That Dodges entire Command reinforced by all that can be spared from Corinth move at once rapidly to
~~Corinth~~ Florence Tuscumbia Russelville to Glasgow Miss, there cross ~~the~~ Tombigbee and break up that Rail road all the way back to Corinth and then resume

his place near Decatur. Third, That I proceed to Memphis after a very short visit
to Ohio and organize a force to go up Yazoo river and attack Grenada from the
south. That McPherson be allowed to manage things on the lower ~~Mississippi~~
river according to his own judgement subordinate to the general plan. Fourth,
That the GunBoats patrol the Tennessee very closely and let Genl Walker ram-
page at pleasure in West Tennessee until the people are sick and tired of him
when the Cavalry as already ordered can get on his heels and chase him to the
walls   I deem Genl W. S. Smith to mistrustful of himself for a leader against
Forrest   Mower is the better man for this duty. I be back to lead this army in
the field before the plan of grand Campaign is determined. I will come to Nashville on tomorrow by train and merely telegraph this in advance that you may be
prepared to answer   I will bring my report of past events in field. I shall leave
my adjutant General here with officers of the General Staff to transact business
until *our* meets again." Telegram received, DNA, RG 94, War Records Office,
Military Div. of the Miss.; copies, *ibid.*, RG 393, Dept. of the Tenn., Telegrams
Sent; *ibid.*, Military Div. of the Miss., Telegrams Received. *O.R.*, I, xxxi, part 3,
445. See *ibid.*, pp. 459–60; *Memoirs of Gen. W. T. Sherman* (4th ed., New York,
1891), I, 414. On Dec. 27, Sherman, Lancaster, Ohio, telegraphed to USG. "Arrived home all safe   Will be at Cairo January 2nd Memphis about 5th. That
the Mississippi should be made safe we should have the fifteenth corps & the river
down to the Baleze. Will write to Halleck a strong letter & send you a copy   If
you think you should have McPherson up the Tennessee I can place some inferior
Officer at Vicksburg & make up a command for him out of Dodges & some other
detachments   Let me know about the time you want me back at Huntsville   Saw
Anderson at Louisville & arranged for pushing the Decatur road with all possible
dispatch"   Telegram received, DNA, RG 94, War Records Office, Military Div.
of the Miss.; copy, *ibid.*, RG 393, Military Div. of the Miss., Telegrams Received.
O.R., I, xxxi, part 3, 511. See *ibid.*, pp. 497–98.

On Dec. 29, Sherman wrote to USG. "I got home Christmas day. . . . I hardly
realized till I got here the intense interest felt for us. Our army is on all lips, and
were you to come to Ohio, you would hardly be allowed to eat a meal, from the
intense curiosity to see you and hear you. I have got along as quietly as possible,
and expect to leave on Friday for Cairo as noiselessly as possible. I will . . . be at
Cairo the day appointed, viz, January 2, or 3 at furthest. I have dispatches from
Hurlbut which satisfy me that all things will be in readiness for my coming. I
have written to Admiral Porter to collect accurate accounts of all damages to
steam-boats on the Mississippi, with the localities where they occurred. I think
that we can hold the people on Yazoo and back responsible for all damages above
Vicksburg, the country on Ouachita for all damages between the mouth of Red
and Arkansas on the west bank, and finally the rich country up Red River for
the more aggravated cases near the mouth of Red River. We should make planters
pay in cotton not only for the damages done, but the cost of our occupation, and
in case of failure to pay we should inflict exemplary punishment. I think we have
force enough on the river to do all this. Hurlbut can spare 5,000 men and Mc-
Pherson 3,000, and I will order Hawkins with his whole negro force to go to the
Ouachita. No part of this force should remain longer than is necessary to produce
these results, and leave general notice that similar visitations will be repeated on
every attack upon the boats navigating the Mississippi. I will surely be back to
Huntsville to resume command of the force there before the railroads are done,
and before you can accumulate at your base the supplies needed for an advance

south and east of the Tennessee. I wish you would urge on Halleck to give you the whole Mississippi from Cairo to the mouth, for we must treat the river as one idea. As long as the enemy held any part of it the case was different, but now the navigation is one and should be controlled by one mind. I will do nothing risky or useless. Admiral Porter heartily sanctions. If Joe Johnston is now at Dalton, it is proof that the army of the Mississippi is all there, and you are right in preparing to get from the base of the Tennessee. We may then be able to draw more men from Hurlbut by neglecting Corinth and the railroad. If you have gone to Knoxville, I cannot expect to hear from you again until I reach Huntsville, but if you are at Chattanooga I should like to hear from you. In relation to the conversation we had in General Granger's office the day before I left Nashville, I repeat, you occupy a position of more power than Halleck or the President. There are similar instances in European history, but none in ours. For the sake of future generations risk nothing. Let us risk, and when you strike let it be as at Vicksburg and Chattanooga. Your reputation as a general is now far above that of any man living, and partisans will maneuver for your influence; but if you can escape them, as you have hitherto done, you will be more powerful for good than it is possible to measure. You said then you were surprised at my assertion on this point, but I repeat, that from what I have seen and heard here I am more and more convinced of the truth of what I told you. Do as you have heretofore done. Preserve a plain military character, and let others maneuver as they will. You will beat them not only in fame, but in doing good in the closing scenes of this war, when somebody must heal and mend up the breaches made by war." *Ibid.*, pp. 527–28.

3. See letter to Maj. Gen. Henry W. Halleck, Dec. 7, telegram to Halleck, Dec. 11, 1863.

4. See telegram to Maj. Gen. John G. Foster, Dec. 20, 1863.

5. On Dec. 23, USG telegraphed to Halleck. "Despatch from Foster just received gives no particulars of situation in East Tennessee   Longstreet I presume has not left the State   As soon as I can get some necessary munitions forwarded to Knoxville will go there in person—" Telegram received, DNA, RG 107, Telegrams Collected (Bound); copies, *ibid.*, RG 393, Military Div. of the Miss., Hd. Qrs. Correspondence; DLC-USG, V, 40, 94. *O.R.*, I, xxxi, part 3, 472. See telegram to Maj. Gen. John G. Foster, Dec. 25, 1863.

To Col. John C. Kelton

Dec. 23 1863[1]

I have the honor to submit the following report of opperations of the Armies of The Ohio, The Cumberland and The Tennessee since ~~since~~ being assigned to the Command of this Military Division.

The Secretary of War delivered the order consolidating the three Departments into one, at Indianapolis Ia. on the   of October.² He then ~~fully~~ informed me of the difficulties under which the Army of the Cumberland was laboring to supply itself, over a long ~~and~~ mountainous and almost impassable road, from Stevenson Ala. to Chattanooga, and of the necessity for speedy relief by shortening this line. From Louisville Ky. I telegraphed the order assuming the new command given me, to Chattanooga, and followed as rapidly as possible. On arrival, the 23d of October, I found that Gen. Thomas had, immediately on being placed in Command of the Department of the Cumberland, ~~taken steps to secure the river from Bridgeport to Brown's Ferry, and the railroad and wagon road, between the same points, on the South side of the river.~~ ordered the concentration of Hookers, command at Bridgeport preparitory to securing the river and main wagon road between that place and Brown's Ferry, immediately below Lookout Mountain.

After a reconnoisance made by Gen. W. F. Smith, Chief Eng. and then by Gen. Thomas & myself, in company with the Chief Eng. The plan agreed upon was to ~~assemble all of~~ cross all of Gen. Hooker's force that could be spared from the rail-road, at Bridgeport, ~~ready to cross to the South side of the Tennessee River, and by a rapid march secure the road and line into Lookout Valley.~~ and march it up the main road to where it immerges into Lookout Valley, at Wauhatchie. To further secure the success of this enterprise one Division was sent from here, Palmer's, over the road North of the river, to Whiteside, where they crossed and held the road passed over by Gen. Hooker.

It was known that the enemy held the North end of Lookout Valley, with a Brigade of troops, and the road leading around near the foot of the mountains from their main camps into the valley. ~~It~~ The enemy holding these advantages would have found no difficulty in concentrating a force sufficient to have driven Hooker back, or to have defeated him in a battle. To remedy this advantage possessed by the enemy it was necessary to secure a route from Chattanooga to Lookout Valley, by the North bank of the river, ~~and~~ crossing on pontoon bridges at the town and again at Brown's Ferry. These secured ~~and~~ we would hold a shorter line (across Moccasin Point & Brown's Ferry) by which to reinforce our troops in the valley than the enemy did by the narrow and tortuous road leading around the foot of the mountain. ~~from their camps~~. To secure this advantage sixty pontoon bridges, capable of holding thirty armed men each, were constructed. On the night of the   of October[3] these loaded with Eighteen hundred men, under Brig. Gen. Hazen,[4] sailed quietly down the river past the enemy's pickets at the point of Lookout Mountain, to the South side of the river at Brown's Ferry; landed without ~~but few casualties~~ the loss of a man killed, and but four or five wounded. The whole number of men detailed for this expedition was four thousand men, Hazen's Brigade and details from other troops to make up the number, the whole placed under the command of Brig. Gen. Wm. F. Smith. Those not transported in boats, together with the material for a Bridge, were transported to the North bank of the river at Browns Ferry, by the North shore, across Moccasin Point, without attracting the attention of the enemy. Before day dawned the whole force was ferried to the south bank of the river and secured the almost inaccessable hights rising from the valley at ~~the~~ its outlet to the river. By 10 O'Clock a. m. an excellent bridge was laid. Thus was secured to us the end of the desired road nearest the enemys forces. A short line was secured ~~over~~ over which to ~~send~~ pass troops, if a battle became inevitable. Positions were taken from which troops could not have been driven except by vastly superior forces, and then only with great loss. The roads for the enemy from his camps into Lookout Valley were completely commanded by our Artillery. On the following day Hooker imerged into the valley by the direct road from Whiteside to Chattanooga, with the 11th Army Corps and Geary's Division of the 12th Corps. This secured a comparatively good road of but twenty-eight miles from the terminous of the rail-road.

The advantages given us by this move were of vast importance. Already near ten thousand animals had pereshed in the vain attempt to supply half rations to the troops by the long and tedious route from Stevenson [& Bridgeport] to Chattanooga, over Waldron's Ridge. They could not have been supplied another week.

The enemy were evidently fully apprised of the necessity of this line to us and lost it by the surprize of our taking the North end of Lookout Valley in a manner they had not dreamed of. So fully were they impressed with the importance of keeping from us this route to supplies that a night attack was made by a portion of Longstreet's forces on a portion of Hooker's troops, Geary's Div. 12th Corps, the first night after their arrival. This failed however, and Howard's Corps, finding their assistance no longer required by Geary, carried all the hights West of Lookout Creek, still held by the enemy. This gave us quiet possession of the short and comparitively good road on the south side of the river from the terminous of the rail-road to Chattanooga. The enemy had, very considerately, left two steamboats at Chattanooga which fell into our hands. One more had been built at Bridgeport. With these the distance over which supplies had to be teamed was reduced to about Nine miles. The capacity of the rail-road and steamers were not sufficient to fully supply all the wants of the Army, but actual suffering was relieved.

Gen. Thomas' reports of this important move, and those of his subordinate commanders, were made direct to Washington, without passing through the proper Military channel. No copies of these reports being furnished these Hd Qrs. I have no oppertunity of commending or condemning them.

Up to this period the Army at Chattanooga was practically invested. True they held possession of the country North of the river. But it was from ~~fifty~~ sixty to ~~sixty~~ seventy miles, over the most impracticable of roads, to any supplies, Artillery horses and mules had become so reduced by starvation they could not have been relied on for moving anything. An attempt at retreat must have been with men alone, and they only with ~~what~~ such supplies as ~~they co~~ they could carry. A retreat would have been almost certain annihilation. ~~of the Army, pursued as it would have been by the forces under~~ Bragg, occupying positions within gun shot of our very fortifications, and would unquestionably have pursued a retreat made by our forces.

About this time it became known that Bragg was detaching

portions of his force and moving it ~~into~~ ~~Tennessee~~ towards Knoxville. I felt restless beyond any thing I had before experienced in this War, at my inability to either move to reinforce Burnside, or to attack the enemy in his position, ~~and~~ to make him feel the necessity of retaining at Chattanooga, all his troops. But the condition of the animals belonging to the Army of the Cumberland was such that to move was impossible. I was forced to leave Burnside to contend alone, against vastly superior forces, until Sherman could arrive with his men and means of transportation. This gave time however to fully ~~ma~~ examine the ground and mature plans of opperation when he did arrive.[5]

An examination of the country North of the river showed good roads from Brown's Ferry, up the river and back of the ~~hil~~ first range of hills, out of view from the enemy's positions on Lookout Mountain and Missionary Ridge. All troops crossing at the ferry could be seen by the enemy, and the battalions counted, but not seeing anything further of them they must have been at a loss to know whether they were moving to Knoxville or simply held on the North side of the river for future use.

An examination, with glasses, showed that the North end of Missionary Ridge was only imperfectly guarded, and that the banks of the river from the mouth of Chicamauga Creek Westward was only watched by a small cavalry picket. It was determined therefore that Sherman should march his forces up the North bank of the Tennessee to near the mouth of the Chicamauga, keeping them concealed from the enemy until they were ready to force a crossing. Pontoons for ~~building~~ throwing a bridge over the river were built and placed in North Chicamauga, a few miles further up, without attracting the attention of the enemy. By the night of the 23d of Nov. three Divisions of Sherman's Army were up ready for opperations. He was strengthened by Davis' Division of the 4th Corps which had been stationed all along on the on the North bank of the river and convenient to where they were to cross. At an hour sufficiently early to secure the south bank of the river, just below the mouth of south Chicamauga, by day dawn, the pontoons were loaded with thirty armed men each, who sailed quietly down past the enemy's pickets, landed and captured all but one of the guard, twenty in number, before they were aware of the presence of a foe. The steamer Dunbar, with a barge in towe, was sent up to aid in the ferriage of the Artillery and remainder of the troops. By ~~10~~ (see Shermans report for the time of day) O'Clock[6] a good pontoon brid[g]e was laid, the army crossed; and very well fortified. This secured and soon the whole of Missionary Ridge was in Sherman's possession, from the extremity next to the river to ~~the~~ near the tunnel. During the night Sherman fortified making his position equal to that held by the enemy for strength.

In connection with the battle of Chattanooga Col. Long crossed the pontoon bridge at the mouth of ~~Chattanooga~~ Chicamauga Creek on the night of the 24th and made a raid on the enemy's lines of communications. He first burned Tyners station with many stores, cut the road about Cleveland, captured near a hundred wagons ~~of~~ from the enemy and over two hundred prisoners. His loss was but small.[7]

It was intended that Hookers move upon the point of Lookout Mountain, and Thomas' on the enemy's first line in Chattanooga Valley, should be made simultaneously with Sherman's crossing the river. But a deserter from the rebel army who came in ~~th~~ to our lines the morning of the 23d reported Bragg falling back.[8] I was not willing that he should get his Army off in good order. Gen. Thomas was therefore ordered to get out his troops stationed in Chattanooga, attack and drive in the enemy's pickets, and make him develop his lines. This was done by Sheridans & Woods Divisions, and the 11th Corps, in the most gallant style, driving the enemy from his first line and securing to us what is known as Orchard Knoll, and a low range of hills south of it. These points were fortified during the night and Artillery moved to them.

The report of this deserter was evidently not intended to deceive but he had mistaken Braggs movements. It was afterwards ascertained that one Division of Buckner's Corps had gone to join Longstreet ~~towards~~ ~~Knoxville~~ and a second Division of the same Corps had started, but were brought back in consequence of our attack.

~~During the 24th,~~ The center having done on the 23d what was intended for ~~that~~ the 24th ~~done but~~ advanced none, but strengthened and bettered their position during the day. Hooker carried out the part assigned him for this day almost beyond the most sanguine expectations. With Geary's[9] Division of the 12th Corps, Osterhaus' of the 15th Corps, and two Brigades of Stanley's Div. of the 14th Corps he scaled the Western slope of Lookout Mountain, drove the enemy from his rifle pits ~~at the foot of the Mountain and on the Northern point~~, on the Northern extremity and slope of the Mountain, capturing many prisoners and without serious loss. During the night of the 24th the enemy made a feint of attempting to drive Hookers forces from the point of Lookout Mountain, but this was evidently intended for nothing more than to cover their retreat from the Mountain top. Hooker's forces had got near the only road by which they could descend the Mountain and join the balance of the rebel forces, except by a circuitous and roundabout way, endangering their being cut off from the main force.

On the morning of the 25th Hooker took possession of the mountain top, with a small force. With the balance of his command he swep across Chattanooga Valley, ~~to Rossville~~ now abandoned by the enemy, to Rosville. In this march he was detained ~~some~~ four hours by the necessity of building a bridge across Chattanooga Creek. At Rossville he ~~was to~~ ascended Missionary Ridge and moved Northward towards the center of the now shortened line. ~~Sherman's~~

Sherman's attack upon the enemy's most Norther, strongest, and to him most vital, point was vigerously kept up all day. The assaulting column advanced to the very rifle pits of the enemy and held their position firmly without wavering. The right ~~being exposed~~ of his assaulting column being exposed to the danger of being turned, two small brigades were sent to their support. These advanced in the most gallant style, over an open field on the mountain side, to near the works of the enemy, and ~~lay there~~ laid there partially covered from fire, for some time. The right of these two brigades rested near the crest of a ravine, or gorge in the mountain side, which the enemy took advantage of to send troops, covered

from their view, below them and to their right rear   Being unexpectedly fired into from this ~~right rear~~ direction they fell back
across the open field below them and reformed in good order in the
edge of the timber. The column which attacked them were speedily
driven to their intrenchments by the assaulting column proper.—~~I~~
~~have been thus particular in noticing this matter because public~~
~~notices prints have, unintentionally no doupt, given accounts of~~
~~this part of the battle of Chattanooga, caculated to do injustice to~~
~~as brave and gallant troops as fought in that battle.~~

Sherman's position not only threatened the right flank of the
enemy, but from him occupying a line across the mountain and to
the rail-road bridge over ~~Chattanooga~~, [Chicamauga Creek] their
rear and stores at ~~Chattanooga~~ [Chicamauga] station. This made
the enemy mass heavily against him. The movements of the enemy
were plainly seen from the position I occupied on Orchard Knoll.
Taking advantage of the enemy weakening his center I directed
Gen. Thomas to move his center, composed of A Bairds[10] Division
14th Corps, and Sheridan's & Woods Divisions of the 4th Corps,
forward, with a double line of skirmishers thrown out, followed
within easy supporting distance by the whole force, and to carry
the rifle pits at the foot of Missionary Ridge. Hooker was at this
time anxiously looked for ~~coming down~~   I expected every moment
to see his column moving North on the ridge, with his left in Chattanooga Valley and right east of the ridge. It was intended that
his approach should be the signal for storming the ridge in the
Center with strong columns. But the troops in the center moved
forward driving the enemy like bees from a hive from the line of
rifle pits, at the base of the hill, stopped but a moment until the
whole were in line, and commenced the ascent of the mountain,
from right to left, almost simultaneously, ~~and without orders~~
~~from me.~~

The orders as given were for a double line of skirmishers to be
thrown forward to press the enemy, followed closely by the whole
force, until the line of rifle pitts at the foot of Missionary Ridge
were carried. Hookers appearance was momentarily looked for on
the top of the ridge, coming from Rossville, and then it was my

intention to order the assault upon the rifle pitts in the Center and on top of the ridge. The order apparently was not understood to contemplate a halt until the entire position of the enemy was carried[11] They encountered a fearful volley of grape & canister from near thirty pieces of Artillery, and musketry from still well filled rifle pits on the summit of the ridge. Not a waver however was seen in all that long line of brave men. Their progress was steadily onward until the summit was in their possession. In this charge the casualties were remarkably few for the fire encountered. I can ~~only~~ account for ~~it by the~~ this only on the theory that the enemy's ~~confusion and~~ surprise at the audacity of such a charge, ~~and amazement~~ caused confusion and purposless aiming of their pieces.

Night ~~had soon set in and pursuit had to be defered until morning. Sheridan however did go some distance, I believe near~~ being near at hand, and the enemy still offering resistence to Bairds Division and the left of Grangers Corps, no ~~organ~~ general pursuit could take place that night. Sheridan with his Div. however followed to Mission Mills. ~~To the left, enemy's right, in front of Sherman and Division~~ the enemy ~~kept up a resistence until after night fall.~~ The 11th Army Corps was brought into Chattanooga before the battle commenced and formed the left of Thomas' forces in the advance made on the 23d. They occupied like position on the 24th. On the 25th they effected a crossing of Citico Creek and joined Sherman where they continued during the battle, pursuit and advance on Knoxville.

On the morning of the 26th the force under Sherman was advanced in pursuit of the enemy by way of Chicamauga station, crossing the creek by a pontoon bridge near the mouth. Hooker advanced by Rossville towards Graysville and Ringgold. ~~The 14th Corps which had been partly engaged with him in the battles from the time the point of Lookout Mountain was carried to the end, and partly with the center, two brigades also having been engaged with him in the assault of that apparently impregnable point.~~ The force with him consisted of Geary's Division 12th Corps, a portion of the 14th Corps commanded by Gen Palmer in person, Osterhaus' Division of the 15th Corps, and two Brigades of the 4th

Corps. Osterhauses' Division and the Brigades from the ~~fou~~ 4th Corp, also operated under Gen. Hooker in the assault on Lookout mountain.

Previous to the battle I ~~had~~ ~~designated Gen.~~ ~~Granger to go~~ ~~to the relief of Burnside as soon as the battle was fought, taking~~ ~~with him enough men from other commands to make his force~~ ~~up to twenty-thousand.~~ directed Gen. Thomas to hold Granger in readines with with his Corps, and detachments enough from other commands to make his force 20,000 men, including the force available at Kingston which was to be gathered and carried along, to go to the relief of Knoxville so soon as the battle was fought. The two Divisions with him therefore were not sent in pursuit of Bragg.

The pursuit was continued the second day to near Tunnel Hill, a distance of ~~eighteen~~ over twenty miles from Chattanooga. Howards Corps was detached and sent to Red Clay to destroy the railroad between Dalton & Cleveland and thus to cut off the enemy's communications with Longstreet. Had it not been for the imperative necessity for relieving Burnside I would have pursued the broken and demoralized retreating enemy as long as supplies could have been found in the country. But my advices were that Burnsides supplies would only last until about the 3d of December. Unless, as I had been advised, Longstreet had been ordered back on the commencement of our attack, (and it would not do to rely on reports obtained entirely from prisoners) it was already geting late to afford the necessary relief. I determined therefore to pursue no further. Hooker was directed to hold the position he then occupied until the night of the 30th going no further south at the expense of a fight. Sherman was directed to march to the rail-road crossing of the Hiwassee to protect Granger's flank until he was across that stream, and to prevent further reinforcements being sent by that route into East Tennessee. Returning from the front to Chattanooga I found that Granger had not taken the number of men with him I had directed. ~~probably~~ This was unavoidable however because one Division of his Corps was with ~~Sherman,~~ Hooker and ~~finding further~~ that between Lookout Valley & Bridgeport. He was one day later in starting than I thought he should be, and ~~that~~ he moved with great reluctance and many complaints. I therefore determined, ~~although two Divisions with Sherman had marched all the way from Memphis, had commenced a battle immediately on their arrival at Chattanooga, had pursued the enemy two days after the battle, and had no rations except what such as they got from the country, to send him.~~ notwithstanding the fact that two Divisions of Sherman's forces had marched from Memphis, and had gone into battle immediately on their arrival at Chattanooga and had been without rations except such as they could gather from the country already for several days to send them, and Sherman to command. Accordingly orders were sent Gen. Sherman ~~on the~~ to Calhoun, to assume command of the troops with Granger in addition to those with him, and to releive East Tennessee of the presence of the enemy.

In connection with the pursuit after Longstreet Gen. Elliott was ordered with his Cavalry Division on the 25th of November. He was at Alexandria Ten.

~~For some reason which I have never yet been fully able to ascertain he only reached Kingston on the 11th of December and Knoxville on the 16th. His starting point was Alexandria.~~

~~Owing to mistakes in telegraphing his first orders were uninteligable. Being some distance from a telegraph office and having to call for a repetition of his orders he did not start until the 28th. The Caney Fork being much swollen much detention~~

Failing to receive his orders at first inteligably over the wires and finding Caney Fork much swollen, ~~he was~~ a difficult to cross he did not reach Kingston in time to follow Longstreet whilst he was retreating.[12]

I have not spoken particularly of the result of the pursuit of the enemy because the more detailed reports accompanying this does this subject justice. For the same reason I do not particularize the part taken by Corps & Division commanders. It would be unfair however if I should fail to make special mention of the services rendered by Brig. Gen. W. F Smith who before the ~~action~~ battle acted as Chief Engineer and during the battle as a staff officer with me   To him is due the most excellent system of fortifications

which defend Chattanooga   To his energy and skill is due our
having the pontoons ~~with~~ which ~~the~~ were so necessary for securing
the route which alone saved the Army and enabled it to fight a
battle; and he commanded the troops, in person, that secured the
entrance into Lookout Valley. Gen. Smith also made all the recon-
noisances first alone, and afterwards in company with Gen. Thomas
and myself, which led to both the plans for securing a route to supplies and for gaining a footing on Missionary Ridge by crossing
the Tennessee River where we did. To make the pontoons logs had
to be cut in the woods, sawed in the mills, anchors had to be made
in the shops and all kept running to the greatest advantage to get
them in time. I feel personally under more than usual obligations
to him for his services and desire that they should be fully appreciated by higher authority.

To the officers of my staff, Brig. Gen. J. A. Rawlins, Chief of
Staff, Brig. Gen. J. H. Wilson Inspector Gen. Brig. Gen. W. F.
Smith, Chief Eng, Lt. Col.   Duff Chief of Artillery, and aides
Maj.   Rowley, Capts, Ross & Hudson much credit is due for
their services during the battle and pursuit.

Accompanying this I send reports of Department and their
subordinate Commanders, to which I refer you for minuter details.
~~of the action~~[13] The recommendations made by them for promotions
I endorse.

ADf, DLC-USG, III. Substantial additions as well as minor corrections, reformu-
lations, and other changes were made in the final report. LS, DNA, RG 94, War
Records Office, Union Battle Reports. *O.R.*, I, xxxi, part 2, 27–37.

On Dec. 7, 1863, 2:30 P.M., Maj. Gen. Henry W. Halleck telegraphed to
USG. "Please telegraph your losses & captures, in round numbers, in your recent
battles near Chattanooga." ALS (telegram sent), DNA, RG 107, Telegrams
Collected (Bound); copies (misdated Nov. 28), *ibid.*, RG 393, Military Div. of
the Miss., Hd. Qrs. Correspondence; DLC-USG, V, 40, 94. On the same day,
7:00 P.M., USG telegraphed to Halleck. "Our losses in killed wounded and missing in recent battle about four thousand (4000)   Enemys loss in killed about
the same. We took over six thousand well prisoners, forty two pieces of artillery,
caisson and battery wagons for a larger number of pieces. Number of small arms
collected about five thousand (5000)   Many have no doubt been collected by
Regiments and not accounted for." Telegram received, DNA, RG 107, Telegrams
Collected (Bound); copies, *ibid.*, RG 393, Military Div. of the Miss., Hd. Qrs.
Correspondence; DLC-USG, V, 40, 94. *O.R.*, I, xxxi, part 2, 27. See *Memoirs*,
II, 95, 97.

On Dec. 4, USG, Chattanooga, telegraphed to John B. Anderson, Nashville. "The wants of this Army will require at least four more cars fitted up for the removal of sick, and arrangements made to move the Hospital trains over the Nashville and Louisville road. The Quartermaster at Nashville will give you any facilities necessary to carry this into effect." Copies, DLC-USG, V, 34, 35; DNA, RG 393, Military Div. of the Miss., Letters Sent. On the same day, USG telegraphed to Col. Robert C. Wood, asst. surgeon gen., Louisville. "It has been suggested to me that in view of the fact that the sick from the Dept of the Cumberland do or should occupy more of the Hospitals in Louisville than the sick from the Dept of the Ohio & should therefore be under the supervision of the Medical Dir of the Cumberland Army   you have a much better opportunity of Judging of this matter than I have   I will leave it for such orders as you choose to make or will make such orders as you may suggest"   Telegram received, DLC-U.S. Army: Civil War Miscellany; copies, DLC-USG, V, 34, 35; DNA, RG 393, Military Div. of the Miss., Letters Sent. Also on Dec. 4, Wood telegraphed to USG. "Telegram received   I enclose order for your approval   Asst. Surg. Gen'ls Office Louisville Ky. December 4th 1863. First—the Medical Director of the Dept. of the Cumberland will exercise supervision over all the Hospitals in Louisville   Second—The Medical Director of the Dist. of Kentucky Surg. George G. Shumard U. S. V. in addition to his other duties will report to Surg. Glover Perin U. S. A. for instructions and will continue to have the immediate control of the Hospitals in Louisville Jeffersonville and New Albany Reporting to Surg. Perin the state of the Hospitals & the condition of the sick and wounded weekly for the information of the Commanding General and receive his instructions"   Copy, ibid., Telegrams Received. On the same day, USG telegraphed to Wood. "The order telegraphed by you defining duties of Med. Dir. Dept of the Cumbd & district Ky recd & approved"   Telegram received, DLC-U.S. Army: Civil War Miscellany. On Jan. 4, 1864, Wood wrote to USG. "In accordance with your views, as expressed to me, I have the honor to enclose an order in reference to Medical Inspectors, which I think the interest of the service requires, and which I trust will meet with your approbation." LS, DNA, RG 393, Military Div. of the Miss., Letters Received.

1. Not in USG's hand. The final report is datelined Chattanooga, although USG was in Nashville on Dec. 23, 1863. Assuming that he began his draft at that time, it was not completed until several weeks later. See letter to Maj. Gen. Henry W. Halleck, Jan. 20, 1864. On Feb. 9 and 15, 1864, Brig. Gen. John A. Rawlins, Nashville, wrote to his wife. "I shall begin to-morrow in connection with Colonel Bowers to copy up General Grant's official report of the battles of Chattanooga. . . ." "Colonel Bowers and I are very busily engaged of evenings on the General's official report of the battles of Chattanooga, which I assure you is a very unpleasant and I might say thankless undertaking, for the General is very tenacious of the claim that he writes his own reports, and it is necessary for us to follow the text as nearly as possible. With the transposition of sentences, even pages, and the writing out too of the very plans of the battles, this is difficult." James Harrison Wilson, *The Life of John A. Rawlins* (New York, 1916), pp. 397, 399. On March 3, Rawlins wrote to Brig. Gen. James H. Wilson. "General Grant's official report of the battle of Chattanooga has gone forward. It is full and complete, written in his usual happy, narrative style, void of pomposity or parade. . . ." *Ibid.*, p. 187. Insertions by Rawlins in USG's draft report have been bracketed.

2. USG met Secretary of War Edwin M. Stanton at Indianapolis on the morning of Oct. 18, 1863. See General Orders No. 1, Oct. 18, 1863.

3. Oct. 26–27. See first telegram to Maj. Gen. Henry W. Halleck, Oct. 28, 1863.

4. William B. Hazen, born in Vt. in 1830, brought to Ohio in 1833, USMA 1855, was promoted to capt., 8th Inf., as of May 14, 1861. Commissioned col., 41st Ohio, as of Oct. 29, he was appointed brig. gen. as of Nov. 29, 1862. He participated in the battles of Shiloh and Chickamauga, and commanded the 2nd Brigade, 3rd Div., 4th Army Corps, at Chattanooga. See *O.R.*, I, xxxi, part 1, 82–85; W. B. Hazen, *A Narrative of Military Service* (Boston, 1885), pp. 154–64.

5. For USG's order to advance, which was delayed pending Maj. Gen. William T. Sherman's arrival, see letter to Maj. Gen. George H. Thomas, Nov. 7, 1863.

6. In the final report, the time noted is "12 o'clock M."

7. In the final report, this paragraph appears at this point, although USG originally wrote it in between his acknowledgments at the end of his draft. See letter to Maj. Gen. William T. Sherman, Nov. 18, 1863, note 3.

8. The final draft contains an insertion at this point: "The following letter from Bragg, received by flag of truce on the 20th, tended to confirm this report: Headquarters Army Tennessee   In the field, 20th November, 1863   MAJ. GEN. U. S. GRANT   Com'd'g U. S, Forces, &c. Chattanooga. GENERAL: As there may still be some non-combatants in Chattanooga, I deem it proper to notify you that prudence would dictate their early withdrawal   I am, General, very respect. your ob't serv't. BRAXTON BRAGG, General Comdg." Copies of Gen. Braxton Bragg's letter are in DNA, RG 109, Braxton Bragg, Letters and Telegrams Sent; *ibid.*, RG 393, Military Div. of the Miss., Miscellaneous Letters Received. See *O.R.*, I, xxxi, part 2, 63.

9. On Dec. 4, 1863, Maj. Gen. Joseph Hooker wrote to Stanton recommending that Brig. Gen. John W. Geary be promoted. Typescript, Atwood Collection, InU. *O.R.*, I, xxxi, part 3, 328–29. On the same day, USG endorsed this letter. "The recommendation of Brig. Gen. Geary for promotion is concured in by me. The services of Gen. Geary in resisting a night attack in Lookout Valley, Oct. 29th, and in the battles around Chattanooga commencing on the 23rd of Nov. prove him eminently deserving of this recognition." Typescript, Atwood Collection, InU. Maj. Gen. George H. Thomas added a similar endorsement on Dec. 5. *Ibid.* Geary was not promoted.

10. Absalom Baird, born in 1824 in Pa., graduated from Washington College, USMA 1849, and spent more than six years teaching mathematics at USMA. He accompanied the Army of the Potomac until appointed brig. gen. as of April 28, 1862, when he received a command in the Army of the Ohio, and remained in the West, distinguishing himself at Chattanooga. At Chattanooga he commanded the 3rd Div., 14th Army Corps. See *O.R.*, I, xxxi, part 2, 507–11.

11. USG inserted this paragraph into his draft at this point.

12. These paragraphs regarding Brig. Gen. Washington L. Elliott are represented in the final report as a single sentence. In his draft, USG wrote the first paragraph in between his acknowledgments and the latter two paragraphs as a separate insertion. See letter to Maj. Gen. William T. Sherman, Dec. 12, 1863, note 5.

13. On Jan. 13, 1864, Lt. Col. Cyrus B. Comstock, Nashville, telegraphed to

Hooker. "Maj. Genl. Grant directs me to state that your official report of the battle of Lookout Valley has appeared in the papers before its receipt by him, and to request that you furnish him with the names of the persons by whose action or neglect this report has become public, with such specifications, that they may be properly punished." Copy, DNA, RG 94, Letters Received, 75H 1864. On Jan. 19, Hooker, Lookout Valley, Tenn., wrote to Col. John C. Kelton. "I have the honor to forward herewith a copy of a telegram received from the Head quarters of the Division of the Mississippi, which explains itself. Soon after its receipt I addressed the Head quarters of the Department concerning it, and was informed in reply that my official report of the battle of Lookout Valley had been forwarded direct from that office to your Head quarters, and had no reason to suppose that a copy of it had found its way to the public prints through the action or neglect of any person or persons connected with his Head quarters. I request that you will inform me whether or not it was received by you, and if so, furnish me with the names of any person or persons, if any, by whose action or neglect the report became public." LS, *ibid.* On Jan. 30, Halleck endorsed this letter. "I am informed by the Secty of War that after the official reports were sent to Congress, he gave to a friend of Genl Hooker (he thinks Mr. Wilkes Editor of the Spirit of the Times) permission to publish a copy of Genl Hooker's report." AES, *ibid.* On the same day, Col. Edward D. Townsend, AGO, wrote to USG stating at Halleck's direction the substance of this endorsement. Copy, *ibid.,* Letters Sent.

On Jan. 13, USG telegraphed to Thomas, Chattanooga. "Have the kindness to send as early as possible your reports of the battle of Chattanooga, so that I may send them to Washington" Copies, DLC-USG, V, 34, 35; DNA, RG 393, Military Div. of the Miss., Letters Sent. On the same day, Thomas telegraphed to USG. "I have only been waiting for the reports of Genls Hooker & Granger to forward mine—Have not recd either of them yet but will forward my report to-morrow" Telegram received, *ibid.,* Dept. of the Tenn., Telegrams Received; copy, *ibid.,* Military Div. of the Miss., Telegrams Received. On Feb. 9, USG telegraphed to Thomas. "Direct Gen'ls Hooker and Granger to prepare their reports and forward them through the proper channel to these Hd. Qrs, by the twentieth inst." Copies, *ibid.,* Dept. of the Cumberland, Telegrams Received; *ibid.,* Military Div. of the Miss., Letters Sent; DLC-USG, V, 34, 35. On Feb. 22, USG wrote to Kelton. "I have the honor to transmit herewith the following sub-reports of Department, Corps, Division and Brigade Commanders of the part taken by them respectively in the Battle of Chattanooga. . . . The reports of Major General Hooker, comdg 11th & 12th Corps, and the report of Major General Granger commanding 4th Corps have not yet been received, but will be forwarded as soon as they come to hand." LS, DNA, RG 94, War Records Office, Union Battle Reports. On March 5, Kelton wrote to USG. "I have the honor to acknowledge the receipt of the reports of the Battle of Chattanooga. With one exception those recd. correspond with those described in your letter. The Report of Maj Genl Sherman, Comdg Dept of the Tennessee was not in the box with the others and has not been recd." ALS, *ibid.,* RG 108, Letters Sent (Press). On March 9, Lt. Col. Theodore S. Bowers telegraphed to USG. "Col Kelton reports the report of Gen Sherman missing. It was enclosed in a bundle of photographic views & forwarded with the others. No dispatches from the front for three days." Telegrams received (2), *ibid.,* RG 107, Telegrams Collected (Bound). On March 10, USG telegraphed to Kelton. "Col Bowers says Sherman's report was Enclosed in a bundle of photographic views & forwarded with the other reports." Telegram received, *ibid*. On March 11, Thomas forwarded through USG's former hd. qrs. the reports of Hooker, Maj. Gen. Oliver O. Howard, Maj. Gen. Gordon Granger, and Elliott. DLC-USG, V, 37. On March 13, Hooker wrote to Stanton submitting a slightly revised copy of his report, dated Feb. 4. *O.R.*, I, xxxi, part 2, 313–25. On March 25, USG, Culpeper Court-House, Va., endorsed this report. "Respectfully forwarded to Maj. Gen. H. W. Halleck, Washington D C. I know of no objection to the substitution of this for Maj. Gen. Hookers original report of his operations in the battle of Chattanooga. Attention is called to that part of the report giving from the reports of his subordinate commanders, the number of prisoners and small arms captured, which is greater than the number really captured by the whole Army" ES, DNA, RG 94, War Records Office, Union Battle Reports. *O.R.*, I, xxxi, part 2, 325. On March 26, Townsend wrote to USG. "A Resolution of Congress calls for your report of Battle of Chattanooga—The report of General Hooker which I handed you the other day in the Secretary's office is one of the sub-reports—Can I get it—and is it to be sent with yours? The other reports are nearly ready—" ALS (telegram sent), DNA, RG 107, Telegrams Collected (Unbound); copy, *ibid*., RG 94, Letters Sent. On the same day, Comstock telegraphed to Townsend. "Lt. Gen. Grant directs me to say that Gen Hookers report of the battle of Chattanooga will be sent up to morrow & that it should accompany his report." ALS (telegram sent), *ibid*., RG 107, Telegrams Collected (Unbound); telegram received, *ibid*., RG 94, Letters Received, 317C 1864; (press) *ibid*., RG 107, Telegrams Collected (Bound). USG's report was published in the *New-York Tribune* on April 13.

To Col. Henry R. Mizner

Nashville December 23d 1863

COLONEL MIZNER COMDG
COLUMBIA TENN

Return to Mr Hillman[1] such of his property, teams &c taken by Col Downey, from Aetna furnace, as can be collected   Any of his Negroes desiring to return, will be allowed to do so. Mr Hillman being vouched for as a loyal citizen, and being at the time this property was seized, protected by a safe guard from the Dept of the Cumberland

U S GRANT
Major General

Telegram, copies, DLC-USG, V, 34, 35; DNA, RG 393, Military Div. of the Miss., Letters Sent. Henry R. Mizner, born in N. Y. in 1828, was appointed capt., 18th Inf., as of May 14, 1861, and col., 14th Mich., as of Dec. 22, 1862.

In Dec., 1863, he was post commander at Columbia, Tenn. On Dec. 15, Col. Thomas J. Downey, 15th U.S. Colored, Columbia, "under orders of General Dodge, . . . to press all able-bodied negroes, horses, and mules, . . . the negroes to be put in my regiment now forming at this place," reported to Maj. Gen. George H. Thomas that "after a five days' hard scout, Colonel Mizner, commanding the post, without any knowledge or consent of me, released 13 negroes and sent them back to their owners. I ask, for information, what is to be done in this case?" *O.R.*, I, xxxi, part 3, 414–15.

On Nov. 17, J. S. Golladay, Nashville, wrote to USG seeking the return of seven Negro men presently employed in government service in Clarksville, Tenn., so that he might fulfill his contract to cut wood for the Nashville and Kentucky Railroad. ALS, USG 3. Golladay attached a copy of a letter of Sept. 3 from Brig. Gen. Jeremiah T. Boyle, Louisville, to Brig. Gen. Andrew J. Smith asking that Golladay, a "loyal citizen" of Todd County, Ky., be permitted to bring his cotton out of Miss. Copy, *ibid.* On Nov. 23, 2:30 P.M., USG telegraphed to Brig. Gen. Robert S. Granger, Nashville. "The negroes Mr Gollady of Ky will returned to him unless they go by their own free will & not then if they have been sworn into the service" Telegram received, DNA, RG 393, Military Installations, Nashville, Telegrams Received; copies, *ibid.*, Military Div. of the Miss., Letters Sent; DLC-USG, V, 34, 35.

1. Daniel Hillman, Jr., born in N. J. in 1807, had been involved in the coal and iron business since the 1820s in Ky., Tenn., and Ala. He became part owner of the Etna Furnace, in Hickman County, Tenn., about twenty miles west of Columbia, in the late 1840s. Operation of the furnace was suspended in 1855, resumed in 1862, and ended permanently after U.S. forces seized the property in 1863. See W. Jerome D. Spence and David L. Spence, *A History of Hickman County Tennessee* (Nashville, 1900; reprinted, n. p., 1969), p. 119; Ethel Armes, *The Story of Coal and Iron in Alabama* (Birmingham, 1910; reprinted, Birmingham, 1972), pp. 210–11. On Jan. 13, 1864, Lt. Col. Theodore S. Bowers wrote to Brig. Gen. Grenville M. Dodge. "You will take prompt measures to restore to Mr Daniel Hillman all property taken from him by forces of your command and in cases where the property is necessary for the use of Government, you will cause proper vouchers to be executed in favor of Mr Hillman for it. You will please give this matter such personal attention as may be necessary to secure a full adjustment of Mr Hillman's claim" LS, Dodge Papers, IaHA.

On Feb. 12, USG telegraphed to Rear Admiral David D. Porter, Mound City, Ill. "Captain Fitch is said to be moving iron from Wheatley' Ferry, Tenn River. The iron belongs to minor heirs, and will no doubt be adjudged their property, I am requested to inquire if it is removed by your authority." Copies, DLC-USG, V, 34, 35; DNA, RG 393, Military Div. of the Miss., Letters Sent. *O.R.* (Navy), I, xxv, 746. On Feb. 13, Francis B. Fogg, Nashville, wrote to USG. "At the request of the acting Trustee of the Minor Heirs and Devisees of the late Anthony W. Vanleer deceased, Mr Daniel Hillman, I send you a statement of the facts in relation to a quantity of Iron which has been taken from the Banks of the Cumberland River by certain Gun-Boats under the command of Rear Admiral David D. Porter. . . . Mr Daniel Hillman has acted as Trustee at the request of the friends of the Children and has endeavoured to protect and secure the property for the grandchildren. We have, owing to our unfortunate condition, no Court of Chancery or rather no Chancellor in this District otherwise a Bill would have

been filed several months ago, to authorize a sale of all the iron, and an investment of the proceeds in United States Stock or Bonds that interest might be obtained for those entitled under the Will." ALS, John M. Taylor, Rangoon, Burma.
On the same day, USG endorsed this letter to Porter. "This will be handed to you
by Mr. Hillman, act. guardian of the minor children who own the iron of which
I telegraphed you yesterday. Mr. H. has been represented to me as a man loyal
to this Govt. He will explain all the circumstances connected with this iron and
ask your advice how to proceed to obtain possession of it." AES, *ibid.*

To Maj. Gen. John G. Foster

By Telegraph from Nashville [*Dec.*] 25 186[3]
To MAJ GENL FOSTER,

Ammunition has left Chattanooga for you   Averill[1] succeeded
in making a raid on Longstreets rear at Salem[2] and destroyed much
of the road some locomotives and Cars three large Depots and an
immense amount of stores[3]   this will give you a great advantage

U S GRANT M G

Telegram received, DNA, RG 94, War Records Office, Dept. of the Ohio; copies,
ibid., RG 393, Military Div. of the Miss., Letters Sent; DLC-USG, V, 34, 35.
O.R., I, xxxi, part 3, 488. On Dec. 24, 1863, Maj. Gen. John G. Foster, Blain's
Cross-Roads, Tenn., telegraphed to USG. "The enemy is still in force   no engagement yet   a movement is in progress which will bring on a partial one
soon   I will telegraph more fully to day in cipher"   Copy, DNA, RG 393, Military Div. of the Miss., Telegrams Received. *O.R.*, I, xxxi, part 3, 479. On the
same day, 12:30 P.M., Foster, Strawberry Plains, Tenn., telegraphed to USG.
"Longstreet is moving his 'Regt' (Came regt—probably intended for force) across
the 'Holston' in the direction of Morristown—where prisoners state he intends to
make a stand—I have crossed the Cavalry under Genl Sturgis and advanced him
to feel the enemy. He engaged them this morning early near 'Massy Creek' and
drove in the force at that point. I am pushing forward the Rail-road bridge at this
place and as soon as it is done can advance—We want ammunition and Cannot
fight a general engagement until supplied—We have more reports that reinforcements have arrived from Virginia—but as I have no proof of it I discredit
the report—Longstreets force is twenty six thousand men—exactly what mine
is—" Telegram received, DNA, RG 94, War Records Office, Union Battle Reports. *O.R.*, I, xxxi, part 1, 285. On Dec. 25, 8:00 A.M., Foster, Knoxville, telegraphed to USG. "Yesterday the cavalry was warmly engaged with the enemys
cavalry beyond New Market   Genl Sturges reports that on the Dandridge road
Col. Campbells brigade met a superior force of the enemy & had a severe
fight   They at once charged on his rear and captured two guns but he recaptured them by a counter charge   The enemy lost eighty killed & wounded   Col
Campbell   Col Garrards Brigade was also on the Dandridge & Morristown road

while Sturges with the main body drove the enemy beyond Massey Creek   Sixty one prisoners have been brought in"   Telegram received, DNA, RG 393, Dept. of Mo., Telegrams Received; copy, *ibid.*, Military Div. of the Miss., Telegrams Received. *O.R.*, I, xxxi, part 1, 625.

On Dec. 26, 5:30 P.M., Foster telegraphed to USG. "Despatch recd   As soon as the Rail road bridge at Strawberry plains is completed and ammunition arrives we can advance in force. In consequance of injury to my wounded leg from the fall of my horse on the 23d I am disabled for a time for field service & have therefore felt it to be my duty to ask to be relieved"   Telegram received, DNA, RG 94, Generals' Papers and Books, John G. Foster; copy, *ibid.*, RG 393, Military Div. of the Miss., Telegrams Received. *O.R.*, I, xxxi, part 3, 503. On Dec. 29, noon, Maj. Gen. Henry W. Halleck telegraphed to USG. "Major Genl Foster has asked to be relieved from his command on account of disability from old wounds. Should his request be granted, who would you like as his successor? It is possible that Genl Schofield will be sent to your command." ALS (telegram sent), DNA, RG 107, Telegrams Collected (Bound); copies, *ibid.*, RG 393, Military Div. of the Miss., Hd. Qrs. Correspondence; DLC-USG, V, 40, 94. *O.R.*, I, xxxi, part 3, 529.

On Dec. 27, 28, 5:00 P.M., and 29, Foster telegraphed to USG. "Great majority of the old regiments have decided to reenlist as veteran Volunteers provided they can be assured them that as soon as the present emergency is passed one third of their Regiments enlisting as Veterans shall go home at the end of thirty days. Another third and the remainder as soon as the first third returns to duty   Gen Sturgis has been and is almost constantly employed with enemys Cavalry in front   he has attained and maintained the morals over them   I have as yet no report of to day's fight." "Gen'l Sturgis with his own & Elliotts Cavalry have been almost constantly engaged with the enemys Cavalry for the past few days. He has gallantly driven them from every position and is now in the country between Mossy Creek & Morristown. One of his brigades made a dash into Martens Camp last night and put to flight three rebel brigades & captured their Camp with provisions and Cooking utensils   Longstreet is unhappy about his communications" "At eleven A. M. to day the whole of the enemys cavalry supported by a Division of Infantry and two batteries of attacked Genl Sturgis near Mossy Creek. The fight was severe and general and lasted until five P. M.   Sturgis held his ground and ended by driving the enemy entirely off the field achieving a complete victory" Copies, DNA, RG 393, Military Div. of the Miss., Telegrams Received. *O.R.*, I, xxxi, part 3, 509, 519; *ibid.*, I, xxxi, part 1, 625–26, 646. See *ibid.*, p. 287.

1. William W. Averell of N. Y., USMA 1855, was badly wounded in a skirmish with Indians in N. M. Territory in 1858. Appointed col., 3rd Pa. Cav., as of Aug. 23, 1861, he participated in the peninsular campaign. Appointed brig. gen. as of Sept. 26, 1862, he commanded the 2nd Cav. Div. during the action of Kelly's Ford, Va., March 17, 1863. Transferred to the Dept. of West Va. in May, he led a successful cav. raid (Dec. 8–25) destroying C.S.A. supplies at Salem, Va.

2. Salem, Va., approximately 110 miles from the Tenn. border on the East Tennessee and Virginia Railroad.

3. On Dec. 23, 3:30 P.M., Halleck telegraphed to USG. "Reports have just reached here that Genl Averill has destroyed the depot locomotives, trains, &c., at Salem, on the East Tenn & Va R. R. He may be able to injure the road

so as to prevent any supplies or reenforcements being sent to Longstreet. I am directed to call your attention particularly to Longstreet's army. Fears are expressed that Foster and Wilcox are not able to cope with it, and that unless it is driven out of Tenn., new raids will be made into Kentucky." ALS (telegram sent), DNA, RG 107, Telegrams Collected (Bound); copies, *ibid.*, RG 393, Military Div. of the Miss., Hd. Qrs. Correspondence; DLC-USG, V, 40, 94. *O.R.*, I, xxxi, part 3, 472. On Dec. 24, USG telegraphed to Secretary of War Edwin M. Stanton. "I will go to Knoxville in person immediately. If Longstreet is not driven from Tennessee soil it shall not be my fault." Telegram received, DNA, RG 107, Telegrams Collected (Bound); copies (addressed to Halleck), *ibid.*, Telegrams Received in Cipher; *ibid.*, RG 393, Military Div. of the Miss., Hd. Qrs. Correspondence; DLC-USG, V, 40, 94. Printed as addressed to Stanton in *O.R.*, I, xxxi, part 3, 479. See telegram to Maj. Gen. Henry W. Halleck, Dec. 31, 1863.

To Lt. Gen. William J. Hardee

Chattanooga December 28th 1863

LIEUT GENERAL W. J. HARDIE
COMDG C. S. FORCES, DEPT. TENN.

Your communication of the 23d December, relative to Captain F. Gurley, who is now on trial for the murder of General McCook, I found here on my return from Nashville where I have been spending a few days.

Captain Gurley, being an officer in the Confederate Army does not preclude the possibility of his having committed a foul murder for which he can be held fully amenable by the laws of war and if found guilty, punished with death.

Captain Gurley has been charged with murder not justified by any position he can possibly hold. He will receive a fair and impartial trial. If acquitted of murder, he will be held as a prisoner of war, if found guilty, not being the reviewing officer myself I am not prepared to say what action will be taken.

Whilst at Nashville I received a communication from Gen Forrest making the same statement of Captain Gurley's position that you do. That communication I refered to the commission which is trying his case.[1] The same desposition will be made of your communication.

This is addressed to you at Rome Ga, your letter having nothing to guide me as to where it was written from and supposing that to be your present Headquarters.

U S Grant
Major General U. S. A.

Copies, DLC-USG, V, 34, 35; DNA, RG 393, Military Div. of the Miss., Letters Sent. *O.R.*, II, vi, 771. On Dec. 23, 1863, C.S.A. Lt. Gen. William J. Hardee wrote to USG. "I have been informed that Captain Frank Gurley, of the 4th Ala. Cavalry, Confederate States Army, now a prisoner of war in your hands, has been tried at Nashville by the United States Authorities, for the alleged murder of Brig Genl. R. L. McCook, late of the United States Army. I deem it my duty to inform you that at the time Genl McCook was killed, Capt. Gurley was an officer in the Confederate Army, and was serving, at that date, under the immediate orders of Capt. J. M. Hambrick, of Forrest's Command. When Genl McCook was killed, he was riding in a wagon, between his advance guard and the main body of his forces. Capt Hambrick, with his command and that of Capt Gurley, attacked the advance and drove it back, and coming upon General McCook, demanded his surrender. He refused to surrender, and endeavored to escape. Capt. Hambrick directed his men to fire upon him and his retreating command, and during this firing General McCook fell. These are the facts of the case, and can be fully sustained by proof   I have been further informed that Capt Gurley has been treated as a felon, having been heavily ironed and his head shaved. The alleged procedure against Capt. Gurley is in conflict with the laws of war and humanity, and believing that the facts of the case have been misrepresented to you, I have deemed it my duty to make this statement, and, at the same time, respectfully and earnestly to protest against any action towards Capt Gurley, on the part of the authorities of your Government, inconsistent with that due to a prisoner of war." LS, DNA, RG 153, MM 1326. On Jan. 4, 1864, C.S.A. Gen. Joseph E. Johnston, Dalton, Ga., wrote to USG. "I enclose you the statement of Lieut. Col: J. M. Hambrick, 4th Ala. Cavalry, in relation to the case of Capt Frank Gurley, of his Regiment, now on trial before a military commission in Nashville, for the murder of Genl McCook. A communication on the same subject was sent you on the 23d ult, by Lieut Genl Hardee. I request that you will submit the statement of Lieut Col Hambrick to the military commission; and, in the event of that body having adjourned, to the revising Officer." LS, *ibid.* Frank B. Gurley or Gurly, captured on Oct. 20, 1863, was tried as a guerrilla and murderer, and sentenced to be hanged. After Maj. Gen. George H. Thomas recommended commuting the sentence to five years in prison, which President Abraham Lincoln approved and then cancelled "because made by mistake," Gurley was inadvertently exchanged as a prisoner of war. AES, *ibid.* Lincoln, *Works*, VIII, 541–42. See letter to Andrew Johnson, April 10, 1866; O. Edward Cunningham, "Captain Frank B. Gurly, Fourth Alabama Cavalry, C. S. A.: Murderer or Victim," *Alabama Review*, XXVIII, 2 (April, 1975), 83–103.

1. On Dec. 12, 1863, Brig. Gen. Nathan B. Forrest wrote to Maj. Gen. Stephen A. Hurlbut stating that Gurley was properly enrolled in C.S.A. service. LS, DNA, RG 153, MM 1326. *O.R.*, II, vi, 691–93. On Dec. 23, Lt. Col. Theodore S. Bowers endorsed this letter. "Respectfully referred to Col Miller, President of G. C. M. in session at Nashville Tenn" ES, DNA, RG 153, MM 1326.

To Julia Dent Grant

———

Chattanooga Tennessee,
December 28th 1863,

DEAR JULIA,

I just arrived here this afternoon traveling steadily ever since I left you. I will leave in the morning for Knoxville and probably reach there on New Years day. If I get there in the morning will remain but a few hours and push on up the valley towards where the two Armies are confronting each other. How long I may be compelled to remain there it is impossible to tell. It may be but a day or it may be a week. I shall stay no longer than is necessary. You need not look for me earlyer than the 10th. of January and, I think, not later than the 15th.

Wilson, Dr. Kittoe, Bowers, Duff & Dunn[1] go with me. We will have a hard time of it with the present state of the roads and at this season of the year. But I always feel well when I can get a plenty of out of doors exercise. The fact is hard labor is the easyest duty I have to perform.

I have a greatdeel of writing to do to night and will therefore cut this short by sending a greatdeel of love and many kisses to you and Jess. Remember me to Mrs. Smith,[2] Mr. & Mrs. Cameron[3] and all at the house.

ULYS.

ALS, DLC-USG.

1. William M. Dunn, Jr., enlisted as a private, 6th Ind., on April 18, 1861. Appointed 2nd lt., 83rd Ind., as of Nov. 19, 1862, and promoted to 1st lt. as of Oct. 4, 1863, he began service as act. aide to USG during the siege of Vicksburg. On Nov. 22, Capt. George K. Leet issued Special Field Orders No. 15, Military Div. of the Miss. "Lieutenant William M. Dunn, Junior, Company F, 83rd Indiana Volunteers, is hereby detached from his company and regiment, and assigned to Staff duty on the Staff of the Major General Commanding, to date from the 4th day of October 1863." Copy, *ibid.*, V, 38. See *General Grant. An Interview with Major W. M. Dunn, U. S. A. Published in the "San Francisco Call."* (n. p., n. d.).

2. Most likely the wife of Brig. Gen. William Sooy Smith. See John Y. Simon, ed., *The Personal Memoirs of Julia Dent Grant* (New York, 1975), p. 125.

3. James and Emma S. Cameron. Cameron and three others owned a dry-goods store in Nashville, where his wife was secretary of the ladies' aid association. In a letter to Secretary of the Treasury Salmon P. Chase, Feb. 15, 1864, James Cameron mentioned having protection papers from USG. ALS, DNA, RG 366, Correspondence of the General Agent. See letter to Emma S. Cameron, Aug. 9, 1864.

To Maj. Gen. Henry W. Halleck

Knoxville Tenn
Dec 31st 1863 11 A M

MAJ GEN H W HALLECK
GENL IN CHIEF

Have just arrived [at] this place. Will go to the front [this] evening or in the morning   [The] Fourth (4th) and Ninth (9th) Corps are at Blains Cross Roads, the Twenty Third (23d) at Strawberry [Pla]ins with one Brigade & Sturgis cavalry at Mossey Creek & Talbot [Station]   Longstreet is at Morristown[1]

U S GRANT
Maj Genl

Telegram received, DNA, RG 107, Telegrams Collected (Bound); copy, *ibid.*, Telegrams Received in Cipher. *O.R.*, I, xxxi, part 3, 542.

On Dec. 29, 1863, Brig. Gen. James H. Wilson, Chattanooga, wrote to Maj. Gen. George H. Thomas. "General Grant directs the 'Lookout' to be prepared at once to go to Loudon with one assorted cargo for General Fosters command   He suggests that the Commissary stores now on board be allowed to remain, and that the other part of the cargo, be made out from stores you have on hand at this place. He wishes the boat to be ready as soon as possible as it is his intention to go on her to Loudon. Be good enough to have him notified of the time when she leaves—" Copies, DLC-USG, V, 34, 35; DNA, RG 393, Military Div. of the Miss., Letters Sent. *O.R.*, I, xxxi, part 3, 529. Probably on Dec. 30, USG, Kingston, Tenn., telegraphed to Maj. Gen. John G. Foster, Knoxville. "Please send Cars to Loudon for myself and staff   will be at Loudon about 11 P M   have seven horses with me" Telegram received, DNA, RG 94, War Records Office, Dept. of the Ohio. See *Memoirs*, II, 101.

1. Strawberry Plains about fifteen miles, Mossy Creek and Talbott's Station nearly thirty miles, and Morristown nearly forty miles northeast of Knoxville, all points on the East Tennessee and Virginia Railroad.

Calendar

1863, JULY 7. USG endorsement. "Respectfully returned to Major Hendrickson U S A. Mr Sampson Wolff was arrested and sent north after I left Millikins Bend on the recent Campaign. And no report of his arrest was made to my Provost Marshal General. Consequently I have no means of knowing the Cause of his arrest. I shall have the matter investigated. I suppose however the arrest was made for good and sufficient reasons. You will please release Mr Wolff and permit him to return to the place where he was arrested, requiring of him only his parol of honor to remain neutral as between the Contending parties."—Copies, DLC-USG, V, 25; DNA, RG 393, Dept. of the Tenn., Endorsements. Written on a letter of Maj. Thomas Hendrickson, military prison, Alton, Ill., enclosing a petition of Samson Wolff.—*Ibid.* On Dec. 21, Wolff, Tensas Parish, La., wrote to Secretary of War Edwin M. Stanton asking for compensation for losses caused by his arrest, noting that ". . . from what I learned of Maj. Genl. Grants Order of my release, there is no offense recorded against me at Headquarters."—ALS, *ibid.*, RG 94, Letters Received, 1170 1864. On Feb. 11, 1864, Col. Edward D. Townsend, AGO, referred the letter to USG.—ES, *ibid.* On Feb. 17, Maj. William R. Rowley, provost marshal, Nashville, wrote to Lt. Col. Theodore S. Bowers. ". . . In his communication he states having been paroled within the limits of the Picket lines— that he visited the house of a Mr James which was then in use as a Commissary Depot, that he was there arrested and placed in close confinement   The fact of his being at or in the vicinity of this Depot of supply, was perhaps sufficient to establish a strong suspicion: upon which he was sent north by a Division or Corp Commander   I am also informed of instances of the arrest of 'Aliens' during during the seige of Vicksburg under circumstances sufficient to justify confinement for the time being."—ALS, *ibid.* On Feb. 20, Brig. Gen. Peter J. Osterhaus, Woodville, Ala., wrote to Lt. Col. Theodore S. Bowers. "Enclosed I have the honor to return the complaint of Mr. Samson Wolff, together with Major Rowleys opinion—I distinctly recollect that my cavalry arrested near Lake St Joseph a rather deaf individual of the Jewish persuasion on or about the 27th of April, on suspicion of communicating with the enemy   After a preliminary examination before the Provost Marshal of my division I concluded to detain him until the movement across the Mississippi should be accomplished. When the last of my division had been placed on the transports said Wolff was on April 29th 62 released on parole to remain at home; here my connection with Mr. Wolff ceased as my division took part in all the operations before Vicksburg commencing with the attack on Grand Gulf   I cannot understand how Mr Wolff came to look for clean linen at Mr. Jame's who lives at Ion near New Carthage a direction exactly opposite to that which he should have taken to go home from Perkins landing at which latter place he was detained by me . . ."—LS, *ibid.* On July 9, Asst. Secretary of War Charles A. Dana endorsed Wolff's letter. "The action of Brigadier General Osterhaus in arresting this claiment was perfectly justifiable, and his imprisonment was no more than his character and acts as a public enemy, made proper. No indemnity can be paid him"—ES, *ibid.*

1863, JULY 8. USG endorsement. "Respectfully forwarded to Head Quarters of the Army, Washington, D. C., and the granting of the request asked for urgently recommended. I have no record of the Majors dismissal, but believe from my acquaintance with Col. O'Meara he would not make the request unless it was just. The other officers too, are among the first in character and bravery in this command."—Copies, DLC-USG, V, 25; DNA, RG 393, Dept. of the Tenn., Endorsements. Written on a letter of Brig. Gen. William Sooy Smith *et al.* asking for the reinstatement of Maj. Owen Stuart, 90th Ill., dismissed by AGO Special Orders No. 160.— *Ibid.* Stuart was mustered in as a lt. col. on Sept. 27.

1863, JULY 8. Medical Purveyor Henry Johnson, Washington, D. C., to USG. "I have the honour to Congratulate you on your Successes. The news of the fall of Vicksburg came to me yesterday direct from the War Deptment. At 12 oclock the cannons from the Surrounding fortifications boomed forth their loud rejoicings Shaking the very foundation of the City. A great Speech was made here last night by Senator Wilkinson   He gave your history from your youth up till the 4th July. after he got through with that the crowd were not Satisfied, they wanted to hear more of General Grant, 'give us more of Grant.' So you See Grant has maintained his position as A No 1 as I predicted one year ago. Mrs. Johnson joins me in my hearty congratulations. The children do not forget you and your family. Little Aggie gave a party to Some of her little playmates most of whom are of Secession families (they are thick here)   She made them all drink to the Success of Genl. Grant. Mrs. Johnson wrote to Mrs. G. Sometime ago, directed to Covington Ky. She would like to have a Photograph for her album of yourself. It is rumored at this moment Port Hudson is taken. I hope it is true."—ALS, USG 3. Answering a list of questions from the surgeon gen. office about his professional qualifications, probably during the summer of 1862, Johnson noted that he ran a pharmacy for eighteen months in Galena, Ill., in 1859–60. The business failed and he returned to Philadelphia, Pa., to run another pharmacy.—ADS, DNA, RG 94, Personal Papers, Medical Officers and Physicians. On May 19, 1862, USG wrote to Johnson that he would be glad to assist him in securing an appointment if a bill passed Congress.—*PUSG*, 5, 126. USG probably referred to the Medical Storekeeper Bill which was signed by President Abraham Lincoln on May 20. Johnson was nominated for the position of medical storekeeper on Jan. 19, 1863, and confirmed on Feb. 19, to date from Aug. 13, 1862. The medical storekeeper performed the duties of the medical purveyor, allowing Surgeon Gen. William A. Hammond to use the regular army medical purveyors, trained military surgeons, in the field.—*U.S. Statutes at Large*, XII, 378–79, 403–4; *HED*, 37-3-1, IV,

50–58. On April 27, 1864, Act. Medical Purveyor Johnson, Washington, wrote to USG. "I sent you some time ago two petitions similar to the one enclosed, for your signature to a hearty approval. I presume they have been overlooked amidst your multitude of cares & business. I would again beg that you will not overlook this little request. I think it a just one, and puts us on an equal footing with others as to rank. We ask for simply that of Captain, although I think that we are entitled to some thing more than this, but yet I will be satisfied, so that I stand upon a firmer basis than the one I now stand upon. I am confident that your approval pass the bill through Congress, and I shall ever feel greatful to you."—ALS, USG 3.

1863, JULY 9. USG endorsement. "Respectfully forwarded to Head Quarters of the Army, Washington D. C., with the recommendation that the application to have that part of Special Orders No. 105, A. G. O., within referred to revoked, be not granted."—Copies, DLC-USG, V, 25; DNA, RG 393, Dept. of the Tenn., Endorsements. Written on a letter of Brig. Gen. James C. Veatch requesting the reinstatement of five lts. of the 55th Ill., which Lt. Col. John A. Rawlins had referred on June 1 to the commanding officer of that regt. "for his remarks."—*Ibid.* On July 29, Maj. Thomas M. Vincent, AGO, wrote to USG. "In accordance with your endorsement upon the papers of Lieutenants Roberts, McIntosh, Keyes, Fellmore and Merritt of the 55th Illinois Volunteers, their application to be reinstated in the service is denied."—Copy, *ibid.*, Military Div. of the Miss., War Dept. Correspondence. On July 17, Maj. Samuel Breck, AGO, wrote to USG concerning irregularities in the muster rolls of other officers of the 55th Ill.—Copies, *ibid.*, RG 94, Enlisted Branch, Letters Sent; *ibid.*, RG 393, Military Div. of the Miss., War Dept. Correspondence.

1863, JULY 9. Lt. Col. James A. Hardie, AGO, to USG. "I have the honor to enclose herewith eighty copies in three packages, of No. 1. of the Army and Navy Gazette, and to request you will please take such steps as will ensure their delivery to the officers for whom they are intended: Viz: One copy to the commander of the Department of the Tennessee. One copy to the commander of each of the four corps. One copy to the commander of each of the twenty Divisions. One copy to the Commander of each of the three Districts. One copy to the Commander of each of the fifty two Brigades."—LS, DNA, RG 393, Dept. of the Tenn., Letters Received. Similar letters and forms followed routinely, transmitting to USG new issues of the *Army and Navy Official Gazette* for distribution in the Dept. of the Tenn.—LS, *ibid.*

1863, JULY 9. Maj. Gen. Stephen A. Hurlbut, Memphis, to USG. "I shall require within this command about 6000 stand of arms. If they can be had of good quality & complete with accouterments—say English Enfields—I will distribute to old Regiments & give their arms to Colored troops—If not of this quality I wish to issue them direct to Colored Regiments. You will greatly oblige me by ordering from 6 to 10,000 furnished to Capt Harper at once"—ALS, DNA, RG 393, Dept. of the Tenn., Letters Received.

1863, JULY 9. William White Williams, New York City, to USG, after reading about the battle of Waterloo, suggesting that each cavalryman carry nails to spike captured art. in the event that they were later driven off from the guns. "Did my physical health permit," Williams continued, "I would gladly enter our national Army as a Chaplain with the expess understanding that after caring for my men out of battle I was to be permitted to share with them the the privilege of using carnal as well as spiritual weapons in behalf of our beloved America, . . ."—ALS, USG 3.

1863, JULY 10. General Orders No. 42, Dept. of the Tenn., announcing the conviction by court-martial on March 27 of 1st Lt. Effingham T. Hyatt, 35th Mo., for advocating the overthrow of the government by Maj. Gen. George B. McClellan.—Copies, DLC-USG, V, 13, 14; DNA, RG 393, Dept. of the Tenn., General and Special Orders; (printed) USGA. On July 10, the sentence of dismissal from the service was overturned by Lt. Col. John A. Rawlins because the judge advocate was improperly sworn.— ES, DNA, RG 153, MM988. On Oct. 7, USG forwarded the case to hd. qrs.—ES, *ibid.* On Oct. 28, Judge Advocate Gen. Joseph Holt reported to President Abraham Lincoln. "Lieut. Hyatt of the 35th Mo. Vols. was convicted of Violation of the 5th article of war. Specification, In that while in the presence of officers and enlisted men he stated in substance that Genl McClellan ought to have marched his army into Washington, and driven Abe Lincoln, and those damed abolitionists out, and taken the reins of government into his own hands. The proof fully established the averment set forth, but the Judge Advocate not being sworn the sentence of dismissal declared by the Court is inoperative. It is there fore recommended that this officer be dishonorably dismissed by order of the President."—ES, *ibid.* On Feb. 15, 1864, Lincoln endorsed the proceedings. "Recom. of Judge Advocate General approved & ordered"—AES, *ibid.*

1863, JULY 10. Alfred B. Safford, Cairo, to USG. "Allow me to congratulate you for the great success of your noble Armey in your every effort to put down this rebellion & more particularly in the crowning effort the taking of Vicksburg. I see that the President has promoted you to Maj Gen of the regular Armay and I assure you *the People* are unanimous in rejoicing at this act of Justice ~~to~~ to you. With the hope that you may be spared to see the end of this Conflict and rewarded for you great sacrifises and service"—ALS, USG 3. See *PUSG*, 4, 212, note 3.

1863, JULY 12. USG endorsement. "Respectfully forwarded to Col. J. C. Kelton, Asst Adjt. Genl."—ES, DNA, RG 109, Taliaferro Papers. Written on a letter of July 9 from Col. William F. Wood to Brig. Gen. Elias S. Dennis enclosing a cipher dispatch of June 26 from Gen. Joseph E. Johnston to Lt. Gen. John C. Pemberton.—ALS, *ibid.*

1863, JULY 12. R. Crowley, Saratoga, N. Y., to USG. "I have just learnt of the Serender of Vixburgh & as your early friend and in the name of a greatfull country I congratulate you You will perhaps be somewhat supprised at receiveing a line from me one whom you have probably long since forgotten But I havenot forgotten you & your early fellow Graduate Richey. do you remember me at Cincinnati & Alexandria I have often thought of that ride on your horse from the camp to the Town, but little did I then think ~~the~~ that God had disigned you to become in the future allmost the Saviour of your country—I trust that you have only just commenced your course of distinction & yousefullness & that God may spair your life through the many perrils you may have to pass through and at lenth restore you to your dear Family amidst the applause & gratitude of your country. I am happy to inform you that a Kind Providence has blessed me in a pecuniary point of view for I often thought of your unsolicited kindness to me when sincear friendship is most praised I have traveled much since I parted from you and am now very plesantly situated in Brooklyn with a plesant convenient home & should be most happy to recipocate in some friendly way your past kindness to me. If any of your Family or Friends should visit new York I should be most happy to extend the hospitality of my house to you or any of your friends myself & Family are makeing a short sogurne at this place for a change but leave for home to morrow.—I would much like to see your Family & become acquainted with them for I am shure your Wife would like to see one of your earlyest friends do you remember our visit to Mr. McMechents country house on the Hill side. Time has produced wonderful changes. You, then a graduate of West Point, now the first General in the U S. I was then what they called a *Pedlar* nevertheless I have been a successfull one thank God & all by my own industery.—If consistant with ~~y~~ your inclination & conveniences I would be most happy to receve a line from you mearly to say that you havenot forgotten your old Friend . . . P S May God Bless you"—ALS, USG 3.

1863, JULY 12. U.S. Representative Elihu B. Washburne, New York City, to USG. "I need not congratulate you on the taking of Vicksburg, because you will imply such congratulation. I was at Washington when I heard the news, and you can form no adequate idea of how it was received there and over the whole country by loyal men. I send you some slips from newspapers to give you some idea. I leave for home to-morrow. The copperheads have been determined not to believe the news and were batling up to yesterday. The enclosed slip from the copperhead Express shows how they tried to reason themselves into the belief that Vicksburg had not fallen. One curious thing—half the class who were hounding you a year ago now swear they always believed in you and were original Grants men. God bless you. Give my kindest regards to your military house-hold."—ALS, USG 3.

1863, JULY 14. James L. Crane, Springfield, Ill., to USG. "Allow your old Chaplain of the 21st to congratulate you upon your recent victory at Vicksburg. Of course, as an american citizen I would follow your success with a great deal of interest, but that interest has been heightend by the fact that I was so pleasantly associated with you in the beginning of the war, & from the further fact that I have repeatedly felt called upon to from my previous acquaintance with you to defend your good name from the aspersions of some of the little souls who are always jealous of a man that surpasses them in the faithful discharge of his duty. I know very well that you need no defence of mine at any time, but I could never find it in me to sit quietly by & hear a friend underrated when I had an opportunity to speak in his favor. But enough of this. May Heaven prosper your forever. I want to speak to you about another item." Crane then asked USG to contribute money to a church-supported women's college.—ALS, USG 3. See *PUSG*, 2, 56.

1863, JULY 15. USG endorsement. "I would strongly urge the appointments herein recommended, and the dismisal from service of the officers named, who, from their negligence cannot be trusted to do Quartermasters duty in this Department."—Copies (dated July 14), DLC-USG, V, 25; DNA, RG 393, Dept. of the Tenn., Endorsements. Written on a letter of July 14 from Lt. Col. Judson D. Bingham to USG. "I have the honor to report that I have been very much embarrassed in directing the business of the Quartermaster Department, in consequence of the inefficiency of several of the Assistant Quartermasters. I respectfully request that the following named Officers may be appointed to the rank of Captain and Assistant Quartermaster, and ordered to report to me as soon as possible. viz: 1st Lieut. C. H. Irvin, 9th Mich. Vols. now at Nashville, Tenn   Lieut. H. W. Janes, 55th Illinois Vols. Lieut. J. T. Conklin, 14th Wisconsin Vols. Lieut. W. C. Hurlbut, 56th Illinois Vols. I wish to relieve from duty the following named officers, who have given satisfactory evidences of their incapacity: Capt. H. S. Clubb A. Q. M. for continued neglect of public property under his charge, resulting in loss and damage of the same. Capt. R. T. Gill, A. Q. M. for abandoning the Ponton train under his charge, when it was ordered to the front, and applying for quarters in the City after the train had left. In reply to his application for quarters, I notified him that he was expected to accompany his train: he then tendered his resignation. Capt. B. J. F. Hanna, A. Q. M. has been occupied since first of June in organizing a supply train of Sixty teams for the 17th Army Corps. The teams, wagons & harness were ready for transfer when he applied for them: he has succeeded up to the present time, in organizing a train of thirteen teams only." —ALS, Goodspeed's Book Shop, Inc., Boston, Mass.

On July 10 and 13, Capt. Richard T. Gill had written to Bingham and to Lt. Col. J. Condit Smith tendering his resignation.—Copy and LS, DNA, RG 94, ACP, G479 CB 1863. On Aug. 1, USG endorsed a letter of July 29 from Gill to Bingham requesting a leave of absence for sixty days due to illness. "Respectfully forwarded to Hd Qrs of the Army Washington D C and the acceptance of this resignation recommended."—ES, *ibid.* On the same day, Col. Edward D. Townsend issued AGO Special Orders No. 343 dismissing Gill "for neglect of duty."—Copy, *ibid.* On May 27, 1864, Gill, Atlanta, Ill., wrote to President Abraham Lincoln resigning because of "poor Health not having a constitution to stand the Climate of the South."— ALS, *ibid.* On July 19, Lincoln endorsed this letter. "Let this resignation be accepted at once, setting aside the order mustering him out."—AES, *ibid.* Col. James A. Hardie accordingly had War Dept. records amended to show Gill resigning on the date of his dismissal.—AES, *ibid.*

1863, JULY 15. Brig. Gen. William K. Strong, St. Louis, to USG. "It is now almost a year since I passed a very pleasant night with you at your hospitable home then in Corinth. I have never ceased to watch with the most friendly interest your steady and onward progress ever since, and words can hardly express the great joy I experienced in common with all loyal citizens upon the announcement of your complete and glorious success at Vicksburg. your faithful, endurring valor and your brilliant successes every where since you entered upon the command of the army of the Tennessee have won for you an imperishable name upon the page of our countrys history and may you long live to enjoy the honors and blessings which have been secured by your valor & the faithfulness of the officers and troops under your command. we had a very pleasant little episode at the Planters last evening. I enclose you a newspaper report of it. On Saturday afternoon and evening 11th inst. we had a great jubilee commemorative of the fall of Vicksburgh & other triumphs of our arms. the display of flags and extent of illumination presented a grand appearance, and full honor was done to the Heroes who have led our armies to victory both in the west & in the east—If my friend C A Dana Esq is still with you please present him my kind regards."—ALS, USG 3. On July 14, at the Planters' House in St. Louis, a brass band led a crowd in congratulating Mrs. Grant on her husband's victories, and Strong spoke in acknowledgment.—*Missouri Democrat,* July 15, 1863. An undated letter in which Maj. Gen. Francis P. Blair, Jr., urged USG to assist in promoting Strong was sold at the American Art Association auction, Jan. 21–22, 1926. Strong, however, was not promoted and resigned as of Oct. 20, 1863.

1863, JULY 15. Governor Samuel J. Kirkwood of Iowa to USG. "Permit me to congratulate you upon your great triumph in the capture of Vicksburg. Your campaign resulting in that great success stands unrivalled in the history of this war for boldness of plan, thoroughness of execution and brilliancy of success. In the name of the people of Iowa whose brave boys aided in achieving this great result I tender you their hearty thanks."— ALS, USG 3.

1863, JULY 15. Charles A. Trowbridge, New York City, to USG. "I cannot forego the privilege that our old acquantance gives me, to drop you a line, for the purpose of thanking you for the Great victory you have achieved over Rebeldom, in the capture of their 'Sabastapol' of the South-west, as well as congratulate you that by your perseverance and courage you have written your name on the highest border of the scroll of fame. Your old Michigan friends—who regard you to a certain extent as one of them, are proud of you! and I particularly am more than delighted; for shortly after your gallant conduct at Fort Donoldson I had on more than one occasion to defend you from the vile attacks of some of your jelous compeers, who had failed to make their '*marks*,' as 'captains' of a high order of merit and ability. Let me also congratulate you that the Govern-mnt has duly appreciated your services, in making you a Major General of the Regular army! May your life be spared to wipe out the last vestage of the Rebellion in the South-west, & may you also live to enjoy to a ripe old age, your laurels so justly earned, on so many a hard fought field—God bless you—"—ALS, USG 3. On Nov. 27, Trowbridge wrote to USG a similar letter of congratulation after the battles at Chattanooga.—ALS, *ibid.* Born in 1817, and raised near Elmira, N. Y., Trowbridge moved to Mich. as a young man, living at first with his uncle, Charles C. Trowbridge, a prominent Detroit businessman. The younger Trowbridge opened a wholesale grocery and, in 1845, was capt. of the Brady Guards, a local military co. USG probably knew him while stationed in Detroit, 1849–51, and in 1864 reportedly asked a Detroiter, "Have you seen Charley Trowbridge lately?" Silas Farmer, *History of Detroit and Wayne County and Early Michigan* (Detroit, 1890), p. 106. See *ibid.*, p. 317. Becoming interested in various mining and railroad ventures, Trowbridge moved to New York City. Michigan Pioneer and Historical Society, *Historical Collections . . . 1889*, XIV (Lansing, 1890), 162.

1863, JULY 20. Col. William Hoffman, commissary gen. of prisoners, to USG. "I have the honor to enclose herewith a list of rebel prisoners of war, captured by the forces under Maj Genl. Sherman and paroled by his order at Jackson Miss   Rolls of paroled prisoners of war cannot be used in making exchanges, unless there is on them the receipt of the authorized agent or officers who receives them and as there is nothing on these rolls to show that the rebel authorities had any knowledge of the transaction, they are of no value   Genl order No 49, of Feby 28, and the subsequent order No 100, prescribe the mode of paroling, which does not seem to have been followed in this case   Par. 2 of Genl. order 207, applies particularly to cases of this kind"—Copy, DNA, RG 249, Letters Sent. *O.R.*, II, vi, 133.

1863, JULY 21. Act. Rear Admiral David D. Porter to USG. "It has been reported to me that a man by the name of Jamison, who was pilot on board the rebel steamer 'Charm' up Big Black and who set fire to her, is now on board the 'Des Arc' he received permission from Gen'l Pemberton to get out of our lines from Vicksburg and did so. came in with the army and is now a pilot on the above named vessel. Also, one Clarke, an Engineer on board the 'Charm' while in the rebel employ is on board 'Des Arc' and I thought these men are traitors and may meditate some treachery."—ALS, DNA, RG 45, Correspondence of David D. Porter, Mississippi Squadron, General Letters (Press).

1863, JULY 21. Col. George H. Crosman, Philadelphia, to USG. "Permit an old friend to join with the multitude in heart-felt congratulations for your great victories which have added such lustre to your name and filled the country with joy and gratitude to Him who has granted such glorious achievements to our arms. God bless you! . . . P. S.—I should have long since sought a share of the work in the field, but for for the wound received in my left leg, when the old Steamer Drayton exploded her boiler, as you may remember, in Corpus Christi Bay, in the summer of 1845, which occasionally cripples me for active service."—ALS, USG 3. George H. Crosman, USMA 1823, was a q. m. in the Mexican War and fought in the battle of Palo Alto, May 8, 1846. He was appointed asst. q. m. gen. on Feb. 26, 1863, in charge of the q. m. dept. in Philadelphia.

1863, JULY 22. USG endorsement. "Respectfully refered to Maj. Gen. Hurlbut. Now that the papers of Memphis have been allowed to recommence their issue I have no objection to any number of being started. The authority and controll in this matter will be left entirely with the Comd.r of the 16th Army Corps."—AES, DNA, RG 109, Union Provost Marshals' File of Papers Relating to Two or More Civilians. Written on a letter of July 13 from Thomas Leonard *et al.* to USG. "We, the undersigned, being *unconditional* union men, and feeling the urgent necessity for an organ to disseminate such principles in Memphis and vicinity; also suffering from the usual effects of a monopoly, do most respectfully pray you for permission to allow Mr. *Thomas Moffet* to establish a daily Union News-paper for the purposes above mentioned. Hoping that the importance of having a *truly* loyal journal in circulation will induce you to grant our request—" —ALS, *ibid.*

1863, JULY 22. Lt. Francis Tunica, "Big Black," to USG. "Just returned from Jackson Should like personal interview with you Have the battle ground of Champion Hills complete including Edwards Station Bolton & Raymond & vicinity of this place with my entrenchments & must have opportunity to plot the work. Shall I come on to Vicksburg. If so please send your ~~or~~ address"—Telegram received, DNA, RG 393, Dept. of the Tenn., Telegrams Received. An answer is written on the telegram.

"Come to Vicksburg. Enquire at Depot for Hd Qrs"—AN, *ibid.* See *O.R.*, I, xxiv, part 1, 186–89.

1863, JULY 23. USG endorsement. "Any action the Com'r of the 17th Army Corps may take in this matter will be sustained."—Anderson Galleries Sale No. 2146, March 16, 1927, No. 31. Written on a letter of Brig. Gen. Jeremiah C. Sullivan to Maj. Gen. James B. McPherson complaining of mistreatment by Col. Robinson while in Vicksburg. On July 12, Lt. Col. Loren Kent wrote to Lt. Col. John A. Rawlins. "I respectfully submit the following statement as [a]n act of Official duty. Yesterday Brig-Genl J. C. Sullivan, and Major Watts C. S. A drank whiskey together [a]t the Court House to such an extent that they became [v]ery much intoxicated, so much so that each in turn [m]ade speeches from the windows to Soldiers gathered about. General Sullivan had previously informed me that Major [G]eneral McPherson would not be there that day and he would officiate in his place. I also heard him at about [t]hat time tell Citizens that they must be ready to leave [t]own next week as an Order to that effect would be issued   I cannot discern that a General Officer has more right [un]der existing Orders, or the revised regulations to be [in]toxicated than a subordinate Officer or private Soldier   I also consider such an example more than usually pernicious when every effort is being made to entirely stop the [s]ale of Liquor by those whose business it is to enforce orders prohibiting such traffic,   while I am unwilling to make common mention of such matters I feel called upon to do so when the reputation of the Army is involved. It may be proper to add that I have no personal feelin[g] against General Sullivan, but that the same motive that first induced me to Volunteer as a Soldier actuates me now in reporting the delinquincies of Officers of any rank. I make this statement officially and am prepared to su[s]tain what I have here stated"—LS, DNA, RG 393, Dept. of the Tenn., Provost Marshal, Letters Sent. On Aug. 1, Maj. Theodore S. Bowers issued Special Orders No. 208 granting Sullivan a twenty-day leave.—Copies, DLC-USG, V, 27, 28; DNA, RG 393, Dept. of the Tenn., Special Orders. On Aug. 28, Maj. Robert Williams, AGO, acknowledged receipt of a disability report for Sullivan.—DS, *ibid.*, Letters Received. On Sept. 23, Bowers issued Special Orders No. 261. "Brig. General Jer. C Sullivan U S. Vols, on his own application and for honorable reasons is hereby relieved from duty in this Department and will proceed, taking with him his personal Staff, to Baltimore Md and from there report by letter to the Adjutant General of the Army, Washington D. C. for orders"—Copies, DLC-USG, V, 16, 28.

1863, JULY 23. Rear Admiral David D. Porter to USG. "As there no longer exists any necessity for the further use of the troops you were kind enough to lend me, and most of them wishing to be returned to their regiments, I propose to return them. Will you please inform me where I am to deliver them."—LS, DNA, RG 393, Dept. of the Tenn., Letters Received. *O.R.* (Navy), I, xxv, 320.

1863, JULY 23.   Governor David Tod of Ohio to USG. "I have been slow in sending you my congratulations; but rest assured, no man in America feels more grateful to you, for your splendid achievements, than I do—The kind relations that ~~have~~ existed between our parents, were alone sufficient to make me feel a lively interest in every thing concerning you—Aside from this, however, the faithful manner in which you have discharged the responsible duties committed to your hands has won for you my profound respect and regard—I have taken the liberty of sending to your address, by express, six boxes of Legislative documents, which I beg you to have distributed to the Ohio Regiments under your command—"—LS, USG 3.

1863, JULY 24.   USG endorsement. "Col. Olivar is a gallant young soldier and good Colonel and I would heartily recommend his appointment at the foot of the list of 2d Lieuts. of one of the regiments in the Regular Army, with permission to retain his Colonelcy to the end of the rebellion, or to a Captaincy should any such vacancy exist subject to being filled outside of regular promotion, with the same liberty of retaining his present position."—AES, DNA, RG 94, ACP, 580 CB 1863. Written on a letter of July 18 from Col. William S. Oliver, 7th Mo., to Brig. Gen. Lorenzo Thomas requesting an appointment in the regular army.—ALS, *ibid.* Although recommended by Brig. Gen. John D. Stevenson, Maj. Gen. John A. Logan, and USG, Oliver was not appointed.

1863, JULY 24.   Rear Admiral David D. Porter to USG. "I am going to commence, tomorrow to raise the Cincinnati. My negroes have most all run away to join the army. Will you do me the favor to order a detail of (50) fifty negroes until I can get the ship afloat which will be about three days work."—AL, DNA, RG 45, Correspondence of David D. Porter, Mississippi Squadron, General Letters (Press). On July 25, Maj. Theodore S. Bowers issued Special Orders No. 201 ordering Col. Herman Lieb, 9th La. A. D., to supply fifty men to the navy for fatigue duty.—Copies, *ibid.*, RG 393, Dept. of the Tenn., Special Orders; DLC-USG, V, 27, 28.

1863, JULY 24.   Col. Albert J. Myer, chief signal officer, to USG, stating that Capt. Ocran H. Howard would report as a member of the board of examiners of the act. Signal Corps in USG's dept.—LS, DNA, RG 111, Chief Signal Officer, Letters Sent.

1863, JULY 27.   USG endorsement. "1st Lieut. William Sinclair is now Acting Inspector General of the 13d Army Corps. I would respectfully recommend his appointment to fill the vacancy now existing."—AES, DNA, RG 94, ACP, O65 CB 1863. Written on a letter of July 26 from Maj. Gen. Edward O. C. Ord to Col. Delos B. Sackett, inspector gen., requesting the appointment of 1st Lt. William Sinclair, USMA 1857, as asst. inspector gen., 13th Army Corps.—ALS, *ibid.* On Sept. 24, 2:45 P.M., Brig. Gen. George W. Cullum, War Dept., telegraphed to USG. "Lieut Sinclair, detached for duty at the Military Academy, is much wanted there—Send him as soon as possible."—ALS (telegram sent), *ibid.*, RG 107, Telegrams Collected (Bound); copy, *ibid.*, RG 94, Letters Received. However, Sinclair served as act. asst. inspector gen., 13th Army Corps, until appointed lt. col. and asst. inspector gen. on Ord's staff on Oct. 12.

1863, JULY 27.   Maj. Robert Williams, AGO, to USG. "I am directed to instruct you to discharge Charles D. Snow, Co. "K." 20th Mich. Vols. from the Military service of the United States, when the substitute furnished by him is accepted and placed on duty in the Regiment to which this Soldier belongs."—Copies, DNA, RG 94, Enlisted Branch, Letters Sent; *ibid.*, RG 393, Military Div. of the Miss., War Dept. Correspondence.

1863, JULY 28.   Maj. Theodore S. Bowers to Maj. Gen. James B. Mc-Pherson. "As this army will probably be inactive for a short time and the General Commanding knowing that it is almost absolutely necessary that many Volunteer Officers be permitted to visit their homes for a short time, he has determined to grant leaves of absence to meritorious Officers, under section 31 of the act of Congress approved March 3d. 1863. One Field Officer for each Regiment and one company officer to each company must remain with their commands. No leaves of absence however will be granted under this act, unless the approval of the Corps Commander is endorsed on the application."—LS, DNA, RG 94, War Records Office, Dept. of the Tenn. *O.R.*, I, xxiv, part 3, 557. Bowers addressed identical letters to Maj. Gens. Edward O. C. Ord and William T. Sherman. On Aug. 1, Sherman wrote to Bowers. "Yours of July 28th is received. I have anticipated the instructions of the General in Chief, and have endorsed no Leaves of absence to Officers unless assured that at least a Field officer & enough for Staff remained to each Regimt, and in case of soldiers Furloughs to 5 per cent of those actually present for duty. The quicker we get over this infliction the better, and I feel satisfied it will in the end enure to the good of the Service."—ALS, DNA, RG 393, Dept. of the Tenn., Letters Received.

1863, JULY 29.   Col. John C. Kelton to USG. "If possible please furnish for the use of these Hd Qr's two files of General Orders issued from Head Qrs Dept. Tennessee during 1862."—LS, DNA, RG 108, Letters Sent (Press).

1863, JULY 29.   Resolution of Thomas J. Durant, president, and James Graham, secretary, Friends of Universal Suffrage, New Orleans, praising recent U.S. military successes and favoring emancipation in La. by state convention, as in Mo.—ADS, USG 3.

1863, JULY 30.   USG endorsement. "Respectfully forwarded. Not approved."—Copies, DLC-USG, V, 25; DNA, RG 393, Dept. of the Tenn., Endorsements. Written on a letter of 1st Lt. John A. Savage, Jr., adjt.,

28th Wis., enclosing a petition for the promotion of Brig. Gen. Frederick W. Salomon.—*Ibid.* Salomon, a brother of Governor Edward Salomon of Wis. and of Col. Charles E. Salomon, 9th Wis., formerly county engineer, St. Louis, was not promoted during the war.

1863, JULY 31.   To Brig. Gen. Elias S. Dennis. "Send Mrs. Clarke's carriage horses and effects immediately to these Head Quarters, driver also, with protection that they are traveling on orders from the Gen. Commanding."—ALS, DNA, RG 393, Dept. of the Tenn., Telegrams Received.

1863, [JULY ?].   To Maj. Gen. Edward O. C. Ord. "Send all prisoners to Provost Marshal General at these Hd Qrs"—Telegram received, DNA, RG 393, Dept. of the Tenn., Telegrams Received.

1863, [JULY–OCT. ?].   USG letter recommending Dr. George B. Bailey, Georgetown, Ohio, for appointment as provost marshal.—*The Collector*, XLIX, 12 (Oct., 1935), No. 32180. See *PUSG*, 1, 3.

1863, AUG. 2.   Maj. Gen. John M. Schofield, St. Louis, to USG requesting that his brother, Capt. George W. Schofield, 1st Mo. Art., be transferred to his staff.—Copies, DLC-John M. Schofield; DNA, RG 393, Dept. of Mo., Letters Sent. On Aug. 19, not having received a reply, Schofield wrote to USG repeating this request.—Copy, *ibid.* USG ordered this transfer, "subject to the approval of the General-in-Chief," by Special Orders No. 218, Aug. 11.—Copies, DLC-USG, V, 27, 28; DNA, RG 393, Dept. of the Tenn., Special Orders.

1863, AUG. 2.   2nd Lt. Albert Sabin, 1st Inf., Vicksburg, to USG requesting a twenty-day leave of absence due to illness.—ALS, DNA, RG 391, 1st Inf., Letters Received. The request was granted by Special Orders No. 210, Aug. 3.—Copies, DLC-USG, V, 27, 28; DNA, RG 393, Dept. of the Tenn., Special Orders.

1863, AUG. 5.   To Maj. Gen. John G. Parke. "The papers in case of Dr. Wolfolke have been refered to me, and your action approved. Lieut Bryan must give up the mules identified. When your orders are complied with, he had better be released from Arrest, unless charges are preferred, as it will be difficult to replace him in charge of Contrabands, and like many others, may have acted under a mistaken notion of whose orders are to be obeyed." —Telegram, copies, DLC-USG, V, 19, 101, 103; DNA, RG 393, Dept. of the Tenn., Letters Sent. Earlier on the same day, Parke, Milldale, Miss., wrote to USG. "Believing Dr Woolfolk to be a loyal citizen from his protection papers', a copy of which I am enclosed I gave him this morning, an order to ~~sach~~ search and sieze his mules stolen from him two nights since (This order I enclose)   I sent an orderly and one sergeant of cavalry with him   They have just returned without the mules and with my order en-

dorsed as you will see   I have sent over one of my staff to place Lt Bryan
in arrest. I shall charge him with receiving Known stolen property and
harboring the thieves   The mules were probably stolen by Dr Woolfolks
negros who have fled to Mrs Blake plantation to seek protection in the contraband camp there—at least as Dr Woolfolk so represents the case"—Copy,
ibid., 9th Army Corps, Letters Sent.

1863, Aug. 5.   Act. Vol. Lt. Joseph P. Couthouy, Vicksburg, to USG requesting forty or fifty contrabands to assist his crew, diminished one-third
by illness, in coaling the *Osage*, ordered by Rear Admiral David D. Porter
to the mouth of Red River.—ALS, DNA, RG 393, Dept. of the Tenn., Letters Received.

1863, Aug. 6.   USG endorsement. "Respectfully forwarded to the Adj. of
the Army."—AES, DNA, RG 94, Letters Received, 288T 1863. Written
on a letter of Aug. 5 from Maj. Gen. William T. Sherman, "Camp on Black
River," to Brig. Gen. John A. Rawlins. "With this letter I send to my Chief
Quarter Master Lt Col J Condit Smith a Box marked for the Adjutant
General U. S. Army Washington D. C. and in one corner 'The Davis papers.' This Box came into my possession through Brig Genl Hugh Ewing
who obtained it at a house near Jackson Mississipi called 'Hurricane' a
residence formerly used by Joe Davis, brother to the Hon Jefferson Davis
President of the Southern Confederacy. It is represented to me that the box
was found by some soldiers ~~who~~ in the garret of the Building, which garret
could only be reached through a trap door of the ceiling, and therefore it
was supposed to be hidden. I am satisfied many papers have been abstracted,
and that it is idle to search for them, but it still contains very many letters
addressed to the Hon Jeff Davis runig through the past ten years some of
which I have examined. Indeed I did commence to assort arrange and endorse them for more convenient Examination, but soon found the task
beyond the limits of my time and patience, and therefore I send them to you
marked for shipment to the Adjutant General of the Army, so that the Commanding General ~~of the Army~~ may make such use of them as he may deem
justifiable under the circumstances."—ALS, *ibid.*

1863, Aug. 7.   USG endorsement. "Col. E. W. Rice has been serving directly under Gen. G. M. Dodge. I know no officer whos judgement I would
more readily endorse than that of Gen. Dodge, I therefore heartily recommend, the within recommendation."—AES, DNA, RG 94, R254 CB 1863.
Written on a letter of July 29 from Brig. Gen. Grenville M. Dodge, Corinth,
Miss., to USG urging the appointment as brig. gen. of Col. Elliott W. Rice,
7th Iowa.—ALS, *ibid.* On Sept. 28, USG endorsed a letter of Sept. 15
from Rice to Secretary of War Edwin M. Stanton regarding his promotion.
"Respectfully forwarded to Head Qrs. of the Army, Washington D. C. and
again recommended"—ES, *ibid.* Rice's letter attributes to USG a separate
letter of recommendation and to President Abraham Lincoln two notes di-

recting his promotion.—ALS, *ibid.* On Jan. 9, 1864, Lincoln endorsed a copy of Dodge's letter. "Col. E. W. Rice above named, was ordered to be appointmented, and, by mistake, a brother, also in the service & worthy, was appointed—It is now urged by the friends of the former, that he should have the preference, over Col. Caldwell, on a contest between them."—AES, *ibid.* Lincoln referred to Brig. Gen. Samuel A. Rice. See also Lincoln, *Works,* VII, 379. Elliott W. Rice was confirmed as brig. gen. on June 20, 1864.

1863, AUG. 7.   Col. William Hoffman, commissary gen. of prisoners, to USG, and to six other gens. commanding depts. "I have the honor to inform you that the following instructions have been given by the Secretary of War in relation to the discharge of Prisoners of War. Prisoners of War who have been impressed into the rebel service, and who wish to take the Oath of Allegiance and join our Army, may be permitted to do so, when the examining Officer is satisfied of the applicants good faith, and that the facts of his Case, are as he represents them. . . ."—LS, DNA, RG 94, War Records Office, Dept. of the Tenn. *O.R.,* II, vi, 186. On Aug. 30, Hoffman wrote to USG and to nine other gens. commanding depts. "I am instructed by the Secretary of war to say that hereafter deserters from the rebel army will be disposed of primarily, at the discretion of the commander of the Department in which they may be found . . ."—Copies, DNA, RG 249, Letters Sent; (dated Aug. 29) *ibid.,* RG 393, Military Div. of the Miss., War Dept. Correspondence. *O.R.,* II, vi, 242. On Dec. 12, Lt. Col. Theodore S. Bowers issued General Orders No. 10. "To obtain uniformity in the disposition of deserters from the Confederate Armies, coming within this Military Division, the following order is published: All deserters from the enemy, coming within our lines, will be conducted to the Commander of the Division or detached Brigade, who shall be nearest the place of surrender. If such Commander is satisfied that the deserters desire to quit the Confederate service, he may, he may permit them to go to their homes, if within our lines, on taking the following oath; . . . Employment at fair wages will, when practicable, be given to deserters by Officers of the Quartermasters and Engineer Departments. To avoid the danger of recapture of such deserters by the enemy, they will be exempt from military [*service*] in the armies of the United States."—Copies, DLC-USG, V, 14; DNA, RG 393, Military Div. of the Miss., General Orders; (printed) USGA. *O.R.,* I, xxxi, part 3, 396.

1863, AUG. 7.   Governor Richard Yates of Ill. to USG. "I desire to recommend to your favorable consideration Mr. Henry A Clubb who desires a position as clerk in the Qur. Master's Department at Vicksburgh. Mr Clubb has been highly recommended to me as a worthy & reliable gentleman and well qualified to fill such a position with credit."—Copy, Yates Papers, I-ar.

1863, AUG. 8. USG endorsement. "Respectfully refered to Maj. Gen. Hurlbut. Comd.g 16th Army Corps, who will please examin[e] into the merits of S. Mansfield & Co. case and report to these Hd Qrs, whether the company should be restored in whole, in part or not atall to what they ask." —AES, DNA, RG 109, Union Provost Marshals' File of Papers Relating to Two or More Civilians. Written on a letter of the same day from Samuel Mansfield & Co. to USG.—ALS, *ibid.* Maj. Gen. William T. Sherman, who had ordered the co.'s goods seized on Sept. 30, 1862, had initially endorsed the letter. "The store & contents of S Mansfield & Co were confiscated by my order in Memphis about one year ago, for their beig engaged in selling to men drugs for smugglig beyond our Lines. The case was designed to be severe and exemplary to check a pernicious system hurtful to the Cause and interests of the United States. I am willing to admit that the change which time and circumstances have brought in Memphis warrant a remission in part or whole. 1st that Mr Mansfield be permitted to resume possession of his store & business which was purposely left to the management of one of his favorite clerks. 2nd that he be permitted to ~~apply~~ use the proceeds in Cash now in the hands of the Quarter Master arising from sales of Drugs &c to be applied to the paymt of debts justly chargeable to the stock of goods then on hand & in store. 3rd That he make up a Bill of the Medicines delivered on the orders of the Medical Directors & Purveyors of the Army and submit it for adjustmt to the Surgeon General of the Army, and to a Board to be assembled in Memphis to hear and determine the merits of the Case."—AES, *ibid.* Earlier in 1863, before carrying his case to Washington, Mansfield acquired several testimonials to his Unionism and business integrity.—Copies, *ibid.*; *ibid.*, Union Provost Marshals' File of Papers Relating to Individual Civilians. On May 2, William Whiting, War Dept. solicitor, wrote to Mansfield. "In regard to your claim that a quantity of Drugs, Medicines &c. seized by Genl Sherman, should be surrendered, I have to say that the Secretary of War declines to interfere in the matter, & refers you to the Commander of the Department of the Mississippi."— ALS, *ibid.*, Union Provost Marshals' File of Papers Relating to Two or More Civilians.

On July 14, Dr. A. J. Park, Memphis, wrote to USG enclosing a petition in Park's hand from Mansfield and David Jennings to USG which noted their arrest on Sept. 27, 1862, imprisonment at Alton, Ill., and release; explained their business transactions after the U.S. occupation of Memphis on June 6; and pleaded for relief.—ALS, *ibid.* On Aug. 19, 1863, Park wrote to Lt. Col. Loren Kent, provost marshal, alleging that Mansfield & Co. had circumvented an agreement to pay Park $5,000 for negotiating the return of their $60,000 inventory, and asking Kent to delay return of the property: "if you will control it, so it shall *come through me,* I will give you $3000. of the fee."—Copy, *ibid.*, Union Provost Marshals' File of Papers Relating to Individual Civilians. On Aug. 23, Kent wrote to Lt. Col. John A. Rawlins enclosing a copy of Park's letter and requesting that he be punished for attempted bribery.—LS, *ibid.* On Sept. 1, Rawlins endorsed this letter to Maj. Gen. Stephen A. Hurlbut ordering Park arrested and sent under guard to USG's hd. qrs.—ES, *ibid.* On Sept. 23, Kent ordered Park confined until he forfeited $3,000.—Copy, *ibid.*, RG 393, Dept. of the Tenn., Provost Marshal, Letters Sent.

On Sept. 12, Rawlins endorsed to Hurlbut a letter of Mansfield and Jennings again seeking to recover their goods. "The manner in which these parties have persisted in trying to evade the just penalty inflicted on them for violation of law and the means employed by their agent in proposing to bribe an Officer in the discharge of his duty only tends to establish the justness of General Shermans acts"—Copies, DLC-USG, V, 25; DNA, RG 393, Dept. of the Tenn., Endorsements. On Oct. 24, Mansfield & Co. wrote to USG disavowing responsibility for Park's actions and pleading at length for relief: "although we violated the Laws of Trade we did not do it for the purpose of Aiding the rebellion   we *never* had any thing to do with Smugling in any manner . . ."—ALS, *ibid.*, RG 109, Union Provost Marshals' File of Papers Relating to Individual Civilians. At about the same time, ten Memphis citizens petitioned USG to have Mansfield and Jennings "reinstated in business."—ADS, *ibid.* On Oct. 27, Brig. Gen. Joseph D. Webster, Memphis, wrote to USG stating his "opinion that Dr. Mansfield did not authorize or expect Dr. Park to offer any bribe in order to further his object of getting possession of his property. . . ."—ALS, *ibid.* On the same day, Mansfield and Jennings signed a statement describing and disclaiming responsibility for Park's misrepresentations.—ALS, *ibid.* On Nov. 11, Capt. George K. Leet referred these papers to Sherman, who endorsed them on Dec. 19: "Let Mansfield be restored to the actual possession of his Store, but no other relief is granted"—AES, *ibid.*

1863, AUG. 8. USG endorsement. "Any steamer going to New Orleans is authorized to land at Grand Gulf for the purpose of taking on board Mr. Green and family."—AES, DNA, RG 109, Union Provost Marshals' File of Papers Relating to Individual Civilians. Written on a pass of July 26, of Maj. Gen. James B. McPherson. "Permission is hereby given to A. A. Green wife, six children & servant to go to New Orleans La, to remain if consistent, with the orders & instructions of the commanding officer of the Dist.—Mr. Green is a citizen of New Orleans, & is at present residing in Port Gibson Miss"—ADS, *ibid.*

1863, AUG. 8. To Peter J. Sullivan, formerly col., 48th Ohio. "Permit me to add my testamonials to those you have already received from your more immediate commanders, first at the battle of Shiloh where you received an honorable wound, then at Memphis where you were for months retained as president of the Board of Claims and Commandant of the Fort, which positions were filled with credit to yourself and the service. For the part you have since taken, with your regiment, in the Campaign terminating with the Capture of Vicksburg you have my thanks. In your retirement to Civil life my well wishes for your success and prosperity accompanies you."

—ALS, Goodspeed's Book Shop, Inc., Boston, Mass. USG made a copy of
this letter on Nov. 8, 1865.—ALS, PPRF. See *O.R.*, I, xxiv, part 2, 236–
40. Sullivan had resigned as of Aug. 7, 1863, to practice law, and on Oct.
7, Maj. Gen. William T. Sherman, Memphis, wrote a letter of recommendation.—Copy, DLC-John Sherman. On Oct. 14, USG, Memphis, wrote:
"Col. P. J. Sullivan, late of the 48th Ohio Vols. is hereby authorized to remain within this Department and to practice his profession or engage in any
business consistent with existing orders. This is to recommend Col. Sullivan to the Dist. & Post commanders for such facilities as are allowed to
loyal men."—ALS, Tyson Collection, Eleutherian Mills Historical Library,
Greenville, Del. On Nov. 20, 1866, Sullivan, Cincinnati, wrote to Bvt. Maj.
Gen. John A. Rawlins. "I respectfully ask to be promoted to the rank and
pay of Brigadeer General of U. S. Volunteers for meritorious conduct, on
both days, at the battle of Shiloh: to date from April the 6th 1862. . . ."
Sullivan detailed his services and enclosed a copy of USG's letter of Aug. 8,
1863.—ALS, DNA, RG 94, ACP, S1312 CB 1866. On Nov. 23, 1866,
USG endorsed Sullivan's letter. "Respectfully forwarded to the Secretary
of War. Col. Sullivan was a gallant officer, and I recommend that he be
brevetted Brigadier General of Volunteers"—ES, *ibid.* Sullivan was appointed bvt. brig. gen. as of March 13, 1865.

1863, AUG. 9. USG endorsement. "Reffered to Major General McPherson. All the hides taken from beef furnishd to the Army, are property of
the Subsistence Department and cannot be given to parties as compensation
for collecting and removing them."—Copies, DLC-USG, V, 25; DNA, RG
393, Dept. of the Tenn., Endorsements. Written on a letter of Aug. 8, of
Lt. Col. John C. Cox, chief commissary, 17th Army Corps, Vicksburg,
stating that citizens, with Brig. Gen. John E. Smith's permission, were collecting and shipping hides of slaughtered animals belonging to the government.—*Ibid.*; DLC-USG, V, 22. On July 27, T. E. Clifford had informed
USG that these citizens were gathering such hides for sale without paying
the government and offering to pay one dollar each.—*Ibid.*, V, 99. On July
28, Lt. Col. Loren Kent had endorsed this letter. "Respectfully forwarded:
Mr. Cadwallader of Chicago Times has the permission referred to, from
General Smith   Mr. Clifford is I think, a reliable man"—Copy, *ibid.*

On Sept. 26, Brig. Gen. John A. Rawlins endorsed a letter of Sept. 25
of Lt. Col. James H. Wilson, asst. inspector gen., reporting that Kahn and
Rice, beef contractors, Cincinnati, had furnished cattle unfit for use. "Respectfully referred to Col. Cox, Chief. Commissary, for his information
and action"—Copies, *ibid.*, V, 25; DNA, RG 393, Dept. of the Tenn., Endorsements. On Oct. 4, Cox referred to USG a letter of the preceding day
of Sgt. H. R. James reporting that these cattle were almost all "in good
condition for beef."—AES and ALS, *ibid.*, Letters Received.

1863, AUG. 9. To Private Alfred E. Mathews, 31st Ohio. "I have examined the Lithographs of views taken by you of the 'Siege of Vicksburg,'

and do not hesitate to pronounce them among the most accurate and true to life I have ever seen. They reflect great credit upon you as a delineator of landscape views."—*Steubenville Herald*, Jan. 20, 1865. On the same day, Maj. Gen. James B. McPherson wrote a similar letter to Mathews.—ALS, MOLLUS Mass. Collection, PCarlA. Mathews circulated these and other testimonials at his "Grand Topographical Panorama of the War," an exhibition in Steubenville, Ohio, on Jan. 18–21, 1865.—*Steubenville Herald*, Jan. 19, 20, 21, 1865. See Elizabeth R. Martin, "The Civil War Lithographs of Alfred Edward Mathews," *Ohio History*, 72, 3 (July, 1963), 241. See also illustrations, *PUSG*, 5, between pp. 18–19; *ibid.*, 8, 417–20.

1863, AUG. 10. USG endorsement. "Respectfully forwarded"—Copies, DNA, RG 94, ACP, F250 CB 1863. Written on a letter of Aug. 10 from Maj. Gen. James B. McPherson *et al.* to President Abraham Lincoln recommending John C. Ford for an appointment as q. m. or commissary because of bravery and wounds received in battle.—Copy, *ibid.* Lincoln endorsed the letter favorably on both Sept. 9 and 24.—Lincoln, *Works (Supplement)*, p. 202. Ford was appointed capt., Veteran Reserve Corps, to date from Dec. 14. On Dec. 13, 1867, Ford wrote to USG. "In connection with my application for an appointment,—which goes herewith—endorsed by Generals A. J. Smith, Hoffman Morgan, Easton and various others—I take the liberty of recalling to your recollection the fact: that,—at the surrender of Colonel Murphy at Holly Springs (when and where every thing was burned except one train) the Engine 'Washington' and twenty eight cars were safely brought out by *myself*—without any assistance whatever—from Holly springs to Oxford:—as you may remember—taking Gen: McCarthy and Brigade from below Oxford to Holly Springs; afterward taking Gen. Grant and family to Holly Springs (on which expedition we had to carry *rails* for fire, while you and I threw *sand* on the track!) by which proceeding vast amounts of property were saved for our government. However, thinking 'tis unnecessary to occupy your time in this way, I proceed to make known my business on the other side of this paper. My friends—both Civil and Military—have suggested that,—if a collectorship cannot now be had, the position of Military Storekeeper (*or even Suttler*) at some one of the various military posts of the U. S. west of the Missouri River would be suited to my crippled condition: and that should I be so fortunate as to receive the apptmt of storekeeper—or Suttler either Forts *Dodge* or *Wallace* in Kansas: or—Reynolds or Lyon in Colorado would prove most satisfactory! General: nothing but my *necessities* prompt me to write and trouble you in this way; but, being totally unable to perform the ordinary duties of Civil Life I have asked this much in order that I may obtain support for myself and family. Asking your favorable notice of my application and the accompanying recommendations of various officers at Fort Leavenworth . . ." —ALS, DNA, RG 108, Letters Received. USG endorsed this letter. "Refer this to Gen. Sherman or Augur to see if trade appointment at one of the posts named can be given."—AE, *ibid.*

1863, AUG. 10.   To Brig. Gen. Lorenzo Thomas. "I have the honor here-with to return papers in the case of Augustus C. Graff 11th Ohio Battery referred to me from your office, under date of July 7th inst., for report, and in reply to respectfully invite your attention to the endorsement hereon of Major W. R. Rowley A. A. D. C., and mustering officer. Upon referring to the records of my office, I find the original papers in this case which are herewith transmitted and afford all the information I possess on the sub-ject."—Copies, DLC-USG, V, 6, 8, 24, 94; DNA, RG 393, Dept. of the Tenn., Hd. Qrs. Correspondence.

1863, AUG. 10.   USG endorsement. "Respectfully returned disapproved. Knowing of no power that members of Congress are competent to exercise in Military matters, save and excepting the nominations of Cadets for West Point, it is simply impossible that I recommended this officer to apply to a member of Congress to secure a leave of absence. An officer who so far de-parts from Military usage as to seek to further his end through politicians does not deserve to succeed."—Copies, DLC-USG, V, 25; DNA, RG 393, Dept. of the Tenn., Endorsements. Written on a letter of U.S. Representa-tive Owen Lovejoy of Ill. forwarding a letter of Lt. Col. John H. Howe, 124th Ill., requesting a sixty-day leave of absence.—*Ibid.*

1863, AUG. 11.   USG endorsement. "If the accounts of Lieut. John F. Neville are satisfactory I would urgently recommend the appointment herin asked. Lt. Neville has had a great amount of experience in the Subsistence Dept. and is a man of great energy and purseverance."—AES, DNA, RG 94, ACP, 79N CB 1863. Written on a letter of Aug. 6 from 1st Lt. John F. Neville, 7th Mo., act. q. m., 3rd Brigade, 3rd Div., 17th Army Corps, Vicksburg, to Brig. Gen. Lorenzo Thomas requesting, in light of his ser-vice "as Commissary and Quartermaster" since June 1, 1861, an appoint-ment as q. m. or commissary in the U.S. Army.—ALS, *ibid.* No appoint-ment was made.

1863, AUG. 11.   To Lt. Col. Judson D. Bingham, dept. q. m., Vicksburg. "I have just seen the instructions to Capt. Reno, A. Q. M. and find nothing in them contemplating his assuming any functions of his office at this place, or anything els improper. It would seem from his instructions that Gen. Burnside had called on the Quartermaster at St. Louis for transportation for 7500 men and four batteries. That Capt. Reno was sent down the river to bring certain boats that had been loaded for Helena, and points above, to this place, or as many of them as might be necessary to supply this transportation. In justice to Capt. Reno, and the officer who sent him, I will revoke the order requiring that he should exercise no functions here." —ALS, deCoppet Collection, NjP.

1863, AUG. 11.   USG protection paper. "A safeguard is hereby granted to the house, family and plantation property of Mrs. M. S. Jones situated on the Raymond and Bolton road, four miles west of Raymond. All Officers and Soldiers belonging to the army of the United States are therefore commanded to respect this safeguard and to afford, if necessary, protection to the persons and property aforementioned"—DS, DNA, RG 217, Southern Claims Commission, Miss., Hinds County, No. 2786. In 1877, Mrs. Mary S. Jones, as administratrix of her husband's estate, was allowed $3,306.25 on a claim of $17,245.50 by the Southern Claims Commission.—*HMD*, 45-2-4, p. 58.

1863, AUG. 11. Maj. Theodore S. Bowers to Maj. Gen. Stephen A. Hurlbut. "Please send the Companies of the Engineer Regiment of the West, now serving in your command to this place, as soon as transportation can be provided for them."—Copies, DLC-USG, V, 19, 101, 103; DNA, RG 393, Dept. of the Tenn., Letters Sent. *O.R.*, I, xxx, part 3, 3.

1863, AUG. 13. Maj. Gen. John Pope, Milwaukee, to USG. "In answer to application for recall of Surgeon George Hutchinson 27th regt Wis Vols from detached duty forwarded by you July 22d and received this A. M. I have the honor to transmit copy S. O. No 107 of these Head Quarters,"—Copy, DNA, RG 393, Dept. of the Northwest, Letters Sent.

1863, AUG. 14. Governor Oliver P. Morton of Ind. to USG. "I have appointed Miss C. Annette Buckel a lady of education and respectability to visit and look after the condition and wants of Indiana's Sick and wounded Soldiers in your Department. Having graduated at a Medical School, she is admirably adapted to the labor and arrangement of Hospitals, and giving attention to the distressed. I respectfully ask for her every facility in your power for the furtherance of her mission in your Army."—LS, Buckel Papers, California Historical Society, San Francisco, Calif. On Aug. 23, Lt. Col. John A. Rawlins issued Special Orders No. 230 permitting Dr. Buckel to travel throughout the Dept. of the Tenn.—DS (2), *ibid.*

1863, AUG. 16. Mrs. E. R. Allen, Ingleside Plantation, La., to USG. "It is painful to me to disturb you again with my affairs, but the ergency compels me; The paper which you gave me, dated Feb 26th,/63, would have prote[c]ted me in every case, with white men of principle, or honour, but a Cap, Greely at the head of a band of negroes come here in the beginning of June, pleased with my house, seemed to regret that I had you[r] protection, acted very rudely, asked me if I had any musical instruments; Three days after, he returned, 4 men had stopped, and saying that they were hungry, went into my citchen, and cooked themselves something to eat. I never had seen them before, learned subsequently that they were citizens, and that they were taking some negroes back, and that they cook also for them, I had lost more than half my mules, when my negroes left; the men asked me if I would sell them some, as I still had 10 and a mare, and colt left, and only an old negro man of at least 70 years; I refused to sell, but

said that I would like to exchange some for sugar, as I must have something
for my children to live on. they said that they would do it for me, with
pleasure, seeing my desolate helpless situation, leaving me enough for all
the purposes of my small force for grinding meal, hauling wood; Just as
they were leaving, the call to halt, sounded from behind some fodder stacks;
but the men proceded on thei[r] way, about 50 shots were fired, from Greelys
company which it proved to be,   A white man then come up to the house,
and into my presence, in a state of nature, without a particle of covering,
took my parour rug, and threw it round himself, and left,   I heard
Greely insist on his coming up again to get something else, but he would
not come; Greely then come up, accosted me in the rudest manner, and
exultingly said that my protection would do me no good that he intended to
report me; I told him that I would report him, for his rudeness, explained
every thing to him, but nothing but my ruin, seemed to fill his hearts desire,   He gathered ropes, and even ordered me to get them, and secured
every mule I had, and took them, shot my mare, in the stable, went out and
took his pocket knife, and cut my carriage gears to pieces, as my old man
told me he saw him do it,   He then come in; and told me that he was hungry, and that he supposed that I could get him something to eat, as well as
the rebels whom I had fed; I told him again, that they had cooked for themselves, that I did not even know what they had, but that had I done so, I
would have only obeyed the teaching of my Heavenly Father, (If thine
enemy hunger, feed him, if he thirst, give him drink; but that I had not
been required to do so, in this case,   he then said abruply *I dont care any
thing about your God*, Im hungry.   so I went and prepared him the best
I had, with my own hands,   When I brought it before him, he express
suspicions that I had drugged the coffee and desired me to drink some
which I did, but still he was not satisfied, but asked my old man, whose
testimony satisfied him,   he then wished me to carry the bread to to the
landing to the negroes, which I did, but they seemed ashamed and would
not have it. What does this mean?   that we are to get that protection from
the negro, that we ought or have aright to expect from our own race?   in
amazement, I express no opinion, but merely give a simple statement of
facts; he told me that I would have to move, that if I come to the River,
he would be the best friend I had, with a great deal of unwarranted freedom of speech,   I told him that this was my home, and that I would remain
here.   by his instructions, 3 day after, a man by name, OFlaherty, at the
head of a company of negroes, come here,   he did not seem to have any
control over them, as they scattered all over the place, seek such things
as they fancied, while some took possession of the house with as little ceri-
mony as if it had been a kennel,   poultry, of all description, was appropri-
ated to themselves,   they broke into my storeroom, where to be sure there
was not much,   the front of my house was locked up, but they brok in, and
went into my closets   a big negro a perfect stranger to me, (for none of
my own would have served me so, nor have has one of them come back or
tried to damage me in the least) was on a chairs in a high shelf, pulling

out my dead husbands clothes, and my little sons clothes who is dead,   the whole house was in such a state of confusion, as I do not believe I could have made in a days time,   they took all they fancied, of my childrens, and my clothes leaving us destitute of any thing for the winter,   all my husbands best clothes are gone, and my little sons which were sacred treasures to me; and some of the Ambrotypes of my children, and they robbed the beds of bed clothes, and ripped up ticks, and pillows and took the clothe and cases, and drove off every hoof of my stock, even two cows, which I had up trying to milk, they drove from their little calves; which I have contrived by care to keep alive, untill last week, when I was in Vicksburg wishing to see you, before you went to N. O. but was disappointed,   while I was absent, Cap Greely was here, and I suppose took, or had taken, my two calves, the last of at least 300 head of the finest stock in the country, which my husban[d] had gathered, and reared and taken care of by his own exertions, and sickness in my family, has detained me untill now, from seeking an interview with you, and redress of my grievances,   My little boy would cry for milk, while my negroes would send me word from the Bend, that they were *doing finely, milking cows,* and *selling butter*; Greely during my abscence, suffered his negroes to rob one of my bed rooms, of bed clothes again, and he himself took my Parish map, which I had told him was *sacred*, as it was the property of my husband; two of the mules from which he had taken from me, in June last, came back, and we needed them badly, but he took them again, in spite of the intreaties of my son, about 14 years of age, and my old man who told him that it would be impossible for us to haul wood for the winter, grind meal, ~~and~~ or any thing else,   he said that I would have to have my protection renewed, before he would respect it,   he threatened to report me,   this is a true though brief representation of facts so far as they go, though paper cannot be equal to the aggravation of the circumstances attending; Though much reduced, I am cheerful, and confident, that the God of the widow and fatherless will hear thier cry,   For he who sitteth on the throne,   Hath ever claimed their cause his own,   The softest cry from infant lips,   Is heard by him who Isreal keeps,   Any assistance which you render me, will be remembered with gratitude unbounded as life, . . . P. S. Please excuse this wretched scrawl as I had a pen that made me nervous, it was so bad"—ALS, DNA, RG 393, Dept. of the Tenn., Letters Received. Referred by Lt. Col. John A. Rawlins to Brig. Gen. John P. Hawkins, the letter was returned with letters of explanation from Capt. John O. Flaherty and Capt. Dennis P. Greeley, 10th La.

1863, AUG. 18.   Maj. Samuel Breck, AGO, to USG. "I have the honor to acknowledge the receipt of the Communication of Capt. O. W. Pollock Co. F. 63d Reg't O. V. I. referred by you to this Office, relative to Priv. Geo. T. Cole, of that command, & to inform you that the Provost Marshal has been directed to arrest him as a Deserter, as he has been discharged on forged papers."—Copies, DNA, RG 94, Enlisted Branch, Letters Sent; *ibid.*, RG 393, Military Div. of the Miss., War Dept. Correspondence.

1863, AUG. 19.   USG endorsement. "Respectfully forwarded to Head
Quarters of the Army Washington D. C. and recommend that this officer
be discharged."—Copies, DLC-USG, V, 25; DNA, RG 393, Dept. of the
Tenn., Endorsements. Written on a letter of Maj. Carlos J. Stolbrand,
chief of art., 3rd Div., 17th Army Corps, stating that 2nd Lt. Nott Smith,
Battery G, 2nd Ill. Light Art., act. q. m., Springfield, Ill., had not complied
with a War Dept. order to rejoin his co.—*Ibid.* Smith was discharged on
Sept. 22.

1863, AUG. 21.   Col. Edward D. Townsend, AGO, to USG and to five
other maj. gens. "The following is substance of General Orders number
two hundred eighty six. No prisoner of war, after having been reported
to the Commissary General Prisoners, will be discharged except on order
from Commissioner for Exchange of Prisoners. All applications and recommendations for discharge will be forwarded to Commissary General of
Prisoners. The mere desire to be discharged on taking oath of Allegiance is
not sufficient ground for discharge without other cause."—Copy, DNA, RG
94, Letters Sent. See *O.R.,* II, vi, 212.
    On Sept. 14, USG endorsed a letter of Col. Greenville M. Mitchell,
54th Ill., reporting that men in his regt. who were captured and paroled by
C.S.A. Brig. Gen. Nathan B. Forrest in west Tenn. in Dec., 1862, had not
yet been exchanged. "Respectfully forwarded to Head Quarters of the
Army Washington D. C. for the action of the General-in-Chief. There are
quite a number of men in parole Camps at St. Louis, captured in West.
Tennessee by Forrest in his raid last December on the Mobile and Ohio
R. R. not yet exchanged. The paroles of these men were not given in ac-
cordance with the terms of the cartel."—Copies, DLC-USG, V, 25; DNA,
RG 393, Dept. of the Tenn., Endorsements.

1863, AUG. 24.   USG endorsement. "Respectfully forwarded to Head
Quarters of the Army Washington D. C. approved"—Copies, DLC-USG,
V, 25; DNA, RG 393, Dept. of the Tenn., Endorsements. Written on a
letter of 1st Lt. George W. Williford, Co. F, 9th Ill., regarding Private
Marellis Ballow of his command.—*Ibid.* On Oct. 9, Maj. Samuel Breck,
AGO, wrote to USG. "I have the honor to acknowledge the receipt of the
papers in the case of Private, M. I. Ballowe, Co. "F," 9th Illinois Cavalry,
forwarded by you to this Office, requesting that he may be discharged
from the Military service of the U. S. to enable him to accept the appointment of Pilot in the U. S. Navy. I am directed to inform you that no action
for his discharge can be taken by this Department, as it appears that no
request has been made to the Navy Department for his appointment, by the
proper officer (Rear Admiral Porter.). His papers are returned herewith."
—Copy, *ibid.,* RG 94, Enlisted Branch, Letters Sent.

1863, AUG. 24.   Maj. Samuel Breck, AGO, to USG. "I have the honor
to inform you that many communications from your Department, request-

ing the discharge of enlisted men, and for other purposes, with the endorsement—'Respectfully forwarded to the Head Quarters of the Army,' have been received at this Office. The General-in-Chief directs me to instruct you, that on all these communications, the approval or disapproval of the Department Commander, should be made to appear, before any action can be taken thereon. . . . P. S. Please find enclosed three comns ret'd for approval or disapproval"—Copy, DNA, RG 94, Enlisted Branch, Letters Sent.

1863, AUG. 25. USG endorsement. "Respectfully returned to Head Quarters of the Army Washington D. C. and for report attention invited to enclosures"—Copies, DLC-USG, V, 25; DNA, RG 393, Dept. of the Tenn., Endorsements. Written on a letter of Col. Powell Clayton, 5th Kan. Cav., concerning Co. K.—*Ibid.* On Sept. 17, Maj. Samuel Breck, AGO, wrote to USG. "I am directed to acknowledge the receipt of applications and reports, refered to by you to this Office relative to the complaint of members of the 5th Kansas Cavalry that they were enlisted for 3-months and fraudulently mustered into the service for 3 years and therefore request to be discharged In reply, I have the honor to inform you that from the reports accompaning the complaint, & also from the records of this Office, it appears that these men have been properly mustered into the service of the U. S. for the period of three years, and will be held to serve out the time for which they were mustered in   The Major General, Commdg, will please have this decision communicated to the men and also instructed that no further communications, upon the subject, will recei[ve] consideration at this Office unless new facts are presented."—Copies, *ibid.*, Military Div. of the Miss., War Dept. Correspondence; *ibid.*, RG 94, Enlisted Branch, Letters Sent.

1863, AUG. 25, 4:35 P.M. Secretary of War Edwin M. Stanton to USG and to others. "Richmond dispatches just received state that Fort Sumpter is in ruins and General Gilmore had given notice that he would shell Charleston yesterday."—ALS (telegram sent), DNA, RG 107, Telegrams Collected (Bound); telegram received, *ibid.*, RG 393, Dept. of the Tenn., Telegrams Received. *O.R.*, I, xxviii, part 2, 63; *ibid.*, I, xxx, part 3, 159.

1863, AUG. 26. USG endorsement. "Col. J. W. Fuller, 27th Ohio has commanded one of the largest Brigades in this Dept. for more than one year. He has distinguished himself both upon the battle field, and, for the discipline of his command, in the Camp. Col. Fuller has before been recommended for promotion and I think was once nominated by the President for the position of Brig. Gen. I would no very respectfully renew the recommendation for Col. Fuller's promotion and that it be for 'gallant and merritorious services' at the 'battle of Corinth' on the 3d & 4th of October, 1862."
—AES, DNA, RG 94, ACP, F255 CB 1864. Written on a letter of Aug. 22 from Col. Wager Swayne, Memphis, to Maj. Gen. Stephen A. Hurlbut reviewing the military career of Col. John W. Fuller, 27th Ohio, which

Hurlbut endorsed on Aug. 25 with a recommendation for promotion.—ALS and AES, *ibid*. Fuller was appointed brig. gen. as of Jan. 5, 1864.

1863, AUG. 26. Capt. Andrew Gallfy, 58th Ohio, to Lt. Col. John A. Rawlins. "This Regiment having been relieved from the Gunboats except Companies H & J and ordered on Provost Guard duty at Vicksburg Miss, I would most respectfully ask whether it would be possible to have those men belonging to this Regiment, and at present on detached service with the 1st Mo Battery 15 Army Corps, relieved and ordered to join their Regiment."—ALS, DNA, RG 393, Dept. of the Tenn., Letters Received. USG endorsed this letter, his signature being affixed by someone else. "Details for filling batteries must come from the Divisions, or at least the Army Corps, to which the batteries belong. If therefore this regiment does not belong to the 15th A. C. the men spoken of will be ordered to their regiments."—AE, *ibid*.

1863, AUG. 26. William Hall, Canton, Mo., to USG. "In my letter of the 15th Inst. I gave you no references, as to my own antecedents. You will then allow me to say, that I have ever been a faithful Sentinel on the Watch Towers of my Country, Ever cherishing her Institutions as the most inestimable gift of our Fathers, a Testament sealed with their Blood and the great anxiety in relation to my Son, is the apology for intruding this letter upon your notice. Then I would say that I have long had the honor of knowing Major Gen. Jon A Dix who was for some years a resident of my native County, Major Gen John E. Wool, who for two years were near near neighbors at Troy N. Y. he may remember somewhat of me. Major Gens. Todd, & Hallack, Hon D. S Dickinson of Binghamton N. Y. His Excellency Horatio Seymour. Now my great desire is that you save my Son the severity of a Military Court Martial, and me from disgrace. Mr. Wilson, is inclined to the belief that he was not sincere, but said what he did say in his letter rather to amuse himself than to do an act of injustice to the Goverment, this is my opinion, for, in no instance to my knowledge during his life has he betrayed a trust or done a dishonorable action. You had evidence of his integrity while in your employ   save him. . . . I have written my Son many letters to prevent him being caught in a Man Trap. These I suppose and hope he has preserved and that you will see them."—ALS, DNA, RG 109, Union Provost Marshals' File of Papers Relating to Individual Civilians. On Sept. 9, W. H. Hall, Memphis, wrote to USG explaining at length that he had been arrested for writing four disloyal letters to a citizen of Memphis while employed as a telegraph operator at Cairo in early 1863, but that his political views had since changed.—ALS, *ibid*.

1863, AUG. 29. USG endorsement. "I would respectfully ask the appointment of Rowland Cox, Pvt. L. Co. 14th Pa. Cav.y as Asst. Adj. Gen. with the rank of Capt. and that he be assigned to duty with me. To the present time I have never had the assistance of but one Asst. Adj. Gen. whilst the office requires the constant services of two."—AES, DNA, RG 94, ACP, 493C CB 1863. Written on a letter of Lt. Col. John C. Cox, commissary, 17th Army Corps, to Secretary of War Edwin M. Stanton asking an appointment as adjt. and capt. for his son, Private Rowland Cox, Co. L, 14th Pa. Cav.—LS, *ibid.* On Sept. 7, John C. Cox wrote to Brig. Gen. John A. Rawlins that his son was a private, Co. A, 15th Pa. Cav.—ALS, *ibid.,* 506C CB 1863. On Sept. 8, USG's name was signed to an endorsement. "Respectfully forwarded to Head Qrs. of the Army, Washington D. C. The recommendation in this case was forwarded Aug. 29th 1863."—ES (forgery), *ibid.* Cox was appointed as of Sept. 19.

1863, AUG. 29. To Col. William Hoffman, commissary gen. of prisoners, urging the release of a young Confederate soldier whose grandfather was a staunch Union supporter.—*The Month at Goodspeed's Book Shop,* II, 7 (March, 1931), 207. On Sept. 26, in a similar letter, USG wrote to the commanding officer, Indianapolis, asking for the discharge of a Confederate soldier "whose father has been a staunch & unflinching Union man from first to last . . . and his son went into the service solely for the purpose of saving his family . . ."—William D. Morley Catalogue, Nov. 17, 1941, No. 176; Lincoln, *Works,* VI, 514. On Oct. 15, President Abraham Lincoln favorably endorsed the letter.—*Ibid.* Possibly related to this matter is a letter of Nov. 13 from Capt. Wilson T. Hartz to Col. Conrad Baker, act. asst. provost marshal, Indianapolis. "I am directed by the Comy. Genl. of Prisoners, to request that he may be furnished with a copy of Genl. Grants, order for the release of Thomas W. Weller, a prisoner of war now confined at Camp Morton Ind."—Copy, DNA, RG 249, Letters Sent.

On Oct. 7, Lt. Col. Loren Kent wrote to Lt. Col. Theodore S. Bowers. "Mr John. E. Brick Co "G" 1st Miss Light Artillery was taken Prisoner at Black River about June 16th 1863   He is now confined at Indianapolis, Ind. Mrs Brick is very anxious for his Liberat[ion] upon taking the Oath of Allegiance. He has written her a letter showing that he is duly penitent and anxious to show his loyalty by returning to his home within our lines and leading the life of a peaceable citizen. I would respectfully request that this be forwarded to the Commissary General of Prisoners at Washington, and that he be released upon taking the Oath of Allegiance."—Copy, *ibid.,* RG 393, Dept. of the Tenn., Provost Marshal, Letters Sent. On the same day, USG endorsed the letter. "Respectfully forwarded to Col Wm Hoffman Commissary General of Prisoners Washington D C"—Copies, DLC-USG, V, 25; DNA, RG 393, Dept. of the Tenn., Endorsements.

1863, AUG. 30. To Lewis Ashmead, Philadelphia. "Your request of the 4th inst. for my 'Autograph' is just received. Feeling that the honor done me in making this request is due more to the brave soldiers, and harmonious officers, whom I have the honor to command, than to any merit of my own, I reman"—ALS, DLC-Breckinridge Long.

1863, AUG. 31. Maj. Gen. John M. Schofield, St. Louis, to USG. "I have been requested by the family of Lieut Mitchell 1st Mo Artty. who was killed by the late disaster on the Steamer City of Madison, at Vicksburg, to enquire what disposition has been made of his effects"—Copy, DNA, RG 393, Dept. of Mo., Letters Sent. On Sept. 10, Brig. Gen. John A. Rawlins endorsed this letter. "Respectfully referred to the General Comdg Post for investigation and report"—Copies, DLC-USG, V, 25; DNA, RG 393, Dept. of the Tenn., Endorsements.

[*1863*, AUG.]. Lt. Col. John A. Rawlins endorsement. "If I mistake not this order was made while we were investing Vicksburg & is of record. Whether it reached its destination I cannot say. Those recruited for General service, as well as those for Artillery were directed to be assigned to the Battery of Regular Artillery in 16th Corps   Those recruited for the Cavalry were assigned to the 3d U. S. Cavalry. Such is my recollection."—ES, DNA, RG 393, Military Div. of the Miss., Letters Received. Written on a memorandum of Maj. Robert Williams. "I have the honor respectfully to submit to the General in Chief the following statement,—By Special Orders 121—paragraph 16 Adjutant General's Office of March 14th 1863, Maj. Genl. U. S. Grant was directed to transfer to the Regular Companies in his Department, certain enlisted men belonging to the 3rd U. S. Cavalry, 4th U. S. Artillery, and General Service, who were then serving in Battery "M" 1st Missouri Light Artillery. That order not having been complied with, it is respectfully recommended that Genl. Grant be ordered to have it carried into effect as soon as practicable."—LS, *ibid.* On Aug. 7, Maj. Gen. Henry W. Halleck endorsed this memorandum. "Respectfully referred to Major Genl Grant to be carried into effect by him."—AES, *ibid.* On Nov. 12, USG wrote to Col. John C. Kelton. "In reply to the memorandum from the Adjutant Generals Office (referred to me by the General in Chief) complaining of my noncompliance with paragraph 16 of Special Orders No 121, A. G. O., directing the transfer of certain enlisted men of the General Service, I have respectfully to state that the order was executed as Soon as the exigencies of the service would permit. Herewith I respectfully submit an official copy of my Special Order on the subject, which I trust will prove satisfactory."—LS, *ibid.*, RG 94, Letters Received. USG enclosed Special Orders No. 178, section XII, July 2, 1863.—Copies, DLC-USG, V, 27, 28; DNA, RG 94, Letters Received; *ibid.*, RG 393, Dept. of the Tenn., Special Orders. On Nov. 13, USG wrote a similar letter to Kelton regarding alleged "non-compliance with paragraph 69 of Special Orders No 121 A. G. O."—Copies, DLC-USG, V, 40, 94; DNA, RG 393, Military Div. of the Miss., Hd. Qrs. Correspondence.

1863, SEPT. 3. To Col. Henry W. Birge, 13th Conn. "Will you do me the favor to enquire if a gentleman by the name of Fulford now Resides in your town   if not if his Family is there"—Copy, DNA, RG 109, Union

Provost Marshals' File of Papers Relating to Individual Civilians. USG apparently sought J. D. Fulford, Thibodeaux, La.

1863, SEPT. 3. Maj. Gen. Henry W. Halleck to USG concerning overdue returns from his dept.—LS, DNA, RG 108, Letters Sent. This letter follows a series of letters from the AGO to USG about missing and incomplete returns, and precedes acknowledgment of the receipt of these returns.—Copies, *ibid.*, RG 94, Enlisted Branch, Letters Sent.

1863, SEPT. 3. Maj. Gen. Lovell H. Rousseau, Louisville, to USG. "Max Dinklespiel, of this place, will hand you this. Please excuse my troubling you with it, but I cannot well refuse his request to say a word of and for him, to the Authorities of our Government. He wishes to engage in some sort of buisness in Vicksburg. He read law in my office, and though but a boy when the rebellio[n] began, he rendered invaluable service to the country. His youth enabled him to obtain facts, and to learn the conduct and designs of the secessionists, which as a man he could not have ascertained: and during several months of the most critical period of our troubles, he kept me fully posted as to men and things here. He has always been true, vigilant and faithful. Because of his services and sterling loyalty, I ask for him such permission to trade, as the authorites in their discretion, grant to other loyal citizens. He is in every way reliable. I congratulate you on your brilliant achievements and the high and honorable estimate in which the country holds you. I am just from the Eastern States where your services are fully appreciated. May God speed you in your glorious work."—LS, DNA, RG 366, First Special Agency, Supply Store Applications.

1863, SEPT. 4. Iowa AG Nathaniel B. Baker to USG. "It has been reported that you recommended Capt Frederick S. Washburn Co. G. 9th Iowa Infantry for the position of Brig. Genl. He died soon after his return to this state, and it now becomes a matter of some importance to his widow what your recommendations or intentions were in the case. We can obtain no information from the War Department and therefore have to trouble you with these inquiries"—ALS, DNA, RG 94, ACP, B95 CB 1863.

1863, SEPT. 10. Maj. Gen. Stephen A. Hurlbut to Brig. Gen. John A. Rawlins. "This communication is respectfully forwarded to Maj. Genl. Grant. Some time since at the request of the Naval Officer, A. Q. M. Eddy by order of Maj Genl Grant assigned to their use for Hospital purposes the Commercial Hotel. It was selected by Surgeon Pinckney U. S. N. and these Stores below were expressly stated not to be required. Since that time application has been made for the Stores but disallowed by me & that disallowance approved by Maj Genl Grant. Rear Admiral Porter in my judgment has no right to give such an order as is pretended & if he wants the buildings must negotiate with these men who are loyal. I shall not permit this order to be Executed until I hear from you"—ALS, DNA, RG 109, Union Provost Marshals' File of Papers Relating to Two or More Civilians. Written on a letter of the same day from five Memphis businessmen to Hurlbut protesting verbal orders from Rear Admiral David D. Porter to vacate their stores in the Commercial Hotel.—LS, *ibid.* On Sept. 21, Rawlins endorsed this letter. "Respectfully returned and action of Maj. Genl. Hurlbut approved"—ES, *ibid.* On Sept. 18, Porter, Cairo, wrote to USG. "The number of sick in the Hospital at Memphis requiring us to have a little more room, I request that you will do me the favor to turn over to me such of the ground floor rooms as we may require. The owner of the property is a Mr. Andrews who has been bothering the Department about 'his rights as an American Citizen,' so I took the trouble to institute some enquiries about him. I received a letter from General Hurlburt yesterday in which he informs me that he has proof that Andrews took the oath of allegiance to the Rebel Government, and on that ground he had seized the building and I suppose it will be confiscated to the Government. While there was a doubt about Andrew's principles I did not think it worth while to do any thing more in the matter, but now that he is placed in the ranks of the rebel sympathyzers, I request that you will give such orders as will enable me to extend the hospital arrangements."—LS, *ibid.*, RG 393, 16th Army Corps, Letters Received. On Sept. 26, USG endorsed this letter. "Respectfully refered to Gen. Hurlbut or Comd.g officer Memphis Ten. who will grant the within request if not inconsistent with contracts already made with private parties. If the stores refered to have been rented out by Govt. the contract should be held good unless the exigencies of the service should imperatively require it to be broken. Should it not be practicable to give the rooms asked by Admiral Porter then give him, or the Naval Medical Officer at Memphis, buildings suitable to their wants."—AES, *ibid.*

1863, SEPT. 11. R. J. Howard, surveyor of customs, St. Louis, to USG. "The Revenue officer, on a late trip of the Steamer War Eagle, to Vicksburg, seized, for a violation of revenue laws, a quantity of watchmakers tools that were shipped without a permit and, of course without paying the 5 per cent tax riquired to be charged by regulations of Treas Dept on Shipments to states heretofore declared in rebellion. These goods were taken from the seizing officer & returned to the owner by order of Brig Gen Smith. The law requires the goods to be reported to U. S. Surveyor or Collector to be proceded against in the Courts for violation of law. I inclose order of Genl Smith returning goods."—ALS, DNA, RG 109, Union Provost Marshals' File of Papers Relating to Individual Civilians. On Sept. 3, Brig. Gen. John E. Smith had ordered: "Mr L T Sherp has permission to land from Str 'War Eagle' pkg containg Watchmakers tools & articles required for repairng Watches"—Copy, *ibid.* On Sept. 19, Brig. Gen. John A. Rawlins endorsed Howard's letter. "Respectfully referred to Brig. Genl. McArthur, commdg. Post, for investigation and report"—ES, *ibid.* On Sept. 26, Maj. Gen. John A. Logan endorsed the letter. "After the most searching hunt for the within named Sherp I am unable to find any thing of him or his whereabouts"—AES, *ibid.*

1863, SEPT. 12. To Brig. Gen. Lorenzo Thomas. "In pursuance of Army Regulations and General Orders No 98. A. G. O. series 1861, I have the honor to make application for the admission of Private John D Brown Company "F" 1st Regiment Missouri Lt Artillery who is insane, into the Government assylum at Washington D. C. established for the treatment of such cases. Accompanying this please find a copy of his 'descriptive list and account of pay and clothing' also the certificate of the Surgeon in charge of of the Hospital where he was sent for treatment and where his insanity appears first to have developed itself   The company or battery to which he belongs has been ordered to and is now in the Department of the Gulf, rendering it impracticable to procure in time to accompany this the certificate of the surgeon who attended it."—Copies, DLC-USG, V, 6, 8, 24, 94; DNA, RG 393, Dept. of the Tenn., Hd. Qrs. Correspondence. Someone else may have written and signed this letter, unless USG did so after returning from New Orleans to Vicksburg.

1863, SEPT. 12. Brig. Gen. William K. Strong, St. Louis, to USG. "I enclose you herein a letter received by me this morning from Mrs. M. E. Fitz, a most excellent loyal woman from Miss. She is living here upon the pittance which Government allows to loyal refugees because she has no other means of support. Brig General H. T. Reid, of your command, made the acquaintance of Mrs. Fitz when he was stationed in the neighborhood of her residence and can inform you of he[r] steadfast loyalty and excellent qualities as a lady and true patriot. I would most earnestly beg that you send up for this lady's corn at the locality she describes, and have it taken for Government use and the proper vouchers made for the same to her, and enclosed to me here and I will see that she gets them."—LS, DNA, RG 393, Dept. of Mo., St. Louis District, Letters Sent (Press). Strong enclosed a letter of the same day from Mrs. Martha E. Fitz of Issaquena County, Miss., regarding the disposition of about nine thousand bushels of corn.— LS, *ibid.* About June 20, Mrs. Fitz had reached St. Louis with a pass from USG, which was stolen from her attorney on Jan. 8, 1864.—DS, *ibid.*, RG 217, Southern Claims Commission, Miss., No. 10,510. In 1874, Mrs. Fitz was allowed $7,125 for the corn taken on Brig. Gen. Hugh T. Reid's orders.—DS, *ibid.*; *HMD*, 43-2-18, p. 16; Frank W. Klingberg, *The Southern Claims Commission* (Berkeley and Los Angeles, 1955), pp. 121–23.

1863, SEPT. 14. USG endorsement. "Respectfully forwarded to Head Quarters of the army Washington D. C. with the request, if deemed proper, Col. Scott be furnished with a copy of such part of the proceedings as interest him."—Copies, DLC-USG, V, 25; DNA, RG 393, Dept. of the Tenn., Endorsements. *O.R.*, I, xxii, part 1, 177. Written on a letter of Sept. 1 from Col. John Scott, 32nd Iowa, Columbus, Ky., to Brig. Gen. John A.

Rawlins. "A Military Commission, of which Brig. Gen. W. K. Strong was President, was convened in St Louis in February last by order of Maj. Gen. Halleck, to investigate as to the evacuation of New Madrid, and destruction of property there and at Island No. 10. Grave charges were preferred against me as Commanding Officer for the evacuation of New Madrid under alleged 'pretended orders,' and I was in arrest for two months. On the finding of that Commission I was ordered to duty by Gen Curtis, but the finding was not made public, nor has been to this time, to my knowledge. Feeling that my arrest was an outrage, and that the Commission fully justified my action, I deem myself entitled to a copy of the finding. I have applied for it heretofore in vain. I respectfully ask that the Maj. Genl. Commanding Department will secure me a copy of the *finding* of said Commission."—ALS, DNA, RG 94, Letters Received. *O.R.*, I, xxii, part 1, 177. The commission found that Scott had destroyed the guns under direct orders from Brig. Gen. Thomas A. Davies.—*Ibid.*, p. 176.

1863, SEPT. 14. USG endorsement. "Respectfully referred to Major General John Pope Comdg Dept of the North west with the request that this man be sent to his regiment"—Copies, DLC-USG, V, 25; DNA, RG 393, Dept. of the Tenn., Endorsements. Written on a letter of Sept. 5 of Capt. John Lynch, Co. E, 6th Ill. Cav., requesting the return of Private Thomas Mount of his co. from the U.S. hospital at Keokuk, Iowa.—*Ibid.* On Oct. 28, Maj. Samuel Breck, AGO, wrote to USG reporting that Mount was unfit for duty in the field.—Copies, *ibid.*, Military Div. of the Miss., War Dept. Correspondence; *ibid.*, RG 94, Enlisted Branch, Letters Sent.

1863, SEPT. 15. Col. Edward D. Townsend, AGO, to USG. "It has been reported to this Department that some of the Commissaries of Subsistence of the Department of the Tennessee are inefficient. The Secretary of War, in consequence, directs that each Corps Commissary be instructed to report to the Chief Commissary those who are inifficient, for examination by a Board of Officers to be detailed by the Department Commander. The report to be forwarded to this office, through the Commissary General of Subsistence, for the information and action of the War Department."—LS, DNA, RG 393, Dept. of the Tenn., Letters Received. On Oct. 1, Brig. Gen. John A. Rawlins forwarded copies of this letter to Maj. Gens. Stephen A. Hurlbut, James B. McPherson, and William T. Sherman, adding: "You will take immediate steps to have the above requirements carried out."— Copies, DLC-USG, V, 19, 103; DNA, RG 393, Dept. of the Tenn., Letters Sent.

1863, SEPT. 17. Maj. Robert Williams, AGO, to USG. "I am directed to request, that you will cause a list to be furnished to this Office, of those Officers of the 13th U. S. Infantry (not to exceed six in number) whom you consider, either on account of their services in the field, or from impaired health, to be best entitled to be relieved from active duty in the field, and detailed upon Regimental Recruiting Service."—LS, DNA, RG 94, Letters Received, 1269S 1863.

1863, SEPT. 17. Maj. Gen. George Stoneman, Cav. Bureau, to USG requesting information concerning horses needed in the Dept. of the Tenn.— LS, DNA, RG 393, Dept. of the Tenn., Letters Received. On Oct. 19, Maj. Gen. Stephen A. Hurlbut wrote to Brig. Gen. John A. Rawlins reporting his needs.—ALS, *ibid.*, 16th Army Corps, Letters Received. *O.R.*, I, xxx, part 4, 472. On Sept. 17, Stoneman wrote to USG concerning monthly cav. reports.—LS, DNA, RG 393, Dept. of the Tenn., Letters Received. On Oct. 8, USG wrote to Stoneman. "In compliance with Your favor of Sept. 21st, I have the honor to transmit herewith the requested list."—LS, *ibid.*, RG 94, War Records Office, Cav. Corps. Docketing indicates that USG enclosed names of gen. and staff officers of cav.

1863, SEPT. 18. USG endorsement. "Respectfully returned. Jackson was occupied after a severe battle on the 14th of May 1863 by Federal forces, and it may be true that they goods were taken by our Soldiers but the General Government certainly cannot be expected to investigate every case of loss under similar circumstances with the view to making payment where parties of their own volition remain in a beseiged city depending upon the strength of the garrison to defend them. Strict orders against pillaging have been enforced in this Army, this case does not come within such Orders"— Copies, DLC-USG, V, 25; DNA, RG 393, Dept. of the Tenn., Endorsements. Written on a petition of Isaac Bloom, owner of a wholesale grocery in Jackson, Miss., sacked as Maj. Gen. William T. Sherman's forces approached and occupied the town.—*Ibid.*; *SRC*, 45-2-180. In 1878, the U.S. Senate Committee on Claims upheld the decision of the Southern Claims Commission against compensating Bloom because he had not satisfactorily proven his loyalty or shown that the goods he had lost had been taken by military authority or for the benefit of Sherman's army.—*Ibid.*

1863, SEPT. 18. Governor Richard Yates of Ill. to USG. "I have had many letters from Commanding Officers of Ills. regts requesting transfer of their commands to Brigades commanded by Ills General Officers I have invariably declined to take an active part in such matters, but occasionally, would desire, if consistent with public good, to second efforts of some of our Colonels in making, an attempt at least, to change Brigade or Div. Commanders At this time I have good reason for asking that the 107th Ill may be placed in some Brigade where other Ills regts are assigned and would esteem it a favor if you will give the matter early notice."—LS, DNA, RG 393, 16th Army Corps, Letters Received. On Sept. 28, Brig. Gen. John A. Rawlins endorsed this letter. "Respectfully referred to Major Genl. Hurlbut for his action. The Brigading of troops by States, is not approved of, but there may be some special reason why this regiment should be transferred to another, than the Brigade it is in"—ES, *ibid.*

1863, Sept. 20. USG endorsement. "Respectfully forwarded to Head Qrs. of the Army, Washington, D. C., and urgently recommended. Capt. R. M. Sawyer is one of the most faithful Asst. Adjt. Generals' in this Department. In all that is said of him by General Sherman I can most cordially concur. He was the Asst. Adjt. Genl. on duty with Maj. Genl. C. S. Hamilton and would no doubt have received promotion on his recommendation had not that officer resigned the service"—ES, DNA, RG 94, ACP, 735S CB 1863. Written on a letter of Sept. 14 from Maj. Gen. William T. Sherman to Brig. Gen. Lorenzo Thomas urging the promotion to maj. of Capts. Roswell M. Sawyer and James C. McCoy of his staff.—ALS, *ibid.* The promotions were confirmed on Feb. 29 and March 8, 1864, to date from July 4, 1863, as Sherman had requested.

1863, Sept. 21. USG endorsement. "Respectfully forwarded to Head Quarters of the Army Washington D. C. and urgently recommended. Lieut. Miller entered the service as 1st Sergeant in Sept. 1861 and was soon after promoted to a 2d Lieutenancy. He was in the movement against Fort Henry and in the battle of Fort Donelson, behaved most gallantly. In the first days fight at Shiloh he was very seriously and dangerously wounded and for meritorious conduct in that battle he was promoted to a 1st Lieutenancy. Since his recovery from his wounds he has served with his regiment and on staff duty and has borne a conspicuous part throughout the entire Vicksburg Campaign, winning the expressed approval of his immediate commanding officers. He has good sound sense and a liberal education—A better or more deserving appointment could not be made"—ES, DNA, RG 94, ACP, M549 CB 1863. Written on a letter of Sept. 11 from Brig. Gen. Jasper A. Maltby to Brig. Gen. Lorenzo Thomas requesting that 1st Lt. J. Warren Miller, 45th Ill., be appointed capt. and assigned as adjt. to Maltby.—LS, *ibid.* Miller received the appointment.

1863, Sept. 21. Maj. Samuel Breck, AGO, to USG. "I am instructed by the President to direct you to discharge Private John C. Hughes, Co "B," 114th Illinois Volunteers, from the Military service of the U. S. upon receipt of this communication."—Copies, DNA, RG 94, Enlisted Branch, Letters Sent; *ibid.*, RG 393, Military Div. of the Miss., War Dept. Correspondence.

1863, Sept. 21. H. J. Hall, chief of scouts, 4th Div., 15th Army Corps, Goodrich's Landing, La., to USG. "Allow me the honor to report the capture of six additional confederate prisoners also Seven (7) horses and one mule in addition to prisoners and stock heretofore reported. four of the prisoners above named were captured west of bayou Mason and are a portion of a company of (25) twenty five engaged in keeping open a line of communication between the east and west. I have evry reason to believe that I will be able to break the up within the next ten days as I have captured nine out of thirty five"—ALS, DNA, RG 94, War Records Office, Dept. of the Cumberland. *O.R.*, I, xxx, part 3, 757. On Sept. 28, Hall, "Camp Sherman Black River," wrote to USG. "allow me to hand you the Report of my late *scout* contained in exibett ('A' and 'B') annexed   I ocupied (15) fifteen days, had six men, passed over something like four hundred miles of the Enemyes teritery, captured (13) thirteen Prisoners of War (11) Eleven stand of arms (20) twenty Horses   have deranged if not destroyed the line of his communication running *Monroe* in *Horses* to *Jacksons* feint as indicated on map marked Exibet (A) annexed   the information was obtained (on) the ninth of the numbers and position and and reported by Despach to Brig Gen Corse Comdg 4th Division 15th Army Corps on the morning of the tenth of September   for vouchers for Prisoners captured se Exibet (B) annexed (which is a copy)   I find Rifle pits on the McCown Brig. comanding the ferryes and about (300) three hundred men this side of *Beff River*   they hold the ground bettwene that Rivver and *Bayou Macon*   there is however a strong Union feeling wherever I have been   this I ascertain beyond a doubt assuming frequently the guise of the Texean Cavalery   the destruction of a large Six board Boat in *Collins Bayou* used by Couriers will inpeade their crossing the Yazoo for some time to come the whole of my labors in this Departm sinse my arrival at Sniders Bluff with *Gen Smith* may be sumed up (48) forty eight Prisoners (53) fifty three Horses a large number of mules sadles Bridles missellaneous arms & also much valuable information . . . P S my party numbers ten men   the duty has been performed by from (6) six to (8) eight men.   if (these men) armed with *Spensers Repeating* Rifle and otherwise properly equiped I should have no hesitancy in, if under your imediate orders attempting any enterprise the exicution of which you might desire"—ALS, DNA, RG 94, War Records Office, Dept. of the Cumberland. The map and vouchers are *ibid.*

1863, SEPT. 23.   USG endorsement. "Respectfully referred to the commandant of the Military Prison, Alton, Illinois who will please release the prisoner whose name is subscribed to the within on parole to report in person to these Head Quarters"—Copies, DLC-USG, V, 25; DNA, RG 393, Dept. of the Tenn., Endorsements. Written on a letter of Henry W. Sauls asking to be released or paroled.—*Ibid.*

1863, SEPT. 23.   B. D. Whitney, Vicksburg, to USG, expecting charges against him to be "dismissed" and requesting "liberty to visit New Orleans for the purpose of procuring such letters from parties high in authority as will remove all doubt of my loyalty . . ."—ALS, DNA, RG 393, Dept. of the Tenn., Letters Received. Whitney had been jailed and tried by USG's orders.—Lt. Col. Loren Kent to Maj. Theodore S. Bowers, Aug. 1, copy, *ibid.*, Provost Marshal, Letters Sent; Special Orders No. 216, Aug. 9, copies, *ibid.*, Special Orders; DLC-USG, V, 27, 28. On Aug. 10, Maj. Gen. William T. Sherman had forwarded to Kent an intercepted letter of Whitney stating his intention to remain in Vicksburg to "furnish Johnson all that is requisite" —*Ibid.*, V, 99.

1863, SEPT. 24. USG endorsement. "Respectfully forwarded to Brig. Genl. L. Thomas, Adjutant General, for the necessary action to cover this case"—Copies, DLC-USG, V, 25; DNA, RG 393, Dept. of the Tenn., Endorsements. Written on a letter of Sept. 16 from Brig. Gen. John P. Hawkins, Goodrich's Landing, La., to Brig. Gen. John A. Rawlins. "There is a class of people in this District, known as government Lessees of Plantations, who, with very few honorable exceptions, have acted in a very unprincipled manner to the negroelabourors they have employed. Every day I have complaints of their treatment. There are no Commissioners present to correct the evils, and I have no time to act as a justice of the Peace to rectify matters. I understand that Mr Montague has been appointed a Commissioner, and if so, he is hardly the man to do justice in affairs as he is largely interested himself, and more disorganization exists on his plantation than any other. How he can decide a matter between Montague Planter, & Montague Commissioner, is hard to see. As matters now stand, the Lessee is a petty tyrant, and does as he pleases in his conduct towards These people. I hope the matter will be brought to the attention of Gen. Thomas as soon as he returns from New Orleans."—Copy, *ibid.*, District of Northeastern La., Letters Sent.

1863, SEPT. 24. Maj. Thomas M. Vincent, AGO, to USG. "I am directed to enclose herewith a copy of a letter to the Governor of Ohio, embracing a plan adopted by the War Department, with the view of securing recruits for the regiments in the field, from that State, and to instruct you to furnish the recruiting parties therein referred to when the Governor may call for them. His Excellency is confident that by the plan he will be able to secure many recruits."—LS, DNA, RG 94, War Records Office, Dept. of the Tenn.; copy, *ibid.*, RG 393, Military Div. of the Miss., War Dept. Correspondence. Vincent enclosed a letter of Sept. 23 of Col. James B. Fry, provost marshal gen., to Governor David Tod of Ohio.—Copies, *ibid.* On Nov. 11, Capt. George K. Leet endorsed a letter from Tod regarding recruiting circulars from Fry. "Respectfully referred to Maj. Genl. W. T. Sherman, Comd'g Dept. Tenn, who will order such details as are authorized by the enclosed circular and letter to be made as soon as practicable."—Copies, *ibid.*, Endorsements; DLC-USG, V, 39.

1863, SEPT. 25. USG endorsement. "Respectfully forwarded to Head Quarters of the Army Washington D. C. In all that is said of Col. Bane by the Officers of his Brigade and the enclosed copys of recommendations of his superiors Officers, I most heartily concur. He would fill with credit the position to which he is recommended"—Copies, DLC-USG, V, 25; DNA, RG 393, Dept. of the Tenn., Endorsements. Written on a letter of Lt. Col. George T. Allen, medical inspector, enclosing a petition of officers of the 3rd Brigade, 3rd Div., 16th Army Corps, to President Abraham Lincoln urging that Col. Moses M. Bane, 50th Ill., be appointed brig. gen.—*Ibid.* On Nov. 16, Brig. Gen. Grenville M. Dodge, Pulaski, Tenn., wrote to USG recommending the promotion of Bane, Col. August Mersy, 9th Ill., and Lt. Col. Jesse J. Phillips, 9th Ill.—ADfS, Dodge Papers, IaHA. On Dec. 14, USG endorsed this letter. "Respectfully forwarded for the consideration of the Genl.-in-Chief. Though I am not personally acquainted with the within named officers, General Dodge under whose command they have served is entirely capable of judging their merits and peculiar qualifications, and in making further promotions I would therefore respectfully that their cases receive due consideration."—Copies, DLC-USG, V, 39; DNA, RG 393, Military Div. of the Miss., Endorsements. These officers were not promoted during the war.

1863, SEPT. 25. Maj. Samuel Breck, AGO, to USG. "I have the honor to acknowledge the receipt of the communication (forwarded to this office by you on the 8th ulto.) from Priv. H. E. Jefferson Co. "K." 3 Iowa Inft'y, applying for his discharge from the service, that his pay may be increased, and to inform you, by direction of the Genl.-in-Chief, that the present exigencies of the public service will not permit of his being discharged."—Copies, DNA, RG 94, Enlisted Branch, Letters Sent; *ibid.*, RG 393, Military Div. of the Miss., War Dept. Correspondence.

1863, SEPT. 26. USG endorsement. "Respectfully referred to Brig. Genl. L. Thomas. I have no doubt the appointments recommended would be good ones"—Copies, DLC-USG, V, 25; DNA, RG 393, Dept. of the Tenn., Endorsements. Written on a letter of Capt. Embury D. Osband, 4th Ill. Cav., urging that certain members of Co. A of his regt. be commissioned in a regt. of cav. of African descent.—*Ibid.*

1863, SEPT. 26. USG endorsement. "Approved and respectfully forwarded to Head Qrs. the Army Washington D. C."—Copies, DLC-Robert T. Lincoln; DLC-USG, V, 25; DNA, RG 393, Dept. of the Tenn., Endorsements. Written on a letter of Sept. 20 of Maj. Gen. John A. Logan to Secretary of War Edwin M. Stanton urging the promotion of 1st Lt. Logan H. Roots, q. m., 81st Ill.—Copy, DLC-Robert T. Lincoln. Roots was confirmed as capt., commissary of subsistence, on May 20, 1864.

1863, SEPT. 27. To commanding officer, Cairo. "The order expelling James McGuire now in Cairo from all points of this Dept south of Cairo, is hereby revoked, and he will be put on the same footing with other loyal Citizens so far as regards traveling and doing business within the Department is concerned."—Copies, DLC-USG, V, 19, 103; DNA, RG 393, Dept. of the Tenn., Letters Sent. On Aug. 3, Lt. Col. Loren Kent, provost marshal, Dept. of the Tenn., had written to Col. Wager Swayne, provost marshal, Memphis. "Mr. James P Maguire has been ordered to proceed to Cairo, Ills. or a point north of that place not to return under penalty of imprisonment in the Military Prison at Memphis, Tenn. I am directed to inform you of the Order, that he may not be allowed to [s]top in Memphis. He is medium size, rather thick [s]et, one eye, and a heavy sandy moustache. Your detectives will know him. You will see that he does not remain in Memphis"—Copy, *ibid.*, Provost Marshal, Letters Sent.

1863, SEPT. 28. USG endorsement. "I would respectfully represent that the order herein applying for exemption have contributed largely of their services to the support of the war, and if any class is to be exempt from the present or any future draft, they have fully entitled themselves to such benefit. Respectfully referred for the consideration of the President, hoping that, if not inconsistent with law or the policy of the Government, that the favor asked will be granted."—*O.R.*, III, iii, 845. Written on a petition of the same day of officers of the Order of the Holy Cross, Notre Dame, Ind., to President Abraham Lincoln seeking exemption from military service and noting the service of certain members as chaplains and nurses.—*Ibid.*, pp. 844–45.

1863, SEPT. 30. USG endorsement. "Respectfully forwarded to Head Quarters of the Army Washington D. C. and for report, attention invited to the enclosed statement of the company commandant, whom it appears furnished the duplicates in these cases in pursuance of an order from Maj. Genl Curtis & in ignorance of the Army regulations and orders on the subject"—Copies, DLC-USG, V, 25; DNA, RG 393, Dept. of the Tenn., Endorsements. Written on a letter of July 20 of John F. Clements & Co., Washington, requesting duplicate discharges for Privates George W. Babcock and James M. Babcock, Co. F, 15th Ill.—*Ibid.*

1863, SEPT. 30. Maj. Gen. John M. Schofield to USG. "Lieut R. C. Wilson Regtl. Quarter Master 5th Ills Cavalry has been reported at these Head Quarters, as having failed to make proper returns to the Quarter Master Department. of vouchers issued by him in June 1862, at which time he was in this Department. Please order him to make proper returns without delay"—Copy, DNA, RG 393, Dept. of Mo., Letters Sent.

1863, OCT. 1. USG endorsement. "Respectfully returned to Head Quarters of the Army Washington D. C. and attention invited to the endorsement of my Chief of Artillery hereon which is concurred in by me."—Copies, DLC-

USG, V, 25; DNA, RG 393, Dept. of the Tenn., Endorsements. Written on a letter of 2nd Lt. Charles Meinhold, asst. commissary of musters, refusing to muster in Maj. Peter Davidson, 2nd Ill. Light Art.—*Ibid.* On July 30, Ill. AG Allen C. Fuller had endorsed this letter to Secretary of War Edwin M. Stanton requesting special authority to muster in Davidson.— Copy, *ibid.*, RG 94, 2nd Ill. Light Art., Letterbook. On Aug. 18, Maj. Thomas M. Vincent, AGO, had endorsed the letter. "Respectfully referred to Maj. Genl. Grant, to know if another Field officer for this Regt. is necessary for the good of the service. The rgt. is not serving together."—Copy, *ibid.* On Aug. 29, Brig. Gen. John A. Rawlins had referred this letter to Lt. Col. William L. Duff, chief of art., who endorsed and returned it on Sept. 18. "Although it is true that the 2nd Ills. Regt. is not at present serving together; during the campaign preceding & at the seige of Vicksburg eight batteries of it were in the different Army Corps before the city; Maj. Davidson has always had command of at least four batteries, although not all of his own Regt. & in my humble opinion it would be of advantage to the Regt. & to the service generally that he should be mustered as a Maj."— Copy, *ibid.* Davidson was mustered in as of Sept. 10.

1863, OCT. 1. USG endorsement. "Approved and respectfully forwarded to Head Quarters of the Army Washington D. C."—Copies, DLC-USG, V, 25; DNA, RG 393, Dept. of the Tenn., Endorsements. Written on a letter of Sept. 1 of 1st Lt. John C. Neely, act. ordnance officer, Memphis, requesting that Private Norman F. Hazen, Co. E, 50th Ill., and Private Frank Neely, Battery I, 1st Ill. Art., be discharged to accept clerkships in the Ordnance Dept.—*Ibid.*; DLC-USG, V, 23. On Oct. 19, Maj. Samuel Breck, AGO, wrote to USG rejecting this request.—Copies, DNA, RG 94, Enlisted Branch, Letters Sent; *ibid.*, RG 393, Military Div. of the Miss., War Dept. Correspondence.

1863, OCT. 1. To Brig. Gen. James M. Tuttle. "There is a man by the name of Wm. Grant, staying some place within your lines, probably with the troops nearest Black River Bridge. I wish you would have him notified to report to me tomorrow."—Copies, DLC-USG, V, 19, 103; DNA, RG 393, Dept. of the Tenn., Letters Sent. On Sept. 13, Lt. Col. Loren Kent, provost marshal, wrote to Brig. Gen. John A. Rawlins that William L. Grant, W. B. McGeorge, Richard M. Robinson, and Leander C. Mitchell were allegedly speculating in cotton and recommended that they be ordered beyond the limits of the dept.—LS, *ibid.*, Letters Received.

1863, OCT. 2. Maj. Gen. John M. Schofield, St. Louis, to USG. "Herewith I respectfully return Copies of General Orders from your Head Quarters, received at these Head Quarters without any letter of advice or transmittal. It is not Known at these Head Quarters why they were sent here but is presumed to have been a clerical error. The prisoners mentioned have never been received at any of the Military Prisons of this Dept."—Copy, DNA, RG 393, Dept. of Mo., Letters Sent.

1863, OCT. 3. Maj. Gen. Henry W. Halleck to USG. "If Brig Genl T. T. Garrard can be spared from your command direct him to report to Genl. Burnside."—ALS (telegram sent), DNA, RG 107, Telegrams Collected (Bound); copies, *ibid.*, RG 94, Letters Received; *ibid.*, RG 393, Dept. of the Tenn., Letters Sent; DLC-USG, V, 6, 8, 24, 94. Brig. Gen. Theophilus T. Garrard became commanding officer, Somerset District, Ky., 23rd Army Corps, under Maj. Gen. Ambrose E. Burnside.

1863, OCT. 4. USG endorsement. "The Rev. H. B. Hibben, Chaplain 11th Ia Vols. is an applicant for the position of Hospital Chaplain. I would respectfully recommend him for that position in the Memphis Gen. Hospitals."—AES, DNA, RG 94, ACP, H1888 CB 1863. Written on a letter of Oct. 4 of Surgeon Henry S. Hewit, Vicksburg, recommending Chaplain Henry B. Hibben, 11th Ind., who was detailed at the time as religious superintendent of hospitals, Memphis.—ALS, *ibid.* On Oct. 16, H. S. Lane, Crawfordsville, Ind., wrote to Secretary of the Interior John P. Usher, adding to "very many Other reccommendations" in Hibben's behalf.—ALS, *ibid.*, H1156 CB 1863. Usher endorsed this letter on Oct. 23. "Respectfully referred to the Secretary of War. It is the wish of the President that Mr Hibben be appointed if there be any propriety or need for a Chaplain at the place indicated"—ES, *ibid.* On July 2, 1864, Hibben was confirmed as U.S. Navy chaplain.

1863, OCT. 4. To [Judson D. Bingham]. "The Chief Quartermaster will turn over to Lt. Col. L. Kent, Provost Marshal Gn, the sum of Twelve Thousand (12000) dollars of Provost Marshal funds now in his hands."—DS (facsimile), Kenneth W. Rendell, Inc., *Autographs and Manuscripts: the American Civil War* (Catalogue No. 46), p. 16. This may relate to a matter brought up by Lt. Col. Loren Kent. On Sept. 18, Kent was relieved as provost marshal, Dept. of the Tenn., to return to regt. command, and replaced by Maj. William R. Rowley, aide-de-camp to USG, who later served as provost marshal, Military Div. of the Miss.—General Orders No. 56, copies, DLC-USG, V, 13, 14; DNA, RG 393, Dept. of the Tenn., General and Special Orders; (printed) Rowley Papers, IHi; USGA. See Special Orders No. 2, Oct. 19, 1863, DLC-USG, V, 38. On Sept. 17, Kent had written to Brig. Gen. John A. Rawlins. "I desire to submit the following statement that it may be forwarded through the proper channels for report: Colonel W S. Hillyer late Provost Marshal General when he resigned left a statement with me of his Cash Receipts and Expenditures that Exhibits the receipt by him of Lieut Col C. A. Reynolds then Chief Quarter Master on February 24, 1863, the sum of twenty thousand dollars ($20.000) and on March 12th, 1863 ten thousand dollars, (10.000) turned over as required by General Orders No. 5. Headquarters Department of the Tennessee current Series ~~of 1863~~. f[or] Secret Service and Hospital fund, which had been previously collect[ed] under that Order and to remain in the hands of the Chief Quar[ter] Master subject to the Order of the Major General Commanding   When Lieut Col Reynolds was relieved he did not leave the m[oney] with his Successor Lieut Col J D. Bingham, neither did he leave any books or papers showing what disposition had been m[ade] of it, but his receipts are on file in my Office for the full amount. On August 2d I addressed Lieut Col Reynolds asking for information but have received no reply. In order that the matter may be set right and the money appropriated to its p[rop]er use, I respectfully request that this communication be forwar[ded] to the proper Officer for investigation and report."—Copy, DNA, RG 393, Dept. of the Tenn., Provost Marshal, Letters Sent. On Sept. 18, Rawlins endorsed this letter. "Respectfully referred to Lieut Col. C. A. Reynolds with the request that he furnish the information required"— Copies, DLC-USG, V, 25; DNA, RG 393, Dept. of the Tenn., Endorsements. On Sept. 22, Capt. Charles A. Reynolds, asst. q. m., Rock Island, Ill., wrote to Brig. Gen. Montgomery C. Meigs pursuant to Q. M. gen. orders of July 22, making "a short and meager report" of his administration as q. m., Dept. of the Tenn., due to the loss of his records at Holly Springs, Miss., Dec. 20, 1862.—ALS, *ibid.*, RG 92, Reports of Q. M. Officers.

1863, OCT. 5.   To Brig. Gen. Lorenzo Thomas. "I have the honor to transmit herewith copies of my special orders from Septr 1st to include Sept. 30th 1863, also abstract of same accepting resignations"—Copies, DLC-USG, V, 6, 8, 24, 94; DNA, RG 393, Dept. of the Tenn., Hd. Qrs. Correspondence. On Oct. 12, Maj. Samuel Breck, AGO, wrote to USG. "I have the honor to request, that Copies of Special Orders, issued from the Head Quarters of the Department under your command, may be forwarded to this Office, hereafter, as soon as issued; instead of forwarding them at the end of each month."—LS, *ibid.*, Unregistered Letters Received.

1863, OCT. 5.   USG endorsement. "Disapproved, and respectfully forwarded to Headquarters of the Army, Washington D. C."—Copies, DLC-USG, V, 25; DNA, RG 393, Dept. of the Tenn., Endorsements. Written on a letter of Sept. 6 of Surgeon Samuel C. Plummer, 13th Ill., of Rock Island, Ill., requesting that he be assigned to duty at a military prison about to be established at Rock Island.—*Ibid.*; DLC-USG, V, 23. On July 15, Maj. Thomas M. Vincent, AGO, had written to USG. "I am directed to inform you that the application of Surgeon Samuel C. Plummer, 13th Illinois Volunteers, for 30 days leave of absence, has been submitted to the General-in Chief and returned by him endorsed 'not approved' "—Copy, DNA, RG 393, Military Div. of the Miss., War Dept. Correspondence. On July 29, however, Plummer was given a twenty-day leave of absence.— Special Orders No. 205, *ibid.*, Dept. of the Tenn., Special Orders; DLC-

USG, V, 27, 28. Yet, on Sept. 3, Plummer was ordered to receive full pay for the period as it was necessary that he remain on duty.—Special Orders No. 241, *ibid.*, V, 16, 28. Plummer was mustered out with his regt. on June 18, 1864.

1863, OCT. 5. USG endorsement. "Respectfully forwarded to Head Quarters of the Army Washington D. C. with the recommendation that Private Charles P. Hasiltine be discharged the service, that he may be employed as draughtsman in the Engineer Department"—Copies, DLC-USG, V, 25; DNA, RG 393, Dept. of the Tenn., Endorsements. Written on a letter of Brig. Gen. Joseph D. Webster and others recommending Private Charles P. Haseltine, Chicago Mercantile Battery, for this position.—*Ibid.* On Oct. 19, Maj. Israel C. Woodruff, Engineer Dept., Washington, returned this letter to the AGO noting "No present need in this office for the service of a draughtsman beyond the number employed—" but recommending that Haseltine be "employed in the Eng. Dept. of the Army of the Tennessee which is believed to be the intention of Maj Gen. Grant—. . ."—Copy, *ibid.*, RG 77, Papers Referred. On Oct. 27, Maj. Samuel Breck, AGO, wrote to USG regarding Haseltine. ". . . the interests of the Public Service, will not permit of his discharge. If his services are required by the Engineer Dep't. he can be detailed for that purpose."—Copies, *ibid.*, RG 94, Enlisted Branch, Letters Sent; *ibid.*, RG 393, Military Div. of the Miss., War Dept. Correspondence. On Nov. 10, Lt. Col. Theodore S. Bowers, Nashville, referred this letter to Haseltine "for his information"—Copies, *ibid.*, Endorsements; DLC-USG, V, 39.

1863, OCT. 5. To Brig. Gen. James M. Tuttle. "Is there any Cotton remaining on Black River to be sent in on Government account? Is so leave it until ownership can be determined."—Copies, DLC-USG, V, 19, 103; DNA, RG 393, Dept. of the Tenn., Letters Sent.

1863, OCT. 7. USG endorsement. "Respectfully returned to Head Quarters of the Army Washington D. C. with the recommendation that the prayer of the petitioner be not granted"—Copies, DLC-USG, V, 25; DNA, RG 393, Dept. of the Tenn., Endorsements. Written on a letter of Governor Richard Yates of Ill. enclosing a petition of officers of the 90th Ill. asking USG to support their effort to reinstate Capt. Mathew Leonard, Co. E, who had been dismissed on March 26.—*Ibid.*

1863, OCT. 7. USG endorsement. "Approved"—Copy, DNA, RG 94, ACP, A308 CB 1865. Written on a letter of Sept. 16 from Governor Richard Yates of Ill. to President Abraham Lincoln recommending William H. Ashburn for a position in the regular army.—Copy, *ibid.*

1863, OCT. 10.   To Maj. Gen. Nathaniel P. Banks requesting that Sgt. Abraham R. Bander, Battery E, 2nd Ill. Art., having received a commission, be ordered to report to Lt. Col. William L. Duff, chief of art., Dept. of the Tenn.—DNA, RG 393, Dept. of the Gulf, Register of Letters Received.

1863, OCT. 10.   USG endorsement. "Respectfully referred to Comdg Officer of Gun Boat stationed near Rodney Miss who will please have the enclosed letter delivered if practicable."—Copies, DLC-USG, V, 25; DNA, RG 393, Dept. of the Tenn., Endorsements. Written on a letter of Oct. 9 of Maj. Thomas D. Maurice, Vicksburg, requesting that an enclosed letter be forwarded to W. R. Dent.—*Ibid.*

1863, OCT. 10.   Col. William F. Lynch, Cairo, to USG. "on assuming Command at this Post I was instructed by Brig Gen Buford whom I releived to endorse upon the leaves of absence of all Officers reporting here the date of their arrival at this Post and to inform them that they were allowed the full time mentioned in their leaves, from the date on which they reported at these Head Quarters. I do not feel exactly right in regard to this Matter and would therefore respectfully request definite instructions in regard to it. Gen Buford informed me that you had given him the instructions given me but I can find no orders relative to the Matter. Please send me instructions that will guide me hereafter"—Copy, DNA, RG 393, Dept. of Ky., Cairo, Letters Sent.

1863, OCT. 13.   Alfred J. Bloor, asst. secretary, U.S. Sanitary Commission, Washington, to USG reporting his election as an associate member of the commission.—DS, USG 3.

1863, OCT. 14.   Maj. Robert Williams, AGO, to USG noting irregularities in his dept. return for July and requesting that existing directions for preparing such returns be followed in the future.—Copy, DNA, RG 94, Enlisted Branch, Letters Sent.

1863, OCT. 16.   To Brig. Gen. Lorenzo Thomas. "I respectfully request that an order be issued consolidating the 131st Regiment Illinois Infantry Vols. (which has been ordered from Paducah to Vicksburg) with the 29th Regiment Illinois Infantry Vols., and that authority be given Maj Gen J. B. McPherson, commanding 17th Army Corps, to convene a Board of Examiners with a view to the mustering out of the Officers in both Regiments who are found upon examination to be inefficient   In its present condition the 131st Illinois is of but little value to the service."—LS, DNA, RG 94, Letters Received by Thomas, G7 AG 1863. On the same day, USG, Cairo, endorsed a letter of Oct. 10 from Lt. Col. Loren Kent to Ill. AG Allen C. Fuller requesting a commission as col., 29th Ill. "Approved and earnestly

recommended. The 131st Ill. is reduced to so low a number and under its
present commanders is so inefficient that it has been ordered to Vicksburg
for consolidation with the 29th, an order for which will come from the Sec.
of War."—AES, Records of 29th Ill., I-ar. On Oct. 30, Thomas issued
Special Orders No. 90 consolidating the 131st Ill. with the 29th Ill.—*Ill.
AG Report*, VI, 608.

1863, OCT. 17. USG endorsement. "Respectfully forwarded to The Hd
Qrs. of the Army Washington D C"—AES, DNA, RG 94, ACP, 492W
CB 1863. Written on a petition of Sept. 3 of twenty officers to Brig. Gen.
Lorenzo Thomas urging that Col. Oliver Wood, 22nd Ohio, be promoted
to brig. gen.—LS, *ibid.* Although not nominated to this rank, Wood be-
came col., 4th U.S. Veteran Vols., Dec. 29, 1864.

1863, OCT. 17. USG endorsement. "Respectfully forwarded to the Hd
Qrs of the Army Washington D C with recommendation that the resignation of this Officer be accepted"—ES, DNA, RG 94, Vol. Service Div.,
Letters Received, T706 (VS) 1876. Written on a letter of Sept. 26 from
Brig. Gen. John M. Corse to Brig. Gen. John A. Rawlins reporting the
result of an investigation of the case of 2nd Lt. John W. Loucks, 15th
Mich.—ALS, *ibid.* On Aug. 18, Loucks had written to Rawlins tendering
his resignation because of his "utter incompetancy to perform the duties
appertaining to the office of 2d Lieut. by reasons of ignorance and distaste
of military life"—ALS, *ibid.* On Sept. 22, Loucks testified to the commission reviewing his case that he resigned because Col. John M. Oliver, 15th
Mich., "did not respect him."—DS, *ibid.* Although the commission recommended that he be reinstated, Maj. Gen. William T. Sherman on Aug. 19
had written: "An officer should be made ignominious by such a confession
and such a Record—But as the service should be rid of such material the
quicker he is disposed of the better."—AES, *ibid.* Loucks received an honorable discharge for disability as of Nov. 20, 1863.

1863, OCT. 17. To Maj. Gen. Henry W. Halleck from Cairo. "Allow me
to ask a suspension of the order relating to Col Martin from the command
at Paducah until a full report can be made. There are factions in West
Kentucky who will make every effort to remove every officer they cannot
control"—Telegrams received (2—dated Oct. 19), DNA, RG 107, Telegrams Collected (Bound); copies (dated Oct. 17), *ibid.*, RG 393, Dept.
of the Tenn., Letters Sent; DLC-USG, V, 6, 8, 24, 94. Datelined Louisville, Oct. 19, in *O.R.*, I, xxx, part 4, 471. See letter to Brig. Gen. Lorenzo
Thomas, April 14, 1863. On Oct. 21, 2:30 P.M., Halleck telegraphed to
USG. "No order has been issued here removing Lt Col Martin from command at Paducah. He was ordered before a board for overstaying his leave,
and exhonorated."—ALS (telegram sent), DNA, RG 107, Telegrams Collected (Bound); copies (misdated Oct. 23, 4:30 P.M.), *ibid.*, RG 393,

Military Div. of the Miss., Hd. Qrs. Correspondence; DLC-USG, V, 40, 94. See *O.R.*, I, xxxi, part 3, 25.

1863, OCT. 17.   Brig. Gen. John A. Rawlins, Cairo, to Brig. Gen. Henry M. Naglee. "I am instructed by Major Gen'l U. S. Grant, to say that the troops of his command are at present considerably scattered, and many of them on the move and under Division Commanders, which he would dislike to displace. You are therefore at liberty and so directed to take up your quarters in any city you may select, reporting to him for further orders by letter."—Copies, DLC-USG, V, 19, 103; DNA, RG 393, Dept. of the Tenn., Letters Sent. On Sept. 29, Maj. Gen. Henry W. Halleck had written to USG. "Brig General H. W. Naglee U. S. Vols., has been placed on duty in several Depts; but seems to nowhere give satisfaction   The Secretary of War has just ordered him to report to you at Vicksburg. I thought it was rather unfair to impose on you an officer, who makes trouble wherever he goes, and the Sec'y. has authorized me to say to you that you are under no obligations to give General Naglee a command. You can put him on duty or not, as you may deem proper"—Copy, *ibid.*, RG 108, Letters Sent. On April 4, 1864, Naglee was honorably mustered out.

1863, OCT. 19.   Dr. Winston Somers, Natchez, to USG urging at length that soldiers suffering from diarrhea be sent home on furlough. Somers had come "from central Illinois" to see his sick son.—ALS, DNA, RG 393, Military Div. of the Miss., Letters Received. On Nov. 11, Capt. George K. Leet referred this letter to Maj. Gen. James B. McPherson who, returning it on Nov. 30, noted that "No restrictions have been put upon the orders granting sick furloughs. . . . Many good men are lost to the service by being sent prematurely up the River and consequently die on the way or very soon after reaching home"—ES, *ibid.*

1863, OCT. 21.   USG protection paper. "All United States forces are commanded to respect the property & persons of the families of Mrs Irene Smith—&—Bullitt residing on the Mississippi River, in the State of Mississippi, at what is known as the Ky. bend. The Stock, utensils & provisions will not be taken for military purposes from either of the three plantations of Mrs Smith, or from the plantations of Mr Bullitt, but all practicable protection will be given them by the Military"—Copies (dated Oct. 20), DNA, RG 217, Southern Claims Commission, Claims Files, Miss., Washington County, File 36,895; *ibid.*, RG 366, Second Special Agency, Unarranged Correspondence. On Oct. 27, 1864, Irene Smith, for herself and for Alexander C. and Irene S. Bullitt, petitioned Secretary of the Treasury William P. Fessenden for permits to sell cotton from their plantations and to buy food and clothing, alleging that they were loyal citizens who had lost at least $100,000 in property taken or destroyed by U.S. forces, had educated their slaves, and had cared for about 250 of them who had returned after having been taken off by the government to contraband camps.—DS, *ibid.* On March 24, 1875, the Southern Claims Commission allowed Bullitt $5,440 for supplies furnished during the war.—*Ibid.*, RG 217, Southern Claims Commission, Claims Files, Miss., Washington County, File 36,895.

1863, OCT. 21.   Brig. Gen. Jeremiah T. Boyle, Louisville, to USG. "The eighth 8th Iowa Cavalry eleven hundred and fifty strong have just arrived en route for Dept. of the Cumberland. Genl Rosecrans directed them to remain here until fully equipped and paid which will require Several days. Shall they be sent through by rail or as escort for wagon train"—Telegram received, DNA, RG 94, War Records Office, Dept. of Ark.; copy, *ibid.*, RG 393, Military Div. of the Miss., Telegrams Received. On the same day, 3:00 P.M., USG, Tullahoma, Tenn., telegraphed to Boyle. "Leave the cavalry at Louisville as directed by Genl Rosecrans unless otherwised directed by Gen Thomas or myself"—Telegram received, *ibid.*, RG 94, War Records Office, Remount Station. On Oct. 28, Boyle telegraphed to USG. "The eighth Iowa Cavalry now here en route for the Department of the Cumberland will be ready to move on the first of November—they are deficient in arms and none can be obtained here. They have sabres and pistols but very few Carbines. Shall they be sent by rail to Nashville or sent as escort for a large wagon train from here"—Copy, *ibid.*, RG 393, Military Div. of the Miss., Telegrams Received. See *O.R.*, I, xxxi, part 3, 28. Also on Oct. 28, Boyle telegraphed to USG. "The twenty third Mo. Vols. and first Kansas Battery ordered by Gen. Schofield to report to me will arrive at Louisville to day. The 23d Mo. has 850 men for duty   where shall they be sent—please send your orders in regard to them to me at Louisville—" —Copy, DNA, RG 393, Military Div. of the Miss., Telegrams Received. See *O.R.*, I, xxxi, part 3, 558.

1863, OCT. 23.   Col. Edward D. Townsend, AGO, to USG. "I am directed by the Secretary of War to inform you, that a recruiting detail consisting of one commissioned officer from each Regiment, and one Non Commissioned officer or Private from each company, is hereby authorized for the following Regiments of Illinois Volunteers, last reported as serving in the Department of the Tennessee. . . . The details will be made as above, provided the exigencies of the service will permit. They will be ordered to report to the Superintendent Vol. Recruiting Service at Springfield Ills. at the earliest moment they can be spared from their companies"—LS, DNA, RG 393, Military Div. of the Miss., Letters Received. On Nov. 13, USG telegraphed to Maj. Gen. James B. McPherson, Vicksburg. "In pursuance of instructions from the Secretary of War, you will at once detail One Commissioned Officer from each of the following Illinois Regiments and One Non Commissioned officer or private from each company of said Regiments, to report without delay to Supt of Volunteer recruiting service at Springfield Illinois, viz. 8th 11th 14th 15th & 17th Illinois Infantry—"—Copies, DLC-

USG, V, 34, 35; DNA, RG 393, Military Div. of the Miss., Letters Sent. On the same day, Capt. George K. Leet sent a similar telegram to Maj. Gen. Stephen A. Hurlbut, Memphis.—Telegram received, *ibid.*, 16th Army Corps, Letters Received; copies, *ibid.*, Military Div. of the Miss., Letters Sent; DLC-USG, V, 34, 35. On the same day, Leet wrote to Maj. Gen. George H. Thomas, Chattanooga, enclosing a copy of Townsend's letter.—Copies, *ibid.* Also on Nov. 13, Leet wrote to Maj. Gen. William T. Sherman, enclosing a copy of Townsend's letter.—ALS, DNA, RG 393, Dept. of the Tenn., Unregistered Letters Received. On Nov. 22, McPherson wrote to USG. "I have the honor to acknowledge the receipt of your telegram of the 12th and 14th inst. in relation to sending recruiting details to Wis. and Ill's. and to inform you that these details have already been sent, some of them having started ten days since. The authority for sending them was based on Circulars from the Govenors of Ohio, Ills. Mo. Iowa and Wis. sent to the Com'd'g Officers of respective Regiments. I did not wait for orders from the War Department, for the reason that we have received no General Orders for several weeks, but took it for granted on seeing the Circulars that orders had been issued, and sent the recruiting parties accordingly. Particular instructions were given to select for the details Officers and men in the line of promotion, especially those who have received Commissions, but who could not be mustered in consequence of their Command being below the minimum. These men have gone to recruit, with the determination to fill up their Cos and Reg'ts. in order that they may receive the promotion to which they feel themselves entitled. Already news of good success in recruiting in the several States where it has been authorized, has been received   Since the date of my last letter nothing material has transpired . . ." McPherson continued, describing troop locations in his command and problems with cotton speculators.— Copies, *ibid.*, RG 393, 13th and 17th Army Corps, Letters Sent; *ibid.*, 17th Army Corps, Letters Sent. *O.R.*, I, xxxi, part 3, 226–28. See *Calendar*, Nov. 12, 1863.

1863, OCT. 23.   Col. Edward D. Townsend, AGO, to USG. "On the requisition of Governor Morton of Indiana, the General in Chief directs that you send from each Company of Indiana Regiments, designated by him, one noncommissioned officer or private to be selected by the Regimental Commander, who, if there be a vacancy for a commissioned officer in his Company will be entitled to promotion on recruiting his Company to the minimum standard; if there be no vacancies of Commissioned Officers to fill in any Company, the Comdg Officer of the Regiment will select at his discretion either one commissioned officer or one enlisted man to recruit and report to the Governor of the State. It is important that these details be made at the earliest moment that military operations will permit the service of the men to be spared from their Companies."—Telegram, copies, DLC-USG, V, 40, 94; DNA, RG 107, Telegrams Collected (Unbound); *ibid.,* RG 110, Letters Received. An identical telegram went to five other gens. On the same day, Townsend sent a copy of this telegram to Governor Oliver P. Morton of Ind.—Copy, Morton Papers, In. Also on Oct. 23, Morton, Indianapolis, telegraphed to USG repeating the authorization received from Townsend and concluding: "I trust that this may be done immediately as the time is favorable for recruiting and I am anxious to have it performed without delay."—Copies, *ibid.;* (dated Oct. 24) DNA, RG 393, Military Div. of the Miss., Telegrams Received. On the same day, USG sent identical telegrams to Maj. Gen. Ambrose E. Burnside, Maj. Gen. Stephen A. Hurlbut, Maj. Gen. James B. McPherson, and Maj. Gen. William T. Sherman. "Detach one man from each Company of Indiana troops to report immediately to Gov Morton for recruiting service where vacancys will exist for commissioned officers by filling the companies men will be selected who it is desired by their commander shall be promoted in case of vacancy—Col of regiment will mak the selections."— Telegram received, *ibid.,* RG 94, War Records Office, Dept. of the Ohio; (dated Oct. 27) *ibid.,* RG 393, 16th Army Corps, Letters Received; (dated Oct. 27) *ibid.,* Dept. of the Tenn., Unregistered Letters Received; copies (dated Oct. 24), *ibid.,* Military Div. of the Miss., Letters Sent; DLC-USG, V, 34, 35. On Oct. 25, USG telegraphed to Morton. "Your dispatch received. I have made the order for the detail you ask"—Copy, Morton Papers, In. On Oct. 26, Capt. Ely S. Parker wrote to Sherman enclosing copies of the telegrams from Townsend and Morton.—LS, DNA, RG 393, Dept. of the Tenn., Unregistered Letters Received.

1863, Oct. 23. Maj. Gen. Ambrose E. Burnside, Knoxville, to USG. "Will you please have Maj L A Gratz 6th Ky cavalry now at stevenson Ala detained for duty on staff of Brig Genl Carter & ordered to report at this place if consistent with the interests of the public service."—Telegram received, DNA, RG 94, Dept. of the Ohio; copy, *ibid.,* RG 393, Military Div. of the Miss., Telegrams Received.

1863, Oct. 27. 1st Lt. Stephen C. Lyford, Ordnance Office, Washington, to USG. "I should have written to you long ago in relation to my leaving you in such an unexpected manner—But various circumstances have conspired to prevent me until now. I am very glad to have the opportunity of congratulating you upon your new and large command,—and wish very much that I was back again with you—I did not come here of my own desire nor will I stay long if at any time I can have the choice of staying or leaving—Old Ramsey is now Chf and keeps us all in hot water—He tries to do too much & succeeds in doing nothing—By the way, Callender wished me to say to you at some time, that he would like very much to go into the field again—I expect you could get him by asking for him—I suppose you still retain your old staff with additional officers that you have found in Tennessee—It is rumored here that Meade is to be removed and

Sedgwick take his place—another rumor says Rosecrans—Thom says that he has not yet forgiven you for those *pants* I hope General that I shall again be allowed to serve with you for I am very well convinced that I could not find a kinder commanding officer—If at any time your time will permit you to drop me a line I would be much pleased— . . . I am a captain or will be officially as soon as the war Dept fills the existing vacancy by promotion—"—ALS, USG 3. See letter to Brig. Gen. Thomas J. McKean, Sept. 16, 1862, note 2; letter to Maj. Gen. Henry W. Halleck, Nov. 26, 1862. On July 6, 1863, by Special Orders No. 182, Lyford had been given a twenty-day leave of absence due to illness.—Copies, DLC-USG, V, 27, 28; DNA, RG 393, Dept. of the Tenn., Special Orders. On Jan. 26, 1864, Lyford wrote to USG. "The vouchers which I enclose, have been stopped against me in the 2n Auditors office, for not having your approval— Will you do me the kindness to approve these and return to me?—There is no hurry about the matter, so you can take your leisure and postpone it until you have nothing else to do, if you ever expect such a time to come— Wilson arrived here yesterday and takes charge of the cavalry Bureau, the same position that Stoneman occupied—I think he will soon tire of it— I see by the papers that one of your boys is ill—I hope it is nothing serious—I wish very much I was back again in the field and am heartily disgusted for ever having left the agreeable position I had—My kindest regards to your lady and family—"—ALS, USG 3.

1863, OCT. 27. John B. Gray, Mo. AG, to USG. "I am directed by His Excellency, the Governor of Missouri to forward to you the annexed copy of Telegram this day recieved, from Washington. Washington Oct 26 4.30 P. M. To GEN'L GRAY. ADJUTANT GEN'L OF MISSOURI You can at once commence raising troops for organizations whose term expires in eighteen sixty four (1864) or eighteen sixty five (1865) and give each recruit so raised bounty, premium and advance: pay of three hundred & two (302) dollars for new recruits for such organizations, or four hundred & two (402) dollars for veterans. Please acknowledge receipt. (signed) JAS. B FRY Pro. Mar. Gen'l The object of this communication is to request you to direct that details of recruiting parties be made from such Mo. Regiments under your command as have not already been allowed to consist of two officers and four enlisted men (one non-commissioned officer) and ordered to report immediately to Col B. L. E. Bonneville Superintendent Gen'l Recruiting service Mo. Vols. at Benton Barracks St Louis Mo. for recruiting duty under the terms of this dispatch. Although existing orders from the War Department touching the recruiting service, permit the detail of a greater number of a greater number of enlisted men from each regiment, still Col Bonneville is of opinion that the number above stated will be sufficient for all practical purposes, and as our Mo. Regiments are already so greatly reduced, it is desirable that as few men as possible should be taken from the field at this time. Under the terms of this dispatch, the Governor feels confident that we can soon fill up our depleted regiments, provided that we can have your co-operation and prompt action in the matter. It is proper to state that the term of service of all of the Missouri Regiments under your command will expire during the years of 1864 and 1865. May I ask that you will reply to this communication, stating in how far you will be able to comply with the terms of its request."— LS, DNA, RG 393, Military Div. of the Miss., Letters Received. On Nov. 2, USG telegraphed to Gray. "I have the honor to acknowledge the receipt of your communication of the 27th Ult. with regard to recruiting in Missouri. The Generals commanding the several Departments composing my command have been instructed to furnish the details requested"—Copies, DLC-USG, V, 34, 35; DNA, RG 393, Military Div. of the Miss., Letters Sent. *O.R.*, I, xxxi, part 3, 23.

1863, OCT. 28. To Maj. Gen. Henry W. Halleck. "In relation to the Medical Dept &c."—DNA, RG 108, Register of Letters Received; *ABPC*, 1950–51, p. 560.

1863, OCT. 28. Brig. Gen. George L. Andrews, Port Hudson, La., to USG. "I have the honor to report that I have had this day delivered to me by Captn. Foster of U. S. Steamer Lafayette two deserters from Co. "A" 2nd Battalion Sixteenth U. S. Infantry, they having shipped on board said U. S. vessel. Their names are Benjamin Lewis and Wm. Stevens. I now hold said deserters, subject to your orders."—Copy, DNA, RG 393, Dept. of the Gulf, Port Hudson, Letters Sent. On Nov. 13, Lt. Col. Theodore S. Bowers, Nashville, endorsed this letter to Maj. Gen. Stephen A. Hurlbut, "with whom the 16th Regulars are serving for action."—Copies, *ibid.*, Military Div. of the Miss., Endorsements; DLC-USG, V, 39.

1863, OCT. 29. Maj. Samuel Breck, AGO, to USG. "I am instructed by the General in chief, to direct you upon receipt of this communication, to discharge Serg't. Andrew J. Kincaid Co. "H" 19th Ky. Vols. from the Military Service of the U. S."—Copies, DNA, RG 94, Enlisted Branch, Letters Sent; *ibid.*, RG 393, Military Div. of the Miss., War Dept. Correspondence. On Nov. 3, pursuant to this request, Lt. Col. Theodore S. Bowers, Nashville, issued Special Orders No. 5.—Copy, DLC-USG, V, 38.

1863, OCT. 30. USG endorsement. "Respectfully forwarded to Headquarters of the Army Washington D C."—ES, DNA, RG 94, ACP, 553H CB 1863. Written on a letter of Col. Sylvester G. Hill, 35th Iowa, to Secretary of War Edwin M. Stanton, favorably endorsed by Maj. Gen. James B. McPherson, Maj. Gen. John A. Logan, and three others, urging the appointment of 1st Lt. Heiskell Loftland, regt. q. m., 35th Iowa, as capt. and asst. q. m.—ALS and AES, *ibid.* Loftland was not appointed.

1863, OCT. 30. To Ernest M. Bement, Nashville. "Gen Thomas commands the Department and will not be interfered with in making all needful regulations looking to supplying the wants of citizens of Nashville. My signature is not necessary and I am not willing to give it without knowing more than I now do of the merits of the enterprise proposed"—Copies, DLC-USG, V, 34, 35; DNA, RG 393, Military Div. of the Miss., Letters Sent. On the same day, USG endorsed a letter of F. T. Foster, Nashville, asking permission to sell wood and coal in that city. "Respectfully referred to Maj. Gen. G. H. Thomas Comd'g. Dept. Cum."—Copies, *ibid.*, Endorsements; DLC-USG, V, 39. On Oct. 8, Bement had written to Governor Andrew Johnson of Tenn. requesting that the enterprise be exempt from military impressment and promising not to charge exhorbitantly, as another supplier allegedly did.—ALS, DLC-Andrew Johnson. On Nov. 2, Bement wrote to Lt. Col. Theodore S. Bowers, Nashville, stating that Johnson approved his plan for the Nashville Coal Co. to supply the city with fuel during the coming winter, and that the co. would supply the deserving poor free.—ALS, DNA, RG 109, Union Provost Marshals' File of Papers Relating to Individual Civilians. Lt. Col. Calvin Goddard, for Maj. Gen. George H. Thomas, to whom Bowers referred this letter on Nov. 5, endorsed it to Maj. Gen. Lovell H. Rousseau, commanding District of Nashville, on Nov. 14. "The exemption from impressment of teams & laborers and from seizure of wood and coal will be granted the Company. They must however, be directed to give certificates of employment to their hands."—AES, *ibid.* On Jan. 15, 1864, Bement presented Johnson with a load of coal.—ALS, DLC-Andrew Johnson. Before this venture, Bement, formerly maj., 3rd Pa. Cav., had attempted to recruit in New York City a regt. known as the Andrew Johnson Cav. for service in eastern Tenn., but the War Dept. order which permitted this out-of-state recruitment was revoked in mid-June, 1863.—See Johnson to Bement, June 17, 1863, ALS, *ibid.*; Clifton R. Hall, *Andrew Johnson Military Governor of Tennessee* (Princeton, 1916), p. 180.

1863, OCT. 31. AGO to USG asking for additional information regarding certain officers reported absent in USG's return for Aug.—Copy, DNA, RG 94, Enlisted Branch, Letters Sent.

1863, OCT. 31. Col. William Given, 102nd Ohio, Nashville, to USG. "The 102. O. V. I was ordered by Gen'l Williams to march from Cowan & Elk River bridge to Nashville It is now at Tullahoma without rations and can't get them there I have but three teams. I respectfully ask an order to put the Regt. on some empty train coming to Nashville will wait answer here."—Telegram, copy, DNA, RG 393, Military Div. of the Miss., Telegrams Received. On Nov. 1, USG telegraphed to Given. "Call on J. B. Anderson Supt of Rail Roads for transportation of your regiment. I have directed him to furnish it."—Copies, *ibid.*, Letters Sent; DLC-USG, V, 34, 35. On the same day, USG had telegraphed to John B. Anderson.

"Direct empty cars going to Nashville to take on the 102d Ohio Infantry at Tullahoma and take them into Nashville"—Copies, *ibid.* On Nov. 2, Anderson telegraphed to USG. "Your dispatch rec'd.   will bring up the 102d Ohio Regt. to Nashville to morrow by return trains   will you please instruct the officers in Com'd. have his regt. ready at Eight thirty A. M. to load promptly so as not to detain the train—"—Copy, DNA, RG 393, Military Div. of the Miss., Telegrams Received. See *O.R.*, I, xxxi, part 1, 672, 716, 769.

1863, Nov. 1.   William W. Leland, Chicago, to USG. "Having traveled with your friend of the 'Illinois Central R Road' Mr Dougllass He fully agrees with me in the *theory broached*, to you the last time, I was at Coreanth. I am *Confident* of *Success*,   I have been in Mexico since then untill June, and have been Intersted in 'Wilkes Spirit of the Times'   The daily Times & Post. are Strong Grant Papers; while in Matameras I saw Genl. McGruder & Bos & other   all Enquired after you   I told them you would be soon Down to see them after Taking *Vixburgh*. They said if that was the Case, you would never see Texas, &c &c. they were very Clever to me on *Nuteral Grounds* but Inform me Frankly if Caught the other side of the River I should be *Promptly Shot*   I told them should be in good compay and under the Protectin of the old Flag & such Generals as you   I came near being captured at Galveston by McGruder   was the Last Stemer over the Bar. My Brothers & Host of frieds are anxious to give that. *Imense Staff* dinner at the Metropolitan Hotel agreed upon befor I left.   be sure & bring with you My Boys & Mrs Grant for I wish to Show you my Seven Girls that the '*Gay Old Coon*' is father off. Col. Lagow & Com. [Glenn] Dined with my Family while in N. York & Grant Stock Ran High. I mett [Hatsh]   he will *not do* to *Field*. I am as ever your friend till Death"—ALS, USG 3. See letter to Brig. Gen. Lorenzo Thomas, July 25, 1862.

1863, Nov. 2.   Capt. William P. Hargrave, commanding at Smithland, Ky., to USG. "Was Col. Wm. S. Hillyer Pro. Mar. in field before Vicksburg May 29th 1863   Did he give pass to f that date to J. W. Hempfield, deserter from Lynch's Artillery East Tenn. vols confederate Army—"—Copy, DNA, RG 393, Military Div. of the Miss., Telegrams Received.

1863, Nov. 2.   Manorah F. Lowe, Indianapolis, to USG requesting that her son, 1st Lt. William R. Lowe, 19th Inf., son of USG's friend, the late Col. John W. Lowe, 12th Ohio, be detached for service under USG's "more direct supervision."—ALS, USG 3.

1863, Nov. 3.   Maj. Samuel Breck, AGO, to USG. "I have the honor to acknowledge the receipt of a communication of the 14th Ulto. from Major General W. S. Rosecrans, enclosing Extracts of Special Field Orders No.

272 Dept. of the Cumberland, assigning Commissaries and Ass't Commissaries of of Muster, for the troops in that Dep'tm't: and to inform you that the appointments are approved, and the Pay Master General has been notified accordingly."—Copies, DNA, RG 94, Enlisted Branch, Letters Sent; *ibid.*, RG 393, Military Div. of the Miss., War Dept. Correspondence.

1863, Nov. 5. USG General Orders No. 4. "The habit of raiding parties of rebel cavalry visiting towns, villages and farms, where there are no Federal forces, and pillaging Union families having become prevalent, Department Commanders will take immediate steps to abate the evil or make the loss fall upon secessionists and secession sympathizers of the neighborhood where such acts are committed For every act of violence to the person of an unarmed Union citizen, a secessionist will be arrested and held as hostage for the delivery of the offender. For every dollars' worth of property taken from such citizens, or destroyed by raiders, an assessment will be made upon secessionists of the neighborhood, and collected by the nearest military forces, under the supervision of the commander thereof, and the amount thus collected paid over to the sufferers. When such assessments cannot be collected in money, property useful to the Government may be taken, at a fair valuation, and the amount paid in money by a disbursing officer of the Government, who will take such property up on his returns. Wealthy secession citizens will be assessed in money and provisions for the support of Union refugees, who have and may be driven from their homes, and into our lines, by the acts of those with whom such secession citizens are in sympathy. All collections and payments under this order will be through disbursing officers of the Government, whose accounts must show all money and property received under it, and how disposed of."—Copies, DLC-USG, V, 14; DNA, RG 393, Military Div. of the Miss., General Orders; (printed) USGA. *O.R.*, I, xxxi, part 3, 58. On Dec. 10, USG telegraphed to Lt. Col. Theodore S. Bowers. "Give union Refugees every indulgence you can"—Telegram received, DNA, RG 393, Dept. of the Tenn., Telegrams Received; copy, *ibid.*, Military Div. of the Miss., Telegrams Received.

1863, Nov. 5. USG endorsement. "Respectfully referred to Hd. Qrs. of the Army Washington D. C."—ES, DNA, RG 94, ACP, L200 CB 1863. Written on a letter of Sept. 29 of Brig. Gen. Walter Q. Gresham, concurred in by Brig. Gen. Marcellus M. Crocker, Brig. Gen. Jacob G. Lauman, and Maj. Gen. James B. McPherson, recommending the promotion of Col. John Logan, 32nd Ill.—ALS, *ibid.* No promotion resulted.

1863, Nov. 5. USG endorsement. "Respectfully forwarded to Hd Qrs. of the Army Washington D. C—"—ES, DNA, RG 94, ACP, G724 CB 1864. Written on a letter of Oct. 2 from Brig. Gen. Michael K. Lawler, Berwick Bay, La., to USG urging the promotion of Col. Samuel L. Glasgow, 23rd Iowa.—ALS, *ibid.* The letter, favorably endorsed by Maj. Gen. Cadwallader C. Washburn, was enclosed in a letter of Oct. 2 from Glasgow to USG.—ALS, *ibid.* Glasgow was appointed bvt. brig. gen. as of Dec. 19, 1864.

1863, Nov. 5, 4:00 P.M. To Brig. Gen. Jacob D. Cox, commanding District of Ohio, Cincinnati. "Send Capt C Bartons Company of sharpshooters to this place immediately via Louisville & Nashville"—Telegram received, DNA, RG 393, Dept. of the Ohio, District of Ohio, Telegrams Received. On the same day, USG telegraphed to Maj. Gen. Ambrose E. Burnside, Knoxville. "I have ordered Captain Barton's Company of Sharpshooters from Cincinnati to this place."—Copies, *ibid.*, Military Div. of the Miss., Letters Sent; DLC-USG, V, 34, 35. On Nov. 6, Capt. William P. Anderson telegraphed to USG that Capt. Charles A. Barton's 8th Independent Ohio Co. had "been ordered to report as directed."—Copy, DNA, RG 393, Dept. of the Ohio (Cincinnati), Telegrams Sent.

1863, Nov. 5, 1:30 P.M. Lt. Col. Robert Macfeely, St. Louis, to USG. "I am here at request of Genl. Sherman forwarding supplies up Tennessee river   Am I still on your staff   Would like to remain with you."—Telegram received, DNA, RG 107, Telegrams Collected (Unbound). On Nov. 7, USG telegraphed to Macfeely. "Your dispatch received. Chief Staff Officers of each Department, remain with Department Commanders. If I think it necessary to have a Commissary, I will transfer you from Department to Division Headquarters."—Copies, *ibid.*, RG 393, Military Div. of the Miss., Letters Sent; DLC-USG, V, 34, 35. Macfeely, appointed chief commissary, Dept. and Army of the Tenn., April 14, continued in that position until Sept. 20, 1864.

1863, Nov. 9. Lt. Col. James A. Hardie, AGO, to USG, Maj. Gen. Ambrose E. Burnside, and Brig. Gen. Jeremiah T. Boyle. "The Secretary of War directs that a General Court Martial be convened for the trial of Captain Samuel Black A Q. M of Vols. late in charge of Forage Dept. at Louisville, Ky, the court to be as full and of as high grade of officer as the exigencies of the public service may admit. The charges against Captain Black prepared by Major J M Wright, Acting Judge Advocate General together with all original papers in this Department will this day be forwarded to Brig Genl. Boyle"—Copy, DNA, RG 107, Letters Sent, Military Affairs.

1863, Nov. 12. Maj. Thomas M. Vincent, AGO, to USG. "The Secretary of War directs that a detail of one Commissioned Officer from each of the following Wisconsin Regiments and Batteries, and one Non-Commissioned Officer or Private from each Company, be ordered to report without delay to Supd't Recruiting Service at Madison Wis. viz: Eighth 8th, Twelfth 12th, Fourteenth 14th, Sixteenth 16th, Seventeenth 17th, Eighteenth 18th, Twen-

ty-fifth 25th and Twenty-seventh 27th Infantry   Second 2d Cavalry. Sixth
6th Seventh 7th and Twelfth 12th Batteries"—Telegram, copies, DNA, RG
107, Telegrams Collected (Unbound); *ibid.*, RG 393, Military Div. of
the Miss., Letters Received; *ibid.*, War Dept. Correspondence; *ibid.*, Hd.
Qrs. Correspondence; DLC-USG, V, 40, 94. On the same day, Capt.
George K. Leet implemented these instructions.—Telegrams, copies, *ibid.*,
V, 34, 35; DNA, RG 393, Military Div. of the Miss., Letters Sent; telegram
received, *ibid.*, 16th Army Corps, Letters Received. On Dec. 3, Vincent sent
USG a similar telegram regarding recruitment for the 31st Wis.—Copy,
ibid., Military Div. of the Miss., War Dept. Correspondence.

1863, Nov. 13.   To Col. William Hoffman, commissary gen. of prisoners.
"I am informed by Gen Thomas, that an arrangement was entered into between Gen Rosecrans of [*and*] Bragg for a mutal release on parole of the
wounded of both armies that in pursuance of said arrangement there was
paroled by Gen Rosecrans one Brig Genl 1 capt & 27 enlisted men of the
Confederate army & Genl Bragg one major eleven captains Thirty nine
subalterns & sixteen hundred ninety one enlisted men."—Telegram received, DNA, RG 249, Letters Received. *O.R.*, II, vi, 511. On Nov. 12,
10:35 A.M., Hoffman had telegraphed to USG. "Was any arrangement
made between Genl. Rosecrans and Genl. Bragg by which prisoners on
both sides were released on parole."—ALS (telegram sent), DNA, RG 107,
Telegrams Collected (Unbound); telegram received, *ibid.*, RG 393, Military Div. of the Miss., Letters Received. *O.R.*, II, vi, 504. On Dec. 23,
Hoffman wrote to USG. "After the battle of Chickamauga there were some
seventeen to eighteen hundred wounded prisoners of War, belonging to
Gen'l Rosecran's Army paroled and delivered within our lines by the enemy.
Rolls of these men have been furnished to this office but with the exception
of a few who have reported at Camp Chase, I have no information of
where they may now be found. Many of them I presume are in hospitals
and many have perhaps gone to their homes, while many doubtless have
died. May I request of you to direct that rolls be furnished to this office
from the various hospitals to which they may have been sent, giving the
names of all men received with the rank, regiment, and company; the time
and place of capture; and the time and place of parole, and stating what has
become of those not now present. Gen'l Order No 72, of June 28th, '62 requires that all paroled troops in the west shall be assembled at Camp Chase
or Benton Barracks according to the States which they come from."—LS,
DNA, RG 249, Letters Received. On Jan. 6, 1864, Capt. George K. Leet
endorsed this letter to Maj. Gen. George H. Thomas "who will cause
to be made out and forwarded to Washington the rolls required by the War
Department."—AES, *ibid.* On Jan. 29, Surgeon Glover Perin, medical director, Dept. of the Cumberland, endorsed the letter. "Respectfully returned
with the remark that an effort will be made to furnish the list required
as soon as practicable; but it will be impossible to complete it within a

period of three (3) months."—ES, *ibid*. On Feb. 5, USG endorsed the letter. "Respectfully forwarded to Head Quarters of the Army Washington. D C."—ES, *ibid*.

1863, Nov. 13.   USG endorsement. "Respectfully forwarded to the Provost Marshal General Washington D. C. withe the request that this man be returned to his regiment if consistent with the good of the service."— Copies, DLC-USG, V, 39; DNA, RG 393, Military Div. of the Miss., Endorsements. Written on a letter of Maj. William D. Williams, 89th Ill., requesting the return of Musician William Furman, Co. G, to his regt.— *Ibid*. On Dec. 9, Maj. Samuel Breck, AGO, wrote to USG reporting that Furman had been sent from Camp Distribution, Va., to his regt. on Aug. 17.—Copies, *ibid*., War Dept. Correspondence; *ibid*., RG 94, Enlisted Branch, Letters Sent.

1863, Nov. 13.   To Maj. Gen. Henry W. Halleck. "Officers sent to Ohio, pursuant to instructions from the War Department, to conduct back drafted men, have none of them returned. Should they not be ordered back forthwith?"—Telegram received, DNA, RG 107, Telegrams Collected (Bound); copies, *ibid*., RG 393, Hd. Qrs. Correspondence; DLC-USG, V, 40, 94. On Nov. 14, Halleck telegraphed to USG. "All officers sent to Ohio for drafted men, except a few placed on recruiting service, were ordered back some days ago,—9th of November."—ALS (telegram sent), DNA, RG 107, Telegrams Collected (Bound); copies, *ibid*., RG 393, Hd. Qrs. Correspondence; DLC-USG, V, 40, 94.

1863, Nov. 14, 2:15 P.M.   Maj. Thomas M. Vincent, AGO, to USG. "Order Major George H. Chandler, Ninth (9.) New-Hampshire Volunteers, now at Paris, Kentucky, to report to General Hinks at Concord, N.-H. for Recruiting Service."—ALS (telegram sent), DNA, RG 107, Telegrams Collected (Unbound); copies (misdated Nov. 15), *ibid*., RG 393, Military Div. of the Miss., Hd. Qrs. Correspondence; DLC-USG, V, 40, 94. Brig. Gen. John A. Rawlins sent an identical telegram to Maj. Gen. Ambrose E. Burnside, Knoxville, dating it Nov. 6.—Copies, *ibid*., V, 34, 35; DNA, RG 393, Military Div. of the Miss., Letters Sent.

1863, Nov. 14.   Governor Oliver P. Morton of Ind. to USG. "Co'l. Jno. T. Wilder of the Seventeenth Indiana Regt. is here unfit for duty in the field by reason of debility but is able to render me very valuable service in recruiting. I respectfully ask that leave be granted him to remain here for this purpose till the twentieth of next month by which time he expects to be able for duty with his com'd."—Copies, DNA, RG 393, Military Div. of the Miss., Telegrams Received; Morton Papers, In. On the same day, USG telegraphed to Morton. "Leave of Col J. T. Wilder, 17th Inda. is extended to the 20th of December, for the purpose of aiding the recruiting service"—Copy, *ibid.*

1863, Nov. 15.   Col. Friedrich Hecker, Lookout Valley, Tenn., to USG requesting the appointment of a paymaster for the 80th and 101st Ill.— LS, DNA, RG 393, 11th Army Corps, 3rd Div., 3rd Brigade, Letters Received. Endorsed on Nov. 17 to Paymaster William Smith, this letter was returned to Hecker the following day.—Copies, *ibid.*, Military Div. of the Miss., Endorsements; DLC-USG, V, 39.

1863, Nov. 16.   Maj. Samuel Breck, AGO, to USG. "I have the honor to acknowledge the receipt of the communication of Sept. 27th from Brig. Gen'l. M. M. Crocker, comd'g 4th Divn. 17th A. C. forwarded by you to this Office on the 8th Ulto. with the recommendation that Lieut Gerald Russell, 3d U. S. Cavalry be declared exchanged, and ordered to report for duty, or relieved as Asst. Coms'y of Musters of the 4th Div. 17th A. C., that an Asst. C. of M. may be appointed in his stead. From a personal report received at this Office, from Lieut Russell, a copy of which is herewith enclosed, it appears that he is stationed at Natchez Miss. to 'resume his duties as Asst. Comms'y of Musters' &c. I am therefore instructed to request you, to inform this Office, with the least practicable delay, whether the removal of Lieut Russell as A. C. M. is desired and a different Officer substituted; If so please name a suitable officer."—Copy, DNA, RG 94, Enlisted Branch, Letters Sent. On Dec. 1, USG endorsed this letter stating that he had not known when recommending 2nd Lt. Gerald Russell's replacement that he ". . . had not reported for duty from his capture. His removal from the Division to which he is appointed as Asst. Comsy of Musters is not desired."—Copies, *ibid.*, RG 393, Military Div. of the Miss., Endorsements; DLC-USG, V, 39. Endorsements regarding this matter on Sept. 30, Oct. 6, and Oct. 8 are *ibid.*, V, 25; DNA, RG 393, Dept. of the Tenn., Endorsements.

1863, Nov. 17.   Reverend Edward P. Smith, gen. field agent, U.S. Sanitary Commission, Chattanooga, to USG. "The United States Christian Commission is a combination of the young men's Christian Associations in all the loyal cities of the country. Its object is to bring aid & comfort, material and moral, to the Army and Navy. The agents employed are mostly pastors of churches who give each at least six weeks gratuitous labor in the field. They come to supplement the work of chaplains & when there are none to do their work in camps & hospitals   Moving constantly among the soldiers, . . . they bring hospital stores in limited quantity—not to undertake the work of the Sanitary Commission but to have something in hand with which to minister personal relief to the suffering. But the main work of the Commission is that of a moral & religious help to the army. . . ."—ALS, DNA, RG 393, Military Div. of the Miss., Miscellaneous Letters Received.

On Nov. 18, Smith wrote to Reverend W. E. Boardman, secretary, Christian Commission, Philadelphia. "I went to the headquarters of the Division of the Mississippi this morning, with fear and trembling. . . . The General received me easily: read my papers with attention; said an order should be issued, covering the points made, as soon as he had leisure to prepare it; . . ." —Lemuel Moss, *Annals of the United States Christian Commission* (Philadelphia, 1868), p. 149. On Dec. 12, Capt. George K. Leet issued Special Field Orders No. 32. "All officers holding commands in the Military Division of the Mississippi are hereby required to extend every facility, not inconsistent with the public service, to all delegates of the United States Christian Commission, and aid them, by every legitimate means in their power to the accomplishment of the benevolent and charitable purposes of the Commission. . . ."—*Ibid.*, p. 141; *United States Christian Commission . . . Second Annual Report* (Philadelphia, 1864), pp. 114–15; copy, DLC-USG, V, 38.

1863, Nov. 20.   Asst. Surgeon John W. Brewer, Louisville, to Lt. Col. Theodore S. Bowers seeking USG's recommendation that he be promoted. —ALS, USG 3. Bowers forwarded this letter to Brig. Gen. John A. Rawlins, noting that Brewer, who had been medical purveyor of the Army of the Tenn., "felt a delicacy about applying to the General direct."—ANS, *ibid.* On March 4, 1864, Bowers wrote to Brewer. "Herewith I have the pleasure of handing you a letter from Gen Grant to the Secretary of War in your behalf. His delay in writing it has been a source of annoyance to me. But it resulted purely from the terrible pressure upon his time. Although he turns off an incredible amount of work, yet not unfrequently matters of this kind are neglected. You can well understand the imminse labor that he has to perform. I can candidly assure, you, however, of his high appreciation of you, and his sincere desire to do you any favour in his power. In this the whole Staff concur with him and you have but to Command any of us to secure our greatful services. If a letter from Gen Rawlins and myself could be of any advantage to you we will gladly furnish it. Hoping that your success may be as certain as my wishes for it are sincere,"—ALS, DNA, RG 108, Letters Received. On Aug. 6, 1866, Brewer, Fort Leavenworth, Kans., wrote to USG. "I have the honor to enclose you a copy of a letter written to me by you in regard to a bill which has now become a law— also a letter from Gen Sherman to the same end—may I ask your interference in my behalf—During the war I held the position of Med Purveyor —the importance of which the law recognizes—what I ask is that my claims to the rank of Surgeon & Major be represented—I can expect nothing from the head of my corps—my services were too remote from his office."—ALS, *ibid.* Brewer was not promoted.

1863, Nov. 20.   Alexander D. Bache, superintendent of the U.S. Coast Survey, Philadelphia, to USG. "It has been found that when the Coast Survey officers are serving in the field their work is much more effective if a local military rank is given to them by which soldiers and officers recognize them and civilians such as clerks and other army outsiders are separated from them. General Foster made trial of this assigning the local rank of Captain or Major as their age in the Coast Survey service seemed to require and the duties to which he assigned them rendered expedient. As they receive their pay and allowances from the Coast Survey there is no question of that kind comes up to make the arrangement inconvenient. I would respectfully request that you issue a general order assigning to Coast Survey Officers serving in your military Department the assimilated rank of Captain, or higher if their pay and emoluments require it."—LS, DNA, RG 393, Military Div. of the Miss., Letters Received. On the same day, Bache wrote to Brig. Gen. Montgomery C. Meigs thanking him for suggesting this letter to USG.—ALS, *ibid.*, RG 92, Letters Received by Gen. Meigs at Chattanooga. See *O.R.*, I, xxxi, part 2, 75.

1863, Nov. 21. USG endorsement. "Respectfully returned to Hd. Qrs of the Army Washington D. C. and attention invited to Copy of Genl. Order No 105 and endorsement of Genl. McLean Provost Marshal General Department of the Ohio as the only report that can be furnished."—ES, DNA, RG 107, Letters Received. Written on a letter of Oct. 26 from Sterling King, a Cincinnati lawyer, to President Abraham Lincoln denying that he supported Clement L. Vallandigham, for which he had been court-martialed, found guilty, and sentenced to six months of hard labor and then exile to the South.—ALS and General Orders No. 105, Dept. of the Ohio, June 15 (printed), *ibid.* On Nov. 17, Brig. Gen. Nathaniel C. McLean endorsed King's statement as "*false.* Since he has been in custody he made his escape from prison & having been rearrested is now fulfilling the sentence of the court. The circumstances attending his escape & recapture led to an investigation from which it appears that King has been acting as a spy and doing all p[os]sible injury to the Federal cause and hence his professed willingness to serve as a soldier without pay in order that he may the more readily carry out his disloyal designs. Prior to the expiration of his present sentence it is the intention to prefer charges against him as a *spy* & no doubt is entertained as to his conviction. My belief is that he is a *bad man* a *miserable traitor* and unworthy of the Executive clemency"—ES, *ibid.* King, who later claimed to have participated in the attempted assassination of Secretary of State William H. Seward, committed suicide in 1866.—*Louisville Daily Courier*, March 14, 21, 22, May 12, 1866.

1863, Nov. 23, 10:00 A.M. To Col. Edward D. Townsend, AGO. "Despatch directing that Gen Mitchell be ordered to Washn recd and will be complied with at once"—Telegram received, DNA, RG 94, Letters Received; copies, *ibid.*, RG 393, Military Div. of the Miss., Hd. Qrs. Correspondence; DLC-USG, V, 40, 94. *O.R.*, I, xxxi, part 3, 231. On Nov. 22,

11:00 A.M., Townsend had telegraphed to USG. "The Secretary of War directs that Brig Gen R. B. Mitchell be ordered here immediately for temporary duty. Please acknowledge"—Copies, DLC-USG, V, 40, 94; DNA, RG 94, Letters Sent; *ibid.*, RG 393, Military Div. of the Miss., Hd. Qrs. Correspondence. *O.R.*, I, xxxi, part 3, 222. Brig. Gen. Robert B. Mitchell, who had been relieved as chief of cav., Dept. of the Cumberland, on Nov. 9, due to ill health resulting from earlier wounds, became commander, Dept. of Neb., in Jan., 1864.—See *ibid.*, I, xxxi, part 2, 62–63.

1863, Nov. 23. Lt. Col. Osborne Cross, deputy q. m. gen., Pittsburgh, to Brig. Gen. John A. Rawlins. "Have you ever issued special Order No. 22 dated Vicksburg Miss Oct. 7th 1863 to a Maj. C. E. Foster 11th Iowa Vols A. D. C. to Maj. Gen'l. McPherson on secret service? please reply" —Telegram, copy, DNA, RG 393, Military Div. of the Miss., Telegrams Received. On Nov. 24, 8:15 A.M., Rawlins telegraphed to Lt. Col. Theodore S. Bowers, Nashville, "No such Order was ever issued   the man is an impostor"—Telegram received, *ibid.*, Dept. of the Cumberland, Telegrams Received. Bowers referred this telegram to Bvt. Lt. Col. James L. Donaldson, q. m., Nashville, "for his further information."—AES, *ibid.* On the same day, Cross telegraphed to USG. "Telegraph rec'd. Have you ever given to Capt. C. E. Compen Co. "I," 11th Iowa Regt. special order thirty nine to proceed to Washington City on public business   please reply—" —Copy, *ibid.*, Military Div. of the Miss., Telegrams Received. On Nov. 25, Cross wrote again "In regard to C. E. Foster, C. E. Compton, and J. B. Dawson, imposters."—DLC-USG, V, 37. On Dec. 12, USG endorsed a letter of Col. Benjamin L. E. Bonneville regarding a special order affecting Lt. J. B. Dawson, 11th Iowa. "Respectfully returned to Head Quarters of the Army with remark that the within order is a base forgery. The books show that S. O. No. 28. was of date Nov. 24th and not 25th. The words 'Army of West Tennessee' were never used, the style being 'Head Q'rs. 13th Army Corps, Dep't. of the Tennessee, Lagrange Tenn. Nov. 24th, 1862, S. O. No. 28.' This order is not on the books at all, and was not written by any Clerk at my Head Qrs."—Copies, *ibid.*, V, 39; DNA, RG 393, Military Div. of the Miss., Endorsements. On Dec. 14, W. D. Spinking, chief clerk, q. m. dept., Pittsburgh, wrote that "the man who has represented himself as Major C. E. Foster, and Capt. C. E. Compton has been arrested. his name is J. B. Dawson,"—DLC-USG, V, 37.

1863, Nov. 26. Capt. John C. Van Duzer, asst. superintendent, U.S. Military Telegraph, Nashville, to USG. "Second line completed to Elk river to night will reach Decherd tomorrow noon. Have much difficulty in getting necessary transportation for materials. Can probably reach Bridgeport on Friday if cars for poles and wire are furnished—"—Copy, DNA, RG 393, Military Div. of the Miss., Telegrams Received.

1863, Nov. 30. USG pass for Gen. Hamilton and Lt. Strong to Louisville.—Anderson Galleries, Inc., Sale No. 1363, Oct. 31, 1918, p. 19.

1863, Nov. 30. Governor Oliver P. Morton of Ind. to USG. "Lieut. W H. Bracken, 4th Ind. Cavalry, now on sick leave, is unfit for duty in the field, but can do much service in recruiting Please extend his leave of absence"—Copy, Morton Papers, In. On Dec. 1, Capt. George K. Leet referred this request to Maj. Gen. George H. Thomas, who denied it.— Copies, DLC-USG, V, 39; DNA, RG 393, Military Div. of the Miss., Endorsements. See Thomas to Morton, Dec. 2, copy, Morton Papers, In.

1863, DEC. 1, 10:10 A.M. To Brig. Gen. Jeremiah T. Boyle, Louisville. "Releive Colonel Mundy from duty in Louisville and order him to his Regiment. He must leave Louisville to morrow."—Copies, DLC-USG, V, 34, 35; DNA, RG 393, Military Div. of the Miss., Letters Sent.

1863, DEC. 1. Col. Edward D. Townsend, AGO, to USG. "A paper in the following case was referred to the Com'dg General Department of the Missouri for investigation and report on the 7th of May 1863 Copy of a communication from Lord Lyons relative to the case of Henry E. Green, who claims to be a British subject and who represents that he is almost totally ruined by the destruction of his property near Napoleon, Ark, by U. S troops. Major General Schofield informs this office September 13th, that the above paper was referred to you as the troops complained of were of your command Your early attention is invited to this case If the paper has not been received please report the fact, that a copy may be sent to you."—Copy, DNA, RG 94, Letters Sent. On Jan. 17, 1864, USG wrote to Brig. Gen. Lorenzo Thomas. "I have the honor to return herewith papers referred to me from your Office, in the case of Henry E. Green, and respectfully invite attention to accompanying reports of Major General W. T. Sherman and Brigadier General A P. Hovey, as all the information I have been able to obtain on the subject. The delay in returning the papers has been occasioned by the fact of General Hovey having by mistake, taken them with him to the Department of the Gulf."—LS, *ibid.*, RG 107, Letters Received from Bureaus. USG enclosed letters of June 17, 1863, from Maj. Gen. William T. Sherman and of June 22 from Brig. Gen. Alvin P. Hovey to Lt. Col. John A. Rawlins stating that their troops were not in the vicinity of Napoleon, Ark., on Dec. 16, 1862, when the alleged losses occurred.—ALS, *ibid.*

On Dec. 11, 1863, Townsend wrote to USG. "Papers in the following case were referred to you for investigation and report, one on the 13th of July and another on the 22d of July 1863 1st. 'A copy of a communication from Lord Lyons relative to the case of Mr Charles Bane Rose, who states himself to be a British subject and claims compensation for losses sustained in May last, at the hands of soldiers belonging to the Army of

General Grant' 2d. 'A copy of a communication from Lord Lyons, who transmits an affidavit in confirmation of the losses sustained by Mr Ross' Your early attention is invited to the above case, If any of the papers have not been received, please report the fact, that copies may be sent to you."—Copies, *ibid.*, RG 94, Letters Sent; *ibid.*, RG 393, Military Div. of the Miss., War Dept. Correspondence. The documents described, with an undated endorsement from Rawlins to Maj. Gen. James B. McPherson, were received at Vicksburg on March 29, 1864.—Copies, *ibid.*, Dept. of the Cumberland, Q. M. Records, Cotton Claims.

1863, DEC. 2. Maj. Thomas M. Vincent, AGO, to USG. "The Secretary of War directs that you order a detail of one Commissioned officer from each regiment, and one non Commissioned officer or private from each Company, of the following Illinois Regiments, now serving in the Department of the Tennessee, Viz:—7th, 9th, 12th, 20th, 28th, 29th, 30th, 31st, 32nd, 40th, 41st, 43rd, 45th, 46th, 47th, 48th, 49th, 50th, 52nd, 55th, 57th, 64th 66th regiments of Infantry, and the 9th and 11th, Cavalry. The details will be ordered to report without delay, to the Superintendent of Volunteer Recruiting service, at Springfield, Ill."—LS, DNA, RG 393, Military Div. of the Miss., Letters Received. On Dec. 15, Brig. Gen. Grenville M. Dodge, Pulaski, Tenn., telegraphed to Brig. Gen. John A. Rawlins. "Adjt. Gen'l. Fuller of Ills. calls upon me for recruiting details from 7th 9th 12th 50th 52nd 57th & 66th Ills. Infy says orders were sent to you on second of month and desires me to anticipate receipt of orders time is short Please instruct."—Copies, *ibid.*, 16th Army Corps, Telegrams Sent, Left Wing; (misdated Nov. 15) *ibid.*, Military Div. of the Miss., Telegrams Received. On Dec. 15, USG telegraphed to Dodge. "Make recruiting details from the 7th 9th 12th 50th 52d 57th and 66th Regiments Illinois Infantry, as requested by Adjutant General Fuller."—Copies, *ibid.*, Letters Sent; DLC-USG, V, 34, 35.

On Dec. 16, Ill. AG Allen C. Fuller telegraphed to USG. "Capt Barrett [*Barnett*] Batty "I" 2nd. Ills Arty. now here on leave of absence. I think can fill his battery in a few days if he can be assigned to recruiting service here please authorize him to report to the Supt recruiting service here."—Copy, DNA, RG 393, Military Div. of the Miss., Telegrams Received. See Clyde C. Walton, ed., *Behind the Guns: The History of Battery I 2nd Regiment, Illinois Light Artillery* (Carbondale and Edwardsville, 1965), pp. xv–xvi, 72, 76.

1863, DEC. 4. To Governor David Tod of Ohio. "Capt Straaks leave is extended to the [t]wenty fifth (25) Instant—"—Telegram received, AGO Records, Ohio Archives, Columbus, Ohio.

1863, DEC. 4. Lt. Col. James A. Hardie, AGO, to James M. McKim, Philadelphia, enclosing letters of introduction to USG and to Maj. Gen.

Nathaniel P. Banks.—ADf, DNA, RG 107, Letters Received; copy, *ibid.*, Letters Sent, Military Affairs. On Nov. 25, McKim, an antislavery leader, had written to Secretary of War Edwin M. Stanton proposing "a tour of observation through Tennessee, and down the Mississippi as far as New Orleans," for the Pa. Freedmen's Relief Association.—ALS, *ibid.*, Letters Received.

1863, DEC. 6, 9:30 A.M.   To Brig. Gen. Grenville M. Dodge, Pulaski, Tenn. "I have received a letter from Mr Lumpkins who, I believe is now with you, desiring a pass for himself and horse to this place where he thinks he can be of service. Say to him that I do not know where I shall be two weeks hence; he had therefore better remain where he is until General Sherman returns from Knoxville, and settles down when you are authorized to give the desired pass."—Copies, DLC-USG, V, 34, 35; DNA, RG 393, Military Div. of the Miss., Letters Sent. On Dec. 26, Maj. Gen. George H. Thomas authorized George W. Lumpkins to organize a body of home guards for protection against C.S.A. "depredations and attacks" in McLemore's Cove, Ga., the valley south of Chattanooga between Missionary Ridge and Pigeon Roost Mountain.—*O.R.*, I, xxxi, part 3, 508–9.

1863, DEC. 7.   USG endorsement. "Approved and respectfully forwarded to HeadQuarters of the Army Washington D. C."—ES, DNA, RG 94, ACP, F26 CB 1863. Written on a letter of Dec. 7 from Capt. Henry C. Freeman, Chattanooga, to Brig. Gen. John A. Rawlins submitting his resignation to attend to business affairs.—ALS, *ibid.*

1863, DEC. 7.   To Reverend J. F. Marlay. "Through you permit me to express my thanks to the society of which you are the honored secretary, for the compliment they have seen fit to pay me by electing me one of its members. I accept the election as a token of earnest support, by members of the Methodist Missionary Society of the Cincinnati Conference, to the cause of our country in this hour of trial."—Julian K. Larke, *General Grant and his Campaigns* (New York, 1864), p. 433. On Nov. 25, Theodore Baur, recording steward, Third Methodist German Church, Cincinnati, wrote to USG stating that on Aug. 16 USG had been made a life member of the Cincinnati Conference Missionary Society.—ALS, USG 3. On Dec. 16, Brig. Gen. James H. Wilson acknowledged a similar letter of Dec. 9, in which Reverend Lewis R. Dunn, Methodist Episcopal Church, Morristown, N. J., wrote that USG had been made a life director of its missionary society.—*New York Times*, Jan. 10, 1864.

1863, DEC. 8.   Governor Oliver P. Morton of Ind. to USG. "I request that Dr. Alexander Mullen Surgeon 35th Indiana Vols. now here on leave of absence may be detailed on recruiting service for his regiment"—Copy, Morton Papers, In.

1863, DEC. 11. USG endorsement. "Respectfully forwarded to Head Quarters of the Army Washington D. C. and recommended."—Copies, DLC-USG, V, 39; DNA, RG 393, Military Div. of the Miss., Endorsements. Written on a letter of Capt. William A. Warren, asst. q. m., Stevenson, Ala., requesting that Private F. A. Bettis, 5th Iowa, be discharged to accept a clerkship in his office.—*Ibid.* On Dec. 31, Maj. Samuel Breck, AGO, wrote to USG denying the request.—Copies, *ibid.*, War Dept. Correspondence; *ibid.*, RG 94, Enlisted Branch, Letters Sent.

1863, DEC. 11. USG endorsement. "The character of the officers who speak from personal knowledge of this officer induces me to urgently recommend his promotion"—ES, DNA, RG 94, ACP, H6 CB 1864. Written on a letter of Oct. 31 of Col. John Shane, 13th Iowa, recommending the appointment as paymaster of Capt. George B. Hogin, Co. D, and act. asst. inspector gen., 1st Div., 17th Army Corps.—ALS, *ibid.* Confirmed on Feb. 23, 1864, Hogin on April 7 wrote to Col. James A. Hardie, AGO, declining the appointment because of wounds received near Vicksburg in Feb., 1863.—ALS, *ibid.*

1863, DEC. 11. To Brig. Gen. Grenville M. Dodge. "By a Communication from Capt B. H. Chenoworth to Genl Wilson of my Staff I learn that the Capt is Offered a Lieut Colonelcy of an African Regiment at New Orleans. You are authorized to give him leave to proceed to that point In view of the facts Set forth I think it best for him to accept. I will gladly do anything I can to further advance his intrests"—Telegram received, DNA, RG 59, Letters of Application and Recommendation, B. P. Chenoweth. Bernard P. Chenoweth forwarded this telegram to Secretary of State Hamilton Fish with a letter of March 16, 1869, in which he requested appointment as minister to Japan or to an Asiatic consulate. Chenoweth stated that when the Civil War began, he was publishing a Republican newspaper at St. Joseph, Mo., and was forced to flee to Kans. where he raised a co. of the 1st Kans. After Chenoweth served on Dodge's staff for some time, Brig. Gen. Albert L. Lee arranged a promotion, but USG reversed his original approval after Brig. Gen. James H. Wilson argued that Chenoweth was needed as inspector.—ALS, *ibid.* On March 9, 1866, USG wrote to Mrs. Chenoweth. "It gives me pleasure to learn, as I do from your letter of the 27th of Feb'y, that your husband, after giving his services to his country during the great struggle through which we have just passed, is likely to receive an appointment in one of the educational institutions of the country suitable to his tastes and agreeable to him. Whilst serving at my Head Quarters as Asst. Inspect. Gen. he won the respect and confidence of all the officers associated with me. Hoping that the appointment asked will be given your husband,"—Copy, *ibid.* See General Orders No. 7, Feb. 27, 1864. In 1869, Chenoweth was appointed consul at Canton.

1863, DEC. 11.   Jeremiah Clemens and six others, Huntsville, Ala., to USG. "The undersigned citizens of Huntsville respectfully request that Mr. John O. Noble may be appointed President of the Board of trade if one is established here."—DS, DNA, RG 366, First Special Agency, Nashville, Letters Received. This petition was endorsed: "Rascal—see Lindsley"— AE, *ibid.* Clemens had been a Democratic U.S. Senator from Ala. (1849– 56).

1863, DEC. 12.   USG endorsement. "Respectfully forwarded to Head Qrs. of the Army Washington D. C., and recommended"—ES, DNA, RG 94, ACP, J144 CB 1863. Written on a letter of Dec. 7 from Col. Thomas E. Champion and twenty others, 96th Ill., to President Abraham Lincoln urging the appointment of 1st Lt. Stephen Jeffers, regt. q. m., as capt., commissary of subsistence.—DS, *ibid.* Jeffers was so appointed on March 2, 1864.

1863, DEC. 12, 10:30 A.M.   To Maj. Gen. Ambrose E. Burnside. "Detail a non commissioned officer who will be entitled to promotion on the filling up of his company, or a commissioned officer who has been appointed but cannot be mustered until his Company is filled, from every Michigan Company where a vacancy exists, and order them to report to the Superintendent of Recruiting Service of their State, forthwith. No details need be made from Companies having their full complement of Officers already mustered in. The 2d 8th 17th 20th 23d and 25th regiments of Infantry are the only ones to make details from."—Copies, DLC-USG, V, 34, 35; DNA, RG 393, Military Div. of the Miss., Letters Sent.

1863, DEC. 12.   Capt. Nicholas J. Rusch, asst. q. m., Louisville, to Brig. Gen. Robert Allen, Louisville, proposing to engage up to 6,000 German and Irish immigrants at New York City, and others not liable to the draft, to supply fuel for navigation on the Mississippi River.—ALS, DNA, RG 94, Letters Received, 59Q 1864. On Dec. 21, Allen wrote to USG. "The enclosed communication I deem of sufficient importance to instruct the writer, Capt. N. J. Rusch, to proceed in person to Nashville and lay the matter before you . . . Capt Rusch has been Commissioner of German Emigration and Lieutenant Governor of the State of Iowa. . . ."—ALS, *ibid.* On Dec. 23, USG endorsed this letter. "The plan herein proposed by Capt. N. J. Rusch for supply fuel on the Miss. river I deem feasible and advantageous to the Govt. I hope the War Dept. will authorize the employment of such a force of wood chopers as is here recommended and the issue of arms and rations to them."—AES, *ibid.* On Dec. 28, Brig. Gen. Mont-

gomery C. Meigs, Chattanooga, endorsed the letter. "Approved & respectfully forwarded to the Secretary of War The plan appears to embody
the elements of usefulness & success. . . ."—AES, *ibid.* In Jan., 1864, Rusch
submitted a detailed outline of his plan to Meigs.—ALS, *ibid.* Although
authorized by War Dept. General Orders No. 124 on March 28, Rusch's
plan was incompletely realized before his death on Sept. 22.

1863, DEC. 13.   USG General Orders No. 11. "All Quartermasters within the Military Division of the Mississippi, who now have, or may hereafter receive, monies for rents accruing from abandoned property, or property known to belong to secessionists within this Military Division, are
hereby directed to pay said monies into the hands of the nearest Treasury
Agent, . . . Any property now held by any Quartermaster, and upon which
rents are collected by him, shall, when satisfactorily proven to belong to
loyal citizens, be restored to the possession of the owners, . . ."—Copies,
DLC-USG, V, 14; DNA, RG 393, Military Div. of the Miss., General
Orders; (printed) *ibid.*, RG 366, Book Records; USGA. Supervision and
control of abandoned property within U.S. military lines had been assigned
to U.S. Treasury Dept. agents on Oct. 9 by War Dept. General Orders No.
331. On Nov. 16, Col. Charles Thomas, act. q. m. gen., wrote to USG regarding the collection of rents on certain houses in Memphis owned by
allegedly loyal citizens.—LS, DNA, RG 56, Div. of Captured and Abandoned Property, Letters Received (Press). On Dec. 22, Lt. Col. Theodore
S. Bowers endorsed Thomas's letter. "Respectfully forwarded to Capt
A. R. Eddy, Depot Quartermaster Memphis Tenn., who will turn ove[r]
to the Special Agent of the Treasury Department at Memphis Tenn., the
administration of the property concerned and to deposit in the Treasury all
moneys received from the rents of the property, subject to the orders of the
Treasury Departm't as within directed by the Secretary of War."—ES, *ibid.*
On Dec. 16, U.S. Treasury Special Agent Charles A. Fuller wrote to USG
seeking protection of his housewares store in Nashville.—ALS, *ibid.*, RG
109, Union Provost Marshals' File of Papers Relating to Individual Civilians. On Dec. 24, in response to a letter of Dec. 21 of Bvt. Lt. Col. James
L. Donaldson, q. m., Nashville, Bowers issued Special Orders No. 28
appointing a board of three officers to set rents on buildings owned by
Unionists and occupied for government use in that city.—Copy, DLC-
USG, V, 38.

1863, DEC. 14.   USG endorsement. "Respectfully forwarded to the General in Chief with the recommendation that Dr Palmer, and Lieut Eggleston
be Mustered out of the U. S. Service, their conduct being prejudicial to
Military propriety. The Woman has been ordered released."—Copies, DLC-
USG, V, 39; DNA, RG 393, Military Div. of the Miss., Endorsements.
Written on a letter of Maj. De Witt C. Fitch, president, military commission, Louisville, regarding the arrest of a Negro woman dressed in a soldier's

uniform.—*Ibid.* On the same day, Capt. George K. Leet wrote to Brig. Gen. Jeremiah T. Boyle, Louisville, stating that at the time of the woman's arrest she was "in charge of 1st Lieut Henry B Eggleston 11th Michigan Regt. to whom she had been entrusted by Dr Palmer of the same Regt. to be taken to the parents of the latter in Michigan, he claiming to have bought her in Alabama. The General comdg directs that said negro woman be immediately released from arrest and confinement."—Copies, *ibid.*, Letters Sent; DLC-USG, V, 34, 35. On Jan. 18, 1864, USG's adjt. endorsed a letter from Fitch, as provost marshal, stating that the woman was at work for private parties. "Respectfully returned. The within order from these Head Quarters, will be obeyed without explanation or equivocation."— Copies, *ibid.*, V, 39; DNA, RG 393, Military Div. of the Miss., Endorsements.

1863, DEC. 14. USG endorsement. "Respectfully forwarded to his Excellency the Gov. of Mo. Lieut. Patton has been kept on engineer duty because of efficiency and worth, and thereby deprived of promotion. I believe merit would be rewarded by making him a Field officer in the new organization."—Copies, DLC-USG, V, 39; DNA, RG 393, Military Div. of the Miss., Endorsements. Written on a letter of 1st Lt. James G. Patton, Co. E, 33rd Mo.—*Ibid.* Patton was promoted to capt., Co. B, as of Nov. 29, 1863.

1863, DEC. 16. USG General Orders No. 12. "To prevent and suppress irregularities in the matter of private buildings taken by military authority for public store-houses, offices or quarters within this Military Division, the following orders are issued: All seizures of private buildings will be made by the Quartermasters Department, on the order of the commanding officer. The buildings of disloyal persons alone, will be taken to furnish officers with quarters, and the need for the public offices and storehouses must be supplied in preference. When the urgent exigencies of the service require it, the buildings of loyal persons may be taken for store-houses and offices, but only after all suitable buildings belonging to disloyal persons have been seized. In the seizure of buildings, the owner will be allowed to retain all movables except the means of heating. All officers will remain in the immediate vicinity of their commands, and if having a less command than a division or post, when the command is in tents they will occupy tents themselves. Commanding officers are prohibited from quartering troops in houses, without the special, written authority of the General Commanding the Corps or Department to which they belong. In furnishing quarters to officers not serving with troops, the Quartermaster's Department, will be governed by existing regulations. Ten days after the receipt and distribution of this order Corps Commanders will cause an inspection of their commands to be made by their Assistant Inspectors General, and will arrest and prefer charges against every officer who may be occupying quarters not assigned to him by the Quartermaster's Department, or in violation of paragraph 4 of this order."—Copies, DLC-USG, V, 14; DNA, RG 393, Military Div. of the Miss., General Orders; (printed) USGA.

1863, DEC. 16. Maj. Samuel Breck, AGO, to USG. "I have the honor to inform you, in reply to communications forwarded by you to this Office, from Officers under your command, requesting the return of men to their Regiments who have been detached, detailed &c. that: Private Wm. Degg, Co. "C" 32d Reg't. Ind Vols. was returned to his Regt. Oct. 19th 1863. Private Mathias Fritsch, was transferred to the 2d Battl'n Invalid Corps, Oct. 17th 1863. Corporal Thomas W. Curren Co "I" 150th Ohio Vols was transferred to the Invalid Corps, Oct. 17th 1863, (2d Battl'n.)"—Copies, DNA, RG 94, Enlisted Branch, Letters Sent; *ibid.*, RG 393, Military Div. of the Miss., War Dept. Correspondence. On Feb. 2, 1864, Breck wrote to USG repeating the information about Fritsch and Curren.—Copy, *ibid.*, RG 94, Enlisted Branch, Letters Sent.

1863, DEC. 19. Maj. Thomas M. Vincent, AGO, to USG. "The second (2), third (3), Battalions ninth (9) Ohio Cavalry, now at Camp-Dennison, Ohio, are ready for the field. The General in Chief directs that you inform the Governor, and Colenel E. D. Powell at Columbus, by telegraph where you desire they shall be sent."—Telegram received, DNA, RG 107, Telegrams Collected (Unbound).

1863, DEC. 20. Lt. Col. John T. Sprague, N. Y. AG, Albany, to USG referring to a report in the Albany *Times and Courier*, Dec. 19, that USG's health was "precarious and that his friends are apprehensive for his life." "The enclosed Scrap I cut from a Newspaper. The substance of it I hope is not true, but I was forcibly struck with the truthfulness of the remarks made by the Editor. What the Country wants, and what it demands, is a General in whom the Government will but its trust, when the Nation will back him up to the utmost point. You have earnt this position, and no part of this Country has followed your carreer with more interest than the State of New York. To this, I can add with confidence, the best wishes of Governor Seymour, who has watched your progress with great interest, and has often spoken to me earnestly in your behalf. You being of t[he] old Army, you must well know that I have taken great pride in your successes, and I most sincerely hope that you will not be compelled to retire from indisposition until the *Scamps*, who brought on this War, are crushed, and driven from the country. It will not be finished until they are. I see you have Hardee as an antagonist. I know him well, we were two years together in Texas. He is a good soldier, and a man of much industry, with a good share of active administrative ability, but I suppose you know him as well as I do. Bragg has found his level. He was always an overrated man in the Army. It is strange that Davis should have been so long decieved. I should be much pleased to have a line from you, as much for your friends here, as for myself, for several have wished me to ask as to the truthfulness of the enclosed scrap. Governor Seymour wishes me to congratulate you upon your success, in which I most cordially concur, wishing you a continuance of them, and health to carry them through."—ALS, DNA, RG 393, Military Div. of the Miss., Letters Received. For a similar report of USG's ill health, stemming from his fall at New Orleans on Sept. 4, see *New York Herald*, Dec. 19.

1863, DEC. 21, 4:40 P.M. Lt. Col. James A. Hardie, AGO, to USG. "Col Williamson, 4th Iowa Vol Inftry applies here for an extension of his leave of absence for forty days, urging important private business at stake. Please communicate your approval or disapproval of same."—Telegram, copies, DLC-USG, V, 40, 94; DNA, RG 393, Military Div. of the Miss., Hd. Qrs. Correspondence.

1863, DEC. 24. To Brig. Gen. Montgomery C. Meigs asking him to investigate a new type of tent and expressing his own opinion of it.— Parke-Bernet Galleries Inc., Sale No. 82, Jan. 18, 1939, p. 25.

1863, DEC. 25. USG endorsement. "Respect forwarded to the Sec. of War and the appointment recommended. Judge John W. King I have known well from *our* earlyest recollection we having been raised in the same village and attended the same ~~schools~~ schools for at least eight years. He has always borne a good character and would fill the position of Pay Master with credit to himself and benefit to the Govt."—AES, DNA, RG 94, ACP, K206 CB 1863. Written on an undated petition of Lt. Col. De Witt C. Loudon, 70th Ohio, Brig. Gen. Jacob Ammen, and Brig. Gen. William Sooy Smith recommending the appointment as additional paymaster of John W. King, Georgetown, Ohio, formerly 1st lt., 89th Ohio, "until disabled by physical debility from the performance of active field duty."— ALS, *ibid*. King was confirmed on Feb. 23, 1864. See *Memoirs*, I, 36.

1863, DEC. 25. USG statement. "The object I think most praiseworthy, and I hope will succeed. Anything I can do for its advancement, your Comittee may command me in."—DNA, RG 393, 17th Army Corps, Letters Received (Unarranged). Printed in a circular of Jan. 18, 1864, asking for funds for the erection of a monument at West Point in memory of U.S. Army officers and men killed in battle during the Civil War.—*Ibid*.

1863, DEC. 26. C. J. Field, Cairo, to USG stating that troops of the U.S. Mississippi Marine Brigade had stolen property from his home near Bolivar Landing, Miss., and had also mistreated and robbed his brother, Dr. E. J. Field.—ALS, DNA, RG 109, Union Provost Marshals' File of Papers Relating to Individual Civilians. Endorsements indicate that the letter was forwarded for investigation but the culprits were not identified.—*Ibid.*

1863, DEC. 29, 3:00 P.M.   Maj. Gen. Henry W. Halleck to USG. "Mr Dana wants to know if the pontoon bridge train which W F Smith is having prepared in New York had better be sent by sea to New Orleans or forwarded by the land route. Please answer"—Telegram, copies, DLC-USG, V, 40, 94; DNA, RG 393, Military Div. of the Miss., Hd. Qrs. Correspondence. See *O.R.*, I, xxxi, part 3, 404. On Jan. 13, 1864, 11:00 A.M., USG telegraphed to Halleck. "I will write full directions for pontoon train   Want it at New Orleans."—Telegram received, DNA, RG 107, Telegrams Collected (Bound); copies, *ibid.*, Telegrams Received in Cipher; *ibid.*, RG 393, Military Div. of the Miss., Hd. Qrs. Correspondence; DLC-USG, V, 40, 94. *O.R.*, I, xxxiv, part 2, 70. On Feb. 8, USG telegraphed to Brig. Gen. William F. Smith. "Give your personal attention to forwording to Chattanooga in the shortest possible time the pontoon train ordered from the east"—Telegram received, Smith Papers, Vermont Historical Society, Montpelier, Vt. On Feb. 9, Smith, Seymour, Ind., telegraphed to USG. "The Pontoon train at Cincinnati has already been ordered forward. I will attend to the others at once. There is a train of French boats parked in Nashville. I have missed the connection here but will be at the Spencer House some time this A. M."—Copy, DNA, RG 393, Military Div. of the Miss., Telegrams Received.

1863.   Orville H. Browning to USG. "I believe I have presented applications on behalf of several others for the same appointment. They are all good men."—William Evarts Benjamin, Catalogue No. 27, Nov., 1889, p. 5.

1863.   Robert Dale Owen to USG. A letter written as chairman of the Freedmen's Inquiry Commission.—William Evarts Benjamin, Catalogue No. 27, Nov., 1889, p. 8.

Index

All letters written by USG of which the text was available for use in this volume are indexed under the names of the recipients. The dates of these letters are included in the index as an indication of the existence of text. Abbreviations used in the index are explained on pp. xvi–xx. Individual regts. are indexed under the names of the states in which they originated.

Burnside, Ambrose E. *(cont.)*
404*n*, 405*n*, 406*n*, 409, 409*n*–10*n*,
413, 423, 424*n*, 425 and *n*, 426*n*,
427*n*, 428*n*, 433–34, 434*n*, 436–37,
437*n*, 438*n*, 439*n*, 445*n*, 449*n*–50*n*,
451*n*, 466*n*, 467, 468*n*, 474 and *n*,
475*n*, 480, 485*n*, 486*n*, 494, 494*n*–
95*n*, 497*n*, 499*n*, 559, 564; telegram
to, Oct. 28, 1863, 337–38; telegram
to, Oct. 30, 1863, 341; supplies for,
341, 341*n*–42*n*, 344*n*, 353*n*–54*n*,
359, 362*n*, 364*n*, 384*n*, 391–92, 402
and *n*, 403*n*, 428*n*, 450*n*, 485*n*, 506*n*,
513, 520*n*; telegram to, Oct. 25,
1863, 341*n*; telegram to, Nov. 1,
1863, 342–43; telegram to, Oct.
30, 1863, 343*n*; telegram to, Oct.
27, 1863, 344*n*; telegram to, Oct. 28,
1863, 344*n*; telegram to, Nov. 3,
1863, 353; cav. expedition of, 353,
364, 366*n*, 369*n*–70*n*, 513*n*; telegram to, Nov. 3, 1863, 353*n*; telegram to, Nov. 5, 1863, 359; telegram
to, Nov. 9, 1863, 359*n*; telegram to,
Nov. 6, 1863, 362*n*; telegram to, Nov.
7, 1863, 368–69; telegram to, Nov.
6, 1863, 369*n*; telegram to, Nov. 8,
[*1863*], 374–75; telegram to, Nov.
14, 1863, 391–92; telegram to, Nov.
14, 1863, 392*n*; telegram to, Nov.
14, 1863, 393; telegram to, Nov. 14,
1863, 393–94; telegram to, Nov.
14, 1863, 395; telegram to, Nov. 15,
1863, 401; telegram to, Nov. 15,
1863, 402; telegram to, Nov. 16,
1863, 402*n*; telegram to, Nov. 17,
1863, 403*n*; plans to relieve, 404,
444 and *n*, 445*n*, 449, 450, 451,
453*n*, 456, 457–58, 458*n*, 459 and
n, 464–65, 473, 474*n*, 485*n*, 494,
496, 505*n*, 506*n*, 513*n*–14*n*, 517*n*,
520*n*; telegram to, Nov. 17, 1863,
404–5; telegram to, Nov. 17, 1863,
405; telegrams to, Nov. 15, 1863 (2),
405*n*; relieved of command, 451*n*,
506*n*, 533*n*; letter to, Nov. 29, 1863,
465; telegram to, Dec. 8, 1863, 506*n*;
telegram to, [*Dec.*] 10, 186[3], 512–
13; deals with personnel, 620, 628,
634, 636, 645; telegram to, Oct. 23,
1863, 628; telegram to, Nov. 5, 1863,
634; telegram to, Dec. 12, 1863, 645;
mentioned, 20*n*, 460*n*, 600
Burnsville, Miss., 281*n*
Burton, James H. (superintendent,
C.S. Armory, Macon), 290*n*

Burwell, Armistead (of Miss.), 419,
420*n*–21*n*
Buschbeck, Adolphus (Pa. Vols.),
436*n*
Bussey, Cyrus (Iowa Vols.), 37*n*, 45*n*,
57*n*, 58*n*, 204 and *n*
Butler, Benjamin F. (U.S. Army),
527*n*
Butler, Mr. (merchant), 178*n*, 179*n*
Butterfield Memorial Library, Julia L.,
Cold Spring-on-Hudson, N.Y.: docu-
ments in, 460*n*, 461*n*
Buzzard Roost, Ala., 296*n*
Byington, LeGrand (of Iowa): tele-
gram to, Aug. 4, 1863, 213*n*
Byrd, Robert K. (Tenn. Vols.), 338*n*,
427*n*–28*n*, 466*n*, 468*n*, 486*n*, 506*n*

Cadwallader, Sylvanus (newspaper
correspondent), 223*n*, 598
Cahawba Iron Co., Irondale, Ala., 290*n*
Cairo, Ill.: dispatches sent via, 31, 81*n*,
167, 168*n*, 235*n*, 236*n*, 261, 265,
274*n*, 303*n*, 312*n*, 315*n*, 463*n*; prisoners at, 74*n*, 153*n*; troops at, 102*n*,
152*n*; business at, 105 and *n*; gens.
confer at, 114*n*, 115*n*, 233*n*; railroad
at, 165*n*, 464*n*; boats at, 182*n*, 236*n*,
402, 473*n*, 492*n*; USG at, 195, 198
and *n*, 199, 200, 207, 226*n*, 253*n*,
260*n*, 276*n*, 277 and *n*, 279*n*, 281
and *n*, 283, 284*n*, 295, 623, 624;
dispatches delayed from, 233 and *n*,
234*n*; U.S. Sanitary Commission at,
250 and *n*, 251*n*; USG papers stored
at, 339; supplies at, 345*n*, 471*n*; signal stations at, 528*n*; commanding
officer instructed at, 617, 618; mentioned, 46*n*, 95*n*, 183, 189*n*, 195*n*,
262*n*, 362*n*, 363*n*, 472*n*, 492*n*, 512*n*,
515*n*, 533*n*, 554*n*, 555*n*, 584, 606,
610, 623, 625, 649
Caldwell, Henry C. (Iowa Vols.), 595
Calhoun, Miss., 45*n*
Calhoun, Tenn., 457*n*, 468*n*, 518*n*,
565
California Historical Society, San Francisco, Calif.: document in, 601
Callender, Franklin D. (U.S. Army),
628
Callender, Horace S. (Iowa Vols.),
168*n*
Cameron, Daniel (Ill. Vols.), 495*n*
Cameron, Emma S. (of Nashville),
576, 577*n*

Longstreet, James *(cont.)*
Ambrose E. Burnside, 368, 375*n*, 376*n*, 391, 392*n*, 393, 394*n*, 400 and *n*, 402*n*, 403*n*, 405, 413, 560; strategy against, 400*n*, 401, 404, 405, 410, 424 and *n*, 439*n*, 454*n*, 458 and *n*, 459 and *n*, 465, 466*n*, 467, 502*n*, 534, 545–46, 564, 574*n*; reported strength of, 400*n*, 427*n*, 428*n*, 435*n*, 445*n*, 497*n*, 505 and *n*, 513*n*, 526, 526*n*–27*n*, 546*n*, 552*n*, 553*n*, 572*n*; besieges Knoxville, 425*n*, 426*n*, 427*n*, 444*n*, 455, 457 and *n*, 467, 473, 474*n*, 485*n*, 494*n*, 497*n*; reported movements of, 455, 461*n*, 467, 532*n*, 543*n*, 545, 572*n*, 577; expedition against, 458 and *n*, 459 and *n*, 465, 468*n*, 481, 496, 498*n*, 506*n*, 513*n*, 517*n*, 519, 520*n*, 521*n*, 526 and *n*, 532*n*, 546*n*, 565, 572, 574*n*; retreats from Knoxville, 466*n*, 484 and *n*, 485 and *n*, 486*n*, 498*n*, 499*n*, 505*n*, 526 and *n*, 531*n*, 547*n*, 552, 555*n*; mentioned, 431*n*, 573*n*
Lookout (steamboat), 577*n*
Lookout Mountain (Tenn.): C.S.A. forces occupy, 255, 371, 559; U.S. plans to capture, 300*n*, 320, 333*n*, 336*n*, 364, 374–75, 377, 391, 400, 406, 411, 413, 426, 560; assault on, 436*n*, 439–40, 441*n*, 442*n*, 443*n*, 446 and *n*, 451*n*, 491, 503*n*, 558, 561, 564, 569*n*
Lookout Valley (Tenn.), 349, 364, 391, 409, 412, 422, 556, 569*n*, 637
Lord, William W. (of Vicksburg), 77*n*
Loring, William W. (C.S. Army), 238, 272*n*, 283, 314*n*
Loucks, John W. (Mich. Vols.), 624
Loudon, De Witt C. (Ohio Vols.), 649
Loudon, Thomas J. (U.S. Army), 127*n*
Loudon, Tenn.: U.S. forces at, 305*n*, 306*n*, 325, 326*n*, 343*n*; threatened, 307*n*, 325, 326*n*, 337, 349, 376*n*, 392*n*, 394*n*, 402*n*; located, 337*n*; evacuated, 338*n*, 369*n*, 468*n*; recaptured by U.S., 460, 474*n*, 530; supplied, 530, 546*n*, 547*n*, 548*n*, 577*n*; mentioned, 520*n*
Louisiana, 5*n*, 40*n*, 71*n*, 196, 222, 224*n*, 225, 464*n*, 501*n*, 591, 592, 603
Louisville, Ky.: railroad at, 165*n*, 367*n*; bank in, 240*n*; USG goes to,

277, 295, 296 and *n*, 297*n*, 298*n*, 300*n*, 302, 303*n*, 309*n*, 317*n*, 534, 556; troops sent to, 296*n*, 626, 641; supplies at, 327*n*, 334, 345 and *n*, 356, 367*n*, 488*n*; prisoners sent to, 330, 331*n*; command of, 339*n*, 343, 344*n*, 445*n*; politics in, 348*n*; telegraph at, 354*n*, 382*n*, 413, 433; Julia Dent Grant in, 397; fair in, 479–80, 480*n*; hospitals at, 567*n*; mentioned, 25*n*, 232*n*, 246*n*, 318*n*, 347*n*, 357*n*, 387*n*, 398, 399*n*, 417*n*, 429, 438*n*, 471*n*, 476*n*, 508*n*, 540*n*, 554*n*, 571*n*, 609, 634, 638, 645, 646, 647
Louisville, Tenn., 466*n*, 486*n*
Louisville and Nashville Railroad, 345, 356*n*, 445*n*, 567*n*, 634
Love, Mary (of Tenn.), 466*n*
Love, Mrs. Walter, Flint, Mich.: documents owned by, 47*n*, 138, 348*n*, 477, 477*n*, 511*n*
Lovejoy, Francis E. (Ill. Vols.), 168*n*, 169*n*
Lovejoy, Owen (U.S. Representative), 600
Lowe, John W. (Ohio Vols.), 632
Lowe, Manorah F. (of Indianapolis), 632
Lowe, Robert F. (Iowa Vols.), 168*n*
Lowe, William R. (U.S. Army), 632
Lowe, William W. (Iowa Vols.), 374*n*, 381*n*
Lum, Ann (of Vicksburg), 77*n*–78*n*, 481
Lumpkins, George W. (of Ga.), 643
Lyford, Stephen C. (U.S. Army), 628–29
Lyman, Charles W. (U.S. Army), 154*n*, 163*n*, 189*n*, 194, 194*n*–95*n*
Lyman and Cooledge (of St. Louis), 141*n*–42*n*
Lynch, John (Ill. Vols.), 612
Lynch, William F. (Ill. Vols.), 250*n*–51*n*, 623
Lynchburg, Va., 484*n*, 513, 514*n*
Lyon, Nathaniel (U.S. Army), 26*n*, 27*n*
Lyons, Richard B. P., Lord (minister of Great Britain), 641–42
Lytle, William H. (U.S. Army), 255, 256*n*

McArthur, John (U.S. Army): in Jackson expedition, 37*n*, 41–42, 42*n*, 43, 45*n*, 47, 48*n*; letters to, July 17,